I Am
LeBron James

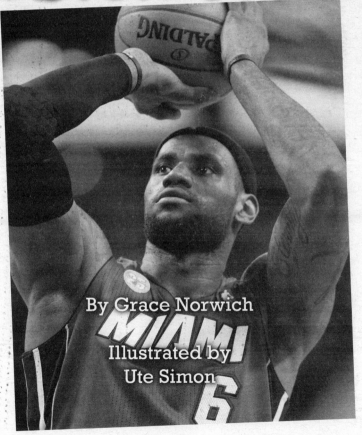

By Grace Norwich

Illustrated by
Ute Simon

SCHOLASTIC INC.

PHOTO CREDITS

Photographs © 2014: Akron Beacon Journal: 8 bottom left, 9 top, top right, 45 top right, bottom right, 46 (Robin Sallie); AP Images: 101 (Alex Menendez), 4, 8 bottom left, 44, 92 (Amy Sancetta), 50, 57 (Bruce Schwartzman), 83 (Charles Krupa), 107 (David Santiago), 117 (Eric Gay), 6 (Matt Slocum), 1 (Michael Dwyer), 110 (Mike Segar), 9 center (Paul Sancya), 52 (Paul Sancya), 8 top left (Phil Long), 17 (Phil Long); AP Images: 8 top (Tom DiPace), 9 bottom left, bottom, 95, 98, 114 (Tom DiPace), 102, 105 (Wilfredo Lee); Dreamstime: 54 (Agent87), 48 center right (Cugianza84), 70 (Nmarques74), 67 (Ratmandude), 11 (Spopho), 84 (Spopho), 69 (Zhuangmu); Getty Images: 118 (Al Bello), 9 center left, 87 (Alexander Tamargo), 113 (David Liam Kyle/NBAE), 96 (Gregory Shamus), 23 (J.D. Pooley), 42, 58 (Linda Spillers), 91 (Michael J. LeBrecht II/Sports Illustrated), 41 (Sergio Perez-IOPP Pool), 31, 49 (Stephen Dunn); iStock 48 (dell640), top right (Francesco Santalucia), 27 (Henryk Sadura), 61 (herreid), 24 (JaysonPhotography), 20 (Jitalia17), 32 (joebelanger),14 (JonGorr), 74 (littleny), 34 (lutherhill), 78 (Randall Esulto), 77 (sierrarat); LeBron James Foundation: 8 left center, 35, 38; Newscom: 62 (Phil Masturzo KRT); The Official White House Photo: 13 (Sonya N. Hebert).

ISBN 978-0-545-67350-1

10 9 8 7 6 5 4 3 2   14 15 16 17 18 19/0

Printed in the U.S.A.   40
First printing, September 2014

Cover illustration by Mark Fredrickson
Interior illustrations by Ute Simon

CONTENTS

INTRODUCTION

I've been a pretty good basketball player ever since I was a teenager—well, maybe more than pretty good. My nickname, "King James," is used by my teammates, fans, and the media. But if you knew me before I was famous, that title might seem like a joke.

While I was growing up, my mom and I were so poor that we often found ourselves without a roof over our heads. We found shelter with friends and family in my hometown of Akron, Ohio. We slept on couches until it was time to move on. During this difficult time, my mom kept me on track. She isn't just the only parent I've ever had—she's also my best friend.

Long before I became one of the greatest basketball players, Kobe Bryant and Shaquille O'Neal were among the thousands of fans who showed up to watch me play power forward for my high-school team. I was just a shy kid with a special talent. Not even my mom, who believed in me from day one, could imagine the success that was waiting for me.

I didn't do it alone. I had the help of devoted coaches, who gave me a shot at greatness as well as a place to live when I really needed it. With *a lot* of hard work, I went from a gangly boy who liked to ride his bike alone around

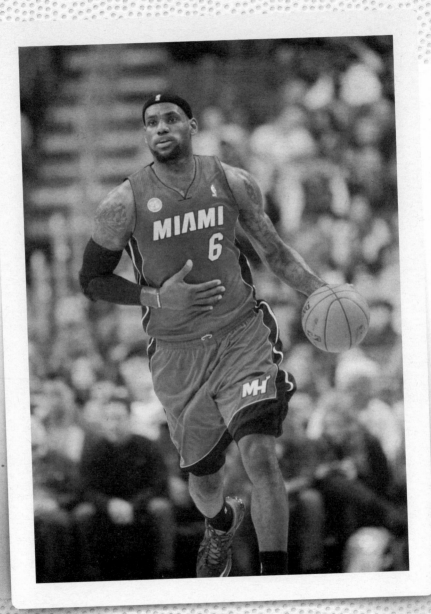

the crumbling streets of Akron to a celebrated athlete on the cover of *Sports Illustrated* magazine.

The early lessons I learned about loyalty can be seen on the basketball court. I pass the ball as often as I shoot. My commitment to teamwork has helped me win championships as well as gold medals at the Olympics.

I may be basketball royalty, but I worked hard to earn my crown. I am LeBron James.

PEOPLE YOU WILL MEET

LEBRON JAMES
One of the best professional basketball players of all time. He overcame many obstacles to become a champion.

Gloria James: LeBron's mother, who lives in Ohio, was a single mom at a young age, and his biggest supporter.

Frankie Walker Sr.: A youth football coach who took in LeBron until he was ten and became an inspiring figure in LeBron's life.

Dru Joyce II: Coach of the Shooting Stars, who helped develop LeBron's on-court skills.

Dru Joyce III: LeBron's good friend and teammate on the Shooting Stars, known for his short height and shy demeanor.

Sian Cotton: LeBron's friend and teammate on the Shooting Stars, known for his practical jokes.

Willie McGee: LeBron's third friend and teammate on the Shooting Stars, known for his maturity and gifted ball handling.

Keith Dambrot: The head basketball coach at St. Vincent-St. Mary High School who helped LeBron learn discipline on and off the court.

Savannah Brinson: LeBron's high-school sweetheart, who became his wife when they married in 2013.

Chris Bosh: Power forward and center who currently plays with LeBron for the Miami Heat.

Dwyane Wade: Guard for the Miami Heat who—along with LeBron and Chris Bosh—is part of the group known as the "Big Three."

TIME LINE

- **December 30, 1984** – LeBron Raymone James is born to Gloria James in Akron, Ohio.

- **1994** – LeBron discovers organized team sports, playing Pee Wee football with the South Rangers and rec league basketball with the Summit Lake Hornets.

- **1996** – LeBron joins the Amateur Athletic Union, playing for the Shooting Stars. There he meets three players who become his lifelong friends.

- **1996–1999** – The Shooting Stars win an amazing six national championships.

● **September 1999 –** Along with his three best friends from the Shooting Stars, LeBron begins attending St. Vincent-St. Mary High School, where he plays basketball *and* football.

● **1999-2003 –** During his freshman, sophomore, and senior years, his high-school basketball team wins the state championships, and LeBron becomes a national star.

● **June 26, 2003 –** The Cleveland Cavaliers select LeBron as the first pick in that year's NBA draft, held at Madison Square Garden in New York City.

2004 – LeBron is named NBA Rookie of the Year.

August 28, 2004 – LeBron plays on the U.S. Men's Olympic Basketball team in the Athens Olympic Games.

October 6, 2004 – LeBron James, Jr., is born to LeBron and his girlfriend, Savannah Brinson.

June 7–14, 2007 – The Cavaliers make it to the NBA Finals for the first time in the team's history.

June 14, 2007 – LeBron and Savannah's second son, Bryce Maximus, is born.

August 10–24, 2008 – LeBron and the U.S. Men's Olympic Basketball Team win gold at the Beijing Olympic Games.

July 8, 2010 – As a free agent, LeBron announces that he will sign with the Miami Heat, a decision that angers fans in his home state of Ohio.

June 21, 2012 – The Miami Heat win the NBA championship and LeBron wins the Most Valuable Player (MVP) award.

August 12, 2012 – LeBron and the U.S. Men's Olympic Basketball Team win gold at the London Olympic Games.

June 20, 2013 – The Heat win the NBA championship and LeBron is MVP for a second time.

September 14, 2013 – LeBron and Savannah get married in San Diego, California.

LeBron with Michelle Obama, Olympics 2012

Akron, Ohio

CHAPTER ONE

THE HOUSE ON HICKORY STREET

LeBron James and his mother, Gloria, have always been close. In fact, he likes to call her his best friend. Their connection began on the cold winter morning of December 30, 1984, when Gloria gave birth to LeBron in the working-class city of Akron, Ohio.

Life wasn't easy. Gloria was only sixteen years old when she had LeBron. LeBron's father was already gone when LeBron entered the world. As LeBron later put it, Gloria was

Gloria always took care of LeBron.

"my mother, my father, everything." At that time, their community was filled with crime, drugs, and **poverty**. Unemployment was high in Akron. "We had some tough times," the basketball star has

Gloria James

admitted, "but she was always there for me."

For the first few years of his life, LeBron and Gloria lived in a big house their family owned on Hickory Street. They lived with his grandmother, great-grandmother, and two uncles on a dirt road next to the railroad tracks. Grandmother Freda spent a lot of time taking care of little LeBron, but everyone helped, even his nine-year-old uncle, Curt. Although the James family didn't have much money, they showered LeBron with love, and he grew into a bouncy, athletic toddler.

A Life-Changing Christmas

In 1987, the year LeBron turned three, Christmas was marked by both joy and pain. Gloria and her boyfriend, Eddie Jackson, bought LeBron a child's basketball set. When Eddie and Gloria raised the level of the hoop as high as it would go, LeBron didn't shoot the ball into the basket like they thought he would. Instead, he took a running start, leapt up, and slam-dunked the ball. When Eddie saw this, he must have thought, *This toddler really has game.*

However, LeBron's world changed on the night of Christmas Eve. At three a.m., LeBron's beloved grandmother suffered a massive heart attack and passed away at their Hickory home.

Tough Times

Soon, the family really began to struggle. Gloria and her brothers tried to maintain the house on Hickory Street, but it was too old, too

LeBron showed an early talent for basketball.

VACATE
DO NOT ENTER

THE DEPARTMENT OF BUILDINGS HAS DE-
TERMINED THAT CONDITIONS IN THIS PREM-
ISES ARE IMMINENTLY PERILOUS TO LIFE.

THIS PREMISES HAS BEEN VACATED AND
REENTRY IS PROHIBITED UNTIL SUCH CONDI-
TIONS HAVE BEEN ELIMINATED TO THE SATIS-
FACTION OF THE DEPARTMENT.

VIOLATORS OF THIS COMMISSIONER'S
VACATE ORDER ARE SUBJECT TO ARREST.

An eviction notice
on a home

big, and too expensive. Even with food and
babysitting help from neighbors, Gloria and
her brothers couldn't afford to pay for the heat,

and the house started to fall apart. There was a hole right in the middle of the floor, which was getting bigger by the day. Eventually, the city **condemned** the house, and the James family had to move. With only a single suitcase and his favorite blue stuffed elephant, LeBron and his mom left the only home he had ever known.

THE CITY THAT RUBBER BUILT

Located approximately forty miles south of Cleveland, Akron, Ohio, was once known as the "rubber capital of the world" because big companies such as Goodyear and Firestone made millions of tires in the city's factories. By the time LeBron was born, most of those companies had moved their business elsewhere. When the tire industry of Akron moved its business overseas, thousands of manufacturing jobs were lost overnight. That negatively affected the entire city. Without jobs, people didn't have money to shop in stores or buy houses. Many people had to move away from Akron in search of work and those who stayed had little opportunity. The damaging effects on the city were lasting and it changed LeBron and his family's everyday life.

Goodyear factory,
Akron, Ohio

CHAPTER TWO

NOWHERE TO CALL HOME

When a kind neighbor offered Gloria and LeBron a place to sleep on her couch, it was a temporary solution to an immediate problem. They stayed on the neighbor's couch for a few months. Then they stayed at a cousin's place. They never imagined that they would spend six long years moving from one house or apartment to another. They stayed anywhere they were invited, until they wore out their welcome. They lived in one building that was so run-down, the city **evicted** everyone living there and tore it down.

Eventually, their travels took them to the Elizabeth Park projects, a gritty apartment complex near Akron's downtown. Gloria had a lot of friends they could stay with there. On the downside, there was also a lot of crime. LeBron's mind raced with worry as he lay awake in a strange bed at night, listening to the loud wails of sirens outside his window. He imagined violent gang fights taking place outside. In his **memoir** entitled *Shooting Stars*, LeBron described these as his "darkest days growing up."

Dark Days

In the spring of 1993, Gloria and LeBron moved five times in only three months. It was the most difficult time in LeBron's childhood. All the moving around was exhausting and made

Akron, Ohio

LeBron rode his bike to get away from bad situations.

getting to school—let alone doing homework or studying for tests—next to impossible. In the fourth grade, he missed 82 out of 160 days of school.

LeBron often rode his bike through the streets of Akron with nowhere in particular to go, and he always kept his head down. Many people mistook this for shyness. But LeBron was simply doing his best to stay out of trouble.

ALWAYS ON THE GO

Between the ages of five and eight,
LeBron and his mother moved a dozen
times! It's especially hard to make
friends when you keep moving around.
Although it was incredibly difficult
for him, LeBron found strength in the
source he always had: his mother. He
has said, "It's really all I cared about
when I was growing up, waking up and
knowing that my mom was still alive
and still by my side."

LeBron's mother wearing a jersey in support of her son

CHAPTER THREE

TEAM PLAYER

For the most part, LeBron succeeded in avoiding trouble. Although he was doing poorly in school, he didn't join a gang or sell drugs like some people around him. Despite the crime, LeBron has said that Akron was also the kind of place where people "found you and protected you and treated you like their own son even when you weren't."

But in order to stay on the right path, LeBron needed an even stronger **community**, which he found in organized sports. In 1994, LeBron joined the South Rangers, the local youth football team. Former NFL players and coaches often came out to watch the middle schoolers play, led by Coach Frankie Walker Sr. While coaching LeBron, Walker took note of both the boy's talent and his difficult home

Football was a good escape for LeBron.

life. Frankie Walker and his wife, Pam, who already had two daughters and a son, invited LeBron to live with them until Gloria found a permanent place for them to live.

Frankie Walker Sr.

A New Beginning

It was difficult for Gloria to be separated from LeBron, but she knew the Walkers were able to provide the stable home environment that LeBron needed. They treated him like a son, which meant chores, homework, and regular meals for LeBron. Gloria was invited to spend as much time at the house as she liked.

The Walkers quickly became like family to LeBron. "The Walkers were disciplined, and they plunged me right into that **discipline**," he said of the life-changing experience. It paid off. After years of struggling with schoolwork and absences, LeBron was able to maintain a B average and achieve a perfect attendance record during fifth grade.

Fifth grade was also the year LeBron started playing basketball.

A Rising Star

LeBron joined the Summit Lake Hornets, the youth rec league basketball team that Frankie Jr. played on and Frankie Sr. coached. LeBron's natural athleticism was immediately obvious to everyone. He was able to learn new plays with lightning speed. When Walker showed the team how to dribble and shoot with their opposite hand, LeBron was the only one able to use the new skill right away in the heat of competition. "You'd tell him something once," Walker recalled, "and then you'd see him do it in a game."

LeBron quickly became a star for the Hornets.

LeBron also demonstrated incredible instinct and the skill of **anticipation**. He seemed to know what was going to happen on the court three or

LeBron (second from left) with Coach Walker

four plays before it actually occurred. LeBron also had a remarkably positive attitude. Losing didn't make him mad; it made him

practice harder. He loved being part of a team, which provided him with another **surrogate** family. Coach Walker was so impressed that he made LeBron assistant coach of the younger grade team.

The qualities that promised to make a champion out of LeBron James were starting to take shape.

TO THE LEFT

Frank Walker Sr. may have taught LeBron the importance of discipline and routine, but he also taught him something else: the left-handed layup. Walker forced LeBron to practice his left-handed layups, encouraging him to be as good with his left hand as he was with his right. Frankie Sr. has said, "He used to cry about it. He used to say 'I can't do it.'" After winning games with last-second left-handed layups, LeBron has said, "I give credit to my little league coach, Frank Walker Sr. I've been doing that since I was eight years old."

LeBron using his left-handed lay-up skills

LeBron wore No. 23, the famous number of Michael Jordan.

CHAPTER FOUR

A FAB START

By 1996, life was much better for the James family. Gloria had found a good job and was finally able to get a place of her own. Their two-bedroom apartment in Spring Hill, was only 300 square feet—but it was all theirs. LeBron, now almost twelve, moved back in with his mother and lived with her until he graduated from high school. He proudly wore the key to the front door around his neck. "Having your own key to your own crib—

Dru Joyce II

that's the greatest thing in the world," he told the *New York Times*.

LeBron joined a new basketball team: the Shooting Stars. Dru Joyce II, the coach of the national-level Amateur Athletic Union (AAU) team, could see that LeBron was a star. At only twelve years old, LeBron was already close to six feet tall, with a gift for controlling the action on the court. When LeBron played, it seemed as if everyone else was moving in slow motion. His coach knew that LeBron was good enough to play alone against five other players and win. But instead of putting a spotlight on LeBron, Dru helped him see the reward in helping his teammates to score rather than just dunking the ball himself.

THE FAB FOUR

During this time, LeBron built powerful friendships with some of his teammates. The coach's son, Dru III (known as "Little Dru"), Willie McGee, and Sian Cotton became LeBron's friends for life. Little Dru was the quiet one. Sian liked to joke around. Willie was mature for his age, like LeBron. Together, the four became like brothers on and off the court. They even gave their group a name: the Fab Four. And they lived up to their name. In the five years that the Fab Four played in the AAU, the Shooting Stars

Dru III

Willie McGee

Sian Cotton

45

The Fab Four

won more than two hundred games and six
national championships.

LeBron received attention from his coach,
teammates, and the fans of the Shooting Stars,
and soon his ability earned him national

recognition. His name was known throughout the country as one of the best young players anyone had ever seen. As he prepared to go to high school, everyone in Akron assumed he would attend John R. Buchtel High School, which had a top-notch basketball program.

However, deciding where to attend high school was complicated for LeBron. The Fab Four didn't want to split up, but it was doubtful that Little Dru was tall enough to be on the team at Buchtel. LeBron faced a serious **dilemma**. Should he join the most competitive team, or stick with the guys? Would this be the end of the Fab Four?

EARNING HIS WINGS

The Shooting Stars expanded LeBron's world in many ways. He improved as a player and made lifelong friends. He also got to travel for the first time in his life. Competing in a national league meant the team went to other states for games, sometimes by plane. The first time LeBron had to fly for a national tournament in Salt Lake City, he was terrified. "He was scared stiff," Coach Dru told the *Akron Beacon Journal.* "He cried the entire time. He wanted his mother."

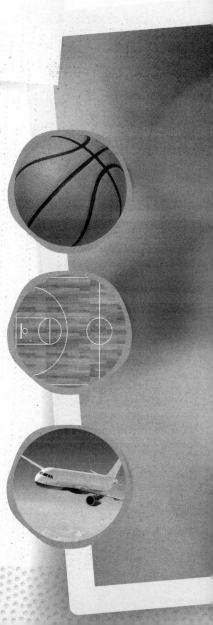

In later years, LeBron would travel the world for work and play.

LeBron at St. Vincent-
St. Mary High School, 2003

CHAPTER FIVE

RISING STAR

When LeBron started his first day of high school, Little Dru, Sian, and Willie were right by his side.

The Fab Four had made the collective decision to attend St. Vincent-St. Mary High School, which was known as "St. V." Many people were surprised by LeBron's choice. St. V was a small Catholic school with a reputation for strong academics, but it was not strong in basketball.

LeBron was in shock when he started school in the fall of 1999: culture shock. St. V had a dress code, a golf team, and without a scholarship tuition cost $8,000 a year, and many of his new classmates were white. "I had never spent any time with white Americans, and I didn't know anything at all about their culture," he told the *New York Times*. "It was a big **transition**."

At St. V, LeBron had a new coach, but he was a familiar face. St. V's Coach Keith Dambrot taught Sunday clinics at the local Jewish community center, which LeBron and the other Shooting Stars attended almost every weekend during eighth grade. Just as Coach Dru Joyce II had taught LeBron the value of passing the ball, Coach

Keith Dambrot

Dambrot kept the six-foot-four, 170-pound rising star humble by putting him in his place. "Coach Dambrot would yell at me, tell me all the time that I'm not as good as I think I am," LeBron said. "I needed that." LeBron practiced long and hard every day—a normal practice session included as many as 800 jump shots— and the work paid off. In his freshman year, the St. V "Irish" won the Ohio state championship. The Fab Four had done it again!

During LeBron's sophomore year, he worked hard to improve his skills. Out of twenty-eight games, the Irish lost only one game that year—they ended the season 27–1 and were state champs again. With a personal average of 25.2 points per game, LeBron was the first sophomore to receive Ohio's Mr. Basketball award, given to the top high-school player in the state. He was also named to *USA Today*'s All-American team, another first for a sophomore.

BETTER THAN THE REST

That summer, LeBron joined a basketball camp called Five-Star, which famous players like Michael Jordan, Moses Malone, Stephon Marbury, and Carmelo Anthony had all attended. Even at camp, LeBron stood out. Howard Garfinkel, the scout who started Five-Star in 1966, said he'd never seen anything quite like it. Usually Five-Star players were divided into two leagues by age. After only four games, Garfinkel decided LeBron's skills were far greater than the other players in his age group and suggested he move up to the league for older players. However, the loyal LeBron didn't want to leave his league team, and got permission from Garfinkel to play in both leagues. That meant he was in four games a day instead of two, and he still made it to the All-Star games for both leagues! Garfinkel said that no one had ever played in both leagues before.

TAKING NOTICE

Back in high school for his junior year, LeBron continued to draw attention. Standing six feet seven inches tall and weighing 225 pounds, LeBron had the height and the strength to push his skills to the next level. His high-school basketball games became major sporting events. As his fame grew, St. V's gym didn't have enough seats for everyone who wanted to watch LeBron and the Irish beat their competitors. Soon, the Irish started playing many of their home games at the University of Akron basketball court.

Famous NBA players like Kobe Bryant and Shaquille O'Neal, as well as professional scouts, came to check him out. One scout deemed him the best high-school player of all time. Everyone agreed that LeBron would be the first pick in the NBA draft if he left high school at the end of his junior year. Immediately, rumors

LeBron going
in for a slam dunk

LeBron and Shannon Brown sharing the MVP trophy at the Jordan Capital Classic, 2003

started to fly that he was going to quit school to join the pros before graduation. In February 2002, when LeBron was still in eleventh grade, he appeared on the cover of *Sports Illustrated* with the headline "The Chosen One." But LeBron made his graduation plans clear to the press when he said: "That is not going to happen. I can do more to get my brain and my game ready if I finish school."

FOOTBALL STAR

During his junior year, LeBron also played high-school football as a wide receiver. He was so good that he made the all-state team. But Gloria didn't want him to play. She was concerned that LeBron could hurt himself and risk his chance at a career in the NBA. Although he did quit football after his junior year, LeBron never lost his love for the game. In 2013, LeBron bought cutting-edge, all-black uniforms for St. V's football team.

LeBron and Dru at their
high school graduation

CHAPTER SIX

UNDER THE MICROSCOPE

Senior year is a stressful time for many kids, and for LeBron, it was a pressure cooker. He still went to the movies with friends, played video games, ate big bowls of cereal for dinner, and had to clean his room. But at the same time, LeBron had basketball scouts breathing down his neck as well as companies asking him to sign **endorsement** deals as soon as he went into professional basketball. Endorsement deals are when companies pay people (usually celebrities or athletes) to put their names on, appear in commercials for, or help to design a product.

The more famous LeBron got, the more people watched and judged his actions. He had to be especially careful about the rules that banned student athletes from taking any money or gifts. LeBron knew just how seriously the **regulations** were enforced. He refused to sign any copies of his *Sports Illustrated* covers for strangers, because he knew copies could be sold on eBay for large sums of money.

However, in May 2002, he did accept a special invitation from the Cleveland Cavaliers to work out with its players. That broke with the policy stating that NBA teams are not to have contact with amateur players unless they are **eligible** to play professionally. Cavaliers coach John Lucas was suspended for the first

LeBron practiced with
the Cleveland Cavaliers.

two games of the 2002–2003 season, and the team was fined $150,000.

UNDER FIRE

In January 2003, LeBron created his own controversy when he arrived at school in a customized Hummer H2, which was worth about eighty thousand dollars. He said it was a present from Gloria for his eighteenth birthday. The story was hard to believe. How could his mom afford to buy him such an expensive car? The press speculated that the car was a gift from a sporting goods company as an **incentive** to sign an endorsement. The accusations threatened LeBron's amateur athletic status and his chances of finishing the season with his high-school team. Two weeks after the initial accusations, Gloria shared copies of the paperwork for the bank loan she'd taken out to buy the car, proved LeBron's innocence, and the scandal died down.

A Hummer H2

Unfortunately, Gloria soon found herself defending her son again. In return for autographed pictures of himself, LeBron accepted a few vintage sports jerseys as a gift from the owner of a clothing store in Cleveland. Regulators said he couldn't finish his high-school season although the store owner insisted the jerseys were simply a thank-you gift. LeBron was heartbroken at being benched and letting his teammates down. "I love them to death and I can do nothing without my teammates," he said in an interview.

Gloria hired an attorney to fight the ruling, which was eventually reversed. LeBron came back to the court ready to win. He was so pumped during his first game back that he scored 52 points, the most he'd ever scored in a single game. The Fighting Irish became the first Ohio team to get to the finals four years

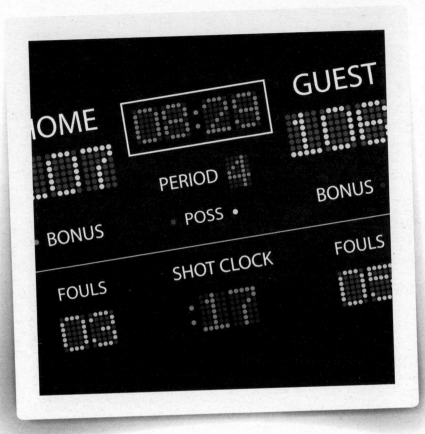

in a row. They won the state championship, and were ranked the number one high-school team in the country by *USA Today*.

BY THE NUMBERS

Although the Hummer H2 his mom bought him during his senior year got him in a lot of trouble, LeBron continued to enjoy the tricked-out ride long after he went pro. In 2007, the massive vehicle underwent a serious makeover on *Unique Whips*. The Speed Channel TV show outfitted the car with 28-inch custom rims, a touch-screen computer, a Sony PlayStation 2, a custom audio system, a bunch of TV monitors, and more. "I might as well live in here," James said on air. "All I need is a pillow and a blanket." Maybe so, but he didn't drive it much. When a Cleveland auto dealer put the infamous car up for auction on eBay in 2014 for $64,800, it only had 28,117 miles.

TV TIME

During LeBron's senior year, ESPN2 decided to broadcast one of his games—it was the first time a high-school game had been broadcast live in prime time. Twelve thousand people were in the stands at the Rhodes Arena to watch the Fighting Irish compete against the Oak Hill Warriors. With 31 points, 13 rebounds, and 6 assists, LeBron helped his team win 65-45.

The TV crews didn't bother LeBron.

Madison Square
Garden

CHAPTER SEVEN

A ROOKIE IN NAME ONLY

By the time LeBron and Gloria arrived for the NBA draft at Madison Square Garden in New York City on June 26, 2003, he was already a multimillionaire. Everyone knew what was going to happen in the draft and that LeBron was going to be a huge pro basketball star. Nike was so certain of his future success that they made a deal worth a lot of money for LeBron to sell their sneakers right after he finished high school. Dressing the part,

LeBron wore an all-white ensemble with huge diamond earrings and a diamond watch to the draft.

For weeks leading up to the NBA draft, the world's biggest sneaker companies had been **wooing** the high-school senior in the hope he would sign an exclusive endorsement deal with them. Adidas chartered a private jet for LeBron and his friends to travel to a meeting in Los Angeles, and put them up at a Malibu mansion with a view of the Pacific Ocean. The only bummer was that the meeting took place during the same weekend as their senior prom, which he missed to take the meeting in L.A. Adidas's campaign was **elaborate**. They even bought billboards and bus signs with messages directly for LeBron! But despite Adidas's efforts, LeBron signed a seven-year contract with Nike worth a staggering $90 million. This deal trumped sneaker endorsements of the

past. When Michael Jordan signed his first endorsement deal with Nike in 1984, it was worth $7 million.

ROOT FOR THE HOME TEAM

The draft pick at the Garden was obvious,

LeBron's line of Nike sneakers has outsold the next most popular NBA star's sneakers by 6 to 1. In 2012, his line of sneakers earned Nike $300 million. He named one pair of sneakers after his first basketball team: the Nike LeBron 9 Summit Lake Hornets. The Nike Zoom LeBron VI has "Gloria" hidden in the midsole, while the Nike Air Max LeBron VII has an image of Gloria and LeBron on the tongue.

since LeBron was clearly number one. The lucky team that landed him was none other than his home state's Cleveland Cavaliers, who were then tied for the worst record in the NBA. Fans of the struggling franchise were counting on LeBron to turn things around. All eyes were on him. For his debut game of the

2003–2004 season against the Sacramento Kings, the Kings' press office gave out twice the normal number of press passes. When asked how LeBron, only eighteen, was handling the pressure, he answered, "As long as you've got friends, you've got nothing to worry about." With confidence that the Fab Four, his mom, and the rest of his close circle would always have his back, LeBron played his heart out during his first season. Although the Cavaliers didn't make the playoffs, he was named Rookie of the Year.

A NEW ROLE

Becoming a pro basketball player wasn't the only big change in LeBron's life. Eight days before the first preseason game of 2004–2005, his girlfriend, Savannah Brinson, gave birth to their son LeBron James Jr. LeBron missed three practices so that he could be with Savannah for the birth of his first child in Akron. Although he never grew up with a father, LeBron was thrilled to become one.

LeBron and Savannah had known each other since high school, although she went to a rival school. After meeting her at a football game, LeBron asked the pretty softball player and cheerleader to come to his school to watch one of his basketball games. She knew he really liked her after their first date at the Outback Steakhouse, because he later brought her the leftovers she forgot in his car. "He just wanted another excuse to come and see me," she said.

LeBron was interested in Savannah from the beginning.

USA, USA!

During the summer after his first NBA season, LeBron went to the Olympics in Athens, Greece, with the U.S. Men's Basketball Team as the youngest player ever to be on Team USA. Unfortunately he spent most of his time during the games on the bench—which might have had something to do with the team bringing home the bronze. Luckily, LeBron had another chance in Beijing during the 2008 Olympics, when the U.S. team went undefeated all the way to the finals, where they beat Spain to win a gold medal. In the London games of 2012, Team USA found itself up against Spain again in the final game, where LeBron had 19 points to win gold. During those three Olympics, LeBron made history by becoming the all-time leading scorer in U.S. Men's Basketball history.

London Olympic
Games, 2012

LeBron on the court,
2007

CHAPTER EIGHT

HERE COMES THE CAVALRY

In spite of a few winning seasons since the team's start in 1970, the Cavaliers had been on a losing streak for many years before LeBron's arrival. Over the next four years, LeBron helped the Cavaliers improve their record, and fan attendance at home games soared. Yet while LeBron was picked for the NBA All-Star Game every year he was with the team, the Cavs' failure to get to the championship finals was a constant disappointment to the team's managers.

Before the 2005–2006 season, the team hired Mike Brown as the new head coach and **acquired** several top-tier players through trades. The Cavs made the playoffs that year for the first time since 1998, but ended up losing in the second round to the Detroit Pistons. Meanwhile, LeBron continued to be a powerful leader on the court, becoming the youngest player to score 4,000 career points.

In the 2006–2007 season, the Cavs avenged their loss to the Pistons and made it all the way to the NBA Finals. Unfortunately, they were outmatched by the San Antonio Spurs, who swept the Cavs 4–0.

LeBron couldn't be upset over the loss for long. Early in the morning on the day of the last game, Savannah gave birth to their second child, named Bryce Maximus James. (Maximus is the name of the lead character in LeBron's favorite film, *Gladiator*.)

Savannah with their two children

But his ultimate goal of a league championship still seemed out of reach. In 2007–2008, the Cavs failed to make it to the Finals. But they made some key changes in the off-season, including adding an awesome point guard named Mo Williams.

A FRESH SEASON

With Mo and LeBron as a team, the 2008–2009 season would be one of the best for the Cavs, who finished 66–16, their best record ever. LeBron was a powerhouse all the way. After a game against the Milwaukee Bucks, during which he scored 55 points (including eight three-pointers), one teammate said that playing with him was "like watching a video game." He was again named MVP at the end of the season. But once again, the Cavaliers couldn't close the deal, and lost to the Orlando Magic in the Eastern Conference Finals.

The Cavs still lacked the support LeBron needed on the court, so the Cavaliers acquired Shaquille O'Neal in 2009. The NBA veteran helped bring the team to the championships the following year, but again they lost—this time to the Boston Celtics in the second round of the playoffs.

LeBron was named MVP, went to the All-Star Game, and became the youngest player ever to score 15,000 points in his career.

But none of that was enough. LeBron wanted to be a champion.

COVER BOY

Between 2002 and 2013, LeBron appeared on the cover of *Sports Illustrated* twenty times. Making the cover of the magazine, which is more than fifty years old and has over three million readers, is most athletes' dream. But LeBron had no clue what an honor it was. "I didn't know till I was like twenty-one years old how big *Sports Illustrated* was," he said. "Then I was like, Wow! I was pretty big in high school!" If he didn't learn what a big deal *Sports Illustrated* was from the other players in the NBA, then he might have figured it out from how much autographed copies of his 2002 cover cost collectors. More than ten years later, an autographed and framed copy of LeBron's first cover had a starting bid of $475 on eBay!

Sports Illustrated
Winter Olympics
WHAT MAKES THESE GAMES SO SPECIAL
U.S. SNOWBOARDERS RULE THE HALFPIPE
THE CHOSEN ONE
High school junior LeBron James would be an NBA lottery pick right now
FEBRUARY 18, 2002 www.cnnsi.com
AOL Keyword: Sports Illustrated

LeBron and his mother holding
the 2009 MVP trophy

CHAPTER NINE

THE HEAT IS ON

Fans of the Cleveland Cavaliers were devastated by their team's loss to the Boston Celtics in the 2010 NBA playoffs. They also had bigger worries. LeBron's contract was up at the end of the season, making him eligible for free agency. In other words, he could play for any team he wanted. He could leave Cleveland.

Theories swirled as to what team LeBron would choose. Many assumed he would stay in Cleveland in order to finally win an NBA championship with the Cavs. Others guessed he would go to a bigger city like New York or Los Angeles.

On the evening of July 8, 2010, LeBron added to the suspense by appearing on a live television special called *The Decision*, which aired on ESPN. With the cameras rolling and basketball fans everywhere on the edge of their seats, LeBron announced: "In this fall— this is very tough—in this fall, I'm going to take my talents to South Beach and join the Miami Heat."

THE DECISION

Some 13 million viewers had tuned in to watch *The Decision*. And many of them were very unhappy about his choice. It was a very **controversial** decision, especially for his fans back home in Ohio, who were counting on LeBron for a championship title. They ripped

LeBron in his Miami
Heat jersey

Cavaliers fans were outraged by LeBron's decision to leave their team.

up LeBron posters in the streets, and some even set fire to the player's No. 23 jersey. In a public letter, the team's majority owner Dan Gilbert called LeBron "selfish" and "heartless."

LeBron had **agonized** over the decision. He didn't just want to be a star. He wanted to be a champion. And in the Miami Heat, he saw just that: a collection of players with the potential to win multiple championships. Yet when reporter Jim Gray asked LeBron about leaving his hometown team, LeBron admitted, "It's very tough, because you feel like you let a lot of people down . . . I never wanted to leave Cleveland. And my heart will always be around that area."

A NEW START

But LeBron was embraced by a new family in Miami. In particular, he found friends in two other Heat players: Chris Bosh and Dwyane

Chris Bosh

Dwyane Wade

Wade. It was similar to his high-school days, when LeBron had such incredible chemistry with his teammates at St. V. Only instead of the Fab Four, in Miami it was the "Big Three."

As the 2010–2011 season got under way, the Heat struggled to find its rhythm, though LeBron was playing well. It was going to take the team some time to come together. Eventually, the Heat hit its stride and made it to the playoffs. They breezed through the early rounds, defeating the Philadelphia 76ers, the

Boston Celtics, and the Chicago Bulls. But then the Heat lost in the championship to the Dallas Mavericks. It was a stinging loss for LeBron and the team.

The media was quick to blame LeBron. They said that the pressure was getting to him and that his team wasn't behind him. And of course, fans in Cleveland delighted in the Heat's defeat.

THE GIFT OF GIVING

Many people criticized LeBron for dramatizing his team choice on TV in *The Decision*. But LeBron has said that his motivation for making his announcement on national TV was driven by his desire to help others. The $2.5 million that LeBron and his business team made from selling ad time went to the Boys & Girls Clubs. "When I found out I had an opportunity to do that for those kids, it was a no-brainer for me," LeBron said afterward. Giving back has always been on LeBron's agenda. The year he went pro, he started the LeBron James Family Foundation, which gives aid to single-parent families. In 2005, he donated $200,000 to efforts to help victims of Hurricanes Katrina and Rita. He pledged $1 million to the foundation ONEXONE, a global organization that supplies children with food, clean water, health care, and education. He has donated thousands of backpacks filled with school supplies to the Ohio school system, and sporting equipment to local community centers.

LeBron James Family
Foundation event in Florida

LeBron holding the
2012 MVP trophy

CHAPTER TEN

A CHAMPION AT LAST

The 2011–2012 NBA season offered LeBron yet another chance at his dreams. He had been working hard to improve his game and he was determined to win the championship. Unfortunately, the start of the season was delayed by a lockout as the league's owners and players struggled to agree on a new contract.

The season finally got under way on December 25, 2011, reducing the number of games from 82 to 66. For LeBron, it was a long and painful wait. But once play finally resumed, he was ready to go. The Heat finished the season with a 46–20 record, good enough for a first-place finish in the division.

PLAYOFF PRESSURE

The Heat started the playoffs against the New York Knicks, beating them easily, four games to one in the five-game series. Next up was the Indiana Pacers, who were coming off a very strong season. The Heat took Game 1, but then Chris Bosh suffered an abdominal strain and had to be sidelined, possibly for the rest of the season. The Pacers then won Games 2 and 3, throwing the Heat for a loop.

The pressure was on LeBron. Would he buckle under the weight or would he rise to the occasion? LeBron answered his critics with one of the greatest games of his career,

LeBron in action, 2012

tallying 40 points, 18 rebounds, and 9 assists in the pivotal Game 4. The last player to post those kinds of numbers in the playoffs was Elgin Baylor, NBA Hall of Famer, in 1961! It was a huge performance and a huge win, giving the momentum back to the Heat. They took the next two games and moved on to the Eastern Conference Finals, where they beat the Boston Celtics.

WE ARE THE CHAMPIONS

That sent LeBron back to the championship, against the close-knit Oklahoma City Thunder that was playing at the top of its game, and was led by star forward Kevin Durant. The Thunder took Game 1 of the series thanks to Durant scoring 36 points. For a moment, it looked like LeBron and the Heat were going to fall short yet again. But that's when LeBron took over.

Even though he was suffering from bad leg cramps, LeBron never stopped pushing. The Heat took the next three games. In Game 5, with victory within reach, LeBron led the charge on offense as well as defense. The Heat won the championship! LeBron was unanimously voted the NBA Finals MVP. "I can finally say that I'm a champion, and I did it the right way," he would later reflect. "I didn't shortcut anything. You know, I put a lot of hard work and dedication in it, and hard work pays off."

Dwyane Wade, Chris Bosh, and LeBron show off their championship rings.

ROUND 2

LeBron's next question was: *What now?* He had spent his career striving for a championship, and he wanted to avoid a post-victory letdown. He worked even harder on his game in the off-season to prepare for a repeat in 2012. It paid off, with LeBron playing the best basketball of his life. The Heat dominated the league, ending the 2012–2013 season with a 66–16 record. At one point, they had won 27 games in a row.

The Heat opened the playoffs against the Milwaukee Bucks, sweeping the series with four straight wins. They won five games to beat the Chicago Bulls in the Eastern Conference Semifinals. In the Conference Finals, the Indiana Pacers gave the Heat more of a challenge, pushing the series to a decisive seventh game. But the Heat were victorious in the seventh game, with LeBron scoring an impressive 32 points.

In the 2013 NBA Finals, the Heat faced the incredibly tough San Antonio Spurs, which were led by Tim Duncan and Tony Parker. The momentum swung back and forth throughout the series, with the Spurs taking Games 1, 3, and 5, and the Heat winning Games 2, 4, and 6. Game 6, which some call the greatest game in NBA history, has been dubbed the "Headband Game" because LeBron lost his trademark headband on a dunk in the fourth quarter and played the rest of the game without it.

The Heat took on the Spurs again in Game 7, which was played in Miami. It was a chance for LeBron to capture another championship in front of the hometown crowd. He did not disappoint, scoring 37 points, including a 17-foot jumper in the closing seconds that sealed the victory for his team.

NBA Finals, 2012

BORN TO BE KING

Once again, LeBron was named the NBA Finals MVP. He later gave a short speech that went right to the heart of his long journey. "I'm LeBron James, from Akron, Ohio," he said. "From the inner city. I'm not even supposed to be here. That's enough."

LeBron is here, and he's here to stay. How many more championships will he win? How many more MVP awards? Only time will tell. But one thing is certain: There is no better player on the basketball court today.

WEDDING BELLS

LeBron proposed to his high-school sweetheart, Savannah Brinson, on New Year's Eve in 2011. In September 2013, they married in San Diego. LeBron wrote on Instagram, "When u have someone that's always there for you no matter the ups and downs in life, it makes it all worth living for!" Savannah obviously feels the same way. She has said, "I just love him so much. We're soul mates." Hundreds of guests gathered at San Diego's Grand Del Mar resort for the wedding, including LeBron's teammate Dwyane Wade and fellow NBA players Chris Paul and Carmelo Anthony.

LeBron enjoying a moment with his family

10 THINGS YOU SHOULD KNOW ABOUT LEBRON JAMES

1 LeBron was born on December 30, 1984, in Akron, Ohio.

2 He started playing organized sports when he was ten, first football and then basketball.

3 Between the ages of twelve and sixteen, LeBron won six national championships with the Shooting Stars, the team he played with in the Amateur Athletic Union league.

4 He attended St. Vincent-St. Mary High School, leading the team to three state championships.

5 LeBron was picked in the first round of the 2003 NBA draft by the Cleveland Cavaliers; he spent his first five seasons with the team.

6 He won gold medals with Team U.S.A. in the 2008 Beijing Olympics and the 2012 London Olympics.

7 In a nationally televised event known as *The Decision*, LeBron announced on July 8, 2010, that he would be moving from the Cleveland Cavaliers to the Miami Heat.

8 LeBron won his first NBA championship in the 2011–2012 season, when the Heat defeated the Oklahoma City Thunder. They repeated as champions in the 2012–2013 season, this time beating the San Antonio Spurs in the Finals.

9 He is a nine-time NBA All-Star, four-time NBA Most Valuable Player, and two-time NBA Finals MVP.

10 LeBron married his high-school sweetheart, Savannah Brinson, in 2013. They have two sons, LeBron James Jr. and Bryce Maximus James.

10 MORE THINGS THAT ARE PRETTY COOL TO KNOW

1 LeBron chose No. 23 for his Cavaliers jersey because 23 belonged to his favorite player, Michael Jordan, when he played for the Chicago Bulls. But LeBron prefers that comparisons to his hero end there. LeBron once tweeted, "I'm not MJ, I'm LJ."

2 LeBron has about thirty tattoos, including one of his mom's name on his arm. During high-school games, he had to cover it up with tape or bandages because tattoos aren't allowed on the court. His biggest tattoo says "Chosen 1" across his back.

3 LeBron was awarded the Most Valuable Player award at the Jordan Capital Classic in Washington, D.C., in 2003, but insisted that he share it with teammate Shannon Brown, because Brown played a key role in helping the team win.

4 LeBron and Kobe Bryant have both said in interviews that they were annoyed at how often they had been compared to each other in the media when LeBron was in high school.

5 Kobe Bryant gave LeBron a pair of sneakers as a gift when he came to see him play in high school.

Kobe Bryant and LeBron play in the All-Star Game.

6 LeBron has been on the cover of *Sports Illustrated* twenty times.

7 LeBron's Miami Heat jersey is the league's top seller, with more than 2.2 million sales to date—nearly a million more than the next best seller.

New York, 2014

8 LeBron's line of Nike sneakers has outsold the next most popular NBA star's sneakers by 6 to 1.

9 LeBron and Michael Jordan are the only two players ever to win the NBA League MVP, NBA Finals MVP, and an Olympic gold medal all in the same year.

10 LeBron fulfilled another dream when he hosted NBC's *Saturday Night Live* in 2007.

GLOSSARY

Acquired: to have gotten something so that you own it or have it

Agonized: experienced severe pain or suffering

Anticipation: a feeling of excitement about something that is going to happen

Community: a place and the people who live in it

Condemned: labeled as unfit for use

Controversial: causing a great deal of disagreement

Dilemma: a situation in which any possible choice has some disadvantages

Discipline: control over your own or someone else's behavior

Elaborate: complex and detailed

Eligible: having the right abilities or qualifications for something

Endorsement: showing support or approval of someone or something; payment exchanged for support and approval of products

Evicted: to have forced someone to move out of a place

Incentive: inspiration to do something

Memoir: a story of personal experience

Poverty: the state of being poor

Recognition: appreciation or acknowledgment of someone or something

Regulations: official rules or orders

Surrogate: one that serves as a substitute

Transition: a change from one form, condition, or place to another

Wooing: seeking, gaining, or bringing about

PLACES TO VISIT

Find your own inspiration from LeBron James by visiting places from his life, either online or in real life.

American Airlines Arena, Miami, Florida

aaarena.com

Naismith Memorial Basketball Hall of Fame, Springfield, Massachusetts

hoophall.com

The official Miami Heat NBA website

nba.com/heat

LeBron James's personal website

lebronjames.com

The LeBron James Family Foundation website

lebronjamesfamilyfoundation.org

BIBLIOGRAPHY

LeBron James (Revised Edition)(Amazing Athletes), Jeff Savage, Lerner Publications, 2012.

LeBron James (Sports Illustrated Kids: Superstar Athletes), Joanne Mattern, Capstone Press, 2011.

LeBron James: The Rise of a Star, David Lee Morgan, Jr., Gray & Company, 2003.

On the Court with . . . LeBron James, Matt Christopher, Little, Brown, 2008.

Shooting Stars, LeBron James and Buzz Bissinger, Penguin Books, 2009.

INDEX

Also Available:

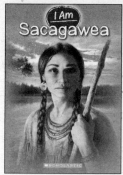

I Am Sacagawea

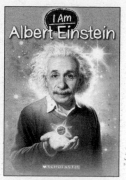

I Am Albert Einstein

I Am Helen Keller

I Am Martin Luther King, Jr.

I Am George Washington

I Am Harriet Tubman

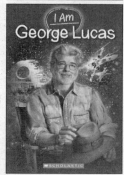

I Am George Lucas

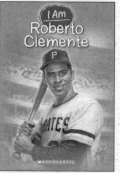

I Am Roberto Clemente

I Am John F. Kennedy

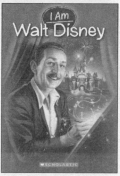

I Am Walt Disney

I Am Cleopatra

Leddy & Pepper's Conceptual Bases of Professional Nursing

Leddy & Pepper's Conceptual Bases of Professional Nursing

SEVENTH EDITION

Lucy Jane Hood, RN, PhD
Professor
St. Luke's College
Kansas City, Missouri

Wolters Kluwer | Lippincott Williams & Wilkins
Health
Philadelphia • Baltimore • New York • London
Buenos Aires • Hong Kong • Sydney • Tokyo

Senior Acquisitions Editor: Hilarie Surrena
Product Manager: Helen Kogut
Vendor Manager: Beth Martz
Director of Nursing Production: Helen Ewan
Art Director, Design: Holly McLaughlin
Art Director, Illustration: Brett McNaughton
Manufacturing Coordinator: Karen Duffield

7th Edition

9 8 7 6 5 4 3 2 1
Printed in China

Library of Congress Cataloging-in-Publication Data

Hood, Lucy J.
  Leddy & Pepper's conceptual bases of professional nursing / Lucy Jane Hood. — 7th ed.
       p. ; cm.
  Includes bibliographical references and index.
  ISBN 978-0-7817-9248-6 (hard copy : alk. paper)
  1. Nursing. 2. Nursing—Philosophy. I. Leddy, Susan. II. Title. III. Title: Leddy and Pepper's conceptual bases of professional nursing. IV. Title: Conceptual bases of professional nursing.
  [DNLM: 1. Nursing Theory. 2. Nursing–trends. WY 86 H776L 2010]
  RT41.H66 2010
  610.73—dc22   2009015953

Care has been taken to confirm the accuracy of the information presented and to describe generally accepted practices. However, the authors, editors, and publisher are not responsible for errors or omissions or for any consequences from application of the information in this book and make no warranty, expressed or implied, with respect to the currency, completeness, or accuracy of the contents of the publication. Application of this information in a particular situation remains the professional responsibility of the practitioner; the clinical treatments described and recommended may not be considered absolute and universal recommendations.

The authors, editors, and publisher have exerted every effort to ensure that drug selection and dosage set forth in this text are in accordance with the current recommendations and practice at the time of publication. However, in view of ongoing research, changes in government regulations, and the constant flow of information relating to drug therapy and drug reactions, the reader is urged to check the package insert for each drug for any change in indications and dosage and for added warnings and precautions. This is particularly important when the recommended agent is a new or infrequently employed drug.

Some drugs and medical devices presented in this publication have Food and Drug Administration (FDA) clearance for limited use in restricted research settings. It is the responsibility of the health care provider to ascertain the FDA status of each drug or device planned for use in his or her clinical practice.

LWW.COM

To all professional nurses who have a passion for nursing that enables them to share their values, beliefs, and skills to make differences in the lives of others and to shape the nursing profession. To Dr. Susan Leddy and Dr. Mae Pepper who saw the need for a textbook for registered nurses who were continuing their educational endeavors. To all the readers of this text who have the courage to take the risk of returning to school. To the following persons whose actions, values, and beliefs enabled me to live out my dream of being a professional nurse: my parents, Bob and Helen Chamberlin; Mary Belle Hickey, RN, my first nurse manager, who always challenged me to be the best possible nurse and gave me the confidence to pursue higher education; my dear mentor, Dr. Susan Leddy, professor of nursing who showed me the essence of nursing scholarship; and my loving husband, Michael, who willingly gave me the time, support, and humor to live out my dreams.

L.J.H.

IN MEMORY
J. Mae Pepper
January 18, 1936–March 19, 1997

For 20 years, Mae was Susan Leddy's colleague, coauthor, mentor, and friend. In 1977, Mae joined the faculty at Mercy College in Dobbs Ferry, New York. Mae's previous teaching experience at the University of North Carolina-Chapel Hill, New York University, and Bronx Community College, as well as her vision, wisdom, and dedication, was crucial to the development and accreditation of the new baccalaureate program for registered nurses and to the subsequent development of the first master's program at the College.

Mae held the position of Chairperson of the Nursing program from 1981 until her sudden death in March 1997 from a ruptured aortic aneurysm. Although she talked for years about leaving administration in order to do more scholarly work, she continued to serve as Chair out of a sense of duty and responsibility. She was devoted to the students and faculty, and very conscientious in her service to the College and many civic and professional organizations.

Mae found time to read voraciously, listen to music, care for animals, and to enjoy outdoor white-water rafting, camping, and bird watching. She loved her garden, was a careful craftsperson in her furniture refinishing, and liked to go to garage sales and flea markets looking for collectibles. Mae had a good sense of humor and loved a good time. Devoted to her friends and family, she willingly gave time and attention to anyone who asked. She was a great listener, and her counsel was always wise and kind. Mae lived her belief in mutuality, genuineness, and respect for others.

IN MEMORY
SUSAN KUN LEDDY
February 23, 1939–February 23, 2007

For 14 years, Susan was my mentor and friend. We met in 1993 when I became a doctoral student at Widener University. Susan had a long distinguished career in nursing education. She set high academic standards for herself and also expected her students to attain them. Her favorite question posed to us was "So what?" thereby forcing us to verify the significance of what we said or wrote.

Susan earned a bachelor of science nursing degree from Skidmore College in New York in 1960. In 1965, she completed a master of science in nursing degree from Boston University. She completed a doctor of philosophy degree in 1973 at New York University. Never wanting to stop learning, she did post-doctoral work at Harvard University in 1985 and the University of Pennsylvania from 1996-1998.

During her first four years as a nurse educator, Susan taught in diploma schools and taught in the baccaluareate program at Columbia University prior to completing her doctoral studies. She and 3 other faculty founded the RN-BSN program at Pace University. In 1976, she was asked to do a feasibility study and generate a proposal to the State of New York to develop a new RN to BSN nursing program at Mercy College. As program chair, Susan and Mae Pepper both opened the program in 1977. The two of them realized the need for a textbook to meet the needs of registered nurses returning to school for baccalaureate educationand cowrote *Conceptual Bases for Nursing Practice* that was first published in 1981. After a trip to Wyoming, Susan became enthralled with the mountains. She moved to the state and became the first dean of the School of Nursing at the University of Wyoming in 1981. In 1984, she was appointed as the Dean of the reconstituted Colleges of Health Sciences at the University of Wyoming. In 1988, she returned to the East Coast as the Dean of the School of Nursing at Widener University in Chester, Pennsylvania until 1993 when she gave up her administrative position to assume teaching responsibilities mainly in the doctoral program.

Susan was a prolific scholar and has many journal publications. After her retirement and while battling breast cancer, Susan continued to write. In addition to previous editions of this text, she authored *Integrative Health Promotion: Conceptual Bases for Nursing Practice* and *Health Promotion: Mobilizing Strengths to Enhance Health, Wellness & Well-Being*. Both of these books, received Book of the Year Awards from the *American Journal of Nursing*.

Susan made time to travel and visited nearly every place in the world. She found her trips exhiliating and stimulating. She incorporated many of the ideas from her travels into her Human Energy Model and into books on health promotion. Susan also enjoyed quilting, weaving and dabbling in watercolors. She was very energetic and always had a project to accomplish.

Susan deeply loved her daughters, Deborah and Erin, and made certain that they had what they needed to pursue successful lives. She adored her granddaughter, Katie, who always got her to laugh and smile even through some very rough times.

Susan explemplied the life of a true scholar, superb teacher, and devoted mother. It is my hope to live up to to the standards of my beloved mentor and friend. I miss her great words of wisdom and support.

Reviewers

Daryl Boucher, MSN, RN, CCEMTP, PNCCT
Nursing Faculty – Adjunct and Nursing Coordinator (FT)
St. Joseph's College & Northern Maine Community College
Presque Isle, Maine

Kristina M. Childers, BSN, MSN, ARNP
Lecturer
West Virginia University School of Nursing, Charleston Division
Charleston, West Virginia

Jessie M. Colin, PhD, RN
Professor & Director of Nursing PhD, Nursing Administration and Nursing Education Programs
Barry University Division of Nursing
Miami Shores, Florida

Sherrill Conroy, RN BN MEd, DPHIL
Assistant Professor, Faculty of Nursing
University of Alberta
Edmonton, Alberta, Canada

Elizabeth J. Diener, RN, PhD, CPNP
Assistant Professor
D'Youville College
Buffalo, New York

Denise R. Doliveira, RN, MSN
Associate Professor
Community College of Allegheny County, Boyce Campus
Monroeville, Pennsylvania

Jane E. Donovan, RN, BSN, MS
Associate Professor of Nursing
Pennsylvania College of Technology
Williamsport, Pennsylvania

Sally H. Eberhard, BSN, MSN, DNS, RN
Associate Professor Emeritus and Senior Adjunct Lecturer
West Liberty State College
West Liberty, West Virginia

Margie Eckroth-Bucher, DNSc, APRN-BC
Associate Professor
Bloomsburg University, Department of Nursing
Bloomsburg, Pennsylvania

Lucille C. Gambardella, PhD, RN, CS, APRN-BC, CNE
Chair/Professor, Department of Nursing
Wesley College
Dover, Delaware

Margaret J. Halter, PhD, APRN
Associate Professor
University of Akron
Akron, Ohio

Karla Haug, MS, RN
Assistant Professor of Nursing
North Dakota State University
Fargo, North Dakota

Henry Henao, MSN, ARNP, FNP-BC
Director, Nursing Resource Center
Barry University
Miami Shores, Florida

Sandra P. Hirst, RN, PhD, GNC(C)
Associate Professor
Faculty of Nursing, University of Calgary
Calgary, Alberta, Canada

Eileen Kaslatas, MSN, RN
Professor
Macomb Community College
Clinton Township, Michigan

Patricia Minton Kennedy
Professor of Nursing
Westmoreland County Community College
Youngwood, Pennsylvania

Maxine Kilstrom, MS, RN
Nursing Instructor
Briar Cliff University
Sioux City, Iowa

**Dr. Daniel J. Little, PhD, MBA, MSN,
ARNP, FNP, ACNP**
Assistant Professor of Nursing
Barry University School of Nursing
Miami Shores, Florida

**Carol Lundrigan, PhD, MSN, BSN,
Diploma, FNP Certificate**
Associate Professor
NCA&T State University
Greensboro, North Carolina

Louise C. Sealanders, EdD, RN, FAAN
Professor – College of Nursing
Michigan State University
East Lansing, Michigan

Rita Smith, RN, BScN, MEd
Faculty
Grant MacEwan College
Edmonton, Alberta, Canada

Lois Tschetter, EdD, RN
Associate Professor
South Dakota State University
Brookings, South Dakota

Michele J. Upvall, PhD, CRNP
Associate Dean & Director
Carlow University School of Nursing
Pittsburgh, Pennsylvania

Rita K. Young, MSN, RN, CNS
Nursing Instructor
The University of Akron College of Nursing
Akron, Ohio

Sharon Wallace, MSN, RN, CCRN
Assistant Dean, Senior Level, Instructor
Thomas Jefferson University, Jefferson
    School of Nursing
Philadelphia, Pennsylvania

Preface

Close to thirty years ago, Susan Leddy and Mae Pepper realized the need for a professional development textbook for registered nurses who were returning to school to earn baccalaureate degrees in nursing. This edition builds on the previous contributions that Leddy and Pepper made in earlier editions of *Conceptual Bases of Professional Nursing*. Continued efforts have been made to make the book more "user-friendly" and to engage the reader in the learning process by continued use of vignettes based on real life experiences, reflection questions scattered throughout the chapters, Internet exercises and end-of-chapter activities that link chapter content to professional practice. To promote the use of nursing research in practice, research briefs appear in most chapters. So that the memory of Susan Leddy and May Pepper will live on, their names have appeared as part of the book title since 2003.

 ## ORGANIZATION

The seventh edition is organized into the following sections:

- Section I, Exploring Professional Nursing
- Section II, The Changing Health Care Context
- Section III, Professional Nursing Roles
- Section IV, Glimpsing the Future of Professional Nursing

Revisions to this seventh edition include:

- Chapter 1: The presentation of a model that depicts the contributions that professional nurses make in health care delivery.
- Chapter 4, Establishing Helping and Healing Relationships (previously Chapter 7, in the 6th edition) was moved forward because of the importance of the nurse-client relationship.
- Chapter 9: New content on health care systems from geographically diverse nations and the effects of inflation on health care delivery.
- Chapter 19: Information linking the Institute of Medicine, Quality and Safety Educaton for Nurses, and Joint Commission Patient Safety Goals
- Chapter 20: The Professional Nurses Role in Public Policy (previously Chapter 16 in the 6th edition) has been updated to present the Kingdon Model for Political action to provide a conceptual approach to professional nurse participation in the formation of public policy. The chapter was moved to later in this edition because political issues presented in the chapter require a working knowledge of the health care system, evidence-based practice and quality improvement.
- Chapters 1, 22, and 23: Revised information on the future of nursing education based on the American Association of Colleges of Nursing.

Visit the Point at http://thePoint.lww.com to learn about a variety of resources that are available for students and instructors.

As Mae Pepper and Susan Leddy noted in the preface to the third edition, "During these changing times, we have been pleased with the utilization of our book in many educational settings, particularly in baccalaureate and graduate programs. Although the first edition of the book was targeted for upper division RN baccalaureate programs, we have become aware of its utilization in generic baccalaureate programs, masters programs, and practice settings...." It is my hope that this seventh edition of *Conceptual Bases of Professional Nursing* will carry on the tradition of previous editions and continue to make a meaningful contribution to the profession.

L.J.H.

Contents

To persons outside of the profession, being a nurse means taking care of persons who are ill or injured in a variety of complex and sometimes chaotic situations. Since its beginning, nursing has struggled to attain professional status. Professional nurses make key contributions in the delivery of health care. The therapeutic relationship that nurses establish with clients plays a significant role in making differences in the lives of the persons who nurses serve. Learning the art and science of nursing requires time and perseverance. When nurses provide solid evidence of the impact they make on client outcomes, the unique contributions they make become apparent to other members of the health care team and to the public. Professional nurses engage in lifelong learning to remain competent in areas of clinical practice. Sometimes, unfortunately, nurses place their own health in jeopardy in order to help others in need.

SECTION I

Exploring Professional Nursing

CHAPTER 1

The Professional Nurse

KEY TERMS AND CONCEPTS

Nurse
Professional nurse contributions model
Caregiver
Client advocate
Teacher
Change agent
Coordinator
Counselor
Colleague
Socialization
Resocialization
Role theory
Role
Role conflict
Returning-to-school syndrome
Transitions
Professional self-concept
Novice-to-expert model
Characteristics of a profession
Associate's degree
Diploma
Baccalaureate degree
Differentiated competencies
Graduate nursing education
Postgraduate nursing education
Critical thinking
Creative thinking
Reflective thinking
Autonomy
State boards of nursing
Licensure
Professional organizations
General-purpose nursing organizations
Specialized nursing organizations
National League for Nursing (NLN)
American Association of Colleges of Nursing (AACN)
National Council of State Boards of Nursing (NCSBN)
American Nurses Association (ANA)
International Council of Nurses (ICN)
Sigma Theta Tau International (STTI)
National Student Nurses' Association (NSNA)
Ethical codes

LEARNING OUTCOMES

By the end of this chapter, the learner will be able to:

1 Identify strategies for thriving in the nursing education environment.

2 Specify a process for socialization into the profession.

3 Discuss methods to facilitate socialization and resocialization into the nursing profession.

4 Outline a process to develop a professional self-concept.

5 Identify characteristics of a profession.

6 Explain how the nursing profession meets the characteristics of a profession.

7 Discuss ways for nursing to attain professional status.

Sue graduated from an associate's degree nursing program and has been working as a night charge nurse on a medical-surgical unit. Her nurse manager has hired a new nurse with a bachelor of science in nursing (BSN) who has been working with Sue as an unlicensed care provider. Sue thinks that perhaps she should go back to school and earn a BSN in order to feel secure about her current position. While speaking with a friend, Sue says, "I am a good nurse, even though I don't have a BSN. I don't see how more education will make me more professional or improve my patient care, but I see where it may make my charge nurse position secure." What assumptions has Sue made related to the importance of education in nursing practice? How would you respond to her? What are your assumptions about the BSN and higher education for nurses?

The words "nurse," "nourish," and "nurture" all come from the Latin root "nutrire." The word **nurse** may be used as either a noun or a verb (Agnes, 2005). Some persons consider all caregivers "nurses." The logical confusion stems from the fact that persons who tend to the sick, injured, disabled, or aged frequently have the word "nurse" in their position title, such as nursing assistants or licensed practical/vocational nurses (LPN/LVNs). However, professional nurses assume ultimate accountability for client outcomes. Professional nurses supervise and educate LPN/LVNs and unlicensed assistive personnel (UAP) as they assist in nursing care delivery. Although professional nurses frequently perform tasks that could be done by other health team members, they bring an ability to improvise while individualizing client care in a variety of settings. Nurses use science as a basis for professional practice and art when modifying care approaches. Thus, is nursing an art, a science, or both? The profession of nursing struggles with defining itself as an art or a science.

Professional nursing offers a specialized service to society. Professional nurses use a broad approach when considering client holistic health needs. Nurses fulfill a multifaceted role while providing professional health care services. In *Nursing's Social Policy Statement*, the American Nurses Association (ANA, 2003) identified the following "six key essential features of professional nursing" (p. 5), which include that nurses:

1. Provide a "caring relationship" that promotes health and healing.
2. Assess and attend to the full range of human responses and experiences to health and illness "within physical and social environments."
3. Integrate subjective and objective data about individual clients or a client group while appreciating their personal interpretation of their experiences.
4. Use professional judgment and critical thinking while applying scientific knowledge to diagnose and treat human responses and experiences.
5. Use scholarly inquiry to advance the nursing profession.
6. Strive for social justice by influencing social and public policy.

Thus, professional nurses provide a very comprehensive approach to client care.

CHARACTERISTICS OF PROFESSIONAL NURSING PRACTICE: THE HOOD PROFESSIONAL NURSE CONTRIBUTIONS MODEL

Professional nurses make multiple and unique contributions to client care as interdisciplinary health team members. Figure 1-1 presents a visual diagram of the contributions professional nurses make to health care delivery in clinical settings. The **Professional Nurse Contributions Model** attempts to synthesize the affective cognitive, behavioral, and psychomotor domains of professional practice. The circular form designates how the interprofessional health care team surrounds health care consumers. A solid outer circle

Figure 1-1
Hood's Professional Nurse Contributions Model.

emphasizes the importance of all team members working cohesively for the benefit of care recipients. Table 1-1 outlines definitions of the concepts that are integrally connected to each other and result in a unified whole.

In an ideal world, all health care team members share an altruistic attitude toward the persons they serve. Many persons enter the nursing profession because they genuinely care (caring) about other persons and have a desire to help others in time of need (compassion). *Caring*, *compassion*, and *commitment* are key affective domains for optimal professional nursing that are intricately linked and comprise the outer circle of the model. Two additional attributes of the nurse that are closely linked are competence and confidence. Clients expect *competence* from health care providers. Likewise, health care providers expect competence from each other. Before competence can be achieved, however, professional nurses must have *confidence* in their ability to execute the clinical, communication, and cognitive skills for effective practice. Competence also breeds confidence. As an individual's confidence improves, the nurse becomes willing to question orders and actions by others that may not appear to be logical or safe.

The innermost circle depicts the overlapping skills and circumstances with which professional nurses must work and cope. The roles assumed by professional nurses require that they have a repertoire of *clinical, cognitive, and communication skills*. The professional nurse must always have sound reasons behind clinical decisions and actions and be able to communicate them well. Well-refined clinical, cognitive, and communication skills delineate professional nurses from all other members of the health care team.

Nurses deliver health care in *complex systems* so it is important that they understand the nature of these systems and be able to manipulate them. Nurses frequently encounter complicated client situations and must adapt to *change* as new scientific evidence

TABLE 1-1

Table of Definitions for Hood's Professional Nurse Contributions Model

Concept	Definition
Caring	Genuine love, interest, concern for another
Compassion	Sorrow for the troubles of another accompanied by a desire to help
Commitment	Pledge or promise to act because of passion and/or deep dedication
Competence	Possessing knowledge and skills
Confidence	Belief in one's personal abilities
Clinical Skills	Tasks performed by nurses as they engage in client care
Cognitive Skills	Critical, creative, logical, and reflective thinking
Communication Skills	Listening, verbal, written, and nonverbal methods to interact with others
Change	An alteration or transformation
Chaos	Disorder with an underlying pattern of order
Complex Systems	Intricate, complicated arrangement of closely related or connected things that form a whole

emerges. Finally, professional nursing practice has an element of unpredictability that can result in *chaos*. Even though a clinical setting may have a well-defined organization, nurses must adapt to and work in an ever-changing, highly complex, and sometimes chaotic environment.

 ## THE MULTIPLE ROLES OF THE PROFESSIONAL NURSE

Nurses assume multiple roles while meeting health care needs of clients. They serve as **caregivers** when providing direct client care. The **client advocate** role emerges in professional practice when the nurse intervenes on behalf of the client to ensure that adequate information and resources to make decisions are provided and that the client's wishes are respected at all times. Nurses assume the role of **teacher** when providing education to UAP, clients, family members, students, each other, and interprofessional colleagues. When working to reform public policy, modify work processes, or transform workplace environments, nurses become **change agents**. They accept the role of **coordinator** when assuming supervisory and managerial responsibilities. Nurses also act as **counselors**, providing emotional and spiritual support to clients. Finally, because professional nurses work with others, they assume the role of **colleague** among all health team members. Nurses execute all the roles competently, and with genuine compassion. To execute the multiple roles of professional nursing effectively, many nurses commit themselves to lifelong learning.

 ## CHALLENGES TO THE RETURNING PROFESSIONAL NURSING STUDENT

Nurses who return to school assume the role of student, which results in many lifestyle changes. The added responsiblities of returning to school may result in chaos and personal sacrifices. Money once used for recreation is spent on tuition, student fees, books, and other school supplies. Nurses in school find that they have much less time to spend with family and friends. Families and friends have different reactions to the nurse returning to school. They may feel neglected at times and do things to derail the educational process. Sometimes family members enjoy their new independence and view it as an opportunity to become more self-sufficient. Communication between the new student, family, and friends enables all involved parties to understand how roles will be altered and what lifestyle changes will need to occur (Dunham, 2008; Quan, 2006).

Along with families and friends, meeting job and school responsibilities may also be challenging for employed students. Employers may not support educational endeavors. Coworkers may add to the difficulties by refusing, or complaining loudly about, work schedule changes, although some coworkers may express pride in their colleague. However, some coworkers may become jealous of the nurse's academic accomplishments.

Part of the toll of returning to school is entering into unfamiliar learning situations. The once-confident professional nurse may question the ability to survive in an academic setting. The educational process is designed to change persons. During times of change, persons frequently encounter feelings of discomfort.

Skills for Educational Success

In ideal educational situations, students and faculty interact with each other as colleagues. Faculty design educational experiences, and students bear the responsibility for learning. In traditional education, faculty serve as authoritarian experts who impart knowledge to students and may create oppressive climates. In educative-caring education, faculty hold equal status with students and strive to create learning climates based on active and participative learning (Bevis & Watson, 2000). Egalitarian interactions with faculty members provide students with experience in collegiality.

When students assume responsibility for learning, they reap maximum benefits from the educational process. To make professional transitions, nurses focus their educational efforts on refining previously learned skills while establishing theoretical foundations for professional practice. Theory-based practice enables professional nurses to understand complex situations and anticipate potential complications in clinical settings. Learners need a variety of skills to be successful in the educational process.

Reading

Reading constitutes a major component of the continuing education experience. Success in any program requires reading assigned material. Along with academic success, reading stimulates the release of neurotrophins, which are growth factors that stimulate neuron proliferation and brain vascularization and also may be responsible for strengthening neural pathways (Martinez, 2000).

Finding time to read remains a challenge in today's busy world, especially as nursing students juggle multiple roles. Effective reading skills streamline the studying process. Trying to read and digest each word printed on a page (or screen) is inefficient reading. When students master the skill of reading for major ideas within a passage, reading becomes more efficient (Dunham, 2008).

Listening and Speaking

Returning nursing students come with well-refined listening skills. In educational settings, effective speaking and listening are essential. Students listen to faculty members as they share their nursing expertise. When faculty ask questions, students are forced to think and respond. Taking time to think before responding to questions enables thought organization and selection of the best words to convey an answer. Many programs require that students give oral classroom presentations to facilitate refinement of public speaking skills.

Asking questions is essential to avoid making errors in the education and health care settings. Most persons (especially faculty) welcome questions from students. However, fear prevents some students from asking questions. Question formulation also requires having the skills to communicate what is not fully understood. Sometimes, the most difficult task to master is learning what questions need to be asked and having the courage to ask them.

Writing

Professional nurses use writing skills to document client care, develop clinical practice policies, compose e-mail messages and letters, publish articles, develop budgets, and submit change proposals. Writing requires nurses to use critical and reflective thinking (Broussard & Oberleitner, 1997).

Written course assignments provide opportunities to polish writing and thinking skills. Most writers make multiple drafts of their works. Success on written assignments requires understanding the purpose of the assignment, setting a timeline for completion by the designated deadline, allowing time for multiple drafts, and having a trusted friend or family member proofread the work. Finding relevant resources for a written assignment may be challenging, especially with the vast amount of available information. However, collegiate nursing programs typically have reference librarians with whom students may consult (Dunham, 2008; Stebbins, 2006).

Perhaps the most difficult part of preparing an assignment is narrowing the topic appropriately to fit assignment criteria and enabling a realistic approach for gathering essential reputable resources. Librarians and faculty welcome the opportunity to help students secure reliable resources such as books, peer-reviewed journal articles (online, in print form, or on microfilm), nursing experts, government documents, and online information from academic, nonprofit organizational, nurse specialty group, and government websites (Stebbins, 2006).

Caution should be exercised when considering information from for-profit sources and some special interest organizations. If an assignment requires detailed information about a particular medication, then, perhaps, the drug manufacturer's website might contain appropriate information. However, some websites serve as a "virtual soapbox" for any person, organization, or company. Health professionals and students must evaluate information from websites used for personal, professional, and client education. Alexander and Tate (1998) proposed using the following criteria to determine the quality of information from a website:

1. Accuracy: freedom from error and reliability (look for inconsistent posted information)
2. Authority: the qualifications of the author(s) and whether or not any fact-verifying procedures are used
3. Objectivity: freedom from biases or attempts to sway the viewers such as selling a product or advocating a specific viewpoint
4. Currency: dates of initial postings and updated information entries
5. Coverage: the breadth and depth of topic coverage
6. Verification that information on the website does not conflict with other scientific-based publications

Hyperlinks appearing within a website may send viewers to websites of lesser quality. Website home pages usually provide information about the origin and date of posted content. Some website information can disappear without warning, and unless the website has security mechanisms, the information may be susceptible to unauthorized and accidental changes (Alexander & Tate, 1998; Stebbins, 2006). For example, any person who accesses the online encyclopedia Wikipedia has the capability to change posted information.

There are various ways to secure reliable resources for written assignments. The availability of computerized databases provides a rich and sometimes overwhelming amount of information. Online library catalog and journal databases are more effectively used by entering Boolean operations (combining concepts by using "and," "or," and "not") along with keywords and subject headings. To limit results, specifying language preferences, delineating publication dates, requesting the format (books or journals), and determining location of resources are useful strategies (Stebbins, 2006). Some relevant material may be found serendipitously when writers browse available printed materials in the library (books and bound journals). Not all material obtained from a literature search may be used in a written assignment. Combining similar ideas from a variety of resources produces a synthesis of information about the topic. Frequently, outlining key points facilitates the writing process (Fondiler, 2007; Dunham, 2008; Stebbins).

Writing style for student written work varies according to assignment criteria. Authors develop nonfiction prose using description, narration, exposition, and argumentation. Description is used to create a dominant impression. When storytelling is the goal, narration serves as an effective tool. Exposition is used when authors want to show the how and why of something. Authors use the following tools for expository writing: (1) exemplification (provide illustrations or examples for a concept), (2) process analysis (give step-by-step instructions to do something), (3) compare and contrast (outline similarities and differences), (4) analogy (compare something unknown with something familiar), (5) classification (place into groups based on common features), (6) definition (explain the meaning of something), and (7) causal analysis (outline cause-and-effect relationships). Finally, writers use arguments to present objective rationale to support a position (Fondiller, 2007).

Effective writing requires that authors select words to convey messages clearly. Reading serves as a vehicle to expand vocabulary that can be used in writing (Fondiller, 2007; Martinez, 2000). Dictionaries and thesauri provide a rich source of words for use in writing. Many dictionaries provide summaries of grammatical rules for written language. When writing is done using a word-processing program, many writers use the spelling and grammar check features. Some writers find it useful to read aloud written passages (Dunham, 2008). Most educational programs have a standard format for written assignments. Students enrolled in specific programs should purchase the publication manual for the selected format. Students also may find Internet sites that provide assistance with questions about frequently encountered formats such as the American Psychological Association (APA) guidelines for manuscript preparation. However, nothing supersedes proofreading by another person to verify that what is written clearly communicates desired ideas and that the proper writing guidelines have been followed.

In recent years, much attention has been paid to plagiarism. The Internet and computers entice students to cut and paste large pieces of text into assignments and then pass it off as their own work. Ways to avoid plagiarism include citing all sources used within an assignment, paraphrasing and summarizing information carefully, limiting the use of direct quotations, avoiding too many citations, and never purchasing a paper from a friend or paper mill (Stebbins, 2006).

Professional Image and Physical Appearance

Besides effective communication, physical appearance plays a role in projecting a professional image. Nursing caps became obsolete in the 1970s, and nurses quickly abandoned their white uniforms for colorful scrub suits and dresses. Clean, pressed scrub suits and dresses present a professional appearance. However, when nurses wear printed scrubs with cartoon characters, they may fail to project a desired professional image.

Cleanliness and safety become priorities when preparing for professional practice. Clean clothing, well-manicured natural nails, and clean shoes decrease the spread of infections. Dangling earrings and necklaces serve as hazards for nurses if they encounter confused or combative clients. Tongue piercing impairs the clarity of a nurse's speech. Visible body piercing and extensive tattooing might create distress for some clients. Clients have more confidence in nurses who display a professional appearance.

Organizational Skills for Educational and Professional Success

Scholastic success requires organizational skills. Previously learned organizational skills transfer readily for effective balancing of personal and professional responsibilities. Work–life–school balance means simply to have a feeling of control, achievement, and enjoyment in daily life (Malloy, 2005). Key organization skills for success include managing information, refining test-taking skills, and managing personal time.

Managing Information

Sifting through volumes of information in printed or electronic media is challenging for everyone, not just students. Scientific discoveries and changes in health care delivery systems surface quickly. The enormous amount of information that one must study to remain current in today's professional practice environment challenges all nurses, not just students.

Students and professional nurses spend much time sorting through large volumes of mail, e-mail, publications, advertisements, and professional information. Going through information immediately as it arrives eliminates clutter. Setting priorities for action facilitates meeting professional, personal, and school deadlines. Time spent organizing personal libraries and files saves time by making available resources easier to find (Dunham, 2008; Quan, 2006). To stay abreast of the latest information, some nurses subscribe to online newsletters and service lists (listservs) that offer summaries of new developments in the health care arena.

Refining Test-Taking Skills

Testing serves as a means for assessing student learning. Many nursing students find test taking stressful. Past testing experiences may affect current test performance. Adequate test preparation increases the chance of a favorable performance. Many students find establishment of a study schedule helpful. Optimal test preparation includes reading all required class readings, attending class, asking questions during class, taking notes, reviewing learning objectives for each class, reviewing class materials frequently, attending test reviews (if available), and talking with faculty members to clarify content before exams. Some students also find participating in a peer study group helpful, while others prefer to study alone. Some students make audiotapes of class sessions (if permitted), outline readings, recopy notes, and create study cards (Dunham, 2008). Nothing allays test anxiety better than adequate preparation.

Some students become overly anxious during examinations, which may result in poor performance. Some ways to alleviate test anxiety include arriving 15 minutes early to the testing site, practicing relaxation techniques (deep-breathing exercises, visualizing success, and guided imagery), skimming notes and textbooks, and talking with classmates. Quan (2006) suggested that study groups offer the opportunity to talk with others about content covered in courses, while beginning to establish new friendships,. Some students find that peer interaction immediately prior to an exam increases test anxiety (Dunham, 2008). Complementary health practices such as aromatherapy (smelling the essential oil of mandarin [citrus reticulate], which evokes feelings of calmness, thereby allaying anxiety) may be useful (Leddy, 2003). For some students, a bit of stress may be needed for optimal performance.

Managing Personal Time

Time becomes a premium for nurses returning to school because of role conflicts. Balancing professional, student, and family responsibilities is an art. Family members may often feel neglected. Scheduling time to attend to the needs of family and friends may provide a welcome study break and facilitate the maintenance of optimal mental and spiritual health (Dunham, 2008; Malloy, 2005).

Learning to say no and asking for help without feeling guilty are essential time management techniques. Delegation of household tasks (such as cooking, cleaning, and laundry) to others frees time for study while providing the family member with an opportunity to learn or refine life survival skills (Dunham; Malloy, 2005; Quan, 2006). Success in education requires a team effort. Finally, networking with one's colleagues can result in time-saving techniques. For example, students enrolled in a BSN program published a book containing quick, easy recipes.

SOCIALIZATION AND RESOCIALIZATION INTO THE NURSING PROFESSION

When nurses assume a different role, the processes of socialization and resocialization occur. **Socialization** is the process of making someone ready for a particular societal role. Professional socialization expands the definition of socialization to include the "formation and internalization of a professional identity congruent with the professional role" (Lynn, McCain, & Boss, 1989, p. 232). **Resocialization** occurs when someone adapts a role to a new setting. Throughout a nursing career, the professional nurse has many socialization and resocialization experiences when a new job or educational endeavor is pursued.

Many authors (Conway, 1984; Hinshaw, 1976; Kozier & Erb, 1988) have referred to socialization as a continuing, interactive, lifelong process. They describe socialization as adaptation to the changing roles that characterize human development and professional growth. This view emphasizes the longitudinal and fluid nature of socialization and implies that educational programs merely provide learners with basic initial professional practice skills. These skills will be further developed or modified in the course of continuing education and clinical practice.

Traditionally, the study of socialization emphasizes how external factors, such as family, peers, school, and other institutions, affect a person's development. Professional socialization addresses the processes by which a person develops a professional identity along with how a profession accepts an individual into its ranks. Significant environmental changes (changing a job, moving to a different practice setting, or returning to school) stimulate a resocialization process. Thus, resocialization is a lifelong occurrence. Nurses can reduce the discomfort of resocialization by understanding all aspects of change processes required for successful professional transitions.

For example, some nursing students select a path of educational mobility as their route to enter the nursing profession. These students start health careers as UAP, then become LPN/LVNs or become technical nurses before pursuing a baccalaureate or higher nursing degree. At each level of education, resocialization is needed to help the nurse synthesize a changed theoretical foundation for practice, adapt to new professional role expectations, and form a new professional identity.

Returning nursing students bring a rich source of information to educational programs. Because of previous client care experiences, they possess a sense of self as a nurse; know how to use current health care–related technology; understand governmental and accrediting agency regulations; know how to interact with other health care team members; have encountered human suffering and death; have coped with personal fears, anxiety, concerns, and shortcomings; have worked within complex organizations; have seen others who model lifelong learning; and acknowledge the inevitability of change (Diekelmann & Rather, 1993).

Although nurses returning to school bring much knowledge and expertise with them, they still face the process of resocialization. Most of the time nurses experience a transformation in the way they practice after earning a new degree. However, in some cases, resocialization may be ineffective and students may finish programs with more knowledge, but without changes in an internalized professional self-image.

Role Theory

Role theory serves as the basis for socialization. As a concept, roles link persons and society. Linton (1945) proposed that a **role** contains three key pieces: values, attitudes, and behaviors. Professional socialization focuses on preparation for a particular role that offers service to society rather than life in general. Because roles are viewed as separate and discontinuous, it is assumed that stress occurs when a person assumes a new role or new expectations within an existing role (Bradby, 1990). For example, when getting married, a woman assumes the new role of wife, and new expectations might be assumed in an existing homemaker role. As adults, nursing students often hold multiple roles that sometimes compete for attention such as the roles of employee, spouse, and parent. When a new role is assumed (becoming a "student" again), students must adjust how they meet all current life roles. **Role conflict** arises when roles assumed by a person compete with each other for time and attention (Bradby). The newly acquired student role competes with other roles because of school demands.

Most students enter nursing with a service orientation. They want to do things that will help others. In contrast, the professional educational image of the nurse differs somewhat from societal views. These differences include an increased emphasis on health maintenance and promotion, the establishment of analytic and therapeutic nurse–client relationships, the establishment of a viewpoint of technical mastery along with a strong scientific knowledge base to guide professional interventions, the use of critical inquiry processes to creatively individualize nursing care to address client concerns and needs, and the assumption of responsibility and accountability for patient care decisions (Hinshaw, 1976, p. 5). Clearly, the socialization process involves changes in knowledge, attitudes, values, and skills that may trigger strong negative emotional reactions.

Questions for Reflection 1-1

1. What potentially competing roles may surface as I return to school?
2. Why is it important to identify potentially competing roles?
3. List your roles in order of priority. Why do you think you listed them in this order?

Shane's Returning-to-School Syndrome

Shane (1980) described a **returning-to-school syndrome** encountered by registered nurses (RNs) returning to earn higher nursing degrees. Although the syndrome was described decades ago, it still has current relevance. The first phase, the honeymoon, is positive. Nurses identify similarities between previous education and the present experience that reinforce the original role identity as a nurse. The nurse feels energetic about learning new things.

The next stage, conflict, is characterized by turbulent negative emotions. Conflict arises during the first nursing theory or clinical nursing course when faculty challenge the nurse to change ways of thinking and/or practicing. Feelings of professional inadequacy may emerge during this stage and may be expressed by angry outbursts, feelings of helplessness, or depression.

Successful resolution of conflict results in the next stage, the beginning of reintegration. In this stage, nurses struggle to hold on to cherished beliefs about practice and frequently wonder why they decided to pursue a higher degree. Hostile feelings toward the nursing program and faculty are common during this phase.

Once the nurse works through the first three stages, the final stage of integration emerges, which is characterized by the ability to blend the original culture of work with the new culture of school. Integration of the old with the new results in a positive resolution of the returning-to-school syndrome. Nurses recognize that a transformation has occurred. They notice that their clinical practice has forever changed, and they incoporate the newly acquired theoretical knowledge into practice. Learning new things and using them in practice stimulate these nurses and foster a new curiosity to learn more.

Throughout a nursing career, every time a nurse changes positions a process of resocialization into another working environment is required. Changing to a new practice arena or position may mean, despite years of clinical experience and specialized education, that an expert nurse becomes a novice again. By recognizing the various stages of socialization and resocialization processes, nurses can identify sources of actual and potential feelings of discomfort and work effectively by steering rather than reacting to the processes of change.

Questions for Reflection 1-2

Thinking back to Sue in the vignette, answer the following questions:

1. What assumptions can you identify that Sue has made about the benefit of seeking a baccalaureate degree in nursing?
2. What personal transitions will be required of Sue to successfully work through resocialization using Shane's Returning-to-School Syndrome? Why are these transitions important?

Bridge's Managing Transitions

Bridges (2003) offered an explanation for understanding the psychological impact of returning to school. He proposed that persons undergo **transitions** (psychological adaptations to changes) whenever they are exposed to changes, and he developed a three-step process to facilitate transitions that "starts with an ending and finishes with a beginning" (p. 5). Persons do not move sequentially through the phases; instead, they experience the phases, at times, simultaneously. The first phase is "letting go" of previous ways and identities. Professional nursing students frequently encounter distress as they embark on a new educational program because they realize that what they have done in past practice may not have always been the best practice.

The second phase Bridges called "the neutral zone," which is the phase when the old identity has vanished, but the new one is not fully developed. In this phase, persons experience a very unsettled feeling because they may not know how to act or what questions to ask. They try new ways of looking at and doing things without discarding old ways. When starting a new course or educational program, students sometimes do not know how to begin. In a beginning nursing program (AD or BSN), students assume a new role of nurse. For nurses returning to college for a bachelor's or advanced nursing degree, they must assume the role of student and reconcile the new role of professional or advanced practice nurse. Feelings of fearful uneasiness surface as the person tries to reconcile the new with the old. If a person leaves the neutral zone prematurely before repatterning is solidified, the successful change most likely will not occur. Because "the neutral zone is a lonely place" (Bridges, 2003, p. 47), communication is critical. Creative use of the neutral zone involves setting short-term goals, spending time in personal reflection to examine the meaning of change, discovering new ways of doing things, experimenting with the new role, taking time to embrace setbacks and losses, and networking with others in similar transitions. Students enrolled in the same program frequently and effectively support each other while experiencing the neutral zone. After working through the uncertainty and obscurity of the neutral zone, an emotional commitment has been made to start anew.

Bridges (2003) called the final phase the new beginning, which is a mental image or experience hallmarked by "a release of new energy in a new direction" (p. 57). A new beginning means a new commitment and identity. Bridges specified that new beginnings require 4 P's: "the purpose, a picture, the plan and a part to play" (p. 60). Quick successes such as the accomplishment of small goals facilitate the process of internalizing a new identity. For example, professional nursing students who actually use theories to guide clinical practice may see the positive effects of a theoretically based practice.

DEVELOPMENT OF A PROFESSIONAL SELF-CONCEPT

As a person develops patterns of behavior, the self-system becomes organized and strives to actualize itself, although it is continually undergoing change, being repatterned, and affecting the environment in a significant way. The self-system interacts symbiotically with the environment. These interactions with the environment provide the conditions from which a personal view of the self emerges—the self-concept. The self-concept encompasses all beliefs about oneself and personal interpretations about the past, present, and future (Jones, 2004). Because human beings develop personal selves first, those personally organized sets of behaviors form the basis of the selves brought into the profession. Thus, the personal self highly influences the emerging professional self.

The development of the **professional self-concept** (how a person perceives oneself as a nurse) follows the same path as that of development of the personal self. In every profession, the professional has significant others. During various stages of professional growth and development, nurses have different significant others that helped them during times of transitions. When initially starting a career, beginning nursing students may view faculty members as significant others. Novice nurses may identify experienced nursing colleagues and/or nurse managers as significant others.

The identified significant others in professional self-development serve as role models or mentors to nurses as they adjust to changing situations. As nurses moves in and out of new situations, they try to be the kind of person capable of meeting situational demands. Role models provide nurses with examples of how to be, and mentors provide guidance and emotional support. Professional self-concept development also requires that individual nurses engage in episodic self-appraisal along with a willingness to accept challenges and criticisms of mentors and role models. The personal self-concept cannot be separated from the professional self-concept, although the professional significant others are different from the personal significant others.

The Professional Self

To a great extent, the kind of professional a person becomes depends on the person's self-system. The professional self-system emerges from the personal self. Successful implementation of professional nursing roles and tasks reinforces one's perception of the professional self. Repeated successes in practice solidify the concept of being a competent professional nurse, resulting in increased self-confidence. Because the development of a professional self requires interactions with others in the profession, separating the developmental from the socialization processes may be impossible.

Benner's Novice-to-Expert Model

Benner (1984) devised a model of stages from novice to expert that has relevance for experienced nurses. Benner's **novice-to-expert model** describes stages in the progression of patient care expertise that can result from practice nursing experience (Table 1-2).

This model, based on work by Dreyfus and Dreyfus (1996), suggests three general aspects of skilled performance:

1. Movement from reliance on abstract principles to use of past concrete experience as paradigms
2. Change in perception of the demand situation from a compilation of equally important bits of information to a more or less complete whole in which only certain parts are relevant
3. Passage from a detached observer to an involved performer who is engaged in the situation

Stage I, the novice stage, corresponds to the student experience in nursing school. Because no background understanding exists, the novice depends on context-free rules to guide actions. Although this approach enhances safety, "rule-governed behavior is extremely limited and inflexible" (Benner, 1984, p. 21). When nursing students encounter a situation that does not conform to the rules learned, they become highly critical of what happened and cling steadfastly to what they learned in class.

TABLE 1-2

Benner's Stages from Novice to Expert

	Stage I	Stage II	Stage III	Stage IV	Stage V
Title	Novice	Advanced beginner	Competent	Proficient	Expert
Experience level	Graduate	New graduate	2–3 years in same setting	3–5 years	Extensive
Characteristics of performance	Is inflexible Exhibits rule-governed behavior	Formulates principles Needs help with priority setting	Plans Feelings of mastery	Perceives "wholes" Interprets nuances	Has an intuitive grasp

Source: Benner, P. (1984). *From novice to expert* (pp. 21–34). Menlo Park, CA: Addison-Wesley.

The new nursing graduate demonstrates marginally acceptable performance as an advanced beginner in stage II. The advanced beginner relies on basic theory and principles and believes that "clinical situations have a discernible order" (Benner et al., 1996, p. 54). The advanced beginner can formulate principles for actions, but because all actions are viewed as equally important, help is needed for priority setting. Advanced beginners typically become very uncomfortable when they encounter chaotic clinical situations.

The competent practitioner, who has reached stage III, typically has worked in the same setting for 2 to 3 years. The competent practitioner has conscious awareness of long-range goals and can engage in deliberate planning based on abstract and analytical contemplation. As a result of this planning activity, the practitioner has a feeling of mastery and the ability to cope with contingencies and feels efficient and organized. Competent practitioners typically must think about what can be done before acting in novel or chaotic situations.

By stage IV, which requires 3 to 5 years of experience, the nurse is a proficient practitioner. The proficient nurse perceives situations as "wholes," rather than as accumulations of aspects, and performance is guided by maxims. Actions do not need to be thought out, and meanings are perceived in relation to long-term goals. In addition, the proficient practitioner can interpret nuances in situations and recognize which aspects of the situation are most significant. Proficient practitioners automatically use creative adaptive strategies when they encounter complex, unfamiliar, or chaotic clinical situations.

Finally, the fifth stage, that of the expert practitioner, is achieved only after extensive experience. The expert has an intuitive grasp of situations and thus does not have to think through actions analytically. In fact, experts are so skilled at grasping the situation as a whole that they often are unable to think in terms of steps. When expert nurses encounter any clinical situations, they instinctively act effectively for the client's welfare.

Professional Nursing Roles

Benner (1984, p. 6) identified that nurses use 31 different competencies as they engage in clinical practice. She organized them into the following seven domains upon which **professional nursing roles** are based:

1. "The helping role" provides the foundation for the roles of caregiver (provider of direct client care), colleague (helpful team member), and client advocate (person looking out for the client's best interests).
2. "The teaching–coaching function" provides the foundation for the roles of teacher (provider of education and information) and counselor (one who provides emotional support and encouragement).

3. "The diagnostic and patient monitoring function" provides the foundation for the caregiver and critical thinker (someone who uses complex thought processes) roles.
4. "Effective management of rapidly changing situations" provides the foundation for the caregiver, change agent (person who initiates and guides the change process), and coordinator (person who manages, leads, and verifies that things get done) roles.
5. "Administration and monitoring of therapeutic interventions and regimens" provide the foundation for the caregiver and change agent roles.
6. "Monitoring of and ensuring the quality of health care practices" provide the foundation for the roles of coordinators, client advocates, and change agents.
7. "Organizational and work role competencies" provide the foundation for the client advocate, change agent, and coordinator roles.

Benner stated that experience is absolutely necessary for the development of professional expertise.

CHARACTERISTICS OF A PROFESSION

Characteristics of a profession (what differentiates a professional from a technician) have been debated for many years. The Flexner Report issued by the Carnegie Foundation in 1910 served as the criteria for determining medicine as a profession. Since the 1950s, the nursing profession has been analyzed using sociological theories that define a "profession." To be classified as a profession, the following characteristics should be met:

1. Authority to control its own work
2. Exclusively unique body of knowledge
3. Extensive period of formal training
4. Specialized competence
5. Control over work performance
6. Service to society
7. Self-regulation
8. Credentialing systems to certify competence
9. Legal reinforcement of professional standards
10. Ethical practice
11. Creation of a collegial subculture
12. Intrinsic rewards
13. Public acceptance (Freidson, 1994; Miller, Adams, & Beck, 1993)

Although considered a profession for many years, an assessment of the characteristics of a profession reveals that nursing fails to meet all required criteria. Nursing is more accurately classified as an "emerging profession." Table 1-3 outlines the characteristics of a profession and how the profession of nursing fulfills them. The nursing profession does use a specialized knowledge base, has autonomy and control over its work, requires specialized competence, regulates itself, possesses a collegial subculture, and has public acceptance (Freidson, 1994; Miller et al., 1993). However, nursing fails to have a standardized education for entry into the profession.

Currently three levels of education qualify persons to take the licensing exam for professional nurse registration. The **associate's degree in nursing (ADN)** consists of 2 years of concentrated study focused on clinical skills in the community college setting. The **diploma nursing program** offers 3 years of nursing education focused on learning nursing skills in a hospital-based setting. In diploma nursing programs, students typically receive the most clock hours of clinical instruction. **Baccalaureate degrees in nursing (BSNs)** offer 4-year nursing degrees in institutions of higher learning (4-year colleges and universities). Along with education focused on the art

TABLE 1-3

How Nursing Meet Characteristics of a Profession

Professional Characteristic	How Nursing Meets the Criteria or Characteristic
Authority to control its own work	Nurses work for physicians or health care agencies unless engaged in private advanced nursing practice.
Exclusive body of specialized knowledge	Nursing pulls from a variety of fields to provide holistic nursing care. Nursing research generates new scientific knowledge for practice.
Extensive period of formal education and training	Currently, there are three levels of education entry into professional nursing practice: associate degree, diploma, and baccalaureate nursing programs.
Specialized competence	Nurses demonstrate assessment skills; possess an understanding of pharmacology, various branches of physical sciences, pathophysiology, diagnostic tests, surgical procedures; and have skills to manage the technical equipment used in client care. Many nurses hold certification in specialized areas of nursing practice.
Control over work performance	Nurses make independent judgments based on client situations and area of practice. Some nurses work in organizations that use shared governance and quality management frameworks.
Service to society	Nursing care focuses on the client system. Caring for others serves as a major theme for most nursing theories. Nurses receive middle-income pay for taking care of others.
Self-regulation	Nurses abide by the Nurse Practice Act of the state in which they practice. Individual state boards of nursing regulate nursing practice.
Credentialing systems to certify competence	Nurses take the National Certification Licensing Exam developed by nurses, which measures minimum competence for safe nursing practice. Nurses obtain certification in specialized areas of nursing practice from nurse specialty organizations. Some states require continuing education for continued licensure.
Legal reinforcement of professional standards	All nurses are held liable for their actions based on what the reasonable and prudent nurse would do in a given client care situation. Individual state boards of nursing have the power to restrict the practice of nursing within a state.
Ethical practice	The American Nurses' Association has published *The Nurses' Code of Ethics,* last updated in 2001.
Creation of a collegial subculture	Professional nursing organizations offer networking opportunities, shared governance and clinical practice partnership models, and they enhance collegiality among staff nurses and nursing administration.
Intrinsic rewards	Many nurses derive a deep personal satisfaction from making a difference in the lives of clients and families one person at a time. Some nurses view the profession as an opportunity to practice religious beliefs on a daily basis.
Public acceptance	Nursing was ranked as the most honest and ethical profession of all the professions (The Gallup Organization, 2003).[a]

[a]The Gallup Organization (2003). Nursing ranks first as the most honest and ethical profession. Available online at http://www.gallup.com/poll/content/login.aspx?ci=14236. Accessed Feb. 1, 2004.

and science of nursing, BSN programs also emphasize the importance of a liberal education, nursing research, and community health nursing.

In the 1960s, diploma nursing programs educated 84% of newly licensed professional nurses. ADN programs blossomed from 1960 until 1991, when they educated 65% of new professional nurses. BSN programs enjoyed substantial growth in this time frame, and 37% of newly licensed nurses graduated from them in 1997. Over the past decade, ADN programs have prepared around 60% of all new graduates, BSN programs accounted for approximately 36% of new nurses, and diploma nursing program graduates accounted for 3–4% of all newly licensed nurses (National Council of State Boards of Nursing, 2007).

Intellectual Characteristics

Because nurses make decisions that affect clients' lives, nurses need the intellectual capability to master scientific concepts, understand the impact of self on others, use this information in clinical practice, and understand potential consequences for alternative actions (American Association of Colleges of Nursing [AACN], 2007). Professional nurses possess the following three intellectual characteristics:

1. A body of knowledge on which professional practice is based
2. A specialized education to transmit this body of knowledge to others
3. The ability to use the knowledge in critical and creative thinking

Because of the global nature of professional nursing to meet client care needs, nurses frequently use knowledge that originated in other professional disciplines. However, they use the cognitive skills of critical and creative thinking to adapt this knowledge to the realm of professional nursing practice.

Body of Knowledge

Professional practice is based on a body of knowledge derived from experience (leading to expertise) and research (leading to theoretical foundations for knowledge and practice). Most state boards of nursing (SBN) specify that an ADN serves as the minimal educational qualification for practice as a registered nurse. Most states require advanced education and professional certification for nurses who assume advanced practice nursing. Professional nurses make clinical judgments based on solid, scientific rationales. They modify plans and action to meet the demands of specific client situations. ADN programs tend to emphasize technical skills and scientifically established methods to respond to specific client situations, and may contribute to a dependent nurse role in clinical practice. ADN nurses may tend to seek the "right" answer and do things the way they have always been done. For example, pain medications may be withheld because "4 hours have not passed since the last dose of medication."

Liberal arts education serves as a hallmark of professional education. A liberal education provides a knowledge base that enhances a person's ability to practice effective citizenship, communicate effectively, appreciate advantages of diverse viewpoints, and understand more deeply the artistic aspects of what it means to be human. Liberal arts courses foster the development of thinking and communication skills, cognizance of historical contributions, understanding of science, exploration of personal values, appreciation of the fine arts, and sensitivity of human diversity (AACN, 2007). Knowledge and skills derived from a liberal education enhance the nurse's ability to adapt knowledge and skills to novel situations through the use of global rather than narrow thinking.

Whether nursing has a unique body of knowledge or applies knowledge borrowed from the fields of medical, behavioral, or physical science has been a matter of debate. In the early days of nursing, nurses derived knowledge through intuition, tradition, and experience, or by borrowing it from other disciplines (Kalisch & Kalisch, 2004). However, the nursing profession uses nursing models and frameworks as a foundation for practice. The models and frameworks have provided guidance for nurse researchers to substantiate scientifically the unique contributions that nurses make in health care delivery.

Specialized Education

The National Council of State Boards of Nursing (NCSBN) coordinates efforts to license registered and practical nurses. The NCSBN Nursing Licensure Examination for Registered Nurses (NCLEX-RN) provides computer adaptive testing that measures minimal competence for safe professional nursing practice. Exam content includes health promotion, pharmacotherapeutics, nursing assessment, clinical decision making, nursing interventions, and evaluating client care outcomes.

Education for other health care professions (pharmacists, social workers, physical therapists, occupational therapists, chaplains, and physicians) requires postbaccalaureate education. Some leaders in nursing have proposed requiring a master's degree (or even a doctorate) as the educational entry level for professional nursing. The recent approach of offering interdisciplinary education by some collegiate health sciences programs provides nursing students an opportunity to collaborate with other future interprofessional health team members.

Efforts during the mid-1980s resulted in **differentiated competencies** for ADN- and BSN-prepared nurses. The agreed-upon role competencies appear in Table 1-4 (Primm, 1987). ADN competencies tend to center around caregiver, counselor, and educator roles, while BSN competencies expand to include the roles of client advocate, colleague coordinator, and change agent. ADN nurses are educated to provide nursing care to persons with similar health alterations in structured settings, whereas BSN-prepared nurses are educated to engage in independent thinking and to provide nursing care to persons with complex and differing health alterations within a variety of settings, including the community. BSNs also assume responsibility for developing research-based care protocols, assume nursing management positions, and coordinate care for persons with complex, interactive health care needs.

Questions for Reflection 1-3

1. Do I agree with the table of differentiated competencies for associate degree- and baccalaureate degree-prepared nurses?
2. Why or why not?

In the 1990s, the PEW Health Professions Commission (1995, p. 34) proposed focusing "associate preparation on the entry-level hospital setting and nursing home practice, baccalaureate on the hospital-based care management and community-based practice, and master's degree for specialty practice in the hospital and independent practice as a primary care provider." The Commission also emphasized the importance of strengthening career mobility paths within the nursing profession (PEW Health Professions Commission, 1998). Aiken, Clarke, Cheung, Sloane, and Silber (2003) have the only published study to date comparing surgical patient mortality with the educational level of registered nurses caring for them. The study findings suggest that when clients receive care in an acute care unit staffed with 50% BSN-prepared nurses, mortality is reduced by 5% and there are substantial reductions in incidences of failure to rescue, nosocomial pneumonia, and pulmonary failure. In 2007, the Agency for Healthcare Research and Quality examined the findings of multiple studies using meta-analysis techniques. The findings are presented in Research Brief 1-1. Unfortunately, there is little published research information about the impact of educational level on the quality and safety of client care.

Graduate nursing education programs offer advanced education for nurses interested in pursuing careers as advanced practice nurses (certified nurse midwifery, nurse practitioners, or clinical specialists), or in nursing education, nursing administration, or nursing informatics. Most graduate nursing education programs offer a master's degree. A master's degree in nursing can usually be completed within 3 years if a student assumes a full-time plan of study. Most programs give students up to 7 years to complete graduate work.

The AACN (2004) cited problems with current educational preparation of advanced practice nurses (APNs). First, the amount of time spent by nurses engaged in nursing graduate study surpassed the amount of time spent by members in other disciplines earning master's degrees (45 versus 60 credit hours). Second, APNs with current

TABLE 1-4

Differentiated Practice for AD- and BSN-Prepared Nurses

AD-Prepared Nurses	BSN-Prepared Nurses
Provide direct care to individual clients with common, well-defined nursing diagnoses while considering clients' familial relationships.	Provide direct care to clients with many different nursing diagnoses using nursing process to define individualized and complex interactive nursing diagnoses while considering the client relationships within a family and community.
Practice within a structured setting that is a geographic or situated environment where policies, procedures, and protocols provide provisions for health care.	Practice within structured or nonstructured settings for families, groups, aggregates, and communities. The lack of formalized policies and protocols necessitates the use of independent nursing decisions.
Use basic therapeutic communication skills with a focal client group and coordinate efforts with other health team members to meet client-focused needs.	Use complex communication skills with clients, collaborate with other health team members, and assume an accountable charge role for client care in a variety of settings.
Recognize the focal client's need for information and modify standardized teaching plans.	Assess client information needs and design individualized client teaching plans.
Acknowledge that nursing research influences nursing practice and assist in standardized data collection procedures.	Collaborate with nursing researchers to incorporate nursing research findings into nursing practice. Develop research-based nursing protocols.
Organize client care aspects for which the nurse is responsible.	Manage comprehensive client care for clients for whom the charge nurse is responsible.
Maintain accountability for own practice and aspects of care delegated to peers, licensed practical (vocational) nurses, and unlicensed assistive personnel.	Maintain accountability for own practice and aspects of care delegated to other nursing personnel consistent with their levels of education, licensure, and expertise.
Plan and implement nursing care consistent with the overall admission to post-discharge plan within a specified work period.	Plan nursing care on identified needs of clients from admission until after discharge.
Practice within the legal and ethical parameters of nursing.	Practice within the legal and ethical parameters of nursing.

master's degrees specified a need for more education to meet the demands of advanced practice. The AACN proposed that all future APNs would earn a doctor of nursing practice and that a new nurse role, the clinical nurse leader (CNL), would be the new model for graduate nursing education. The CNL would be a nurse generalist (not an advanced practice nurse) who would be capable of providing care in all health care arenas. AACN envisions the CNL as a nurse who would provide "care in all health settings at the point of care, and assumes accountability for client care outcomes by coordinating, delegating, and supervising the care provided by the health care team" (AACN, 2004, p. 10).

Postgraduate nursing education leads to a doctorate in nursing. Nurses enrolled in these programs generate new nursing knowledge by executing original nursing research studies. Traditional doctoral nursing programs offer a philosophy degree (PhD) to prepare nurse researchers and collegiate faculty. Some doctoral nursing programs offer clinical doctorates such as doctor of nursing (DNS), doctor of nursing science (DNSc), or doctor of nursing practice (DNP) to prepare nurses for a specific area such as advanced clinical practice and nursing education. Grants and scholarships are available for nurses interested in doctoral work.

Research Brief 1-1

Kane, R. L., Shamlian, T., Mueller, C., & Wilt, T. (2007, March). Nursing staffing and quality of care (Evidence Report/Technology Assessment No. 151, AHRQ Publication No. 07-E005, prepared by the Minnesota Evidence-Based Practice Center under Contract No. 290-02-0009). Rockville, MD: Agency of Healthcare Research and Quality.

The authors reviewed 94 studies published between 1999 and 2006 in the United States and Canada. Using the meta-analysis technique, they examined patient care unit factors, hospital-related factors, nursing organization factors, nursing staffing policies, and individual nurse factors on the outcomes of client care in acute care hospitals. They found only one published study that addressed the educational level of the nurses and multiple articles related to RN staffing patterns on client outcomes.

Some of the key findings of the study revealed that individual nursing factors and years of clinical experience positively affected client care outcomes, with BSN preparation and increased years of nursing experience (greater than 7.85 years) improving the mortality rate of hospitalized clients. When the RN-to-client ratio was reduced from 1:5 to 1:4 clients, on a given shift there were statistically significant reductions in failure to rescue falls, urinary tract infection, nosocomial pneumonia, and pulmonary failure. The length of stay for clients in intensive care and surgical units also decreased. The reduction in nurse client loads resulted in a 6% reduction in mortality for all hospitalizations. When nurses have a voice and autonomy over their practice as well as a reduced workload, there is an increase in RN job satisfaction and retention. When nurses and physicians collaborated as equal professionals, client adverse outcomes were also reduced. The study also found that medication and treatment error increased threefold when RNs worked shifts exceeding 12.5 hours.

When multiple studies are analyzed together, the results have increased likelihood of accuracy and validity. However, this study captured data that failed to take into account the support systems offered to the nurses such as the skills mix of UAP and LPN/LVNs; the use of rapid response teams; access to resources such as pharmacists, advanced practice nurses, clinical nurse specialists, and nurse managers; and individual nurse factors such as competence, leadership abilities, organizational skills, and job performance. More research is needed to establish evidence demonstrating differences in client outcomes based on staffing patterns and mixes, the educational level of the registered nurse, the availability of support systems and resources, and the effects of the length of shifts that nurses work.

Using Knowledge by Critical Thinking

Critical thinking has cognitive and affective characteristics. Critical thinking imposes standards (Paul, 1992) and prevents illogical thinking. As critical thinkers, nurses "exhibit these habits of mind: confidence, contextual perspective, creativity, flexibility, inquisitiveness, intellectual integrity, intuition, open-mindedness, perseverance and reflection. Practicing nurses have cognitive skills of analyzing, applying standards, discriminating, information seeking, logical reasoning, predicting, and transforming knowledge" (Scheffer & Rubenfeld, 2000, p. 357). Professional nurses use critical thinking as they practice in order to make optimal clinical decisions.

Creative Thinking

Considered an essential component of critical thinking (Scheffer & Rubenfeld, 2000), creative thinking generates alternative approaches to clinical situations. **Creative thinking** requires an ability to think outside of what usually is done and results in novel approaches to client care. If not tempered with critical thinking, solutions generated with creative thinking may be hazardous. For example, nurses follow care standards when providing client care. Suppose a nurse uses an alternative health treatment such as therapeutic touch (TT) to reduce client pain that results in deep relaxation and hypotension.

If the hypotension results in the client fainting when getting out of bed after the TT session and sustaining an injury, the nurse is accountable for the adverse outcome. Nurses engage in creative thinking when confronted with clients who have complex integrative health problems that require individually designed plans to attain desired outcomes.

Reflective Thinking

Reflective thinking is engaging in purposeful analysis about what one is currently doing and about what one has done (Schon, 1987). Reflection plays a key role in professional nursing practice. Consider the following clinical situation: Ms. S. has advanced cancer and lives in constant pain. Because the pain is unbearable, Ms. S's physician orders patient-controlled analgesia (PCA) with morphine. Ms. S is fearful that the morphine will not ease her pain, will result in addiction, and will produce a loss of consciousness. Her fear and anxiety cause increased muscle tension. As the nurse initiates the morphine drip, she remembers the pharmacologic action and potentially adverse effects of the morphine. She educates Ms. S about morphine and how best to use the PCA device for optimal pain control. As the nurse talks with Ms. S., she performs a back massage, knowing the theoretical benefits of human touch and the physiologic response to muscle massage. When thinking about and using theory in daily practice, nurses engage in reflection in action (Schon, 1983). Reflection in action occurs when nurses think about theoretical and scientific principles while delivering client care (Clarke, James, & Kelly, 1996; Kim, 1999; Powell, 1989).

Schon (1983, 1987) advocated for reflection on action, another form of professional reflection. Reflection on action occurs when the professional practitioner conducts a retrospective analysis of action taken (Clarke et al., 1996; Schon, 1987). The nurse analyzes care given to Ms. S, considering what interventions were implemented and which were or were not successful. Reflection on action enables the practitioner to develop a deeper understanding of practice and provides a vehicle to learn from experience (Clarke et al.; Schon). Journal writing also provides practice with reflection on action. Cognitive skills such as critical, creative, and reflective thinking help nurses make sound clinical decisions when providing client care.

Independent Clinical Decision Making

Professional nurses make independent decisions to solve problems in clinical practice. Sometimes, nurses act prematurely because of inadequate information and insufficient time to generate alternative approaches. Consider the following situation.

Problem: Which of the following actions would you take with a patient whose visitors insist on staying beyond the visiting hours established by hospital policy?

1. Possible Action 1: Tell the patient and the visitors that the visitors must leave.
2. Possible Action 2: Allow the visitors to stay for an additional hour.
3. Possible Action 3: Explore the reasons why the visitors want to stay and the significance of having the visitors spend time with the patient. Base the decision on the result of information generated.

Discussion: The nurse uses critical thinking to realize that collecting more information surrounding the situation will result in an optimal decision. Perhaps the visitors have arrived from out of town and have no place to stay. Maybe the client has not seen them in a long time or the client may be afraid to be left alone in the hospital the night before a potentially life-threatening procedure. When nurses use critical thinking and logical reasoning to support actions taken, they make effective clinical decisions.

Nursing Process

Nurses use nursing process, a systematic thinking method to process information about specific client care situations. Basically, nursing process is a problem-solving approach that consists of five steps: assessment, diagnosis, planning, implementation, and evaluation. Figure 1-2 depicts the steps of nursing process. Assessment consists of collecting subjective (what clients say) and objective (measured or verifiable by another) information about clients. Nurses then categorize data into clusters to determine nursing diagnoses (an actual or potential client response) upon which a care plan is developed. After the care plan is implemented (executed), nurses evaluate the effectiveness of the plan and start the process again with assessment. Effective use of nursing process requires critical, creative, and reflective thinking.

Service to Society

Since its beginning, nursing has been associated with serving others. Many students still enter nursing "to help people," an image of the nurse shared with the public. However, the intrinsic motivation "to care" is only one way to look at caring. Morse, Bottorff, Neander, and Solberg (1991, p. 122) have identified the following five conceptualizations of caring: (1) caring as a human trait, (2) caring as a moral imperative, (3) caring as an affect, (4) caring as an interpersonal interaction, and (5) caring as a therapeutic intervention. Obviously, caring encompasses more than just intuitive concern for others. Several nursing theories use caring as a major concept or central theme.

Professional service to society requires impeccable integrity, individual responsibility for ethical practice, and lifelong commitment. Some nurses view nursing as a job,

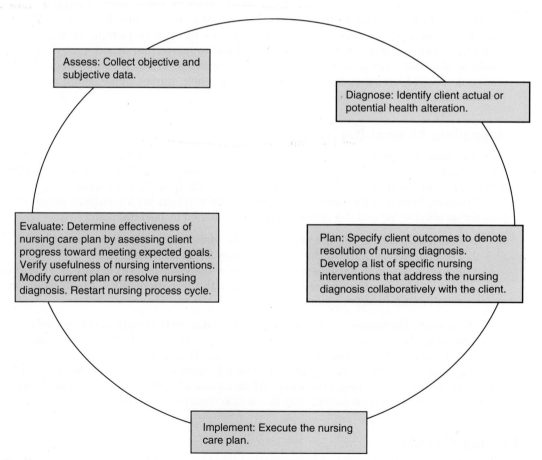

Figure 1-2
Nursing process as a continuous cycle.

rather than a professional career. Two and a half million registered nurses are employed, and 59% of these nurses are employed by acute care hospitals (Bureau of Labor Statistics [BLS], 2008). The BLS (2008) reported that approximately 21% of currently employed nurses work part-time and that 10% of all employed nurses work in more than one job. Many nurses leave the profession (permanently or temporarily) to pursue personal interests or to raise a family. Some nurses work to supplement family income, and others work because they are sole or primary income providers for a family. Nurses needing job security avoid confronting less-than-ideal nursing practice situations. Employing agencies sometimes exploit these nurses. Regardless of high client-to-nurse ratios, rotating shifts, and floating, some nurses make do and maintain the status quo. However, other nurses confront poor working conditions and always do what is best for clients.

Service to others involves ethical and legal responsibilities. Nurses must have the integrity to do what is right, especially in situations that cause moral dilemmas. Codes for nurses have been developed by the International Council of Nurses (ICN) and the ANA. These codes emphasize that nursing care recipients have basic rights and that the nurse's primary responsibility is to the client.

Service to society requires legal assurances that practitioners are competent. Credentialing systems, such as licensure, provide a means to certify minimal competence for safe practice by a person legally permitted to use the title "registered nurse." State nurse practice acts also provide legal reinforcement against incompetence by specifying the legal definition of nursing practice, the minimal education preparation for licensure, and penalties for illegal, unethical, or negligent practice. Upon initial state licensure, the nurse receives a copy of a state Nurse Practice Act (NPA). Copies of a specific NPA can be obtained in print form from the state board of nursing (a fee usually is charged), or copies may be downloaded from state board of nursing websites. When litigation occurs, courts of law hold nurses accountable for what a usual and prudent nurse would do in a particular client care situation.

Autonomy and Self-Regulation

Autonomy means that professionals have control over their practice. Autonomy involves independence, a willingness to take risks, and accountability for one's actions, as well as self-determination and self-regulation. In the United States, each state has a nursing board that governs practice that occurs within its borders. **State boards of nursing** (SBNs) regulate professional nursing practice by issuing professional licenses to qualified individuals. SBNs have legal authority to ensure that all nurses follow the state's Nurse Practice Act.

The NPA in each state defines various levels of nursing practice, determines rules that guide each level of nursing practice, and specifies guidelines for continued licensure. The SBN has legal authority and accountability to implement the NPA. Most SBNs are composed of a group of persons with nurses holding most of the positions. The state governor typically appoints persons to serve on the SBN. Requirements for licensure as a RN appear in each state's NPA. Most NPAs contain information related to reasons for licensure, nursing definitions, minimum standards for nursing education programs, licensure requirements, licensure exemptions, reasons for license revocation, endorsement provisions for nurses licensed in other states, development of a state board of examiners, nursing board responsibilities, and penalties for practicing nursing without a license or not in accordance with the state NPA. Each SBN has the responsibilty for carrying out activities covered in its NPA.

In 1978, all 50 SBNs saw a need for a united approach to nursing licensure and education. They formed the NCSBN, which has developed licensure examinations for professional and practical nursing, a mutual compact for interstate nursing licensure, and educational materials for new and experienced nurses.

As in the United States, Canadian legislation to regulate nursing practice is passed by the provincial and territorial governments. In all provinces (except Ontario), the regulation of professional nurse registration lies with the provincial or territorial professional nursing associations. In Ontario, the College of Nurses of Ontario assumes responsibility for the regulation of professional practice. Canadian nursing regulatory bodies determine educational and practice standards along with defining the scope of nursing practice. They also specify who may use the title of RN and outline mechanisms for professional discipline. Finally, the regulatory bodies also approve educational programs to prepare persons for entry into practice and establish continuing educational and competency requirements for members of the nursing profession (Brunke, 2003).

Because the profession of nursing defines nursing practice, sets practice standards, and has established mechanisms to discipline members failing to meet practice standards, nursing fulfills the element of autonomy and self-regulation. In some cases, the regulatory bodies also provide a means for professional nurses to engage in activities resulting in the creation of a collegial subculture, another hallmark of a profession.

A Collegial Subculture (Accrediting, Professional, and Student Nursing Organizations)

Professions also have a collegial subculture in order to support each other and ensure continuance. Professional nurses have a variety of professional nursing organizations that create a collegial subculture.

Professional Nursing Organizations

Like other professions, nursing has **professional organizations** that set standards, advocate, and provide networking opportunities for members. Professional nursing organizations foster the development of collegial relationships among nurses. International and national professional nursing organizations develop standards for professional practice. American nursing organizations offer certification programs for advanced nursing practice. Professional nursing organizations can be divided into two categories: **general-purpose nursing organizations** (that address the issues and concerns of all nurses) and **specialized nursing organizations** (that address specific issues and concerns of nurses practicing within a specific specialized practice arena). Participation in a specialty nursing organization links nurses who practice in a particular area and creates subcultures of nurses with common interests within the nursing profession. Each nursing organization specifies its mission, goals, and constituency. The *"American Journal of Nursing* 2008 Career Guide" (*American Journal of Nursing*, 2008) lists 122 nurse specialty organizations. Some nurses believe that membership in specialty organizations better fits their professional needs than membership in a general nursing organization. Unfortunately, only about 10% of professional nurses belong to the ANA (DeLeskey, 2003). Some (DeLeskey, 2003; Milstead, 2008) have argued that if all professional nurses would join a single, general-purpose nursing organization, nurses would become more influential in health care delivery and policy formation. The following discussion presents some of the major broad-purpose organizations.

National League for Nursing

The **National League for Nursing (NLN)** strives to improve and advance the quality of nursing education so that the nursing workforce will be prepared to meet the health care needs of diverse populations in the continuously changing health care environment. The NLN mission statement (2007) denoted, "The National League for Nursing promotes excellence in nursing education to build a strong and diverse nursing workforce" (p. 2). In 2007, the NLN adopted the core values of caring, integrity, diversity, and excellence to guide its work and services. The organization's Strategic Plan 2007–2012 specifies the following goals: to (1) become the recognized national and international leader in nursing education; (2) construct a sustainable, diverse membership that leads the organization; (3) represent nurse educators and champion to uphold their interests in the areas of politics, academics, and professional issues; and (4) "promote evidence-based nursing education and the scholarship of teaching" (NLN, p. 3). The NLN Accrediting Commission accredits associate's degree, diploma, baccalaureate, and upper-degree nursing programs.

Along with its accreditation activities, the NLN provides consultation services, continuing education programs, analysis of statistical data related to nursing education and nursing workforce resources, various examination and testing services, information about legislative affairs affecting nursing, journals, continuing education seminars, grants for nurse educators conducting research, nurse educator certification, and a variety of information packages to promote recruitment and the image of professional nursing. NLN membership is available to nursing education institutions, nurses, other health care professionals, and anyone interested in improving the quality of nursing education.

American Association of Colleges of Nursing

American Association of Colleges of Nursing (AACN) membership consists exclusively of deans and directors of baccalaureate and higher-degree nursing programs. In 1997, AACN established two separate entities: a commission for baccalaureate and higher-degree program accreditation called the Commission on Collegiate Nursing Education, and an alliance of all professional nursing organizations to streamline the credentialing of advanced practice nurses. Criticisms of AACN include aggravating tensions among education programs offering various nursing degrees, limiting membership to deans and directors, and emphasizing the importance of the baccalaureate degree as a minimal entry level for professional nursing (Gelman, Bellack, & Berkman, 1999).

National Council of State Boards of Nursing

The **National Council of State Boards of Nursing (NCSBN)** and individual State Boards of Nursing bear the responsibility for protecting the public from fraudulent and unsafe nursing practice. The NCSBN assumes the responsibility for development and administration of the nursing licensing examination (NCLEX) for professional and practical/vocational nurses (Bower, 1999). Along with licensure examination, the NCSBN keeps records on nursing license suspensions, tracks professional nursing demographics, and spearheads an effort toward interstate licensure. In collaboration with the ANA and other advanced nursing practice groups, the NCSBN and SBNs set guidelines for licensure of advanced practice nurses at state levels (Bower).

American Nurses Association

The **American Nurses Association**, the oldest professional nursing organization in the United States, was officially established in 1911 (Flanagan, 1976). Membership criteria require professional nursing licensure. When professional nurses join the national organization, they obtain membership at the state and local district levels. The ANA represents nurses in all 50 states, the District of Columbia, Guam, and the Virgin Islands. The ANA offers a wide variety of services to members and plays a key role in promoting healthy workplaces for nurses. The ANA participates in the following activities: continuing education programs for nurses; certification programs for specialized and advanced practice; nurse workforce data; political activism and public policy analysis; programs to promote the economic and general welfare for nurses; and the development and publication of nursing practice standards, handbooks, journals, newsletters, social policy statements, and an ethical code. Membership provides discounts on nurse liability insurance, publications, journal subscriptions, conferences, and online educational programs.

Through the ANA's Congress on Nursing Economics and Nursing Practice, standards and programs are developed for nursing education, practice, research, organized nursing services, economic security, employment, and human rights. ANA participates in national nursing issues through membership in various national nursing councils that meet regularly to discuss issues and concerns about nursing practice. The ANA also sponsors activities of the American Academy of Nursing, a group of distinguished nurses who have made major contributions to the nursing profession, and the American Nurses Foundation, a program that provides funding for nursing research and other projects to advance the nursing profession. The ANA is also a member organization of the International Council of Nurses.

The International Council of Nurses

The **International Council of Nurses (ICN)** unites national nursing organizations from 128 nations into a single confederation and is located in Geneva, Switzerland. The founders included nurses from nursing organizations in Great Britain, Canada, Germany, Scandinavia, and the United States. Since 1899, the ICN has worked to preserve the professional welfare of nurses, address interests of women, and improve global health. The mission of the ICN is "to represent nursing worldwide, advancing the profession and influencing health policy" (ICN, 2001). The ICN strives to advance the profession and practice of nursing globally while bringing nurses from across the world together and influencing health care policies. The ICN addresses a wide array of nursing concerns including nursing regulatory issues, the global standardization and credentialing of nurses, human rights, ethics, the socioeconomic welfare of nurses, occupational safety, health policy formation, career development, and position statements on health issues.

The ICN serves as an advocate for nurses and for all people of the world. Current efforts by the ICN focus on establishing a global definition of professional nursing practice, addressing the global shortage of nurses, credentialing nursing competence, measuring the value of professional nursing contributions on client outcomes, addressing a variety of global health issues, and furthering advanced nursing practice. The organization has advised the United Nations on global health issues. The ICN has published position statements that have been presented to governments to consider when making health care policy decisions.

Sigma Theta Tau International

Four nursing students at the University of Indiana formed Sigma Theta Tau in 1922. **Sigma Theta Tau International (STTI)** became an international honor society for nurses in 1985. The organization has 405,000 members in more than 463 chapters; members reside in 75 countries. International chapters are located in 22 countries located on all continents except Antarctica. STTI holds membership in the Association of College Honor Societies (STTI, 2007).

To become a member, a nurse must demonstrate superior scholastic achievement, professional leadership potential, or marked achievement in the nursing field. STTI contributes to the advancement of nursing via research grants, conferences, and publications. The organization publishes the printed journal *The Journal of Nursing Scholarship* and the electronic journal *The Online Journal of Knowledge Synthesis*. STTI also sponsors writers' seminars, has a media development program, and bestows awards for outstanding contributions to the nursing profession. Local chapters also present educational programs, awards, and scholarships. STTI runs the Center for Nursing Scholarship and the Virginia Henderson International Nursing Library, a state-of-the-art electronic library and information resource center (Vance, 1999). The database of the electronic library holds more than 30,000 abstracts of research studies and nursing conferences (STTI, 2007).

National Student Nurses' Association

The **National Student Nurses' Association (NSNA)** is an inclusive student association from all types of nursing educational programs. Student members finance and run the organization. As an autonomous organization, NSNA goals, according to the group's mission statement (2008), are to:

- Mentor nursing students preparing for initial licensure as registered nurses;
- Convey the standards, ethics, and skills that students will need as responsible and accountable leaders and members of the profession.

NSNA offers a variety of activities and services to implement its mission. The Association participates on committees of the NLN, ANA, and ICN. The NSNA Foundation administers a scholarship program and publishes the journal *Imprint*, the newsletter *NSNA News*, and a variety of reports and handbooks. As members of NSNA, students enjoy discounts on health insurance, publications, conference attendance fees, and state board review courses.

Questions for Reflection 1-4

1. Am I currently a member of a professional nursing organization? Why or why not?
2. If you are a member of an organization: How would I go about recruiting another nurse to join a professional nursing organization?
3. If you are not a member of an organization: What factors prevent you from joining one?
4. Is a nurse more professional if he or she holds membership in a professional organization? Why or why not?

Ethical Practice

Ethical professional practice has been defined by several of the broad-purpose nursing organizations (ICN, ANA, and NSNA) by published **ethical codes** (statements defining honest, honorable, humane, and fair practice). Ethics permeates all areas of professional practice. Nurses with solid professional identities possess strong individual and professional values. Values provide the foundation for ethical dimensions of professional practice. Caring emerges as a shared value within the nursing profession. Clients trust nurses with their lives. Professional nurses must never violate this sacred trust. Sometimes, professional duties conflict with each other. Nurses have individual, professional, and societal duties (Bandman & Bandman, 1995; Bower, 1999; Fowler, 2008). As science and technology advance and resources dwindle, nurses confront ever-increasingly difficult, complex, and conflicting issues in daily practice. Ethical systems provide nurses with a set of values and behaviors to use when situations without clearly right or wrong answers arise. By studying ethics, nurses identify and examine personal biases and values. A code of ethics assists nurses to make decisions when confronted with ethical dilemmas.

Bandman and Bandman (1995) stated, "Effective nurses function as moral agents" (p. 46). When acting as moral agents, nurses assume responsibility and accountability to do no harm. Nurses assume responsibility for action when they assume blame or credit for their own actions. Accountability encompasses the ability to provide sound reasons, explanations, and defenses for actions taken (Sullivan & Christopher, 1999). Nurses encounter many practice situations with multiple correct actions and answers. When this occurs, nurses agonize about which of the imperfect and alternative choices would serve the best interests of the client. Table 1-5 identifies some common ethical dilemmas encountered by nurses in clinical practice.

TABLE 1-5

Ethical Issues Encountered by Professional Nurses in Practice

Ethical Principle	Definition	Practice Dilemma(s)
Sanctity of human life	Human life as the most important characteristic of being human	Quality versus quantity of life Pro-choice versus pro-life Capital punishment Withholding life-saving treatments Euthanasia and assisted suicide
Autonomy	Individual freedom to make rational and unconstrained decisions	Lack of client knowledge about available treatments Coercive power Paternalism Cognitively impaired individuals Individual decisions that interfere with another person's rights
Veracity	Truth-telling	Whistleblowing Concealing a chemical or physical abuse pattern Falsification of legal document to cover errors Covering up reasons Informed consent
Distributive justice	Allocation of limited resources	Managed care Reduced access to care based on inability to pay for services Judicious use of high-tech equipment for prolonging life Deciding who gets resources based on fitness, cost-benefit analysis, equal chance, equal share, or equal consideration
Respect for personal beliefs	Accepting individual beliefs as a basis for decision making	Religious preferences not to subject self or family to "impure" acts Conflicts of research evidence on personal health habits
Nonmalfeasance	Do no harm	Securing court orders for life-saving therapies Withholding therapy Assisted suicide Right to leave clients alone
Beneficence	Do only good	Balancing what is morally right with what is legal and practical. Highly individualized for each situation and shares actions with many of the principles presented above.
Confidentiality	Keeping privileged information private	Reporting health problems that interfere with safe driving to state officials Telling families about poor prognoses before informing clients Disclosing alternative lifestyles
Fidelity	Keeping promises	Not keeping one's word Failing to follow up with what one says one will do
Justice	Treating people fairly	Treating clients differently based on their ability to pay or other sociocultural characteristic Singling out special clients for extra nursing care Denying health care access to anyone

For ethical decision making, nurses use several codes of ethics. Common principles appear in original versions of the ICN *Code for Nurses: Ethical Concepts Applied to Nursing* (2003) and the ANA *Code for Nurses with Interpretive Statements* (ANA, 2001). Nurses can read specific ethical codes online. Despite recent updates to ethical codes, all contain the following common principles: (1) respect for human dignity and uniqueness, (2) protection of confidential information, (3) acts to safeguard persons receiving nursing care, (4) responsibility and accountability for nursing actions, (5) maintenance of nursing competence, (6) use of informed judgment, (7) participation in research and other activities to generate new nursing knowledge, (8) participation in activities to improve and implement nursing standards, (9) integrity of the nursing profession, and (10) collaboration with other health care professionals and consumers. Ethical codes are morally, not legally, binding.

Societal Acceptance: Legal Reinforcement of Professional Standards

Society holds professional nurses accountable for abiding by standards of professional nursing practice. The legal system protects consumers from unsafe nursing practice. Along with licensure, the legal system holds nurses responsible for professional actions. **Licensure** refers to "a form of credentialing whereby permission is granted by a legal authority to do an act, without such permission, action would be illegal, trespass, a tort, or otherwise not allowable" (Loquist, 1999, p. 105). A professional nursing license is a legal document that certifies that an individual has met minimal standards for qualified practice. As a state function, licensure protects citizens from unsafe or incompetent health care providers. Upon licensure, nurses become registered in a particular state to practice professional nursing. Registration denotes the "enrolling or recording the name of a qualified individual on an official roster by an agency of government" (Loquist, p. 15). Although licensure is permanent (unless it is revoked for illegal or immoral behavior), registration must be renewed periodically (usually every 1 to 2 years) by paying a fee to each state in which current registration is desired.

Licensure as a RN carries with it the responsibility for safe and competent practice. If injury, unnecessary suffering, or death should occur as a result of care delivered by a nurse, the nurse may be held legally responsible. States expect all licensed professional nurses to act reasonably and prudently and judge their actions compared with a nurse with the same education and experience within a given situation.

Nurses must know and function within the legal parameters of nursing practice in the state where nursing services are offered. If nurses have ethical or legal concerns about medical treatment or client situations, they must share them with medical and institutional authorities. Because nurses are responsible for client well-being, they may refuse to execute a treatment, but must not attempt to circumvent the physician by interfering with treatment without the physician's knowledge. Nurses and physicians must collaborate, not compete with each other.

Future Work for the Nursing Profession to Attain Full Professional Status

Because the nursing profession fails to meet all characteristics of a profession, nursing can be thought of as an emerging profession. Several barriers to fulfilling all criteria for professional stature have occurred. First, professional nursing has multiple levels of education for entry into the profession. Most professions have a single, specialized plan of study before persons can enter them. Many recipients of nursing services do not know the differences in educational preparation. To them, a nurse is a nurse.

Along with an inconsistent educational entry level, many nurses have become specialists in a particular area of practice (e.g., oncology, cardiology, or critical care). Frequently, some of these nurses find themselves having to choose between joining a specialty or general-purpose nursing organization because of limited time and monetary resources.

Other nurses may not even join a professional organization (DeLeskey, 2003). By failing to unite, nurses reduce their political effectiveness and collective identity. The lack of working collectively also may create opportunity for others to exploit nurses.

In addition, society tends to devalue nurses more than other health team members. Although nurses hold the lives of other persons in their hands when they practice, some clients view them as "hired" help. In a capitalistic society, the amount of money received for a service is based on its perceived value. Professional nurses tend to receive much less compensation when compared to other interprofessional health team members. According to the U.S. Bureau of Health Professions (BHPR; 2006a), the average salary for full-time employed RNs was $57,785 (including generalist and advanced practice nursing). In 2006, Mee (2007) surveyed 1100 RNs about their salaries. Mee found that RNs with ADs earned less than RNs with a BSN ($50,100 to $53,300) and nurses with graduate nursing degrees earned an average of $60,500. In comparison, based on 2006 data from the BHPR, physician generalists earned a mean income of $149,850 (mean salaries for some specialty physicians topped $200,000), pharmacists earned $93,500, physical therapists earned $68,050, and dental hygienists earned $63,430 (BHPR, 2006b). The disparity in salary could be related to the fact that all of the above health team members (with the exception of dental hygienists) have received at least a master's degree in their practice area (BHPR, 2006b).

Professional nurses must work together to showcase the contributions they make to society while developing methods to overcome the barriers from attaining full status as a profession. Currently, 2.53 million RNs make contributions to health care delivery in the United States (BLS, 2008). Professional nursing has more numbers than any of the other members of the interdisciplinary health team. If efforts by the profession were channeled toward cooperation rather than competition, nurses could make substantial contributions toward the betterment of health for all.

 ## SUMMARY AND SIGNIFICANCE TO PRACTICE

Because the nursing profession fails to meet all criteria for a profession, nursing is sometimes referred to as an emerging profession. The process of becoming a professional nurse involves change and growth throughout various stages of a career. Over time, being a professional nurse may become embedded into one's personal identity and being. The profession calls upon nurses to engage in moral and ethical practice to provide what is best for clients. Through educational and occupational experiences, the nurse develops attitudes, beliefs, and skills as knowledge expands and deepens. A professional nurse should expect to commit to a life of continuous learning, growth, and development. Any change in clinical specialty practice area and formal education results in resocialization. The professional nurse assumes many roles when engaged in clinical practice. Effective implementation of the roles associated with professional nursing practice requires deep commitment; authentic caring; genuine compassion; technical competence; self-confidence; cognitive, clinical, and communication skills; along with an ability to work in and cope with nonstop change, highly complex systems, and chaos.

FROM THEORY TO PRACTICE

1. What advice would you give to Sue as she enters a baccalaureate nursing program? Why do you think each piece of advice you will give her is important?
2. Has your perception of professional nursing changed since reading this chapter? Why or why not?
3. What do you think is a major barrier to nursing achieving status as a profession? Why do you think this is a major barrier? What steps could the nursing profession take to eliminate this barrier to attaining full status as a profession?
4. Do you belong to a professional nursing organization? Why or why not?

WWW INTERNET EXERCISES

This chapter has provided a broad overview of the profession of nursing. These Internet exercises will enhance your understanding of the chapter material and help you appreciate what it means to be a professional nurse.

1. Visit the website http://www.nursingworld.org, the official website of the American Nurses Association. Analyze the benefits and costs of membership. Would you join the ANA? Why or why not?

2. Using the search engine of your choice, type in any specialized area of nursing practice and see if you can find a professional nursing organization to support nurses practicing in that field of nursing. Analyze the benefits and costs of membership. Compare and contrast two professional nursing organizations.

3. Visit the website http://www.ncsbn.org. Identify key issues surrounding safe nursing practice. Discover what states have enacted the multistate compact for professional nursing practice. While there, visit your state board of nursing website using the hyperlinks and identify key information about license renewal, announcements, and news.

WWW INTERNET RESOURCES

American Nurses Association: http://www.nursingworld.org
Sigma Theta Tau International: http://www.nursingsociety.org
National League for Nursing: http://www.nln.org
American Association of Colleges of Nursing: http://www.aacn.nche.edu
The National Council of State Boards of Nursing: http://www.ncsbn.org
The International Council of Nurses: http://www.icn.ch

REFERENCES

Agnes, M. (Ed.). (2005). *Webster's new world college dictionary* (4th ed.). Cleveland, OH: Wiley.

Aiken, L. H., Clarke, S. P., Cheung, R. B., Sloane, D. M., & Silber, J. H. (2003). Educational levels of hospital nurses and surgical patient mortality. *Journal of the American Medical Association*, *290*, 1617–1623.

Alexander, J., & Tate, M. A. (1998). *Web resource evaluation techniques*. Chester, PA: Widener University.

American Association of Colleges of Nursing. (2004, October). *AACN position statement on the practice doctorate in nursing, October 2004*. Available at http://www.aacn.nche.edu/DNP/pdf/DNP.pdf. Accessed March 14, 2008.

American Association of Colleges of Nursing. (2007). *The essentials of baccalaureate education for professional nursing practice*. Washington, DC: Author.

American Journal of Nursing. (2008). *American Journal of Nursing* 2008 career guide. *American Journal of Nursing*, 109(1, Suppl.).

American Nurses Association. (2001). *Code for nurses with interpretive statements*. Washington, DC: American Nurses Publishing.

American Nurses Association. (2003). *Nursing's social policy statement* (2nd ed.). Silver Spring, MD: Author.

Bandman, E. L., & Bandman, B. (1995). *Nursing ethics through the life span* (3rd ed.). East Norwalk, CT: Appleton & Lange.

Benner, P. (1984). *From novice to expert*. Menlo Park, CA: Addison-Wesley.

Bevis, E. O., & Watson, J. (2000). *Toward a caring curriculum: A new pedagogy for nursing*. Sudbury, MA: Jones & Bartlett.

Bower, F. L. (1999). The role of professional organizations. In E. J. Sullivan (Ed.), *Creating nursing's future* (pp. 345–354). St. Louis, MO: Mosby.

Bradby, M. (1990). Status passage into nursing: Another view of the process of socialization. *Journal of Advanced Nursing*, *15*, 1220–1225.

Bridges, W. (2003). *Managing transitions, making the most of change*. Cambridge, MA: Perseus.

Broussard, P. C., & Oberleitner, M. G. (1997). Writing and thinking: A process to critical understanding. *Journal of Nursing Education*, *7*, 334–336.

Brunke, L. (2003). Canadian provincial and territorial professional organizations and colleges. In M. McIntyre & E. Thomlinson (Eds.), *Realities of Canadian nursing* (pp. 143–160). Philadelphia: Lippincott Williams & Wilkins.

Bureau of Labor Statistics (BLS). (2008). *Occupational outlook handbook 2008–2009*. Available at http://stats.bls.gov/oco/ocos083.htm. Accessed March 14, 2008.

Clarke, B., James, C., & Kelly, J. (1996). Reflective practice: Reviewing the issues and refocusing the debate. *International Journal of Nursing Studies, 33*, 171–180.

Conway, M. E. (1984). Socialization and roles in nursing. In H. H. Werley & J. J. Fitzpatrick (Eds.), *Annual review of nursing research* (Vol. 1, pp. 183–208). New York: Springer.

DeLeskey, K. (2003). Factors affecting nurses' decisions to join and maintain membership in professional associations. *Journal of PeriAnesthesia Nursing, 18*, 8–17.

Diekelmann, N. L., & Rather, M. L. (Eds.). (1993). *Transforming RN education: Dialogue and debate*. New York: National League for Nursing.

Dreyfus, H. L., & Dreyfus, S. E. (1996). The relationship of theory and practice in the acquisition of skill. In P. Benner, C. A. Tanner, & C. A. Chesla (Eds.), *Expertise in nursing practice: Caring, clinical judgment, and ethics* (pp. 29–47). New York: Springer.

Dunham, K. S. (2008). *How to survive and maybe even love nursing school!* (3rd ed.). Philadelphia: F. A. Davis.

Flanagan, L. (1976). *One strong voice*. Kansas City, MO: Lowell Press.

Fondiller, S. H. (2007). *Health professional style manual*. New York: Springer.

Fowler, M. D. M. (2008). *Guide to the code of ethics for nurses, interpretation and application*. Silver Spring, MD: American Nurses Association.

Freidson, E. (1994). *Professionalism reborn: Theory, prophecy and policy*. Chicago: University of Chicago Press.

Gelman, S. B., Bellack, J. P., & Berkman, A. K. (1999). Educational accreditation. In E. J. Sullivan (Ed.), *Creating nursing's future* (pp. 226–240). St. Louis, MO: Mosby.

Hinshaw, A. S. (1976, November). *Socialization and resocialization of nurses for professional nursing practice* (National League for Nursing Publication No. 15-1659). New York: National League for Nursing.

International Council of Nurses (ICN). (2001). About ICN. Available at http://wwwicn.ch/abouticn.htm. Accessed June 25, 2007.

International Council of Nurses (ICN). (2003). *Code for nurses: Ethical concepts applied to nursing*. Geneva: Author.

Jones, R. (2004). The science and meaning of the self. *Journal of Analytical Psychology, 49*, 217-233.

Kalisch, P., & Kalisch, B. (2004). *The advance of American nursing: A history* (4th ed.). Philadelphia: Lippincott Williams & Wilkins.

Kane, R. L., Shamlian, T., Mueller, C., & Wilt, T. (2007, March). Nursing staffing and quality of care (Evidence Report/Technology Assessment No. 151, AHRQ Publication NO. 07-E005, prepared by the Minnesota Evidence-Based Practice Center under Contract No. 290-02-0009). Rockville, MD: Agnecy of Healthcare Research and Quality.

Kim, H. S. (1999). Critical reflective inquiry for knowledge development in nursing practice. *Journal of Advanced Nursing, 29*, 1205–1212.

Kozier, B., & Erb, G. (1988). *Concepts and issues in nursing practice*. Menlo Park, CA: Addison-Wesley.

Leddy, S. K. (2003). *Integrative health promotion*. Thorofare, NJ: Slack.

Linton, R. (1945). *The cultural background of personality*. New York: Appleton.

Loquist, R. S. (1999). Regulation: Parallel and powerful. In J. A. Milstead (Ed.), *Health policy and politics: A nurse's guide*. Gaithersburg, MD: Aspen.

Lynn, M. R., McCain, N. L., & Boss, B. J. (1989). Socialization of RN to BSN. *Image, 21*, 232–237.

Malloy, A. (2005). *Stop living your job, start living your life*. Berkeley, CA: Ulysses.

Martinez, M. E. (2000). *Education as the cultivation of intelligence*. Mahwah, NJ: Lawrence Erlbaum.

Mee, C. (2007, January). A closer look at nurses' salaries. *Nursing 2007 Career Directory*, 8–10.

Miller, B. K., Adams, D., & Beck, L. (1993). A behavioral inventory for professionalism in nursing. *Journal of Professional Nursing, 9*, 290–295.

Milstead, J. A. (2008). *Health policy and politics: A nurses guide* (3rd ed.). Sudbury, MA: Jones & Bartlett.

Morse, J. M., Bottorff, J., Neander, W., & Solberg, S. (1991, Summer). Comparative analysis of conceptualizations and theories of caring. *Image, 23*, 119–126.

National Council of State Boards of Nursing. (2007). 2006 number of candidates taking NCLEX examination and percent passing by type of candidate. Available at http://www.ncsbn.org/Table_of_Pass_Rates_2006.pdf. Accessed April 20, 2009.

National League for Nursing (NLN). (2007, Summer). National League for Nursing Strategic Plan 2007–2012. *NLN Report: The Member Newsletter of the National League for Nursing*, (1), 2–3.

National Student Nurses Association. (2008). About us. Available at http://www.nsna.org/about_us.asp. Accessed April 20, 2008.

Paul, R. (1992). *Critical thinking: What every person needs to survive in a rapidly changing world* (2nd rev. ed.). Santa Rosa, CA: Foundation for Critical Thinking.

PEW Health Professions Commission. (1995). *Critical challenges: Revitalizing the health professions for the 21st century*. San Francisco: University of California, San Francisco Center for the Health Professions.

PEW Health Professions Commission. (1998). *Recreating health professional practice for a new century*. San Francisco: University of California, San Francisco Center for the Health Professions.

Powell, J. H. (1989). The reflective practitioner in nursing. *Journal of Advanced Nursing, 14*, 824–832.

Primm, P. L. (1987). Differentiated practice for ADN- and BSN-prepared nurses. *Journal of Professional Nursing, 3*, 218–225.

Quan, K. (2006). *The everything new nurse book*. Avon, MA: Adams Media.

Scheffer, B. K., & Rubenfeld, M. G. (2000). A consensus statement on critical thinking in nursing. *Journal of Nursing Education, 39*, 352–359.

Schon, D. (1983). *The reflective practitioner*. London: Temple Smith.

Schon, D. A. (1987). *Educating the reflective practitioner: Toward a new design for teaching and learning in the professions*. San Francisco: Jossey-Bass.

Shane, D. L. (1980). The returning-to-school syndrome. In S. Mirin (Ed.), *Teaching tomorrow's nurse* (pp. 119–126). Wakefield, MA: Nursing Resources.

Sigma Theta Tau International (STTI). (2007). Organizational fact sheet. Available at http://www.nursing society.org/aboutus/mission/Pages/facsheet.aspx. Accessed March 14, 2008.

Stebbins, L. F. (2006). *Student guide to research in the digital age*. Westport, CT: Libraries Unlimited.

Sullivan, M. C., & Christopher, M. M. (1999). Ethical issues. In E. J. Sullivan (Ed.), *Creating nursing's future* (pp. 241–251). St. Louis, MO: Mosby.

U.S. Bureau of Health Professions. (2006a). RN salaries. Available at http://bhpr.hrsa.gov/healthwork-force/rnsurvey04/appendixa.htm. Accessed March 22, 2008.

U.S. Bureau of Health Professions. (2006b). Salaries for healthcare professionals and technicians. *2006 Healthcare workforce reports*. Available at http://bhpr.hrsa.gove/healthworkforce/reportsMay2006 stimates/current/ones_nat.html#b29-0000. Accessed April 7, 2008.

Vance, C. (1999). Nursing in the global arena. In E. J. Sullivan (Ed.), *Creating nursing's future* (p. 334). St. Louis, MO: Mosby.

CHAPTER 2

The History Behind the Development of Professional Nursing

LEARNING OUTCOMES

By the end of this chapter, the learner will be able to:

1 Trace the history of nursing from ancient to current times.
2 Outline key societal trends that affected recruitment and retention of nurses in the workforce.
3 Explain the parallels of past history to current nursing practice.
4 Describe how history could be used to address current and future nursing issues.

VIGNETTE

Martha, Carol, and Joe received an assignment to give a class presentation on nursing history that could be used to prepare the nursing profession for a future challenge. At first, they view this assignment as just more busywork. However, as they explore the history of nursing, they come to appreciate historically significant events and persons. They acknowledge that the profession may need to look at history to solve current and future problems.

As current health care increases in scientific and technological complexity, people realize its limitations. Advances in technology permit measurement of previously unmeasured dimensions of the world. Increasingly, the field of health care has initiated targeted efforts to explain the interrelationships of health, longevity, multiculturalism, socioeconomics, and spirituality. In many ways, nursing forged a path to holistic health care. An examination of nursing history provides professional nurses with an understanding of the profession's unique place within the health care arena and how history may have answers for today's problems and future challenges.

NURSING IN ANCIENT CIVILIZATIONS (BEFORE AD 1)

Humans learned how to care for each other from observing animals tending to each other. People observed uninjured animals bringing food to injured companions and helpless off-spring. By watching animals, humans learned therapies such as licking wounds (a form of an antiseptic dressing), applying pressure to control bleeding (from apes), amputating extremities when ensnared in traps (from rats), licking salt (from deer, cows, and ante-lope), wrapping wounds in a spiral fashion (from birds), applying splints (from snipe), traveling great distances to soak in healing water (from deer), and entombing the dead (from bees). Ancient humans saw how the animals relied on each other in times of need (Nutting & Dock, 1935a).

Primitive Man

The earliest of men believed in a spirit world. Early cultures believed that a person's soul (or life-giving spirit forces) existed independently of the body. Human tragedy, including illness, was blamed on the spirit world. Certain societal members possessed special powers that could ease suffering, enhance healing, and cure diseases by appeasing the spirits. Techniques used by early healers included pummeling (a form of massage), administering herbs, exposing persons to smoke, squeezing, starving, purging, applying roots or balms to the skin, or twisting the body into various positions. Along with touch, medicine magicians frequently applied warm applications and held other healing ceremonies using drumming, smoking, and chanting to drive out evil spirits (Nutting & Dock, 1935a).

The East

As persons organized societies, the need for someone to care for the very young, injured, infirmed, and aging members arose. The ancient Hindi linked hygiene to health. Details of nursing are recorded in Lesson IX of the *Charada-Samhita*. This Indian record describes the following four qualifications for a nurse: (1) knowledge of drug preparation, (2) cleverness, (3) devotion to patients, and (4) purity of body and mind (Nutting & Dock, 1935a). These early nurses were primarily men, and nursing was viewed as a sacred serv-ice that only the purest of body and mind could perform (Nutting & Dock, 1935; Kalisch & Kalisch, 2004; Jamieson & Sewall, 1954).

In the third century BC, King Asoka developed community institutes to care for sick travelers. These precursors of hospitals were described as spacious and roomy mansions protected from strong winds, breezes, smoke, sun, dust, and rain. In **ancient nursing practice**, the sick were cared for by a body of attendants (men) noted for their purity and cleanliness of habits who were full of kindness, were clever, and possessed great skills in providing service to others. Along with good nutrition, ventilation, and a clean environ-ment, the attendants read stories, chanted hymns, played musical instruments, and con-versed with the infirmed while attending to all their needs (Nutting & Dock, 1935a). In many cases, nursing interventions that occurred in ancient times serve as the **roots of holistic nursing practice**.

Ancient Buddhist texts from Ceylon possess equally touching accounts of good deeds and philanthropy. These texts contain allusions to "thousands" of priestesses (women) whose duties included the care of the sick (Nutting & Dock, 1935a).

China

Chinese civilization began around 3000 BC on the banks of the Yellow River. The Chinese set the worth of women as the number of sons produced. Old women who bore many sons were revered and given high societal positions. The ancient Chinese developed the concept of yin (the passive, negative, feminine energy force) and yang (the active, positive, masculine energy force). They defined health as a balance of the two energy forces. Before 2000 BC, the Chinese practiced dissection, performed acupuncture, and prescribed herbal therapies to enhance health and cure illness. They used baths to reduce fever, used bloodletting to remove evil spirits from the body, and outlined detailed principles of physical examination (look, listen, ask, and feel) (Jamieson & Sewall, 1954).

Egypt

The oldest written recordings about medicine and nursing come from Egypt on papyrus and date to 3000 BC. The Ebers Papyrus outlines over 700 therapies derived from minerals, plants, and animals. The compounded prescriptions were made up in the forms of decorations, pills, tablets, injections, infusions, lozenges, powder, potions, inhalations, lotions, ointments, and plasters (Kalisch & Kalisch, 2004; Nutting & Dock, 1935a). The art of medicine in ancient Egypt consisted of two branches: the theurgic class devoted themselves to magical cures, and the practitioners used natural cures. Along with disease treatment, the Egyptians practiced public hygiene and sanitation. In all records from Egypt, there is no evidence of hospitals and nursing. However, there is mention of temple priestesses without reference to their duties (Nutting & Dock, 1935).

Babylonia

The Babylonians experienced a vastly different lifestyle than the Egyptians. They believed that numbers possessed magical powers and displayed a great interest in astrology (Jamieson & Sewall, 1954). Illness was viewed as punishment for displeasing or sinning against the gods. The Babylonians left records outlining surgical procedures, methods to banish demons, and ways to avoid evil spirits. In 1900 BC, Hammurabi developed a code that provided the first sliding scale for payment of fees for goods and services. The law specified that citizens compensate each other for transgressions equally. Therefore, a surgeon could have his hands amputated if he performed unsuccessful surgery (Nutting & Dock, 1935a; Jamieson & Sewall).

Assyria

The Assyrian civilization began about 2300 BC. Like other ancient cultures, the Assyrians credited the good and evil spirits for human conditions. Failure to abide by cultural mandates resulted in severe punishment, including mutilation and death. Medical practices centered on sacred rites for banishment of evil spirits or severe punishment for sins (Jamieson & Sewall, 1954).

Persia

In a Persian epic dated 642 BC, three kinds of physicians were mentioned. One healed by the knife, another by exorcism and incantations, and a third by using plants. Although there is no mention of nurses, there are descriptions of many procedures, many of which fall within the domain of current nursing practice (Nutting & Dock, 1935).

Palestine

The Hebrew culture adopted sanitary measures from Egypt during the period of enslavement. The ancient Hebrews adopted natural cures, but rejected the magical therapies. The Old Testament outlines food inspection, vital statistics records, and infectious disease quarantine followed by fumigation. Rabbis declared that every Hebrew had an obligation to show sympathy, cheer, and aid to the sick. One of the seven acts of charity mentioned in rabbinical literature is to visit the sick. They developed sick houses that were connected to rest houses for travelers and the destitute (Nutting & Dock, 1935a).

Greece

Like Egypt, Greece traced medical arts to divine myths. In the *Iliad*, Homer identifies Asklepios, the father of Machaon and Podalirius, as the "blameless physician." The Greeks also divided the healing arts into two branches, with one retaining priestly powers and the other having medical functions. Temples of Asklepios were reported to exist as early as 1134 BC. Hospitality was a sacred obligation in Greek culture. The "xenodochion" served as a municipal inn for strangers, the poor, and the sick in large Greek cities (Nutting & Dock, 1935a).

Besides the public xenodochion, the Greeks established "iotrions" (temples for healing services) where surgery was performed and dispensaries were located. Only persons who could be cured were admitted to the iotrions. Temples had a place devoted to the sick called the "abaton." Ruins reveal that the abaton contained a large room with an altar surrounded by smaller rooms that could accommodate one person. Along with priests, the abaton was staffed with a variety of persons including physicians, bath attendants, slaves, and priestesses. They believed that birth and death caused permanent pollution where they occurred. Therefore, the terminally ill were left on the street to die (Nutting & Dock, 1935).

The great physician Hippocrates outlined the role of physician as assisting nature to bring about a cure. Hippocrates set standards for bathing, bandaging, and other cures. Although he provided no treatise on nursing, his work specified that he used assistants (Nutting & Dock, 1935; Kalisch & Kalisch, 2004).

Rome

The Greeks introduced the Romans to medicine sometime in the third century BC. Before then, Romans believed that lost health could only be restored by the gods. The Romans constructed drains, aqueducts, good roads, sewage systems, and proper cemeteries, as well as an organized system of medicine that enhanced public health. Nero organized a Roman medical service and appointed a superintendent of court physicians. Slaves of rich families cultivated knowledge of practical medicine. Many slaves earned freedom by curing owners with their skills. The Romans reserved the best medical and nursing care for the soldiers (Nutting & Dock, 1935; Kalisch & Kalisch, 2004).

Northern Europe

In northern Europe, the ancient Teutons revered their wise women. These ancient women gathered herbs, which they knew had medicinal and remedial qualities. These women may have been the earliest prototypes of witches. As time progressed, various superstitions followed both wise women and the medicine men. According to Finnish mythology, the ancient healers practiced **white magic** that was primarily medicinal in nature. However, society grew to believe that these persons with special healing powers also had connections to evil spirits and could use "black magic" that caused natural catastrophes or human illness and injury (Nutting & Dock, 1935).

Germany

Like the northern Europeans, the Gauls and Germans highly regarded women. They believed that women could communicate with the gods more easily than men. These women possessed great knowledge and skill in medicine and surgery. German women established expertise in treating wounds from war, providing obstetrical care, and treating animals (Nutting & Dock, 1935).

Questions for Reflection 2-1

1. Are any ancient nursing interventions used to tend to the ill and infirmed today?
2. Why do you think that some ancient nursing interventions and medical therapies had to be "rediscovered"?

NURSING IN THE EARLY CHRISTIAN ERA (AD 1–500)

Roman Matrons

Women from well-established Roman families enjoyed dignified and respected positions in society. Wives were considered as equal to their husbands. The earliest women workers in the church that were concerned with nursing were the deaconesses and widows. The virgin, presbyteress, canoness, and nun appeared later. Men also performed nursing duties. Early converts to Christianity, especially the ladies of leisure, viewed comforting the afflicted as a sacred duty. Women joined the **deaconess movement** and attended to the sick in their homes. In AD 60, Phoebe became the first parish worker, friendly visitor, and district nurse and is credited as the mother of visiting nursing (Nutting & Dock, 1935a).

Early church deacons and deaconesses sought out those in need, established a system of visiting nurses, and sometimes brought the ill into their homes. As home hospitals were organized, the deaconate became associated with the work of nursing. Eventually, the bishops followed their example, and opened their homes to tend to the sick. As congregations grew and more poor persons joined them, the church established the Christian xenodochium, or home for strangers. The xenodochium contained a section for the ordinary traveler and another section for the poor and infirmed. As early as the second century, Roman converts to Christianity transformed their homes into places to care for the sick and poor. **Roman matrons** organized and delivered care to these persons in need. Nutting and Dock credited this work to the matrons named Marcella, Paula, Eustochia, Blesilla, Proba, Laeta, Lucina, Fabiola, Principia, Ansella, Lea, Melanie, Albina, and others. Nursing the sick was seen as proper penance for past sins and solace for unhappy lives (Nutting & Dock, 1935a).

Between the years of AD 249 and 263, an extensive epidemic hit Rome, resulting in many deaths of the deaconate. In AD 350, another epidemic hit the city of Edessa, where wealthy inhabitants in desperation freely gave money to Ephren to provide care for the ill. St. Ephren used the donations to build the first hospital. Along with the matrons, widows, old men, and the disenfranchised provided nursing care.

In the fifth century, Justinian granted the bishops authority over hospitals. With great zeal, the bishops built shelters, hospices, foundling asylums, and nosocomials (nursing hospitals) within the confines of monasteries. A glorious record of the religious nursing orders of men and women flourished for a thousand years. Through religious order life, women found freedom from social fetters and distasteful arranged marriages. They were free to conduct satisfying work and cultivate intellectual desires (Nutting & Dock, 1935a; Jamieson & Sewall, 1954).

Advances in Greece

Although the **early Christian nurses** were instrumental in the development of modern nursing, other groups played a key role in the advancement of nursing practice. In AD 100, Areateus emphasized the necessity of strict cleanliness of bedclothes, the use of powders on moist skin, and mouthwashes for patients who were not allowed to drink. For fevers, the room should be light and airy and the patient should be lightly covered and receive only liquids for nourishment. Excitable patients should be kept in a small, undecorated room, with constant temperature. He outlined strategies for pain control that included hot baths, fomentations, hot-water bladders, light massage, plasters, and salves. Music was also used to soothe and lull persons in distress. In AD 138, the Greeks established a maternity hospital and a home for the dying (Nutting & Dock, 1935a).

 ## NURSING IN THE MIDDLE AGES (500–1500)

As the church gained influence and power, the monasteries proliferated. Religious men and women gained social status by serving others. The first mention of a nursing uniform surfaced in 1190, when a Bavarian monk insisted that religious women wear distinctive dress in order to be recognized when out in public as they performed charitable acts. As monasteries flourished as centers of learning, nuns became distinguished for work in academia and service. By the 13th century, monks and nuns were said to have more medical knowledge than the rest of society (Nutting & Dock, 1935a).

The Lateran Council in 1123 forbade monks and priests to practice medicine. The Benedictine sisters, however, actively continued to expand the knowledge of medicine and practiced medicine and nursing. Monks and nuns conjointly cared for the sick. The monks cared for men; the nuns cared for women. The nuns took charge of the hospital while the monks served as priests (Nutting & Dock, 1935a).

Perhaps Hildegarde, a nun, heralded the beginning of female dominance in nursing. She possessed extraordinary intellectual powers and amassed great knowledge of medicine through her nursing experiences. Between 1151 and 1159, she wrote volumes devoted to medical works that include accurate physiology related to reproduction, circulation, and the nervous system (Nutting & Dock, 1935a).

The Crusades and Nursing Knights

During the Crusades, hospitals were built on the routes to and in Jerusalem where men delivered care to travelers and battle-scarred warriors. The Knights Hospitallers of St. John of Jerusalem started as an exclusive nursing order. The Teutonic Knights had both nursing and military duties. The Knights of St. Lazarus were a nursing order from the great hospital built by St. Basil in AD 329. Along with the Knights of St. Lazarus, there were Sisters of St. Lazarus. In England, the Order of St. John consisted of men devoted to charitable work, including the formation of cottage hospitals, convalescent homes, and nurse's training for the poor (Nutting & Dock, 1935a; Kalisch & Kalisch, 2004).

In the 11th century, two hospitals were built in England: one to care for lepers, and another to care for other persons. Brothers attended to the sick men, and sisters attended to the sick women. The hospital for lepers (St. Giles) was run by an order of nuns known as the Poor Clares. Around 1148, ladies of noble birth added attending to the sick as a social duty (Nutting & Dock, 1935a).

Religious Orders of Nursing for Women

In the 12th century, French nursing became part of the manual labor performed by several orders of Roman Catholic sisters. There were also secular orders of sisters who engaged in nursing. One French hospital staffed itself with women who were either widowed or repenting from sins of impurity (Nutting & Dock, 1935a). **Nurses from religious orders** provided a more structured approach to the care of the ill and infirmed.

In Paris, the Augustinian order of nuns provided nursing care for the hospital. Those in the Augustinian order shared with one another information on how to care for the sick. In 1212, the church passed statutes to regulate the nursing orders. To join the nursing orders, both men and women took permanent vows of poverty, chastity, and obedience.

By 1368, conflict among the various orders resulted in corruption and greed. The men and women caring for the sick became demoralized because of no respite from the unrelenting toil. Religious orders, especially the sisters, accumulated much money and many possessions and focused their efforts to manage them. An epidemic of syphilis spread, and hospitals became centers of infection. During this time, many persons left monasteries and convents taking whatever they could carry, further depleting resources for the care of the infirmed (Nutting & Dock, 1935a).

NURSING IN THE RENAISSANCE AND COLONIAL AMERICA (1500–1860)

In 1505, King Louis XII decreed that jurisdiction of the hospitals be temporarily removed from the church and be governed by secular directors. In 1526, the rectors of a hospital (located in Lyons, France) directed hospital staff to wear a white uniform because the women came to work in scandalous apparel. In 1562, the dress changed from white to a black dress, white linen apron, and unstarched white cap. By the middle of the 16th century, the rectors introduced stringent regulations and required nursing service members to become part of a religious order. The male nurses (who were brothers) wore a blue robe and a silver cross. Women could only leave nursing to marry or to care for aging parents. Two notable nursing orders of men also flourished. They worked in hospitals, visited the sick at home, and distributed herbal medications (Nutting & Dock, 1935a).

Similar degeneration of religious life occurred in England. The control of hospitals became the responsibility of the cities. Philanthropy and state aid became the major funding sources. Religious orders were replaced with ordinary lay servants and attendants who had little knowledge of caring for the infirmed. A matron with some knowledge of how to run a hospital supervised them and had the responsibility for finding staff. Frequently, the matron found the care attendants from jails and debtor prisons. City hospitals became like crowded prisons with small rooms, undecorated walls, and small windows. Patients received care from heartless attendants and sisters (also called servant nurses) who were required to work 12 to 48 hours without a break. In some cases, patients nursed each other as the servant nurses slept (Nutting & Dock, 1935a).

As the New World was settled, French and Spanish religious orders opened hospitals. The Jesuits opened a hospital for settlers and the Canadian Indians. The Indians shared remedies for scurvy with the French. Likewise, the Jesuits shared their knowledge of medicines with the Indians. As hospital labors for the nuns grew heavier, the native women quickly grasped the concept of charitable practice and provided patient care (Nutting & Dock, 1935b).

Before 1524, Cortez built the hospital of the Immaculate Conception in the current location of Mexico City. Nursing staff consisted primarily of a brotherhood. In 1531, the second oldest hospital of the New World was founded in Santa Fe, where a community of over 30,000 Native Americans practiced hospitality and charitable works (Nutting & Dock, 1935b).

In New England, growth of hospitals was slow. The ship captain assumed the role of religious deacon, and frequently his wife assumed midwife responsibilities. Early treatment for illness in the English colonies consisted of prayer and superstitious practices. When hospitals opened in New York and Philadelphia, inmates provided nursing services (Jamieson & Sewall, 1954; Kalisch & Kalisch, 2004).

The 1700s marked the beginning of the hospital reform movement. John Howard worked on reforming hospitals, which evolved from his crusade to reform prisons (Jamieson & Sewall, 1954). In his 1789 notes on the state of hospitals throughout Europe and England, Howard wrote that hospitals staffed by members from religious orders tended to be quiet, neat, and clean with careful attention to patient hygiene and infection prevention. When describing secular hospitals, he wrote that patients were dirty, pest infested, and without bed linens (Nutting & Dock, 1953b).

THE MOVEMENT OF NURSING TO A RESPECTABLE PROFESSION (1820–1917)

Twenty-five years after Howard's death, Stephen Grellet (a French American) became appalled at the living conditions of children who had been born in prison. He consulted Elizabeth Fry, an English friend, to help the infants. Mrs. Fry developed a program for the women prisoners to make and sell goods. As Mrs. Fry traveled throughout Europe setting up similar programs, she became acquainted with **Kaiserworth**, a German training program for nurses. Mrs. Fry referred **Florence Nightingale** to Kaiserworth upon learning of Florence's interest in nursing (Jamieson & Sewall, 1954; Nutting & Dock, 1935b).

In 1821, Pastor Fliedner arrived in Kaiserworth, Germany, to find himself the pastor of a financially depressed congregation. Pastor Fliedner founded a hospital for two purposes. First, he wanted to care for the sick, and, second, he wanted to provide a field for deaconess instruction. In 1836, Gertrud Reichardt, a physician's daughter who helped with her father's practice, became the first probationer. Under the leadership of Fredrike Fliedner (the pastor's wife), the hospital tended the sick and probationers received clinical and theoretical instruction on the art of nursing. Upon completion of their education, the newly ordained deaconesses provided services to the poor, imprisoned, and infirmed (Jamieson & Sewall, 1954; Nutting & Dock, 1935b).

The deaconesses from Kaiserworth established an honorable reputation that spread worldwide. In 1850, Fliedner took several deaconesses to Pittsburgh, Pennsylvania, where they staffed a hospital. The movement progressed to Milwaukee, where the Deaconess Home and Hospital was founded (Jamieson & Sewall, 1954; Nutting & Dock, 1935b).

In 1831, a group of Irishwomen under the leadership of Catherine McAuley formed the Religious Sisters of Mercy and provided nursing services throughout Ireland and the world. The Irish sisters devised a system of **careful nursing** that comprised "physical care and emotional consolation provided from a spiritual perspective" (Meehan, 2003, p. 99). In the realm of careful nursing, nurses provided nursing services using great tenderness, gentleness, kindness, and patience with each client encounter. Patients received highly skilled care from nurses who practiced with spiritual love, sought to create an environment of calmness, created restorative environments, strove for perfection in keeping patients safe and comfortable, provided health education, collaborated with physicians and other health care providers, and took care of themselves. During the Asian cholera epidemic of 1832, there was a substantially lower mortality rate among recipients of nursing services from McAuley and her colleagues (Meehan).

At the end of the 18th century, nursing manuals began to appear. Some contained commonsense information, and some were scientifically based. J. D. Phahler's manual gave specific instructions on how to arrange and maintain a sick room, procedures for various treatments, instructions for use of equipment, and maintenance of written records. Along with procedures, Dr. Phahler's manual emphasized the importance of attending to patients' psychological needs. Dr. Franz May's manual provided more general approaches to patient care and also emphasized the importance of maintaining the health of caregivers. An evangelical hospital in Germany supplied nurses' training. In 1836, Pastor Gossner favored the word "Pfelegerin" (nurse) to title care attendants in Prussia (Nutting & Dock, 1935b).

During the American Revolutionary War, Catholic nuns were the only organized group of nurses. Women followed husbands to the battlegrounds and provided nursing care to soldiers who were either wounded or infirmed. Many homes and barns became hospitals. In 1786, the Quakers established the Philadelphia Dispensary, where physicians practiced disease prevention. In New York, a residential insane asylum was founded in 1798. In Canada, the Augustinian nuns from France established hospitals, visiting nurse programs, schools, and orphanages (Nutting & Dock, 1935b; Jamieson & Sewall, 1954).

The Nursing Society of Philadelphia was founded in 1836 and primarily provided home maternity services. The Nursing Society selected its nurses from applicants who displayed stable character. In 1850, the Nursing Society opened a home and school where systematic instruction was given on cooking and obstetrics. Students received clinical instruction in client homes (Jamieson & Sewall, 1954).

The Birth of Nursing as a Profession

Efforts at social reform flourished in the late 19th century. The reform of nursing evolved from efforts to reform prisons and hospitals. Florence Nightingale led the efforts to reform patient care and established nursing as a profession. Florence Nightingale was born into an affluent English family. Mr. Nightingale delighted in teaching Florence Latin, Greek, and other languages, as well as mathematics, science, and reading. According to her diary entries, Florence identified nursing as her life passion from her experiences accompanying her mother on hospital visits. However, Mrs. Nightingale expressed concern about her daughter keeping company with drunken, immoral nurses and tending to the needs of people with unhealthy bodies in prison-like, dirty, smelly hospitals. Florence's parents allowed her to attend a British hospital-based nurse's training program in an English hospital when she turned 25 years old. Florence did not practice nursing full-time after her training, but continued to travel with her parents.

During European trips, Florence explored the option of starting a community of trained nurses after visiting with nuns in Rome. Mrs. Fry, a friend of the Nightingale family, informed Florence about Kaiserworth upon learning about her interest in nursing. She attended Kaiserworth in 1850 and 1851, where she was instructed in the art of nursing (Kalisch & Kalisch, 2004; Jamieson & Sewall, 1954; Nutting & Dock, 1935b).

At the age of 34, Florence became the superintendent of a small institution on Harley Street in London that provided shelter to homeless women and nursing services to sick governesses. After a cholera epidemic, the British became involved with the Crimean War and discovered that they had no sisters to assist with injured and infirmed troops. In 1854, the British government appointed Florence as the Superintendent of the Nursing Staff. She and 38 other women (including Joanna Bridgeman, a colleague of Catherine McAuley) went to Scutari, Turkey, where they found two hospitals in deplorable condition. Florence obtained funding and supplies from friends and transformed the hospitals into clean, well-ventilated buildings that provided nutritious meals for the patients. The mortality rate of 40% declined to 2% after the implementation of Nightingale's reforms (Kalisch & Kalisch, 2004; Jamieson & Sewall, 1954; Meehan, 2003).

Power, admiration, and fame came to Florence. Before long, army nursing under Florence Nightingale evolved into a health service valued by the British government. Nightingale considered the physical and psychosocial needs of the ill and injured. She wrote letters for soldiers, employed wives who had accompanied spouses to the battlefield, and made night rounds in the wards with a lamp.

During the Crimean War, Nightingale met **Mary Seacole**, a Jamaican nurse volunteer who also nursed the soldiers. Seacole also saw the need for holistic outreach nursing services to civilians who had been injured or displaced. She set up a hotel where she provided shelter, relaxation, and excellent food. When guests became ill, she prescribed medicines. After the war, Mary Seacole dedicated her life to elevating nursing to a respectable profession (Wheeler, 1999).

In 1855, prominent British citizens established the "Nightingale fund" to enable Florence to establish a school to train women in the art of nursing. Nightingale expected these women to teach nursing to the entire world. Besides establishing a formalized program of nursing education, Florence continued her efforts at reforming hospitals, public health, and nursing (Jamieson & Sewall, 1954; Nutting & Dock, 1935b).

Along with Florence Nightingale, several American women influenced the reform of health care and nursing. In 1893, Lillian Wald and Mary Brewster opened a Nurses' Settlement House in New York City. They used the term "public health nurse" to describe the trained nurses who responded to nursing needs outside of the hospital. These nurses responded to calls from individuals as well as physicians to provide home nursing services. The program provided services regardless of the ability of recipients to pay. In 1895, Wald and Brewster moved to larger accommodations that became known as the Henry Street Settlement House. By 1900, 20 district nursing organizations employed 200 nurses across the United States (Roberts, 1954).

Questions for Reflection 2-2

1. Did you know about the contributions of others to professional nursing in the 19th century?
2. Why do you suppose these contributions were overlooked?

The Birth of Formal Nursing Education

Efforts to standardize training for nursing occurred in the Victorian era. Upper- and middle-class women led circumscribed lives, were considered property of their fathers or husbands, had no independent rights, and were considered incapable of intellectual development. Some even thought that education would damage women's reproductive organs. Women from lower classes, who had to work, found socially acceptable employment as retail clerks, factory workers, governesses, or domestic servants. Nursing, on the other hand, was considered an unacceptable profession and reserved for women paupers from workhouses or those who served prison time for drunkenness, vagrancy, or prostitution.

However, the example of Florence Nightingale's service in the Crimean War elevated the profession. Society began thinking of nursing as an art that "must be raised to the status of a trained profession" (Kjervik & Martinson, 1979, p. 22). Although Nightingale established a theoretical model for nursing practice, she proposed that nurses should follow protocol rather than use independent thinking. She emphasized that nurses should be taught how to carry out physicians' orders. To maintain discipline among nurses, Nightingale delineated a strict nursing service hierarchy. Good character superseded intellectual ability when the Nightingale nursing school selected students. Education received by nurses in Nightingale's school focused on teaching nurses what to do and how to do it, following physicians' orders, knowing why, training the nurse's senses, and linking these things with reflection to decide what should be done (Kalisch & Kalisch, 2004).

Civil War Nursing

As nursing became more acceptable, women volunteered during the Civil War to be nurses. American women transformed the ballrooms of their homes into wards for the injured and infirmed soldiers, resulting in the birth of **Civil War nursing**. Dorothea Dix was appointed as the Superintendent of Female Nurses in the Union Army, founded the first American Army Nursing Corps, and was given full power to organize human and material resources to care for sick and injured soldiers.

Along with nurses from the Army Nursing Corps, female volunteers and family members also provided nursing services to Civil War casualties. Louisa May Alcott wrote about her tragic experiences caring for soldiers. Mother Bickerdyke diligently searched to find living soldiers who had been wounded in battle but had been mistakenly placed among the dead. Clara Barton used her own resources to provide supplies to care for those injured or displaced on both sides of the battle, and she founded the American Red Cross. In her writings, Jane Stuart Woolsey noted that the hospitals run by Roman Catholic nuns were cleaner and had better outcomes, but praised the devotion and virtue of all nurses (Kalisch & Kalisch, 2004). Along with female volunteers, Young Men's Christian Association (YMCA) members volunteered to serve as nurses (Jamieson & Sewall, 1954).

In Confederate states, most of the nursing care was delivered by Southern "matrons" who volunteered their services. Efforts made by these women focused on cooking, making bandages, and sewing. Slaves and plantation mistresses and daughters worked together at times to provide care to injured and infirmed soldiers (Kalisch & Kalisch, 2004).

American Hospital Training Programs and Diploma Schools

In the United States, nursing training programs started simultaneously when society accepted and provided college education for upper-class women. As medical education moved into the postgraduate university, nursing education became established as apprenticeship training under the control of physicians and hospitals. The first nursing training programs were established in 1872 and 1873 in Boston, New Haven, and New York City. By 1880, 15 programs existed. Within a decade, programs proliferated to 432 and had graduated 3,465 nurses (Burgess, 1928).

The early hospital training schools had some autonomy in determining the nursing program of study. They rapidly became dependent on hospitals for financial support. Eventually, they became nursing service departments within the affiliated hospitals. Students worked 7 days a week, 50 weeks annually, for 1 to 2 years in exchange for on-the-job training, a few lectures, and a small allowance. Staffing the hospitals with students and faculty proved financially advantageous, and hospitals without training programs quickly established them. From 1880 to 1926, the number of hospital-based nursing programs increased from 15 to 2,155 (Burgess, 1928).

The United States was not the only nation that offered formal nursing education in hospitals. Australia and Great Britain also educated nurses within the confines of hospitals. Training hospital nursing programs became the dominant form of nursing education in the early part of the 20th century. However, untrained nurses continued to practice nursing, especially in rural areas (Kalisch & Kalisch, 2004; Madsen, 2005). Untrained nurses filled a need in rural areas, and many had the respect of the members of their communities. Unlike trained nurses, the untrained nurses willingly provided housekeeping services along with patient care. They also filled the void of caretakers in chronic care institutions (Madsen).

Research Brief 2-1

Madsen, M. (2005). Early 20th century untrained nursing staff in the Rockhampton district: A necessary evil. *Journal of Advanced Nursing, 51*(3), 307–313.

This historical study addresses the use of untrained nurses during the time from 1900 to 1949 in Rockhampton, Queensland, Australia. Using primary sources, the investigators collected information about the use and effectiveness of untrained nurses in this time. The investigators found that the untrained nurses provided nursing services to facilities that did not have a training school, including a small public hospital, a nursing home, a tuberculosis sanitorium, charity-based institutions (including a maternity hospital), small lying-in hospitals (owned by nurses), a maternal-child welfare service, and client homes. Untrained nurses were provided an opportunity to attain registration as part of the 1911 Health Amendment Act that required small lying-in hospitals to be run by board-registered nurses. Care outcomes were similar for persons receiving nursing care from trained and untrained nurses. Untrained nurses and nurse midwives had private practices or owned their own small hospitals. As time progressed, some untrained nurses became assistants in nursing and worked under the supervision of trained nurses. Despite national legislation that worked against them, untrained nurses worked in government-funded facilities offering nursing home services and tuberculosis care. The demographic profile of untrained nurses shifted from a woman with family responsibilities to a single woman who sometimes would live in the institution that provided residential care.

This historical study presents only the use of untrained nurses in a small rural district in Australia. In this study, the autonomy of untrained nurses declined substantially.

In addition, evidence suggests that many untrained nurses in this study offered high-quality nursing services, thereby dispelling the myth that all untrained nurses were marginalized members of society frequently with financial and alcohol problems. Untrained nurses provided care in areas where trained nurses preferred not to practice. When they practiced alongside trained nurses, they frequently performed many of the same tasks, but were required to be supervised. Key findings from this study present some of the same issues confronted in today's practice such as the need for delineation of a clear role for professional nurses and the increasing use of unlicensed care providers in expanded capacities in acute care hospitals.

The American Public Health Movement

As the field of **public health nursing** grew, basic principles specific to the specialty emerged. Reform efforts indicated a need to provide nursing services to all who were sick without considering ability to pay, religious affiliation, or ethnic background. District nurses identified the need to keep formal client records to facilitate consistency in service. To avoid duplication of services and prevent gaps in fulfilling client needs, the nurses learned the importance of cooperation with other groups providing community care. During the public health movement, the family became the basic care unit (Spradley, 1990). Some public health nurses acknowledged the limitations of their hospital-based education and sought additional education in institutions of higher learning to develop a global approach for community nursing.

Public health nursing prospered from 1900 until the outbreak of World War I. The patient home served as the major location for nursing practice, as hospitals had become places to receive charity, contract infection, and die.

Other Social Reform Movements

Other social reform movements impacted the nursing profession. William Booth founded the Salvation Army to protect the poor, ex-prisoners, the old, the young, and any who were miserable and had fallen from the grace of God. Jane Addams established the Hull House in Chicago, which provided day care, kindergarten, and library services to immigrant women and children. Christian Associations of young men and women were formed to build character and provide community services. Medicine experienced reforms that emphasized science and invention over superstitious practices. Finally, word of these and many more movements became known throughout the world from the invention of the telegraph and telephone (Jamieson & Sewall, 1954; Kalisch & Kalisch, 2004).

 NURSING DURING THE EARLY 20TH CENTURY, THE WORLD WARS, AND THE POST–WORLD WAR II ERA (1890–1960)

The hospital and medical reform movement resulted in changes in the nursing practice. Physician demand for educated nurses resulted in the replacement of untrained attendants with nursing students. Graduates of nursing programs found themselves in hospital supervisory positions, or in homes as private duty nurses. Hospitals with nursing students used them as staff or contracted their services with families and pocketed the money for services rendered. Typical private duty nursing cases required the nurse to live with families in order to be available 24 hours a day. The average wage earned was $120 per month. The nurse remained idle if not on a private case. As nurses aged, they lacked the stamina required for all-night vigils and the hard work required for safe, effective patient care (Goldmark, 1923).

North Carolina led the efforts to **state registration** of nurses in 1903 by establishing guidelines for professional registration. Requirements included graduation from an established diploma nursing school. New Jersey and New York quickly followed. By

1912, 29 states and the District of Columbia had registration requirements for nurses. To renew initial registration, nurses were given a 3-year grace period to practice, then they were required to write a licensing exam that emphasized dietetics, patient comfort, skilled handling of patients, and general management (Dock, 1912).

As the United States entered the First World War in 1917, unmarried trained nurses entered the Army and Navy Nurse Corps. Volunteers from well-to-do families served as nurses' aides at their own expense. The government launched a publicity campaign to recruit women into nursing. Advertisements glamorizing nursing appeared in newspapers and magazines. However, on the battlefields, the nurses encountered the horrors of battlefield injuries. At times, the ratio of nurse to patient rose to as high as 1 to 60. Nurses were required to perform surgery to save lives. Finally, the flu epidemic of 1918–1919 compounded the need for more nurses (Kalisch & Kalisch, 2004).

Nursing sustained an image problem in the 1920s. Movies portrayed nursing in ways that were unrealistic and unflattering to the profession. Reduced prestige for the profession resulted from the fact that 95% of nurses were women, the fact that most nursing leaders were unmarried, a renewed societal expectation of the woman's place in the home as a devoted wife and mother, and the portrayal of nursing as an altruistic, self-sacrificing profession in a time that focused on frivolity and self-indulgence.

Proliferation of Nursing Education Programs

The proliferation of nursing programs resulted in widespread variance in nursing education quality. Linda Richards, a graduate of a Canadian nursing program and the first trained American nurse, led reforms at major American nursing programs (Jamieson & Sewall, 1954). Isabel Hampton Robb questioned the qualifications of nursing faculty and spearheaded the first educational program for nursing faculty at Teacher's College in New York in 1901 (Dock, 1912). Widespread concerns about the safety of nursing and medical care arose among the public. Reforms in nursing education followed reforms in medical education. In 1910, the Flexner Report broadcasted problems with the quality of medical education and resulted in drastic reforms (Flexner, 1910). Nursing leaders of the time hoped that results from the Flexner Report would result in nursing education reforms. The Goldmark Report of 1923 and other studies and surveys done at the time indicated that the root of most of the difficulties related to nursing training stemmed from the nursing schools' dual purpose of providing education and nursing service. Unfortunately, these studies resulted in limited reform.

Baccalaureate Programs

In 1893, the School of Medicine at Howard University established the first nursing diploma program within a university setting. The program, designed for African American students, lasted only 1 year before being assumed by Freedmen's Hospital. The University of Texas recognized nursing in the early 1890s and gave an endowed professorial chair to Hanna Kindborn, who lectured to both nursing and medical students (Dock, 1912). In 1909, the University of Minnesota established a 3-year diploma nursing program within the College of Medicine. In subsequent years, colleges adopted the pattern of combining academic and professional courses that led to both a diploma and a bachelor of science degree in nursing. Students attended academic courses at the university and received professional nursing courses using the apprenticeship model at the hospital (Dock; Jamieson & Sewall, 1954). In 1909, Dr. Richard Olding Beard instituted a plan to make nursing a college major at the University of Minnesota (Jamieson & Sewall).

In 1923, Yale University established a nursing program that had its own dean and endowed funds. Other universities that established baccalaureate nursing programs included Case Western Reserve University (in 1923), the University of Chicago (in 1925), and Vanderbilt University (in 1930). As nursing education moved to the collegiate setting, physicians voiced opposition because they thought that higher education and theoretical knowledge might question their authority (Kalisch & Kalisch, 2004). By the 1920s, most trained nurses were employed as private duty nurses. However, with the advent of technological advances in patient care and improvements in hospital facilities, more patients were being hospitalized for treatment and surgery. Public acceptance of going to the hospital for acute and serious illnesses reduced the demand for private duty nurses who worked in home settings (Kalisch & Kalisch). The hospitals relied on student nurses for patient care, leaving program graduates unemployed. In 1939, the National League for Nursing (NLN) reported that the typical hospital connected with a school of nursing during 1938 employed only an average of 10 graduate nurses for general duty (p. 898).

During the Great Depression, trained nursing graduates willingly worked for room and board. As the economic state improved, hospitals kept these trained nurses as staff while paying them an hourly wage. Scientific advances in medicine increased the demand for educated registered nurses. A few nurses found employment with the new aviation industry as nurse-stewardesses. Other nurses participated in the Civil Work Administration (CWA) and Works Progress Administration (WPA) programs and became employed in public hospitals, clinics, and public health agencies. Empty public hospital beds soon were filled. Cinematographers portrayed nurses as attractive young women who placed professional duties over personal desires (Kalisch & Kalisch, 2004).

By World War II, graduate and registered nurses had become accepted members of hospital staffs. When hospitals discovered that hiring registered nurses could cut costs, many nursing schools closed. However, as news of war loomed in Europe, the government took steps to promote the entry of young women into nursing. Recruitment methods included advertisements in printed media and the Nurse Cadet Program (Kalisch & Kalisch, 2004). As registered nurses joined the military, a civilian nurse shortage resulted. Hospitals employed civilian workers who held certificates from the Red Cross and hired the volunteers who had been helping nurses with nonprofessional duties.

After World War II, the United States experienced a great time of economic growth. Companies offered health insurance as a fringe benefit for workers and a concession for not increasing wages. Insurance reimbursement of hospital care resulted in an increase in the number of hospital beds. Hospitals also became profitable and provided a central location for proliferating medical technology. However, the nursing shortage increased as more hospital beds became available. Workplace reforms led to an 8-hour day and a 40-hour workweek. Also, many nurses left practice to pursue marriage, better-paying jobs outside the profession, and more autonomous positions in industry or public health.

Associate Degree Programs

The Brown Report (Brown, 1948) and the Ginzberg Report (Ginzberg, 1949) specified that professional nursing education should be removed from hospitals and transferred to the collegiate setting. In 1951, Mildred Montag published a doctoral dissertation that proposed education for the technical nurse to occur in community college settings. She proposed that the technical nurse education would be a terminal degree and that technical nursing would attain a unique and semiprofessional identity (Montag, 1951). Upon graduation, the technical nurse would be completely prepared for hospital or nursing home employment. Community college nursing programs flourished. Graduates of associate degree programs wrote the same professional nursing licensure examination as did graduates from diploma and baccalaureate nursing programs.

 NURSING IN THE MODERN ERA (1960–1999)

The 1960s

The 1960s ushered in a time of great change in American culture. A variety of movements occurred in the 1960s. The Civil Rights Movement to end racial segregation accelerated (although the court decision *Brown v. the Board of Education* had occurred in 1954). In hopes to end discrimination, many Civil Rights marches happened, and acts of civil disobedience (mostly peaceful, but some violent) increased the awareness of all Americans about the inequalities that were happening in everyday life. In 1965, Congress enacted legislation proposed by President Lyndon Johnson to create a Great Society in which all citizens would have equal access to employment, education, and health care. Many of today's current social programs such as Medicare and government grants for education grew out of the Civil Rights Movement. Equal rights meant equal rights for all, including all women.

After the Civil Rights Movement, individuals began to question the status quo of American society and the government. The Peace Movement protested American involvement in the Vietnam War. Again, acts of civil disobedience occurred. The American public questioned the intentions of the government and governmental agencies. The Peace Movement emphasized the power of individuals to make their own choices. Some young American men opted to flee to Canada to avoid the military draft. Other young Americans chose to protest against the war, thereby creating confusion for troops returning home. However, many young men and women (who served as nurses) remained patriotic and served in the military. At times, demonstrations for peace became festivals for "free love" and to do whatever felt good. Thus, persons experiencing a "bad trip" from using illicit substances sometimes found their way to an emergency room. Sexual promiscuity resulted in the rise of sexually transmitted diseases.

In the early 1960s, the health care system consisted primarily of independent, not-for-profit hospitals; small independent physician offices; and neighborhood pharmacies and medical supply stores. By working independently or in small practices, physicians enjoyed autonomy and control over patient care. Hospitals recruited physicians to join medical staffs. Private insurance companies or patients reimbursed physicians based on fee-for-service payment systems. Persons unable to afford care sought health care services in local government-managed hospitals and clinics. Society and nurses viewed nursing as being subservient to the physician.

Because of an increased demand for professional nurses for hospital care from the newly initiated Medicare program, ways to increase the nursing workforce were examined. Associate degree nursing programs were viewed as a means to provide a quick way to increase the number of nurses capable of hospital practice. Many hospitals that provided diploma programs in nursing found they were struggling to maintain their nursing programs because of the financial costs. The U.S. Public Health Service (1963) issued a report, *Toward Quality in Nursing: Needs and Goals*, which outlined the following concerns: severe deficiencies in the current nursing education, not enough young persons entering the nursing profession, high turnover within the nursing profession, the need for collegiate and university-based nursing programs, the persistent low socioeconomic status of nurses, the ineffective use of available nursing personnel, and not enough research being conducted to advance the practice of professional nursing. The report served as evidence for the Nurse Training Act of 1964, which provided federal funding for diploma nursing schools to defray nursing education costs. The act also provided federal monetary support for associate degree programs in community colleges and baccalaureate degrees in colleges and universities (Kalisch & Kalisch, 2004).

In the 1960s, the NLN denied accreditation of hospital diploma schools that used students to staff hospitals. Hospital-based diploma schools remained the dominant educational pattern for registered nursing until the early 1970s. Table 2-1 highlights historical events that have resulted in multiple entry points into the nursing profession.

In 1965, the American Nurses Association (ANA) published the *ANA Position Paper on Education for Nursing*. The paper specified that the minimum educational level for beginning professional nursing practice should be at the baccalaureate degree level, the minimum educational preparation for technical nursing practice should be at the

TABLE 2-1

Historical Events Resulting in Multiple Educational Programs for Entry Into Professional Nursing

Event	Date
First school for training practical nurses opens	1897
Daughters of the American Revolution serve as the examining board for military nurses	1898
North Carolina becomes the first state to require registration of nurses	1903
1,006 hospital-based nursing training programs and 90 mental health institution–based nursing programs	1911
The Goldmark Report proposes that additional education beyond the basic diploma is needed for the practice areas of public health, nursing education, and supervision	1923
University of Minnesota starts a baccalaureate degree nursing program	1909
Apprenticeship approach dominates nursing educations	1920s
25 programs of nursing granted A.B. or B.S. degrees in nursing with Yale opening the first separate university nursing department in 1924	1926
11 practical nursing programs in the United States	1930
1,472 hospital-based education programs, 70 collegiate nursing education programs, 36 practical nursing programs	1936
Development of crash programs to train nursing aides to alleviate nursing shortage of World War II	1941
The Brown Report ranked nursing as important to society as teachers; ranks collegiate nursing education as equal to other professional education programs	1948
Accreditation programs for practical and professional nursing schools	1952
296 practical nursing programs	1954
Birth of associate degree nursing programs in community colleges	1958
Toward Quality in Nursing Needs and Goals. A Report of the Surgeon General's Consultant Group in Nursing is released by the Public Health Service	1963
The Nursing Training Act is enacted	1964
The American Nurses' Association *Position Paper on Education for Nursing*	1965
797 hospital-based, 218 associate degree, and 210 baccalaureate degree nursing education programs	1966
288 hospital-based, 742 associate degree, and 402 baccalaureate degree nursing programs	1982
60 hospital-based, 890 associate degree, and 661 baccalaureate degree nursing programs	2003

Sources: Kalisch, P. A., & Kalisch, B. J. (2004). *The advance of American nursing* (4th ed.). Philadelphia: Lippincott Williams & Wilkins.

associate degree level, and all unlicensed care assistants should receive education in vocational education centers instead of on-the-job training. The proposal assumed that hospital diploma nursing schools would collaborate with either baccalaureate degree–granting institutions or community colleges to develop either professional or technical nursing programs. However, instead of collegial collaboration among hospitals and other educational institutions, the paper resulted in a deep division among members of the nursing profession (Kalisch & Kalisch, 2004; Flanagan, 1976).

The 1960s also was a time of biomedical advancements leading to expensive technologies to save lives. Complex surgical procedures, new pharmaceuticals, and new technology increased the cost of health care delivery. This increased the need for highly skilled and educated nurses. By this time, employers offered health care insurance as a standard benefit to workers. In 1965, the government introduced Medicare and Medicaid to provide health care coverage to the elderly and poor. Improved insurance coverage meant improved access to health care services for the employed and for elderly citizens. Demand for hospital care and physician services increased. Hospital admissions rose and along with it the need for highly educated, clinically competent professional nurses for patient care.

With the growing popularity of television, two fictional medical programs, *Ben Casey* and *Dr. Kildare*, attracted viewers. In these programs, nurses primarily were depicted as physicians' handmaidens.

The 1970s

Inflation and unemployment increased in the 1970s. Consumers revolted against tax increases. To decrease the economic burden of supplying health care, the government employed mechanisms to monitor health care delivery to Medicare and Medicaid recipients. Although ineffective, mechanisms such as utilization review to reduce lengths of hospital stays and physician peer review programs became common practice. Hospitals and physicians were required to participate in these programs or lose Medicare and Medicaid reimbursement.

Insurance providers also carried increased risks as consumers and employers exerted pressure on them to keep premiums from rising. In 1974, the Employment Retirement Security Act added incentives to business to self-insure employees. A few for-profit investor hospitals were established, but medical and hospital care proceeded as usual. Therefore, the need for professional nurses continued.

During this era, community colleges prospered as society placed emphasis on equal opportunity for all American citizens to education. Associate degree–prepared nurses successfully passed the professional nursing licensure examination and soon filled vacant nursing positions, where they provided effective nursing care services. Costs for hospital-based nursing education programs continued to rise.

The 1970s also saw increases in graduate nursing education. Graduate nursing education programs proliferated and offered advanced study in clinical specialty areas, nursing education, and nursing administration. Nurse practitioner programs were started to improve health care delivery while reducing costs. Nursing research became a hallmark of advanced nursing education and practice.

Compared to medical research, nursing research has also been hampered by inadequate financial support. Between 1971 and 1981, the government awarded the National Center for Nursing Research $40 million. During the same period, the National Institutes of Health (NIH) received $1.7 billion for general biomedical research. However, the NIH noted the importance for nursing research and established the National Center for Nursing Research.

Television and movies increased in popularity. Positive images of nurses surfaced on television shows such as *Julia, Nurse, Emergency*, and *M*A*S*H*. In *Emergency*, Nurse Dixie, a fictional emergency department nurse, had collegial relationships with paramedics, physicians, and fellow nurses; performed telephone triage and complex nursing procedures; and even disagreed with physicians. Margaret Houlihan of *M*A*S*H* was portrayed as a competent, caring professional who had many personal problems. Nurses as persons with rigid and cold personalities were depicted in the 1975 movie *One Flew Over the Cuckoo's Nest*. Some less-than-flattering images of nurses in the media appear in Table 2-2.

The 1970s also ushered in the women's movement, called Women's Liberation, the modern feminist movement, or second-wave feminism (Malka, 2007). Equality of all oppressed persons became a dominant societal theme. Women fought for equal rights, pay, and access to jobs and education. Women strove to discover their authentic selves, find personal meaning in their existence, and enjoy social equality. Women could pursue other careers besides nursing and teaching (Malka).

TABLE 2-2

Less-than-flattering Images of Nurses in the Media

Image	Example(s)
Rigid and cold personality	Nurse Ratchet in *One Flew Over the Cuckoo's Nest* (1975 movie) Major Margaret Houlihan in *M*A*S*H* (1969 movie and 1972–1983 TV show)
Intense drive to satisfy sexual needs	"Hot Lips" Houlihan in *Mash* (movie and TV show) *Nightingales* (1988–89 TV show) Margaret on *Becker* (2000–04)
Sex objects	*Nightingales* (1988–89 TV show) *Pearl Harbor* (2001 movie) Various soap operas
A goal to marry a physician and flirtatious relationships with male physicians	Nurse Hathaway in *ER* (1993–2005 TV show) Nurse characters in *Diagnosis Murder* (1994–2001 TV show) Nancy Nichol, clinic nurse in *Doc* (2001–2005 TV show)
Dysfunctional lives	Suicide attempt by Nurse Hathaway during the *ER* TV show pilot *ER's* Nurse Abby, a chain smoker and alcoholic *M*A*S*H's* Major Houlihan's intermittent drinking binges Margaret's marital woes on *Becker* (2000–04 TV show)
Selfless martyr	Hanna in *The English Patient* (1996 movie)
Complicity	Phillip Seymour Hoffman in *Magnolia* (1999 movie)
Men in nursing as being effeminate	Ben Stiller's role as the male nurse in *Meet the Parents* (2000 movie)
Nurses kill or injure patients	*Dateline* (TV show) Series of three articles published by *The Chicago Tribune* in September 2000
Temporary and agency nurses as engaging in illegal and unethical behavior	Bogdanich's 1991 report in the *The Wall Street Journal*

Sources: Berens, M.J. (2000), accessed March 18, 2001. Nursing mistakes kill, injure thousands. *The Chicago Tribune.* Available online http://www.chicagotribune.com/news/specials/chi-000910nursing1,1,2682439.story?ctrack-1?cset=true Bogdanich, W. (1991, November 1). Danger in white: The shadowy world of 'temp' nurses. *The Wall Street Journal,* pp. B1, B4; Muff, J. (1988). Of images and ideals: A look at socialization and sexism in nursing. In A.H. Jones (Ed.), *Images of nurses: Perspectives from history, art, and literature* (pp. 197–220). Philadelphia: University of Pennsylvania Press).

A shift also occurred in women's behavior from one of pleasing men toward an opportunity for self-expression and fulfillment. Medicine, a male-dominated profession, dictated how health care was delivered, resulting in further oppression of some nurses. However, other nurses saw the feminist movement as a means to assert themselves and use female empowerment as a means to transform the role of nurses from that of a dutiful servant to that of a competent professional with an obligation to question physician orders when needed to protect patients. Many nurses asserted their rights as persons and professionals. Changes became prevalent in practice settings, and nurses no long stood when physicians entered nursing units, gathered charts for rounds, and got coffee for them. However, other nurses found second-wave feminism as antithetical toward their profession of service. Early years of the feminist movement resulted in further divisions within the nursing profession (Malka, 2007). Nurses began to assert themselves with physicians, administrators, and each other.

The 1980s

Costs for health care continued to skyrocket during the 1980s, despite a weak economy. More expensive and sophisticated diagnostic equipment and treatments became common as new advances in health care were discovered and consumers demanded them. In 1983, Medicare introduced a prospective payment system known as "diagnosis-related groups." The goal of the program was to reduce cost rate increases for hospital care by reducing the length of hospitalization. Employers selected health insurance programs offering preferred provider organizations that negotiated discounted services from participating health care organizations. By the end of the decade, hospitals experienced decreased profits, as beds remained empty. Hospitals consolidated, resulting in a decreased demand for hospital nurses.

In attempts to alleviate the high cost of health care, the nursing profession embarked on expanding the roles of professional nursing. Collegiate nursing programs offered education for nurse practitioners, clinical nursing specialists, and certified nurse midwives along with established advanced education to prepare nursing faculty.

As the number of hospital beds declined, inpatient acuity increased substantially, thereby requiring that highly skilled nurses care for patients. Primary nursing became the dominant nursing care delivery system. Primary nursing brought the professional nurse back to the bedside. In primary nursing, the registered nurse planned individualized care, implemented the plan, and also provided health education for hospitalized patients and families. Persons were sent home to recover from surgery and illnesses once their conditions stabilized. In response, the demand for nurses working in home health and ambulatory health care increased.

Media portrayals of nurses were less than flattering. Soap operas and the prime-time television show *Nightingales* depicted nurses and nursing students as sex objects. In a coordinated effort with the ANA, professional nurses instituted a boycott of sponsors of *Nightingales*, which resulted in its cancellation.

Feminism flourished in the 1980s. Carol Gilligan (1982) published *In a Different Voice*, which highlighted key differences between the communication styles of men and women and presented key differences in the socialization of boys and girls. Gilligan emphasized that women preferred to be connected to each other. Various approaches to feminism arose. The liberal feminist view, although devised in the 19th century, grew in popularity because of its continued commitment toward achieving equality between men and women. Marxist feminist theory taught that the introduction of private property led to female oppression. Therefore, sexism would disappear if property would be distributed equally among all members of society. Socialist feminist theory looks at societal institutions such as patriarchal families, the rise of consumerism, and the invisible contributions of women (such as housework and motherhood). Radical feminism gets its principles from a women-centered world perspective with the aims of ending oppression from men and other cultural institutions. Female oppression would end when gender roles and discrimination no longer exist (Chinn, 2007; Chinn & Wheeler, 1985; McPherson, 1983; Speedy, 1987). Nursing education embraced feminist traditions. Educators and students alike strove to become their authentic selves, use intuition as one means of clinical decision making, and embark on teaching-learning partnerships.

However, some professional nurses still could not accept the feminist movement. Because of the movement's derogatory comments about the nature of the work of nursing, nursing contributions to client care remained invisible (Malka, 2007). For example, persons cannot see nursing assessments and surveillance activities. Nursing omissions, however, become visible, such as the failure to reposition bedfast patients resulting in pressure ulcer development. Therefore, showing the differences that nursing care made to client outcomes was difficult to describe. Only the presence of the adverse effects of poor nursing care was visible. The feminist movement also devalued nursing as a profession because of its subservient status to the medical profession (Malka).

The 1990s

By 1990, "95% of insured employees were enrolled in some form of managed care, including fee-for-service plans with utilization management, preferred provider organization or HMOs" (Bodenheimer & Grumbach, 1995, p. 87). Hospitals, physicians, and insurance companies joined forces and created integrated health care networks. Large surpluses of specialist physicians with a shortage of generalists were predicted. Physicians increasingly formed large practices, while commercial companies dominated insurance coverage through managed care plans. For-profit companies took control of many nursing homes, home health care companies, and multihospital system networks. Physicians lost control of medical practice. Third-party payers dictated reimbursement rates to hospitals. Eighty-five million Americans remained uninsured, underinsured, or enrolled in Medicaid (Ginsberg, 1995). Insurance providers employed management tactics to avoid enrolling potentially high users of health care services.

As hospital and home health care agencies lost profits, efforts to control costs of services resulted in reducing professional nursing staff even as the acuity level of inpatients continued to rise. Use of unlicensed assistive personnel (UAP) became popular despite evidence that registered nurses improved patient care quality (Brooten & Naylor, 1995). The change in skill mix reduced professional nurse positions and further devalued the contributions of registered nurses to client care (Buerhaus, 1995).

Patient-focused care and **work redesign** efforts were developed. Greenberg (1994) outlined the following four key elements of patient-focused care:

1. Patients with similar diagnoses are grouped on the same units.
2. Ancillary and support services are decentralized to the nursing unit.
3. Staff are cross-trained shifting from specialized to generalized care providers.
4. Patient care teams of cross-trained providers give the majority of care for the specified patient group.

In efforts to improve quality of care by minimizing variance in care-providing procedures, hospitals instituted clinical pathways. The clinical paths also standardized the hospital length of stay for persons having the same procedures or hospital admissions for the same illness. Standardized paths reduced the individualization of nursing care plans.

Work redesign effort expanded the responsibility and job scope for nonprofessional staff. UAP replaced registered and licensed vocational (practical) nurses. With minimal on-the-job training, UAP perform the basic tasks of patient hygiene, ambulation, vital signs, and intake–output determination while assuming phlebotomy, electrocardiogram (EKG) testing, bladder catheterization, and simple dressing changes in some institutions. In addition, some institutions assign social workers, housekeeping personnel, dietary workers, respiratory therapists, and clinical laboratory staff to a nursing department under the supervision of a nurse manager. As a result, the registered nurse (RN) role changed from one of direct care provider to one requiring delegation of patient care to others. Instead of spending time with patients, the RN now supervised care provided by

UAP. The RN role shifted to one of manager who focused efforts at patient outcome evaluation.

To ensure efficient and effective use of health care resources without sacrificing client satisfaction and care quality, health care providers and insurers developed **case management** systems. Case management systems varied in setting and implementation. Table 2-3 outlines seven common components contained in all case management models.

Social workers served as the first case managers. However, when they realized their limitations to see the entire patient situation, health care institutional administration and social workers turned to nurses for assistance. In addition, case management required thought processes frequently used by nurses in clinical practice. Early efforts at case management improved patient outcomes, increased consumer satisfaction with care, and decreased health care costs (Cohen & Cesta, 2001).

Research in nursing continued to be hampered by inadequate financial support. In 1993, the National Institute for Nursing Research (NINR) was established with the purpose of identifying nursing research priorities, distributing grants to nurse researchers, and disseminating findings of nursing research to the public and other health professions. In 2000, NINR received $90 billion to achieve its mission.

TABLE 2-3

Common Components of Case Management Systems

Component	Description
Client identification and outreach services	Case managers receive clients through referrals, interviews, and networking.
Client assessment and diagnosis	Case managers perform comprehensive holistic client assessments to identify physical, psychological, sociocultural, and spiritual problems.
Planning of services and resource identification	Case managers determine what services will be used in collaboration with the client. The case manager then assumes the responsibility for planning and coordinating the services.
Linking clients to required services	Case managers serve as brokers to expedite and follow through with the coordination and planning of services for the client.
Coordination and implementation of services	Case managers verify that the identified needs are met and abide by formal agreements made with the service-providing agencies by keeping extensive documentation and records focused on the efficiency, effectiveness, and quality of case-managed care services.
Service delivery monitoring	Case managers collaborate with interdisciplinary team members who are providing client services and verify that the client is receiving appropriate, quality services from the agencies.
Client advocacy	Case managers work on behalf of the client to ensure that the client is receiving services contracted for, making progress in the delineated program, and receiving satisfactory services.
Evaluation of services and outcomes	Case managers bear responsibility for specific and general client outcomes. They continuously monitor and reassess services being provided. Prompt identification of need for change or problems ensures timely intervention and replanning.

In the 1990s, most American women had attained equality with men. However, the profession of nursing continued to have difficulty in attracting the best and brightest women. Ironically, successful and highly educated nurses moved away from the bedside. Advanced practice nurses worked in collaborative partnerships with physicians. Some physicians began to see nurse practitioners and certified nurse midwives as competitors rather than partners (Malka, 2007). Nurses attended to all ranges of human responses to health and illness while providing a caring relationship to facilitate health and healing according to the 1995 ANA *Social Policy Statement*.

Despite federal government recognition of unique professional nursing contributions to health care, the American public continued to see mixed pictures of professional nursing. Prime-time news programs became popular. *Dateline* featured a story about a nurse who had murdered several patients in a veteran's hospital. The show *ER* debuted with an episode featuring the suicide attempt of an emergency department employee, Nurse Hathaway. In future episodes, Nurse Hathaway became the epitome of the caring nurse who secretly provided health care services to persons without the ability to pay for them. Unlike previous portrayals of oppressed nurses, Nurse Hathaway never let fear get in the way of confronting potential errors or injustices.

 ## NURSING IN THE POSTMODERN ERA (2000–BEYOND)

Scholars debate when the postmodern era actually began. Some acknowledge that the postmodern era began in the 1960s; others claim it began with the introduction of the computer and Internet. Another group of scholars heralds the beginning of the postmodern age with questioning of scientific method as the best approach for discoveries to answer the questions surrounding humanity, the environment, and health-related issues. Wilson (1998) introduced the term **consilience**, a term to describe the unity of knowledge. Consilience represents the point where scientific, artistic, ethical, spiritual, social, environmental, and personal knowledge intersect. Recent research has discovered that spirituality plays a key role in health and healing, and qualitative research methods hold the same status as quantitative research methods.

Currently, professional nursing finds itself in a state of flux. Scientific advances promise increased complexity and costs of health care. Limited resources for health care drive its delivery. As the population of the United States grows older and lives longer, nursing services are in high demand. The gap between the rich and poor continues to widen, resulting in an increase in governmental funding for health care services. Sources of health care insurance for consumers of health care come from employment, private purchase, or the government. Nearly 47 million Americans have joined the ranks of the uninsured. Twenty-eight million persons participate in Medicaid programs. By virtue of education and practice, nurses are the best-equipped health team members to assume the gatekeeper and advocacy roles required of case managers. Nurse practitioners have demonstrated the ability to deliver high-quality health care economically without compromising care quality. Hospitals currently employ 66% of working RNs, and nurses work in extended care facilities, homes, clinics, and community health settings (Bureau of Labor Statistics, 2008).

Along with different settings for professional nurse employment, nurses find that the complexity of information in any given practice area requires continuous education. Professional nursing organizations provide opportunities for further education in a specialized practice field. An Internet search revealed over 130 professional nurse organizations. Specialty areas include critical care, oncology, neuroscience, holistic, parish, maternal-child, psychiatric, and administration, to name only a few. Although certification by a recognized nursing specialty organization attests to knowledge and skill in the special area of practice, few positions require certification, and many fail to provide financial rewards for professional certification. However, many individuals consider certification prestigious and view it as a means to improve the image of nursing.

Along with specialty certification, nurses in a variety of practice settings participate in improving the quality of health care. Evidence-based standards for client nursing care assessments and interventions reduce client injuries and complications. Regulatory and accrediting agencies require that certain standards are met before designating them as accredited centers. For example, the Joint Commission (formerly JCAHO) sets national and international care standards for client care that must be met prior to accreditation. All Joint Commission–accredited organizations must have quality improvement programs in place (see Chapter 19). The Center for Medicare and Medicaid Standards (CMMS) has determined that all Joint Commission–accredited organizations meet all requirements to receive reimbursement for rendered services. If an organization fails to meet criteria for accreditation, it loses the ability to receive federal monies for delivered health care services. In addition, the CMMS has identified 11 hospital-associated complications for which Medicare and Medicaid reimbursement will be denied.

Besides being knowledgeable in a specific practice area, informatics, and quality improvement, nurses realize the importance of being versed in current consumer health care practices. Many alternative or complementary health care practices affect current medical therapies. Some complementary therapies such as aromatherapy, guided imagery, therapeutic touch, and massage ease some adverse effects of conventional medical and surgical therapies. The NIH has added research on alternative and complementary health care practices to its list of research priorities. Thus, the knowledge required for effective nursing practice continues to expand and increase in complexity.

The image of nurses in a postmodern society has yet to be determined. Current mainstream media tend to ignore the role of nurses in health care delivery, thus continuing the invisibility of the contributions that professional nurses make in health care.

SUMMARY AND SIGNIFICANCE TO PRACTICE

The development of recognizing nursing as a respected profession continues in the ever-changing, complex, and chaotic world. Three entry levels of education continue to be a major barrier for nursing to attain professional status. Advances in science are providing an opportunity for the nursing profession to establish its own scientific body of knowledge as well as increasing the need for highly educated nurses. Hard science continues to become intertwined with ethics, spirituality, and philosophy and points to the validity of individualized holistic nursing care. Professional nurses must focus efforts toward looking at all aspects that affect human health and healing For many generations, nurses have made remarkable, but invisible, contributions to the delivery of health care. Hopefully, as a result of nurses exhibiting compassion, confidence, and competence, current and future societies will value the contributions that nurses make to health care. By showcasing their clinical, cognitive, and communication skills with confidence, nurses can shape the image of the nursing profession.

FROM THEORY TO PRACTICE

1. What are some current issues in health care that might be solved by looking at nursing history?
2. What are the similarities among current and ancient nursing practice?
3. Why is it important for nurses to have knowledge about nursing history?
4. How does current professional practice compare to nursing in various stages of human history?
5. How did the feminist movement affect the nursing profession?
6. How could nurses use history to guide current and future nursing practice?

WWW INTERNET EXERCISE

This chapter has provided you with a broad overview of the history of nursing. Visit http://www.internurse.com. View pictures, and read more about the nurses who shaped the profession of nursing. Listen to the voice of Florence Nightingale. Write a paragraph or two describing your thoughts and feelings on visiting the site. Please also include information related to your perception of nursing history since reading and visiting this website. Share with your nursing colleagues in class or at work.

WWW INTERNET RESOURCES

Internurse: http://internurse.com/history.htm. Listen to a voice recording of Florence Nightingale and see many historical nursing photographs.

American Association for the History of Nursing: http://www.aahn.org. Read about organizational membership and view nursing history archives.

The Center for the Study of the History of Nursing: http://www.nursing.upenn.edu/history. Visit the gravesites of historical nursing figures and read about their contributions to the profession.

Men in American Nursing History: http://www.geocities.com/Athens/Forum/6011/. Trace the historical role of men in professional nursing and discover current issues confronting men in nursing.

Women's History: http://womenshistory.about.com/homework/womenshistory/cs/nurses. Read about key historical nursing figures and learn about contributions of minority nurses to the profession.

American Nurses Association (ANA): http://www.nursingworld.org. Read about ANA history, membership services, and current issues affecting professional nursing.

Sigma Theta Tau International: http://www.nursingsociety.org. Read about Sigma Theta Tau history, membership criteria, membership services, and efforts to promote nursing scholarship, and visit the Virginia Henderson Library.

National League for Nursing (NLN): http://www.nln.org. Learn about NLN history, membership services, standards for professional and vocational nursing program accreditation, testing services, and research initiatives.

American Association of Colleges of Nursing (AACN): http://www.aacn.nche.edu. Read about the AACN history and mission, and get a hyperlink to the Commission for Credentialing of Nursing Education for program accreditation standards for baccalaureate and graduate nursing educational programs.

Check out past and current media images of professional nurses by visiting http://www.truthaboutnursing.org.

REFERENCES

American Nurses Association. (1965). *ANA position paper on education for nursing*. Kansas City, MO: Author.

American Nurses Association. (1995). *Social policy statement*. Kansas City, MO: Author.

Bodenheimer, T., & Grumbach, K. (1995). The reconfiguration of U.S. medicine. *Journal of the American Medical Association, 274*, 85–90.

Brooten, D., & Naylor, M. D. (1995). Nurses' effect on changing patient outcomes. *Image, 27*, 95–99.

Brown, E. L. (1948). *Nursing for the future (Brown report)*. New York: Russell Sage Foundation.

Buerhaus, P. I. (1995). Economic pressures building in the hospital employed RN labor market. *Nursing Economics, 13*, 137–141.

Bureau of Labor Statistics. (2008). Occupational outlook handbook, 2008–2009 edition. Available at http://www.bls.gov/oco/ocos083.htm. Accessed April 20, 2009.

Burgess, M. A. (1928). *Committee on the grading of nursing schools: Nurses, patients and pocketbooks*. New York: Commonwealth Fund.

Chinn, P. L. (2007). *Peace and power, creativing leadership for building community* (7th ed.). Sudbury, MA: Jones & Bartlett.

Chinn, P. L., & Wheeler, C. E. (1985). Feminism and nursing. *Nursing Outlook, 33*(2), 74–77.

Cohen, E. L., & Cesta, T. G. (2001). *Nursing case management from essentials to advanced practice applications* (3rd ed.). St. Louis, MO: Mosby.

Dock, L. L. (1912). *A history of nursing* (Vol. 3). New York: Putnam.

Flanagan, L. (1976). *One strong voice: The story of the American Nurses Association*. Kansas City, MO: American Nurses Association.

Flexner, A. (1910). *Medical education in the United States and Canada*. The Carnegie Foundation for the Advancement of Teaching. Boston: Merrymount Press.

Gilligan, C. (1982). *In a different voice*. Cambridge, MA: Harvard University Press.

Ginsberg, E. (1995). A cautionary note on market reforms in health care. *Journal of the American Medical Association, 274,* 1633–1634.

Ginzberg, E. (1949). *A pattern for hospital care*. New York: Columbia University Press.

Goldmark, J. (1923). *Nursing and nursing education in the United States*. New York: Macmillan.

Greenberg, L. (1994). Work redesign: An overview. *Journal of Emergency Nursing, 20,* 28A–32A.

Jamieson, E. M., & Sewall, M. F. (1954). *Trends in nursing history* (4th ed.). Philadelphia: W. B. Saunders.

Kalisch, P. A., & Kalisch, B. J. (2004). *The advance of American nursing* (4th ed.). Philadelphia: Lippincott Williams & Wilkins.

Kjervik, D. K., & Martinson, I. J. M. (1979). *Women in stress: A nursing perspective*. New York: Appleton-Century-Crofts.

Madsen, W. (2005). Early 20th century untrained nursing staff in the Rockhampton district: A necessary evil? *Journal of Advanced Nursing, 51*(3), 307–313.

Malka, S. G. (2007). *Daring to care*. Urbana: University of Illinois Press.

McPherson, K. I. (1983). Feminist methods: A new paradigm for nursing research. *Advances in Nursing Science, 5*(2), 17–25.

Meehan, T. C. (2003). Careful nursing: A model for contemporary nursing practice. *Journal of Advanced Nursing, 44,* 99–107.

Montag, M. (1951). *The education of nursing technicians*. New York: Putman.

National League for Nursing. (1939). More graduate duty nurses. *American Journal of Nursing, 39,* 898.

Nutting, M. A., & Dock, L. L. (1935a). *A history of nursing: Vol. 2. The evolution of nursing systems from the earliest times to the foundation of the first English and American training schools*. New York: Putman.

Nutting, M. A., & Dock, L. L. (1935b). *A history of nursing: Vol. 3. The evolution of nursing systems from the earliest times to the foundation of the first English and American training schools*. New York: Putman.

Roberts, M. M. (1954). *American nursing: History and interpretation*. New York: Macmillan.

Speedy, S. (1987). Feminism and the professionalisation of nursing. *Australian Journal of Advanced Nursing, 4*(2), 20–28.

Spradley, B. W. (1990). *Community health nursing: Concepts and practice*. Glenview, IL: Scott Foresman/Little Brown.

U.S. Public Health Service. (1963). *Toward quality in nursing: Needs and goals*. Washington, DC: Author.

Wheeler, W. (1999). Florence: Death of an icon? *Nursing Times, 95,* 24–26.

Wilson, E. O. (1998). *Consilience: The unity of knowledge*. New York: Alfred A. Knopf.

CHAPTER 3

Contextual, Philosophical, and Ethical Elements of Professional Nursing

KEY TERMS AND CONCEPTS

Values

Beliefs

Context

Philosophy

Contextual elements of nursing practice

Mission

Morality

Ethics

Principalism

Care

Contextualism

Ethical decision-making process

Ethical competence

LEARNING OUTCOMES

By the end of this chapter, the learner will be able to:

1 Identify environmental factors that constitute the context for nursing practice.

2 Outline the essential elements of a nursing philosophy.

3 Develop a personal nursing philosophy.

4 Outline key steps for effective analysis of ethical dilemmas.

5 Use a structured method for making ethical decisions.

6 Specify fallacies that might occur when making ethical decisions.

7 Explain how demographic, cultural, economic, environmental, and ethical factors influence professional practice.

8 Incorporate knowledge, freedom, and choice while using nursing process.

VIGNETTE

Jane has been in nursing for 15 years. She yearns for the "good old days" when client care was focused on persons rather than on business. Currently, Jane feels detached from her clients and perceives herself as a client care machine. However, she knows in her heart that she does make a difference in her clients' lives, and she derives profound satisfaction from helping others through times of pain and suffering. Jane is considering a career change, but she feels passionate about helping other people.

As a science, nursing focuses on humanity in a highly objective manner using interventions based on scientific evidence. As advances in technology create a more complex world, making sense of the world becomes more important. A well-defined set of **values** (principles, or what things are important) and **beliefs** (ideas regarded as truths) provides a firm foundation for nursing practice. Nurses who rely exclusively on thinking and approach nursing using only the hard sciences would appear cold and distant to their clients. However, professional nurses also connect emotionally and spiritually with clients, thereby allowing genuine warmth and authentic compassion to guide clinical practice. Values and beliefs influence perceptions, thoughts, and feelings.

Values and beliefs directly interact with the environment. All environmental and situational conditions create the context of nursing practice. One definition states that **context** refers to "the whole situation, background, or environmental relationships to a particular event, personality, creation, etc." (Agnes, 2005, p. 315). Each nurse brings a personal set of beliefs about people, the world, health, and nursing. This set of beliefs constitutes a **philosophy** of nursing. When providing nursing care, nurses interact with the environment, which is composed of contextual factors in which a nurse's philosophy plays a key role. The pragmatic professional self focuses on using nursing for a practical purpose such as solving client health-related problems. The idealistic professional self pays serious attention to the ideal conceptualizations of nursing practice and views nursing as a means for forming authentic and caring relationships with others to help them achieve their maximal health potential. The realistic professional self emphasizes facts and scientific principles during nursing practice. The existentialist professional self shows great regard for who individuals are and respects their choices with an acceptance of responsibility for those choices made as nursing care is delivered. Pragmatic professional nurses look for the practical nature of nursing and how it can be used to solve issues that arise in daily clinical practice. They also seek to find cause-and-effect relationships. Some degree of congruence with the vastly different world views is desirable for authentic, humane, scientific-based, nonpaternalistic nursing practice.

Development of an individual nursing philosophy helps nurses come to terms with diverse world views. However, to begin developing a personal nursing philosophy, nurses need to be cognizant of contextual elements of nursing practice. **Contextual elements of nursing practice** are all of the demographic, economic, environmental, and ethical factors that surround a client care situation. Contextual elements surrounding a clinical situation affect the professional roles assumed by nurses and the clinical decisions they make. These elements, along with a personal nursing philosophy, help nurses develop a meaningful and thoughtful practice.

 ## CONTEXTUAL BASIS OF NURSING PRACTICE

What is the world of nursing like today? Before that question can be answered, we must look at the world environment, the place where nursing occurs. Professional nursing practice does not occur in isolation; rather, nursing is one piece of the health care delivery system. When one area of health care experiences a change, all areas of health care delivery experience change. Dramatic changes have occurred in health care over the past 2 decades that have profoundly affected professional nursing practice. Future changes may occur so quickly that nurses (and other persons) may have difficulty in fully comprehending the effects of change and coping with the implications of nonstop change (Porter-O'Grady & Malloch, 2003, 2007). Professional nursing is a complex phenomenon. Many contextual elements affect professional practice, making it impossible to present all of them in a single chapter. To capture an accurate picture of current professional practice, the following discussion focuses on quantum science that requires relational and whole-systems thinking, technology and consumerism, the global community, communication, and the desire for equality while maintaining personal identity.

Quantum Science: Relational and Whole-Systems Thinking in Health Care

Because change is constant, no one can avoid it (Hawking, 2002). To survive, humans must learn new ways of thinking. The world is a complex place full of chaos. Everything is interconnected. Structure becomes defined by wholes rather than individual parts

(Hawking; Porter-O'Grady & Malloch, 2003, 2007). When looking into a hologram, the entire large picture is seen on any size fraction of the entire picture. Such is the nature of overall structure. The smallest structural unit of a system mirrors its entire system in terms of organization pattern and behavior. Systems work continuously to renew and reinvent themselves while maintaining their basic integrity. Systems are composed of multiple interacting feedback loops. Structure has disorder, and disorder has structure. Quantum science eliminates dualistic or "either-or" thinking, and envisions new possibilities of combining ideas through the use of synthesis. Synthesis involves putting ideas or things together in a new way. For example, Porter-O'Grady and Malloch (2003, 2007) defined competence as using one's skills to attain a desired outcome rather than just having skills. As caregivers, coordinators, and change agents, nurses are frequently called upon to look for new ways of delivering client care to meet optimal outcomes.

Relational thinking involves recognition of the interconnectedness of all things. All things become interdependent. A complex algorithm (series of steps or events) is required for things to occur or exist (Porter-O'Grady & Malloch, 2003, 2007). For example, human health is a complex process that involves a safe environment, intact physical and mental capabilities, meaningful interpersonal relationships, and spiritual dimensions. The link between a person's psyche and health has been extensively studied in the field of psychoneuroimmunology. Studies have established relationships among health status, mental outlook, and finding meaning in life (Antonovsky, 1987; Ferreira & Sherman, 2008; Hatala, 2008; Iwarrsson, Horstmann, & Slaug, 2007; Lewis, 2008a, 2008b). As client advocates, caregivers, coordinators, teachers, and counselors, nurses look at the client holistically to determine what resources are required to promote health.

The holistic approach also requires whole-systems thinking. Whole-systems thinking envisions the "whole." Many smaller interacting systems create the larger (or whole) system (Porter-O'Grady & Malloch, 2003, 2007). For example, a hospital consists of many departments (surgery, radiology, laboratory, central supply, pharmacy, nursing, dietary, rehabilitation services, etc.). Each department assumes responsibility for an integral part of client care. In the case of nursing departments, client care is delivered 24 hours a day, 7 days a week. Thus, different teams of nursing personnel staff the hospital during the different shifts. Each nursing unit also represents another system. The nursing team on a unit may be broken down even further to represent the professional nurse, a vocational (or practical) nurse, and unlicensed care providers. Each person providing client care is also a complex system with many personal needs. When engaging in whole-systems thinking, persons look at the complex nature of all the interacting systems. To further emphasize the nature of whole-systems thinking, consider the hospital as being only a smaller system of the larger health care delivery system. Various nations have different forms of health care delivery systems. How health care is delivered has an impact on whether persons use an organized system or rely on other modes to keep themselves healthy. Waste by-products of health care therapies must be either discarded or recycled. The impact of waste affects the global environment. Nurses use whole-systems thinking frequently in daily clinical practice. As coordinators, nurses look for ways to use resources optimally to meet client care needs (e.g., staffing nursing units to meet client care needs and judicious use of medical supplies). When assuming the role of client advocate, nurses frequently refer clients to community agencies for assistance when needed.

Because of the complex nature of practice and health care delivery, nurses consider many factors when providing client care. Quantum science and relational and systems thinking provide nurses with the ability to consider the impact of clinical decisions not only on clients but also on the institutional, national, and global communities. Because change remains constant, nurses must stay abreast of factors that influence professional practice. The ability to use relational and systems thinking enables the nurse to appraise the entire client care situation before making decisions focused on the client's best interest. The following discussion provides a broad overview of factors that affect professional nursing practice.

Technology, Safety, Communications, and Consumerism in Health Care

Technology has transformed human lives. Increased use of technology in health care has resulted in people surviving illnesses once thought of as untreatable, enabled instant access to information, increased the cost of health care, and created more savvy health care consumers. Pharmaceutical companies post new information about medications on the Internet and target consumers with advertising. In the United States, consumers drive the delivery of health care. Frequently, health care consumers rely on information obtained from the Internet. When assessing client knowledge of health-related information, nurses must find out what clients know and the source of the information. As educators, professional nurses should assist clients in determining the quality of information accessed from various Internet sites (see Chapter 15, "Informatics and Technology in Nursing Practice"). Clients sometimes demand the newest (not always the best) health care treatments from providers (Herzlinger, 2004). Because of the array of sources of health information on the Internet, professional nurses must stay abreast of developments in health promotion and disease management to remain effective caregivers and educators.

In some instances, clients may know more about their health problems than health care providers (Herzlinger, 2004). For example, a young woman, newly diagnosed with myasthenia gravis (MG), finds detailed information about her disease from visiting the National Myasthenia Gravis Foundation website. She learns what medications may result in increased muscle weakness. When she needs surgery that requires hospitalization, she brings the long list of medications known to increase muscle weakness in persons with MG to the hospital so that she will not receive them. However, her action may have been unnecessary because nurses and physicians providing her care have access to the same information via the Internet using a desktop or handheld computer.

Constant connections to cellular telephones and pagers serve as distractions to focusing on persons with whom one is interacting and frequently result in ineffective interpersonal communication. Nurses have always valued developing therapeutic relationships with clients. Clients expect nurses to care for them by assuring their safety, being competent in nursing, taking action that is in their best interests, and listening to them. Some health care organizations provide nurses with pagers (or cellular telephones) so nurses can receive instant messages (in case of client emergency or other client needs). These devices can prevent nurses from devoting their entire attention to the client whom they are helping. In addition, some clients become distracted when their own cellular telephones ring while receiving health care and may miss critical information on how to best manage their health (Herzlinger, 2004).

Along with the latest developments in traditional medical care, many clients have knowledge of alternative and complementary health care therapies. Some consumers expect health care professionals, including nurses, to have knowledge of, and provide them with, these therapies or to offer advice about them (Herzlinger, 2004; Ross, Wenzel, & Mitlyng, 2002; Porter-O'Grady & Malloch, 2003, 2007). Professional nurses must inquire as to all health care practices used by clients to ensure the safety of prescribed, traditional medical therapies and to determine if any complementary or alternative therapies may pose client health hazards.

In today's health care, the client and health care providers work as partners toward common goals. Looking out for one's own safety or the safety of a loved one has become a factor in care delivery. Accrediting agencies, health care facilities, and health care professionals provide clients and families with information about how to remain safe while hospitalized by providing them with educational materials about fall prevention and the importance of handwashing. The media also share information with consumers about unsafe health care practices. Professional nurses and all health team members strive to keep clients safe. Technological devices such as bar-coding machines reduce the incidence of errors in medication and bedside acquisition of blood and body fluid specimens for laboratory testing. Because of the complex nature of health care delivery, various members of the health care team assume different aspects of care. Thus, effective communication becomes crucial in ensuring that all health team members involved in the client's care are aware of specific needs and anything that might adversely affect the client (as in the aforementioned case of the woman with MG). Breakdown in communication frequently results in client care errors, and, when errors occur, the system involving the entire team bears the blame rather than a single person (Porter-O'Grady & Malloch, 2007).

The Global Community and Health Care

Besides technology, the emergence of a single world economy and the acknowledgment of finite earth resources for all persons have resulted in a changed context for professional practice. Disparities in the quality of life and health care have surfaced. Whereas undeveloped and overpopulated nations are looking for ways to combat malnutrition and infectious diseases, citizens of highly developed nations suffer from health problems related to a life of excess, such as obesity, diabetes mellitus, and cardiovascular disease. Developed nations have well-refined health care delivery systems along with access to sophisticated treatments, while undeveloped nations (especially those in political turmoil) may have no organized systems to meet the health care needs of residents (Fried & Gaydos, 2002; U.S. Census Bureau, 2008b).

Along with differences in health problems related to wealth, the nations of the world are connected as a global economic community. Companies looking to reduce labor costs set up manufacturing and service centers in countries where there are fewer regulations to protect workers, and where persons just want income to provide the basics (food, clothing, and shelter) for their families. Outsourcing of jobs decreases the tax revenue that would have been generated to finance governmental health care programs, and newly unemployed workers find themselves without health insurance coverage (Fried & Gaydos, 2002). According to the U.S. Census Bureau (2008a), 47 million Americans lack health insurance coverage.

Political and social unrest in one nation have the potential to disrupt the economies of many nations. Fried and Gaydos (2002) characterized the current global phenomena that threaten the health of the world population:

1. The exacerbation of old infections (e.g., multidrug-resistant tuberculosis [TB], and smallpox as a potential biologic weapon)
2. The emergence of new infections (e.g., the HIV/AIDS pandemic)
3. Environmental devastation (natural or manmade disasters)
4. Lowering of occupational and environmental standards for workers (especially in underprivileged countries)
5. Global drug trafficking
6. War
7. Terrorism
8. Domestic violence
9. Suicide

According to infectious disease experts, their worst nightmare would be the birth of a new, highly contagious lethal flu virus. Because of worldwide air travel, the virus could spread to many areas of the world within 100 days of its emergence. In this scenario, clusters of cases would pop up simultaneously in Sydney, London, Toronto, and Los Angeles, and hundreds of persons would die as their lungs filled with fluid. In actuality, public health officials cooperating globally prevented a pandemic of severe acute respiratory syndrome (SARS) in 2003 (Enserink, 2004) and a TB epidemic in 2007 (when an American with active tuberculosis flew across the Atlantic Ocean twice).

Desire for Equality While Maintaining a Personal Cultural Identity

Despite globalization and access to information from around the world, persons strive to maintain ties to their culture. Current geopolitical unrest stems from the perception that

democracy, capitalism, and freedom are best for, and wanted by, all persons. Many persons immigrate to developed wealthier nations to escape political persecution or less-than-ideal economic situations. Others may come to developed nations to secure treatment for diseases. Many persons born in developed nations value their cultural heritage. As caregivers, nurses who deliver culturally sensitive nursing care acknowledge the cultural needs of clients. Culturally sensitive health care enables the health care system to accommodate client needs to abide by specific cultural practices. Some health care facilities use computers that permit printing of discharge instructions in more than one language and have interpreters for staff to use when working with clients from diverse cultures. In some cases, folk healers are permitted to practice in inpatient settings (Dossey, Keegan, & Guzzetta, 2005). As client advocates, sometimes nurses have to question specific cultural practices that might be detrimental to client health. (More detailed information on multicultural issues in professional practice is presented in Chapter 11.) When questioning client health practices, nurses use personal values and belief systems. Determining if and when a client's health practices are questionable depends on the individual nurse's knowledge and beliefs systems. Part of education involves discovery of things unknown about oneself. The next section offers a discussion about philosophy and its significance for professional nursing practice.

PHILOSOPHY

Philosophy is a conceptual discipline and involves things that cannot be directly touched or observed. The word philosophy is derived from the following Greek words: philia (love or friendship) and sophia (wisdom). Philosophers strive after wisdom, not necessarily to possess it. "Wisdom is used inclusively to cover the sustained intellectual inquiry in any area, the understanding and practice of morality, and the cultivation of such enlightened opinions and attitudes as lead to a life of happiness and contentment" (Earle, 1992, p. 2). People have been searching for meaning and happiness in their lives for centuries. Development of a personal philosophy requires examination of beliefs and values about life and requires a little time. However, development of a collective philosophy (group philosophy) requires much time and consolidation of individual beliefs and values. Philosophies may change as people gain new knowledge and skills through life journeys.

Anyone can be a philosopher. Tools used by philosophers include analyzing concepts (in terms of necessary and sufficient conditions and specific criteria, and by counterexamples), doubting everything, and describing our inner lives (phenomenology or lived experience). When describing lived experiences, persons capture the essence of the situation (Earle, 1992; Law, 2005). Finding meaning in one's life enables persons to survive harsh conditions (Frankl, 1963) and promotes health (Antonovsky, 1987; Church, 2007; Lewis, 2008b).

Building the Foundation

The discipline of philosophy consists of nine major areas, each of which is summarized as follows:

1. Logic: the systematic study of arguments for logical or illogical reasoning. Does this make sense?
2. Epistemology: the study of knowledge. What is knowledge? How do people acquire it?
3. Philosophy of science: the explanation of the successes of science. How is science used? What are the benefits of hard sciences to humans?
4. Metaphysics (ontology): the analysis of issues surrounding the ultimate nature of existence, reality, and experience. What is there? This branch also addresses the reality of abstractions (from mathematical constructs such as numbers, to religious concepts such as God, angels, and the human soul), and the existence of abstractions in the absence of human thought.

5. Philosophy of mind: the study of the nature of the mental dimension of people. What is the mind? How should we understand intentions, desires, beliefs, emotions, pleasure, and pain? How do mental processes explain human behavior?
6. Ethics (moral philosophy): the study of the appropriateness of possible courses of action based on a system of moral principles and values. What is morality? What actions are obligatory, morally permissible, or impermissible?
7. Sociopolitical philosophy: the study of the control and regulation of persons living in a society, and the means to improve their lives. Where do states come from? What does it mean to be a citizen of a state? Must we obey laws, and why? When should laws be changed?
8. Philosophy of religion: the study of the meaning of human life. Is religious language meaningful? Does God exist? Is there good and evil? What other basis can give meaning to life if the religious assumptions were to be proven false?
9. Aesthetics: the study of what constitutes beauty. What is beauty? What makes something a work of art? Why are art and other forms of artistic expression important?

Philosophy focuses on conceptual clarity and requires an individual journey while providing a foundation for human action (Earle, 1992; Law, 2005). For clarity, philosophy of nursing is defined as the intellectual and affective outcomes of the professional nurses' efforts to:

1. Understand the ultimate relationships between humans, environment, and health.
2. Approach nursing as a scientific discipline.
3. Integrate a sense of values into practice.
4. Appreciate aesthetic elements that contribute to health and well-being.
5. Define the mission of nursing.
6. Articulate a personal belief system about human beings, environment, health, and nursing.

Significance of Philosophy for Nursing

Achievement of intellectual enlightenment is considered better protection against calamitous mistakes than ignorance. Thus, over time, the study of philosophy has accrued great benefits for individuals, societies, and, particularly, specific sciences. Pursuing the objectives of philosophy provides individuals an opportunity to develop an understanding of the world around them and to exercise value judgments. The quest for reason develops understanding. Development of a personal system of values requires making ethical and aesthetic decisions. Science benefits from philosophy essentially because philosophy governs scientific methods through logic and ethics.

The nursing profession needs nursing philosophers who articulate visions for nursing as a scientific discipline, emphasize concern for the ultimate good of humankind, develop belief systems reflecting sound ethics, reflect upon the meaning of nursing, and conduct periodic review of philosophies of nursing. Never carved in stone, a nursing philosophy remains a constant work in progress.

Practitioners of the profession of nursing need personal philosophies that reflect a belief in recasting the health system to benefit all humankind rather than ensuring institutional survival. Nursing philosophers analyze current health care systems and conceptualize the bases for nursing practice, research, and education. These nursing philosophers also concern themselves with moral issues surrounding nursing and health care while promoting behavior based on a professional code of ethics.

Rafael (1996) coined the term "empowered caring" to denote leadership as a unity of power and caring that values the characteristics and experiences of women, and a system of ethics that "stems from a heightened awareness of interrelatedness and emerges as a sense of responsibility toward others" (p. 15). Rafael's writing demonstrates the work of a nursing philosopher who provides novel thinking and uses this to shift from a hierarchical approach to nursing to one where nurses and nurse leaders share knowledge and expertise with clients (and each other).

Finally, nurse leaders have identified a system of values to guide the nursing profession. The American Association of Colleges of Nursing (AACN) in 1986 defined values as "beliefs or ideals to which an individual is committed and which guide behavior" (p. 5). According to AACN (1986), values should be "reflected in attitudes, personal qualities, and consistent patterns of behavior" (p. 5). The AACN has identified altruism, equality, aesthetics, freedom, human dignity, justice, and truth as values that underpin the practice of professional nursing. Although these values were developed nearly 2 decades ago, they remain relevant today.

Developing a Personal Nursing Philosophy

A nursing philosophy provides a personal perspective for nursing practice, research, and scholarship (Salsberry, 1994). A philosophy combines the way of doing with the way of being (Rew, 1994). Development of a nursing philosophy requires that the nurse embark on a journey of self-discovery. As knowledge and experience in nursing expand, a personal nursing philosophy may change. A personal nursing philosophy is never complete, but always remains a work in progress. Because the profession of nursing concerns itself with human beings, health, nursing, and the environment, most personal philosophies of nursing address these key concepts. Carper (1978) identified four patterns of knowing in nursing: personal knowledge, empirics, aesthetics, and ethics (presented in more detail in Chapter 4). A well-developed nursing philosophy represents personal knowledge related to professional nursing.

To construct a personal philosophy of nursing, one must engage in reflective thinking about one's relationship to the universe. Discovery of a personal **mission** or goal within the realm of nursing solidifies the decision to practice professional nursing. Because nursing focuses on individuals and the environment, a beginning nursing philosophy should minimally address these concepts.

From a nursing perspective, to develop a nursing philosophy, the individual nurse should examine and answer the following questions:

1. What is the environment, and what is the nature of the relationship between humans and the environment?
2. What is your central belief about the individual person and that person's potential?
3. What is your central belief about the family and its potential?
4. What is your central belief about the community and its potential?
5. What are your central beliefs about the relationship between society and health?
6. What is your view on health? Is it a continuum? A state? A process?
7. How do illness and wellness relate to health?
8. What is the central reason for the existence of nursing?
9. Who is the recipient of nursing care?

From the perspective of a philosopher's concern with knowledge, the individual nurse should look at the following questions that consider essential elements of the scientific discipline:

1. Is nursing a science or art? Or both?
2. From what cognitive base does the professional nurse operate?
3. What is nursing process? How is it implemented?
4. What is necessary to apply nursing knowledge?
5. How is the theory base for nursing derived?
6. What is the theoretical framework for the profession? Or is there more than one theoretical framework?
7. What are the purposes and processes of nursing research?

A Sample Nursing Philosophy   DISPLAY 3-1

Nursing is like a diamond ring. Special conditions must exist for a diamond ring to be created, and special care must be taken to maximize its luster.

Nurses hold a sacred trust with their clients when clients put their lives in the nurse's hands. The nurse **has a mission** to focus on what is best for the client when making decisions concerning care. When possible, the nurse and clients work as partners to promote health. **Together they carve out a multifaceted** **plan of care that integrates the needs of body, mind, and spirit. The nurse always considers client choices for care. However, when the client is no longer able to choose, the nurse abides by information left previously by the client or by the family's wishes.** Along with caring for individuals, the nurse cares for families and communities. A diamond ring never shows its luster if left in a box; **a nurse fails to shine when unable to care for others.**

From the philosopher's concern with ethics and aesthetics, the professional nurse must attempt to answer the following questions reflecting the valuation elements of nursing:

1. What are the essential rights and responsibilities of the professional nurse?
2. What are the essential rights and responsibilities of recipients of nursing care?
3. What are the governing ethical principles in the delivery of nursing care and the conduct of nursing research?
4. What are your beliefs about the educational requirements for the practice of the profession?
5. What are your beliefs about the teaching–learning process?
6. What is the ultimate goal of professional nursing care?

The greatest opportunity to begin developing answers to the preceding questions begins with the first nursing course. However, as nurses attain higher levels of education, beginning a new course becomes an opportune time to evaluate and modify a professional nursing philosophy. A nurse's professional self-concept is built on the foundation of personal life, and educational and clinical practice experiences. As a nurse progresses on his or her life journey, finding meaning in one's personal and professional existence remains a constant challenge. Articulation of a personal nursing philosophy helps the nurse find purpose, create meaning, and increase commitment to the profession of nursing. A sample and abbreviated nursing philosophy is found in Display 3-1. In the sample philosophy, the author uses an analogy to present her philosophical views about nursing. Analogies are useful to some when presenting deeply held beliefs. However, a nursing philosophy does not require using an analogy; statements about personal beliefs serve just as well. As you develop your philosophy, realize that there is no "right" nursing philosophy. You may also find that your nursing philosophy may change.

Once you have an established nursing philosophy, you can use it in many ways. When seeking employment, ask to see the potential employer's organizational philosophy and see how closely it matches your own. A recent trend in health care is the development of a unit-based philosophy. To engage in the process, all unit staff meet and draft a philosophy. This process is time-consuming and creates some interesting debates among staff members. When organizational and personal philosophies match, people have more commitment to work processes and increased job satisfaction.

 MORALITY AND ETHICS IN NURSING PRACTICE

Within any practice context, nurses feel compelled to do what is "right" for their clients. **Morality**, as defined by O'Neill (1995, p. 224), encompasses "the oughts of a given society." Ethics is "the philosophical study of morality" (Noddings, 1984, p. 1). Nurses confront many situations in which they rely upon their consciences for decision making. When working with coherent clients, nurses provide information and share decision making with them.

By virtue of being a nurse, individual nurses are expected to care. Caring permeates the profession of nursing. Early Indian and Christian nurses tended to the infirmed as a way to express altruism. Nurses provide holistic health care services in a caring manner. Persons acknowledge that a desire to care for others stimulated them to enter the nursing profession (Boughn, 1994, 2001; Okrainec, 1994; Streubert, 1994). The science and art of nursing center around the concept of caring. Experts in caring theory emphasize that before one can effectively care for others over a lifetime, the person must be able to care for the self (Benner, 1994; Benner & Wrubel, 1989; Watson, 1988, 1999, 2005). Watson (1988, 2005) proclaimed that caring is a moral imperative. Nurses enter the nursing profession with an intention to care, and society expects them to care.

Recent changes in health care delivery prevent nurses from having the time to express caring in practice. Some institutions treat nurses as replaceable technicians who have sophisticated skills. Clients become consumers. Instead of individualized care, health care consumers receive care from standardized plans. Nurses feel pressure to streamline care to maximize use of health care resources.

The shift of nursing care to a "trade service" rings true, especially when managed care looks for cost-cutting measures such as increased use of unlicensed care providers. Health insurers limit covered health care services and an individual's right to choose health care providers. Access to and justification for care supersede the more important, close interpersonal relationships that nurses build with clients. Therefore, the main stimulus for entering nursing, caring, becomes less valued by health care providers.

Gilligan (1982) identified two ways of thinking about moral development. She associated these conceptions of morality with male and female modes of describing relationships between others and self (Gilligan, p. 19):

1. Fairness: connecting moral development to the understanding of rights and rules (male mode)
2. Concern with the activity of care: connecting moral development to the understanding of responsibilities and relationships (female mode)

Traditional views of moral development emphasize "rights" over relationships and responsibilities (Kohlberg, 1981). Noddings (1984) proposed that morality and **ethics** should be "rooted in receptivity, relatedness and responsiveness" (p. 2). Haegert (2004) adapted Noddings, work on the ethics of caring to professional nursing practice. For Noddings, caring involves two aspects of human nature in the embodied and ethical self. The first encompasses an ideal self that is "synonymous with caring" and the "vision that implied a picture of goodness toward the one caring (the nurse) and the one cared for (the patient)" (Haegert, p. 434). As nurses practice, much energy is devoted to the development of authentic, therapeutic, and caring relationships with clients. Nurses also consider legal and institutional standards of care, along with client rights for self-determination and the equal access to care. Therefore, nursing presents a unique opportunity for blending different approaches to morality and ethics. However, as long as society values fairness and responsibility over receptivity, relatedness, and responsiveness, contributions made by professional nurses may not be as valued as those made by members of other health professions.

Morality supersedes status when persons entrust their lives, a sacred trust, to others. Therefore, moral principles guide health care providers in practice. Several moral principles central to nursing include beneficence, fidelity, and veracity. According to Flynn (1987), the principle of beneficence is to do only good. This principle also requires that persons act to prevent harm. Aroskar (1987) viewed fidelity as undisputed and primary loyalty and faithfulness to the client. Finally, veracity requires absolute truth telling. Professional nurses use these principles daily when providing care to clients.

Moral and ethical principles create dilemmas for nurses. Disagreements surface regarding what is good for a client, depending upon the situation (Flynn, 1987). Individual members of health care teams may disagree on what is best for a terminally ill person.

Fidelity specifies that nurses should always remain loyal and faithful to the client and to abide by the client's wishes. Sometimes, nurses encounter situations that require them to deceive or withhold information from clients to protect the institutions in which they work, or physicians whom they serve. Most institutions require nurses to report errors using some form of incident reporting. However, many institutional policies specify that the nurse should not document completion of an incident report.

When nurses encounter situations in which there is no good outcome, the principle of double effect (known as choosing the "lesser evil") guides practice. Keegen (1995, p. 140) outlined that the following four conditions should be met to justify actions:

1. The act itself must be morally good or at least indifferent.
2. The good effect must not be achieved by means of the bad effect.
3. Only the good effect must be intended, although the bad effect is foreseen and known.
4. The good effect intended must be equal to or greater than the bad effect.

As client advocates, nurses must act on behalf of clients. To assess a particular clinical situation, nurses use critical thinking skills to collect and analyze information, and to formulate possible courses of action. As critical thinkers, nurses also anticipate consequences of actions before choosing the best course to take. Professional nurses use values and philosophical beliefs to set priorities and establish action plans in ethically and morally charged situations. For example, Mrs. G is a 96-year-old woman in a coma from a head injury from an automobile accident in which she was the driver. Before the accident, she lived independently and volunteered at the library teaching adults to read. Mrs. G has been unresponsive and ventilator dependent for 3 days. She has shown no improvement, but her son is insisting on a tracheotomy so that his mother can be maintained on the ventilator until she regains consciousness. In this situation, nurses caring for Mrs. G turn to ethics when having to make value-based decisions about how to provide the best care for Mrs. G and her son.

 ETHICAL DECISION-MAKING PROCESS

According to Bandman and Bandman (1995), nursing ethics focus on doing good and avoiding harm. Ethical behavior relies on the ability to make choices. The nurse bears responsibility for valuing choices that clients make. Choices may be clearly articulated when persons complete living wills before becoming incapacitated. However, when persons fail to make desires known before they are unable to do so, health care professionals rely on families for treatment-related decisions. In the absence of family, health care professions use moral and ethical tenets to guide actions.

Nurses, like all other scientists and philosophers, base decisions on outcomes of inquiry. Munhall (1988) linked nursing inquiry to ethical reflection with the ultimate ethical question being "[T]oward what goal and what end?" (p. 151). Munhall added that "many of our research endeavors focus on facilitating 'health.' The search for a means to produce a desired health outcome requires critical ethical reflection" (p. 152).

Different Perspectives

Traditionally, three perspectives provide a foundation for and influence ethical thinking: principalism, care, and contextualism. Of the three, the most prevalent framework is **principalism**, which is "an orientation incorporating duties, rights, and principles" (O'Neill, 1995, p. 232); this perspective values rationalism. However, O'Neill acknowledged the importance of incorporating analysis of individual situations, sensitivity to the needs of others, and relationship dynamics when principalism guides ethical decision making.

The **care** perspective values dialogue to discover the particular needs of the person(s) involved in the decision. Finally, in **contextualism**, individual situations become the paradigm cases that provide "rules of thumb" to follow. In the contextualist perspective, practical experience in patient care is highly valued (O'Neill, 1995). Nursing based on contextualism supports detailed analysis of individual nursing situations and determines the best approaches to fit each situation.

In a postmodern world, persons tend to discount the simpler, monolithic approach to life and prefer pluralism. McCarthy (2006) proposed a pluralistic view of nursing ethics that blends the traditional and theory views of nursing ethics. The traditional view espouses that nursing ethics is indeed a subcategory of health care ethics. With the traditionalist approach, nurses engage in identifying, analyzing, and making decisions using the concepts of deontology (acting on the basis of moral duty and obligations), utilitarianism (acting to bring about the greatest good), or principalism (using duties, rights, and rules based on truth, laws, or doctrine) to navigate ethical challenges encountered in daily practice. On the other hand, the theory view of ethics espouses a nursing-focused, ethical approach based on philosophical appoaches derived from "virtue ethics, care ethics, or feminist ethics" (McCarthy, 2006, p. 160). This approach also uses ethical standards developed by international, national, and specialty nursing organizations. The theory view of ethics is contextual and emphasizes the power relationships among persons, societies, and organizations. In a pluralistic view of nursing ethics, nurses use a combination of approaches to reflect upon and make decisions about encountered ethical dilemmas.

Typically, ethical dilemmas are messy, heart-wrenching situations with no clear-cut answers. In practice, nurses (and other health care professionals) must make decisions with which they can live and, perhaps, make a better decision in the future. However, some persons may experience confusion in how to figure out life and find meaning in it when rules are abandoned. They may desire to find the "right" way to approach a given situation and develop radical, steadfast approaches that fuel political debates and conflict. Consider the following example of the nursing profession. For years, nursing scholars have debated if nursing is an art or a science. Emphasis on technology, scientific evidence, and quality improvement suggests that nursing is a science. However, considering the beauty of the deep, meaningful, interpersonal relationship among nurses and clients and capturing how it unfolds suggest that nursing may really be an art. Conventional thinking would require a decision to be made. However, a pluralistic view would suggest that, perhaps, nursing could simultaneously be both an art and a science.

Questions for Reflection 3-1

1. What are my beliefs and values about human life?
2. How strong are these beliefs and values?
3. What would I do if I encountered a client care situation in which decisions were made that were against my values and beliefs? Why would I act this way?

An Ethical Decision-Making Process

Nurses frequently encounter moral and ethical problems in practice, thereby creating a need for a workable method with which to analyze and resolve ethical dilemmas. Fowler and Levine-Ariff (1987, pp. 183–184) proposed a systematic **ethical decision-making process** that incorporates principalism, care, and contextualism to help nurses thoughtfully address moral problems in practice. Fowler's steps are outlined in Table 3-1, and Display 3-2 provides an example of how the process is used. Consistent use of a sequential process for ethical decision making enables nurses to consider all aspects surrounding a situation before taking action. Once the situation has resolved, engagement in evaluation allows the nurse to reflect on actions taken, and to generate ideas for ways to manage a future, similar situation.

TABLE 3-1

Process for Ethical Decision Making

Step	Thoughts and Actions
Identify the problem.	Analyze the situation to clearly identify the problem. Determine the presence of more than one ethical concern. Look for any conflict of duties with personal or professional values. Determine if the ethical conflict rightly belongs to you.
Identify the morally relevant facts.	Examine the complete context of the dilemma (how it occurred, likelihood of arising again). Identify the key players and their views and vested interest(s). Identify administrative, political, economic, legal, medical, and aesthetic concerns.
Evaluate the ethical problem.	Examine the ethical norms by reviewing the literature, code of ethics for nursing, and moral traditions in the profession. Based on information from the review, identify guides for moral actions that are appropriate for the situation. Consider broader ethical principles, such as justice and autonomy, to provide directions for action. Consider aspects that are unique to the dilemma. Examine the dilemma using each ethical principle. Assign priorities to each of the ethical principles (Chapter 1) according to professional and personal values.
Identify and analyze action alternatives.	Determine all possible options for action. Create new options not found elsewhere. Analyze each alternative action for potential harms and benefits. Speculate on the possible outcomes of each action for the key players. Identify which actions will produce subsequent dilemmas. Analyze each alternative according to institutional procedures.
Choose and act.	Choose a course of action (preferably in consultation with others). Modify the plan in accordance with legal, institutional, or other values while remaining true to your moral values and norms. Implement the action selected.
Evaluate and modify the plan.	Identify the result of action taken. Clarify your moral feelings about your actions. Generate modifications to the plan used if you encounter similar situations in the future. Modify the current plan if the ethical dilemma persists.

Adapted from Fowler, M.D.M., & Levine-Ariff, J. (Eds.) (1987). *Ethics at the bedside: A source book for the critical care nurse* (pp. 183; 184). Philadelphia: J. B. Lippincott.

Bandman and Bandman (1995, pp. 110) discussed the pitfalls that may occur when nurses use an ethical decision-making process. They labeled these pitfalls "fallacies," or errors in reasoning. Such errors in reasoning include the following:

1. Arguing that because something (X) is the case, therefore, something else (Y) ought to be the case
2. Making someone accept the conclusion of another based on force alone (appealing to force)
3. Abusing the person rather than addressing the person's reasons for making a particular decision
4. Arguing that because everybody does something, that something must be good
5. Appealing to inappropriate authority to justify a decision
6. Assuming that if one exception is made to a rule, then uncontrolled events with unwanted circumstances will occur (called the "slippery slope fallacy")
7. Refusing to allow evidence to be shared if it contradicts one's personal position

An Example Using Fowler's Process

DISPLAY 3-2

Mary is a nurse who works the night shift on an acute general surgical unit. Because of budget cuts, the hospital has eliminated two night shift professional nursing positions, resulting in a consistent staffing pattern of one professional nurse for 15 patients. Mary has always valued her ability to provide individualized nursing care to postoperative patients. However, since she has been working under the new staffing pattern, Mary knows that patients are receiving substandard care (problem identified). Mary realizes that the hospital has been losing revenue, but she also feels that the staffing pattern is unsafe. Her recent complaints to her nurse manager have been futile. Because of unsafe care situations, Mary knows that she will have to inform her nurse manager's supervisor and possibly the director of nursing and hospital administration to analyze the entire situation (morally relevant facts identified). Mary reads current literature and identifies serious gaps in the accepted standards of practice and examines the effects of the new staffing practice on each ethical principle (ethical problem evaluated). After sharing her concerns with her coworkers and manager, Mary and her colleagues work as a team to develop three action plans. They discuss the pros and cons of each plan (alternatives identified and analyzed). The nursing team decides to meet with the director of nursing to share their concerns about unsafe patient care (course of action chosen and implemented). The director of nursing thanks the nurses for informing her of the situation and promises action to increase the number of professional nurses for the night shift on the unit. Two months pass and no change in staffing results. The nurses decide to meet with hospital administration to voice their concerns (plan evaluated and modified).

Bandman and Bandman (1995) offered suggestions for ways to avoid fallacies by using the following principles for ethical decision making:

1. Valuing and respecting the client's self-determination
2. Serving the client's well-being in practice in a manner that prevents harm and does good
3. Treating clients fairly and equally by respecting their rights and treatment options and by making them equal partners in shared health care decisions

Nursing practice, education, and research provide many opportunities for the professional nurse to make ethical decisions and to experience the satisfaction of resolving ethical dilemmas. Situations that generate ethical dilemmas arise from the nurse's efforts to determine what is right. In dealing with each of these ethical issues, the primary responsibility of the professional nurse in caring for the client is always to respect the person as a unified being. Despite variations in the definition of responsibility in nursing, most nurses would probably agree that the goal for resolving ethical issues is to achieve what is best for clients while attending to the responsibility to self, professional colleagues, and the profession.

Feeling confident and competent in ethical decision making takes time and practice. Examples of ethical concerns of nurses include the quality of client care, unfair organizational practices, poor-quality work environments, disagreements about end-of-life issues, and conflicts with physicians. When ethical issues arise, nurses may act with power or be powerless. Displays of passivity include silence, "submission, obedience[,] and powerlessness" (Peter, Lunardi, & McFarlane, 2004, p. 403). Empowered nurses directly confront ethical issues through the exercise of resistance. Examples of resistance include whistleblowing, refusal to follow physician orders, acts of disobedience, and direct confrontation. Failure to abide by one's moral principles has been identified as reasons for nurses leaving a job and, in some cases, leaving the profession. Nurses who use resistance for solving ethical dilemmas display great courage because of possible retaliation against them from persons (or the organization) with whom they disagree (Peter et al., 2004).

Achieving Ethical Competence

Achieving ethical competence takes time and practice. **Ethical competence** means that nurses have the knowledge, confidence, and courage to take action to do what is right in an ethically charged situation. In nursing education programs, curricula allot time to the presentation of ethical concepts and discussion of ethical dilemmas. Cultural aspects related to defining what is right and wrong are also covered in most professional nursing programs. For example, American news broadcasts (in May 2008) about babies being tossed off the roof of a temple in India shocked and horrified many Americans despite the fact that no infants sustained injury. However, the religious beliefs in India specified that the rite actually served as a blessing and protection against future harm. Therefore, nurses must possess a strong knowledge base and value system to provide ethically correct professional services.

Key concepts related to nursing ethics include understanding of basic theoretical approaches to ethics such as principalism, utilitarianism, and deontology. In addition, professional nurses need to understand the key ethical principles outlined in Table 3-2. Without basic knowledge of ethical principles, nurses may be unaware of ethical dilemmas and how to handle them when they occur.

Before nurses can address ethical dilemmas, they need to have confidence in nursing knowledge and clinical decision-making skills. They also need to have refined communication skills to collect information about the events and to share professional nursing ideas to manage the ethically charged situation. Research Brief 3-1 outlines how professional ethics is an important factor in the professional nurse's clinical competence. As nurses gain experience in handling ethical issues, their confidence increases in their ability to manage them. Confident nurses have the courage to tackle ethical issues as they arise in clinical practice.

Research Brief 3-1

Memarian, R., Salsali, M., Vanaki, Z., Ahmadi, F., & Hajizadeh, E. (2007). Professional ethics as an important factor in clinical competency in nursing. *Nursing Ethics, 14*(2), 203–214.

The investigators used audiotaped semistructured interviews and a purposeful sample to collect data from 36 employed professional nurses in Tehran, Iran, in 2005 to develop a model for gaining and using clinical competency. By using grounded theory methodology, the investigators identified key factors contributing to clinical competence in nursing.

Results revealed that internal and external factors contribute to professional nurses' clinical competency. The internal factors included the personal factors of knowledge and skills, ethical conduct, professional commitment, and respect for self and others. Work experiences, another aspect of internal factors, included effective relationships, interest in the nursing profession, and responsibility and accountability. External factors were composed of professional factors such as effective management, licensure, control, and supervision along with environmental factors including provision of an effective educational system and adequate technology. Ethical conduct in all areas of practice was identified as an essential element of professional competency.

Although this study was executed in Iran, the findings may hold true for professional nurses worldwide. Nurses can make more effective decisions about client care when they understand the ethical elements associated with professional practice. More research is needed to see if the same elements would be present in nurses from different nations.

 ## MAJOR CONTEXTUAL ELEMENTS AFFECTING NURSING PRACTICE

To understand the moral or ethical dimension of nursing more fully, the nurse needs to understand the contextual elements of nursing practice that either reinforce or challenge belief and value systems. Contextualism refers to the constellation of all factors that impact

TABLE 3-2

Key Ethical Principles

Principle	Definition	Examples
Nonmaleficence	To do no harm to others	*Due diligence*: Exercise care in a situation so that one does not harm another, e.g., carefully checking medications before administering them *Double effect*: The outcomes outweigh the potential harm, e.g., the administration of chemotherapy (adverse effects) to kill cancer cells
Beneficence	To do only good for others	*Compassion*: Caring with a desire to help others, e.g., attending to the psychological needs of a person who has a new colostomy *Veracity*: Being honest and telling the truth, e.g., informing clients about all options for the treatment of a health condition *Fidelity*: Being faithful in relationships and in matters of trust, e.g., maintaining the confidentiality of personal health information and disclosing information when obtaining informed consent *Proportionality*: Choosing the option that produces more good than harm, e.g., determining the best treatment options for clients
Autonomy	The right for persons to make free and informed choices	*Privacy*: Respecting another's personal space and business, e.g., asking for permission prior to touching a client *Confidentiality*: Keeping personal information about clients secret, e.g., not holding an end-of-shift report within earshot of visitors and other clients *Advocacy*: Hearing and respecting client wishes, needs, and values, e.g., abiding by a terminally ill client's desires not to be connected to life support *Informed consent*: Ensuring that clients receive all pertinent information surrounding a prescribed treatment so they can make the best possible decision, e.g., explaining all potential hazards of a surgical procedure
Justice	Fairness and impartiality to provide equality of service according to individual needs and contributions	*Respect*: Preserving or maintaining personal dignity and rights, e.g., providing equal services for all clients despite their ethnicity or culture *Allocation of resources*: Fairly distributing limited services based on need rather than ability to pay, e.g., using complex life-saving technology on persons with the potential for survival

Sources of information:
Agnes, M. (2005). *Webster's new world college dictionary* (4th ed.). Cleveland, OH: Wiley.
Bosek, M., & Savage, T. (2007). *The ethical component of nursing education, integrating ethics into clinical experience*.
   Philadelphia: Lippincott Williams & Wilkins.

the current situation. In contextualism, the nurse analyzes a whole situation including background, environmental, and personality factors and relationships. Display 3-3 briefly summarizes selected demographic, economic, cultural, environmental, and ethical factors that characterize the contexts of nursing practice that are discussed subsequently. Public policy, another significant contextual element, is discussed in Chapter 20. The following discussion aims to provide a general overview of factors chosen as being most influential to professional nursing practice.

Five Major Contextual Elements Affecting Professional Nursing Practice

DISPLAY 3-3

Demographic: These characteristics reflect social and economic conditions. The demographics of a population influence the opportunities an individual has to form or maintain cooperative and interdependent relationships with fellow human beings.

Economic: Economics primarily focuses on the considerations of costs and return for provided services. In cultures in which health services are viewed as commodities, providers must be reimbursed for their services. However, when societies view health care as a basic right, governments usually provide a national health insurance plan for all citizens.

Cultural: Provides organization and structure for groups of people. Within a culture, people share common values, beliefs, norms, and practices (Giger & Davidhizar, 1999). Culture plays a key role in the development of human behavior patterns. Some-

times cultural beliefs clash with scientifically based health care practices.

Environmental: These elements consist of global health influences. Along with safe food sources, the human species requires clean air and water for survival. Kleffel (1996) presents an ecocentric view of the world by describing that "the environment is considered to be whole, living, and interconnected" (p. 1).

Ethical: These elements encompass the moral obligations and duties that emerge from an individual's struggle with good and bad, and right and wrong. Ethical nurses act in accordance with approved standards or codes for professional behavior. Nurses confront ethical issues in daily practice. Ethical dilemmas occur when nurses confront situations in which alternatives for action produce unsatisfactory results. Sometimes, what is ethically right can be legally or morally wrong.

Demographic Elements

Within the next decade, Americans will be living longer and growing older. By 2015, over 53 million Americans will be 65 years old or older. The life expectancy for American women will be 81 years, and for American men, 79 years. By 2025, one in five Americans (70 million persons) will be older than 65 years (U.S. Census Bureau, 2008b). The percentage of elderly will also increase in Europe, Asia, and Latin America, with China having close to 290 million persons older than age 60 in 2030 (U.S. Census Bureau, 2008a). Elderly persons use more health care resources and have different care needs than younger persons. Nurses need to consider specific needs of the elderly when providing care to them.

The increased elderly population may strain current health care resources because this age group has an increased risk for chronic illness. Persons older than 65 have higher rates of hospital admittance and may have greater need for assistance with activities of daily living. In 2004, the National Center for Health Statistics reported that 51% of Americans older than the age of 75 years had mobility limitations, and 23% relied on family members for assistance.

According to Horrigan (2004) at the U.S. Department of Labor Bureau of Labor Statistics, 623,156 new nurses will be needed to meet the demand for registered nurses in 2012 (an increase of 25.2%). The increased numbers stem from nurses needed to care for the aging population and to replace aging nurses who currently practice.

Perhaps the most important health care need for the American population is the need for health promotion and disease prevention services. Nurses need to look for ways to promote healthy aging. Efforts should target persons of all ages, especially adults and adolescents whose current lifestyles and health habits will significantly affect their future wellness (U.S. Department of Health & Human Services, 2000). Middle-aged adults find themselves torn between meeting career obligations, raising teenagers, and caring for aging parents. In the role of counselor, professional nurses can provide clients (and their children or spouses) support by inquiring about the stresses associated with fulfilling multiple role responsibilities.

Cultural Elements

The U.S. population will continue to become more diverse. In 2007, the U.S. Census Bureau reported that 73.9% of the population considered themselves to be white (this included persons of Middle Eastern ancestry and some Hispanics). The distribution of ethnic groups is not equal in all areas of the United States. The Hispanic population represents 14.8% of the U.S. population, and became the largest minority group. Persons of African American heritage represented 12.2% of the population. Asian Americans accounted for 4.4% of the population; American Indians and Alaskan Natives represent 0.8% of the population. Finally, Native Hawaiians and Pacific Islanders account for 0.8% of the population. Many Americans counted in the updated figures reported having more than one racial background. The western states and Texas had the highest percentage of Hispanics (24–25%). Increasing diversity increases the complexity of providing effective nursing care.

In locations with large Hispanic populations, nurses may need to communicate with clients who may not be fluent in English. In addition, many immigrant groups tend to settle in a specific community. Nurses need to be aware of culturally diverse population clusters and their usual health practices to provide effective nursing care. Meeting the health care demands of a culturally diverse population means that nurses need to understand biophysiologic variations related to risk for specific health problems, development, and medication metabolism, along with specific cultural values, beliefs, and health practices (see Chapter 11 for more specific information).

Economic Elements

The economic gap between the wealthy and the poor in the United States continues to expand. Factors associated with increased poverty levels include age, ethnicity, and education. In 2007, the U.S. Census Bureau reported that 12.3% of Americans lived in poverty. Poverty level is defined as an annual income of $20,614 for a family of four, $16,079 for a family of three, and $13,167 for a family of two. The minority group with the highest poverty level is African Americans (24.3%), followed by Hispanics (20.6%).

Along with ethnicity, educational level also contributes to increased incidence of poverty. The median income of persons with some high school education is $20,321. For high school graduates, the median income is $26,505. The median incomes for persons with higher education are as follows: bachelor's degrees, $43,143; graduate degrees, $52,390; professional degrees, $82,473; and doctorates, $70,853. Close to 8% of adults without high school diplomas are unemployed. Low incomes mean less money to purchase health insurance when money is spent on the basic needs for survival (food, shelter, and clothing) and transportation costs for getting to a job (U.S. Bureau of Labor Statistics, 2008).

Unfortunately, projections for access to health care will be three-tiered, with 38% being empowered, 43% being worried, and 28% being excluded. Consumers excluded from accessing health care will be the poor, uninsured, unemployed, and uneducated, with the poor and uneducated having the poorest access. Currently, 47 million persons (16.1%) in the United States do not have health insurance (U.S. Census Bureau, 2007). The worried consumers include early retirees and persons dependent on employer-provided health insurance. As health expenditures continue to escalate, employers may have to reduce health care benefits or pass on increased costs to employees to afford any form of health insurance coverage. Empowered health care consumers have discretionary income that can be used to cover health care costs. They also tend to be well educated and frequently use technology (especially the Internet) as a source for health care information. Empowered consumers frequently actively participate when making health-related decisions with physicians and other health care professionals.

Health care spending is expected to increase. In 2007, health care expenditures accounted for 15.4% of the GDP. Companies providing health care insurance to employees have seen 12–15% increases in premiums over the past 3 years. Within the next 5 years, company costs for providing health insurance are expected to double. Increased costs for health insurance will be passed on to employees who then may not be able to afford the increased copayments, thereby increasing the numbers of uninsured Americans.

According to the Institute for the Future (2003), the following factors determine personal health status: access to care (10%), genetics (20%), personal health behaviors (50%), and uncontrollable factors (30%). Uninsured Americans have limited access to health care. Personal health-promoting habits require that individuals know what lifestyle behaviors promote health and that they have the resources to obtain them. Persons without health insurance may use free clinics and public health departments for primary health care services. In these settings, an advanced practice nurse assumes the role of caregiver. Other clients may prefer a more holistic approach to health care. These consumers may turn to nurses rather than physicians for primary care services. As educators, professional nurses can teach clients health-promoting strategies. However, if clients do not have the ability to practice them, then nurses can refer them to social or governmental agencies to help them (nurse as client advocate). As change agents, nurses can engage in efforts to change the health care system by actively participating in public policy development (see Chapter 20).

 ## SUMMARY AND SIGNIFICANCE TO PRACTICE

Professional nursing centers on caring for others. When delivering care to individuals, groups, and communities, professional nurses use individual value systems as a basis for some clinical decisions. Many contextual elements affect health care delivery and clinical practice. Sometimes the contextual elements create ethical dilemmas that need to be resolved. Nurses who have examined their beliefs and have developed a personal nursing philosophy have a basis for finding meaning in professional practice. By becoming cognizant of ethical principles and the multiple factors contributing to ethical dilemmas in clinical practice, nurses can readily identify them as they arise. Nurses who have a strong value system and philosophical stance are armed with effective tools to confront ethically charged situations directly and with confidence.

FROM THEORY TO PRACTICE

1. What does it mean to be a professional nurse?
2. How do nurses make differences in the lives of others?
3. After reading this chapter, how would you help Jane, the nurse in the vignette? Outline a plan for you to help Jane make a decision whether or not to continue in her current job or to be a professional nurse.
4. Stephen is often the only registered nurse on duty during the evenings in a nursing home in which he works. Lately, he has become increasingly concerned about one of his patients. Mrs. Moore is a 77-year-old woman with advanced Parkinson's disease who has to be restrained to keep her from pulling out her feeding tube. Whenever Mrs. Moore speaks, she begs to be allowed to die. Mrs. Moore's son and daughter refuse to let the physician remove the feeding tube. Stephen agonizes about what he should do. Analyze this case using the guidelines for the ethical decision-making process outlined in this chapter, and decide what decision should be made about Mrs. Moore.
5. Look at your nursing program's philosophy and the developmental and organizational philosophies at your place of employment. Compare these to your own personal philosophy, and outline key similarities and differences.

WWW INTERNET EXERCISES

1. Search the Web for any college- or university-based nursing program and see if they have the philosophy of the school of nursing posted on the home page.
2. Visit the home page of the American Holistic Nurses Association (AHNA) and read this organization's philosophy of nursing at http://www.ahna.org.

3. Select a nursing organization that interests you. Use the search engine of your choice to get the home page of the organization. Visit the site and see whether you can find the organization's values, mission, and philosophy. Based on a review of available information, outline reasons why you might or might not join the organization.

WWW INTERNET RESOURCES

For an example of an integrated health system: Visit the website of Saint Luke's Health System in Kansas City at http://www.saint-lukes.org. View the mission, vision, and value statements.

For a sample nursing department philosophy, view the nursing department philosophy of Barnes Jewish Hospital in St. Louis, Missouri, at http://www.barnesjewish.org/groups?NavID=636.

Sample nursing organization philosophy: the New Jersey State Nurses Association at http://www.njsna.org/about.htm.

REFERENCES

Agnes, M. (Ed.). (2005). *Webster's new world college dictionary* (4th ed.). Cleveland OH: Wiley.

American Association of Colleges of Nursing (AACN). (1986). *Final report: Project on the essentials of college and university education for professional nursing.* Washington, DC: Author.

Antonovsky, A. (1987). *Unraveling the mystery of health.* San Francisco: Jossey-Bass.

Appleton, C. (1993). The art of nursing: The experience of patients and nursing. *Journal of Advanced Nursing, 18,* 892–899.

Aroskar, M. A. (1987). Fidelity and veracity: Questions of promise keeping, truth telling, and loyalty. In M. D. M. Fowler & J. Levine-Ariff (Eds.), *Ethics at the bedside: A source for the critical care nurse.* Philadelphia: Lippincott Williams & Wilkins.

Bandman E. L., & Bandman, B. (1995). *Nursing ethics through the lifespan* (3rd ed.). Stamford, CT: Appleton & Lange.

Benner, P. (1984). *From novice to expert: Excellence and power in clinical nursing practice.* Menlo Park, CA: Addison-Wesley.

Benner, P., & Wrubel, J. (1989). *The primacy of caring: Stress and coping in health and illness.* Menlo Park, CA: Addison-Wesley.

Boughn, S. (1994). Why do men choose nursing? *Nursing and Health Care, 15,* 406–411.

Boughn, S. (2001). Why women and men choose nursing. *Nursing and Health Perspectives, 22,* 14–19.

Carper, B. A. (1978). Fundamental patterns of knowing in nursing. *Advances in Nursing Science, 1,* 13–23.

Church, D. (2007). *A vision of the future of medicine, the genie in your genes: Epigenetic medicine and the new biology of intention.* Santa Rosa, CA: Elite Books, Energy Psychology Press.

Dossey, B., Keegan, L., & Guzzetta, C. (2005). *Holistic nursing: A handbook for practice* (4th ed.). Sudbury, MA: Jones & Bartlett.

Earle, W. J. (1992). *Introduction to philosophy.* New York: McGraw-Hill.

Enserink, P. M. (2004). Looking the pandemic in the eye. *Science, 306,* 392–394.

Ferreira, V., & Sherman, A. (2007). The relationship of optimism, pain and social support to well-being in older adults with osteoarthritis. *Aging and Mental Health, 11*(1), 89–98.

Flynn, P. A. R. (1987). Questions of risk, duty, and paternalism: Problems in beneficence. In M. D. M. Fowler & J. Levine-Ariff (Eds.), *Ethics at the bedside: A source for the critical care nurse.* Philadelphia: Lippincott Williams & Wilkins.

Fowler, M. D. M., & Levine-Ariff, J. (Eds.). (1987). *Ethics at the bedside: A source for the critical care nurse.* Philadelphia: Lippincott Williams & Wilkins.

Frankl, V. (1963). *Man's search for meaning.* New York: Washington Square Press.

Fried, B. J., & Gaydos, L. M. (Eds.). (2002). *World health systems, challenges and perspectives.* Chicago: Health Administration Press.

Giger, J. N., & Davidhizar, R. E. (1999) *Transcultural nursing assessment and intervention* (3rd ed.). St. Louis, MO: Mosby.

Gilligan, C. (1982). *In a different voice: Psychological theory and women's development.* Cambridge, MA: Harvard University Press.

Haegart, S. (2004). The ethics of self. *Nursing Ethics, 11,* 434–443.

Hatala, A. (208). Spirituality and Aboriginal mental health: An examination of the relationship between Aboriginal spirituality and mental health. *Advances in Mind-Body Medicine* (electronic version), *23*(1), 6–12.

Hawking, S. (2002). *The theory of everything.* Beverly Hills, CA: New Millennium Press.

Herzlinger, R. (2004). *Consumer-driven health care.* San Francisco: Jossey-Bass.

Horrigan, M. (2004, February). Employment projections to 2012: Concepts and context. *Monthly Labor Review*, 3–22.

Institute for the Future. (2003). *Health and health care 2010* (2nd ed.). San Francisco: Jossey-Bass.

Iwarrsson, S., Horstmann, V., & Slaug, B. (2007). Housing matters in very old age—yet differently due to ADL dependence level differences. *Scandinavian Journal of Occupational Therapy*, *14*, 3–15.

Keegan, L. (1995). Holistic ethics. In B. M. Dossey, L. Keegan, C. E. Guzzetta, & L. G. Kolkmeier (Eds.), *Holistic nursing: A handbook for practice* (2nd ed.). Gaithersburg, MD: Aspen.

Kleffel, D. (1996). Environmental paradigms: Moving toward an ecocentric approach. *Advances in Nursing Science*, *18*, 1–10.

Kohlberg, L. (1981). *The philosophy of moral development: Moral stages and the idea of justice*. New York: Harper & Row.

Law, S. (2007). *Eyewitness companions: Philosophy, first American edition*. New York: DK Publishing.

Lewis, S. (2008a). Helping people live between office visits: An interview with Bernie Siegel, MD. *Advances in Mind-Body Medicine* (electronic version), *23*, 24–27.

Lewis S. (2008b). The emerging field of spiritual neuroscience: An interview with Mario Beauregard, PhD. *Advances in Mind-Body Medicine* (electronic version), *23*, 20–23.

McCarthy, J. (2006). A pluralist view of nursing ethics. *Nursing Philosophy*, *7*, 157–164.

McKay, M. L. (2001). The growth of health care. *American Journal of Nursing*, *101*, 24F–24H.

Memarian, R., Salsali, M., Vanaki, Z., Ahmadi, F., & Hajizadeh, E. (2007). Professional ethics as an important factor in clinical competency in nursing. *Nursing Ethics*, *14*, 203–214.

Munhall, P. (1988). Ethical considerations in qualitative research. *Western Journal of Nursing Research*, *10*, 150–162.

National Center of Health Statistics. (2004). National health care expenditures projections: 2002–2012. Available at http://www.cms.hhs.gov/statistics/nhe/projections-2002/proj2002.pdf. Accessed June 25, 2005.

Noddings, N. (1984). *Caring: A feminine approach to ethics and moral education*. Berkeley: University of California Press.

Okrainec, G. D. (1994). Perception of nursing education held by male nursing students. *Western Journal of Nursing Research*, *16*, 94–107.

O'Neill, J. (1995). Ethical decision making and the role of nursing. In G. L. Deloughery (Ed.), *Issues and trends in nursing* (2nd ed.). St. Louis, MO: Mosby-Year Book.

Peter, E., Lunardi, V., & McFarlane, A. (2004). Nursing resistance as ethical action: Literature review. *Journal of Advanced Nursing*, *46*, 403–416.

Porter-O'Grady, T., & Malloch, K. (2003). *Quantum leadership: A textbook of new leadership*. Sudbury, MA: Jones & Bartlett.

Porter-O'Grady, T., & Malloch, K. (2007). *Quantum leadership: A resource for health care innovation* (2nd ed.). Sudbury, MA: Jones & Bartlett.

Rafael, A. R. (1996). Power and caring: A dialectic in nursing. *Advances in Nursing Science*, *19*, 3–17.

Rew, L. (1994). Commentary. In J. F. Kikuchi & H. Simmons. (Eds.), *Developing a philosophy of nursing* (pp. 20–31). Thousand Oaks, CA: Sage.

Ross, A., Wenzel, F., & Mitlyng, J. (2002). *Leadership for the future: Core competencies in healthcare*. Chicago: Health Administration Press.

Salsberry, P. J. (1994). A philosophy of nursing: What is it? What is it not? In J. F. Kikuchi & H. Simmons (Eds.), *Developing a philosophy of nursing* (pp. 11–19). Thousand Oaks, CA: Sage.

Streubert, H. (1994). Male nursing students' perceptions of clinical experience. *Nurse Educator*, *19*, 28–32.

U.S. Bureau of Labor Statistics. (2008). Education and employment: April 2008 updates. Availabe at http://bls.gov/web/cpseea5.pdf. Accessed May 3, 2008.

U.S. Census Bureau. (2007). 2007 current population survey. Available at http://www.census.gov.prod/2007pubs/pd60-223.pdf. Accessed May 3, 2008.

U.S. Census Bureau. (2008a). International data base. Available at http://www.census.gov/ipc/www/idb/worldpopinfo.html. Accessed May 3, 2008.

U.S. Census Bureau. (2008b). World population clock. Available at http://www.census.gov/popclock world.html. Accessed May 3, 2008

U.S. Department of Health and Human Services. (2000). *Healthy people 2010*. Washington, DC. U.S. Government Printing Office.

U.S. Department of Health and Human Services. (2004). National health care expenditures projections: 2002–2012. Available at http://www.cms.hhs.gov/statistics/nhe/projections-2002/proj2002.pdf. Accessed June 25, 2005.

Watson, J. (1988). A case study: Curriculum in transition. In *National League for Nursing. Curriculum revolution: Mandate for change* (pp. 1–8). New York: Author.

Watson, J. (1999). *Postmodern nursing and beyond*. London: Harcourt Brace.

Watson, J. (2005). *Caring science as sacred science*. Philadelphia: F. A. Davis.

CHAPTER 4

Establishing Helping and Healing Relationships

KEY TERMS AND CONCEPTS

Helping relationships
Communication
Metacommunication
Verbal communication
Nonverbal communication
Interpretation
Perception
Collaborative relationships
Principles of communication
Nurses as helpers
Stages of the nurse–client relationship
Mutuality
Anxiety
Caring interaction
Noncaring behaviors
Healing relationships
Professional partnerships

LEARNING OUTCOMES

By the end of this chapter, the learner will be able to:

1 Compare and contrast helping and healing relationships.

2 Specify the importance of communication in professional nursing.

3 Outline major purposes of communication.

4 Discuss principles to establish helpfulness in nurse–client communication.

5 Outline the stages of nurse–client relationship development.

6 Identify the mutuality in helping relationships.

7 Differentiate therapeutic from nontherapeutic communication strategies and relationships.

8 Discuss how nurses use relationships to promote client healing.

9 Explain how health team members can develop meaningful professional partnerships.

VIGNETTE

Margie, an emergency department nurse, has just arrived at work. As she finishes receiving reports and her assignment to be the triage nurse, a middle-aged man with severe chest pain and dyspnea arrives with his family. Margie gets immediate help for the man, who is rushed to the cardiac catheterization laboratory. Margie notices that the family members seem very anxious and distressed. When she asks them if they would like anything, they reply, "No," but the wife tries to hold back tears as she wrings her hands, the daughter's hands shake, and the son paces. Margie notes that the nonverbal behavior of the family is incongruent with the verbal message and wonders what would be the best course of action to help this distressed family.

Many nurses enter the profession with a desire to help others. As a commonly used verb, the word "help" can mean (1) to assist or make things better for another person, (2) to give something necessary to someone in need or trouble, (3) to do part of the work, (4) to assist another person moving from one position or location to another, (5) to aid the growth of or promote, and (6) to serve or wait on another person (Agnes, 2005, pp. 662–663). Professional nurses help clients, colleagues, and other team members in many different ways as they engage in clinical practice. Communication is an essential element of helping others. The human need for relatedness binds people together, and communication serves as the exchange medium in these relationships. The verbal and nonverbal messages exchanged during human relationships determine the structure and function of interpersonal relationships. Communication enables persons to share information, thoughts, and feelings. Indeed, the whole existence and the health status of human beings depend on communication because the affective dimension of life cannot be separated from the biologic or spiritual dimensions.

COMMUNICATION AS INTERACTION

Nurses and clients rely on communication during nurse–client, collegial, and interprofessional interactions. Without communication, nurses cannot effectively provide safe, effective client care.

The Interpersonal Component of Professional Nursing

Effective use of nursing process requires that nurses and clients communicate with each other. When nurses and clients interact, they experience emotions as they communicate. Nurses strive to maximize the client's potential for optimal health. To live out this commitment, nurses must clearly understand the power of communication in shaping professional relationships. Without well-refined communication skills, nurses cannot establish therapeutic relationships with clients. **Helping relationships** occur when nurses communicate with clients with the aim of assisting them to attain optimal health or supporting them through difficult situations. The quality of **communication** between the nurse and the client is an essential determinant of the success of the professional, helping relationship. Mutual goals cannot be defined or achieved in the relationship without effective communication. This chapter focuses on communication as a key factor in the effective use of nursing process and an essential element of helping relationships.

Assuming that humans possess all the characteristics of an open system, the nurse concludes that people are influenced by and influence all human beings with whom they are associated. Indeed, this reciprocal process suggests that the most important human attributes are not only openness to interpersonal experiences but also power to influence self and others. Sullivan (1953, p. 32) assumed that "everyone is more simply human than otherwise."

Human beings influence others primarily through communication. Communication is described as the "exchange of meanings between and among individuals through a shared system of symbols that have the same meaning for both the sender and the receiver of the message" (Vestal, 1995, p. 51). Through communication during nursing interactions with a client, the nurse hopes to create new client attitudes and situations that will influence the client to live in a healthier manner. This goal can be achieved only if the nurse is knowledgeable about the content and process of the nurse–client relationship.

To understand content in nursing situations, the nurse must have knowledge of the person as a human system interacting with the environment and striving for health, and of specific factors that promote positive change in human systems. To understand the process in the nurse–client relationship, the nurse must have knowledge of communication and experience in developing helping relationships. Thus, to participate effectively in nurse–client relationships, intradisciplinary or interdisciplinary relationships, and personal relationships, the nurse must understand the structure and the functions of communication.

Nursing, as an organized body of professionals, has not always been successful in portraying an image of being an autonomous professional discipline. Disagreement among nursing theorists, practitioners, and educators about the purpose and meaning of nursing and key concepts such as nursing diagnosis has led to multiple, and sometimes conflicting, images of nursing. Currently, nurses generally agree that contemporary nursing practice addresses the client holistically to address the full range of human responses and illness. Nurses also agree that assessment of objective and subjective factors related to client health is essential. They concur that that evidence (scientific, intuitive, or mystical) may be used to guide practice. Finally, most nurses in practice acknowledge that in establishing authentic, caring relationships with clients is essential to promote health and healing.

Nursing's unique service to society consists of dealing with human responses in health and illness. These responses are the substance of communication. Thus, professional nursing's business is communication and the purposeful use of communication in nurse–client relationships. The relationship should be "characterized by compassion, continuity, and respect for the client's choice. The focus is on the process: the process of the client–environment interaction and the process of the nurse–client relationship" (Newman, Lamb, & Michaels, 1991, p. 406).

The Structure of Communication

Not only does human communication convey information and influence another throughout a relationship, but also "communication is the relationship" (Sundeen, Stuart, Rankin, & Cohen, 1994, p. 94). It is the dynamic interaction between two or more persons in which ideas, goals, beliefs and values, feelings, and feelings about feelings are exchanged. Experiencing even a minute communication exchange effects change in all parties in the communication process.

Communication is defined only in the context of process. Because human beings are continually and irrevocably exchanging energy with the environment, and life is continually being repatterned, it can be assumed that the individual human being reflects only dynamic actions. Each person is always affected by others and is always affecting others. One constantly communicates, thereby generating change in others and experiencing change in self.

Although communication is a dynamic process, it is possible to identify components and to analyze the interrelationships among the components. Berlo (1960), a noted authority on communications, traced the various models of communication from Aristotle to the 1960s. Aristotle identified the related components as the speaker, the speech, and the audience. After analyzing behavioral science research and several points of view, Berlo (pp. 30–32) postulated a communication model that is generally accepted today:

1. An (interpersonal) source: some person(s) with ideas, needs, intentions, information, and a reason for communicating
2. A message: a coded, systematic set of symbols representing ideas, purposes intentions, and feelings.
3. An encoder: the mechanism for expressing or translating the purpose of the communication into the message (in human beings, these are the motor mechanisms—the vocal mechanism for oral messages, the muscles of the hands for written messages, and the muscle systems elsewhere in the body for gestures)
4. A channel: the medium for carrying the message
5. A decoder: the mechanism for translating the message into a form that the recipient can use (in human beings, the sensory receptor mechanisms)
6. A receiver: the target or recipient of the message

In this model, the transmission of meaning occurs via a dynamic process in which:

1. A person has an intention or purpose (the communication source).
2. The purpose is translated into a communicable form by the person's set of motor mechanisms and skills (encoder).
3. The message is transmitted through a channel.
4. The message is translated into receivable form by the recipient's sensory mechanisms and skills (decoder).
5. The recipient receives the message (the communication receiver).

Since this model was postulated, system theorists have further explained the reciprocal relationship between the participants in the communication process. At any time, the individual person is both an active initiator and a recipient of meanings in an interpersonal situation. Thus, it is important for nurses to understand that they are simultaneously acting and reacting by using nursing processes and that clients' meanings have an equal effect on the outcome of purposeful relationships. The process just described has been labeled "transactional."

The dynamic nature of the communication process dictates the need for nurses to evaluate their actions and reactions when using the nursing process with a client. Without such awareness and evaluation, the professional will be less likely to experience successful communication with the feeling of satisfaction associated with transmitting clear meanings and the validation that the message intended was the message received. Validation of meanings is essential to achieving any therapeutic goals in helping relationships.

Functions and Types of Communication

Synthesizing from several communication models, Ceccio and Ceccio (1982) proposed four major purposes of communication: to inquire, inform, persuade, and entertain. The nurse may attempt to achieve any of these purposes with clients, the health care delivery system, peers, interdisciplinary team members, and even the self. In attempts to achieve one or more of these purposes, the nurse transmits messages.

People transmit messages verbally and nonverbally. In addition, implicit in all models of communication is the concept that communication has two interacting components:

1. The content value of the message
2. The interactional or perceptual value of the message and its participants

The informational aspect of the message, the content value, is expressed in verbal or nonverbal forms. The interactional or perceptual value of the message (referred to as **metacommunication**) identifies how the participants interpret content and how they perceive the interpersonal relationship. Metacommunication may be expressed in verbal and nonverbal forms.

Verbal Communication

Verbal communication consists of the spoken word. Verbal communication requires functional physiologic and cognitive mechanisms that produce, recognize, and receive speech. Although a major influence, specific words are not the greatest influences on communication. Nonverbal communication may override verbal communication. Language comprises an elaborate system of symbols. Words symbolize actual objects or concepts. Lack of congruence in language between the nurse and the client usually interferes with initiating relationships and creates obstacles to validation of meanings—the essential characteristic of an effective message.

Two primary influences on verbal communications are developmental age and cultural heritage. Developmental age affects verbal abilities through the person's physiologic ability to change sounds into words and cognitive ability to symbolize through language. Through the process of acculturation, the person develops culture-based variations from others in defining meanings for words. Although denotative meanings are equal among different persons (i.e., the concrete representations of words are the same), connotative meanings often vary among persons of different cultures and their accompanying acculturation.

Three types of problems with which the nurse needs to be concerned are associated with words being symbols of communication (Ceccio & Ceccio, 1982):

1. The technical problem: How accurately can one transmit the symbols of communication?
2. The semantic problem: How precise are the symbols in transmitting the intended message?
3. The influential problem: How effectively does the received meaning affect conduct?

The verbal content of communication can be used to evaluate the content theme of the communication process. If one evaluates the seemingly varied topics of discussion, the words that underlie or link together several ideas will reflect the "what" (or content) of the communication.

Nonverbal Communication

Nonverbal communication usually exerts more influence on communication than the words said. **Nonverbal communication** consists of all forms of communication that do not involve the spoken or written word. Perception of nonverbal communication involves all the senses, especially hearing, that are used for the perception of verbal messages. Kinesics (facial expressions, gaze, gestures, and all body movements that are not specific signs), objects (all intentional and unintentional display of material things), and proxemics (the use of space) are powerful nonverbal messages perceived by the senses (Hosley & Molle, 2006; Northouse & Northouse, 1998).

Besides receiving verbal messages, Sundeen and colleagues (1994) identified the additional purposes of nonverbal communication: expressing emotion and interpersonal attitudes; establishing, developing, and maintaining social relationships; presenting the self; engaging in rituals; and supporting verbal communication (p. 99).

The tactile senses represent the most primitive sensory process developed by humans. Bonding between the infant and the parent figure (important to infant development) occurs largely through nonverbal tactile communication. Touch remains a powerful communication tool throughout life.

Deprivation of tactile stimulation in infancy may impair the achievement of some developmental tasks. Young children orients themselves to space through touch. As a child develops into an adult, touch as nonverbal communication takes on specific cultural meanings.

Nurses must understand taboos concerning touch and distance if they desire to be purposeful in nonverbal and verbal communication. For example, to one person, a touch on the knee might mean concern, whereas to another it may be interpreted as seduction. Used sensitively at the proper time and within the context of the client's culture, touch is a powerful nonverbal tool for the nurse.

All the sensory processes become powerful components of the communication process as human beings exchange nonverbal and verbal messages with others throughout life. For example, the olfactory (smell) and gustatory (taste) senses make it possible for the person to distinguish pleasant from not-so-pleasant odors and tastes. When persons have adequate smelling and tasting capacities, odor and taste become significant nonverbal messages in the communication process. The nurse needs to manipulate the health care environment to control odors.

The sense of hearing the spoken word also has a nonverbal component: that of interpreting the qualities of the voice. Hunsaker and Alessandra (1980) identified the following voice qualities as strong determinants of effective communication: resonance (the intensity with which the voice fills the environmental space), rhythm (the flow, pace, and movement of the voice), speed (how fast the voice is used), pitch (the highness or lowness of the voice that relates to the tightening of the vocal cords), volume (or loudness), inflection (the change in pitch or volume of voice), and clarity (the articulation and enunciation capacity of the voice).

People move during communication, and these motor or kinesic actions are perhaps most often performed with little or no awareness. Body movements are largely determined through socialization. Developed in a particular psychosocial and cultural setting, motor actions vary according to gender, socioeconomic status, age, and ethnic background. Misinterpretations of culturally variable kinesic behaviors produce barriers to effective communication. For example, eye motions involved with eye contact communicate culturally specific messages. If the nurse and client assign different meanings to this nonverbal communication, the effectiveness of the nurse–client relationship is likely to be reduced.

Hunsaker and Alessandra (1980) suggested that 90% of meaning comes from nonverbal communication; thus, nonverbal behavior has a significant impact on the recipient of the communicated message. Therefore, nonverbal behavior has great significance for nurses as they engage in all professional nursing roles, especially leadership roles. It conveys the greatest meaning to persons involved in leadership processes. For example, the following motor actions (which are commonly observed) may be highly influential in the communication process (Hunsaker & Alessandra):

1. Gently rubbing behind the ear with the index finger—interpreted as doubt
2. Casually rubbing the eye with one finger—interpreted as the recipient in the communication process not understanding what is being communicated
3. Cupping hands over the mouth—interpreted that the gesturer is trying to hide something
4. Leaning back with both hands supporting the head—interpreted as confidence or superiority
5. Pinching the bridge of the nose with eyes closed—interpreted as thoughtful evaluation
6. Moving eyeglasses to the lower bridge of the nose and peering over them—interpreted as a powerful negative evaluation

Kinesics, the meaning of motor actions, and proxemics, or the function of space in nonverbal communication, also play important roles in all aspects of life. Space is a constant. It may be perceived either as surrounding persons or as existing between them. Nurses must strive purposefully for congruence among their own nonverbal behaviors and the verbal communications they intend to convey. In addition, nurses must recognize that culture affects all aspects of nonverbal communication (Hosley & Molle, 2006; Leininger & McFarland, 2002). For example:

- Proximity/spacing. Persons from various cultures define appropriate personal space differently. For example, Americans prefer more personal space (6 inches to 4 feet) than Latin Americans. Nurses must abide by client preferences for personal space to facilitate effective communication.
- Touching. Any physical contact or touching that is part of an individual's communication style can create problems or discomfort for people from many cultures. Nurses need not abandon hands on a shoulder or arm to show support and caring. Rather, clients should feel empowered to tell the nurse if such touching makes them feel uncomfortable.
- Gestures. People from some cultures may be more animated than others, using gestures and body language to communicate their message. In addition, gestures that have a positive meaning in one culture may be insulting and rude in another.
- Eye contact. Traditionally, Americans have valued direct eye contact as a sign of confidence and respect, whereas not making eye contact has negative connotations. However, in many cultures, making eye contact with an authority figure is considered an insult.

- Use of silence. People from some cultures prefer active verbal interaction and are uncomfortable with silence. Other cultures may value periods of contemplative silence, leading to the potential for misunderstanding of communication style and motivation.
- Body language. The body is one of the more subtle ways people communicate meaning and sincerity. The nurse may say all the right things but communicate tension through body language.

With an awareness of what a client perceives as acceptable use of space and how body position and direction affect the meaning of the relationship, the nurse can manipulate personal and environmental space for the benefit of the client during clinical practice.

Metacommunication
Occurring on both verbal and nonverbal levels, metacommunication represents an integrative level that defines the "what," the "who," and the relationship between the "what" and the "who" of the communication process. Because this level of communication is influential in determining the effectiveness of relationships, the nurse must evaluate communication in terms of its context and the relationships among its parts. Understanding themes of the relationship helps the nurse evaluate the metacommunication occurring in the nursing process. The nurse searches for the content theme (the central underlying idea or links), the mood theme (the emotion communicated—the how of the message), and the interaction theme (the dynamics between the communicating participants).

Knowing that change occurs more readily and more effectively if congruence exists between the verbal and nonverbal components of communication, the nurse must be alert to indicators of the degree of agreement on the meaning of the content and on the process of the relationship. When a discrepancy arises between verbal and nonverbal components, the nonverbal component usually is the more accurate indicator. However, nonverbal behavior is more open to subjective meaning and variations; thus, it must be verbally validated. This validation process plays an important part in effectively using metacommunication in the nursing process.

Interpretation and Perception
The capacity for interpretation makes communication between humans possible. When engaged in interpretation, persons assign meaning to the interpersonal interaction. **Interpretation** involves perception, symbolization, memory, and thinking. Perhaps the most important of these is perception, the basic component after which the others follow. Taylor (1977) defined **perception** as the selection and organization of sensations so that they are meaningful. Taylor proposed that humans learn perceptions and that what they learn depends on socialization experiences. Perceptual expectations are influenced by emotions, language, and attitude, and vary widely from one individual to another. Thus, one's interpretation ability highly depends on individual perceptual ability.

Factors affecting perception in the nurse–client relationship are the capacity for attention (reception of sensations) by the nurse and client, the perspective each brings to the relationship, and the physical condition of the receptors. Anxiety (the tension state resulting from the actual or anticipated negative appraisal of the significant other in the communication process) in the nurse or the client limits the ability to be attentive in the communication process, interferes with the validation of individual perspectives, and decreases physical capacities. Therefore, anxiety must be controlled in the nurse–client relationship. Validated perceptions between nurse and client are essential to goal setting and achievement. The nurse must constantly be aware of the power and influence of perception on the outcomes of a communication, regardless of its form.

Self-Concept and Interpersonal Relationships
The relationships among participants greatly affect communication. The self-concept of each participant largely determines the nurse–client relationship. Clients receiving care

from a nurse with low self-esteem will question the nurse's competence and actions more frequently, whereas clients will feel more comfortable when receiving care from a confident, self-assured nurse.

According to Brill (1990), "In dealing with people it is essential that workers possess awareness of themselves, their own needs, the ways in which they satisfy these needs, [and] the ways in which they use themselves in relationship with others" (p. vii). In addition to self-awareness, other factors involved in the self-concept are essential to effective communication:

- Ability to share with individuals (a function of achievement of interpersonal developmental tasks)
- Ability to establish, maintain, and terminate the kind of relationship in which one is comfortable (a function of the human need to perpetuate a personal self-concept)
- Ability to share power (a reflection of the person's view of self and others)

If the major reason for nurses' communication with clients is to influence clients toward better health, nurses must develop concepts of self that are most effective in facilitating the potential of the client for growth. These concepts include an awareness of one's perceptions of and feelings about self, the ability to derive satisfaction by sharing with the client the responsibility for the nurse–client relationship, the ability to view the self as the therapeutic tool for implementing the nursing process, and an appreciation of the value of shared power in activities directed toward change.

Questions for Reflection 4-1

1. When I see nonverbal behavior not matching verbal messages of clients, what do I do? Why is it important to act when I see this incongruence?
2. How do I come across as a professional nurse? (You may have to ask a colleague for the answer to this one; it may surprise you.) Why is it important to know how others perceive me as a professional nurse?

Principles of Communication in Collaborative Relationships

When engaged in communication with clients, nurses empathize with, demonstrate respect for, and respond genuinely to them. When nurses and clients equally share the responsibility and authority for steps of the nursing process, they enter into collaborative relationships. **Collaborative relationships** promote client sharing of essential information as the nurse performs a health assessment. During diagnosis, the nurse must verify conclusions with the client so that accurate conclusions based on client data related to human response have been drawn. The nurse and client work together to plan and implement nursing care. Finally, the client reports success or failure of nursing interventions or proposes alternative courses of action during evaluation. Collaboration of this magnitude cannot occur without presence, empathy, respect, and genuineness. Presence, empathy, and respect are **principles of communication** that facilitate collaboration.

Presence

Presence is an important part of several nursing conceptual models, including those of Parse (1996), Paterson and Zderad (1988), and Watson (1996). "The core element in presence is 'being there'…. It is described as a gift of self and is equated with a use of self that is conveyed through open and giving behaviors of the nurse" (Osterman & Schwartz-Barcott, 1996, p. 24). Characteristics of four ways of "being there" are described in Table 4-1. These ways "reflect degrees of intensity in the context of another" (Osterman & Schwartz-Barcott, p. 29).

TABLE 4-1

Presence: Characteristics of Four Ways of Being There

Characteristics of Presence	Presence	Partial Presence	Full Presence	Transcendent Presence
Quality of being there	Physically present in context of another	Physically present in context of another	Physically present (there) (physical attending behavior—eye contact, leaning toward) Psychologically (present with) (attentive listening behavior)	Physically present Psychologically present (metaphysical beliefs) Holistic
Focus of energy	Self-absorbed	Objects or tasks in environment, relevant to the other individual but none of the energy is directed at the other	Self/Other (focusing on another influences response—reciprocal)	Centered (drawing from universal energy) Subject/subject—leads to oneness
	Personal, subjective reality	Mechanical/technical reality	Present oriented (here and now)—anchoring in present reality	Transcending and oriented beyond here and now—sustaining while transforming reality
Nature of interaction	No interaction; self-absorbed, intra-personal encounter	Interaction with part of other encounter	Interactive; essential communication; boundaries—role constraints; professional relationship; dyad caring	Relationship; high degree of skilled communication; role free; human intimacy/love; humanistic caring, no boundaries, monad relationship
Positive outcomes	Reduces stress; reassurance that someone is there; may be quieting and restorative; facilitates creative thinking	Reduces stress; solving a mechanical problem; reduces amount of stimuli in an encounter	Solving of a human problem; relief of a here-and-now distress	Transformations decreased loneliness expansion of consciousness; spiritual peace, hope and meaning in one's existence (love/connectedness); nice feeling generated in the environment; transpersonal (oneness)
Negative outcomes	No interpersonal engagement—missed communication; isolation, withdrawn, increased anxiety	Not interpersonal connectedness	May be too much energy for recipient or feel negative to a recipient; energy not always available for full presence; increased anxiety	Fusion and possible loss of objective reality; danger of taking on recipient's problems

Source: Osterman, P., & Schwartz-Barcott, D. (1996). Presence: Four ways of being there. *Nursing Forum,* 31, 25. Used with permission of the publisher.

By synthesizing these theoretical conceptions of presence, the nurse focuses all his or her energy on a client when being with the client. The nurse can be present without speaking. Clients and nurses engaged in true presence during an encounter describe an experience that cannot be effectively captured with words. In my experience, presence with a client results in a deep, personal connection for both participants with possible resultant personal transformations. Presence is integrally related to genuineness and a necessary antecedent to empathy.

Questions for Reflection 4-2

1. Why is it important for me to be truly present with clients?
2. What factors in my clinical practice setting prevent me from being truly present with clients?
3. How could I proceed with changing the clinical practice setting?

Empathy

Empathy, the ability to understand, sense, share, and accept the feelings of another, enables the nurse to develop helping relationships with clients. Therapeutic helping relationships focus on change. Understanding the potential impact of change on clients enables the nurse to identify obstacles for clients to change behaviors and attitudes. When using an empathetic approach, the nurse becomes more tolerant of behaviors, attitudes, and values that differ and could impede progress toward goal attainment. Empathy is defined as "the art of communicating to others that we have understanding [of] how they are feeling and what makes them feel that way" (Keegan, 1994, p. 127). Wiseman (1996, p. 1165) identified four defining attributes of empathy: seeing the world as others see it, being nonjudgmental, understanding another's feelings, and communicating the understanding.

Nurses possessing empathy show awareness of the uniqueness and individuality of clients. They listen and respond as clients share feelings and concerns. They care about clients as sentient beings like themselves. If clients perceive that nurses care about them and how they feel, the benefits include the following (Keegan, 1994):

- More trusting relationships with open communication
- Increased feelings of being connected to another
- Enhanced client and nurse self-esteem
- Genuine acceptance of others just as they are
- Increased self-awareness for both the nurse and the client
- Increased self-caring and less self-criticism on the part of the client

To be truly empathic, **nurses as helpers** have to listen carefully so that they can act as intended, perceive and accept the inner feelings and experiences of clients as the clients experience them, and paraphrase feelings, ideas, and intentions accurately. Two essential actions are necessary for a nurse to develop empathy:

1. Awareness and acceptance of self as a feeling person open to one's experiences
2. Ability to listen to each message of the client, to identify the client's feelings associated with it, and to respond to those feelings

Thus, empathy involves far more than the cognitive or thinking part of the self. It involves the acceptance that we are feeling beings, commonly experiencing multiple emotions simultaneously. In effective communication, the nurse and the client know that the nurse perceives and accepts the client's feelings.

Respect

Respect is feeling or showing deferential regard or esteem (Agnes, 2005, p. 1221). Respect is the nonpossessive caring for and affirmation of another's personhood as a separate individual. Respect builds self-esteem and positive self-image. In the nurse–client relationship, respect is demonstrated by equality, mutuality, and shared thinking.

Certain behaviors display respect toward others. Nurses act respectfully toward clients when they look directly at them when providing care; give them full, undivided attention; maintain eye contact, if culturally appropriate; smile appropriately; determine how each client wants to be addressed; call clients by name; introduce themselves to clients; and make physical contact such as a handshake or gentle touch. Clients who are members of a cultural group unlike that of the nurse may have special needs for respect, and sometimes the aforementioned actions should be avoided because they conflict with cultural norms and values (Leininger & McFarland, 2002).

According to Bradley and Edinberg (1990), nurses may be "viewed as being powerful, one-up, and, if from a different racial group, nonempathic.... In addition, it can be the nurses who view the clients as powerless, one-down, and different" (p. 226). Respecting the client's dignity is critical to therapeutic communication, "even when the client is in dire social, economic, or health circumstances" (Bradley & Edinberg, p. 226). Respect toward the client facilitates the development of effective helping relationships.

Genuineness

Genuineness is the state of being real, honest, and sincere. Clients readily detect dishonesty and insincerity when interacting with health care providers. Frequently, genuineness is used synonymously with authenticity.

When defining authenticity, phrases such as "being actually and precisely what is claimed," "genuine," "good faith," and "sincere" are used. Genuine nurses display their real selves to clients. They do not let themselves become distorted or different because of thought or emotions. Genuine nurses act from their hearts and do not need to rehearse or contrive actions. In previous times, nurses were expected to be neutral to attain and maintain a helping relationship (Rogers, 1951). However, neutral behavior often seems depersonalized and sends messages of ambiguity. Ambiguous messages may cause client anxiety because clients may not understand their roles or positions in a relationship.

Nurses take risks to be genuine because it frequently involves expressing negative thoughts and confronting others. However, there may be even more risk when incongruence surfaces between nurse intentions and behaviors. When clients detect incongruence in the nurse–client relationship, feelings of distrust, confusion, and suspicion may arise. Clients may begin to question the credibility of the nurse and the value of the health information being shared. They may only believe the nonverbal messages sent and discount the verbal ones. Finally, therapeutic rapport erodes if clients believe that the nurse is attempting to impress them rather than connect with them.

When a nurse is genuine, action occurs spontaneously. "Being real does not mean being overly familiar"; what the client wants "is an emotionally available, calm, caring proficient resource that can protect, care about, and above all, listen to him or her" (Arnold & Boggs, 1989, p. 439).

Internalizing the principles of empathy, respect, and genuineness makes it possible for the nurse to demonstrate these behaviors and experience satisfaction in professional nursing practice. These principles also help nurses to establish healthy, helping relationships with clients and their significant others.

HELPING RELATIONSHIPS: THE NURSE AS HELPER

The nurse–client relationship is a special helping relationship. Nurses tailor this private, platonic relationship to fit the needs of individual clients. The nurse–client relationship

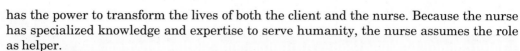

has the power to transform the lives of both the client and the nurse. Because the nurse has specialized knowledge and expertise to serve humanity, the nurse assumes the role as helper.

Rogers (1958) set the following essential conditions of a helping relationship, which are applicable to professional nursing:

1. The individual is capable of and expected to be responsible for himself.
2. Each individual (nurse and client) has a strong drive to become mature and to be socially responsible.
3. The climate of the helping relationship is warm and permits the expression of both positive and negative feelings.
4. Limits, mutually agreed on, are set on behavior only, not on attitudes.
5. The helper communicates understanding and acceptance.

The characteristics of helping as developed by Rogers have positively influenced many health professionals and serve as criteria for nurses as they develop effective helping relationships.

The nurse bears the responsibility to fulfill a helper role, regardless of the specific parameters and purposes of each relationship. The nurse must validate that the client knows why help was sought. The nurse also assumes that both the client and nurse will share the responsibility for the outcomes of the nursing encounter. The helping role is viewed as a facilitative one, in which the nurse uses self and expertise as therapeutic tools to assist the client to overcome threats to health and well-being or obtain optimal health.

The nurse and client bring unique talents, skills, and characteristics that affect the development of a helping relationship. The nurse uses client strengths to facilitate the helping relationship. Table 4-2 displays what the client and the nurse bring to their relationship (Benner, 1984; Northouse & Northouse, 1998; Riley, 2000). When the client is confused or unresponsive, the client's significant others (such as family members, close friends, or those having durable power of attorney) bring these attributes into the therapeutic relationship. At times, as the nurse delivers physical care to the client, efforts are made to fulfill the psychosocial and spiritual needs of the client's significant others.

Nature of Helping in Progressive Stages of the Nurse–Client Relationship

The nurse–client relationship evolves over time. The purposes and functions of the nurse–client relationship vary as the relationship proceeds through predictable sequential stages. Although the nurse in a helping relationship always assumes the roles of facilitator, advocate, and coordinator, specific functions and purposes evolve throughout the relationship. **Stages of the nurse–client relationship** vary according to the purpose of the helping relationship. For example, the facilitator helps the client move toward improved health. The advocate protects the client from stress inherent in the petitioner role and acts on behalf of the client in promoting access to and use of health care delivery services. The coordinator attempts to organize and articulate all the services related to meeting the client's health care needs.

The knowledge base needed to act as a helper in professional nursing was largely developed and shared by Dr. Hildegard Peplau over 50 years ago. Her book, *Interpersonal Relations in Nursing* (Peplau, 1952), presented a thorough analysis of Harry Stack Sullivan's (1953) interpersonal theory in psychiatry and gave nursing a sound conceptual model for practice. Although other nurse scholars have developed other models and changed forms of the interpersonal model, Peplau's phases of the nurse–client relationship remain applicable. Following is a brief summary of the phases and their purposes, with associated functions of the nurse in each phase.

TABLE 4-2

Interchange of Knowledge, Attitudes, and Skills Between Client and Nurse in the Helping Relationship

What the Client Brings to the Client–Nurse Relationship	What the Nurse Brings to the Client–Nurse Relationship
Cognitive	**Cognitive**
• Individual ways of perceiving the world	• Individual ways of perceiving the world
• Preferred ways of making judgments	• Preferred ways of making judgments
• Knowledge and beliefs about health and illness in general	• Knowledge and beliefs about health and illness in general
• Specific knowledge related to current health status of illness in general and of the current illness in particular	• Knowledge about his/her clinical specialty
	• Knowledge about what should help this particular client
• Knowledge and beliefs about health promotion and maintenance in general and information about own health care routines and activities	• Knowledge and beliefs about health behaviors that prevent illness and promote, regain, and maintain health
• Ability to solve problems and knowledge of preferred methods of doing so	• Ability to solve problems and knowledge of preferred methods of doing so while using nursing cognitive and clinical skills
• Ability to learn	• Knowledge about factors that increase client compliance with treatment regimens
• Preferred ways to learn based on individualized learning style	
• Preferred communication patterns	• Expectations of client based on previous encounters with other clients
• Knowledge of how current health affects role responsibilities	• Knowledge of available resources to assist client with this particular health problem
• Expectations of encounter with this nurse based on previous encounters with nurses	• Ability to perceive if help is needed for effective nursing management of client health problem
Affective	**Affective**
• Cultural and spiritual values	• Cultural and spiritual values
• Self-perceptions	• Professional nursing values
• Feelings about seeking help from a nurse	• Self-perceptions
• Attitudes toward nurses in general	• Feelings about being a nurse–helper
• Attitudes related to previous encounters with nurses	• Attitudes toward clients in general
• Attitudes toward previous and currently prescribed treatment regimens	• Attitudes toward this particular client system
	• Intuitive feelings about the client system
• Values regarding illness prevention	• Biases about nursing treatment regimens
• Attitude of either being willing to or fighting actions to take the required measures to improve health status at this time with this particular nurse	• Values placed on being healthy
	• Values placed on people actively preventing illness or enhancing well-being
• Personal meaning of current health status and encounter with this nurse	• Willingness to help client take positive action to improve his/her well-being
	• Personal meaning of current client encounter
Psychomotor[a]	**Psychomotor**
• Ability to relate and communicate with others	• Ability to relate and communicate with others using therapeutic communication techniques
• Ability to carry out own health care management	• Proficiency in administering general and specialized nursing interventions (in some cases the nurse has developed expertise)
• Ability to learn new methods of self-care	• Ability to teach nursing interventions to client

[a]Client may not always be capable of these if health problem has impaired cognitive or motor abilities.

Adapted from Riley, J. B. (2000). *Communications in nursing* (4th ed., p. 28). St. Louis: C.V. Mosby. Used with permission of the publisher.

Additional information gathered from Benner (1984) and Northouse & Northouse (1988).

Peplau's Phases of the Relationship

Orientation Phase

The purposes of the orientation phase include:

- Introduction of nurse and client
- Elaboration of the client's need to recognize and understand his or her difficulty and the extent of a need for help
- Acceptance of the client's need for assistance in recognizing and planning to use services that professional personnel can offer
- Agreement that the client will direct energies toward the mutual responsibility for defining, understanding, and meeting productively the problem at hand
- Clarification of limitations and responsibilities in the delivery system environment

When the nurse and the client validate understanding of the client's need for help and acceptance of resources to meet those needs, and they do so with feelings of shared responsibility and a sense of trust, they move into a new phase of the relationship.

Identification Phase

The purposes of the identification phase include:

- Provision of the opportunity for the client to respond to the helper's offer to assist
- Encouragement for the client to express feelings, reorient those feelings, and strengthen positive forces
- Provision of the opportunity for the nurse and the client to clearly understand each other's preconceptions and expectations

When the client and nurse articulate agreement that the nurse may help the client, the relationship moves to a different level. The nurse assumes responsibility and accountability to act in a helping manner. The nurse asks the client questions related to how to best help the client meet health-related goals.

Exploitation Phase

The purposes of the exploitation phase include:

- Full utilization of the nurse–client relationship to mutually work on the solution to problems and the changes needed to improve health
- Provision of opportunities for the client to explore earlier experiences and behaviors and to have emerging needs met

This phase represents the working stage of the therapeutic relationship. In an ideal therapeutic relationship, the nurse and client connect and work together to help the client transcend his or her current health status (in growth models of nursing) or attain a stable state (in stability models of nursing). Nurses use a variety of resources, including client referrals to others, during this stage.

Resolution Phase

The purposes of the resolution phase include:

- Provision of opportunity to formulate new goals
- Encouragement of gradual freeing of the client from identifying with the nurse
- Promotion of the client's ability to act more independently

Other Approaches to Therapeutic Relationship Development

Since Peplau (1952), other persons have established phases of the development of a helping therapeutic relationship. Travelbee (1966, 1971) designated five phases of the client–nurse relationship, starting with the phase of original encounter. During the original encounter, the client and nurse work to view each other as individual human beings, rather than "nurse" and "client." Once the nurse and client transcend their respective roles, they enter the phase of emerging identities, in which both perceive the other's uniqueness, value each other, and decide to make an emotional investment to begin the therapeutic relationship. Once the client and nurse have established their identities in the relationship, they enter the phase of empathy, during which they predict the behavior of each other but fail to genuinely share feelings. Travelbee proposed that after the phase of empathy, the nurse and client enter the phase of sympathy, when the nurse translates sympathy into helpful nursing actions. After the phase of sympathy is complete, the nurse and client enter the phase of rapport, in which the nurse and client enter into a personal, meaningful relationship in which they genuinely communicate deeply with each other (Travelbee, 1964, 1966, 1971). Unlike Peplau, Travelbee never addressed the need to end a helping relationship with the client.

Hames and Joseph (1980) outlined the following four stages in the development of a professional helping relationship that is not specific to nursing:

Stage 1: Trust formation, in which the client trusts the nurse because of being the recipient of honesty, respect, positive regard, and empathy as the nurse displays consistent behavior.

Stage 2: Resistance, in which the client pulls away from the relationship, but the nurse continues to show concern.

Stage 3: Working, in which the client and nurse become actively involved in working together to help the client achieve health-related goals.

Stage 4: Termination, in which the client and nurse end the relationship by engaging in closure activities, such as saying goodbye, shaking hands, and extending good wishes for the future.

Northouse and Northouse (1998) designated four phases of the nurse–client relationship that differ slightly from those of Peplau (1952) and Hames and Joseph (1980). They also proposed that each phase may overlap, depending upon various contextual factors. The following summarizes the phases of the professional helping relationship as viewed by Northouse and Northouse.

1. Preparation: Before the client and nurse can establish a therapeutic relationship, both undergo a preparation phase. For the nurse, this phase involves preparing the setting and oneself for client interactions. The client prepares by making plans to actively seek assistance from a health care provider, such as making an appointment or arranging for a hospital stay.

2. Initiation: During this phase, the nurse uses a variety of therapeutic communication techniques and demonstrates genuine concern, compassion, and respect for the client. The nurse and client also clarify client needs and establish mutual agreement on expected outcomes for the professional encounter.

3. Exploration: During this phase, the client and nurse examine and work on client needs and concerns. The nurse creates an environment to foster client sharing of needs and concerns. The nurse also helps the client to manage anxiety resulting from discussion of sometimes potentially embarrassing personal issues. The nurse and client work together to outline a plan to help the client. Finally, the nurse helps the client develop new skills to learn how to live with or resolve the concern (or need) for which the client sought assistance.

4. Termination: The nurse assesses the client's ability to independently manage and cope with the health-related issue. During this phase, the nurse summarizes client issues and accomplishments. The client and nurse mutually agree upon ending the relationship.

Most of the approaches to developing a helping relationship address the need for the nurse to establish trust with clients by demonstrating the utmost respect for them. The nurse also works with the client so that a mutual plan can be established. Finally, terminating the relationship with adequate closure ends the therapeutic relationship.

Sometimes, the therapeutic relationship has permanent life-changing effects on clients. Occasionally, the nurse may encounter a former client in a social setting (shopping mall, church, or community event) or the client may return to the health care setting for a brief visit. When this happens, memories of previous encounters may surface, resulting in an affirmation of the benefits of the helping relationship.

The Roles of the Nurse in Therapeutic Relationships

The nurse assumes various roles, depending upon the stage of therapeutic relationship development. Because the stages of therapeutic relationship overlap, the roles assumed by the nurse vary. Table 4-3 outlines roles assumed by the nurse throughout the various phases of therapeutic relationship behavior. Success of the therapeutic relationships relies on nurse consistency in demonstrating deep respect, listening intently, and affirming client thoughts, concerns, and needs throughout all phases. As the relationship unfolds, client dependence on the nurse decreases, and the professional nurse role changes primarily to one of offering support. The relationship ends when the client assumes independence, responsibility, and accountability for meeting his or her own health care needs.

During the various therapeutic relationship phases, the nurse moves back and forth in some of these roles, depending on the client's needs. The nurse uses client responses as a guide to determine which role to assume at a particular time. Role selection requires that the nurse analyze the client response, weigh the pros and cons of the best role to assume, and anticipate consequences of nursing actions. Thus, the nurse constantly assumes the role of critical thinker. However, as the client's needs are met, the nurse essentially

TABLE 4-3

Various Roles Assumed by the Professional Nurse During the Therapeutic Relationship

Therapeutic Stage or Phase	Professional Nursing Roles
Peplau (1952)	
1. Orientation stage	1. Stranger (someone who may or may not be trusted)
2. Identification stage	2. Unconditional mother surrogate, resource person, teacher, counselor, and surrogate
3. Exploration stage	3. The above roles and those of support person or coach
4. Resolution stage	4. Primarily a support person as client has attained independence in managing own health
Travelbee (1971)	
1. Original encounter phase	1. Stranger
2. Emerging identities phase	2. Listener and information giver
3. Empathy phase	3. Physical caregiver, but client remains uncomfortable sharing deep personal concerns with nurse, early counselor
4. Sympathy phase	4. Caregiver, counselor, facilitator, coach, support person, client advocate
5. Rapport phase	5. All professional nursing roles include that of change agent
Names & Joseph (1980)	
1. Trust formation stage	1. Stranger
2. Resistance stage	2. Counselor (especially in offering self continuously despite rejection)
3. Working stage	3. Caregiver, counselor, facilitator, leader, resource person, coach, support person, client advocate, change agent
4. Termination	4. Counselor and support person
Northouse & Northouse (1998)	
1. Preparation	1. Critical thinker in deciding how to prepare self and setting for client
2. Initiation	2. Stranger and counselor
3. Exploration	3. Caregiver, counselor, resource person, coach, client advocate, change agent, support person, teacher
4. Termination	4. Counselor and support person

assumes the roles that promote client independence. The following discussion outlines characteristics of the helping roles assumed by the nurse.

In the role of stranger, the client perceives the nurse as an unknown individual who may or may not be trustworthy and competent. Peplau (1952) pointed out how it is essential for the nurse in this role to accord the client respect and positive interest to promote open communication. A surrogate is a substitute figure who, in the client's mind, reactivates the feeling generated in earlier relationships. The nurse's responsibility in this role is to help the client to become aware of likenesses and differences and to differentiate the nurse as a person. By permitting clients to reexperience old feelings, the nurse who is acting as surrogate sets up the opportunity for growth experiences.

The resource person role involves the nurse in providing specific information, usually formulated in relation to larger problems. When clients cannot perform activities of daily living or complex care procedures independently, the nurse assumes the role of caregiver. The teacher role involves the nurse sharing information and promoting the client's learning through experience, and requires the development of novel alternatives with open-ended outcomes in the nurse–client relationship. The leader role involves the nurse facilitating the client's work on the solution of problems and coaching the client to continue when obstacles are encountered. (The nurse also assumes the leader role when working with other members of the nursing and interdisciplinary health care teams.) For clients to become independent in meeting health care needs, they experience change in behavior or attitude. When the nurse facilitates change, the professional role of change agent emerges.

The counselor role incorporates all of the activities associated with promoting experiences leading to health. The counselor helps the client to become aware of health behaviors, to evaluate them, and to plan how to improve them. Counseling focuses primarily on how clients feel about themselves and what is happening to them (Peplau, 1952). Throughout the entire relationship, nurses frequently assume the counselor and critical thinker roles.

Mutuality in Responsibility and Decision Making

Every person involved in a communication process affects and is affected by every other person involved in the communication field. Rogers (1970, p. 97) called this phenomenon "reciprocity." Reciprocal relationships are the basis of the nursing process. The nurse having the potential to affect the client and to be affected by the client offers the nurse the potential to assist the client to change behaviors in the direction of improved health. Such nurse–client exchanges can be powerful in problem-solving and decision-making situations that determine the nature and direction of change.

Reciprocity is a concept that is similar to the concept of mutuality. Reciprocity "is characterized as an interpersonal exchange, customarily expected to be symmetrical or equivalent" (Mendias, 1997, p. 435). The state of being mutual serves as a lexicon definition of **mutuality**. *Webster's New World College Dictionary* (Agnes, 2005) defined mutual as "a) done, felt, etc. by each of two or more or toward the other or others; reciprocal. b) of, or having the same relationship toward, each other or one another, c) shared in common, joint" (pp. 951–952). Mutuality appears as a concept in Peplau's (1952), Watson's (1996), and Leddy's (2004) conceptual models in terms of mutual gain in a client–nurse relationship. Leddy expanded the use of the term "mutual" in terms of shared and connected processes humans have with environments.

Developing these ideas of mutual exchange and gain, Marck (1990) discussed the concept of therapeutic reciprocity as

one phenomenon of caring, [which] allows both the nurse and the client to benefit from their relationship in a mutually empowering manner…. Therapeutic reciprocity is a mutual, collaborative, probabilistic, instructive, and empowering exchange of feelings, thought, and behaviors between the nurse and client for the purpose of enhancing the human outcomes of the relationship for all parties concerned. (pp. 49, 57)

All of the previously specified roles represent elements of presence, empathy, respect, and genuineness. Communication in these role relationships evolves from diagnostic interactions to therapeutic interactions including educative and supportive interactions as the client moves toward achievement of optimal health. The absolute element of all of these roles is mutuality in responsibility and decision making if both the nurse and the client are expected to grow and experience satisfaction from the nursing process.

Communication and the Phenomenon of Anxiety

Nursing process results in change. The nature of change includes alternatives of cognitive repatterning (using new information to increase understanding), affective adjustment (using the relationship to become aware of, accept, and express feelings), and synthesis of cognitions and feelings in interpersonal repatterning (using the relationship to learn to interact with others in the social system). The direction of change can be toward health enhancement or deterioration. Obviously, the nurse wants to direct change toward enhanced health.

Every social system has role behaviors for constituents to follow. The way a person communicates is greatly affected by his or her perceived role in the system. Roles "are structures that are imposed on behavior" (Berlo, 1960, p. 153). Three aspects of roles must be understood in trying to positively affect the other person in a relationship: role prescription, role description, and role expectations. Berlo defined these aspects as follows:

1. Role prescription: the formal, explicit statement of what behaviors should be performed by persons in a given role.
2. Role description: a report of the behaviors that are performed by persons in a given role.
3. Role expectations: the images that persons have about the behaviors that are performed by persons in a given role. (p. 153; enumeration added)

In the ideal nurse–client relationship, there is congruence among these three aspects. Together, the nurse and the client agree on the structure and dynamics of their purposeful communication. When there are differences regarding the prescriptions, descriptions, and expectations of role behavior between the nurse and the client, communication breakdowns occur and create uncertainty.

Uncertainty and ambiguity create increased tension and discomfort in the system. Such tension in human systems leads to dissipation of energy and less ability to use the energy to improve. In interpersonal systems, such tension often is called "anxiety."

Anxiety is the tension state resulting from the actual or anticipated negative appraisal of the significant other in the communication process. Prolonged or intensive anxiety ties up available energy that could be better used for decision making or problem solving aimed to change behavior and attitudes toward enhanced health.

The tension state of anxiety in one person is readily communicated, thus engendering anxiety in the other person(s). Sullivan (1953) attributed great power to the tension of anxiety in a person's interpersonal growth, development, and ability in all stages of life. The actual or anticipated negative appraisals by others that lead to anxiety are perceived as threats to one's self-image. If the anxiety is limited in amount and duration, it simply leads to an increased state of alertness, mediated through physiologic reactions and behavior to reduce the tension. However, if the state of anxiety is unduly prolonged or intense, the level of alertness and successful tension-reducing behaviors are decreased.

Sullivan (1953) postulated that learning occurs through an anxiety gradient extending from mild to severe. A client with mild anxiety can focus energy on most of what is really occurring. A client with moderate anxiety has limited ability to focus on what is really occurring and tends to distort reality. A client with severe anxiety cannot focus energy on what is really happening and thus cannot participate effectively in problem solving or decision making. Because the effective nursing process requires that both the nurse and the client focus on what is really happening, it is essential to control anxiety in the communication process.

Nurses have two primary responsibilities in controlling anxiety:

1. To be aware of their own feelings of anxiety and to structure interactions in such a way that limited anxiety is transferred to the client.
2. To use effective strategies for intervening in the client's anxiety. Therapeutic intervention for anxiety relies on the ability of nurses to recognize client anxiety as well as monitor and relieve their own.

Clinical practice settings often place nurses in stressful situations. Clients find themselves on unfamiliar turf when they enter the health care system. Nurses realize the importance of learning stress reduction strategies for themselves that they can share with clients. Techniques to help clients (and nurses) recognize, gain insight into, and cope with threats of anxiety are discussed in the following section.

Caring and Noncaring Nursing Practices: Therapeutic and Nontherapeutic Communication Techniques

Many nurses identify caring as the essence of nursing. Because of its abstract nature, the concept of caring is difficult to define. However, certain behaviors used by others demonstrate caring. The following actions are frequently used by nurses to show that they care: presencing (being physically, emotionally, and spiritually with another to enter the world of the other), sharing (giving of one's skills, thoughts, and knowledge to help another), supporting (providing fortifying help, displaying concern, trusting others, and affirming persons in their actions), and competence (education and clinical skill). Caring creates the uplifting effects for persons involved in a **caring interaction**: feelings of being respected, feelings of belonging, personal growth, personal transformation, wanting to learn to care, and desire to care (Beck, 2001). In daily client interactions, nurses primarily use communication to demonstrate the presence of caring or noncaring. Caring communication strategies empower clients while being therapeutic. In contrast, noncaring communication typically creates a power-over relationship, with the nurse (or health care provider) dominating the client as well as being nontherapeutic. Selected therapeutic and nontherapeutic communication strategies are presented in Table 4-4 and provide an opportunity to see how they differ. Noncaring communication creates feelings of ill will among clients, nurses, and other members of the health care team.

Listening is perhaps the most important therapeutic technique in the process of effective communication and in demonstrating caring. Sundeen and colleagues (1994) stated that it is devastating to the formation of a helpful relationship if the nurse fails to listen. Listening transmits the message "I value and am interested in you." Effective listening requires the use of various techniques (Sundeen et al., 1994; Hosley & Molle, 2006; Schiavo, 2007; Videbeck, 2008). All of these techniques include strategies of learning how to ignore internal and external environmental distractions. Guidelines for engaging in effective listening include the following:

1. Give the other person your full attention, by facing him or her directly.
2. Focus solely on the current interaction by resisting all external distractions that cause your mind to stray.
3. Listen for central ideas and validate them with the client.
4. Ignore gut-feeling traps that confirm prejudices and/or produce biases.
5. Do not become defensive.
6. Watch for nonverbal and verbal messages.
7. Do not prejudge worth based on appearance or delivery of the speaker.
8. Listen for ideas and underlying feelings.
9. Do not interrupt the person as he or she speaks or when brief pauses in the conversation occur.
10. Try to see the situation from the other person's point of view.
11. Do not try to have the last word.

Questions for Reflection 4-3

1. As a health care consumer, what caring behaviors have I experienced?
2. What caring behaviors have I seen in a clinical practice setting?
3. What caring behaviors do I display as a nurse?

TABLE 4-4

Therapeutic and Nontherapeutic Communication Techniques: Descriptions and Outcomes

Therapeutic Communication Techniques	Description and Outcome(s)	Non therapeutic Communication Techniques	Description and Outcome(s)
Focused Listening	Focusing only and intently on what the client is saying; results in reception of client message, equal power, and genuine interest in the client	Inattentive Listening	Failure to receive intended message, perception of disinterest in client and perception of nurse power over client
Silence	Periods of no verbal communication signifies client acceptance	Uncomfortable Silence	Makes client feel very ill at ease
Guideline Establishment	Clarifies roles, responsibilities, purposes and limitations so client understands his/her expectations	Provider Constantly Talking	Nurse perceived by client as being superior or perhaps even uninterested in what client has to say
Open-ended Questions or Broad Opening	Comments or questions that require more than 1 to 2 word responses let client determine what should be shared	Closed Questions or Comments	One- or two-word responses facilitate data collection, but fail to get at the entire story, resulting in the client's impression that the nurse may be rushed
Distance Reduction	Decreasing the amount of physical space between provider and client conveys desire to become involved	Inappropriate Use of Space	Too close invades client's personal space; too far away conveys not wanting to touch or be involved with the client
Acknowledgement or Acceptance	Recognition of the client demonstrates importance of client role in the interaction, thereby equalizing the power balance	False Reassurance	Attempting to solve or soothe client with words or platitudes, thereby negating the client's feelings or fears
Restating	Repeating the provider's perception of the main point to enhance validity of provider's interpretation of what was said	Parroting	Restating word for word what the client says conveys that the provider is not listening or may be incompetent with verbal communication skills

(continued)

Therapeutic and Nontherapeutic Communication Techniques: Descriptions and Outcomes (Continued)

Therapeutic Communication Techniques	Description and Outcome(s)	Non therapeutic Communication Techniques	Description and Outcome(s)
Reflection	Stating back client ideas, thoughts, questions, and perceptions, thereby showing importance of client ideas	Rejection	Refusal to discuss topics with clients conveys potential client rejection or the nurse is disinterested or uncomfortable with the topic of concern, thereby enhancing the nurse's power
Clarification	Request for more information to fully understand client views	Giving Advice	Telling the client what should be done negates partnership in decision making and emphasizes nurse power over the client
Consensual Validation	Attempt to attain a mutual direct and underlying meaning of what was said shows provider's desire to understand client more fully	Judging	Approval or disapproval of what is said promotes a client's dependent relationship on the provider and results in the nurse having power over the client
Focusing	Question of statement that invites client to expand ideas in more detail conveys true interest	Failure to Probe	Inadequate data collection resulting in lack of individualization of client care and chance for errors
Summarizing	Statements of key points raised in an encounter helps to distinguish relevant from irrelevant, provides a review, validates accuracy of interpretation, and closes the interaction	Defensiveness	Protection of someone or something against negative feedback negates the client's right to question thereby giving the perception of nurse having power over the client
Collaboration	Mutual decision making about future actions fosters equality	Giving Advice	Telling the client what should be done negates client participation in decision making, resulting in shifting power balance to the nurse
Stating observations, the implied	Statements of direct observation or verbalizing what client says indirectly might remove communication barriers for client when he/she may be avoiding or may feel fearful to express thoughts	Introduction of an Unrelated Subject or Changing Topics	Nurser directs the nature of the interaction, thereby determining what is useful information and negates the concerns or important issues of the client; gives perception of nurse having power over client

Therapeutic and Nontherapeutic Communication Techniques: Descriptions and Outcomes (Continued)

Therapeutic Communication Techniques	Description and Outcome(s)	Non therapeutic Communication Techniques	Description and Outcome(s)
Offering Self	By making oneself available, the nurse presents an unconditional offer to be with, understand, and meet client perceived needs and lets the client know that the nurse is available	Patronization	Condescending comments by the provider place the provider in a superior position
		Stereotypical Comments	Use of trite, meaningless, perhaps fashionable verbal expression negates the importance of what the client has said
General Leads	Statements or phrases that invite clients to express ideas or feelings facilitates client sharing of information and ideas	Relentless Probing	Insisting that the client talk about a particular issue or concern sets a tone of nurse power over client and negates client's right to privacy
Concentrating on a Single Point	Focuses the interaction to refine information while preventing the overwhelming nature of the multiple factors contributing to a client care siutation	Interpreting	By telling the client the hidden meaning behind thoughts and feelings, the nurse blocks understanding them because only the client can identify or confirm his or her thoughts and feelings.

Sources of information:

Sundeen, S. J., Stuart, G. W., Rankin, E. A. D., & Cohen, S. A. (1998). *Nurse–client interaction* (6th ed., pp. 124–132). St. Louis, MO: Mosby.

Hosley, J., & Molle, E. (2006). *A practical guide to therapeutic communication for health professionals*. Philadelphia: Saunders Elsevier.

Schiavo, R. (2007). *Health communication from theory to practice*. San Francisco: Wiley.

Videbeck, S. L. (2008). *Psychiatric-mental health nursing* (4th ed.). Philadelphia: Wolter Kluwer Health/Lippincott Williams & Wilkins.

To listen effectively and to get clients to share thoughts and feelings, the nurse must use verbal communication techniques that facilitate the client's verbal and nonverbal expressiveness. Such techniques generally are referred to as "therapeutic communication techniques." Nurses spend time learning caring communication techniques very early in their nursing careers. Some nursing students find some of the techniques artificial and phony at first because our current culture values speed and multitasking. They need time to refine the use of each technique so that it becomes natural and genuine.

To be helpful, the nurse must respond empathetically, attempt to understand the meaning of health and illness for clients, and respond with respect and authenticity. What does a nurse do to show empathy? The empathetic nurse attends carefully, listens intensely, responds reciprocally to verbal and nonverbal messages, uses appropriate language, times responses appropriately, clarifies and confirms ideas, explores the world from the client's viewpoint, and paces verbal and nonverbal behavior to the client's abilities.

What does a nurse do to show caring? The caring nurse spends time with clients, identifies relationships, makes connections based on knowledge, conceptualizes trends and patterns, summarizes appropriately, explains purposes of activities, and identifies nonverbal meanings while engaging in clinical practice activities. Some nurses, especially in inpatient or residential settings, make unexpected visits to client rooms to offer professional nursing services. Caring nurses make clients feel as though they are the most important persons in the world.

What does a nurse do to show respect? The respectful nurse verbalizes a clear commitment to understand, conveys acceptance, and clearly affirms the client's worth as a unique person while affirming the client's strengths and ability to assume self-responsibility. By offering oneself unconditionally and allowing clients when feasible (in situations in which the client is not at risk for harming self or others) to direct the nurse–client interactions, the nurse shares power with the client and enhances client self-worth and personal identity. The nurse who displays the utmost respect toward clients works actively to maintain client dignity at all times.

Research Brief 4-1

Coenen, A., Doorenbos, A., & Wilson, S. (2007). Nursing interventions to promote dignified dying in four countries. *Oncology Nursing Forum*, *34*, 1151–1156.

A convenience sample of 560 nurses from Ethiopia, India, Kenya, and the United States completed the International Classification for Nursing Practice Dignified Dying Survey that included an open-ended item to address what intervention they used to promote a dignified death in terminally ill cancer clients. Along with identifying the holistic nature of the dying experience, the nurses identified key nursing interventions for use to promote a dignified death.

A thematic analysis of data generated in the study revealed three key areas of concern addressing illness, a dignity-conserving repertoire, and a social-dignity inventory. Illness concern interventions included addressing symptom relief (pain, dyspnea, and nausea) and providing psychological comfort (education about the death process) and reassurance that comfort would be maintained. Nursing interventions included in the dignity-conserving repertoire included providing psychological or spiritual comfort, maintaining hope and faith, accepting clients' feelings, facilitating grief work and reminiscence, praying with and for the client, fostering autonomy and control by enabling clients to participate in end-of-life care and treatment decisions, and enabling culturally based spiritual practices. The interventions identified in the theme of the social-dignity inventory focused on interpersonal interactions and included the following actions: encouraging the presence of family members, involving family members in the dying person's care, reassuring and supporting family members, providing education and explanations to families about the condition of the dying clients, helping the family accept death, supporting beliefs of life after death, providing a peaceful or home-like environment, treating clients and families with utmost dignity and respect, and being present with the client and family.

This study clearly shows nurses how to maintain the dignity of terminally ill clients with cancer as they engage in the dying process. The survey also revealed cultural differences in nursing approaches to end-of-life care, even though the issues across the countries were comparable. The results of this study should be exercised with caution because a convenience sample was used, inequivalent numbers of nurses from each country were included in the study, there was a poor response rate from American nurses (32% compared with 75% for Kenya), and there was a possibility of loss of consistency of meaning in the survey items because of issues. Future research using a random sample along with including nurses from many more nations would facilitate understanding the needs of terminally ill clients and how nurses intervene to help them achieve a dignified death.

How does the nurse respond with authenticity? The authentic nurse consistently responds with genuine thoughts and feelings, and resists all urges to play-act; assumes ownership of ideas and feelings; and freely shares emotions with clients. Other expressions of authenticity include extending a hand for the client to grasp in times of loneliness or distress, being present with the client in times of need, and connecting with the client on a spiritual level. Authentic nurses do not assume the role of imposter and acknowledge their limitations.

Therapeutic and caring professional nursing activities require the ability to listen. Listening demonstrates genuine concern and prioritizes client needs over the nurse's needs. Nurses frequently overlook the nursing intervention of therapeutic listening and communication techniques in client care documentation. The use of therapeutic techniques facilitates the client's efforts at problem solving, self-expression, and health improvement. Therapeutic communication distinguishes professional nurses from health care technicians.

In contrast, noncaring or nontherapeutic communication strategies typically make clients feel inferior to the nurse. Unfortunately, at times, nurses may demonstrate noncaring behaviors. **Noncaring behaviors** communicate the following attitudes: "You have no value"; "I am not interested—actually, I'm bored"; or "I have more important things to do than to spend time listening to you." Failing to listen to clients is perhaps the most noncaring behavior a nurse can exhibit. Other nurse behaviors that are not helpful to clients include being judgmental (i.e., putting personal values, beliefs, or expectations above the client's), making stereotyped responses (i.e., negating the uniqueness of the client by using platitudes or clichés as responses), and changing the subject (verbally directing the interaction to a new topic of importance to the nurse or by nonverbally signaling that the topic being discussed is not important). Noncaring or nontherapeutic communication strategies are contrasted with caring communication in Table 4-4. When nurses distinguish the main differences between caring and noncaring communication strategies, they can determine how to avoid the strategies that disvalue clients.

Nurses display noncaring behaviors for several reasons. In today's current health care system that values cost over care, some nurses find themselves overwhelmed by professional care tasks and have little time to spend engaged in caring interactions with clients. In addition, some nurses may enter the profession with a need for regressive behavior. This need, accompanied by increasing anxiety, sometimes leads nurses to adopt an attitude of superiority that is expressed in negative actions, such as moralizing, rejecting, or reacting with hostility.

Defensive behavior commonly occurs in regressive states. For example, a person might demonstrate denial, unconsciously evading or negating the real factors in a situation. Regressive states also may be marked by distortions, rote habitual actions, dogmatic responses, loss of control, invalidated assumptions (jumping to conclusions), parroting, inappropriate timing, and poor judgment. These behaviors represent important components of noncaring and nontherapeutic nursing strategies.

Because therapeutic communication is essential for effective professional nursing practice, nurses should periodically evaluate their communication techniques. Techniques for evaluating professional communication strategies include taking time to reflect on how and what is said during nurse–client interactions or keeping a written journal. If a pattern of nontherapeutic behaviors is identified, the nurse should seek help from a colleague or counselor or attend classes or workshops to improve communication techniques. Nurses should let their own feelings be a guide to evaluate the effectiveness of communication during nurse–client interactions. A persistent feeling of anxiety or tension is perhaps the best cue that the nurse may be unwittingly communicating in a noncaring and unhelpful way.

Although there are different views on the advantages and disadvantages of nurses (as professionals) being characterized as caring persons, the fact is that nurses do care about their fellow humans. One dilemma for nurses is that they are not always permitted to care for clients to the best of their knowledge or ability. Many factors in clinical environments (such as short staffing, increased focus on cost reduction, and ineffective working relationships with other health team members) impede the ability of nurses to care for clients as they would like. This results in feelings of frustration. However, when nurses have the opportunity to share their specialized knowledge and compassion, all involved in health care delivery become enriched as desired outcomes are attained.

Questions for Reflection 4-4

1. As a health care consumer, what noncaring behaviors have I experienced?
2. What noncaring behaviors have I seen in a clinical practice setting?
3. What noncaring behaviors have I displayed as a nurse? What were the factors that contributed to my noncaring behaviors?
4. How could I go about changing characteristics of my practice setting to keep me from displaying noncaring behaviors to clients and families?

Outcomes of Helping Relationships

The nurse–client relationship has three major desired outcomes:

1. Increased client understanding of how better personal responsibility and accountability for health can be achieved (learning)
2. Attainment of optimal health
3. Perceived satisfaction in the relationships

In terms of nurse outcomes, knowing that clients have adequate knowledge and skills to solve problems or take steps to adopt a healthy lifestyle is the desired outcome. When clients have adequate preparation, they can make educated choices, expend the required energy, and assume greater responsibility for their own health.

In the nurse–client relationship, change occurs in two ways: as an outcome of learning in terms of the information gained and understood, and as an outcome of learning in terms of the interpersonal experience in the nursing process. The quality of communication plays the paramount role in change. When change and its effects are not communicated clearly, the change cannot be understood. Lack of understanding leads to resistance.

Hunsaker and Alessandra (1980) have proposed a schema for self-evaluation of communication patterns of persons in management positions that apply to nurses when working with clients. They proposed several questions that are clearly applicable to the evaluation of communication in the professional practice and can serve as questions for nurse reflection and journaling.

1. Did I comprehend each point made?
2. Did I make judgments of the words before the speaker was through speaking?
3. Did I make decisions in my own mind while he or she was still speaking?
4. Did I hunt for evidence that would prove the speaker right? Wrong?
5. Did I hunt for evidence that would prove myself right? Wrong?
6. Did I become upset while listening?
7. Did I generally jump to conclusions while listening?
8. Did I let the client speak at least 50% of the time?
9. Did I understand the words in terms of their intended meanings?
10. Did I restate ideas and feelings accurately?
11. Did I study voice, posture, actions, and facial expressions as the client talked?
12. Did I listen between the lines for unspoken meanings behind the words?
13. Did I really try to listen to the client?
14. Did I really want to listen to the client?
15. Did I really show the client I was, in fact, motivated and interested in listening to him? (Hunsaker & Alessandra, pp. 140–141; enumeration added)

Nurses should continually evaluate their own communication behaviors. In addition to self-evaluations such as the preceding questions, the nurse should consistently evaluate the effectiveness of communication with the client. Feedback should be sought from the client about what has been said and about how the client feels the relationship is going. The value of the nurse–client interactions should be explored at intervals to promote mutual benefits to nurse and client. A focus on asking the client, "How are we doing in terms of meeting your needs and expectations?" states to the client that the nurse values him or her and cares how the communication affects him or her. In addition, effective therapeutic communication enables clients to feel free to speak out when they have questions or concerns about their care and may result in error reduction (Finkelman & Kenner, 2007).

Along with individual evaluations of nurse–patient relationships, much work needs to be done to validate the benefits of helping relationships built by nurses. Therapeutic communication is an independent nursing intervention. However, nurses frequently fail to make entries on client records such as "therapeutic listening" or "explored feelings about the meaning of (client health concern)" when documenting delivered care. Most nursing research studies addressing caring are qualitative or descriptive in nature. Client satisfaction data offer potential to identify the benefits of caring communications and helping relationships from only recipients of nursing care. Nursing job satisfaction studies have potential to explore provider benefits of being a helper. Perhaps a nursing research program exploring the positive outcomes of helping relationships needs to be established.

HEALING RELATIONSHIPS: THE NURSE'S ROLE IN HEALING

A **healing relationship** might be considered a special type of helping relationship. Because "to heal is the activity of becoming whole" (Kritek, 1997, p. 11), healing has been defined as "a process of bringing parts of one's self together at deep levels of inner knowing, leading to an integration and balance, with each part having equal importance and value" (Dossey, Keegan, & Guzzetta, 2005, p. 6), and as "an inner process through which a person becomes whole" (Lerner, 1994, p. 13). Healing occurs within the person, and external interventions mobilize the client's inner healing resources (Micozzi, 1996). Healing is not synonymous with curing, because persons with terminal illness can become whole in the process of dying (Dossey et al., 2005).

Healing encompasses the improvement of the whole person (body, mind, and spirit). Dossey et al. (2005) identified many healing modalities used by nurses in practice, including the following:

- Body–mind healing (cognitive therapy, self-reflection, and relaxation techniques)
- Nutritional healing (healthy diets, dietary restrictions, herbs, and vitamin and mineral supplements)
- Exercise and movement therapy (tai chi, walking, dance, and yoga)
- Spiritual healing (faith healing, miracles, play, humor, and use of fine arts)
- Energetic healing (meridians, chakras, aura, smells, sounds, colors, magnets, therapeutic touch, and healing touch)
- Environmental healing (reducing toxins, recycling, and feng shui)

Along with these integrative healing modalities, nurses engage in healing activities based on traditional scientific medicine when administering medications to clients and following pre- and postprocedure protocols.

Lerner (1994) differentiated among universal, common, and unique conditions of healing. Examples of universal conditions are inner peace and a deep experience of love. Attention and care from friends and family, deeply enjoyed work, laughter, moving music, and great art are examples of common conditions. However, Lerner indicated that the unique conditions of healing are some of the most important. Unique conditions are those that apply only to a single individual and may be the result of life experiences or personal relationships. As a healer, the nurse must assess clients as individuals to iden-tify the particular needs that are most meaningful for each client.

Given that healing occurs within the client, the nurse healer's role is to facilitate another person's growth and life processes toward wholeness or to assist with illness recovery, with a more healthy lifestyle, or with transition to peaceful death (Dossey et al., 2005). The nurse assists and responds to the client, who is the central force in the healing process. "Nurses assume that their actions, as professionals, aim to facilitate wholeness in others through an interaction based on a mutuality of purpose" (Kritek, 1997, p. 14). Kritek (p. 21) stated that four fundamental elements are always present in the healing encounter:

1. Nurse and client interact within a given context.
2. The encounter is in response to a health experience.
3. The nurse works in a pattern of mutuality with the client.
4. Healing is facilitated in response to a client's elicitation of nursing involvement and expertise.

Healing is facilitated within a helping relationship, which is characterized by principles such as presence (being rather than doing), intention and purpose, empathy, guiding, cre-ativity, imagery, and spirituality (Dossey et al., 2005; Keegan, 1994; Lerner, 1994).

As a healer, the nurse must assess all life dimensions for potential positive and nega-tive forces that might influence the energy available to use when healing another. Effec-tive healers have heightened sensitivity and awareness as they act with conscious intent. Nurses must recognize that healing not only is a unique life gift, but also must be nur-tured. Before healing another, some nurse healers practice preparation rituals. Healing fosters personal growth and the ability to live life to its fullest for both client and nurse (Conti-O'Hare, 2002; McKivergin, 2005).

Healing relationships with clients produce interpersonal connections. Nurses often display intensity and unconditional love when acting as instruments of healing. Nurse healers usually perceive "that healing does not come from them, but through them" (McKivergin, 2005, p. 243). The potential healing does not come from the healer, but rather it is a mysterious phenomenon involving a higher power and energy within the environment. McKivergin offered the following factors to increase the nurse's capacity as "an instrument of healing" (p. 245):

- Self-care in all of life's dimensions to ensure a personal flow of energy and healing
- Personal interpretations of life's lessons and meanings
- Rootedness and expansiveness: balancing grounded approaches with intuitive inspirations
- Understanding of the complex dynamics of holographic nature, the systems metaphor, and the essential nature of life, health, and healing
- Expansion of consciousness: broaden one's thinking, shift perspectives, and embrace new approaches to life
- Growth in love
- Courage
- Alignment with the Divine
- Openness to being an instrument of the Creator's healing grace
- Ability to detach self from the outcomes
- Groundedness and reliability
- Patience
- Authenticity
- Mindfulness
- Integrity

The healing process requires exchange of energy and truth during authentic communi-cation to create an environment of support while helping others become attuned to their own healing capabilities. Outcomes of healing include deep relaxation, and the profound change of becoming more whole.

Questions for Reflection 4-5

1. Which of Keegan's types of healing have I used in my clinical practice?
2. What would be the consequences for me if I used one of Keegan's healing techniques with clients that were not compatible with the traditional medical model?

HELPING AND HEALING RELATIONSHIPS WITH COLLEAGUES AND OTHER HEALTH TEAM MEMBERS

Professional nurses and other health team members work together to achieve the common mission of providing the absolute best care possible for clients. Each member of the interdisciplinary team brings a unique perspective to and skill set for providing health care to clients. Since the beginning of health care delivery, various conflicts among health team members have surfaced. Physicians have exerted power over nurses. Professional nurses have competed with other health team members, such as pharmacists, laboratory technologists, radiology technicians, and dietitians, for scarce resources. Unlicensed personnel have experienced a lack of respect from professional nurses. As health care professionals find fewer resources for client care, they sometimes turn against each other, instead of working effectively together to provide the best possible care for clients.

With the increasing complexity of client health care needs, members of the health team need to establish professional partnerships to meet client needs and concerns. Currently, many health care organizations do not have healthy working environments for health care providers. Health team members tend to blame each other for shortcomings in client care. The needs of the clients, physicians, and organizational administrators frequently supersede the needs of the nursing staff. In today's fast-paced environment, persons communicate with each other just to get jobs done. Civility and politeness have become icons of the past. The profession of nursing fails to attract young bright persons, and many practicing nurses leave the profession because of intense frustration with practice settings.

Members of the health care team need to establish professional partnerships to dispel competition, exploitation, and frustration in the delivery of health care in the ever-changing health care system. A **professional partnership** is a relationship based on mutual respect to achieve a common mission while each participant lives out his or her life's purpose. "Partnerships join hearts and minds around a common purpose" (Wesorick, Shiparski, Troseth, & Wyngarden, 1997). In health care, the common mission is client care. For a physician, a life purpose may be curing illness in the sick. For a professional nurse, a life purpose may be to care for and help persons as they respond to health alterations. For an unlicensed nursing staff member, a life purpose may be helping persons incapable of caring for themselves. All of these life purposes play essential parts in a common mission: client care.

Theoretical foundations and concepts presented related to the development of healthy helping relationships with clients also apply to interdisciplinary health team members. Healthy working relationships among health care providers require meaningful conversations. Wesorick and Shiparski (1997, paraphrased from p. 40) said that meaningful conversations result when persons use the following principles for communication:

- Intention: creation of a safe place to foster collaborative learning and to share and listen to the thinking of others to connect at a deeply human level (body–mind–spirit)
- Listening: truly hearing oneself and others using physical, mental, and spiritual connections to learn exclusively

- Advocacy: willingness to share spontaneous personal thinking along with reasons behind the thinking, with the intention only to disclose thoughts, not to defend them
- Inquiry: willingness to ask others questions to discover new insights and learn by connecting diverse ideas and feelings
- Silence: time of quiet reflection to learn lessons from unspoken words; personal awareness of "the quiet of the Soul" (p. 40)

Taking time to abide by these principles could foster the development of more respectful and healthy working relationships among health team members. Development of professional partnerships might facilitate team members to help each other, bolster team member esteem, and heal wounds.

Questions for Reflection 4-6

1. How could I develop professional partnerships with health team members in my clinical practice setting?
2. What personal behaviors/attitudes would I have to change to develop these professional partnerships?

SUMMARY AND SIGNIFICANCE TO PRACTICE

Professional nurses develop helping and healing relationships with clients. All people have visions of what they would like to accomplish and noble intentions about acting on their dreams. Mastery of communication is necessary for carrying out the agendas of life and promoting health and healing of clients and members of the interdisciplinary health team, including professional nurses.

FROM THEORY TO PRACTICE

1. Reread the vignette at the beginning of the chapter. What would you do if you were Margie? What would be the consequences of your proposed actions? Are there other actions that you could take?
2. Think about encounters you have had with health care providers as a consumer. Make a list of positive ones and negative ones. Compare the lists. What are characteristics of caring encounters? What are characteristics of noncaring encounters? Has this exercise changed you as a professional nurse? Why or why not?

INTERNET RESOURCES

The Clinical Practice Model Resource Center: http://www.cpmrc.com.
American Holistic Nurses Association: http://www.ahna.org.
American Psychiatric Nurses Association: http://www.apna.org.
American Psychiatric Association Help Center: http://helping.apa.org.
Healing Touch International: http://www.healingtouch.net.
Therapeutic Touch: http://therapeutictouch.com.

REFERENCES

Agnes, M. (Ed.). (2005). *Webster's new world college dictionary* (4th ed.). Cleveland, OH: Wiley.
Arnold, E., & Boggs, K. (1989). *Interpersonal relationships: Professional communication skills for nurses.* Philadelphia: W. B. Saunders.
Beck, C. T. (2001). Caring within nursing education: A metasynthesis. *Journal of Nursing Education, 40,* 101–109.

Benner, P. (1984). *From novice to expert*. Menlo Park, CA: Addison-Wesley.

Berlo, D. K. (1960). *The process of communication*. New York: Holt, Rinehart & Winston.

Bradley, J. C., & Edinberg, M. A. (1990). *Communication in the nursing context* (3rd ed.). East Norwalk, CT: Appleton & Lange.

Brill, N. I. (1990). *Working with people: The helping process* (4th ed.). New York: Longman.

Ceccio, J. F., & Ceccio, C. M. (1982). *Effective communication in nursing theory and practice*. New York: Wiley.

Coenen, A., Doorenbos, A., & Wilson, S. (2007). Nursing interventions to promote dignified dying in four countries. *Oncology Nursing Forum, 34*, 1151–1156.

Conti-O'Hare, M. (2002). *The nurse as wounded healer: From trauma to transcendence*. Sudbury, MA: Jones & Bartlett.

Dossey, B., Keegan, L., & Guzzetta, C. (2005). *Holistic nursing: A handbook for practice*. Sudbury, MA: Jones & Bartlett.

Finkelman, A., & Kenner, C. (2007). *Teaching IOM: Implications of the Institute of Medicine reports for nursing education*. Silver Spring, MD: American Nurses Association.

Hames, C. C., & Joseph, D. H. (1980). *Basic concepts of helping: A holistic approach*. New York: Appleton-Century-Crofts.

Hosley, J., & Molle, E. (2006). *A practical guide to therapeutic communication for health professionals*. Philadelphia: Saunders Elsevier.

Hunsaker, P. L., & Alessandra, A. J. (1980). *Art of managing people*. Englewood Cliffs, NJ: Prentice-Hall.

Keegan, L. (1994). *The nurse as healer*. Albany, NY: Delmar.

Kritek, P. B. (1997). Healing: A central nursing construct—reflections on meaning. In P. B. Kritek (Ed.), *Reflections on healing: A central nursing construct* (pp. 11–27). New York: National League for Nursing.

Leddy, S. K. (2004). Human energy: A conceptual model of unitary nursing science. *Visions: The Journal of Rogerian Scholarship, 12*, 14–27.

Leininger, M., & McFarland, M. (2006). *Cultural care diversity and universality: A worldwide theory for nursing* (2nd ed.). Sudbury, MA: Jones & Bartlett.

Lerner, M. (1994). *Choices in healing*. Cambridge, MA: MIT Press.

Marck, P. (1990). Therapeutic reciprocity: A caring phenomenon. *Advances in Nursing Science, 13*, 49–59.

McKivergin, M. (2005). The nurse as an instrument of healing. In B. Dossey, L. Keegan, & C. Guzzetta (Eds.), *Holistic nursing: A handbook for practice* (pp. 233–254). Sudbury, MA: Jones & Bartlett.

Mendias, E. P. (1997). Reciprocity in the healing relationship between nurse and patient. In P. B. Kritek (Ed.), *Reflections on healing: A central nursing construct* (pp. 435–451). New York: National League for Nursing.

Micozzi, M. S. (Ed.). (1996). *Fundamentals of complementary and alternative medicine*. New York: Churchill Livingstone.

Newman, M., Lamb, G. S., & Michaels, C. (1991). Nurse case management: The coming together of theory and practice. *Nursing & Health Care, 12*, 404–408.

Northouse, L. L., & Northouse, P. G. (1998). *Health communication: Strategies for health professionals* (3rd ed.). Stamford, CT: Appleton & Lange.

Osterman, P., & Schwartz-Barcott, D. (1996). Presence: Four ways of being there. *Nursing Forum, 31*, 23–30.

Parse, R. R. (1996). The human becoming theory: Challenges in practice and research. *Nursing Science Quarterly, 9*, 55–60.

Paterson, J. G., & Zderad, L. T. (1988). *Humanistic nursing*. New York: National League for Nursing.

Peplau, H. (1952). *Interpersonal relations in nursing*. New York: G. P. Putnam's.

Riley, J. B. (2000). *Communications in nursing* (4th ed.). St. Louis, MO: Mosby.

Rogers, C. R. (1951). *Client-centered therapy: Its current practice, implications, and theory*. Boston: Houghton Mifflin.

Rogers, C. R. (1958). Characteristics of a helping relationship. *Personnel and Guidance Journal, 37*, 6–16.

Rogers, M. E. (1970). *An introduction to the theoretical basis of nursing*. Philadelphia: F. A. Davis.

Schiavo, R. (2007). *Health communication from theory to practice*. San Francisco: Wiley.

Sullivan, H. S. (1953). *The interpersonal theory of psychiatry*. New York: Norton.

Sundeen, S. J., Stuart, G. W., Rankin, E. A. D., & Cohen, S. A. (1994). *Nurse–client interaction* (5th ed.). St. Louis, MO: Mosby.

Sundeen, S. J., Stuart, G. W., Rankin, E. A. D., & Cohen, S. A. (1998). *Nurse–client interaction* (6th ed.). St. Louis, MO: Mosby.

Taylor, A. (1977). *Communicating*. Englewood Cliffs, NJ: Prentice-Hall.

Travelbee, J. (1964). What's wrong with sympathy? *American Journal of Nursing, 64*, 68–71.

Travelbee, J. (1966). *Interpersonal aspects of nursing*. Philadelphia: F. A. Davis.

Travelbee, J. (1971). *Interpersonal aspects of nursing* (2nd ed.). Philadelphia: F. A. Davis.

Vestal, K. W. (1995). *Nursing management: Concepts and issues* (2nd ed.). Philadelphia: J. B. Lippincott.

Videbeck, S. L. (2008). *Psychiatric-mental health nursing* (6th ed.). Philadelphia: Wolters Kluwer Health/ Lippincott Williams & Wilkins.

Watson, J. (1996). Watson's theory of transpersonal caring. In P. H. Walker & B. Neuman (Eds.), *Blueprint for use of nursing models: Education, research, practice and administration* (pp. 141–184). New York: National League for Nursing.

Wesorick, B., & Shiparski, L. (1997). *Can the human being thrive in the work place? Dialogue as a strategy of hope*. Grand Rapids, MI: Practice Field Publishing.

Wesorick, B., Shiparski, L., Troseth, M., & Wyngarden, K. (1997). *Partnership Council field book*. Grand Rapids, MI: Practice Field Publishing.

Wiseman, T. A. (1996). A concept analysis of empathy. *Journal of Advanced Nursing, 23*, 1162–1167.

CHAPTER 5

Patterns of Knowing and Nursing Science

KEY TERMS AND CONCEPTS

Certainty

Relativity

Rationalism

Empiricism

Intuition

Historicism

Postmodernism

Empirical knowing

Empirical knowledge

Aesthetic knowing

Aesthetic knowledge

Personal knowledge

Personal knowing

Ethical knowledge

Ethical knowing

Nursing science

Concepts

Theories

Nursing conceptual models

Four central concepts of nursing

LEARNING OUTCOMES

By the end of this chapter, the learner will be able to:

1 Discuss the evolution of three systems of thought about how to organize developing knowledge in science.

2 Describe the differences among logical empiricism, historicism, and postmodernism in their philosophic approaches to the development of knowledge.

3 Explain the differences among the four patterns of nursing knowledge.

4 Compare and contrast concepts, theories, and conceptual models.

5 Identify the four central concepts of nursing that are the focus for scientific inquiry in nursing.

VIGNETTE

Paul, a registered nurse (RN) for 7 years, is taking a nursing research course while working on his bachelor of science in nursing (BSN) degree. He believes that knowledge from "hard science" is the only way nursing can become as respected as other health care professions. He also believes that research is only useful if it directly improves patient care, and he disregards conceptual or explanatory research. Last week, one of his assigned clients with pancreatitis went into shock and was transferred to the intensive care unit. Surprisingly, his colleague Jill (a nurse with 15 years of clinical experience) happened to enter the client's room just as the client started to hemorrhage. At the end of the shift, Paul thanked Jill and asked her how she was able to detect that the client needed help. Jill replied, "I just knew. I cannot explain it other than nurse's intuition. I just get this little voice that tells me to check on clients and I do." Based on this experience, Paul decides to pursue the topic of the scientific validation of nurse intuition as the topic of his research class.

Understanding nursing's body of knowledge is essential for competent professional practice. Knowledge can be obtained from a number of sources, including experience, reflection, and values. Science is "a unified body of knowledge about phenomena that is supported by agreed-on evidence" (Meleis, 1997, p. 10; Meleis, 2007, p. 36). "Since nursing is a learned profession, it is both a science and an art. The practice of nurses, [therefore], is the creative use of [this] knowledge in human service" (Rogers, 1992, pp. 28–29). For many years, nursing scholars have debated whether professional practice is a science, an art, or both (Meleis, 1997, 2007; Rogers, 2005; Roy, 2007; Watson, 2007).

The science of nursing incorporates the study of relationships among nurses, clients, and environments within the context of health. It also is the result of interrelationships among theory, practice, research, and education. Theory provides the tools to direct nursing practice. Practice provides the professional individual with the setting to apply nursing knowledge and develop and test nursing theories. Research provides the means to test theories. Education provides the means to shape belief systems and to synthesize and disseminate knowledge.

Nursing science is emerging as an autonomous, distinctive professional discipline that is valued by society. As an emerging science, nursing uses and builds on knowledge developed in many disciplines through centuries of evolution.

Questions for Reflection 5-1

1. What are the benefits of establishing a base of nursing science for the profession of nursing?
2. What consequences arise for the nursing profession if it fails to generate a specialized knowledge base?

THE EVOLUTION OF SCIENTIFIC THOUGHT

Human life has greatly changed since prehistoric times, and many of the changes have been the result of the advancement of science. To a large degree, science accounts for humankind's progress. This chapter addresses three systems of thought about organizing and developing human knowledge because it is impossible to cover each era of human history and the entire evolution of human knowledge (Spradlin & Porterfield, 1984).

At first, ancient humans knew about the world through magical beliefs, and they believed that they were controlled by forces beyond human understanding or control. A second way of trying to know about the world began during the scientific revolution (around 1500). Science emphasized observations, measurement, and quantification as the means for understanding the world. Since Einstein's discovery of relativity in the early 20th century, humans began to accept uncertainty and focused on processes that have influenced human thought.

Ancient Humans

Early humans differentiated the world into two parts: me (internal) and not me (external). They viewed the external world as being populated by spirits, demons, and gods, who assumed both good and evil characteristics of humans. Because gods were believed to be irrational and to be moved by whims and passions, humans tried to influence the gods' behavior, instead of trying to figure out rational causes of events.

Through trial and error, humans discovered that some patterns of action led to predictable outcomes, which could be reproduced as long as the procedure was followed exactly (as one would with recipes from a cookbook). Thus, in an elementary way, humans studied and observed phenomena sufficiently to gather many isolated facts. However, the facts remained isolated, rather than being organized into a body of data that could form the basis for scientific conclusions. To the extent that nursing functioned primarily from protocols and procedures based on tradition for many years, nursing also somewhat followed the methods of science that existed until approximately 2 centuries ago.

Because disease, aches, and pains were assumed to be caused by gods and evil spirits, early medicine was associated with religion or magical beliefs. However, time and attention to cause and effect led to practical approaches and logical sequencing of steps of treatment. Hippocrates (460–377 BC) was followed by Aristotle (384–322 BC), who emphasized classification of signs and symptoms. Increasingly, attention was paid to exploring the mechanisms of the human body (Spradlin & Porterfield, 1984).

Questions for Reflection 5-2

1. What current superstitions have I encountered in my professional practice?
2. How do these superstitions affect my practice and the profession?
3. What are the consequences of relying on superstitions to guide professional practice?

The Search for Certainty

By the 1500s, the development of mathematics coincided with increasing interest in the scientific study of humans and nature. The ability to count made relationships appear more logical and the world more predictable. The philosophy of logical positivism drove the search for **certainty**. This was based on a belief that the world was like a simple machine, but only God understood the laws by which it operated. Time and space were absolute. Time flowed smoothly and uniformly. A reductionist approach was used to identify causes to predict effects.

Scientific scholars "became engulfed in a spiral of logic and increasing certainty about quantification of relationships among absolute entities that led to concepts of truths that could be validated.... We could, with the use of observation, measurement, and logical reasoning, know the laws of nature.... All the entities that composed the whole of nature could be reduced to their smallest parts, studied and understood, and rebuilt" (Spradlin & Porterfield, 1984, p. 106).

Reduction of humans into separate psyche and soma (Cartesian dualism), both of which could be measured physically, was advanced by Descartes (1596–1650), who saw the human being as a machine ruled by the same laws as all of nature (Spradlin & Porterfield, 1984, p. 108). The separation of mind from matter (body) and the emphasis on the human being as the sum of minute parts have dominated medical and nursing science ever since.

Four basic assumptions about humans and the universe are inherent in this kind of mechanistic world view: determinism, quantity, continuity, and impersonality. Leaving no room for uncertainty, the principle of determinism reflects the belief that "nature proceeds by a strict chain of events from cause to effect, the configuration of causes at any instant fully determining the event in the next instant, and so on forever" (Ware, Panikaar, & Romein, 1966, p. 127). The ability to predict comes out of this principle, whereas lack of predictability and the presence of uncertainty represent ignorance.

The quantitative principle expresses the exact nature of science. It reflects the belief that science consists of "measuring things and setting up precise relations between the measurements" (Ware et al., 1966, p. 129). In this view, humans and the universe are described by numbers (e.g., spatial coordinates, time, position, amounts, and locations) that quantify physical properties and by relations among these quantitative characteristics.

Continuity, the third principle, is concerned with the "transitions of nature from one state to another [and] express[es] the sense, deeply engrained in the outlook of the age, that the movements of nature are gradual" (Ware et al., 1966, p. 129). This principle reflects the belief that the processes involving humans and the universe are continuous.

In the fourth principle, impersonality, the scientist is viewed as an instrument, not a person. The scientist uses observation rather than imagination, passively finds order in phenomena rather than creating it, and does not permit personal influence on the phenomena under observation (Ware et al., 1966, p. 129).

Belief in these principles led Galileo (1564–1642) and Sir Isaac Newton (1642–1727) to develop the scientific method, based on a particular method of reasoning: logic. Logic encompasses principles of reasoning applicable to any branch of knowledge. Because logic is based on reason and sound judgment, it can be convincing.

Inquiry is a technique of science. It seeks truth, information, or knowledge to solve problems. A problem is any question or matter involving doubt, uncertainty, or difficulty that needs solution. Solution is the act of solving a problem by finding the answer or explanation. The most extensive investigative process of science is the systematic inquiry of research.

Questions for Reflection 5-3

1. How do I use logic, science, and inquiry in my professional practice?
2. What are the consequences of using logic, science, and inquiry in my professional practice and for the profession?

The Relative World of Process

By the 20th century, scientists realized that the physical world consisted of matter and forces that interact with matter, such as gravity, magnetism, and electricity. By exploring the cell, genetic mechanisms and mechanisms that influenced cellular structure and function were explained. It appeared that "the immutable laws which governed the world" were being discovered.

Then, in the early 20th century, Albert Einstein demonstrated that the world was composed not of events, but of observations, which were relative to the place and velocity of the observer. "Any absolutes or cause and effect sequences [are] illusions … testable only in a retrospect organization of events" (Spradlin & Porterfield, 1984, p. vi). Heisenberg's (1971) and Bertalanffy's (1968) work in quantum physics led to postulation that mass, energy, time, and space coordinates are interchangeable. All systems are considered interrelated and interdependent on a continuum of **relativity** and probability, and thus uncertainty.

The implications of this different conceptual system are enormous. Continuity is replaced by discontinuity, and probability (determined statistically) replaces certainty. Emphasis is placed on patterning, rather than on discrete entities, and on interactions, rather than on isolated events. The scientist is no longer an isolated objective observer of events. "Man came to be seen not as a detached observer but as an irremovable part of his observations" (Ware et al., 1966, p. 148). In addition, awareness of the limitations and biases of individual perception has increased, implying that truth and meaning are not absolute but are relative to history and context.

Nonetheless, "while physicists have become increasingly concerned with … a relative world of process, biologists have until recently tended to be even more involved in the reductionistic approach to life" (Spradlin & Porterfield, 1984, p. 189). Because one's belief system is critical to determining sources and methods of discovering knowledge, the following section discusses differing approaches to the philosophy of science that currently influence nursing science.

Questions for Reflection 5-4

1. How does relativism affect nursing practice?
2. How have I used relativism to justify some nursing actions that I have taken?
3. What are the consequences of the use of relativism for patients, myself as a professional nurse, and the nursing profession?

PHILOSOPHY OF KNOWLEDGE

Based on Plato's concepts, knowledge is considered to be belief that has been justified through reason (Stumpf, 1993). What constitutes adequate justification is the concern of the discipline of philosophy. Philosophy considers questions such as whether there is such a thing as truth and how one can be certain that something is true. It is necessary to accept that some things can be true to question the truth or falseness of any particular thing. But must certainty be beyond all possible doubt, or is certainty sufficient if it is beyond logical and reasonable doubt? How does an individual acquire knowledge? What are the roles of intellect, perception, and intuition in the process of knowing?

Processes of Knowing

The three primary processes of knowing are rationalism, empiricism, and intuition. **Rationalism** involves belief in the possibility of knowing truth by thinking and by use of reason that is a priori, or independent of experience. **Empiricism** involves belief that the only source of certainty about knowledge is immediate experience. However, because raw experience is subject to individual perception, the emphasis must be on verification and on confirmation or refutation of observations. **Intuition** is sometimes described as "just knowing." The source of the knowing is internal to the individual and often is perceived as occurring independently of experience or reason. It is subjective and personal in origin, although it can be validated through experience and interaction with others.

Approaches to Knowing

Logical Empiricism

Logical empiricism, a philosophic approach to the development of knowledge accepted since the 16th century, is based on the following assumptions:

1. A body of facts and principles that explain the way the world operates is waiting to be discovered. These include abstract, general, and universal principles. Theories provide alternative explanations of how the body of facts is ordered and systematically unified.
2. Cause-and-effect (linear) relationships can be established by using deductive processes and experimental methodology. The results are context-free generalizations that can be applied to all individuals. Truth is achieved through sensory data and controlled experiments.
3. It is necessary to control values and biases to achieve "objective" knowledge; therefore, the observer must be separated from the observed world. Science is value free. Social relevance is unimportant.
4. Theoretical reduction is an important scientific goal. It is assumed that the ultimate character of reality will be best explained using the logic and simplicity of the fewest possible theoretical concepts and laws.
5. The whole is the sum of its parts. Circumscribing (reducing) observations to small parts of the whole gives better control of the data and stronger explanatory power.

Logical empiricism is synonymous with logical positivism. Logical empiricism provides guidelines for the scientific process and criteria for scientific rigor. Under logical empiricism, the goal of science is "to predict, explain and control" world events, situations, and occurrences. To identify "pure facts," scientists must remain value free while engaging in scientific methods. Nursing knowledge based on the "hard sciences" has its roots in logical empiricism (Rogers, 2005).

Historicism

Historicism, advanced since the 1930s under the influence of concepts such as relativity and process, is based on the following assumptions:

1. Because "truth" is dynamic and constantly changing, what is important is the effectiveness of a theory for solving problems.
2. The whole is more than the sum of its parts. Reducing the whole to parts is counterproductive. Interrelationships and interactions are part of what must be studied.
3. An individual or a phenomenon must be studied as a whole in a natural setting. The observer is part of the setting, so interactions between the observer and the setting should be described, rather than controlled. Emphasis is on process, rather than fact.
4. Multiple research traditions are desirable (e.g., theories from psychology, physiology, education, and so forth) to explain different dimensions of the same phenomenon. Synthesis and development of multiple theories are encouraged.
5. Knowledge is related to context. Values, subjectivity, intuition, history, and tradition are useful for discovery.

Unlike logical empiricim, historicism emphasizes the "importance of the context and processes in which scientific activity takes place" (Rogers, 2005, p. 99). Truth and knowledge are related to context, and multiple approaches can be used to generate knowledge. In professional nursing, historicism provides a value-laden approach to nursing knowledge. Kuhn's (1970) perspective of science as a way to "solve puzzles" and Laudan's (1981) perspective of science as a means to "solve problems" provide a practical approach to the generation of nursing knowledge. Also, in historicism, theories become dynamic rather than static (Rogers, 2005; Watson, 2007). For example, a complete client family history served as the standard for determining client risk for specific diseases prior to the completion of the human genome project. For persons with no access to genetic testing, perhaps a detailed family history may be beneficial in determining future risk of disease.

Postmodernism

Postmodernism is a social movement and a philosophy that originated in Europe in the 1960s (Reed, 1995). Postmodern perspectives on knowledge development are based on the following assumptions:

1. There is a focus on understanding multiple meanings and ways of knowing reality, rather than "a single, transcendent meaning of reality" (Reed, 1995, p. 71). As a result, conceptual models and grand theories are considered irrelevant.
2. Because "multiple truths" are accepted, knowledge is considered to be uncertain and provisional (Holmes & Warelow, 2000). Contradictory positions have value for generating alternative meanings.
3. Statements "reflect a concern for context rather than universality, specificity rather than generalization, uniqueness rather than sameness, and relativism rather than absolutism" (Holmes & Warelow, 2000, p. 90).
4. The emphasis of knowledge development shifts "from concern over the truth of one's findings to concern over the practical significance of the findings" (Reed, 1995, p. 72).

5. Problems are not "solved," but rather are "deconstructed," which means that efforts are made to disentangle or separate concerns from underlying values and beliefs. Language is analyzed for the meanings of words and assumed power structures.

6. With lack of concern about generalization is a shift toward lived experience, and toward "creativity, flexibility, uniqueness, and local value" (Holmes & Warelow, 2000, p. 96). Instead of probable "truth," relevance and usefulness for practice and the potential to generate additional study are the criteria for research.

There is no single definition for postmodernism. Structuralism recognizes the role that language, rituals, social structures (including male and female roles), and traditions play in influencing the discovery of what it means to be fully human. Poststructuralism challenged the dominant thoughts of unity, uniformity, and one-ness (Rogers, 2005; Watson, 1999). Deconstruction aims to reverse hierarchies and acknowledges the importance of power in relationships. From a poststructualist view, persons have no subjective identity, but reveal themselves through various forms of communication along with their actions and behaviors. In postmodernism, "a belief in a single reality that provided a unifying and stable center is discarded" because "it is indefensible" (Rogers, 2005, p. 135). According to a postmodern perspective, all persons have different perspectives and experiences about the world (Rogers, 2005; Watson, 1999).

Until recently, nursing research and theory were dominated by logical empiricism and positivistic philosophy. However, beginning with Rogers (1970) and increasing in the 1980s, nurse scientists incorporated principles of historicism and process into theory, research, and practice. In the mid-1990s, principles of postmodernism began to appear in the nursing literature.

Currently, a debate about the appropriate methods for developing nursing knowledge is being waged in the nursing literature. Some authors in support of qualitative methods have maintained that "human behaviors cannot be isolated and quantified and that the attempt to do so results in misleading and dehumanizing outcomes rather than in knowledge that is useful for nursing practice" (Campbell & Bunting, 1991, p. 2). Others have suggested that quantitative and qualitative methods can be used at different times to serve different purposes. Meleis (1997) advocated development of a world view [Weltanschauung] that includes an integration of norms emanating from different theories of truth. It combines rigor and intuition, sensory data as they exist and as they appear, perceptions of the subject and of the theoretician, and logic with observable clinical data. (p. 87)

Such a synthesis of philosophical approaches would encourage various methods for the development of nursing science, thereby capturing the complexity of the discipline of nursing.

The next section discusses patterns (ways) of knowing and methods for their use.

PATTERNS OF NURSING KNOWLEDGE

Chinn and Kramer (1999, pp. 1, 7) described knowing as "ways of perceiving and understanding the self and the world.... Nursing's patterns of knowing are interrelated and arise from the whole of experience."

Gender differences have been identified in the ways in which men and women may develop frameworks for the organization of knowledge. Perry (1970) identified four positions through which men make sense of their educational experiences:

1. Basic dualism: Authorities hand down the truth, and the learner is passive. Choices are perceived as either right or wrong, black or white, good or bad, and we or they.

2. Multiplicity: The teacher may not have the right answer. A personal opinion is acceptable and may be valid.

3. Relative subordinate position: Evidence is sought for opinions. The emphasis is on analysis and evaluation of information.

4. Full relativism: Truth is relative. The meaning of knowledge depends on its context.

Perry suggested that the positions occurred in a linear sequence, with each position an advance over the previous one.

In a study of women's perceptions, Belenky, Clinchy, Goldberger, and Tarule (1986) described five major categories used for the organization of knowledge:

1. Silence: The individual is subject to the whims of an external authority and perceives herself to be mindless and voiceless.

2. Received knowledge: External authority is all-knowing. The individual is capable of receiving and even reproducing knowledge, but not of creating it.

3. Subjective knowledge: Truth and knowledge are personal, private, and subjectively known or intuited.

4. Procedural knowledge: The individual is invested in learning and in applying objective procedures for obtaining and communicating knowledge.

5. Constructed knowledge: The individual experiences herself as a creator of knowledge. She views knowledge as contextual and values both objective and subjective strategies for knowing.

Additional study is needed to identify whether these categories develop sequentially.

Gender has been linked to the distribution of power and privilege in society (Marecek, 1995). Doering (1992, p. 26) stated that knowledge reinforces and supports existing power relations that "subtly support male dominance and reinforce female submissiveness." "When the male model is assumed to be the human model, women are viewed as the 'other,' deviant from the male norm or prototype" (Doering, p. 31). However, Doering continued, "since power is always exercised in relation to a resistance" (p. 31), ways of knowing (such as intuitive knowing and contextual, phenomena-centered knowledge) that are not based on a male world view "may alter the balance of the nursing–medicine power relation" (p. 32).

Carper (1992), in "an effort to understand the kinds of knowledge comprising the discipline of nursing" (p. 73), analyzed the nursing literature published between 1964 and 1975. Her results, which were published in a seminal 1978 article, identified four fundamental patterns, or ways, of knowing in nursing: empiricism, aesthetics, personal knowledge, and ethics. These ways of knowing have been extended by Chinn and Kramer (1999) and White (1995). Although they were devised over 30 years ago, most nursing scholars agree they encompass ways of knowing for the nursing profession (Meleis, 1997, 2007; Rogers, 2005; Roy, 2007; Watson, 2007).

Empirical Knowledge

The pattern of **empirical knowing** constitutes the science of nursing. It "encompasses publically verifiable, factual descriptions, explanations, and predictions based on subjective or objective group data" (Fawcett, Watson, Neuman, Walker, & Fitzpatrick, 2001, pp. 115–116). "Empirical data, obtained by either direct or indirect observation and measurement … are formulated as scientific principles, generalizations, laws, and theories that provide explanation and prediction" (Carper, 1992, p. 76) or enrich understanding through interpretation or description (White, 1995). **Empirical knowledge** is obtained through the senses, can be verified, is credible, and is used to impart understanding. Processes related to creating empiric knowledge include explaining and structuring (Chinn & Kramer, 1999).

Aesthetic Knowledge

Aesthetic knowing in nursing "is that aspect of knowing that connects with deep meanings of a situation and calls forth inner creative resources that transform experience"

(Chinn & Kramer, 1999, p. 183). This knowledge is not universal but is uniquely experienced and expressed and has subjective meaning. Aesthetic knowing involves the creative processes of rehearsing and envisioning (Chinn & Kramer).

"Art begins with the assumption of a common, generalizable human experience … and seeks expression of the infinite creative possibilities for experiencing or responding to the human experience" (Chinn, 1994, p. 30). Intuition, defined as "an immediate apprehension, or the power of gaining knowledge without evidence of rational thought" (Mitchell, 1994, p. 2), can be an important component of **aesthetic knowledge** in nursing practice.

Benner and Tanner (1987) discussed six aspects of intuitive judgment previously identified by Dreyfus and Dreyfus (1985). These aspects are not sequential but rather are used in combination by the practitioner:

1. Pattern recognition is the ability to recognize patterns and relationships without prior consideration of the separate components.
2. Similarity recognition is the ability to see similarities and parallels among patient situations, even when there are marked dissimilarities in objective features.
3. Commonsense understanding is "a deep grasp of the culture and language, so that flexible understanding in diverse situations is possible. It is the basis for understanding the illness experience, in contrast to knowing the disease" (Benner & Tanner, 1987, p. 25). It is a way of "tuning in" to the patient and grasping the patient's experience.
4. Skilled know-how is based on a combination of knowledge and experience that permits flexibility of actions and judgment.
5. A sense of salience makes it possible to differentiate what is particularly significant in a situation.
6. Deliberative rationality involves the use of analysis and past experience to consider alternative interpretations of a clinical situation.

Carper (1978) emphasized the importance of integrating aesthetic knowledge into the nursing process. The experience of helping and caring "must be perceived and designed as an integral component of its desired result rather than conceived separately as an independent action imposed on an independent subject" (Carper, p. 17). The result is a richness and appreciation of the practice of nursing as an art as well as a science.

Personal Knowledge

Personal knowledge involves a "person's individualized and subjective ways of learning, storing, and retrieving information about the world" (Rew, 1996, p. 96). "The pattern of **personal knowing** refers to the quality and authenticity of the interpersonal process between each nurse and each [client]" (Fawcett et al., 2001, p. 116). Both the nurse and the client are considered to be "integrated, open system(s) incorporating movement toward growth and fulfillment of human potential" (Carper, 1978, p. 19). In the process of mutually establishing a nurse–client relationship, there must be efforts toward "receptive attending" (Moch, 1990, p. 155) and engagement, rather than detachment and a manipulative impersonal orientation. The result is an authentic knowing of an individual apart from the category of nurse or client. The creative processes of personal knowing include opening and centering (Chinn & Kramer, 1999).

Because personal knowing "concerns the inner experience of becoming a whole, aware, genuine self" (Chinn & Kramer, 1999, p. 5), the individual needs to accept ambiguity, vagueness, and discrepancies in what is essentially a subjective and existential process. There is no specific methodology that can be used consistently. The individual must be open to experience and intuitive feelings, be honest with self, and make efforts to acknowledge the responses of others. This is an ongoing process, because the self is constantly changing.

Belenky and colleagues (1986) stated that educators can help women develop their own authentic voices if they emphasize connection over separation, understanding and acceptance over assessment, and collaboration over debate; if they accord respect to and allow time for the knowledge that emerges from firsthand experience; if instead of imposing their own expectations and arbitrary requirements, they encourage students to evolve their own patterns of work based on the problems they are pursuing (p. 229).

Moch (1990, pp. 156–159) described three overlapping components of personal knowing:

1. Experiential knowing involves becoming aware through participation in which the knower learns through self-observation, by observing others, through feeling, and through sensing.
2. Interpersonal knowing is increased awareness through connectedness or interaction, which can involve intense attending, opening oneself to another, and conveying feelings to another.
3. Intuitive knowing involves the immediate knowing of something without the use of reason. The knower often describes this as a "hunch" or as a "feeling about something."

Moch (1990) believed that personal knowing can be viewed only from within a context of wholeness; includes a process of encountering, passion, commitment, and integrity; and entails a shift in connectedness at the conscious or unconscious level (p. 159).

In identifying implications for research and knowledge development, Moch (1990, p. 162) suggested the following assumptions for capturing and transmitting personal knowing:

1. All perceptions are involved in data gathering.
2. The process of the experience may take precedence over the product.
3. The product of knowing is validated by the knower with both internal and external validation criteria.
4. No attempts are made to reproduce the process or the product because each situation is unique.

"The processing may consist of any combination of human and environmental interaction, rational intuiting, appraisal, active comprehension, and personal judgment" (Sweeney, 1994, p. 917).

Ethical Knowledge

Ethics in nursing focuses on an obligation, or "what ought to be done" (Chinn & Kramer, 1999, p. 5). Sarvimaki (1995) described four aspects that represent different ways of organizing and expressing moral knowledge. Theoretical or **ethical knowledge** "stands for an intellectual conception of what is good and right. It is organized into concepts and propositions that are formulated into judgments, rules, principles, and theories" (Sarvimaki, p. 344). Moral action knowledge means "having the skill necessary for performing the act as well as having good judgment.... Values and principles are manifested in action" (Sarvimaki, p. 345). Personal moral knowledge "refers to the way in which morality is organized in the person, that is, in his motives, inclinations, emotions and commitments" (Sarvimaki, p. 346). Situational knowledge "means being aware of the moral significance of the situation and being able to identify its morally significant traits" (Sarvimaki, p. 347).

Biomedical ethics are derived from models of patient good, rights-based notions of autonomy, or the social contract of medical practice (Fry, 1989). However, it has been argued (Fry; Sarvimaki, 1995; White, 1995) that nursing ethics should be based on an ethic of caring and must consider the nature of the nurse–client relationship. A caring orientation is based on the moral ideal of doing what is good, rather than that which is just.

Mutuality, not autonomy, is foundational (White). "Creative processes of **ethical knowing** in nursing include clarifying and valuing" (Chinn & Kramer, 1999).

White (1995) proposed that a fifth way of knowing, sociopolitical knowing, needs to be added to the original patterns identified by Carper (1978). "The pattern of sociopolitical knowing addresses the 'wherein'" (White, p. 83), a broader context that includes the context of nurse and client (including cultural identity), and the context of nursing as a practice profession. White stated that "a sociopolitical understanding in which to frame all other patterns of knowing is an essential part of nursing's future in an increasingly economically driven world" (p. 85).

In addition, Munhall (1993) proposed "unknowing" as another pattern of knowing in nursing. She argued that the state of mind of unknowing is a condition of openness, and "a de-centering process from one's own organizing principles of the world" (p. 125). The intent is to "come to know the patient's world" (Munhall, p. 126), and "lead to a much deeper knowledge of another being, of different meanings, and interpretations of all our various perceptions of experience" (p. 128).

Three different perspectives, each described as reflecting a different point of view (paradigm) of the way to develop nursing knowledge, have been identified (Newman, Sime, & Corcoran-Perry, 1991, p. 4):

1. Particulate-deterministic perspective: Phenomena are viewed as "isolatable, reducible entities having definable properties that can be measured." Knowledge includes facts and universal laws that can be used to predict and control change.
2. Interactive-integrative perspective: Phenomena are viewed as having multiple, interrelated parts. Reality is assumed to be multidimensional and contextual. Relationships may be reciprocal (rather than linear and causal), and knowledge may be context dependent.
3. Unitary-transformative perspective: Each phenomenon is viewed as a unitary self-organizing field embedded in a larger self-organizing field. It is identified by pattern and by interaction with the larger whole. Change is unpredictable. Knowledge is personal and involves pattern recognition. Both the viewer and the phenomenon are involved in a process of "mutuality and creative unfolding."

Patterns as ways of knowing are not mutually exclusive; rather, they "are interrelated and arise from the whole of experience" (Chinn & Kramer, 1999, p. 7). Different ways of knowing are not judged against one another. Each of the ways of knowing and of creating knowledge are useful. Because each pattern adds only one specific component, none alone is a sufficient source of knowledge for nursing science. Comprehensive nursing knowledge must be based on an integration of all the ways of knowing. "Nursing depends on the specific knowledge of human behavior in health and in illness, the aesthetic perception of significant human experience, a personal understanding of the unique individuality of the self and the capacity to make choices within concrete situations involving particular judgments" (Carper, 1978, p. 22).

 ## THE DEVELOPMENT OF NURSING SCIENCE

Because of the complexity of the discipline of nursing and competing world view perspectives (particular-deterministic, interactive-integrative, and unitary-transformative), defining **nursing science** poses a challenge. However, attaining a clear definition of nursing science would provide a foundation for the profession's unique body of knowledge. Specialized branches of science develop knowledge and theories. First come the ideas and theories. Scientists then test the theories, and depending upon the results, the ideas and theories are refined. Nursing contributes uniquely to health care delivery, but failure to articulate exact contributions may place the profession at risk.

Concepts

For a discipline to have growth of knowledge, the **concepts**—highly abstract and general "word[s] or phrase[s] that summarize the essential characteristics or properties of a phenomenon" (Fawcett, 2000, p. 3)—that are important for the discipline must be identified, and there must be a shared acceptance of conceptual definitions. Fawcett (2005) defined the term "concept" as "a word or phrase that summarizes ideas, observations, and experiences" (p. 4). Four concepts have been commonly accepted as central to the discipline of nursing: human beings (who may be a nurse or client individual, a family, a group, or a community), the environment (which may be alive or inanimate), health (which may include well-being and illness), and nursing (which may include all the interactions among the nurse, client, and environment in the pursuit of health as well as what nurses do). These four concepts represent the metaparadigm of nursing that encompasses all phenomena of interest in a value-neutral way to identify a distinctive domain for the profession of nursing (Fawcett, 2005).

Since its creation, various nurse scholars have proposed additional concepts that should be included such as the concepts of caring. Newman and colleagues (1991) even asserted that "nursing is the study of caring in the human health experience" (p. 3). However, others have expressed concern that "caring is relatively underdeveloped as a concept, has not been clearly explicated and often lacks relevance for nursing practice" (Morse, Bottorff, Neander, & Solberg, 1991, p. 119). Watson (2007) conceptualized caring as a value and ideal that also encompasses a "philosophy of action" (p. 32). At least five conceptualizations of caring have been identified: a human trait, a moral imperative, an affect, an interpersonal interaction, and a therapeutic intervention (Morse et al., 1991). Caring seems to be part of content and relationship (Knowlden, 1991) and associated with varying outcomes, such as the client's physical response and the client's or the nurse's subjective experience (Morse et al., 1991). When effective, some concepts including care can be directly measured using empirical indicators that take the form of clinical practice tools (Fawcett, 2005) (such as the McGill pain rating scale) or research instruments (Fawcett, 2005).

Melies (2007) offered a different approach to the nursing paradigm and proposed the following seven central concepts:

1. Nursing client (recipient of professional nursing services)
2. Transitions (changes in health status, role relationships, expectations, or abilities)
3. Interaction (instrument for assessment and constructing relationships)
4. Nursing process (steps that nurses use to deliver services, including assessment, diagnosis, planning, implementation, and evaluation)
5. Environment (not well defined, but relates to the setting, context, and properties or dimensions of the world that affect human health; see Chapter 6 for various nursing approaches to this concept)
6. Nursing therapeutics (deliberate nursing activities and actions nurses use while caring for clients)
7. Health (goal of nursing services, but not limited to the absence of disease; see Chapters 5 for various nursing approaches to this concept)

Because of their abstract nature, concepts can pose problems within a single discipline or across disciplines. Other issues arise when a particular phenomenon is incompletely understood or lacks procedures to explain or measure it (Fawcett, 2005; Rogers, 2005; Meleis, 2007). Because the profession of nursing is highly complex and has various specialty areas of practice, attaining a "single" definition for nursing concepts is extremely difficult. At present, in the absence of a consensus on definitions for the concepts of human beings, environment health, and nursing, multiple definitions coexist (see Chapter 6).

Theories

Theories communicate links or relationships among concepts in an organized, coherent, and systematic way and vary in levels of abstraction and scope (Fawcett, 2005; Meleis,

2007). Theories symbolize reality and can either be discovered or invented (Meleis, 2007). Meleis (2007) specified that theories can describe, explain, predict, or prescribe phenomena, including relationships, events, situations, responses, or conditions (p. 37). Fawcett (2005) explained that propositions are statements that either define or describe a concept (nonrelational) or specify a relationship or linkage between multiple concepts. Grand theories for professional nursing provide a broad characterization of professional nursing and typically are highly abstract. Thus, they fail to provide specific information to guide research and clinical practice (Fawcett, 2005; Meleis, 2007; Rogers, 2005; Walker & Avant, 2005). When theories become able to describe, explain, or predict certain relationships between or among concepts, nursing scholars categorize these as middle-range theories, which serve as theoretical frameworks for nursing research and practice (Fawcett, 2005; Meleis, 2007; Rogers, 2005; Walker & Avant). Theories help nurses understand how and why the phenomena of nursing are associated with one another.

Theories in nursing may be unique to the discipline of nursing, or borrowed from or shared with another discipline that has interest in similar human phenomena (Fawcett, 2000; Meleis, 2007). For example, the concept of self-esteem is borrowed from the field of psychology but plays a key role when nurses establish therapeutic relationships with clients and interprofessional relationships with members of the health care team. Before questioning a physician order, the nurse must have the self-esteem to have confidence in his or her knowledge of pharmacology to confront the physician in order to avoid a serious event for a client. After successfully confronting the situation, the nurse's self-esteem becomes enhanced because he or she did the right thing.

Effectiveness in practice is directly related to the ability to understand, describe, explain, and anticipate human responses concerning health. Theoretically based professional practice enables nurses to anticipate client complications before they occur and determine the best approaches to use in specific client care situations.

Theoretical Frameworks

A theoretical or conceptual framework has been defined as "a logical grouping of related concepts or theories" (Chinn & Kramer, 1999, p. 258). A model is composed of abstract and general concepts and propositions that are linked together in a distinctive way. Fawcett (2000) stated that a conceptual model "provides a unique focus that has a profound influence on individuals' perceptions" (p. 16). Theoretical frameworks provide guidance and direction for nursing research endeavors (Meleis, 2007). Rogers (2005) distinguished theoretical frameworks from theories in that the theoretical framework is broader than a theory and typically has not been validated through scientific testing. Theoretical frameworks tend to address phenomena more global in nature. Developing theoretical frameworks for nursing ensures practice that considers the complex nature of professional practice. Nurses who use theoretical frameworks in professional practice typically have some sort of method to provide holistic care rather than just focusing on client physiological issues.

Models for Nursing

Several nurse scientists have proposed individual and distinctive models about the interrelationships of concepts that form the nature and processes of nursing. Each nurse scholar who has proposed a conceptual model has based the model on empirical observation, intuitive insights, or deductive reasoning "that creatively combine[s] ideas from several fields of inquiry" (Fawcett, 2000, p. 16). Although they may present diverse views of nursing phenomena, each conceptual model is useful for professional nursing because of the organization it provides for thinking, observing, and interpreting in nursing practice. Some **nursing conceptual models** provide an illustrative diagram to depict relationships among concepts (e.g., Fig. 1-1, Chapter 1; and see Chapter 6 for a discussion of selected conceptual models). Nursing conceptual models identify the interventions that nurses use in practice while explaining the **four central concepts of nursing**: human beings, environment, health, and nursing (Fawcett, 2005; Meleis, 1997, 2007; Rogers, 2005; Walker & Avant, 2005).

SUMMARY AND SIGNIFICANCE TO PRACTICE

Because of the complexity of client care, nurses use a variety of methods of knowing when providing professional nursing services. Nursing science encompasses more than the physiological aspects of client care. Most nurses encounter practice situations in which they rely on personal and ethical knowing to make effective clinical judgments and decisions. Understanding and appreciating the patterns of knowing in nursing sharpen the cognitive skills of professional nurses as they engage in daily practice.

Most nursing scholars have a general agreement on the central concepts of the discipline of nursing. The central concepts help to describe the phenomenon of professional nursing practice and guide nurses in clinical practice, research endeavors, and educational programs. Explication of the central concepts and tenets of professional nursing remains a challenge because of the various approaches to patterns of knowing available to nurses in the postmodern era.

FROM THEORY TO PRACTICE

1. How do you use the empirical, aesthetic, personal, and ethical ways of knowing in your professional practice? How do your attitudes about the ways of knowing affect your professional practice? Why are the ways of knowing important for professional nurses?
2. How has reading this chapter affected your views about nursing science and nursing theory?
3. What suggestion would you give Paul as he explores the phenomenon of nursing intuition as the topic of his class research project? How do you think Paul would respond to each of your points? What are the consequences of having a narrowly defined perception of what constitutes nursing knowledge?

REFERENCES

Belenky, M. F., Clinchy, B. M., Goldberger, N. R., & Tarule, J. M. (1986). *Women's ways of knowing: The development of self, voice and mind*. New York: Basic Books.

Benner, P., & Tanner, C. (1987). Clinical judgment: How expert nurses use intuition. *American Journal of Nursing, 87*, 23–31.

Bertalanffy, L. von. (1968). *General system theory*. New York: Braziller.

Campbell, J. C., & Bunting, S. (1991). Voices and paradigms: Perspectives on critical and feminist theory in nursing. *Advances in Nursing Science, 13*, 1–5.

Carper, B. A. (1978). Fundamental patterns of knowing in nursing. *Advances in Nursing Science, 1*, 13–23.

Carper, B. A. (1992). Philosophical inquiry in nursing: An application. In J. F. Kikuchi & H. Simmons (Eds.), *Philosophic inquiry in nursing* (pp. 71–80). Newbury Park, CA: Sage.

Chinn, P. L. (1994). Developing a method for aesthetic knowing in nursing. In P. L. Chinn & J. Watson (Eds.), *Art and aesthetics in nursing* (pp. 19–40). New York: National League for Nursing.

Chinn, P. L., & Kramer, M. K. (1999). *Theory and nursing: Integrated knowledge development* (5th ed.). St. Louis, MO: Mosby-Year Book.

Doering, L. (1992). Power and knowledge in nursing: A feminist poststructuralist view. *Advances in Nursing Science, 14*, 24–33.

Dreyfus, H., & Dreyfus, S. (1985). *Mind over machine: The power of human intuition and expertise in the era of the computer*. New York: Macmillan Free Press.

Fawcett, J. (2000). *Analysis and evaluation of contemporary nursing knowledge: Nursing models and theories*. Philadelphia: F. A. Davis.

Fawcett, J. (2005). *Contemporary nursing knowledge: Analysis and evaluation of nursing models and theories* (2nd ed.). Philadelphia: F. A. Davis.

Fawcett, J., Watson, J., Neuman, B., Walker, P. H., and Fitzpatrick, J. J. (2001). On nursing theories and evidence. *Journal of Nursing Scholarship, 33*, 115–119.

Fry, S. T. (1989). Toward a theory of nursing ethics. *Advances in Nursing Science, 11*, 9–22.

Heisenberg, W. (1971). *Physics and beyond*. New York: Harper & Row.

Holmes, C. A., & Warelow, P. J. (2000). Some implications of postmodernism for nursing theory, research, and practice. *Canadian Journal of Nursing Research, 32*, 89–101.

Knowlden, V. (1991). Nurse caring as constructed knowledge. In R. M. Neil & R. Watts (Eds.), *Caring and nursing: Explorations in feminist perspectives* (pp. 201–208). New York: National League for Nursing.

Kuhn, T. (1970). *The structure of scientific revolutions* (2nd ed.). Chicago: University of Chicago Press.

Laudan, L. (1981). A problem solving approach to scientific growth. In I. Hacking (Ed.), *Scientific revolutions*. Oxford: Oxford University Press.

Marecek, J. (1995). Gender, politics, and psychology's ways of knowing. *American Psychologist, 50*, 162–163.

Meleis, A. (1997). *Theoretical nursing: Development and progress* (3rd ed.). Philadelphia: Lippincott.

Meleis, A. (2007). *Theoretical nursing: Development & progress* (4th ed.). Philadelphia: Lippincott Williams & Wilkins.

Mitchell, G. J. (1994). Intuitive knowing: Exposing a myth in theory development. *Nursing Science Quarterly, 7*, 2–3.

Moch, S. D. (1990). Personal knowing: Evolving research and practice. *Scholarly Inquiry for Nursing Practice, 4*, 155–170.

Morse, J. M., Bottorff, J., Neander, W., & Solberg, S. (1991). Comparative analysis of conceptualizations and theories of caring. *Image, 23*, 119–126.

Munhall, P. L. (1993). "Unknowing": Toward another pattern of knowing in nursing. *Nursing Outlook, 41*, 125–128.

Newman, M. A., Sime, A. M., & Corcoran-Perry, S. A. (1991). The focus of the discipline of nursing. *Advances in Nursing Science, 14*, 1–6.

Perry, W. G. (1970). *Forms of intellectual and ethical development in the college years*. New York: Holt, Rinehart and Winston.

Reed, P. G. (1995). A treatise on nursing knowledge development for the 21st century: Beyond postmodernism. *Advances in Nursing Science, 17*, 70–84.

Rew, L. (1996). *Awareness in healing*. Albany, NY: Delmar.

Rogers, B. L. (2005). *Developing nursing knowledge philosophical traditions and influences*. Philadelphia: Lippincott Williams & Wilkins.

Rogers, M. E. (1970). *An introduction to the theoretical basis of nursing*. Philadelphia: F. A. Davis.

Rogers, M. E. (1992). Nursing science and the space age. *Nursing Science Quarterly, 5*, 27–34.

Roy, C. (2007). Advances in nursing knowledge and the challenge for transforming practice. In C. Roy & D. Jones (Eds.), *Nursing knowledge development and clinical practice* (pp. 37). New York: Springer.

Sarvimaki, A. (1995). Aspects of moral knowledge in nursing. *Scholarly Inquiry for Nursing Practice, 9*, 343–358.

Spradlin, W. W., & Porterfield, P. B. (1984). *The search for certainty*. New York: Springer-Verlag.

Stumpf, S. E. (1993). *Socrates to Sartre: A history of philosophy* (5th ed.). New York: McGraw-Hill.

Sweeney, N. M. (1994). A concept analysis of personal knowledge: Application to nursing education. *Journal of Advanced Nursing, 20*, 917–924.

Walker, L. O., & Avant, K. C. (2005). *Strategies for theory construction in nursing* (4th ed.). Upper Saddle River, NJ: Pearson Prentice Hall.

Ware, C. F., Panikaar, K. M., & Romein, J. M. (1966). *History of mankind, cultural and scientific development: Vol. 6. The twentieth century*. New York: Harper & Row.

Watson. J. (1999). *Postmodern nursing and beyond*. Edinburgh: Churchill Livingstone.

Watson, J. (2007). *Nursing human science and human care: A theory of nursing*. Sudbury, MA: Jones & Bartlett.

White, J. (1995). Patterns of knowing: Review, critique, and update. *Advances in Nursing Science, 17*, 73–86.

Nursing Models and Theories

LEARNING OUTCOMES

By the end of this chapter, the learner will be able to:

1 Compare and contrast systems, adaptation, caring, and complexity theories.
2 Outline differences in how nursing's metaparadigm concepts are defined in each of the nursing models presented.
3 Explain the key differences among rote, stereotypical, and theoretically based nursing practice.
4 Identify assumptions in the various nursing models presented in the chapter.
5 Determine the strengths and weaknesses of current nursing models and theories.
6 Apply each of the presented nursing models and theories to a clinical practice situation.

VIGNETTE

Nancy and Ann are two nurses working the night shift. Tonight, Ms. Green uses the call light every 5 minutes because she cannot sleep. Her nurse, Nancy, asks Ann for help because Ann always seems to know just what to do. After Ann spends 5 minutes with Ms. Green, she goes to sleep. Nancy asks, "How do you always know what to do to help the restless patients?" Ann shares her knowledge about Parse's human becoming theory emphasizing being truly present with clients. Ann also summarizes key concepts and approaches presented by other nursing theorists that she learned in her undergraduate nursing program. Ann mentions that although she prefers to use Parse's model, she finds that other nursing models help in different client care situations.

MODELS AND THEORIES FOR PROFESSIONAL NURSING

The discipline of nursing is highly complex. Over the years, most nursing scholars have adopted the following four key concepts to serve as a metaparadigm: human beings (recipients of nursing care), environment (physical and social), health (a process or state), and nursing (goals, roles, and functions) (Fawcett, 2005). The term **metaparadigm** comes from "the Greek prefix 'meta,' which means more comprehensive or transcending, and the Greek word 'paradigm,' which means an overall concept accepted by most people in an intellectual community" (Agnes, 2005). Hardy (1978) introduced the idea of paradigms to the nursing profession as a means to offer a comprehensive description and possibly a method of unifying professional nursing (Fawcett, 2005; Meleis, 2007; Rogers, 2005; Roy, 2007). All existing nursing models and theories address these four concepts. In fact, four of the models presented in this chapter contain the word "human" in their titles. Each model also uses a different philosophical view of the world. Although nursing models and theories vary according to philosophical world views, all flow from the metaparadigm of nursing.

NURSING MODELS

Before 1950, the writings of Florence Nightingale served as the primary source of nursing theory, and nursing science was derived principally from social, biologic, and medical science theories. Nursing science started to emerge as part of the profession in the 1950s and continues to flourish as nursing theorists develop and refine models of nursing. Some nursing theories and models arose when nurses tried to generate a clear, concise definition of nursing.

A model, as an abstraction of reality, provides a way to visualize reality to simplify thinking. For example, a spaceship model provides a representation of a spaceship. A **conceptual model** gives structure to and shows how various concepts are interrelated. Conceptual models serve as a foundation for theory development or can also apply theories to predict or evaluate consequences of alternative actions. According to Fawcett (2000), a conceptual model "gives direction to the search for relevant questions about the phenomena of central interest to a discipline and suggests solutions to practical problems" (p. 16). **Nursing models** tend to be more abstract than nursing theory.

Nursing Theory

Chinn and Kramer (1999) defined **theory** as "a creative and rigorous structuring of ideas that projects a tentative, purposeful, and systematic view of phenomena" (p. 83). Professional nurses apply concepts, principles, and theories from many disciplines. For example, nurses use physics when placing cardiac monitor electrodes on client chests, pharmacology when monitoring clients receiving medications, psychology when providing emotional support, microbiology when using asepsis, family theory when assessing effective mother–infant bonding, and human development theory when caring for clients of all ages. However, these borrowed theories and principles fail to capture the essence of professional nursing. Theories create a different way of looking at a particular phenomenon by interrelating concepts in a logical manner and provide a framework for describing, explaining, and predicting practice. They also provide a relatively simple, yet generalizable, view for testable hypothesis development. Once validated through research, theories expand discipline-specific knowledge while identifying other questions for future investigation.

Many nurses base their practice on intuition, experience, or "how I learned it in nursing school." These methods lead to rote and stereotypical practice. Nurses rely on memorization and habit when engaging in rote practice. Rote practice enables nurses to provide care while in an "autopilot" or robotic mode. When nurses use long-standing traditions and incorporate the expectations of others in practice, they engage in stereotypical practice. In the stereotypical practice mode, nurses try to fulfill expectations others may have of them such as blindly following physician orders or willingly assuming the role of the self-sacrificing angel of mercy.

However, practice based on models or theories allows for hypotheses about practice, which make it possible to derive a rationale for nursing actions. When using a specific nursing model or theory, nurses use key concepts and relationships to direct client assessments and interventions. Testable theories provide a knowledge base for the science of nursing. As the science of nursing develops, nurses will be able to more accurately understand and explain events, and to provide a basis for predicting and controlling future events. In addition, practice based on science fosters the recognition of nursing as a professional discipline. Looking at philosophical differences helps to explain why nursing models and theories vary in approaches to professional practice.

Questions for Reflection 6-1

1. How do I rely on traditions and personal experience when I practice nursing?
2. What consequences have resulted when I used traditions to guide my nursing practice?
3. What is my personal attitude toward nursing models and theories? Why do I feel this way about them?

Categories of Nursing Models and Theories

Because many nursing conceptual models and theories exist today, this chapter presents nine models that provide a foundation of professional practice for many individual nurses, nursing research studies, and nursing departments in some health care organizations (Fawcett, 2005; Meleis, 2007; Watson, 2007). The nine models selected present a multiplicity of philosophical world views in the hope of capturing reader interest and, perhaps, stimulating dialogue among present and future nurses about the essence of professional nursing. To distinguish differences among them, the models and theories have been classified according to the following criteria:

1. The world view of change reflected by the model (growth or stability)
2. The major theoretical/conceptual classification with which the model seems most consistent (systems, stress/adaptation, caring, or growth/development)

Providing a structure for grouping the models and theories should provide the reader with a basis for understanding conceptual similarities and differences.

Many nurses fail to appreciate nursing models and theories. By revealing the essence of each model or theory, from original sources as much as possible, the chapter aims to provide concise summaries so that the reader can appreciate similarities and differences among them and identify points of congruence with the world views on which the model or theory is based. Some nurse theorists coin words, define family words in different ways, and develop new concepts. This chapter aims to clarify the models, rather than critique them or to select a single best model or theory for use. The selection of a nursing model or theory to guide practice is an individual decision. Interpretations of the professional nursing processes based on these models will be presented in Chapter 7, "Professional Nursing Processes."

Growth and Stability Models of Change

Two basic philosophical world views exist about the nature of change. Change remains constant; however, perceptions of change differ among people. In 1989, Fawcett presented world views according to perceptions of change. One world view recognizes change as continuous, a desired opportunity for growth to attain maximum human potential.

The other world view is persistence, which maintains that human beings strive for stability and that endurance results from "a synthesis of growth and stability" (p. 12). The persistence world view focuses on continuing and maintaining patterns by emphasizing balance and equilibrium. Although the world views differ, they are not mutually exclusive. However, the selected nursing models in this chapter approach change differently and provides a means to classify them.

THE STABILITY MODEL OF CHANGE

The **stability model of change** proposes that the natural order of things revolves around consistency. Although change is inevitable and may be undesirable, it forces adaptation. Stability means that the organism attains a new and stable equilibrium.

Questions for Reflection 6-2

1. Which world view seems more compatible with my personal philosophy, the change or persistence world view?
2. Why is this world view more compatible with my philosophy?
3. Is it possible to embrace both world views? Why or why not?

Systems Theory

Systems theory is concerned with elements and interactions among all the factors (variables) in a situation. Interactions between the person and the environment occur continuously, thereby creating a complex, constantly changing situation. Systems theory provides a way to understand the many influences on the whole person and the possible impact of change on any part of the whole. This theory can help nurses to understand, predict, and control the possible effects of nursing care on the client system and the concurrent effects of the interaction on the nurse system and environment.

Auger (1976) defined a system as "a whole with interrelated parts, in which the parts have a function and the system as a totality has a function" (p. 21). Within the systems framework, single systems (subsystems) form more complex systems (suprasystems). Subsystems may be smaller than the tiniest cell of an organism. Suprasystems extend beyond what humans know as the universe.

A human being is composed of cells, organs, and physiologic systems—the subsystems of humans. These subsystems are continuously interacting and changing. As the person eats, the blood supply to the gastrointestinal organs increases. Absorption of carbohydrates increases the blood glucose level, which results in increased insulin secretion. Simultaneously, changes in the blood circulation and blood glucose level affect the attention level and the feeling of hunger. The person may feel satisfied and contented.

The whole person is the suprasystem for multiple interacting subsystems. The person's internal environment consists of interacting subsystems that are contained within bodily boundaries. People have membership in a subsystem called family (which is a suprasystem of the person, which is a subsystem of the community system, and so on). Subsystems may be isolated for study, but human beings are more than and different from the sum of their parts (Rogers, 1970). Thus, a person cannot be characterized by describing physiologic, psychological, and sociocultural subsystems. A person's behavior is holistic, a reflection of the person as a whole. The focus of systems theory is on understanding the interaction among the various parts of the system, rather than on describing the function of the parts themselves (Auger, 1976).

As open systems, people exchange matter, energy, and information across their boundaries with the environment (Sills & Hall, 1977). A human being's internal environment interacts constantly with an ever-changing external environment. Changes occurring in one affect the other. For example, walking into a cold room (change in the external environment) affects various physiologic and psychological subsystems of the internal environment, which in turn reduces blood flow to the periphery, the ability to concentrate, and the feeling of comfort. Similarly, a human being's angry outburst (change in the internal environment) may have a demonstrable effect on the moods of others. This openness of human systems makes nursing intervention possible. Under general systems theory, nurses interact with clients to help them attain homeostasis, defined as the constancy of the internal environment caused by action of regulatory mechanisms. Constancy does not mean that the internal environment is static, but rather constantly changing. This relative equilibrium is maintained by homeodynamics (Cannon, 1932).

Systems analysis assumes that structure and stability can be measured during an arbitrarily frozen period. The system seeks equilibrium, or a steady state, in which a balance exists among the various forces operating within and on the system. Factors from the environment impinge on the system across the system boundary. These factors cause tension, stress, strain, or conflict that may upset system balance. Change is a process of tension reduction and dynamic equilibrium, which restores a new position of system balance after a disturbance (Chin, 1976).

Energy, information, or matter provides system input. The system "transforms, creates, and organizes input in the process known as throughput, which results in a reorganization of the input" (Sills & Hall, 1977, p. 21). Thus, each system modifies its input. Simultaneously, energy, information, or matter is given off into the environment as output. When output is returned to the system as input, the process is known as feedback.

For example, information about a therapeutic diet given to the client by the nurse is system input for the client system. What the client eats would be one type of system output, based on the throughput related to assimilation and acceptance of the information originally given. The nurse, using the client's reported food intake as feedback, can help reinforce or modify the client's future behavior (Figure 6-1).

A person (or human being) can be viewed as "an interrelated, interdependent, interacting, complex organism, constantly influencing and being influenced by [the] environment" (Sills & Hall, 1977, p. 24). Because the person is in constant interaction with the environment, many interrelated factors, including the nurse, affect the human being's health status. The human being's response, in turn, results in environmental change. Because of these interactions, a change in any part affects the whole human–environment system.

Using systems theory to guide nursing process directs assessment of the relationships among all variables that affect the client–environment interaction, including the influence of the nurse. While intervening, the nurse must anticipate the system-wide impact from change in any part of the system and appreciate the simultaneous, rather than cause-and-effect, nature of change in open systems.

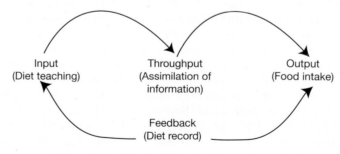

Figure 6-1
An example of systems interaction.

Systems theory provides one approach for nursing practice. Imogene King and Betty Neuman developed nursing models based on systems theory that are described subsequently.

Imogene King's Systems Interaction Model (Theory of Goal Attainment)

Imogene King stressed interactions and mutuality in her nursing model known as **King's systems interaction model (theory of goal attainment)**. King developed her model when she was trying to outline essential content for a new graduate nursing program (Fawcett, 2001). According to Imogene King's systems interaction model, the purpose of nursing is to help people attain, maintain, or restore health, primarily by mutual goal setting. King described the nurse–patient interaction as transaction, which means the following: nurse–patient mutual understanding of events, mutually set goals, and agreement on means to achieve the goal.

King's (1989) model has its roots in sociology and focuses on "individuals whose interactions in groups within social systems influence behavior within the systems" (p. 152). King defined humans as "open systems interacting with environment" (1981, p. 10) and as "rational, sentient, reacting, social, controlling, purposeful, time-oriented, and action-oriented" (1987, p. 107). The human "perceives the world as a total person" (King, 1981, p. 141), resulting in environmental interactions to which he or she must constantly adjust. King (1981) delineated the environment as internal (within the body/person) and external. King proposed that the personal system underlies each person as a whole system who interacts with one or more persons, thereby creating interpersonal systems. When interpersonal systems expand to include large groups of human beings, social systems are developed. King (1999) emphasized that the three systems interact with the other and "represent organized wholes in constant interaction in one's environment" (p. 292). As humans interact with their environment, their perceptions influence their behavior and health. Nurses interact with clients to facilitate achievement of mutually determined health-related goals.

Perception is the comprehensive concept in personal systems. It is "a characteristic of a human process of interaction, and along with communication provides a channel for passage of information from one person to another" (King, 1989, p. 153). Concepts of self, growth and development, learning, body image, time, and space also relate to individuals as personal systems.

Interaction is the comprehensive concept in interpersonal systems. Related concepts include communication, transactions, roles, stress, and all the concepts identified in personal systems. Organization is the comprehensive concept in social systems, with related concepts of power, authority, status, decision making, and control (King, 1989).

Health assumes achievement of maximum potential for daily living and an ability to function in social roles. It is the "dynamic life experiences of a human being, which implies continuous adjustment to stressors in the internal and external environment through optimum use of one's resources to achieve maximum potential for daily living" (King, 1981, p. 5). "Illness is a deviation from normal, that is, an imbalance in a person's biological structure or in his psychological makeup, or a conflict in a person's social relationships" (King, 1989, p. 5).

"The goal of nursing is to help individuals and groups attain, maintain, and restore health" (King, 1981, p. 13). "Nursing's domain involves human beings, families, and communities as a framework within which nurses make transactions in multiple environments with health as a goal" (King, 1996, p. 61). Nursing care is accomplished within goal-oriented nurse–client interactions "whereby each perceives the other and the situation, and through communications, they set goals, explore the means to achieve them, [and] agree to the means, and their actions indicate movement toward goal achievement" (King, 1987, p. 113). The emphasis of health-related goal attainment provides the name of theory of goal attainment.

King (1987) identified the following 10 concepts relevant to understanding the dynamic interacting systems delineated in her model:

1. Interaction: "a process of perception and communication between person and environment and between person and person, represented by verbal and non-verbal behaviors that are goal-directed"
2. Perception: "each person's representation of reality"
3. Communication: "a process whereby information is given from one person to another"
4. Transaction: "an observable behavior of human beings interacting with their environment … [in which] valuation is a component of human interaction"
5. Role: "a set of behaviors expected of persons occupying a position in a social system"
6. Stress: "a dynamic state whereby a human being interacts with the environment to maintain balance for growth, development, and performance"
7. Growth and development: "continuous change in individuals at the cellular, molecular, and behavioral levels of activities"
8. Time: "a continuous flow of events in successive order that implies change, a past, and a future"
9. Self: "a personal system defined as a unified, complex whole"
10. Space: "existing in all direction and the same everywhere" (pp. 109–110).

King (1995) has proposed the theory of goal attainment in which these concepts are interrelated in a number of propositions and hypotheses that indicate "the nature of nurse–client interactions that lead to goal attainment" (p. 27). Decision making is "a shared collaborative process in which client and nurse give information to each other, identify goals, and explore means to attain goals; each moves forward to attain goals. This is identified in the theory as a critical independent variable called mutual goal setting" (King, 1989, p. 155). From the theory, a transaction process model has been designed to lead to goal attainment when practiced (King, 1999). Examples of testable hypotheses generated from King's theory include the following: the process of mutual goal setting with clients, the strengths of mutual goal setting, and role conflict between client and nurse in nursing situations (King, 1987).

King's model and the theory of goal attainment provide a "theoretical base for applying the traditional nursing process … aimed at maintaining or restoring health" (Magan, 1987, pp. 129, 132). King's model has provided theoretical foundation for international nursing practice, nursing departments, nurse empowerment, and client satisfaction (Fawcett, 2005). A 2007 computerized literature search using the Cumulative Index of Nursing and Allied Health Literature (CINAHL) reveals that over 85 research articles have been published that use King's model. Published studies using King's model have been performed internationally and include the areas of client decision-making processes and effectiveness of client education. Besides research, King's model serves as a foundation for undergraduate and graduate nursing programs and nursing service departments (Fawcett, 2005). The King International Nursing Group formed in 1998 and publishes an annual newsletter. Table 6-1 presents the major concepts of this model. Despite being originally conceptualized over a quarter of a century ago, King's model offers a systems approach that is compatible with the perception of health care delivery as a system with the goal of helping others to attain optimal health status while coping with internal and external stressors by using available resources.

Betty Neuman's Health Care Systems Model

Betty Neuman also has used systems theory to provide a foundation for her nursing model known as **Neuman's health care systems model**. She developed her model while she attempted to help nursing students organize their thinking and look at clients holistically (Neuman, 2002). Neuman's health care systems model specifies that the

TABLE 6-1

Major Concepts as Defined in King's Model

Human beings	A personal system that interacts with interpersonal and social systems
Environment	A context "within which human beings grow, develop, and perform daily activities" (King, 1981, p. 18)
Health	"dynamic life experiences of a human being, which implies continuous adjustment to stressors in the internal and external environment through optimum use of one's resources to achieve maximum potential for daily living" (King, 1981, p. 5)
Nursing	A process of human interaction

purpose of nursing is to facilitate optimal client system stability by reducing the impact of environmental stimuli or stressors.

Neuman described human beings as having a core that is protected by buffering systems. The following four key concepts describe the interaction of human beings with environmental stressors that determine health status:

1. Central core: the basic structure and energy reserves of the human that make life possible
2. Flexible lines of defense: adaptive responses that fluctuate and protect the core from stressor penetration
3. Normal line of defense: a conscious adaptation response usually used by an individual to protect the core from stressor penetration
4. Lines of resistance: protection factors activated when stressors have penetrated the normal line of defense that are usually unconscious in nature

Neuman's model focuses on stress reduction and addresses how stress and individual response to it affect the development, maintenance, and restoration of health. Human beings are composites of physiologic, psychological, sociocultural, developmental, and spiritual variables that act harmoniously and simultaneously when encountering stressors from either the internal or external environments. Neuman defined clients as individuals, families, groups, or communities who interact constantly with the environment.

The environment includes "all internal and external factors or influences surrounding the identified client or client system" (Neuman, 2002, p. 18). The internal environment is composed of interacting elements within the human body. The external environment consists of anything outside of the human body. The created environment encompasses individual perceptions of the internal and external environments.

Human beings constantly encounter stressors from the internal, external, or created environment. Stressors are tension-producing stimuli that have the potential to disturb a human being's equilibrium or normal line of defense. This normal line of defense is the human being's "usual steady state." It is the way in which an individual usually deals with stressors. Stressors may be positive (eustress) or negative (distress). Stressors may be of three types: intrapersonal (arising from within the human being), interpersonal (arising between two or more human beings), or extrapersonal (arising from the external environment rather than other human beings).

According to Neuman (1982, 2002), the basic structure and energy resources of humans need protection from encountered stressors. Reactions and resistance to stressors are provided by lines of defense. Neuman (1982, 2002) called the outermost line of defense the flexible lines of defense. This dynamic protective buffer consists of physiologic, psychological, sociocultural, developmental, and spiritual variables affecting a human being at any given moment. These variables may include a person's current physiologic state, mood, beliefs, cognitive state, nutritional status, spiritual beliefs, developmental state, and cognitive ability. If the flexible line of defense is no longer able to protect the human being against a stressor, the normal lines of defense work to buffer the effects produced. The normal lines of defense encompass the usual response used by the human being. Examples of normal lines of defense include exercise regimens, health habits (such as basic hygiene), typical methods of relaxation, and conscious coping methods. The final protections for the core are the lines of resistance. Examples of lines of resistance include immunologic responses and unconscious emotional defense mechanisms. Obvious reactions to stress become visible when lines of resistance are penetrated. The reaction to stressors may lead to restoration of balance or to death. Three factors influence the human being's reaction and recovery to encountered stressors: the number and strength of the stressor(s) affecting the human being, the length of exposure to the stressor(s), and the meaningfulness of the stressor(s) to the human being.

Neuman (1996) intended for the nurse to "assist clients to retain, attain, or maintain optimal system stability" (p. 69). Thus, health (wellness) seems to be related to dynamic equilibrium of the normal line of defense, where stressors are successfully overcome or avoided by the flexible line of defense. Neuman (2002) defined illness as "a state of insufficiency with disrupting needs unsatisfied" (p. 25). Illness appears to be a separate state when a stressor breaks through the normal line of defense and causes a reaction with the human being's lines of resistance.

Nurses use primary, secondary, or tertiary prevention to help clients attain optimal wellness. Primary prevention covers interventions to promote health. Secondary prevention occurs once a stressor has penetrated the normal lines of defense or lines of resistance (e.g., pain medication). Tertiary prevention focuses on restoration of balance (e.g., rehabilitation). When restoration is complete, nursing interventions return to primary prevention.

Neuman's systems model has compatibility with the traditional medical model. Over 400 research articles using Neuman's systems model have been published, including research conducted by nurses in the Pacific Rim and Europe according to a 2007 CINAHL literature search. The model serves as the framework for the World Health Organization project "Nest of Love" and for delivery of mental health services in Holland (Fawcett, 2004). The Neuman Trustee Group promotes utilization of the Neuman systems model. Table 6-2 summarizes major concepts as defined in Neuman's model. By offering a systems approach, looking for ways to reduce the impact of stressors, and using prevention as intervention, the Neuman health care systems model remains a relevant approach to professional nursing practice.

Stress/Adaptation Theory as a Framework

In contrast to systems theory, stress and adaptation theories view change in terms of accommodation. People adjust to environmental changes to avoid disturbing a balanced existence. Adaptation theory provides a way to understand both how the balance is maintained and the possible effects of disturbed equilibrium. This theory has been widely applied to explain, predict, and control biologic (physiologic and psychological) responses of human beings and serves as traditional medical therapy.

TABLE 6-2

Major Concepts as Defined in Neuman's Model

Human Beings (client system)	A composite of physiological, psychological, sociocultural, developmental, and spiritual variables in interaction with the internal and external environment
Environment	All internal and external factors of influences surrounding the client system
Health	A continuum of wellness to illness
Nursing	Prevention as intervention

The regulatory systems operate by way of compensation. Any change in the internal environment automatically initiates a response to minimize or counteract the change. For example, when the blood glucose level drops, the endocrine system responds with increased cortisol secretion, which decreases the rate at which cells use glucose and stimulates the conversion of amino acids into glucose. These compensatory actions cause the blood glucose level to increase. If it should increase above acceptable limits, insulin secretion would increase the rate of glucose uptake by cells, tending to reduce the blood glucose level.

Compensation occurs constantly as the body adjusts to stimuli that tend to disturb equilibrium. Stimuli may be anything that creates change in the internal environment and thus places demands on the body to compensate. Examples of stimuli include changes in external environmental temperature or sleep pattern, hunger, joy, and infection. Stimuli, either beneficial or harmful, all require the body to adapt.

A human being's ability to adapt to changes in life events may determine the potential for health or disease. One way that a human being adapts is through coping mechanisms that aim "to master conditions of harm, threat, or challenge when a routine or automatic response is not readily available" (Monat & Lazarus, 1977, p. 8). Some regard coping methods primarily as psychological barriers when stimuli are perceived as threats. Thus, a human being's reaction to stimuli involves cognitive appraisal and psychological coping methods, in addition to physiologic reactions. One of the best-known nursing models that uses adaptation theory is the model developed by Sister Callista Roy.

Callista Roy's Adaptation Model

Sister Callista Roy developed the adaptation model as a graduate nursing student when confronted with the challenge of defining nursing (Fawcett, 2002a; Meleis, 2007). Although initially concerned with the focus and target of and indications for nursing care, the model has evolved to incorporate her religious views (Meleis). In 2008, Roy specified that the philosophical view underlying her model is cosmic unity that proposes that humans and "the earth have common patterns and integral relationships" (p. 139). She also incorporated the concept of verativity, defined as "a common purposefulness of human existence," which translates into persons finding meaning in life (Meleis). The **Roy adaptation model** outlines the purpose of nursing as promoting a human being's adaptation, the process and outcome by which thinking and feeling human beings use conscious awareness and choice to create human and environmental integration. Roy used the following five key terms in her model:

1. Stimulus: point of interaction of the human system and environment. Stimulus produces a response.
2. Adaptive modes: ways that human beings adapt (e.g., through physiologic needs, self-concept, role function, or interdependent relations).
3. Classes of stimuli: focal (immediately confronting the human being), contextual (all other stimuli present), and residual (nonspecific stimuli, such as beliefs or attitudes).
4. Adaptation level: range of a human being's ability to adapt and create changes in the integrated, compensatory, and compromised environments.
5. Coping: ways of responding to the changing environment.

Roy organized her model around adaptive behaviors that encompass the set of processes by which human beings adapt to environmental stimuli. The human being as a unified system is viewed as a "set of parts connected to function as a whole" (Roy & Andrews, 1999, p. 36) through homeostatic and homeodynamic systems. The human being constantly interacts with an ever-changing environment. The human being's ability to respond positively reflects the level of adaptation.

Environmental stimuli affect the human being. A focal stimulus is an environmental change that requires an immediate adaptive response from the human being. Accompanying the focal stimulus are contextual stimuli (all other stimuli present) and residual stimuli (other relevant factors such as nonspecific stimuli), which mediate and contribute to the effect of the focal stimulus.

The pooled effect of the three classes of stimuli establishes the human being's adaptation level. The human being's adaptation level determines a zone that indicates the range of additional stimulation that will have a positive or adaptive response. If additional stimuli fall outside of the zone, the human being cannot respond effectively, and compromised adaptation ensues. Effective adaptation results in free energy available for use in subsequent adaptation to stimuli.

According to Roy and Roberts (1981, p. 56), "Coping refers to routine, accustomed patterns of behaviors to deal with daily situations as well as to the production of new ways of behaving when drastic changes defy the familiar responses." The two major coping mechanisms for individuals are the regulator subsystem, composed mainly of automatic neural, endocrine, and chemical activity, and the cognator subsystem, which includes cognitive-emotive channels and provides for perceptual and information processing, learning, judgment, and emotion (Andrews & Roy, 1986, p. 7).

In 2008, Roy redefined adaptation as the "process and outcome whereby thinking and feeling persons, as individuals or in groups, use conscious awareness and choice to create human and environmental integration" (p. 138). Roy (1987) identified four adaptive modes: physiologic-physical, self-concept–group identity, role function, and interdependence. The desired result is a state in which conditions promote the human being's goals, including survival, growth, reproduction, mastery, and personal and environmental transformations.

Health "is viewed in light of human goals and the purposefulness of human existence. The fulfillment of this purpose in life is reflected in becoming integrated and whole" (Roy & Andrews, 1999, p. 54). Thus, health is viewed as both "a state and a process of being and becoming an integrated and whole human being" (Roy & Andrews, p. 54).

The goal of nursing is "to promote adaptation by the use of the nursing process, in each of the adaptive modes, thus contributing to health, quality of life, and dying with dignity" (Roy, 1987, p. 43). Nursing assessment and intervention foster the goal of adaptation with the client actively participating in the processes. The criteria for goal attainment encompass generally any positive response by the human being that creates free energy that can be used for responding to other stimuli (Riehl & Roy, 1980). The goal of adaptation is fostered through nursing assessment and intervention, with the client as an active participant.

Roy's model provides a classification system for stimuli that may affect adaptation, as well as a system for classifying nursing assessment. The model "has been useful in supporting the traditional concept of nursing practice within the medical model perspective" (Huch, 1987, p. 63). According to a CINAHL literature search done in 2007, 1,337 articles have been published, about half of them research articles using Roy's model as a theoretical framework, some in Spanish and Japanese. The Roy Adaptive Association based in Boston offers support to nurses conducting research using the model. Nurses use Roy's model as a framework for nursing education in baccalaureate and higher degree programs, as a foundation for health assessment in clinical practice, and as guidance for application in nursing service departments. Roy also advocated the use of the model by other health care professionals (Fawcett, 2002a, 2003a). Table 6-3 summarizes the major concepts defined in Roy's model. The Roy adaptation model has also been used as a theoretical framework for the development of tools for research and clinical practice, to develop nursing interventions to promote empowerment, in undergraduate and graduate nursing programs, and in nursing services departments (Meleis, 2007).

THE GROWTH MODEL OF CHANGE

Unlike the previous models, which focus on achievement or restoration of stability, nursing models based on the **growth model of change** tend to focus on helping human beings grow to realize and attain their full human potential. The models of nursing that

TABLE 6-3

Major Concepts as Defined in Roy's Model

Human Beings (human system)	"a whole with parts that function as a unity" (Roy & Andrews, 1999, p. 31)
Environment	"the world within and around humans as adaptive systems" (Roy & Andrews, 1999, p. 51)
Health	"a state and process of being and becoming an integrated and whole human being" (Roy & Andrews, 1999, p. 54)
Nursing	Manipulation of stimuli to foster successful adaptation

espouse the growth change model tend to use caring theory or complexity theory as an underlying framework.

Caring Theory as a Framework

Nursing practice focuses on caring for and about others. No single, universally accepted definition exists for **caring** in the nursing context as it can be used as a verb or noun (e.g., "The nurse cared for the client," and "Nursing care was given"). Morse, Solberg, Neander, Bottorff, and Johnson (1990, p. 2) pointed out that the literature includes references to care or caring as actions performed (as in to "take care of"), as well as concern demonstrated (as in "caring about"). An analysis of the literature reveals at least five perspectives or categories of caring, including caring as a human trait (Benner & Wrubel, 1989; Gaut & Leininger, 1991), caring as a moral imperative (Watson, 1985, 1999, 2007), caring as an interpersonal relationship (Parse, 1987), caring as a therapeutic intervention (Orem, 1980), and caring as an affect (Morse et al., 1990).

Clients perceive as caring "those nursing ministrations that are person-centered, protective, anticipatory, physically comforting, and that go beyond routine care" (Swanson, 1991, p. 161). Kyle (1995, p. 509) concluded that there is a "marked difference between the patients' perceptions of caring and those of nurses, with the nurses focusing on the psychosocial skills and the patient on those skills which demonstrate professional competency." Caring outcomes may be demonstrated in terms of either subjective experiences or objective client outcomes.

Several classifications of the components of caring have been published. Swanson (1991, p. 162) defined caring as "a nurturing way of relating to a valued other toward whom one feels a personal sense of commitment and responsibility." She identified the five caring processes:

1. Knowing: striving to understand an event as it has meaning in the life of another
2. Being with: being emotionally present for the other
3. Doing for: doing for others as they would do for themselves if it were possible
4. Enabling: facilitating the other's passage through life transitions and unfamiliar events
5. Maintaining belief: sustaining faith in the other's capacity to get through an event or transition and face a future with meaning

Koldjeski (1990) also described the five "essences" of caring as:

1. Interpersonal valuing and involvement
2. Being there for and experiencing with the other
3. Instilling faith
4. Concern and love for the other
5. Actualization

TABLE 6-4

A Comparison of Components of Caring

Swanson	Koldjeski
Knowing	Interpersonal involvement
Being with	Experiencing with concern and love
Doing for	Nursing actions
Enabling	Actualization
Maintaining belief	Instillment of faith

Table 6-4 compares Swanson's and Koldjeski's theoretical components of caring. The concept of caring permeates the nursing literature and appears in many nursing models. Orem's self-care deficit theory uses the term "care" primarily as action, whereas Watson used the term to describe an attitude or display of compassion that is a moral imperative for nurses.

Questions for Reflection 6-3

1. What are the characteristics that I identify when I have been the recipient of a caring interaction?
2. What results from a caring interaction between two human beings?
3. Why is caring an important aspect of professional nursing?

Dorothea Orem's Self-Care Deficit Theory

Orem (1980, 1985, 1990, 1995) proposed that the purpose of nursing is to help people meet their self-care needs. She suggested that nurses do for others what they cannot do for themselves. She observed nurses as they engaged in clinical practice to develop the theory. **Orem's self-care deficit theory** uses the following five key concepts:

1. Self-care: learned behaviors that a human being performs for self (when able) that contribute to health
2. Self-care deficit: a relationship between actions that a human being should take for healthy functioning and the capability for action
3. Self-care requisites: needs that are universal or associated with development of or deviation from health
4. Self-care demand: therapeutic actions to meet needs
5. Agency: capability to engage in self-care

The essence of Orem's three-part nursing theory "focuses on a human being in relations. The theory of self-care focuses on the self, the I; the theory of self-care deficit focuses on you and me; and the theory of nursing systems focuses on we, human beings in community" (Orem, 1990, p. 49). Orem's general theory, the self-care deficit theory, integrates the theory of self-care, the theory of self-care deficit, and the theory of nursing systems (Orem, 1995).

Orem (1995) defined self-care as the "voluntary regulation of one's own human functioning and development that is necessary for individuals to maintain life, health, and well-being" (p. 95). People learn self-care activities as they mature. Culture, society, and family customs play key roles in determining individual self-care activities. Age, developmental state, or health status can affect the ability to perform self-care activities. For example, parents or guardians must provide continuous care for infants and toddlers.

Orem (1980) specified that nursing is concerned with the human being's need for self-care action to "sustain life and health, recover from disease or injury, and cope with their effects" (p. 6). In Orem's view, nursing care may be offered to individuals and groups. However, Orem emphasized that only people have self-care requisites. The nurse cares for, assists, or does something for the client to achieve client-desired health outcomes (Orem, 1980).

Orem (1985) implied that health is "a state of a human being that is characterized by soundness or wholeness of developed human structures and of bodily and mental functioning" (p. 179). Orem proposed that individual perception (well-being) affects health.

Orem addressed the physical, psychological, interpersonal, and social aspects of health but indicated that they are inseparable in the human being: "Health describes the state of wholeness or integrity of human beings" (Orem, 1995, p. 96). "If there is acceptance of the real unity of individual human beings, there should be no difficulty in recognizing structural and functional differentiation within the unity" (Orem, 1980, p. 180). Orem viewed individuals as moving "toward maturation and achievement of the individual's human potential" (Orem, 1985, p. 180) rather than organisms seeking a steady state.

Orem suggested that some people may have self-care requisites (needs) associated with development or with health deviations. Self-care requisites are essential enduring needs, whereas other needs may surface because of internal or external conditions that alter the ability to care for oneself. Orem (1980) identified the following universal self-care requisites (p. 42):

1. Maintenance of sufficient air, water, and food intake
2. Provision of care associated with elimination processes and excrements
3. Maintenance of a balance between activity and rest and between solitude and social interaction
4. Prevention of hazards to life, functioning, and well-being
5. Promotion of human functioning and development within social groups in accord with potential, known limitations, and the desire to be normal

Identified self-care requisites require actions known as "therapeutic self-care demands." Therapeutic self-care demands can be determined by:

1. Identifying existing or potential self-care requisites.
2. Developing methods for meeting self-care requisites by considering basic factors (e.g., developmental state, general health status, and living patterns) that "condition the values of patients' self-care agency and therapeutic self-care demands as well as the means that are valid for meeting self-care requisites and in regulating self-care agency at particular times" (Orem, 1985, p. 78).
3. Designing, implementing, and evaluating a plan of action. Orem tended to use nursing process as a way to develop a system of nursing.

The theory of nursing systems involves "an interpersonal unity in a particular time–space localization. This unity is formed by nurses, persons who have entered into an agreement to accept and participate in nursing, and the relatives or persons who are responsible for the individuals who require nursing" (Orem, 1990, p. 54). Thus, candidates for nursing care are clients who have insufficient current or projected capability for providing self-care. "It is the need for compensatory action (to overcome an inability or limited ability to engage in care) or for action to help in the development or regulation of self-care abilities that is the basis for a nursing relationship" (Orem, 1980, p. 58). Other concepts and theories that have been derived from the self-care deficit theory include self-care agency, dependent care, and dependent care agency (Taylor, Geden, Isaramalai, & Wongvatunyu, 2000).

TABLE 6-5

Major Concepts as Defined in Orem's Theory

Human Beings (patient)	A person under the care of a nurse
Environment	Physical, chemical, biologic, and social contexts within which human beings exist
Health	"A state characterized by soundness or wholeness of developed human structures and of bodily and mental functioning" (Orem, 1995, p. 101)
Nursing	Actions to overcome or prevent the development of a self-care deficit or provide therapeutic self-care for a patient who is unable to do so

Orem's theory specifies that nurses help clients when they are is unable to provide for their own self-care requisites. Nursing interventions may be aimed at maintaining health, preventing illness, or restoring health, and they may involve actions for or with the client. The theory, which is compatible with the traditional medical model, has been widely used in practice and education and recently has been the basis for research. According to a 2007 CINAHL search, more than 1,260 research-based journal articles have used Orem's theory; most of the research tends to be descriptive in nature. Major concepts defined in Orem's model are summarized in Table 6-5. Unlike many of the nursing models and theories, Orem incorporates traditional medical approaches while carving out a unique place for nursing in health care delivery. Orem's nursing theory has been used to guide acute and chronic care nursing departments, for utilization review programs, and in undergraduate and graduate nursing programs (Meleis, 2007).

Jean Watson's Human Science and Human Care Theory

Jean Watson developed **Watson's human science and human care theory** while writing a book about a BSN-integrated nursing curriculum (Fawcett, 2002b, 2005). Watson proposed that the purpose of nursing is to help human beings gain greater harmony within the mind, body, and soul. Key concepts in Watson's model are the phenomenal field, which is the totality of past, present, and future influences on each human being, and carative factors, which are interventions that demonstrate caring as a moral ideal of nursing.

Watson's theory blends Eastern philosophy while representing phenomenological, existential, and spiritual orientations. The model arises from her conception of "transpersonal caring" as "a moral ideal of nursing, rather than an interpersonal technique, and it entails a commitment to a particular end" (Watson, 2007, p. 58). Watson (2007) further explained the particular end as "the protection, enhancement, and preservation of the person's humanity, which helps restore inner harmony and potential healing (p. 58). Caring also demands action. Watson (1999) proposed the use of the term "caritas" to promote a deeper form of caring for the nursing profession.

Watson (2007) stated, "Human life ... is defined as (spiritual–mental–physical) being-in-the-world which is continuous in time and space" (p. 47). Although the soul, mind, and body are explicitly identified as spheres of the human being, they are viewed as integrated and inseparable until the time of death, when the soul transcends and continues to exist (Watson, 2007).

Watson described health as "a unity and harmony within the mind, body, and soul" (Watson, 1985; Watson, 2007, p. 48). She expanded health to include congruency between the perceived self and experienced self, and summarized health as "I = Me—Health (harmony, with the world and open to increased diversity)" (Watson, 2007, p. 48). In contrast, illness becomes a state of I not equaling me and can occur in varying levels of intensity, there may be continuous time periods, and the person is "less open to diversity" (Watson, 2007, p. 48). Watson did not equate illness with disease. However, illness is a state of disharmony between the I and me.

Watson viewed each human being as having a unique phenomenal field that encompasses "the totality of human experience as one's being-in-the-world" (Watson, 2007, p. 55). Although not equivalent to human consciousness, the phenomenal field is the entire constellation of internal and external factors that shape all human experiences (past, present, and future). She described human behavior as being goal directed with the aim of seeking harmony within body, mind, and soul, resulting in self-integration, enhancement, and actualization. When two or more persons come together, they share a phenomenal field and experience a transpersonal event. For a caring event to occur, the nurse and patient must each make a choice to enter the relationship. The nurse enters the experience of the patient, and the patient enters into the experiences of the nurse.

Watson (2007) used the word "nurse" as a noun (a person caring for another) and a verb (actions related to caring for another). She described caring as "the moral ideal of nursing" (p. 54) consisting of "transpersonal human-to-human attempts to protect, enhance, and preserve humanity by helping a person find meaning in illness, suffering, pain, and existence; to help another gain self-knowledge, control and self-healing wherein a sense of inner harmony is restored regardless of the external circumstance" (Watson, 1985, p. 54; Watson, 2007, pp. 53–54).

Caring is "a moral ideal, rather than an interpersonal technique" (Watson, 1985, p. 58; Watson, 2007, p. 58), which can be demonstrated through the carative factors (nursing interventions) that "allow for contact between the subjective world of the experiencing persons" (Watson, 1985, p. 58; Watson, 1989, p. 227). The following carative factors are all presupposed by a knowledge base and clinical competence (Watson, 2007, p. 75):

1. Humanistic-altruistic system of values
2. Faith–hope
3. Sensitivity to self and others
4. Helping–trusting, human care relationship
5. Expressing positive and negative feelings
6. Creative problem-solving caring processes
7. Transpersonal teaching–learning
8. Supportive, protective, and/or corrective mental, physical, sociocultural, and spiritual environment
9. Human needs assistance
10. Existential-phenomenologic-spiritual forces

During the human care process (nursing), the nurse and person engage in a mutual endeavor, a specific level of space and time. The nurse and client together embark on a journey to discover new meanings and understanding that require "serious study, reflection, and action" (Watson, 2007, p. 29). The nurse uses the carative factors to facilitate the human care process.

Watson's theory provides one framework for the study of caring that has served as the foundation for many nursing research studies across the world. A current literature search using CINAHL retrieved 763 articles using Watson's framework. Watson (2007) proposed that descriptive phenomenology along with transcendental or depth phenomenology and poetic results may be the most effective ways to generate evidence and knowledge about specific caring processes for professional nursing practice. Despite the abstract nature of caring, 18 instruments have been designed using the human science and human care theory as a theoretical approach to measure caring in studies related to patient satisfaction, nursing student perceptions of caring, intercollegial relationships among professional nurses, and caring behaviors of nursing faculty (Watson, 2002). Smith (2004) outlined four categories addressed by nurse researchers using Watson's theory: the nature of nurse caring, client and nurse perceptions of the nurse

TABLE 6-6

Major Concepts as Defined in Watson's Theory

Human beings	Unities of mind, body, soul, and environment with souls that are not confined to the physical world but exist following physical death
Environment	Referred to as the world, described as all universal forces that affect a person, including the person's immediate environment and situation, "be they internal, external, human, humanmade, artificial, natural, cosmic, psychic, past, present or future" (Watson, 2007, p. 56)
Health (healing)	"Unity and harmony within the mind, body and soul" that is congruent with the person's perceived and experienced self" "Health is I = me" (Watson, 2007, p. 48)
Nursing	A transpersonal process of "human-to-human attempts to protect, enhance, and preserve humanity by helping a person find meaning in illness, suffering, pain and existence; to help another gain self-knowledge, control and self-healing within; a sense of inner harmony is restored regardless of the external circumstances" (Watson, 2007, pp. 53–54)

caring experience, human experiences, and human caring needs. Nurses use Watson's theory to measure caring behaviors, attitudes, and efficacy; in practice across various specialty areas; and in nursing education research (Smith, 2004). The University of Colorado hosts the Center for Human Caring, where nurses study and practice the human science and human care theory. Table 6-6 summarizes the key concepts as defined in Watson's theory. Watson has developed an international consortium for her human science and human care theory that provides consultations to health care organizations for the implementation of her model and theory in practice settings. Human science and human care theory provide a theoretical foundation for nursing service departments, nursing research studies, and nursing educational programs (Fawcett, 2005).

Complexity Theory as a Framework

Like stability theory, complexity theory assumes that reality continuously changes. However, change occurs with irregularity and cannot be predicted. **Complexity theory** "emphasizes change over time, long-term unpredictability, and openness to the environment with mutual simultaneous interactions.... The complexity perspective seeks to understand patterns of phenomena as wholes within their contexts" (Maliski & Holditch-Davis, 1995, p. 25). In complexity theory, change occurs spontaneously when many individual factors interact interconnectedly and interdependently. Change becomes dynamic and unpredictable, and co-evolves with the environment (Leddy, 2006). Unlike systems theory, interacting systems cannot be separated because they are one.

Complexity theory replaces the metaphors of separation and interaction (reductionistic) with the metaphor of participation (holistic) (Porter, 1995). The whole cannot be known from the sum of the parts, nor can the sum of the parts be more than the whole because everything is unitary.

Assumptions of complexity theory include:

- Nonlinear change over time
- Long-term unpredictability
- Openness to the environment
- Mutual, simultaneous interactions
- Continual fluctuations that reveal patterns
- Variable patterns that appear at critical points

Because the theory assumes mutual change of human being and environment, which provides potential for restructuring in new patterns, linear cause and effect is difficult to infer. The theory suggests that multiple, dynamic, mutual relationships, rather than enduring "causes," influence change. Thus, change of an individual, because it is related to initial conditions, is not generalizable.

Nursing models and theories with complexity theory as their foundation emphasize how persons become more fully human (human becoming) in terms of potential for change. Some nurses find models based on complexity theories difficult to understand because complexity theory challenges them to think in multiple dimensions.

Martha Rogers' Science of Unitary Human Beings

Martha Rogers developed **Rogers' science of unitary human beings** while searching for a specific and unique body of knowledge for nursing during the late 1970s (Fawcett, 2003b). In Rogers' science of unitary human beings, the purpose of nursing is to foster health potential. Rogers incorporates the following three key concepts in her model:

1. Unitary human being: an irreducible, indivisible, pandimensional energy field identified by pattern
2. Unified energy field: a pandimensional nonlinear domain without spatial or temporal attributes
3. Mutual process: changes within the human and environmental fields that occur simultaneously

Rogers' model builds on an assumption of the human being as a unified energy field that continuously exchanges energy with an environmental energy field. Rogers proposed that "man is a unified whole possessing his own integrity and manifesting characteristics that are more than and different from the sum of his parts" (Rogers, 1970, p. 47). Physical, biologic, psychological, social, cultural, and spiritual attributes are merged into behavior that reflects the total human being as an indivisible whole. Rogers believed that it is impossible to describe humans by combining attributes of each of the parts. Only as the parts lose their particular identity is it possible to describe the human being.

The human being is an organized energy field that has a unique pattern. The continuous mutual process of energy field with environmental energy field results in continuous pattern manifestation changes in both the human being and the environment (Rogers, 1970). This results in increasing complexity and innovativeness of the human being. Rogers believed that this life process "evolves irreversibly and unidirectionally along the space–time continuum" (Rogers, 1970, p. 59). She conceptualized this unidirectionality as a spiral, with self-regulation "directed toward achieving increasing complexity of organization—not toward achieving equilibrium and stability" (Rogers, 1970, p. 64). The human being also is characterized by "the capacity for abstraction and imagery, language and thought, sensation and emotion" (Rogers, 1970, p. 73).

Rogers believed that health serves as an "index of field patterning" (Maliski & Holditch-Davis, 1995, p. 27). Health and illness are not separate states, good or bad, or in a linear relationship. "Ease and disease are dichotomous notions that cannot be used to account for the dynamic complexity and uncertain fulfillment of man's unfolding" (Rogers, 1970, p. 42). Thus, observable manifestations are all "manifestations of patterning (that) emerge out of the human/environmental field mutual process and are continuously innovative" (Rogers, 1990, p. 8).

Rogers conceptualized nursing as both an art and a science. Nursing science includes knowledge specific to the domain of nursing that has an abstract nature and has been generated by scientific research and logical analysis. The art of nursing emcompasses how nurses creatively use knowledge in professional practice (Rogers, 1992, cited in Fawcett, 2005). Nursing intervention is aimed toward promoting the betterment of humans wherever they may be (Rogers, 1992). Rogers also specified that nurses must address health promotion with consumers because disease and pathology may always be a potential manifestation of human patterns. Rogers (1992) viewed caring in nursing as "simply a way of using knowledge" (p. 46).

Rogers (1990, p. 333) has described three principles that explain change: integrality, helicy, and resonancy. The principle of integrality emphasizes that the human energy field and the environmental energy field are continuous and must be perceived simultaneously. The relationship is one of constant interaction and mutual simultaneous change. In other words, "they are reciprocal systems in which molding and being molded are taking place at the same time" (Rogers, 1970, p. 97).

The principle of helicy predicts that change occurs as a "continuous innovative, unpredictable, increasing diversity of human and environmental field patterns" (Rogers, 1990, p. 8). The human field becomes increasingly diverse with time. As the human being ages, behavior may not be repeated but may recur at ever more complex levels. The principle of resonancy indicates that change in pattern and organization toward increased complexity of the field occurs by way of waves, "manifesting continuous change from lower-frequency, longer wave patterns to higher-frequency, shorter wave patterns" (Rogers, 1980, p. 333).

Rogers believed that an understanding of the mechanisms that affect the life process in humans makes it possible for the nurse to purposefully intervene to affect client pattern manifestations in a desired direction. In the process, the nurse also is changed. She saw the future as "one of growing diversity, of accelerating evolution, and of non-repeating rhythmicities" (Rogers, 1992, p. 33). Rogers' emphases on holism and on the simultaneity and mutuality of humans and the environment are concepts that have been widely accepted in nursing. Rogers proposed that the science of unitary human beings would serve as a foundation for future theory development to make this abstract science applicable to practice (Fawcett, 2003a, 2005). Parse (1987), Newman (1986), and Leddy (2004, 2006) have used the science of unitary human beings as the foundation for practice. Barrett developed a theory of power using the science that nurses use to guide nursing service departments (Fawcett, 2003b). Over 1,040 nursing articles have been published addressing Rogerian science according to a 2007 CINAHL computer database search. Nurse researchers use Rogers' theory as a foundation in validating effectiveness of complementary and alternative health practice (e.g., therapeutic touch, guided imagery, and other energy therapies). Research Brief 6-1 provides an example of how the science of unitary beings is used to identify the effects of meditation. Table 6-7 presents major concepts as defined in Rogers' model. Despite its complexity, the science of unitary beings provides a theoretical foundation for undergraduate and graduate nursing education programs, guidelines for administration of nursing services in health care organizations, knowledge for the development of clinical practice guidelines, and foundation for research instrument development. Instruments have been developed using the science of unitary beings for nursing research and clinical practice (Fawcett, 2005).

TABLE 6-7

Major Concepts as Defined in Rogers' Theory

Human beings	A unitary energy field with a unique pattern
Environment	An energy field in mutual process with the human being
Health	An expression of the complexity and innovativeness of patterning of the energy field that is the person
Nursing	Compassionate concern for human beings by using independent science and practice art in which nurses intervene to improve pattern manifestations and the environment to achieve maximum health potentials

Research Brief 6-1

Kim, T. S., Park, J. S., & Kim, M. A. (2008). The relation of meditation to power and well-being. *Nursing Science Quarterly*, *21*(1), 49–58.

The investigators used a quasi-experimental controlled research design to study the effects of meditation on perceptions of power and well-being in Korean adults (students and employees of a university). A total of 63 participants engaged with the study comparing the effects of chakra meditation conducted in group settings over 4 weeks. Thirty-one participants were in the meditation group, and 32 participants were in the control group. The study used Rogers' science of unitary human beings to provide reasoning behind the theory that each of the seven chakras represents human patterning and responds to specific frequencies of vibration.

Group meditation participation required participants to attend at least two 30-minute sessions (one in the morning and one in the evening each day) during each week. The group meditation session consisted of an introduction to chakras and their significance and learning the art of chakra meditation using Caroline Myss' *Chakra Meditation* CD (Sounds True, 2002). Power was measured using Barrett's 1990 Power as Knowing Participation in Changes Tool, Version II—Korean version (PKPCT). Well-being was measured using the Well-Being Picture Scale, a 10-item scale that assesses four characteristics of human energy fields: frequency, awareness, action, and personal power. Instruments used to collect data had high levels of internal consistency ranging from .83 to .98 at various points in the study. Data were collected at the very beginning of the study, 2 weeks into the study, and at the end of the fourth study week.

Analysis of variance revealed that persons in the chakra meditation program had higher increased perceptions of power than persons in the control group (F (2, 120) 8.944 $p < .001$) and higher increases in perception of well-being (F (2, 120) 3.522 $p < .05$). Results of the study demonstrate that human–environment processes can be enhanced with chakra meditation. Chakra meditation appeared to strengthen power and well-being "in human-environmental field patterning processes" (Kim, Park, & Kim, 2008, p. 57).

Results of this study should be interpreted with some caution. First, the study was done in Korea, an Eastern nation that has differences in cultural and philosophical views than other parts of the world. Second, participants were either university students or employees who may have a higher level of education than that of the typical population. Finally, all but one of the participants were women. More study is needed to demonstrate the effectiveness of human–environmental field patterning processes and how they impact human health and quality of life.

Rosemarie Parse's Human Becoming Theory

Like Rogers, Parse suggested that the purpose of nursing is to improve the quality of life for both the client and nurse in **Parse's human becoming theory**. Parse coined words to describe the essence of nursing and the following three key concepts in her model:

1. Coconstitution: development of patterning through human being–environment interaction
2. Coexistence: dynamic mutual processes between the human being and the environment
3. Situated freedom: freedom of choice in a situation

Parse's model incorporates a combination of Rogers' principles and building blocks "with the tenets of human subjectivity and intentionality and the concepts of coconstitution, coexistence, and situated freedom from existential phenomenological thought" (Parse, 1987, p. 161). The emphasis is on the meaning and values that influence a human being's active choices of behavior. "The human being constructs his or her own meaning" (Parse, 1996, p. 57).

Parse defined the human being as "an open being, more than and different from the sum of parts in mutual simultaneous interchange with the environment who chooses from options and bears responsibility for choices" (Parse, 1987, p. 160). As a human being interacts with the environment, patterns of relating are established that provide insight into his or her patterning and values at that moment. Health is viewed as a "nonlinear entity," a constantly changing process of becoming that incorporates values. Because it is not a state, health cannot be contrasted with disease. "The human becoming nurse's goal is to be truly present with people as they enhance their quality of life" (Parse, 1998, p. 69).

Parse described her key concepts in a highly paradoxical manner (Parse, 1998, pp. 29–51, defines 13).

1. Human becoming: human participation with the environment to create health and quality of life (p. 32)
2. Meaning: human interpreted, linguistic, and imaged content of something (p. 29)
3. Rhythmicity: The paradoxical patterning of the human–universe mutual process (p. 29)
4. Transcendence: Reaching beyond with possibility—the hopes and dreams envisioned in multidimensional experiences and powering the originating of transforming (p. 30)
5. Imaging: Reflective-prereflective coming to know that explicit-tacit all-at-once (p. 36)
6. Valuing: Confirming–not confirming cherished beliefs in light of a personal world view (pp. 37–38)
7. Languaging: Signifying valued images through speaking–being silent and moving–being still (p. 39)
8. Revealing–Concealing: Disclosing–not disclosing all-at-once (p. 43)
9. Establishing–Limiting: Living the opportunities–restrictions present in all choosings all-at-once (p. 44)
10. Connecting–Separating: Being with and apart from others, ideas, objects, and situations all-at-once (p. 45)
11. Powering: The pushing–resisting process of affirming–not affirming being in light of nonbeing (p. 47)
12. Originating: Inventing new ways of conforming–nonconforming in the certainty–uncertainty of living (p. 49)
13. Transforming: Shifting the view of the familiar–unfamiliar, the changing of change in constituting anew in a deliberate way (p. 51)

Parse (1998) combined these 13 concepts into the following three principles:

1. Structuring: meaning multidimesionally is cocreating reality through the languaging of valuing and imaging (p. 35).
2. Cocreating rhythmical patterns of relating is living the paradoxical unity of revealing–concealing and enabling–limiting while connecting–separating.
3. Contrascending (being one) with the possibles is powering unique ways of originating in the process of transforming (p. 46).

Parse (1996) stated that "the way of living the belief system is through true presence" (p. 57), "which is a non-routinized, unconditional loving way of being within which the nurse witnesses the blossoming of others" (p. 57). Practicing within this model, the nurse would provide an empathic sounding board for clients and families to express and therefore uncover the meaning of thoughts and feelings, values, and changing views. In the process of expression through language and movement, and in "dwelling with" the rhythm of the client and family, new possibilities for change in the quality of life would become apparent. "The new insights shift the rhythm and all participants move beyond the moment toward what is not-yet. This is mobilizing transcendence" (Parse, 1989, p. 257). In this model, the nurse connects with clients through focused interactions rather than doing things for them (Phillips, 1987). Therefore, Parse blended caring with Rogers' science of unitary human beings.

Parse (1998) also has developed a phenomenological-hermeneutic research methodology to test relationships suggested by the model. The methodology uses "dialogical

TABLE 6-8

Major Concepts as Defined in Parse's Theory

Human Beings	An open being, more than and different from the sum of parts
Environment	In mutual process with the person
Health	Continuously changing process of becoming
Nursing	Use of true presence to facilitate the becoming of the participant

engagement," a researcher–participant encounter, to uncover the meaning of the live experience being studied (Parse, 1989, p. 256), and serves as the research methodology for many qualitative nursing studies. A CINAHL search done in 2007 retrieved 860 published nursing research studies that used Parse's human becoming theory as a conceptual framework. In 2003, Parse expanded her model by introducing the following community change concepts (again using paradoxes): (1) moving–initiating, (2) anchoring–shifting, and (3) pondering–shaping. She perceived that human becoming could be done at a community level in addition to the individual level.

Parse's theory emphasizes the importance of the meaning that underlies behavior and provides a structure for the identification and clarification of "manifestations of whole people as they interrelate with the environment" (Phillips, 1987, p. 188). Hansen-Ketchum (2004) specified that outcomes for nursing practice using Parse's theory include opportunities for multidimensional client healing, enhanced personal growth (for the client and nurse), and continued professional growth (for the nurse). Table 6-8 summarizes the major concepts defined in Parse's theory. Parse's theoretical approach enables nurses to practice nursing differently because the human becoming theory brings a multidimensional approach, incorporates the use of paradoxes, and fosters deep connections among nurses and nursing care receipients. Parse's theory of human becoming provides a theoretical framework for undergraduate and graduate nursing programs, for individual nurses, and in descriptive applied research projects (primarily in Canada; Fawcett, 2005).

Margaret Newman's Theory of Health as Expanding Consciousness

Like Parse, Newman uses principles from Rogers' science of unitary beings in **Newman's theory of health as expanding consciousness**. Margaret Newman stated that the purpose of nursing in this theory is to promote a higher level of consciousness in both client and nurse. Newman used the concept of consciousness as the capacity of the system (human beings) to interact with its environment, the informational capacity of the system in her nursing model.

Newman's theory incorporates Rogers' concept of a unitary human being as a center of energy in constant interaction with the environment. Human beings are characterized by patterning that is constantly changing. According to Newman (1994), "[T]he focus of nursing is the pattern of the whole, health as pattern of the evolving whole, with caring as a moral imperative" (p. xix).

"The total pattern of the human being-environment can be viewed as a network of consciousness" (Newman, 1986, p. 33) that is "expanding toward higher levels: the patterns of interaction of human being-environment constitute health.… Health is the expansion of consciousness" (Newman, 1986, pp. 3, 18), and "health and the evolving pattern of consciousness are the same" (Newman, 1990, p. 38). "Consciousness is defined as the information of the system: the capacity of the system to interact with the environment" (Newman, 1994, p. 38).

Health is viewed as a process that encompasses both disease and "non-disease." Instead of the familiar linear relationship between health as good and disease (or illness)

TABLE 6-9

Major Concepts as Defined in Newman's Theory

Human Beings	"unitary and continuous with the undivided wholeness of the universe" (Newman, 1994, p. 83)
Environment	"undivided wholeness of the universe" (Newman, 1994, p. 83)
Health	Expansion of consciousness
Nursing	Facilitating repatterning of the client to higher levels of consciousness

as bad, Newman conceptualized disease as a meaningful component of the whole and a possible facilitator of health. "Sickness can provide a kind of shock that reorganizes the relationships of the human being's pattern in a more harmonious way" (Newman, 1994, p. 11). As the human being interacts with the environment, "the fluctuating patterns of harmony–disharmony can be regarded as peaks and troughs of the rhythmic life process" (Newman, 1986, p. 21).

Newman posited four major ways in which human being–environment patterning is manifest: movement, time, space, and consciousness. Consciousness is expressed in patterns of rhythmic movement toward higher levels that can be described in time and space. Manifestations of these patterns include exchanging, communicating, relating, valuing, choosing, moving, perceiving, feeling, and knowing (Newman, 1986, p. 74). The task for nursing intervention is to recognize patterning and relate to it in an "authentic" (genuine, sincere) way.

The new paradigm is relational. The professional enters into a partnership with the client with the mutual goal of participating in an authentic relationship, trusting that in the process of its evolving, both will grow and become healthier in the sense of higher levels of consciousness (Newman, 1986, p. 68).

Nursing facilitates the process of evolving to higher levels of consciousness by "rhythmic connecting of the nurse with the client in an authentic way for the purpose of illuminating the pattern and discovering the new rules of a higher level of organization" (Newman, 1990, p. 40).

Newman's theory contributes to the development of a body of knowledge about manifestations of healthy patterning of unitary human beings. Newman has described a methodology for using practice as the basis for research within the model, and recently, over 800 research studies based on the theory have been reported in the literature according to a 2007 CINAHL computerized database search. Areas for research based on Newman's theory include nurses as cancer survivors, use of nursing spiritual interventions, empowerment of cancer patients, nurse–family relationships with medically fragile children, family caring, and perceived health of men with human immunodeficiency virus. Table 6-9 lists major concepts defined in Newman's theory. Along with providing a theoretical framework for graduate and undergraduate nursing programs, Newman's theory guides professional nursing practice in substance abuse settings, pattern recognition for members of a faith congregation, and pattern assessment in a woman with hyperthyroidism. Application of the theory has been useful in the following clinical situations: school-aged children with insulin-dependent diabetes mellitus, the elderly living alone, family caregivers, and persons with cancer (Fawcett, 2005).

Susan Leddy's Human Energy Model

Leddy's human energy model was influenced by Rogers' science of unitary human beings, Eastern philosophy, and quantum physics and complexity theories. This model identifies three aspects of universal essence—matter, information, and energy—which constitute an undivided whole. In the human energy model, Leddy (2004) proposed that the purpose of nursing is to facilitate the harmonious pattern of the essence fields of both client and nurse. Leddy (2004) used five key concepts in her model.

1. Self-organization: the structure of the human being demonstrated by pattern and its manifestations
2. Energy field: a dynamic web of energy interactions
3. Awareness: an energy that links humans with the environment
4. Energy: manifested by movement and change
5. Pattern: a web of relationships

Leddy (1998, p. 192) viewed the human being as "a unitary energy field that is open to and continuously interacting with an environmental universal essence field" that can only be understood as a whole. "Sensitivity to complementary facets and vantage points for observation provides a view of the whole from different perspectives" (Leddy, 1998, p. 192; Leddy, 2003, p. 68). "Self-organization distinguishes the human energy field from the environmental field with which it is inseparable and intermingled" (Leddy, 2003, p. 68). "Self-organization is a synthesis of continuity and change that provides identity while the human evolves toward a sense of integrity, meaning, and purpose in living" (Leddy, 1998, p. 192). Humans also have awareness that enables the development of self-identity, the construction of meaning, and the capability to influence change by making choices (Leddy, 2004).

Leddy (2004) viewed the environment as the context in which the human is embedded. People are one with the environment. Change can be partially predicted and partially unpredictable. She explained that the universal essence environment is ordered, and has a rhythmic pattern while constantly changing "through continuous transformation of matter and information" (Leddy, 2004, p. 14). However, change "is also influenced by the inherent order of the universe" (Leddy, 2003, p. 68). Along with the order of the universe, history, pattern, and choice also shape change.

Leddy (2003) defined health as being "the pattern of the whole" (p. 68). This pattern is rhythmic, varying in quality and intensity over time. Health is characterized by a changing pattern of harmony and dissonance.

Knowledge-based consciousness in a goal-directed relationship with the client is the basis for nursing. "A nurse–client relationship is a commitment characterized by intentionality, authenticity, trust, respect, and genuine sense of connection. The nurse is a knowledgeable, concerned facilitator. The client is responsible for choices that influence health and healing" (Leddy, 1998, pp. 192–193). The facilitation of harmonious health patterning for both client and nurse is identified as the purpose of nursing.

Leddy (2004) has derived three theories from the model: the theory of healthiness, the theory of participation, and the theory of energetic patterning. In the theory of healthiness, healthiness is defined as a manifestation of a health pattern. It is a process characterized by purpose, connections, and power to attain goals. The theory proposes that healthiness acts as a resource that influences the ongoing patterning that is reflected in health (Leddy & Fawcett, 1997). Leddy derived her theory empirically. The pattern of healthiness consists of a constellation of connection, purpose (challenge viewed as change, goals, meaningfulness, choice–possibilities, confidence–competence, and control), and power (choice–creativity, capability, capacity, change–curiosity, and confidence–assurance). The theory emphasizes the importance of goals and meaningfulness in life (Leddy, 2006).

The Leddy Healthiness Scale (LHS) (Leddy, 1996) includes items that measure meaningfulness, connections, ends, capability, control, choice, challenge, capacity, and confidence. In studies with the LHS (Leddy, 1996, 2006; Leddy & Fawcett, 1997), healthiness has been found to be moderately and negatively related to fatigue and symptom experience in women with breast cancer; and moderately and positively related to mental health, health status, and satisfaction with life in a sample of healthy people.

In the theory of participation, participation is defined as the experience of continuous human–environment mutual process. Leddy (2004) defined participation as the

TABLE 6-10

Major Concepts as Defined in Leddy's Theory

Human Beings	A unitary, self-organized field of matter, energy and information that constantly interacts with an environmental universal essence field
Environment	A dynamic, ordered, connected web in continuous transformation of energy, matter, and information with the human being (environmental universal essence)
Health	The rhythmic pattern of harmony/dissonance of the whole
Nursing	Knowledge-based consciousness involved in a mutual, connected, and goal-directed relationship with clients

experience of expansiveness (fullness and activity) and ease (smoothness and calmness of the mutual process of the human and environmental fields). The Person–Environment Participation Scale (PEPS; Leddy, 1995) measures expansiveness and the ease of participation. In studies with the PEPS to date, participation has been found to be moderately and positively correlated with healthiness, sense of coherence (Antonovsky, 1987), and power (Barrett, 1990), and moderately and negatively correlated with fatigue and symptom experience in healthy people.

The theory of energetic patterning proposes that nursing interventions to facilitate the harmonious pattern of both client and nurse are accomplished through health pattern appraisal, recognition of patterns, and energy-based nursing interventions (Leddy, 2004, 2006). Nursing healing interventions promote healing by surrounding, supporting, or penetrating the human body. The six domains of energetic patterning are:

1. Coursing: to reestablish free flow of energy
2. Conveying: to foster redirection of energy away from areas of excess to depleted areas
3. Converting: to augment energy resources
4. Collecting: to reduce energy depletion
5. Clearing: to facilitate the release of energy tied to old patterns
6. Connecting: to promote harmony within the human field and with the environmental field

A number of types of interventions are consistent with this theory, including nutrition, exercise, touch modalities, bodywork, light therapy, music, imagery, relaxation, and stress reduction (Leddy, 2003, 2004).

Leddy's conceptual model offers a unique and modern perspective for nursing; however, because it is a newer model, its usefulness for practice and research remains to be demonstrated. Table 6-10 presents major concepts defined in Leddy's model. Leddy's model and theories have yet to be empirically tested; however, they show great promise for providing a framework to guide future research on healthiness and energetic patterning.

NURSING MODELS IN RESEARCH AND PRACTICE

Model Use in Nursing Research

Most published nursing research studies fail to use conceptual nursing models as study foundations. Currently, three kinds of research related to models of nursing are being conducted: testing the relationships predicted by a model, using a model as a framework for descriptive analysis, and attempting to modify nursing care through use of a model.

For example, Leddy and Fawcett (1997) interpreted the results of a study to explain relationships among theoretical variables (participation, change, energy, and healthiness) derived from the human energy model as being supportive of the model. In another example, Hart (1995), in a study of pregnant women, derived research variables from Orem's general theory and tested the relationships between the variables. The results were interpreted as supporting Orem's model.

Models also have been used as a framework for descriptive analysis. For example, concepts from Watson's science of human caring and Newman's health as expanding consciousness were used to describe personal (DeMarco, Picard, & Agretelis, 2004) and professional (Picard, Agretelis, & DeMarco, 2004) experiences of nurses who survived cancer. Picard and colleagues' (2004) study demonstrates how nursing models may be used to guide clinical research. Scura, Budin, and Garfing (2004) used the Roy adaptation model to organize and categorize data in a pilot study using telephone social support and education to promote adaptation in men with prostate cancer. Roy's adaptation model was also used to organize study variables in a study looking at change in exercise tolerance, activity and sleep patterns, and quality of life in cancer patients who participated in a structured exercise program (Young-McCaughan et al., 2003). Bauer (2001) demonstrated how Newman's theory may be helpful in establishing patterns common to human beings with similar health problems.

A few studies attempt to modify nursing care through use of a model. For example, Kelly, Sullivan, Fawcett, and Samarel (2004) tested the effects of therapeutic touch, quiet time, and dialogue on women's perceptions of breast cancer using Rogerian science. They found that only women receiving therapeutic touch experience bodily sensations of tingling, magnetic pull, or being touched. Experimental and control groups both found quiet time and dialogue with the nurse as calming and relaxing. Therefore, nurses should not overlook therapeutic results from just spending time with clients.

Model Use in Practice

As more nurses receive baccalaureate degrees and graduate nursing education, model use in practice may become more prevalent. Nursing models and theories provide guidance to nurses engaged in practice for holistic assessments, rationale for various nursing interventions, and delineation of professional nursing roles in health care delivery. Some hospitals identify a particular theory as a basis for use of nursing process. For example, nurses at St. Luke's Hospital of Kansas City, Missouri, use Orem's self-care deficit theory as a foundation and guide for nursing practice. The American Nurses Association requests that nursing departments specify nursing model and theory use by the organization as part of the Magnet Hospital application process.

However, nursing model use in professional practice seems irrelevant to some nurses. Do models make real differences in nursing care delivered to clients? Does it matter if the client need is called a "noxious influence" affecting a behavioral subsystem, a "self-care deficit" leading to a "self-care demand," or a "focal stimulus" that is a stressor? How is the care given any different if its purpose is labeled to "limit self-care deficits," "reduce stressors," or "foster coping"? Why does the profession need specific nursing models and theories?

Although nursing science remains in an early stage of development, nursing scholars agree on categories of concepts (human beings, environment, health, and nursing) that are central to nursing knowledge. Nursing science must attain distinction from medical science. Much discussion about whether there should be one model for nursing has occurred, but the popularity of a growing number of models within different paradigms and frameworks indicates that disagreement still exists about how professional nursing should be described and how its goals can best be achieved. Perhaps multiple approaches and definitions of nursing would be advantageous due to the complex nature of nursing.

However, the profession continues to progress in defining nursing, identifying the unique nursing contributions to health care, developing nursing theory, and using nursing models and theories in practice. As health care evolves, nursing must demonstrate an ability to articulate its important and unique contribution to client care, and perhaps new models and theories may be needed.

Questions for Reflection 6-4

1. What is my personal attitude toward nursing models and theories?
2. Has my attitude changed since reading this chapter?
3. Why do I feel this way about them?
4. What are the consequences of my attitudes toward nursing models and theories?

SUMMARY AND SIGNIFICANCE TO PRACTICE

The nursing models discussed in this chapter use the metaparadigm concepts of human beings, environment, health, and nursing. Philosophical differences between the change as stability paradigm and the change as growth paradigm are pronounced. Professional nurses have the freedom to select which models to use in clinical practice based on personal philosophy and world views. Sometimes, a particular nursing model may fit a clinical situation better than others. Nursing models do not compete with each other but provide a variety of approaches and explanations for the phenomena associated with professional nursing practice.

A comparison of concepts in selected theories is presented in Table 6-11.

The major differences and similarities among models can be seen by comparing Table 6-12 with Table 6-13. More research is needed to see if the models provide an effective description of nursing and make differences in client care outcomes.

FROM THEORY TO PRACTICE

Reread the vignette at the beginning of the chapter and answer the following questions:

1. Do you believe that because Ann uses theory to guide her nursing practice, she is a better nurse than Nancy? Why or why not?
2. Which of the nursing models or theories presented in this chapter appeals to you the most?
3. How would you incorporate the theory identified in question 2 into your professional practice?
4. What are the consequences of using a nursing model or theory to guide clinical practice?

INTERNET EXERCISE

1. Visit one of the nursing theory websites listed below or found on the Clayton College and State University Nursing Theory websites, and answer the following questions:
   a. Can you contact the nursing theorist?
   b. Who maintains the nursing theory website?
   c. What materials are available on the website to explain the nursing theory?
   d. Where can you go to find additional information about the nursing theory?
   e. Would you recommend the website to a colleague interested in the selected nursing theory? Why or why not?

TABLE 6-11

Comparison of Concepts in Selected Theories

Theory	Human	Human–Environment Interaction	Health	Examples of Nursing Implication
Systems	Multiple interacting subsystems that form the human system	Simultaneous change in both systems	Tendency toward increased complexity	Nurse system and client system are mutually affected
Stress and adaptation	Multiple subsystems that share an internal environment	Humans cope and compensate for environmental change	Constancy of the internal environment within normal parameters	Support coping mechanisms of client
Complexity	Unitary whole	Mutual simultaneous interaction; nonlinear	Pattern of the whole	Stimulate repatterning

TABLE 6-12

Similarities and Differences of Conceptualization in Nursing Models within the Change as Stability Paradigm

Model	Person		Health	Environment	Nursing	
	Goal	Composition			Nature	Purpose
King	Functioning in social roles	Open system	Dynamic state of well-being	Internal and external stressors	Goal-oriented interaction	Attainment maintenance, or restoration of health
Orem	Constancy	Whole with physical, psychological, interpersonal, social aspects	Meeting self-care needs	External forces	Systems that address self-care requisites	Help people to meet self-care needs
Roy	Become integrated and whole	System with biopsychosocial components	Adaptation	External conditions	Manipulation of stimuli to foster coping	Promotion of adaptation
Neuman	Balance	Composite of physiologic, psychological, sociocultural, developmental of spiritual variables	Equilibrium	Internal and external stressors	Stress-reducing activities	Promotion of equilibrium

TABLE 6-13

Similarities and Differences of Conceptualization in Nursing Models Within the Change as Growth Paradigm

Model	Person		Health	Environment	Nursing		Purpose
	Goal	Composition			Nature		
Peplau	Equilibrium	System with physiologic, psychological, and social components	Forward movement of the personality	Significant others	Therapeutic interpersonal process		Helping people to meet needs and to develop
Watson	Sense of inner harmony	Integrated and inseparable spiritual, mental, and physical spheres	Unity and harmony	Energy field external to the person	Transpersonal caring		Promoting harmony
Rogers	Increased complexity of pattern	Indivisible energy field	Increasing innovativeness of patterning	Contiguous, continuously interacting energy field	Promotion of repatterning		Facilitating health potential
Newman	Expansion of consciousness	Center of energy	Patterns of person–environment interaction expanding toward higher levels	Energy field in continuous interaction with the person	Repatterning partnership		Promoting higher level of consciousness
Parse	Process of becoming	Open being	Process of becoming	Energy field in continuous interaction with the person	Interpersonal processes		Improving quality of life
Leddy	Harmony, integrity, meaning, and purpose	Unitary energy field	Pattern of the whole	Energy field and person are one	Goal-directed relationship		Facilitation of harmonious health patterning

WWW INTERNET RESOURCES

Clayton College and State University Department of Nursing's Nursing Theory: http://www.healthsci.clayton.edu/eichelberger/nursing.htm.

Neuman's health system model: http://www.neumansystemsmodel.com.

Newman's health as expanding consciousness: http://www.healthasexpandingconsciousness.org.

Orem's self-care deficit nursing theory: http://www.muhealth.org/~nursing/scdnt/scdnt.html.

Parse's human becoming theory: http://www.humanbecoming.org.

Roy's adaptation model: http://www2.bc.edu/schools/son/faculty/theorist/Roy_Adaptation_Association.html.

Rogers' science of unitary human beings: http://medweb.uwcm.ac.uk/martha.

Watson's theory of caring and the Colorado Center for Human Caring: http://www2.uchsc.edu/son/caring/content/sprim.asp.

REFERENCES

Agnes, M. (Ed.). (2005). *Webster's new world college dictionary* (4th ed.). Cleveland, OH: Wiley.

Andrews, H. A., & Roy, C. (1986). *Essentials of the Roy adaptation model*. Norwalk, CT: Appleton-Century-Crofts.

Antonovsky, A. (1987). *Unraveling the mystery of health*. San Francisco: Jossey-Bass.

Auger, J. R. (1976). *Behavioral systems and nursing*. Englewood Cliffs, NJ: Prentice-Hall.

Barrett, E. A. M. (1990). A measure of power as knowing participation in change. In O. L. Strickland & C. F. Waltz (Eds.), *Measurement of nursing outcomes* (pp. 159–180). New York: Springer.

Bauer, D. J. (2001). Common patterns of person-environment interaction in persons with rheumatoid arthritis. *Western Journal of Nursing Research, 23*(4), 414–430.

Benner, P., & Wrubel, J. (1989). *The primacy of caring: Stress and coping in health and illness*. Menlo Park, CA: Addison-Wesley.

Cannon, W. B. (1932). *The wisdom of the body* (Rev. ed.). New York: Norton.

Chin, R. (1976). The utility of systems models and developmental models for practitioners. In W. G. Bennis, K. D. Benne, K. E. Corey, & R. Chin (Eds.), *The planning of change* (3rd ed., pp. 90–122). New York: Holt, Rinehart & Winston.

Chinn, P. L., & Kramer, M. K. (1999). *Theory and nursing: Integrated knowledge development* (5th ed.). St. Louis, MO: Mosby-Year Book.

DeMarco, R., Picard, C., & Agretelis, J. (2004). Nurse experiences as cancer survivors: Part 1—personal. *Oncology Nursing Forum, 31*, 523–530.

Fawcett, J. (1989). *Analysis and evaluation of conceptual models of nursing* (2nd ed.). Philadelphia: F. A. Davis.

Fawcett, J. (2000). *Analysis and evaluation of contemporary nursing knowledge: Nursing models and theories*. Philadelphia: F. A. Davis.

Fawcett, J. (2001). The nurse theorists: 21st-century updates—Imogene M. King. *Nursing Science Quarterly, 14*, 311–315.

Fawcett, J. (2002a). The nurse theorists: 21st-century updates—Callista Roy. *Nursing Science Quarterly, 15*, 308–310.

Fawcett, J. (2002b). The nurse theorists: 21st-century updates—Jean Watson. *Nursing Science Quarterly, 15*, 214–219.

Fawcett, J. (2003a). Conceptual models of nursing: International in scope and substance? The case of the Roy adaptation model. *Nursing Science Quarterly, 16*, 315–318.

Fawcett, J. (2003b). The nurse theorists: 21st-century updates—Martha E. Rogers. *Nursing Science Quarterly, 16*, 44–51.

Fawcett, J. (2004). Conceptual models of nursing: International in scope and substance? The case of the Neuman systems model. *Nursing Science Quarterly, 17*, 50–54.

Fawcett, J. (2005). *Contemporary nursing knowledge: Analysis and evaluation of nursing models and theories* (2nd ed.). Philadelphia: F. A. Davis.

Gaut, D., & Leininger, M. (1991). *Caring: The compassionate healer*. New York: NLN Press.

Hansen-Ketchum, P. (2004). Parse's theory in practice. *Journal of Holistic Nursing, 22*, 57–72.

Hardy, M. (1978). Perspectives on nursing theory. *Advances in Nursing Science, 1*, 37–48.

Hart, M. A. (1995). Orem's self-care deficit theory: Research with pregnant women. *Nursing Science Quarterly, 8*, 120–126.

Huch, M. H. (1987). A critique of the Roy adaptation model. In R. R. Parse (Ed.), *Nursing science: Major paradigms, theories, and critiques* (pp. 47–66). Philadelphia: W. B. Saunders.

Kelly, A., Sullivan, P., Fawcett, J., & Samarel, N. (2004). Therapeutic touch, quiet time, and dialogue: Perceptions of women with breast cancer. *Oncology Nursing Forum, 31*, 625–631.

Kim, T. S., Park, J. S., & Kim, M. A. (2008). The relation of meditation to power and well-being. *Nursing Science Quarterly*, *21*(1), 49–58.

King, I. M. (1981). *A theory for nursing: Systems, concepts, process*. New York: Wiley.

King, I. M. (1987). King's theory of goal attainment. In R. R. Parse (Ed.), *Nursing science: Major paradigms, theories, and critiques* (pp. 107–113). Philadelphia: W. B. Saunders.

King, I. M. (1989). King's general systems framework and theory. In J. P. Riehl-Sisca (Ed.), *Conceptual models for nursing practice* (pp. 149–158). Norwalk, CT: Appleton & Lange.

King, I. M. (1995). The theory of goal attainment. In M. A. Frey & C. L. Sieloff (Eds.), *Advancing King's systems framework and theory of nursing* (pp. 23–32). Thousand Oaks, CA: Sage.

King, I. M. (1996). The theory of goal attainment in research and practice. *Nursing Science Quarterly*, *9*, 61–66.

King, I. M. (1999). A theory of goal attainment: Philosophical and ethical implications. *Nursing Science Quarterly*, *12*, 292–296.

Koldjeski, D. (1990). Toward a theory of professional nursing caring: A unifying perspective. In M. Leininger & J. Watson (Eds.), *The caring imperative in education* (pp. 45–57). New York: National League for Nursing.

Kyle, T. V. (1995). The concept of caring: A review of the literature. *Journal of Advanced Nursing*, *21*, 506–514.

Leddy, S. K. (1995). Measuring mutual process: Development and psychometric testing of the person-environment participation scale. *Visions: The Journal of Rogerian Nursing Science*, *3*, 20–31.

Leddy, S. K. (1996). Incentives and barriers to exercise in women with a history of breast cancer. *Oncology Nursing Forum*, *24*, 885–890.

Leddy, S. K. (1998). *Leddy & Pepper's conceptual bases for professional nursing* (4th ed.). Philadelphia: Lippincott.

Leddy, S. K. (2003). *Integrative health promotion*. Thorofare, NJ: Slack.

Leddy, S. K. (2004). Human energy: A conceptual model of unitary nursing science. *Visions: The Journal of Rogerian Scholarship*, *12*, 14–27.

Leddy, S. K. (2006). *Health promotion: Mobilizing strengths to enhance health, wellness and well-being*. Philadelphia: F. A. Davis.

Leddy, S. K., & Fawcett, J. (1997). Testing the theory of healthiness: Conceptual and methodological issues. In M. Madrid (Ed.), *Patterns of Rogerian knowing* (pp. 75–86). New York: National League for Nursing.

Magan, S. J. (1987). A critique of King's theory. In R. R. Parse (Ed.), *Nursing science: Major paradigms, theories and critiques* (pp. 115–133). Philadelphia: W. B. Saunders.

Maliski, S. L., & Holditch-Davis, D. (1995). Linking biology and biography: Complex nonlinear dynamical systems as a framework for nursing inquiry. *Complexity and Chaos in Nursing*, *2*, 25–35.

Meleis, A. (2007). *Theoretical nursing development and progress* (4th ed.). Philadelphia: Lippincott Williams & Wilkins,

Monat, A., & Lazarus, R. (Eds.). (1977). *Stress and coping: An anthology*. New York: Columbia University Press.

Morse, J. M., Solberg, S. M., Neander, W. L., Bottorff, J. L., & Johnson, J. L. (1990). Concepts of caring and caring as a concept. *Advances in Nursing Science*, *13*, 1–14.

Myss, C. (2002). *Carolyn Myss' chakra meditation* [CD]. Louisville, CO: Sounds True.

Neuman, B. (1982). *The Neuman systems model: Application to nursing education and practice*. Norwalk, CT: Appleton-Century-Crofts.

Neuman, B. (1996). The Neuman systems model in research and practice. *Nursing Science Quarterly*, *9*, 67–70.

Neuman, B. (2002). The Neuman systems model. In B. Neuman & J. Fawcett (Eds.), *The Neuman systems model* (4th ed.). Upper Saddle River, NJ: Prentice Hall.

Newman, M. A. (1986). *Health as expanding consciousness*. St. Louis, MO: Mosby.

Newman, M. A. (1990). Toward an integrative model of professional practice. *Journal of Professional Nursing*, *6*, 167–173.

Newman, M. A. (1994). *Health as expanding consciousness* (2nd ed.). New York: National League for Nursing.

Orem, D. E. (1980). *Nursing: Concepts of practice* (2nd ed.). New York: McGraw-Hill.

Orem, D. E. (1985). *Nursing: Concepts of practice* (3rd ed.). New York: McGraw-Hill.

Orem, D. E. (1990). A nursing practice theory in three parts, 1956–1989. In M. E. Parker (Ed.), *Nursing theories in practice* (pp. 47–60). New York: National League for Nursing.

Orem, D. E. (1995). *Nursing: Concepts of practice* (5th ed.). St. Louis, MO: Mosby.

Parse, R. R. (1987). *Nursing science: Major paradigms, theories, and critiques*. Philadelphia: W. B. Saunders.

Parse, R. R. (1989). Man-living-health: A theory of nursing. In J. P. Riehl-Sisca (Ed.), *Conceptual models for nursing practice* (pp. 253–257). Norwalk, CT: Appleton & Lange.

Parse, R. R. (1996). The human becoming theory: Challenges in practice and research. *Nursing Science Quarterly, 9*, 55–60.

Parse, R. R. (1998). *The human becoming school of thought*. Thousand Oaks, CA: Sage.

Phillips, J. R. (1987). A critique of Parse's man-living-health theory. In R. R. Parse (Ed.), *Nursing science: Major paradigms, theories, and critiques* (pp. 181–202). Philadelphia: W. B. Saunders.

Picard, C., Agretelis, J., & DeMarco, R. (2004). Nurse experiences as cancer survivors: Part II—professional. *Oncology Nursing Forum, 31*, 537–542.

Porter, E. J. (1995). Non-equilibrium systems theory: Some applications for gerontological nursing practice. *Journal of Gerontological Nursing, 21*, 24–31.

Riehl, J. P., & Roy, C. (1980). *Conceptual models for nursing practice*. New York: Appleton-Century-Crofts.

Rogers, B. L. (2005). *Developing nursing knowledge: Philosophical traditions and influences*. Philadelphia: Lippincott Williams & Wilkins.

Rogers, M. E. (1970). *An introduction to the theoretical basis of nursing*. Philadelphia: F. A. Davis.

Rogers, M. E. (1980). Nursing: A science of unitary man. In J. P. Riehl & C. Roy (Eds.), *Conceptual models for nursing practice* (pp. 329–337). New York: Appleton-Century-Crofts.

Rogers, M. E. (1990). Nursing: Science of unitary, irreducible human beings: Update 1990. In E. A. M. Barrett (Ed.), *Visions of Rogers' science-based nursing* (pp. 5–11). New York: National League for Nursing.

Rogers, M. E. (1992). Nursing science and the space age. *Nursing Science Quarterly, 5*, 27–34.

Roy, C. (1987). Roy's adaptation model. In R. R. Parse (Ed.), *Nursing science: Major paradigms, theories, and critiques* (pp. 35–45). Philadelphia: W. B. Saunders.

Roy, C. (2007). Advances in nursing knowledge and the challenge for transforming practice. In C. Roy & D. Jones (Eds.), *Nursing knowledge development and clinical practice* (pp. 3–38). New York: Springer.

Roy, C. (2008). Adversity and theory: The broad picture. *Nursing Science Quarterly, 21*, 138–139.

Roy, C., & Andrews, H. A. (1999). *The Roy adaptation model* (2nd ed.). Stamford, CT: Appleton & Lange.

Roy, C., & Roberts, S. L. (1981). *Theory construction in nursing: An adaptation model*. Englewood Cliffs, NJ: Prentice-Hall.

Scura, K., Budin, W., & Garfing, E. (2004). Telephone social support and education for adaptation to prostate cancer: A pilot study. *Oncology Nursing Forum, 32*, 335–338.

Sills, G. M., & Hall, J. E. (1977). A general systems perspective for nursing. In J. E. Hall & B. R. Weaver (Eds.), *Distributive nursing practice: A systems approach to community health* (pp. 22–43). Philadelphia: Lippincott.

Smith, M. (2004). Review of research related to Watson's theory of caring. *Nursing Science Quarterly, 17*(1), 13–25.

Swanson, K. M. (1991). Empirical development of a middle range theory of caring. *Nursing Research, 40*, 161–166.

Taylor, S. G., Geden, E., Isaramalai, S., & Wongvatunyu, S. (2000). Orem's self-care deficit nursing theory: Its philosophic foundation and the state of the science. *Nursing Science Quarterly, 13*, 104–110.

Watson, J. (1985). *Nursing: Human science and human care*. Norwalk, CT: Appleton-Century-Crofts.

Watson, J. (1989). Watson's philosophy and theory of human caring in nursing. In J. P. Riehl-Sisca (Ed.), *Conceptual models for nursing practice* (pp. 219–235). Norwalk, CT: Appleton & Lange.

Watson, J. (1999). *Postmodern nursing and beyond*. Edinburgh: Churchill Livingstone.

Watson, J. (2002). *Assessing and measuring caring in nursing and health science*. New York: Springer.

Watson, J. (2007). *Nursing human science and human care: A theory for nursing*. Sudbury, MA: Jones & Bartlett

Young-McCaughan, S., Mays, M., Arzola, S., Yoder, L., Dramiga, S., Leclerc, K., et al. (2003). Research and commentary: Change in exercise tolerance, activity and sleep patterns, and quality of life in patients with cancer participating in a structured exercise program. *Oncology Nursing Forum, 30*, 441–454.

CHAPTER 7

Professional Nursing Processes

KEY TERMS AND CONCEPTS

Critical thinking

Nursing process

Assessment

Diagnosis

Planning

Implementation

Evaluation

Nursing diagnosis

Goals

Outcomes

Nursing Outcomes Classification (NOC)

Nursing interventions

Nursing Interventions Classification (NIC)

Intuition

Reflection

Reflection-in-action

Reflection-on-action

Research-based model of clinical judgment

Interpersonal processes

Psychomotor processes

Patterning nursing processes

LEARNING OUTCOMES

By the end of this chapter, the learner will be able to:

1 Outline cognitive processes nurses use in clinical practice.

2 Specify the steps of nursing processes.

3 Appraise the strengths and weaknesses of using nursing process in practice.

4 Discuss variances in the use of nursing process when practice is based upon a selected nursing model.

5 Compare and contrast critical thinking, reflection, and intuition.

6 Differentiate among the stages of the novice-to-expert model of clinical practice.

7 Distinguish between linear and integrated cognitive nursing processes.

8 Discuss interpersonal nursing processes consistent with selected nursing conceptual models.

9 Outline psychomotor processes for patterning of health.

Carol, a nurse employed in a university-based health clinic, serves as a preceptor for community health nursing students from a local baccalaureate nursing program. Today is her first day working with Jane, a senior nursing student. Carol receives a telephone call from the University Campus Police informing her that they are bringing an obese student who fell and has a very swollen ankle. Before the student arrives, Carol asks Jane, "What is the first thing we should do when the injured student arrives?" Jane replies, "I think we should find out her name and how the accident happened." Carol responds, "OK. What other information do we need?" Jane begins to shake and answers, "I never had a client with an orthopedic problem, so I really don't know where to begin. It seems like I always get confused in the clinical setting what I should do first. Maybe I should not be a nurse." Knowing the frustration she experienced as a nursing student, Carol replies, "Once I understood nursing process, it seemed as though what to do in the clinical setting fell into place for me when I was a nursing student. Can you tell me the steps of nursing process and what nursing theorist you use?" "I get the steps of nursing process confused all of the time, and the program has us use Rogers' nursing theory," replies Jane. Carol sighs and thinks to herself, "How can a nursing student get this far in her education without understanding how to use nursing process? What can I do to help Jane master nursing process quickly?" Carol instructs Jane just to observe while she handles the injured student and tells Jane that the two of them will talk about nursing process and Rogers' nursing theory later.

Questions for Reflection 7-1

1. How would I explain nursing process to someone else?
2. Why is nursing process important to practice?

Beliefs about nursing shape the way nurses practice. Consider the nature of nursing when nurses practice using the medical model. Much of nursing, as taught and practiced, is standardized according to medical diagnoses and supports medical intervention. The physician does the assessment needed for the medical diagnosis, and this information serves as the basis for the medical orders. Nursing focuses on human responses to health status and the medical plan of care. When so-called nursing knowledge is actually borrowed from medicine, nurses focus on detailed knowledge of pathophysiology, symptoms of disease, standard medical interventions, and a single "best" way to perform treatments and procedures.

In contrast, nursing practice differs greatly when the nature of nursing is based on a model of autonomous professional practice. In an autonomous nursing model, nurses focus on supporting the client to improve well-being status and develop human potential. Nursing knowledge includes detailed understanding of the client as a whole person, health and the factors that promote health, the environment and the mutual and ongoing interaction between environment and humans, and the purpose and functions of nursing. Nurses perform their own client assessments, gathering information about each client's well-being status, including client

1. Strengths and weaknesses.
2. Whole responses to health concerns.
3. Analysis of circumstances associated with well-being status.
4. Knowledge related to health and well-being.
5. Beliefs and values about health.
6. Lifestyle.

7. Health-related goals.
8. Support systems.

Because nurses view clients as whole persons and consider themselves key partners in an interdisciplinary health care team, they also have knowledge about the care regimens of the other providers, such as physicians, pharmacists, and physical therapists. Understanding care regimens outlined by other health team members helps nurses to appreciate the global health care plan and acknowledge its impact on the whole client. By sharing knowledge about the plan, nurses help clients assume mutual and equal responsibility for setting health-related goals and participating as equal members of the health care team.

The knowledge projected by the model of nursing, accepted by the nurse, provides the basis for all nursing processes. Skill in the integrated use of cognitive, interpersonal, and psychomotor processes in client care is basic to the practice of professional nursing. This chapter emphasizes the relationship between nursing processes and the practice of professional nursing according to the nursing models discussed in Chapter 6.

CRITICAL THINKING

Many different definitions of critical thinking appear in the nursing and higher education literature. Table 7-1 outlines some of the more common definitions of critical thinking used in nursing and higher education. Although they vary somewhat, elements that consistently appear in the definitions include that **critical thinking** appears to be a highly complex thinking pattern that requires higher order thinking. Persons who think critically take time to examine situations in terms of content and context, instead of jumping into action to make personal judgments and clinical decisions or to solve problems. Critical thinkers also take time to examine consequences of anticipated actions. Finally, critical thinking also demands that persons have solid, logical reasons for judgments and actions.

Critical thinking scholars debate whether the critical thinking process is a general skill that applies to all areas of life. If viewed as a general life skill, critical thinking must be learned by everyone to survive in a rapidly changing world (Paul, 1993). Fortunately, skills can be taught. However, basic elements of critical thinking may have to be altered to "fit" the context of the situation (Paul). When a nurse encounters a person without a pulse and respirations, spending time critically thinking about the situation would cause great harm; immediate action is warranted. However, after the emergency has been handled, the professional nurse could spend some time engaged in critical reflection about why the arrest occurred, how it could have been avoided, and the effectiveness of professional actions.

Other authors, such as Facione (2006) and Facione, Facione, and Sanchez (1994), proposed that critical thinking may be a personal quality and relies on attitude in addition to cognitive skills. Before persons can engage in regular critical thinking, they must value truth seeking, open-mindedness, analyticity (recognizing potential problems, anticipating results, and prizing the use of reason), systematicity (the orderly, focused approach to inquiry), and inquisitiveness (natural curiosity) while having the maturity to make honest, reflective judgments and self-confidence in reasoning processes (Facione, Facione, & Giancarlo, 1996). This view of critical thinking fits well with Benner's novice-to-expert model (Benner, 1984), which illustrates the idea that experts develop certain characteristics related to practice (confidence, competence, and maturity) that enable them to quickly make correct clinical judgments that seem to simultaneously spring into action. Critical thinking is integrated throughout the cognitive nursing processes.

COGNITIVE NURSING PROCESSES

The Nursing Process

Clients rely on nurses to make effective clinical decisions. Kataoka-Yahiro and Saylor (1994) suggested that the nursing process, as a method for problem solving and decision

TABLE 7-1

Some Commonly Used Definitions of Critical Thinking

Author(s)	Definitions
Bandman & Bandman (1995)	"The rational examination of ideas, inferences, assumptions, principles, arguments, conclusions, ideas, statement, beliefs and action" (p. 7)
Brookfield (1987)	"Reflecting on the assumptions underlying our and others' ideas and action and contempative alternative ways of thinking and living." (p. 18) Reflective skepticism
Turner (2005)	"A purposeful self-regulatory judgment associated with clinical decision making, a diagnostic reasoning, the nursing process, clinical judgment and problem solving, characterized by reasoning, inference, interpretation, knowledge, and open-mindedness." (p. 276)
Kennedy, Fisher, & Ennis (1991)	"Reasonable and reflective thinking that is focused upon deciding what to believe or do" (p. 46)
Facione (2006)	"The process of purposeful self-regulatory judgment. This process gives reasoned consideration to evidence, context, conceptualization, methods and criteria." (p. 21)
Kurfiss (1998)	"An investigation whose purpose is to explore a situation, phenomenon, question, or problem to arrive at a hypothesis or conclusion about it that integrates all available information and that, therefore, can be convincingly justified" (p. 37)
McPeck (1981)	"The propensity and skill to engage in an activity with reflective skepticism" (p. 8)
National League for Nursing Accrediting Commission (2000)	"The deliberative nonlinear process of collecting, interpreting, analyzing, drawing conclusions about, presenting and evaluating information that is both factual and belief based" (p. 8)
Paul (1983)	"A unique kind of purposeful thinking in which the thinker systematically and habitually imposes criteria and intellectual standards upon the thinking, taking charge of the construction of thinking, guiding the construction of the thinking according to the standards, and assessing the effectiveness of the thinking according to the purpose, the criteria and the standards" (p. 21)
Scheffer & Rubenfeld (2000)	"In nursing is an essential component of professional accountability and quality nursing care." Critical thinkers display the following habits of the mind: "confidence, contextual perspective, creativity, flexibility, inquisitiveness, intellectual integrity, intuition, open-mindedness, perserverance and reflection." They also use " the cognitive skills of analyzing, applying standards, discriminating, information-seeking, logical reasoning, predicting and transforming knowledge." (p. 357)
Watson & Glaser (1990)	Problem definition Decision making about pertinent information for problem solving Identifying and recognizing overt and convert assumptions Hypothesis formation and selection Drawing valid conclusions and judging validity of inferences (p. 1)

making in nursing practice, represents a discipline-specific version of critical thinking. **Nursing process** consists of the following five steps:

1. **Assessment**: comprehensive data collection of factors related to client health status
2. **Diagnosis**: a judgment that identifies actual or potential client health strengths and weaknesses
3. **Planning**: a two-phase step that determines health-related goals (or outcomes) and specifies a series of actions to be taken to attain them

   4. **Implementation**: execution of the action plan outlined in step 3
   5. **Evaluation**: determining the effectiveness of the implemented action plan to either make needed revisions or restart nursing process with step 1

Nursing process has been compared with the scientific method and problem solving. Effective problem solving relies on extensive data collection for proper problem identification. Nurses assess clients holistically to determine actual and potential health-related problems or strengths (nursing diagnoses). Problem solving, the scientific method, and nursing process incorporate planning as a key step. When determining ways to solve the problem, test hypotheses, or deliver individualized nursing care, people generate action plans consisting of a desired goal and steps for attainment. After execution of action plans, problem solving, scientific method, and nursing process evaluate the effectiveness of predetermined action plans in meeting the desired outcome.

The nursing process provides a logical and rational way for the nurse to solve problems and make decisions so that the care given is appropriate and effective. Nurses use critical thinking skills while using all steps of the nursing process. Critical thinking enables nurses to collect relevant data from a variety of sources, sift out irrelevant pieces of data, determine what data are important, and validate the meaning of data with others if uncertain. Nurses use critical thinking to organize data into meaningful patterns, determine if more data are required, compare data patterns with norms and known theories, examine assumptions about the client situation, and identify the major client health concerns to arrive at a **nursing diagnosis**. Critical thinking helps nurses to set safe care priorities, set realistic care outcomes, determine appropriate nursing interventions, and generate a rationale for interventions while considering client needs and concerns. Nurses use critical thinking while applying knowledge for intervention performance, testing the efficacy of interventions, updating and revising care plans as needed, noting changes in client status, and determining when to consult other health team members. Finally, critical thinking is used by nurses to evaluate the effectiveness of the care plan, determine alternative approaches and interventions, monitor the quality of care delivered, track client progress toward desired outcomes, and revise the plan as needed. Although nursing process has its roots from the scientific process, nurses execute it in a sensitive and caring manner when working with human beings. Nurses consider client individual needs and preferences when providing client care. Nurses use creativity to individualize nursing care for clients. Thus, the nursing process is an artistic and scientific process.

Invariably, the nursing process is presented as a series of four or five phases, with a number of steps within each phase. The net effect is a procedure that appears linear (or, at best, overlapping or circular) and cumbersome. However, all parts of the process are interrelated and influence the whole. The parts or phases of the nursing process occur sequentially, but they are not linear. Planning may lead to intervention, or evaluation during planning may result in more assessment. Figure 7-1 depicts the nursing process viewed from an interactional perspective. The following discussion presents an overview of each phase of the nursing process.

The Assessment Step

During assessment, the nurses collect subjective and objective data about the client's health status. Subjective data consist of information that the client or significant other shares with the nurse. Objective data consist of information that can be directly measured or observed. For example, a client's report of right flank pain (particularly the presence of pain, its location, its intensity, and aggravating and alleviating factors) represents subjective data. Increased blood pressure, pulse, and respiratory rates represent objective data. Other forms of objective data include diagnostic test results. Nurses collect data systematically and verify their accuracy with clients. If unable to collect desired data, nurses use critical thinking to determine reasons for obstacles and devise alternative approaches to collect it. When working with clients, nurses continuously

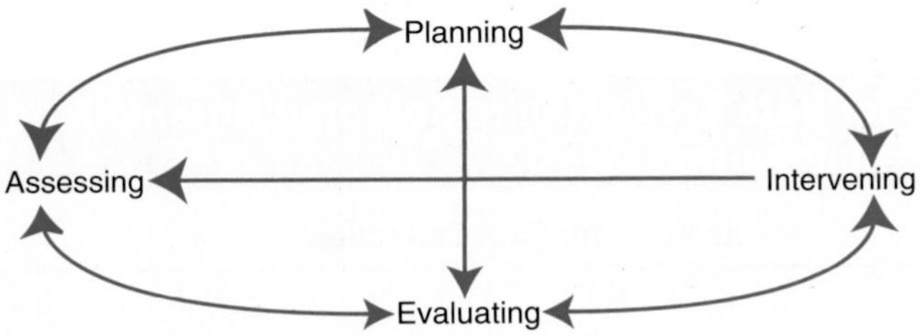

Figure 7-1
An interactional approach to the nursing process.

collect data and analyze them to make nursing decisions. Nurses document data collected to provide a legal record of their surveillance activities and so that members of the interprofessional health care team have access to it.

Before nurses can begin collecting data, clients must trust them. Usually, nurses initiate client relationships. When possible, nurses and clients work together as partners to outline specific care **goals** and specify responsibilities and ways to tailor nursing care to meet individual client needs. Nurses use critical thinking to evaluate client responses and determine ways to facilitate communication.

Most nurses use an organized process for data collection. They decide which data are desirable and significant to collect in a particular situation and determine what sources and methods would be best to obtain these data. Data provide evidence for determining nursing diagnoses and planning nursing care. Nurse-collected data should supplement, rather than duplicate, data collected by other health professionals (e.g., history) and should focus on information needed for nursing care. During data collection, nurses review all data to determine if more needs to be collected. When data collection is complete, nurses organize and begin planning nursing care.

First, the nurse must know who the client is, why the client needs nursing care, and what factors currently influence the client's health status. Therefore, the nurse must collect key data, such as the client's name, age, gender, marital status, occupation, education, economic status, existing knowledge about health–illness status, and family (and significant other) attitudes toward health care. Second, to individualize care, the nurse collects data regarding the client's personal habits, communication styles, cultural influences, growth and development status, learning capacity, supports and resources, previous experience with the health care system, medical diagnosis and regimen, coping patterns, personal values, and desired changes. Finally, the nurse uses a preferred conceptual nursing model to guide and organize data collection using suggestions outlined in Table 7-2.

As data are collected, the nurse validates the findings with the client and other sources. If discrepancies are noted, they should be clarified. Nurse evaluation of the data should consider accuracy and whether all relevant factors have been included. As data collection continues, the organization and analysis of patterns within the data proceed concurrently, which may identify additional data collection needs. When all of this is completed, the nurse moves to the second phase of the nursing process.

The Diagnosis Step

Nurses derive nursing diagnoses from client data. Using all the data collected during the assessment, nurses organize data into clusters and interpret what they reveal about the client. Effective data analysis and synthesis require that nurses remain objective, engage in thoughtful deliberation, make sound judgments, and discriminate relevant from irrelevant pieces of information. Nursing diagnoses represent the professional nurse's judgment about human responses within a contextual situation that may either threaten or strengthen health and well-being, The concept of nursing diagnosis started in professional nursing practice in the early 1970s (Webber, 2008) in North America and has now expanded to all continents. The North American Nursing Diagnosis Association International (NANDA-I;

TABLE 7-2

Implications for Data Collection in Selected Nursing Models Organized by Theoretical Frameworks

Nursing Models	Implications for Data Collection
Systems Theory	
King	Perceptions of self, level of growth and development, level of stress, abilities to function in usual role, decision-making abilities, and abilities to communicate
Neuman	Stressors, indications of disruption of the lines of defense, resistance factors
Stress/Adaptation	
Roy	Adaptation level (related to three classes of stimuli), coping in relation to modes of adaptation, position on the health–illness continuum
Caring	
Orem	Therapeutic self-care demand, presence of self-care deficits, ability of clients to meet self-care requisites
Watson	Phenomenal field (self within life space and motivational factors for health), values, needs for information, problem-solving abilities, developmental conflicts, losses, feelings about the human predicament
Complexity	
Peplau	Physiologic and personality needs, illness symptoms, relationships with significant others, influences on establishment and maintenance of the nurse–client relationship
Rogers	Characteristics of patterning, health potential, rhythms of life, simultaneous states of the individual and environment
Parse	Thoughts and feelings about the situation, the synchronizing rhythms in human relationships, personal meanings, ways of being alike and different, and values
Newman	Person–environment interactions, patterns of energy exchange, client's responses to symptoms, transforming potential, client's feelings and what he does because of those feelings, patterns of life
Leddy	Characteristics of human universal essence field and enviornmental essence field

2007) identified five types of nursing diagnoses: actual, risk, possible, wellness, and syndrome. Nursing diagnoses exclusively address care situations for which the professional nurse has responsibility. Although nursing practice may vary across state and national boundaries, nurses make independent judgments when clustering data to formulate nursing diagnoses. Professional nursing responsibility means that the nurse has the legal qualifications and accountability to take action. Nursing diagnoses may apply to individuals, families, or communities (NANDA-I, 2007).

When defining characteristics of a nursing diagnosis are present, nurses work with an actual nursing diagnosis. Actual nursing diagnoses are written using a three-phrase clause: the client problem, followed by the words "related to," then the etiology. Proper formatting of actual nursing diagnoses forbids the use of the name of a disease or surgical procedure as the related-to clause. NANDA-I has other classifications of nursing diagnoses to fit a variety of clinical situations. Wellness diagnoses occur when a person, family, or community experiences a transition to a higher level of wellness. When persons or groups are at risk to develop a specific human response, but the signs and symptoms (diagnostic cues) are absent, nurses formulate at-risk nursing diagnoses. Nurses use a syndrome diagnosis when a particular clinical situation results in a predictable cluster of commonly encountered actual or at-risk nursing diagnoses. Finally, nurses may encounter a clinical situation in which insufficient data are present to designate an actual, at-risk, wellness, or syndrome diagnosis. The possible nursing diagnosis presents a nurse with an option to address the human response despite insufficient data. Finally, when nurses monitor for possible complications from medications or an invasive procedure, nurses use collaborative problem statements (NANDA-I, 2007). The number of clauses in a nursing diagnosis varies according to its classification. Table 7-3 offers definitions, specific formats, and examples of the various classifications of nursing diagnoses.

Ideally, nurses develop nursing diagnoses in collaboration with clients. When nurses involve clients in the generation of nursing diagnoses, clients validate that the nurse has the complete story, become more aware of the goals, and have the opportunity to determine desired **outcomes** of nursing care. Human response patterns and functional health patterns of health perception provide different ways for nurses to collect and organize

TABLE 7-3

Definition, Format, and Examples of Nursing and Collaborative Diagnoses

Nursing Diagnosis Classification	Definition	Format	Examples
Actual	A clinical judgment identifying a problem with major defining characteristics being present with identified contributing factors influencing the health status change	Three clauses: 1. The human response 2. Etiology (or contributing factors) 3. Clinical signs and symptoms	Altered nutrition less than body requires (1) related to persistent nausea and vomiting (2) as evidenced by no food intake for 1 week, refusal to eat, weight loss of 10 pounds within 2 weeks, (3) prealbumin of 14.8 mg/dl and c/o "feel tired all the time" and statement "I am afraid to eat because I will throw up."
Risk	A clinical judgment identifying a potential problem because of increased vulnerability to developing it	Two-clause statement designating the potential human response and the etiology	Risk for infection related to compromised host defenses from the potentially immunosuppressive effects of chemotherapy and presence of Groshong central venous catheter
Syndrome	A clinical judgment identifying health-altering situation resulting in the likely presence of multiple nursing diagnoses	One-clause statement designating the type of altered health	Battered child syndrome
Wellness	A clinical judgment identifying a transition from a current wellness level to a higher one	One-clause statement designating a human response with the possibility of moving toward greater wellness	Potential for enhanced spiritual well-being
Possible	A clinical judgment describing a suspected problem not validated by available data	Two-clause statement designating the human response and possible etiology	Possible death anxiety related to recent cancer diagnosis
Collaborative problems and diagnostic statements	Potential complications arising from a disease process or medical interventions	Two-part phrase including the words: Potential complication	Potential complication: hemorrhage Potential complications of cardiac catheterization

Adapted from Carpenito, L. J. (2002). *Nursing diagnosis application to clinical practice* (9th ed.). Philadelphia: Lippincott Williams & Wilkins. NANDA-I (2007). Nursing diagnoses: Definitions and classifications. Philadelphia: Author.

data to compile a nursing diagnosis. Gordon's (1995) functional health patterns provide an internationally coherent method to identify nursing diagnoses. Gordon (1995) outlined the following 11 functional health patterns that apply to all persons:

1. Health perception–health management
2. Nutritional-metabolic
3. Elimination
4. Activity–exercise
5. Sleep–rest
6. Cognitive-perceptual
7. Self-perception–self-concept
8. Role–relationship
9. Sexuality–reproduction
10. Coping–stress tolerance
11. Value–belief (NANDA-I, 2007)

Although the more commonly used nursing diagnoses tend to be problem oriented only, nurses help clients to enhance their health and address potential health concerns. Nursing diagnoses focusing on enhancing wellness and preventing potential health problems enable nurses to focus on client strengths and use them to improve client health. Nursing diagnoses have created a language for professional nurses. Because of its esoteric nature and rigid formatting, other professionals (especially physicians) find nursing diagnostic terminology confusing and view it as an impediment to effective interprofessional communication in and across health care settings (Gordon, 2005; Finkelmann & Kenner, 2007; Webber, 2008). Failure of members of the interprofessional health team members to communicate with each other has resulted in errors (sometimes fatal) in health care delivery (Finkelman & Kenner). In a systematic review of the published literature on nursing diagnoses, Müller-Staub, Lavin, Needham, and von Achtenberg (2006) outlined the following benefits of using nursing diagnoses: improved quality of client assessments, increased client satisfaction, and improved documentation of assessments. However, the literature review failed to provide substantiated evidence that the use of nursing diagnoses in clinical practice resulted in improved client outcomes.

In recent years, some nurses perceive nursing diagnosis as a highly esoteric and rigid method to identify and communicate client health issues. Specific rules presented in Table 7-3 may limit independent thinking, especially in client care situations that fall outside of a typical nursing care situation. Professional nurses may use nursing diagnostic statements when following standardized clinical paths and when generating computerized care plans. Some agencies promote the use of nursing diagnoses when nurses give end-of-shift reports to each other. However, in reality, professional nurses rarely use nursing diagnositic statements when communicating to each other (Webber, 2008). They never use them when communicating client problems to other interprofessional health team members because nursing diagnoses tend to describe something very simple using complex, circular language. Safe, effective health care requires that communication among health team members be clear, concise, and understood by all.

The Planning Step

Once a comprehensive list of nursing diagnoses has been generated, professional nurses develop a plan of care to communicate specific client care needs to nursing personnel so that desired outcomes are attained. Care plans guide and direct client care efforts to ensure continuity of care when different nurses assume client care responsibilities. In addition, care plans designate specific interventions to meet client care goals. Finally, nursing care plans outline contributions that nurses make to client health care delivery.

Nurses follow certain guidelines to generate effective nursing care plans. When planning client care, nurses establish a set of nursing diagnoses in priority order, designate desired nursing goals and client outcomes, and prescribe specific nursing interventions.

Nurses set priorities based on preserving client functional status (except in the terminally ill), promoting client comfort, and meeting mutually agreed-on client goals.

Because of the need to streamline care and improve client outcomes, some nurses rely on standardized care plans. Standardized nursing care plans provide less variance in care delivered to clients with similar health problems. They address all critical assessments and customary interventions for medical therapies, invasive procedures, and diagnostic tests. When nurses follow standardized care plans, they may forget to include clients in care decisions or neglect client preferences.

The nursing care plan includes the priorities and the prescribed nursing interventions to achieve desired goals (the global desired state) derived from the nursing diagnoses. Ideally, nurses and clients work together to develop desired goals and outcomes of nursing care. Once goals are defined, specific outcomes can be generated. Outcomes are end results that, when measured, determine client progress toward resolution of the nursing diagnosis. These expected outcomes must be realistic and stated clearly and concisely as they provide the basis for evaluating nursing care plan effectiveness. Broad guidelines for goal setting in selected nursing models are presented in Table 7-4. Because the nursing models vary, the foci of nursing goals differ.

Nursing Outcomes Classification

The **Nursing Outcomes Classification (NOC)** provides an alternative approach to delineating client outcomes. Since the 1990s, increased importance has been placed on determining the effectiveness of nursing care. To meet this challenge of developing measurable client outcomes, nurse researchers at the University of Iowa developed NOC, a research-based classification of nursing care outcomes. Currently, NOC provides nurses with more than 200 scales to measure outcomes of holistic nursing care. For example, NOC has a scale to measure personal safety behaviors. Nurses can use this scale to identify client risk for injury. After client education about personal safety or correction of metabolic disorders, nurses can reassess the client using the scale to determine if improvement in behavior has occurred. NOC facilitates the development of computerized information systems for tracking nursing care outcomes across health care settings. NOC

TABLE 7-4

Broad Guidelines for Goal Setting in Selected Nursing Models Organized by Theoretical Frameworks

Nursing Models	Broad Guidelines for Goal Setting
Systems Theory	
King	Achievement of goals and solution of problems related to personal, interpersonal, and social systems
Newman	Maintenance or restoration of dynamic equilibrium by reducing stressor penetration or strengthening the normal line of defense
Stress/Adaptation	
Roy	Promotion of adaptation from successful coping
Caring	
Orem	Restoration of external and internal constancy
Watson	Meeting human needs and solving problems in a caring interpersonal relationship
Complexity	
Rogers	Help people design ways to attain optimal rhythmic patterns
Parse	Illuminating meaning, synchronizing rhythms, and mobilizing transcendence
Newman	Transformation of patterns of life and facilitation of evolving consciousness
Leddy	Mutual process to define meaningful goals to attain an optimal pattern of the whole

also facilitates comparable data collection, substantiates nursing care contributions, creates uniform nursing data sets, provides nurses with outcome measurement tools, facilitates electronic documentation of client care, improves reimbursement for nursing services, and standardizes ways nurses can evaluate nursing care innovations. Through the process of determining measurable, standardized outcomes, professional nurses clearly articulate the contributions they make to client care while developing a unique body of nursing knowledge (Johnson, Maas, & Moorhead, 2000).

Not all nurses use the NOC in clinical practice. However, the planning phase requires that goals, objectives, or outcomes are determined within the client plan of care. After the goals and outcomes for care have been established, priorities must be set among them. When survival is threatened, physical needs must take precedence. Cost, available personnel and resources, and time may influence priorities. For example, for the overweight student who has a broken leg, weight loss may be considered an important goal, but because of the time needed to accomplish substantial weight loss, it may be assigned a lower priority than learning how to use crutches, which is needed immediately for mobility. The theory or model being used to organize care also can influence determination of priorities. For example, use of Maslow's (1962) theory would assign higher priority to physiologic, safety, and security needs, and lower priority to love, self-esteem, and self-actualization needs. In addition, as always, the client must be closely involved in priority setting.

Once the priorities among goals and outcomes have been determined, alternative options for care can be generated and their probability for success predicted. The possible solutions or approaches are heavily influenced by availability of resources and by factors in the client's lifestyle and cultural background. For example, the student's weight loss could be achieved by 2 weeks of residence at a health spa, or a self-monitored weight reduction program consisting of weighing portions of food and following a prescribed exercise program. However, financial constraints may make the spa trip unfeasible, and time and lifestyle constraints may influence the desirability of the exercise or food-weighing approaches. With NOC, nurses working with the client would look at adherence to the outlined dietary regimen, compliance, knowledge and use of health-promoting behaviors, knowledge about prescribed diet, and specific weight control behaviors along with weight reduction measurements. The NOC provides a standardized method to track client progress toward care objectives across inpatient, community, and home settings (Johnson et al., 2000).

Unfortunately, today's nurses care for increased numbers of clients with higher levels of acuity. Time pressures prevent them from developing multiple approaches to address client situations (Gordon, 2005; Finkelman & Kenner, 2007). As a result, nurses quickly generate a plan of care without taking the time to analyze interventions for appropriateness and likelihood of success in the particular clinical situation. Time constraints, an instilled belief in a single best way for goal attainment, and the need for rapid closure result in a tendency for nurses to avoid collaborative brainstorming.

Nurses must make conscious efforts to avoid choosing a prescribed "cookbook recipe" approach to delineating care outcomes. To preserve nursing as a collaborative partnership with clients, the nurse and client together must select from alternative goals that have the best likelihood of success within a specific nursing situation. The individualized and collaborative approach then can be translated into specific actions, the desired frequency of the actions, who will be assigned to carry them out (e.g., the nurse, the client, or other health team members), and the timetable for expected achievements.

Along with the establishment of goals, outcomes (or objectives) for nursing care, the nursing care plan outlines specific nursing interventions. **Nursing interventions** are actions nurses take to attain care goals and outcomes. Frequently, nursing students find written nursing care plans challenging and complex. Recently, some nurse educators have replaced traditional nursing process papers (that include written care plans) with concept mapping, which enables students to make connections among multiple nursing diagnoses, pathophysiology nursing interventions, and desired client outcomes (Fonteyn,

2007; Rubenfeld & Scheffer, 2006; Schuster, 2002; Shelton, 2008; Taylor & Wros, 2007). Unlike practicing nurses, student care plans usually require written rationales for proposed nursing interventions. However, conscientious nurses take time to reflect and recall rationales behind clinical interventions. For each nursing diagnosis, nurses determine priority lists for each identified nursing diagnosis, determine expected outcomes and goals, and prescribe specific interventions (with established frequencies and time for each action). Computerized software for care plan generation offers nurses a series of checklists to complete individualized care plans.

As part of the care plan, the nurse can prescribe independent interventions (those not requiring a physician order, such as using a pillow under a client's foot to keep the heels off the mattress), designate collaborative interventions (those requiring a physician order, such as the administration of prescription medications), and outline specific interventions to screen for potential complications associated with medical or surgical treatments. Ideally, another nurse should be able to follow the care plan exactly as written by the nurse who developed it. Nurses can find published care plans in books, in journal articles, in computer programs, and on the Internet.

Nursing Interventions Classification

In 1987, the University of Iowa developed the **Nursing Interventions Classification (NIC)** system as a means to standardize all possible nursing interventions. NIC contains over 486 standard nursing interventions and outlines 12,000 nursing activities. Most interventions contain 10 to 30 specific activities that include information related to assessing and assisting clients in managing health-related issues, maintaining safe care environments, providing client and family education, offering psychosocial and spiritual support, engaging in consultation with professionals, and referring clients to community support services. NIC facilitates nursing professionalism by standardizing nursing treatment nomenclature; strengthening links between nursing knowledge, diagnoses, interventions, and outcomes; facilitating electronic documentation of nursing care; assisting in determining costs and resources needed for nursing interventions; providing a theoretical foundation to help beginning nurses learn clinical decision making; and increasing nursing-specific knowledge (McCloskey & Bulechek, 2000).

To explicate the use of NIC and compare it to traditional nursing process, the example of a client on a weight reduction plan continues. The NIC contains two interventions related to weight reduction and management. The NIC uses the label "weight reduction assistance" for the nursing intervention for the following nursing diagnosis: alteration in nutrition: more than body requires, related to reduced activity secondary to nonbearing weight status for fractured leg. Nursing activities for the intervention include assessment of eating patterns, reasons for overconsumption, and weekly weight determinations. Development of weight loss goals, an exercise program, and a daily eating plan with the client appears as a nursing activity. Teaching activities include appropriate energy-expending activities, nutritional needs to promote fracture healing without increasing caloric intake, and calculation of fat content in food. Food selections to stay within predetermined daily caloric limit when eating out or participating in social gatherings also appear as a desired client outcome. The NIC suggests other tips, such as posting weekly weight loss goals in a strategic location (such as the refrigerator), charting weight loss weekly, referring to community weight reduction support groups, and rewarding the client for meeting goals. Because NIC designates a framework for nursing interventions that can be computer coded (and clients can be charged for them), NIC use in clinical practice has become standard practice in some health care organizations. Evaluation of the care plan occurs by using NOC (McCloskey & Bulechek, 2000).

Client Care Paths

Since the 1990s, many acute care and outpatient centers have developed client care paths. The nursing care plan for commonly encountered human responses to a specific illness, surgery, or procedure and potential complications is outlined on the client care path. Client care paths have reduced variation of nursing care received by clients with the same clinical problem, streamlined care to reduce costs, reduced care errors and oversights (health team members become specialists in care protocols), and decreased the time nurses spend in documentation (paths frequently contain checklists, instead of requiring nurses to write detailed narrative notes). Clients receive a copy of the care path so they can track progress toward health restoration. In addition, care paths outline specific instructions to follow when they assume self-care responsibilities. Most care paths have methods to accommodate instances when care delivery fails to follow the path exactly because of an unexpected client response. Criticisms of care paths include reduced individualization of client care plans and decreased critical thinking by nurses because of feeling the need to follow the path exactly as outlined.

The Implementation Step

During implementation, nurses execute proposed nursing care plans. Nursing actions support and complement the medical plan of care. Ideally, professional nurses use interventions based on scientific evidence. For successful care plan implementation, nurses use the following skills: teaching clients (and significant others), managing others, facilitating group process, resolving conflicts, performing technical skills, and, above all, communicating effectively with others.

All client–nurse interactions should be goal directed and purposeful. As nursing actions are performed, nurses collaborate with the clients and their significant others to involve them appropriately in the care. Nurses perform interventions with sensitivity to the client's feelings and individual preferences in mind. Conceptual models play a role in the organization of nursing care. Table 7-5 outlines how conceptual models may be used to organize care along with possible implications for nursing interventions.

TABLE 7-5

Implications for Nursing Interventions in Selected Nursing Models Organized by Theoretical Frameworks

Nursing Models	Implications for Nursing Interventions
Systems Theory	
King	Emphasis is on exploration of the situation, shared information, mutually set goals, and explored means to resolve problems, achieve goals, and move forward.
Neuman	Emphasis is on primary, secondary, or tertiary prevention to reduce stressors or strengthen the lines of defense.
Stress/Adaptation	
Roy	Emphasis is on increasing, decreasing, or maintaining focal contextual, or residual stimuli.
Caring	
Orem	Emphasis is on self-care actions for or with the client if he is unable to perform them for himself.
Watson	Emphasis is on caring that reflects interpersonal teaching–learning, mutual formulation of the problem, joint appraisals, shared need for problem solving, joint planning, provision of cognitive information, and evaluation of helpfulness for learning and coping.
Complexity	
Rogers	Emphasis is on mobilization of the client's resources and repatterning of the human–environment interaction.
Parse	Emphasis is on guidance to relate the meaning of the client's situation, to share thoughts and feelings with one another, and to change the meaning of the situation by making it more explicit.
Newman	Emphasis is on the process of growth in which the nurse focuses on the client's evolving capacities, diversity, and complexity in the process of expanding consciousness.
Leddy	Emphasis is on the mutual process of transforming energy to create change.

An important part of implementation is the documentation of the results of nursing interventions. Documentation provides a means to track client progress toward desired outcomes as well as a legal record of rendered health care services. More importantly, documentation serves as a key method for communication among interprofessional health team members. Nurses continually assess clients to determine responses to nursing interventions. When interventions are determined to be ineffective, the nurse revises the nursing care plan. Changes in a client's condition may mean an alteration in the frequency of prescribed interventions, modification of the current one, prescription of new ones, or consultation with another health care professional. The process of intervention is integrally involved with the final phase of nursing process, evaluation.

The Evaluation Step

During evaluation, nurses and clients collaborate to determine if progress is being made toward the attainment of the health-related goal in ideal client care situations. Processes included in the evaluation of care include reassessment, reviewing and reordering (if necessary) care priorities, establishing new goals, and revision of the care plan. Evaluation occurs continuously throughout each phase of the nursing process. However, during evaluation, the main purpose is to compare changes in client behavior or health status with the determined goals or expected outcomes specified in the nursing care plan. Results of evaluation may reveal one or a combination of the following:

1. Goals and outcomes were fully met and future client contacts are needed to reaffirm that the health status change remains permanent.
2. Goals and outcomes were partially met, revealing that the health problem or desired health status change has not been resolved. However, progress continues. Continued monitoring is warranted; more time may be needed with the current plan before considering modification.
3. Goals and outcomes were not met. The client has little or no evidence of change in health status or health problem since the initial assessment. The care plan needs revision.
4. New problems have emerged and the entire care plan needs to be revised to address them.

Because not all client-related health goals are amenable to quantification, nurses sometimes have difficulty finding valid and reliable tools to objectively measure progress toward some goals. It may be helpful to consider whether there are appropriate tools to measure progress toward goals when the goals are established. For example, weight loss and blood pressure reduction are easily validated. However, it is difficult to assess improved self-concept or attitudes toward a more healthful lifestyle. Sources for instruments to measure progress may be found in NOC, journal articles, websites, and instrument handbooks. However, not all goals may be effectively quantified.

Because the nursing process is systematic, logical, and goal directed, it is assumed that adherence to the process will result in desired attainment of goals. When evaluation of progress indicates that the problem is not resolved, it is necessary to consider possible reasons. Nurses explore possible reasons by collaborating with clients, their significant others, and members of the interprofessional health care team. Depending on the outcome of evaluation, the nurse and client may need to modify the goals or interventions, continue the planned strategies with a modified timetable, or, if the goals have been met and no new ones have emerged, terminate the relationship. Both the client and the nurse may have difficulty terminating the relationship. Clients may be unsure of their ability to maintain the changes in health behavior or well-being status on their own. The nurse may have ambivalence about not being needed any longer. Awareness and an open sharing of these feelings can lead to satisfaction in having accomplished the desired goals and acceptance of the need to end the relationship.

Despite the extensive attention given to nursing process, many nurses continue to intervene using standardized procedures based on medical diagnoses. Perhaps nursing process may not be how experienced nurses practice. Efforts to standardize client care have resulted in the development of client care paths. In many institutions, professional nurses helped develop client care paths that incorporate nursing assessments and interventions to address commonly encountered nursing diagnoses for specific health problems. These nurses tend to engage in rote practice.

However, when nurses use nursing models to guide care, they engage in critical thinking because models provide solid reasoning behind clinical practice. In the following section, two brief examples illustrate that nurses can approach the nursing process differently when they use conceptual nursing models to guide practice.

Questions for Reflection 7-2

1. How does my clinical practice setting promote or discourage the use of nursing process in clinical practice?
2. What are the barriers to developing individualized nursing care plans for clients in my current practice setting?
3. Why do I perceive these as barriers?
4. How could I change the practice setting to facilitate individualization of client care?
5. What are the consequences of not individualizing client care in practice?

Conceptual Models Emphasizing the Nursing Process

Roy and Neuman have addressed nursing process specifically in their nursing models. Instead of keeping with the five-step process, they refined it. Roy (Roy & Andrews, 1999) kept nursing process focused on nursing practice, whereas Neuman (Neuman & Fawcett, 2002) proposed use of nursing process for all health care professionals because it is based on the scientific method.

The Roy Adaptation Model

In the Roy adaptation model, the goal of nursing is to promote adaptation. The nurse manipulates stimuli to move the client in the desired direction of change toward adaptation. The process of nursing is described as a six-step problem-solving method (Roy & Andrews, 1999).

1. First-level assessment: Examine client behaviors in the adaptation modes and make a judgment about whether behaviors in the four modes are adaptive or ineffective.
2. Second-level assessment: Analyze stimuli that influence ineffective behaviors and determine nursing care priorities.
3. State problem areas as nursing diagnoses.
4. Determine specific goals.
5. Determine interventions.
6. Evaluate as behavior changes, and modify as needed.

The Neuman Systems Model

In the Neuman systems model, the purpose of nursing action is "to best retain, attain and maintain optimal client health or wellness using the three preventions as intervention to keep the system stable" (Neuman & Fawcett, 2002, p. 25). Client stability depends upon the depth of stressor penetration. Nurses assess for actual and potential effects of environmental stressors before making judgments of taking action. Neuman proposed a modification of the nursing process to incorporate the following three steps:

1. Determine a nursing diagnosis.
2. Establish nursing goals.
3. Determine nursing outcomes with interventions classified as primary (wellness retention), secondary (attainment of health), or tertiary (maintenance of health) prevention (Neuman & Fawcett, 2002).

Benefits and Criticisms of the Nursing Process

The American Nurses Association, the National Council of State Boards of Nursing, and other nurse specialty organizations incorporate the five phases of nursing process in professional nursing practice standards. Many professional nurses use nursing process daily in clinical practice and many organizations have documentation forms based on the steps of nursing process. Research has demonstrated that nurses hold a relatively positive attitude toward the nursing process (Martin et al., 1994). In addition, nursing process provides an organized way of thinking about client care and fosters deliberate nursing actions.

However, some nurses report that they do not use nursing process in daily practice (Webber, 2008). Benner (1994) suggested that many nursing experts do not follow the steps of nursing process as they engage in professional nursing practice. Henderson (1987), Lindsey and Hartrick (1996), Rew (1996), Varcoe (1996), and Webber (2008) offered the following concerns that the nursing process:

1. Is inconsistent with real-world practice because it is a linear, rational problem-solving process.
2. Is focused on problems rather than client strengths and potential.
3. Is time-consuming and requires elaborate nursing jargon for its use.
4. Prefers rules over interaction.
5. Is antithetical to a holistic approach to client care.
6. Labels clients by nursing diagnoses.
7. Minimizes disallowance of nursing intuition.
8. Is a questionable approach for expert nursing practice.

The formulaic structure of the nursing process has been useful to teach rules to novice learners. However, many nurses treat the nursing process as if it were the only process in nursing practice. Research has demonstrated that the nursing process is inadequate "when sensory data are changing rapidly or are ambiguous, uncertain, or conflicting" (Rew, 1996). Interestingly, a relationship between critical thinking ability and professional competence has not been demonstrated (Maynard, 1996). In addition, Benner, Tanner, and Chesla (1996) found that clinically proficient and expert nurses use intuitive cognitive processes, rather than rule-based thinking, to make clinical judgments.

Integrated Models for Clinical Judgment

Along with nursing process, nurses use other models to make clinical judgments. Benner and colleagues (1996) suggested that "the clinical judgment of experienced nurses resembles much more [the] engaged, practical reasoning ... than the disengaged, scientific, or theoretical reasoning ... represented in the nursing process" (p. 1). Experienced nurses tend to bypass some steps of nursing process, whereas novice nurses comply with each of the five steps.

Intuition

Studies of expert clinical practice have identified intuition, knowing the patient, and reflection as important characteristics. **Intuition** has been described as "another way of knowing wherein facts or truths are known or felt directly rather than arrived at through a linear process of rational analysis" (Rew, 1996, p. 149), or as "an instantaneous, direct grasping of reality" (Mishlove, 1994, p. 32). In a study that supported the novice-to-expert model, Polge (1995) found that "as the level of nursing proficiency increases from advanced beginner to expert, there is a significant increase in the use of intuitive critical thinking to make clinical nursing judgments" (p. 8). Young (1987) proposed that intuition is multidimensional. The functional dimension of intuition is composed of cues and judgment, in which actions do not have a logical link with data. Intuition as a personal way of knowing relies on direct patient contact, self-receptivity, experience, energy, and self-confidence. Many nurses have saved lives by acting on intuitive feelings. In some cases, physicians have been known to come and see hospitalized clients because the nurse identified intuition as the reason for contacting the physician.

Questions for Reflection 7-3

1. How have I used intuition to guide personal or professional actions?
2. What were the consequences of using intuition in the situation(s) identified above?
3. What advice would I give to someone about using intuition to guide action?
4. Would the advice I give be different for a professional colleague than if I were giving it to a friend? Why or why not?

Reflection

Reflection is a process of thinking about concerns associated with an experience. Reflection develops the affective domain of learning and allows nurses to relate to the aspects of their experience that are the most profound at the time. Consequently, reflection has the potential to provide for personal growth. Reflective learning is multidimensional and may be triggered by a sense of inner discomfort. When things do not go according to plan, nurses engage in reflection to identify and clarify concerns surrounding a clinical situation. Effective reflection requires that the nurse be open to new information that may arise from non-empirical sources. Sometimes reflection results in the resolution (or "aha moment") in confounding situations, or with the feeling that one has learned something that is personally significant. Reflection may result in profound changes in attitudes or behaviors.

The Pew Health Professions Commission (1998) identified reflection as one essential skill that health professionals must be able to perform along with critical thinking and rational problem solving. Health care professionals need to develop skills in reflective and critical thinking to identify and respond to new situations and practice dilemmas. Professionals also use reflection during practice and afterward to evaluate professional performance. Schon (1987) identified two ways in which professionals use reflection: reflection-in-action, and reflection-on-action. During **reflection-in-action**, health care practitioners think about the purposes and reasons behind actions being performed. **Reflection-on-action** thinking is a self-evaluative process in which practitioners analyze personal performance in a given clinical situation, think of what could have been done better, and determine plans to improve performance the next time a similar clinical situation is encountered.

Brookfield (1995, p. 8) proposed that reflection becomes critical reflection when it "questions assumptions and practices" as well as seeks to understand power forces behind current practice. Reflection also provides opportunities for professionals to find meaning in practice (Brookfield, 1995; Schon, 1987). Reflection takes time to master, especially in today's fast-paced society. A variety of means help persons to develop skills in reflection, including writing one's autobiography, keeping professional logs, auditing self-performance, constructing criteria for role model profiles, developing survival advice memos, videotaping oneself in professional action, having peer evaluations, identifying critical incidents, and engaging in meaningful dialogues with others (Brookfield, 1995).

A Research-Based Model of Clinical Judgment

Tanner (2006) reviewed over 200 studies that addressed clinical judgments made by nurses in practice that substantiate the use of intuition and reflection by professional nurses. Professional nurses bring knowledge and experience to clinical practice situations. As nurses gain more experience, they learn to identify patterns that indicate impending deterioration in client status requiring rapid action. Quick pattern identification occurs rapidly and sometimes intuitively. When nurses work in clinical settings, most typically reflect upon what they are currently doing and the outcomes of interventions. When a situation fails to unfold as planned, many nurses review their actions (or lack of action) to see what went wrong. Thus, reflection-on-action becomes a mechanism for nurses to refine clinical practice strategies. According to Tanner (2006), what nurses bring to practice situations may be more important than the objective data available to the nurse when clinical judgments are made. Within the practice context, experienced nurses notice (i.e., perceptually grasp) the global situation. Nurses interpret the situation by using reasoning, pattern identification, analysis, intuition, and personal narratives. After the nurses interpret the situation, they respond by taking action to help clients. Immediately following action, they assess the client outcomes. The process of interpreting and responding requires reflection-in-action. The final step in the clinical judgment model is reflecting, in which the nurse reflects-on-action and solidifies knowledge learned from the clinical experiencee.

Effective professional nurses constantly engage in complex thinking processes while performing basic nursing care tasks. Research Brief 7-1 provides an example of cognitive processes nurses use when administering medications.

Research Brief 7-1

Eisenauer, L., Hurley, A., & Dolan, N. (2007). Nurses' reported thinking during medication administration. *Journal of Nursing Schaolarship*, *39*(1), 82–87.

The investigators wanted to document nurse reports of the thinking process used while administering medications prior to and after implementation of barcode/MAR, a computerized point-of-care medication administration system. Forty nurses employed in inpatient units of a large tertiary-care teaching hospital participated in the study. Data were collected using semistructured interviews and nurse recordings of their thinking while they administered medications.

The following categories of professional nurse thinking were identified (listed highest to lowest in frequency): communication (sharing client data with others to verify safe administration), dose time (making a judgment about the timing of prn medications), checking (verifying the appropriateness and correctness of part of the medication administration process), assessment (monitoring key client signs and symptoms to substantiate the need for the medication), evaluation (determining if the desired therapeutic effects were obtained), teaching (providing the client or family information about the need for the ordered medication and strategies for safe use), side effects (monitoring the client for potential adverse effects), work around (determining ways to bypass the standard protocols for medication administration for either the client's benefits or the nurse's convenience), anticipatory problem solving (considering the best future course of events based on client responses, scheduled diagnostic testing, or invasive medical interventions), and drug administration (determining the best way to actually give the medication). The investigators found no changes in nurse thinking after the implementation of the barcode/MAR medication delivery system.

The results of this study reveal that there is much more than just the psychomotor skills to administer medication safely to clients. Nurses must also use their cognitive skills, including knowledge and assessment processes, to safely deliver medications to clients and monitor them for potentially adverse effects and desired therapeutic effects. When giving medication, nurses must be vigilant to the task at hand and minimize interruptions and multitasking. Findings of this study should be interpreted with caution because of the small sample size, fast-paced nature of acute care nursing, and potential failure of some of the nurses to share all key thinking related to medication administration. More study needs to be done to determine the depth of knowledge and cognitive processes needed for safe medication administration across the health care delivery continuum.

Intuition and reflection are professional nursing processes that integrate experience with cognition. Cognitive processes receive more attention during discussions related to nursing process, intuition, and reflection. Without attention to interpersonal processes, nursing practice may become impersonal, dominated by technology, and self-serving. Therefore, the next section showcases interpersonal processes as guided by selected nursing conceptual models and theories.

INTERPERSONAL PROCESSES

The practice of professional nursing cannot occur without the use of interpersonal processes. The nurse–client relationship (which may perhaps be the most important aspect of nursing practice) requires that nurses use interpersonal processes. **Interpersonal processes** can be defined as interactions between two or more persons. The following content provides brief examples of different approaches used by selected nursing conceptual models and theories in the use of interpersonal processes.

King's Theory of Goal Attainment

In King's (1995) theory, the goal of nursing is to help individuals maintain their health so they can function in their roles. Nursing is a process of action, reaction, and interaction that results in goal attainment. Although the process proposed by this theory is classified according to the steps in the nursing process, the emphasis is on interpersonal processes within the steps. Assessment incorporates perception, communication, and interaction of the nurse and the client. Planning includes mutual determination of goals and agreement on means to attain them. Implementation is the process in which transactions are made. Finally, evaluation is the process in which nurses ask, "Was the goal attained?"

Peplau's Interpersonal Relations Model

In Peplau's model (Reed, 1996), nursing is a therapeutic, interpersonal process. Nurses use the interpersonal process as an educative instrument, a maturing force that aims to promote forward movement of the personality. The interpersonal process is the method by which nurses facilitate useful transformation of the client's energy or anxiety. The interpersonal process is based on a participatory relationship between the nurse and client, in which the nurse governs the purpose for and the process in the relationship and the client controls the content. The process consists of the following four phases.

1. Orientation: Clients become aware of the availability of and trust in the nurse's abilities.
2. Identification: The nurse facilitates expression of feelings without rejection.
3. Exploitation: The client derives the full value from the relationship.
4. Resolution: The client is gradually freed from identification with the helping professional. The client's ability to meet his or her needs is strengthened.

Paterson and Zderad's Humanistic Theory

In the humanistic nursing practice theory, nursing is perceived as a lived experience between human beings. "Nursing is a response to the human situation. One human being needs a kind of help and another gives it" (Paterson & Zderad, 1988, p. 11). The humanistic nursing effort is directed toward increasing the possibilities of making responsible choices. The process, which is labeled the "phenomenologic method of nursology" (science of nursing), consists of five phases.

Phase I: The nurse knower prepares for coming to know.
Phase II: The nurse intuitively knows the "other."
Phase III: The nurse scientifically knows the other by:

- Analyzing the situation.
- Considering relationships between components.
- Synthesizing themes or patterns.
- Conceptualizing or symbolically interpreting a sequential view of this post-lived reality.

Phase IV: The nurse complementarily synthesizes known others by:

- Comparing similarities and differences.
- Synthesizing the similarities and differences to create an increased knowing.

Phase V: Succession occurs within the nurse from the many to the paradoxical one—"a conception or abstraction that is inclusive of and beyond the multiplicities and contradictions" (Paterson & Zderad, 1988, p. 74).

Parse's Human Becoming Theory

In Parse's (1996) theory, the goal of practice is quality of life from the client's perspective, with the focus on the meaning constructed by the client. The nurse is present in a nonroutine, unconditional, loving way of being with the client. The full attention of the nurse is with the client "as they move beyond the moment." The methodology in this theory consists of three processes:

1. Explicating (illuminating meaning): making clear what is appearing now through languaging.
2. Dwelling with (synchronizing rhythms): giving of self over to the flow of the struggle in connecting–separating.
3. Moving beyond (mobilizing transcendence): propelling with visioned possibles in transforming.

Newman's Theory of Health as Expanding Consciousness

Newman described nursing as "caring in the human health experience" (Newman, 1994, p. 139). "The responsibility of the nurse is not to make people well, or to prevent their getting sick, but to assist people to recognize the power that is within them to move to higher levels of consciousness" (Newman, p. xv). The focus of nursing in this theory is the pattern of the whole that is clarified through a praxis (practice) method. The method starts with the establishment of a partnership with the client with a mutual goal of participating in an authentic relationship that requires meeting and forming connections. The nurse and client then form a shared consciousness that serves as the basis for increasing awareness. When client and nurse goals are met, they move apart. Each participant in the nursing encounter tells his or her story in his or her way.

The nurse is free to be authentic and fully present. "Awareness of being, rather than doing, is the primary mechanism of helping" (Newman, 1994, p. 104). To develop a sequential pattern over time, the nurse organizes data in chronological order as a narrative.

 ## PSYCHOMOTOR PROCESSES

In addition to cognitive and interpersonal processes, nursing care includes psychomotor processes. **Psychomotor processes** are defined as the manual dexterity, coordination, and ability to use equipment effectively while performing nursing procedures. Skill in the performance of physician-ordered, often invasive, disease- or problem-related interventions is a major emphasis in much of nursing clinical practice. Associate degree programs emphasize these technical aspects of nursing, whereas baccalaureate and higher degree programs focus on cognitive and interpersonal processes. Health care consumers and organizations expect nurses to have the ability to carry out complex procedures smoothly and efficiently.

PATTERNING NURSING PROCESSES

Patterning nursing processes use energy to enhance health and well-being. Patterning processes are more compatible with a unitary approach to nursing practice. Some complementary and alternative health care interventions incorporate manipulation of human–environment energy fields. Table 7-6 presents some noninvasive nursing interventions to promote self-patterning.

Rogers' Science of Unitary Human Beings

Nursing from an interaction perspective delineates structure in qualities and persons in the environments. Rogers' science of unitary human beings proposes that separations do not exist, but rather all things form a single constellation. Rogers (1988, 1992) specified that the purpose of nursing is to create optimal health and well-being for all persons. The science of unitary human beings defines health not as a separate state or as the result of lifestyle choices or an encounter with illness. Instead, health is viewed as "an index of field patterning" (Malinski, 1986, p. 27). "Pattern is concerned with qualities and is expressed by the map of the configuration of relationships" (Bartol & Courts, 2005, p. 114). Only manifestations of patterns can be accessed by humans (Leddy, 2004, 2006).

In Rogerian science, behavior patterns are viewed as manifestations of the human–environment field. Field manifestations may include lifestyle parameters, such as nutrition, work, and play; exercise; sleep–wake cycles; safety; interpersonal networks; and decelerated-accelerated field rhythms.

TABLE 7-6

Noninvasive Nursing Interventions to Promote Self-Patterning

Intervention	Example(s)
Imagery	Guided imagery in which client visualizes healing occurring
Relaxation	Progressive relaxation exercises or warm bath
Affirmations	Positive self-talk
Sound	Listening to 60 beats/second cycle music
Exercise	Yoga or Tai Chi
Wave modulation	Color or light therapy
Nutrition	Special diet or herbal, vitamin, or mineral supplements
Meaningful presence	Being with another
Humor	Clowning, sharing appropriate jokes
Authentic dialogue	Guided reminiscence
Wellness counseling	Health education
Therapeutic touch	Centering and altering energy fields
Movement therapy	Dance or imposed motions
Journaling	Diary writing or critical incident written records
Balancing	Finding balances between activity rest, work, and fun
Bibliotherapy	Reading self-help or inspirational literature
Body therapy	Acupressure, massage, or healing touch

Examples of field rhythm manifestations might include diversity (from greater to lesser), motion (from slower to seemingly continuous), time (from slower to timelessness), and creativity (from pragmatic to visionary). The client is a knowing participant in change in this model. Through being aware, having choices and the freedom to act intentionally, and being involved in creating changes, the client is a mutual participant with the nurse in the patterning process. A healing relationship is characterized by certain principles.

1. The focus is on strengths and skills.
2. Nurse and client are involved in creating changes and influencing outcomes.
3. Nurse and client are equal partners, but the client has the major responsibility for change decisions.
4. A balance of exchange or reciprocity occurs.
5. Presence and involvement or connectedness emerge.
6. Flow and harmony exist.

The patterning process has two phases, appraisal and deliberative patterning. The elements of appraisal in Phase 1 include:

1. Using multiple modes of awareness, including recognizing, being aware, and being sensitive
2. Tuning into a person's unique patterns
3. Appreciating manifestations of the human field in the form of experience, perception, and expressions
4. Constructing pattern knowing through synthesis
5. Verifying with the client

Phase 2 involves the mutual deliberative patterning of behavior, which is possible because of the integral connectedness of the person–environment. Although diversity is considered a norm, patterning of each individual is unique. Each individual has an intrinsic potential for growth, which can be identified through exploring the meaning of experiences for the individual. The client and nurse are viewed as connected, and the healing milieu is as important as the particular modality selected as a treatment. Because change is viewed as inevitable, the challenge is to reframe problems into opportunities for positive becoming. By tuning in to the client's rhythms, the nurse can help the client to free energy for self-patterning through a number of possible noninvasive interventions:

- Imagery
- Relaxation
- Affirmation
- Sound (music)
- Exercise
- Color/light (wave modalities)
- Nutrition (diet, vitamins, minerals, and herbs)
- Meaningful presence
- Humor
- Authentic dialogue (guided reminiscence)
- Wellness counseling (health education)
- Therapeutic touch (centering)
- Movement (dance, and imposed motion)
- Journal keeping
- Balance between activity and rest
- Bibliotherapy
- Acupressure
- Bodywork (massage, and touch for health)

The science of the unitary human being seems highly compatible with traditional and integrative approaches to health care. As clients become more aware of complementary and alternative health care treatments, professional nurses need the knowledge to help them make wise choices for health enhancement.

Questions for Reflection 7-4

1. How do I feel about using energy to promote healing and health?
2. Which of the patterning processes would I like to try to enhance my health? Why would I like to try this one?

SUMMARY AND SIGNIFICANCE TO PRACTICE

Cognitive, interpersonal, and patterning nursing processes provide methods by which the nurse sensitively and systematically approaches practice to achieve mutually determined health goals with the client. Nurses use a variety of cognitive skills (knowledge, nursing process, intuition, and reflection) when delivering client care. Critical thinking enables nurses to effectively use nursing cognitive processes in clinical practice. Although nursing process arises out of scientific foundations, nurses can be artistic when developing individualized client care plans. In addition to nurse cognitive processes, the nurse–patient relationship facilitates data collection (assessment) and collaborative goal setting between clients and nurses. and goal setting for nursing care plans. Recent efforts to standardize nursing diagnoses, outcomes, and interventions may interfere with the ability to provide individualized client care developed in partnership with clients. The use of interactive processes may provide enriching relationships for the client and the nurse because authenticity provides the basis for therapeutic partnerships. Patterning processes provide a complex holographic approach to nursing care, in which nurses focus on maximizing client human potential. The various nursing models and theories presented in the chapter guide nursing practice. However, the individual nurse decides the approaches and processes used to implement nursing care effectively and in collaboration with clients and interprofessional health team members.

FROM THEORY TO PRACTICE

1. Why is it important for professional nurses to use cognitive, interactive, and patterning processes when engaging in clinical practice?
2. Which of the professional nursing processes do you use most frequently in clinical practice? Why? What assumptions underlie your most frequently used professional nursing process?
3. Based on the vignette, how would you respond to the nursing student having difficulty using nursing process? Why is it so important that beginning nurses understand nursing process?
4. Obtain a clinical path (or standardized care plan) from a clinical setting. Analyze it for the presence of nursing process. Outline the rationale behind all the nursing interventions. Does the path facilitate all aspects of nursing care delivery? Why or why not?

WWW INTERNET EXERCISE

Read Phillipa O'Reilly's online article, "Barriers to Clinical Decision Making in Nursing." To access the article quickly, perform a Google search using the terms "Barriers to Clinical Decision Making in Nursing" and hit the "I Feel Lucky" tab, or do a basic Internet search using the search engine of your choice. The article is housed in a New South Wales, Australia, government website that does not permit a hyperlink. The article appears in the hospital policy section of St. Vincent's Hospital in Sydney, Australia.

1. What did you think of the article?
2. List the factors for effective decision making that you commonly use in your clinical practice.
3. List the factors that impede your decision making in your clinical practice.
4. Outline a plan to improve your clinical decision-making process.
5. Would you forward this article to a colleague? Why or why not?

INTERNET RESOURCES

Critical Thinking Consortium: http://www.criticalthinking.org.
California Academic Press: http://www.insightassessment.com.
North American Nursing Diagnosis Association-International (NANDA-I): http://www.nanda.org.
Center for Nursing Classification and Clinical Effectiveness: http://www.nursing.uiowa.edu/cncce.

REFERENCES

Bartol, G., & Courts, N. (2005). The psychophysiology of body mind healing. In B. Dossey, L. Keegan, & C. Guzzetta (Eds.), *Holistic nursing: A handbook for practice* (4th ed., pp. 111–133). Sudbury, MA: Jones & Bartlett.

Benner, P. (1984) *From novice to expert*. Menlo Park, CA: Addison-Wesley.

Benner, P., Tanner, C. A., & Chesla, C. A. (Eds.). (1996). *Expertise in nursing practice: Caring, clinical judgment, and ethics*. New York: Springer.

Brookfield, S. D. (1995). *Becoming a critically reflective teacher*. San Francisco: Jossey-Bass.

Eisenauer, L., Hurley, A., & Dolan, N. (2007). Nurses' reported thinking during medication administration. *Journal of Nursing Scholarship*, *39*(1), 82–87.

Facione, N. C., Facione, P. A., & Sanchez, C. A. (1994). Critical thinking disposition as a measure of competent clinical judgement: The development of the California Critical Thinking Disposition Inventory. *Journal of Nursing Education, 33*, 345–350.

Facione, P. A. (2006). *Critical thinking: What it is and why it counts*. Millbrae, CA: California Academic Press.

Facione, P. A., Facione, N. C., & Giancarlo, C. A. (1996). *The California Critical Thinking Disposition Inventory test manual*. Millbrae, CA: California Academic Press.

Finkelman, A., & Kenner, C. (2007). *Teaching IOM, implications of the Institute of Medicine reports for nursing education*. Silver Spring, MD: American Nurses Association.

Fonteyn, M. (2007). Concept mapping: An easy teaching strategy that contributes to understanding and may improve critical thinking. *Journal of Nursing Education*, *46*(5), 199–200.

Gordon, M. (1995). *Manual of nursing diagnosis, 1995–1996*. St. Louis, MO: Mosby-Year Book.

Gordon, S. (2005). *Nursing against the odds*. Ithaca, NY: Cornell University Press.

Henderson, V. (1987). Nursing process: A critique. *Holistic Nursing Practice, 1*, 7–18.

Johnson, M., Maas, M., & Moorhead, S. (2000). *Nursing outcomes classification (NOC)* (2nd ed.). St. Louis, MO: Mosby.

Kataoka-Yahiro, M., & Saylor, C. (1994). A critical thinking model for nursing judgment. *Journal of Nursing Education, 33*, 351–356.

King, I. M. (1995). The theory of goal attainment. In M. A. Frey & C. L. Sieloff (Eds.), *Advancing King's systems framework and theory of nursing* (pp. 23–32). Thousand Oaks, CA: Sage.

Leddy, S. (2004). Human energy: A conceptual model of unitary nursing science. *Visions: The Journal of Rogerian Scholarship*, *12*, 14–28.

Leddy, S. K. (2006). *Health promotion mobilizing strengths to enhance health, wellness, and well-being*. Philadelphia: F. A. Davis.

Lindsey, E., & Hartrick, G. (1996). Health-promoting nursing practice: The demise of the nursing process? *Journal of Advanced Nursing, 23*, 106–112.

Malinski, V. M. (1986). *Explorations on Martha Rogers' science of unitary human beings*. Norwalk, CT: Appleton-Century-Crofts.

Martin, P. A., Dugan, J., Freundl, M., Miller, S. E., Phillips, R., & Sharritts, L. (1994). Nurses' attitudes toward nursing process as measured by the Dayton Attitude Scale. *Journal of Continuing Education for Nurses, 25*, 35–40.

Maslow, A. H. (1962). *Toward a psychology of being*. Princeton, NJ: Van Nostrand.

Maynard, C. A. (1996). Relationship of critical thinking ability to professional nursing competence. *Journal of Nursing Education, 35*, 12–18.

McCloskey, J., & Bulechek, G. (2000). *Nursing interventions classification (NIC)* (3rd ed.). St. Louis, MO: Mosby.

Mishlove, J. (1994). Intuition: The source of true knowing. *Noetic Sciences Review, 29*, 31–36.

Müller-Staub, M., Lavin, M., Needham, I., & von Achtenberg, T. (2006). Nursing diagnoses, interventions and outcomes-application and impact on nursing practice: Systematic review. *Journal of Advanced Nursing, 56*(5), 514–531.

Neuman, B., & Fawcett, J. (2002). *The Neuman systems model* (4th ed.). Upper Saddle River, NJ: Prentice Hall.

Newman, M. A. (1994). *Health as expanding consciousness* (2nd ed.). St. Louis, MO: Mosby.

North American Nursing Diagnosis Association International (NANDA-I). (2007). *Nursing diagnoses: Definitions an classification, 2007–2008*. Philadephia: Author.

Parse, R. R. (1996). The human becoming theory: Challenges in practice and research. *Nursing Science Quarterly, 9*, 55–60.

Paterson, J. G., & Zderad, L. T. (1988). *Humanistic nursing*. New York: National League for Nursing.

Paul, R. (1993). *Critical thinking: What every person needs to survive in a rapidly changing world* (3rd ed.). Santa Rosa, CA: Foundation for Critical Thinking.

Pew Health Professions Commission. (1998). *Recreating health professional practice for a new century*. San Francisco: University of California, San Francisco Center for the Health Professions.

Polge, J. (1995). Critical thinking: The use of intuition in making clinical nursing judgments. *Journal of the New York State Nurses Association, 26*, 4–9.

Reed, P. G. (1996). Peplau's interpersonal relations model. In J. J. Fitzpatrick & A. L. Whall (Eds.), *Conceptual models of nursing: Analysis and application* (3rd ed., pp. 55–76). Stamford, CT: Appleton & Lange.

Rew, L. (1996). *Awareness in healing*. Albany, NY: Delmar.

Rogers, M. E. (1988). Nursing science and art: A prospective. *Nursing Science Quarterly, 1*, 99–102.

Rogers, M. E. (1992). Nursing science and the space age. *Nursing Science Quarterly, 5*, 27–34.

Roy, C., & Andrews, H. A. (1999). *The Roy adaptation model* (2nd ed.). Stamford, CT: Appleton & Lange.

Rubenfeld, M., & Scheffer, B. (2006). *Critical thinking tactics for nurses*. Sudbury, MA: Jones & Bartlett.

Schon, D. A. (1987). *Educating the reflective practitioner: Toward a new design for teaching and learning in the professions*. San Francisco: Jossey-Bass.

Schuster, P. (2002). *Concept mapping: A critical-thinking approach to care planning*. Philadelphia: F. A. Davis.

Shelton, D. (2008). Beyond tests: Other ways to evaluate learning. In B. Penn (Ed.), *Mastering the teaching role: A guide for nurse educators* (pp. 287–297). Philadelphia: F. A. Davis.

Tanner, C. (2006). Thinking like a nurse: A research-based model of clinical judgment in nursing. *Journal of Nursing Education, 45*(6), 204–211.

Taylor, J., & Wros, P. (2007). Concept mapping: A nursing model for care planning. *Journal of Nursing Education, 46*(5), 211–216.

Varcoe, C. (1996). Disparagement of the nursing process: The new dogma? *Journal of Advanced Nursing, 23*, 120–125.

Webber, P. (2008). Facilitating critical thinking and effective reasoning. In B. Penn (Ed.), *Mastering the teaching role: A guide for nurse educators* (pp. 361–384). Philadelphia: F. A. Davis.

Young, C. E. (1987). Intuition and nursing process. *Holistic Nursing Practice, 1*, 52–62.

CHAPTER 8

The Health Process and Self-Care of the Nurse

KEY TERMS AND CONCEPTS

Interaction world view

Disease

Illness

Sickness

Well-being

Wellness

Integration world view

Health promotion

Health protection

Alternative health practices

Complementary health practices

Lifestyle behavior change

Health patterning

Burnout

Health-enhancing techniques

LEARNING OUTCOMES

By the end of this chapter, the learner will be able to:

1 Differentiate wellness from health.

2 Distinguish illness from disease.

3 Compare and contrast the interaction and integration world views of health.

4 Identify factors that contribute to individual variability in wellness.

5 Describe how health/illness can be explained as a unitary concept.

6 Differentiate health protection from health promotion.

7 Outline strategies for changing lifestyle behaviors and health patterning.

8 Identify signs and symptoms of work-related stress, role underload, role overload, and burnout.

9 Describe strategies for managing work-related stress and enhancing personal wellness.

VIGNETTE

After an exhausting shift, two nurses, Michael and Jane, discuss how ironic it seems that they have worked all day to help others get better at the expense of their own health. Michael states, "The hospital doesn't seem to care about the health and well-being of the staff. We never have time to eat or even take bathroom breaks. Within a few months we will all be ready to occupy one of the beds." Jane continues the discussion, "You know, I have never thought about the toll this job is taking on my health. I wonder what we could do to make this place a more healthful place in which to work?"

Many nurses enter the nursing profession "to help people." Most persons have the perception that nurses help sick people. Because nurses are linked to the discipline of medicine, most people define health using the medical definition, "the absence of disease." Throughout history, persons outside of the medical field have characterized the nurse as the physician's handmaiden.

Curing diseases remains the major focus of medicine despite high costs and sometimes futile efforts. Recently, the public has become aware of the importance of disease prevention and health promotion. Reports on the role of nutrition and exercise in preventing debilitating and fatal illness permeate the airways, Internet, and printed media. Through roles designed to (1) promote health, (2) capitalize on the healthy outlook of people, and (3) reinforce their strengths, the nursing profession has the potential to change societal beliefs about health and health care delivery. Health promotion and patterning are essential nursing activities in all settings for nursing care (including acute care).

This chapter presents the interaction and the integration world views of health, organizing frameworks for alternate views of the concepts of health, well-being, wellness, disease, illness, and sickness. Later sections of the chapter consider models and nursing interventions for the protection, promotion, and patterning of health. Finally, strategies for nurses to attain optimal health are presented.

✦ WORLD VIEWS OF HEALTH

Basic philosophic assumptions about the nature of reality, including human beings and the human–environment relationship, are referred to as paradigms or world views. World views that have been described by nursing scholars include change/persistence (Hall, 1981), totality/simultaneity (Parse, 1987), particulate-deterministic/interactive-integrative/unitary-transformative (Newman, 1992), and reaction/reciprocal interaction/simultaneous action (Fawcett, 1993). Elements of these classifications have been synthesized into the interaction and integration world views of health, which are summarized in this chapter.

The Interaction World View

In the **interaction world view**, as in the totality world view (Parse, 1987), the human being usually is conceptualized as a whole, comprising parts who interacts with a physically separate environment. The environment exerts stressors on persons to which they must react. The interaction world view supports a belief in linear, predictable, and quantifiable cause-and-effect relationships.

In this world view, persons strive to maintain a balance or state of stability. Whenever the environment changes, persons must change. Environmental changes may pose threats for persons. Effective reactions to environmental changes result in personal changes without negative effects to well-being, wellness, or health. However, ineffective reactions to environmental changes may result in disease, illness, or sickness that affects personal well-being, wellness, or health.

Disease

Disease is a medical term consistent with the interaction world view. Benner, Tanner, and Chesla (1996) defined **disease** as a "dysfunction of the body" (p. 45). The objective of the physician is to classify observable changes in the body structure or function (signs) into a recognizable clinical syndrome. A correct label, or diagnosis, implies disease course and duration, communicability, prognosis, and appropriate treatment. Medical intervention is aimed at curing the disease. Many nursing interventions support and promote the medical regimen as nurses administer medications, perform treatments, encourage rest, and evaluate the effects of medical and nursing interventions.

Historically, diseases were believed to be attributable to one agent that in a sufficient dose caused certain predictable signs and symptoms. However, a variety of factors related to the person (host), agent, and environment increasingly are viewed as being interrelated in the cause and effective treatment of disease. All these interactions must be considered in determining a plan for care.

Illness

Illness is a subjective feeling of being unhealthy that may or may not be related to disease. A person may have a disease without feeling ill and may feel ill in the absence of disease. For example, a person may have hypertension (a disease), controlled with medication, diet, and exercise, and be symptom-free (no illness). Another person may have pain and feel ill but may not have an identifiable disease. What is important is how people feel and what they do because of those feelings.

Nursing intervention focuses on the human response to illness, the identification of reasons for symptoms, and efforts to decrease symptoms, if possible. In contrast, medical interventions focus on efforts to label and treat the symptoms and cure disease. When a person's illness is accepted by society and thus given legitimacy, it is considered "sickness."

Sickness

According to Twaddle and Hessler (1977), in a classic reference, **sickness** is "a status, a social entity usually associated with disease or illness, although it may occur independently of them" (p. 97). Once the person fulfills criteria for being sick, others condone various dependent behaviors that otherwise might be considered unacceptable. When working with persons who are sick, nursing roles focus upon assisting the persons until they can reassume responsibility for decision making or independent functioning.

Well-Being

Well-being is a subjective perception of vitality and feeling well that is a component of health within the interaction world view. Although well-being is a variable subjective trait, it can be described objectively, experienced, and measured. Experienced at the lowest degrees, people might feel ill. Experienced at the highest levels, people would perceive maximum satisfaction with life, understand what it means to be in harmony with the universe, and feel as though they have made a significant contribution to humanity. Thus, well-being status can be plotted on a continuum, as shown in Figure 8-1.

Health as Wellness

Health is difficult to define. Health is described in various sources as a value judgment, a subjective state, a relative concept, a spectrum, a cycle, a process, and an abstraction that cannot be measured objectively. In many definitions, physiologic and psychological components of health are dichotomized. Other subconcepts that might be included in definitions of health include environmental and social influences, freedom from pain or disease, optimum capability, ability to adapt, purposeful direction and meaning in life, and a sense of well-being.

In the interaction world view, health indicates the absence of disease and the presence of normal functioning in roles or tasks. In this book, health has been defined as a state or

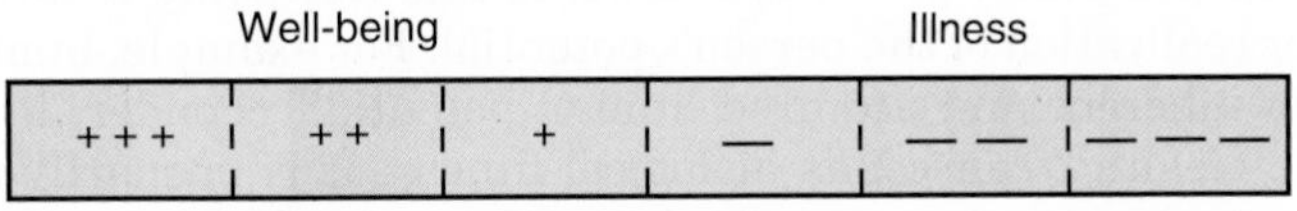

Figure 8-1
The well-being continuum. (Modified from Terris, M. (1975). Approaches to an epidemiology of health. *American Journal of Public Health, 65,* 1039. Used with permission from the publisher.)

condition of integrity of functioning (functional capacity and ability) and perceived well-being (feeling well). As a result, a person is able to:

- Function adequately (can be observed objectively).
- Adapt adequately to the environment.
- Feel well (as assessed subjectively).

Wellness, as defined in the literature, is similar to the open-ended and eudaimonistic models of health described in this chapter, and in this book will be considered synonymous with health. Dunn (1977), in his classic work on high-level wellness, described wellness as "an integrated method of functioning which is oriented toward maximizing the potential of which the individual is capable, within the environment where he is functioning" (p. 9). Others have characterized wellness–illness as "the human experience of actual or perceived function–dysfunction" (Jensen & Allen, 1994, p. 349). Indications of wellness (health) might include:

- A person's capacity to perform to the best of his or her ability.
- The ability to adjust and adapt to varying situations.
- A reported feeling of well-being.
- A feeling that "everything is together."

Smith (1981), in a seminal publication, presented four models of health consistent with the interaction world view that "can be viewed as forming a scale—a progressive expansion of the idea of health": the clinical model, the role performance model, the adaptive model, and the eudaimonistic model (p. 47).

The clinical model is the narrowest view. People are seen as physiologic systems with interrelated functions. Health is identified as the absence of signs and symptoms of disease or disability, as identified by medical science. Thus, health might be defined as a "state of not being sick" (Ardell, 1979, p. 18) or as a "relatively passive state of freedom from illness … a condition of relative homeostasis" (Dunn, 1977, p. 9). Much of the current health care delivery system, which is based on this model of health, is designed to deal with disease and illness after they occur. In the clinical model of health, the opposite end of the continuum from health is disease.

Next on the scale is the idea of health as role performance. This view adds social and psychological standards to the concept of health. The critical criterion of health is that the person has the ability to fulfill societal roles effectively. If a person becomes unable to perform expected roles, this inability can mean illness, even if the individual appears clinically healthy. For example, "Somatic health is … the state of optimum capacity for the elective performance of valued tasks" (Parsons, 1958, p. 168). In the role performance model of health, the opposite end of the continuum from health is sickness.

The adaptive model combines the clinical and role performance health models. In the adaptive model, health is perceived as a condition in which the person can engage in effective interaction with the physical and social environment. This model addresses continuous and simultaneous growth and change in persons and the environment. For example, McWilliam, Stewart, Brown, Desai, and Coderre (1996) defined health as "the individual's ability to realize aspirations, satisfy needs, and respond positively to the challenges of the environment" (p. 1). The adaptive model suggests that health may be a process rather than a state of being. In the adaptive model of health, the opposite end of the continuum from health is illness.

The eudaimonistic model provides an even more comprehensive conception of health than the previously presented views. In this viewpoint, health is a condition of actualization or realization of the person's potential. For example, human health is "the actualization of inherent and acquired human potential" (Pender, Murdaugh, & Parsons, 2002, p. 22). Health "transcends biological fitness. It is primarily a measure of each person's ability to do what he wants to do and become what he wants to become" (Dubos, 1978, p. 74). In the eudaimonistic model, health is consistent with high-level wellness and at the opposite end of the continuum from disabling illness.

Examples of nursing conceptual models that are consistent with the interaction world view are King's systems interaction model, Neuman's health care systems model, Roy's adaptation model, and Orem's self-care deficit model (see Chapter 6).

The Integration World View

In the **integration world view**, as in the simultaneity world view (Parse, 1987), the human being is considered to be a unitary, indivisible whole. Humans, although distinct, are embedded in and inseparable from their environment. Because the person is in mutual process, multiple "causes" and "effects" and nonlinear changes make prediction probabilistic and sometimes imprecise.

In this world view, the goal for people is to develop their potential toward increased diversity. Change is inevitable and provides an opportunity for growth. Health is viewed as a unitary pattern, with manifestations of health reflecting the whole of the human.

Disease and Illness as Manifestations of Health

In the integration world view, health is viewed as encompassing both disease and "non-disease" (Newman, 1994). Disease can be considered to be "a manifestation of health … a meaningful aspect of health" (Newman, 1994, p. 5) and "a meaningful aspect of the whole" (p. 7). Illness and health are viewed as a single process of ups and downs that are manifestations of varying degrees of organization and disorganization. Disputing that death is the antithesis of health, Newman (1994, p. 11) proposed that disease and nondisease are not opposites, but rather are complementary, to determine health, a unitary process. Illness, like health, simply represents a pattern of life at a particular moment. The tension characteristic of disease throws one off balance, which promotes growth toward a new level of evolving capacities, diversity, and complexity. The person may transform into a new pattern of being.

Therefore, health can be conceptualized as an actively continuing process that involves initiative, ability to assume responsibility for health, value judgments, and integration of the total person. It is a goal, a fluid process, rather than an actual state. Thus, health is difficult to quantify for objective evaluation. In clinical practice, nurses collaborate with clients while trying to help them attain optimal health. Nurses help clients by focusing on client strengths while getting them to acknowledge factors impeding growth toward maximal health potential. Client goals and feelings direct nursing interventions.

Nursing models and theories that are consistent with the integration world view include Rogers' science of unitary human beings, Parse's theory of human becoming, Neuman's theory of health as expanding consciousness, and Leddy's human energy model (see Chapter 6). These models and theories describe health as an evolving or emerging process, a forward movement with mutual person–environment patterns.

Questions for Reflection 8-1

1. Which of the following world views on health appeal to me the most?
2. Do I view health as a state or a process?
3. How do my views about health affect my professional practice?

HEALTH PROTECTION AND PROMOTION

Health promotion has been defined as "activities directed toward increasing the level of well-being and actualizing the health potential of people, families, community, and society" (Hravnak, 1998, p. 284). Pender et al. (2002) distinguished health promotion from disease prevention. According to Pender et al. (2002, 2005), health promotion is the process of increasing well-being and actualizing an individual's maximal health potential. Individual motivation plays an important role in health promotion. Whereas **health protection** focuses on efforts for active disease or injury avoidance, and early detection or optimal functioning within the confines of an illness, health promotion expands the potential for health.

Goals for Health Promotion and Protection

The U.S. health care system remains disease oriented, despite increased efforts toward health promotion and fitness. The United States spends more on health care than all other nations with the goal of curing and controlling illness. Health promotion, disease prevention, and health education receive less funding. Efforts for health education mainly address illness prevention. For example, children are taught to brush their teeth to avoid cavities (not because the mouth will feel, look, taste, and smell better) and to eat properly and exercise to prevent diabetes (rather than because they will feel better).

In 2000, the U.S. Department of Health and Human Services published *Healthy People 2010*. This report described national objectives for health promotion and disease prevention, including the following two major goals: "increase quality and years of healthy life" (p. 8) and "eliminate health disparities" (p. 11). The government report specified the following 28 focus areas for improvement in the health of American citizens:

1. Access to quality health services
2. Arthritis, osteoporosis, and chronic back conditions
3. Cancer
4. Chronic kidney disease
5. Diabetes
6. Disability and secondary conditions
7. Educational and community-based programs
8. Environmental health
9. Family planning
10. Food safety
11. Health communication
12. Heart disease and stroke
13. Human immunodeficiency virus
14. Immunization and infectious diseases
15. Injury and violence prevention
16. Maternal, infant, and child health
17. Medical product safety
18. Mental health and mental disorders
19. Nutrition and overweight
20. Occupational safety and health
21. Oral health
22. Physical activity and fitness
23. Public health infrastructure
24. Respiratory diseases
25. Sexually transmitted diseases
26. Substance abuse
27. Tobacco use
28. Vision and hearing (p. 17)

Because all these objectives specify illnesses, conditions, or injuries to be avoided, the plan represents an extensive program of health protection rather than health promotion. Unfortunately, since the implementation of *Healthy People 2010*, the rates of obesity, diabetes, and heart disease have continued to rise (Leddy, 2006; Logan, 2007; O'Keefe & O'Keefe, 2006).

In contrast, the United Nations Millennium Development Goals (UNMDG; 2002) appeared more health promoting. Papp (2007, p. 8) outlined the goals as follows:

- Eradication of extreme poverty and hunger
- Promotion of gender equality and empowerment for women
- Reduction of child mortality
- Improvement of maternal health
- Prevention and elimination of HIV/AIDS, malaria, and other infectious diseases

Most UNMDG relate to improving society and the general quality of life except for the fifth goal, thereby creating a world society capable of providing basic human needs for all persons, which should translate into improved health and well-being for all global citizens.

The concepts of health protection and promotion are consistent with the interaction world view. To guide nurses in interventions targeted for health promotion and protection, the next section discusses various models and strategies for use in clinical practice.

Questions for Reflection 8-2

1. Think about the last time you engaged in clinical practice. Write down examples of when your practice focused on health protection. Write down examples of when your practice focused on health promotion. Why is it important for professional nurses to engage in client health protection and promotion?
2. Do I have any of the unhealthy conditions or habits outlined in the *Healthy People 2010* initiatives? How can I work to become a role model of health for my clients?

Models for Changing Lifestyle Behavior

Health Belief Model

Why do people behave in certain ways in certain situations? What kinds of nursing intervention would be most effective in modifying a person's behavior to reduce risk of disease? Rosenstock (1966), in his "health belief" model, which still applies in today's health care situations, included the following factors:

1. Perceived susceptibility: the client's perception of the likelihood of experiencing a particular illness
2. Perceived severity: the client's perception of the seriousness of the illness and its potential impact on his or her life
3. Benefits of action: the client's assessment of the potential of the health action to reduce susceptibility or severity
4. Perceived threat of disease
5. Costs of action: the client's estimate of financial costs, time and effort, inconvenience, and possible side effects, such as pain or discomfort
6. Cues that trigger health-seeking behaviors, such as information in newspapers or on television; internal signals, such as symptoms; and interpersonal relationships with the health care provider and significant others

The health belief model, called a "rational model," explains how persons work toward improving their general well-being and health. The model assumes that all persons value well-being and that differences vary according to differing perceptions in interactions and motivation. Kasl and Cobb (1966) extended the basic model by specifying a relatively positive variable, the "perceived importance of health matters," in addition to perceived value and perceived threat. Becker and Maiman (1975) expanded the model further by

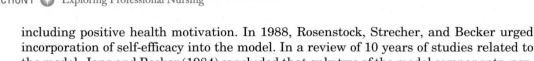

including positive health motivation. In 1988, Rosenstock, Strecher, and Becker urged incorporation of self-efficacy into the model. In a review of 10 years of studies related to the model, Janz and Becker (1984) concluded that only two of the model components, perceived barriers and perceived susceptibility, explained or predicted preventive behaviors. Perceived susceptibility has been found to be strongly related to compliance with medical advice (Vincent & Furnham, 1997).

Revised Pender Health Promotion Model

The health promotion model (HPM; Pender, Murdaugh, & Parsons, 2002, 2005) was developed in the early 1980s and has undergone several revisions based on research findings. The HPM provides a framework for combining professional nursing and behavioral science outlooks on various determinants of health behaviors. Pender categorized the determinants of health-promoting behavior into cognitive-perceptual factors (individual perceptions), modifying factors, and variables affecting the likelihood of action. Pender distinguished the HPM from other models explaining health action because it eliminates the "fear" and "threat" perceptions for health action.

Based on extensive research, the HPM was revised in 1996 (Figure 8-2; Pender, 1996; Pender et al., 2002, 2005) and has not undergone subsequent revisions. The revised model proposes that health-promoting behavior is related to direct and indirect influences among the 10 determinants of individual characteristics and experiences (e.g., previous related behavior and personal factors), behavior-specific cognitions and affect (e.g., perceived benefits of action, perceived barriers to action, perceived self-efficacy, activity-related affect, interpersonal influences, and situational influences), commitment to a plan of action, and immediate competing demands. Pender (1996) considered the behavior-specific cognitions and affect category of variables "to be of major motivational significance ... [and to] constitute a critical 'core' for intervention, because they are subject to modification through nursing actions" (p. 68).

Research has supported the predictive validity of some of the constructs in the revised HPM, such as perceived benefits of action, perceived barriers to action, perceived self-efficacy, interpersonal influences, and situational influences. A review of studies testing the HPM by Pender et al. (2002, 2005) reveals that the following factors contribute to health-promoting behaviors:

1. Perceived benefits of action
2. Perceived barriers to action
3. Perceived self-efficacy
4. Interpersonal influences
5. Situational influences

Additional research is needed to validate the contributions of the role of affect during health-promoting activities, the commitment to action, and the competing demands and preferences (Pender et al., 2002, 2005).

The Transtheoretical Model

The transtheoretical model assumes that change requires movement through discrete motivational stages over time, with the active use of different processes of change at different stages. The model has been supported in studies of a number of lifestyle behaviors, including smoking cessation, weight control, sunscreen use, exercise acquisition, mammography screening, and condom use (Prochaska, Velicer, et al., 1994).

According to Prochaska, Redding, Harlow, Rossi, and Velicer (1994), the stages of change in this model represent a continuum of motivational readiness for behavior change. The stages include:

- Precontemplation: not intending to change
- Contemplation: intending to change within 6 months

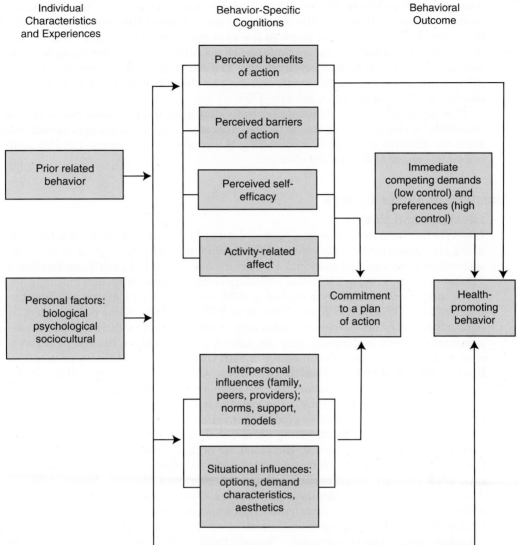

Figure 8-2
Health promotion model. (From Pender, N. J., Murdaugh, C. L., & Parsons, M. A. (2002). *Health promotion in nursing practice*, 4th ed. Reprinted with permission of Pearson Education, Inc. Upper Saddle River, NJ.)

- Preparation: actively planning change
- Action: overtly making changes
- Maintenance: taking steps to sustain change and resist temptation to relapse

Westberg and Jason (1996, p. 147) described steps of successful change that are consistent with the stages of the transtheoretical model. The steps are:

1. Acknowledging that something is not right in one's life
2. Deciding that a change is wanted
3. Setting a goal or goals
4. Exploring options for the achievement of goals
5. Deciding on and trying to implement a plan
6. Assessing progress
7. Guarding against backsliding

Also included in the transtheoretical model is the concept of decisional balance. The model proposes that part of the decision to move toward the action stage of change is based on the relative weight given to the pros and cons of changing behavior to reduce risk. "The pros represent the advantages or positive aspects of changing behavior, and may be thought of as facilitators of change. The cons represent the disadvantages or negative aspects of changing behavior, and may be thought of as barriers to change" (Prochaska, Redding, et al., 1994, pp. 478–479).

This model provides a rationale for individualizing interventions based on a client's readiness for change. It remains to be demonstrated whether stage-appropriate interventions are effective not only in encouraging behavior change progress but also in promoting maintenance of the desired change.

Lifestyle Behavior Change

Lifestyles and Health

Lifestyle has been described as a "general way of living based on the interplay between living conditions in the wide sense and individual patterns of behavior as determined by sociocultural factors and personal characteristics" (World Health Organization Health Education Unit, 1986, p. 118). Many scholars on health promotion and disease prevention have suggested that lifestyle makes a 33% contribution to a person's health status (Logan, 2007; O'Keefe & O'Keefe, 2006; Rau & Wyler, 2007). Some persons elect to incorporate habits that fall outside of traditional scientific-based medicine. When these health practices are used exclusively, they are known as **alternative health practices**. However, when they are used in combination with traditional scientific-based medicine, they become **complementary health practices**. Cuellar, Rogers, and Higshman (2007) reported that 2.1% of Americans use one or more forms of complementary health practices, with 88% of these persons being over the age of 65 years. Examples of complementary health practice include isopathic remedies (disarming viruses and bacteria by pairing them up with a neutralizing agent), chelation therapy (giving intravenous medication that binds body toxins to the blood for renal excretion), ozone therapy (exposing the client's own blood to ozone and reinfusing it), chiropractics (spinal manipulation), myoreflex therapy (acupressure points and meridian theory), homeopathy (usually diluted preparations to stimulate the immune system), cleanses (detoxifying programs with specific diets, juices, and colonic irrigations), and hyperthermia or sauna treatment (Rau & Wyler). Health promotion "is motivated by the desire to increase well-being and actualize human health potential" (Pender, 1996, p. 7). Thus, health-promoting lifestyle activities might promote feelings of vitality, vigor, improved mood and affect, flexibility, relaxation, confidence, and harmony.

Recent evidence reports that modifying simple lifestyle habits can increase the length and improve the quality of life. Table 8-1 presents attainment strategies for selected lifestyle modifications for health protection and promotion.

Pender (1996) suggested that a healthy lifestyle incorporates both health-protecting behaviors and health-promoting behaviors. Health-protecting behaviors include activities such as:

- Optimal nutrition
- Perceived self-efficacy
- Supportive relationships
- Regular exercise
- Adequate sleep

People select their lifestyles. Many assume responsibility for their own lifestyle choices; however, some persons may refuse to accept the consequences of personal actions that contribute to a perceived less-than-optimal lifestyle. The nurse can facilitate behavioral change for persons who believe that personal actions determine lifestyle and who exhibit

TABLE 8-1

Lifestyle Modifications and Attainment Strategies

Lifestyle Modification	Attainment Strategies
Getting adequate sleep (7–8 hours nightly)	Establish a sleep routine. Use the bed and bedroom exclusively for sleeping.
Maintaining a body mass index between 19 and 25 square meters	Weigh at least on a weekly basis. Monitor food intake and exercise patterns on a daily basis. Chew each bite of food 20–30 times before swallowing it. Use any opportunity available to engage in physical activity. Avoid eating before retiring for sleep.
Consuming a healthful diet containing at least nine servings of fruits and vegetables daily that includes breakfast	Strive to eat mainly fresh produce. Bake or poach foods rather than frying them. Avoid fast food or eating on the run. Avoid bringing calorie-dense foodstuffs into the house—consider going out for sweet treats rather than storing them at home. Schedule mealtimes and eat with another person.
Exercising on a regular schedule	Determine what form of exercise gives you pleasure. Schedule exercise time daily. Seek out companionship during exercise. Engage in aerobic exercise (e.g., walk 10,000 steps per day, run, treadmill, or dance) for at least 5 days a week. Lift weights every other day. Perform flexibility (stretching) exercises after each exercise routine.
Participating in recreational activities	Discover what you like to do. Make time to play each day. Try something new and different.
Drinking 64 or more ounces of water daily	Drink water instead of soda, fruit juice, dairy drinks, or caffeinated beverages. Get a water bottle or commuter cup, and wash it daily. Consume a glass of water between other beverages.
Scheduling quiet time for reflection, prayer, or relaxation techniques	Schedule quiet time by learning to say, "No." Turn off cell phones and other paging devices. Inform other household members of the need for quiet time alone.
Brushing teeth twice and flossing them once daily	Establish the routine of brushing your teeth each morning upon arising and each evening prior to bed. Keep toothbrush, toothpaste, and dental floss in a visible location. Floss either in the morning or in the evening.
Maintaining an optimistic attitude	Try to always look at the bright side of life. Take time to inventory life's pleasures.
Securing an integrated approach between allopathic and complementary health practices	Follow governmental guidelines for health screenings. Communicate all health-promoting and -protecting practices to health care providers. Practice skepticism of any health care device or preparation that makes unsubstantiated claims to improve health and well-being.
Keeping in touch with social support network	Schedule time to meet with persons who uplift you. Establish meaningful relationships with family and friends.

Sources of information:
Leddy, S. K. (2006). *Health promotion: Mobilizing strengths to enhance health, wellness and well being.* Philadelphia: F. A. Davis.
Logan, A. C. (2007). *The brain diet revised and expanded.* Nashville, TN: Cumberland House.
O'Keefe, J., & O'Keefe, J. (2006). *The forever young diet & lifestyle.* Kansas City, MO: Andrews McMeel.
Pender, N., Murdaugh, C., & Parsos, M. (2005). *Health promotion in nursing practice* (5th ed.). Upper Saddle River, NJ: Pearson Prentice-Hall.
Rau, T., & Wyler, S. (2007). *The Swiss secret to optimal health.* New York: Berkley.

sufficient motivation. Thus, the nurse must understand the meaning of health promotion to the client and the client's expectations of outcomes of health promotion interventions. The nurse must shift thinking from using professional expertise to overcome client weaknesses to empowering clients to help themselves by building on their strengths.

Health Strengths

A large body of literature associates stress with illness. Stress is assumed to arise when a situation is appraised as threatening or otherwise demanding and an appropriate coping response is not immediately available (Lazarus & Folkman, 1984). When an event is appraised as stressful, emotionally linked responses occur that result in vulnerability to illness.

Certain characteristics, including social support, self-efficacy, and internal locus of control, seem to decrease the relationship between stress and illness. Two models explain the process by which these characteristics might influence well-being. One model suggests that the person is protected, or buffered, from the potentially pathogenic influence of stressful events. In this case, these characteristics would be related to well-being only (or primarily) for persons under stress (Cohen & Wills, 1985, p. 310). The alternative model suggests that health strengths have a beneficial effect, regardless of whether the person is under stress.

Some research suggests that certain personality characteristics reduce the perception of stress or increase resistance to stress and thus may be considered health strengths. In her theory of hardiness, Kobasa (1979) assumed that life is always changing and thus is inevitably stressful. However, people who have a sense of commitment (an overall sense of purpose), control (a belief that one can influence the course of events), and challenge (a view of change as opportunity and incentive for personal growth) are thought to be more resistant to stress. In the sense of coherence theory, Antonovsky (1987) proposed that confidence in comprehensibility (a cognitive sense that information is consistent, clear, and ordered), manageability (a belief that resources are adequate to meet demands), and meaningfulness (a motivational commitment and engagement) provides generalized resistance resources and promotes health. These two theories are compared in Table 8-2.

Strategies for Lifestyle Behavior Change

A **lifestyle behavior change** means that people assume different activities in multiple aspects of their lives. The idea of changing health behavior is uncomfortable for many people. Deeply ingrained habits, even harmful ones, can be difficult to change, and most people have difficulty making even minor changes. According to Westberg and Jason (1996, pp. 147–148), people tend to resist change because change of behavior may:

- Require giving up pleasure (e.g., eating high-fat ice cream)
- Be unpleasant (e.g., doing certain exercises)
- Be overtly painful (e.g., discontinuing addictive substances)

TABLE 8-2

Comparison of the Subconcepts of the Sense of Coherence and Hardiness Models

Antonovsky	Kobasa
Sense of coherence	Hardiness
Comprehensibility: cognitive sense	Challenge: change is normative
Manageability: adequate resources	Control: internal locus of control
Meaningfulness: motivation	Commitment: self-involvement

- Be stressful (e.g., facing social situations without alcohol)
- Jeopardize social relationships (e.g., engaging in unprotected adolescent sex)
- Not seem important anymore (e.g., in the case of older individuals)
- Require alteration in self-image (e.g., in the case of a hard-working executive learning how to play)

As a result, giving up long-standing habits and attitudes is not easy for most people.

Given that health behavior change is difficult for most people, Westberg and Jason (1996, pp. 148–150) suggested that to promote "what it takes" to make meaningful, lasting changes in lifestyle, the individual should:

- Endorse the need for change.
- Have "ownership" of the need for change.
- Feel that there is more to gain than to lose.
- Develop an enhanced sense of self-worth.
- Identify realistic goals and workable plans.
- Seek gradual change, rather than a "quick fix."
- Have patience.
- Address starting new behaviors, instead of just focusing on what behaviors should be stopped.
- Practice new behaviors.
- Seek the support of family, friends, colleagues, and/or health professionals.
- Gain positive reinforcement for the desired behavior.
- Have a strategy for monitoring progress and making needed changes.
- Seek constructive feedback.
- Have a mechanism for follow-up to reduce backsliding.

Learning how to help people adopt and sustain healthy attitudes and habits is a challenge for health professionals. "There are no miracle drugs available for helping people change long-standing patterns of living. Simply telling people to stop smoking, eat less fat, have safe sex, exercise more, discontinue their abusive practices, or reduce their life stresses seldom works" (Westberg & Jason, 1996, p. 146). Clients often do not follow the advice of nurses or physicians, particularly when authoritarian "orders" are given. Clients must be actively involved as collaborative partners who assess their current health, develop a health promotion plan, and monitor plan effectiveness. Rewards facilitate adherence to health promotion plans. The nurse can best assist in promoting and changing health behaviors by providing education (e.g., hazards of the latest health fad), facilitating changes (e.g., positive reinforcement for adhering to a plan), and sustaining positive health behaviors (e.g., reminding clients of how they were before they started the health promotion plan).

According to Prochaska, Redding, and colleagues (1994), some of the most frequently replicated strategies and techniques to help clients modify their behavior include:

- Consciousness raising
- Self-reevaluation
- Environmental reevaluation
- Self-liberation
- Social liberation
- Helping relationships
- Stimulus control
- Counterconditioning
- Reinforcement management

During the contemplation stage of behavior change, consciousness raising occurs as the individual seeks information. The nurse can provide potential information resources so that the individual can be actively involved. The client's perceived incentives and barriers to change can be clarified, and the nurse can help explain and interpret often conflicting or unclear information. In addition, the knowledge and interest of family members can be assessed. It may be helpful for the individual to talk with others who have successfully made the contemplated changes.

As movement occurs toward the preparation and action stages of change, individuals engage in self- and environmental reevaluation. They consider how the current problem behavior (or lack of positive behavior) affects their physical and social environment and personal standards and values. Questions that might be asked include "Will I like myself better as a (thinner, nonsmoking, less stressed) person?" "Is my environment supportive of the proposed changes?" and "Do I believe that I am able to make and continue the changes needed?" The assumption is that changes will not occur unless they are congruent with a person's self-concept.

A strategy that can assist with self- and social liberation is cognitive restructuring. "Cognitive restructuring focuses on client's thinking, imagery, and attitudes toward the self and self-competencies as they affect the change process" (Pender, 1996, p. 171). The nurse can help clients clarify the messages they give themselves about their health and health-related behaviors. Certain beliefs can be irrational. Positive affirmations and imagery, repeated several times daily, can help clients to believe that they have the power to think positively and make desired lifestyle changes.

Helping relationships with family members, friends, colleagues, or health care professionals can be critical in helping to move the individual through the preparation, action, and maintenance stages of change. A self-help group is a strategy that has been found to be helpful for modeling, support, and reinforcement of desired behavior.

Stimulus control, emphasizing activities that precede the desired behavior, can be helpful during the action and maintenance stages of change. The activities, which must be personally relevant for the individual client, might include a postcard reminder for a mammography screening, a personal call from the nurse to encourage continued exercise, or a scheduled group meeting to practice relaxation. To encourage the development of a desirable behavior habit, it may be helpful to promote the behavior in the same setting or context and time on a daily basis. For example, the client can be encouraged to exercise in a consistent place, early each morning before other activities intervene.

Counterconditioning to break an undesirable association between a stimulus and a response can be desirable during the latter part of the action stage and during the maintenance stage. Undesirable associations can occur that create a negative emotional response to the behavior. For example, many people indicate that exercising can become boring. The nurse can encourage a varied routine, walking outside when the weather permits, and at least occasional exercise with a partner to counteract boredom.

Reinforcement management is an effective strategy, especially during the preparation and action stages of change. "It is based on the premise that all behaviors are determined by their consequences. If positive consequences occur, the probability is high that the behavior will occur again. If negative consequences occur, the probability is low for the behavior's being repeated" (Pender, 1996, p. 172). Immediate reinforcement of the desired behavior is important, especially in the early phases of change. Personalized attention and positive verbal feedback are helpful. Eventually, a desirable consequence of the behavior can become an intrinsic reward. For example, a weekly scale reading indicating decreasing weight can be a reward in itself for continuing a weight reduction diet.

The object of these strategies is to decrease barriers and increase incentives to change behavior. Barriers to change include lack of:

- Knowledge
- Skills
- Perception of control
- Facilities
- Materials

- Clear goals
- Social support
- Time
- Motivation

Incentives to change behavior include:

- Expectation of benefit
- Sense of personal responsibility
- Enjoyment of the activity
- Previous experience
- Guilt
- Support from family, peers, and/or professionals (Leddy & Fawcett, 1997)

The nurse and the client should base the choice of appropriate strategies to foster incentives and reduce barriers and thereby promote behavior change.

This section has addressed models and strategies for health promotion consistent with the interaction world view of health. In the next section, models and strategies for health patterning consistent with the integration world view for health are discussed.

 ## HEALTH PATTERNING

Models for Health Patterning

For centuries, the concept of vital life energy, or chi, has been a part of Eastern religion and culture. For example, the ancient Chinese originated the belief that chi circulates through invisible channels called meridians that can be blocked by stressors or by living excesses. A blockage in energy flow results in energy imbalances and areas of the body with energy deficits, producing symptoms or disease.

Leddy's (2004, 2006) practice theory of energy (see Chapter 6) proposes that consciousness or focused attention by the nurse can pattern client–nurse energy by clearing (transforming), conveying (carrying), coursing (reestablishing free flow), conserving (decreasing disorder), converting (amplifying resonance), or connecting energy (promoting synchronization to promote harmony).

Martha Rogers introduced the concept of the person as an energy field interacting with an environmental energy field to nursing (see Chapter 6). She conceptualized that **health patterning** of the human energy field occurs simultaneously and mutually with changes in the environmental energy field. The nurse (part of the environmental energy field) can influence the client's health by redistributing energy and thus repatterning the client's energy field. Nurses work with manifestations of health patterns (Leddy, 2003). Viewing persons as energy fields provides a rationale for nontraditional healing modalities that enhance health patterns.

Health-Patterning Modalities

Leddy (2003, 2006) identified integrative nursing interventions to promote health and healing. The following interventions act on the human energy field and can be used by nurses in clinical practice:

1. To relinquish bound energy: herbal preparations and aromatherapy
2. To reestablish energy flow: physical activity, tai chi, qigong (chigung), and aerobic and strengthening exercises
3. To release blocked energy: touch, massage, acupressure, reflexology, applied kinesiology (touch for health), jin shin do, self-massage, the Alexander technique, the Feldenkrais method, the Trager psychophysical integration, and structural integration (Rolfing)

4. To reduce energy depletion: meditation, autogenic training to elicit the relaxation response, progressive muscle relaxation, deep-breathing exercises, yoga, biofeedback, and guided imagery

5. To regenerate agent's optimal nutrition: foodstuffs, vitamin and mineral supplements, a high-fiber diet, ingestion of phytonutrients (soy, garlic, onions, and deep-colored fruits and vegetables), and antioxidants (vitamins A, C, and E; selenium; coenzyme Q 10; and beta carotene)

6. To restore energy field harmony: centering, chromatherapy (color therapy), music therapy, polarity therapy, prayer, Reiki, and therapeutic touch

Other complementary forms of interventions aimed at strengthening or restoring energy harmony include feng shui and life energy therapies such as yoga and chakra cleansing, strengthening, and healing. Healing modalities using interventions to balance, release, or restore energy have been used for centuries in Eastern cultures. Feng shui works on the assumption that persons have an emotional energy field running through and around their bodies, thereby creating an external aura and concentrated internal energy centers called chakras. Chakras within the human body flow with energy outside the human body. Personal ideas, thoughts, and feelings mix with the world, and the energy fields interact and become one. Feng shui incorporates chi ("the subtle change in electromagnetic energy that runs through everything, carrying information from one thing to another"; Brown, 2005, p. 25). Brown (2005) and Rosen (2007) explained that the chi in the seven chakras relates to aspects of a person's character. The location of the chakras is presented in Table 8-3 along with a color that may be used for the strengthening or healing of each chakra (Brown, 2005; Rosen, 2007). Persons also have an aura or outer energy field that projects the energy within the inner body, thereby enabling the life energy within to connect with the world and "tap into the vast array of cosmic information" (Brown, p. 26). Here is an example of how using chakras can result in a positive outcome: I experienced writer's block when I was trying to create an example of using

TABLE 8-3

The Seven Chakras

Name	Location	Color	Influences
Crown	Top of head	Pale violet	Spirituality, peace, bliss, and enlightenment
Brow or midbrain	Between the eyebrows	Indigo	Intelligence, inspiration, intuition, insight, and wisdom
Throat	Throat	Blue	Expression in all forms, integrity, creativity, and listening
Heart	Center chest	Green	Emotional feelings, giving and receiving love, empathy, compassion, acceptance, and forgiveness
Solar plexus or stomach	Midway between the chest and naval	Yellow	Responsibility, motivation, power, prosperity, and gut feelings
Sacral or abdomen	8 cm (3 in) below the navel	Orange	Vitality, sexual pleasure, generation of new ideas, flexibility, and ability to give and receive nurturance
Root or reproductive organs	Spinal base near genitals	Red	Survival, stability, assertiveness, self-worth, good judgment, desire, and grounding

Sources: Gerber (1988), Brown (2005), and Rosen (2007).

chakras. I stopped writing, closed my eyes, and visualized my throat chakra turn from a pale to a vivid, iridescent peacock blue, thus achieving my desire for an example.

Chi has two opposing but complementary forms: yin and yang. Yin is slower, cooler, and more dispersed, whereas yang is hotter, faster, and more compressed. Most of the time, it is healthy being more of one form. However, should one form become too dominant, then an imbalance occurs, resulting in health problems. Chi energies interact with each other in a positive or negative manner. In feng shui, complex interactions (e.g., a person's position, the location of objects within the envronment [such as a room or even a building], and the magic nine patterns of chi [the magic square determines the flow of chi]) serve as the basis for timing events, arranging a home or work space, decorating, and remediating personal problems (Brown, 2005). For example, I am seated facing the north as I write. According to feng shui, facing north is a good position to access deep creativity and to produce individualistic, original work.

Many of the aforementioned interventions that act on the human energy field have yet to be scrutinized through double-blind controlled scientific studies. However, any disruption in today's fast-paced world that requires continuous multitasking does reduce the effects of stress on current frantic lifestyles.

The literature contains increasing evidence that these kinds of therapies, most of which are noninvasive and involve the client as an active participant in the process, have tangible and highly desirable outcomes for health and healing. In fact, nursing licensing examinations in Europe contain information about the safe use of herbs and essential oils. Before using complementary interventions with clients, however, the nurse must be educated about how each may affect physiology and potential adverse effects (Dossey, Keegan, & Guzzetta, 2005). In the future, nurses will be increasingly expected to incorporate patterning methods as an integral part of clinical practice.

IMPLICATIONS OF THE NURSE'S VIEW OF HEALTH FOR ROLE PERFORMANCE

A positive model of health emphasizes personal strengths and power that are resources for health, wellness, and well-being. Personal strengths include having meaning, goals, and connections (with other persons or a higher being) in life. Personal power includes self-perceptions of capability, control, choice, and the capacity to cope with life challenges with confidence (Leddy, 2006). The integrative world view supports the belief that nurses work with persons who display areas of strength and weakness in health pattern manifestations at a specific time. The effects of the nurse on client manifestations of patterns are complex and nonlinear. Persons entrenched in reductionism or who espouse an interaction world view may find this approach confusing, and perhaps even nonscientific. However, recent studies have shown that even thinking about or praying for clients may enhance health and healing (Burkhardt & Nagai-Jacobson, 2005).

In trying to improve the quality of health of clients and self, the nurse is obligated to fulfill roles that incorporate promoting health, systematically and strategically planning changes, and using the strengths displayed by the client. Note that the term "promotion and maintenance of health" was missing. "Maintenance" is an obsolete concept because wellness (health) is an active process in which life moves forward, and the client is always evolving. The nurse may promote well-being and may restore perceptions of well-being, but the process of health does not permit the status quo that maintenance implies.

If health is a process, and if nurses believe that nursing focuses on the person's responses, as a whole, to the environment and to a perception of well-being, then nurses have a basis for a variety of professional roles when clients perceive a sense of harmony, vitality, and ability; when they can learn most effectively how to enhance their personal strength and gain greater control of their lives; and when they perceive a lack of harmony, feel consumed by weakness, and feel vulnerable (the illness state).

This chapter has described strategies the nurse can use to help promote or protect the health of the client. In the next section, the emphasis is on self-care strategies nurses can use to promote their own health.

 ## SELF-CARE OF THE NURSE

The Stressful Work Environment

A stressful work environment refers to the pressure that is put on nurses by the external organizational forces that determine work conditions. The health care system contributes to nurse burnout through multiple regulations, lack of adequate staffing, mandatory overtime, reimbursement issues, lack of perceived support for quality nursing care at the bedside, and failure to seek nurse input into clinical practice issues. At times, a nurse's work environment could be compared to assembly line work with the goal of moving clients in and out of the system as quickly as possible to reduce costs. Client care protocols that streamline care and reduce chances for error leave little room for individualization of nursing care. Little time is available to develop therapeutic client relationships and do the small things for clients that make big differences. With reduced client contact, nurses usually cannot see evidence of how their interventions positively affect client outcomes. Being put in the position of having to lower standards to accommodate the employer's financial agenda (especially in for-profit institutions) creates distress for some professional nurses. If left alone, the distress becomes the state of emotional and physical apathy and exhaustion known as **burnout**.

The more conscientious nurses, who have a need to give their very best, are most vulnerable to burnout. Cullen (1995) suggested that one of two things happens when nurses work in a system in which they are never able to give their best. Either the nurses lower their standards and work apathetically or they may continue trying to give their best, while constantly bucking a system that fails to have excellence in nursing as a top priority, until they finally experience burnout.

Stress and Burnout

A person becomes overstressed when demands exceed perceived resources. Some stress is inevitable and even positive in energizing the person. However, more stress than can be managed may be associated with physical, mental, emotional, and behavioral symptoms in health care providers. Some of the more common symptoms of stress in nurses and other practitioners include:

- Sleep disturbance and fatigue
- Appetite changes: increases or loss
- Reduced abilities to think and concentrate
- Frequent tardiness or absences from work
- Overeating or increased smoking
- Sudden mood swings
- Deep resentment of clients (Bartholomew, 2006; Gordon, 2005; Mitchell & Cormack, 1998)

If a nurse is constantly exposed to a situation in which demands exceed resources, the nurse's energies gradually will deplete, culminating in burnout. Stressful events may be perceived as either challenges that lead to positive growth or threats that can lead to negative consequences (Wells-Federman, 1996). Escalating and continual emotional overload is a common factor in burnout (Bartholomew, 2006; Gordon, 2005; Kahn & Saulo, 1994; Sutton, 2006). When nurses experience constant exposure to clinical practice situations that demand that they continually work in overloaded and stressful conditions, they experience reduced efficiency, irritability, a sense of constant pressure against time, diminished motivation, poor judgment, accidents, and care errors. In professional nursing practice, care errors may sometimes be fatal. The threat of potentially making a fatal error exacerbates stress levels in clinical practice.

The best time to think about burnout is before it happens. Answers to questions such as "Do I feel little enthusiasm for doing my job?" "Do I feel tired even with adequate sleep?" and "Do I have too much to do and too little time in which to do it?" can help the nurse to identify symptoms and sources of job stress and signs of impending burnout (Davis, Eshelman, & McKay, 2000). Selected suggestions for ways to manage nursing job stress are listed in Display 8-1. Many of the strategies require that the nurse take time to evaluate current working conditions and require attitudinal and behavioral changes.

The following section presents a number of techniques for managing job stress, preventing burnout, and promoting well-being.

Techniques to Enhance Well-Being

This section emphasizes positive techniques that can be used to avoid burnout, promote health, and reframe stressors into challenges. **Health-enhancing techniques** promote personal well-being. Techniques such as stress management, affirmations, refuting irrational ideas, social support, values clarification, and taking care of oneself are presented.

Stress Management

In human life (and clinical nursing practice), perfection is a human impossibility. However, given that stressors are an inevitable part of personal and professional interactions, a number of techniques have been proposed in the literature as positive ways to build strengths, avoid burnout, and promote well-being. First, it is necessary to identify sources

---

Managing Job Stress

DISPLAY 8-1

- Identify sources of job stress
- Set realistic goals and priorities to respond effectively to job stress and demands
- Avoid procrastination
- Say no when offered special projects or opportunities
- Toss out clutter in your work environment
- Develop and maintain trusting, mutual, and meaningful collegial relationships with coworkers (and persons outside of the work setting)
- Adopt an attitude that change is a challenge rather than an inconvenience
- Cast off the perception of the nurse being victimized by more powerful members of the health care team
- Inject fun and humor in the work setting
- Create a positive environment by looking at the bright side of adversity
- Take control over nursing work processes
- Participate in decision making
- Schedule time to eat a healthy meal or snacks each day while at work

- Consume a healthy diet (a balanced diet with moderation in refined sugars)
- Take responsibility for successes and failures
- Take a 15–20 minute mini-vacation daily while on the job. Go to a quiet place in the work setting to relax (progressive relaxation, deep breathing exercises, meditation, or prayer with your beeper and/ or cell phone turned off)
- Confront work issues directly with persons involved
- Engage in a daily regimen of physical exercise that you find enjoyable (stretching, strength building, and aerobic exercises)
- Take vacations and personal days when needed
- Get an adequate amount of sleep (for most persons this is 7–8 hours)
- Balance your work and personal life

Sources: Bost, 2005; Boucher, 2004; Cherewatenko & Perry, 2003; Covey, 2004; Davis, Eshelman, & McKay, 2000; Dossey, Keegan, & Guzzetta, 2005; Ellis & Harper, 1961; Kendall-Reed & Reed, 2004; McGraw, 2004; Neuharth, 2004; Sachs, 2001; Schaffner & Ludwig-Beymer, 2003.

Organizing Time to Achieve Goals

DISPLAY 8-2

- Control situations as much as possible; schedule to avoid too many changes or events happening at the same time.
- Organize your time to accomplish the most important goals; identify values and goals and goal priorities as a framework for time management.
- Set limits; be assertive.
- Say no to demands that are unrealistic or of low priority; imagine yourself protected inside of a bubble.

- Reduce tasks into smaller parts to allow mastery and feelings of competence.
- Delegate responsibilities to others and enlist their assistance; use the skills of others; you don't have to be "all things to all people"; differentiate between time urgencies that are valid and others that are needlessly created; overinvolvement leaves little time for fulfillment of personal needs and often leads to resentment and blame (Wells-Federman, 1996).

of stress and be aware of tension buildup and situations that are likely to prove stressful. Nurses should try to get in touch with their bodies and learn their bodily reactions to and manifestations of stress (e.g., sweaty palms, tightening of back and neck muscles, and dry mouth). If signs of stress are recognized early, it is possible to start stress-relieving exercises that can keep the effects of stress from increasing (Eliopoulos, 1999).

It is important for the nurse to take care of herself or himself first before attempting to meet someone else's needs (Elder, 1999). Organization of time is one way to focus on the most important goals. Suggestions for ways to organize time are provided in Display 8-2. Goal achievement requires setting time aside to set realistic goals, determining an action plan, using personal values to determine priority goals, and delegating tasks to others.

Enhancement of self-esteem is another way to avoid burnout and promote well-being. Increasing self-awareness of one's positive characteristics can enhance self-esteem. In addition, the nurse should assertively express his or her thoughts and feelings; share feelings, troubles, and opinions with others; accept shortcomings and imperfections; and maintain a positive and tolerant attitude toward others and the world at large. One way to do this is to change the way a stressor is viewed by putting it in proper perspective to help make the stressor manageable.

To help avoid worrying, it may be helpful to practice the serenity prayer, authored by a medieval monk, St. Francis of Assisi: "God grant me the serenity to accept the things I cannot change, the courage to change the things I can, and the wisdom to know the difference" (quoted in Mauk & Schmidt, 2004, p. 98). In addition, it is helpful for the nurse to try to reduce the "shoulds" and "should nots." It is reasonable, legitimate, and healthy for clients to express their needs and do what is best for themselves; why do nurses perceive themselves as being different?

"I should take care of my own needs and I should not worry about what others may think" (Eliopoulos, 1999, p. 311). Display 8-3 lists selected stress reduction or supportive noninvasive modalities. Many of these strategies fall within the realm of health-promoting behaviors.

Additional strategies that might be helpful in achieving a balance between threatening and challenging stress are listed in Display 8-4. Like the other display strategies, these also may require that the nurse ask for help from others.

Affirmations

Another strategy that can contribute to healthful self-care is to promote affirmations, a positive declaration aimed at producing a desired effect (Carter, 2006; Clark, 1996a). Affirmations are positive self-statements that become healthy alternatives to negative self-talk. An affirmation is simply a positive thought, a short phrase, or a saying that has meaning for the person. It can help change assumptions and beliefs that have negative

Selected Stress Reduction and Supportive Noninvasive Modalities

- Make the environment conducive to relaxation, rather than overstimulating, by adjusting the noise, room temperature, and lighting.
- Follow good health practices by eating a sound diet, avoiding caffeine, avoiding simple carbohydrates ("junk food") and food additives, and supplementing vitamins A, C, E, and the B-complex group.
- Have regular physical activity (exercise).
- Get ample and regular rest and sleep.
- Instead of coffee and cigarette breaks, enjoy short relaxation exercises, recline in a quiet area, or listen to relaxing music.
- Have a pet.
- Practice mindfulness and relaxation.
- Get in touch with nature.
- Build leisure activities into the day; develop a hobby.

- Take vacations and breaks from routine work.
- Use alternative therapies, such as therapeutic massage, guided imagery, progressive relaxation, meditation, yoga, herbs, or aromatherapy.
- Use herbs (e.g., Echinacea or ginseng) to protect the immune system if subjected to chronic or high levels of stress.
- Learn how to center. "The skill of relaxing in the face of stress, taking a deep breath, loosening some of the tension in your neck and shoulders, and quieting your mind for a few moments is called centering. Centering is simply regaining your physical, mental, and emotional balance in order to proceed with the task at hand" (Achterberg, Dossey, & Kolkmeier, 1994, p. 62).

consequences. Affirmations are important in reinforcing new ways of thinking and behaving from moment to moment. They are statements that can be selected to reaffirm new intentions, and they can help to increase the clarity of goals and help the nurse assume responsibility for actions. When starting to feel upset, anxious, frustrated, sad, or overwhelmed, the nurse can stop and examine her or his internal monologue and simply challenge that monologue with language that is more affirming, such as:

- I can ask for what I need.
- I can take care of myself.
- I'm doing the best I can.
- I can find alternatives to problems.
- I can meet my needs.
- I care for myself, and I care for others.

Additional Strategies to Balance Threatening and Challenging Stress

- Develop a sense of balance among physical, mental, and spiritual dimensions.
- Get personal and social support during times of stress and distress; develop personal support systems at work.
- Find ways to maintain interest, enthusiasm, and knowledge at work by remaining alert to new ideas; avoid isolation by attending conferences and discussing your practice with other people; hear and accept the praise from clients and colleagues.

- Leave work behind when you go home.
- Set limits and have priorities other than work.
- Be interested. "Everyone wants to be interesting, but the vitalizing thing is to be interested.... Keep a sense of curiosity.... Discover new things" (Gardner, 1996, p. 11).
- Avoid unfulfilling or burdensome relationships; minimize contact with people who add more stress, rather than joy, to your life.
- Risk failure.

Guidelines for the Use of Affirmations

DISPLAY 8-5

- Find a relaxing, sharing atmosphere. Consider using a relaxation exercise before the affirmation process.
- What health issues are you concerned about?
- Is the affirmation best stated in the attitude, feeling, or action mode? Are you ready for action?
- State the affirmation in your own words. Affirmations are best stated in the becoming mode ("It's getting easier," "I'm becoming more comfortable").
- Once you have selected an affirmation, write or say the affirmation 10 to 20 times each day while listening to your inner, gut response to hearing it said or writing it.

- Carry your chosen affirmation with you on an index card and place it in a briefcase, purse, or car dashboard where it will be read throughout the day. Hearing oneself on tape, viewing oneself saying the affirmation, or writing and reading it back provides two kinds of feedback and thus is more powerful than simply saying the affirmation to oneself.
- Provide an ongoing method of reinforcement for continuing the affirmation.
- Try not to become frustrated or expect too much.

Source: Clark, 1996b.

Initially this may seem superficial and uncomfortable, but as the internal monologue is changed, the nurse will begin to notice changes in behavior and in the environment (Carter, 2006; Wells-Federman, 1996). Do not allow the negative thought patterns of others to distract you from your mission. The guidelines in Display 8-5 are suggestions for the use of affirmations.

Refuting Irrational Ideas

In a system called rational emotive therapy, Ellis and Harper (1961) proposed that emotions are not caused by actual events. In between the event and the emotion, they said, is realistic or unrealistic self-talk that produces the emotions. Accordingly, the person's own thoughts, directed and controlled by the individual, are what create anxiety, anger, and depression. But irrational self-talk can be changed, and the stressful emotions changed with it (Davis et al., 2000).

At the root of all irrational thinking is the assumption that things are done to someone. Statements that interpret experience as catastrophic (e.g., a momentary chest pain is a heart attack) or absolute (e.g., I should, must, ought, always, or never) are examples of irrational thinking. Other examples of irrational ideas are listed in Display 8-6.

Examples of Irrational Ideas

DISPLAY 8-6

- It is possible to please all persons all of the time.
- Complete competence and perfection is possible in everything.
- Things can always be as I want them to be.
- Misery is created from external factors.
- The unknown, uncertain, and potential dangers instill great fear in me.
- I need to rely upon others at all times.
- Avoiding life's difficulties and responsibilities is easier than facing them.
- The past directs the present and the future.
- Constant relaxation and leisure leads to happiness.
- I am the only one capable to do the job properly.

- Life situations and other persons are the source of pressure.
- It is possible to have it all, all of the time.
- I am responsible for everything that happens.
- Genetics dictate my reactions and life outcomes.
- It is impossible to control my emotions.
- Just getting over things is easy.
- Contributions I make to the world are unimportant.
- All my problems are my fault.
- There is one single best approach to life.

Sources: Bost, 2005; Davis, Eshelman, & McKay, 2000; Dossey, Keegan, & Guzzetta, 2005; Ellis & Harper, 1961; McGraw, 2004; Neuharth, 2004.

Irrational ideas can be disputed and eliminated through a process of rational thinking that includes (Davis et al., 2000; Ellis & Harper, 1961):

1. Writing down the objective facts of the event
2. Writing down your self-talk, rational and irrational
3. Focusing on your emotional response
4. Questioning the rational support (e.g., evidence) for and against an irrational idea
5. Identifying the worst and best things that could happen
6. Substituting alternative self-talk

Social Support

Fellow colleagues can provide the insights and perspectives necessary to cope with commonly shared experiences. "Acknowledging the pain and seeking support from others are the most enduring long-term coping strategies. Practicing collegiality is a way of fostering this social support network. It is a way of building an atmosphere at work where you can support your colleagues and they you" (Wells-Federman, 1996, p. 15).

Building a supportive work environment requires conscious awareness of and action toward valuing yourself and your colleagues. The following are some suggestions (Wells-Federman, 1996) for shaping the quality of the atmosphere in which you work and developing a stronger support network:

- Find someone doing something right, and acknowledge him or her.
- Expect the best from yourself and those with whom you work.
- Model the values you believe. Take responsibility for your health and well-being, and encourage others to do the same.
- Establish a mentoring or buddy system.
- Make decisions based on nursing's ethical values.
- Establish a support group to help deal with the feelings that can arise from professional practice.
- Be supportive, but refer colleagues to professional support when needed.

Values Clarification

It may be helpful to consider why, despite the drawbacks, nursing can be so rewarding. Editors at *Nursing 2000* magazine ("Nursing Top Ten Rewards," 2000, pp. 42–43) compiled the following list of 10 values, or "qualities that make nursing great," based on interviews with 20 seasoned nurses. Some of these values may be helpful in considering personal strengths of practicing nursing:

- A way to make a difference
- The human connection
- Flexibility
- The chance to use all of yourself
- Long-term security
- The chance to mentor
- A connection between technology and humanity
- Respect
- Personal growth
- Personal rewards

A procedure known as values clarification can be used to try to identify values that are most significant for an individual. This process also can be helpful in focusing self-care priorities for the nurse. Clark (1996b, p. 19) described three steps in a values clarification process:

1. Prizing
   a. Prizing and cherishing. Learn to set priorities, become aware of what the nurse is for or against, begin to trust inner experiences and feelings, and examine why he or she feels as he or she does.

b. Clearly communicate personal values, and actively listen to others as they share theirs.

2. Choosing
   a. Choosing freely by examining values that others have imposed on the nurse.
   b. Choosing thoughtfully between alternatives by examining the process by which the nurse chooses and considering the possible consequences of each choice.

3. Acting
   a. Trying out the value choice by developing a plan of action and trying it out.
   b. Evaluating what happened when action was taken, and making plans to reinforce actions that support the values.

Taking Care of Oneself

Nurses have a responsibility to take care of themselves because they can be in a position to give only when their own needs have, at least to some extent, been acknowledged and satisfied. Mitchell and Cormack (1998, p. 142) have suggested ways for the nurse to protect herself or himself from burnout, including:

- Do some honest soul searching to determine whether you're the kind of nurse who needs to express creativity and excellence, and who values and displays originality and enthusiasm in your work.
- Objectively evaluate your workplace, and respond proactively to achieve a more positive outcome for yourself.
- Don't assume responsibility where you have none.
- Be honest about what you can and can't do in your role, given the constraints on your time and resources.
- Remember that you're not on duty 24 hours a day and that nursing is one part of the whole of your life.
- Remember that a good job doesn't love you back, and get your priorities straight.
- Find your own outlets for creativity.
- Don't stay in a situation that consistently fails to meet your needs; give yourself permission to leave.
- Give yourself a break.
- Create support for yourself.
- Love yourself; heal your wounds.
- If the problem is a feeling of helplessness, the solution is to develop personal power.
- Try approaching each task as a challenge.
- Remember that you are here to serve, not to rescue.

Focusing on the positive sides of giving care to others can be helpful. Helping others as professional nurses provides great rewards. The work is challenging and fulfilling, especially when nurses can see the effects of interventions. Some nurses find problem solving thrilling, especially when they have success with creative methods never used. Some nurses derive a deep intrinsic pleasure just by knowing that they helped another person. The personal pleasure becomes enhanced when clients express gratitude, and nurses see the results of efforts to reduce human suffering (Mitchell & Cormack, 1998).

Annoyances that trigger stress also affect eating habits. Some nurses engage in "emotional" or "stress" eating. Consumption of carbohydrate-rich, protein-poor foods increases the amount of tryptophan that reaches the brain, thereby stimulating serotonin production. Serotonin release makes people "feel good." In addition, the sympathetic nervous system is stimulated, and additional cortisol is released during times of acute and chronic stress. Very few North Americans consume the recommended three to five servings of vegetables and two to four servings of fruits on a daily basis. Fiber associated with intake of fruits and vegetables blocks the absorption of fat in the gastrointestinal tract. A poor diet has been associated with oxidative stress and inflammation, which are contributing factors to many disorders, such as diabetes mellitus, cardiovascular disease, depression, dementia, fibromyalgia, Alzheimer's disease, anxiety disorders, amyotrophic lateral sclerosis, chronic fatigue syndrome, and depression (Logan, 2007).

Poor sleep also hampers a person's ability to combat the effects of stress. Sleep deprivation is associated with reduced leptin levels, resulting in poor appetite control in humans. The average hours of sleep that Americans get nightly have declined 1.5 hours over the past century. More than one third of Americans get fewer than 6.5 hours of slumber per night. Sleep deprivation also stimulates the sympathetic nervous system and cortisol production and release. Sleep deprivation triggers the desire to consume sweet and starchy foodstuffs. Chronic stress interferes with sleep, and sleep deprivation alters a person's moods and cognitive processes (Logan, 2007; O'Keefe & O'Keefe, 2006). Tips to promote effective sleep include using the bedroom solely for slumber; keeping a regular sleep schedule (even if working nights and during days off); exercising in the daylight or early evening; avoiding consumption of caffeine, alcohol, or a large meal within 6 hours of bedtime; purchasing a comfortable mattress; scheduling a relaxing activity (e.g., a warm bath, reading, or meditation) right before bedtime; and providing a room with optimal darkness (to stimulate melatonin release) and quiet. Logan (2007) suggested using mindful meditation (focusing on the positives of the here and now instead of worrying about tomorrow), drinking any form of milk (the milk protein alpha-lactalbumin is high in tryptophan, which increases brain serotonin levels), or consuming a small carbohydrate snack such as whole-grain toast (or crackers) or a small bowl of cereal (which also stimulates brain serotonin).

In summary, nurses need to care for themselves to provide effective care to others. Lifestyle patterns and behaviors of nurses affect their ability to extend themselves to help others. Because nurses are people, they must assume responsibility for personal health promotion.

Research Brief 8-1

Nemcek, M. (2007). Registered nurses' self-nurturance and life and career satisfaction. *American Association of Occupational Health Nursing Journal, 55*(8), 305–310.

The investigator used a descriptive correlational design to reexamine the relationships among self-nurturance, life satisfaction, and career satisfaction. One hundred thirty-six nurses participated in the study, which required them to complete the Modified Self-Nurturance Scale (MSNS), Satisfaction With Life Scale (SWLS), and Nursing Career Satisfaction Scale (NCSS). Statistically significant correlations were found between the nurses' mean scores on the MSNS and SWLS ($r = .43, p < .01$), MSNS and NCSS ($r = .42, p < .01$), and SWLS and NCSS ($r = .37, p < .01$). The investigator found no significant correlations of sample demographic variables on MSNS, SWLS, and NCSS scores. The nurses in this study had life satisfaction and self-nurturance scores consistent with those of prior studies of well adults. Persons who practice self-nurturing behaviors have increased life satisfaction and typically experience fewer injuries and illnesses.

The results of this study could be used to promote self-nurturing behaviors in professional nurses. Occupational health nurse managers and nurses could educate and support colleagues on ways to engage in health-promoting behaviors such as thinking positively about oneself, exercising regularly, and consuming healthy foods. In addition, personnel policies of health care organizations could be implemented to promote nurse self-nurturance, health, and safety. Nurses who are satisfied with their careers and life tend to stay in their current clinical practice areas. The study's results should be viewed with caution because a convenience sample was used, correlations were used to analyze data (making predictions impossible), and the NCSS had low internal consistency (.63) and test–retest reliability (.54) between the first and second administration, which occurred 2 weeks apart from each other. More research is needed to refine the NCSS. Additional studies using a random national sample would eliminate the increased chance of biased findings.

Barriers to Self-Care

One example of a barrier to self-care is the belief "It can't happen to me," in which nurses may feel that they will not be in danger of burnout because they are too smart or too aware to let negative feelings progress to burnout. Another issue may be rooted in the altruistic nature of many nurses, in which the client or the job may take precedence over considering the nurse's health. So, for example, the nurse may feel, "I don't deserve to be cared for in the same way as others," "I can't get sick because others depend on me," or "My job is to take care of others, not to look after myself." The essence of this section has been the message that the nurse must take care of herself or himself first. Then, the nurse will be better able to continue to deal with the stresses of the work environment, and advocate for the needs of clients.

SUMMARY AND SIGNIFICANCE TO PRACTICE

In our society, responsibility for illness has been delegated to health professionals who have been prepared and are rewarded for delivering care to the sick. Short-term incentives and rewards to maintain health do not exist for the recipient; in addition, the health care system is not organized to reward providers for keeping clients well.

Clients must be encouraged to assume an increased concern and responsibility for their health potential. Nurses can support, facilitate, and encourage those positive skills, qualities, and plans that will promote health. The client and the nurse, based on goals and a timetable determined by the client, can then devise interventions collaboratively.

In addition, nurses need to take responsibility for self-care. Approaches to managing job stress and techniques such as stress management, affirmations, refuting irrational ideas, social support, values clarification, and taking care of oneself are positive techniques that can be used to avoid burnout, reframe stressors into challenges, and enhance well-being.

FROM THEORY TO PRACTICE

1. Identify factors within your current lifestyle that fall into the categories of health promotion and health protection. What are the consequences of a lifestyle focused on health protection rather than health promotion?
2. Thinking about Jane and Michael in the vignette, identify factors in their (or your) work environment that are not health promoting. Why is having a colleague to share common experiences important for promoting health?
3. Did you find some of the tips for caring for yourself helpful? If so, which ones do you plan to use? If not, why not?

WWW INTERNET EXERCISES

1. Visit the American Holistic Nurses Association (AHNA) at http://www.ahna.org. Click on the icon "About AHNA." Read the information. Would you be interested in joining the AHNA? Why or why not?
2. Using the search engine of your choice, type in one of the nursing interventions for the human energy field identified by Leddy (2003, 2006). Come prepared to participate in a class discussion about the information you find. Do you think other health team members would agree that the identified intervention would be beneficial to clients? Why or why not?

WWW INTERNET RESOURCES

American Association of Retired Persons: http://www.aarp.org. Access information related to healthy living and aging and a wide array of information addressing the special sociocultural concerns of the elderly.

Centers for Disease Control and the National Center for Chronic Disease Prevention and Health Promotion: http://www.cdc.gov. Learn the latest information related to the prevention of communicable diseases along with health promotion information to reduce the incidence of chronic diseases.

American Institute for Cancer Research: http://www.aicr.org. Consult this site for research-based information for the prevention of cancer and healthy lifestyle information.

National Institutes of Health: http://www.nih.gov. Read information about the latest government-sponsored health research along with opportunities for funding health promotion research. Read about the National Center for Complementary and Alternative Medicine: www.nccam.nih.gov.

Alternative Medicine Home Page: http://www.pitt.edu/~cbwaltm.html. Jump to a variety of alternative and complementary health care websites from this website maintained by the Falk Library for the Health Sciences at the University of Pittsburgh.

Association for Applied and Therapeutic Humor: http://www.aath.org. Tickle your funny bone by visiting this website, and jump to other health care humor sites to lift your spirits.

National Health Information Center: http://health.gov/nhic. Obtain educational materials for clients and yourself using this website.

American Heart Association: http://www.americanheart/org. Visit this site to learn the latest on cardiovascular disease. Because this is a client-oriented site, refer clients and their families to this site.

The American Holistic Nurses Association: http://www.ahna.org.

Get a free subscription to *The Wellness Newsletter*, a research-based e-newsletter: http://www.carolynchambersclark.com.

REFERENCES

Antonovsky, A. (1987). *Unraveling the mystery of health*. San Francisco: Jossey-Bass.

Ardell, D. B. (1979). The nature and implications of high level wellness or why "normal health" is in a rather sorry state of existence. *Health Values, 3*, 17–24.

Bartholomew, K. (2006). *Ending nurse-to-nurse hostility: Why nurses eat their young and each other*. Marblehead, MA: HCPro.

Becker, M. H., & Maiman, L. A. (1975). Sociobehavioral determinants of compliance with health and medical care recommendations. *Medical Care, 13*, 10–24.

Benner, P., Tanner, C. A., & Chesla, C. A. (Eds.). (1996). *Expertise in nursing practice: Caring, clinical judgment, and ethics*. New York: Springer.

Burkhardt, M. A., & Nagai-Jacobson, M. G. (2005). Spirituality and health. In B. Dossey, L. Keegan, & C. Guzzetta (Eds.), *Holistic nursing: A handbook for practice* (4th ed., pp. 137–172). Sudbury, MA: Jones and Bartlett.

Carter, D. (2006). *10 smart things women can do to build a better life*. Eugene, OR: Harvest House.

Clark, C. (1996a). Career fitness guide: Stress management. *Nursing Spectrum, 5*, 65–68.

Clark, C. (1996b). *Wellness practitioner: Concepts, research and strategies* (2nd ed.). New York. Springer.

Cohen, S., & Wills, T. A. (1985). Stress, social support and the buffering hypothesis. *Psychological Bulletin, 98*, 310–357.

Cullen, A. (1995). Burnout: Why do we blame the nurse? *American Journal of Nursing, 95*, 22–28.

Cuellar, N., Rogers, A., & Higshman, V. (2007). Evidence-based research of complementary and alternative medicine (CAM) for sleep in the community-dwelling older adult. *Geriatric Nursing, 28*(1), 46–51.

Davis, M., Eshelman, E. R., & McKay, M. (2000). *The relaxation and stress reduction workbook* (5th ed.). Oakland, CA: New Harbinger.

Dossey, B. M., Keegan, L., & Guzzetta, C. (2005). *Holistic nursing: A handbook for practice* (4th ed.). Sudbury, MA: Jones and Bartlett.

Dubos, R. (1978). Health and creative adaptation. *Human Nature, 1*, 74–82.

Dunn, H. H. (1977). What high-level wellness means. *Health Values, 1*, 9–16.

Elder, A. (1999, March 1). Nurturing the caregiver in today's health care arena. *Advance for Nurses*, 7.

Ellis, A., & Harper, R. (1961). *A guide to rational living*. North Hollywood, CA: Wilshire Books.

Eliopoulos, C. (1999). *Integrating conventional and alternative therapies: Holistic care for chronic conditions*. St. Louis, MO: Mosby.

Fawcett, J. (1993). *Conceptual models of nursing* (3rd ed.). Philadelphia: F. A. Davis.

Gordon, S. (2005). *Nursing against the odds*. New York: Cornell University Press.

Hall, B. A. (1981). The change paradigm in nursing: Growth versus persistence. *Advances in Nursing Science, 3*, 1–6.

Hravnak, M. (1998). Is there a health promotion and protection foundation to the practice of acute care nurse practitioners? *AACN Clinical Issues, 9*, 283–289.

Janz, N. K., & Becker, M. H. (1984). The health belief model: A decade later. *Health Education Quarterly, 11*, 1–47.

Jensen, L. A., & Allen, M. N. (1994). A synthesis of qualitative research on wellness-illness. *Qualitative Health Research, 4*, 349–369.

Kahn, S., & Saulo, M. (1994). *Healing yourself: A nurse's guide to self-care and renewal*. Albany, NY: Delmar.

Kasl, S., & Cobb, S. (1966). Health behavior, illness behavior and sick role behavior. *Archives of Environmental Health, 12*, 246–266.

Kobasa, S. C. (1979). Stressful life events, personality and health: An inquiry into hardiness. *Journal of Personality and Social Psychology, 37*, 1–11.

Lazarus, R. S., & Folkman, J. (1984). *Stress appraisal and coping*. New York: Springer.

Leddy, S. K. (2003). *Integrative health promotion: Conceptual bases for nursing practice*. Thorofare, NJ: Slack.

Leddy, S. K. (2004). Human energy: A conceptual model of unitary nursing science. *Visions: The Journal of Rogerian Nursing Science, 12*, 14–27.

Leddy, S. K. (2006). *Health promotion: Mobilizing strengths to enhance health, wellness, and well-being*. Philadelphia: F. A. Davis.

Leddy, S. K., & Fawcett, J. (1997). Testing the theory of healthiness: Conceptual and methodological issues. In M. Madrid (Ed.), *Patterns of Rogerian knowing* (pp. 75–86). New York: National League for Nursing.

Logan, A. C. (2007). *The brain diet, revised and expanded*. Nashville, TN: Cumberland House.

Mauk, K., & Schmidt, N. (2004). *Spiritual care in nursing practice*. Philadelphia: Lippincott Williams & Wilkins.

McWilliam, C. L., Stewart, M., Brown, J. B., Desai, K., & Coderre, P. (1996). Creating health with chronic illness. *Advances in Nursing Science, 18*, 1–15.

Mitchell, A., & Cormack, M. (1998). *The therapeutic relationship in complementary health care*. Edinburgh: Churchill Livingstone.

Newman, M. A. (1992). Prevailing paradigms in nursing. *Nursing Outlook, 40*, 10–13, 32.

Newman, M. A. (1994). *Health as expanding consciousness* (2nd ed.). St. Louis, MO: Mosby.

"Nursing top ten rewards." (2000). *Nursing 2000, 30*(5), 42–43.

O'Keefe, J., & O'Keefe, J. (2006). *The forever young diet & lifestyle*. Kansas City, MO: Andrews McNeel.

Papp, E. (2007). *Occupational health and safety management programme for nurses*. Geneva, Switzerland: International Council of Nurses.

Parse, R. R. (1987). *Nursing science: Major paradigms, theories, and critiques*. Philadelphia: W. B. Saunders.

Parsons, T. (1958). Definitions of health and illness in the light of American values and social structure. In E. G. Jaco (Ed.), *Patients, physicians, and illness* (pp. 165–187). Glencoe, IL: Free Press.

Pender, N. J. (1996). *Health promotion in nursing practice* (3rd ed.). Stamford, CT: Appleton & Lange.

Pender, N. J., Murdaugh, C. L., & Parsons, M. (2002). *Health promotion in nursing practice* (4th ed.). Upper Saddle River, NJ: Prentice Hall.

Pender, N. J., Murdaugh, C. L., & Parsons, M. (2005). *Health promotion in nursing practice* (5th ed.). Upper Saddle River, NJ: Pearson Prentice Hall.

Prochaska, J. O., Redding, C. A., Harlow, L. L., Rossi, J. S., & Velicer, W. F. (1994). The transtheoretical model of change and HIV prevention: A review. *Health Education Quarterly, 21*, 471–486.

Prochaska, J. O., Velicer, W. F., Rossi, J. S., Goldstein, M. G., Marcus, B. H., Rakowski, W., et al. (1994). Stages of change and decisional balance for 12 problem behaviors. *Health Psychology, 13*, 39–46.

Rau, T., & Wyler, S. (2007). *The Swiss secret to optimal health*. New York: Berkley.

Rosen, B. (2007). *A Gaia busy person's guide to chakras, finding balance and serenity in everyday life*. London: Gaia.

Rosenstock, I. M. (1966). Why people use health services. *Milbank Memorial Fund Quarterly, 44*, 94–127.

Rosenstock, I. M., Strecher, V. J., & Becker, N. H. (1988). Societal learning theory and the health belief model. *Health Education Quarterly, 25*, 175–183.

Smith, J. A. (1981). The idea of health: A philosophical inquiry. *Advances in Nursing Science, 3*, 43–50.

Sutton, R. (2006). *The no asshole rule*. New York: Warner Business Books.

Terris, M. (1975). Approaches to an epidemiology of health, *American Journal of Public Health, 65*, 1039.

Twaddle, A. C., & Hessler, R. M. (1977). *A sociology of health*. St. Louis, MO: Mosby.

U.S. Department of Health and Human Services. (2000). *Healthy people 2010*. Boston: Jones & Bartlett.

Vincent, C., & Furnham, A. (1997). *Complementary medicine: A research perspective*. Chichester, UK: John Wiley & Sons.

Wells-Federman, C. L. (1996). Awakening the nurse healer within. *Holistic Nursing Practice, 10*, 13–29.

Westberg, J., & Jason, H. (1996). Fostering healthy behavior: The process. In S. H. Woolf, S. Jonas, & R. S. Lawrence (Eds.). *Health promotion and disease prevention in clinical practice* (pp. 145–162). Baltimore: Williams & Wilkins.

World Health Organization Health Education Unit. (1986). Lifestyles and health. *Social Science and Medicine, 22*, 117–124.

Providing access to health care for all persons, delivering nursing care based on strong science and evidence, addressing specific cultural preferences when providing care, balancing accountability to clients in the era of cost containment, creating healthy environments, caring for communities, and using technology effectively are challenges for today's professional nurses. In addition, spiraling health care costs have led to increased consumer discontent with the health care system, which places health care providers at risk for litigation. This section provides an overview of these challenges while reinforcing professional nursing's goal of doing what is best for clients.

SECTION II

The Changing Health Care Context

CHAPTER 9

Health Care Delivery Systems

KEY TERMS AND CONCEPTS

Primary care

Secondary care

Tertiary care

Entrepreneurial insurance model

Mandated insurance model

National Health Service insurance model

Medicare

Medicaid

Prospective payment

Interdisciplinary health care team

Nursing care delivery models

LEARNING OUTCOMES

By the end of this chapter, the learner will be able to:

1   Explain the differences among primary, secondary, and tertiary care.

2   Identify key concerns and pressures for all health care delivery systems.

3   Specify the three major ways that health care is financed.

4   Explain how history shaped current American and Canadian health care systems.

5   Explain the major forces that influence change in the health care system.

6   Identify the impact of changes in health systems on nurses.

7   Explore practical and ethical issues associated with health care delivery systems on professional nurses.

VIGNETTE

Jane is a registered nurse employed by a hospital owned by a for-profit company. When Jane's father had hip replacement surgery, he received generic medication instead of his regular medicines during his hospital stay. He got quite upset because he was convinced that he was receiving the wrong medication. Two days after surgery, the case manager informed Jane's parents that her father would be transferred to an extended-care facility for rehabilitation the next day. Jane's parents became distraught because they had promised each other that they would never put each other in a nursing home. Jane's parents bombarded her with questions about why her father did not receive the same medications that he took at home and why he had to leave the hospital before he was well enough to care for himself.

In recent years, health care delivery has undergone radical transformation because of the explosion of scientific knowledge, integration of technology in health care, emphasis on health promotion, resource limiations, and shortages of health care professionals (especially professional nurses, primary care physicians, and pharmacists) (Andersen, Rice, & Kominski, 2007; Sanders, 2002). Health care delivery systems provide **primary care** for health promotion and illness prevention, **secondary care** for treatment toward the early detection and cure of illness, and **tertiary care** for chronic rehabilitative and end-of-life services. These changes impact the availability of and access to health care for many persons. This chapter explores current challenges for health care delivery, highlights selected countries that use different strategies to provide health care services, and outlines specific challenges for professional nurses.

CHALLENGES OF HEALTH CARE DELIVERY IN THE 21ST CENTURY

All health care delivery systems in the world struggle to provide optimal services for the persons that they serve. Display 9-1 outlines current challenges for all health care delivery systems. Access and cost seem to be the most prevalent current issues. Different countries because of different values, beliefs, wealth, history, and politics use different approaches for health care delivery. For example, is health care a right, responsibility, or luxury? Who should assume responsibility for health: the individual? The employer? The state?

Health Care Access

When the United Nations (UN) was chartered in 1945, the aim was to provide a global agency for international cooperation and collaboration. World health and the provision of health care services quickly emerged as key issues. The World Health Organization (WHO) was established as a UN unit whose early efforts included the eradication of infectious diseases and provision of health services for mothers and children (Jamieson & Sewall, 1954). By the middle of the 20th century, the WHO focused attention on providing essential health services to all. The UN and WHO held conferences to address the global environment, population, trade, and women's rights. By the late 1970s, the need to change global health care delivery became apparent (Zakus & Cortinois, 2002).

In 1978, the WHO and UNICEF held a joint conference at Alma-Ata, Kazakhstan during which a declaration was issued that affirmed that health and health care were

---

Challenges for Health Care Delivery Systems	**DISPLAY 9-1**

Ensuring access to care for all

Operating within the confines of available health care resources

Providing both preventive and curative services

Determining the optimal balance between health promotion, disease prevention, illness treatment, and quality of life

Attaining an effective system using governmental support and private resources

Providing and maintaining a qualified, competent health care workforce

Achieving a balance between health care needs with all other human needs

Responding to actual and future epidemics and other potential health threats

Allowing consumer participation in the provision of health care services

Enabling optimal health essential for a high quality of life

Sources of information:
Fried, B. J., & Gaydos, L. M. (2002). *World health systems: Challenges and perspectives.* Chicago: Health Administration Press.
Andersen, R., Rice, T., & Kominski, G (2007). *Changing the U.S. health care system* (3rd ed.). San Francisco: Wiley.

fundamental human rights. The conference report emphasized that social and economic development were key to supporting health care initiatives. In 1981, the World Health Assembly expanded the initiatives to promote and coordinate social and economic efforts to promote the general health and welfare of all persons (Zakus & Cortinois, 2002).

Despite international efforts to secure health care services for all, serious gaps persist. Wealthy developed nations have fully developed health care systems, while many poorer countries lack basic infrastuctures for health care delivery. Typically, rural residents have less access to health care services (in both wealthier developed and poorer undeveloped nations).

Countries differ in their approach to health care delivery. Some nations aspire to a business/market approach to health care delivery that relies on an individual's ability to pay for rendered services. Other nations use government-sponsored programs because for them health care is a basic human right and the government has the obligation to provide it. Although access is guaranteed under this approach, care may be delayed because of government funding shortfalls. Whichever approach is used, funding is needed to provide the basic infrastructure and qualified health care professionals.

Health Care Funding

American culture values individualism, independence, innovation, and capitalism. American health care is a big business. Pharmaceutical and health care equipment vendors bombard Americans with advertisements for the newest medications and therapies. Because American health care delivery has been based on a free enterprise system, some Americans believe that if the government controls the system, there might be a reduction in the quality of and access to health services (Sanders, 2002; Fifer, 2007). In contrast, Canada and Great Britain hold the belief that health care is the right of all citizens and fair access should be provided to all (Andersen et al., 2007; Fried & Gaydos, 2002; McIntyre & Thomlinson, 2003; Storch, 2005).

Funding of health care delivery challenges many nations (Andersen et al., 2007; Fischer, 2006; International Council of Nurses [ICN], 2006; O'Donnell, Smyth, & Frampton, 2005; Rosen & Haglund, 2005). People tend to spend money on things that have value to them. Unless they are extremely wealthy, most persons have some form of health insurance. Three different models of funding health care expenditures exist.

The **National Health Service model** funds health care by guaranteeing access to health care services through a national health insurance plan usually funded by general tax revenues. The citizens or government either own or control the factors for health care delivery and/or production of health care goods (Andersen et al., 2007; Sanders, 2002). The United Kingdom, Canada, and Japan are some of the nations that have adopted this model (Fried & Gaydos, 2002). Under the National Health Service model, some nations prohibit citizens from purchasing private health insurance. Promotion of equal access to and quality of services to all persons justifies the limitation (Sanders; McIntyre & Thomlinson, 2003; Storch, 2005). On the other hand, other countries enable citizens to purchase private insurance. A citizen's right to choose drives the justification for permitting private insurance purchase even though disparities in services may result (Fifer, 2007).

The **mandated insurance model** requires compulsory universal health care insurance. Nonprofit insurance funds provide resources for persons and employers to purchase health insurance (Andersen et al., 2007; Sanders, 2002). Some of the nations that have adopted this model include Germany, Brazil, Italy, Jamaica, and South Africa (Fried & Gaydos, 2002).

The **entrepreneurial insurance model** consists of voluntary health insurance coverage that relies upon purchase of health insurance by individuals. In this model, employment-based insurance occurs frequently. Employers provide group coverage and employees pay part of the insurance premium (Andersen et al., 2007; Sanders, 2002).

The United States, China, South Korea, Mexico, Nigeria, and India are some of the nations that espouse this model (Fried & Gaydos, 2002). The entrepreneurial health insurance model encourages persons to purchase private health insurance. For example, in the United States, federal- and state-sponsored programs provide access to all citizens who lack resources to buy health insurance, provided that they meet strict income and asset guidelines. **Medicare** is a federal program funded by income taxes that provides health care insurance for elderly and disabled Americans (Foster & Clemens, 2006). Many elderly opt to purchase private insurance to fill the gaps in Medicare coverage. **Medicaid** offers health care insurance coverage to persons who qualify for federally supported, but state-managed, welfare programs. States determine Medicaid eligibility requirements, but all states must provide coverage for persons who receive federal aid to families and children. To cover the health care costs of children whose parents cannot afford health insurance, the U.S. Congress enacted the State Children's Health Insurance Program (SCHIP). Thus, the U.S. government relies on states to manage federal health care programs for persons meeting eligibility criteria (Andersen et al., 2007).

Health Care Workforce

The 2006 World Health Report (WHO, 2007) estimated critical shortages of physicians, nurses, and midwives in 57 of 192 reporting countries. Europe was the only region that did not report a shortage of health care personnel. The report documented an estimated global shortage of over 2 million health care professionals. Currently, the world needs a 70% increase in the number of health care personnel to meet global health care needs (WHO, 2007).

According to the U.S. Bureau of Labor Statistics (2006–2007), there is a shortage of registered nurses (RNs). In 2006, there were 2.4 million RNs. American hospitals employ close to 60% of all working RNs. Of the working RNs, 23% work part-time and 7% hold more than one job. Because of the projected growth of the elderly in the next decade, 27% or more nurses will be needed by 2014 (U.S. Bureau of Labor Statistics, 2006–2007).

As a global phenomenon, the current shortage differs from cyclical shortages of the past. Nursing traditionally has been equated with women's work. Since the women's movement, more career opportunities have become open to women, resulting in younger women pursuing more lucrative and respected careers. The current nursing workforce is also aging. As these RNs retire, there are not enough replacements and nurses from poorer nations migrate to wealthier nations in order to live a better life (ICN, 2006). Unfortunately, some migrant nurses have been exploited by being forced to work to pay for relocation in sometimes unfair conditions (Kennedy, 2007).

Along with nurses, the need for American physicians is also expected to grow. However, the rate of growth is estimated to be somewhere between 18 and 26% by 2014. Currently, 40.8% of physicians practice primary care, with 12.8% of physicians being engaged in general/family practice. American physician salaries range from $156,010 to $321,616, with specialists earning substantially more (Bodenheimer, 2005; U.S. Census Bureau, 2006–2007). High physician salaries increase health delivery costs and open the door for increased use of nurse practitioners for primary care services.

Some nations simply do not have adequate funding to pay for professional services, thereby resulting in unemployed health care professionals (Andersen et al., 2007; ICN, 2006; WHO, 2007). Many unemployed health care professionals would rather stay safely at home than provide services in areas without stable goverments, safe food, effective sanitation, and reliable utilities.

In most nations, well-equipped and staffed hospitals are located in larger urban areas. Rural areas have special challenges to overcome to attract qualified health care personnel. Despite incentive programs, health care professionals (including nurses) prefer to work in work environments that offer them a voice in decision-making processes, provide support for continued professional development, and pay them a life-sustainable wage (ICN, 2006; WHO, 2007).

 SELECTED CURRENT HEALTH CARE DELIVERY SYSTEMS

Health care delivery systems arose as people identified a need to care for the infirmed and injured. Societal beliefs about the nature of the world provided the for early health delivery systems and continue to guide their evolution. Many different approaches to health care delivery occur around the world. Because of the impossibility to cover all systems within the confines of a single chapter, selected nations that have different approaches to health care delivery and represent various geographical locations are presented.

The American Health Care Delivery System

The American health care delivery system was largely influenced by Europe because European immigrants quickly became the dominant American cultural group. The evolution of the American health care delivery system explains its emphasis on market competition and individualism.

The Evolution of the American Health Care Delivery System

Early expeditions to the New World provided health care services to sailors and passengers. The Spaniards sent priests with health care expertise on missions to the New World even though the purpose was to convert Native Americans to Christianity. The priests provided public health services to Native Americans when they contracted contagious diseases (e.g., smallpox and influenza). While helping them, the priests kept detailed records of daily activities that included health-related information shared by the Native Americans. Other religious orders established missions to set up places for worship, trade, agriculture, and health care (Jamieson & Sewall, 1954).

The Franciscans built the first American hospital in 1531 as part of the Mission of Santa Fe (Spanish for "holy faith"). The hospital and monastery offered comprehensive services to the Native Americans and European settlers. The missions provided education and training centers. When outbreaks of European diseases occurred, Native Americans sought care within the confines of the missions (Jamieson & Sewall, 1954).

The British were less successful in establishing health care delivery. The captain of the ship, his spouse, or a minister typically provided health care to sailors and passengers. Prayer and various forms of quackery became the mainstay of health care in the British colonies, where any educated man could provide health care services (Jamieson & Sewall, 1954).

As in Europe, funding for health care in the Americas came from philanthropic and government sources. Physician learned medicine through an apprenticeship process. Hospitalization meant almost certain death (Jamieson & Sewall, 1954).

Until the middle of the 19th century, most American physicians had only a high school education and a minimal apprenticeship with a European-trained physician. Medical education focused on the new scientific discovery of germ theory. Epidemics of acute infectious diseases caused by contaminated food and water, poor sewage, and crowded conditions of urban housing were the predominant health problems. No organized health programs existed because the predominant ethic of the time was that of self-sufficiency, and accepting charity was seen as a sign of grave, personal weakness (Torrens, 1978). Thus, the seeds for the American value of independence were sown into health care delivery.

Most early American hospitals were actually almshouses or pesthouses where the socially marginal fragments of society resided (Vogel, 1979). Because hospitals were supported by the philanthropy of the wealthy, class distinctions were considered to be justified, and hospital patients were stigmatized as dependent and somehow unworthy of societal membership. By 1873, the United States had 178 established hospitals (Jonas, 1998) and formal education in nursing began (Torrens, 1978).

Scientific Advancements

In the mid- to late 1800s, scientific discoveries revolutionized health care. Anesthesia was introduced in 1847 and antisepsis became prevalent by 1865, leading to the need for centralized facilities to support expensive equipment for surgery. Germ theory became accepted for the transmission of infectious diseases, and the typhus vaccine became available in 1896. By 1860, the thermometer, ophthalmoscope, and laryngoscope were in use, joined by the gastroscope, cystoscope, hypodermic needle, and sphygmomanometer by 1883. X-rays were discovered in 1895. Hospitals improved hygiene measures. People went to hospitals for advanced diagnostic tests and treatment. Hospitals became places of healing rather than death (Jamieson & Sewall, 1954).

Health Care Becomes a Flourishing Industry

As urbanization increased, hospitals flourished. Hospital-owned schools of nursing provided an inexpensive source of nursing care. Hospitalized patients provided rich learning experiences for nursing and medical students. An apprenticeship approach dominated nursing and medical education. Medical education moved to university settings and developed independent prestige based on increased scientific knowledge, whereas nursing became associated with a medically dependent scope of practice, with an apprenticeship type of education totally dominated by hospitals.

Health Care in the Early 20th Century

Hospitals and physicians enjoyed high profits by providing services to wealthy, private patients who could afford their services. However, "the poor and penniless, whom the institution had originally been meant to serve, became a liability" (Vogel, 1979, p. 115). A two-tiered system of private and public institutions arose. Public institutions met the health care needs of the poor; physician-dominated private hospitals met the needs of the affluent. The nuclear family replaced the extended family and health care moved from being home oriented and family centered to institutionally centered. Health care became a stratified and localized system administered by municipalities (as in the British and French traditions).

In 1901, the American Medical Association (AMA) was restructured, and "doctors sought to assure their financial security and power through their own organization and reform of medical education" (Markowitz & Rosner, 1979, p. 186), thereby eliminating competition from other persons as health care providers. Private foundations supplied additional resources to the AMA, thereby creating a central power source for medical practice and education. Efforts focused on replacing the haphazard art of medical practice with new scientific-based knowledge. As new treatments and technology developed, more hospitals were needed. By 1910, the number of hospitals in the United States expanded to 4,400 (Jonas, 1998).

Concerned with the impact of illness on worker productivity, Montgomery Ward and Company, in 1910, provided group insurance for illness and injury. This plan frequently is regarded as the first group health insurance coverage in the United States. The Ladies' Garment Workers' Union provided the first union medical care services after a fatal accident that killed 146 women (Public Broadcasting Service [PBS], 2007).

World War I (WWI) provided an opportunity for Americans to learn about different health care approaches. Health care personnel shortages also increased. The global influenza epidemic of 1918 and pneumonia killed more soldiers than combat. Because of contagious disease fatalities (including physicians and nurses), public health efforts focused efforts on containing and preventing infectious diseases. Because of hospital overcrowding, families assumed responsibility for nursing care at home and physicians made home visits (Jamieson & Sewall, 1954). Between 1915 and 1920, 16 states introduced, debated, and rejected legislation mandating health insurance coverage for all (PBS, 2007).

The Depression of the 1930s had a devastating effect on the developing American health care system. Without employment, many American adults could not feed or clothe their families, much less even think about paying for health care services if needed. Therefore, illness prevention and health promotion became top priorities for government-sponsored health programs (Jonas, 1998). The government increasingly assumed responsibility for providing and funding health care services. In 1935, the Social Security Act included provisions for financially supporting the indigent and the infirmed elderly, thereby carving out a role for the federal government in providing health care services (PBS, 2007).

Accident and life insurance companies started offering insurance covering hospital services. The first hospitalization insurance plan, Blue Cross, covered a group of teachers from Dallas, Texas, in 1929 (Scofera, 1994). In 1939, a Blue Shield plan for medical and surgical expenses was sponsored by the California Medical Society. Prior to World War II, less than 20% of Americans had any form of health care insurance (Scofera).

Many medical care advancements were made during World War II (WWII, 1939–1945). Penicillin and sulfonamides successfully treated infections. Blood transfusions became commonplace to treat blood loss. Insect- and rodent-borne diseases were virtually eliminated with dichloro-diphenyl-trichloroethane (DDT). During WWII, the War Labor Board froze wages to divert resources to the war effort. To appease unions and workers, employers added health insurance to fringe benefit packages (PBS, 2007). Vaccines were proven safe as WWII soldiers received vaccines prior to deployment and few adverse effects occurred. Rehabilitation and psychiatric medicine advanced as war-injured soldiers returned home. To assume responsibility for war-related injuries (physical or psychological), the U.S. government set up the Veterans Administration (VA) program (Jamieson & Sewall, 1954). The VA health care system still offers extensive rehabilitation programs and health care services to all veterans.

Following WWII, workers expected reasonable wages, employers, and hospitalization insurance. Because of problems arising in the health insurance industry, the McCarran-Ferguson Act was enacted that provided state regulation of all forms of insurance (PBS, 2007). By 1951, 100 million Americans had some form of health care insurance coverage (Scofera, 1994), enabling many people to reap the benefits of scientifically developed medications and surgical interventions. Because of the technical skills required to administer new therapies, hospitals expanded and became places where persons got well.

Health Care in the Mid- to Late 20th Century

Health care vastly changed in the mid- to late 20th century. Increased scientific knowledge resulted in an information explosion that led to the era of specialization for health care delivery, which resulted in fragmentation and increased cost (Jonas, 1998; Kovner & Jonas, 1999). Infectious diseases were eradicated because of the widespread use of antibiotics. Chronic diseases became prevalent, and complex regimens to control them were developed.

"The percentage of Americans covered by some form of health insurance rose from less than 20% prior to World War II to more than 70% by the early 1960s" (Torrens, 1978, p. 13). The increased demand for health care resulted in the passage of the Hill-Burton Act (1946) that stimulated hospital construction. The Department of Health, Education and Welfare was formed in 1953 to provide a mechanism to coordinate health research and service programs. The Civil Rights Movement (equal rights for all) espoused the belief that equal health care is a basic right and encouraged the government to became more involved in health care. In 1965, Congress amended the Social Security Act to provide Medicare and Medicaid, thereby creating a role for the federal government in health care delivery for the elderly and poor.

By 1960, 320 million Americans were covered by some form of health care insurance (Scofera, 1994). Whereas the 1960s had emphasized equity and cohesion of services, the 1970s concentrated on access, with tremendous growth in the number of hospitals, ancillary services, and sophisticated technology. The emphasis on research and technology led to specialization and depersonalization, as well as rapidly escalating expenses (Jonas, 1998; Kovner & Jonas, 1999). Expenditures on health care services were essentially unmonitored. Increased demand for services led to more hospitals, extended-care facilities, and health-related research facilities.

By the late 1970s, spiraling and unacceptable health care costs became impossible to ignore. The federal government established new regulations to monitor delivered services along with reductions in funding. The changes rewarded efficiency over equity, quality, and access. Prospective payment reimbursement for hospital expenses for Medicare patients was introduced in 1981 as an effort to reduce hospital costs. **Prospective payment** set prearranged reimbursement amounts (by diagnostic category) known as diagnosis-related groups (DRGs) that the federal government paid hospitals for care given to Medicare recipients. The hospital received the prearranged amount, regardless of accrued costs.

Under the prospective payment system, big profits could be made, resulting in a business approach to health care. Detailed documentation of medical services and supplies used became crucial as insurance providers looked for reasons to deny reimbursement. For-profit insurance companies and hospital chains grew. Not-for-profit hospitals invested increased profits back into expanding and improving hospital services for the community, thereby increasing consumer access to sophisticated health care services. However, by the late 1980s, the federal government progressively reduced the amount of reimbursement for specific DRGs, which added financial pressure to struggling smaller (and usually rural) hospitals.

Managed care plans started in the 1970s and flourished as health care costs continued to rise. Enrollment in managed care plans rose from 2 million persons in 1970 to more than 39 million persons in 1992. Managed care plans believed that they could reduce health care costs by promoting health (Scofera, 1994; Andersen et al., 2007). The following three models of managed care emerged: health maintenance organizations (HMOs), preferred provider organizations (PPOs), and point-of-service plans (POS). Table 9-1 highlights the differences among the plans.

Because of the economic downslide of the 1980s, many persons lost their jobs and, along with it, their health care coverage. In 1985, the Consolidated Omnibus Budget Reconciliation Act (COBRA) was enacted. COBRA requires that employers (with more than 20 workers) partially subsidize health insurance coverage offered to former employees (and their dependents) for 18 months after terminating employment. Because of the high costs associated with COBRA, many unemployed Americans could not afford to continue health care coverage (Andersen et al., 2007).

The 1990s brought many changes in the health care delivery system. During the 1990s, health care expenditures rose close to twice the rate of inflation between 1990 and 1995. Between 1950 and 2000, health care costs rose, on the average, 3.4%. At the same time, inflation rose 2.5%. Health care costs increased at twice the rate of inflation in 2001–2002 and slowed to less than twice the inflation rate in 2002–2003. Since 2003, American expenditures for health care rose from 15% of the gross domestic product (GDP) to 16.1% (U.S. Department of Health and Human Services, 2008). They are expected to increase to 18.7% of the GDP by 2014 (Andersen et al., 2007).

Multiple efforts in hopes to contain health care costs in the late 20th century included reductions in prospective payments, consolidation of health care services, and hospital closures. Hospital costs fell because of reduced lengths of inpatient stays. Only the medically unstable were hospitalized. Once stabilized, people were expected to leave the hospital. Medicare and insurance companies provided coverage for rehabilitation in extended-care facilities (if patients were too weak to return home safely). When possible, family members would provide care to relatives at home. Insurance companies also shifted the burden of rising health care costs to consumers by increasing premiums, co-payments, and deductibles (Andersen et al., 2007).

TABLE 9-1

Differences in Managed Care Models

Health Maintenance Organization	Preferred Provider Organization	Point-of-Service Plan
Group-model HMOs contract directly with a single medical group to care for members. Staff-model HMOs contract with individual physicians to serve members. Network HMOs contract with a network of physicians to provide services for members.	Network of preferred health care providers contained within an insurance plan who agree to follow insurance company's utilization guidelines and accept deeply discounted fees for provided services.	Network of preferred providers who contract to provide services for a managed care company and follow guidelines set by the insurance carrier while accepting discounted fees for rendered services.
Open-panel HMOs permit physicians to treat non-HMO members. Closed-panel HMOs require physicians under contract to see members only.	Members can access physicians not on the list of preferred providers, but they have substantially higher co-payments for services.	Members select the level of managed care services: 1. Use of a primary care provider gatekeeper for specialist referrals 2. Self-referral to specialists within the provider network 3. Self-referral to specialist of choice
Cheapest of all forms for consumer because of limitations of covered services.	Costs for co-payments higher than those for HMOs.	Graduated co-payments with members using a gatekeeper having the lowest out-of-pocket expenses and members with ability to self-refer to their specialist of choice having the highest co-payment.
Members must receive authorization for care from a specialist, usually a primary care physician.	Members can self-refer for specialist services.	
In the 1990s, some HMOs offered self-referral to specialists, but members had higher co-pays.	Preferred providers agreed.	

Information adapted from Andersen, R., Rice, T., & Kominski, G (2007). *Changing the U.S. health care system* (3rd ed.). San Francisco: Wiley, pp. 552–553.

Increased competition as a cost-containment mechanism provided an opportunity for nurse practitioners to expand primary and secondary health care services despite opposition by many physicians. The free market approach dominated the health care industry in the 20th century and continues today (Jonas, 1998; LeBow, 2003; Feldstein, 2004).

American Health Care Costs

Health care providers continue to explore new methods for health care delivery to provide high-quality and cost-effective client care. The late 20th century saw an explosion of technology and scientific advances. Many health care leaders debate the benefits of a market-driven health care system based on the premise that competition controls the costs of health care delivery. These changes have resulted in a highly complex, multifaceted health care delivery system in the 21st century, which has resulted in the United States using over 15% of its GDP for health care (Andersen et al., 2007).

According to the U.S. Federal Health Care Financing Administration (HCFA), health care expenditures fall into the following categories: health-related research, facility construction, or payment for personal health care services and supplies. Costs for individual health care services and supplies supersede those of new construction or research, with hospital costs being the greatest single health care expense (Andersen et al., 2007; Thorpe & Knickman, 1999; Sultz & Young, 2004).

Provider Costs

American hospital costs surpass those of all developed nations. The amount of money charged for an acute-care hospital patient day in the United States is more than twice the Canadian costs and three times higher than those of most other developed countries. Hospitalized Americans undergo more sophisticated diagnostic procedures and intensive medical regimens. The increased use of highly technical equipment and expensive medications fuels rising health care costs. Because of the litigious nature of the American culture, the threat of malpractice suits adds to the costs (Bodenheimer, 2005).

Physician income in the United States (on average) is 1.5 to 3 times higher than that of physicians in other developed countries. The United States tends to have a surplus of specialist physicians because they earn substantially more than general practice physicians (Bodenheimer, 2005). Advanced practice registered nurses (APRNs) offer an alternative to the high costs of physician services. Despite resistance by organized medicine, in 1996, all states allowed third-party reimbursement to APRNs (Sultz & Young, 2004). Services rendered by APRNs cost substantially less, and consumers report high satisfaction.

Insurance

In 2008, the U.S. Census Bureau reported that there were 44.8 million uninsured persons in the United States, approximately 15.3% of the American population. The Census Bureau also estimated that over 250 million Americans were underinsured (Hellander, 2008). The rate of uninsured Americans tends to fluctuate with the unemployment rate. However, 83% of employed adults cannot afford the employee contribution to their employer-sponsored health insurance plan (Andersen et al., 2007). Twenty-eight percent of Americans aged 18 to 35 years have no health insurance and represent the fastest-growing group of the uninsured in the United States (U.S. Census Bureau, 2004). The lack of affordability of private health care insurance serves as an impetus to mandated national health insurance and other health care reform measures.

Corporations represent the largest purchasers of private health insurance. Employer-offered health insurance accounts for 60.36% of privately funded health care insurance coverage (U.S. Census Bureau, 2004). In an effort to contain costs, companies have:

- limited consumer choice of providers through HMOs or PPOs;
- increased premiums, deductibles, and out-of-pocket charges;
- required authorization for hospitalizations and second opinions;
- substituted ambulatory and home care to reduce hospital stays; and
- encouraged reduced use of services.

Pressures for change in insurance policies have potential opportunities for nursing. Nurses serve as competitive alternatives for providing primary care services. Nurse actions reduce care costs while improving care quality. Nurses educate consumers about ways to practice healthful living, monitor them for adverse effects of medical and invasive interventions, make referrals to community resources, and ensure effective use of health care resources. As responsible client advocates, nurses need to become active participants in the creation of new health care delivery systems.

The Canadian Health Care Delivery System

Like the United States, Canada enjoys much wealth. Both countries share a similar history, but different historical decisions resulted in Canada adopting a very different form of health care delivery.

Historical Development of the Canadian Health Care System

The French established colonies in Canada. In May 1639, Mme. de la Peltrie, along with Augustinian and Ursuline sisters, established a trading post infirmary. The Augustinian sisters established the Hôtel Dieu in Quebec City, Quebec in 1639. They dispensed medications and offered cheerful encouragement to ill persons who preferred to stay at home. In 1645, Jean. Mance established the Hôtel Dieu in Montreal as a hospital for wounded French and British soldiers during the Seven Years' War. In 1693, the Jesuits built another hospital in Canada using the support of the wealthy Duchess d'Aigillon, who obtained land and permission to establish a hospital (Jamieson & Sewall, 1954).

In Canada the Fathers of Confederation laid out terms of the British North America Act of 1867 that specified responsibilities of the Canadian government, which included taking a census, collecting vital statistics, determining quarantine regulations, providing hospitals for persons in quarantine, and caring for Canadian natives. Along with these basic responsibilities, a section of the act provided for the establishment of provincial hospitals, asylums, and charities (Goldsmith, 2002; McIntryre & Thomlinson, 2003; Storch, 2005).

Rising health care costs also plagued Canadians, resulting in federal efforts to provide coverage for health expenditures for everyone. In 1947, the Province of Saskatchewan enacted the Hospital Insurance Act, which provided hospital insurance for all its residents. At the same time, the Canadian government offered grants to the provinces and public health agencies for hospital construction and provision of health care services. In the 1960s, Saskatchewan expanded insurance coverage to include outpatient health care, and by 1968 the Medical Care Act was enacted, thereby providing national health insurance for all Canadians (Goldsmith, 2002; McIntyre & Thomlinson, 2003; Storch, 2005).

Canada also experienced problems with skyrocketing health care costs and limited public funding. The Canada Health Care Act of 1984 resulted in provincial administration of health care programs. All Canadians have equal access to a specific list of health care services under provincial policy plans. Additional costs cannot be incurred by citizens for services covered by these plans. Finally, the Canadian plan is portable and covers citizens if they move from province to province or travel abroad. However, non-emergency and out-of-province services require preauthorization (McIntryre & Thomlinson, 2003; Storch, 2005).

Principles of the Canadian Health Care System

Health care in Canada is directed by five key principles. First, a public, nonprofit authority administers provincial health insurance plans and answers to the provincial government. Second, each insurance plan covers all eligible residents using uniform terms and conditions. Third, Canadians have health insurance coverage when they travel abroad or across provinces. However, the plans have limited out-of-country coverage and provincial plan approval is required for non-emergency services when receiving care out of the province in which a citizen resides. Fourth, each plan covers "all medically necessary services" citizens may need from physicians and hospitals. Finally, the plans provide reasonable access to health services without discrimination. Provincial plans may require premiums from citizens, but care cannot be denied based on inability to pay for coverage (Goldsmith, 2002).

Funds for the Canadian health care system come from taxes (primarily payroll), health insurance premiums, and consumer out-of-pocket expenses. Tax credits offer relief for high out-of-pocket health care expenditures. For services not covered by government plans, some Canadians may purchase private health care policies. Approximately 65% of Canadians have private insurance that covers dental, chiropractic, and some complementary health care services (Goldsmith, 2002; Jost, 2005).

Because of citizens' complaints about getting required health care in a timely fashion, the provincial premiers agreed to the Health Renewal Accord in 2003. Principles outlined by the accord include 24-hour-a-day, 7-day-a-week access to a health provider; timely access to procedures for diagnosis and treatments; elimination of the need to repeat health histories or diagnostic tests for each provider seen; and access to home and community health care. Although the Canadian health care system is perceived as being efficient, it responds slowly in addressing needed reforms. Increased collaboration among the federal and provincial governments and the sharing of best practices based on solid evidence have resulted in improvement of Canadian health care outcomes (Storch, 2005).

The Mexican Health Care Delivery System

Unlike Canada and the United States, Mexico has less wealth. Rapid industrialization with increasing environmental pollution along with increasing tobacco and alcohol use, poor diet, sedentary lifestyle, and infectious diseases (in crowded urban areas) pose challenges to the health status of Mexicans. Not all Mexicans have equal access to health care services. The affluent purchase private health insurance plans; workers are covered through a social security system or purchase employment-based health insurance. The poor rely on a public services system. The Ministry of Health (MOH) manages health promotion and disease prevention for Mexican citizens. In addition, the MOH monitors and tests medications made by and sold in Mexico for quality, safety, and efficacy (Johnson, Carillo, & Garcia, 2002).

Affluent Mexicans receive the same quality of care and services enjoyed by Canadians and Americans. The Mexican health care system consists of hospitals, outpatient facilities, and long-term care facilities. Modern medical centers are located in urban areas. Health care in rural areas frequently has problems with understaffing and relies on medical students as providers. In recent years, health delivery to Mexicans covered by public services has become decentralized, and emphasis has been placed on a healthy municipalities program. Shifting the emphasis to health promotion rather than disease treatment for public health services has increased access to health care services for the poor (Johnson et al., 2002).

The Chinese Health Care Delivery System

China was established as a nation in 221 BC under the auspices of the Qin Dynasty. China has been a communist state since 1949. Chinese health policy and services are guided by universal health care. Health care personnel goals center around maximal output. Health services focus on prevention rather than treatment (Williams & Jian, 2002).

The central government has various governmental departments to address all aspects of health. Because of concerns for contagious disease epidemics, China has a Nationwide Anti-epidemic Computer Telecommunication Network that disseminates information about disease outbreaks to the entire nation. Priorities for health care services are aimed at reducing tobacco use, preventing sexually transmitted diseases, overcoming the effects of poverty, ensuring proper diet and safe food sources, and fostering exercise in the general population. The government enacted a one-child-per-family policy to curtail population growth (Williams & Jian, 2002).

The government acknowledges the need for effective health care services because healthy workers mean increased productivity. The recent transformation of the economy to a partial free-market approach has resulted in cost-of-living variations across provinces. Thus, provinces and counties determine wages for health care personnel. The central government tightly controls the number of health care professionals and professional mobility. Independent associations for health care workers do not exist (Williams & Jian, 2002).

The state owns most of the Chinese hospitals and health clinics. Provincial and county governments, cities, village resident committees, and the MOH administer hospitals and clinics. Few clinics and fewer hospitals are owned and operated by joint ventures, collectives, and the private sector (Williams & Jian, 2002).

Four principles guide the delivery of health care in China. First, health care and medicine comprise a service for workers, peasants, and soldiers. Second, preventive medicine supersedes curative medicine. Third, traditional Chinese medicine should be blended with Western medicine to attain the benefits of both approaches. Finally, health services should be available to all people (Williams & Jian, 2002).

China has a three-tiered health care delivery system with expanding services based on the size of the facility and the number of people each serves. According to health care protocols, persons should seek care at the lowest level before using hospital services. In urban locales, lane and street health stations serve neighborhoods and provide health promotion, family planning, and maternal-child health care using health care personnel similar to physician assistants and nurse practitioners. District hospitals offer a full range of inpatient and outpatient services and employ the most highly educated and experienced physicians, nurses, and technicians (Williams & Jian, 2002).

In rural locations, the levels of service are composed of village health stations, township health centers, and county hospitals. Village stations are staffed by a medical doctor, several midwives, and health aides, and offer preventive health, maternal-child, and first-aid services. Township health centers provide similar services, but are staffed with a highly trained physician who supervises assistant physicians, village doctors, and nurses. County hospitals offer inpatient and outpatient services to the more seriously ill and are staffed with assistant doctors, nurses, and technicians (Williams & Jian, 2002). Lack of access to power in rural Chinese areas has prevented the ability of the Chinese to use computers, telemedicine, and sophisticated equipment requiring electricity (Toffler & Toffler, 2007).

The Indian Health Care Delivery System

India attained independence from Great Britain in 1947. As the second most populous country in the world, and without much wealth, communicable diseases remain a major cause of death and disability (Shah, 2002).

Hallmarks of the Indian health system include the following: (1) privatizing medical services, (2) permitting user fees for rendered services, (3) allowing private investment in public hospitals, and (4) creating technologically centered interventions. The central Indian government determines policies, has a national strategic delivery framework, finances health care partially, and regulates medical education, pharmaceuticals, and immunization programs. The Ministry of Health and Family Welfare (MOHFW) supervises these functions. Each state and union territory has its own MOHFW to implement governmental health policies (Shah, 2002).

Health care funding comes from the national, state, and local branches of government; combined governmental and private insurance pools; and out-of-pocket expenditures. Insurance covers allopathic and traditional Indian treatments. The Central Government Health Scheme (GHS) and the Employer State Insurance Scheme (ESIS) are two government-based insurance plans. The GHS covers national government employees, pensioners, and their families. The ESIS covers private citizens who meet income eligibility requirements. Persons with incomes exceeding ESIS income caps purchase employer-based or private health insurance coverage. Consumers pay providers directly for services and receive retrospective reimbursement from insurance providers according to an established fee-for-service schedule. Hospitals also offer health care plans that provide services similar to those of American managed care programs. Many employers opt for this form of coverage for their workers because hospitals tailor plans based on employer specifications. Most plans cover inpatient and outpatient services (Shah, 2002).

Most of the health care resources in India are located in urban areas. However, most of the population resides in rural areas. An integrated network of rural health care consisting of community health centers, primary health centers, and subcenters provides services to rural citizens. Over half of the hospitals are privately owned. More than three fourths of the allopathic physicians practice medicine in the private sector. Privately owned hospitals contain start-of-the-art equipment and are staffed with highly qualified nurses and physicians. Religious-affiliated and voluntary agency–sponsored hospitals charge lower fees for high-quality care and frequently reserve beds for charity care. Government hospitals frequently deliver substandard care, and have ill-kept wards and less than optimal sanitation (Shah, 2002).

The Turkish Health Care Delivery System

In 1923, Mustafa Kemal Ataturk founded the Republic of Turkey, which is ruled as a parliamentary democracy. The government strove to make health care services available to all starting in the 1960s. However, because of economic woes, Turkey never quite attained this goal. Many huge disparities exist in regard to urban and rural health care in Turkey (Tansel, 2002).

The Turkish government bears legal responsibility for providing preventive and curative health services. The State Planning Organization plans health services, develops objectives, sets health care policies, and controls capital expenditures for public hospitals. The MOH designs and implements plans for health care delivery and operates hospitals. Health care funding is approved by Parliament. The MOH receives funding for health care services from the national budget and tax revenues. Insurance companies and individual users of health care services also provide revolving funds that add to the funds available for health care. The MOH decides how allocated funds are to be spent (Tansel, 2002).

University hospitals receive funding for rendered health care services from allocations from the Higher Education Board and the MOH along with funds received from insurers and individual consumers. The Social Insurance Organization (SSK) is a social security program for all private-sector employees and blue-collar state workers. Employers and employees both contribute to the system, which provides retirement and health care benefits. Bag-Kur is a health insurance program for the self-employed. Bag-Kur contracts for health care services for inpatient and outpatient care using a standardized fee schedule.

Government employees and retirees are entitled to health care through the Government Employees Retirement Fund. Active civil servants receive free preventive health services through governmental health care units. When additional health care needs arise, they are referred to other health care providers. Private insurance offers coverage for anyone who wishes and can afford to purchase it. To attract employees, many private firms offer private health insurance as a fringe benefit. Poor citizens who are unable to afford care or insurance receive a green card from the government that is used for free services at any MOH or university health center (Tansel, 2002).

Turkey delivers health care in a variety of settings. Care access and quality differ between urban and rural locations, with increased availability and options in larger cities. The government does not offer incentives for health care personnel to work in rural settings. The health post (the smallest center) typically serves persons in rural areas. Because the government typically pays for the education of physicians and nurses, graduates of medical and nursing programs are required to spend time (1–2 years) staffing the rural health care posts.

Health centers comprise the next level, serve 500 to 1,000 persons, and are staffed by a physician, nurse, midwife, health technician, and medical secretary. Health centers offer family planning, health education, environmental health, statistical data collection, immunizations, communicable disease prevention and therapy, and maternal-child care services. Along with health centers, Turkey has dispensaries dedicated to special care needs for infectious diseases and mental health. Hospitals serve as the final tier of health care. Over half of the hospitals are owned and operated by the MOH. The remaining hospitals are owned and operated by the SSK (10%), the private sector (18%), the Ministry of Defense (4%), and universities (3%). Most health care personnel work for the public sector and have civil service status. However, some physicians combine part-time public service work with private practice. Turkish nurses usually work in secondary and tertiary health care settings.

The Nigerian Health Care Delivery System

Nigeria is a very poor African nation consisting of a federation of 36 states with a central capital federation known as the Capitol Territory. Nigerian residents come from 380 different ethnic groups. As a rapidly developing nation, Nigeria has experienced a rapid rate of urbanization (Lacey, 2002).

Accurate data about Nigerian health and use of health care services are difficult to obtain because 60% of Nigerians use private sector health care that includes local traditional healers. Basically, Nigerians have little access to modern health care services (Lacey, 2002).

Local governments assume primary health care services for Nigerian citizens. Primary health care services are organized using a three-tiered system composed of village, district, and local government levels. Each tier has its own health care committee composed of representatives from the state MOH, nongovernmental organizations, professional health staff, local community leaders, and elected council members. The state MOH coordinates health care efforts with the federal MOH. Local councils of elected members make decisions about primary health care services. The health committees develop project proposals, collect data about basic health data, and implement health care services.

The Nigerian government expanded the health services initiated by the British. A federal MOH coordinates payments for health services using petroleum tax revenues. A school of health technology provides training for community health workers who staff local health facilities run by the government (Lacey, 2002).

The primary health care system is composed of village health posts that serve about 500 persons, dispensaries that provide services to 10,000 persons, health clinics that provide health services to 20,000 to 50,000 persons, and primary health care centers that offer services to 20,000 to 80,000 persons. Along with primary health care centers, Nigeria has state hospitals that are managed by the Hospital Management Board. State hospitals are frequently overcrowded and understaffed, and have few supplies.

Local governments receive financial support from six sources: (1) the Nigerian Federation Account (a national account with funds approved by the legislature for health care delivery), (2) grants from the model local government authority, (3) state revenues, (4) local taxes, (5) nonprofit donor organizations, and (6) community members. Local authorities base decisions typically on how to do the most good for the entire community. Most funding for health care is spent on staff salaries rather than medications and supplies (Lacey, 2002).

The private sector and nongovernmental agencies in Nigeria deliver approximately 60% of the services. Along with traditional tribal medicine, private firms own and operate hospitals, clinics, chemist shops, and other health organizations. Traditional medical services include herbalists, bonesetters, birth attendants (similar to midwives), and spiritual healers. Religious-based organizations also provide health care services in churches and schools. The Christian Health Association of Nigeria (CHAN) collaborates with the federal MOH to coordinate all church-sponsored health care services. CHAN-affiliated health care facilities serve the urban and rural poor by running hospitals, freestanding clinics, maternal centers, and mobile clinics (Lacey, 2002).

Local health care delivery uses the efforts of "a chief medical offer, physicians, community health supervisors, public health nurses, midwives, nurses, a community health superintendent, laboratory technicians, dispensary/pharmacy technicians, record officers, community health assistants and a family planning manager (typically a nurse)" (Lacey, 2002, p. 512). The primary health care team offers health education; supplies adequate food, safe water, and basic sanitation; delivers maternal-child health care (including family planning); administers immunizations; manages contagious diseases; maintains health records (of commonly encountered illnesses and injuries); and provides essential medications and supplies (Lacey).

Comparing and Contrasting the Selected Health Care Delivery Systems

Various health care systems are used to provide health care services to different populations. Access to a clean water source, effective sanitation, and adequate food supply clearly separate health care needs for developed and undeveloped nations. For example, in developing nations malnutrition, infant and child mortality, and communicable diseases are frequently the major health concerns. However, in wealthy, developed nations, diseases of affluence (obesity, and chronic diseases such as diabetes mellitus and degenerative joint diseases) emerge as major health concerns.

National wealth also results in the amount of funding available to build and maintain health facilities, along with providing them with adequate human and material resources. Wealthy persons have resources to spend on health care services even if they live in undeveloped countries. Not all citizens of a wealthy nation have resources to access and receive required health care services. 2007 WHO data on the presented countries reveals that the United States spends 15.4% of its GDP on health care compared with Canada (9.8%) and Turkey (4.7%). India has 63 hospitals per 10,000 persons compared to Mexico, which has 10 hospitals for the same number of persons. The Canadian government supplies 69.8% of funding for health services, and 69.9% of Nigerian health care services are funded by the private sector. Nations with a history of British or communist influences tend to approach health care delivery as a state, rather than as a personal responsibility.

The number of health care professionals also varies according to the development and financial status of a country. 2007 WHO data reveal that the United States reported the highest concentration of physicians, pharmacists, and managerial and support staff. Fifer (2007) and Bodenheimer (2005) proposed that the high level of management and support staff greatly increases the cost of American health care delivery. Canada ranks highest in the concentration of nurses, 9.95 per 10,000 persons. India and Mexico have fewer than one nurse for 10,000 persons. Turkey and the United States both reported 1.63 dentists per 10,000 persons, thereby addressing the link of dental health to general health. Less affluent nations report having shortages of health care professionals.

Although the United States and Canada offer similar health care services but use different sources of funding, citizens of both nations tend to be satisfied with the services that they receive. Research Brief 9-1 is a landmark study comparing the health status between these two countries.

 ## HEALTH CARE DELIVERY SETTINGS

Persons seek health care services in a variety of settings. Table 9-2 outlines various types of facilities and explains the differences. Organizations offering health care services differ according to mission and philosophy. Although they exist to offer health care services, organizations differ in being proprietary (privately funded and for profit), governmental (publicly funded and not for profit), or voluntary (privately funded and not for profit) (Jonas, 1998). For-profit organizations tend to emphasize providing services while achieving a high profit margin.

To avoid the high costs associated with hospital-based care, more outpatient facilities have opened. Some examples of alternative ambulatory care systems include diagnostic, urgent care, surgery, birthing, substance abuse, and rehabilitation centers. Health care consumers also can receive health care services in outpatient clinics and urgent care centers located in shopping malls or pharmacies. Some clinics may be affiliated with an integrated health care delivery system or hospital. Consumers also may get annual influenza vaccinations at grocery stores, pharmacies, and/or places of business. In addition, home health agencies and hospices provide nursing services in home settings. Recognizing the need to offer more outpatient services, some hospitals have built plush outpatient centers complete with food courts and small shops. To promote health within the community, hospitals hold classes on health-promoting topics, such as smoking cessation, various types of exercise, weight reduction, and basic life support.

Primary Care Options
Persons seeking allopathic medical care typically consult physicians. Physicians tend to practice in either individual practice associations (IPAs) or preferred provider organizations

Research Brief 9-1

Sanmartin, C., Ng, E., Blackwell, D., Gentleman, J., Martinez, M., & Simile, C. (2004). *Joint Canada/United States survey of health*. Washington, DC: Centers for Disease Control. Available at http://www.cdc.gov/nchs/data/hsis/jcush_analyticalreport.pdf.

This landmark multinational study sought to compare the quality of health and satisfaction of health care delivery in the United States and Canada. In 2002–2003, a random sample of 5,000 Americans and 3,500 Canadians participated in telephone interviews.

Results revealed that Canadians and Americans report having similar access to a variety of health care services. Canadians and Americans rely on insurance for dental care. Eighty-five percent of Americans and 88% of Canadians described their health as being good or excellent. Persons with low incomes in both countries reported poorer health status. Ninety percent of Americans and 87% of Canadians reported being very or somewhat satisfied with their current health care. Similarities in health status were noted in mobility, depressive episodes within the last 12 months, percentage of persons seeing a physician within the previous 12 months, number of dental visits, and dental insurance coverage. Differences occurred in the following areas: Canada had a slightly higher percentage of daily smokers, more Americans were found to be obese, poor persons in the United States reported more difficulty in accessing health care services, more Canadians reported having regular medical appointments, American women aged 50–69 years were more likely to have had annual mammograms, and Americans between the ages of 45 and 64 reported using more prescription drugs.

The investigators reported the following study limitations: data collection exclusively at the national level, participants had household telephones, potential inaccuracies from self-reported information, potential misinterpretation of survey questions by respondents, potential sampling error, and no available data of characteristics of nonparticipants.

This study clearly highlights the perceived high levels of satisfaction and health status of Americans and Canadians. However, citizens of both nations with low incomes had perceived levels of reduced health status. The study findings could be used to improve the health care delivery systems of both nations. Implications for professional nursing practice vary for Canadian and American nurses. American nurses may need to improve efforts aimed at obesity prevention and treatment, the dangers of using multiple prescription medications, and advocating for health care services for Americans with low incomes. Canadian nurses might want to look for ways to plan and execute smoking cessation programs.

(PPOs). IPAs consist of a group of physicians who independently negotiate for set fee schedules with hospitals and insurance providers. Physicians employed in an IPA enjoy freedom to practice medicine as they desire. Physicians working in PPOs follow specific fee payment schedules and clinical utilization guidelines determined by the PPO. Integrated health care delivery systems employ physicians and some may even own the group practice.

The HMO (health maintenance organization) was designed to focus efforts and resources on health promotion, preventive care, and consumer education to reduce health care costs. HMOs provide capitated payments (a set amount of money) for each member rather than paying only for rendered services. The traditional group- or staff-model HMO is a vertically integrated organization that operates its own physical facilities in different geographic locations and whose salaried physicians work solely for the HMO. A physician group may also contract services to a HMO. In order to increase practice revenues, some physicans employ nurse practitioners (NPs) and physician assistants (PAs). The practice gets to keep surplus payments when care is delivered below the capitated payment (Gabel, 1997).

Growth in retail clinics continues to expand. NPs provide health care services in clinics located in drug, grocery, and discount chain stores. NPs treat commonly occurring illnesses that can be diagnosed by simple tests (strep throat, and urinary tract and ear infections) following standardized care regimens. In 2005, only a handful of convenience clinics existed. By 2007, there were 500 with the potential to increase in numbers to

TABLE 9-2

Settings for Health Care Delivery

Setting	Definition
Public hospital	Nonprofit, government-owned institution that provides inpatient care
1. Federal hospital	1. Owned and operated by the United States government
2. Nonfederal hospital	2. Owned and operated by a state or local government
Community hospital	A locally owned institution that offers short-term services that are accessible to the public
Specialized hospital	An institution that offers services in one specialty area of health care (e.g., oncology, mental health, orthopedics, maternal–child health, children services)
General hospital	Offers a full scope of short-term services, including obstetric care
Teaching hospital	Provides medical education to undergraduate or graduate medical students, residents, or postgraduate medical fellows
Extended care facility	Institution that offers long-term care, also known as nursing homes (75% owned by for-profit companies)
Long-term care homes	Small group homes that provide a home setting for persons with chronic mental illness or dementia
Rehabilitation center	Institution that offers services to persons with a disability to become independent
Chemical dependence center	Institution that offers detoxification and rehabilitation for persons with drug or alcohol addiction
Neighborhood health center	Outpatient facility offering comprehensive primary care health services
Retail store–based health clinic	Clinic designed for episodic care of frequently occurring illnesses staffed by nurse practitioner
	Care recipient frequently able to purchase treatment for the illness in the store where the clinic is located
Private physician office	Comprehensive ambulatory patient medical care provided by a single physician
Physician partnership office	Comprehensive ambulatory medical care provided by a pair of physicians
Group physician office practice	Comprehensive ambulatory medical care services provided by a group of three or more physicians
Managed care clinic	Comprehensive ambulatory medical care provided within the confines of an office or clinic operated by a managed care company
Public health clinics	State-, county-, or city-funded health services that focus primarily on prevention of or controlling communicable diseases
Ambulatory surgery center	Outpatient center where minor surgical procedures are performed
Specialty care centers	Outpatient offices or centers that offer full scope of ambulatory care services to persons with specific health problems (renal failure, cancer, diabetes, pain); may have for-profit status
Emergency department	Outpatient facility linked to a hospital where life-threatening health problems can be managed. Some emergency facilities have designated trauma center certification. Frequently used by persons to receive health care after office or clinic hours
Urgent care center	Outpatient facility (may be linked to a hospital) for health care consumers to receive medical care services for health-related problems when clinics or offices are closed or when they do not have an established health care provider. Usually have for-profit status. Some emergency rooms may dedicate a specific location to provide urgent care for non-life-threatening health problems.
Hospital-based clinics	Outpatient comprehensive medical care services that are linked with a specific hospital. Many teaching hospitals hold resident clinics to provide health care to the poor

(continued)

Settings for Health Care Delivery (Continued)

Setting	Definition
Hospital outpatient departments	Ambulatory diagnostic testing or rehabilitation services that have connections to a specific hospital
Diagnostic testing centers	Ambulatory diagnostic testing services. Some have connections to nonprofit hospitals and others are run by for-profit companies
Industrial health service units	Employment-based health services to address job-related illnesses and injuries. Some industrial health service units provide health-promotion activities and health screenings for employees
School health clinics	Health care services offered to students in academic settings (health rooms in primary or secondary schools or university health clinics)
Home health care	Medical care and nursing services offered for persons who are homebound
Hospice	Comprehensive service to assist persons in receiving a "good" death. Services may be given in the home, extended-care, or acute care facility

Sources: Jonas, S. (1998). *An introduction to the U.S. health care system* (4th ed.). New York: Springer Publishing; Kovner, A.R., & Jonas, S. (Eds.). (1999). *Jonas Kovner's health care delivery in the United States* (6th ed.) New York: Springer Publishing; McGinn, D. & Springen, K. (2007). Express-lane medicine. *Newsweek, CL* (4), 44.

5,000 by the year 2012. Consumers appreciate the convenience of securing a diagnosis and treatment in one location (McGinn & Springen, 2007).

Many consumers opt to receive routine vaccinations at public health departments or immunization clinics held in churches, retail establishments, or shopping centers. Local public health departments may waive fees for local residents who are unable to pay for services or if local taxes cover immunizations. Sometimes fees may be reduced if the health department has a fee schedule based on resident incomes.

The Hospital Industry

Hospitals provide acute inpatient and outpatient services. Inpatients undergo many expensive (and frequently invasive) procedures for diagnosis and treatment for their reason for admission. Highly technical equipment and qualified nurses monitor patients to detect abnormal conditions, progress of ordered treatments, and potential complications associated with diagnostic procedures and therapies. The hospital industry employs more than 50% of RNs. Although occupancy rates have been decreasing, the severity of illness of clients who are admitted to the hospital has been increasing.

Hospitals vary in size and scope of service. Large medical centers may have hundreds (or thousands) of inpatient beds, whereas small community hospitals may have less than 50 beds. Hospitals may be owned by a for-profit corporation, a nonprofit organization, or the government (state, military, or Veterans Administration). Sometimes, a hospital may be part of a larger integrated health care delivery system. Along with providing inpatient care, hospitals offer emergency room services for persons who sustain traumatic injuries or become seriously ill. Sometimes persons without health insurance or a primary care provider use emergency rooms for health care needs that arise. Inappropriate use of emergency rooms increases the cost of health care delivery (Andersen et al., 2007).

Hospitals offer a variety of health services. Some hospitals also offer outpatient services such as surgery and specialized diagnostic testing. Hospitals may furnish a single specialized service such as cancer care, orthopedic surgery, burn care, pediatrics, or rehabilitation. Acute-care hospitals provide services to persons who have episodic health care needs. Subacute-care hospitals care for patients who no longer need the intensity of care provided by acute-care hospitals, but have complex medical needs above the services offered by extended-care or rehabilitation facilities. The intensity of required nursing care is less acute, but professional nursing care services are still needed.

Questions for Reflection

1. How do I define quality health care?
2. What strategies do I follow to keep myself healthy?
3. How much have I spent during the last year on health care? Is the amount of money that I spend worth it? Why or why not?

Integrated Health Care Delivery Systems: A Choice for Today's Consumer

Integrated health care delivery systems provide consumers with a high continuity of care by providing primary, secondary, and tertiary health care services within a single health care system. The health care system combines dimensions of consumer preference, expert providers, and economic reimbursement into a single package. The system offers a variety of local health care centers that are typically linked to a large urban health care center that offers comprehensive, sophisticated, and the newest therapies. Some systems may offer complementary therapies. The system may be part of one of the following organizations: a national proprietary (for-profit) chain, a national or regional nonprofit organization (frequently religious based), or an arm of the local, state, or federal government.

To provide effective health care in today's world, there appear to be three key factors: cost, access, and quality. In the United States, health care costs continue to rise and outpace the rate of inflation. High costs result in consumer inability to access needed health services. Some consumers with low-paying jobs cannot afford health insurance copayments offered by their employers. Some health care organizations charge higher fees for rendered services when consumers do not have health care coverage. When consumers know that they bear the responsibility for full payment of medical services, they frequently hesitate to seek care until a condition becomes life-threatening, impedes the ability to engage independently in activities of daily living, or prevents their ability to work.

THE INTERDISCIPLINARY HEALTH CARE TEAM

The science behind health care is highly specialized. In order to best meet the physical, psychological, social, and spiritual health care needs of persons seeking care, a multidisciplinary approach is commonly used. Table 9-3 specifies the various members of the interdisciplinary health care team and the contribution of each member. Sometimes, care is coordinated by a case manager, who may be a nurse or social worker. Professional nurses usually coordinate care delivery in inpatient care environments.

As members of the interdisciplinary health care team, nurses provide key information for holistic client care. When clients and families become overwhelmed with the complexity of health care, nurses guide them through the system while offering them emotional support. Nurse navigator programs have surfaced in the field of oncology nursing. The nurse navigator meets with clients on a regular basis to discuss questions about and barriers to care, provide individualized client education, offer special emotional support, and facilitate referrals to needed community resources and other health care professionals. Identified strengths of nurse navigator programs include facilitation of continuity across the continuum of care, and timely treatment and prevention of clients in today's ever complex delivery of health care (Bruce, 2007).

NURSING CARE DELIVERY MODELS

Management of nursing care for clients has always fallen within the purview of professional nurses. On a daily basis, nurses make decisions about how to organize client care. They consider a variety of factors when choosing the best way to deliver care to a group of

TABLE 9-3

Members of the Interdisciplinary Health Care Team

Member	Role
Client (consumer or patient)	Seeks out various health care services and makes decisions related to plan of care
Board of Directors (or Trustees)	Responsible for organizational mission, service quality, strategic planning, medical staff credentialing, evaluation and selection of the chief executive officer, self-evaluation and education, and financial status. For-profit companies report to stockholders. Nonprofit organizations usually have a variety of persons from the community with specialized expertise (e.g., lawyers) and philanthropists as board members
Chief Executive Officer (or Administrator)	Responsible for overall daily operation of the organization, including implementation of board policies, addressing of health care concerns within the local community, and preparation and delivery of board reports
Administrative staff (managers or directors)	In large organizations, each department usually has someone responsible for its overall daily operations. In nursing, the head of the nursing department has the title of Chief Nursing Executive or Director of Nursing
Medical staff	Physician, who may be independent practitioner or organizational employee, diagnoses and treats clients using medical therapies.
Nursing staff 1. Registered nurses 2. Licensed practical/vocational nurses 3. Unlicensed assistive personnel (care assistants) 4. Clerical assistants (unit clerk, secretary)	Responsible for execution of direct and indirect client care services. Registered nurses assess clients, diagnose human responses to illness, outline a care plan, implement the plan (including the delegation of tasks to others), and evaluate the effectiveness of nursing care
Case manager (for managed care organizations)	Advanced practice nurse or social worker who follows clients across the spectrum of health care settings. Most start the discharge process as soon as clients are admitted to acute care facilities
Dietitians	Baccalaureate-prepared nutritionists who have had internships to learn clinical nutrition. They outline specific client therapeutic diets and verify that client nutritional needs are met. They also provide client and family education related to therapeutic diets. Inpatient facilities have food service departments that prepare client and cafeteria meals
Pharmacists	Prepare and dispense medications, educate other team members about medications, monitor controlled substance use, monitor client allergies, work to prevent medication errors, and monitor potential drug interactions
Paramedical personnel or technologists	Highly trained experts who have specialized education or training. Examples include medical technologist (lab tests), radiology technologist (x-ray, CT scan, PET scan, etc.), respiratory therapist (breathing therapies, ventilator management, and oxygen therapy)
Social workers	Assist clients with social concerns that arise from illness, injury, or surgery. Help clients with financial issues resulting from disruption of work and insurance benefit gaps. Also refer them to community support agencies
Therapists	Physical therapists assess function and provide restorative therapy for body movement, ambulation, and safety. Occupational therapists assess and provide restorative therapy for problems with activities of daily living as well as skills for employment. Speech therapists assess for swallowing difficulties and speech problems, and provide restorative therapy related to these areas
Medical Records or Health Information Services	Keep detailed and accurate medical records on clients
Business manager or office staff	Coordinates client appointments (outpatient settings) and keeps financial records for services rendered

Members of the Interdisciplinary Health Care Team (Continued)

Member	Role
Central supply or central products services	Warehouse and distribute client care products (not pharmaceuticals) per ordered request
Linen services	Provide client linen and gowns
Environmental or house-keeping services	Maintain a clean, safe physical environment
Biomedical engineering services	Maintain proper functioning of electronic client care machines (IV pumps, bed-side monitors, thermometers, etc.) and verify electrical safety of client care equipment
Information services	Develop integrated computer systems and provide user support services (some may offer computer and software staff education)
Quality management	Monitors the quality of rendered services. Includes the risk management department, which monitors actual and potential client care errors and financial losses. Outlines a plan for continuous quality improvement
Third-party payer	Pays for all or part of health care services used by the consumer. Various levels of government are third-party payers for tax-supported health insurance plans. Private insurance companies provide funding for plan enrollees. Frequently audit client records to verify rendered services
Utilization review	Set up in the late 1970s by the federal government to verify effective utilization of health care resources and avoid fraud
Spiritual support service (chaplain)	Inpatient settings usually have chaplain support services to provide spiritual and other support to clients and their significant others
Human resources (personnel department)	Hires new employees, tracks employee incidents, and coordinates employee fringe benefits. Payroll departments that issue employee paychecks may fall under this category
Foundation	Nonprofit organizations usually have services to coordinate private donations to the organization
Alternative care providers	Persons who provide alternative or complementary therapy to clients, such as chiropractors, herbalists, acupuncturists, massage therapists, reflexologists, and folk healers

Adapted from Jonas, S. (1998). *An introduction to the U.S. health care system* (4th ed.). New York: Springer Publishing; Kovner, A. R., & Jonas, S. (Eds.). (1998). *Jonas & Kovner's health care delivery in the United States* (6th ed.) New York: Springer Publishing; and American Hospital Association. (1999). *Welcome to the board: An orientation for the new health care trustee.* Chicago: AHA Press.

clients. Decisions are based on client factors (acuity, and specialized needs), staff factors (number of available staff, licensure status, clinical experience, and staff preferences), and organizational factors (the usual nursing care delivery system). A nursing care delivery model is a system used by nurses to organize and deliver nursing services to best meet client care needs. Effective nursing care delivery models match client care needs with available human resources to attain the best possible outcome (Porter-O'Grady & Malloch, 2007).

Traditional methods of nursing care delivery models include case method (total patient care), functional nursing, team nursing, district nursing, primary nursing, case management, and client-focused (patient-focused or modular) care. Table 9-4 outlines the origins with the rationale of each model, describes clinical decision making, outlines the scope of responsibility and authority, delineates team titles (when appropriate), presents the level of nurse and client satisfaction, and presents major advantages and disadvantages of each model. Prior to industrialization and employer-based insurance, professional nurses practiced case nursing, during which they performed all intervention, to meet all the client's needs. The case method is still used in home health and private duty

Comparison of Nursing Care Delivery System Models

TABLE 9-4

Nursing Care Delivery Model	Case Method (Total Patient Care)	Functional	Team	District	Primary	Case Management	Client Focused (Patient Focused or Modular)
Date of origin and reason designed	1880s; patients were at home	1940s in response to nursing shortage	1950s in response to movement in management away from tasks to human relations	1950s–1960s to decrease the amount of leg work required for team nursing	1960s to facilitate movement of nurses toward independence and autonomous practice	1980s in response to diagnosis-related grouping (prospective payment system), budget awareness, and total quality management philosophy	1990s in response to increased efficiency with escalating costs and as a response to the nursing shortage
Clinical decision making	Done per shift	Done per shift	Shift based	Shift based	24-hour accountability of the primary nurse	24-hour accountability of the case manager	Shift based
Responsibility and authority	One or a small group of patients	Autonomous to a large group of patients	Large group of patients	Group of patients located in close proximity to each other	Autonomous for a small group of patients as a primary nurse	Coordination of care with members of the interdisciplinary health care team	Coordination with case manager common for plan of care Individual actions are autonomous and shift-based for a large group of patients
Work allocation	Total care to all assigned patients	Each member assigned specific tasks for all patients	Tasks for entire team with some being assigned according to skills or license requirements	Same as in team nursing	Total care of own primary patients along with care of small number of patients with a different primary nurse	May serve as coordinator or actual provider of direct client care May be required to see caseloads of clients with similar health problems at more than one clinical site	Tasks assigned according to on-the-job training and licensure requirements

Nursing team titles	Nurse	Charge nurse Medicine nurse Treatment nurse Education nurse Admissions and discharge nurse Nurse's aide Orderly	RN becomes the team leader and delegates tasks to team member Team members: LPN/LVNs and unlicensed care providers	RN becomes the district nurse with team members having the same titles as in team nursing	Primary nurse Associate nurse No LPN or LVN Nursing assistants and orderlies assigned to unit to help RNs	Case managers Care manager Registered nurses and LPNs are nurses Unlicensed personnel titles may be the same as in team nursing or client-focused care	Care pairs or care partners consisting of an RN with an unlicensed assistive personnel (UAP) member called a patient care technician (PCT) or patient service associate (PSA)
Professional nurse satisfaction	Yes	No	Yes	Yes	Yes	High for the case manager and nursing staff	Mixed results for nurses Higher for unlicensed personnel than team
Client satisfaction	Yes	No	Yes	Yes	Yes	Mixed results	Yes
Major advantages	Care received from one nurse per 8-hour shift Holistic care provided Clear lines of responsibility No complex assignment planning required	Highly cost-effective Clear lines of responsibility Development of technical experts if assigned the same task daily Useful with severe staffing shortages	Cost-effective and staff satisfaction with working with small patient groups Comprehensive holistic care possible Development of better staff relationships	Same as with team nursing except less exhaustion by nursing staff from reduced walking	Very satisfied nurses and patients Comprehensive holistic nursing care delivered	Cost-effective care coordinated to achieve client outcomes Holistic care orientation Continuity of care across the spectrum of health care settings Client knows who to call for assistance	Cost-effective and clients seem to be satisfied Clients can ask anyone for help Staff develop technical competence in a variety of skills

(continued)

Comparison of Nursing Care Delivery System Models (Continued)

Nursing Care Delivery Model	Case Method (Total Patient Care)	Functional	Team	District	Primary	Case Management	Client Focused (Patient Focused or Modular)
Major disadvantages	No continuity of care Very expensive by today's standards Potential overloading of ancillary departments with multiple requests for the same supplies in a short time frame	Task-oriented system resulting in fragmentation of care Staff boredom from repetitive work Limited communication among staff members	Team leaders may not be available to lead the team Poor communication may lead to tasks being omitted Team leader needs time to supervise team members, which decreases time available to clients	No district nurse available to lead team Same as in team nursing	Not cost-effective to have all RN staffing Some primary nurses not available 7 days a week for 24-hour-a-day consultation Not all nurses want to assume primary nursing responsibilities Requires large numbers of RNs Sense of loss by ancillary workers	High costs required for successful implementation Critical pathways reduce individualization of client care Physician resentment about being called for consultation by a nurse Chief executive officer complaints of expenditures requested for care by case managers	Expensive to develop and provide technological support Blurs the distinctions of nursing roles from those of other interdisciplinary team members Nurses may lose essential elements of nursing practice
Areas where currently used	Home care Private duty Intensive care units Nursing student assignments	Hospitals Extended care facilities Rehabilitation centers Operating rooms Outpatient surgical centers Physician offices	Hospitals Extended care facilities Rehabilitation centers Home health agencies	Hospitals Extended care facilities Rehabilitation centers	Hospitals Intensive care units Specialty centers such as dialysis, oncology, and diabetes outpatient centers Hospice Home care	Hospitals Home health agencies Health departments Anywhere managed care is practiced	Hospitals Home health agencies Transport teams

Information adapted from:
Manthey, M. (1991). Delivery systems and practice role models. *Nursing Management, 22*(1), 28–30.
Tappen, R. M. (2001). *Nursing leadership and management: Concepts and practice.* Philadelphia: F. A. Davis.
Wise, P. S. Y. (1995). *Leading and managing in nursing.* St. Louis, MO: Mosby-Year Book.

nursing as well as in clinical nursing education when faculty assign beginning nursing students to care for a client.

In the functional team and district nursing care models, nursing staff members with different skills and licensure status care for a group of patients. Functional and team nursing models work well when there is a shortage of nursing staff. When either model is used, care may become fragmented, and without effective communication, little attention is paid to client needs for rest and privacy.

During the 1980s, job satisfaction of nurses plummeted and hospitals had high levels of nurse turnover (McGillis-Hall, Doran, & Petch, 2005). Increased responsibility for supervision of others for direct client care was cited as a major factor. Primary nursing emerged as a way to reconnect professional nurses with direct client care. A primary nurse for each patient develops and revises the nursing care plan. In the event of the primary care nurse's absence, nursing care is delivered by another RN, who is the designated associate nurse. Continuity of client care also increased because the same nurses provided care services to the client. However, some nurses and hospital administrators frown on using professional nurses to perform tasks that could be done by UAP.

The economic crunch of the early 1990s experienced by acute-care facilities gave rise to redesigned care delivery systems. Quality improvement efforts focused on optimal client outcomes and satisfaction. Work redesign efforts resulted in a model that placed the client (or patient) in the center. The following names are used to identify the new model of nursing: client-focused care, patient-focused care, or modular nursing. Some institutions expanded the roles of the UAP and provided them with intensive on-the-job training so that they could perform sterile urinary catheterization, phlebotomy, and electrocardiograms. Professional nurses were then freed to engage in holistic assessment, advanced nursing procedures, and client education. However, supervision of UAPs was added to the professional nurse's role.

Modular nursing represents a unique form of client-focused care. In modular nursing, UAPs and professional nurses receive assignments to work continuously as "care partners." Members of the care partners receive cross training to perform basic respiratory therapy treatments, physical therapy, phlebotomy, and electrocardiography. Under this delivery system, clients receive almost instantaneous therapy as they do not have to wait for ancillary personnel to arrive.

Case management provides a system of patient care delivery that focuses on the achievement of outcomes within effective time frames and with appropriate use of health care resources. Key elements of case management involve a case manager (CM) (who may be a bachelor's-prepared RN, advanced practice nurse, or social worker) and a standardized method for managing a particular disease process. The predetermined path for specific care delivery (critical path, clinical path, or care map) is followed during the duration of client care. The path outlines typical interdisciplinary clinical problems with desired outcomes, maps out daily expected interventions, and specifies discharge client instructions and education. Staff nurses and the CM frequently monitor client progress toward desired outcomes. Some paths cross the health care settings, enabling a seamless continuum of care. The CM assumes responsibility for matching client care needs so that appropriate services are rendered. The CM may use standardized clinical protocols, guidelines, and third-party payer criteria to ensure optimal outcomes with the most efficient use of resources.

The CM executes multiple roles that require critical thinking. As a clinician, the CM communicates effectively with the multidisciplinary health care team. The CM also coordinates care among all professionals and consultants. To ensure that economic constraints do not affect quality of client care, the CM justifies expenditures and care variances. The CM sometimes troubleshoots conflicts that might arise between health care providers, third-party payers, and consumers and acts as a client advocate. Some CMs maintain an ongoing relationship with clients using the telephone or Internet technology (Mahn-Dinicola & Zazworsky, 2005).

Innovative Patient Care Delivery Systems

Porter-O'Grady and Malloch (2007) specified that delivery of patient care encompasses more than nursing care and proposed that the care delivery system models should encompass the entire multidisciplinary patient care team. Such models have the client at the center of the circle and members of the interdisciplinary care team surrounding the client. The direct client caregivers (the nursing staff) constitute the first tier of service. Surrounding the nursing team that provides direct patient care are nursing support systems consisting of nursing directors, resources nurses, rapid response teams (to support nurses with patient care crisis situations), phlebotomy services or admissions staff, clinical nurse specialists, and staff development personnel. The outermost circle includes all members of the interdisciplinary client care team. Models such as these are useful in depicting the interdisciplinary approach to client care, but offer little help for nursing staff in deciding exactly how to deliver client care or achieve job satisfaction. The following research brief, however, does provide evidence of how a patient care delivery model may improve nurse job satisfaction.

Research Brief 9-2

Allen, D., & Vitale-Nolen, R. (2005). Patient care delivery model improves nurse job satisfaction. *Journal of Continuing Education in Nursing*, 36(6), 277–282.

Seventy RNs employed in a psychiatric nursing unit participated in a quasi-experimental longitudinal study to measure the effects of a staff-developed relationship-based primary nursing care model on job satisfaction (JS). The staff developed a relationship-based nursing model that empowered the nurses who best knew the clients to make decisions on how best to provide care for them.

Results of the study revealed that for the participating nurses, pay was the most important component of JS. However, autonomy, interactions, task requirements, professional status, and organizational policies also played key roles in JS. Although implementation of the model did not affect salaries, the participating nurses reported higher levels of JS ($p < .05$) in the areas of autonomy, collegial interactions, task requirements, professional status, and organizational policies over a 6-month time frame.

Implications for practice are that when nurses have a voice in designing a nursing care delivery system and have support from administration, their JS increases. JS also increases when nurses are allowed to perform their professional roles in an environment where their contributions are appreciated and they have the opportunity to provide direct client care. Caution must be exercised when attempting to generalize the results of this study to other settings because psychiatric nursing may differ from other nursing practice areas and because of the study's small sample size.

NURSING CHALLENGES RELATED TO HEALTH CARE DELIVERY SYSTEMS

Health care delivery systems offer challenges to professional nurses. As major health care providers, nurses face challenges created by health care delivery systems on a daily basis. Challenges occur at both the practical and ethical domains of clinical practice.

Practical Challenges

Two key practical challenges encountered by nurses involve the supply of professional nurses and the structure of the work environment. The current nursing shortage and changes within practice settings offer key daily challenges for all employed nurses.

The Nursing Shortage

A nursing shortage or an insufficient number of nurses to meet the health care needs of clients exists currently and is expected to worsen. The U.S. Department of Health and Human Services Resources and Services Administration (2002) predicted a 12% shortfall of professional nurses in 2010, 20% in 2015, and 29% in 2020 in the United States. The supply of professional nurses also looks bleak in Canada, where there has been a 5% decline in the number of registered nurses from 1990 to 2000 (Fried & Gaydos, 2002). Currently, there are 126,000 unfilled registered nurse positions in the United States (Inglis, 2004). Many factors contribute to the current global nursing shortage, including:

- Reduced number of young persons (18–24 years) entering the profession
- Decreased interest in a professional nursing career because of other career options for women (91% of the current nursing workforce are women)
- Compressed salary and fewer promotions throughout a nursing career
- Increased labor intensity from increased client acuity and numbers of clients
- Chronic understaffing in acute- and extended-care settings
- Poor collegial relationships with other health team members
- Widespread fear of contracting medication-resistant infectious diseases
- Increased chance of sustaining musculoskeletal injuries because of increased client body mass index (in the United States) and lack of enforceable policies related to lifting limitations for nursing staff
- Reduced job satisfaction
- High turnover
- Unfavorable stories about the profession being shared with potential nursing recruits
- Nursing faculty shortage
- Aging workforce (in 2004, the average age of a RN was 45.2 years according to the U.S. Bureau of Health Professions)

If the RN shortage persists, health care facilities will be forced to explore other staffing mix options, which may mean having RNs assume more supervisory responsibilities (ICN, 2006; Porter-O'Grady & Malloch, 2007; Seago, Spetz, Chapman, & Dyer, 2007). Historically, the nursing shortage has been perpetuated by external factors such as problems with recruitment, retention, negative image, and poor working environments. In addition, internal factors such as job dissatisfaction, role overload, poor collegial relationships, and professional disillusionment exacerbate the shortage (West, Griffith, & Iphofen, 2007). However, the current projected nursing shortage is linked to the aging nursing workforce with a reduced number of persons entering the nursing profession (ICN, 2006).

Alleviating the nursing shortage requires that the nursing profession attack all factors associated with it. Nurses must believe that they have the power to change work environments to promote professional autonomy and safety. Empowering nurses begins with nursing education programs and continues through an entire career. All areas of nursing (practice, administration, and education) must collaborate rather than compete with each other to shape the nursing profession.

Challenges Resulting from Changes in Hospital Care Delivery

Recently, the new role of hospitalist has emerged for physicians. Hospitalists are physicians (some of whom have direct employment status or contracts with the hospital) who manage client care in acute-care settings for primary care physicians. Hospitalists devote 25–100% of their time managing inpatient client care. When clients are admitted to the hospital, a hospitalist rather than their private physician manages their hospitalization. The hospitalist refers clients for follow-up care with a primary care physician. Hospitalists enable primary care physicians to focus on client health promotion and maintenance. Some acute-care facilities have reported reduced inpatient length of stay and substantial cost savings since introducing the hospitalist role (McDonald, 2001).

The emergence of hospitalists has created the need for professional nurses in hospitals to educate clients about the advantages of receiving medical care from a physician who specializes in the complex nature of acute care. Along with educational efforts, the hospital RN may receive the effects of angry clients who are very disappointed about not having their usual physician take care of or even visit them while they are hospitalized. Some hospitalists develop a list of standardized orders that outline protocols for managing commonly encountered reasons for and health problems arising from hospitalization (e.g., electrolyte replacement and constipation), thus reducing the need to interrupt the daily routine of client care to contact the physician for orders. Sometimes nurses and hospitalists develop close, collaborative working relationships.

Current structural changes within the health care system may erode the power of physicians in the practice of medicine. Business managers and facility administrators continue to have more powerful voices in health care delivery. Recent reductions in the length of hospitalization mean that nurses care for more acutely ill clients. Nurses must be more vigilant to notice small changes in client status that may foreshadow a catastrophic health event. They also must have detailed knowledge about potential adverse effects of complex interactions among medications. For example, contrast dye used in magnetic resonance imaging may cause permanent renal failure in persons receiving certain oral hypoglycemic agents. Nurses also must possess the capability to perform sophisticated procedures such as central line management, intravenous medication drips, and complicated dressings. New medications and technology demand increased knowledge, skills, and time.

Ethical Challenges

Ethical concerns have been raised by an increasing life span, the development of health care technology, and the increasing cost of delivering care. For decades, the ability of persons to pay for health care determines who has access to services and the quality of service that can be received (Andersen et al., 2007; Curtin, 1996; ICN, 2006; WHO, 2007).

Because it is not possible to meet all goals of accessibility, equity, and quality given available resources, difficult choices must be made among competing values and multiple desirable alternatives. One basic issue is the relative valuing of containment of health care costs versus the access to health care for all persons.

Ethical questions raised by these choices include:

1. What will some people willingly do to assume the costs of health care for persons unable to pay so that quality health care is available to everyone?
2. Is health care a basic right or a privilege?
3. What is the basic acceptable level of health care?
4. Who has priority for health care services if there are access limitations and finite resources for health care delivery?
5. What governmental and/or social programs should be cut to increase health care resources for better access to health care?
6. How much choice should people have in deciding from whom and where they can receive health care?
7. Should the wealthy be able to purchase private health care services or insurance coverage?
8. How would rationing of health care be determined?
9. Who would determine rationing criteria?
10. What criteria would be used for rationing of health care services?
11. Should expensive technology and advanced life support measures be made available to all persons?
12. What (and when) is death?
13. How much is the prolongation of life worth?
14. What rights do clients have?

15. Is cure of all disease possible and desirable?
16. Who needs professional nursing services?
17. How do we use health care resources and personnel for the best interest of the human race?

"Treating health care primarily as a business and a commodity to be sold like cars is an impoverished notion of health care in relation to the concept of health care as a human service created by society to meet the needs of vulnerable people who are ill or at risk of becoming ill" (Aroskar, 1987, p. 65). It is critical that the voice of the nursing profession be added to that of the public in discussions of the philosophic considerations and values that will shape the decisions concerning the size, shape, and direction of all future health care delivery systems.

✦ SUMMARY AND SIGNIFICANCE TO PRACTICE

As a result of significant demographic, economic, attitudinal, and available manpower forces, health care delivery systems are in the process of massive structural change and reorganization, raising multiple ethical and practical considerations. Health care delivery systems are primary shaped by history, cultural values, and resource availability. Nurses should assume leadership in shaping future health care delivery by using their cognitive skills and compassion so that all persons will have access to optimal health care services.

FROM THEORY TO PRACTICE

1. Identify the strengths and weaknesses of the American and Canadian health care delivery systems. Why have you listed items as strengths and weaknesses?
2. How can nurses work to improve health care delivery? What are the consequences if nurses do not get involved with changes in the health care delivery system?
3. Reflecting on the vignette, how should Jane explain to her father the benefits of receiving generic medication and a temporary stay in an extended-care facility on his recovery? How would you explain the complex web of health care delivery to elderly clients? What type of help do they need to navigate their way through the health care system?

WWW INTERNET EXERCISES

1. Visit the Health Insurance Association of America at http://www.ahip.org to learn about the complexity of the health insurance industry. The website contains the latest updates on legislative efforts to reform health insurance and provides consumers with information about the types of health insurance plans and how to enroll in them.
2. To learn about issues confronting physicians in today's health care environment, visit the American Medical Association (AMA) at http://www.ama-assn.org. Look for the listing of a physician you know.
3. Visit the ANA at http://www.nursingworld.org to learn about issues confronting professional nurses in the health care system.
4. Compare and contrast the ANA and AMA websites. How could ANA improve its website?

WWW INTERNET RESOURCES

Agency for Healthcare Policy and Research: http://www.ahrg.gov.
American Nurses Association: http://www.nursingworld.org.
American Hospital Association: http://aha.org.
Health Care Financing Administration (Medicare and Medicaid): http://www.cms.hhs.gov.
National Health Information Center: http://health.gov/nhic.
Health Insurance Association of America: http://www.ahip.org.
American Association of Retired Persons: http://www.aarp.org.
International Council of Nurses: http://www.icn.ch.

REFERENCES

American Nurses Association. (1995). *Social policy statement.* Kansas City, MO: Author.

Andersen, R.M., Rice, T. H., & Kominski, G. F. (2007). *Changing the U.S. health care system: Key issues in health services policy and management* (3rd ed.). San Francisco: John Wiley.

Aroskar, M. A. (1987). Fidelity and veracity: Questions of promise keeping, truth telling, and loyalty. In M. D. M. Fowler & J. Levine-Ariff (Eds.), *Ethics at the bedside: A sourcebook for the critical care nurse* (pp. 72–83). Philadelphia: J. B. Lippincott.

Bodenheimer, T. (2005). High and rising health care costs: Part 3: The role of health care providers. *Annals of Internal Medicine, 142*, 996–1002.

Bruce, S. D. (2007). Taking the wheel, oncology nurses help patients navigate the cancer journey. *ONS Connect, 22*(3), 8–11.

Bureau of Health Professional Resources. (2004). The registered nurse population: Findings from the national sample survey of registered nurses. Available at http://hrsa.gov/healthworkforce/reports/nursing/samplesurvey00/chapter2.htm. Accessed April 26, 2009.

Curtin, L. L. (1996). The ethics of managed care—part I: Proposing a new ethos. *Nursing Management, 27*, 18–19.

Feldstein, P. J. (2004). *Health policy issues: An economic perspective* (3rd ed.). Chicago: Health Administration Press.

Fifer, J. J. (2007). A healthcare mystery. *Healthcare Financial Management, 61*(2), 28.

Foster, R. S. & Clemens, M. K. (2005). Medicare financial status, budget impact and sustainability—which concept is which? *Health Care Finance Review, 27*, 127–140.

Fried, B. J., & Gaydos, L. M. (Eds.) (2002). *World health systems: Challenges and perspectives.* Chicago: Health Administration Press

Gabel, J. (1997). 10 ways HMOs have changed in the 1990s. *Health Affairs, 16*, 134–135.

Goldsmith, L. (2002). Canada. In B. J. Fried & L. M. Gaydos (Eds.), *World health systems: Challenges and perspectives* (pp. 227–248). Chicago: Health Administration Press.

Hellander, I. (2008). The deepening crisis in U.S. health care: A review of the data, spring 2008. *International Journal of Health Sciences, 38*, 607–623.

Inglis, T. (2004). Nursing the trends. *American Journal of Nursing Career Guide 2004,* (2), 25–32.

International Council of Nurses (ICN). (2006). The global nursing shortage: Priority areas for intervention. Available at http://www.icn.ch/global/report2006.pdf. Accessed August 6, 2007.

Jamieson, E. M., & Sewall, M. F. (1954). *Trends in nursing history* (4th ed.). Philadelphia: W. B. Saunders.

Johnson, A., Carillo, A., & Garcia, J. (2002). Mexico. In B. J. Fried & L. M. Gaydos (Eds.), *World health systems: Challenges and perspectives* (pp. 421–444). Chicago: Health Administration Press.

Jonas, S. (1998). *An introduction to the U.S. health care system* (4th ed.). New York: Springer.

Jost, T. (2005). Chaoulli v. Quebeck: Charter rights, private health insurance and the future of Canadian Medicare. *Health Affairs, 25*(3), 878–879.

Kennedy, M. (2007). An American dream gone wrong. *American Journal of Nursing, 107*(8), 17–18.

Kovner, A. R., & Jonas, S. (Eds.). (1999). *Jonas & Kovner's health care delivery in the United States* (6th ed.). New York: Springer.

Lacey, L. (2002). Nigeria. In B. J. Fried & L. M. Gaydos (Eds.), *World health systems: Challenges and perspectives* (pp. 507–520). Chicago: Health Administration Press.

LeBow, R. H. (2003). *Health care meltdown.* Chambersburg, PA: Alan C. Hood & Company.

Mahn-Dinicola, V., & Zazworsky, D. (2005). The advanced practice nurse case manager. In A. Hamric, J. Spross, & C. M. Hanson (Eds.), *Advanced practice nursing: An integrative approach* (3rd ed., pp. 617–675). St. Louis, MO: Elsevier-Saunders.

Manthey, M. (1991). Delivery systems and practice role models. *Nursing Management, 22*(1), 28–30.

Markowitz, G. E., & Rosner, D. (1979). Doctors in crisis: Medical education and medical reform during the Progressive era, 1895–1915. In S. Reverby & D. Rosner (Eds.), *Health care in America: Essays in social history* (pp. 185–205). Philadelphia: Temple University Press.

McDonald, M. D. (2001). The hospitalist movement: Wise or wishful thinking? *Nursing Management, 32*(3), 30–31.

McGillis-Hall, L. Doran, D. M., & Petch, T. (2005). Measurement of nurse job satisfaction using the McCloskey/Mueller Satisfaction Scale. *Nursing Research, 55*, 128–136.

McGinn, D., & Springer, K. (2007). Express-lane medicine. *Newsweek, 150*, 44.

McIntyre, M., & Thomlinson, E. (2003). *Realities of Canadian nursing: Professional, practice and power issues.* Philadelphia: Lippincott, Williams & Wilkins.

O'Donnell, J. Smyth, D., & Frampton, C. (2005). Prioritizing health care funding. *Internal Medicine Journal, 35*, 409–412.

Porter-O'Grady, T., & Malloch, K. (2007). *Managing for success in health care.* St. Louis, MO: Mosby.

Public Broadcasting Service (PBS). (2007). *The Online NewsHour: The uninsured in America, timeline: Insurance in the U.S.* Available at http://www.pbs.org/newshours/indepth_coverage/health/uninsured/timeline/inde.html. Accessed August 5, 2007.

Rosen, M. & Haglund, B. (2005). From healthy survivors to sick survivors–Implications for the 21st century. *Scandinavian Journal of Public Health, 33*, 151–155.

Sanders, J. (2002). Financing and organization of national health systems. In B. J. Fried & L. M. Gaydos (Eds.), *World health systems: Challenges and perspectives* (pp. 25–38). Chicago: Health Administration Press.

Sanmartin, C., Ng, E., Blackwell, D., Gentleman, J., Martinez, M., & Simile, C. (2004). *Joint Canada / United States survey of health.* Washington, DC: Centers for Disease Control. Available at http://www.cdc.gov/nchs/data/hsis/jcush_analyticalreport.pdf.

Scofera, L. (1994). The development and growth of employer-provided health insurance. *Monthly Labor Review, 117*(3), 3–10.

Seago, J., Spetz, J., Chapman, S., & Dyer, W. (2007). Can the use of LPNs alleviate the nursing shortage? *American Journal of Nursing, 106*(7), 40–49.

Shah, O. (2002). India. In B. J. Fried & L. M. Gaydos (Eds.), *World health systems: Challenges and perspectives* (pp. 495–506). Chicago: Health Administration Press.

Storch, J. L. (2005). Country profile: Canada's health care system. *Nursing Ethics, 12*(4), 413–418.

Sultz, H. A., & Young, K. M. (2004). *Health care USA: Understanding its organization and delivery* (4th ed.). Sudbury, MA: Jones & Bartlett.

Tansel, A. (2002). Turkey. In B. J. Fried & L. M. Gaydos (Eds.), *World health systems: Challenges and perspectives* (pp. 357–368). Chicago: Health Administration Press.

Tappen, R. M. (2001). *Nursing leadership and management: Concepts and practice.* Philadelphia: F. A. Davis.

Thorpe, K. E., & Knickman, J. R. (1999). Financing for health care. In A. R. Kovner & S. Jonas (Eds.), *Jonas & Kovner's health care delivery in the United States* (6th ed., pp. 32–63). New York: Springer.

Toffler, A., & Toffler, H. (2007). *Revolutionary wealth.* New York: Doubleday.

Torrens, P. R. (1978). *The American health care system: Issues and problems.* St. Louis, MO: Mosby.

U.S. Bureau of Labor Statistics. (2006–2007). The occupation outlook handbook. Available at http://bls.gov/OCO. Accessed August 4, 2007.

U.S. Census Bureau. (2004). Health insurance statistics. Available at http://pubdb3.census.gov/macro/032004/health-hol_001.htm. Accessed August 4, 2007.

U.S. Census Bureau. (2008). Income, poverty and health insurance coverage in the United States: 2007. Available at http://www.census.gov/prod/2008pubs/p60-235.pdf. Accessed April 25, 2009.

U.S. Department of Health and Human Services. (2008). National health expenditure data. Available at http://www.cms.hhs.gov/NationalHealthExpendData/02_national-HealthAcoountsHistorical.asp. Accessed July 20, 2008.

U.S. Department of Health and Human Services Health Resources and Services Administration. (2002). New HRSA report predicts deepening nursing shortage. Available at http://archive.hrsa.gov/newsroom/NewsBriefs/2002/nurseshortagereport.htm. Accessed April 25, 2009.

Vogel, M. J. (1979). The transformation of the American hospital, 1859–1920. In S. Reverby & D. Rosner (Eds.), *Health care in America: Essays in social history* (pp. 105–116). Philadelphia: Temple University Press.

West, E., Griffith, W., & Iphofen, R. (2007). A historical perspective on the nursing shortage. *MEDSURG Nursing, 16*, 124–130.

Williams, P., & Jian, Z. (2002). China. In B. J. Fried & L. M. Gaydos (Eds.), *World health systems: Challenges and perspectives* (pp. 343–356). Chicago: Health Administration Press.

Wise, P. S. Y. (1995). *Leading and managing in nursing.* St. Louis, MO: Mosby-Year Book.

World Health Organization (WHO). (2007). The 2006 world health report. Available at http://www.int/entitiy/whr.2006. Accessed August 4, 2007.

Zakus, D., & Cortinois, A. (2002). Primary healthcare and community participation: Origins, implementation and the future. In B. J. Fried & L. M. Gaydos (Eds.), *World health systems: Challenges and perspectives* (pp. 39–54). Chicago: Health Administration Press.

CHAPTER 10

Developing and Using Nursing Knowledge Through Research

KEY TERMS AND CONCEPTS

Research

The research process

Quantitative research

Qualitative research

Research critique

Variable

Independent variable

Dependent variable

Research ethics

Informed consent

Anonymity

Institution review board (IRB)

Research utilization

Diffusion

Innovation

Diffusion of innovations

Stetler research utilization model

Research utilization facilitators

Research utilization barriers

Evidence-based nursing

Scholar

National Institute for Nursing Research (NINR)

LEARNING OUTCOMES

By the end of this chapter, the learner will be able to:

1   Describe how professional nurses contribute to research in nursing.

2   Outline the sequential steps of the research process.

3   Differentiate qualitative and quantitative research.

4   Debate the ethical considerations of nursing research.

5   Compare and contrast research utilization models.

6   Discuss the key elements of a research study critique.

7   Identify barriers to research utilization by nurses in the clinical setting.

8   Identify strategies to facilitate clinical research utilization.

9   Differentiate research utilization from evidence-based nursing practice.

10 Specify how using nursing research affects the public image of professional nursing.

Joan and Sandy work together on a surgical unit. Sandy has been practicing for 12 years, takes pride in her expertise, and practices nursing "the way that I was taught." Joan has read several research articles substantiating the effectiveness of noninvasive nursing interventions on reducing client need for postoperative narcotics for pain control. Joan is unsure if she should use these findings in practice and how Sandy will react if she suggests implementing these findings on a unit-wide scale. Joan also knows that current federal guidelines related to postoperative pain control specify that nurses should use other methods besides pain medication.

Questions for Reflection 10-1

1. How do I feel about nursing research?
2. What research-based interventions have I used in my clinical practice?

In today's world, health care professionals and consumers rely on research-based interventions for health promotion and disease management. Discipline-specific **research** enables a profession to develop and validate its unique knowledge base. Research also validates principles and techniques of clinical practice. Because nursing primarily is a practice discipline, nurses need to understand research principles, critically analyze research study results, and use research findings to guide client care.

Florence Nightingale (1860) conducted research and published her findings in her book, *Notes on Nursing*. The information generated by her research transformed health care, changed nursing practice, and provided a theoretical foundation for her nursing school in London. However, serious efforts to conduct nursing research and develop theory to guide practice began about 40 years ago, when nursing scholars began the pursuit of establishing theoretical- and factual-based nursing practice, instead of perpetuating nursing practice based on personal opinions, longstanding traditions, and prescribed protocols from other disciplines. Martha Rogers (1967), one of the nursing visionaries, said more than 40 years ago, "Only the most uninformed and those endeavoring to maintain a long obsolete hierarchal control would propose that in today's world society is better served by ignorance than by knowledge" (p.). However, a study of medical-surgical nurses found that many rely on information from individual patients, personal experience, and information gained during nursing school far more than on facts from journal articles (Baessler et al., 1994). Clinicians must appreciate that incorporation of research findings into practice is not an optional activity in which to engage when there is time, but is a critical element of professional practice.

Science seeks the truth and humans create science through research (Barrett, 2002). Therefore, nursing research should result in the creation of nursing science. Research is the "careful, systematic, patient study and investigation in some field of knowledge undertaken to discover or establish facts or principles" (Agnes, 2005, p. 1219). Therefore, nursing research focuses on generating knowledge for the profession and practice of nursing. Scholars debate over which of the following situations can be categorized as nursing research: a nurse or group of nurses conducting research, or studies based on nursing theories or to generate new nursing knowledge. Heitkemper and Bond (2003) identified two commandments, perhaps three, for nursing science: "contribute to science and contribute to patient care," and "contribute to theory development" (p. 152). When research-generated nursing knowledge results in improved client outcomes, enhances the professional practice environment, or contains health care costs, the research has practical applications for client care. When unresolved client care or professional nursing issues arise, nurses can conduct research to solve the problem. Therefore, research guides practice and practice generates new ideas for research.

The baccalaureate-prepared nurse can contribute to nursing research in several ways, including:

1. Reading and critiquing nursing research studies
2. Using nursing research findings to guide nursing practice
3. Valuing a sense of inquiry about the phenomena of nursing
4. Participating in research projects as opportunity allows
5. Refining the ability to collect, organize, categorize, and analyze data
6. Suggesting nursing research questions that need to be addressed to improve practice

To participate in these ways, the nurse must have an understanding of the research process and of strategies to overcome barriers and facilitate research utilization.

 ## RESEARCH PROCESSES IN NURSING

This section serves as an overview to facilitate understanding of the components of the research process. The **research process** consists of a series of logical steps of inquiry. Familiarity with the research process enhances the nurse's understanding of nursing research studies. Complete understanding of the research process and expertise in its execution improve as one develops as a nurse researcher, a process that requires much time and commitment.

Beginning with the nurse's query about some aspect of nursing, the research process structures the systematic investigation of that question and the reporting of the answers and new questions about that aspect of nursing. The research process follows the methods of science, which essentially means that the process:

- Has an identifiable order.
- Includes controls over factors not being investigated.
- Includes the gathering of evidence about the question.
- Is built on a theoretical framework.
- Operates for the purpose of applying results to improve nursing practice.

Raising Questions

The most significant step in the nursing research process may be the first one—the nurse's identification and articulation of a question to be answered. When nurses seek to find the best way to practice, they become accountable for asking questions that reflect the sensitivity needed to better understand all that falls within the domain of nursing. Nurses identify potential research questions when they encounter clinical practice problems. Because nursing theory and practice are deeply intertwined, research questions also may arise when nurses identify a gap in theory and practice. Concrete examples for research studies include, but are not limited to, client health experiences; nursing professional procedures, characteristics, and responsibilities; facilitating factors for nurse–client relationships; and environmental factors to promote health, health promotion, and client adjustment to illness and other life transitions. Clearly and concisely stated questions provide direction for studies. The chance of executing clinically relevant nursing research studies increases when clinical nurses and nurse researchers collaborate.

Quantitative and Qualitative Approaches

Two research approaches to developing nursing knowledge have emerged in recent years: the quantitative approach and the qualitative approach. In the earliest years of nursing research, valuing of the scientific method led to the use of quantitative approaches to develop objective information. However, nurse researchers currently accept qualitative approaches to develop subjective information while remaining open to quantitative approaches.

According to Haase and Myers (1988), quantitative and qualitative research approaches have a common purpose: to gain understanding. The difference between the approaches is one of emphasis. **Quantitative research** focuses on the "confirmation of theory by explaining," demonstrating an empirical analytical emphasis; **qualitative research** focuses on the "discovery and meaning of theory by describing," demonstrating a human science emphasis (Haase & Myers, p. 131).

According to Guba and Lincoln (reported by Haase & Myers, 1988), the differences between the two approaches can be categorized in three ways according to the assumptions made by each approach: the nature of reality, the nature of relationships, and the nature of truth. The following comparison of quantitative and qualitative assumptions according to the three categories is presented from the work of Haase and Myers (pp. 130–134).

1. View of reality
   Quantitative: Researcher focuses on objective reality seen as singular, the process for discovering reality is reductionistic, and it is believed that knowledge of the whole can be gained through knowledge of the parts.
   Qualitative: Researcher focuses on subjective realities seen as multiple and related, the process for understanding reality is ecologic, and it is believed that "the whole is greater than the sum of its parts" (p. 132).
2. View of relationships
   Quantitative: Researcher objectively distances self from subjects and believes that boundaries must exist to ensure objectivity.
   Qualitative: Researcher interacts with the subject and believes that a unity exists between them and that both are integral to the research process.
3. View of truth
   Quantitative: Researcher sees the world as stable and predictable and believes that the truth is discovered in common laws, principles, and norms. Thus, the researcher's goal is generalization.
   Qualitative: Researcher sees the world as dynamic and believes that truth is discovered in the changing patterns of the world. Thus, the researcher's goal is to discover uniqueness, valuing differences as well as similarities.

Appreciating the complexity of nursing phenomena and valuing subjective experiences as legitimate foci of nursing research, Artinian (1988) noted that nurses willingly use qualitative approaches, all of which use participant observation and in-depth interviewing. Cohen and Tripp-Reimer (1988, p. 226) supported ethnography as a significant qualitative research approach to help nurses understand cultural differences, stating that "ethnography is a method designed to describe a culture. The ethnographer seeks to understand another way of life from the native's point of view."

Grounded theory methodology seeks to outline a basic social process or generate a new theory based on participant data. Using grounded theory methodology, Artinian (1988, pp. 138–149) described four modes of inquiry the qualitative researcher can use:

1. Descriptive mode, which "presents rich detail that allows the reader to understand what it would be like to be in a setting or to be experiencing the life situation of a person or group" (p. 139).
2. Discovery mode, which "enables the researcher both to identify patterns in the life experiences of the subjects and to relate the patterns to each other" (p. 141).
3. Emergent fit mode, which is "used when a substantive theory has already been developed about the phenomenon under study" from which a research question "is formulated to extend or refine the previously developed theory" (p. 142).

4. Intervention mode, in which the researcher tries to answer the fundamental question of how to make something happen after the "phenomenon has been adequately conceptualized so that the conditions under which the basic social process takes place are understood" (p. 139).

The researcher decides which of the four modes of inquiry to use only after clarifying the purpose of the research and evaluating knowledge that is available on the topic.

Along with ethnography and grounded theory, nurse researchers use other qualitative research processes. Phenomenology looks at the "lived experience" of a particular life transition, a clinical experience, or having a specific illness or surgery. Hermeneutic inquiry seeks to find the deep, personal meaning of an experience. Qualitative research enables nurses to discover individualized and human phenomena surrounding health and illness. Historical studies examine artifacts from a particular era to determine what persons did in the past that might have application for today.

Steps in the Research Process

Whether the nurse researcher chooses the qualitative or the quantitative approach, the overall steps in the research process remain essentially the same. The research process is a sequence of 11 steps during which researchers make decisions to plan and execute a study. While engaged in the research process, the investigator may not necessarily complete a step, but rather may revisit steps while planning and executing a study. The study question determines which approach would be best. Knowledge of the research process steps discussed in the subsequent sections will facilitate the nurse's use of findings in practice.

Focus on the Clinical Problem Area

From where do the questions that need to be answered about nursing arise? Of these questions, which require research for adequate response? Which have sufficient data already available for effective problem solving? All nurses have the ability to identify problems in professional practice. While engaging in clinical practice, nurses frequently identify gaps between what is and what could be. The identified gaps become clinical problems that may be solved through nursing research.

Nurses also can focus on a problem area by reviewing the current research and other information in the literature on a topic of interest, by deriving questions from the theories or conceptual models used to guide practice in the nurses' practice setting or educational program, or by getting ideas from external sources such as faculty, peers, or priorities established for practice.

For example, some nursing organizations have determined areas of priority for research. The Oncology Nursing Society has ongoing research initiatives on pain control, prevention of nausea, optimal nutrition, and fatigue in persons with cancer. The American Nurses Association has ongoing studies related to workplace hazards for nurses. The American Association of Critical Care Nurses' priorities for clinical research focus on client pain, nosocomial infections, and ventilator weaning. Often, nursing organizations provide grants to researchers who conduct studies in the determined priority areas.

The development of the research problem, according to Polit and Beck (2004), incorporates the following sequential steps:

• Note a general area of interest about which you have some questions.
• Narrow the topic through critical evaluation of ideas with a mentor or expert. That evaluation must address feasibility and worth.
• Establish the benefit of the investigation of the selected problem to nursing by addressing who will benefit, what are the applications, what is the potential for the results to be relevant to theoretical bases of practice, and how important are the findings (in other words, so what?).

- Make certain that the selected problem is amenable to scientific methodology.
- Verify that the problem is not primarily a moral issue.
- Critique the feasibility of studying the problem in terms of time factors, availability of subjects, cooperation required, facilities and equipment needed, and costs.

The initial review of the literature helps researchers accomplish these steps in the early development of the problem.

Initial Review of the Literature

Nurse researchers obtain a broad understanding and general background on the problem to be studied from an initial review of the literature. Once the researcher has raised a question, an initial review of the literature is helpful in:

- Identifying the major variables in the area of interest.
- Finding out what is already known.
- Gathering feasibility data on the needs for investigation of the question.
- Refining the focus of the problem to be investigated.

A review of the literature should make the researcher aware of all the possible relevant material available regarding a problem of interest. Along with reading the literature available on the research topic, researchers must appraise each research study by assessing its strengths and weaknesses. A **research critique** points out the strengths and weaknesses of a study and helps researchers discover gaps in the current literature. Helpful sources for locating resource materials include indexes from nursing, related disciplines, and popular literature; abstracting services from nursing and related disciplines; computer searches of appropriate databases; dictionaries; encyclopedias; guides; and directories. Reference librarians in most libraries provide tremendous help to the beginning nurse researcher in locating and using these materials.

In summary, the initial review of the literature should answer some questions about the topic of interest, describe other people's interests in the topic, and help the researcher develop a strong knowledge base of what has been written and reported on the topic. Frequently, qualitative research studies avoid reviewing the literature before collecting data to avoid developing preconceived ideas about the topic area. In quantitative research, such a knowledge base makes it possible for the researcher to proceed to the next stage of research: specifying the problem and defining the variables.

Specification of the Problem and the Defining Variables

When the researcher has completed the initial review of the literature, and gained a general understanding of the research topic and a sense of what is known about the topic, the researcher proceeds to more clearly delineate the problem to be investigated.

Decisions are made about exactly what is to be investigated or what part of the nursing domain is to be studied. The nurse researcher may be investigating some client aspect that is clearly important to understand in the nursing process, some client health phenomenon, some client outcomes associated with particular nursing interventions, some aspect of the nurse–client relationship, some aspect of the delivery of nursing care services, some aspect of the environment that affects the health status, or any combination of these factors in the nursing domain.

Clear articulation of the problem incorporates the identification of the phenomenon to be investigated. In quantitative research, a phenomenon of interest generally is called a "variable." A **variable** is a characteristic, a trait, a property, or a condition. If the variable is purposefully manipulated by the researcher to have a direct effect on another variable, it is an **independent variable**. The variable that is observed, measured, and presumed to be influenced by or related in some special way to the independent variable is the **dependent variable**. Variables do not exist in qualitative research because the purpose may be to identify key phenomena surrounding a client or nurse experience.

An example of an investigative problem with one variable that is manipulated and another that is observed and measured is as follows: What is the relationship between specific parenting guidance by the professional nurse and the development of positive nutritional habits of the toddler? In this investigation, the independent variable is the specific parenting guidance, the dependent variable is the toddler's nutritional habits, and the approach to studying the variables is quantitative.

To make these variables measurable, the researcher must determine exactly what is meant by each variable: what constitutes parenting guidance and what constitutes positive nutritional habits in the toddler. The statement of the problem may be in the form of a question or a declaration. In both cases, this problem statement also must clearly identify who is to be studied and what is to be studied.

Establishment of Tentative Propositions: Hypotheses and the Second Review of the Literature

After the nurse researcher has clarified the problem under investigation, studied the available data, and recalled observations from professional experience, he or she may formulate a hypothesis, a formal statement that predicts or explains the relationships between two or more variables (Polit & Beck, 2004). Not all studies require that the researcher generate a hypothesis; for example, descriptive, qualitative, and exploratory natured questions do not need hypotheses. However, for studies requiring manipulation of an independent variable and measurement of a dependent variable, hypotheses must be stated and tested.

Nurses have excellent opportunities to form some hunches about the relationships among variables they observe in practice. Thought of as bridges, hypotheses connect theory with observation and are derived from observations, reasoning, and theoretical bases.

Hypotheses in quantitative studies are tested statistically in relation to the laws of chance. Thus, they are based on statistical probability and incur an element of risk of reaching an incorrect conclusion. How much risk can be afforded is a judgment of the investigator, but when permanent or serious consequences are involved, the investigator cannot afford to take too many risks. Because hypotheses sometimes force the investigator to infer from the sample findings to an interpretation about the population, the researcher uses probability statistics (level of significance) to determine the likelihood that the relationship between the variables results from something other than chance.

When the researcher is determining hypotheses, additional review of the literature is used to evaluate testing procedures and to project a research design appropriate for investigating the variable(s). The review of the literature can be used to learn what investigative methods have been used, how data have been collected and analyzed, and what has and has not been successful in previous research.

In summary, in quantitative studies, hypotheses declare the researcher's proposition about the relationship between variables and then serve as the means for testing the proposed relationship. Hypotheses do not appear in descriptive, correlational, or qualitative research studies.

Determination of a Suitable Research Design

The nurse researcher selects the type of research design suitable for the study based on the research question(s) or hypothesis(es). The descriptive design answers questions about the nature of presently occurring events. The experimental design tests the effects of manipulating one or more specific variables on other variables. The historical design is based on the desire to describe or evaluate past events. The researcher frequently acts as a member of or observes a group in ethnographic research. Detailed interviews followed by participant validation of data serve as the means to capture the essence of an experience in phenomenology.

Development of Measurement Methods and Instruments

After the approach is selected for a particular study, the nurse researcher must decide on the appropriate method for gathering data about the variables. The investigator then selects instruments for data collection; the instrument chosen depends on the purpose of the research. Instruments generally are categorized under three methods: observation, questioning, and measurement.

Examples of data collection instruments from these categories include critical incidents, tests, interviews, questionnaires, checklists, records, scales, and physical measurement techniques. The researcher strives to select a measurement tool that is appropriate to answer the research question, that is not biased, and that has precision in measuring the variables being studied. For quantitative studies, the researcher carefully analyzes available measurement tools to determine instrument validity (the extent that it actually measured the variable of interest) and reliability (consistency of variable measurement). In qualitative studies, the researcher exercises caution to eliminate any personal biases that could interfere with objective data collection. The quality of data generated for a study relies on careful selection of data collection methods.

Knafl and Webster (1988, pp. 196–203) pointed out how the researcher's data collection, analysis of those data, and reporting are likely to vary, according to the purpose of the study. They described four purposes of qualitative research:

1. Illustration, in which the researcher aims to identify qualitative examples of specific quantitative variables
2. Instrumentation, in which the researcher aims to collect data that serve as the basis for developing an instrument to describe and measure perceptions of some phenomenon of interest to nursing
3. Description, in which the researcher aims to "translate the data into a form that would facilitate an accurate, complete description" (p. 200) of a phenomenon of interest to nursing by identifying and delineating the major themes
4. Theory building, in which the researcher aims to conceptually explain the phenomenon under study

Knafl, Pettengill, Bevis, and Kirchhoff (1988) reported that, although debate continues about the credibility of using either qualitative or quantitative approaches to study particular nursing phenomena, some nurse researchers are beginning to use both qualitative and quantitative methods in single studies. This process is known as method triangulation and it is believed that by integrating the two approaches, researchers can capitalize on the strengths of each approach while minimizing the weaknesses of each. For example, a nurse studying the effects of specific parenting guidance on positive toddler nutritional habits might want the mother's attitudes about specific guidance given to her by the nurse.

In addition to selecting instruments for data collection during this stage of research, the nurse must determine the composition of the sample; establish a process for collecting data from the sample; and prepare a format for data collection (which may include designing specific forms), data classification, and data storage for later analysis. The sample subjects must be clearly described, and the method for choosing the subjects must be appropriate. The number of sample subjects must meet statistical requirements for the nurse to draw appropriate conclusions about the findings.

Assurance of an Ethical Process

Research requires honesty and integrity. **Research ethics** are principles by which researchers abide to ensure truth in scientific studies, protect the human rights of participants, balance risks and benefits of a study, and prevent exploitation of vulnerable persons. Research ethics became important after reports of inhumane and unethical treatment sustained by prisoners during Nazi Germany medical experiments. In 1949, the Nuremburg Code was established to protect human subjects in biomedical experiments. The researcher bears the responsibility for protecting human rights when persons participate in a research study. This protection is provided primarily through informed consent and protection from harm.

Informed consent means that the researcher provides subjects with a clear description about the study, how they meet study criteria, requirements for participation, and potential hazards. The subjects must understand and consent to their role in the study. Having given informed consent does not keep any subject from changing his or her mind anytime during the study and withdrawing from it.

Protection from harm means just that: the investigator will not knowingly do anything that will harm or abuse the subjects. Investigators also work to preserve subject **anonymity** (keeping the identification of all subjects confidential).

Most institutions where research is conducted have a formalized process for approving research proposals before implementation. An **institution review board (IRB)** meets on a regular schedule to review research proposals to verify that investigators have considered research ethics and that the study meets scientific standards. In health care settings, nurses sometimes hold IRB membership. Because they are client advocates and have holistic views of health care, nurses sometimes identify potentially harmful research treatments that other IRB health team members may overlook.

To ensure truth in research, the researcher assumes responsibility for honesty when collecting and analyzing data and when reporting research findings. For-profit and non-profit organizations frequently fund research studies. When corporations fund research projects, a conflict of interest may arise. Researchers have taken funds from sponsors for many years while remaining neutral when performing scientific studies. Corporations frequently fill in gaps in required funding so that research studies can be performed. When extramural funding has been received for the research study, the investigator has an obligation to report the source of funds within the written report (Blumenstyk, 2001).

Collection of Data

After protection of human rights for all subjects has been ensured, data collection can begin. However, before any subject associated with an institution can be approached, the researcher must have approval from appropriate agency personnel.

The researcher or a specified data collector orients each subject clearly and concisely to the data collection method, then administers the data collection instrument to each subject in the same manner. Throughout this implementation stage, the researcher follows the written proposal (in the methodology) as closely as possible. While collecting data, the researcher records the data on the prepared forms. The data then are classified and organized for analysis.

Analysis of Data and Report of Findings

Once data are collected, the researcher organizes data in a manner that makes them amenable to analysis. If the researcher's goal is simply to display the data collected, no analysis other than the narrative description of the displayed data is needed. However, if the researcher aims to infer some characteristics about a population or to evaluate some relationship among variables, the organized data must be subjected to statistical analysis. Computations are done. If hypotheses have been stated, statistical testing, by hand or by computer, of those hypotheses must be done.

Based on accurate data analysis, the researcher must report the findings exactly as they occurred. Summaries of the data must reflect the subjects' findings exactly. All data collected for purposes of testing the hypotheses must be reported. Tables, charts, and graphs used to present data should be pertinent, clear, and well labeled, and they should be discussed in the text of the research report. The reports of the findings are then used to draw conclusions.

Conclusions and Implications

For quantitative research studies, the researcher must determine the meaning of the findings and their value to nursing with use of the theoretical foundation guiding the study. Findings are analyzed first by inspecting the statistical tests performed to test the hypotheses or evaluate the data. The researcher then interprets what the numerical analysis means. With hypothesis testing, the findings may support the predicted relationship with demonstrated statistical significance (the findings were not attributable to chance alone), the findings may not be in the predicted direction, the findings may be contradictory, or the findings may indicate an unpredicted relationship. Sometimes statistical significance has little practical significance. Practical significance indicates that the results add to the body of nursing knowledge or result in major changes in clinical outcomes. For example, the tobacco industry argued in the court system that cigarette smoking failed to cause lung cancer with statistical significance. However, research studies revealed a high degree of correlation (strong relationship) between smoking and the development of lung cancer.

For qualitative studies, the researcher determines the meaning of the study and its value to professional nursing by identifying the significance of the new knowledge generated by the study. The conceptual overview generated by a qualitative study may have profound importance when working with clients with similar conditions. Qualitative studies frequently provide a foundation for hypothesis generation and research instrument development for future quantitative research studies.

Based on the analysis and interpretation of data, the researcher might make generalizations about what the data mean and whether the data can be applied to groups different from the sample. Generalizations should emerge only from the findings, and the researcher should not go beyond the data as a result of the excitement generated by scientific discovery.

Study implications usually relate to one of the four aspects of professional nursing: clinical practice with clients, professional education, clinical practice environments, and ideas for additional nursing research. Researchers generally report implications in a section of a research study called "Recommendations." The implications for practice (that is, how they affect the nursing process with clients) are discussed. Recommendations for the education of practitioners and for future research are also usually given. If the recommendations are clearly and concisely stated and derived logically, clinical nurses can find the study valuable and consider using the findings in practice.

The Written Report

Research completed but not compiled into a report is wasted. Some research experts argue that the research process is not complete until it is shared in writing or some other public medium. Characteristics of an effective research report are brevity, clarity, and complete objectivity.

Although there are variations on the form of the report that may be determined by faculty, a particular style manual, or other institutional requirements, the usual report follows the outline of the research process presented in this chapter. Most outlines include the problem statement, review of literature, methods of investigation, presentation of findings, discussion of the analyses and conclusions, bibliographic data, and appendixes. The reader is directed to a nursing research book or a writing style manual for specific guidance in developing each part of the written research report.

Questions for Reflection 10-2

1. What questions do I have related to the research process and how to critique nursing research studies?
2. Who would be able and willing to help if I had questions when reading a nursing research report? How can I reach them?
3. Would I be interested in starting or participating in a nursing research journal club? Why or why not? If so, how could I make journal club participation a reality?

UTILIZATION OF NURSING RESEARCH

Nurses have used nursing research in practice for more than a century. Florence Nightingale used a systematic approach to collect data and presented detailed statistics using bar graphs, pie charts, and color-coded tables to highlight key points. She used these to present evidence of the benefits of sanitation and trained nurses when she pleaded her case for increased funding for ill and infirm soldiers during the Crimean War. She published her findings in *Notes on Nursing* (Nightingale, 1860) so that the knowledge she generated could be used in practice (McDonald, 2001). Nurses have been using research in practice for years but frequently overlook its use. **Research utilization** is a systematic process used by nurses to incorporate research-based knowledge into professional nursing practice.

Every time nurses administer medications in the United States, the medication is subjected to randomized clinical trials. Because new knowledge is being generated rapidly, what nurses learn in an academic program may become obsolete within a few years. Professional nurses cannot plead ignorance of new knowledge and practices because part of professional accountability requires keeping up with new practice developments (Rambur, 1999). To stay abreast of new practices, professional nurses must read the research nursing literature and apply new knowledge appropriately in practice.

The use of a scientific base for clinical practice has a number of benefits, including:

- A sound foundation for practice.
- Enhanced self-confidence, autonomy, critical thinking skills, and professional self-concept.
- Cost-effective patient care.
- Increased patient and job satisfaction and quality of care.
- Improved patient outcomes.
- A stimulus for collaborative practice, retention, and recruitment.
- An improved image of nursing.
- An ever-increasing scientific nursing knowledge base. (Goode et al., 1991, pp. 8–9)

Research utilization may be as simple as one nurse changing the way in which care is given (Gennaro, 1994). However, despite the significant amount of available nursing research, there is a well-documented gap in the use of research findings to improve practice. This section describes two major theories of research utilization, with Display 10-1 as an illustrative example, presents possible barriers, and describes strategies to facilitate the use of research findings in practice.

Theories and Models of Research Utilization

The professional nurse can select from a variety of nursing research utilization models and theories to provide a conceptual basis for integrating research findings into practice. Since the 1970s, several nursing research models have appeared and have been useful for nurses who want to use nursing research findings in practice. Various research

---

Case Study for Research Utilization	DISPLAY 10-1

Tony works on a rehabilitation unit with a variety of clients who have problems with activities of daily living, such as ambulation and feeding themselves. Because of staff shortages, he has noticed that there has been an increase in client impaired skin integrity. He would like to use the Braden scale, a research-based tool, to screen clients at risk for impaired skin integrity. When he suggests using research findings as the basis for nursing care protocols on the unit, his colleagues tease him and call him "professor". His work setting does not permit him time to prepare a proposal for using research-based findings on the job.

utilization models target different nurses. Research utilization theories that have been used with some success have been borrowed from the corporate world or developed by nurse researchers and collaborative nursing research projects. Some nursing research utilization models, such as the Iowa model, contain paths for nurses to follow when they cannot find adequate research upon which to base practice changes (Polit & Beck, 2004). The American Association of Critical Care Nurses has an ongoing collaborative research effort, the Thunder Project, to develop critical care nursing protocols based on research conducted at multiple clinical sites (Beyea & Nicoll, 1998). Because no single model fits each nurse's needs, nurses can find a variety of models for research utilization in nursing research texts, in professional journals, and on nursing specialty organization websites.

Tony, the nurse presented in the vignette, knows the key elements specified by many nursing research utilization models. To illustrate how to use them, the factors identified using the vignette appear in parentheses after each of the key areas to be addressed by nursing research utilization models. The following key elements appear in most of the nursing research utilization models:

1. Identifying a gap between desired outcome (skin integrity maintenance)
2. Articulating the clinical problem clearly and concisely (increased incidence of client impaired skin integrity)
3. Reviewing research literature (securing, reading, and critiquing research literature based on client risk factors for impaired skin integrity)
4. Preparing a comprehensive report outlining key research findings (preparing a table outlining the research findings from literature reviewed on risk factors for impaired skin integrity, and drawing conclusions and forming clinical implications for a specific practice setting)
5. Selecting from one of the research-based innovations found in the literature review (selection of the Braden scale to monitor client risk for impaired skin integrity)
6. Developing specific practice outcomes for the proposed innovation (incidence of client impaired skin integrity will be reduced by 50% within 1 month of using the Braden scale to monitor clients at risk for impaired skin integrity)
7. Establishing an implementation plan for the innovation (staff education on the use and documentation of the Braden scale, securing staff acceptance of using the Braden scale, and printing and distributing Braden scale assessment forms)
8. Creating an evaluation plan development to assess the effects or practice outcomes of the innovation (chart audits to verify staff use of Braden scale and identify episodes of skin development, summarize findings of audits, and note any changes from current incidence rate)
9. Implementing the innovation within a practice setting (using the Braden scale twice weekly to assess client risk for impaired skin integrity)
10. Evaluating the clinical effects of the innovation (seeing if Braden scale use reduced the incidence of client impaired skin integrity)

Once the effectiveness of the innovation has been demonstrated, agency policy and procedures may be revised to make using the innovation standard practice. To facilitate change and innovations to practice, many nurses desiring to make practice changes find using theories and models of research utilization helpful.

Rogers' Theory of Diffusion of Innovations

According to Rogers (1983, p. 5), "**Diffusion** is the process by which an innovation is communicated through certain channels over time among the members of a social system." Rogers (1983, p. 11) defined an **innovation** as "an idea, practice, or object that is perceived as new." In Display 10-1, changing the method for screening clients for increased risk for skin integrity would be considered an innovation.

Rogers (1983) suggested that **diffusion of innovations**, a five-stage process, is useful for deciding whether to adopt an innovation (something perceived as new by those who are considering adoption). The knowledge stage is the first awareness of the existence of the innovation (Tony's awareness of the Braden scale as a research-validated instrument to assess impaired skin integrity risk that he shares with his colleagues). The persuasion stage occurs when the individual forms an attitude toward the innovation (Tony's willingness to ask his colleagues what they would think about trying the Braden scale twice weekly for skin assessment). A decision occurs when the individual makes the choice for adoption or rejection of the innovation (Tony's staff decides to give the Braden scale a try to see if it makes a difference). In the implementation stage, the individual uses the innovation (staff use the Braden scale twice weekly for skin assessment and documentation), and in the confirmation stage, the individual seeks reinforcement of the decision (client incidence of skin breakdown decreases and staff like using the Braden scale). Reversal of the decision can occur at any time during the implementation and confirmation stages.

For an individual to consider adoption of an innovation, the person must be aware of the innovation. Rogers (1983) used the term "diffusion" to describe the dissemination of an innovation. The theory proposes that diffusion of an innovation is enhanced by face-to-face and mass media communication channels, time, and interaction within the social system. Adoption of an innovation is enhanced by persuasion by a peer colleague or by influence from opinion leaders within the social system. An outside change agent also may facilitate diffusion and adoption of an innovation.

The perceived characteristics of the innovation affect favorable or unfavorable attitudes toward the adoption. The probability and speed of adoption are enhanced if the staff perceives the innovation as being superior to current practice; the innovation is consistent with current values, experience, and priority of needs; the innovation is easy to learn, understand, or use, or can be tried out on a limited basis with the option of returning to previous practices; and the innovation causes visible results (Burns & Grove, 2004).

The Stetler/Marram Decision-Making Model

Although Rogers' theory addresses the structure of diffusion of any innovation, including research findings, the revised Stetler/Marram model, now commonly called the **Stetler research utilization model** (Stetler, 1994), refers to a six-phase, critical-thinking and decision-making process to assist the individual practitioner in using published research.

In Phase 1, preparation, the nurse determines the purpose for the research review (Tony identifies the problems of increased impaired skin integrity and decides to review research on risk factors for it). The purpose influences the development of measurable outcomes later in the process (desired outcome is to reduce the incidence of impaired skin integrity). In Phase 2, validation, the strengths and weaknesses of a research study are assessed to accept or reject findings based on their potential for applicability (Tony analyzes the research studies, and based on his findings he decides that the Braden scale may be a feasible way to screen clients on the rehabilitation unit for impaired skin integrity problems).

Phase 3, comparative evaluation, determines whether it is desirable or feasible to apply findings in practice. Criteria include similarity of the study sample and environment to the population and setting of the nurse; assessment of the effectiveness of current practice and whether or not theory would be an improvement; assessment of risk, need for resources, and readiness; and substantiating evidence. Multiple research articles with congruent findings or a meta-analysis are, of course, more desirable than one study. Table 10-1 presents considerations for examining the fit, flow, and feasibility of reported research that fits with Phases 2 and 3. (Tony looks at the research findings on the Braden scale use in long-term and rehabilitation settings, and uses criteria found in the table to determine desirability and feasibility of using the Braden scale in his clinical practice setting.)

Phase 4, decision making, may result in the decision to use the new knowledge to change practice or modify a way of thinking without waiting for additional data. Another

TABLE 10-1

Considerations for Preliminary Evaluation of Nursing Research for Use in a Particular Clinical Setting

Fit to Clinical Setting	Flow of Research Study	Feasibility of Adoption
Purpose of study fits the clinical area where findings may be adopted	Research questions or hypothesis flows from the study's stated purpose	Innovation proposed legally permitted by State Nurse Practice Act
Study sample represents clientele of clinical setting	Researcher follows all steps outlined in the research process	Innovation is ethical practice
Sample size is appropriate	Variables are well defined	Acceptable costs to clients, third-party payers or institution
Enhances the fulfillment of the clinical area's mission	Measurements for the variables make sense	Enough staff and time to fully execute the proposed innovation
	Validity and reliability of variable measurements presented	Innovation is congruent with nursing philosophy of the organization or unit
	Efforts made to control factors that might affect the results	Any risks to clients, nurses or the organization?
	Data presented accurately	Available resources needed are obtained
	The correct statistics are used to answer the research question(s) or test the hypothesis(es): • research purpose • number and type of variables • level of measurement for each variable	Staff ready to adopt the proposed innovation
	Sample size is large enough to support the statistical test or researcher reports power level	
	Weaknesses of the study are reported	
	Logically and accurately generated study conclusions	
	Implications for practice logically flow from findings	

Source: Liehr, P., & Houston, S. (1993). Critiquing and using nursing research: Guidelines for the critical care nurse. *American Journal of Critical Care, 2*, 407–412; Burns, N., & Grove, S. (2004). *The practice of nursing research: Conduct, critique and utilization* (5th ed.). Philadelphia: Saunders.
Important Note: Do not change practice on the basis of the findings of one study. Similar findings from multiple studies indicate that the findings were more likely not to be the result of chance.

alternative is to consider use but continue to collect additional data. A third option might be to delay use until additional research has been conducted. A fourth alternative might be to reject or not use the information because of the risks or costs involved, lack of consistent, strong findings, or the strength of current practice (Stetler, 1994). (Tony decides that the research evidence provides a solid foundation to propose using the Braden scale on his unit.)

Phase 5, translation/application, involves generalization of the similarities or differences in the sources that were reviewed, and identification of implications for practice (the "so what"). See Figure 10-1.

In Phase 6, evaluation, the expected outcomes are compared with the purpose that was defined in the preparation phase. Following this decision-making process, the nurse

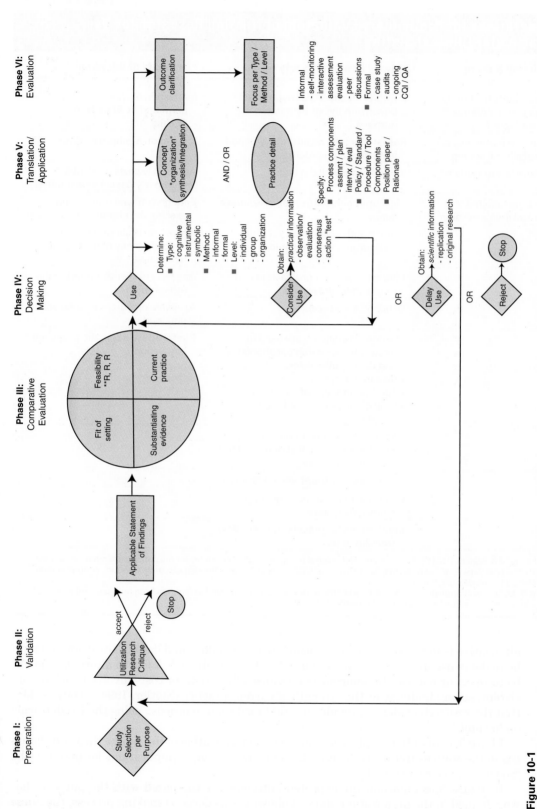

Figure 10-1

The Stetler/Marram research utilization model. (Stetler, C. B. [1994]. Refinement of the Stetler/Marram model for application of research findings to practice. *Nursing Outlook, 42,* 18–19. Used with permission.)

would implement a planned change model, such as Rogers' diffusion of innovations or other planned change models presented in Chapter 18.

The process of research utilization is a continual one. Advances in the health science arena mean that nurses must stay abreast with changes in their clinical practice areas. New theoretical developments in nursing result in different approaches to client assessments, nursing interventions, and outcome evaluation. Nursing research utilization success relies on a variety of factors that facilitate use of research findings in practice.

Facilitators to Research Utilization

Many factors influence the utilization of nursing research in clinical practice. **Research utilization facilitators** are any factors that promote the use of research-based knowledge into clinical practice. Individual nurse and employing organization factors can facilitate research utilization in clinical practice setting. Estabrooks, Floyd, Scott-Findlay, O'Leary, and Gushta (2003) identified the following six categories of possible individual factors that promoted research utilization from a review of 22 studies:

1. Beliefs and attitudes toward nursing research
2. Involvement in nursing research activities
3. Information-seeking behavior
4. Education level
5. Professional characteristics
6. Socioeconomic factors

Estabrooks, Midodzi, Cummings, and Wallin (2007) developed a three-tiered multilevel model to predict research utilization and discovered that individual nurse factors (increased Internet usage and lower levels of emotional exhaustion) were contributing factors for research utilization. They also discovered that nurses employed in larger hospitals tended to use research more than nurses employed in other settings. Table 10-2 summarizes facilitators of utilization of nursing research based on individual nurse factors. Cultivating these characteristics in all professional nurses remains a challenge for the profession.

Organizational factors also serve as facilitators to research utilization by nurses. Research utilization efforts require use of human and financial resources. Research utilization projects are time intensive. Nursing research utilization requires organizational commitment. The following strategies to facilitate research utilization have been used with some success in nursing departments:

1. Clear expectation of research utilization as part of a job description
2. Staff educational programs on the process of research utilization
3. Incentives, such as promotions or salary increases
4. Formation of nursing research/research utilization committees
5. Provision of time for nurses to read research reports while on duty
6. Clinical career ladders requiring research utilization as criteria for promotion and maintenance of organizational position
7. Organizational support to defray expenses for research utilization projects
8. Formalized collaboration between nursing service and academia
9. Library services for nurses to use to perform computerized literature searches and access needed materials
10. Nursing unit–based libraries and nursing journal subscriptions
11. Sponsorship of nurses to attend professional nursing conferences

Characteristics of published research studies also serve as facilitators of research utilization in nursing practice. Because many nurse researchers may not engage in clinical practice on a regular basis, performing clinically relevant studies may be challenging. However, nothing captures the interest of professional nurses better than a study that

TABLE 10-2

Individual Nurse Facilitators for Utilization of Nursing Research

Main Category	Facilitator
Beliefs and attitudes	Positive attitude toward nursing research Self-expectation to use nursing research in practice Interest in nursing research Lower levels of emotional exhaustion
Involvement with research activities	Perceived availability of research findings Current collaboration or past participation on a research project Collecting data for other researchers Participation in a research study as a subject or participant Previous use of nursing research Experience with the research process
Information-seeking behaviors	Reading nursing journals as the top information source to stay current in practice Regular reading of professional journals (*Nursing Research, American Journal of Nursing*) Subscribing to professional journals More time spent studying while off duty Use of nursing school as a resource for nursing research materials and information Increased use of the Internet
Education	Education preparation in the research utilization process Attendance at professional nursing conferences Attendance at more staff in-services Bachelor of Science in nursing or higher degree Perception of being well prepared in education process Completion of a research and/or statistics course
Professional characteristics	Perceived organizational support for research utilization activities Perception of an organizational policy for research use Increased number of years experience in a nursing specialty areas or clinical unit Nursing leadership or advanced practice nursing role Membership in the American Nurses Association Certification from the Oncology Nursing Society
Socioeconomic factors	Younger-aged nurses

Adapted from Estabrooks, C., Floyd, J., Scott-Findlay, S., O'Leary, K., & Gushta, M. (2003). Individual determinants of research utilization: A systematic review. *Journal of Advanced Nursing*, 43, 506–520; Estabrooks, C., Midodzi, W., Cummings, G., & Wallin, L. (2007). Predicting research use in nursing organizations: A multilevel analysis. *Nursing Research, 56*(4, Suppl. 1), S7–S23.

demonstrates substantial improvements in client outcomes or working environments. A well-written research study using clear, concise language enhances the ability of all nurses to read and understand published nursing research studies.

Barriers to Research Utilization

Research utilization barriers are any factors that block or impede the use of research findings in clinical practice. Goode et al. (1991); Rutledge, Mooney, Grant, and Easton (2004); and Funk, Champagne, Wiese, and Tornquist (1991) identified a number of barriers to research utilization, including barriers from the researcher, the clinician, and the administration. Barriers to research utilization because of the nature of disseminated research studies include the following:

- Insufficient current research with solutions to address today's complex clinical problems
- Failure of replicated research studies

- Research reports that are difficult to read
- Many unpublished or nondisseminated research reports (especially studies done to meet graduate and postgraduate program requirements)
- Lack of a central depository for nursing research studies

Nursing practice should not be changed on the basis of a single study because of potential confounding factors that may have caused the study results. Unfortunately, few replication studies appear in the nursing literature. Either nurses are not performing replication studies or they are not being accepted for publication when they are submitted.

Barriers to research utilization based on characteristics of the clinician include the following:

- Lack of education in how to read, critique, conduct, and use research (most new nurses are being educated in associate degree programs that focus on technical skills)
- Negative attitudes among practicing nurses about using research findings in practice
- Not enough time or commitment to implement research utilization projects
- Failure of nurses to read nursing research articles or journals
- Inability of nurses to understand statistical analyses contained within studies
- Comfort with practice based on tradition, which is difficult to change, even if it is ineffective
- Difficulty determining if studies are well designed and scientifically sound
- Isolation from knowledgeable colleagues who could assist them in understanding research studies

Nursing research utilization requires much time and commitment. In today's society, many nurses assume multiple roles that compete for their attention. Even though practice based on sound science is preferred, changing personal attitudes and the status quo remains difficult.

Barriers arising from nurse researcher characteristics include the following:

- Submission of studies for publication to journals not read widely by most nurses
- Use of research jargon in publications that is not understood by clinicians
- Failure to offer realistic implications for clinical practice because of either lack of patient care experience or current clinical experience
- Presentation of findings in a format not conducive to clinical implementation

Failure to understand statistics serves as another barrier for using research clinical practice. Researchers sometimes manipulate statistics to distort the truth (Best, 2001). Because the average nurse does not comprehend statistical tests presented in a research study, the nurse accepts the study's reported findings, even though the authors might make implausible claims. A common misconception related to statistics is that they "prove" something. A crucial approach to statistics avoids the extreme of naïve acceptance and cynical rejection. When reading statistics, the consumer of research must realize that researchers choose variable definitions, instruments for data collection, and samples for a variety of reasons (Best). Reported statistics represent a compromise among various choices that researchers make during a study. Critical analysis of a statistic found in a research report involves asking the following questions:

- Do they answer the question or issue outlined in the purpose of the study?
- What is the level of measurement of the research variables contained in the study?
- How many independent and dependent variables appear in the study?
- Is the sample size large enough to effectively use the statistical test?
- What instruments were used to collect data, and what is the level of measurement that these generate?
- How might the sampling techniques affect the study results?
- Are comparisons appropriate if comparisons are being made?

- How have the figures been generated, and have any techniques been used to alter the appearance of the data?
- What stakes does the researcher have if the statistical tests used are not significant?

Instead of being awestruck or overwhelmed by complex statistical tests found in research reports, nurses should read for logical, feasible, and appropriate findings. Many advanced practice nurses find great rewards in helping staff nurses understand research reports.

Barriers to research utilization from the health care agency administration include the following:

- Minimal value placed on research by many administrators and managers
- No provision made for resources such as time, financial support, and education
- Lack of nursing autonomy within a bureaucratic structure to implement data-based solutions to problems
- Lack of incentives for nurses to participate in research utilization activities
- Reliance on established policy and procedures, rather than openness to change
- Lack of support for implementation of research findings by physicians and other staff

Unfortunately, many clinicians are not familiar with research methods, language, and statistical methods because associate degree nursing programs do not offer instruction in research methodology and critique. However, baccalaureate-educated clinicians should be able to raise questions during practice and recognize effective and ineffective interventions from experience. Strategies to address barriers and facilitate the utilization of research must build on basic professional education. The following section presents some strategies to facilitate research utilization in clinical practice settings.

Strategies to Facilitate Research Utilization

In baccalaureate-degree nursing programs, students are exposed to the basic steps of the research process and how to effectively critique studies for use in clinical practice. Most baccalaureate graduates have a basic understanding of research terminology, and some (though not all) can read and understand published research reports containing basic statistical analysis techniques (Hunt, 2001). Nursing students and professionals gain confidence and expertise in reading and understanding research with continuous practice. Upon graduation, beginning nurses focus on acquiring clinical competence, and they spend little or no time reading nursing research reports. Rutledge et al. (2004) found that when nurses received formal education in research utilization, oncology nurses could master the process well enough to design and implement nursing research utilization projects in a clinical settings course.

Researchers should make an effort to write for practicing nurses and to emphasize the meaning of the findings for practice in language that is understandable by most clinicians (Hunt, 2001). Consultation with a master's degree–educated nurse serves as a useful method for understanding and interpreting complex statistical analyses. The clinical setting may employ a master's-prepared research facilitator who is available for consultation. Another source might be graduate students or faculty from a local school of nursing. Possibly a group of nurses could work together with a consultant in locating and interpreting relevant literature.

To use research findings, practicing nurses must read professional journals, including research journals. A number of journals, including *Applied Nursing Research* and *Clinical Nursing Research*, now focus on the use of research for practice. Many nursing specialty journals have adopted the practice of publishing research articles. Other means of finding research articles pertinent to one's areas of nursing practice is to use electronic databases such as Medline or Cumulative Index of Nursing and Allied Health Literature (CINAHL). Many hospitals have a basic medical (or health sciences) library that includes a core collection of nursing journals. Nurses also may visit a local college or university library. As state taxpayers, nurses may use public university and college libraries.

Research Brief 10-1

Rutledge, D., Mooney, K., Grant, M., & Easton, L. (2004). Implementation and refinement of a research utilization course for oncology nurses. *Oncology Nursing Forum, 31*, 121–126.

The investigators sought to determine the effectiveness of a short research utilization (RU) course presented at annual Oncology Nursing Society conferences from 1997 to 2001. The course covered information about systematic RU, research article critique techniques, RU models, strategies for computerized database literature searches, and preparation of a RU project. Participants presented proposals for RU projects during the course. The course was primarily held using director-led discussions. Twenty-two nurses attended the course, and course evaluations were collected at 6-month and 12-month intervals, and in summer 2002.

Findings from the interviews of 21 participants revealed that the nurses benefited more when they had precourse-mentored experiences in preparing a literature search and completing a set research critique tool for some of the articles. They identified the following facilitators for RU in clinical practice: institutional, peer, and interdisciplinary health team member support; nursing research departments within the work setting; role autonomy; and course knowledge and resources. Barriers to RU included lack of support in the clinical setting, staffing changes, increased client acuity or loads, competing time obligations, and difficulty of getting staff to learn and use new ideas from research in practice. Twelve participants reported that they either had completed or continued to work on their RU projects, six never completed them, two partially completed them, and seven began new projects. Of the nurses failing to complete their projects, two had taken medical leave, three had changed positions, and one nurse worked on a unit that had undergone restructuring.

Implications for practice identified by the investigators include the following: RU is hard to sell to nurses, and most nurses fail to have a good grasp of the RU process, have no idea of RU models, find generating a literature review cumbersome, seem naïve about processes to facilitate practice changes, and become anxious when publicly presenting RU projects and proposals. However, attending a RU course seems to increase confidence and skill to promote RU in practice. Because of the small size of the study sample, more research is needed to determine the most effective ways to help nurses use research findings in clinical practice.

Nominal fees may be charged for book checkout privileges and for photocopying journal articles of interest. To save time, nurses should look for integrative reviews or meta-analyses that review a number of studies and provide information about the quality of the results.

Other ways of gaining access to research findings include a research bulletin board, newsletters, or research grand rounds, but these strategies need to be organized, maintained, and supported. Many institutions have a research committee that can take responsibility for coordinating the review of literature, exploring ideas, pilot-testing innovations, and developing and disseminating research-based protocols and policies.

Nurses also may find the inservice education or nursing staff development departments useful when seeking to establish nursing practice based on research. Master's-prepared clinical educators could evaluate and synthesize knowledge across studies and provide direction for clinicians. Practitioners need continuing inservice education to help with identifying and locating appropriate literature, evaluating the quality of research, understanding data analysis, and determining the relevance of research findings for practice modifications.

Even if resources are available to nurses, agency managers and administration must create an atmosphere where nurses are encouraged and supported to question and evaluate current practice protocols, to use research study findings as a basis for protocol revisions, and to be valued (and even rewarded) for using research in practice. Without a supportive environment, nurses who use research in practice may become discouraged and rely on agency traditions, or they may leave the work setting for an agency that supports research utilization. Managers and administrators who use research in their roles serve as role models for research utilization. They also should provide adequate funding for staff to have access to computerized databases, health sciences libraries, and research-based education programs (Hunt, 2001). When research is valued as a way of knowing, positive attitudes and tangible resources for research utilization become standard practice. Incentives and rewards for risk taking and creativity promote research utilization. Fostering peer collaboration and networking with other colleagues also provide impetus for research use in practice. Most of all, the atmosphere must be one of respect and encouragement for professional practice and delegation of authority so that nurses control nursing practice.

However, in the final analysis, the clinician has to value the use of research as the basis for practice enough to provide the effort and make the time for research utilization activities. When a significant number of nurses value scholarship enough to participate in creation, dissemination, and utilization, then and only then will nursing be viewed as a true profession.

EVIDENCE-BASED PRACTICE

Evidence-based practice (EBP) has nearly become a standard mode of care delivery among the interprofessional health care team. Evidence-based medicine, evidence-based physical therapy, evidence-based nutrition, and **evidence-based nursing** provide a mechanism for the delivery of best practices for health care. Nursing research provides nurses with the opportunity to supply evidence, and nursing research utilization facilitates the nursing research based on scientific findings. However, the evidence for evidence-based practice does not rely solely on research findings. Sources of evidence used for evidence-based practice include research findings, clinical experience, quality improvement data, logical reasoning, recognized authority, and client satisfaction, situation, experience, and values (Boswell & Cannon, 2007; Burns & Grove, 2004; DiCenso, Guyatt, & Ciliska, 2005; Glanville, Schirm, & Wineman, 2000; Malloch & Porter-O'Grady, 2006; Polit & Beck, 2004). Table 10-3 presents a comparison of research utilization with evidence-based practice.

Some health care organizations encourage and support nurses to implement evidence-based nursing projects. Malloch and Porter-O'Grady (2006) outlined a model of disciplined clinical inquiry (DCI) to guide the process of evidence-based patient care (EBPC). According to Malloch and Porter-O'Grady, EBPC is patient centered, resource efficient, knowledge driven, and clinically appropriate. EBPC the model (Malloch & Porter-O'Grady, p. 37) outlines the following five phases:

1. Phase 1: Needs Assessment & Environmental Scan
2. Phase 2: Learning & Knowledge Generation
3. Phase 3: Knowledge Assimiliation
4. Phase 4: Knowledge Application
5. Phase 5: Appraisal/Evaluation

Melnyk and Fineout-Overholt (2005) outlined a different approach to EBPC using the following five steps:

1. Identifying, formulating, and raising a key clinical question using a format that outlines all key aspects of the issue.
2. Obtaining and assembling key evidence appropriate to the identified issue.
3. Evaluating the assembled evidence critically to ascertain its validity, relevance, and applicability to the current practice situation.
4. Assimilating the evidence identified as applicable to the situation into the practice setting.
5. Assessing and evaluating the results of the changes resulting from the use of the best evidence.

Ironically, both approaches use five steps and appear to be congruent with steps of problem-solving strategies. Malloch and Porter-O'Grady (2006) emphasized the importance of

TABLE 10-3

Comparison of Nursing Research Utilization and Evidence-Based Practice

	Nursing Research Utilization	Evidence-Based Practice
Purpose	Establish nursing practice based on scientific evidence	Establish best practice guidelines for various clinical problems
Participants	Professional nurses	Interdisciplinary health team
Sources of evidence	Quantitative or qualitative research study findings	Research study findings Quality improvement data Retrospective and concurrent chart audits Risk management data Infection control data Local, national and international standards Pathophysiology of clinical problem Cost-effective analysis data Benchmarking data Expert opinions Logical reasoning Clinical experience Individual patient situations Client preference data
Processes	Critiques of research reports of topic of interest Integrative review of research reports Innovation subjected to a planned change process Evaluation of results of care innovation	Group meetings of one component of the health care team for issues related to a specific discipline Group meetings of interdisciplinary health team members to develop critical paths or other care pathways Interdisciplinary review of current clinical needs, practices, established guidelines and care principles Extensive systematic review of published research on issue to be addressed from all health care disciplines if the guideline will be interdisciplinary or from one health care discipline if guideline will be specific to a special group Guideline review by experts, clinicians and clients Guidelines are tested for effective clinical use Guidelines are subjected to continuous review
Outcomes	Improve client outcomes Improve professional practice Research-based nursing care and clinical practice protocols	Improve client outcomes Clinical guidelines for client care based on solid evidence that yield the most benefit for the least possible cost
Dissemination of information	Agency newsletter Letters to staff Staff electronic mail Electronic or printed agency clinical policy manual Staff inservices Nursing publications Nursing specialty organization websites	Agency newsletter Staff electronic mail Electronic or printed agency policy manuals Professional publications Websites of professional organizations, large health care agencies, Agency for Healthcare Research & Quality, and the National Guideline Clearinghouse American Medical Association, American Association of Health Care Plans

Sources: Burns, N., & Grove, S. K. (2004). *The practice of nursing research: Conduct, critique & utilization*, 5th Ed. Philadelphia: WB Saunders; Glanville, I., Schirm, V., & Wineman, N. M. (2000). Using evidence-based practice for managing clinical outcomes in advanced practice nursing. *Journal of Nursing Care Quality, 15* (19), 1–11. Beyea, S. C., & Nicoll, L. H. (1998). Developing clinical practice guidelines as an approach to evidence-based practice. *AORN Journal*, 67, 1037–1038; Goode, C. J., & Piedalue, F. (1999). Evidence-based clinical practice. *Journal of Nursing Administration, 29*, 15–21; Jennings, B. M., & Loan, L. ?A. (2001). Misconceptions among nurses about evidence-based practice. *Journal of Nursing Scholarship, 33*, 121–127.

creating an organizational culture that supports nurses as they embark on learning how to assess evidence and executing EBPC clinical practice changes.

Proponents of evidence-based practice view it as a means to solve clinical practice problems by making the best possible decisions related to care based on client reports, clinician observations, and research data. Systematic review of all research literature on a particular health topic provides the best form of evidence for clinical practice (Boswell & Cannon, 2007; DiCenso et al., 2005; Malloch & Porter-O'Grady, 2006). Cinical practice guidelines fall into this category. In the United States, the Agency for Health Care Research and Quality (AHRQ; then the Agency for Health Care Policy and Research) created the National Guideline Clearinghouse (NGC) in 1998 to offer interprofessional health team members a rich source of evidence-based clinical practice guidelines. NGC publishes free guidelines that have been generated through synthesis of recent, valid research findings along with expert commentary for each guideline. The NGC offers high-quality information on disease management and prevention. Some health care insurance companies use NGC as a basis for reimbursement (NGC, 2008). The Cochrane Collaboration is an international organization that also provides information for health care providers based on systematic integrative reviews of controlled clinical trials. The Cochrane Collaboration charges a fee to access evidence based solely on disease management. Currently, many health care professionals use evidence-based clinical practice guidelines developed by the AHRQ for the treatment of urinary incontinence, low back problems, pain, depression, and prevention of and treatment for pressure ulcers (Boswell & Cannon; DiCenso et al.; Malloch & Porter-O'Grady). When research data are not available on a specific clinical problem, professional experts who specialize in a specific area develop practice guidelines using consensus. Health care providers can access clinical practice guidelines from a variety of websites, such as the NGC, professional specialty organizations, and large health care organizations. Evidence-based practice also enables health care providers to use objective and subjective ways of knowing when to make client care decisions.

Opponents of evidence-based practice in medicine and nursing suggest that the development of clinical practice guidelines, critical care pathways, and protocols entices practitioners of medicine and nursing to adopt a "cookbook recipe" approach to client care. The basic tenet to quality improvement initiatives specifies that elimination of variation in practice decreases the chance for error and improves quality (Glanville et al., 2000). Because quality improvement has its roots in industrial production, perhaps standardization may not be as desirable because clients have unique characteristics and needs that may be overlooked when practitioners adhere strictly to clinical practice guidelines. In addition, consumers and third-party payers may hold health care providers accountable for actions in addition to or for not strictly following established clinical practice guidelines (Glanville et al.; Goode & Piedalue, 1999).

Health care organizations and individual health team members hold the key to the successful implementation of evidence-based practice. Organizations must display commitment to developing evidence-based care pathways and provide health care team members with the time and required resources. Time periods as long as 6 months may be required for the development of a single evidence-based pathway (Kirrane, 2000; Malloch & Porter-O'Grady, 2006).

Questions for Reflection 10-3

1. What forms of evidence do I use to provide a basis for clinical decision making?
2. How are client care policies, protocols, and pathways developed where I engage in clinical practice?

CREATING A PUBLIC IMAGE OF THE NURSE AS SCHOLAR

A **scholar** is someone who is an intellectual and who has advanced study in a given field. Public perceptions of nurses tend toward the nurse as a person with technical expertise, a subordinate to physicians, and someone who cares for others. However, a visit to a college or university today reveals the strides that the nursing profession has made in developing a unique research base and expert researchers. In recent years, many nursing journals have become devoted to dissemination of research findings and nursing theory. Some journals devote space for research findings and methodological issues (*Nursing Research*, *Western Journal of Nursing Research*, and *International Journal of Nursing Research*), and others have space for publication of research and nursing theory (*Journal of Nursing Scholarship*, *Journal of Advanced Nursing*, and *Nursing Science Quarterly*). Some journals have print and online versions (*Evidence-Based Nursing* and *Nursing Research*). The journal published by the American Nurses Association, *The American Journal of Nursing*, recently has included original research studies as a regular feature. These journals reflect the advancing body of knowledge unique to nursing, an important element for an emerging profession.

Advanced technology offers great support for the nurse researcher today. The storage, retrieval, and analysis of data afforded by computer support make conducting research much faster and achievable by nurses. In most educational and practice settings, a researcher should not have to manually manage data. Another great help to research is the computer's ability to manipulate numbers, which allows almost unlimited analysis of data and the ability to use research findings to a fuller capacity.

In addition, it is anticipated that the word-processing support and electronic transmission of information offered by computers will be helpful in sharing more research findings with clinicians in practice. Thus, nursing is moving into a period of valuing and conducting research at a time when technology greatly supports many aspects of the research process.

Traditionally, nurses have not been viewed as scholars. Nurses themselves sometimes fail to acknowledge advanced education of colleagues. Sometimes, health care–providing agencies refuse to place academic credentials on nurses' employment name badges. The public perception of nursing is highly affected by individual experience with nurses. With approximately 70% of nurses having less-than-baccalaureate preparation, nurses remain among the least educated members of the interdisciplinary health care team. Nurses and clients tend to value clinical practice over nursing scholarship. However, when (and if) nurses communicate to others the contributions of nursing research to health outcomes, the nursing profession will attain recognition as a scholarly, rather than an exclusively practice, discipline.

As nursing has developed its own theory base during the past 35 years, nurses have begun to value the scholarship role of the nurse. Most nurses today probably would agree that a practice based on research is desirable. Capitalizing on that consensus, the profession can begin to present a different image to the public. To help actualize the motivation to base nursing practice on research, educational programs need to prepare students in scientific inquiry while preparing them to apply theory in the conduct of professional roles.

Research in nursing also has been hampered by inadequate financial support. Between 1971 and 1981, the government awarded the National Center for Nursing Research $40 million. During the same period, the National Institutes of Health (NIH) received $1.7 billion for general biomedical research. Originally, the National Center for Nursing Research was established within the NIH. In 1993, the **National Institute for Nursing Research (NINR)** was established. The NINR identifies nursing research priorities, distributes grants to nurse researchers, and disseminates nursing research findings to health professionals and the public. Current focus areas for research for the NINR include health promotion, disease prevention, quality-of-life improvement, health disparities elimination, and directions for end-of-life research (NINR, 2008a). Funding for the

NINR has risen steadily since its inception. The NINR is funded through section 301, title IV of the National Public Service Act. In 2008 the NINR received $137,800,000 in federal funding. Public funding of nursing research acknowledges the valuable contributions it makes (NINR, 2008b).

As nurses begin to feel and act like scholars, the public will begin to see a scholarly side of nursing. If the profession nourishes this scholarship in nurses, it undoubtedly will help change the image of the nurse. Because scholars accept that research is a vital component of nursing, the development of scholars will increase the supply of researchers to better serve the profession and the public.

Questions for Reflection 10-4

1. How can I promote the image of nurses as scholars?
2. What are the potential consequences of changing the image of the nurse from caregiver to scholar?

⊕ SUMMARY AND SIGNIFICANCE TO PRACTICE

In the 1960s through the 1990s, many researchers and scholars provided a beginning theoretical base for nursing. By the beginning of the 21st century, nurses identified the benefits of evidence-based practice in order to provide the best possible health care to the most persons at the least possible expense. Nurses use multiple cognitive skills to navigate through the vast complex web of information and decide how to use available research findings and various forms of evidence in clinical practice. With practice, nurses gain confidence in the ability to analyze, critique and decide how and when to use evidence in clinical practice. Qualitative and quantitative research findings provide evidence that captures the complex, holistic nature of clients, nurses, and health care delivery. Recent public funding of nursing research initiatives shows that the public values nursing research. As nurses assume the roles of researchers and scholars, they make discoveries, generate evidence, and determine how to incorporate the best possible evidence to guide and change clinical practice in today's complex and sometimes chaotic health care delivery systems.

FROM THEORY TO PRACTICE

1. Reread the vignette at the beginning of the chapter. What strategies would you suggest to Joan to use in her attempts to integrate the research-based knowledge about alternative forms of pain control on her unit?
2. Outline a research utilization project for Joan to follow.
3. What forms of evidence are used as a foundation for currently used clinical policies and procedures in your area of clinical practice?
4. Who do you have available to help you if you encountered difficulty making sense of a published research study?

WWW INTERNET EXERCISES

1. Visit The Royal Windsor Society for Nursing Research at www.geocities.com/researchnurses. Click on the icon "Research Fun," and play Research Jeopardy. Learn about some interesting health care research findings.
2. Visit the National Institute for Nursing Research (NINR) at http://ninr-nih.gov/ninr/. Read about the mission and strategic plan of the NINR. Identify the research priorities of the Institute and bring them to class for discussion.

3. Peruse the online version of the journal *Evidence-Based Nursing* at http://www.evidencebasednursing.com. Read one or two selections from the journal. Answer the following questions:
    a. Do you believe the content contained in the summary of each research article and the commentary that follows it?
    b. What are the advantages of reading an entire research report?
    c. What are the disadvantages of reading an entire research report?
    d. Would you use information found in this journal in your clinical practice? Why or why not?

WWW INTERNET RESOURCES

National Institute for Nursing Research: http://ninr-nih.gov/ninr/.
National Guideline Clearinghouse: http://www.guideline.gov.
The Canadian Health Services Research Foundation: http://www.chsrf.ca/.
The Royal Windsor Society for Nursing Research: http://www.geocities.com/researchnurses.
Nursing Effectiveness, Utilization and Outcomes Research Unit (NRU), a joint project of the University of Toronto and McMaster University School of Nursing in Ontario, Canada: http://nhsru.com/www.fhs.mcmaster.ca/nru.
American Nurses Foundation (ANF): http://www.nursingworld.org/anf.
Midwestern Nursing Research Society: http://www.mnrs.org.
Southern Nursing Research Society: http://www.snrs.org.
Agency for Healthcare Research and Quality: http://www.ahrq.gov.
Centers for Disease Control and Prevention: http://www.cdc.gov.
The Cochrane Collaboration: http://www.cochrane.org.
Integrity in Science: http://www.cspinet/org.integrity. (Find the list of what corporations are currently funding or have funded research.)

REFERENCES

Agnes, M. (Ed.). (2005). *Webster's new world college dictionary* (4th ed.). Cleveland, OH: Wiley.

Artinian, B. A. (1988). Qualitative modes of inquiry. *Western Journal of Nursing Research, 10*, 138–149.

Baessler, C. A., Blumberg, M., Cunningham, J. S., Curran, J. A., Fennessay, A. G., Jacobs, J. M., et al. (1994). Medical-surgical nurses' utilization of research methods and products. *MEDSURG Nursing, 3*, 113–117, 120–121, 141.

Barrett, E. A. M. (2002). What is nursing science? *Nursing Science Quarterly, 15*, 51–60.

Best, J. (2001). Telling the truth about damned lies and statistics. *The Chronicle of Higher Education, 47*, B7–B9.

Beyea, S. C., & Nicoll, L. H. (1998). Developing clinical practice guidelines as an approach to evidence-based practice. *AORN Journal, 67*, 1037–1038.

Blumenstyk, G. (2001). A new web site details the corporate ties of some researchers. *The Chronicle of Higher Education, 47*, A25.

Boswell, C., & Cannon, S. (2007). *Introduction to nursing research: Incorporating evidence-based practice.* Sudbury, MA: Jones & Bartlett.

Burns, N., & Grove, S. K. (2004). *The practice of nursing research: Conduct, critique, and utilization* (5th ed.). Philadelphia: W. B. Saunders.

Cohen, M. Z., & Tripp-Reimer, T. (1988). Research in cultural diversity: Qualitative methods in cultural research. *Western Journal of Nursing Research, 10*, 226–228.

DiCenso, A., Guyatt, G., & Ciliska, D. (2005). *Evidence-based nursing: A guide to clinical practice.* St. Louis, MO: Elsevier/Mosby.

Estabrooks, C., Floyd, J., Scott-Findlay, S., O'Leary, K., & Gushta, M. (2003). Individual determinants of research utilization: A systematic review. *Journal of Advanced Nursing, 43*, 506–520.

Estabrooks, C., Midodzi, W., Cummings, G., & Wallin, L. (2007). Predicting research use in nursing organizations: A multilevel analysis. *Nursing Research, 56*(4, Suppl. 1), S7–S23.

Funk, S. G., Champagne, M. T., Wiese, R. A., & Tornquist, E. M. (1991). Barriers to using research findings in practice: The clinician's perspective. *Applied Nursing Research, 4*, 90–95.

Gennaro, S. (1994). Research utilization: An overview. *JOGNN, 23*, 313–319.

Glanville, I., Schirm, V., & Wineman, N. M. (2000). Using evidence-based practice for managing clinical outcomes in advanced practice nursing. *Journal of Nursing Care Quality, 15*, 1–11.

Goode, C. J., Butcher, L. A., Cipperley, J. A., Ekstrom, J., Gosch, B. A., Hayes, J. E., et al. (1991). *Research utilization: A study guide* (Video recording). Ida Grove, IA: Horn Video Productions.

Goode, C. J., & Piedalve, F. (1999). Evidence-based clinical practice. *Journal of Nursing Administration,* 29, 15–21.

Haase, J. E., & Myers, S. T. (1988). Reconciling paradigm assumptions of qualitative and quantitative research. *Western Journal of Nursing Research, 10,* 128–137.

Heitkemper, M., & Bond, E. (2003). State of nursing science: On the edge. *Biological Research for Nursing, 4,* 151–164, 170.

Hunt, J. (2001). Research into practice: The foundation for evidence-based care. *Cancer Nursing, 24,* 78–87.

Kirrane, C. (2000). Evidence-based practice in neurology: A team approach to development. *Nursing Standard, 14,* 43–45.

Knafl, K. A., Pettengill, M. M., Bevis, M. E., & Kirchhoff, K. T. (1988). Blending qualitative and quantitative approaches to instrument development and data collection. *Journal of Professional Nursing, 4,* 30–37.

Knafl, K. A., & Webster, D. C. (1988). Managing and analyzing qualitative data: A description of tasks, techniques, and materials. *Western Journal of Nursing Research, 10,* 195–218.

Malloch, K., & Porter-O'Grady, T. (2006). *Introduction to evidence-based practice in nursing and health care.* Sudbury, MA: Jones & Bartlett.

McDonald, L. (2001). Florence Nightingale and the early origins of evidence-based nursing. *Evidence-Based Nursing Online, 3,* 68–69. Available at http://ebn.bmjjournals.com/content/vol4/issue3/. Accessed June 15, 2004.

Melnyk, B., & Fineout-Overholt, E. (2005). *Evidence-based practice in nursing and healthcare: A guide to best practice.* Philadelphia: Lippincott Williams & Wilkins.

National Guideline Clearinghouse (NGC). (2008). About us. Available at http://www.guideline.gov.

National Institute of Nursing Research (NINR). (2008a). Fiscal year 2008 budget, congressional justification. Available at http://ninr.nih.gov/ninr/budgetappropiation_2008/CJ2008.pdf. Accessed June 14, 2008.

National Institute of Nursing Research (NINR). (2008b). Mission and strategic plan. Available at http://ninr.nih/AboutNINR/NINRFAQs/Mission&StrategicPlan.

Nightingale, F. (1860). *Notes on nursing.* New York: Appleton.

Polit, D. F., & Beck, C. (2004). *Nursing research: Principles and methods* (7th ed.). Philadelphia: Lippincott Williams & Wilkins.

Rambur, B. (1999). Fostering evidence-based practice in nursing education. *Journal of Professional Nursing, 15,* 270–274.

Rogers, E. (1983). *Diffusion of innovations* (3rd ed.). New York: Free Press.

Rogers, M. E. (1967, February 3). Nursing science: Research and researcher. Paper presented at the annual Conference on Research and Nursing, Teachers College, Columbia University, New York.

Rutledge, D., Mooney, K., Grant, M., & Easton, L. (2004). Implementation and refinement of a research utilization course for oncology nurses. *Oncology Nursing Forum, 31,* 121–126.

Stetler, C. B. (1994). Refinement of the Stetler/Marram model for application of research findings to practice. *Nursing Outlook, 42,* 15–25.

CHAPTER 11

Multicultural Issues in Professional Practice

KEY TERMS AND CONCEPTS

Culture

Transcultural nursing

Multicultural nursing

Culture-universal care

Culture-specific care

Cultural competence

Ethnocentrism

Cultural relativism

Cultural assessment

Culturally congruent care

International nursing practice

Folk illnesses

Variations in physical appearance

Variations in physiology

Multicultural profession of nursing

Culture shock

Multicultural health care team strategies

LEARNING OUTCOMES

By the end of this chapter, the learner will be able to:

1 Discuss diversity and assimilation issues for a shrinking world.

2 Compare and contrast theoretical frameworks addressing cultural competence in nursing practice.

3 Differentiate transculturalism and multiculturalism.

4 Specify strategies to address special cultural needs of nursing care consumers.

5 Outline strategies to create a multicultural nursing profession.

6 Specify ways to enhance working relationships among multicultural health team members.

VIGNETTE

Judy, a nurse administrator, cannot get American nurses to work in the small rural hospital where she's employed. The hospital has decided to send her and a group of nurses to the Philippine Islands to recruit Filipino nurses. Although she has reservations about hiring Filipino nurses and paying them for relocation, educational, and licensure expenditures, Judy knows that she must have enough staff to provide effective client care. Judy wonders how her current nursing personnel will respond to having to work with foreign nurses, especially if her staff finds out that the hospital has spent a lot of money to attract the Fillipino nurses. She also worries about the potential language and cultural barriers.

Technology and transportation systems create opportunities for persons to experience the world. Technology, such as the Internet and fiber-optic cables, enables people to communicate instantly with each other despite vast differences in geographic locale. Within less than 24 hours, people can travel halfway around the world. This creates situations in which persons from different nations can meet each other. Sometimes persons from different nations meet and develop meaningful relationships that result in one person moving to another's country temporarily or permanently. Persons must abide by the laws of the country when they visit or establish residency.

Health care in the United States is highly consumer driven. In response to a more culturally diverse population, the Joint Commission along with the Office of Minority helped establish National Standards for Culturally and Linguistically Appropriate Services in Health Care (NSCLASHC) in 2006. The standards require health care organizations (HCOs) to provide culturally sensitive health care that includes appropriate language interpreters for persons who do not speak English. In addition, HCOs must also periodically survey the communities they serve and aim for employing health care providers that mirror the local community demographics. The NSCLASHC also holds HCOs accountable for educating staff about culturally sensitive care, posting signs in the languages of frequently encountered clients, working toward promoting persons from diverse backgrounds into leadership positions, and monitoring the effectiveness of culturally sensitive and interpreter services. These standards also set criteria for the involvement of persons of local cultural groups to assist in designing and implementing cultural and linguistic services. HCOs are required to inform the culturally diverse consumer about available language interpretation services, and provide written materials about available services and how to proceed with conflict resolution and grievance processes if culturally insensitive care or inappropriate situations should arise (U.S. Department of Health and Human Services, 2001). Therefore, effective nursing care includes meeting special cultural care and language needs of clients.

DIVERSITY AND ASSIMILATION IN A SHRINKING WORLD

American culture values unity and equality. The United States consists of many immigrants who became assimilated into one culture. American national diversity has been represented on coins with the phrase "e pluribus unum" (out of many: one). In the United States, people tend to identify themselves in terms of economic status and geographical locale. However, sometimes as persons lose their ethnic identity, they yearn for it more. Some persons from immigrant backgrounds often return to their native language when they are at home or with persons from the same background.

Before 1930, immigrants frequently anglicized their surnames to hide their ethnic roots because Eastern Europeans were considered inferior to Western Europeans (Cose, 2000). With time, people from other areas of the world sought refuge in the United States. After World War II, many persons from Eastern Europe and the Soviet Union came to the United States to escape communism. The American withdrawal from Vietnam resulted in increased immigration from Southeast Asian nations.

In recent years, persons from Mexico and South America have sought economic refuge in the United States. The U.S. Census Bureau (2008) estimated the cultural configuration of the U.S. population in July 2007 to be approximately 65.7% Caucasian/non-Hispanic, 14.5% Hispanic or Latino origin, 13.5% Black/African American, 4.5% Asian, 1.5% American Indian/Alaskan Native, and 0.3% Hawaiian/Pacific Islander. This estimate did include persons of multiracial origin. Johnson (2004) reported that from 2000 to 2050, cultural diversity of the American population will increase by 30%, with projected increases in the Asian/Pacific Islander population by 213.9%, the Hispanic population by 187.8%, the nonwhite Latino population by 217.1%, the African American population by 71.7%, and the White/non-Hispanic population by 7%. In 2004, the Sullivan Commission on Diversity in the Healthcare Workforce identified that only 9% of nurses, 6% of physicians, and 5% of dentists came from diverse cultural groups. To provide effective nursing care to diverse cultural groups, nurses need to consider cultural and ethnic differences of the clients they serve. Because persons feel more comfortable with people like themselves, the nursing profession must identify ways to recruit and retain persons from different cultural backgrounds.

Basic Terminology to Understand Culture

Recently, confusion has arisen about the meaning of various terms to denote inclusion of culture in nursing care. In 1871, Sir Edward Taylor, a British anthropologist, first used the term **culture** to refer to the complex whole, including knowledge, belief, art, morals, law, custom, and any other abilities and habits people acquired as societal members. In 1935, Margaret Mead expanded the definition of culture to include technological systems, political practices, and habits of daily life. Culture serves as a guide for determining the values, beliefs, and practices of individuals or groups of people.

Transcultural nursing uses the Latin prefix "trans," which means across, thereby referring to nursing across cultures. **Multicultural nursing** uses the Latin prefix "multi," which means many, denoting nursing of many different cultures. Finally, intercultural nursing uses the Latin prefix "inter," which means between, thereby meaning nursing between cultures (Andrews & Boyle, 2008).

Specific terminology must be understood to comprehend transcultural nursing principles. These terms come from the fields of sociology and anthropology and are summarized in Table 11-1. Most persons use a culture-based health practice before entering the formal health care system (Andrews & Boyle, 2008; Giger & Davidhizar, 2008; Leininger, 1995; Leininger & McFarland, 2002, 2006). Culture may include large numbers of persons, as in the example of global or national culture, or it may incorporate small numbers of persons, such as a single-family unit or gang. Culture also can be differentiated by age, such as the youth culture and the old-age culture. Analysis of culture enables health care providers to understand the impact of lifeways (a way of life distinctly different in anthropology from lifestyle), rituals, and taboos when providing care.

As a nurse with advanced education in anthropology, Madeline Leininger founded the transcultural nursing movement and Transcultural Nursing Society. Leininger (1995) defined transcultural nursing as "a formal area of study and practice in nursing focused upon comparative holistic cultural care, health, and illness patterns of individuals and groups with respect to differences and similarities in cultural values, beliefs, and practices" (p. 4). The goal of transcultural nursing is "to provide culturally congruent, sensitive, and competent nursing care to people of diverse cultures" (Leininger, p. 4). Leininger's writing justifies transcultural nursing by saying persons have rights and expectations to have their cultural values and beliefs respected. In addition, nurses have the obligation to meet the cultural needs of clients. Leininger suggested that efforts at being kind, relying on common sense, and ignoring prejudices do not foster culturally relevant care to clients of various cultural backgrounds. She proposed that nurses should receive formal education in transcultural nursing that begins with an analysis of one's own cultural values and beliefs.

Transcultural nursing blends nursing and anthropology in theory and practice. A provision of cultural-specific and cultural-universal care serves as the aim of transcultural nursing. "Care" refers to providing nursing services with consideration to particular values, beliefs, and behavior patterns unique to a specific group. These tend not to be shared with persons from other cultures. **Culture-universal care** denotes the commonly shared values, behaviors, and life patterns that appear among most cultures (Andrews & Boyle, 2008; Leininger & McFarland, 2002, 2006). Examples of culture-universal care include the formation of family, the socialization of children into society, and basic physical survival needs.

TABLE 11-1

Basic Terminology to Understand Culture

Cultural Term	Definition
Acculturation	Blending of two cultures by taking the best of each and combining them into one
Cultural accommodation	Allowing specific cultural practices within another culture
Cultural assimilation	Adoption of group culture by a member or members of a different culture
Cultural blindness	Ignoring cultural differences and acting as though they fail to exist
Cultural diffusion	Spreading out of cultural traits, patterns, and beliefs
Cultural competence	Integration of knowledge, attitudes, and skills that enable effective and appropriate communications and behaviors when working with persons from one or more cultures different from one's own
Cultural diversity	Differences in groups
Cultural empathy	Expressive concern and the ability to see the experiences as the client sees them
Cultural group	Two or more persons sharing the same ancestry, nationality, values, beliefs, or behavior
Cultural identity	Professed membership within a group
Cultural imposition	Forcing cultural beliefs, values, and patterns onto another from a different background
Cultural lifeways	Group beliefs about activities of daily living, inherited traits, and behaviors
Cultural maintenance	Continued practice of a specific culture
Cultural negotiation	Working with a person from another culture to determine what cultural practices can be used without jeopardizing effects
Cultural norms	Acceptable behaviors and practices
Cultural pluralism	Maintaining cultural differences after being assimilated into another culture
Cultural preservation	Continued practice of a specific culture
Cultural relativism	Acknowledging that other ways of doing things are different, but they are valid and may be superior
Cultural repatterning (or restructuring)	Changing unhealthy cultural behavior patterns to promote better health
Culture shock	State in which one feels totally disconnected from the group because of extreme differences
Cultural values	Prevalent, powerful forces that provide meaning and direction to group actions, decisions, and lifeways
Culture	An integrated pattern of socially transmitted behaviors that includes all products of human work and thoughts specific to a group of persons that guide formulation of worldviews and decision-making processes
Emic perspective	An insider's view
Enculturation	Attempting to get one group to accept the ways of another group
Ethnicity	Sharing the same ancestral, physical, racial, and national origins along with the same language, lifestyle, religion, or other characteristics misunderstood by others
Ethnocentrism	Believing that one's way is best
Etic perspective	An outsider's view
Generalization	Oversimplified assumption about a group of persons
Rituals	Routine practices
Stereotype	Oversimplified idea, opinion, or belief about all members of a particular group of persons
Taboo	What is absolutely forbidden by a group

Basic Terminology to Understand Culture (Continued)

Cultural Term	Definition
Transcultural nursing	Providing physical, psychological, and spiritual nursing care while considering specific cultural beliefs and practices when providing nursing services to clients from a different cultural background
International nursing	Providing nursing care services outside one's country of legal residence
World view	Personal perception of the universe that provides a foundation for values and beliefs about the world and life

Adapted from Andrews & Boyle, (2008); American Association of Colleges of Nursing, (1998); Giger & Davidhizar, (2008); Leininger, (1995); Leninger & McFarland (2006); Pedersen, Draguns, Lonner, & Trimble, (1996); and Purnell & Paulanka, (2003).

Culture-specific care includes idiosyncratic practices of a particular cultural group. Cultural-specific care practices may be similar across groups, but each group has slight differences in either the manner in which practices are implemented or the meaning behind them. Individuals from many cultural groups use folk (or generic) remedies and healers before seeking care from the medical health care system; sometimes they use folk care in conjunction with medical care. Table 11-2 lists some culturally based healers and folk remedies and compares them to the culture of the American health care system. The table only briefly summarizes cultural practices. Great differences may occur across various ethnic groups. Health care practitioners frequently impose their own cultural values, beliefs, and practices on clients receiving care. However, competent transcultural care blends the culturally based practices with empirically based medical practices. When these practices conflict with each other, the nurse (or other health care provider) works with the client from another culture to accommodate cultural practices with the medical plan of care so that the combination of remedies does not cause harm (Leininger & McFarland, 2002, 2006).

Questions for Reflection 11-1

1. Have I used any folk healers or healing practices to enhance my health or recover from an illness or injury? How did I learn about these practices?
2. Have I ever encountered a folk healer in my professional practice? How did I react? How would I react if a family member or client insists that a folk healer practice folk medicine on a client to whom I am delivering nursing care?
3. What are the policies related to the use of folk healers in my clinical practice setting?

ESTABLISHING CULTURAL COMPETENCE

Attainment of **cultural competence** is a lifelong journey that requires the elimination of **ethnocentrism** (belief that one's way is best) and an unconditional acceptance of cultural diversity unless the practice places another person in harm's way. Establishment of cultural competence requires contact and interaction with persons from other cultures. Kavanagh and Kennedy (1992) proposed that minority status is given to those who do not have power, status, and wealth within a given society (or situation), rather than being established by sheer numbers. Those with power, status, or wealth frequently may be viewed as being worthy of receiving health care services. In American culture, the ability to pay for the services rendered defines who is given access to health care services. In addition, some health care providers may view the working poor as being more worthy of health care than the nonworking poor because persons who are employed contribute some service and pay

TABLE 11-2

Cultural Healers and Folk Remedies

Cultural Group	Healer Title	Healer and Folk Remedies
Traditional Chinese	Physician Acupuncturist Herbalist	Physician diagnoses health problems by listening, questioning, and palpating, including feeling quality of pulse and sensitivity of body parts Acupuncture Herbal preparation (have used 5,767 documented herbs)
Eastern Indian	Ayurvedic medicine	Drugs used come from vegetable and mineral raw materials Yoga Meditation Herbal preparations
Native American	Shaman Singer or chanter (highest position in the Navajo tribe) Crystal gazer, hand trembler, or diagnostician (one step below singer in the Navajo tribe) Singer for healing ceremonies Medicine man (Hopi tribe) Herbalist	Sweating and purging usually done in a lodge Herbal remedies from local environment Healing ceremonies using the medicine wheel, sacred hoop, and singing (Lakota, Dineh, and Navajo tribes) Stargazing and hand trembling for diagnosis (Navajo) Herbalist prescribes herbs for symptomatic relief while members await healing ceremony (Navajo)
Latin American	Curanderismo	Foods with qualitative (not literal) properties of "hot" and "cold" Persons with "hot" diseases should receive "cold" foods and vice versa to restore a balance of hot and cold
Muckleshoots (Northwest Native Americans)	Nuclear and extended family	Mothers, grandmothers, and aunts are source of information related to pregnancy, birth, and childhood illnesses Health care decisions are made by consensus of the family
American Jewish	Mohel Mother	Performs the bris ceremony (infant male circumcision) Traditional folk remedies are passed down from many generations, such as cupping or charms to symbolize the "hands of God" No consumption of meat and milk at the same meal
Mexican American	Family member Curandera Sobadora (massage and bone and joint manipulation specialist) Espiritualista (spiritualist) Yebero (herbalist)	*Curanderismo* is an eclectic, holistic, and syncretic compilation of beliefs from the Mesoamerican Spanish, spiritualistic, homeopathic, and modern medical beliefs System is based on herbal preparations, Spanish prayers, altered states of consciousness, and healing rituals that blend Indian traditions and Catholic rituals Herbal teas, ingestion or application of powdered substances, massage with warm oils, and skin Popping on the small of the back
African American	Extended family members, friends and neighbors Old Lady (experienced woman who successfully raised a family) Folk practitioners Faith healers (spiritualist) Hougan (Voodoo priestess or priest)	Health clinic and physician visits occur when all folk remedies have been exhausted Herbal remedies, potions, applications of heat and cold, crystals, massage, meditation, oils, powders, tokens, rites, and ceremonies Oils, candles, soaps, and aerosolized sprays are used to repel evil forces

Cultural Healers and Folk Remedies (Continued)

Cultural Group	Healer Title	Healer and Folk Remedies
Philippine American	Family traditions Folk healers	Based on hot/cold theory that requires persons to consume hot foods for a cold illness and cold foods for a hot illness Widely use herbal remedies Very quiet and passive when seeking health care
Japanese American	Kampo practitioners Family members	*Kampo* is a holistic approach to illness and uses acupuncture, herbal medicines, moxibustion, and spiritual exercises For colds, use of ginger, sake, and egg; herbal teas for "cure-all"; headaches are treated by rubbing head with sesame or ginger oil; finger massage and exercise are used to stay well Hot/cold (yin and yang) theory apply to health- related situations
Korean and Vietnamese American	Shamans	Serve as the mediator between people and the spiritual world to prevent, diagnose, and treat health problems Principles of yin and yan (hot and cold) Infections are hot and should be treated with a cold food such as fruit; cancers are cold and should be treated with hot food such as chicken soup Strong herbal teas that may be dangerous if concurrently used with Western medicine Dermabrasion, massage, acupressure, acupuncture, and moxibustion Spiritual healing rituals (more commonly used by Vietnamese)
South African	Medicine men Isangoma (diagnostician) Inyanga (healer) Midwives Herbalists	*Ukincinda* (licking), *ukubhema* (inhalation of snuffing substances), *ukuhlanza* (emetics), *ukuchatha* (enemas), *ukugguma* (steaming), and *ukugcaba* (incisions made and medicine rubbed into them) are forms of traditional healing methods Herbal preparations Spiritual ceremonies and sacrifices to spirits Goal of health is to achieve a balance with nature
Professional	Physician	Scientifically validated medication and therapies
American health care system	Nurse practitioner Nurses Physical, occupational, and respiratory therapists Social worker Chaplain	Complex technological equipment for diagnosis and treatment Some reliance on intuition Effectiveness based on cost–benefit ratio High degree of concern for timeliness of treatments and appointments Spiritual needs of clients usually referred to chaplain
Puerto Rican American	Santiguadora Spiritual healers	Herbal teas Massage with warm oils Spiritual rituals
Amish	Brauch or brauch-doktor Lay midwife	Combination of many modalities, including manipulation of body parts, massage, herbs, herbal teas, reflexology, and other folk healing remedies Midwife provides prenatal, birthing, and postpartum care
Greek American	Magissa Bonesetters Greek Orthodox priest	Magician, usually a woman, who cures "evil eye" and other disorders caused by spells Bonesetters specialize in setting uncomplicated fractures Ordained priest consulted for advice, direct healing, or exorcism

taxes. Health care professionals often expect minorities to adapt to the established norms and policies of the institution, rather than the institution adapting to the needs of the minorities. To become minority friendly, health care institutions must have their professionals learn about the social organization and processes of each minority group served (Kavanagh & Kennedy). However, some persons who do not have societal power may find the term "minority" offensive. The term "minority" might lead to perceptions of diminished status by the majority or dominant group. Perceptions of reduced status (being less than a full person who deserves respect, dignity, and equality) may move the dominant group to exclude others unlike themselves from full participation in society.

Steps to Acquiring Cultural Competence

Being culturally competent does not happen overnight, but rather takes time and commitment. Burchum (2002) defined cultural competence as a developmental process that builds continuous increases in knowledge and skill development in the areas of cultural awareness, knowledge, understanding, sensitivity, interaction, and skills. The following six steps outline a process for nurses to follow to acquire cultural competence.

Step 1: Examination of Personal Values, Beliefs, Biases, and Prejudices

The journey to cultural competence begins with an examination of personal values, beliefs, biases, and prejudices. Attitudes result from evaluative judgments that may have developed over time. Some attitudes become embedded in persons when they are children, and others result from experience. Attitudes reflect personal values, beliefs, and biases. A variety of self-report tools such as the Cultural Attitude Scale, developed by Bonaparte in the late 1970s and modified by Rooda in 1991 and 1992 (Giger & Davidhizar, 2008); the Cultural Self-Efficacy Scale, developed by Forman in 1987 (Giger & Davidhizar); Randall-Davis's checklist *How Do You Relate to Various Groups of People in the Society?* (Andrews & Boyle, 2008); and Terrence Freeman's 1987 Cross-Cultural Interaction Scale (Hughes & Hood, 2007) can be used to measure cultural sensitivity (the degree to which someone has awareness and demonstrates positive responsiveness to cultural differences). Many times people are unaware of either their own or those of the dominant culture's specific values, beliefs, biases, and prejudices. For self-report tools to be effective, persons completing them must be honest in their answers rather than answering items in a socially acceptable manner. Once the person identifies areas for attitudinal and/or behavioral change, even longstanding negative attitudes and beliefs may be changed. However, sometimes a personal experience with a person (or persons) from a cultural group may be required to eliminate biases and prejudices held by an individual (Giger & Davidhizar; Purnell & Paulanka, 2003). Identification of one's personal values, beliefs, biases, and prejudices moves these thoughts into conscious awareness and serves as the first step toward establishing cultural competence.

Step 2: Cultural Awareness

To several transcultural nursing specialists, cultural awareness serves as an antecedent toward obtaining specific communication strategies and knowledge about other cultures (Andrews & Boyle, 2008; Giger & Davidhizar, 2008; Purnell & Paulanka, 2003). Results of the self-report methods presented in Step 1 provide a means for individuals to become more aware of values, beliefs, biases, and prejudices which may have been culturally induced. When nurses understand how their cultural beliefs affect care delivery, they can change their behavior and attitudes toward clients from a different culture. For example, health care providers tend to follow cultural values and mores set forth by European cultures. Sometimes, outpatient facilities from clinics to rehabilitation services distribute written materials to clients informing them of operational policies for keeping appointments. For example, a policy might be that all clients must keep scheduled appointments unless they call to inform clinic staff that they will not be coming. If clients fail to come or notify the clinic that they are unable to keep the appointment three times, all scheduled appointments will be automatically cancelled. Policies such as these reflect the American values of being punctual, adhering to a schedule, and keeping appointments. Once health team members are aware of key cultural differences, they can develop specific communication strategies to tear down barriers to cultural and linguistically appropriate health care delivery.

Step 3: Specific Communication Strategies

Learning culturally specific communication strategies serves as the third step toward attainment of cultural competence. Specific communication strategies affirm diversity. Verbal and nonverbal communication patterns indicate how well differences are respected and are a key part of understanding cultural nuances in order to serve persons from different cultural backgrounds (Andrews & Boyle, 2008; Kavanagh & Kennedy, 1992; Leininger, 1995; Leininger & McFarland, 2006). For example, some cultures (Asian and American Native) view that making direct eye contact is rude and demonstrates a lack of personal respect. However, principles of therapeutic communication suggest that making direct eye contact facilitates client assessment, serves as a way to show genuine compassion, and cues persons engaged in a conversation when it is each person's turn to speak (DeVito, 2004).

A key way to foster communication with clients from other cultures is to approach them in a manner that displays authentic empathy and deep respect (Pullen, 2007). Some organizations provide nurses with information about various cultural groups in print (books, pamphlets) or digital (software programs or access to online information) format. The nurse's body language also plays a big role in displaying confidence when working with persons from other cultures. A calm, cheerful, unhurried approach displays a sense of concern across most cultures. The definition of personal space varies across cultures, with persons from North American backgrounds requiring the most distance. However, persons from Middle Eastern, Latin American, and Japanese cultures feel quite comfortable being close to others, and the closeness indicates interest and concern. If uncertain if clients' cultural mores permit touching by another person other than a family member, nurses should ask permission to touch them. Speaking even a few words of the client's native language conveys awareness and respect for his or her culture. Some nurses find using gestures and pantomimes effective to get key assessments completed and to meet clients' basic needs. When nurses hurry while working with clients from another culture, some clients may perceive that the nurse might be indifferent to or biased against them (Pullen).

Step 4: Interactions With Different Cultures

Engaging in interactions with persons from different cultures becomes the fourth step toward cultural competence. This requires risk taking. Respectful engagement during interactions with members of another culture or group provides an opportunity to develop personal and professional expertise in order to work effectively with culturally diverse clients and colleagues. Asking questions before acting serves as a useful tool. Sometimes, persons avoid others who differ from themselves. This practice creates minimization or denial that differences exist across various groups, such as race, class, nationality, or gender (to name a few broad differences in groups). Avoidance enforces the invisibility of sensitive issues (Kavanagh & Kennedy, 1992). However, most persons from different cultures send cues to each other during interactions. If heeded, the cues can guide the transcultural interaction, and errors can be avoided (Andrews & Boyle, 2008; DeVito, 2004; Giger & Davidhizar, 2008; Grossman, 1996; Yoder, 1996, 1997). Some nurses and health team members may be bilingual. However, the extent of their language proficiency may be limited to social conversational use with a poor understanding of medical terminology in both their own and the dominant culture's language. Some nurses may speak enough of the client's language to perform a physical assessment and meet client basic care needs. Occasionally, professional nurses and other health team members rely on families, friends, or nonprofessional members of the health care team who speak the client's language to explain medical procedures to non-English-speaking clients. Reliance on persons who do not have the educational background to fully comprehend the implications of complex diagnostic testing and surgical procedures limits full disclosure of potential complications and accurate client education. The National Standards for Culturally and Linguistically Appropriate Health Care Services (Office of Minority Health Care Resources, 2007) require the use of a qualified interpreter, rather than a translator, when clients and health care providers speak different languages. Family members and friends may be used as interpreters only upon the request of the client.

Questions for Reflection 11-2

1. How have I handled nursing care issues when taking care of clients who did not speak English?
2. What resources, policies, and procedures are available to me in my clinical setting to provide culturally competent care?

Step 5: Mistake Identification and Acknowledgment

Mistake identification and acknowledgment serve as the fifth step toward cultural competence. Most persons from different cultural backgrounds accept sincere apologies when errors occur. Valuable lessons can be learned from communication and behavioral mistakes. Because literature on culturally diverse practices places persons into various groups, resulting in large clumps of cultural categories, errors of similarities may occur. These errors may have devastating effects (Leininger, 1995; Leininger & McFarland, 2002, 2006). For example, demographics related to Pacific Islanders represent 40 different cultural groups who speak 23 languages (Farella, 2001). Within this cultural group, health practices and taboos differ greatly.

Along with errors of similarity, errors of assumption frequently occur. Persons assume things about others based on outward appearances. Racial profiling results when persons assume that others who look alike share specific traits and behaviors. The population of the United States is a melting pot, and citizens often refer to themselves as African American, Japanese American, Italian American, Native American, Mexican American, or some other designation. Second- or third-generation immigrants may or may not abide by cultural practices of their ancestral homelands (Leininger, 1995; Leininger & McFarland, 2006). Likewise, as persons learn about health practices from other cultural groups, culturally based folk practice may become intertwined with traditional Western medicine, resulting in an inability to know what individuals do to achieve and maintain health. For example, an American of German descent may or may not abide by the hot and cold food theory for illness treatment, although this is common practice in Germany. The best way to avoid the error of similarity is to perform a detailed, individually focused client health assessment.

Along with errors of assumption, nurses and other health care providers must understand that they hold membership in the American (or other national) health care provider culture. In the United States, health care delivery organizations value efficiency, quality, and empirical evidence. This culture often expects consumers to hold the same (or similar) values (Andrews & Boyle, 2008; Giger & Davidhizar, 2008; Leininger, 1995; Leininger & McFarland, 2002, 2006). Some clinics that serve diverse client populations hold clients to standards determined by the values of health care providers, for example if a teaching medicine clinic in an urban neighborhood sends clients a certified letter informing them of severing them from clinic services after they have missed three scheduled appointments without informing the clinic staff.

Questions for Reflection 11-3

1. What policies in my clinical setting use American values or cultural values of the health care system as their foundations?
2. How have these policies obstructed culturally sensitive care?

Step 6: Remediation for Cultural Mistakes

Remediation for cultural mistakes serves as the final step toward cultural competence. Correcting mistakes requires communication between both persons (and groups). Genuine dialogues result in the development of ideas for cultural accommodation and preservation. Because nursing focuses on client comfort, cultural-specific nursing interventions enhance client comfort by fostering maintenance of client cultural identity. In addition to enhancing client comfort, culturally competent nurses serve as a means for recruitment of health care consumers for a particular health care institution.

Once transcultural communication has been established, nurses and other health care providers can expand their knowledge related to cultural-specific care practices. Andrews and Boyle (2008) identified examples of skills that are useful in transcultural nursing practice. These are assessment, communication, hygiene, activities of daily living, and religion from the range of engagement with clients. From relationships to assessments, nurses must consider biologic variations in signs of illness and health and ways to avoid cultural taboos when measuring the heads of infants, use separate charts for growth and development for children of Asian descent, modify childhood developmental screening tools, and use appropriate ways to conduct gynecologic examinations of women from various cultures.

Transcultural communication skills include speaking in the client's native language, providing health care information in the client's native language, and providing a language interpreter for clients. For hygiene, the nurse must become cognizant of specific hair and skin care needs for clients of various ethnic backgrounds. Nurses must be aware and capable of coaching clients who require special needs for activities of daily living (such as eating with chopsticks or using special assistive devices such as the West African "chewing stick" for oral hygiene).

Nutritional preferences also play a key role in health care. Providing hot and cold foods to clients whose cultures abide by this practice instills trust between nurses and clients. Finally, permitting clients to engage in their religious practices enhances spiritual well-being. Some religious ceremonies include the anointing of the sick (among Roman Catholics), circumcision and special rituals for the dead (among those of the Jewish faith), and cleansing before daily prayer (among practicing Moslems).

Several theories related to transcultural nursing have been published. Cultural phenomena that address the culturally unique individual vary slightly across these theories. Table 11-3 summarizes the key cultural phenomena addressed by major transcultural nursing theories. Because Leininger began cultural studies in the 1960s, the nursing profession sometimes refers to her as the founder of transcultural nursing. Leininger was the first nurse to bring the importance of culturally sensitive nursing care into nursing practice. As members of the culture of health care providers, value conflicts frequently occur between nurses and health care consumers (Giger & Davidhizar, 2008; Leininger, 1995; Leininger & McFarland, 2006; Spector, 2000). Books written by the theorists cited in Table 11-3 provide more detailed descriptions of cultural traditions and taboos related to health protection, maintenance, and restoration.

Hallmarks of Culturally Congruent Care

At times, nurses may be oblivious of cultural issues surrounding a client care situation. Failure to acknowledge and incorporate culture into client care increases the likelihood of distrust on the part of the health care consumer and antagonism on the part of the

TABLE 11-3

Comparison of Transcultural Nursing Theories

Leininger's Sunrise Model and Theory of Culture Care Diversity and Universality (1991, 1995, 2006)

Describes, explains, and predicts factors within nursing care situations that need to be addressed when providing nursing care to persons from different cultures.

The goal is to provide culturally congruent care for all clients.

Key Elements

1. Interacting and influential factors for client holistic well-being
   Available technology, religion, client personal philosophy, kinship and social relationships, cultural values and lifeways, political and legal factors, educational background, and economic forces
2. The roles of the professional nurse to ensure culturally relevant care
   - Mediator between the Western health care system and the folk health care system used by the client
   - Advocates for maintenance of the client's culture by accommodating folk practices that do not interfere with Western health care system treatments
   - Assesses and educates the client (or community) to establish different patterns and structures to more fully enhance health and general well-being

Highly flexible theory and easily used with individuals, families, groups, communities, and institutions across diverse health care systems

Examines the culture of individuals, groups, families, institutions, regional communities, societies, nations, and global humankind

Outlines three phases for obtaining and using transcultural nursing knowledge:

1. Cultural awareness
2. Use of theory to guide cultural research and explain cultural behaviors
3. Use of cultural knowledge in nursing practice to provide culturally congruent care

Purnell's Model for Cultural Competence (1998, 2003)

Cultural competence requires that the health care provider master the following tasks:

1. Development of a deep self-awareness of personal existence, feelings, ideas, and emotions and hold these from influencing actions and attitudes when working with persons from a different culture
2. Learning and understanding the culture of the health care client
3. Accepting and respecting cultural differences (p. 2)
4. Adapting usual care practices to become congruent with the culture of the client

Cultural competence is seen as a nonlinear conscious process

The individual is seen as the core of an ever-expanding network that includes the family, community, and global society

Twelve Key Elements

1. Cultural overview and heritage includes the country of origin (climate and topography), heritage, residence, reasons for migration, economic factors, educational level, and occupation.
2. Communication encompasses the dominant group language, cultural communication patterns (eye contact, space, touch, facial expressions, separate ways to greet outsiders), temporal relationships (time orientation, social and clock time differences, importance of punctuality), and format for names (formal and informal use, sequencing of family and individual names).
3. Family roles and organization include gender roles, accepted head of household, behaviors that are accepted or restricted, taboos, familial roles, familial priorities, alternative lifestyles, and nontraditional families.
4. Work force issues address immigration, temporary immigration for education, multicultural workplace considerations, acculturation into the work group, native health care practices, issues related to professional autonomy, cultural gender roles, religious issues, perception of authority figures, and language barriers.
5. Biocultural ecology includes skin color, biological variations, culturally prevalent diseases, ethnic health conditions, and variances in medication metabolism.
6. High-risk behaviors include use of tobacco, alcohol, illegal drugs; sedentary lifestyle; and failure to use protective devices.
7. Nutrition considers the meaning of food, commonly consumed food, rituals, health-promoting dietary practices, nutritional deficiencies, and alterations in food metabolism.
8. Pregnancy and childbearing practices include cultural views and practices related to fertility control and pregnancy and any prescriptive practices, restrictions, or taboos related to pregnancy and childbearing.

Comparison of Transcultural Nursing Theories (Continued)

Purnell's Model for Cultural Competence (1998, 2003)

9. Death rituals encompass cultural expectations of death, purposes behind death and mourning rituals, burial practices (including cremation), cultural expectations of grief, and cultural meanings about death and afterlife.
10. Spirituality considers the influence of the dominant religion on persons and families, the meaning of prayer, other religious rites and rituals, faith-based symbols (such as icons, statues, medallions), meaning of life, personal sources of strength, and the linkage of spiritual beliefs with health practices.
11. Health care practices encompass predominant cultural beliefs that influence practices, especially those of health promotion and disease prevention, a curative or fatalistic focus for acute care, responsibility for health care, role of health insurance, over-the-counter medication use, folk practices, health care barriers, cultural responses to health, illness, and rehabilitation; cultural perceptions of the "sick role," and acceptance of blood transfusion and organ donations.
12. Health care practitioners includes an exploration of the roles of traditional, folk, and religious health care providers; acceptance of Western medicine health care providers, significance of health provider age, perception of various members of the health care team, status of various health team members, and perceptions of health team members of each other.

Theory acknowledges that health care providers' cultural competence falls into the following four categories: unconsciously incompetent, consciously incompetent, consciously competent, and unconsciously competent.

Emphasizes the use of interpreters over translators when health care clients do not speak the same language as the health care provider.

The 12 key elements of culture provide a comprehensive assessment of cultural care considerations.

Acknowledges workplace issues and the potential value conflicts between clients and providers and conflicts among health team members.

Spector's Model of Heritage Consistency (1996, 2000)

Heritage consistency refers to the degree that a person's lifestyle reflects his/her traditional culture.

Four Key Elements

1. Culture is a complex phenomenon that includes a connected web of symbols, a means for making and limiting human decisions, an extension of biologic capabilities, a medium for social relationship, and personhood. Only part of culture is conscious and exists in a person's mind as well as in the environment.
2. Ethnicity is the condition of belonging to a particular group that shares common characteristics, such as geographic origin, race, migratory status, religion, kinship, geographic locale, traditions, symbols, institutions, literature and other fine arts, values, food preferences, race, language, and dialect. Ethnicity provides an internal sense of distinctness as well as an external perception of distinctiveness. In the United States, a person may belong to different ethnic groups simultaneously.
3. Religion is the belief in a higher power to be obeyed and to worship that also provides a foundation for beliefs, practices, and ethics.
4. Socialization is the process by which persons are raised within a group and acquire group characteristics. Socialization results from the interactive effects of culture, ethnicity, and religion.

Socialization is the focal point of the model.

Factors indicating heritage consistency:
1. Childhood development within the country of origin or neighborhood of persons sharing same country of origin.
2. Extended family participation in cultural or religious activities.
3. Return visits to country or neighborhood of birth.
4. Regular contacts with extended family.
5. Extended family homes within the same community.
6. Individual participation in cultural and religious events.
7. Engagement in social activities with others from the same ethnic background.
8. Personal knowledge of culture and language of origin.
9. Deep personal pride about heritage.
10. Surname not Americanized.
11. Extended family engaged in childrearing.

(continued)

Comparison of Transcultural Nursing Theories (Continued)

Spector's Model of Heritage Consistency (1996, 2000)

Heritage consistency occurs as a continuum.

Uses Giger and Davidhizar's six cultural phenomena that affect health: environmental control, biologic variations, social organization, communication, space perception, and time orientation

Views health providers as a special cultural group with values that frequently conflict with those of health care consumers

Giger and Davidhizar's Transcultural Assessment Model (1995, 1999, 2004, 2008)

Provides a systematic approach for assessing culturally diverse clients

Six Key Cultural Elements

1. Communication is language spoken, voice quality, pronunciation, use of silence, and nonverbal behavior.
2. Space involves is action with personal space invasion, conversation distance, body movement, role of objects, and perception of space.
3. Social organization is the culture, ethnicity, race, role and function of family, work, leisure, religious practices, and friends.
4. Time includes how time is spent, measurement, definition, social, work, and orientation (future, past, or present).
5. Environmental control is cultural health practices (efficacious, neutral, harmful or uncertain effects), values and cultural definitions of health and illness.
6. Biologic variations include body structure, skin color, hair color, genetic makeup, enzymatic deficiencies, increased susceptibility to disease and chronic illness, nutritional preferences (and if these result in deficiencies) and psychological characteristics, including coping strategies and social support.

health care provider. Trust and comfort, on the part of the client, increase when nurses consider cultural preferences during client care. Transcultural care considerations should not supersede the need for safe, effective client care (Andrews & Boyle, 2008).

Identification of cultural nursing considerations begins with the nursing assessment. Cultural assessment provides the nurse with the opportunity to learn about client lifeways. An individualized cultural assessment prevents the nurse from making cultural errors based on client appearance. Elements of the **cultural assessment** include family and kinship systems, social life, political systems, language, traditions, perception of the world, value orientation, cultural norms, religious and health beliefs, and practices. Table 11-4 presents information on each of these elements and suggests ways for nurses to collect data that may be relevant for nursing care. While performing a cultural nursing assessment, nurses must observe clients for cues that indicate discomfort with any questions asked. Sometimes, the nurse must rely on family members to supply information, especially in cultures in which a particular family member serves as the patriarch.

Along with verbal communication, the nurse can scan the environment for clues related to culture. In the home and inpatient settings, many persons have symbolic objects to signify specific beliefs. Clients place these symbols in a prominent area so that they can be easily spotted. Sometimes, items such as charms or religious medals are worn and should not be removed without first asking the client. Displayed objects, such as statues, prayer beads, shrines, or special candles, may provide clues to nurses that special cultural health needs may surface. Polite inquiries related to unfamiliar objects may begin a dialogue about culture (Grossman, 1996).

Sometimes, a nurse and client may share the same religious beliefs, but come from different cultural groups. For example, a middle-class nurse may practice Roman Catholicism. When performing spiritual assessments on clients of Hispanic or African American descent, the nurse might discover that although she and the clients come from different cultural backgrounds, they share common beliefs. In this example, when clients know that their beliefs are acknowledged and understood, they may feel more at ease when

TABLE 11-4

Elements of Cultural Assessment

Cultural Element	Description	Suggestion to Collect Data
Family and kinship system	Family structure, roles, and relationships	Describe your family to me. Who lives in your home? Describe the roles of each family member. Who provides support to you in the home? Observe the client as he/she interacts with family members.
Social life	Daily routine, group memberships, and recreation	Describe your typical day/week for me. To what groups do you belong? How do you spend your free time?
Political systems	Government, organizational, and economic affiliations	What support systems do you use outside of the home? Describe your work environment. What are your feelings about the government? Please share with me any economic concerns you may have related to this illness/injury or seeking health care. Please tell me what type of support you need at home.
Language	Language spoken inside and outside the home	What is your native language? Do you speak more than one language?
Traditions	Nonverbal communications, personal space, and other rituals that may have passed down from previous generations	Is there anything that I should share with other health team members with regard to your personal space or other aspects of communication? Do you have any rituals or habits that we need to consider in providing health care to you?
Perceptions of the world	Viewpoints on the meaning of existence and how the world operates	How do you view the world and your place in it?
Values orientation	What the person sees as being the most important things in life	What things in life matter the most to you? How can we see that these things are preserved for you?
Cultural norms	Cultural attitudes about food, time, work, and leisure	What are your attitudes about food, time, work, and leisure? (It may be useful to separate this into four separate questions.)
Religion	Spiritual beliefs including special beliefs and rituals surrounding life, health or illness, and death	Please tell me if there are any special spiritual needs that you have related to your life, health, or illness. If you were to have a terminal illness, do you have a living will or advanced directive?
Health beliefs	Group attitudes about health and illness	What are your beliefs about health and illness?
Health practices	Behaviors and rituals surrounding health and illness including the use of folk healers and remedies	Tell me about the things that you do at home to maintain your health. What type of measures did you take to cope with this health problem before you sought health care?

Adapted from Andrews & Boyle (2008).

receiving care from the nurse who practices the same religion. Institutional chaplains serve as invaluable resources for information regarding religious differences and accessing services for various religious rites and practices.

Once the assessment is complete, the nurse proceeds with planning **culturally congruent care**. This may require referring to resources related to specific cultures and detailed information about the medical plan of care. Sometimes, traditional folk remedies may interfere with ordered medications. When this occurs, the nurse must find ways to work with clients so that they understand the hazards of using folk remedies along with prescription medications. Some special rituals, such as providing clients with water for cleansing themselves before daily prayer, present no harm. However, the use of marijuana tea as a treatment for asthma poses great harm (Pachter, 1994). By engaging in respectful conversations, nurses and clients work together to make decisions related to accommodating lifeway practices with health care treatments.

Linguistically appropriate care serves as the final hallmark of culturally congruent care for clients who do not speak the language of health care providers. When possible, interpreters should be used for health teaching unless the provider is fluent in the client's language. Conversational foreign language provides the nurse with an ability to meet the client's basic needs. Most persons who speak English as a second language find comfort with providers who speak to them in their primary language. However, mistakes can be made by the provider, and for critical information, interpreters are essential as preservation of client confidentiality becomes an issue in small cultural communities.

International Nursing Opportunities

Disparities in access to health care occur across the globe. Some countries have socialized and government programs that provide health care to all citizens (McIntyre, Thomlinson, & McDonald, 2006; Fried & Gaydos, 2002). In other lands (e.g., the United States), access to health care is determined by the ability to pay for services either as an individual or through insurance coverage. In 2006, the World Health Organization (WHO) set the following eight developmental goals for attainment by 2015: (1) eradicate extreme poverty and hunger; (2) achieve universal primary education; (3) empower women and promote gender equality; (4) reduce childhood mortality; (5) improve maternal health care services; (6) combat HIV/AIDS, malaria, and other infectious diseases; and (8) develop a global partnership for worldwide development (WHO, 2006). Some developing countries have infant mortality rates exceeding 70% and life expectancies of less than 50 years, whereas other countries enjoy single-digit infant mortality rates and life expectancies that exceed 75 years. Most countries have a disparity in health care access for persons living in poverty. The WHO and many state governments have documented evidence of positive contributions made by nurses in the areas of health maintenance, disease prevention, health promotion, and control of specific health-related problems (WHO). With formal recognition of the contributions that professional nurses can make toward improving the health of all citizens, nurses gain increased social status and reap increased governmental and nonprofit funding for nursing-based health care programs and nursing education.

Governmental, private, and religious organizations offer opportunities for **international nursing practice**. The United Nations has nursing opportunities for nurses in various areas, such as refugee support, immunization programs, AIDS prevention and treatment, and health promotion in developing countries. The Peace Corps provides nurses with the opportunity to improve health in developing countries under the sponsorship of the U.S. government. The U.S. Public Health Service offers assignments abroad. Private organizations, such as Doctors without Borders, CARE, Catholic Relief Services, and Project HOPE (Health Opportunities for People Everywhere), seek the services of professional nurses for long- and short-term programs. The International Red Cross offers worldwide disaster relief, for which nursing services are needed. Various organized religions offer opportunities for missionary nursing.

The United States shares the current nursing shortage with other countries. Saudi Arabia frequently recruits professional nurses across the globe. The ethical issue of "poaching" nurses from underdeveloped countries arises in such recruitment. When nurses accept employment for a foreign assignment, they become bound by the country's laws, cultural values, and norms. Therefore, before embarking on an international nursing experience or career, the professional nurse (or nursing student) should read extensively about the culture, politics and economics, religions, health care system, and laws of the destination country. Scholarly journals and popular media provide sources for this information. If possible, the nurse should meet with host country residents to learn more about the culture. Some nurses find it very useful to develop fluency in the country's language(s) and visit the country as a tourist. Upon arrival to the host country, the nurse should make a visit to his or her native country's embassy or consulate (Herberg, 2008). Lack of knowledge serves as no excuse for breaking laws, and in some cases, nurses have been subjected to corporal punishment for failure to abide by laws related to dress and being in public without escorts.

STRATEGIES FOR MULTICULTURAL NURSING PRACTICE

When taking care of clients from multiple cultural backgrounds, the nurse must treat persons as individuals with unique personal needs. Some persons become assimilated to the culture of the nation in which they reside. Not only are there international differences, but there also may be geographical differences within a country. Differences also may occur within a state (or province), county, or city. Taking time to listen to clients as care is delivered and having a broad knowledge base of cultural preferences enable the nurse to increase client comfort.

Challenges for Multicultural Nursing Practice

In relation to health promotion, knowledge of specific disease risks across various cultural groups provides useful information to the professional nurse. Table 11-5 summarizes some health risks and diseases that occur with higher incidence in various cultural groups in the United States. The governmental publication *Healthy People 2010* (U.S. Department of Health and Human Services, 2000) emphasizes disparities in the quality of health across various cultural groups in the United States, most of which arise from poverty and lack of access to health care. Burggraf (2000) noted that elderly persons of non-European backgrounds hold different attitudes and behaviors about health care. These include the following:

1. General distrust of health care systems, societal disadvantages, language problems, reliance on traditional or spiritual healing practices, and discrimination based on race, ethnicity, gender, or age
2. Reduced satisfaction with health care plans and providers
3. Abuse from family members who became acculturated to the American way of life
4. Exposure to hazards in lower economic living areas and low-paying jobs

Burggraf (2000) noted that language barriers may be a deterrent to seeking health care in populations of older Hispanics and elderly Asian women. These groups of elderly women also tend to rely on folk and spiritual healing practices before entering the health care system (Burggraf). However, because all humans have similar biologic structure and basic physiology, nurses work to achieve cultural-universal care.

Folk Illnesses

In addition to different risks for specific illnesses based on ethnicity, some cultures have **folk illnesses** that may require the use of culturally based healers. Empacho is an infant

TABLE 11-5

Common Health Risks and Diseases Encountered by Various Cultural Groups in the United States

Cultural Group	Health Risks	Diseases
African American	Higher incidence of homicide Lower physical activity levels Obesity Cigarette smoking Alcohol abuse Incarceration Unintended pregnancy Untreated dental caries	Heart disease Stroke High blood pressure Chronic renal disease Cancer Premature deaths associated with breast and prostate cancer Sexually transmitted disease HIV/AIDS Cirrhosis of the liver Arthritis Asthma Black out[a] Low blood[a] High blood[a] Thin blood[a] Disorders caused by spells or hexes (Voodoo)[a]
Native American or Alaskan	Highest infant death rate among cultural groups in the US Unintentional injuries Suicide Cigarette smoking Alcohol abuse 38% lack health insurance coverage Home fire deaths Gingivitis	Heart disease Cancer Diabetes Chronic liver disease Cirrhosis of the liver Pneumonia/influenza Chronic renal disease Ghost affliction[a]
Pacific Island/Asian American	Cigarette smoking Air pollution	Heart disease High blood pressure Diabetes Cancer Cervical cancer (Vietnamese) Hepatitis Arthritis[b] Koroa (Southeastern Asian) Wagamama[a](Japanese) Hwa-byunga (Korean)
Hispanic American	Low birth weight Lower physical activity levels Obesity Cigarette smoking Air pollution 33% lack health insurance coverage Unintended pregnancy Home fire death Untreated dental caries Gingivitis	High blood pressure Diabetes Tuberculosis (20% higher rate than European Americans) Increased rate of cancer deaths Cervical, esophageal, gall bladder, and stomach cancer Increasing rates of breast and lung cancer Sexually transmitted disease HIV/AIDS Asthma Empacho[a] Fatigue[a] Mal ojo (evil eye)[a] Pasmo[a] Susto[b]

Common Health Risks and Diseases Encountered by Various Cultural Groups in the United States (Continued)

Cultural Group	Health Risks	Diseases
European American	Lower physical activity levels with increasing age Obesity Cigarette smoking	Heart disease Alcohol abuse Arthritis Osteoporosis[b] Asthma Anorexia nervosa Bulimia[a] Hysteria[a] (Greek) Evil eye[a] (Greek)

[a]Culturally based syndromes.
[b]Health problem identified in elderly women of specified cultural group.
Adapted from U.S. Department of Health and Human Services (2000); Andrews & Boyle (2008); Andrews & Herberg (1999); and Burggraf (2000).

gastrointestinal condition that occurs in Mexican culture. Empacho results in an obstruction in which food and other matter adhere to the walls of the stomach or intestines. Empacho occurs if the child swallows too much saliva during teething or when parents change formulas that do not mix well with each other. Symptoms include abdominal distention, pain, poor appetite, perceived stomach lump, and diarrhea. Infants are placed on a regimen of clear liquids and herbal teas to "refresh the stomach" (Pachter, 1994, p. 692). If the infant begins to lose too much weight, Latino parents may consult physicians so that they are not perceived by others as being neglectful. Successful blending of conventional medical therapy with folk remedies provides the family with culturally competent care. In addition, persons with medical illnesses go to "physicians" but may seek the advice of a folk healer to discover why the illness occurred. Some persons view medical illnesses as the result of an evil spell and need to seek treatment from a spiritual healer to be fully well (Pachter; Andrews & Boyle, 2008; Giger & Davidhizar, 2008).

Physical Appearance Variations

Along with increased specific health risks, persons from different ethnic backgrounds have **variations in physical appearance** (Andrews & Boyle, 2008; Giger & Davidhizar, 2008; Pachter, 1994). The transculturally competent nurse considers physical appearance variations when performing health assessments. A general appearance scan reveals information related to gender, age, skin color, body structure, consciousness level, facial features, clothing, and behavior. Initial interaction with the client permits the nurse to collect information regarding orientation, speech patterns, facial expression, mood, and cognition. Choice of clothing determines the ability of the person to select appropriate clothing for the weather and social situation. Although a matter of personal preference, grooming also provides the nurse with cues related to client culture.

Clothing styles vary widely across cultures. Amish women usually wear solid-color dresses, held together by pins or snaps, and a bonnet. Mennonite women wear similarly styled clothing, but the dresses may be of printed material and have buttons. Islamic women wear clothing to cover all extremities and a veil. Arab-Muslim men sometimes wear a cloth headdress and long robe. Some Indian women wear saris. In certain instances, cultural and religious clothing may be concealed, as in the case of special white undergarments known as "temple garments" that are worn by members of the Church of Jesus Christ of Latter Day Saints (Mormons) (Andrews & Boyle, 2008; Andrews & Herberg, 1999). Roman Catholics often wear religious medals or pictures of Jesus and the Blessed Virgin encased in plastic around their necks (scapulars). When providing physical care to clients, the nurse should ask permission before removing specific items of clothing or jewelry. Attention should be paid to problems with caregiver gender, with alternate staffing arrangements made when feasible.

Skin color varies among all persons and depends on melanin concentrations. Melanin protects the skin from ultraviolet radiation. Increased quantities of melanin protect persons from skin cancer (Andrews & Boyle, 2008). Because all persons (other than true albinos) have some level of melanin in the skin, all persons are people of color. When assessing for skin changes, the nurse must determine what the usual healthy shade is for the individual, rather than for the ethnic group. Specific skin variations for various ethnic groups may be found in physical assessment and transcultural nursing textbooks. Table 11-6 provides a brief summary of some key aspects for nursing assessments related to variations in ethnic descent. If the nurse relies on assessment data information based on the skin color of whites, critical errors could occur. Along with skin color, specific hair care considerations surface. The hair of persons of African descent requires combing, gentle brushing, and oil application, rather than the frequent shampooing to eliminate hair oil that is practiced by persons of European descent (Andrews & Boyle; Giger & Davidhizar, 2008).

Variations in Physiology

In addition to skin color, genetic traits result in physiology variances across ethnic groups such as the adjustment in "normal" reference laboratory values for blood tests. For example, the hemoglobin levels of African Americans tend to be lower than those of their African counterparts; Native, Japanese, and Hispanic Americans have higher blood glucose levels than do European Americans. African Americans have higher levels of high-density lipoproteins (HDLs) than do persons with European descent, and Hispanic Americans have lower levels of HDLs. The source of these variations may be genetic or environmental. The federal government has identified medical research across gender and ethnic groups as a research priority (U.S. Department of Health and Human Services, 2000; Jarvis, 2008). Current trends indicate that a vast amount of data will be generated by genetic research.

Pharmacogenetics (or pharmacogenics) is the field of study that describes metabolic variations that result in different responses to pharmacologic agents. Some of the known responses are summarized in Table 11-7. Some variations result from an inherited enzyme deficiency, whereas the source of other variations remains unknown. When providing care for a culturally diverse client population, professional nurses should be aware of differing responses to medications to anticipate potential adverse effects and different therapeutic responses that may require dosage alterations (Andrews & Boyle, 2008). Research Brief 11-1 showcases a research study on the biophysiological differences of homocysteine levels, a known risk factor for ischemic cardiac disease and strokes, among Mexican American and non-Hispanic white veterans.

CREATING A MULTICULTURAL PROFESSION OF NURSING

In an ideal health care system, health care providers should mirror the population that they serve. Surveys indicate less than 15% of nurses come from a minority background. According to the U.S. Department of Health and Human Services (2000), only 6.9% of professional nurses are African American, 3.4% are Hispanic or Latino, 3.2% come from Asia, and 0.7% are Native American or Alaskan Natives. The Asian Pacific Island Nurses Association represents 40 nursing subgroups who speak 23 different languages (Farella, 2001). The proportion of minority members in the nursing profession varies across states.

To offer health care services to a diverse population, the creation of a **multicultural profession of nursing** must occur. Attracting persons from different cultural backgrounds to the nursing profession remains a challenge. The best and the brightest students often prefer to enter other professions (such as law, medicine, engineering, or teaching) because nursing sometimes is perceived by outsiders as an oppressed profession that holds a status that is subservient to physicians. Adding membership to one

TABLE 11-6

Nursing Assessment Considerations Based on Ethnicity

Ethnic Group	Assessment Considerations
African	Mongolian spots and vitiligo more common Higher carotene levels in sclera may give them a yellow appearance Pallor appears as ashen or gray Erythema difficult to see, but inflammation is more detectable by palpation for warmth, edema, and hardness Hard and soft palates may be the best place to see a macular rash Petechiae cannot be seen in some cases, and if seen, can be found on the buccal mucosa, conjunctiva, abdomen, buttocks, and volar forearm surface Tend to have stronger body odor Hair and scalp tend to be dry Copper-color hair in children is an indication of severe malnutrition Less susceptible to noise-induced hearing loss Increased incidence of oral hyperpigmentation in older age Increased periodontal disease Highest bone density
Native Americans	Mongolian spots and vitiligo more common Pallor appears yellow brown Mild or absent body odor 18% have cleft uvula Eskimos have the largest teeth 30% of Navajo women have longitudinal vascular pattern on chest Eskimos have lower bone density than do whites
Asian	Mongolian spots and vitiligo more common Areola and genitalia are darker Pallor appears as pasty or nearly white Mild to absent body odor Hair usually silky, black, and straight Delayed hair graying Highest incidence of myopia (Japanese and Chinese) 10% have cleft uvula Lower bone density than whites
European	Persons of Mediterranean descent frequently have blue lips, thereby negating reliance on circumoral cyanosis as a reliable indicator of poor oxygenation Pallor appears as pasty or nearly white Skin wrinkles appear at a younger age Tend to have more moles than other groups Tend to have stronger body odor Hair turns gray at an earlier age Smallest teeth, resulting in more tooth loss
Pacific Island	Higher carotene levels in sclera may give them a yellow appearance Pallor appears yellow brown
Middle Eastern	Vitiligo more common Persons of Mediterranean descent frequently have blue lips, thereby negating reliance on circumoral cyanosis as a reliable indicator of poor oxygenation Pallor appears yellow brown
Hispanic	Pallor appears yellow brown

Adapted from Andrews & Herberg (1999); Andrews & Boyle (2008).

TABLE 11-7

Cultural Variations to Pharmacologic Agents

Cultural Group	Pharmacologic Agent	Variations
African Americans	Analgesics	Reduced sensitivity to therapeutic effects Increased gastrointestinal adverse effects, especially with acetaminophen
	Antihypertensives	Blood pressure responds better to single-agent therepy Less responsive to beta blockers and angiotensin-converting, enzyme-blocking agents Increased mood responses to thiazide diuretics
	Mydriatics	Less pupil dilation
	Psychotropics	Increased chance of extrapyramidal side effects
	Steroids	Increased chance of steroid-induced diabetes (especially with methylprednisolone in renal transplantation)
	Tranquilizers	15%–20% poorly metabolize diazepam
Arab Americans	Antiarrhythmics	Some dose reduction may be needed
	Antihypertensives	Some dose reduction may be needed
	Neuroleptics	Some dose reduction may be needed
	Opioids	Higher doses may be required because this group may have diminished ability to metabolize codeine to morphine
	Psychotropics	Some dose reduction may be needed
Native Americans	Muscle relaxants	Alaskan Eskimos may have prolonged muscle paralysis with succinylcholine administration during surgery and may need mechanical ventilation for respiratory support
Chinese Americans	Narcotic analgesics	Less sensitive to respiratory depressant and hypotensive effects Have a higher clearance of morphine
Asian Americans	Antihypertensives	Best response with calcium antagonists
	Neuroleptics	May need reduced dosage
	Psychotropics	May need reduced dosage and up to one-half the normal dose for tricyclic antidepressants and lithium
	Fat-soluble drugs	Increased dosages of fat-soluble drugs needed because of reduced percentages of body fat (especially vitamin K for Warfa reversal)
Hispanic Americans	Psychotropics	May need to reduce dosage as frequently have a higher incidence of adverse effects to tricyclic antidepressants
Americans of Mediterranean descent with glucose-6-phosphate dehydrogenase deficiency	Oxidating medications	Precipitation of a hemolytic crisis with primaquine, quinidine, thiazolsulfone, nitrofurazone, furazolidine, naphthalene, toluidine blue, phenylhydrazine, chloramphenicol, and aspirin
Jewish Americans (Ashkenazi)	Psychotropics	20% experience agranulocytosis with clozapine treatment for schizophrenia

Adapted from Andrews & Herberg (1999).

Research Brief 11-1

Baldwin, C., Bell, I., Guilano, A., Mays, M., Arambula, A., & Alexandrov, A. (2007). Differences in Mexican American and non-Hispanic white veterans' homocysteine levels. *Journal of Nursing Scholarship*, *39*(3), 235–242.

Two hundred and twenty-nine veterans (109 Mexican Americans [MAs] and 120 non-Hispanic whites [NHWs]) who used an Arizona outpatient Veteran's Administration Health Care Center participated in a cross-sectional study aimed at comparing homocysteine (Hcy) levels and other factors such as the intake of dietary supplements and foodstuffs with their risk factors for stroke. The investigators collected data related to ethnicity using Deyo, Diehl, Hazuda, and Sterns' (1985) acculturation scale with documented validity for use in health care along with the veterans' self-report on cultural identity. The participants completed the Stroke Risk Assessment Form (SRAF) from the Framingham study, the Arizona Food Frequency Questionnaire (AFFQ), the Cutting down, Annoyance by criticism, Guilty feelings, and Eye openers (CAGE) Alcoholism screening index, along with other measures for mood, cognition, and behavior. Hcy levels were measured using fasting blood samples to measure plasma Hcy.

The investigators analyzed data using the Statistical Package for Social Sciences (SPSS), Windows versions 13.0 to 15.0. Results revealed no ethnic group differences on the AFFQ for intake of calories, fat, carbohydrates, protein, alcohol, caffeine, or dietary sources of vitamins B6, B12, or folate. The MA group (n = 55) reported significantly higher levels of supplemental intake of vitamin B12 in comparison to the NHWs (n = 79). The MA group was smaller than the NHW group. Statistically significant ethnic differences were found in the following areas: NHW participants reported higher levels of education, greater numbers of smoking pack years, and lower Hcy levels. MA participants reported lower levels of education, lower annual income, fewer smoking pack years, and higher Hcy levels. Hcy levels for MA remained significant after controlling for age, educational level, diabetes, and smoking history ($F(3,37) = 4.45$, $p = .009$) (p. 239). Stepwise linear regression was performed to determine significant predictors of Hcy levels. Ethnicity was not included in the regression analysis because investigators knew that it was a confounding factor. They discovered three predictors that accounted for elevated Hcy plasma levels. The predictors were less education, reduced blood folate levels, and elevated stroke risk score. When regression equations were run using MA or NHW subgroups, only stroke risk score was a predictor of Hcy levels for the NHW group (52% of the variance).

The clinical significance of this study is that MA veterans have higher Hcy levels when compared to NHW veterans. The elevated Hcy level in the MA veterans was more likely to be in the mild hyperhomocysteinemia range, and this was not influenced by nutritional intake, age-related changes in gastrointestinal absorption of nutrients, or use of lipid-lowering medication. Although the SRAF predicted high Hcy levels in NHW veterans, it failed to predict high Hcy levels in MA veterans. However, Mexican Americans have a higher risk of hemorrhagic rather than ischemic strokes. Because of the small sample size, no differences were detected between the groups for type 2 diabetes and dietary supplement use which have appeared in other studies comparing Mexican Americans and non-Hispanic white groups. Also, because the men volunteered to participate in the study, there may be differences in the sample used in this study. For these reasons, the results of this study should be interpreted with caution. Although elevated Hcy levels are associated with increased incidence of cardiovascular disease (CVD) and stroke (CVA), nurses working in clinical settings serving diverse populations may want to teach clients about risk factors for elevated Hcy levels, including family history of CVD and CVA, prescription medication use, smoking, poor diet, and lack of regular exercise.

more oppressed group may be more than a person can bear. Nursing competes with other professions for the same students.

In addition to the perception of nurses being a less powerful member of the health care team, white women traditionally have dominated nursing. This dominance brings with it values, beliefs, and practices that reflect the socialization of white women. Current efforts to increase cultural diversity in the nursing profession include minority nursing scholarships, grant programs, and targeted recruitment efforts. The National Coalition of Ethnic Minority Nurses serves as a clearinghouse for information related to nursing education, leadership, practice, research, and health care policy initiatives (Farella, 2001).

However, once accepted into a nursing program, some minority nursing students experience **culture shock** (feelings of alienation, difficulty in relationships, loss of excitement, and a general dislike of the nursing program) that stems from an inability to interact with someone like themselves. Most nurse educators come from a dominant group of nurses and expect students to abide by traditional cultural values of nursing. Faculty may make errors when working with students from various cultural groups. For example, punctuality is a highly valued work practice in nursing and education. Students sometimes receive a grade penalty for arriving to class late or submitting assignments late, especially when faculty fail to explore reasons for a late assignment or fail to explain the reasons why punctuality is valued. Nursing students from differing cultures occasionally use different nonverbal behaviors when conversing with persons of authority. Students from Far Eastern countries tend to not make eye contact when conversing with teachers, supervising staff nurses, physicians, and older persons; for the students, this practice is a way of conveying respect, but some faculty and staff may label the student as being cold and distant. They question the student's ability to practice the profession of nursing with genuine compassion.

Upon graduation from a nursing program, the minority nurse may fall victim to incidences of racism and stereotyping, especially when nurses encounter stressful working relationships (Farella, 2001). Countries such as the Philippines produce a surplus of nurses. Many of these nurses seek employment in countries with nursing shortages, such as Canada, Great Britain, Australia, Saudi Arabia, and the United States (Alaniz, 2001). American nurses have a history of being less than hospitable to internationally educated nurses. Leininger (1995) and Farella reported incidents in the 1980s in which Filipino nurses fell victim to racial slurs and stereotyping. Sometimes, European American clients and relatives falsely accuse health team members from different ethnic backgrounds of theft of personal belongings.

Professional nurses have an obligation to be hospitable to nurses and other health team members who are from different ethnic backgrounds. Platz and Wales (1999) outlined the various methods to make others feel welcome. First, culturally competent nurses make all clients and colleagues feel cared for and appreciated. Second, standards for business etiquette include greeting colleagues and all persons with each encounter; respecting the time of others; being prompt for meetings and appointments; calling to inform others if delayed for more than 5 minutes; sending thank-you notes; listening actively to others when speaking; respecting other's religion and culture; and considering other's privacy and the right to a neat, clean, and safe working environment.

Strategies for Working in Multicultural Health Care Teams

The influx of persons from other cultures as health care team members is expected to increase as the cultural diversity in the population occurs. Lack of adequate representation of various cultural groups in health care teams has been identified with disparities in access to care services and health care outcomes. Culturally diverse persons have a key role to play in filling the projected vacancies in the health care team of the future. Professional programs, especially nursing, need to recruit culturally diverse students, commit to admitting them, and offer services to facilitate program success. Steady employment as health care professionals may also serve as a way to reduce income disparities based on cultural background in the United States (Sullivan Commission, 2004). Effective health and nursing care requires a multidisciplinary effort and includes work efforts of licensed professionals and technicians. Unlicensed assistive personnel frequently perform the less mentally challenging and more physically demanding work associated with inpatients in acute or long-term care facilities. Many professional nurses encounter different cultural groups as they work with various members of the health care team. Principles of cultural competency used with clients foster effective teamwork.

Ninety-one percent of professional nurses in the United States come from white, female, Christian, and middle-class backgrounds (Sullivan Commission, 2004). Unlicensed care providers (UCPs) and licensed practical/vocational nurses (LPN/LVNs) frequently come from more diverse backgrounds. Technical education programs frequently attract persons who cannot afford a 4-year college education. Therefore, nurses from the current dominant cultural group (European descent) find themselves supervising nursing care delivered by members of a different cultural group. When working with English as a second language (ESL) team members, the professional nurse can have direct caregivers repeat instructions back to validate they understand what needs to be done for clients. Some nurses when working with ESL team members take advantage of this opportunity to learn a few phrases or how to converse in the foreign language. Culturally competent nurses who are aware of their own biases and prejudices acknowledge and deal with them openly, in order to get to know all team members as individuals rather than as members of the different cultural group. When nurses learn about various cultural group practices and values and when they have positive working relationships with persons from another cultural group, their preconceived myths and stereotypes about a cultural group readily become dispelled. Professional nurses can encourage and support talented UCPs and LPNs/LVNs to pursue a professional nursing career. Because of the nature of client care, some professional nurses, UCPs, and LPN/LVNs have formed life-long friendships.

Sometimes nurses encounter language barriers when working with health team members who come from a foreign country or have been internationally educated. Nurses have the responsibility to provide safe, effective client care and should ask health team members to repeat what they say when they are uncertain about the content of sent messages. For example, a nurse receiving a verbal order from a physician who has limited spoken English skills must have the physician repeat what is said to substantiate that the information or order was correctly interpreted. Likewise, the physician should verify understanding verbal communications from the nurse about the client.

When a group of persons who speak the same foreign language work together, some health care organizations have work policies that prohibit them from speaking their language in clinical practice areas unless they are conversing with clients who speak the same language. The individuals are not prohibited from speaking their language in non–client care areas. In clinical practice, stories have been shared with nurses and nursing students by elderly persons from extended-care facilities about foreign-born UCPs speaking and laughing together while bathing the elderly person.

Culturally diverse health team members sometimes face issues of not being accepted by other team members and the clients whom they serve. Culturally competent health care providers value clients and team members from diverse backgrounds and use strategies to promote their psychological comfort. When the health care team focuses on efforts to provide the best possible client care, attainment of a common goal solidifies the bonds among team members.

Questions for Reflection 11-4

1. What are the benefits of having persons from different cultural backgrounds and identities serving on the health care team?
2. What are the values promoted by the health care system in terms of work habits? Do you see a potential conflict with them based on your cultural background? Why or why not?

SUMMARY AND SIGNIFICANCE TO PRACTICE

As the U.S. population increases in cultural diversity, professional nurses need knowledge and skills to provide culturally relevant care. However, all the knowledge cannot accommodate for nurses who have personal biases and misconceptions about persons who are different. Scientific advances demonstrate genetic differences that alter metabolism across racial groups, thereby increasing the complexity of decision making for the safety and therapeutic effectiveness of various medications and optimal strategies for health promotion/disease prevention as nurses encounter culturally diverse clients. The nursing profession faces challenges to develop a workforce that mirrors population demographics. To establish cultural competence in clinical practice, professional nurses must first become cognizant of personal biases; this requires the cognitive skill of honest self-reflection. Establishing cultural competence requires an attitude of genuine caring toward all humankind as well as personal commitment to make the time to learn about client cultural care considerations. Nurses should take the time to ask questions related to cultural preferences, listen to individuals, consider cues given to them by persons from a different culture, and analyze the benefits (or hazards) of generic (or folk) health practices before outlining care plan strategies. Interacting with persons from cultural backgrounds different from their own sometimes means that nurses must take risks, but nurses can learn from their mistakes. Nurses serve as client advocates when they see that specific client cultural needs are met. Authentic caring and effective communication skills enhance the development of therapeutic relationships with clients and collegial relationships with colleagues from different cultural backgrounds.

FROM THEORY TO PRACTICE

1. Referring to the vignette at the beginning of the chapter, what do you think Judy could do to facilitate the teamwork for a multicultural nursing care team? Why is it important that team members of diverse cultural groups understand each other?
2. If you were Judy, what steps would you take to prepare yourself for nursing practice in a foreign country? Would you help your friend in the health clinic? Why or why not?
3. Think of a time when you worked with someone who was from a different cultural background than your own. What did you learn from this person? Did your personal encounters with this person result in any changes in your thoughts, values, or beliefs? Why or why not?
4. Outline a plan of how you might resolve a dispute in a clinical situation with either a client or coworker.

WWW INTERNET EXERCISES

1. Using a search engine, type in the country or countries of your heritage. Visit a tourist site for the country or countries you identified, and read a description of the people and any legal or cultural issues for which you may be held accountable. Bring these to share with your classmates.
2. Visit the Smithsonian Center for Folklife and Cultural Heritage (http://www.folklife.si.edu/index.html) and experience one of the posted virtual festivals (border festival, Hawaiian luau, or African naming ceremony). Write down your reactions as you proceed through each ceremony and listen to music. Click on the words "Folklife Festival." On the next screen, click on "Virtual Festival."

WWW INTERNET RESOURCES

To learn more about transcultural nursing, visit The Transcultural Nursing Society at: http://www.tcns.org.

To learn more about transcultural health care issues, visit the Center for Cross-Cultural Health (CCCH) careers at: http://www.crosshealth.com.

Visit the International Council of Nurses to find information and opportunities about international nursing and networking at: http://www.icn.ch.

To learn more about minority nursing information, visit: http://www.MinorityNurse.com and the following websites:

The National Black Nurses Association, Inc.: http://www.nbna.org.

National Association of Hispanic Nurses: http://www.thehispanicnurses.org.

For folkway and folklife information, visit one of the following websites:

The American Folklife Center at the Library of Congress: http://www.loc.gov/folklife

The Smithsonian Center for Folklife and Cultural Heritage: http://www.folklife.si.edu/index.html.

For a different look at health and healing, visit the Institute of Noetic Sciences at: http://www.noetic.org.

REFERENCES

Alaniz, J. (2001). Give-and-take. *Nurse Week Midwest*, *2*(3), 14–15.

American Association of Colleges of Nursing. (1998). *The essentials of baccalaureate education for professional nursing practice*. Washington, DC: Author.

Andrews, M. M., & Boyle, J. S. (Eds.). (2008). *Transcultural concepts in nursing care* (5th ed.). Philadelphia: Lippincott Williams & Wilkins.

Andrews, M., & Herberg, P. (1999). Transcultural nursing care. In M. M. Andrews & J. S. Boyle (Eds.), *Transcultural concepts in nursing care* (3rd ed., pp. 23–77). Philadelphia: Lippincott Williams & Wilkins.

Baldwin, C., Bell, I., Guilano, A., Mays, M., Arambula, A., & Alexandrov, A. (2007). Differences in Mexican American and non-Hispanic white veterans' homocysteine levels. *Journal of Nursing Scholarship*, *39*(3), 235–242.

Burchum, J. (2002). Cultural competence: An evolutionary perspective. *Nursing Forum*, *37*, 5–15.

Burggraf, V. (2000). The older woman: Ethnicity and health. *Geriatric Nursing*, *21*, 183–187.

Cose, E. (2000, September 18). What's white anyway? *Newsweek*, *68*, 64–65.

DeVito, J. (2004). *The interpersonal communication handbook* (10th ed.). Boston: Pearson.

Farella, C. (2001). How we hurt our own. *Nursing Spectrum*, *2*(2), 12–13.

Fried, B. J., & Gaydos, L. M. (Eds.). (2002). *World health systems: Challenges and perspectives*. Chicago: Health Administration Press.

Giger, J. N., & Davidhizar, R. E. (2008). *Transcultural nursing assessment and intervention* (5th ed.). St. Louis, MO: Mosby.

Grossman, D. (1996). Cultural dimensions in home health nursing. *American Journal of Nursing*, *96*, 33–36.

Herberg, P. (2008). Perspectives on international nursing. In M. M. Andrews & J . S. Boyle (Eds.), *Transcultural concepts in nursing care* (5th ed., pp. 424–452). Philadelphia: Lippincott Williams & Wilkins.

Hughes, K., & Hood, L. (2007). Teaching methods and an outcome tool for measuring cultural sensitivity in undergraduate nursing students. *Journal of Transcultural Nursing*, *18*(1), 57–62.

Jarvis, C. (2008). *Physical examination and health assessment* (5th ed.). St. Louis, MO: Saunders Elsevier.

Johnson, A. D. (2004). In 2050, half of the U.S. will be people of color. *Diversity Newsletter*. Available at http://www.diversity.com/members/6550.cfm. Accessed March 18, 2004.

Kavanagh, K. H., & Kennedy, P. H. (1992). *Promoting cultural diversity: Strategies for health care professionals*. Newbury Park, CA: Sage.

Leininger, M. (1991). *Transcultural nursing* (1st ed.). New York: McGraw-Hill.

Leininger, M. (1995). *Transcultural nursing* (2nd ed.). New York: McGraw-Hill.

Leininger, M., & McFarland, M. (2002). *Transcultural nursing: Concepts, theories, research and practice* (3rd ed.). New York: McGraw-Hill.

Leininger, M., & McFarland, M. (2006). *Cultural care diversity and universality: A worldwide theory for nursing* (2nd ed.). Sudbury, MA: Jones & Bartlett.

McIntyre, M., Thomlinson, E., & McDonald, C. (2006). *Realities of Canadian nursing: Profession, practice and power issues* (2nd ed.). Philadelphia: Lippincott, Williams & Wilkins.

Office of Minority Health Care Resources. (2007). National standards for culturally and linguistically appropriate services. Available at http://www.omhcr.gov/template/browse.aspx?/v/=2&/v/ID=15. Accessed April 25, 2009.

Pachter, L. M. (1994). Culture and clinical care: Folk illness beliefs and behaviors and their implications for health care delivery. *Journal of the American Medical Association*, *271*, 690–694.

Pedersen, P. B., Dragunus, J. C., Lenner, W. J., & Trimble, J. E. (Eds.). (1996). *Counseling across cultures* (4th ed.). Thousand Oaks, CA: Sage.

Platz, A., & Wales, S. (1999). *Social graces: Manners, conversation and charm for today*. Eugene, OR: Harvest House.

Pullen, R. (2007). Tips for communicating with a patient from another culture. *Nursing 2007*, *37*(10), 48–49.

Purnell, L. D., & Paulanka, B. J. (2003). *Transcultural health care: A culturally competent approach* (2nd ed.). Philadelphia: F. A. Davis.

Spector, R. E. (2000). *Cultural diversity in health and illness* (5th ed.). Upper Saddle River, NJ: Prentice Hall Health.

Sullivan Commission. (2004). Missing persons: Minorities in the health profession, a report of the Sullivan Commission on diversity in the healthcare workforce. Available at http://www.amsa.org/div/Sullivan_-Commission.pdf. Accessed July 13, 2008.

U.S. Census Bureau. (2008). U.S. Hispanic population surpasses 45 million. Available at http://www.census.gov/Press-Release/www/releases/archives/population/011910.html. Accessed July 13, 2008.

U.S. Department of Health and Human Services. (2000). *Healthy people 2010* (Vol. 2, Conference ed. in two vols.). Washington, DC: Government Printing Office.

U.S. Department of Health and Human Services. (2001). Standards for culturally and linguistic appropriate health care. Available at http://www.omhrc.gov/assets/pdf/checked/Executive%20Summary.pdf. Accessed December 31, 2007.

World Health Organization (WHO). (2006). Health in the millennium developmental goals. Available at http://www.who.int/mdg/goals/en/print.html. Accessed January 3, 2008.

Yoder, M. K. (1996). Instructional responses to ethnically diverse nursing students. *Journal of Nursing Education*, 35, 315–321.

Yoker, M. K. (1997). The consequences of a generic approach to teaching nursing in a multicultural world. *Journal of Cultural Diversity*, 4, 77–82.

CHAPTER 12

Professional Nurse Accountability

KEY TERMS AND CONCEPTS

Accountability
Responsibility
Answerability
Autonomy
Authority
Competence
Delegation
Professional standards
Ethical accountability
Nurses as client advocates
Shared governance
Accountability checklist

LEARNING OUTCOMES

By the end of this chapter, the learner will be able to:

1   Differentiate accountability from autonomy and authority.

2   Identify the essential questions the professional nurse must answer to be accountable to the client and public.

3   Relate current standards of professional nursing practice to accountability.

4   Identify some of the positive outcomes of the nurse becoming accountable to clients, profession, self, employing institution, managed care networks, and third-party payers.

5   Evaluate oneself on professional accountability, using this chapter's checklist.

VIGNETTE

Carol is a charge nurse of a neuroscience unit. Mr. Jones, who is 90 years old, has been admitted for altered level of consciousness. Mrs. Jones wants absolutely everything done to make her husband well. She insists that the nursing assistant, Gloria, give him food and fluid to drink. When Gloria refuses, Mrs. Jones insists on seeing the nurse in charge. Carol is busy and cannot talk to Mrs. Jones. Mrs. Jones grows impatient and fixes coffee for her husband, then holds the cup to his mouth for him to take sips. Mr. Jones chokes violently. Carol runs into the room and finds that there are no suction catheters for the wall unit suction apparatus. As she delivers the Heimlich maneuver to Mr. Jones, she sends Gloria to the supply cart to get suction catheters; none are found there. Mr. Jones quits breathing, and Carol "calls a code." Unfortunately, Mr. Jones dies.

Questions for Reflection 12-1

1. List the mistakes and the persons who made them in the vignette.
2. What are the potential consequences of Mr. Jones' death?
3. How would I feel if a situation similar to this happened while I practiced nursing?

Accountability means being able to explain reasons behind and being held responsible for having done something. In the early writings about the nursing profession, the term *responsibility* meant duty. Florence Nightingale's *Notes on Nursing* (1859/1946) frequently emphasizes the responsibilities of professional nurses. She delineated the nurse's responsibility for the state of the sick room (Nightingale, p. 45) and the need for careful observation on the part of the nurse to avoid patient accidents (p. 66), and mentioned the fact that "I have often seen really good nurses distressed, because they could not impress the doctor with the real danger of their patients" (p. 68).

Perhaps private-duty nursing represents the epitome of nursing accountability to clients. In private-duty nursing of the past, a nurse took a "case," lived with the client, and remained until the patient no longer needed nursing services. The nurse assumed responsibility and was held accountable for the patient's life, space, and nursing care.

After the Depression of the 1930s, fewer nurses chose to practice private-duty nursing and nurses sought employment as staff nurses in hospitals or public health agencies (Dachelet & Sullivan, 1979). Nurses focused on care tasks and duties were assigned to others according to functions outlined by job descriptions. The professional nurse was a supervisor of other staff and assumed accountability for the actions of self and others.

The notion of accountability became tied to negative situations and carried a punitive connotation. Although they were unaware, nurses were legally liable for their actions or their omissions. Many nurses believed that the ultimate liability remained with the institution, which would "cover" them in the event of a lawsuit. Accountability in the professional sense did not exist because nurses and society viewed nurses as holding subservient roles and merely following physician orders. True professional accountability in nursing surfaced in the late 1970s (Clifford, 1981). In 1980, accountability first appeared as a free-standing topic heading in the Cumulative Index of Nursing and Allied Health Literature (CINAHL).

● DEFINITION OF ACCOUNTABILITY AND RELATED CONCEPTS

To assume **accountability**, nurses must understand its definition. As an adjective, the word accountable means, "1. obliged to account for one's acts; responsible. 2. capable of being accounted for; explainable" (Agnes, 2005, p. 9). Accountability and **responsibility** are synonymous (Agnes). The term *accountability* carries a negative connotation in today's business environment because the question "Who's accountable or responsible?" tends to surface only when things go wrong (Dethmer, 2006a; Miller, 2004). Accountability "is increasingly confused with and used in place of autonomy and authority, although it is synonymous with neither, but related to both" (Batey & Lewis, 1982, p. 13). The following section attempts to clarify and differentiate this trio of terms.

By dividing the term *accountability* in two parts, Dethmer (2006a) simplified its definition. Dethmer's (2006a) first aspect of accountability incorporates the concept of responsibility, which basically means "to account for what has been done" (p. 46). Accountability for an outcome is assumed by "Who did it?" "Who participated in it?" and "Who started it?" In contrast, the term *responsibility* means "to be able to respond" (Dethmer, 2006a, p. 50). Dethmer (2006a) took the concept of accountability one step further and devised the term *radical responsibility*, which is to take full responsibility for whatever happens in one's life rather than blaming others and have the commitment to learn from each life situation. The beauty of this aspect of accountability is that persons must take credit for successes and failures.

The second aspect of Dethmer's (2006b) conceptual approach to accountability includes making and keeping agreements that he calls impeccable agreements. He defined an agreement as anything persons say that they will or will not do. An impeccable agreement is a commitment that a person really wants to make, is aligned with the person, and is something over which the person has control, and the person acknowledges its importance and keeps a record of it. Once an agreement is made, the person is bound to keep it or renegotiate it should something interfere with its execution because "broken agreements damage trust" (Dethmer, 2006b, p. 80).

Clear agreements involve facts (exactly what the agreement contains), feelings (emotional reactions to agreeing), and reasons (the specific rationale behind the agreement). Renegotiating a deadline involves just giving plain, simple facts and works best if the renegotiation occurs prior to the deadline. When an agreement is broken, all involved parties must identify that the agreement was broken and acknowledge it to all involved persons. The person breaking the agreement needs to take responsibility for the action without providing excuses, justifications, or explanations and also listens to the responses of the affected person(s). The person breaking the agreement should inquire about what can be done to address the consequences of the broken agreement. Finally, when agreements are broken, all involved persons should take the time to analyze what happened, learn from it, and not repeat the same mistake (Dethmer, 2006b).

Thus, accountability is the state of being responsible for agreements and answerable for the behaviors and their outcomes that fall into the realm of one's professional role. When nurses establish a relationship with a person to provide professional services, they enter into a binding agreement with that person. They become accountable for implementing established agreements with consumers, employers, and interprofessional colleagues.

Responsibility and Answerability

Accountability continues to retain its original meaning of responsibility but has an added dimension, that of **answerability**, the necessity of offering answers, reasons, and explanations to certain others. Ethical codes for nurses published by international, national, and nursing organizations contain information related to professional accountability (International Council of Nurses, 2005; American Nurses Association, 2001). As the American Nurses Association (ANA) Code for Nurses states, this accountability refers to being answerable to someone for something one has done. It means providing an explanation to self, to the client, to the employing agency, and to the nursing profession (ANA, 2001).

In 2003, the ANA revised nursing's *Social Policy Statement*, which specified that a social contract provides the basis for the authority of professional nursing practices. The contract gives the nurse professional rights and responsibilities for all actions taken while engaged in clinical practice, including effective delegation of tasks to others. Public protection from unscrupulous and unsafe nurses occurs through legal mechanisms including civil and criminal laws as well as various laws and statutes that govern professional nursing licensure. In the United States, state governments set rules and regulations for professional nursing licensure and practice. When credentialing health care professionals, state governments consider the potential for public harm if the professional fails to follow safe, acceptable practice standards and how much autonomy and accountability for decision making are assumed by the professional (Milstead, 2008).

Currently, discussions of accountability for professional nursing revolve around interventions (nursing care), outcomes (results), and costs (expenditures). Because of legal, accrediting agency, third-party payer, and managed care requirements, documentation frequently serves as evidence that nurses either performed or did not perform specific nursing assessments and interventions. Currently, the health care delivery industry has higher error rates than other industries. Recent efforts by businesses, accrediting agencies, consumers, and the government to expect higher-quality health care based on scientific evidence may result in increased areas of accountability for professional nurses.

Thus, accountability is the state of being responsible and answerable for the behaviors and their outcomes that fall into the realm of one's professional role. Professional nurses display accountability each time they answer questions for reasons behind actions, document interventions and outcomes of delivered care, and participate in clinical competency programs.

Autonomy and Authority

In distinction to accountability, **autonomy** refers to the independence of functioning. Autonomy means that one can perform one's total professional function on the basis of one's own knowledge and judgment and that one is recognized by others as having the right to do so. Obviously, this concept is related to accountability because one who functions autonomously must be accountable for his or her behavior (Holden, 1991; Hylka & Shugrue, 1991).

The final closely related term is authority. **Authority** can be defined as being in a position to make decisions and to influence others to act in a manner determined by those decisions. Again, this term is certainly related to accountability because those who are in authority are accountable for the decisions they make and for the actions of themselves and others who act on the basis of their decisions. In addition, authority relates to autonomy because those in authority often act autonomously in performing all or part of their respective roles.

One can see these relationships further developed in the nursing literature. According to Batey and Lewis (1982),

Responsibility, authority, autonomy, and accountability are inextricably related. Responsibility and authority are necessary conditions for both autonomy and accountability. It is illogical and inappropriate for an organization to hold a department or an individual accountable for those activities over which the department or individual has no authority.... Autonomy within the areas in which nursing service has responsibility is also a necessary condition for accountability.... Accountability is an exercise in futility and an experience in failure unless it is linked to nursing service's autonomy. The process of fulfilling nursing's formal obligation to disclose requires that nursing services have the formal and legitimate power to carry out relevant actions. Without the opportunity to make binding decisions, accountability is a hollow concept. (p. 13)

Webb, Price, and Van Ess Coeling (1996, p. 29) discussed the relationship of accountability as something that professional nurses want and seek:

The professional elements of practice are authority, accountability, responsibility and decision-making; therefore, the professional nurse is described as one who is autonomous and who desires responsibility and accountability.

Professional autonomy has been incorporated as an essential element of a magnetic work environment for nurses. Kramer, Schmalenberg, and Maguire (2008) developed a definition for "clinical autonomy" using transcripts of recorded interviews with 289 nurses employed in Magnet hospitals.

Autonomy is the *freedom* to act on *what you know*, to make independent clinical decisions that *exceed standard nursing practice*, in *the best interest of the patient*. *Freedom* is about trust and organizational sanction for autonomous practice. (p. 25)

This definition empowers nurses to act on all forms of nursing knowledge in order to provide optimal client care. Nurses practicing in hospitals with Magnet status are expected to use evidence-based practice as the standard for professional practice. When nurses encounter a situation that is not based on evidence or is counterintuitive, they are expected to take steps to verify that proposed therapeutic interventions are in the best interest of their clients before proceeding with them. In order to question physician orders, nurses must have the cognitive skills to recognize a discrepancy, the solid knowledge (or evidence) to justify questions, and the confidence to know that they must consult with a physician prior to action. When nurses exercise autonomy, they become accountable for the results (be they positive or negative).

Because professional nurses frequently delegate nursing responsibilities to practical/vocational nurses and unlicensed assistive personnel (UAP), they become accountable for the outcomes of the actions of others. Before delegating a task to anyone, the nurse must ascertain that the person has the **competence** (or ability) to perform the delegated tasks. **Delegation** of tasks requires that nurses use professional judgment to decide what tasks can be safely done by another member of the nursing team. Most state nursing practice acts address the delegation process. Many of the directives regarding delegation leave room for the professional nurse to decide what tasks can be safely delegated to others. The following questions help professional nurses to decide what tasks can be safely done by another member of the nursing care team (ANA and the National Council of State Boards of Nursing, 2005):

1. Are there laws that support delegating the task?
2. Is the task within the scope of the professional nurse's practice?
3. Does the delegating nurse have the knowledge and skill to make competent decisions about delegation (such as determining client risk for each delegated task)?
4. Does the task meet all conditions and criteria for delegation to an unlicensed care provider (including guidelines within the nursing practice act, routinely recurs in daily work, needs no modification, has a predictable outcome, and does not require ongoing assessment, interpretation, or independent decision making)?
5. Does the unlicensed care provider have the knowledge, skill, and ability to perform the task effectively?
6. Do the skills of the unlicensed provider match with client care needs?
7. Does the agency have policies, protocols, and procedures in place for the proposed delegated task?
8. Will appropriate supervision be available during task completion?

When UAP accept delegated tasks, they assume responsibility for completing them. In some instances, such as delegation of a bedbath, UAP can make simple decisions whether to use commercially prepackaged baths or use traditional soap, water, and washcloths. At times, nurses may opt to perform a task usually delegated to an unlicensed care provider when client situations reveal a high potential for harm and quick independent decision making is required to avert a serious complication. For example, a registered nurse may decide to feed a newly admitted client who has difficulty speaking because the nurse can assess for safe swallowing and intervene quickly should the client choke.

The agency that uses UAP has the responsibility to verify they received adequate education and training prior to assuming work duties. Part of the education includes when to report problems to nurses. Nurses who fail to respond to client problems reported by subordinates usually fall out of compliance with their job descriptions and may be violating a state nursing practice act. When professional nurses serve in the capacity of unit charge nurses, they have a duty to report any conditions that keep them from effectively performing their designated roles.

Accountability, responsibility, and autonomy empower professional nurses. Each of these related concepts projects an image of responsible, independent individuals, capable of making decisions and influencing others to act on them. They answer for their own behaviors as well as the behaviors of associates. In the professional nursing context, the nurse becomes an autonomous practitioner who brings a different perspective and fulfills a particular role in the interdisciplinary health team. The nurse assumes responsibility for professional activities (including using research-based nursing actions, maintaining clinical competence, and staying abreast of new developments) and is held accountable for the outcomes of client care. This evolving image of a professional nurse demonstrates how increased accountability for the outcome of actions moves nursing toward the status given to other health care professions.

PROFESSIONAL ACCOUNTABILITY

Porter-O'Grady and Malloch (2007) suggested replacing "responsibility" with "accountability" because responsibility historically has been tied to tasks and work processes, rather than outcomes. To be responsible, workers need to arrive for work and fulfill outlined job description activities. The quality of the work is defined by the error rate and the time it took to accomplish tasks. Responsibility-based work means having to report to someone else (usually a supervisor). The supervisor typically evaluates the performance of workers and determines how well the person met expectations. The supervisor, rather than the worker, determines when exceptional or excellent work occurred. In contrast, accountability facilitates self-assessment of professional role performance.

All persons in a living system such as a workplace ideally assume ownership of job roles and responsibilities that contribute to desired outcomes. In this case, persons designated to fulfill a particular role also have the authority to design their work, have clear expectations of their contributions, and have an attitude to strive to do their absolute best. New relationships blossom among coworkers, and workers create meaningful partnerships with each other to fulfill specified outcomes. Sustainable changes occur when they are generated by persons engaged in the actual work. With this new approach, workers become empowered, shape the workplace, and find more satisfaction in their work (Porter-O'Grady & Malloch, 2007, p. 331). Porter-O'Grady and Malloch described accountability as an internally generated concept that occurs when persons are given "complete ownership of what they are and what they do and on their making a commitment to take their talents, energies, and skills and apply them in ways that make the circumstance of life better for themselves and others" (p. 332). Thus, nurses become accountable to clients, the public, the profession, other professionals and unlicensed health team members, the employing agency, and themselves.

As nursing evolves to fit all criteria for professional status, increased interest in and concern with accountability has arisen. Accountability has always been acknowledged as one of the hallmarks of a profession. Flexner (1915) supported this view when outlining characteristics of a profession. In that work, Flexner indicated that a profession is likely to be more responsive to public interest than are unorganized and isolated individuals.

In terms of nursing's involvement with its professionalization in the 1950s and 1960s, Bixler and Bixler (1959) stated that a profession functions autonomously to form professional policy and control professional activity. McGlothlin (1961) explained that a profession undertakes tasks that require the exercising of judgment in applying knowledge to the solutions of problems and accepts responsibility for the results. However, to be accountable, a profession must know that for which it is accountable. To do this, the profession must establish professional standards and attempt to enforce them. **Professional standards** outline the guidelines and principles of a specific line of work or career. The ANA, nursing's major professional organization, has done this with its standards of nursing practice, service, and education. In doing so, the ANA has complied with one of the functions of a professional organization, according to Merton (1958)—that is, of providing the means by which members of the profession can judge the competence of its members. Through its standards, the ANA has contributed greatly to the ability of the nursing profession to be accountable.

By using the standards of practice (ANA, 2004) as a guide, the nurse can identify the scope and limits of professional nursing practice. Nurses can internalize that for which they are accountable. The National Council of State Boards of Nursing sets standards for "safe nursing practice." Individual State Boards of Nursing develop standards for professional practice and monitor professional nurse performance. In addition, a nursing service department monitors its collective accountability through the process of peer review.

Such monitoring has increased dramatically in recent years through the introduction of systematic nursing quality improvement activities with active participation by staff nurses in many institutions and agencies. In 1991, the Joint Commission on Accreditation of Healthcare Organizations mandated that quality assurance programs are required for accreditation. This action hastened the process of operationalizing the concept of accountability as quality assurance at the nursing service department level. At the beginning of the 21st century, the Joint Commission changed the emphasis on ensuring quality in health care to improving quality in health care (see Chapter 19). Thus, nurses became accountable for continuously improving the quality of health care for consumers.

Nurses have another document to guide them for practice accountability—the Code for Nurses, which also was developed by the ANA. The code for nursing outlines terms for **ethical accountability** for professional nurses. **Nurses as client advocates** base professional decisions on what is best for clients. More in the nature of an ethical code, the ANA Code for Nurses provides a clear framework within which nurses can seek to uphold the standards of care and protect the clients they serve. Should there be any doubt about accountability of the nursing profession, the Code lays this to rest by directly confronting the issue. As stated in item 4 of the code, "The nurse assumes responsibility and accountability for individual nursing judgments and actions" (ANA, 2001, p. 1). Other items in the Code do not address the area of accountability directly but, by discussing various factors that are necessary underpinnings for accountability, indirectly support the concept. These factors include the presumed competence of the nurse, the use of informed judgment, and the use of nursing research.

Because society holds individual nurses accountable for professional actions, the nursing profession is accountable to establish and monitor standards for safe practice. Only nurses can determine the definition of "safe practice" and care standards. In some states, physicians routinely testify in court proceedings that a nurse displayed unsafe practice or deviated from the standard of care. Obviously, nursing is accountable as a profession and its individual practitioners also are accountable. It has been implied throughout this discussion that nurses are accountable to the public and to the profession itself. In addition, with most nurses remaining employed by health care agencies rather than being independently employed, one must consider the area of accountability to the institution (Copp, 1988; Vaughn, 1989). In the current climate of cost control, the notion of accountability to managed care networks and third-party payers of health care has emerged. Finally, in light of the current emphasis on self-actualization and growth, it is important to add that professional nurses must be accountable to themselves.

Accountability to the Public and Clients

A profession exists to provide service to the public. Although it may be personally and intellectually stimulating, gratifying, and exciting to execute professional roles and responsibilities, the ultimate reason for its existence is its service relationship with society. Thus, almost by definition, a profession must be accountable to the public. The consumer has the right to receive the best possible quality of care performed by those who use a specialized knowledge base while applying sound judgments to make decisions within a clear and appropriate value system. In order to provide the best possible care, nurses must stay abreast of current best practices. Nurses become aware of changes in practice by staying employed in nursing, attending continuing education seminars, completing required competency tests, and reading professional literature (in print or online format).

As consumers become more knowledgeable through formal education and access to information from many media formats, they sometimes know more about what the professions are supposed to be doing. The increased knowledge empowers consumers to demand more and to make those demands openly. Instead of assuming authority positions, nurses work collaboratively with clients to determine and attain health-related goals.

Nurses must be aware of increased consumer knowledge and sophistication and be prepared to respond to it in an equally knowledgeable and sophisticated manner. Nurses must demonstrate clearly the principles and concepts on which practice is based. They also need to access current information, use problem solving to effectively evaluate outcomes of care, and revise care strategies if desired outcomes are not achieved.

Society holds nurses legally accountable for professional practice. Each state has a board of nursing that monitors practice according to the Nursing Practice Act (NPA). The NPA defines professional nursing practice, specifies the scope of practice, and distinguishes professional nursing from other health professions. Nurses must practice within these guidelines when working in a state. Thus, securing a copy of the NPA for states in which one practices is essential because ignorance of the law serves as no excuse for a professional nurse. Nurses can use the Internet, telephone, or mail services to secure a copy of a local NPA.

When undesired client outcomes occur in health care, the law holds professional nurses to a standard of safe and prudent practice. Safe and prudent practice means that the nurse exercises reasonable judgment and delivers reasonable care (Kopp, 2001; Milstead, 2008). Examples of reasonable actions and judgments include being competent in the area of current practice, securing help for situations in which one is unqualified to manage, and fulfilling professional duties as a nurse. Negligence occurs when a nurse commits a breach of duty; an example of this would be falling short of an acceptable standard of care through an action or omission (Kopp). When a nurse deviates from approved policies, procedures, or standards, the risk for being accused of malpractice or negligence increases. However, before legal action is taken, the plaintiff must demonstrate that the event caused some form of injury.

Documentation of care delivered serves as legal evidence when legal action is taken against nurses. Meticulous documentation of events enables the nurse to present a highly professional image and serves as one of the best defense resources during legal actions. When on the witness stand, the nurse must be able to formulate and present to others the theoretical and scientific bases for the judgment exercised while fulfilling professional responsibilities.

In addition to legal accountability, nurses must be able to formulate and present to others the ethical code or value system to which they refer when making judgments and using knowledge. They must answer the questions from consumers and others of "Why did you do that?" "How did you come to that decision?" and "What makes you believe that is the most effective course of action?" In addition, nurses must give responses to these questions without becoming defensive. Consumers have the right to know about all aspects of their nursing care, and nurses who are truly professionals have the responsibility to know and provide the answers.

As knowledgeable professionals, nurses share accountability for the nation's health care delivery system with other health team members. When nurses blame others, such as physicians, administrators, or politicians, for the state of the health care delivery system or constantly look to others to improve the system, nurses weaken their position and power base. By accepting an appropriate degree of responsibility for the current situation and actively pursuing methods of improving it, nurses act on a more professional level and make their claim for a piece of the health care pie.

Nursing also is accountable to the public in guarding against ill-prepared UAP. During times of nurse shortages and cost containment, some hospitals provide brief (4- to 6-week) training programs for unlicensed workers to prepare them to assume complex nursing care tasks. In some cases, the quality of care has been seriously compromised.

For example, considering pain as a fifth vital sign and delegating its assessment to UAP deviate from judicious nursing practice. Effective pain management requires a nursing assessment because UAP do not have the knowledge for thorough pain assessments. In addition, a complaint of client pain needs to be managed by some form of independent or collaborative nursing intervention. Poor pain control may result in impaired healing, other potential physical complications (e.g., a postoperative client refusing to move, resulting in the development of atelectasis and pneumonia), and client dissatisfaction with nursing care. Nurses must work collectively and cohesively to protect the public against potential harm and protect aspects of health care delivery that belong to professional nursing.

Accountability to the Profession

The profession of nursing exercises its accountability toward itself in the performance of its duty to formulate its own policy and control its activities. Professional nurses determine standards for nursing licensure (the National Council of the State Boards of Nursing and individual state boards of nursing) and those that exist for entry into a variety of professional groups and associations (such as the Association of Operating Room Nursing and the American Association of Critical Care Nurses). When nurses determine and monitor compliance to professional nursing standards and guidelines, professional autonomy is preserved.

In connection with this aspect of accountability, the individual nurse must understand the necessity of being aware of and accountable for not only the nurse's own actions but also those of colleagues. For example, chemically addicted colleagues pose a danger to clients, themselves, and coworkers. Chemical abuse in nursing is a complex problem (Lillibridge, Cox, & Cross, 2002; Hastings, 2007). Signs of chemical addiction include early arrival to or late departures from work, arriving at work when not scheduled, wearing long-sleeved garments, wasting drugs excessively, volunteering to administer controlled medications to unassigned clients, taking frequent breaks, spending excessive amounts of time close to a drug supply, volunteering for overtime, recordkeeping that is sloppy or suspect (e.g., entering incoherent or sloppy notes or initials), signing out medications for clients who have left the unit, and increasing personal and/or professional isolation (Maer-Brisen, 2007; U.S. Drug Enforcement Agency [DEA], 2005). For every addict, there is an enabler (DEA). Before confronting or reporting suspicions of illegal drug use, nurses should keep a written log (including time, date, and suspicious behavior). Nurses have a professional and legal responsibility to abide by the law and safeguard clients and other members of society, which means they need to report chemically impaired coworkers (DEA).

When confronting a colleague about suspected chemical impairment, the nurse should display genuine empathy and concern, be direct and open, share specific behaviors and incidents, and expect the colleague to deny allegations. Experts in chemical impairment management advocate interventions involving the suspected nurse, colleagues who observed behaviors, the nurse's direct supervisor, and a chemical impairment counselor when confronting chemically impaired coworkers. An intervention provides the suspected nurse with immediately available assistance should he or she want to seek professional help for the alleged problem. Forty state boards of nursing offer alternatives to disciplinary actions that typically involve legally binding programs for detoxification, treatment, peer assistance, and recovery programs that include random monitoring for signs of chemical use (Maer-Brisen, 2007). When nurses police themselves, professional autonomy is enhanced.

Regular peer review programs provide another means for nurses to monitor their own profession. Benefits of peer review include increased self-awareness of practice, quality of client care, professionalism, and accountability. The Joint Commission recommended that nurses engage in peer review as part of professional practice (Roper & Russell, 1997). Peer review processes require that nurses look objectively at a colleague's performance, which sometimes can be difficult when generating a peer evaluation on a friend. Also, some nurses dislike pointing out deficiencies in another nurse's performance. Effective peer evaluations offer constructive suggestions to remedy identified performance deficiencies.

Finally, nurses have accountability for the survival of the profession. As members of a noble and well-respected profession, nurses need to recruit new members, support them through the educational process, mentor them as they enter the workforce, and support them as experienced colleagues.

Accountability to the Interprofessional and Unlicensed Health Care Team Members

As a professional in the interprofessional and multidisciplinary health care team, nurses have accountability for the unique contributions they make to client care. The nurse often spends more time with the client than any other health team member. Nurses who engage in holistic nursing care consider more than just client physiologic needs; they also identify psychological, sociocultural, and spiritual needs. Many times, nurses identify obstacles for client self-care by spending time assessing, teaching, and evaluating client and family responses to what they need to know before discharge.

For example, when working on a rehabilitation unit, one nurse was caring for an elderly woman who was going to perform glucose self-monitoring at home. The diabetes nurse educator who provided the basic instructions documented that the woman could effectively perform required tasks. However, 2 days before the client was to be discharged, the nurse observed that the woman failed to have the manual dexterity to manipulate the glucose-monitoring equipment, the vision to read the results, and the fine hand control to record the results. The nurse discovered that the woman lived alone and that no family members would be available to assist. The professional nurse fulfilled her obligation to document this information and share it with the case manager, who then arranged home health care. The proactive steps taken by the nurse in this situation may have prevented poor blood glucose control, prevented another hospital admission, and thereby reduced health care costs.

Professional nurses also have accountability for informing UAP of potential hazards they might encounter when providing basic care to clients with contagious diseases or the potential for violence. UAP need to know what actions need to be taken to protect themselves. Likewise, UAP have the responsibility to inform professional nurses about changes in client status that indicate a potentially infectious disease or escalation of anger into physical violence. For example, the UAP caring for a post-op client receiving antibiotics should report the incidence of frequent, loose stools to the professional nurse (a possible sign of *clostridium difficile* infection). In addition, the UAP should report to the nurse that a client (or family member) is disgruntled about any aspect of care so the nurse can use therapeutic communication techniques to discover and alleviate the issues to prevent escalation of anger into an episode of verbal abuse or physical assault of staff.

Accountability to the Employing Agency

Nurses also have accountability to employing agencies. Employees, even those with professional status, have responsibilities and must answer for job actions. Although not unimportant, accountability to the agency rightfully takes a back seat to accountability to the client, the public, the profession, and nurses themselves.

A health care agency is accountable to the public for the care provided under its auspices. Agency administration must verify that they have competent persons providing health care to consumers. Thus, the agency has the right to expect the nurse to be accountable to that agency. Dimensions of accountability include quality of work, unsafe practice situations, nurse attitudes toward the employing agency, and professional practice with outside agency staff.

The agency holds nurses accountable for the quality of work (nursing care). This includes their preparation for the job and their fitness each time they report for work. The agency contracts with nurses for a specific job to be done at a specific time and place for a specific wage. Nurses must uphold their end of the bargain in all of these areas. They also have accountability for monitoring peer performance. In addition, professional nurses are accountable for those whom they supervise in the work setting, and must be aware of what they are doing and how they are doing it, to exercise that accountability.

Nurses also have the responsibility to inform their employers about situations that result in actual or potential unsafe nursing practice situations. Recent legislation has resulted in legal protection for nurses who report unsafe practice situations. Sometimes the agency may refuse to correct what the nurses perceive as an unsafe practice situation. Nurses must refuse to work in areas and situations that they consider unsafe. This further fulfills accountability to the agency (as well as self) because such nurses are saying, in effect, "I will not put the agency in the position of giving unsafe care." Not taking action against unsafe practices places clients at risk, who will then tell family members and acquaintances of the poor care received at the employing agency. However, sometimes refusal to provide client care as designated by terms of employment may result in reprimand, demotion, and even dismissal from the agency unless the nurse is employed in a state that offers whistleblower protection.

An additional aspect of the nurse's accountability to the agency involves the attitude toward that agency that the nurse projects to clients. The attitude should be one of objectivity and honesty. Nurses who find joy in working for a particular agency may appropriately and honestly promote the agency's strengths. However, if confronted with an agency shortcoming, nurses must be honest in their responses. Sometimes, in the heat of the moment, when particularly taxed or following a disagreement, a nurse may denigrate an agency. In this case, the nurse has not acted maturely and has no awareness of the impact of such statements on the client, visitors, or the agency.

Concerns have arisen recently regarding accountability to the employer because of a large and growing number of nurses employed by nursing agencies and then essentially "rented" to hospitals on a per diem basis. In most cases, agency nurses possess high levels of clinical competence. However, they may be unfamiliar with an employing institution's policies and procedures. Some agency nurses rely on nurses who are employed by the institution to help them access information and guide them through institutionally set care standards. Agency nurses may have more accountability to the nursing agency, thus diminishing some of the support they might be offering the hospital, or they feel primarily accountable to the hospital's clients. When the allegiance to the employing institution supersedes that to the agency, the nurses may run the risk of being dropped by the agency.

Nurses have, for too long, maintained their accountability to their employing agency above their accountability to all others. This has detracted from a desirable image of nurses as working primarily in the public interest and instead has fostered the impression of the nurse as being subservient to and totally under the control of the employing institution. Now is the time to fully recognize and implement nursing's accountability toward its primary foci (the client and public, the profession, team members, and the self) without losing sight of the nurse's accountability toward the employing agency.

Accountability to Self

Although professional people perhaps display more commitment to their careers, they sometimes can be exploited by systems in which they work. In the early days of the profession, hospitals and clients expected nurses to live on the premises in which they worked. Unlike the days of old, agencies no longer assume ownership of nurses and do not expect them to work long hours without breaks. Employers and clients see nurses as free and independent persons with multiple facets to life other than their professional role.

As persons, nurses owe it to themselves not to agree to participate in any situation that violates their personal or professional values. When personal accountability is lacking, the games of blaming, complaining, and procrastination appear. When persons practice personal accountability, they experience healthier relationships, improved teamwork, and less stress while employers enjoy increased productivity, greater teamwork, and improved customer service. Personal accountability begins with looking at oneself and seeing how things can be changed rather than pointing fingers at others. When things do not go smoothly, two key questions to ask are "What can I do?" and "How can I help?" These questions focus on action and include a role for the individual to make a difference (Miller, 2004).

However, sometimes the job situation may cause nurses and others to overlook these basic facts. Staff shortages may keep nurses from fulfilling their basic needs for nutrition and elimination. In addition, nurses' other life roles may often affect professional performance. Therefore, nurses must be accountable to themselves for their actions both on and off the job because of the potential effects of their actions on themselves and others.

The nurse who appears for work still experiencing the effects of too much celebrating on days off may not be prepared to function as a safe professional. Fatigue, jet lag, minor illness, exhaustion, or the effects of alcohol or drugs make the nurse a liability, rather than an asset, in the work situation. Professional practice also may be hampered by nurses who put in too much overtime, allow themselves to be placed in a position far beyond their abilities and knowledge, and function in a constantly and highly stressed state. These nurses may find themselves too exhausted or unprepared to function ineffectively in professional and personal roles.

Significant others cannot always be expected to have lower priority than one's work, whereas work cannot always be expected to take second place to social and personal relationships. Nurses need to attain a certain balance. Overdoing the amount of time and energy expected on the job often leads to burnout, with the nurse becoming incapable of or unwilling to do adequate work. Burnout also may take a toll on personal and social lives (Chaska, 1983).

The nurse's accountability to self comes across clearly. Nurses must assume responsibility for their own physical, mental, and spiritual health by maintaining a balanced lifestyle. They must decide when to give more energy to work and when to devote more energy to other life areas. When nurses sacrifice wholeness of life, they lose capacity for optimal functioning as professionals and people. They must function at fullest capacity when on the job and yet set a pace to avoid despair and profound fatigue.

The nurse's accountability to self includes refusing to work in situations deemed unsafe. Each nurse defines unsafe situations individually. Some examples of unsafe practice situations include lack of knowledge or experience to work in an unfamiliar specialty area and insufficient staffing. Nurses must learn to see refusal to work in unsafe situations as the ultimate professional service to the consumer despite potential sanctions that may be applied as consequences for this action. Whistleblowing is the act of reporting unsafe or unethical situations or incompetence of another health care team member. Murray (2007) offered the following suggestions for self-protection for nurses who opt to blow the whistle on unsafe client care situations:

1. Hire an attorney for legal advice.
2. Verify the legal status of whistleblower protection at the federal and state levels.
3. Consult with the local state nurses association for answers to or clarification of state laws and regulations.
4. Develop a written, accurate account of all observed events (time, date, and incident).
5. Store all documents in a secure location and have multiple copies of each incident.
6. Follow the facility's chain of command when reporting incidents.
7. Ask for help from experts, including the local state attorney general, legislative bodies (state and federal levels), and other agencies and organizations who have an interest in reducing unsafe health care delivery.
8. Forward all documents to outside agencies using certified mail for proper verification of receipt of records and materials.
9. Maintain professionalism at all times when presenting information to the employing and outside agencies.

Research Brief 12-1

Davis, A., & Konishi, E. (2007). Whistleblowing in Japan. *Nursing Ethics*, *14*, 194–202.

The investigators surveyed 24 nurses (graduate students and clinical faculty) at a Japanese nursing college to identify "experiences, actions and ethical positions' (p. 194) on reporting a colleague or physician for wrongful acts. A questionnaire was translated from English to Japanese and then back-translated. The questionnaire contained items addressing actual experiences and hypothetical situations.

Questionnaire results revealed that 21 respondents would whistleblow depending on the results of direct confrontation of the person involved in the wrongful deed. Twenty-three nurses reported the reason for reporting would be based on the effects of the wrongful act on the client. Twenty of the the nurses responded that the head nurse should receive information of wrongdoing because he or she possesses the ultimate responsibility for unit activities to the hospital. The support of colleagues on the unit for whistleblowing would depend on whom had committed the wrongful act. Seventeen participants reported they would receive support for reporting a physician and 14 reported that they would be supported for reporting another nurse. Perceptions of physician support varied according to the situation, with 16 nurses reporting physician support for reporting a nurse and 11 nurses reporting physician support for reporting another physician. The following number of nurses reported they had blown the whistle on the following persons: physicians (12), a nursing colleague (10), and someone else in the work setting (9).

Results of this study indicate that nurses use a professional judgment to determine whether or not to report acts of wrongdoing. Key considerations for reporting include the extent that the wrongdoing affects the client along with results of directly confronting the person who performed the act. The study also revealed that whistleblowing conflicts with traditional concepts of group loyalty (health team member or nurse) and saving face. Because of the small sample size and educational status of the participants, these findings should be exercised with caution. However, the study adds to professional nursing knowledge by viewing whistleblowing as an act of professional advocacy. More research needs to be done to see if there are commonalities among nurses on an international level related to whistleblowing.

Accountability to self also involves acknowledging one's own limitations and knowing when additional education or assistance from another is needed for effective client care. Questioning physician orders requires confidence and sometimes even courage, but it protects both client and nurse. Deciding when to assume a new nursing position (such as promotion to a nurse manager) should be based on each nurse's appraisal of personal qualifications for the job rather than the opinion of other persons. Completing an academic degree (such as a bachelor's degree in nursing) does not automatically prepare all nurses to assume a managerial role. Other factors such as personality, job description, and career goals also play a role prior to assuming an administrative position.

Because nursing and agency administration make decisions related to daily operations, professional nurses sometimes do not have full control over practice situations. Many agencies carry insurance policies to protect themselves when client care errors and other accidents occur. If professional nurses become involved in incidents in which client harm has occurred, the agency may either support them or use them as scapegoats. Accountability to self involves protecting oneself against financial loss should an unforeseen incident occur. Table 12-1 presents reasons for lawsuits filed against professional nurses. In the United States, client suits involving nurses rose from 307 in 1997 to 586 in 2005. Two thirds of these suits involved registered nurses not practicing in advanced nursing roles (Domrose, 2007). Client suits against nurses fall into two main categories: failing to do what is expected, and doing what is not expected (Aiken, 2003). Lawyers carefully examine client records for signs of breaches in nursing care standards and incidents of nurse failure to respond to, report, and follow up on changes in client status (Domrose). Sometimes, a slight omission in documentation can precipitate legal action when harm comes to clients in a nurse's care. Table 12-2 presents arguments for and

TABLE 12-1

Reasons for Nurse Malpractice Suits

Reason	Example
Failure to document	Procedures, medications, and physician interactions not documented are considered not done in a court of law
Therapy error	Incorrect medication or treatment
Failure to follow standards of care	Using alternative treatments or procedures and/or failing to follow guidelines outlined by institutional policy and procedure manuals
Communication failure	Not listening intently to client concerns, inaccurate discharge instructions, not notifying a physician in a timely manner
Omitted assessment	Not performing routine assessments for various medical conditions or procedures, or forgetting to document a required assessment
Forgetting to be a client advocate	Not questioning physician orders when needed or not providing a safe environment
Breach of confidentiality	Sharing of private information with others
Invasion of privacy	Failure to provide drapes for procedures requiring physical exposure
Release of medical information without permission	Failure to get written permission from clients when sharing medical information with others
Assault and battery	Performing invasive procedures without client-informed consent
False imprisonment	Inappropriate use of physical or chemical restraint
Discrimination	Unequal treatment based on particular group membership or specific disease
Defamation	Harming the reputation of another person
Slander	Saying false statements or misrepresentations that harm the reputation of another
Libel	Any written or oral statement or other representation published without just cause for the purpose of exposing another to public contempt

Adapted from Helm & Kihm (2001); and Croke (2003).

TABLE 12-2

Reasons for and Against Nurses Carrying Individual Liability Insurance

Reasons For	Reasons Against
Employer language may cover the facility but not individual employees.	Attitude of being not at risk for malpractice
Employer policies may be insufficient to cover all claims, leaving the nurse responsible for the amount that exceeds the facility policy limits.	Perceived adequate coverage from employer
Hospital insurer might seek indemnity from nurse after lawsuit is settled.	Clients may file malpractice claims several years after an incident, and the nurse may change jobs, or the facility could close or change its malpractice policy.
Personal policies provide legal defense for the nurse, and some include costs for time off work and transportation during legal proceedings.	Nurse could be caught in a facility's decision to side with a physician during legal proceedings, holding the nurse responsible for malpractice.
Facility policy may have coverage gaps.	Perception that carrying own insurance policy increases the likelihood of being sued.
Most jurors assume nurses carry individual liability insurance.	

Adapted from Helm & Kihm (2001).

against purchasing individual professional liability insurance. Professional liability insurance pays for individual nurse legal defense costs should he or she be named in a malpractice suit or involved in an early settlement program. Liability coverage also pays damages to an injured party if the nurse is found negligent. As supervisors and coordinators of client care, nurses may be held accountable for actions of unlicensed personnel, nursing assistants, other nurses, and clerical staff (Croke, 2003). According to advertisements in a variety of 2008 nursing journals and mailed advertisements, the annual cost of $1,000,000 in professional liability insurance coverage ranges from $98 to $450 for professional nurses. Advanced practice nurses (depending on their specialty) may pay up to $1,250 for liability coverage. Nurses who are self-employed and nurses working in various specialty areas (e.g., critical care and obstetrics) pay higher fees than nurses employed in medical-surgical units and extended-care facilities. In comparison, physician malpractice costs range from $10,836 to $45,550 anually (Gans, 2007).

Coverage terms vary according to the type of policy purchased. Claims-made policies cover the nurse for the time when the plaintiff files a court claim. In contrast, occurrence policies cover the nurse for the time in which the situation happened that resulted in litigation. The nurse should know which type of policy he or she carries. When a nurse has claims-made coverage, the policy needs to be active until all chance of litigation has expired. Each state determines the time when persons can file legal claims for health care providers for undesirable care outcomes.

Recently some health care organizations have adopted early settlement programs when adverse client outcomes arise. Part of the program includes established policies and procedures outlining exactly how appropriate disclosure is made to clients and families when an adverse event occurs. The process may include full apologies and early offers for compensation if deemed appropriate (Greenwald, 2008). Programs such as these have been implemented to reduce litigation against physicians and hospitals. However, no assurances have been made to professional nurses that the health care organization will not take punitive action against them should the adverse event occur because of a nursing error.

Finally, nurses are accountable to themselves to do their own personal best (Styles, 1985). Factors outside nursing can influence this aspect of accountability. Government can aid or hinder nurses' abilities to do their best through legislation, funding (or lack of funding) of health care, education and research, reimbursement policies, and health care priorities. Managed care networks and third-party payers strive to provide health care services to subscribers at the least possible cost. The nurse must consider political activism as a means to the end of accountability to self, as a method of bringing public policy and the most expert care into congruence.

The Groundwork for Accountability

From this complex description of accountability, professional nurses must consciously prepare themselves to develop the skills and attributes that enable its accomplishment. Nurses need to know the latest research, use theroretical bases, display competence in clinical practice, assume leadership, and practice following a personal ethical framework.

Research and the Establishment of a Theoretical Base for Nurse Accountability

One of the major factors in the accelerating pace of nursing's movement toward professional status is the growth of its theoretical and conceptual base for practice. Theory-based knowledge is now available in some practice areas and will be available increasingly in others as the result of nursing research.

Nurses in practice use knowledge generated through research to substantiate nursing actions. Research demonstrates that professional nursing care makes a difference in the lives of clients. Doran (2003) identified the following nursing-sensitive client outcomes: functional status, self-care ability, symptom control, safety, adverse occurrences, and client satisfaction. Nurses have access to online and printed research findings. However, finding time to read and analyze nursing research results poses a dilemma for many nurses. Some nurses (especially those educated in associate degree programs) have received no formal education on how to evaluate research findings for use in practice.

The dissemination of nursing research results to practicing nurses occurs very slowly, as sometimes it may be years before key findings are published. Some nurses use research findings to develop clinical practice policies and procedures. With the advent of evidence-based practice and quality improvement initiatives, the use of research findings has become more desirable and acceptable in many practice settings. Many nurses (especially those prepared by associate degree nursing programs) lack the ability to comprehend and evaluate the research studies they may read. These registered nurses desperately need help to understand available research reports and apply the findings to work situations. Some health care agencies have nursing research committees and offer resources to help nurses use research findings in practice. However, until nurses and health care organizations value nursing research use, nurses will continue to practice on the basis of tradition.

Clinical and Professional Competence

The public, consumers, health care agencies, and physicians expect nurses to have clinical competence. Different specialty areas of practice have different knowledge and skills for competent practice. However, all areas of practice require that nurses understand and apply principles and techniques of asepsis, physical assessment, nursing process, pathophysiology, pharmacology, human growth and development, psychology, sociology, spirituality, and safety. Because all nurses hold their clients' lives in their hands, whatever a nurse does, it must be done well.

Currently, with many levels of nursing being reflected in the composition of the health care team, nurses at each level should have a clear idea of the scope of practice at their level, and responsibly perform to the maximum limit of that level. The nurse's accountability may be called into question if he or she is functioning beyond the scope of practice at a particular level. It is no more appropriate for nurses who have been educated at the baccalaureate level to restrict professional activities to those they may have exercised at the associate degree level than it is for them to assume the role of the master's-prepared practitioner.

The key to expertise in practice lies in both knowledge and skill, a somewhat artificial distinction that nevertheless allows for more clarity in this discussion. Nursing has always had a strong manual skills component. To the extent that the nurse is in a role that calls for these skills, activity, gentleness, quickness, and accuracy remain hallmarks of excellence. Where the skills required are in the areas of communication, teaching, leadership, management, and research (the so-called hands-off skills), the matter of expertise is no less pressing.

Underlying all skills is excellence in terms of command of "nursing knowledge." Nurses can never expect to contribute significantly to health care in its assessment, planning, implementation, and evaluation aspects if they do whatever they do in a mediocre manner. Competence is an absolute prerequisite for accountability.

Leadership Skills

Leadership development frequently brings questions and puzzlement when first introduced to nursing students. A frequent response is "Not everyone can be a head nurse or a supervisor, or wants to be an instructor. I don't want to be a leader; I just want to be a nurse." The fact is that the elements of leadership are inherent in the nurse role.

Leadership ability is one of the most important areas in laying the groundwork for accountability. The nurse's accountability extends into all areas of health care delivery, including health maintenance and promotion, as well as the area of promoting self-care. The nurse is a constant catalyst for change in health care quality and delivery, especially if she or he is "just" a nurse.

To fulfill the leadership role, nurses must be well versed in the theory and practice of change. Nurses are leaders because they influence others, provide others with desired health-related information, participate in the formation of health care and organizational policies, serve as role models of health, and coordinate client care. Accountable nurses cannot function without leadership skills.

Personal Ethical Framework

Nurses are accountable within a personal ethical framework. They cannot be accountable in a moral vacuum. They must have as their guide standards and values in which they believe and to which they refer. To some extent, these are determined by the collective values of the profession, and these, in turn, are partly determined by what the public expects of that profession and partly by what the profession demands of itself.

In nursing, these professional values are formalized by the Code of Ethics for Nurses (ANA, 2001). However, in large measure, this ethical code is a personal one, developed in the course and context of the individual's total life experience. It includes values learned in the home, in schools, from social groups, during religious training, in the work setting, and from the activities and contacts of daily life. It is influenced by the nurse's ethnic and religious background, the area of the country in which he or she lives, and the nurse's personality. It is highly individual.

A personal ethical code often is something of which he or she is relatively unaware. It is unconsciously used in making decisions and running one's life, but is rarely, if ever, pulled out and scrutinized or even acknowledged as existing. It is this code that is so essential in the professional nurse. A nurse must be aware of his or her code, how it affects decisions and actions, and where it is congruent with or departs from standard codes of the profession. Thus, these conflicts must be worked through and compromise sought so that the nurse can feel comfortable with and confident in the ethical basis in which the practice is rooted.

ACCOUNTABILITY IN AN ERA OF COST CONTAINMENT

Health care costs continue to outpace the inflationary rate of other goods and services. Prospective payment systems serve as the major reimbursement method for many health care services. Public support for imposing controls on costs for health care continues to increase. In the United States, the Centers for Medicare and Medicaid predict a staggering shortfall in funding by 2012 (Goldstein, 2006). In efforts to curb costs, Medicare no longer covers costs for hospital-acquired infections, complications, and errors. Thus, nurse accountability for the prevention of adverse effects of hospitalization increases. For-profit health care providers and managed care consistently look for ways to provide cost-effective health care. Health care practices deemed to be effective will be increased and retained, while those determined to be ineffective will be decreased or discarded. Professional nurses must substantiate the benefits of nursing contributions they make to health care delivery.

All too often in health care, "effective" seems to mean "cost-effective." The idea of a universal right to top-quality care for all is being diluted to a standard of adequate care to those who meet specific criteria set by third-party payers. Nurses are now asked to be accountable for the care they give and for giving that care in the least expensive manner possible, often in a setting or time frame severely limiting the comprehensiveness of that care. However, recent disease management programs offer a means to enhance the ability of clients to manage chronic health conditions (e.g., end-stage renal disease, diabetes, and HIV/AIDS) by offering intensive client education and home support services to keep persons with these conditions in their homes rather than in the hospital or an extended-care facility. As key providers of care under this relatively new health care delivery mode, professional nurses making home visits are held accountable for accurate client assessments, effective health education, and appropriate referrals. Because of the complexity of community interventions and algorithms present in the disease management programs, Goldstein (2006) recommended bachelor degree–level preparation as the minimum for nurses working in them.

The Unlicensed Health Care Worker

Increased use of UAP adds layers of accountability for health care delivery. UAP have always been accountable for proper performance of assigned duties and for knowing when other workers must be consulted for situations determined to be beyond the limits of the worker's knowledge and training. Unlicensed workers must earn the trust of the professional nurse, and vice versa. Although the legal doctrine of respondeat superior (let the superior answer) still applies, unlicensed workers do bear some accountability for their actions.

However, principles that have guided nursing care for years still apply. The RN is still accountable for the client's overall care. However, the current situation requires that the RN broaden the scope of supervision and be more vigilant. The RN must be more aware of the UAP's abilities and activities while increasing availability for consultation.

Managed Care and Third-Party Payers

Managed care, government health care plans, and private health insurance companies monitor access to services, strive to eliminate redundancy, look for ways to reduce overuse of services, and control health care costs. Unfortunately, sometimes in managed care and insurance companies, persons without health care experience or education make approval decisions for consumers needing or wanting specific health care services (including health insurance coverage).

With cost-containment efforts, the nurse's role as a client advocate becomes vital. The nurse advocate pays attention to and acts in instances in which clients are being denied access to essential care or seem to be short-changed by policies and actions directed primarily at cost containment (Aroskar, 1992; Stevens, 1992). The issue of access to care has been a legitimate one for nurses to address for years, as succinctly stated in the Code of Ethics for Nurses (ANA, 2001):

> The nurse assumes the responsibility and accountability for individual nursing judgments and actions.... The nurse collaborates with members of the health professions and other citizens in promoting community and national efforts to meet the health needs of the public. (p. 1)

This notion has also been reiterated and emphasized by its inclusion in the ANA's Nursing Policy Statement (2003). There can be no doubt that the nurse's accountability extends into exerting efforts to respond to the health care needs of the public in a collective sense.

Along with doing what is right for clients, nurses play a key role in reimbursement to the employing agency from managed care and other third-party payers. Meticulous documentation of all supplies and interventions provides evidence that consumers received care. Third-party payers frequently audit charts in efforts to disallow charges appearing on consumer bills.

ACCOUNTABILITY IN THE FUTURE

The future relies on current actions. The nursing profession has renewed its interest in accountability, and practice changes have occurred to increase nurse accountability.

Some nurses have assumed control of practice by adopting **shared governance** models that increase nurse participation in shaping professional practice. Nurses assume responsibility and accountability for developing unit-based and institutional-wide procedures for clinical practice and quality improvement.

When adverse client events or failure of work processes arise, accountable nurses complete incident reports that are used to track reasons why errors occur in health care delivery. Although incident reports are used internally to discover reasons for errors, nurses completing them admit that mistakes were made and examine the reasons why they occurred. A just culture approach to care errors uses incident reports as opportunities to identify flawed work processes and as opportunities for employee growth. Health care delivery (especially in hospitals) relies on many team members to execute physician orders. Each member of the health team makes a contribution, and all assume accountability for actions. Nursing may have to learn to be accountable within a more ambiguous, multidisciplinary framework.

Advanced technology has provided the means for nursing to become more accountable. Using technology, nursing can clearly show what it does: the care it delivers, its cost, and its outcomes. Nursing must be rescued from burial in the category of "room and board" in budgets and on client bills. Once nursing services departments control their budgets, they will be empowered to make decisions and be accountable for them.

 ## CHECKLIST FOR ACCOUNTABILITY

Preparation for accountability for action requires that nurses evaluate personal actions periodically. The following sections serve as an **accountability checklist** for nurse self-assessment of professional accountability. The list is not all-inclusive but offers a beginning tool for working the concept of accountability into one's life and work.

Accountability to the Client

- Am I providing the best care of which I am capable?
- Is that care sufficient to meet the needs of the client in this situation?
- Is this client entitled to more than I can offer, and am I turning elsewhere to obtain the needed, additional dimension?
- Am I incorporating what I know of nursing theory and research into my practice in this situation?
- Am I using my leadership skills to encourage others to function at their optimal ability levels in the care of this patient?
- Am I acting in accordance with my own ethical code and that of the profession?
- If, by meeting the needs of this client, I am in conflict with my personal ethical code, am I seeking some alternative method or person to satisfy those needs?
- Have I given clients information that they want or need to know about their health status, while considering the effect on them of that knowledge?

Accountability to the Public

- Am I seeking to improve health and nursing care?
- Am I speaking out against abuses I see in health and nursing care?
- Am I acting as a community resource in the areas of health and nursing?
- Am I remaining an active and contributing member of the profession and to society after using public funds to finance my education?
- Am I attempting to increase the knowledge of the public to enable it to make more knowledgeable choices about health and nursing care?
- Am I recruiting others to enter the profession to have future health care needs of the clients met?
- Am I sharing my knowledge and expertise about health care with elected officials to shape public policy?

Accountability to the Profession

- Am I fulfilling my professional role in accordance with the requirements of the profession?
- Are other nurses in my setting doing the same?
- If I am not performing satisfactorily, or if others are not, am I taking steps to remedy that situation?
- Am I willing to help other nurses in my work setting?
- Am I a participant in professional meetings, organizations, seminars, conferences, and so forth, so that I may express my views on nursing to those in nursing?
- Am I working within the profession to improve practice, education, or research?
- Am I complying with the ethical code of the profession?

Accountability to the Agency

- Am I performing in accordance with the job description for the position for which I was employed?
- If I am not satisfied with that job description, am I seeking appropriate ways to change it?
- Am I seeking to ensure that I am practicing under safe, if not optimal, conditions?
- Am I giving the institution its money's worth in terms of my work?
- Am I working in accordance with the policies and procedures of the institution?
- If I am not satisfied with those policies and procedures, am I seeking to change them using principles of leadership and change and with the total mission of the institution in mind?

Accountability to Self

- Am I satisfied with my chosen profession?
- Am I performing my professional role in the best way I can?
- Should I seek additional preparation for that role?
- Should I withdraw from that role until I receive additional preparation?
- In areas where I am dissatisfied, am I seeking alternative modes of action or thought?
- Am I comfortable, ethically, with the way in which I am performing my professional role?
- Am I shortchanging my patients, my significant others, or myself in the way I am performing my professional role?
- Do I have adequate financial protection for myself and family if I were to be involved in a professional litigation case?
- Am I satisfied with the position this role assumes within my total lifestyle?

Because of the magnitude of this checklist, only a super person could look through this checklist and confidently say he or she fulfills all criteria. Some activities are more appropriate than others for nurses in different settings and at different times. However, nurses who are to act in an accountable manner or increase the accountability of their decisions and actions must consider these and other questions. Those who wish to call themselves professional nurses must consider these questions to live a life of accountability.

 SUMMARY AND SIGNIFICANCE TO PRACTICE

Accountability in professional nursing is a complex phenomenon and requires nurses to look globally at how their actions affect clients, society, employing agencies, colleagues, and themselves. For a long time, nurses have assumed the reponsibility of protecting clients and tending to their needs. Because of the nature of nursing practice, nurses have binding legal and ethical obligations to clients, the public, the employing agency, the profession, and themselves. Nurses need to have confidence in their cognitive skills and themselves to tackle situations with the potential to place clients in harm's way. Sometimes nurses have to make tough decisions such as reporting unsafe acts of a colleague or employer. In today's rapidly changing and chaotic health care environment, nurses become accountable for staying current with new treatments, research findings, cost containment issues, and clinical skills. Because of its breadth and depth, professional accountability takes time to develop. Professional accountability expands as nurses assume more autonomous and leadership career paths.

FROM THEORY TO PRACTICE

1. Review the vignette at the beginning of the chapter. List the persons who made mistakes in the care of Mr. Jones and the mistakes that they made. Who has accountability for their actions? How could this unfortunate incident have been avoided? What steps should be taken by everyone involved in the incident to avoid repeating the same errors with a future patient?
2. Do I currently carry professional malpractice insurance? Why or why not?
3. Answer the questions contained in the chapter accountability checklist. Note areas for future growth in areas of accountability to the client, public, profession, self, and agency for which you work.
4. How are student accountabilities addressed in your professional nursing program? How are they communicated to students? What are the consequences for a student breach of accountability?

WWW INTERNET EXERCISES

1. Visit the National Council of State Boards of Nursing website at http://www.ncsbn.org. Click on "About NCSBN" and read the NCSBN mission, vision, and purpose. Go back one screen. Click on "Boards of Nursing" to access your state board of nursing. Find your state in the list and click on the website address to discover specific information related to professional nursing in your state.
2. View a sample nurse's malpractice insurance policy by visiting the website of the Nurses Service Organization at http://www.nso.com. Click on the words "Professional Liability Insurance." Under "Individuals," select either "Nurses" or "Student Nurses." Select your state. Then Click on NSO's Professional Liability Insurance Program to get a sample of terms of liability coverage from this professional liability insurance provider.

WWW INTERNET RESOURCES

The American Nurses Association: http://www.nursingworld.org.
Code for Nurses with Interpretive Statements: http://www.nursingworld.org/ethics/code/protected_nwcoe303.htm.
International Council of Nurses: http://www.icn.ch.
ICN Code of Ethics: http://www.icn.ch/icncode.pdf.
ICN Scope of Nursing Practice: http://www.icn.ch/psscope.htm.
Nurses Protection Group: http://nursesprotectiongroup.com.
American Association of Colleges of Nursing: http://www.aacn.nche.edu.
National League for Nursing: http://www.nln.org.
National Council of State Boards of Nursing: http://www.ncsbn.org.
American Association of Legal Nurse Consultants: http://www.aalnc.org.
Medical-Legal Consulting: http://www.legalnurse.com.
Nurses Service Organization: http://www.nso.com.

REFERENCES

Agnes, M. (Ed.). (2005). *Webster's new world college dictionary* (4th ed.). Cleveland, OH: Wiley.
Aiken, T. M. (2003). Nursing malpractice: Understanding the risks. *Travel Nursing 2003*, 7–12.

American Nurses Association (ANA). (2001). *Code of ethics for nurses with interpretive statements.* Washington, DC: Author.

American Nurses Association (ANA). (2003). *Social policy statement* (2nd ed.). Washington, DC: Author.

American Nurses Association (ANA). (2004). *Scope and standards of practice.* Washington, DC: Author.

American Nurses Association and the National Council of State Boards of Nursing. (2005). Joint statement on delegation. Available at http://www.ncsbn.org/pdfs/ Joint_Statement.pdf. Accessed June 23, 2008.

Aroskar, M. A. (1992). Ethical foundations in nursing for broad health care access. *Scholarly Inquiry for Nursing Practice, 6,* 201–205.

Batey, M. V., & Lewis, F. M. (1982). Clarifying autonomy and accountability in nursing service: Part 2. *Journal of Nursing Administration, 12,* 10–15.

Bixler, G. K., & Bixler, R. W. (1959). The professional status of nursing. *American Journal of Nursing, 59,* 1142–1147.

Chaska, N. L. (1983). *The nursing profession: A time to speak.* New York: McGraw-Hill.

Clifford, J. C. (1981). Managerial control versus professional autonomy: A paradox. *Journal of Nursing Administration, 11,* 19–21.

Copp, G. (1988). Professional accountability: The conflict. *Nursing Times, 84*(3), 42–44.

Croke, E. M. (2003). Nurses, negligence and malpractice. *American Journal of Nursing, 103,* 54–64.

Dachelet, C. Z., & Sullivan, J. A. (1979). Autonomy in practice. *Nursing Practice, 4,* 15–16, 18–19.

Davis, A., & Konishi, E. (2007). Whistleblowing in Japan. *Nursing Ethics, 14,* 194–202.

Dethmer, J. (2006a). Accountability: Part 1, taking responsibility. In J. Ware, J. Dethmer, J. Ziegler, & F. Skinner (Eds.), *High performance investment teams* (pp. 45–65). Hoboken, NJ: John Wiley.

Dethmer, J. (2006b). Accountability: Part 2, making and keeping agreements. In J. Ware, J. Dethmer, J. Ziegler, & F. Skinner (Eds.), *High performance investment teams* (pp. 67–91). Hoboken, NJ: John Wiley.

Domrose, C. (2007, October–December). Malpractice suits against nurses on the rise. *New Hampshire Nursing News,* 8–9.

Doran, D. (Ed.). (2003). *Nursing-sensitive outcomes: State of the science.* Sudbury, MA: Jones & Bartlett.

Flexner, A. (1915). Is social work a profession? In *Proceedings of the National Conference of Charities and Correction* (pp. 576–590). Chicago: Heldman.

Gans, D. (2007). Malpractice insurance: A necessary but offensive cost. *MGMA Connextion, 7*(7), 20–21.

Goldstein, P. (2006). Impact of disease management programs on hospital and community nursing practice. *Nursing Economic$, 24*(6), 308–314.

Greenwald, J. (2008), Stanford's Medical Center mulls expanding role of captive. *Business Insurance, 42*(17), 36–37.

Hastings, J. (2007). Addiction: A nurse's story. *American Journal of Nursing, 107*(8), 75–77, 79.

Holden, R. J. (1991). Responsibility and autonomous nursing practice. *Journal of Advanced Nursing, 16,* 398–403.

Hylka, S. C., & Shugrue, D. (1991). Increasing staff nurse autonomy. *Nursing Management, 22,* 54–55.

International Council of Nurses. (2005). *ICN code for nurses: Ethical concepts applied to nursing.* Geneva: Author.

Joint Commission on Accreditation of Healthcare Organizations. (1991). *Nursing care accreditation manual for hospitals, 1991.* Chicago: Author.

Kopp, P. (2001). Fit for practice: Legal issues in accountability. *Nursing Times, 97*(5), 45–47.

Kramer, M., Schmalenberg, C., & Maguire, P. (2008). Essentials of a magnetic work environment. In *Nursing 2008 career directory* (pp. 36–37). Philadelphia: Lippincott Williams & Wilkins.

Lillibridge, J., Cox, M., & Cross, W. (2002). Uncovering the secret: Giving voice to the experiences of nurses who misuse substances. *Journal of Advanced Nursing, 39,* 219–229.

Maer-Brisen, P. (2007). Addiction: An occupational hazard in nursing. *American Journal of Nursing, 107*(8), 78–79.

McGlothlin, W. J. (1961). The place of nursing among the professions. *Nursing Outlook, 9,* 214–216.

Merton, R. K. (1958). The functions of the professional association. *American Journal of Nursing, 58,* 50–54.

Miller, J. (2004). *QBQ! The question behind the question.* New York: G. P. Putnam's Sons.

Milstead, J. (2008). *Health policy and politics: A nurse's guide.* Sudbury, MA: Jones & Bartlett.

Murray, J. (2007). Before blowing the whistle, learn to protect yourself. *American Nurse Today, 2*(3), 40–42.

Nightingale, F. (1946). *Notes on nursing: What it is and what it is not.* Philadelphia: J. B. Lippincott. (Originally published in 1859)

Porter-O'Grady, T., & Malloch, K. (2007). *Quantum leadership: A resource for health care innovation* (2nd ed.). Sudbury, MA: Jones & Bartlett.

Roper, K. A., & Russell, G. (1997). The effect of peer review on professionalism, autonomy and accountability. *Journal of Nursing Staff Development, 13,* 198–206.

Stevens, P. E. (1992). Who gets care? Access to health care as an arena for nursing action. *Scholarly Inquiry for Nursing Practice, 6,* 185–200.

Styles, M. (1985). Accountable to whom? *Nursing Mirror, 160*, 36–37.

U.S. Drug Enforcement Agency (DEA). (2005). *Drug addiction in health care professionals*. Available at http://www.deadiversion.usdoj.gov/pubs/drug_hc.htm.

Vaughn, B. (1989). Autonomy and accountability. *Nursing Times, 85*(3), 54–55.

Webb, S. S., Price, S. A., & Van Ess Coeling, H. (1996). Valuing authority/responsibility relationships. *Journal of Nursing Administration, 26*, 28–33.

CHAPTER 13

Environmental and Global Health

KEY TERMS AND CONCEPTS

Environment

Global environment

Anthropocene

Environmental health

Ecocentric

Pollution

Environmental surprises

Discontinuity

Extinct

Synergism

Unnoticed trend

Positive feedback

Cascading effects

Multiple chemical sensitivity

Community environment

Work environment

Home environment

LEARNING OUTCOMES

By the end of this chapter, the learner will be able to:

1 Explain the role that the global, community, work, and home environments play in human health.

2 Identify elements within one's personal environment that are noxious to the global environment.

3 Identify factors within the environment that are health promoting.

4 Integrate personal behaviors that foster a health-promoting environment.

5 Outline noxious environmental factors that may impair human health.

6 Relate environmental quality to the quality of human health.

VIGNETTE

Emily has come to the emergency department of a teaching hospital reporting an intense headache and an inability to concentrate. As the triage and charge nurse, Barbara asks Emily questions related to her medical history. Emily states that she is allergic to a long list of medications, cleaning products, and foods. Emily begins to hyperventilate and whispers when responding to questions. Barbara becomes suspicious of all of Emily's allergies and seeming overdramatization of her symptoms and decides that Emily must be mentally ill. As Barbara searches for the pager number of the psychiatric resident, Emily's allergist arrives, orders epinephrine, and mentions that Emily has multiple chemical sensitivity syndrome, a rare disorder that the allergist says is becoming more prevalent in her practice.

Questions for Reflection 13-1

1. How would I respond if I encountered a client like Emily in my clinical practice?
2. What advice would I give Barbara if she consulted with me about Emily's case?
3. What are the impacts of technology, modernization, and manmade products on the environment?

Objects, conditions, and circumstances create the environment. Living organisms depend on the environment for formation and survival. Not all environments possess the capability of sustaining life. Multiple environmental systems must remain in balance to sustain life. For the purpose of this chapter, **environment** refers to all the conditions, circumstances, etc., that surround and influence life on earth (Agnes, 2005, p. 476). The environment consists of physical domains (air, water, soil) and social domains (land use, industry, housing, transportation, agriculture). Depending on the context, environments may be miniscule or enormous. The **global environment** refers to the conditions on the planet earth. The current geological era has been named the **anthropocene**, a term coined by Paul Crutzen, a Nobel Prize–winning atmospheric scientist from the Netherlands (Pearce, 2007). The anthropocene era started approximately 200 years ago and encompasses the time during which human beings have dominated many of the earth's planetary processes (especially the release of greenhouse gases, the transformation of natural habitat for agricultural and urban development, and various environmental pollutants) (Fagan, 2008; Lynas, 2008; Pearce; Sachs, 2008).

Humans rely on an external environment for air, water, and food. Within a systems framework, interacting groups create a unitary whole. When the balance is altered, the unitary whole experiences changes, some of which may lead to destruction of life. Because humans rely on earth for their existence, air, water, and food quality determine human health status. Fagan (2008), Lynas (2008), Pearce (2007), and Sachs (2008) provide possible scenarios of the effects of global warming on the earth, some of which may result in marked reductions of the population and even the demise of the human race. **Environmental health** refers to conditions in the environment that preserve the balance of nature. This chapter examines the effects of the global, local community, working, and home environments on human health and offers strategies for professional nurses to create a sustainable future.

THE GLOBAL ENVIRONMENT

Florence Nightingale linked environmental quality to the health of soldiers during the Crimean War. As a diligent supporter of germ theory, her writings emphasized the importance of cleanliness and adequate ventilation with fresh air to prevent mortality and promote healing and disproved conventional nursing practices of her time (Dock, 1912). In Victorian times, persons tended to look at local, rather than global, environmental conditions. Nurses lost Nightingale's passion for the environment as they developed the profession and as women fought for equal social status (Kleffel, 1994). In the 1970s and 1980s, nurses again included the environment as part of nursing theories. Fawcett (1984) delineated environment as an essential element when developing a metaparadigm for nursing (man, health, environment nursing). Definitions of the environment depend on the philosophical stance of each theorist. Rogers (1990), Leddy (2004), and Newman (1994) defined the environment as an energy field. However, Watson (1999), Neuman (2002), and Roy (1987) defined the environment as an open system. Neuman further separated the environment into internal and external domains that interact with each other. Humans have come to know much more about the environment through the advancement of scientific technology. When the world saw pictures of the earth from outer space, people acknowledged the interconnectedness of nations and how regulations (or lack of them) could potentially affect everyone. The future of human civilization relies on a safe and clean environment. As people realize the importance of the environment on human health, an **ecocentric** (the perspective of the environment as being whole, interconnected, and alive) approach to health care delivery becomes a societal priority (Kleffel, 1996).

The earth is a delicate planet that has the conditions to support many varieties of life. Balanced ecosystems provide the resources to sustain life. Many times humans cause environmental **pollution** from waste products from manufacturing products, energy production, or burning wood or petroleum products; chemicals used to control pests (animals, insects, or plants); and widespread use of plastic products. Pollution disrupts the usual natural balance. When the balance becomes disturbed, **environmental surprises** emerge. Bright (2000) identified the following three forms of environmental surprises: discontinuity, synergism, and unnoticed trends. An abrupt shift in a trend or steady state constitutes a **discontinuity**. Forest habitat loss causes some animals to seek refuge elsewhere or travel to human-populated areas for food. The species (e.g., bears) becomes a menace to persons by scouring human garbage cans for food; local governments spend money to control them; some people get harmed; and in extreme cases, the species becomes endangered or **extinct** (ceases to exist). Simultaneous changes in several natural phenomena with greater-than-expected environmental effects define **synergism**. The combined effects of a heavy rainstorm, cutting trees on a hillside, and people moving to an identified flood plane resulting in a catastrophe with a high human death toll comprise an example of a synergism. An **unnoticed trend** develops when an event occurs undetected but does considerable damage to an ecosystem. Nonnative weed invasion of fertile farm acreage in the United States displaced native plants that facilitated the balance of natural fire cycles that destroyed 9,884 acres of farmland during a 30-year period before it was detected. To further complicate the earth's balance, synergisms can produce discontinuities (ozone depletion combined with acid rain and other atmospheric aerosols results in increased depth penetration of ultraviolet radiation in water, which results in the destruction of microorganisms essential for the survival of coral reefs and fish). Alternatively, discontinuities can produce synergisms, such as pesticide-resistant insects carrying plant viruses that destroy crops (Bright).

Along with the three types of environmental surprises, positive feedback loops can create discontinuities. In a **positive feedback** loop, the cycle of change continues to amplify itself. Global warming provides a prime example of the positive feedback loop. The Arctic ice cap is melting as the result of global warming. Even a thick ice cap absorbs only 10% of the sunlight, and the ocean absorbs the rest. As the ice mass dwindles, the ocean becomes warmer, which results in accelerated global warming (Bright, 2000; Lynas, 2008; Pearce, 2007; Sachs, 2008).

In addition to positive feedback loops, cascading effects occur, leading to more environmental changes. **Cascading effects** happen when a change in one component of a system results in a change in another component, which sets up a change in yet another component, with multiple changes occurring throughout various components. Cascading effects can produce discontinuities and synergisms. The Alaskan coastline provides an example of a cascading effect. When the Alaskan perch and herring population declined, sea lions and seals starved. As the population of sea lions and seals declined, killer whales had to resort to finding new prey to survive. The sea otter was the ideal candidate. However, the sea otter feasted on sea urchin. As the sea urchin population exploded, they demolished kelp forests. Now, many species of fish, marine invertebrates, marine mammals, and birds are at risk because they rely on kelp for food (Bright, 2000; Lynas, 2008; Pearce, 2007; Sachs, 2008).

Sachs (2008) identified six trends of the 21st century that shape the future of humankind. These are (1) the age of convergence (when the per capita income of poorer nations rises to, catches up with, and even exceeds that of rich nations), (2) increased population growth of persons with higher incomes (increased demands for goods, services, and energy), (3) Asian dominance of the world economy, (4) more people living in urban locales from migration, (5) environmental challenges (how to mitigate the effects of human environmental destruction), and (6) the poverty trap (large gaps between the incomes of the rich and poor) with self-reinforcing and perpetual cycles of poverty. In addition to these issues, Pearce (2007) and Lynas (2008) shed more light on the future environmental issues resulting from the exploding human population, such as rising global temperatures, falling water tables, declining croplands, diminishing fisheries, shrinking forests, and the loss of plant and animal species. The population is expected to increase from 6.6 billion in 2007 to 9.2 billion by 2050 with current population growth trends (Sachs). With increased carbon dioxide emissions from the Industrial Age, the global temperature has risen 0.8° Celsius (C) (1.4° Fahrenheit) over the past 150 years (Lynas). Because of the uncertainty and complexity of the earth's ecosystem, projections for global warming by 2050 vary from 1°C to 12.7°C (1.7–21°F). As global temperatures warm, infectious diseases (especially those associated with insects) typically encountered in tropical climates may be encountered in temperate climate zones (Greer & Fisman, 2008; Lynas; Pearce). Many unknowns exist among the climate change models, such as the long-term effects of manmade pollutants on the environment. For example, ozone promotes the conversion of hydoxyl to a compound that oxidizes air pollutants such as sulfur dioxide, carbon monoxide, and methane so they can be washed away from the air by rain. However, when carbon dioxide does not oxidize out of the atmosphere, it diffuses into the ocean, with resultant elevation in ocean temperatures (Lynas; Pearce; Sachs). Sachs, Pearce, and Lynas have attributed the following natural disasters to global warming: Hurricane Katrina, the 2003 European heat waves, the 2003 Midwestern U.S. flooding, droughts in Africa and Australia, the intensification of bush fires in Australia, grass fires in Florida, and forest fires in the western United States.

The rising population creates more demand for food, water, space, and goods. China, India, North Africa, and the United States pump more water than what can be replenished through snow and rain. Farmers overpump water for crops, and many industries (such as the paper industry) use enormous amounts of water for production. Crop, livestock, and consumer goods and production result in an increased release of nitrogen and phosphorus into the atmosphere and trigger acid rain. Trees become more susceptible to disease and damage from extreme temperatures, effects of acid rain, and reduced rainfall. Deterioration of dead trees results in the release of more carbon dioxide and methane into the atmosphere, resulting in even more global warming (Lynas, 2008; Pearce, 2007). The canopy of leaves absorbs carbon dioxide as well as moisture from the air. The consolidation of air moisture facilitates the development and falling of rain in tropical forests. Rainfall and snowfall account for most sources of freshwater for drinking (Lynas; Pearce; Sachs, 2008). Recent reports have identified various levels of human pharmaceuticals (analgesics, lipid regulators, beta-blockers, antidepressants, oral contraceptives, and antibiotics) being present in water treatment effluents, surface waters, groundwater, seawater, and some drinking waters around the world (Fent, Weston, & Caminada, 2006; Hemminger, 2005). In addition, urban sprawl impinges on available cropland and results in deforestation. Burning harvested trees releases more carbon and methane into the atmosphere, which increases global warming and also reduces rainfall (Lynas; Pearce; Sachs).

Urbanization increases the consumption of fossil fuels, which also contributes to global warming. Higher global temperatures result in increased ocean temperatures and acidity that destroy plankton and coral that fish rely on for survival (Lynas, 2008; Pearce, 2007; Sachs, 2008). From 1957 to 1997, the annual oceanic fish catch increased by 71 million tons, from 19 to 90 million tons. Many marine biologists theorize that the ocean cannot sustain an annual fish catch of more than 95 million tons (O'Meara, 2000). In addition, rising atmospheric carbon dioxide levels contribute to increased ocean acidity and temperatures, which further deplete fish supplies linked to the loss of plankton (the main diet for many fish) (Lynas; Pearce; Sachs).

As a global society, international efforts for global preservation have been formed by governmental, international, and private organizations. Governmental agencies and nongovernmental organizations frequently exert pressure on companies to clean up their acts. In 1992, the United Nations Framework Convention for Climate Change, an initiative to stabilize greenhouse gas emissions, was adopted. The U.S. Senate ratified the agreement in 1994 after President George H. W. Bush signed it. The Kyoto Protocol sought to reduce greenhouse emissions by 5% worldwide from 1997 to 2012. The protocol carried different guidelines for nations based on their wealth. Although adopted by the rest of the world, the United States never accepted it because of the perceived economic hardships that it would cause. In 2005, the Earth Institute of Columbia University sponsored a Global Roundtable on Climate Change (GRTOCC) as a means to combat global warming on an international scale. A scientific consensus statement arising from the GRTOCC specifies that "global warming is real and that it is caused by greenhouse gas emissions and primarily caused by our consumption of fossil fuels" (Sachs, 2008, p. 110). The GRTOCC outlined three methods to combat the issue of global warming: "mitigation, adaptation and research, development and demonstration (RD&D) of new technologies" (Sachs, p. 110). Genome pioneer Craig Ventner proposed making a bacterium that would eat carbon dioxide and produce fuel, which would be an excellent way to combat the impact of anthroponetic effects on the environment (Zakaria, 2008). However, safety concerns arise if the bacterium would mutate and produce disease or another toxic effect. Tough national standards can be undermined by less vigorous standards abroad. Deforestation in South America and Asia results in local and global environmental changes. Wood burning in China results in acid rain in Japan (Pearce, 2007; Sachs).

American hospitals produce approximately 6,000 tons of medical waste per day. According to the Environmental Protection Agency (2008), the health care industry is one of the major sources of mercury (found in medical equipment such as thermometers, sphygmomanometers, and endoscopes) and dioxin (from polyvinyl plastic materials) pollution. Other pollutants attributed to health care organizations include dead batteries, old computers, hazardous chemicals (cleaning products), and pharmaceuticals (chemotherapy, and radioactive isotopes) (Shaner & Botter, 2003).

In addition to formal governmental and international global efforts, nongovernmental organizations serve as environmental caretakers. Table 13-1 outlines several global environmental networks. Global networking among environmentalists provides the opportunity for global solutions to global problems. In addition to special interest groups, research universities such as the University of Michigan devote resources to ecosystem toxicology. By exploring microscopic changes in the environment, such as measuring the content of specific pesticides in marine life and avian eggshells, damage to the environment can be discovered before deformed animals are found and freshwater sources become hazardous to drink (Scully, 2001). Nurses can use information from these organizations to increase their awareness of global pollution, take steps to minimize pollution-promoting behaviors, and educate others about behaviors that may contribute to global pollution and destruction.

Environmental degradation indicates that the earth has undergone and is currently undergoing many changes as the result of human habitation. Ancient Greeks, Romans, Asians, and Native Americans viewed the world as a living organism. Traditional Native American and Eastern philosophies still espouse this belief. The Gaea hypothesis proposes that the difference between living and nonliving things is one of graded intensity and that the Earth remains the sole provider of resources for humans. Many environmentalists profess a world view of wholeness, in which each cell has equal value and is reflective of the entire cosmos. All cells within the environment interact and achieve a balance. Because everything is interconnected, all parts of the universe are equally important, and no organism should receive special status (Kleffel, 1994; Pearce, 2007). Unfortunately, human beings have appropriated a special status for themselves, and the environment has become the casualty of our self-interests.

TABLE 13-1

Global Environmental Organizations and Networks

Organization/Network	Purpose	Website
Environmental Defense Fund	Monitors and communicates the status of the environment. Creates an online data scorecard that ranks facilities, revealing the most offending polluters	www.scorecard.org
Association for Progressive Communications	Links nongovernmental organizations that promote human rights and environmental concerns with each other	www.apc.org
OneWorld Online	Links many websites to provide information on economic development	www.oneworld.net
UNEPnet	United Nations Environmental Programme (UNEP) offices are linked with other partner institutions by satellite to improve the flow of environmental data	www.centre.nep.net
Global Urban Observatory	Links researchers to a global network of data, statistics, and examples of best practices in urban management	http://www.unhabitat.org/programmes/guo/
HORIZON Solutions	Case studies on solutions related to water, waste, energy, transportation, toxic pollutants, public health, industrial, biodiversity, air pollution, and agricultural issues	www.solutions-site.org

Adapted from O'Meara, M. (2000). Harnessing information technologies for the environment. In L.R. Brown, C. Flavin, H. French, S. Postel, & L. Starke (Eds.), *State of the world 2000* (pp. 138–139). New York: W.W. Norton & Company.

Global Environmental Factors Threatening Health

Many global environmental factors threaten the health of people, plants, and animals. Professional nursing practice focuses on health promotion, as well as caring for the infirm. Nurses must become aware of environmental health risks. Many people drink chemical soups when they partake of water from local water supplies. Persons living in urban locales inhale chemical vapors, which results in an increased incidence of asthma, lung cancer, and other chronic pulmonary diseases. Agricultural workers have an increased incidence of lymphoma and other cancers that are linked to herbicide and pesticide exposure (McGinn, 2000).

Infectious diseases also pose health risks to persons. Many diseases have a higher prevalence in various geographical locations. For example, over 35 million persons have the human immunodeficiency virus (HIV). Of these, 23 million reside in sub-Saharan Africa. Women account for nearly half of the persons living with HIV. In sub-Saharan Africa, women constitute 60% of persons with HIV. Over 6 million persons residing in South and Southeast Asia are HIV positive. Unprotected sex and contaminated needles serve as the primary means of HIV infections for Asians and Africans (Quinn & Overbaugh, 2005).

Besides HIV, other infectious illnesses threaten humans. African mosquitos have evolved to bite only humans, resulting in a high incidence of malaria. In areas without medication for treatment or chemically treated nets for sleeping places, malaria infects over a billion and kills over a million persons (many of them children) annually (Sachs, 2008). Human Ebola virus outbreaks over the past 4 years have been confined to the Republic of Congo, Sudan, and Gabon, where hunters were infected by handling dead primates and subsequently spread it to other humans (LeRoy et al., 2004). The West Nile virus originated in Africa, but appeared in the United States when infected birds migrated to the United States. The birds transmitted the virus to mosquitoes, which then transmitted the virus to humans. However, documented cases of infection with West Nile virus have been linked to blood transfusions, organ donation, and breast milk (Bender & Thompson, 2003). Severe acute respiratory syndrome (SARS) is a human form of an avian flu that originated in the Chinese province of Guangdong. SARS spread rapidly across the globe because it is transmitted from human to human by inhaling respiratory droplets from infected persons. The close contact of humans during air flights facilitated its spread in 2003. Antibiotic-resistant bacteria (methicillin-resistant *Staphylococcus aureus* and vancomycin-resistant enterococcus) have arisen because of indiscriminate use of and client noncompliance with antibiotic therapy. Professional nurses and all health care workers bear the responsibility to contain the spread of infectious disease.

Along with infectious disease detection and containment, nurses and other health care providers must be aware of potential environmental health hazards. Table 13-2 outlines some environmental health hazards and potential remedies. Awareness of exposure to environmental toxins provides nurses with the ability to teach clients about ways to avoid long-term exposure to pollutants that sometimes result in devastating health consequences.

Global industrialization and urbanization affect the quality of the air and water. People become exposed to a variety of chemicals no matter where they live. The quality of air and water relies on international efforts. Irrigation and the use of herbicides and pesticides along the Colorado River in the Rocky Mountains affect the quality of water in Mexico. Industrial pollutants, medical waste, and other garbage dumped into the ocean near the United States may wash onto Canadian coastlines.

Some persons experience severe reactions to chemical exposures. Ordinary persons experience chemical injuries, environmental illnesses, and chemical hypersensitivities and allergies. Some persons experience sensitivities to many chemicals found in the environment; this condition is known as **multiple chemical sensitivity** (MCS) and is a recognized form of physical disability (Gibson, 2000; Cooper, 2007). For unknown reasons, persons with MCS have sustained "systemic damage that causes them to react negatively to common chemicals in ambient air" (Gibson, p. 8) and typically have a heightened sense of smell (Cooper). Reactions range from slight drowsiness or nasal congestion to potentially fatal asthmatic attacks. Display 13-1 outlines the criteria for MCS as determined by group consensus of 34 researchers and clinicians who treat MCS. Sensitivities frequently result from exposure to solvents, pesticides, formaldehyde, fresh paint, new carpets, gas exhaust (diesel, car, propane, and natural gas appliances), perfumes, scented cleaners, air fresheners, and food additives. Even processed lumber products used in new construction and electromagnetic fields from appliances can trigger reactions (Gibson). Gibson estimated that 11 million Americans have MCS and that 2% of these persons have lost jobs because of it. Persons with MCS frequently receive psychiatric diagnoses from health care providers. Reports of chemical sensitivity have been published in Denmark, Sweden, Norway, Finland, Germany, Holland, Belgium, Greece, and Great Britain (Gibson).

The cause of MCS appears to have a physiologic basis. For unknown reasons, the human body becomes damaged in response to repeated chemical exposures. The following physiologic theories related to the etiology of MCS have been proposed:

1. Nervous system damage as a result of repeated exposures
2. Limbic kindling through the olfactory-limbic system, resulting in triggered responses to repeated chemical exposure
3. Depletion of or damage to enzymatic production within the body
4. Repeated immunologic insults
5. Airway and neurogenic inflammation
6. Chronic candidiasis
7. Carbon monoxide poisoning
8. Electrical changes in the brain

TABLE 13-2

Environmental Health Hazards and Potential Remedies

Health Hazard	Geographical Locale(s)	Potential Remedy
Overpopulation	Ethiopia, Pakistan, Nigeria, India, South and Central America	Education about birth control Limitations on number of children Sterilization Abortion Drugs to prevent conception or induce abortion
Human immunodeficiency virus (HIV-AIDS)	Sub-Saharan Africa	HIV prevention education
Shrinking crop lands from soil erosion, persistent plant disease, and soil pollution	Worldwide	Environmentally sound agricultural practices
Deforestation	Brazil, Indonesia, Malaysia	Reduce demand for paper, lumber, and fuel wood
Increasing carbon dioxide atmospheric concentrations	Worldwide	Human population control Reduce demand for fossil fuel Reforestation
Global warming	Worldwide	Reduce demand for fossil fuel Reforestation Reduce demand for paper, lumber, and fuel wood
Reduced fish population	Worldwide with profound implications in the East	Curb release of industrial waste chemicals into oceans, lakes and waterways Judicious use of pesticides Reduce global warming Enforce fishing catch limits
Falling water tables	China, India, North Africa, Saudi Arabia, United States	Find ways to reduce use of water in industrial production; water conservation efforts; paper recycling; and reduce agricultural crop irrigation
Ozone depletion	Worldwide	Limit demand for fossil fuel Avoid use of aerosol products containing fluorocarbons Eliminate freon from air conditioning and refrigeration systems
Air pollution	Worldwide	Reduce use of coal, wood, and petroleum products for fuel sources Use hydrogen as an alternative fuel source Use solar and wind power plants Consider taxation for usage of polluting fuels
Malnutrition Undernourished	Africa, Asia, Latin America, the Caribbean, and especially Bangladesh, India, Ethiopia, Vietnam, Nigeria, Indonesia	Promote breastfeeding efforts, improve pre-natal care, find a way to alleviate poverty, examine and correct food distribution problems
Overnourished	United States, Russian Federation, United Kingdom, Germany, Columbia, Brazil (adults)	Educate about health hazards of fast and highly processed foods, reduce food portion sizes, limit advertisements of food aimed at children, adopt a "junk food" tax

(continued)

Environmental Health Hazards and Potential Remedies (Continued)

Health Hazard	Geographical Locale(s)	Potential Remedy
Persistent organic pollutants (dioxins, polychlorinated biphenyls, and furans)	Russia, Japan, Holland, Belgium	Intensive recycling of batteries, electrical wiring, transformers, computers; limit use of incinerators; institute laws for business and agricultural use of these products; paper recycling; autoclaves for sterilization; barriers such as nets or steel meshes for insect control; larvae-eating fish, selected natural pests for agriculture; use of environmentally friendly pesticides
Chlorine (plastics, polyvinyl chloride)	Worldwide	Recycle products containing plastic and reduce demand for products made from plastic
Latex	Health care institutions, day care centers, schools	Latex-free health care products; ban latex balloons
DDT	Central Asia, India, China, Columbia, Ecuador	Crop rotation and use of environmentally friendly pesticides and herbicides

Adapted from Brown, L.R., Flavin, C., French, H., Postel, S., & Starke, L. (Eds.). (2000). *State of the world 2000.* New York: W.W. Norton & Company.

Along with the physiologic theories, the following psychological theories have surfaced:

1. Psychological and behavioral conditioning
2. Odor conditioning
3. Increased vulnerability related to preexisting anxiety and depression
4. Amplification of symptoms
5. Negative affectivity
6. Personality disorders
7. Somatization disorder
8. Childhood trauma
9. Excessively focused thought patterns and cognitions on chemicals

Practitioners who espouse a physiologic theory think that avoidance of chemicals is the only way to avoid continued health deterioration. Some health care professionals believe that MCS is a psychiatric disorder. They think that chemical avoidance enables persons with MCS to obsess about their disorder and become socially isolated. However, personality disturbances and panic attacks have been documented in workers exposed to organic solvents, and these problems may be the result of nervous system injury (Gibson, 2000; Cooper, 2007).

Criteria for Multiple Chemical Sensitivity Diagnosis

DISPLAY 13-1

Identical symptoms are reproduced with repeated exposure to the same chemical.
Reactions are chronic.
Low levels of exposure to the offending chemical produce manifestations of the reactive symptoms.
When the offending chemicals are removed, the symptoms lessen or resolve.

Reactions occur to multiple, unrelated chemical substances.
Reaction symptoms affect multiple organ systems.

Adapted from Gibson, P. R. (2000). *Multiple chemical sensitivity: A survival guide* (p. 9). Oakland, CA: New Harbinger.

Foods consumed by humans (especially those in developed countries) contain an array of additives and contaminants. To increase crop yields, many farmers use a variety of herbicides and pesticides; farmers also genetically manipulate crops. To improve meat production, some farmers use bovine growth hormone feed to maximize livestock growth and development. Many preservatives protect the consumer from foodborne infections. Persons who try to lose weight consume artificial sweeteners, such as aspartame and saccharin. To increase the visual appeal of food, some manufacturers use artificial dyes. Some foods contain flavor enhancers such as monosodium glutamate. Although some food chemicals reduce the risk of foodborne disease, others merely create another human chemical exposure (Gibson, 2000).

The Professional Nurse's Role in Promoting a Healthy Global Environment

Sachs (2008) and Papp (2007) identified nurses as key human resources to confront the future challenges of improving the health and well-being of all. Nurses possess communication and clinical skills to help persons understand ways to promote a healthy global environment. The profession of nursing has global nurse leaders who have made key differences in the well-being of persons around the world. Research Brief 13-1 identifies factors that contribute to the successful endeavors of global nurse leaders. As current global nurses retire, the profession needs to develop future ones.

Research Brief 13-1

Kim, J., Woith, W., Otten, K., & McElmurry, B. (2006). Global nurse leaders: Lessons from the sages. *Advances in Nursing Science, 29*(1), 27–42.

Using literature to develop a survey of 17 nurse leaders, the investigators used a descriptive survey design to identify major factors associated with the development of nurse global leaders. Seventeen nurses participated in the study interviews, which consisted of four open-ended items that addressed life experiences that shaped them as leaders, their first international nursing experience, other experiences that prepared them for international leadership, and childhood events that they believed contributed to their effectiveness as international nurses.

The audiotaped interviews were transcribed, and content analysis was performed by each member of the research team with a group team meeting to review and verify the interpretations. The team discovered the following factors that influenced the participants' perceptions of factors contributing to their success as global nurse leaders: (1) being open-minded and flexible; (2) learning continuously from others, displaying cultural awareness, sensitivity, and interest; (3) dealing with complexity effectively; (4) setting high aspirations; (5) displaying resiliency, optimism, and energy; (6) being honest; (7) having integrity; (8) coming from a stable personal family life in which they experienced lots of encouragement and support; (9) sharing nursing knowledge and expertise with others; (10) being politically savvy; (11) having the patience to wait for others to assume responsibility; (12) participating in leadership roles as a child; (13) having a mentor who challenged them to excel; (14) having informal and formal education and training for global competencies; and (15) believing with conviction and passion the importance of their work.

Results of this study should be viewed with caution because of the small sample size; however, the study does shed light on how to develop future global nurse leaders. This is important because all nurses, no matter where they practice, encounter similar situations and dilemmas in professional practice.

Musker (1994) proposed a life of voluntary simplicity—a holistic, ecologically based lifestyle—to create a healing environment. In the voluntary simplicity outlook, "less is more," and persons focus on the quality of life, rather than the quantity of consumer products (contrary to Western culture, in which some think "more is better"). Voluntary simplicity consists of inner and outer processes. The inner process consists of the process of "mindfulness" and requires deep self-reflection to attend to personal needs and to separate them from personal desires. In this inner process, persons discover their genuine, authentic self and discard the illusion of their preconceived self. Some persons keep journals to discover patterns of behavior. The external process consists of the process of "doing," which results in responsible life behaviors that serve the world, rather than pure self-interest. As the inner and outer processes fuse, being becomes doing, and doing becomes being. Voluntary action involves purposeful life choices by eliminating automatic ones. Simplification of life involves reducing overall consumption, purchasing durable and easily repaired products, consuming a more natural diet, pursuing work that contributes to the world while using more individual creativity and capacities, and changing transportation habits. Simplification also means releasing mental clutter, emotional baggage, useless worries, and other concerns that distract from enjoying the present.

As individual global citizens, professional nurses can model environmentally friendly behaviors. Table 13-3 offers some suggestions for preventing pollution and conserving environmental resources. When possible, nurses should look for ways to reduce energy consumption, recycle discarded products, and limit purchases to reusable items.

THE COMMUNITY ENVIRONMENT

Multiple environmental factors affect the health of the community. Community services that enhance health include public health departments, disease prevention services, and social support services. The individual health status of community residents relies on the quality of the physical and social community environments. For the purposes of this discussion, the **community environment** refers to the geographical location where people live and work.

Questions for Reflection 13-2

1. Do I have any personal habits that may be potentially toxic to the global environment?
2. What could I do differently to change my environmentally unsafe behaviors?

Community Environmental Factors Threatening Health

Although the local community provides health services to promote community health, most communities also have environmental factors that threaten the health of citizens. Heavy traffic and industrial fumes pollute the air. Some municipalities and counties use pesticides to prevent the spread of insect-borne illnesses. High-tension power lines and power stations emit electromagnetic fields (Gibson, 2000; Pearce, 2007; Sachs, 2008).

Along with business and industry, the level of affluence within the community affects the health of individuals and families. The income of citizens enables communities to maintain infrastructure and provide services to enhance health. However, affluence can negatively affect health. Since 1980, Americans have increased the annual mileage on their cars by 80%. Many persons have long commutes from their suburban homes to their workplaces. In 2008, skyrocketing gasoline and diesel fuel prices have resulted in the decreased use of motor vehicles and the increased use of mass transit systems. Traffic jams contribute to road rage and increased pollution.

Automobiles make it convenient to drive short distances, resulting in individuals getting less exercise from walking or cycling. For many Americans, the ease of obtaining high-calorie foods quickly contributes to an unhealthy diet. The combination of physical

TABLE 13-3

Suggestions to Curb Pollution and Conserve Resources

Environmental Goal	Suggestions
Clean air	Reduce gasoline vapors by replacing cracked gas caps and do not top off fuel tanks Refuel vehicles in the evening, decreasing exposure of gas vapors to sun Repair any systems in vehicles or appliances that leak Carpool Avoid purchasing products with chlorofluorocarbons, polystyrene, methyl chloroform, and freon Use a push or electric-powered lawn mower Mow lawn in the evening Use water-based rather than latex paints
Oil conservation	Use fuel with octane rating recommended for vehicle and not a higher one Limit vehicle warm-ups to 30 seconds Recycle oil and purchase recycled oil Keep tires inflated to manufacturer's specifications Carpool Purchase vehicles with best available mileage ratings Keep vehicles tuned up Fit vehicles with radial tires
Land	Purchase products containing at least 25% recycled materials Buy canned soup instead of instant soups Buy products made of wood, cotton, or wool instead of plastics Use a durable shopping bag Reuse shopping bags Choose cloth instead of paper napkins and cleaning rags Wrap sandwiches in wax paper instead of plastic wrap Use reusable food containers, plates, and utensils Purchase a reusable coffee filter rather than paper ones Compost vegetable scraps with yard waste Use unbleached paper items when paper products are used Buy pet food in bulk
General resources	Consume less meat and eat foods lower on the food chain Use durable coffee mugs and drink containers
Energy	Seal any appliance seals that contain cracks Bake in glass or ceramic dishes Thaw frozen foods in the refrigerator Cool leftovers before refrigeration Use self-cleaning oven cycle immediately after baking Clean clothes dryer filter and hoses regularly Dry several loads of clothes in succession or hang clothes outside to dry Use natural sunlight or fluorescent bulbs for lighting Close blinds, shades, and curtains during the summer Place air conditioners in a shady location Keep air conditioner vents free of debris Service furnaces and air conditioners regularly Change furnace and air conditioner filters every 4 months Keep freezers full of food Cap stored liquids in the refrigerator Install a hot water tank timer Wrap an insulation blanket around hot water heater Attach a timer to home thermostat Install solar panels Turn off unused lights and appliances

(continued)

Suggestions to Curb Pollution and Conserve Resources (Continued)

Environmental Goal	Suggestions
Energy (continued)	Install compact fluorescent bulbs in light fixtures Tighten and insulate cooling and heating ducts Keep attic well ventilated by using turbine or screen vents Repair foundation cracks Use air drying setting on dishwasher Use short cycles for laundry and dishwasher loads whenever possible
Forests	Recycle paper Buy recycled paper products Use durable cups and drinking containers Use both sides of paper Institute a sharing program for books, magazines, and other periodicals Store information on computers rather than on hard copies Check out books and periodicals from the library
Water	Water lawn only when absolutely necessary and use a deep soak watering technique Drip irrigate gardens Mulch around trees and plants Use natural pesticides and herbicides Leave grass clippings on lawn Turn off water when brushing your teeth Install low-flow shower heads and aerators on faucets Rinse razor in a filled sink rather than a running tap Inspect toilets and faucets for leaks and fix them promptly Clean driveways and garages with a broom instead of a hose

Adapted from *Simple Steps for Individuals*, a publication from Choose Environmental Excellence, which is part of Bridging the Gap Inc., Kansas City, MO.

inactivity and excessive food intake has resulted in 23% of adults and 16% of children in the United States having a body mass index of 30% or higher than the criteria for obesity. Reasons for obesity include heredity, metabolism, behavior, environment, culture, and socioeconomics (U.S. Department of Health and Human Services, 2000).

The U.S. Department of Health and Human Services (2000) reported that 120 million Americans lived in areas where exposure to air pollutants, including ozone-exceeded governmental health standards. The same report indicated that a disproportionate number of Hispanic and Pacific Islanders lived in these areas.

Although pesticides may result in environmental pollution, they play a key role in preventing infectious disease epidemics. Surveillance and control of insect-borne illnesses require expenditures of public revenue. Revenue for epidemic prevention comes from federal, state, and local sources. In recent years, the West Nile virus has been linked to insects that infect birds, and Lyme disease has been linked to insects that infect deer (Enserink, 2001). Professional nurses frequently participate in the development of community educational programs or community service announcements to help citizens avoid contracting these infectious diseases. The proper application of pesticides limits environmental damage. Responsibility for the proper use of pesticides lies with companies who secure community contracts and homeowners.

To eliminate the risk of foodborne illness, local health departments license businesses and organizations that serve food. Poor handwashing by persons handling food has led to outbreaks of hepatitis A, salmonella, and *Escherichia coli* infections. Foodborne illnesses also occur when persons fail to abide by guidelines for food storage and safe preparation.

The potential for the spread of infectious illnesses, such as tuberculosis, influenza, and viral or bacterial meningitis, is increased in persons subjected to overcrowded conditions. College dormitories, schools, and child day care centers also provide residence for a variety of disease-causing organisms.

In addition to the threats to the physical integrity of communities, social problems also threaten human health. Poverty, substance abuse, incivility, and moral decay have led to a decline in communities. Violence occurs in urban, rural, and suburban settings. In urban areas, violence is the leading cause of death in young African American men. Among industrialized nations, the United States has the highest rate of childhood homicides (U.S. Department of Health and Human Services, 2000). In most instances, victims of homicide know their killers. Domestic, child, and elder abuse occur in all socioeconomic groups but occur more frequently when families struggle to have basic human needs met (food, water, and shelter). In addition to economic factors, the media expose persons to acts of violence in movies, fictional television programs, cartoons, and newscasts, and some computer and video games use violence as entertainment. As individuals are repeatedly exposed to images of violence, victims of violent crime become depersonalized, and violence becomes a part of life.

School shootings have occurred across the United States (Colorado, Oregon, Arkansas, Tennessee, Georgia, Kentucky, and Mississippi). Most of the shooters came from middle-class homes with two parents, and most used guns found in their homes. Preventive measures against teen violence focus on parents and include limiting teen exposure to violent movies, television programs, and video games. Experts place emphasis on parents spending quality time with their children, serving as role models for them, and teaching them ethical and moral behavior (Steger, 2000).

Social interactions vary according to the type of communities in which persons reside. Persons tend to socialize more with persons who share similar life situations. In working-class neighborhoods (especially when adults of households are both employed), relationships tend to be more casual. Time constraints present challenges for maintaining relationships with neighbors. Schools and churches provide opportunities for persons with similar values to develop relationships.

The Professional Nurse's Role in Promoting a Healthy Community Environment

Professional nurses play key roles in promoting a healthy community environment. Nurses assess communities for actual and potential factors that are noxious to human health and well-being. When noxious factors are identified, nurses can inform community members, provide community education, and take action to eliminate them. Nurses can also inspire other community members to incorporate health promotion activities into their lives. Reporting local health hazards, such as deteriorating road conditions, the need for reduced speed limits, or dangerous intersections that need traffic signs or signals, helps to prevent motor vehicle and pedestrian accidents. Nurses, like all citizens, have the freedom and obligation to attend local governmental meetings to express concerns related to community development projects. By participating in community cleanup programs, nurses reduce the community's risk of injury from exposure to broken glass, used needles, and sharp metal objects, and risk of infectious illnesses from exposure to rotting food.

Nurses also can become active participants in local school, civic, and church activities to foster mental health and offer safe recreation for persons of all ages. As an act against societal violence, nurses can refuse to purchase products that use violence as entertainment, buy products from companies that advertise their products during violent television programs, or attend movies or plays that glorify violence. When working with teens, nurses should be alert to any precursors of imminent violent acts, including inappropriate angry outbursts, cruelty to animals, essays with violent themes, fascination with weapons (especially firearms), obsession with playing violent computer games, threats to harm self or others, vandalism (even of their own property), assumption of the victim role, involvement in fringe groups or gangs, behavior with the goal of getting suspended or expelled, and incidents of bringing weapons to show to other students. Teaching violence awareness, stress management, self-esteem, gun safety, substance abuse prevention, and cultural diversity classes in the community serves as a means to eliminate violence in society (Steger, 2000). Nurses also can serve as resources to local schools for violence prevention, violence recovery, and other health promotion programs. Finally, nurses can lobby local, state, and federal legislative bodies to protect environmental health.

Questions for Reflection 13-3

1. How would I rate the health of my local community based on the information presented previously?
2. What community resources are available to me as a citizen and professional nurse to improve the environment of my local community?
3. What strategies could I use to promote a healthy community environment?

THE WORK ENVIRONMENT

Many persons spend more time in the workplace than they do at home. The quality of the **work environment** relies on physical and cultural factors. National, state, and local laws protect worker safety. Individual organizations have policies that guide worker behaviors and inform workers of potential health hazards.

Work Environmental Factors Threatening Health

Many offices and work settings contain factors that threaten the physiologic, psychological, and spiritual health of employees and consumers. Some industries and manufacturers rely on chemicals and solvents to produce products. Some jobs require workers to perform repetitive movements. According to the U.S. Occupational Safety and Health Administration (OSHA, 2007), each year 1.8 million workers in the United States experience work-related disabling musculoskeletal disorders. Nelson, Fragala, and Menzel (2003) reported that nursing-related back pain occurs in 47% of all American nurses. They also project that nurses will have more back pain as they care for more obese clients. Other common injuries sustained by nurses in clinical practice include overexertion (including lifting too much), falls or slips, twisting injuries, bruises or lacerations from being struck by or against objects, injuries from violent acts, harmful substance exposure, transportation accidents, repetitive motion insults, and compression injuries. Nurses also have a six times higher suicide rate than the general population (Belanger, 2000).

Tasks required for patient care performed by professional nurses in hospitals create an "ergonomic nightmare" (Trossman, 2000, p. 1). Many nurses work 12-hour shifts and experience repetitive movement stress from lifting and turning patients, entering data into computers (for electronic documentation systems), drawing up parenteral medications, pumping up sphygmomanometers, resetting monitor alarms, and moving heavy equipment.

In addition to the potential for disabling musculoskeletal disorders, nurses are exposed to dangerous chemicals in the work setting. In recent years, an increase in latex allergies in health care providers, ancillary personnel, and clients has been reported. Currently, there are more than 40,000 consumer products containing latex, including gloves, clothing, intravenous supplies, medication vials, urinary catheters, feeding tubes, endotracheal tubes, carpeting, furniture, blood pressure cuffs, tape, balloons, condoms, and chewing gum (Dyck, 2000; Kellet, 1997; Kim, Graves, Safadi, Alhadeff, & Metcalfe, 1998; Lee & Kim, 1998). Since 1998, most medical devices containing latex must be appropriately labeled to protect persons sensitive to latex (Kim et al., 1998). Just using a latex-containing product exposes the professional nurse at risk for latex sensitization and future latex allergy (Lee & Kim). Kim, Wellmeyer, and Miller (1999) reported that as many as 17% of health care workers may have a latex allergy. Most have cutaneous allergic responses, but 1.3% of health care workers with latex allergy have allergic asthmatic responses with exposure. However, vinyl gloves tend to tear more readily than do latex ones. In addition, vinyl gloves release toxic environmental substances such as dioxin. Nitrile, neoprene, and thermoplastic gloves offer protection equal to that offered by latex gloves. However, like latex, these products may trigger allergic reactions, because their chemical composition is similar (Worthington, 2000).

Depending on their practice area, nurses are exposed to dangerous chemicals other than latex. These are summarized in Table 13-4. OSHA has published standards for safe handling of all dangerous chemicals used in the workplace. In addition, nurse specialty organizations publish guidelines for safe practice use, which usually are covered in nurse specialty certification examinations. Antineoplastic agents may cause birth defects, allergic reactions, and skin, eye, and mucous membrane irritation. Chemicals used for sterilization and anesthesia have been associated with cancer development, birth defects, spontaneous abortion, respiratory tract irritation, central nervous system symptoms, dermatitis, eye irritation, liver dysfunction, and renal disorders (Papp, 2007).

In addition to chemical and radiation exposure, infectious diseases pose a hazard to nurses and other health care workers. Nurses have the potential to contract hepatitis B and HIV from a percutaneous stick with a contaminated needle or other sharp implement. Strategies for preventing such an event include strict adherence to OSHA Bloodborne Pathogen Standards and hepatitis B vaccination. Nurses may encounter hepatitis A if they work in places where personal hygiene may be poor. Effective handwashing serves as the best method for preventing contraction of this virus. In recent years, nurse exposures to pulmonary illnesses such as SARS and tuberculosis (TB) have increased. Contributing factors for resurgence in cases of TB include the acquired immunodeficiency syndrome (AIDS) epidemic, immigration, homelessness, and the development of drug-resistant strains. Diligent attention to isolation procedures and wearing special ventilation masks decrease the chance of contracting TB. SARS is contracted from infected persons via inhaled respiratory droplets. Measles, rubella, mumps, and influenza also threaten the health of nurses as they engage in professional practice. To protect nurses, determination of immune status and offering appropriate immunizations eliminate the risk of contracting most of these diseases (Papp, 2007). However, nurses bear the responsibility for protecting their health by following specific isolation techniques and using protective devices when caring for clients with potentially contagious diseases.

Along with contracting illnesses from clients, nurses come into contact with many organisms that cause nosocomial infections. Vancomycin-resistant enterococcus and methicillin-resistant *S. aureus* thrive in hospital environments. Frequently, nurses may be colonized with these organisms, but because of immunocompetence, infection does not develop. Other infections that threaten the health of nurses include herpes zoster and *Clostridium difficile*. Diligent isolation practices, meticulous handwashing, and habits to promote immunocompetence protect nurses from catching infectious diseases from clients or the work environment.

Nurses also experience stress in the workplace. The following workplace factors contribute to the work-related stress encountered by nurses:

1. Making decisions that may result in life or death
2. Working with clients in pain
3. Working with demanding clients
4. Understaffing

TABLE 13-4

Strategies to Prevent Health Hazards in Nursing Environments

Health Hazard	Prevention Strategies
Needle stick injuries	Use needleless systems for IV therapy when possible Use syringes with recapping devices for intramuscular, subcutaneous, and intradermal injections Replace containers for used needles before they become more than two-thirds full
Back and shoulder injuries	Evaluate all clients for weight-bearing status and mobility before moving or lifting them Use assistive devices (such as mechanical lifts, slide boards, and sheets) and engineering controls properly Verify that enough help is present before lifting, transferring, or ambulating clients Take time to raise beds and equipment to a comfortable working level Provide training on proper body mechanics from physical therapy departments for employees Redesign work stations to provide ergonomically sound charting stations for standing and sitting Provide supportive chairs for seated activities Negotiate for ergonomically sound workplace practices Lobby state legislators to enact ergonomic legislation
Repetitive stress injuries	Increase worker and administrator awareness on how repetitive movements may result in musculoskeletal injury
Carpal tunnel syndrome	Avoid long time periods for computer data entry Provide wrist support devices for computer mouse and keyboards Teach employees wrist-stretching exercises
Blood-borne infections	Use needleless and recapping syringe devices
Air-borne infections	Use and change masks Provide respirator masks for specific infections Separate ventilation units for isolation rooms
Other infections	Make soap and water accessible for handwashing Make alcohol-based hand cleansers accessible
Latex	Persuade employer to remove as many latex-containing supplies from the organization as possible Use latex-free gloves exclusively Follow extensive rinse procedures for any equipment rinsed with gluteraldehyde solutions and wear gloves not containing vinyl or latex Encourage coworkers to refrain from touching telephone, intercom, and other equipment buttons and light switches while wearing latex gloves
Hazardous chemicals Antineoplastics	Follow OSHA and Oncology Nurses Society guidelines for safe handling of chemotherapeutic agents
Ethylene oxide, formaldehyde and glutaraldehyde (sterilization chemicals)	Follow OSHA guidelines
Anesthetic gases (especially nitrous oxide)	Follow National Institute of Occupational Safety and Health recommendations for exposure limits
Mercury	Do not touch mercury with hands. Request published standards for mercury disposal from environmental services or housekeeping departments
Bleach and other disinfectant cleaners	Wear gloves when cleaning surfaces using bleach and be certain that the work location is well ventilated

Strategies to Prevent Health Hazards in Nursing Environments (Continued)

Health Hazard	Prevention Strategies
Radiation	Limit exposure by using lead shields, keeping distance between self and radiation source, and limiting time spent in areas where radiation exposure may occur. The Nuclear Regulatory Commission (NRC) has set maximum exposure at 3 rem every 3 months for safe exposure. If radiation dose exceeds exposure limit, workers are to be reassigned to work without radiation exposure risk. OSHA has guidelines for workers not covered by the NRC
Suicide	Monitor self and others for addictive behaviors (including cigarettes) Talk to colleagues when intensively critical situations arise or when they are resolved Be alert for colleagues who appear preoccupied with death or say they wish they were dead Practice stress management and relaxation techniques Do not be afraid to confront colleagues when suicidal warning signs occur and refer them to mental health professionals

Adapted from Shaner, H. (1994). Environmentally responsible clinical practice. In E.A. Schuster & C.L. Brown (Eds.), *Exploring our environmental connections practice* (pp. 233–251). NLN Publication No. 14-2634. New York: National League for Nursing. Belanger, D. (2000). Nurses and suicide: The risk is real. *RN, 63,* 61–64. Kim, K.T., Graves, P.B., Safadi. G.S., Alhadeff, G., & Metcalfe, J. (1998). Implementation recommendations for making health care facilities latex safe. *AORN Journal, 67,* 615–632. Papp, E. (2007). *Occupational health and safety management programme for nurses.* Geneva, Switzerland: International Council of Nurses.

5. Rotating shifts
6. Working long shifts (12 hours or more)
7. Completing client documentation in a timely fashion
8. Keeping current in the areas of pharmacology, technology, nursing standards, and procedural changes
9. Dealing with authoritative managers
10. Working with unlicensed personnel
11. Being eliminated from participating in decisions that affect nursing care delivery
12. Coping with client deaths
13. Feeling unappreciated by other health team members
14. Practicing nursing without the time to establish meaningful and therapeutic client relationships
15. Delegating tasks that serve as a source of accomplishment
16. Dealing with reduced client length of stay (inpatient settings)
17. Working in uncivil work settings

In any setting, people cannot avoid stress. However, individuals perceive stress differently (Lazarus & Folkman, 1984), and those perceptions may affect physical and mental health (McLean, 1974).

Questions for Reflection 13-4

1. How would I rate the health of my work environment based on the information presented in this chapter?
2. In what ways have I promoted a healthy work environment within the past month?
3. What are factors in my work environment that negatively affect the health of me and my coworkers?
4. What strategies could I take in the future to promote a healthy work environment?

Violence in the Workplace

According to the International Council of Nurses (ICN, 2006), professional nurses world-wide have been victims of violence. Forms of workplace violence encountered by nurses include physical assault, verbal abuse, bullying, mobbing, and sexual harassment. Nurses can be assaulted physically or verbally by clients, family members, their friends, physicians, administrators, and coworkers. On rare occasions, nurses and other health team members have been assaulted or shot by a client visitor when caring for an injured party from an act of gang violence (Carroll, 2004). According to the ICN (2006), the high-est incidence of physical assault occurs in an American emergency department (36% of nurses reported being physically assaulted). Surveys of nurses reveal that incidences of psychological abuse and sexual harassment range from 24% to 91% (Bartholomew, 2006; ICN; Papp, 2007; Sutton, 2006). Forty to 70% of nurses who encounter violence in the workplace suffer from posttraumatic stress disorder (Bartholomew; ICN; Papp). In ear-lier times, nurses considered working with violent persons to be part of the job. Recent initiatives by health care administrators, nurses, and collective bargaining units have resulted in zero tolerance for workplace violence. In the United States, some states have passed legislation requiring health care facilities to provide a safe work environment, including provisions for rapid response teams to handle situations with a high potential to become violent. Efforts to promote a violence-free workplace include zero tolerance for physical violence, sexual harassment, or verbal abuse. Staff education may include the definition of what constitutes an act of violence, triggers of violent acts, causes of violent behaviors, assessment of potentially violent situations, signs and symptoms of anger, phases of the assault cycle, conflict resolution strategies, techniques to disrupt escalating violent behavior, strategies for effective intervention for potentially violent situations, procedures for reporting acts of violence, and techniques of medical and physical restraint (as a last resort). Some health care organizations have rapid response teams to deploy during situations when basic conflict management strategies fail and nurses (and other health care providers) feel threatened. The team consists of persons with advanced education in conflict management and resolution.

Prevention is the best protection against workplace violence. Study results indicate that there is no "reliable tool to predict the potential for violence" (ICN, 2006, p. 15). How-ever, a history of violent behavior seems to be a predictor. Therefore, flagging the charts of clients with a history of assaultive or disruptive behavior alerts staff to the potential for violence should conflict arise. Clearly written policies and procedures offer staff actions to take to avoid and report acts of violence. The organization keeps records of actual and alleged acts of violence. Confidentiality of reports of violence must be ensured so that incidents involving supervisors and/or physicians will be reported. After an act of violence occurs, a debriefing session is useful to determine potential causes of the event, review steps taken, help victims cope with the effects, and determine if follow-up counsel-ing or education is warranted (Bartholomew, 2006; ICN; Papp, 2007; Sutton, 2006).

The Professional Nurse's Role in Promoting a Healthy Work Environment

Before a nurse can promote a healthy work environment, he or she must become cogni-zant of actual and potential hazards in the workplace. The nurse should assess the work setting systematically to identify the quality of the work environment, paying close atten-tion to its impact on worker physical, mental, and spiritual health. When nurses identify actual or potential health hazards, they should educate staff about them and make refer-rals to persons who can eliminate them. The nurse has an ethical obligation to protect the health of all health team members. The nurse should validate that governmental guide-lines to protect workers and clients are followed and take risks to advocate for change when needed.

Along with protecting the physical health of coworkers, nurses play a key role in pro-moting the mental and spiritual health of colleagues and client care team members.

Health team members sometimes encounter ethical dilemmas, especially when they work in health care organizations that emphasize profits over client care quality, find themselves being unable to provide services to all persons in need of health care, and have to make decisions on how best to use new technology in clinical practice. These conditions create an unhealthy work environment characterized by little or no commitment, worker rebellion, deflated morale, workplace anger, worker disengagement, inferior problem solving, and sloppy client care (Wilson & Porter-O'Grady, 1999). Hierarchical relationships among health team members (physicians, nurses, administrators, and unlicensed personnel) compound the problem of unhealthy work environments (Bartholomew, 2006; Watkins & Mohr, 2001; Wesorick, Shiparski, Troseth, & Wyngarden, 1997; Wilson & Porter-O'Grady, 1999). When persons deeply connect with each other to do important work, a healthy work environment emerges (Watkins & Mohr; Wesorick et al., 1997). Client care in any setting is important work. When nurses and other team members focus all efforts on what is best for clients, they become united in purpose. Finding meaning in one's existence nourishes the human spirit (Frankl, 1970). When coworkers share the same meaning in work, they connect on a spiritual level (Wesorick et al.).

Efforts to create this healthy work environment require personal commitment, cooperative efforts with others, and a courageous attitude to express genuine authenticity. Wesorick and colleagues (1997, p. 9) have identified the following three characteristics to connect souls and create healthy work cultures: (1) shared meaning and purpose in work, (2) healthy relationships, and (3) meaningful conversations. Identification of shared meaning and purpose in work requires that everyone working together is aware of and agrees to what matters most in their work. Wesorick and colleagues (pp. 14–15) defined healthy relationships as partnerships and outlined the following six basic partnership principles:

1. Intention: a personal decision to connect with another at the deepest level of humanness
2. Mission: a calling to live out something that deeply matters or is meaningful
3. Equal accountability: mutual ownership of the mission without one person having power over or instilling fear in another
4. Potential: the human capacity of all (including oneself) persons to continuously learn, grow, and create
5. Balance: harmonious relationships with self and others required to attain the mission
6. Trust: synchronous sense on important things or issues that matter

Wesorick and colleagues (1997) outlined meaningful conversation as the vehicle for developing healthy and meaningful relationships in work settings. Participants engaging in dialogue feel welcomed and honored while they share ideas, thoughts, and feelings. In dialogue, messages are deeply listened to and not judged. The partnership approach to clinical practice has the potential to transform a toxic work setting for all health team members to one that promotes health in body, mind, and spirit.

In 1983, the American Academy of Nursing embarked on identifying "magnet" hospitals that deliver excellent client care, recruit and retain professional nurses, and provide an empowering environment for nurses. Using descriptive research methods, the American Academy of Nursing derived eight essential elements that distinguished magnets from other hospitals. According to Kramer and Schmalenberg (2004, p. 50), the eight essentials are (1) support for education, (2) working with other nurses who are clinically competent, (3) positive nurse–physician relationships, (4) autonomous nursing practice, (5) a culture that values concern for the patient, (6) control of and over nursing practice, (7) perceived adequacy of staffing, and (8) nurse manager support (enumeration added). Kramer and Schmalenberg (2002) and McClure and Hinshaw (2007) identified that health care organizations that held Magnet Status had an increased ability to recruit and retain nurses even in the era of health care cost containment. Some nurses apply only for positions in health care organizations that hold Magnet Status because these organizations value nurse contributions to health care delivery.

Questions for Reflection 13-5

1. How would I rate the environment of my home based on the information presented in this chapter?
2. What things could I change in my home to promote a healthy home environment?

THE HOME ENVIRONMENT

The **home environment** plays a key role in human health. A family's home creates a haven for individual autonomy and control. Some consider the home as an extension of their personal identity. The quality of the physical structure, general cleanliness, storage of chemicals, and interpersonal relationships affect the health of individual family members.

Home Environmental Factors Threatening Health

Persons seek safe living quarters. Even the homeless find some way to stay warm and dry. Persons with established residences live in single- or multiple-family dwellings. Homes may be purchased or rented. The home's arranged floor plan provides family members with space for privacy, sleeping, and interaction. In American culture, social status and self-esteem are linked to the home. Homeowners (or landlords) bear the responsibility for repairs to maintain environmental safety.

Accidents occur frequently in the home. The types of accidents vary according to the age and developmental level of family members. The structural integrity of stairs, railings, ceilings, walls, and furniture must be assessed periodically to prevent injury. Safe storage and proper labeling of cleaning products and medications are critical in homes with young children. Homes with throw rugs create hazards for falls, especially for the elderly. Fire safety relies on periodic inspection and maintenance of household appliances, working smoke detectors, storage of paper and flammable materials away from furnaces or other appliances that could generate sparks, and clear home entrances and exits.

The home can be a source of illness, as well as the scene of accidents. Problems with cleanliness and personal hygiene result in outbreaks of infectious disease. An estimated 30 million cases of foodborne illnesses, resulting in 9,000 deaths, occur each year in the United States. Salmonella, *E. coli* (especially *E. coli* 0157:H7 found in raw ground beef), and *P. aeruginosa* thrive on many kitchen counters (Rutala, Barbee, Aguiar, Sobsey, & Weber, 2000). Adequate water supply, plumbing, refrigeration, garbage disposal, and general household cleaning practices reduce infections in the home. Handwashing after using the toilet and before food preparation and eating remains the most effective measure for the prevention of infectious illness in the home. Proper kitchen counter cleaning using commercially prepared disinfectants (such as Lysol, Lysol antibacterial spray, or Mr. Clean) or a 10% bleach solution effectively destroys bacteria when left on surfaces for at least 30 seconds. However, vinegar and baking soda fail to provide effective disinfection (Rutala et al., 2000).

Indoor air pollution and allergens set the stage for the development of allergic disorders, especially asthma. Smoking has been named the main source of indoor air pollution. Sources of indoor allergens include house dust mites, cockroach particles, pet dander, rodent dander, and mold. Limiting smoking to the outdoors and regular house cleaning eliminate these factors that could potentially impair respiratory health.

Pets and insect infestation also may serve as vectors for infectious diseases. To control lawn and household infestations, people use pesticides. Organophosphate insecticides kill insects by inducing muscle paralysis. Organophosphates can be absorbed through inhalation, ingestion, and dermal and optical contact. Symptoms of insecticide poisoning may occur when humans are exposed (Melum & Kearney, 2001). In addition to direct contact, organophosphates contaminate freshwater supplies, especially if applied too heavily.

Many potentially noxious substances can be found in the home. Household chemicals, fixtures, and even construction materials contain organic compounds that contaminate the indoor environment (Gibson, 2000; Davis 2007). Benzene, a known human carcinogen, is present in synthetic materials, plastic, cleaning solutions, and tobacco smoke (Friedman & Morgan, 1992; Gibson). Construction materials such as particleboard and plywood emit formaldehyde, especially during the first year after construction. Most new carpeting contains a latex back, and latex carpet pads also are common. Newly poured concrete, fresh mortar, and paint emit gases (Gibson; Davis). Most commercial cleaners contain petrochemicals, fragrances, dyes, organophosphates, or bleach, which also contribute to environmental pollution. Tap water contains pollutants such as bacterial colonies, nitrates, pesticides, particulates, and metals. Radon gas may seep into basements from rock foundations (Davis).

In addition to indoor pollution, people are exposed to chemicals and vapors used by neighbors. Propane cookers, gas-powered lawn tools, gas appliances, and fresh paint emit fumes (Gibson, 2000). Many people apply dangerous herbicides and pesticides on lawns to make lawns look thicker and greener.

Along with pollutants, the home contains many sources for accidents. Home power sources such as natural gas and electricity can pose health hazards if basic rules for each are not followed. Appliances provide another source for accidents, especially in households where children reside. Hot water may cause burns, especially if the hot water tank is set above 140°F. Along with sources of power and appliances, stairs and throw rugs provide opportunities for falling. Fireplaces and improper storage of paper, rags, and combustible materials may create fire hazards.

Psychological health requires privacy. Persons need to have a place for emotional release, to feel independent, and to express affection toward those they love. When persons have time to recharge emotionally, the threat of domestic violence is reduced.

Factors contributing to domestic violence include household weapons, pregnancy, and drug or alcohol abuse. Many batterers have a history of violent behavior outside the home, depression, chemical dependency, and posttraumatic stress disorders. Children from homes where domestic violence occurs are at risk for being victims or perpetrators of violence. In addition, a history of head trauma has been associated with intense jealousy and violence (Gerard, 2000).

The Professional Nurse's Role in Promoting a Healthy Home Environment

The professional nurse detects home health hazards by performing a comprehensive environmental assessment. When hazards are identified, the professional nurse provides education and support to help clients eliminate them. Sometimes, especially when nurses work with the disabled, community resources can be obtained to assist persons with housekeeping and home maintenance.

Because of the high prevalence of domestic violence, health care providers, including nurses, routinely screen clients during outpatient visits and inpatient stays. Gerard (2000) reported that 35% of emergency department visits had links for domestic violence. Many admission assessment forms contain direct questions to screen for physical and psychological abuse. Once violence has been confirmed, the professional nurse's priority is to ensure the safety of the victim and any dependents. Sometimes immediate referrals to social workers, police departments, or domestic shelters may be needed to protect the victim(s). If there is no threat of immediate danger, the nurse should outline a plan for safety if the violence escalates (Gerard, 2000). In some states, professional nurses have a legal duty to report incidents of child and elder abuse but not domestic violence between intimate partners.

COMPREHENSIVE ENVIRONMENTAL HEALTH ASSESSMENT

Before professional nurses can take action to promote a healthy community environment, they must identify environmental factors that affect health. Shaner (1994) and Pope, Snyder, and Mood (1995) have outlined various elements of an environmental health history (Table 13-5). The age of residences (lead paint was commonly used in home construc-

TABLE 13-5

Elements of a Comprehensive Environmental Assessment

Location or Activity	Key Questions
Home	Where do you live? What is the distance from a major thoroughfare, industrial complex, or military base? If close to an industry, what type of industrial plant is it? What is the drinking water source for your residence? What types of cleaning agents do you use for housework and laundry? What types of chemicals do you use for yard care? What insecticides do you use inside the home? How old is your home structure (house, condo, or apartment)? How is your home heated? How is your home cooled? What is your fuel source for cooking? Have you tested your home for radon gas? Do you have a carbon monoxide alarm and smoke alarms in your home? Do you purify your home air or water? Have you recently acquired new furniture or carpeting? What type of paint is used on the exterior and interior of your home? Have you ever or recently refinished furniture or wood items in your home? What are the occupations of other household occupants? Do household occupants come into contact with chemicals as part of employment or leisure activities? Does anyone living with you smoke?
Work	List your past jobs (including military experience) and if you were exposed to any chemicals. Describe any work-related health problems or accidents. Did any of your co-workers have similar health problems or accidents? Where do you currently work? Are you employed full-time or part-time? How does your employer inform you of potentially hazardous chemicals, equipment, or procedures used in the workplace? Describe your work safety education programs (if any available). What protective devices are available for your use? Do you use the protective devices? How old is the building in which you work? Do you have any symptoms associated with your work setting? If so, please describe them.
Hobbies	What hobbies do you have? Are there any chemical agents used while engaging in the hobby?
Symptom assessment	What symptoms do you currently have? When did they start? When do they occur? Where do they occur? Does anyone who works with you or lives with or near you have the same symptoms?

Adapted from Shaner, H. (1994). Environmentally responsible clinical practice. In E. A. Schuster & C. L. Brown (Eds.), *Exploring our environmental connections practice* (pp. 233–251). NLN Publication No. 14-2634. New York: National League for Nursing; and Pope, A. M., Snyder, M. A., & Mood, L. H. (Eds.). (1995). *Nursing, health, and the environment.* Washington, DC: National Academy Press.

tion prior to the 1970s) and their proximity to military installations and industries provide clues to potential exposure to substances and chemicals that impair health (Davis, 2007). Because persons might be exposed to health hazards within work settings, information about occupations also provides information about environmental health hazards. Workers in many businesses that prepare foods for consumption (restaurants and grocery stores) may use latex gloves to prevent foodborne infections (Dyck, 2000; Kellet, 1997; Kim, Wellmeyer, & Miller, 1999; Lee & Kim, 1998). Along with home and work settings, hobbies such as photography, furniture restoration, and gardening may result in exposure to hazardous chemicals. Household and lawn chemicals used on a regular basis also serve as a source of exposure to substances that may affect health. Finally, nurses should assess persons for being potential perpetrators or victims of violence.

SUMMARY AND SIGNIFICANCE TO PRACTICE

The relationship of the environment to human health is highly complex. Professional nurses who have a solid knowledge about environmental factors affecting human health effectively assess clients for injuries and diseases arising from various forms of exposure. Ecocentric professional nurses act to preserve the environment at the global, community, employment, and home levels by practicing lives of voluntary simplicity. Nurses routinely assess factors that threaten health and provide education to promote environmental health for clients, each other, other health team members, and communities. When nurses become truly committed toward improving the environment, they educate clients, coworkers, and community officials about potential hazards and advocate for change.

FROM THEORY TO PRACTICE

1. After reading this chapter, how would I handle a client like Emily presenting in the emergency department with breathing difficulty? What advice would I give to a nurse providing care to a client like Emily? Why is it important to look for environmental factors contributing to client symptoms?
2. What workplace environmental hazards can I identify in my clinical practice setting? What are the procedures for making changes in my health care organization? Why is it important to know the established policies and procedures for making changes in a workplace setting?
3. What individual behaviors could I change to promote a more healthy global, community, work, and home environment? What would be the consequences for making these changes?

WWW INTERNET EXERCISES

1. Visit the Scorecard Organization at http://www.scorecard.org. Type in your zip code to get answers to the most frequently asked questions about the major polluters and polluting agents found in your community. Click "Get Report" after entering your zip code. Make a list of the top polluters in your county and the top chemicals released in your county. Learn about local lead hazards in houses and if your area has a worst toxic site. Bring this information to share in class with your colleagues.
2. Visit the National Institute of Occupational Safety and Health at http://www.cdc.gov/niosh/homepage.html. Read down the page and click on "Health Care Workers." On the next screen, scroll down to see the various topics covered. Select a topic of interest and click it. Read the information. Compare your current clinical practice agency's policies and procedures on the topic. Also, note the compliance level of health team members with the policies and procedures in your agency. Outline areas of compliance and areas of noncompliance. Develop a report about noncompliant practices to submit to the appropriate administrator in your clinical practice agency.

WWW INTERNET RESOURCES

Resources for Mapping the Environment: Global Digital Data Sets on the Internet

For population distribution, visit http://www.ciesin.org/data.html.

For oceans and sea surface temperatures, visit the University of Wisconsin Space Science and Engineering Center at http://www.ssec.wisc.edu/data/sst.html.

Resources for the Home Environment

For indoor air quality information, visit the Environmental Protection Agency at http://www.epa.gov/iaq/pubs/hpguide.html.

For information about household products, visit http://householdproducts.nlm.nig.gov/products.htm.

Assess your personal knowledge of home environmental hazards at http://uwex.edu/healthyhome/tool/.

Websites for Information Related to Environmental Health

Environmental Protection Agency: http://www.epa.gov.

Health Care Without Harm: http://www.noharm.org.

Center for Disease Control: http://www.cdc.gov.

National Center for Environmental Health: http://www.cdc.gov.nceh.

National Institute of Occupational Safety and Health: http:www.cdc.gov/niosh/homepage.html.

National Library of Medicine: http://www.nlm.nih.gov.

Nightingale Institute for Health and Environment: http://www.nihe.org.

The International Labour Organization's Guidelines for Occupational Safety and Health: http://www.ilo.org/public/english/support/publ/pdf/guidelines.pdf.

Toxnet: http://toxnet.nlm.nih.gov.

Toxic Release Inventory: http://www.epa.gov/tri.

U.S. Environmental Protection Agency, Persistent, Biocumulative & Toxic Chemical Program: http://www.epa.gov/pbt.

Resources for Workplace Safety

Visit http://www.osha-slc.gov/index/html. Type in "workplace violence," then click on the title "Guidelines for Preventing Violence for Health Care and Social Service Workers."

Visit OSHA's ergonomic website at http://www.osha-slc.gov/SLTC/ergonomic/index.html.

Visit the Clinical Practice Model Resources Center to learn more about Partnership, Dialogue and Healthy Workplace Development at http://www.cpmrc.com.

For resources on safer cleaning products and pesticides in work settings, visit Health Care Without Harm at www.noharm.org/us.

REFERENCES

Bartholomew, K. (2006). *Ending nurse-to-nurse hostility: Why nurses eat their young and each other.* Marblehead, MA: HCPro.

Belanger, D. (2000). Nurses and suicide: The risk is real. *RN, 63,* 61–64.

Bender, K., & Thompson, F. (2003). West Nile virus: A growing challenge. *American Journal of Nursing, 103,* 32–40.

Bright, C. (2000). Anticipating environmental "surprise." In L. R. Brown, C. Flavin, H. French, S. Postel, & L. Starke (Eds.), *State of the world 2000* (pp. 22–38). New York: W. W. Norton.

Carroll, V. (2004). Preventing violence in the healthcare workplace. *The Missouri Nurse, 2,* 12–13, 31.

Cooper, C. (2007). Multiple chemical sensitivity in the clinical setting. *American Journal of Nursing, 107*(3), 40-48.

Davis, A. (2007). Home environmental health risks. *Online Journal of Issues in Nursing, 12*(2), 5. Nursing & Allied Health Collection: Comprehensive Database. Available at http://search.ebscohost.com/login.asp?direct-true&db=nyhAN=26283739&loginpage=asp&site=ehost-live. Accessed June 23, 2008.

Dock, L. L. (1912). *A history of nursing* (Vol. 3). New York: G. P. Putnam's Sons.

Dyck, R. J. (2000). Historical development of latex allergy. *AORN Journal, 72,* 27–29, 32–33, 35–40.

Enserink, M. (2001). Infections diseases: West Nile researchers get ready for round three. *Science, 292,* 1289–1291.

Environmental Protection Agency. (2008). Medical waste. Available at http://www.epa.gov/osw/nonhaz/industrial/medical/mwfaqs.html. Accessed May 3, 2009.

Fagan, B. (2008). *The great warming.* New York: Bloomsbury.

Fawcett, J. (1984). *Analysis and evaluation of conceptual models of nursing.* Philadelphia: F. A. Davis.

Fent, K., Weston, A., & Caminada, D. (2006). Ecotoxicology of human pharmaceuticals. *Aquatic Toxicology, 76,* 122–159.

Frankl, V. (1963). *Man's search for meaning.* New York: Washington Square Press.

French, H. (2000). Coping with ecological globalization. In L. R. Brown, C. Flavin, H. French, S. Postel, & L. Starke (Eds.), *State of the world 2000* (pp. 184–202). New York: W. W. Norton.

Friedman, M., & Morgan, I. (1992). The health care function. In M. Friedman (Ed.), *Family nursing: Theory and practice* (3rd ed., pp. 291–313). Norwalk CT: Appleton & Lange.

Gerard, M. (2000). Domestic violence: How to screen and intervene. *RN, 63,* 52–56, 58.

Gibson, P. R. (2000). *Multiple chemical sensitivity: A survival guide.* Oakland, CA: New Harbinger.

Greer, A., & Fisman, D. (2008). Climate change and infectious diseases in North America: The road ahead. *The Canadian Medical Association Journal, 178*(6), 715–722.

Hemminger, P. (2005). Damming the flow of drugs into drinking water. *Environmental Health Perspectives, 13,* A678–A681.

International Council of Nurses. (2006). *Guidelines on coping with violence in the workplace.* Geneva: Author.

International Council of Nurses. (2007). *Occupational health and safety management programme for nurses.* Geneva: Author.

Kellet, P. B. (1997). Latex allergy: A review. *Journal of Emergency Nursing, 23,* 27–36.

Kim, K. T., Graves, P. B., Safadi, G. S., Alhadeff, G., & Metcalfe, J. (1998). Implementation recommendations for making health care facilities latex safe. *AORN Journal, 67,* 615–618, 621–624, 626.

Kim, K. T., Wellmeyer, E. T., & Miller, K. V. (1999). Minimum prevalence of latex hypersensitivity in health care workers. *Allergy and Asthma Proceedings, 20,* 387–391.

Kim, J., Woith, W., Otten, K., & McElmurry, B. (2006). Global nurse leaders: Lessons from the sages. *Advances in Nursing Science, 29*(1), 27–42.

Kleffel, D. (1994). The environment: Alive, whole and interacting. In E. A. Schuster & C. L. Brown (Eds.), *Exploring our environmental connections* (NLN Publication No. 14-2634, pp. 3–15). New York: National League for Nursing.

Kleffel, D. (1996). Environmental paradigms: Moving toward an ecocentric perspective. *Advances in Nursing Science, 18,* 1–10.

Kramer, M., & Schmalenberg, C. (2002). Staff nurses identify essentials of magnetism. In M. McClure & A. Hinshaw, (Eds.), *Magnet hospitals revisited: Attraction and retention of professional nurses* (pp. 25–59). Kansas City, MO: American Nurses Publishing.

Kramer, M., & Schmalenberg, C. (2004). Essentials of a magnetic work environment: Part 1. *Nursing, 34,* 50–54.

Lazarus, R. S., & Folkman, S. (1984). *Stress, appraisal and coping.* New York: Springer.

Leddy, S. K. (2004). Human energy: A conceptual model of unitary nursing science. *Visions: The Journal of Rogerian Scholarship, 12,* 14–27.

Lee, M. H., & Kim, K. T. (1998). Latex allergy: A relevant issue in the general pediatric population. *Journal of Pediatric Health Care, 12,* 242–246.

Leroy, E., Rouquet, P., Formenty, P., Souquiere, S., Kilbourne, A., Froment, J., et al. (2004). Multiple Ebola virus transmission events and rapid decline of central African wildlife. *Science, 303,* 387–390.

Lynas, M. (2008). *Six degrees: Our future on a hotter planet.* Washington, DC: National Geographic.

McClure, M., & Hinshaw, A. (2007). The magnetic matrix: Building blocks of Magnet™ hospitals. *American Nurse Today, 2*(12), 22–24.

McGinn, A. P. (2000). Phasing out persistent organic pollutants. In L. R. Brown, C. Flavin, H. French, S. Postel, & L. Starke (Eds.), *State of the world 2000* (pp. 79–100). New York: W. W. Norton.

McLean, A. (1974). Concepts of occupational stress: A review. In A. McLean (Ed.), *Occupational stress* (pp. 3–14). Springfield, IL: Charles C. Thomas.

Melum, M. F., & Kearney, K. (2001). Organophosphate toxicity. *American Journal of Nursing, 101,* 57–58.

Merriam-Webster's collegiate dictionary (10th ed.). (1994). Springfield, MA: Merriam-Webster.

Musker, K. (1994). Voluntary simplicity: Nurses creating a healing environment. In E. A. Schuster & C. L. Brown (Eds.), *Exploring our environmental connections* (NLN Publication No. 14-2634, pp. 195–212). New York: National League for Nursing.

Nelson, A., Fragala, G., & Menzel, N. (2003). Myths and facts about back injuries in nursing. *American Journal of Nursing, 103,* 32–41.

Neuman, B. (2002). The Neuman system model. In B. Neuman & J. Fawcett (Eds.), *The Neuman systems model* (4th ed.). Upper Saddle River, NJ: Prentice-Hall.

Newman, M. A. (1994). *Health as expanding consciousness* (2nd ed.). New York: National League for Nursing.

Occupational Safety and Health Administration. (2007). 2007 Industry injury and illness data. Available at http://www.bls.gov/iif/oshwc/osh/os/ostab.pdf . Accessed May 3, 2009.

O'Meara, M. (2000). Harnessing information technologies for the environment. In L. R. Brown, C. Flavin, H. French, S. Postel, & L. Starke (Eds.), *State of the world 2000* (pp. 121–141). New York: W. W. Norton.

Papp, E. (2007). *Occupational health and safety management programme for nurses*. Geneva: International Council of Nurses.

Pearce, F. (2007). *With speed and violence: Why scientist fear tipping points in climate change*. Boston: Beacon.

Pope, A. M., Snyder, M. A., & Mood, L. H. (Eds.). (1995). *Nursing, health and the environment*. Washington, DC: National Academies Press.

Quinn, T., & Overbaugh, J. (2005). HIV/AIDS in women: An expanding epidemic. *Science, 308*, 1582.

Rogers, M. E. (1990). Nursing: Science of unitary, irreducible human beings: Update 1990. In E. A. M. Barrett (Ed.), *Visions of Rogers' science-based nursing* (pp. 5–11). New York: National League for Nursing.

Roy, C. (1987). Roy's adaptation model. In R. R. Parse (Ed.), *Nursing science; Major paradigms, theories and critiques* (pp. 35–45). Philadelphia: W. B. Saunders

Rutala, W. A., Barbee, S. L., Aguiar, N. C., Sobsey, M. D., & Weber, D. J. (2000). Antimicrobial activity of home disinfectants and natural products against potential human pathogens. *Infection Control and Hospital Epidemiology, 21*, 33–38.

Sachs, J. (2008). *Common wealth: Economics for a crowded planet*. New York: Penguin.

Scully, M. G. (2001). Taking the pulse of the Kalamazoo. *Chronicle of Higher Education*, 47, B16.

Shaner, H. (1994). Environmentally responsible clinical practice. In E. A. Schuster & C. L. Brown (Eds.), *Exploring our environmental connections practice* (NLN Publication No. 14-2634, pp. 233–251). New York: National League for Nursing.

Shaner, H., & Botter, M. (2003). Pollution: Health care's unintended legacy. *American Journal of Nursing, 103*, 79, 81, 83–84.

Steger, S. (2000). Killed in school! *RN, 63*, 36–38.

Sutton, R. (2006). *The no asshole rule: Building a civilized workplace and surviving one that isn't*. New York: Warner Business.

Trossman, S. (2000). Moving violations: Working to prevent on-the-job injuries. *The American Nurse, 32*, 1, 12–14.

U.S. Department of Health and Human Services. (2000). *Healthy people 2010*. Boston: Jones & Bartlett.

Von der Werf, G., Randerson, J., Callatz, G., Gigio, L., Kesibhatla, P., Arelloro, A., et al. (2004). Continental-scale partitioning of fire emissions during the 1997–2001 El Nino/La Nina Period. *Science, 303*(5654), 73–75.

Watkins, J. M., & Mohr, B. J. (2001). *Appreciative inquiry*. San Francisco: Jossey-Bass/Pfeiffer.

Wesorick, B., Shiparski, L., Troseth, M., & Wyngarden, K. (1997). *Partnership Council field book*. Grand Rapids, MI: Practice Field Publishing.

Wilson, C. K., & Porter-O'Grady, T. (1999). *Leading the revolution in health care* (2nd ed.). Gaithersburg, MD: Aspen.

Worthington, K. (2000). Seeking the perfect fit. *American Journal of Nursing, 100*, 88.

Zakaria, F. (2008). A bug to save the planet. *Newsweek, 151*(24), 40.

CHAPTER 14

Community Health

KEY TERMS AND CONCEPTS

Community
Population
Community health problem
Demography
Epidemiology
Community assessment
Community-based nursing
Community health nursing
General systems theory
Systems model for geopolitical and phenom-
enological communities
Lundy-Barton's general systems model for
community and population assessment
and intervention
Community as partner
Dimensions model

LEARNING OUTCOMES

By the end of this chapter, the learner will be able to:

1 Define the terms community, community health,
and community health nursing.

2 Compare and contrast the following models for
community health nursing: the systems model for
geopolitical and phenomenological communities,
Lundy-Barton's general systems model for
community and population assessment and
intervention, the community as partner model,
and the dimensions model.

3 Outline the roles of the community health nurse.

4 Summarize key elements of professional nursing
within various community settings presented in
the chapter.

VIGNETTE

Paula works as the nursing director of a county public health department that receives 3,000 free flu vaccines annually from a federal government program. Last year, she had to return 1,000 doses because they were not used. She noticed that there were four small towns in the county in which no residents took advantage of the free flu vaccine program. She noticed that these towns were more than 20 miles from the health department office. To make it easier for residents of the small towns, Paula decides to hold a free immunization clinic in each town. She schedules the clinics on a Wednesday from 8:00 am to 4:00 pm. Even though each of the towns has a population of 1,500 persons, only a total of 150 vaccines were given. Paula asks herself, "Why didn't more people come for free vaccines?" What assumptions did Paula make regarding the lack of participation in the free vaccination program? How could she have elicited better participation of these small-town residents in the program?

Community health nursing originated in the Middle Ages, when persons opened their homes to care for the infirm (Anderson & McFarlane, 2006; Jamieson & Sewall, 1954; Lundy & Janes, 2001; Stanhope & Lancaster, 2006). Before 1965, most clients received nursing care in the home. Nursing care delivery shifted primarily to acute care settings during the mid-1960s through 1980. During the 1980s, escalating health care costs resulted in changes in third-party reimbursement to hospitals. The federal government initiated a prospective payment system known as diagnosis-related groups, whereby predetermined reimbursement schedules were set for payment for services rendered by hospitals to persons covered by Medicare and Medicaid. To reduce health care costs, health care services—especially nursing care—have shifted back to community settings. Nurses who work in community settings need to display competence in client physical care, teaching, communication, and management (Hunt, 2008). They also must look beyond individual and family client systems and consider the complex and global nature of community health issues.

KEY CONCEPTS OF COMMUNITY HEALTH

Community health nursing differs from other forms of professional practice because the focus of care shifts from individuals to groups. To develop an understanding of community health nursing, the professional nurse must have a clear understanding of key definitions.

Community

Sources of community health nursing information have varying definitions of the term **community**. *Webster's New World College Dictionary* (Agnes, 2005, p. 233) defined community as "1. *a)* all the people living in a particular city, district, etc.; *b)* the district, city where they live ... 2. a group of people forming a smaller social unit within a larger one, and sharing common interests, work, identity, location etc." Scholars of community health nursing define community in various ways. Leonard (2000, p. 93) defined community as a web of persons "shaped by relationships, interdependence, mutual interests and patterns of interactions." He proposed that a community encompasses "people at a particular time and place" (p. 93). Lundy, Janes, and Hartman (2001, p. 12) defined a community as "a group of people who have something in common, and interact with one another, who may exhibit a commitment to one another and may share a geographic boundary." Hunt (2008, p. 11) defined community as "a people, location, and social system." Smith and Maurer (2000, p. 342) defined community as "an open social system that is characterized by people in a place over time who have a common goal." All these definitions agree that a community consists of a group of persons who share a common interest and interact with each other.

A community need not have specific geographic borders (Hunt, 2008; Leonard, 2000; Lundy et al., 2001). Communities may encompass persons from a particular profession, such as the nursing community; a specific faith community; a specific cultural group, such as the Hispanic community; or persons living within a geographical area, such as a local community. Schools also may be considered a community. As a species, all persons have membership in the global community (Hunt, 2008; Lundy et al., 2001). In community health nursing, professional nurses target a specific group of persons or a geographical locale to serve; this group or location is known as "the **population**." For example, the population served by school nurses includes all persons who provide and receive school services, such as students, parents, teachers, counselors, administrators, clerical workers, and service workers (janitorial, food). The *Healthy People 2010* initiatives of the U.S. Department of Health and Human Services (USDHHS, 2000) target all American citizens.

The holographic community described by Davis (2000) expands the definition of community to one of multiple dimensions that include the following concepts: community consciousness (awareness), community heart (values), community soul (service), community voice (power), community body (structure and relationships), community mind (learning and development), community spirit (celebration and ritual), and community vision (health and survival) (Leddy, 2003).

The profession of nursing fits the definition of a holographic community because its members are connected to each other (belong to a profession), have shared values (caring, compassion, altruism), possess moral integrity (code of ethics), strive for unity (work toward providing the best care possible), create learning environments (client and professional educational programs), and work as individuals and collectively to achieve a better level of health for all.

Other approaches to community define community as place, social interaction, and political and social responsibility. As a place, the essential element includes a specific designated area where persons live and engage in various types of activity. Sharing a common purpose to communicate and work together to attain the goal denotes community as a social interaction. When considered as a political and social responsibility, community involves dynamic interactions and social relationships to form a sense of mutual obligation, solidarity, and responsibility to ensure social survival (Leddy, 2003).

Healthy Community

The healthy city/community movement began in the middle 1980s in Europe. Hancock and Duhl (1986) specified that the following must be present for a community to be classified as healthy:

1. A clean, safe, ecologically stable physical environment
2. Resident access to resources that promote and maintain a healthy, diverse, vital, and innovative economy
3. A strong, supportive, nonexploitative community
4. Basic human needs met for all members (food, water, shelter, income, and safety)
5. Access to a wide variety of experiences and resources (communications, cultural events, diverse contacts, and communications)
6. A connection to community's heritage and past
7. Equal access to public health and illness care services
8. Good health status of citizens
9. High levels of public participation in and control over decisions that affect individual citizens' lives, health, and well-being

Morse (2004) denoted characteristics of successful communities that plan for and adapt to change. Healthy communities have members who understand their relationship and responsibility to others rather than focusing on individual pursuits. By strategically planning for change, communities ensure their survival and brighter futures for members following in their footsteps. Morse identified the following seven key points that result in successful community adaptation to change:

1. Making the right investments/decisions the first time
2. Working together instead of as individuals or special interest groups with specific agendas
3. Building on current community strengths
4. Using a democratic process
5. Preserving the community's history
6. Growing their own leaders
7. Inventing a better and brighter future

In an ideal world, nurses working in community health help communities become better and use nursing skills to help them achieve health for all their members.

Community Health Problem

Hunt (2008, p. 386) defined a **community health problem** as a "health need identified in a community assessment." Lundy and Barton (2001) and Anderson and McFarlane (2006) would equate community health problems to the concept of nursing diagnosis.

When a gap exists between ideal community health and current community health, a community health problem exists.

Demography

Demography, the science of human populations, traces population size, characteristics, and changes. Shifts in demographics may have profound implications for health care delivery and professional nursing, as in the case of the graying and increasing cultural diversity of American citizens (Anderson & McFarlane, 2006; Hunt, 2008; Lundy & Janes, 2001; Agnes, 2005; USDHHS, 2000).

Epidemiology

Along with demographic trends is **epidemiology**, the study of factors that promote wellness or cause illness and help delineate the health of a community. Because illness is easier to measure, the focus of epidemiology tends to be on factors such as morbidity (illness), mortality (death), incidence (number of persons in a population who have a condition develop during a specified time frame), and prevalence (number of persons in a population who have a condition within a given time). Epidemiology views health and disease as a composite state of the three following variables: agent, host, and environment. These three variables create the epidemiologic triangle. In the case of altered health, an agent (or combination of agents) may result in the development of a specific health problem. Before the health alteration occurs, there must be a host, or person who contracts the health problem. Finally, environmental factors contribute to the development of a health problem (Agnes, 2005; Anderson & McFarlane, 2006; Lundy & Janes, 2001; Smith & Maurer, 2000; USDHHS, 2000).

For example, for tuberculosis (TB) to develop, a person must come into contact with the Mycobacterium tubercle. The environment must have conditions for the tubercular bacillus to thrive (crowded conditions), and an available person must be susceptible to contract the illness (host). Many community health nurses spend much time tracking down cases of infectious diseases, and in some cases, they monitor client compliance to prescribed therapies.

Community Assessment

To determine the health of a specific community, community health care nurses assess the community in terms of status, structure, and process. Because of the breadth of **community assessment** in each of the terms, the following list provides brief examples of each:

- Status assessment includes reported statistics related to birth, death, poverty, crime, and incidence of mental and physical illness.
- Structure assessment includes inpatient and outpatient health care facilities, local government structures, schools, law enforcement agencies, retailers, roads, and population demographics (socioeconomic status, gender, age).
- Process assessment includes factors such as member commitment; communication patterns; relationships of the community with the larger society; and how well the community voices need for, accesses, and uses resources (Anderson & McFarlane, 2006; Clark, 1999; Hunt, 2008; Lundy & Janes, 2001; Smith & Maurer, 2000).

Community-Based Nursing

Hunt (2008) defined **community-based nursing** as delivery of nursing care within the context of a family's home and community. Community-based nursing facilitates continuity of care across the spectrum of consumer health care services, thus enabling health care professionals to meet the needs of people as they move from acute care to the community and vice versa. Community-based nursing refers to where nursing care is delivered. Nurses who deliver nursing services away from acute or extended care institutions practice community-based nursing.

Community Health Nursing

Community health nursing encompasses more than where nursing care is delivered, but represents a specialized area of professional practice. As a more comprehensive concept, Anderson and McFarland (2006) expanded the concept of community health nursing to include the following dimensions of nursing practice: (1) assessment of populations; (2) development of partnerships with community members and stakeholders; (3) emphasis on health promotion (primary prevention); (4) creation of health environmental, social, and economic conditions in a community; (5) outreach services for community members in need; (6) focus on the group as a whole rather than individual members; and (7) judicious allocation of resources and wise stewardship.

CONCEPTUAL MODELS FOR COMMUNITY HEALTH NURSING

A variety of nursing models may be used by community nurses to guide clinical practice. Community nurses select models to guide clinical practice based on their world views. Models commonly used by nurses in community settings are the systems model for geopolitical and phenomenological communities (Smith & Maurer, 2000), the Lundy-Barton general systems model for community and population assessment and intervention (Lundy & Barton, 2001), and Anderson and McFarlane's (2006) community as partner model. These models base theoretical relationships on general systems theory.

General Systems Theory

In **general systems theory**, the universe is composed of interacting elements of various sizes known as subsystems, with the individual's cells being the smallest element. Each system has boundaries that separate it from other systems. Subsystems increase in size and complexity; include persons, groups, towns, states, and nations; and expand to encompass the entire universe. All subsystems receive energy, resources, and information (input) that are transformed (throughput) for the maintenance of a steady state or for subsystem growth and development. Results of resource and energy use then return to the system (output). Resources used by subsystems (individuals, groups, or society) may result in waste products that may be beneficial or noxious to the environment and other subsystems. In the general systems theory, a change in one subsystem results in cascading changes for the entire system, thus necessitating adaptation. System disorganization (entropy) results from demands of continuous readjustment for effective adaptation to change. For systems to meet goals, increasing order (negentropy) occurs so the system can attain a steady state. Systems strive for balanced steady states but must experience disorder for growth and development. Subsystems continuously receive feedback from each other when the output of one becomes the input for another (Bertalanffy, 1968).

Systems Model for Geopolitical and Phenomenological Communities

The **systems model for geopolitical and phenomenological communities** uses a systems analysis framework to guide nurses in data collection and organization. Smith and Maurer (2000, p. 348) designated the following seven key components:

1. Boundaries: factors that separate the community from the environment and maintain the integrity of the community
2. Goals: The purpose or reason for which the community exists

3. Set factors: The physical and psychosocial characteristics of the community that affect behavior
4. Inputs: External influences from the suprasystem
5. Throughputs: The internal functioning of the community divided into four functional subsystems (economy, polity, communication, and values)
6. Outputs: The health behavior and status of the community
7. Feedback: The information that is returned to the system regarding its functioning

Nurses using the systems model for geopolitical and phenomenological communities assess these seven components when collecting data about the community that receives professional nursing services. Smith and Maurer (2000) advocated for the following three different approaches to community assessment: the comprehensive needs assessment, in which community members are asked what they need; the problem-oriented approach, in which the nurse addresses a particular health concern; and the familiarization approach, in which the nurse studies existing data about a community to determine the presence of a special group that has specific health care needs.

Once the community assessment is completed, the nurse analyzes the collected data to determine the level of community health according to environmental safety, social structure, available energy and resources, and health status behaviors. When problems arise in any of these areas, the professional nurse works in partnership with community representatives to set priorities and design a plan of care with a goal of maximizing health for all community members. Professional nursing interventions include providing health education, screening persons for health problems, developing and implementing policies, fostering community self-help, and looking for ways to empower the disenfranchised community members. Once the nurse has implemented nursing interventions, the nurse evaluates the community care plan in terms of outcome attainment, appropriateness, adequacy, efficiency, and process. Evaluation of the effectiveness of each is performed.

Lundy-Barton General Systems Model for Community and Population Assessment and Intervention

Lundy-Barton's general systems model for community and population assessment and intervention (Lundy & Barton, 2001) offers a global systematic approach for professional nurses to use when practicing community health nursing. The Lundy-Barton model incorporates the steps of the nursing process to identify community health issues and take action to remedy them. (Table 14-1 summarizes the model in detail.) The Lundy-Barton model provides a comprehensive approach to community health nursing and effectively addresses individual, family, health care delivery, political, social, educational, economic, and religious systems within a community. The model serves as one template that community nurses may use on which to base their professional practice. However, before using the model, professional nurses must define the target community or population that receives nursing services. Then, the nurse considers the subsystems within the community and how the target community interacts with larger systems (suprasystems) and compares with communities of similar size and structure (Lundy & Janes, 2001).

Community as Partner Model

Another nursing model commonly used to direct community health nursing is the **community as partner** model. Anderson and McFarlane (2006) adapted the Neuman systems model (see Chapter 5) to communities. Anderson and McFarlane identify eight areas for community assessment and care: physical environment, health and social services, communication, economics, safety and transportation, politics and government, education, and recreation. Nurses assess community stressors and buffers (flexible lines of defense, normal lines of defense, and lines of resistance) that the community uses to

TABLE 14-1

Summary of the Lundy-Barton General Systems Model for Community and Population Assessment and Intervention

Nursing Process Step/Model Phase	Elements for Nursing Consideration
Assessment/database	Compile a database that includes community demographics, psychological climate, nutritional status, physical fitness, geographical boundaries, location, environmental conditions, safety practices, health care delivery services, political systems, dominant social system, communication patterns, and educational systems
Diagnosis/problem list	Generate a community problem list based on assessment findings
Planning/problem assessment and plan formulation	Determine an action plan for identified community problems in partnership with members of the community. Community members and the nurse work together to set priorities for action, long- and short-term program objectives, and specific actions
Implementation	Execute the action plan with continued community participation while documenting progress notes
Evaluation/progress notes	Review documented progress notes to determine effectiveness of the action plan as the plan is executed so that changes in approaches may be made and again at completion of the action plan to determine its effectiveness
Restart process	Reassess the community and proceed with steps of nursing process

Adapted from Lundy and Janes, 2001.

reduce the impact of stressors. The model considers individual and group reactions to stressors. Based on assessment, nurses generate community-nursing diagnoses in collaboration with community members. Nurses and community members work together to determine primary interventions to promote community health (e.g., *Healthy People 2010* [USDHHS, 2000] or routine vaccinations), secondary interventions to address stressor penetration (e.g., screening people for exposure to an infectious disease, vaccination, or prophylactic antibiotic administration to persons exposed to an infectious illness and treatment of ill community members), and tertiary interventions to promote community recovery from stressor penetration (education, counseling, and support services for members living in fear of the contagious illness for which interventions have occurred). Anderson and McFarlane emphasized that community feedback and changes in community processes provide the basis for evaluating community health nursing interventions.

Epidemiology

Although humans acknowledged the contagious dimension of many illnesses during the time of Hippocrates, William Farr, a London physician, developed a system of tracking births, illnesses, and deaths that started the discipline of modern epidemiology (Harkness, 2001; Jamieson & Sewall, 1954; Anderson & McFarlane, 2006). Florence Nightingale used the epidemiologic principles of cleanliness, fresh air, and optimal nutrition to reduce the fatalities during the Crimean War (Harkness, 2001; Jamieson & Sewall, 1954). Work of pioneers in the field of epidemiology resulted in the development of the epidemiologic triad: host, agent, and environment. The epidemiologic triad evolved into the epidemiologic model that acknowledges that disease is multifaceted and that the three factors—a susceptible host (humans), an offending agent (something that causes a disease or illness), and an environment (physical, chemical, biologic, and social climate)—must all be present before a health-related problem can occur (Harkness, 2001; Parrish, 1969). In recent years, epidemiology has expanded from the study of infectious illnesses to include the critical influences that lead to chronic illnesses, crime, lifestyle, and other factors that result in less-than-optimal health.

Epidemiology, like professional nursing, has a process that is used to solve health-related problems. The following steps occur in the epidemiologic process:

1. Define the problem.
2. Gather information from a variety of reliable sources.
3. Describe the problem by identifying people, time, and places.
4. Formulate a hypothesis to speculate who, what, where, why, and how the problem occurred.
5. Compile descriptive data analysis to test the generated hypothesis.
6. Develop a plan to control the problem.
7. Implement a controlled plan.
8. Evaluate the controlled plan.
9. Prepare a report that includes the scope of the problem, control plan development, implementation, and evaluation, as well as prevention strategies for problem recurrence.
10. Conduct additional research on the identified problem (Harkness, 2001).

The science of epidemiology is divided into two branches: descriptive epidemiology and analytical epidemiology.

Descriptive Epidemiology

Descriptive epidemiology focuses on statistics to describe the state of health for a given population. Persons with particular health problems are identified. Risk factors for a particular health problem result when persons with the problem share common characteristics (e.g., risky sexual practices and the development of sexually transmitted diseases). Epidemiologists frequently use rates, which are fractions, to describe the incidence of a health problem during a specified time (105 cases/100,000 persons). Incidence refers to the occurrence of new cases in a previously disease-free population for a specific time. Prevalence rates indicate the number of persons within a given population who have an existing health problem within a specified time.

Along with rates, epidemiologists become concerned with place and time when the health condition occurs. In 2007, an American lawyer with active tuberculosis (TB) flew across the Atlantic Ocean. Airplane travel results in a large number of persons placed in a closed environment in close proximity to each other. When the authorities learned of the event, international public health officials collaborated with each other, determined health risks encountered by persons who flew on the same plane, contacted them, and monitored them for signs and symptoms of active TB. As a precaution, some passengers and airline staff elected to take prophylactic medications for TB. The knowledge of epidemiology helped identify persons at risk. In addition, epidemiologists track trends or long-term changes to forecast future health care needs.

Analytical Epidemiology

Analytical epidemiology focuses on the why, or determinants, of the health-related problem. Sometimes determinants surface when descriptive data are analyzed. However, analytical epidemiology sometimes reveals that more descriptive data need to be collected. Analytic epidemiologists conduct the following four types of studies:

1. Cross-sectional surveys: Data collected at one point in time to describe current health status and to determine possible hypotheses for a particular health problem.
2. Retrospective studies: Study a group of persons to trace past experiences to determine reasons for a health problem.

3. Prospective, cohort, or longitudinal studies: Determine/compare the incidence of a health-related problem in persons who were exposed to that of persons who were not exposed to a specific factor.

4. Therapeutic, intervention, or prevention trials: Randomized studies to determine the persons who will benefit from specific interventions to prevent the health-related problem.

In tropical climates, malaria kills millions of persons annually. Analytical epidemiology studied how malaria differs among continents, traced the high incidence and mortality to Africa, determined how the disease could be prevented (distribution of bednets and widespread insecticide spraying in affected geographical areas to limit mosquito bites), developed more powerful medications, and instituted a public education campaign to seek health care immediately at the first signs and symptoms for early treatment (Sachs, 2008).

The Dimensions Model

Using concepts derived from epidemiology, Clark (1999) developed the **dimensions model** to guide community health nursing practice. The dimensions model uses dimensions of nursing, health, and health care as interacting elements to determine a state of health or illness. The dimensions of nursing, health, and health care are outlined in Table 14-2. The nurse uses the dimensions of professional nursing outlined by Clark when working with individuals, families, or communities. The dimensions of health determine the quality of individual, family, and community health. Finally, the level of prevention determines specific strategies used by the nurse to prevent health problems, treat them when they arise, and support persons to attain the best possible health state after experiencing a health problem.

The dimensions model emphasizes the importance of the role of the professional nurse in helping persons to obtain and maintain optimal health by providing a holistic approach to care. Along with individual and family factors, the model also incorporates the health care system as a determinant of health status for individuals, families, and communities.

Other nursing models also provide a conceptual basis for community health nursing. Leininger's sunrise model (see Chapter 11) for transcultural nursing focuses on specific considerations when nurses provide professional service to clients from various cultural groups. Pender's health promotion model (see Chapter 8) also provides a solid foundation for promoting wellness when working with individuals and groups.

COMMUNITY-LEVEL NURSING INTERVENTIONS

Health promotion within a community encompasses collective efforts. Community nursing interventions work best when the community assumes ownership of the plan, responsibility for community health program maintenance, and control for planning future programs. Nurses use multiple strategies to help communities improve their health. Nurses empower, collaborate with, build capacity for, and advocate for individual members and the entire community (Leddy, 2003; Lind & Smith, 2008). Nurses empower communities by investing time and resources to enable communities to assume control over their destiny. Community members view the nurse as a health expert who has much knowledge and expertise in developing programs and supporting others to attain better health or as someone who plans to force sometimes culturally incompatible ways on them (Andrews & Boyle, 2008; Leininger & McFarlane, 2006; Lind & Snith, 2008). Poverty-stricken communities perceive a lack of control over their destinies and feel powerless because they may not be valued by others, have few (or no) resources, lack economic and political power, have no experience in making decisions, and have learned helplessness.

TABLE 14-2

The Dimensions Model

Nursing Dimensions	Health Dimensions	Health Care Dimensions
Cognitive dimension	**Biophysical dimension**	**Primary prevention**
Knowledge	Age	Health promotion
	Genetic heredity	Disease prevention
	Physiological function	
Interpersonal dimension	**Psychological dimension**	**Secondary prevention**
Interaction skills	Internal psychological environ-	Early detection of health problems
Affective elements	ment (ideas about self)	Treatment of existing health
	External psychological environ-	problems
	ment (ideas derived from others)	
Ethical dimension	**Social dimension**	**Tertiary prevention**
Ethical decision-making	Social structure	Return to highest functioning level af-
skills and processes	Norms	ter health problem treatment
Client advocacy	Attitudes	Prevent further health deterioration
	Social action	Prevent health problem recurrence
Skills dimension	**Behavioral dimension**	
Manipulative skills (clinical	Diet	
skills)	Exercise	
Intellectual skills	Recreation	
	Substance use (and abuse)	
	Sexual habits	
	Use of protective devices	
Process dimension	**Health system dimension**	
Nursing process	Availability	
Epidemiology	Access	
Health education	Affordability	
Home visits	Appropriateness	
Case management	Adequacy	
Change	Acceptability	
Leadership	Use	
Group process		
Political action		
Reflective dimension		
Theory development		
Research		
Evaluation of care		

Adapted from Clark, 1999.

Sometimes, community members have a history of fighting with each other. Nurses can serve as mediators to settle long-standing disputes so that the community members can determine which programs are needed. Nurses also serve as consultants, coaches, and cheerleaders as community members plan, implement, and evaluate community health programs.

Collaboration with the community requires that the nurse and community members share information and resources with each other, but above all, trust each other. Lind and Smith (2008) proposed the use of appreciative inquiry (AI) as a means to connect with the community and identify community strengths. AI provides opportunities for persons to share their stories and to perceive that they have been heard and that their ideas are valued. In the community health context, AI promotes health and empowers community members. Everyone involved in AI shares ideas and listens intently. Through the use of AI, the community health nurse becomes familiar with traditional folk medicine, key community concerns, and community leaders. AI fosters deep personal connections while fostering the participation of everyone engaged in the development, planning, and implementation of community nursing interventions. The community and nurse work in partnership to promote health rather than merely identify health problems.

Capacity building occurs with individual members, small groups, and the entire community. Capacity building involves building upon the current strengths, resources, and abilities already present in the community. Individual capacity building involves changing personal values for health-enhancing outcomes, having a positive attitude toward collaboration, deciding things using consensus, sharing power and information, showing respect, giving support, participating in egalitarian relationships, perceiving self-efficacy, setting future goals, feeling a sense of coherence, identifying with others with similar problems, feeling able to help others, and understanding community member roles and responsibilities. Small-group capacity building includes interacting with others to help them assume control, fostering a sense of connectedness, establishing trust, and creating positive interactions. Capacity in building communities involves helping members and the community to articulate health problems and potential solutions, providing them access to information, supporting current community leadership, and assisting them to overcome obstacles to action. While building capacity within a community, the nurse may act as a strategist, coach, meeting facilitator, mediator, and developer of community leadership (Leddy, 2003).

Once the community has mobilized its internal human and physical resources, the community shares a group consciousness. With a united purpose, the community becomes capable of taking social and political action to obtain more resources for use in community building and improvement. Disenfranchised persons may not have the ability to independently develop as a community. The nurse helps these persons achieve community-building skills through role-modeling, providing support, and listening to them share their problems and concerns.

 ## CAREER OPPORTUNITIES IN COMMUNITY HEALTH NURSING

Many opportunities for nurses to engage in community nursing exist. Sometimes, as members of a community apart from an employment setting, community members who know the professional nurse ask for health advice and information. Professional nurses may be employed in community settings, such as public health departments, factories, businesses, camps, homes, homeless shelters, prisons, schools, parishes, and the armed forces. However, some nurses elect to use professional skills to serve communities and engage in volunteer nursing. Nurses who give health-related advice to friends and acquaintances are practicing nursing and assume accountability for actions. Thus, the professional nurse should keep a record of nursing actions (including consultations with neighbors) and evaluate outcomes of health education, advice, recommended consultations, and nursing procedures. Nurses have a positive effect on the health and well-being of communities.

Research Brief 14-1

Bigbee, J. (2008). Relationships between nurse- and physician-to-population ratios and state health ranking. *Public Health Nursing, 25*(3), 244–252.

The investigator performed secondary data analysis from the 2006 United Health Foundation's State Health Ranking (SHR) with the 2004 National Sample Survey for Registered Nurses (NSSRN) and the U.S. Health Workforce Profile from the New York Center for Health Workforce Studies (HWP) to see if there was a relationship between nurse-to-population ratio to state population health. The NSSRN data was collected from 35,724 nurses residing across the United States. SHR was determined by the following indices: "personal behaviors, community environment, public and health policies, public health services and outcomes (including both length and quality of life measures)" (pp. 246–247). Two-tailed Spearman's rank order correlations were performed.

Results revealed that the nurse-to-population ratio was positively related to the SHR (rho = −.446, $p <$ .001). The correlation has a negative sign because the state with the best overall health ranking has the top rank of number one. Higher nurse-to-population ratios was related to higher SHR and reduced motor vehicle death, crime rates, incidence of infectious diseases, childhood poverty, uninsured persons, premature deaths, and time off work for poor physical and mental health. Higher nurse-to-population ratios were related to increases in high school graduation rates, recommended immunizations, and prenatal care. Effects of higher nurse-to-population ratios tended to be related to positive aspects of aggregate health, and higher physician-to-population ratios tended to be positively related to aspects of individual health.

Therefore, the study findings "suggest that more RNs per capita may be associated with healthier populations" (p. 250), thereby substantiating the need for effective strategies to alleviate the current and projected future nursing shortage. A critical consideration in interpreting this study is that correlation does not infer causation. Additional research needs to be performed using data sources from the same calendar year, examining the impact of all specialized areas of nursing on population and individual health, seeing if differences in nurse educational level is related to health outcomes, and exploring the effects of all health professionals on community health.

Nurses contribute to community health because of their ability to share their knowledge, skills, and expertise with others. Because of the array of nursing opportunities, the subsequent section briefly describes selected practice areas for community health nursing. More detailed information regarding community nursing opportunities may be found by consulting chapter website resources or references.

Public Health Nursing

Since 1893, public health nurses have been serving individuals, groups, communities, and populations. The Institute of Medicine (2003) defined public health as what a society does collectively to guarantee that conditions occur so that persons can be healthy. Public health nurses respond to societal health needs. Public health nurses focus on promoting and protecting the health of populations. Public health nurses do not work in isolation; rather, they collaborate with interprofessional health care team members, typically within a local government agency (city or county health department). When health issues arise that concern more than the local community, public health nurses find themselves consulting and working with national governments (the United States Public Health Services Department) and even world organizations (United Nations). Health promotion and protection are the top priorities for public health nurses (American Nurses Association [ANA], 2007; Lind & Smith, 2008; Quad Council of Public Health Nursing Organizations, 1999).

Since 1999, the Quad Council of Public Health Nursing Organizations has stipulated the baccalaureate degree as the practice entry level. The ANA offers certification in community/public health nursing. Bekemeir (2007) noted that the certification has intrinsic value for nurses (personal satisfaction, sign of professional growth, evidence of professional accomplishment and specialized knowledge, increased confidence, and professional credibility). However, many nurses report the certification has little extrinsic value such as employer and public recognition. Very few nurses report receiving salary increases by holding community/public health nursing certification (Bekemeir, 2007). Currently, advanced practice of public health nursing requires graduate-level education with a master's degree in either nursing or public health. Most state Nurse Practice Acts fail to recognize advanced nursing practice in the realm of public health nursing (Levin et al., 2008). However, when practice focuses on health and illnesses of individuals, less highly educated nurses may appropriately practice public health nursing.

Public health nurses aim to promote and protect the health of populations thorough the creation of situations and provision of services to help people optimize their health. Along with using foundational nursing knowledge, public health nurses incorporate knowledge from the social and public health science into practice (ANA, 2007). Public health nurses provide services to meet government-specified health objectives as outlined in *Healthy People 2010* (USDHHS, 2000). Essential services offered by public health service nurses include (1) monitoring the health states of a particular population, (2) diagnosing community health problems, (3) identifying community health hazards, (4) investigating community health problems when they arise, (5) developing partnerships with those whom they serve, (6) solving community health problems, (7) developing policies and action plans to support community health, (8) enforcing laws and regulations to ensure public safety and health, (9) linking persons to appropriate health care services, (10) educating current and future public health personnel, (11) evaluating the effectiveness and quality of public health services, (12) identifying future health threats, and (13) researching to find innovative solutions to maximize the health and safety of the public (Bekemeier, 2007; Bender & Salmon, 2001; Clark, 1999; Levin et al., 2008; Smith & Maurer, 2000; Quad Council of Public Health Nursing Organizations, 1999).

Questions for Reflection 14-1

1. Do I know how to contact the closest local public health department?
2. What services does my local public health department offer?

COMMUNITY MENTAL HEALTH NURSING

Promoting the mental health of citizens is extremely important for the quality of life in a community. Many countries, including the United States, provide a full array of mental health services (from acute and long-term residential programs to home health care) for citizens who need them. The civil rights movement of the 1960s transformed the delivery of mental health care in the United States. Many mentally ill persons were freed from institutions that provided chronic mental health services. They became part of local communities and were no longer required to conform to the restrictions required by shelters and group homes. Many homeless persons suffer from mental illness. Many persons with mental disorders cannot hold a job, which means they frequently have no health care insurance. When left to fend for themselves, some mentally ill persons have no access to mental health services to receive the psychotropic medications necessary to function effectively as citizens. Some communities have civil ordinances against persons living on the streets; some provide homeless shelters; other communities rely on private agencies or churches to provide shelter for the homeless. Some homeless shelters provide mental health services for their clients. Community mental health nurses work in a variety of settings such as mental health clinics, public health departments, chemical abuse programs, homeless shelters, group residential homes, prisons, and home health.

When working in community settings, mental health nurses assume the following client care activities: assessing client condition and progress, managing medication, promoting health, supporting clients and families, and intervening to prevent (hopefully) and manage psychiatric emergencies. When signs of mental deterioration occur, community mental health nurses collaborate with physicians for emergency management and make referrals for emergency or immediate care. In life-threatening situations, community health nurses activate the emergency response system. Advanced practice mental health nurses may have prescriptive privileges for psychotropic medications and frequently have education and credentials to offer counseling services (Elsom, Happell, & Manias, 2007; McCardle, Parahoo, & McKenna, 2007; Videbeck, 2008). When working in community settings, community mental health nurses collaborate with and support members as they make autonomous decisions. In addition, community mental health nurses work with other health care professionals to maximize use of available resources for health promotion, such as using a social worker to help secure food stamps or vouchers. Along with working in a variety of settings, community mental health nurses may find themselves working with persons who may have a history of violent behavior or have been victims of violence. Some persons living in high-crime areas become isolated because of their fear for their safety or the safety of their home and its contents. Because of the lack of residential programs, many persons with severe mental illness may live at home. Not all public health departments provide mental health services for their communities. When they do, community health nurses provide mental health services to clients who seek care in public health clinics. If the public health department fails to provide mental health services, community members receive mental health services from free-standing, government-supported, non-profit, or for-profit mental health centers. To access mental health services, community members must be informed of the location and nature of the mental health services offered by each center. They receive such information from nurses or other health care providers. If a major event occurs within a community that has the potential to affect the mental health of its members, coordinated efforts from all facilities offering mental health services are required. For example, community mental health nurses from various mental health facilities may be consulted to support students and teachers in schools after an act of violence or student loss of life has occurred.

The U.S. government specified goals to improve and increase access to quality mental health services in *Healthy People 2010* (USDHHS, 2000). Mental health services targeted for improvement include preventative services for suicide, adolescent suicide attempts, and eating disorders. Increased efforts aimed at providing employment of persons with serious mental illnesses are another goal. The initiative also hopes to improve services for serious mental illnesses among homeless adults. Areas for treatment expansion for mental health and illness include the following: (a) primary care including screening and assessment for mental disorders, (b) pediatric mental health problem treatment, (c) screening for mental disorders in juvenile justice facilities, (d) treatment for adults with mental and co-occurring disorders, and (e) providing adult jail diversion programs (USDHHS). More community mental health nurses are and will be needed to attain these goals.

Healthy People 2010 also challenges the states to track consumer satisfaction with offered mental health services, create means to address cultural competence, and develop plans to address the mental health needs of the future burgeoning elderly population (USDHHS, 2000).

Electronic Community Health Nursing

Internet chat rooms create a gathering place for persons with similar interests or conditions. When a chat room is formed for a specific purpose, such as providing support, education, and resource information for persons with a similar condition or life situation, the purpose is consistent with the American Nurses Association *Scope and Standards of Public Health Nursing Practice* (2007). When nurses participate in chat rooms with the aim of promoting and protecting the health of its members, they could be providing community nursing services. In chat rooms, nurses may provide social support to other members, model therapeutic communication techniques, reinforce positive behaviors among group members, offer self-care or health-promoting advice, provide health-related information, and monitor group dynamics (Copeland, 2002).

Before electronic community health nursing can be recognized, current international, national, and state laws require changes. The following questions about professional nursing practice must also be addressed:

1. How (or will) professional nurses receive compensation for their services?
2. What accountability will the nurse have to the members of the electronic community?
3. What are the roles of the professional nurse providing e-community health nursing services?
4. If the nurse shares a similar condition as other chat room participants, how are professional and personal boundaries delineated?

Disaster Nursing

The education of professional nurses arms them with useful knowledge and skills to help others in times of disaster. In addition, the public perceives nurses as persons with knowledge and expertise with an obligation to provide care to them in times of distress. Nurses have a detailed understanding of first aid principles, helping victims of trauma, and preventing the spread of contagious illnesses. Professional nurses also have well-refined teaching, organizational, and leadership skills that can be put to use in executing and coordinating care during all phases of a disaster. Finally, professional nurses have expertise in therapeutic communication skills to help provide psychological and spiritual support to persons during times of uncertainty. Thus, professional nurses play a key role in helping persons prepare for, survive during, cope with, and adapt to life after a disaster.

Veenema (2003) defined a disaster as "any destructive event that disrupts the normal functioning of a community" (p. 4). Disasters come in many forms. They may arise suddenly without warning (terrorist attack, plane crash, subway accident, earthquake), occur with warning (hurricane, flood, tornado, blizzard), or evolve over a long period (drought, famine). Disasters can be caused by nature (natural) or by humans. Disasters caused by humans fall into three broad categories: complex (e.g., multiple causation, such as a drought leads to a famine that stimulates political unrest and relocation of large numbers of people), technologic (e.g., destruction of community infrastructure, industrial accidents, massive power failure), or human settlement (e.g., migration of an entire ethnic group to avoid persecution). The magnitude of a disaster depends on its location. Disasters in highly populated areas affect more people and strain more resources than those occurring in rural areas. Hurricane Katrina paralyzed the city of New Orleans as well as much of the Louisiana coastal areas. However, in remote areas, getting help to the disaster may be very difficult, as in the 2008 Chinese earthquake. A medical disaster occurs when a catastrophic event creates more casualties than the health care resources within a community can effectively accommodate (Veenema, 2003).

Veenema (2003) and McGlown (2004) outlined a timeline for handling disasters that starts with preparation and ends with recovery. The first phase occurs before the disaster and encompasses planning/preparedness, prevention, and warning. In the first phase, communities identify hazards and make attempts to remove them. If they cannot be removed (such as weather), then the community develops early warning systems, evacuates members at risk, institutes public awareness campaigns, performs disaster drills, develops nursing databases (mass casualty plans), and devises means to evaluate all components of the disaster response. The response phase (phase 2) occurs with disaster onset and lasts 72 hours immediately following its end. The second phase consists of response, emergency management, and mitigation. In the second phase, the disaster response plan is activated; potential and ongoing hazards are identified, and action is taken to relieve human suffering (mitigated); public health needs are anticipated; victims are triaged for effective use of available health care resources; emergency food and water distribution centers are established; and alternatives for sanitation and waste removal are established if the community infrastructure has been damaged. The third and final phase focuses on recovery, rehabilitation, reconstruction, and evaluation. This phase starts after 72 hours of the disaster. In this phase, victims receive medical and nursing care, disease surveillance continues, public health infrastructure is restored, family members are reunited, victims are monitored for long-term physical and psychological injuries, disaster responders attend debriefing and counseling sessions, and the disaster team evaluates the disaster plan and revises the original disaster preparedness plan as needed (Veenema, 2003; McGlown, 2004). In developed countries, most communities have a disaster preparedness plan. However, these plans remain intact only in those with stable governments.

Professional nurses play key roles in each of the disaster states. Professional nurses who are uninjured at the disaster site offer basic first aid to victims. Some nurses, especially those working in emergency departments and as flight nurses, have special certification in trauma nursing and find themselves assisting in the rescue of victims in the field, triaging persons for appropriate treatment, or treating victims in first aid stations or emergency departments. Nurse administrators participate by assisting in communicating information about victims to families. Some nurses may assume the responsibility of reuniting family members and friends who became separated during the disaster. Mental health nurses offer counseling to victims and relatives of victims. Acute care nurses may find themselves mobilizing supplies, adjusting staff assignments, and determining which patients can be discharged early to make room for victims according to the facility's disaster plan. If the prospect of spread of infectious disease surfaces, other nurses may participate in mass vaccination programs. Finally, nurses may become involved with shelter supervision.

In response to American disasters after the September 11, 2001, Twin Towers terrorist attack, the United States has developed the Emergency System for Advance Resigtration of Volunteer Health Professionals (ESAR-VHP) to rapidly mobilize required health care personnel. Under the ESAR-VHP, individual states create a database of 100,000–200,000 qualified volunteer health care professionals. Each state verifies credentials, offers volunteers access to disaster training and drilling, and develops a plan for requesting registration activation. Persons who spontaneously volunteer during disasters may get in the way or be denied participation in response efforts. If used, volunteer skills may not be fully deployed because of lack of verification of professional status (Peterson, 2006). In the event of a disaster, an incident commander could identify and mobilize health care personnel with the skills to handle specific types of incidents (Vogt, 2004). Effective disaster planning for nurses involves the following ways for personal and professional preparation:

1. Personal preparation: being aware of possible or potential disasters, developing a personal household plan (including a 3-day to 3-week supply of food, medication, batteries, and water for all family members), drilling the family on the emergency action plan (including what to do if separated), staying current on immunizations, keeping first aid supplies and skills up to date, learning about wilderness survival (especially if power plants become disabled for prolonged periods), becoming involved in community activities, and supporting leaders who want to pass ordinances that protect the community against floods, mudslides, or collapses. Nurses can access detailed checklists for emergency preparedness from the Red Cross (www.redcross.org) or the Department of Homeland Security (www.dhs.gov).

2. Professional preparation: obtaining disaster nursing certification by a local American Red Cross Chapter or university; providing community education about disaster preparedness, response, and recovery; becoming involved in local disaster plan development; participating in local disaster drills; and making arrangements with employers for work relief if called to serve in a disaster (Gebbie & Qureshi, 2006; Peterson, 2006; Polivka et al., 2008; McGlown, 2004; Veenema, 2003, 2006). Following a disaster, nurses play key roles in screening and assessing community members

for symptoms associated with infectious illnesses and exposure to environmental toxins (Garfield & Yamin, 2006; Polivka et al.; Veenema, 2003, 2006). Nurses also would have valuable contributions to disaster debriefings in order to improve responses to future events (Polivka et al.; Veenema, 2003, 2006).

Camp Nursing

Camps are temporary, small communities. "Like all communities, camps provide basic services for their members, including food, shelter, socialization, protection from harm, meaningful activity, and the other necessities of life" (Lishner & Bruya, 1994, p. 7). Although seen primarily as a form of recreation, camps offer opportunities for nurses to practice first aid skills and care for the injured and infirm in more rustic settings, thereby providing practice in skills that might be required to respond to and care for disaster victims (Erceg & Pravda, 2001).

Camp nurses work toward attaining a healthy camp community. Camping allows individuals of all ages to experience nature; escape the stress of a fast-paced, highly technological society; and learn self-reliance while learning skills for survival and recreation, depending on the type of camp. Camp enables persons to live with others unlike themselves and shows them how to establish a community for a prescribed time. Skills learned at camp transfer to other settings.

Professional nurses have opportunities to participate in a variety of camping experiences. Day camps provide sessions of varying lengths, but the participants and staff return home at night. Resident camps require participants and staff to live on site for a few days or up to 2 months. Resident camps assume great responsibility to ensure the safety and health of participants and staff. Travel camps involve some form of motorized transportation so that participants can move from site to site. Trip camps use individually guided vehicles or animals (such as horses, bicycles, or canoes). Special needs camps serve persons with special physical, cognitive, or emotional needs and provide an opportunity to reap the benefits of camp life. Special needs camps include the various members of the interdisciplinary health care teams on staff to ensure that special health needs are met (Erceg & Pravda, 2001).

Camp nurses confront a variety of health care needs in professional practice. Generally speaking, camp nurses provide the following:

1. Emergency care for accidents and acute care for minor illness and injuries (such as insect bites, sore throats, or cuts)
2. Plans to avoid spread of contagious illnesses (foodborne illness, athlete's foot, plantar warts)
3. Health education for campers and staff
4. Screening and eliminating health hazards from the camp environment (insects; snakes; mice; and poison ivy, oak, and sumac)
5. Verification of healthy diet offerings and daily camp schedules
6. Supervision that persons abide by health-related rules

Nurses working or volunteering in special needs camps find themselves providing direct care to campers by administering medications, performing specialized procedures and therapies, and monitoring the effects of interventions and the camping experience on those with special needs. Camp nurses also must be aware of, develop relationships with, and secure camp contracts for emergency care with health care providers located in the camp's vicinity (Erceg & Pravda, 2001).

Occupational Health Nursing

Because employers and employees in work settings share a common goal and spend time together, workplaces fit the definition of community. Occupational health nursing provides primary, secondary, and tertiary care to persons in the work setting. Occupational health nurses assure employee safety by collaborating with agencies that set standards for safe, healthy working environments. Federal guidelines for worker safety specify that employers bear responsibility for deleterious effects encountered by workers for occupational and environmental hazards (Clark, 1999; Rogers, 2001). Large businesses may have an occupational health department that employs many nurses; small businesses may employ only one nurse or contract with health care providers to provide occupational health services for employees.

In addition to providing direct care services, occupational health nurses may provide health education to employees. They also compile statistical reports summarizing the annual incidence of employee occupational illness and injuries. By law, these reports are submitted to federal, state, and local agencies and made available to employees. Commonly occurring occupational illnesses include repetitive stress injuries, allergic and contact dermatitis, respiratory disorders caused by inhalation of toxic agents, poisoning, hearing loss, low back disorders, hearing loss, traumatic injuries, fertility problems, and pregnancy abnormalities (Clark, 1999; Rogers, 2001).

In 2004, the American Association of Occupational Health Nurses (AAOHN) developed 11 standards for occupational and environmental health nursing practice. These standards are summarized here. The entire document is available from the American Association of Occupational Health Nurses. According to these standards, occupational health does the following in clinical practice:

1. Assesses the health status of clients, workforce, and work environment using a systematic approach
2. Analyzes the health data from the assessment and develops nursing diagnoses that need to be addressed
3. Develops specific expected client outcomes to address identified nursing diagnoses
4. Creates a goal-directed plan with comprehensive interventions and therapies to achieve care outcomes
5. Implements identified interventions to achieve desired care plan outcomes
6. Evaluates the developed care plan systematically and continuously in response to client responses
7. Manages and uses corporate resources to support occupational health and safety programs
8. Assumes responsibility for professional self-development for enhancement of professional growth and competency
9. Collaborates with clients to prevent health issues while promoting and restoring health in the work environment
10. Uses research findings in and contributes to the scientific knowledge base for occupational and environmental health nursing for improving practice and advancing the profession
11. Uses an ethical framework when making practice decisions

The AAOHN identified core competencies based on the results of a Delphi process using Benner's (1984) *Novice to Expert* framework for ranking professional nurse competency levels in the following areas: clinical practice, case management, efforts at keeping the workforce healthy and safe while promoting a safe and healthy workplace and environment; regulatory and legislative efforts (abiding by current regulations and impacting future public policies); management, business, and leadership skills; health promotion and disease prevention; health and safety education and training; occupational and environmental health research; and professionalism (AAOHN, 2007).

Occupational health nursing provides nurses with an opportunity to improve the health of employees and the work environment. By screening employees for various health problems related to their work before symptoms occur, occupational health nurses not only improve the health of workers but also reduce long-term health care costs for employers (AAOHN, 1999, 2007).

Questions for Reflection 14-2

1. What are some of the occupational health hazards that are present in my current work setting?
2. What are some of the health hazards that are present in my position as a student and in the building where I attend classes?
3. How can I reduce health hazards that I find in my work or school setting?

Home Health Nursing

Nurses engaged in home health nursing provide nursing services to a client within the confines of the client's residence. Although home health nursing practice focuses primarily on individuals, the home health care nurse considers the needs of the family and designated caregivers. Home health nurses view the client, family, and designated caregivers as partners when planning and implementing nursing care. The nurse performs a detailed home assessment to determine the safety of the home for the client (Bailey, 2007; Clark, 1999). In addition, the home health nurse performs a community assessment in which the client's home is located to determine access to services and availability of resources for client support. The home health nurse provides direct care; educates the client, family, and caregivers how to independently meet health care needs; counsels the client and family; and coordinates community resources and benefits. Home health nurses continuously evaluate the effectiveness of planned interventions and community resources as nursing care is delivered (American Nurses Association [ANA], 1999; Bailey, 2007).

The nurse–client relationship differs in home health nursing because the client (and family) considers the nurse as a guest (ANA, 1999). This perception of the client sets up vastly different dynamics for the nurse–client relationship. The nurse must diligently work to ensure that he or she is welcome while helping the client and family assume responsibility for meeting individualized health needs. The nurse exercises special care not to offend the host or disaffirm client and family self-determination. Sometimes, the nurse must politely refuse client requests when they fall outside of the arena of professional nursing practice (Clark, 1999). When such requests are made, the nurse might consider referring the client to appropriate community resources or set up visits by a homemaker or unlicensed care provider.

Home health nurses frequently supervise visits by unlicensed care providers and coordinate the schedules of other members of the health care team and home services so that the client has someone making a visit each day of the week. Home health care nurses frequently take calls on weekends and holidays so that homebound clients have access to a nurse should health care problems arise.

Recent advances in technology enable home health nurses to have daily contact with clients. Telehealth and satellite home monitoring systems enable home health nurses to check client weight, blood pressure, pulse, peripheral blood glucose, and prothrombin times. Some home monitoring systems set alarms and verbally prompt clients when it is time to get connected and send physical assessment data to the home health care agency. Certain systems offer direct video monitoring and/or wireless technology to obtain results of client home monitoring. Because of computer technology, the home health agency can create printed records of client data using tables or graphs to detect trends toward meeting expected outcomes or to indicate deteriorating parameters. Some systems even have the capability to ask a client specific questions to assess for potential disease complications. Home health nurses need to stress to clients that home monitoring systems do not replace calling 911 or an ambulance when an emergency arises. Home health nurses use these systems for planning the sequence of daily visits or determining if an additional, unscheduled visit should be made. They also can telephone clients when they fail to perform required, daily monitoring tasks. Medicare covers home monitoring systems as long as clients have been certified for home health nurse visits. Once clients no longer need home health care, the monitoring system may be removed from the home. Some clients with financial resources elect to keep the system in their home using private funds to pay for continued home monitoring.

For home health agencies to be reimbursed for services, the professional nurse maintains detailed records of home health visits. Complete, accurate documentation of the visit serves as data for third-party payer reimbursement, validation of services rendered, and data for nursing research. The professional nurse completes approval and recertification forms to validate the need for nursing services.

Hospice Nursing

Hospice care nurses frequently make home visits. For terminally ill clients who reside in extended care or residential facilities, hospice nurses visit clients where they live and assist care providers with end-of-life care issues. Starting in 1983, Medicare began covering home health services for the terminally ill (Lundy & Janes, 2001; Smith & Maurer, 2000; Stanhope & Lancaster, 2006).

Nurses have a long history of caring for the dying. In 1950, Dr. Cicely Saunders founded the hospice movement at St. Christopher's in London. Hospice aims to add more life to each day when medical science cannot add additional time to a person's life. Hospice uses a team approach to maximize the quality of life for the terminally ill client and caregivers. Hospice provides the following services: (1) intermittent nursing services; (2) physician services aimed at alleviating human suffering; (3) medications for relieving pain, nausea, and other discomforts associated with the dying process; (4) home health aides; (5) medical equipment and supplies; (6) pastoral services for spiritual support; (7) continuous care when crises arise; and (8) follow-up bereavement services for the family for as long as a year after the client has died.

Hospice nurses receive special education on the dying process, grief, and bereavement management. To effectively care for the terminally ill client and caregivers, hospice nurses must have confidence in their clinical skills and spiritual beliefs. Much of the nursing care focuses on helping the terminally ill and their families find meaning in their past, present, and future lives. As a team member, the hospice nurse frequently spends more time with clients and families and shares comprehensive information with other members of the hospice care team (Lundy & Janes, 2001; Smith & Maurer, 2000; Stanhope & Lancaster, 2006).

Nursing the Homeless

Homeless persons are humans who lack a fixed, regular nighttime residence or use a shelter, mission, welfare hotel, or other physical place not designed for human slumber. For some persons, homelessness may be temporary (has no home, but community membership remains), episodic (several bouts of having no home), or chronic (no home as a way of life). Homelessness is not confined to single adults; children appear among the ranks of the homeless. During times of economic recession, the number of homeless families increases. Reasons for homelessness include poverty, lack of affordable housing, unemployment, lack or inadequacy of government financial support, crime, violence, lack of kin support, mental illness, substance abuse, deinstitutionalization of the mentally ill, and socially stigmatized infectious diseases (Anderson & Riley, 2008; Butts, 2001; Clark, 1999). In American life, securing a job, societal privileges, or government-sponsored social services requires a permanent address.

Access to health care services creates problems for the homeless. Frequently, homeless persons use emergency rooms for treatment of illnesses or enter the health care system as victims of crime. They receive emergency and acute care for sustained injuries in acute care facilities. Once they recover, placing them in a safe situation where they can meet the demands of follow-up care poses a great challenge to social workers and case managers.

Homeless persons rarely have a consistent primary care provider because of their inability to pay for rendered services. When health care is needed, some homeless persons rely on community free health clinics or homeless shelters. Unfortunately, some of these health care–providing organizations depend solely on volunteer health care providers, and the consistency of seeing the same client over time becomes problematic. Nurses also see homeless clients in soup kitchens and on urban streets. However, homelessness is not confined to urban settings. Migrant workers also fit the definition of homelessness. Rural county health departments frequently serve as the vehicle for health care for transient farm workers and homeless persons seeking refuge in rural areas.

For effective nursing practice with the homeless, the community health or volunteer professional nurse must develop and maintain a realistic understanding of the world of homelessness. Many times, homeless persons lack the knowledge of available local programs and services to which they are entitled. Sometimes, homeless persons become so overwhelmed in securing food and shelter they lose hope. To survive, some homeless individuals develop street-smart behaviors that include manipulation, lying, and panhandling. Sometimes homeless alcoholics and drug addicts use money received to purchase alcohol or illicit drugs. Some churches give homeless persons food when they ask for cash.

Professional nurses may play a variety of roles when working with and for the homeless. Nurses, when working with persons in clinical practice and in social activities, can work with clients to prevent the factors contributing to homelessness. Nurses also can lobby for legislation that increases services to homeless persons and provide government officials with information about the plight of the homeless. Professional nurses can provide direct care and health screening to persons who seek help at public health departments, free health clinics, homeless shelters, churches, or soup kitchens. Finally, professional nurses can refer the homeless to mobile treatment centers, mental health facilities, and drug and alcohol rehabilitation programs.

Nursing the Incarcerated

As punishment for crimes, individuals become incarcerated in jails, prisons, and juvenile detention facilities. Professional nurses do not participate in procedures exclusively for correctional purposes. However, professional nurses working in such facilities engage in primary, secondary, and tertiary interventions for those who are incarcerated. Professional nursing practice in correctional facilities emphasizes disease prevention, promotes health enhancement activities, and recognizes and treats physical and mental illness and injuries from an accident or act of violence. Nurses also evaluate the effectiveness of care and look for ways to improve prison health services (ANA, 1995). In prisons, nurses make most health care decisions. They work with medically approved care protocols. Correctional registered nurses have the opportunity to work with diseases rarely seen in the general population (such as TB). Before becoming incarcerated, prisoners frequently pursued high-risk lifestyles that included drug and alcohol abuse, poor living conditions, lack of effective parenting, and poor access to preventive health services (Stringer, 2001).

Watson, Stimpson, and Hostick (2004) reported that as many as 90% of incarcerated persons may have mental health problems, 80% smoke, 12% may be infected with HIV, and 8% may have hepatitis. As prison sentences lengthen, nurses in prison encounter older inmates, and as many as 85% of them may have more than one chronic major illness. Although not common, some terminally ill prisoners may be seen by prison hospice workers or volunteers (Watson, Stimpson, & Hostick).

Security systems at correctional facilities apply to health care professionals and other staff members. Security systems protect staff, volunteers, and visitors from acts of violence. Prison officials have corrections officers stand outside examination rooms and accompany nurses to cells as they deliver health care to inmates who have a history of violence (Stringer, 2001). Some inmates receive outpatient care in prison clinics and if 24-hour nursing care is needed, most prisons have an infirmary. Prisons frequently develop partnerships with university health care centers and the private sector to obtain medical staff coverage for clinics. However, prisons staff infirmaries with nurses and other unlicensed care providers are employed by the prison system (Watson, Stimpson, & Hostick, 2004).

The nurse in the correctional institution must display self-confidence and strength. Correctional nurses also must avoid performing favors for inmates because inmates frequently try to take advantage of anyone who displays kindness toward them (Stringer, 2001).

Forensic Nursing

The scientific study of death, or forensics, has been a vital arm of law enforcement. In recent years, the application of forensic science to investigate trauma in emergency departments has created the need to secure reliable evidence and support victims of violent crime. The practice of forensic nursing includes forensic nursing sexual assault examiners, forensic nursing educators/consultants, nurse coroners, nurse death investigators, legal nurse consultants, nurse attorneys, correctional nurses, clinical nurse specialists, forensic pediatric nurses, forensic gerontology nurses, and forensic psychiatric nurses. Forensic nurses use the nursing process to determine the occurrence of sexual assault, homicide, physical assault, spouse abuse, and child abuse (International Association of Forensic Nurses & American Nurses Association, 1997).

Forensic nurses identify injuries with forensic implication. Using strict protocols, they collect evidence when a crime has occurred. Nurses who collect evidence frequently provide expert witness testimony to the integrity of the evidence. They also meticulously document client interactions and evidence collection because the documentation will be used in court as trial evidence. Forensic nurses also interact with the victims of crime and their grieving families. Finally, forensic nurses may consult with other agencies and law enforcement personnel when forensic interests are shared (International Association of Forensic Nurses & American Nurses Association, 1997).

Armed Forces Nursing

The U.S. Armed Forces work and live together for a common purpose: to protect the country. Because each branch of the military has a specific area of expertise, each branch fits the definition of community. Armed forces nursing provides nurses with the opportunity to work with military personnel, their families, and civilians (affected by warfare). The U.S. Army, Navy, and Air Force each have Nursing Corps. Nurses serve the military by enlisting for active duty, for reserve status, or in the National Guard. Military nurses have the opportunity to practice with clients of all ages. Armed forces nurses work in ambulatory clinics, community hospitals, large medical centers, hospital ships, field hospitals, and aircraft. Military nurses receive comparable compensation to nurses in civilian practice settings. Branches of the armed services offer generous signing bonuses, a full array of benefits, and the option to retire with full benefits after 20 years of service. Nurses have lots of upward mobility potential in all branches of the armed forces (Marquand, 2004). Professional practice responsibilities vary according to assignment.

Military nurses confront special personal and professional challenges when deployed into a combat zone. Some of the challenges include long separations from family (a year, or sometimes longer), language and cultural differences, climate issues (temperature extremes, dust, or tropical storms), supply shortages, severe trauma exposure, violent threats from enemy combatants or insurgents, and posttraumatic stress disorder. When serving in a combat zone, military nurses, like soldiers, receive increased pay (Spencer, 2006).

Armed forces nursing provides professional nurses with opportunities for advanced education. Nurses can earn graduate degrees in nursing, receive specialty education, and pursue graduate degrees outside the discipline of nursing. Military nurses have opportunities for teaching patient care skills to corps members and leadership classes to future officers (Marquand, 2004). A recent interest of the armed forces is conducting nursing research related to issues of deployment, the needs of military personnel and their beneficiaries in times of war and peace, and cultural aspects of military nursing (Committee on Military Nursing Research, 1996; Marquand, 2004).

Military nursing provides the opportunity for nurses to work with other health team members as equal partners. The camaraderie among health team members is high because everyone focuses on what is best for the soldier, sailor, airman, or marine receiving care. Physicians and nurses have weapons training together. In some circumstances, nurses may outrank physicians. When armed forces deploy active duty and reserve nurses during times of war, they expend energy and resources to recruit civilian nurses to fill vacancies left in stateside hospitals and clinics (Marquand, 2004).

School Nursing

Schools are organizations that focus on the education of persons of all ages. Within a school, many persons work together to attain the goal of imparting cognitive, affective, or psychomotor knowledge and skills to others. Thus, all levels of schools meet the definition of a community. Many persons tend to view school nursing as confined to the kindergarten through high school levels. However, many colleges and universities also provide health services to students, and some nurses work with college students. The role of the school nurse remains consistent across all levels of education. However, when nurses work with children and minors, they spend much time working with the parents of these younger clients (Lundy & Janes, 2001; Novak, 2002; Smith & Maurer, 2000).

School nurses have various roles in clinical practice. They provide student health care directly when using clinical knowledge and nursing process in meeting the health care needs of students when they have bouts of acute physical illness or chronic illness, or when special health care needs are the result of a disability. In addition, professional school nurses also provide first aid; administer medications; screen students for health problems, general fitness, and signs of abuse; monitor vital signs; participate in case management activities; change dressings; and perform urinary catheterizations. School nurses develop individualized nursing care and health educational plans for students with chronic illness or those who need to learn complex self-care skills to cope with a disability. Along with providing services to students, school nurses engage in enhancing the wellness of teachers; administrators; counselors; and nutritional, janitorial, and clerical staff. School nurses perform periodic environmental assessments to ensure a safe and health-promoting environment of the school. School nurses also may review the daily menu schedules for school cafeterias to verify that healthy meals are being served. When specific health care needs arise, school nurses make referrals to local health care providers (Lundy & Janes, 2001; Novak, 2002; Smith & Maurer, 2000).

In some school systems, nurses frequently develop the health education program in collaboration with school administration, teachers, and parents. Health education programs may be tailored to meet an individual school's needs or be developed to meet health education needs and concerns for a school district. Many times, the school nurse teaches health education classes to students, parents, school staff, or community groups (Lundy & Janes, 2001; Novak, 2002; Smith & Maurer, 2000).

School nurses spend much time maintaining student health records. They verify that all students have received required immunizations and that students have received screening for visual, hearing, and skeletal deformities. When students make visits to the school nurse, the nurse documents the reason for the visit, interventions performed, parental contact (if needed), and referrals made (if required). Most school health programs have protocols indicating actions that can be taken by nurses without parental consent. Many schools have parents sign forms specifying particular over-the-counter medications (such as acetaminophen, antibiotic or steroid ointments, antihistamines, and decongestants) the nurse may administer to their children. School nurses also receive detailed information about routinely prescribed medications that students may require. Because of the prevalence of drug abuse, students taking prescription medications must visit the school nurse to receive their scheduled doses (Lundy & Janes, 2001; Novak, 2002; Smith & Maurer, 2000).

The school nurse serves as a resource of health information for students, faculty, and staff. Sometimes, faculty and staff consult the school nurse when they suspect a potential health-related problem among students. The nurse develops several approaches to the problem and consults with school administration before activating a plan. Sometimes nurses work collaboratively with teachers and administrators to develop plans for students with learning disabilities and mental health problems. In some cases, the school nurse assumes responsibility for monitoring school compliance to specific portions of student disability regulations.

School nursing is a specialized area of nursing practice, and additional education beyond the baccalaureate degree is recommended for optimal clinical effectiveness. School nurses may become certified through the National Association of School Nurses and the ANA. Many states also have certification requirements for school nursing.

In addition to providing nursing services and health education, the school nurse participates in research, investigates cases, and delegates health-related tasks to unlicensed persons. Unfortunately, not every school has a nurse on campus, and certain tasks must be delegated to school staff members. When this happens, the professional nurse must provide the staff members with education to safely accomplish health-related tasks.

College health nursing focuses primarily on the health care needs and concerns of persons between the ages of 17 and 24 years. Nurses working with college students emphasize self-care and wellness. College nursing services vary in size and scope. Some college health programs offer ambulatory care services with scheduled office hours exclusively, whereas others provide an infirmary for acute care staffed by a multidisciplinary health team. The American College Health Association Review Group in collaboration with the ANA has published guidelines for collegiate nursing practice. Many colleges and universities provide clinics for students that have an advanced practice nurse on staff to deliver required health services (ANA, 1997).

Regardless of student age group, school nurses use the nursing process to guide client care activities. They also systematically evaluate the effectiveness of nursing practice and health care services. School nurses also must abide by various state regulations where they practice. They bear responsibility for the following: (1) maintaining competence, (2) remaining current in regard to knowledge and issues affecting their student populations, (3) providing ethical care, (4) using research findings in practice, (5) conducting research studies when gaps in practice are identified, (6) using school resources judiciously, and (7) collaborating with others to develop relevant health care services (ANA, 1997; Lundy & Janes, 2001; Novak, 2002; Smith & Maurer, 2000).

Questions for Reflection 14-3

1. What are the health services offered at the college where I attend classes?
2. What health-promoting factors are present within the college where I attend classes?
3. What are my major health-related concerns as a nursing student? Why are these important to me?

Parish Nursing

Parish nursing provides nurses with an opportunity to practice within faith communities. Faith communities are people who share a common faith tradition and meet in a house of worship (church, mosque, or synagogue) (Berry, 2002). In 1984, Granger Westberg started a parish-nursing program at Lutheran General Hospital in Chicago. The International Parish Nursing Resource Center offered the first continuing education program in parish nursing in 1987. In 1998, the ANA published *Scope and Standard of Parish Nursing Practice*, thereby acknowledging parish nursing as a distinct specialized area of professional practice (ANA, 1998).

Berry (2002) identified two models for parish nursing. In the congregational model, the nurse acts autonomously and nursing and health programs arise from the community in which the nurse serves. The nurse is held accountable to the congregation and the governing body. In the institutional model, the nurse collaborates more closely with local hospitals, medical centers, extended care facilities, and educational institutions. Sometimes the parish nurse holds contracts with the collaborating agencies. The nurse works in partnership with the local health care and educational institutions to meet the needs of parishioners.

Nurses holding membership in a faith-based community frequently serve as the first responder when a congregational member has a health-related problem during a service or activity. However, a parish nurse expands the role and engages in health ministry. Health ministries may or may not need the expertise of a professional nurse and include activities such as visiting homebound congregational members, providing meals for families in times of crises, forming prayer circles or chains, serving healthy church meals and refreshment at congregational activities, and volunteering for local community care groups (Berry, 2002). In some parishes, nurses provide volunteer service. Other parishes have formalized programs staffed by paid directors, coordinators, and nurses. Some parish nursing programs allow the nurse to run clinics to serve poor, marginalized congregations. These clinics are staffed by nurse practitioners (Boss, 1999).

As a specialized area of professional practice, the following factors distinguish parish nursing from other practice areas:

1. The client spiritual dimension is the core and central dimension of parish nursing practice.
2. The parish nurse balances knowledge of nursing science, humanities, and theology as nursing services are delivered.
3. The faith community and its ministry become the focus of practice.
4. The parish nurse emphasizes individual, family, and faith community strengths.
5. Spiritual health, health, and healing are viewed as dynamic ongoing processes (Solari-Twadell & McDermott, 1999).

Nursing skills used when providing care to faith-based communities vary across parish nursing programs. Solari-Twadell (1999) emphasized that "parish nursing cannot be all things to all people" (p. 24). The eight key functions of the parish nurse have been identified: health education, personal health counseling, health care referral services, support group development, volunteer facilitation, volunteer training, faith and health integration, and health care advocate. In 1984, Westberg envisioned the parish nurse as a part-time paid position assumed by a baccalaureate-prepared nurse (Solari-Twadell, 1999).

Education preparation for parish nurses has evolved from a 1- or 2-day continuing education seminar into more formalized programs. Nurses can attend a 1-day continuing education program or take a formal course of study lasting several years to earn a master's degree in nursing or a graduate degree in divinity. In 1996, 50 parish nurse coordinators identified key elements of a standardized curriculum for parish nursing. Curricular content addresses the church's role in health; health theology; the history and philosophy of parish nursing; models of parish nursing practice; the teaching, counseling, referring, and educating functions of the parish nurse; the integration of faith and health; parish community assessment; health promotion and maintenance; families and faith communities as client; parish nurse self-care; working with churches and within a ministerial team; legal and ethical issues; accountability, and documentation techniques; prayer, and worship leadership; and how to start a parish nursing program. Additional content for parish nurse coordinators includes budgeting, writing grants, managing human and fiscal resources, developing spiritually, and planning continuing education for parish nurses (McDermott et al., 1999). Berry (2002) suggested that advanced practice and specialty practice education along with practical experience in community health nursing enrich parish nursing services.

Parish nursing offers an avenue for development of new spiritual (or religious), community, and interpersonal nursing diagnoses and interventions. Proposed new nursing diagnoses include the potential for enhanced acceptance, spiritual concern, altered spiritual development, spiritual isolation, altered spiritual ritual patterns, risk for cultural incongruity, ineffective boundaries, ineffective meditation skills, and communication enhancement. Spiritual nursing interventions focus upon enhancing health through strengthening faith and hope while preventing religious addiction. Parish nurses empower parish communities to engage in unified political actions on health-related legislation, support and teach each other to provide volunteer assistance to ill and frail parishioners, and promote health by enhancing the spiritual dimensions of congregation members (Burkhart & Kellen, 1999).

Volunteer Nursing

Many nurses volunteer to provide nursing services in community settings. Some nurses routinely schedule volunteer activities into life routines. Examples of scheduled volunteer activities may be serving on organizational or institutional boards, monthly or weekly duties at a free health clinic, and regularly scheduled community health screening activities. Other nurses may provide volunteer service for episodic events such as health fairs, camps, community service projects (e.g., nursing services for a Habitat for Humanity group), church activities, and community events. When volunteering, professional nurses have an obligation to have adequate knowledge about actual and potential situations that may arise.

When providing services, the professional nurse assumes responsibility for providing accurate health information and ensuring that those served receive the care they require. In the case of blood pressure screening, the professional nurse must establish guidelines for persons who require emergency treatment, those with dangerously high or low blood pressure measurements, those who need medical referral for abnormal measurements, and those with borderline measurements. While engaging in blood pressure screening, nurses can teach persons about blood pressure and ways to avoid hypertension. Sometimes, nurses provide clients with a form containing the client's blood pressure reading and recommended actions for various readings. The professional nurse cannot force anyone to seek immediate treatment for blood pressure problems or verify that clients participating in the screening follow through with referral recommendations.

Family members, friends, neighbors, and other acquaintances often consult the professional nurse for health-related concerns. When this occurs, the nurse assumes responsibility for health care advice. The nurse must acknowledge his or her limitations to knowledge and expertise. The professional nurse safeguards the person asking questions by giving advice that is more cautious and making referrals when uncertain. When giving out health advice, some nurses keep personal notes as to the advice they give family, friends, and acquaintances. Recordkeeping enables the nurse to make additional inquiries regarding the results of advice given.

 ## SUMMARY AND SIGNIFICANCE TO PRACTICE

Professional nurses have an array of opportunities to engage in community health nursing. Community health nursing requires that the nurse and community members collaborate and establish partnerships with each other to establish effective and relevant health programs. Professional nurses use nursing process, communication skills, and knowledge of the political process to plan, establish, and provide effective programs to promote community health in a variety of community settings.

FROM THEORY TO PRACTICE

1. Reread the vignette at the beginning of the chapter. After reading the chapter, what ideas can you generate as possible reasons for lack of community participation in the annual flu vaccine program developed by Paula?
2. Generate a plan to improve turnout for next year's program. In this plan, include specific details, such as ways to entice each small town community member to participate in the plan.
3. What are some community health problems that you can identify in the community where you live? What community services are available to address the problems that you identify? If no services are available, how would you go about developing a community health program to address them?

WWWW INTERNET EXERCISES

Exercise 1

Visit the CDC Emergency Preparedness and Response home page at http://www.bt.cdc.gov.

1. Click on "Recent Outbreaks & Incidents" to learn about recent public health hazards. Select a topic of interest and prepare a brief summary to share with your colleagues in class.
2. Return to the home page and click on "Bioterrorism Agents" to learn about potential agents that could be used in a bioterrorist attack. Do you think that you would recognize an act of bioterrorism? Why or why not?
3. Return to the home page and read about "Chemical Emergencies" and "Radiation Emergencies." Has your local community had a release of a toxic chemical or radiation?
4. Return to the home page, then click on "Natural Disasters & Severe Weather." List the disasters and severe weather incidents that are possible in your area. Check with your clinical agency to see if the Mass Casualty and Disaster Plan has procedures to follow for each disaster or severe weather incident that might occur in your area.

Exercise 2

Visit the American Public Health Association: http://www.apha.org. Quickly skim the home page. When finished, click on the words "Site Search." Enter the word "nursing" in the blank space provided to search American Public Health Association documents. Once the documents appear, select the latest edition of the *Public Health Nursing Newsletter* and read it. Make a list of the key topics and issues contained in the newsletter. Compare these issues to issues and concerns in your current area of professional nursing practice.

WWWW INTERNET RESOURCES

Healthy People 2010: http://health.gov/healthypeople.
Morbidity and Mortality Weekly Report: http://www.cdc.gov/mmwr.
American Public Health Association: http://apha.org.
The American Red Cross: http://www.redcross.org and http://www.redcross.org/services/disaster.
The International Parish Nurse Resource Center: http://ipnrc.parishnurses.org.
Johns Hopkins University Center for Civilian Biodefense Strategies: http://www.hopkins-biodefense.org.
Department of Homeland Security: http://www.dhs.gov.
American Psychiatric Association: http://www.psych.org.
Association of Camp Nurses: http://www.campnurse.org.

Occupational Safety and Health Administration: http://www.osha.gov.
American Association of Occupational Health Nurses: http://www.aaohn.org.
American Correctional Health Services Association: http://www.org/achsa.
The International Association of Forensic Nurses: http://www.forensicnurse.org.
National Association of School Nurses: http://www.nasn.org.
Armed Force Nursing:
  U.S. Army Nurse Corps: http://www.goarmy.com.amedd/nurse/index.jsp/.
  U.S. Navy Nurse Corps: http://www.navy.com/healthcare/nursing.
  U.S. Air Force: http://www.airforce.com.

REFERENCES

Agnes, M. (2005). *Webster's new world college dictionary* (4th ed). Cleveland, OH:Wiley.

American Association of Occupational Health Nurses (AAOHN). (1999). *Standards of occupational health nursing practice*. Atlanta, GA: Author.

American Association of Occupational Health Nurses (AAOHN). (2004). Standards of occupational and environmental health nursing. *American Association of Occupational Health Nurses Journal, 52*(7), 270–274.

American Association of Occupational Health Nurses (AAOHN). (2007). Competencies in occupational and environmental health nursing: By the American Association of Occupational Nurses, Inc. *American Association of Occupational Health Nurses Journal, 55*(11), 442–447.

American Nurses Association (ANA). (1995). *Nursing social policy statement*. Washington, DC: Author.

American Nurses Association (ANA). (1997). *Scope and standards of college health nursing practice*. Washington, DC: Author.

American Nurses Association (ANA). (1999). *Scope and standards of home health nursing practice*. Washington, DC: Author.

American Nurses Association (ANA). (2007). *Scope and standards of public health nursing practice*. Washington, DC: Nursebooks.org.

Anderson, D., & Riley, P. (2008). The homeless population. In L. L. Ivanov & C. L. Blue (Eds.), *Public health nursing leadership, policy & practice* (pp. 572–590). Clifton Park, NY: Delmar Cengage Learning.

Anderson, E. T., & McFarlane, J. (2006). *Community as partner* (5th ed.). Philadelphia: Lippincott Williams & Wilkins.

Andrews, M. M., & Boyle, J. S. (2008). (Eds.). *Transcultural concepts in nursing care* (5th ed.). Philadelphia: Lippincott Williams & Wilkins.

Bailey, V. (2007). Satisifaction levels with a community night nursing service. *Nursing Standard, 22*(5), 35–42.

Bekemeier, B. (2007). Credentialing for public health nurses: Personally valued … but not well recognized. *Public Health Nursing, 24*(5), 439–448.

Bender, K. W., & Salmon, M. E. (2001). Public health nursing: Pioneers of health care reform. In B. S. Lundy & S. Janes (Eds.), *Community health nursing: Caring for the public's health* (pp. 866–879). Sudbury, MA: Jones & Bartlett.

Benner, P. (1984). *From novice to expert*. Menlo Park, CA: Addison-Wesley.

Berry, R. (2002). Community health nurse as parish nurse. In M. Stanhope, & J. Lancaster (Eds.), *Foundations of community health nursing: Community-oriented practice* (pp. 449–461). St. Louis, MO: Mosby.

Bertalanffy, L. von. (1968). *General systems theory*. New York: George Brazziller.

Bigbee, J. (2008). Relationships between nurse- and physician-to-population ratios and state health rankings. *Public Health Nursing, 25*(3), 244–252.

Boss, J. G. (1999). Parish nursing practice with underorganized, underserved, and marginalized clients. In P. A. Solari-Twadell & M. A. McDermott (Eds.), *Parish nursing: Promoting whole person health within faith communities* (pp. 55–65). Thousand Oaks, CA: Sage.

Burkhart, L., & Kellen, P. (1999). Proposed diagnoses and interventions. In P. A. Solari-Twadell & M. A. McDermott (Eds.), *Parish nursing: Promoting whole person health within faith communities* (pp. 257–267). Thousand Oaks, CA: Sage.

Butts, J. B. (2001). Urban and homeless populations. In K. S. Lundy & S. Janes (Eds.), *Community health nursing: Caring for the public's health* (pp. 594–617). Sudbury, MA: Jones & Bartlett.

Clark, M. J. (1999). *Nursing in the community* (3rd ed.). Norwalk, CT: Appleton & Lange.

Committee on Military Nursing Research. (1996). The program for research in military nursing: Progress and future direction. Available at http://www.nap.edu/catalog/5257.html. Accessed July 5, 2005.

Copeland, M. (2002). E-community health nursing. *Journal of Holistic Nursing, 20*, 152–165.

Davis, R. (2000). Holographic community: Reconceptualizing the meaning of community in an era of health care reform. *Nursing Outlook, 48*, 294–301.

Elsom, S., Happell, B., & Manias, E. (2007). Exploring the expanded practice roles of community mental health nurses. *Issues in Mental Health Nursing*, *28*, 413–429.

Erceg, L., & Pravda, M. (2001). *The basics of camp nursing*. Martinsvlle, IN: American Camp Association.

Garfield R., & Hamid, A (2006). Tsunami response: A year later. *American Journal of Nursing*, *106*(1), 76–79.

Gebbie, K., & Qureshi, K. (2006). A historical challenge: Nurses and emergencies. *Online Journal of Issues in Nursing*, *11*(3), 6-8. Available at http://search.ebscoostcom/login.aspx?direct=true&db=nyh&AN=23 146891&loginpage=Login.asp&site=ehost-live. Accessed June 23, 2008.

Hancock, T., & Duhl, L. (1986). *Healthy cities: Promoting health in the urban context* (Healthy Cities Paper No 1.) Copenhagen: World Health Organization Europe.

Harkness, G. A. (2001). Epidemiology of health and illness. In K. M. Lishner & M. A. Lishner (Eds.), *The camp community* (pp. 100–117). Martinsville, IN: American Camp Association.

Hunt, R. (2008). *Introduction to community-based nursing* (4th ed.). Philadelphia: Lippincott Williams & Wilkins.

International Association of Forensic Nurses & American Nurses Association. (1997). *Scope and standards of forensic nursing practice*. Washington, DC: American Nurses Publishing.

Jamieson, E. M., & Sewall, M. F. (1954). *Trends in nursing history* (4th ed.). Philadelphia: W. B. Saunders.

Leddy, S. (2003). *Integrative health promotion*. Thorofare, NJ: Slack.

Leininger, M., & McFarland, M. (2006). *Cultural care diversity and universality: A worldwide theory for nursing* (2nd ed.). Sudbury MA: Jones and Bartlett.

Leonard, B. (2000). Community empowerment and healing. In E. T. Anderson & J. McFarlane (Eds.), *Community as partner* (3rd ed., pp. 92–115). Philadelphia: Lippincott Williams & Wilkins.

Levin, P., Cary, A., Kulbok, P., Leffers, J., Molle, M., & Polivka, P. (2008). Graduate education for advanced practice public health nursing: At the crossroads. *Public Health Nursing*, *25*, 176v193.

Lishner, K. M., & Bruya, M. A. (Eds.). (1994). *Creating a healthy camp community: A nurse's role*. Martinsville, IN: American Camping Association.

Lind, C., & Smith, D. (2008). Analyzing the state of community health nursing: Advancing from deficit to strengths-based practice using appreciative inquiry. *Advances in Nursing Science*, *31*(1), 28–41.

Lundy, K. S., & Barton, J. (2001). Community and population health: Assessment and intervention. In K. S. Lundy & S. Janes (Eds.), *Community health nursing: Caring for the public's health* (pp. 30–69). Sudbury, MA: Jones & Bartlett.

Lundy, K. S., & Janes, S. (Eds.). (2001). *Community health nursing: Caring for the public's health*. Sudbury, MA: Jones & Bartlett.

Lundy, K. S., Janes, S., & Hartman, S. (2001). Opening the door: Community and public health nursing. In K. S. Lundy & S. Janes (Eds.), *Community health nursing: Caring for the public's health* (pp. 4–29). Sudbury, MA: Jones & Bartlett.

Marquand, B. (2004, Spring). An army (and navy and air force) of opportunities. *Minority Nurse*, 26–30.

McCardle, J., Parahoo, K., & McKenna, H. (2007). A national survey of community psychiatric nurses and their care activities in Ireland *Journal of Psychiatric and Mental Health Nursing*, *14*, 179–188.

McDermott, M. A., Solari-Twadell, P. A., & Matheus, R. (1999). Educational preparation. In P. A. Solari-Twadell & M. A. McDermott (Eds.), *Parish nursing: Promoting whole person health within faith communities* (pp. 269–276). Thousand Oaks, CA: Sage.

McGlown, K. (Ed.). (2004). *Terrorism and disaster management*. Chicago: Health Administration Press.

Minhard, H. A., & Blanchard, M. (2004). Older people with depression: Pilot study. *Journal of Advanced Nursing*, *46*, 23–32.

Morse, S. (2004). *Smart communities*. San Francisco: Jossey-Bass.

Novak, J. (2002). Community health nursing in the schools. In M. Stanhope & J. Lancaster, *Foundations of community health nursing: Community-oriented practice* (pp. 487–510). St. Louis, MO: Mosby.

Parrish, H. M. (1969). Epidemiologic and public health aspects of disaster. In S. Garb & E. Eng (Eds.), *Disaster handbook* (pp. 20–25). New York: Springer.

Peterson, C. (2007). Be safe, be prepared: Emergency system for advance registration of volunteer health professionals in disaster response. *Online Journal of Issues in Nursing*, *11*(7), 7-9. Available at http://search.ebsco.com/loginaspx?direct=true&db=ny&AN=23146892&loginpage=Login.asp&site=ehost-live. Accessed June 23, 2008.

Polivka, B., Stanley, S., Gorden, D., Taulbee, K., Lieffer, G., & McCorkle, S. (2008). Public health nursing competencies for public health surge events. *Public Health Nursing*, *25*(5), 159–165.

Quad Council of Public Health Nursing Organizations. (1999). *Scope and standards of public health nursing practice*. Washington, DC: American Nurses Publishing.

Rogers, B. (2001). Occupational health nursing. In K. S. Lundy & S. Janes (Eds.), *Community health nursing: Caring for the public's health* (pp. 942–967). Sudbury, MA: Jones & Bartlett.

Sachs, J. (2008). *Common wealth: Economics for a crowded planet*. New York: Penguin Press.

Smith, C. M., & Maurer, F. A. (2000). *Community health nursing theory and practice* (2nd ed.). Philadelphia: W. B. Saunders.

Solari-Twadell, P. A. (1999). Nurses in churches: Differentiation of the practice. In P. A. Solari-Twadell & M. A. McDermott (Eds.), *Parish nursing: Promoting whole person health within faith communities* (pp. 249–256). Thousand Oaks, CA: Sage.

Solari-Twadell, P. A., & McDermott, M. A. (Eds.). (1999). *Parish nursing: Promoting whole person health within faith communities*. Thousand Oaks, CA: Sage.

Spencer, B. (2006). Nursing care on the battlefield, how the war in Iraq is changing critical care. *American Nurse Today, 1*(2), 24–26.

Stanhope, M., & Lancaster, J. (2006). Foundations of community health nursing: Community-oriented practice. (2nd ed.) St. Louis, MO: Mosby.

Stringer, H. (2001). Prison break. *Nurse Week, 2,* 24–25.

U.S. Department of Health and Human Services (USDHHS). (2000). *Healthy people 2010* (Conference ed., 2 Vols.). Washington, DC: U.S. Government Printing Office.

Veenema, T. (2003). *Disaster nursing and emergency preparedness for chemical, biological, radiological terrorism and other hazards.* New York: Springer.

Veenema, T. (2006). Expanding educational opportunities in disaster response and emergency preparedness for nurses. *Nursing Education Perspectives, 27*(2), 93–99.

Vogt, R. (2004). Message from the president: Continuing the plan for national security. *Missouri State Board of Nursing Newsletter, 6,* 1.

Watson, R., Stimpson, A., & Hostick, T. (2004). Prison health care: A review of the literature. *International Journal of Nursing Studies, 41,* 119–128.

CHAPTER 15

Informatics and Technology in Nursing Practice

KEY TERMS AND CONCEPTS

Informatics

Electronic health record (EHR)

Personal digital assistant (PDA)

Personal health record (PHR)

Nursing informatics

Informatics nurse specialist

Clinical informatics

Public health informatics

Consumer health informatics

Telemedicine

Telehealth

Educational informatics

Robotics

Genomic medicine

Family health history

Stem cells

Technology in clinical practice

Cyberstalking

LEARNING OUTCOMES

By the end of this chapter, the learner will be able to:

1 Discuss the roles and implications of informatics and technology on professional nursing practice.

2 Specify the educational preparation and roles of the informatics nurse specialist.

3 Identify current technology used in clinical practice.

4 Debate the advantages and disadvantages of complex technology used in clinical practice.

5 Identify key ethical considerations as technological advances become standard practice in professional nursing.

VIGNETTE

John, Susan, and Amy graduated from the same nursing program several years ago. They now work at three different health care facilities. John works at a large university medical center where he enters all information related to client care into a computer. Susan, a director of nursing at a rural hospital, is exploring the feasibility of starting a computerized client care documentation system. Amy works in a home health care agency that uses laptop computers to record home visits as well as computer technology for remote client monitoring. When they meet at a college alumni event, they compare notes about the strengths and weaknesses of the current computer systems and technology that they use in practice. Susan poses the following questions during the discussion: "I know that computers are wonderful, but how can I get my older staff members to overcome their computer phobia? How can we ensure confidentiality of client information with computerized medical records? What are the key elements that need to be included in an employee policy related to computer use and confidentiality of information? How will client care documentation occur when the computer system fails or during a power failure? How much time will be required of staff for computer documentation? What are the legal implications for nurses who use technology for remote client monitoring?"

Like the nurses in the vignette, many professional nurses raise practical questions about the use of computer technology and complex information systems in practice. For optimal professional practice, nurses need to have well-refined computer skills as well as know how to use informatics and complex technology for optimal client care. This chapter provides an overview of the informatics and technology encountered in today's nursing practice while exploring the implications for professional nurses as technology plays an increasingly important role in health care delivery. Key computer competencies for professional nursing and advances in technology for clinical practice are presented. Finally, the chapter challenges professional nursing students to consider the advantages, disadvantages, and ethical issues of technology use for client care.

Changes in technology occur quickly. In fact, by the time this chapter has been published, some information may be obsolete. Faster, improved models of computer equipment seemingly come out just as the latest model has been bought. In 1965, Moore noted that computer chip capacity and speed tended to double on a regular basis. New materials superior to silicon continue to make chips smaller and faster. In fact, purchasing a book such as this may become obsolete in the future because small handheld computers capable of storing over 200 books may very soon become commonplace (Levy, 2007). Soon, nurses may be able to access, record, and store clinically relevant information using handheld devices, thereby eliminating the need for desktop computers and printed materials.

INFORMATICS AND HEALTH CARE

As computers have become a dominant feature in the postmodern world, the average person living today with electrical and telephone services has access to more information than a single person could possibly comprehend. Information science deals with the discovery of "efficient collection, storage and retrieval of information." (Agnes, 2005, p. 733). **Informatics**, known as the science of information (Agnes, 2005), has emerged as the practical application of organizing information for a specific purpose. Because of the wide array of information available to people, a way to organize it must be developed so that information can be used effectively. Essential information in one area of life may be irrelevant to another area. For example, how informatics is used to generate, store, manage, and communicate information for computer gaming most likely has little relevance to health care providers (unless a provider is working in the field of neuroscience and is studying the effects of computer gaming on memory). However, in professional nursing, informatics plays a key role in managing and storing key knowledge essential for professional practice and client care.

Informatics and Professional Nursing

Nurses must know how to use computers and manage enormous volumes of information for effective clinical practice. Nurses use a variety of computers in daily clinical practice. Nurses document various aspects of client care using computers, thereby creating an **electronic health record (EHR)** for each client. An EHR uses computer technology to store client health information in a digitalized format, Some nurses use **personal digital assistants (PDAs)**, which are handheld computers, for managing daily tasks, keeping calendars, calculating medication dosages, performing other complex clinical calculations, and consulting references such as medication information, medical terminology, disease references, and various medical calculation software programs. Some health care organizations place computers on carts that are moved throughout the nursing unit, requiring nurses to scan client identification bracelets and medications prior to administration.

A special EHR known as a **personal health record (PHR)** may soon become readily available to health care consumers. Many individuals keep personal health records in written or digitalized format. As health care consumers become more computer savvy, the demand for PHRs is likely to increase. Nelson (2007) described the PHR as digitalized personal health information housed in a secure electronic database. Already, some consumers have access to their personal health records using cell phones. Benefits of a PHR include error reduction and seamless health care delivery. A PHR enables a new care provider to access specific health information about a client, including actual viewing of diagnostic tests (including digitalized radiographic films), accurate lists of currently prescribed medications, and up-to-date third-party payment information (Nelson, 2007).

Unfortunately, current PHRs have no universal standardized version. The American Health Information Management Association (AHIMA) keeps records of progress toward standardization and policy development about electronic health information on its website (http://www.ahima.org). The "Putting Patients First" initiative from the National Health Council (NHC) calls for health information to be "portable, belong to the patient, and empower the patient to make informed decisions regarding care" (Nelson, 2007, p. 27). The NHC also emphasizes the importance of standardization of electronic platforms used for PHRs so that when a person changes insurance coverage or health care providers there is no loss of health information. Currently, there are over 60 different software programs available for PHRs. Hospitals, outpatient facilities, physician offices, and integrated health care systems currently purchase computer platforms and software for keeping client EHRs. Software development to determine what health-related information should be made available to consumers is also being undertaken so that health care consumers can track personal health information and make informed health care decisions (Nelson, 2007).

Health care informatics is a specialty that looks at the most effective way to integrate data collection, storage, and treatment of a person's health data to facilitate continuity of care. As PHR use grows, health care consumers may consult professional nurses for assistance in deciding what key information should be included in their PHRs and for help in learning how to use PHR systems (Nelson, 2007). **Nursing informatics** is a subspecialty of health care informatics that addresses issues surrounding nursing practice, a major element of current client care. Professional nurses use nursing informatics as a means to integrate the vast amount of knowledge, information, and data required for effective clinical practice (Ozbolt, Nahm, Roberts, & Wilson, 2007).

Questions for Reflection 15-1

1. What are my current skills and abilities with computers and technology?
2. Which of my skills may be useful to me in clinical practice? Why?

Computer and Informatics Competencies for Professional Nurses

Computers and software programs play key roles in the delivery of client care. Consumers of health care expect nurses to know what they are doing. Nurses must display competence in using computer hardware and software. Use of technology has become a critical component of basic and continuing education for nurses. The American Association of Colleges of Nursing (2008) has recommended that professional nurse generalists should be able to:

- Use information and communication technology to document and evaluate patient care, advance patient education, and enhance the accessibility of care.
- Use appropriate technologies in the process of assessing and monitoring patients.
- Work in an interdisciplinary team to make ethical decisions regarding the application of technologies and the acquisition of data.
- Adapt the use of technologies to meet patient needs.

- Teach patients about health care technologies.
- Protect the safety and privacy of patients in relation to the use of health care and information technologies.
- Use information technologies to enhance one's own knowledge base.

The American Medical Informatics Association (AMIA) assembled an expert panel of nurses to develop and refine necessary competencies for nurses. The panel identified 313 different competencies for beginning nurses, experienced nurses, informatics nurse specialists, and informatics innovators. In 2000, the International Medical Informatics Association (IMIA) identified the need for specialists in information technology, health and medical informatics, and clinicians.

According to the IMIA (2000), all health care professionals should have skills to effectively use information processing and communication technology. Sample competencies for the beginning nurse include the use of administrative applications, telecommunication devices, e-mail, database management programs, and the Internet. The beginning nurse also should be able to operate the appropriate devices required to access patient data (e.g., an ability to obtain client information on a health care organization's computer system), know how to enter client data into the same system, evaluate the quality of Internet health information, and find available resources to assist with clinical and ethical decision making as it relates to computing. Along with the knowledge of how to access and record client information, health care professionals must also learn how to use and provide basic maintenance of various handheld devices and computers used in health care organizations (IMIA, 2000).

The experienced nurse must be able to use applications for diagnostic coding, evaluate computerized assisted instruction as a teaching method, and integrate selected resources into a client file. The experienced professional should also be able to define how computerized information affects the nurse's role, assess the accuracy of health information posted on the Internet, and serve as an advocate to client system users. Table 15-1 provides a checklist for nurses to verify their level of competence with informatics and technology in clinical practice.

The **informatics nurse specialist** has a graduate education and can integrate established technologies into clinical practice. The informatics innovator holds a doctorate and designs new technological systems, techniques, and conceptual models for databases. The innovator evaluates the safety, effectiveness, cost, and social impacts of the technological systems and researches theoretical foundations of the specialty itself (Staggers & Gassert, 2000).

In 1999, the IMIA drafted a list of 41 recommendations to integrate informatics into health care delivery. The IMIA suggested that two areas of specialization be developed in medical informatics: one that focuses on informatics, and one that focuses on health care delivery. Since then, additional subspecialties has emerged. **Clinical informatics** has become subdivided into specialty areas of systems and support analysis, systems administrators, training managers, project managers and leaders, and chief information officers. In order to facilitate computer and information systems for nurses, expert or nursing liaision positions have been developed (Ozboltz, Nahm, Roberts, & Wilson, 2007). Informatics specialists design software programs and computer systems to manage information related to clients and health care. Specialists who focus on the health care delivery aspects design software and create integrated systems that facilitate health care delivery.

Because of the complex nature of health care delivery and informatics, it takes many experts with specializations in a variety of fields of health care informatics to create fully integrated systems. Informatics professionals usually fail to have the knowledge of what health care providers need to deliver safe, effective health care, and health care professionals sometimes lack the computer expertise to design and maintain efficient clinical information systems. Currently, the following five subspecialties have emerged in the

TABLE 15-1

Checklist for Professional Nurse Competencies in the Use of Technology and Informatics

Competency	Yes	No
Explain basic concepts of computer hardware, software, and networks.		
Use computer hardware including a keyboard, screen, signing on, and turning on the computer.		
Use computer software including a basic word processing program, spreadsheet, e-mail, and Internet search program.		
Use a computerized database to search professional nursing and other professional health team member literature.		
Access dictated client reports such as history and physicals, radiology and lab reports, operation reports, pathology reports, and consultations.		
Access telemetry, vital signs, and pulse oximetry data (all practice areas); access central venous pressure, cardiac output, pulmonary wedge pressure, and intracranial pressure (intensive care nursing areas); and access nursing and other health team members' electronic documentation (all areas of nursing practice).		
Document client assessments electronically.		
Document independent and collaborative nursing interventions electronically.		
Document evaluation of independent and collaborative nursing interventions electronically.		
Enter electronically a basic care plan for clients and update it as needed.		
Take steps to ensure confidentiality of client personal health information.		
Enter verbal and written (unless program requires physician direct entry) orders.		
Determine safe staffing needs for assigned unit.		
Perform basic maintenance and/or calibration of handheld computer devices.		
Enter and monitor client ordered medication dosages on IV pumps with computer chips.		
Use telecommunication devices effectively (beepers or cellular phones).		
Develop an attitude of confidence when using technological devices in professional practice.		
Outline strategies for continued client care in the event of a situation during which computer systems may not be available.		
Specify the advantages of computers and telecommunication device use in clinical practice.		
List disadvantages when using computers and telecommunication devices in clinical practice.		

Sources of information:
American Association of Colleges of Nursing. (2008). *The essentials of baccalaureate education for professional nursing practice*. Washington, DC: Author.
Nelson, R. (2007). The personal health record. *American Journal of Nursing, 107*(9), 27–28.
Ellerbee, S. (2007). Staffing through web-based open-shift bidding. *American Nurse Today, 2*(4), 32–34.
Lin, J., Lin, K., Jiang, W., & Lee, T. (2007). An exploration of nursing informatics competency and satisfaction related to network education. *Journal of Nursing Research, 15*(1), 54–65.

arena of nursing informatics: "clinical informatics, consumer-health informatics, educational informatics, **public health informatics** and research in nursing informatics" (Ozboltz et al., 2007, p. 34).

The Technology Informatics Guiding Educational Reform Summit

By 2014, the American health care industry will look toward full adoption of electronic health records. Federal legislation supporting this idea was enacted in 2001 and efforts to increase funding continue today. The first national summit on how to begin the process of fully integrating health information technology into the current health care system was held in 2004. Representatives of the entire interprofessional health team members attended the summit. Nursing leaders realized the need for separate arms of the profession (practice, education, industry, government, and administration) to pull together to work toward integrating health care information technology into all nursing practice settings. The Technology Informatics Guiding Educational Reform Summit (TIGER Summit) initiative proposes a vision for how nurses need to be prepared to adapt to the use of electronic health records and the ever-increasing amount of technology in professional practice across the health care continuum (TIGER Summit, 2007).

The TIGER Summit participants outlined the following seven key factors to cohesively attain the TIGER vision: (1) management and leadership, (2) education, (3) communication and collaboration, (4) informatics design, (5) information technology, (6) policy, and (7) culture. The Summit participants also outlined a 3-year action plan to reach the 10-year goal of transforming professional nursing to a profession capable of using evidence and technology to provide the safest and highest quality of care services to patients. Summit participants proposed that information technology would become the nurse's "stethoscope of the 21st Century" (TIGER Summit, 2007, p. 3). Along with increased use of technology, Summit participants envisioned the profession using solid evidence as informatics software was developed. They also developed plans to promote educational strategies to prepare future nurses and teach current ones how to navigate complex health informatics systems. Updated information is posted frequently on the TIGER Summit website (http://www.tigersummit.com).

CLINICAL INFORMATICS

Clinical informatics addresses the needs of nurses and other health care providers to streamline client care documentation, keep accurate client records, and integrate various aspects of client care to improve the quality of care. In an ideal inpatient system, the physician orders a diagnostic test by entering it directly into a computer. The request is received by the department that performs the test. The nurse caring for the client receives a copy of routine client preparation orders and educational materials. When the client leaves the nursing unit for the test, a chip on the client hospital identification bracelet monitors the client location. After the test is completed, computerized postprocedure orders are generated and the client's hospital bill is updated to indicate that the test was performed and what supplies were used. In addition, the institution gathers data about the diagnostic procedure for quality improvement and electronically sends data to a registry collecting information about the procedure for research purposes. Finally, the updated bill is sent directly to the client's health insurance company.

The complex nature of designing, developing, implementing, and maintaining such a system requires many experts. Therefore, many positions in the field of clinical informatics have emerged. Applied/professional roles focus on the design, development, execution, and maintenance of health care clinical information systems. Systems analyst, support analyst, systems administrator, software designer, project leader, and chief information officer are examples of applied/professional job titles. Once an information system is designed and developed, nurses and other health care providers need to learn how to use it. Sometimes, staff within a health care organization find themselves in the position of deciding what health care information system program would best fit their institutional needs. Informatics experts or liaisons focus on performing organizational needs assessments, helping organizations select particular hardware and software programs, implementing selected information systems, and educating users on the newly purchased programs. Organizations frequently employ staff educators and persons well versed in the information system programs (known as "super users") who assist staff in learning the system and troubleshooting it when issues arise. Other expert/liaison positions include informatics coordinator, chief nursing informatics officer, and information technology nursing advocate. Professional nurses with specialization in computer applications are needed to develop nurse-friendly computer systems to support nurses working at the bedside (Ozboltz et al., 2007).

Questions for Reflection 15-2

1. How do I currently use technology in client care?
2. What are the benefits of using complex technology in professional nursing practice?
3. How does the use of technology affect the nurse–client relationship?
4. What is the impact of new technology on the cost and quality of health care?

CONSUMER HEALTH INFORMATICS

Some current health care consumers are highly computer savvy. At times, the health care consumer may know more about his or her current health status than the provider consulted for care. Consumers may receive health care information from reliable sources. Some consumers participate actively in health-related decisions by surfing the Internet and finding a vast amount of information on health promotion, illness prevention, disease management, and information about currently experienced symptoms. They can watch video clips of surgical and other invasive procedures. Consumers can subscribe to online health promotion newsletters and receive checkup reminder text messages. **Consumer health informatics** focuses efforts at delivering health care services to persons who need or want services. The informatics services include telemedicine, telehealth, and telemonitoring.

Telemedicine

Telemedicine provides health care services to persons at a distance. **Telehealth** started as a means to provide persons residing in areas without specialized health care services access to services using video technology. For example, a victim of a motor vehicular accident who is seen in a rural hospital's emergency room can receive a consultation from a trauma team at a larger urban trauma center when both centers are equipped with video technology. Physicians at the trauma center can assess the victim, review all diagnostic tests, consult with the rural emergency physician, and make suggestions of how to deliver the best possible care. If needed, the victim may be transported to the trauma center or the trauma surgeon may walk the rural physician step by step through a life-saving procedure.

In more recent years, telemedicine has expanded to provide a variety of inpatient services. The Electronic Intensive Care Unit (EICU) offers remote monitoring and medical services for persons in the intensive care unit. The EICU team typically is composed of a critical care physician and at least one critical care registered nurse. Using telecommunications, the nurses and physician provide additional monitoring of patients occupying intensive care unit beds. The critical care physician is available for consultation by critical care unit nurses when they pick up a special phone and turn on a video camera. The EICU team also contacts the critical care nurses when they notice a change in a monitored client and order early interventions. Remote monitoring improves critical care patient outcomes as well as lengthening the career spans of intensive care nurses and physicians (Loustau, 2007).

Besides delivering critical care services from a remote location, some physicians use robotic devices to make hospital rounds. Basic robotic equipment includes a two-way video feed, a microphone, speaker, and a bay that enables stethoscope use. The robot and physician's laptop are connected to the Internet using a secure hospital wireless network. The physician uses a laptop computer and joystick to guide the robot to perform a physical assessment as if the physician were actually in the client's room. The physician can also use the robot to monitor critically ill clients several times daily. Clients and physicians can engage in conversations free of interruption (Wilke, 2007).

Telehealth

Telemedicine, although sometimes used interchangeably with telehealth, refers to the actual use of telehealth technology for disease diagnosis and treatment of a patient at a remote location by a physician. Telenursing refers to nursing care delivered to a client at a remote site. The term telemedicine first appeared in the literature in the 1960s, when telephone lines were used to transmit client information, such as facsimiles of test results. Then, technology enabled transmission of electrocardiograph information using telephone lines. Now, a comprehensive telehealth system enables clients to interact in real time with health care providers using computer connections. In the process known as "store forward," images, photographs, and client records become digitalized for transmission from one location to another (Thede, 1999). With telehealth, health care professionals working in remote locations can participate in continuing education programs that occur in large urban health centers. They also can receive step-by-step instructions from specialists in how to perform complex life-saving procedures.

Telehealth enables consumers to use interactive educational materials and self-manage illnesses and health. Interactive websites may be sponsored by proprietary companies or nonprofit organizations. Some hospitals and integrated health care systems offer online educational materials to the public. For example, if a woman is diagnosed with early-stage breast cancer, she can visit the American Cancer Society to learn about treatment options, view information about breast cancer from the National Health of Institute and the National Library of Medicine, and see actual surgical procedures and radiation devices found on websites of medical centers, university-based cancer centers, and treatment product manufacturers. For health care providers, telehealth offers challenges because some clients may have more information about recent advances in the management of a particular disease or have themselves self-diagnosed.

Blogs also provide consumers with health-related information while providing persons with a particular health problem a social network. Facebook© and MySpace© are the two predominant social networking tools (Skiba, 2007). Health information accessed through blogs typically may not have been empirically tested and sometimes may even be harmful for health care consumers.

Telemonitoring

Telemonitoring is another use of telecommunications during which client data are transmitted to health care providers. The earliest example of telemonitoring happened when clients with pacemakers sent information to cardiology offices using the telephone. Telemonitoring systems consist of a video camera, monitor, thermometer, blood pressure cuff, and stethoscope. The nurse calls the client to connect to the system. The nurse receives real-time images and data that can be stored electronically. This system provides client access to a home health nurse on a 24-hour-a-day basis (Reuters Health, 2000).

Some home health organizations offer clients the option of having a video camera installed in their homes along with monitoring devices (e.g., telemetry, blood pressure monitoring equipment, and fetal heart monitoring devices), and clients contact the home health agency using a high-speed Internet connection. The home health nurse and the client hold a video conference with each other. If the conference reveals no problems, the nurse does not have to make a home visit. However, if a client fails to contact the agency at the specified time or, if during the conference the nurse determines that the client needs to be seen in person, the nurse makes arrangements to go see the client. Whether it is telemedicine, telehealth, or telemonitoring, informatics nurses and clinical specialists develop and improve systems (Ozboltz et al., 2007).

 ## EDUCATIONAL INFORMATICS

Educational informatics provides students, health care professionals, and consumers with ways to access information. Health care professionals have the capability to earn continuing education credit by completing online courses. Nursing and other health care professional students have access to online collegiate courses. Students can choose from courses that use either synchronous (faculty and students meet online at the same time for online classes) or asynchronous (students access course information at their own convenience). In a 2007 report published by the American Association of Colleges of Nursing, the following types of nursing programs were offering more than 50% of courses online: 1% entry-level baccalaureate, 24.1% master's nursing programs, 16.5% doctoral programs with a research focus, and 25% doctor of nursing practice programs.

Some nursing programs have developed clinical simulations that use highly advanced mannequins, or media case studies offer interprofessional communication (using role play) and provide virtual client electronic health records. These simulations offer student instruction in complex case scenarios that cover commonly encountered client care situations in a variety of specialized areas of nursing practice (Ozboltz et al., 2007).

Perhaps the course using this text is an online course. Access to distance education becomes available to anyone connected to the Internet. Each institution specifies required hardware and software for online courses and many have vendor contracts for student discounts. Students also need to exercise care when selecting an Internet service provider (ISP) before enrolling in an online course. Some ISPs disconnect users after a specified time, especially during high network congestion (Short, 2000). Also, some web-based course materials (especially those with sound and complex graphics) require digital and high-speed service line connections for complete downloading.

Before enrolling in an online course, a student must possess the skills for success and verify the quality of education. A self-assessment reveals if a student has the ability to connect to the class, engage in online class discussions, download complex documents, manage files, and access help. A student should ask questions related to available technical assistance and provision of a backup computer if problems with technology occur (Mueller & Billings, 2000; Short, 2000).

Asking questions about course content, the number of times the course has been offered online, and faculty experience with online education can lead to clues about the quality of the course and instruction. The following five indicators reflect similarity between on-campus and distance online education: (1) reasonable faculty electronic office hours, (2) online library resources, (3) alternative ways to interact with student colleagues beyond e-mail, (4) online secure examinations, and (5) course content that balances passive lecture with interactive teaching techniques (Short, 2000).

A key benefit of asynchronous online courses is the student's ability to develop an individually tailored class schedule, which is especially important to students juggling multiple roles. When students have access to a 24-hours-a-day, 7-days-a-week technical support services, they can meet program requirements based on individual needs (Short, 2000). However, some online courses require synchronous class meetings.

Because online courses differ from those taught in traditional classrooms, some students may not learn effectively in the online setting. For students who rely heavily on peer contact, the isolation of home study may impede learning. Persons who need structure and strict deadlines to complete course requirements do not fare well with online education (Short, 2000). Because most faculty-to-student and student-to-student interactions occur in written format, students with poorly developed writing skills may find online courses too burdensome (Mueller & Billings, 2000). Some students perceive that because they determine the time of instruction, there is less work associated with an online course, only to be surprised with the time commitment.

Educational informatics also enables practicing nurses to access continuing education programs any time of the day. Some professional nursing associations offer online continuing education programs to their members. Many of the online educational programs charge a fee for processing continuing education credits for the members. However, some programs may be offered free of charge to members while charging a fee for nonmembers. Some hospitals offer continuing education programs using online educational vendors or their own educational platform. For example, a large midwestern health system uses the online platform Health Stream© for employees to access various programs to fulfill annual competency requirements regarding infection control; fire, radiation, and electrical safety; age-related developmental care strategies; and domestic abuse.

Social networking tools also provide an opportunity for nursing students at all levels of education to connect with each other. Online social networks help students connect with other students in similar educational situations. In collegiate settings, online social networking has been used for accessing registration information (checking with other students to find out the best section of a course to take or what section one's friends plan to take), identifying a tutor, participating in a study group, broadcasting classes, orienting freshmen, providing academic advising, establishing partnerships for exchanging languages, as well as developing a social network for persons with the same major (Skiba, 2007). Social networking can be done using online networking tools, accessing a professional nursing organization's website, or employing a discussion board feature found on many online learning platforms (such as Blackboard©, Web CT©, or Angel©). When online discussions are used, faculty must set clear guidelines for student entries. For example, a faculty member may use the Oncology Nursing Society's networking feature for nursing students to share thoughts and feelings about working with oncology clients. A nursing student from another nursing program may enter into the discussion.

Although popular with young students, online discussion using Facebook© or MySpace© also has some disadvantages. First, once a blog has been established, the user must realize that everything posted may be read by almost anyone, even future employers. Deleted information from an individual's profile is cached (or entered) onto multiple search engines. Finally, any person who posts things online may have to assume legal responsibility for the posting (Skiba, 2007).

PUBLIC HEALTH INFORMATICS

The Centers for Disease Control and Prevention and local health departments offer public health information. The goal is to keep the public informed of any health threats such as an infectious disease epidemic, adverse drug events, environmental health hazards, and acts of bioterrorism. Along with informing the public of health hazards, the public health information network most likely will improve data collection, distribution, and security of the nation's vital statistics. By improving the access to information related to public health, policy makers and voters might be able to develop and improve public policies regarding health promotion and health care delivery (Ozboltz et al., 2007).

TECHNOLOGY IN DIRECT CLIENT CARE

Professional nurses use a variety of technological tools in clinical practice. Many pieces of client care equipment have computer chips. Technology has revolutionized client care delivery. For client assessment, nurses use bedside and handheld monitors to collect a variety of information, including blood glucose level, clotting time, electrocardiograph rhythm, cardiac output, blood pressure, oxygen saturation of hemoglobin, and temperature. Some monitoring systems require that the client be connected in some way to the device, and others require a drop or two of blood. Point-of-care testing enables nurses to receive instantaneous results for peripheral blood glucose levels for diabetics and activated clotting time for clients receiving anticoagulation therapy (Nelson, 2001). Client monitoring systems that use wireless technology enable automatic nurse-paging capability when client measurements fall outside normal parameters.

For example, a client connected to a centralized telemetry system experiences a run of multifocal premature ventricular contractions. The monitoring system immediately pages the nurse. If the nurse fails to respond in a specified time, the system sends pages to other nurses working on the unit, thereby enabling a faster response to abnormal findings (McConnell, 2001).

Nurses and other health care providers also have access to computerized clinical decision-making support systems. Decision-making support systems help nurses define clinical problems, generate potential solutions, and select the best solution based on the likelihood of success. Many decision-making models use spreadsheets with formulas to predict the results of specific actions in a given client care situation (Thede, 2003). Nurses also have access to decision-making algorithms when clinical practice guidelines and procedures have been entered into computer systems.

Handheld computers (HHCs) enable nurses in some clinical settings to streamline client care tasks and have access to current information. For example, a nurse could create a worksheet for personal use that has various spaces to indicate when client care procedures are needed. The HHC may also contain software capable of complex clinical calculations such as body mass index, absolute neutrophil count, corrected QT intervals, and formulas to calculate various medication continuous intravenous drips. Many HHCs have alarm features and the nurse can set an alarm to remind him or her that it is time to perform a client care task. Along with scheduling client care activities, the nurse might also have information about medications, client care procedures, and pathophysiology of disease processes loaded onto the HHC (Thede, 2003). Some sophisticated information systems enable the nurse to record client care information onto the HHC and then place the HHC onto a docking station that downloads the entered client data into the client's EHRs.

Along with improved client assessment and access to clinical information, some nurses use computers to plan client care. Some health care institutions have software that enables nurses to enter care plans by selecting a specific nursing diagnosis. The software provides the nurse with expected outcomes and nursing interventions related to the identified nursing diagnosis. Computer software programs also organize client care, and store clinical forms and teaching protocol information. Various software programs offer different features, including the capability to translate client education materials into multiple languages. Some institutions place clinical practice guidelines and employee policies onto a mainframe that can be accessed by using any computer connected to the local area network.

Nurses use HHCs and desktop computers to access institutional electronic mail (e-mail) accounts. Currently, many nurses receive updated policies and key organizational announcements by using e-mail. Clinical units frequently hold team meetings. If unable to attend the meeting, a nurse can access the minutes of the meeting sent to all staff via e-mail. Finally, some nursing organizations (such as the American Nurses Association and the Oncology Nursing Society) send e-mail messages to members routinely to inform them of new developments in clinical practice and legislative issues.

Computerized documentation eliminates the need for nurses to shuffle through lots of paper. Time becomes compressed when computer documentation is used. Instantaneous diagnostic test and assessment findings become available to the interprofessional team as soon as the results are entered into the computerized system. With wireless technology and highly integrated wired information systems, some radiologists have the capability to access X-rays in digital format and then dictate their findings without leaving their homes.

Information generated from a diagnostic test may have implications for nursing care. For example, results of a swallowgram might reveal that a client is at high risk for aspiration. Detailed information about how to promote safe swallowing for a client with poor tongue control and weak throat muscles is received instantaneously. The nurse then creates an individualized client care plan to promote safe swallowing for a particular client. Features of future nursing care planning software programs could include required outcomes as specified by organizational accrediting bodies along with a way to customize the care plan to meet the individual client's needs.

Nurses also use technology for nursing interventions. Most intravenous pumps contain computer microprocessors for effective operation. Computerized intravenous pumps enable nurses to program administration rates for ordered medications without having to perform manual calculations. The IV pumps are also programmed for safe dosage limits over a specified time frame and have features for nurses to start infusions after hanging IV fluids or medications. Pumps with complex features enable nurses to program an infusion of multiple medications for specific timeframes and schedules.

In addition to IV pumps, other nursing care devices use computer technology. Even some air mattresses use computer components and software to regulate the amount of air inflation. Implantable subcutaneous pumps deliver local anesthetic along surgical incisions and have the computer technology to regulate the rate of subcutaneous drug administration. Some diabetics use computer programmed pumps for insulin administration.

Computerized medication-dispensing stations (CMDSs) prevent nurses from making medication errors while automatically notifying the pharmacy when the stocked medications need to be replenished. CMDSs facilitate the work of professional nurses, especially when they are mounted on bases that enable mobility. Portable medication stations equipped with barcoding devices require that nurses scan client identification bracelets and medication prior to medication administration. This safety feature increases the ease of following the "5 rights" of medication administration, thereby reducing potentially costly medication errors. Successful implementation of computerized medstations relies upon the system's ability to be user-friendly, efficient, and well supplied. Some CMDS models offer information about the therapeutic action, pharmacookinetics, adverse effects, and incompatabilities of medications in device software. More sophisticated models offer features such as warning signs for potential drug interactions that require communication between physicians and pharmacists prior to dispensing medications (Hurley et al., 2007). Some CMDSs require biometric identification of users such as fingerprinting.

Along with improving the safety of medication at the bedside, nurses can use computer software for staffing nursing units and making daily staff assignments. Computer programs can be used to determine the number of direct client care hours that are needed based on client acuity levels. Some staffing software allows nurses to look online for vacant staff positions that fall outside of their established schedules and then sign up to work shifts with vacancies. Staffing options include 4-hour and 6-hour work options. By allowing regular employees to sign up for extra shifts, overtime and the use of agency nurses have declined (Ellerbee, 2007).

Applications in Record Keeping and Documentation of Care

Health information systems (HIS) require that nurses become adept with computer technology. Documentation can be performed with a personal computer located in a central area, or with a laptop or handheld computer. However, nurses must also know how to document client care activities and provide care when computers are not functioning because of routine maintenance, software updates, or a power failure. EHRs are computerized client documents that contain complete and accurate data about a client's past and present health. EHRs also may possess practitioner's alerts, reminders, and clinical decision-making systems. In addition, some EHRs have links to bodies of medical knowledge and health information databases (Thede, 2003). In 1992, the Institute of Medicine formed the Computer-Based Record Institute to promote the development of computerized patient records to capture a comprehensive record of an individual's health status over a lifetime. Persons could carry such information on a card no larger than a credit card and have it with them at all times.

As health care delivery complexity increases, universal access to a client's health record by all members of the health care team improves care quality, safety, and efficiency. EHRs can alert care providers to drug incompatibilities, allergies, and scheduled cancer and heart disease screenings. EHRs also can provide information related to regional differences in health care delivery, track health care costs, identify areas of best practices for certain procedures, and provide clients with one health record that could be used anywhere when health care needs arise. Staff members need time to master electronic documentation systems. Notable improvements in client care documentation may not be apparent for as long as one year after an electronic documentation system is introduced (Ammenwerth & Haux, 2000).

Computer information systems (CIS) enable nurses "to collect, process, store, retrieve, and display data and information" (Örlygsdottir, 2007, p. 283). When computer information systems include Nursing Minimum Data Set (NMDS) components, nursing care documentation encompasses all phases of the nursing process. As these phases are included in clinical documentation systems, the potential to report and merge client care information into a large multi-institutional database becomes possible. Thus, a large database may become available for use in nursing research studies and to compare the effects of nursing care across institutions and health care settings. In the United States, the NMDS includes information about patient demographics (personal identification, birth date, gender, ethnicity, and residence), nursing care elements (care intensity, nursing diagnoses, interventions, and outcomes), and service components (unique agency code, client health record, admission dismissal or termination dates, client disposition when leaving the facility, and expected bill payer). Establishment of a large database enables the profession of nursing to develop best practices based on client outcomes.

Applications for Communication

The use of wireless telephones reduces the time spent by health care professionals in trying to reach each other. Wireless telephones also decrease the need for overhead paging, which sometimes disrupts client rest. Physicians can call nurses directly. Alphanumeric pocket pagers and portable phones enable staff members to inform each other of specific events or assistance needs.

Electronic mail also can be used to send messages about patients to physician's offices or inform staff of continuing education opportunities, special institutional events, and personal messages. Clients can be notified of health care appointments using e-mail and also ask their health care providers questions. Because of the confidentiality of health-related information, e-mail messages containing information about clients needs to be encrypted (digitally electronic coded). Encryption keeps personal health information private and accessible only to persons directly involved in the client's care.

Protecting client identity in outpatient settings poses a challenge to health care providers. Technology fosters the protection of clients' personal identities. Some facilities give clients a beeper, cell phone, or lighted handheld device that goes off when it is time to receive care. However, these electronic communication devices can sometimes create confusion for elderly clients seeking health care services.

THE INFORMATICS NURSE SPECIALIST

Because of technological advances, the human species generates vast volumes of information in a relatively short time. Management of this information requires special expertise. To use information effectively, it must be organized, accessible, and relevant. Informatics nurse specialists (INSs) are nurses with special education and experience who develop nursing computer applications, and analyze technology and informatics to improve nursing practice and the quality of care.

Responsibilities of the Informatics Nurse Specialist

The American Nurses Association (ANA; 1994) defined nursing informatics as nursing-related information management. Nursing informatics enables nurses to access databases to improve client care. In 2001, the ANA developed Scope and Standards of Nursing Informatics Practice. INSs work as "project managers, systems specialists, consultants, system educators, researchers, policy developers and product developers" (Thede, 2003). Some INSs work for health care organizations, others are employed by product vendors, and others work as entrepreneurs. Some INSs manage large databases specific to a specialty area of practice. Because of the rapid advances in technology, all INSs must engage in lifelong learning. Knowledge of computers and information systems comes through formal education (collegiate and continuing education programs) as well as practical experience (Thede).

INSs fulfill integral roles in the development of health information systems (HIS). Their perspective gives the technological development team a working knowledge of the nursing profession so client care information can be better managed. Without input of nursing, created HIS may miss critical aspects of client care and may create procedures that reduce nursing effectiveness.

Education of the Informatics Nurse Specialist

The education of nursing informatics specialists varies. Table 15-2 outlines the educational preparation and role description for a nursing informatics expert. The INS needs a thorough understanding of clinical practice and detailed computer expertise. Because nursing informatics is a new area of specialty practice, the preparation and roles vary. The clinical nursing informatics specialist designs and executes network education for nurses. Many organizations require a list of computer-based competencies for staff (Thede, 2003). Because of wide variances in nurse familiarity with computers, the effectiveness of network education must be validated in order to provide staff nurses with key computer skills used in daily practice. The following research brief explores how nurses perceive their competency in nursing informatics and identifies nurse satisfaction in regard to computer network education.

Research Brief 15-1

Lin, J., Lin, K., Jiang, W., & Lee, T. (2007). An exploration of nursing informatics competency and satisfaction related to network education. *Journal of Nursing Research*, *15*(1), 54–65.

A descriptive correlational research study used data from 218 Taiwanese nurses who completed an online questionnaire that addressed nursing informatics competency, computer limitations, attitudes about computers, and personal and social issues.

Analysis of variance (ANOVA) revealed that the following demographic nurse characteristics were related to increased nursing informatics competency: (1) education at the baccalaureate or master's levels, (2) clinical level of practice, with nurse administrators having the highest level of computer competency, (3) high-speed cable Internet access at home, (4) spending 4 or more hours online per week, (5) receiving 4 or more hours of online course experience, (6) being single, and (7) completing more than 3 computer training courses.

Nurses who were most satisfied with network education owned a home personal computer, had previous online course experience of more than 4 hours, commonly used more than 3 computer software applications, and held registered professional nurse positions. Statistically significant correlations were found between nursing informatics competencies and satisfaction with network education.

Implications for practice are that participant-perceived learning plays a key role in satisfaction with online staff educational programs. Older, more professional, experienced, and higher nursing employment status were noted to increase computer competency in this study. Nurses educated at the baccalaureate degree or higher educational levels also tended to report more computer competence than nurses educated at the associate's degree level. Learning results contribute more highly than content to participant satisfaction with computer network education. Results of this study point to the importance of having 4 or more hours of computer network education in order to achieve computer competence and satisfaction with computer education. Because this study was conducted using participants employed at a single Taiwanese hospital, the results may not be the same in other hospitals or in other countries. However, it appears that increased time, increased clinical experience, administrative experience, and educational level may contribute to increased computer competence and satisfaction with computer educational offerings. As computers become a key element in professional nursing practice, increased computer experience must be included in all levels of nursing education.

As a nursing specialty, the ANA offers certification examinations to validate competence in nursing informatics. To stay abreast of changes in the practice of nursing informatics, the ANA requires certified informatics nurse specialists to engage in clinical practice and complete continuing education. Hours of clinical practice vary. An informatics nurse specialist may have 2,000 hours of clinical practice or 1,000 hours with 12 semester hours of academic credit within 5 years. In addition, the specialist must complete 20 contact hours in continuing education in nursing informatics within 2 years to maintain certification (American Nurses Credentialing Center, 2000; Thede, 2003).

Role of the Informatics Nurse

Software developers and computer programmers have expertise in computer systems, but lack familiarity with clinical nursing practice and health care delivery. Thus, to develop software and computer systems that are compatible with nursing care delivery and facilitate, rather than hinder, client care, health care systems and software companies seek nurse consultants or hire nurses with special education in nursing informatics. Nurses contribute critical information that affects client care. They also field-test software programs to determine the ease of use and the feasibility for implementation in client care settings.

Nursing informatics is an exciting nursing specialty practice area. As computer technology and complex information systems permeate health care, more informatics nurse specialists will be needed to verify that systems address key nursing practice considerations and facilitate, rather than hinder, nursing care delivery. Table 15-3 outlines the complex nature of health information systems currently in use. Nearly every application has implications for professional nursing practice. As the need for automated systems to manage health care and document client health information increases, the need for computer analysts and computer support personnel is expected to rise. The U.S. Department of Labor Bureau of Labor Statistics (2007) projected the growth for professional nurses, health systems computer analysts, and computer support specialists will grow by more than 27% between now and 2014 for professional nursing. Nurses with advanced education in informatics will be able to design nurse-friendly systems, direct nurses effectively in their use, and provide support services to nurses when they experience problems using computer and information systems.

TABLE 15-2

Education and Role Description of the Nursing Informatics Specialist

Education	Role Description
At least 2 years of clinical nursing practice[a]	Thorough understanding of clinical practice to develop, implement and maintain information systems that are relevant to clinical nursing practice
Successful completion of the ANA Certification Examination in Nursing Informatics[a]	Provides evidence for competence in the area of nursing informatics
Computer system design and analysis[b]	Develop novel system designs to meet nursing information needs Analyze hardware and software available to design a comprehensive nursing information system Recommend hardware and software to develop a system Develop proposals for acquisition of resources needed for a system or system revisions Program computers to meet the needs of the health care organization
Information and support of systems[b]	Develop, plan and implement education for nurses who use the information system Develop and implement policies and procedures for system use Develop documentation for staff education and support services Maintain collegial relationships with system users Outline strategies for implementation of system Provide ongoing technical and clinical support for system users
Testing and evaluation of systems	Implement testing of system to verify functioning Develop and implement system evaluation plan to detect strengths and weaknesses Assess current system and new products for potential updates
Managing information and databases[b]	Collect and analyze aggregate data Transform data into meaningful presentation format Plan future updates to system
Professional practice, issues and trends[b]	Role components: nurse, information expert, computer expert, educator, and researcher Financial issues related to system development, utilization, and updates Future developments in technology Ethical issues, such as confidentiality of client information Federal regulations Interdisciplinary organizations for health informatics Professional standards for health and nursing informatics
Theoretical foundations for practice[b]	Concepts of nursing informatics Nursing Taxonomy and Nomenclature (e.g., NANDA, Nursing Interventions Classification System/Nursing Outcomes Classification System, Nursing Management Minimum Data Set, Omaha System, Patient Care Data Set, Nightingale Tracker) Mental models of data and information processing Nursing decision making models and decision support systems

[a]Certification requirements from the American Nurses Credentialing Center, 2000.
[b]Topics covered the American Nurses Credentialing Center Examination, 2000.
Information adapted from Thede (1999), *Computers in nursing: Bridges to the future* (pp. 289–293). Philadelphia: J. B. Lippincott; and Turley, J. P. (2000). Informatics and education: The start of a discussion. In B. Carty (Ed.), *Nursing informatics education for practice* (pp. 271–293). New York: Springer Publishing.

TABLE 15-3

Components of a Health Information System Currently Employed by Health Care Providing Institutions

Health Information Component	Function Descriptions
Admission, discharge and transfer application	Tracks patient demographic data, insurance information, responsible parties, medical record number, care provider, and dates of admissions, transfer and dismissals
Financial application	Keeps records related to billing information for medical supplies and services rendered, tracking of accounts receivable, general ledger, and institutional costs for care delivery
Physician order entry application	Provides computer order entry and almost instant notification of orders to ancillary departments. Sometimes, information related to specific test preparation is immediately sent to the unit
Ancillary department application	Shares information among various departments to facilitate scheduling of entered orders. These applications also provide information related to quality control
Documentation application	Consist of pop-up screens that enable care providers to select assessment parameters, document care delivered and evaluate client response by using checklists. These also have the capability of free text entry should the need arise
Care planning application	Allows the nurse to select appropriate nursing diagnoses, expected care outcomes and nursing interventions for any client
Scheduling application	Enables patient scheduling of radiographic, nuclear medicine, and other specialized diagnostic tests and surgery. In addition, provides a means to schedule staff. Both systems are integrated into the financial information system
Acuity application	Provides a summary of the client care needs based upon the acuity of illness and in some cases, the projected hours of nursing care in order to verify adequate staffing levels to fulfill client care needs
Specialty practice application	Provides health care providers within a specific specialty practice area to collect specific client data. Unfortunately, many of these systems fail to integrate data with other components of the health information system
Decision support application	Provides algorithmic decision making related to specific health problems, client demographics, and laboratory test results
Communication application	Provides e-mail and Internet access. Some institutions publish policies and procedures in this system component
Critical pathways applications	Streamline the efforts of the interdisciplinary health team by focusing on specific care outcomes. Because all members document on the same form, a more coordinated approach to care results. When documentation is done by computer entry, comparisons of clinical data related to intervention, outcomes and multidisciplinary approaches become possible.

From Hassert, M. (1999). Information systems. In Thede, L. Q. (1999). Computers in nursing: Bridges to the future (pp. 237–247). Philadelphia: J. B. Lippincott.

TECHNOLOGICAL CHANGES AFFECTING NURSING PRACTICE AND HEALTH CARE

Robotics

With the impending nursing shortage, some nursing tasks may be safely accomplished by machines. **Robotics** is the design of machines to perform tasks usually done by humans. Pharmacy robots have been in use for over a decade to perform mundane tasks associated with preparing and dispensing medications. As described earlier in the chapter, robots equipped with television cameras allow nurses and physicians to see, hear, and talk to clients and staff through a wireless Internet connection. Some nursing tasks performed by robots (nursing bots) include meal tray delivery, filling water pitchers, making routine rounds, and taking vital signs (Jossi, 2004). Increasingly, surgery and other invasive procedures are being performed by robots because robots have better dexterity and eliminate human error when performing delicate procedures. However, for the robots to perform, they must be controlled by an experienced physician. The use of robotics increases access to sophisticated procedures for persons living in rural areas. In Canada, surgeons control a robot from an urban medical center while the procedure is performed by the robot in a local hospital. Surgical costs are reduced as clients who need specialized surgery need not travel to a large metropolitan medical center to have the needed surgery (Jossi).

Genomic Medicine

For many years, health care providers relied on a client's family health history for understanding and predicting many disease processes. A family health history tracks incidences of illnesses that occur in persons who share ancestors. Ideally, three generations worth of data should be collected. Since completion of mapping the human geonome, information generated from a family history can now be scientifically validated.

Mapping the human genome has transformed health care delivery. Knowing the genetic sequence of organisms causing various infectious diseases enables scientists to develop new vaccines against them (Rappouli & Covacci, 2003). **Genomic medicine** applies knowledge generated from human, bacterial, and viral genomes to develop new medical treatments and determine specific regimens for clients based on their particular human genetic sequence. Vastly different approaches to health promotion and disease management surface as more becomes known about how human genes affect health.

Initial publicized findings of the Human Genome Project revealed that humans have approximately 34,000 genes and that people are 99.5% identical. However, the 34,000 genes have the capability to make between 500,000 to 1 million proteins. Results indicate that genes do not cause disease, but proteins do. Implications for disease screening and therapy most likely lie with the study of proteomics (human proteins).

Diseases linked to genomics and proteomics include some cancers (ovarian, breast, and colon), mental illnesses (depression, schizophrenia, chemical addiction, and bipolar disease), birth defects (neural tube defects), preterm birth, obesity, type I and type II diabetes, cardivascular disease, hypercholesterolemia, chronic sinusitis, immune deficiency disorders (X-linked combined immune deficiency), and neurological diseases (Huntington's chorea, Alzheimer's disease, and multiple sclerosis) (Check & Rogers, 2001; Conley & Tinkle, 2007; Dolan, Biermann, & Damus, 2007; Holden, 2003; Sanner & Frazier, 2007). Genetic screening and genetic-based therapies have transformed many disease screening and treatment protocols (Conley & Tinkle).

Estimates indicate that the amount of information generated by the Human Genome Project would take scientists centuries to decipher. However, software companies have developed programs to facilitate data analysis. Genetic testing of malignant tumors is commonplace. These new tools may shorten the development process for new medications and determining what medications would work best for individual clients because of inherited genetic variations. Eventually, physicians may send a genetic sample from a patient and receive a medication plan tailored to the patient's genotype, resulting in better disease management. Newborns may be genetically tested and receive a lifetime plan (including when to begin taking medications designed for their genotypes) to prevent illness (Stone, 2001).

Genetic differences in metabolism explain variations in therapeutic responses of medications based on ancestral heritage (Holden, 2003; Marshall, 2003b). Genetic differences have been identified to explain the lack of effectiveness of angiotensin-converting enzyme inhibitors in controlling blood pressure in some persons of African descent. Persons from India have survived famines that resulted in a "thrifty gene" presentation in approximately one third of the Indian population. This gene is linked to the development of hypercholesterolemia when Indians westernize their diets (Holden). Risky genes have been identified in persons who experience long QT syndrome after receiving specific medications (Marshall, 2003a). Twenty medications have warning labels specifying that fatal reactions may occur in persons with inherited metabolism disorders (Marshall, 2003b; Conley & Tinkle, 2007).

Health care professionals can identify persons at risk for specific illnesses and institute early health screenings. Genetic testing may be offered to persons at risk for a particular illness. However, personal behaviors and environmental factors also play a role in disease development. Once a genetic predisposition to an illness within a family is identified, the professional nurse sometimes becomes a resource for how to tell other family members they are at risk (Giarelli & Jacobs, 2001). Currently, the cost of testing for a single gene that affects drug metabolism or identifying a person at risk for a disease ranges from $100 to $1,000 (Marshall, 2003b). Conley and Tinkle (2007) reported that future costs for personal, complete genome testing may be $1,000 within a decade. Although clients may undergo genetic testing, they may not fully comprehend the meaning and implications of results (Barnoy, Apel, Peretz, Meiraz, & Ehrenfeld, 2006).

In 2006, the National Coalition for Health Professional Education in Genetics established a list of essential professional nurse competencies in genetics. Jenkins and Calzone (2007, p. 13) presented the essential competencies for professional responsiblities and practice. Competent nurses have the following responsibilities:

1. Acknowledge when one's personal values and attitudes about genetics and genomic science could affect client care.
2. Advocate for client access to genetic/genomic services and support groups upon request.
3. Analyze personal competency with genomics and genetic science and get additional education if needed.
4. Include genetics and genomic science as part of routine professional practice.
5. Tailor client education on genetics and genomic science to the client's culture, religious beliefs, literacy level, and preferred language.
6. Advocate for clients as they make autonomous, voluntary, and informed choices for genetic testing and genomic interventions.

Jenkins and Calzone (2007, p. 13) outlined the following professional nurse's clinical practice competencies:

1. Displays an "understanding of the relationships of genetics and genomics to health prevention, screening, diagnostics, prognostics, selection of treatment and monitoring of treatment effects" (p. 13).
2. Collects client family history for a minimum of three generations.
3. Uses standardized symbols and terms to construct a pedigree from a client's family history.
4. Assesses client's personal, health, and developmental histories inclusive of genetic, environmental, and genomic risks and influences on health status.

5. Analyzes health and physical assessment data for the presence of genetic, environmental, and genomic risks and influence on health status.
6. "Assesses clients' knowledge, perceptions and responses to genetic and genomic information" (p. 13.)
7. Creates a nursing care plan that considers genetic and genomic assessment findings.

Along with these competencies, the professional nurse can play a key role in shaping public policy regarding access to genetic testing and therapies for all persons. Nurses also need to build knowledge for evidence-based practice so that effective public and client education about genomics and proteonomics can be implemented. Finally, professional nurses must collaborate with interprofessional team members to evaluate the effectiveness of advances in health care based on new genetic and protein information.

Stem Cell Therapy and Research

Technology has given medical researchers the ability to grow body parts using embryonic or adult stem cells. Approximately 3,000 human illnesses could benefit from stem cell therapies (Lanza et al., 2001). **Stem cells** are immature human cells that have not yet committed to becoming a particular type of human cell. Patients with Parkinson's disease, hematologic disorders, and malignancies currently use stem cell therapies. Stem cells readily multiply and can be "coaxed into creating nearly any type of cell" (Gutterman, 2001, p. A19); however, human progenitor cells can grow into any form of human tissue. With a research team, Charles Vacanti at the University of Massachusetts Medical School has discovered tiny cells (3 to 5 microns across) in human tissue that become activated to repair damaged tissue (Gutterman). This exciting research potentially solves the problem of waiting lists for organ donation, eliminates the need for isolating adult stem cells for growing body parts, and bypasses the ethical issues related to use of embryonic stem cells for laboratory-grown tissue or skin (Gutterman). However, despite the advancements in stem cell research in the early years of the 21st century, using stem cells to grow body parts and organs has not become commonplace.

Because of the advances in the treatment of certain diseases such as leukemia, parents of newborns need to have information related to the storage of stem cells from placentas and umbilical cords. Some obstetricians present this information to women during pregnancy. However, most health insurance companies do not cover storage fees. Parents also have the option of donating stem cells from cord blood to private or public stem cell banks. Cells stored in private stem cell banks are reserved for use by the family. Some labor and delivery nurses routinely collect umbilical stem cell blood for storage. Ethical issues arise, such as equal access to stem cells as well as what is done with stored cells when they are no longer needed.

 ## CHALLENGES MANAGING HEALTH-RELATED INFORMATICS AND TECHNOLOGY

The rapid introduction of **technology in clinical practice** provides a challenge to professional nurses. Once a nurse becomes competent and confident with a new piece of patient care equipment, medical device manufacturers introduce a new version. New generations of client care equipment usually contain features that increase accuracy or efficiency. However, some nurses find it challenging to adapt to constantly changing equipment.

The vast amount of health-related information can create confusion for health care professionals and consumers. Professional nurses, like any other consumer, use the Internet to find information. Many hospital websites offer consumers information about the prevention and treatment of diseases, lists of provided services, and instructions on how to provide a health care provider with practice privileges. Some health care organizations use their websites as marketing tools to attract consumers. The ever-increasing use of technology and computers in health care results in key challenges for professional nurses, who must ensure ethical use of protected health information, determine the quality of health information for use in practice, maintain data security, and struggle to stay abreast of new developments.

Confidentiality

To protect persons from discrimination based on genetic testing, the United States provided legal protection in the Genetic Confidentiality and Non-Discriminatory Act of 1997. When medical and pharmaceutical research centers use biologic material and data to develop new therapies for illnesses, the donors of human tissue and cells have a right to privacy. However, the pharmaceutical company or research center retains the right to ownership of discoveries from human extracted materials (Giarelli & Jacobs, 2001).

The Health Information Portability and Privacy Act (HIPPA) mandates confidentiality of client medical records and other information shared with insurance companies, physicians, hospitals, and other health care providers. Access to private health information (PHI) is limited either to persons who are directly involved in the client's care or to persons designated by the client (U.S. Department of Health & Human Services, 2003). Under the act, health care organizations are required to offer education about PHI to all employees. Documented consent from the health care consumer is required before health care providers can disclose PHI to anyone not involved directly in the client's care (including family members). HIPPA provides health care consumers with the following four rights: (1) to receive written notice related to PHI storage and use changes before they are implemented, (2) to access and view one's health information, (3) to obtain an account of how PHI has been disclosed, and (4) to request a correction or amendment to PHI. Law violators may be fined $25,000 to $250,000 and imprisoned for up to 10 years. Most health care providing organizations employ privacy officers to protect PHI (Huchenski, 2001). Some health care organizations terminate employees for accessing PHI of persons if not involved in their direct care.

Extreme care is taken by health care organizations to ensure confidentiality of PHI. Computer screens, facsimile (fax) machines, and even boards containing client names have been placed in locations accessible only to health care providers. All electronic mail messages containing PHI must be encrypted. Although telecommunications using computer technology have greatly improved over the years, no connection offers complete security and information can be lost in cyberspace.

Computerized or electronic health records contain a lot of personal information. Institutions using computerized records in areas such as academia and health care protect private data with passwords and firewalls. Many health care providers sign binding confidentiality agreements. Most health care organizations have departments devoted to information management that set policies for computer access and for managing violations of computer security policies. Computer hackers anywhere in the world have the capability of infiltrating any system containing private and personal information. Transmission of private medical data to an outside computer or server provides an opportunity for it to be viewed by unauthorized persons (Foster, 2001; Thede, 2003).

Ethics and Technology

Ethical debates frequently occur with the introduction of new technology in health care. For example, stem cell therapy triggers debates on the definition of the beginning of human life (does it begin at conception or when the fetus becomes viable?). Some abortion opponents view the use of embryonic human cells as approval of abortions. Proponents of embyronic stem cell research suggest that clinicians dispose of products of abortion and that using them for stem cell research provides societal benefits. Additional sources of stem cells have also been discovered, such as umbilical cords and adult stem cells.

Other ethical issues surrounding expensive procedures focus on access to services. If insurance companies do not cover the cost (for example, storing umbilical cord stem cells and genetically designed medications), then only persons with personal financial resources reap the benefits of such technology. Thus, in the future, the disparities over the quality of health care for the rich and poor may become more apparent.

Data Security

The potential loss of data is the biggest concern when using individual PHRs. Loss of health data may occur with hardware failures and system programming errors. Through the processes of acquisition, storage, and processing, some data may be lost. Routine data backups and off-site storage protect information against natural disasters (Thede, 2003). Recent evidence reveals that long-term storage of computerized data may be unstable. Recent observations indicate that data stored on CD-ROMs may begin to disintegrate after 5 years. Files and disks can become corrupt at any time (Thede).

Computer systems sometimes quit for no apparent reason. They rely on quality information entry by humans. Bad information input results in poor use of technology. Computers cannot detect many of these errors even though they are capable of performing complex mathematical operations and providing algorithims for complicated decision making (Thede, 2003). Finally, computers rely on a power source (electricity or battery) to work. When the power source is severed, the computer stops. Until a reliable paperless method of storing and accessing client health information becomes standard practice, some clinical practice settings that use computer systems still require nurses to have paper copies of documents.

Struggling to Stay Abreast of New Technologies

The success of high-technology client care devices depends on the ability of the nurse (or consumer) to operate them. If a device is shown to promote client comfort or save time, professional nurses tend to adopt it readily. New devices are more readily accepted by nurses if nurses participate in the decision making to use them.

One of the disadvantages of high-tech care is the inclination of nurses to focus on the machinery rather than clients. Sometimes, nurses attend to machine alarms before observing clients. This practice may result in a nurse being perceived as being cold and aloof. No machine can replace the warmth of a genuine, caring human interaction.

Advances in technology create challenges for professional nurses. Recent predictions suggest that information and technological advancements will expand exponentially during the next five years. With the vast amount of information required for effective client care, professional nurses frequently experience information overload. Because nurses cannot know everything, in order to provide effective client care, nurses must stay abreast of new developments in health care information and technology, be willing to admit knowledge deficits, consult others when uncertain, and stay focused on the ever-increasing importance of authentic therapeutic relationships with clients and their significant others.

Accessing Information

The U.S. Armed Forces started the Internet, which now has become the largest global computer network, in the late 1960s. The Internet is a worldwide computer network that uses digitalized transmission of information. Any computer with required software can connect to the Internet. Information is shared by a network of collected websites that uses the hypertext transfer protocol for communcation. All Web addresses have the same letters and symbols to begin their address (http://), which is automatically inserted when a computer user enters a universal resource locater (Thede, 2003). Internet sites not connected to the Web require that the user type in the complete address, including a transfer protocol abbreviation. To access the Internet, persons need an Internet service provider (ISP) that provides a server (a large computer linked to other computers to share information and provide services). Electronic mail remains the most popular of all Internet services, followed by personal blogs. Blogs enable anyone to share life events and personal views on current events and politics.

A web address starts with the letters www, then the name of the organization or person, followed by the type of organization. For example, the website address of the publisher of this book is www.lww.com. When inputting e-mail or website addresses, there is no margin for error; the address must be entered accurately for a successful link to occur (Akens, 1999).

A website is a collection of pages posted on the Internet (Akens, 1999). A home page is the beginning point of a website, where a browser enters the site and usually views content within the website. Most home pages contain text, graphics, sound, animation, and other interactive features (Akens). In the United States, the following six domains are used to designate the type of server that hosts a website: (1) commercial = .com; (2) educational = .edu; (3) network = .net; (4) nonprofit organization = .org; (5) governmental = .gov; and (6) military = .mil (Thede, 2003).

If a person can type and use a mouse, accessing information on the Internet is a simple task. Many information searches start with the use of a search engine. All Internet software programs contain a search engine, with which the computer user inputs a topic of interest, then hits a key to command the computer to find matches. Sometimes a computer search can retrieve hundreds of thousands of matches on a single topic.

Nurses also can find Internet sites by using publishing guides, reading journal articles, and using bibliographies. Millions of websites exist. Many have long lives, but some become obsolete when organizations merge or disband. Once a site has been accessed and found to be useful, the computer user can file it by using a bookmark or a list of favorites, thereby eliminating the need to enter the complex website address again.

Chat rooms (or discussion boards) connect persons with similar interests. Information can be exchanged through synchronous or asynchronous postings. Typical computer programs contain software for participation in a chat room. Some nursing organizations offer discussion boards and chat rooms. Most professional discussion boards require users to register and sign in before reading and posting entries. Some nursing textbook companies offer online course platforms that include discussion boards or forums. When posting information on a discussion board (or forum), a good rule to follow is not to post information that you would not want broadcasted on a televised news show.

Chatting enables instant communication with persons around the world. Most chatting is text-based. Persons can participate in group conversations. Participation in chat rooms enables persons to keep in touch with friends, colleagues, and relatives who reside in a wide geographical area without paying long-distance telephone fees. When participating in a chat room with unfamiliar persons, chatters tend to use a nickname for personal protection (Maran, 1998). Some nurses use chat rooms as a means for professional networking. Chat rooms enable nurses to identify problems within professional practice that occur across care delivery settings, serve as a means for offering each other moral support, and provide collaborative efforts in solving clinical practice problems.

The Internet also lets you browse through files stored on computers around the world by using the file transfer protocol (FTP), thereby allowing users to download files. Types of files found on FTP sites include text, images, sound, video, and computer programs. Large files from FTP sites are compressed to increase the speed of travel over the Internet. These files must be decompressed using a decompression program (Maran, 1998).

Cyberstalking

Along with information insecurity, computer users connected to the Internet may fall victim to cyberstalking. **Cyberstalking** has three primary forms: harassment, spamming, and phishing. Institutions that provide employee e-mail addresses and office telephone numbers place them at risk for cyberstalking. Harassment includes receiving unwanted ads, pornographic material, and threatening messages (Foster, 2001). Spamming, another form of receiving unwanted information, occurs when a person distributes a piece of advertising to members of a large distribution list. Nurses and others using e-mail sometimes receive hundreds of messages daily, and much time is spent reading or deleting spam.

Internet criminals use phishing to attempt to access personal information about Internet users that is later used to steal identities or drain bank accounts. In addition, some legitimate businesses attach spyware programs to computers when consumers complete product registration forms online (Hartman, 2005). Hartman offered the following suggestions as ways to protect against cyberstalking: (1) use a nonsense password and change it frequently; (2) never post personal information on a website; (3) if female, use computer sign-on entries that prevent gender identification; (4) check websites that collect information about people and request that personal information be removed from them; (5) never use a credit card for a purchase in a nonsecure environment; (6) read and understand security policies before making purchases or registering for services; (7) report any spam to the system administrators of the receiving and sending persons; (8) report any Internet abuse to CyberSnitch, a network that automatically files reports to appropriate law enforcement agencies; (9) use e-mail filtering programs; and (10) invest in and use firewalls, virus protection, and other computer safety programs.

Balancing Technology with Life

For some nurses (and other persons), computers and cellular devices may become an impediment to leading a balanced life. The purchase of each new device when it becomes available serves as a status symbol for some people, but it may be a sign of an addiction to technology. Some people (including nurses) spend hours on computers participating in chat rooms, surfing the Internet, and playing games. Small handheld devices enable persons to be constantly connected to the Internet or to the job. Using technology may become an addiction or serve as an excuse for not interacting with other persons.

Some persons rely heavily on personal pagers and cell phones. Having nearly instantaneous information related to medical emergencies and community health hazards enables nurses (especially those working in emergency departments or community health settings) to act swiftly, save lives, and prepare for victims of a disaster. However, the need to respond to them immediately sometimes impedes a person's ability to engage in deep, meaningful, face-to-face conversations. In addition, some persons assume that because a nurse is issued a pager or an electronic mail account in the workplace, the nurse is available to them 24 hours a day, seven days a week. Nurses need to have time away from their work setting and technology to cultivate personal relationships and outside interests.

However, computers and other handheld technological devices may enhance interpersonal relationships among professional colleagues, health team members, and families. Whitmore (2005) outlined etiquette for computer use and coined the term "netiquette." Table 15-4 offers strategies with rationales for professional nurses to use to foster effective computer use to build and maintain high-quality working relationships with others.

TABLE 15-4

Netiquette Techniques

Technique	Rationale
Denote special dates on electronic calendars.	Send greeting cards acknowledging the important event of a colleague's or client's life.
State the main reasons for the message in the subject line area.	Facilitates prioritization of e-mail messages by receivers.
Consider e-mail messages as business letters.	E-mail has become a formal communication medium in business.
Use proper English grammar and avoid using all uppercase letters.	E-mail is a means of professional communication and using uppercase letters is known as cyber shouting.
Avoid use of fancy or cute decorations.	Detracts recipient's attention from message content.
Keep messages succinct but not abrupt.	Avoid being perceived as being rude when sending a message.
Treat e-mail as a public document.	Recipients can forward, print, or photocopy any message and messages can be retrieved from computers.
Wait until anger passes prior to sending an e-mail message.	Strongly emotional messages can easily be misinterpreted because of the lack of body language and voice characteristics and there is no opportunity to immediately clarify if a misunderstanding should occur.
Save messages praising people until you see them face-to-face or send them a handwritten, personal note.	People usually cherish handwritten notes or greeting cards and these forms of communication are more likely saved.
Proof messages prior to sending them.	Use of automated correction devices for spelling or grammar may not always be accurate, especially when potential homonyms are used within a message.
Use the "Reply to All" feature only when everyone on the list requires a response.	Limits the number of e-mails sent and received, thereby increasing productivity.
Avoid pestering recipients by sending multiple messages if they fail to respond within your expected time frame.	If something is that urgent, contact people via the telephone or stop by their office. Some persons check e-mails only once daily.
Respond as quickly as possible, especially messages that are flagged urgent.	Courtesy goes a long way in the work environment, especially when deadlines for responses are required.
Send attachments only when necessary.	Consider what is actually needed to get business done.
Less is more.	Sometimes an entire message can be sent using only the subject line, but end the line with the letters "EOM" for end of message.
Mark messages to denote whether they are urgent or just FYI (for your information).	Facilitates prioritization of messages by recipients.
Think twice before sending unsolicited advertisements or humorous messages.	What you think might be humorous may not be humorous to others and some organizations may enforce strict e-mail usage policies.
Inform others when you are unavailable by using an out-of-office feature and provide contact information if something occurs during your absence that needs your immediate attention.	Senders of messages will know of your unavailability and contact you only if absolutely necessary.

Information adapted from Whitmore, J. (2005). *Business class etitquette: Essentials for success at work.* New York: St. Martins Press.

Questions for Reflection 15-3

1. How do I balance high tech with high touch in my personal and professional lives?
2. Why is it important to strike a balance between high tech and high touch in client care?
3. Why is it important to strike a balance between technology and other personal life aspects?

SUMMARY AND SIGNIFICANCE TO PRACTICE

Nurses must have competence in managing complex technology and staying abreast of new advances for health care delivery. Increased use of technology may threaten the therapeutic and effective relationships that nurses build with others because of the loss of face-to-face human interactions. However, increased technology and information have the ability to improve health care by providing early disease detection, reducing errors, and facilitating optimal use of limited resources. Effective use of informatics and technology has become a critical clinical skill for nurses practicing in today's complex and chaotic world of health care delivery. Nurses use cognitive skills to determine how to incorporate and evaluate the use of new information and technology in clinical practice. Finally, nurses need to find a way to strike a balance to provide high-tech and high-touch client care while taking time to lead satisfying personal lives.

FROM THEORY TO PRACTICE

1. Reread the vignette in the chapter opener. Based on your current use of computers and technology in clinical practice, what information would you share if you were part of the discussion?
2. Outline a plan to introduce a computerized documentation system to a group of nurses who have never used computers as a routine part of their clinical practice. Justify each portion of the orientation program.
3. What are the advantages of using computers and technology in clinical practice for nurses and consumers? Why are these advantages? What are the disadvantages of using them in clinical practice for nurses and consumers? Why are these disadvantages?

WWW INTERNET EXERCISES

1. Select a topic that interests you as a professional nurse. Using any search engine (http://www.metacrawler.com, http://www.yahoo.com, or whatever search capability is offered by your ISP), enter the topic. Identify the number of potential websites to visit. Select two or three of these websites and compare and contrast them in terms of the type of website, the fees required to use the site information (if they are selling something), when the web page was last updated, and if the information presented is credible.
2. Complete the questionnaire "Are Telecourses for You?" found at the Public Broadcasting Services website (http://www.pbs.org/adultlearning/als/college/quiz.htm). This survey identifies how well distance education courses fit learner needs.
3. For the practical implications of telehealth on nursing practice, visit http://telehealth.hrsa.gov. Click on the "What's new" icon for updates on legislation, privacy issues, and current guidelines.

WWW INTERNET RESOURCES

American Nurses Association: http://www.nursingworld.org.
Nursing Informatics Association: http://www.ania.org.

For information about federal guidelines related to genetically engineered crops, visit the U.S. Department of Agriculture site, http://www.usda.gov, and the Environmental Protection Agency site, http://www.epa.gov.

International Society of Nurses in Genetics: http://www.isong.org.

The Cancer Genetics Genome Project: http://www.ncbi.nlm.nih.gov/ncicgap/.

The National Human Genome Research Institute: http://www.genome.gov.

The Human Genome Project Information Guide: http://www.ncbi.nlm.nih.gov/genome/guide/.

CyberSnitch: http://www.cybersnitch.net.

The American Health Informatics Management Association: http://www.ahima.org

REFERENCES

Agnes, M. (Ed.). (2005). *Webster's new world college dictionary* (4th ed.). Cleveland, OH: Wiley.

Akens, D. S. (1999). *Computers in plain English*. Huntsville, AL: PC Press.

American Association of Colleges of Nursing. (2007). American annual state of schools: Educate, advocate, innovate. Available at http://www.aacn.nche.edu/media/pdf/AnnualReport07.pdf. Accessed May 3, 2009.

American Association of Colleges of Nursing. (2008). *The essentials of baccalaureate education for professional nursing practice*. Washington, DC: Author.

American Nurses Association (ANA). (1994). *Standards of practice for nursing informatics* (NP-100 7.5M 3/95). Washington, DC: Author.

American Nurses Credentialing Center. (2000). Informatics certification catalog [Online]. Washington, DC: American Nurses Credentialing Center. Available at www.ana.org/ancc/certification/catalogs/html. Accessed July 9, 2005.

Ammenwerth, E., & Haux, R. (2000). A compendium of information processing functions in nursing: Development and pilot study. *Computers in Nursing, 18*, 189–196.

Barnoy, S., Apel, D., Peretz, C., Meiraz, H., & Ehrenfeld, M. (2006). Genetic testing, genetic information and the role of maternal-child health nurses in Israel. *Journal of Nursing Scholarship, 38*(3), 219–224.

Bureau of Labor Statistics. (2007), *Occupational outlook handbook 2007–2008*. Available at http://www.bls.gov/oco. Accessed November 24, 2007.

Conley, Y., & Tinkle, M. (2007). The future of genomic nursing research. *Journal of Nursing Scholarship, 39*(1), 17–24.

Dolan, S., Biermann, J., & Damus, K. (2007). Genomics for health in preconception and postnatal periods. *Journal of Nursing Scholarship, 39*(1), 4–9.

Ellerbee, S. (2007). Staffing through web-based open-shift bidding. *American Nurse Today, 2*(4), 32–34.

Foster, A. L. (2001). The struggle to preserve privacy. *The Chronicle of Higher Education, 47*, A37–A39.

Giarelli, E., & Jacobs, L. (2001). Issues related to the use of genetic material and information. *Oncology Nursing Forum, 27*, 459–467.

Gutterman, L. (2001). How to make a kidney, an ear, or even a heart. *Chronicle of Higher Education, 47*(34), A19.

Hartman, R. (2005). Cyberstalking and internet safety FAQ. Available at http://www.sfwa.org/gateway/stalking.htm. Accessed July 8, 2005.

Holden, C. (2003). Race and medicine. *Science, 302*, 594–596.

Huchenski, J. (2001). New federal rule protects individual healthcare information privacy. *Computers in Nursing, 19*, 41, 43–44, 46.

Hurley, A., Lancaster, D., Hayes, J., Wilson-Chase, C., Bane, A., Griffin, M., et al. (2007). The medication administration system—nurses assessment of satisfaction (MAS-NAS) scale. *Journal of Nursing Scholarship, 38*(3), 298–300.

International Medical Informatics Association (IMIA). (1999). The standards for health care informatics. Available at http://www.imia.org. Accessed July 8, 2005.

International Medical Informatics Association (IMIA). (2000). Recommendations of the International Medical Informatics (IMIA) on education in health and medical informatics. *Methods of Information in Medicine, 39*, 267–277.

Jenkins, J., & Calzone, K. (2007). Establishing the essential nursing competencies for genetics and genomics. *Journal of Nursing Scholarship, 39*(1), 10–16.

Jossi, F. (2004). Robostaff. Healthcare Informatics Online. Available at http://www.healthcare-informatics.comissues/2004/04_04/jossi.htm. Accessed July 8, 2005.

Lanza, R., Ciebelli, J., West, M., Dorff, E., Tauer, C., & Green, R. (2001). The ethical reasons for stem cell research. *Science, 292*, 1299.

Levy, S. (2007). The future of reading. *Newsweek, 150*, 22, 56–64.

Loustau, L. (2007, September 24). Working to save lives—from a distance. *Kansas City Nursing News 2007 Guide to Nursing*, 2, 15.

Maran, R. (1998). *Teach yourself computers and the Internet visually* (2nd ed.). Foster City, CA: IDG Books Worldwide.

Marshall, E. (2003a). First check my genome, doctor. *Science, 302*, 589.

Marshall, E. (2003b). Preventing toxicity with a gene test. *Science, 302*, 588–590.

Merikangas, K., & Risch, N. (2003). Genomic priorities and public health. *Science, 302*, 599–601.

Moore, G. E. (1965, April 19). Cramming more components onto integrated circuits. *Electronics, 38*(8). Available at http://www.intel.com/research/silicon/moorespaper.pdf. Accessed December 27, 2007.

Mueller, C. L., & Billings, D. M. (2000). Focus on the learner. In J. Novotny (Ed.), *Distance education in nursing* (pp. 65–84). New York: Springer.

Nelson, L. (2001). Point of care testing: Is it right for everyone? *Nursing Management, 32*, 50.

Nelson, R. (2007). The personal health record. *American Journal of Nursing, 107*(9), 27–28.

Offit, K. (1997). *Clinical cancer genetics: Risk counseling and management*. New York: John Wiley.

Örlygsdottir, B. (2007). Use of NIDSEC-Compliant CIS in community-based nursing-directed prenatal care to determine support of Nursing Minimum Data Set objectives. *CIN: Computer Informatics Nursing, 25*(5), 283–293.

Rappouli, R., & Covacci, A. (2003). Reverse vaccinology and genomics. *Science, 302*, 602.

Reuters Health. (2000). FDA approves system for virtual house calls [Online]. Available at www.phschool.com/atschool/health/health_update/spring2000.pdf.

Short, N. (2000). Online learning: Ready, set, click. *RN, 63*, 28–32.

Skiba, D. (2007). Nursing education 2.0: Poke me. Where's your face in space? *Nursing Education Perspectives, 28*(4), 214–216.

Staggers, N., & Gassert, C. (2000). Competencies for nursing informatics. In B. Carty (Ed.), *Nursing informatics: Education for practice* (pp. 17–34). New York: Springer.

Stone, B. (2001). Wanted: Hot industry seeks supergeeks. *Newsweek, 137*, 54–55, 58.

Thede, L. (1999). Computers in nursing: Bridges to the future. Philadelphia: Lippincott Williams & Wilkins.

Thede, L. (2003). *Informatics and nursing: Opportunities and challenges* (2nd ed.). Philadelphia: Lippincott Williams & Wilkins.

TIGER Summit. (2007). The TIGER initiative: Evidence and informatics transforming nursing: 3-year action steps toward a 10-year vision. Available online at http://www.tigersummit.com/About_Us.html. Accessed May 3, 2009.

Turley, J. P. (2000). Informatics and education: The start of a discussion. In B. Carty (Ed.), *Nursing informatics: Education for practice* (pp. 271–294). New York: Springer.

U.S. Department of Commerce. (2004). Strategic plan for optical technology. Available at http://physics.nist.gov/Divisions/Div844/publications/Strategicplan04.pdf. Accessed July 9, 2005.

Wilke, A. (2007, September 24). With nurses' help REMi brings SMMC doctors to the bedside. *Kansas City Nursing News 2007 Guide to Nursing*, 5, 10.

Professional nurses assume a variety of nursing roles as they engage in the complexities of clinical practice. Frequently, professional nurses assume multiple roles simultaneously while providing nursing services. They consciously choose the roles to be assumed based on the nature of the client system, specific client needs, and the interprofessional team's efforts. Professional nurses aspire to provide the best quality of health care by bringing a constellation of cognitive and clinical skills to empower clients while constantly assessing clinical practice environments for ways to improve the safety and quality of health care.

Professional Nursing Roles

CHAPTER 16

Nursing Approaches to Client Systems

KEY TERMS AND CONCEPTS

Human systems

Clients

Change/growth view of change

Persistence view of change

Change/growth model

Change/stability model

Family

Family as client

Family system

Family functions

Community

Community as client

Health promotion

Risk

Disease prevention

Primary prevention

Secondary prevention

Tertiary prevention

LEARNING OUTCOMES

By the end of this chapter, the learner will be able to:

1 Define individual, family, and community as nursing clients.

2 Outline how various nursing conceptual models differentiate client systems in professional nursing.

3 Outline differences in ethical issues when making decisions while delivering nursing care to an individual as client, family as client, and community as client.

4 Compare and contrast nursing approaches in the realms of family nursing using the change/growth view and the change/stability view.

5 Explain the differences in viewing communities as aggregates of people, human systems, and human field/environmental field process.

6 Outline key differences in how nurses adapt their strategies based on their perceptions and theoretical approaches to the three client systems.

7 Specify advantages of using nursing models when working with individuals, families, and communities.

Lisa is a teenage girl who prides herself on her skill in gymnastics, ballet, and academics. She strives for perfection in all her endeavors because she knows that her parents make great sacrifices so she can pursue her interests. Her ballet teacher has been encouraging her to lose 20 pounds because she carries 125 pounds on her 5-foot 7-inch frame. Today, Gina, a friend of Lisa's who also takes ballet lessons, collapsed during physical education class while running a relay race. Gina had recently lost the 20 pounds as requested by the ballet teacher and secured a starring role in a local ballet production.

Upon hearing the news about Gina, Lisa has come to the Health Room complaining of dizziness. Her friend Cindy helps her to the Health Room. Nancy notices that Cindy also appears to be extremely thin and has sunken eyes. Nancy, an experienced school nurse, gives Lisa and Cindy some orange juice. Nancy suspects that the girls have eating disorders. When she asks Cindy and Lisa about their eating habits, they both say they can eat anything they want without gaining weight. Both girls fail to make eye contact with Nancy when responding to her questions.

Nancy notices that both girls are wearing clothes similar to those worn by the cover model on a magazine. Nancy, concerned for the health of both girls, realizes that families play a key role in eating disorders and that peer pressure sometimes makes teenagers do foolish things. Nancy realizes that this is an opportunity in nursing practice to help individual clients, their families, and the school community.

Human systems are living systems open to interactions with other systems. Interacting systems are characterized by mutual change; that is, each human system can effect change in another and at the same time is influenced (changed) by that other system. Nurses involved in professional practice interact with client systems and the health care delivery system. The nursing profession defines **clients** as the recipients of nursing care. Besides being passive recipients of care, clients assume the important role of active participants, or partners, with nurses when they seek the services of professional nurses. This chapter explores the professional nurse's role with client systems. It presents a beginning in differentiation of the client systems—individuals, families, and communities.

Traditionally, nurses have cared for individuals; conceptual models of nursing have developed their views of "the person" (individual); and nurses have practiced with families and communities. The traditional practice with families and communities usually has been practice with individuals in a collective setting; thus, family and community actually have been treated as contexts of the identified client. The major questions for the professional nurse are: How do I implement processes of nursing with the whole human being, the individual client? With the whole family unit, the family as client? With the community as client?

Change in human beings is lifelong, natural, and evolutionary. As human beings move through their lives, they establish themselves as integral elements of larger and more complex systems. The individual synthesizes the concept of "me" with "my family" and "my community." At times, nurses effectively and appropriately work with "me" in professional relationships. In other instances, the nurse must consider that working with "the family" may be more effective. Finally, nurses sometimes have to work with "the community," especially when the health of a large group of persons may be affected.

According to the paradigm selected for application in this book—the growth or persistence views of change (Fawcett, 1989)—it is the client–environment relationship that is most important. In the **change/growth view of change**, growth serves as the outcome of change. In the **persistence view of change**, the outcome is stability. The way individual nurses think about change determines how they view the client. In the change/growth model, nurses see clients with the ability for continuous growth, and nurses facilitate the change process by focusing the client on the client's strengths and abilities. In the change/stability model, nurses see clients as potentially capable of stability, and they facilitate the process by identifying and assisting with plans for resolving client problems.

When all of the conceptual models of nursing originally were developed, the nursing scholars equated "person" with the individual client. The developers of some models and other thinkers in nursing have attempted to explain how the models can be applied to family and community as client. Some nurse leaders believe that "person" has been redefined in the models to include families as clients, the recipients of care (Anderson & Tomlinson, 1992). Hanchett (1988) declared that community also can be defined as client; thus, "community" replaces "person" as the human being in some conceptual models.

Questions for Reflection 16-1

1. Have I ever encountered a nursing situation that required more than caring for the individual as client?
2. How did I handle the situation?
3. Does consulting with family breach client confidentiality? Why or why not?
4. How does a nurse know when a health-related issue involves more than an individual or family system?

THE INDIVIDUAL AS CLIENT

The philosophy inherent in this book is that a person progresses through life. This progression is characterized by unique evolving patterns of interaction between the person and the environment. Such patterns of interaction determine the person's health. In general, the changes that occur in the developing human being are characterized by higher abilities to organize interactions and deal with more complex levels of interaction. The person's patterns are unique and are continuously evolving from earlier life experiences, including biologic, genetic, cultural, interpersonal, and social influences, as well as current interactions and conceptions of the future.

Because the conceptual models of nursing were developed with persons defined as the client, professional nurses derive directives for nursing practice from the discussion of nursing processes according to both the integration and interaction nursing models. The following section reflects our efforts to differentiate the professional nursing care of families and communities from that of individuals.

FAMILY AS CLIENT

Who is defined as family? This question has evoked many definitions of family, from the conjugal or nuclear family (the family of marriage, parenthood, or procreation) to the extended family (the kinships of biologically related persons—grandparents, aunts, uncles, and cousins). Such definitions have limited applicability and usefulness in today's society. Thus, the definition of family that is accepted is "two or more individuals who depend on one another for emotional, physical, and/or economic support. The members of the family are self-defined" (Hanson, 1996, p. 6).

Curently many words are used to describe family nursing care. Some call it family-centered care, some call it family-based care, others call it family-focused care, and some call it simply family nursing. These different terms reflect confusion about whether the family is the client (the recipient of care) or is the context of care (in which the individual family member is the recipient of care). Family approaches to nursing care have been standard practice in the areas of maternal-child nursing, school nursing, and mental health nursing. In the era of cost containment in health care and early hospital dismissals, families frequently assume caretaker roles. Families also become the recipient of nursing care when they commit to caring for an aging family member in the home instead of an extended care facility (Bailey, 2007; Magnusson & Hanson, 2005; Stadnyk, 2006). The importance of family as client remerges as a key component of cultural competence in professional practice (Andrews & Boyle, 2008; Knoerl, 2007). When providing care to the terminally ill, nurses sometimes find themselves focusing more on families than those persons who are dying (Schumacher, Stewart, & Archbold, 2007). In today's practice settings, nurses indeed frequently view the family as the unit of care or clients.

The family-as-client approach means that the entire family rather than individuals become the recipient of nursing services. For example, in the vignette, the presenting problem is the teenage girl, Lisa, who is complaining of dizziness. If the nurse focuses on the unit of care as the individual, nursing interventions would address only specific interventions for Lisa. However, because of Lisa's age and the nature of eating disorders, a more appropriate unit of care would be the family.

What are the indices and phenomena that represent the family as a holistic unit upon which the professional nurse must focus if the family is to be the client system? One approach is to view the family as a system interacting with subsystems and suprasystems. Artinian (1994) indicated that some of the assumptions of the family systems perspective are:

- A family system is an organized whole; individuals within the family are parts of the system and are interdependent.
- The family system is greater than and different from the sum of its parts.
- There are logical relationships (connectedness patterns) between the subsystems. In some families, the connectedness patterns may reflect rigid and fixed structures and relationships. In other families, the patterns of connectedness may reflect highly flexible structures and relationships.
- Using feedback from the environment, the family system responds (adapts) to change in ways that reduce strain and maintain a dynamic balance.

In the systems approach, the phenomena of interest are wholeness, relationships, belief systems, family rules, family needs, roles, and the tensions between individuation and togetherness. Two family theories that are congruent with the family systems model are the Calgary family assessment model (Hanson, 1996; Wright & Leahey, 1998) and the framework of systemic organization (Friedmann, 1995). A summary of the family systems model is presented in Display 16-1.

Another approach to family as client focuses on the family as a structural-functional social system (Artinian, 1994). The focus is the family structure and its effectiveness in performing its functions. Friedman (1992) identified seven **family functions**: (1) affective support (meeting the emotional needs of family members), (2) socialization and social placement (socializing children and making them productive members of society), (3) reproduction (producing new members for society), (4) family coping (maintaining order and stability), (5) economic (providing sufficient economic resources and allocating resources effectively), (6) providing physical necessities (food, clothing, shelter), and (7) health care (maintaining health).

The Friedman family assessment model (Friedman, 1992; Hanson, 1996) appears congruent with a combination of the structural-functional model and the family systems model. Friedman stated that nurses must view the family in two ways when implementing family nursing: as each individual within the family context and the family as the unit of care. A summary of the structural-functional model is presented in Display 16-2.

A third approach to family as client is the family stress model. Artinian (1994) listed the following assumptions of this model: (1) the family is a system, (2) unexpected or unplanned events usually are perceived as more stressful than expected events, (3) events within the family that are defined as stressful are more disruptive than events outside the family, (4) lack of experience with a stressor leads to greater perceived stressfulness, and (5) ambiguous stressor events are more stressful than unambiguous ones. Artinian

---

The Family Systems Model

Overview: Focuses on interaction between members of the family system and on the family system with other systems. A change in one member of the family system influences the entire system.

Concepts: Subsystems, boundaries, openness, energy, negentropy (energy that promotes order), entropy (energy promoting chaos), feedback, adaptation, homeostasis, input, output, internal system processes.

Assumptions: Family system is greater than the sum of its parts. Subsystems are related and interact with one another, and the whole family system interacts with other systems. Family systems have homeostatic features and strive to maintain a dynamic balance.

Clinical Application: Assess, diagnose, and intervene with family according to major concepts.

Sample Assessment Questions

- How did change caused by the critical illness event affect all the members of the family?
- How are members of the family system relating with one another?
- How is the family system relating to the critical care environment?
- What is the "input" into the family system?
- Is the family system internally processing the input? What is the family system output?
- How open is the family system? Does the family system have homeostasis?
- Determine how family behavior affects the patient.

- Determine how the patient's behavior affects the family.

Interventions

- Encourage nurse–family interactions through establishing trust and using communication skills to check for discrepancies between nurse and family expectations.
- Establish a mechanism for providing family with information about the patient on a regular basis.
- Foster the family's ability to get information.
- Listen to the family's feelings, concerns, and questions.
- Orient the family to the critical care environment.
- Answer family questions or assist them to get answers.
- Discuss strategies for normalizing family life with family members.
- Provide mechanisms for the patient and other family members to interact with one another through pictures, videos, audiotapes, or open visiting.
- Monitor family relationships.
- Facilitate open communication among family members.
- Collaborate with the family in problem solving.
- Provide necessary knowledge that will help the family make decisions.

Source: Artinian, N.T. (1994). Selecting a model to guide family assessment. *Dimensions of Critical Care Nursing, 14*, 6. Used with permission of the publisher.

---

indicated that client assessment should include family resources, the meaning of the situation to the family (e.g., is it viewed as a threat or a challenge?), the level of crisis the family is experiencing, and coping mechanisms.

Patterson (1999) presented a postmodern view of a family and provided an ecological perspective that requires nurses to think in layers with the smallest unit, the person, being in the center, with larger units extending outward until it comprises the entire cosmos. In this model, the family is an integral part of an ecosystem, and many variations in family form exist. Children receive support and protection from family members (parents, grandparents, siblings, and other relatives). The family serves as a unit of the **community** that encompasses schools, child care providers, churches, health care providers, workplaces, locally supportive services (police, fire, city, and county services), neighborhoods, and friends. The community is part of society, which is composed of the military, government, multinational corporations, technology, prisons, research institutions, courts, banks, insurers, transportation systems, media, and welfare systems. Patterson designated the following four family functions:

- Family formation and membership: to provide a sense of belonging, personal and social identity, and meaning and direction for life
- Economic support: to provide basic shelter, food, clothing, and other things to facilitate and enhance human development

---

The Structural-Functional Model

Overview: Focuses on family structure and family function and how well family structure performs its functions.

Concepts: Structural areas include family form, roles, values, communication patterns, power structure, or support network. Functional areas include affective, socialization, reproductive, coping, economic, physical care, and health care functions.

Assumptions: Family is a system and a small group that exists to perform certain functions.

Clinical Application: Assess, diagnose, and intervene with family according to major concepts.

Sample Assessment Questions

- What impact did the critical illness event have on family structure and function?
- How did the critical illness alter the family structure?
- What family roles were changed? What family functions have been affected?
- What are family members' physical responses to the illness event?

Interventions

- Assist the family to modify its organization so that role responsibilities can be redistributed.
- Respect and encourage adaptive coping skills used by the family.
- Counsel family members on additional effective coping skills for their own use.
- Identify typical family coping mechanisms.
- Tell the family it is safe and acceptable to use typical expressions of affection.
- Provide privacy for the family to allow for family expression of affection.
- Provide for family visitation.
- Encourage family members to recognize their own health needs.
- Help family members find ways to meet their health needs while helping them feel their concern for the patient has not diminished.
- Assist the family to use existing support structure.

Source: Artinian, N.T. (1994). Selecting a model to guide family assessment. *Dimensions of Critical Care Nursing, 14,* 6. Used with permission of the publisher.

- Nurturance and socialization: to provide holistic development and support of members while instilling social values and norms
- Protection of vulnerable members: to provide care for the young, disabled, ill, or aging members incapable of self-care or at risk for harm

Patterson (1999) also proposed that each family develops specific functioning patterns that include consistent ways a family displays affection, shows anger, copes with stress, deals with conflict, accomplishes daily routines, disciplines children, seeks health care, and celebrates special occasions. The family alters these patterns as the family experiences developmental transitions (birth, raising children, departing children, aging, and death). Because the familial experience is multidimensional, Patterson suggested that limiting assessment to completing family questionnaires limits data collected by health care providers. Health care professionals should consider observing family interactions when families enter the health care system. Because a family is a system, the conceptualization of family health requires consideration of the individual health status of each member and the health of the family's functioning patterns (Patterson). Alteration in the health of one member usually results in altered family functioning patterns.

Two theories that are congruent with a combination of the family stress model and the family systems model are the family assessment and intervention model (Hanson, 1996; Mischke & Hanson, 1995) and the resiliency model (McCubbin & McCubbin, 1993). A summary of the family stress model is presented in Display 16-3.

Anderson and Tomlinson (1992, p. 61) identifed five realms of family experience that represent elements of the approaches identified and that direct professional practice:

1. Interactive processes: (a) family relationships, (b) communication, (c) nurturance, (d) intimacy, and (e) social support
2. Developmental processes: (a) family transitions and (b) dynamic interactions between stages of family development and individual developmental tasks

---

The Family Stress Model

Overview: Focuses on stressors, resources, and perceptions to explain the amount of family disruption caused by a stressful event.

Concepts: "A"—stressful event with associated hardships; "B"—physical, psychological, material, social, spiritual, informational resources of family; "C"—family's subjective definition of the stressful event; "X"—crisis, the amount of disruption or incapacitation within the family caused by the stressful event.

Assumptions: Family is a system. Unexpected and ambiguous illness events are more stressful. Stressful events within the family are more disruptive than stressor events that occur outside the family. Lack of experience with a stressor event leads to increased perceptions of stressfulness.

Clinical Application: Assess, diagnose, and intervene with family according to major concepts.

Sample Assessment Questions
- Identify the family's understanding and beliefs about the situation.
- What family hardships are associated with the critical illness event?
- What are other situational stressors for the family?
- Did the family have time to prepare for the event?
- Has the family had experience with the event?
- What resources are available to the family?
- Are the resources sufficient to meet the demands of the event?
- What are the family's perceptions of the event?
- Do they perceive the event to be a threat or a challenge?
- Does the family blame themselves for the event?
- How incapacitated is family functioning?

Interventions
- Help the family to cope with imposed hardships.
- If appropriate, provide spiritual or informational resources for the family.
- Introduce the family to others undergoing similar experiences.
- Discuss existing social support resources for the family.
- Assist the family in capitalizing on its strengths.
- Assist the family to resolve feelings of guilt.
- Help the family visualize successfully handling all the hardships associated with the situation.
- If possible, encourage the family to focus on the positive aspects of the situation or cognitively reappraise the situation as positive.

Source: Artinian, N.T. (1994). Selecting a model to guide family assessment. *Dimensions of Critical Care Nursing, 14,* 7. Used with permission of the publisher.

---

3. Coping processes: (a) management of resources, (b) problem solving, and (c) adaptation to stressors and crisis
4. Integrity processes: (a) shared meanings of experiences, (b) family identity and commitment, (c) family history, (d) family values, (e) boundary maintenance, and (f) family rituals
5. Health processes: (a) family health beliefs, (b) health status, (c) health responses and practices, (d) lifestyle practices, and (e) health care provision during wellness and illness

Therefore, nurses need to implement the nursing process in a way that facilitates exploration of all the family realms listed rather than focusing exclusively on health processes. In all the conceptual nursing models, the client system is viewed holistically; thus, the professional nurse cannot extricate the health processes from the other processes (integrity, coping, development, and interaction).

Family nursing interventions depend on the clinical practice context. For example, early discharge planning requires that nurses teach and counsel families as they anticipate taking clients home from inpatient settings. Nurses listen to families as they express concerns about the changes in the family's previous lifestyle. They teach families knowledge and skills so that they can safely provide care, anticipate potential complications, and know what to do in case they occur. In inpatient settings, families frequently find the ability to room-in with their loved one most beneficial. Nurses also assess family dynamics as families interact in all nursing care settings. Nurses collaborate with families in many nursing care settings to design family nursing care plans when needed

(Blanes, Carmagnani, & Ferreira, 2007; Li, Melnyk, & McCann, 2004; Knoerl, 2007; Stadnyk, 2006). Sometimes nurses can use creative arts as an innovation to reduce stress and lower anxiety in family caregivers (Walsh, Martin, & Schmidt, 2004). Nurses in long-term care facilities frequently support spouses of residents as they adapt to living alone in the community. Research Brief 16-1 identifies activities that facilitate spousal separation related to placing one's spouse in an extended care facility.

Sometimes, practice barriers prevent nurses from addressing the relevant realms when the family is the client. Because of laws related to client privacy, nurses must exercise caution when disclosing protected health information about individuals to their family members. Some health care organizations limit the number of persons who may receive client information, which sometimes creates friction among family members. Situations such as decreased length of stay in inpatient settings, inadequate staffing, poor coordination of services across the health care setting continuum, lack of coordinated inpatient and outpatient services, less-than-optimal communication among interdisciplinary health providers, lack of nurse education regarding family structure and processes, and overwhelming complexity of family needs serve as reasons for ineffective family nursing care. In addition, many health care settings emphasize medical care over nursing care (Rose, Mallinson, & Walton-Moss, 2004).

How would nurse theorists explain the family as the client and the application of nursing to the nurse–family relationship? Following is a discussion of how the family may be understood in nursing models within the change/growth paradigm (Orem, 1983; Watson, 1996; Peplau, 1952; Rogers, 1983; Parse, 1996, 1998; Newman, 1983) and those nursing models within the change/stability paradigm (King, 1983; Neuman, 1983; Roy, 1983).

Research Brief 16-1

Stadnyk, R. (2006). Community-dwelling spouses of nursing home residents: Activities that sustain identities in times of transitions. *Topics in Geriatric Rehabilitation*, 22(4), 283–293.

The investigator explored the role of activities that fostered the identity changes experienced by spouses who had placed their partners in an extended care facility using qualitative semistructured interviews. Data were collected from 52 spouses using convenience sampling. Interviews requested information regarding financial issues, daily activities, how activities had changed during placement of the spouse, identification of difficulties, and sharing of their biggest worry or concern.

Key findings included that spouses engaged in marriage-sustaining activities that included visiting at least daily, spending time together, reminiscing with each other, involving the resident in decision making about the outside household life's little pleasures (e.g., eating a meal together), and monitoring the quality of care the spouse received. The spouse living in the community also engaged in identity-sustaining activities that included attending church, participating in community recreational activities (exercise classes, dancing, and playing cards), volunteering, engaging in previous hobbies, reading, seeing friends on a regular basis, and pursuing other pleasurable activities.

Results of this study reveal that spouses of recently admitted extended care residents engage in activities to sustain their identities and marriages. Professional nursing in these settings can affirm and support spouses as they engage in these activities, as well as offer education in these methods to facilitate the transition to living alone in the community. However, results of this study should be exercised with caution for the possible reasons: (1) convenience sampling techniques were used, (2) participants had to be willing to disclose issues about finances, (3) participants had a higher level of education than the Canadian population, (4) they reported poorer health than most Canadians over age 65 years, and (5) the study was done in Canada. However, the findings offer potential effective strategies for nurses to use to support elderly persons when they can no longer care for spouses at home.

The Family in the Change/Growth Models of Nursing

When nurses use the **change/growth models** of nursing, they acknowledge that families experience growth when confronted with change. Like the individual, the family possesses great potential to develop in ways to maximize health for all members. The following section outlines professional considerations for nurses using the change/growth models of nursing.

Orem's Self-Care Deficit Model

According to Taylor and Renpenning (1995, p. 356), Orem viewed family as a multiperson care system, which is

> those courses and sequences of action which are performed by the persons in multiperson units for the purpose of meeting the self-care requisites and the development and exercise of self-care agency of all members of the group and to maintain or establish the welfare of the unit.... The sub-systems of the multiperson system are the self-care systems of the individuals.

Whall and Fawcett (1991, p. 20) indicated that Orem's self-care conceptual framework primarily "views the family as only a backdrop for individuals." In her own words, Orem (1983, p. 368) directed the nurse to "first, accept the system of family living, the physical and social environment of the family, and the family's culture as basic conditioning factors for all the family members." She stressed that the family support system needs to be explored and "adjusted as needed and then incorporated into the system of family living" (Orem, p. 368).

Family is context in self-care, in which family members take actions to create conditions essential for human functioning and development, and for dependent care, in situations when family members need their care provided by others. Both self-care and dependent care are directed toward creating and maintaining conditions that support life and integrated functions and promote human growth. Self-care and dependent care "are forms of deliberate action, learned behaviors, learned within the family and other social units within which individuals live and move" (Orem, 1983, p. 209). However, Orem also considered the family to be a unit, "a complex entity which can be regarded as a whole" (Taylor & Renpenning, 1995, p. 350). Thus, there is concern with the quality of interaction and the outcomes of those interactions on the family as a whole.

Two realms of family can be readily implemented in Orem's self-care model: the interactive processes, particularly the social support systems in the family, and the developmental processes, particularly in the understanding of dependent care needs at various life stages. "Conditions which justify identifying the multi-person unit include a need for protection and prevention, regulation of a hazard, need for environmental regulation, [and] need for resources" (Taylor & Renpenning, 1995, p. 366).

Lapp, Diemert, and Enestredt (1991) stressed the concept of the family as a partner in health care decision making. In keeping with the self-care perspective, they see "the primary responsibility for health and life choices as ultimately resting with the client family" (Lapp et al., 1991, p. 306). Lapp et al. further suggested that the main responsibility of the nurse is "ensuring that those choices were made on the basis of the most complete information possible while facilitating self-discovery of strengths and resources already existing for a family" (p. 306).

Chevannes (1997) specified that Orem's three levels of care enable nurses and family to develop a caring partnership. The nurse and family collaborate to determine the care level needed to fulfill the needs of the incapacitated member. In the wholly compensatory level of care, the nurse provides care to the incapacitated person while beginning to teach family members. The nurse assesses family needs for nursing care or provides episodic care in the home when the family requires partly compensatory nursing care. Finally, when families assume full care responsibilities, the nurse provides support and education as needs arise.

If the nurse in the vignette practiced nursing according to Orem's self-care deficit theory, the nurse would assess Lisa and her family for their ability to access physical and mental health services independently and offer her assistance if the family could not access required services independently, discuss treatment options for Lisa (and the family), and help them select specific services and treatment plans. Once the family obtained the help they needed, the nurse would offer education and support to them.

Watson's Human Science and Human Care Model

Watson's caring model lends itself to a view of the family as client if the nurse redefines the phenomenal field to be the family within the family system's environment. The nurse assesses family values by exploring the five realms of family experience (Anderson & Tomlinson, 1992)—namely, the integrity processes—through the family's shared meanings of experiences, its members' identity and commitment to that family identity, the family history, members' shared values and rituals, and their strategies for maintaining family boundaries.

During actual caring occasions, nurses learn about the family and identify needs for information and problem-solving abilities by identifying the past and current family's coping processes. Nurses and family members are "coparticipants in becoming in the now and the future and both are part of some larger, deeper, complex pattern of life" (Watson, 2007, p. 60). Together, nurses and family members analyze interaction processes, focus on familial relationships and communication patterns, explore the meanings of various transitions occurring within the family, identify support networks, and share feelings and meanings about family life. They also observe how the family members nurture each other and express intimacy, acting as coparticipants. In the human science and human care framework, nurses relate all familial processes to the health processes, clarifying with the family specific health beliefs, responses, and practices, and the patterns of caring for each other during times of wellness and illness.

If the nurse in the vignette used Watson's approach to professional practice, she would offer education about eating disorders and help to access required resources, and provide support during the treatment process. However, she would also pay more attention to the deep meaning of the experience for them, their family health beliefs, and their patterns of caring for each other.

Peplau's Interpersonal Relations Model

Because Peplau based her nursing model on the central concepts of growth and development facilitated by relationships with significant others, the model provides the foundation for the nurse to focus on the family as the unit of care if the patterns of interaction within the family, and the family developmental processes, replace individual needs as the central area of concern. Forchuk and Dorsay (1995, p. 114) stated that Peplau's model and family systems nursing "both share a common focus on interactions, patterns and interpersonal relationships."

Perhaps Peplau's greatest contribution to the family nursing process is the enumeration of the stages of the nurse–client relationship. According to Friedman (1992, p. 42), "trust and rapport-building set the stage for and are the cornerstones of effective family nursing care." In the orientation stage, if the nurse and the family are to have an effective relationship, each member of the family must be able to share his or her concerns so that the nurse and other family members may more fully understand the whole family and the meaning of its experience together. In the planning stage, mutual goal setting—that is, jointly formulated among family members and the nurse—and ways to meet commonly derived goals are directed toward reframing the need for help in the professional relationship to be a learning and growth experience.

It is proposed that, in the intervention stage (called the exploitation stage by Peplau) with families, Peplau's role behaviors originally designated as professional nursing roles could be developed as strategies for the entire family. Family needs replace individual needs, and the roles of resource person, teacher, leader, counselor, and surrogate may be played by both the nurse and various family members. Each role performance in the family should be fully explored in a way that the family learns about its interactive processes and the effect of those interactive processes on health processes.

If the nurse in the vignette used Peplau as a framework for professional practice, the nurse would work to build trust and rapport with the family unit, explore all family members' concerns, work with the family to understand the total experience, and collaborate with the family to set goals. The nurse would primarily assume the roles of teacher and counselor/teacher as the family learns about the daughter's eating disorder, what it means, and treatment options. Emphasis would be placed on how the disorder and treatment regimens would affect performance of family roles and how the overall interactive processes would affect the health of each family member and the family as a unit.

Rogers' Science of Unitary Human Beings

Various analysts agree that Rogers' conceptual model of nursing science lends itself readily to the family as the recipient of nursing care—the client system. As Friedman (1992, p. 62) said, "Rogers's legacy is clearly associated with general systems theory, and because of this orientation there is a good fit between Rogerian nursing theory and family nursing." Rogers herself said that the family system is an energy field that serves as the focus of study and interaction. She asserted that family fields and their respective environmental fields are engaged in a continuously evolving mutual process and that patterns identify this ongoing process (Rogers, 1983, p. 226). Some patterns may represent togetherness, others may represent activity/rest, and still others may represent rhythmicities in the family experience.

Whall and Fawcett (1991, p. 22) suggested that, in the Rogerian model, the family is "viewed as an irreducible whole that is not understood by knowledge of individual family members." Newman, Sime, and Corcoran-Perry (1991, p. 4) pointed out that, from the unitary-transformative perspective (the perspective first described by Rogers), a phenomenon (any client system) is "viewed as a unitary, self-organizing field embedded in a larger self-organizing field … [and] identified by pattern and by interaction with the larger whole." Given this perspective, the family represents a unitary phenomenon embedded in the larger environmental field and a phenomenon that has patterns of energy exchange within its field and within its interactions with the larger environment.

Whall (1986) suggested that, despite Rogers not being completely clear about what assessment strategies are used in the unitary model, she deserves credit for the idea that the nurse providing care must assess the family as a whole. Other nurses have developed some of the tools needed for assessing the whole family. For example, Smoyak developed the idea of using genograms and the identification of family rules of organization as approaches in the nursing process (Whall). The genogram records information about family members and their relationships over at least three generations. It involves mapping the family structure, recording family information, and delineating family relationships. According to McGoldrick and Gerson (1985, p. 1), genograms "display family information graphically in a way that provides a quick gestalt of complex family patterns and a rich source of hypotheses about how a clinical problem may be connected to the family context and the evolution of problem and context over time."

The genogram is one of nursing's most useful tools for studying family patterns because it maps relationships and patterns of functioning and thus "may help clinicians think systemically about how events and relationships in their clients' lives are related to patterns of health and illness" (McGoldrick & Gerson, 1985, p. 2). Using the historical data obtained by completing the genogram, the nurse assesses previous life cycle transitions. This assessment helps the nurse to "picture the important connections between the family and the world" (Wright & Leahey, 1994, p. 49). Readers are referred to McGoldrick and Gerson, and Wright and Leahey, for additional details on constructing and interpreting the genogram as a tool for nursing assessment of the family.

All of the family realms described by Anderson and Tomlinson (1992) and discussed earlier in this chapter represent patterns of the family as a unitary phenomenon. Thus, these realms could be used as a basis for assessment, planning, intervention, and evaluation by nurses practicing on the basis of a Rogerian philosophy of nursing.

If the nurse in the vignette used Rogers' science of unitary human beings to guide practice, she would see that the health status of both girls in her office was a manifestation of the pattern of the whole. The nurse would focus on understanding all mechanisms that affect the life process of the girls, one of which is the family.

Parse's Human Becoming Model

The nursing models of Parse and Newman may be considered Rogerian based. Thus, the nurse practicing within any of these models would incorporate Rogerian concepts in the caregiving process with the family.

For Parse, "since the abstract term 'human' includes all human phenomena, it encompasses family phenomena as inherent in being human" (Cody, 1995, p. 11). Parse, who views the person as an open being always in the process of becoming, probably would describe the family as open and always in the process of becoming. "Family health is co-created by persons as they live family process" (Cody, p. 14). Nurses would direct nursing care most likely at structuring meaning, co-creating rhythmic patterns of relating, and co-transcending with the possibles through the interpersonal processes occurring among family members and the nurse for the purpose of improving the quality of life for the family.

"For each participant family, a multiplicity of views co-creates the reality of the family situation as lived by each person" (Cody, 1995, p. 23). Clearly, the family realms (Anderson & Tomlinson, 1992) that characterize Parse's model are the interactive processes (family relationships, communication, nurturance, intimacy, and social support) and the integrity processes (shared meanings of experiences, family identity and commitment, family history, family values, boundary maintenance, and family rituals).

If the nurse in the vignette used Parse's human becoming model as a framework for professional practice, the approach would be similar to that of Rogers' science of unitary human beings. However, the nurse would expend more energy to uncover the meaning that underlies the behaviors associated with the eating disorders. To discover the true meanings, the nurse would be truly present with the family as they expressed concerns that would ultimately reveal the meaning of thoughts, feelings, values, and changes that may have potentially contributed to Lisa's problems. The nurse would also provide a relationship so that the family can express these things as they engage in the treatment process and recover once treatment is completed.

Newman's Theory of Health as Expanding Consciousness

Newman, who views the individual as a center of energy, views the family the same way—a center of energy in constant interaction with the environment. Newman (1983) made five assumptions about families:

1. Health encompasses family situations in which one or more family members may be diagnosed as ill.
2. The illness of family members can be considered a manifestation of the pattern of the family interaction.
3. Elimination of the disease condition in the identified ill family member will not change the overall pattern of the family.
4. If one person's becoming ill is the only way the family can become conscious of its pattern, then that is health (in process) for that family.
5. Health is the expansion of consciousness of the family. Consciousness has been defined as the informational capacity of the system, a factor that can be observed in the quantity and quality of responses to stimuli.

The nature of nursing with the family would be the repatterning of partnerships between the family and the environment that promote higher levels of consciousness. Newman (1983) said that the purpose of nursing with the family is to facilitate the development of an increased range of responses of family members to each other and to the world outside the family and to facilitate the refinement of those responses (quality). She suggests that the first task is to assess the patterns of movement, space, time, and consciousness in the family. The nurse would consider the following factors to assess movement through observation: (1) the coordinated movement of language between speaker and listener, (2) other coordinated movements (such as dancing, lovemaking, and sports), (3) the freedom of individual movement within the family, and (4) the movement outside the family.

Time is assessed for the quantity and quality of private time, coordinated time, and shared time. Space is assessed for territoriality, shared space, and distancing. Finally, consciousness is assessed by collecting data on the informational capacity of the family system, the quantity and quality of interaction within the family, and the quantity and quality of the interaction of the family with the community.

By completing these assessments, the nurse providing care for the family would be able to analyze the patterns of energy exchange between the family and the environment, and the transforming potential and life patterns of the family. These patterns will identify where the family energy is flowing and where it is blocked, depleted, or diffused and will determine whether there is overload or build-up of energy in the family. Newman (1983, p. 173) said that as these patterns emerge, the family's informational capacity will be increased in the nurse–client relationship. Assessment of these patterns also will reveal the family's evolving capacities, diversity, and complexity. If the nurse in the vignette used Newman's theory of health as expanding consciousness, she would intervene to facilitate repatterning the family into a higher level of consciousness.

Consistent with the models of Rogers, Parse, and Newman is the fact that the family functions as a unitary, open system integrated with its environment. Family functions may be organized around Anderson and Tomlinson's (1992) five realms of family experience; thus, the assessment, planning, implementation, and evaluation of the family as client by nurses practicing from any of the change/growth nursing models should reflect interactive, developmental, coping, integrity, and health processes and the relationship among all of these processes.

The Family in the Change/Stability Models of Nursing

When nurses use **change/stability models** of nursing, they acknowledge that nursing roles focus on assisting families in solving problems. This section presents a brief discussion of how the family may be viewed as the recipient of care in the nursing models in which the changes are directed toward restabilizing the client system.

King's Systems Interaction Model

King (1983, p. 179) viewed the **family** as "a social system that is seen as a group of interacting individuals." Thus, the family is an interpersonal system. In King's model, a theory of goal attainment in the family emphasizes interaction between the family members.

The major concepts in this theory of goal attainment are self, role, perception, communication, transaction, stress, growth and development, time, space, and interaction. Each of these concepts is assessed in the nursing process between the nurse and the family. Communication is the interrelating factor among these concepts. Nurses and families make transactions to attain goals. King said that family movement through space and time may be social (called vertical movement) or physical (called geographic mobility). She also stated that family roles are related to growth and development and stress in the family.

To summarize King's perception of the **family as client**, the nurse assesses the family situation to identify real or potential problems. The nurse "assist[s] family members in setting goals to resolve problems [and] provide[s] relevant information to help families make decisions about those factors that detract from or enhance healthy living" (King, 1983, p. 183). If the nurse in the vignette used King's approach to professional practice, the nurse would assess the family to identify factors contributing to the suspected eating disorders, and help families identify actual and potential issues and concerns regarding having a family member with an eating disorder.

Neuman's Health Care Systems Model

A stress/adaptation-based conceptual model for family nursing is Neuman's health care systems model. The nurse practicing with this model can modify assessment strategies to plan, implement, and evaluate primary, secondary, and tertiary interventions with families.

According to Neuman (1983, p. 241), "the concept of family as a system can be viewed as individual family members harmonious in their relationships—a cluster of related meanings and values that govern the family and keep it viable in a constantly changing environment." Stability is considered to represent the wellness state, instability the illness state, and transition the mixed wellness–illness state. The role of the nurse is "to control vigorously factors affecting the family, with special goal-directed activities toward facilitating stability within the system" (Neuman, p. 243). To understand influences on the stability of the **family system**, Neuman proposed the following points:

1. The nurse must deal with the needs of each family member in terms of his or her developmental age, developmental state, individual differences (strengths and weaknesses), and environmental influences according to his or her perceptions of events.
2. The nurse must determine the structure and process of the family by studying the values and interaction patterns. The significant values and interaction patterns are the decision-making process (how power is distributed), coping style (how differences are negotiated in relation to stress), role relationships (the controlling or facilitating effects of roles in meeting individual and family needs), communication styles and interaction patterns (congruence of verbal and nonverbal messages and the effects of situational or entrenched defense mechanisms in the family), goals (the sharing and supporting of concerns and feelings between members), boundaries (rules that define the type of behaviors that are acceptable or unacceptable to the family), socialization process (the adequacy of resources to support cultural and structural factors in meeting family needs), individuation (the quality of individuality of each family member that defines the wellness or stability of the unit), and sharing (an index for family stability).
3. The nurse must facilitate the meeting of family needs by intervening in the intrafamily stressors (all things occurring within the family unit), interfamily stressors (all things occurring between the family and the immediate environment), and extrafamily stressors (all things occurring between the family and the distal or indirect external environment). These interventions occur as primary prevention, secondary prevention, or tertiary prevention.

Tomlinson and Anderson (1995) described five areas of interface between Neuman's systems model and a general family health system paradigm:

1. Complexity of the system: the "need to consider not only the individual stressor response in relation to the family but also the family's response relative to lines of defense and resistance" (pp. 138–139).
2. Conceptualization of the core of the family: "The core of the family is composed of its individual members, and assessment of the family is done in relation to the dynamics of individual member contributions to the whole within their environmental interactive context … [in comparison] the core of the family systems is viewed as the interface of its members in interaction with the environment" (p. 139).
3. Goal of family health: "Neuman's central concern is to facilitate optimal client system stability or wellness in the face of change … [in comparison] from a family health system perspective, it is most desirable to facilitate family system wellness using strengths to reduce stressor effects and enhance family growth toward positive transformation" (p. 140).
4. Entry point in caring for families: The family becomes partners in health care. "According to Neuman, nursing functions to conserve system energy" (p. 140).
5. Nursing interaction: In the Neuman model, "the nurse role creates an explicit cooperative alliance with the client … [in comparison] based on a family systems perspective … in the family caregiving situation there may be considerable boundary ambiguity" (p. 141).

The nurse's prevention activities are the heart of Neuman's model of care. Primary preventions are the activities aimed at preventing stressors from invading the family. Secondary preventions are the protective activities that follow stressor invasion. Tertiary preventions are the activities during the family's reconstitution from stressors. All of these preventions are aimed at reestablishing stability within the family. If the school nurse in the vignette used the Neuman systems model as a foundation for practice, she would assess the family for stressors using five variables (physiologic, psychological, sociocultural, developmental, and spiritual). She would look for ways to minimize the impact of stressors associated with familial factors that may have contributed to the eating disorder, living with a family member with an eating disorder as well as the stressors associated with treatment.

Roy's Adaptation Model

Roy's adaptation model can be used by the nurse dealing with the family as client. Roy (1983) believed that the family as an adaptive system can be analyzed and that interventions can be organized around enhancing stimuli to the family.

Inputs for family include individual needs and changes within members and among members, and external changes in the environment. These inputs serve as focal stimuli for the family system. Processes handling the inputs are the control and feedback mechanisms. The control mechanisms—supporting, nurturing, and socializing—serve as contextual and residual stimuli to the family system. The feedback mechanisms are the transactional patterns and member control.

Outputs of the family system are the behaviors manifested. Roy (1983) has chosen three goals as proposed output of the adaptive family system: (1) survival, (2) continuity (role function), and (3) growth (the system's self-concept). At the current stage of development, Roy (p. 275) simply said that "family behavior can be observed as it relates to the general family goals of survival, continuity, and growth."

The nurse observes for the outputs of survival, continuity, and growth and for the transactional and member controls that serve as feedback to the family to signal the need to adjust the behavior of a member or the group. Nursing practice emerges from the assessment of the previously described family factors. The nursing process continues to (1) identify and validate with family members the factor that is most immediately affecting their behavior, (2) identify individual family member needs as focal stimuli, (3) make nursing diagnoses and set goals, and (4) intervene to enhance stimuli configuration in the family.

Friedman (1992, p. 61) supported Roy's suggestion that "nursing problems involve ineffective coping mechanisms, which cause ineffective responses, disrupting the integrity of the person" and suggested that "this notion could easily be broadened to the family unit, where ineffective family coping patterns lead to family functioning problems." Whall and Fawcett (1991, p. 24) acknowledged the potential contribution of Roy's model of nursing care to care of the family as an adaptive system but noted that "theories of family adaptation and nursing practice theories of family need to be generated and tested." Family adaptation theories need to be elaborated by identifying specific and concrete inputs, processes, and outputs of the family system.

It can be clearly seen that the family as client, rather than context, is a significant new conceptual basis for nursing. Although the attribution "of wellness and illness to the family unit is a recent phenomenon" (Gilliss, Highley, Roberts, & Martinson, 1988, p. 5), it is anticipated that an eclectic view of family incorporating both the nursing conceptual models and other social systems approaches will continue to be refined.

Nurses frequently integrate family approaches to clinical situations. Family theory and nursing models provide solid foundations for professional practice. Many family assessment tools exist. Most inpatient admission databases collect data surrounding family life. Although family models and theories are not specific to a particular nurse theorist, they complement many current nursing models and theories. Some cases such as the structure provided by Anderson and Tomlinson (1992), cited earlier in this chapter, provides an eclectic approach when working with families as clients. The family plays a key role in its own health and the health of individual members. Current family health practices evolve from previous health practices. When a family unit forms, the health practices of the new family frequently blend health patterns that the family heads learned as children. Women tend to assume primary responsibility for family health, family members have specific health routines, and community and cultural context affect family health (Andrews & Boyle, 2008; Blanes et al., 2007; Denham, 1999; Lundy & Janes, 2001; Schumacher et al., 2007).

THE COMMUNITY AS CLIENT

In this book, the emerging philosophy defines community as a social system with open communication networks between structural and functional subsystems and the greater societal systems. Vertical bureaucratic relationships tie the community to the larger society. A community always has a sense of common identification, even if it does not exist as a common geographic location. Thus, the boundaries of a community can be determined in terms of role relationships as well as geography. As with all open systems, the nurse influences change in the community. The change is directed toward higher levels of wellness in the system. Shuster and Geppinger (2004) specified that the community becomes the client when service providers aim to achieve what is best for the collective good of the population receiving care services instead of focusing on what is best for the individual. In addition, members of the community and nurses work collaboratively to identify community needs and develop programs to meet them.

Basic concepts from community health nursing apply to the care of **community as client**. Various community nursing scholars such as Neuman (1989); Pender, Murdaugh, and Parsons (2005); and Canty-Mitchell, Little, Robinson, and Chandler (2008) have agreed that the following considerations are essential to professional nurses working with the community as client:

- **Health promotion**: improving the well-being and quality of life of the community
- **Risk**: identifying factors that increase the chance the community will either experience or be affected by a particular health problem

- **Disease prevention**: protecting the population from diseases, disabilities, and their consequences
- **Primary prevention**: preventing the occurrence of health problems or diseases
- **Secondary prevention**: identifying and treating health problems and diseases
- **Tertiary prevention**: preventing further deterioration following a health problem or restoring health and functioning after disease occurs

Sometimes, a social change may be needed to address these key considerations. For example, in the vignette, the professional nurse may find the need to confront the societal value that it is impossible to be too thin. Along with educating the girls and their family, the school nurse may find it necessary to consult with teachers, school administration, the parent–teacher organization, students, and the ballet teacher to inform them of the dangers and plan a program to alleviate malnutrition stemming from the desire to be thin.

Definitions of Community

Because community has been thought of primarily as a setting for care, nurses need to explore the various definitions of community to determine how they may view the community as a client for nursing services. Multiple definitions exist for the definitions of community. Clark (1999, p. 6) defined a community as a "group of people who share some type of bond, who interact with each other, and who function collectively regarding common concerns." From a nursing perspective, Hanchett (1988, p. 7) said that community can be considered as an aggregate, a system, or a human–environment field: "As an aggregate, the individual is the basic unit of the community; that is, the community is a number of separate individuals." As a system, one must consider the "relationships among the individuals or groups who constitute the community" (Hanchett, p. 8). As a human–environment field, the community represents a human field integral with its environment and "manifesting correlates of the patterning of that field process" (Hanchett, p. 8).

If the nurse views the community as an aggregate, nursing really is organized around the concept of the community serving as a context for individuals. Clark (1999, p. 56) defined community health nursing as "a synthesis of nursing knowledge and practice and the science and practice of public health, implemented via systematic use of the nursing process and other processes, designed to promote health and prevent illness in population groups. The focus of care is the aggregate." Clark indicated that community health nursing is characterized by the following attributes:

1. Health orientation: health promotion and prevention of disease, rather than cure of illness
2. Population focus: emphasis on aggregates, rather than individuals or families
3. Autonomy: greater control of health care decisions
4. Continuity: providing continuing, comprehensive care, rather than care on a short-term, episodic basis
5. Collaboration: nurse and client interacting as equals
6. Interactivity: awareness of interaction of a variety of factors with health
7. Public accountability: accountability to society for public health
8. Sphere of intimacy: greater awareness of the reality of client lives and situations

Nurses can select from a variety of community nursing and community health models to follow when working with the community as client. Christensen and Kenney (1990) proposed a comprehensive model for implementing the nursing process focusing on the aggregate within the context of a geopolitical environment.

Zotti, Brown, and Stotts (1996, p. 211) differentiated between community-based nursing and community health nursing; community-based nursing "means a philosophy of nursing that guides nursing care provided for individuals, families, and groups wherever they are, including where they live, work, play, or go to school." In contrast, community health nursing "represents a systematic process of delivering nursing care to improve the health of an entire community" (Zotti et al., 1996, p. 212). Characteristics of community-based nursing and community health nursing are compared in Table 16-1.

When the community becomes the client, nurses may find themselves approaching ethical issues in a different manner. Many times ethical practice requires that nurses balance ethical considerations for the individual with those for the community. For example, protecting the community or collective becomes more important, especially when determining the allocation of scarce resources and when the need for community information supersedes the privacy and autonomy of an individual. Professional nurses must also look for ways to ensure social justice and equal access to offered care services while working with culturally diverse and marginalized groups within a designated community. When serving the community, professional nurses may encounter ethical conflicts arising from roles and responsibilities outlined by the profession and employing agency as well as conflicts arising among cultural values and practices from different groups within the community. However, as with all clients, professional nurses must act with honesty, integrity, transparency, loyalty, and truthfulness (Allen & Easley, 2008; Bosek & Savage, 2007; Racher, 2007).

If nurses view the community as a system, then they seek to introduce changes in the community systems and base interventions on their understanding of the impact of these changes on system functioning (Spradley, 1990). Christensen and Kenney (1990) also proposed a general systems assessment model for directing the nursing process with families. Considerable work on viewing the community as a system that is the recipient of nursing care has emerged from Neuman's conceptual model of nursing. This model is discussed later in this chapter. Hanchett (1988) postulated that Roy's adaptation model of nursing and King's general system framework also offer the nurse the opportunity to practice nursing with the community as a client system, in which the focus is on the pattern of relationships among the elements of the system.

Following are brief discussions of (1) a systems model of community as client based on Neuman's conceptual model, in which change is directed toward restoring stability to the system; and (2) a human field–environment model of community as client based on

TABLE 16-1

Community-Based Nursing Compared with Community Health Nursing

Component	Community-Based Nursing	Community Health Nursing
Goals	Manage acute or chronic conditions Promote self-care	Preserve/protect health Promote self-care
Client	Individual and family	Community
Underlying philosophy	Human ecological model	Primary health care
Autonomy	Individual and family autonomy	Community autonomy Individual rights may be sacrificed for good of the community
Client character	Across the life span	Across the life span, with emphasis on high-risk aggregates
Cultural diversity	Culturally appropriate care of individual and families	Collaboration with and mobilization of diverse groups and communities
Type of service	Direct	Direct and indirect
Home visiting	Home visitor	Home visitor
Service focus	Local community	Local, state, federal, and international

From Zotti, M.E., Brown, P., & Slotts, R.C. (1996). Community-based nursing versus community health nursing: What does it all mean? *Nursing Outlook, 44,* 212. Used with permission of the publisher.

Rogerian nursing science, in which change is directed toward increasing capacities and evolving growth, and Parse's perception as community from a human becoming perspective. Despite the different approaches, the presented models tend to agree that community nursing interventions primarily address health promotion, interactions among the domains of space, human relationships, and the environment. When the school nurse in the vignette operates from a community as client perspective, her focus on eating disorders shifts. Once, she intervened with individual students affected by the problem. Now, she considers how the problem affects the entire school community. She plans and executes educational programs for students, faculty, staff, and administration on the detection and prevention of eating disorders. Along with education, she offers her time and attention to listen to concerns and counsels all persons affected by the declining health of students with eating disorders.

A Systems Model of Viewing the Community as Client

Anderson and McFarlane (2006) adapted the Neuman health care systems model in an effort to provide a way for nurses to conceive of the community as the recipient of care. This effort synthesizes public health with nursing. In this systems approach, the community has eight subsystems: (1) recreation, (2) safety and transportation, (3) communication, (4) education, (5) health and social services, (6) economics, (7) politics and government, and (8) the physical environment.

The boundaries of a community are generally geopolitical. The interactive nature of these eight subsystems results in a whole that is more than the sum of its parts. Other nurse leaders have expanded views on this model in terms of the nursing process (Christensen & Kenney, 1990). For example, Beddome (1995) stressed the need to clearly define the client system that is the target of data collection and nursing intervention (geopolitical or aggregate).

The application of Neuman's model to the development of the nursing process with the community as the recipient of care is built around the redefinition of person, environment, health, and nursing. Community nursing scholars have described communities as groups of persons who share common characteristics, such as language or culture, who may or may not live in a specific geographical area (Anderson & McFarlane, 2006; Lundy & Janes, 2001). They redefined the environment to include all conditions, circumstances, and influences that affect the development of the community. Health is equated with competence to function and "a definable state of equilibrium in which subsystems are in harmony so that the whole can perform at its maximum potential" (Saucier, 1991, p. 59).

Nurses participate in the care of the community by participating in community assessment, identifying and diagnosing problems amenable to nursing interventions, planning for and implementing interventions that enhance the interacting forces within the system, and evaluating the outcomes of the interventions on the community's health.

The systems model focuses on prevention. Primary prevention strategies for the professional nurse include (Saucier, 1991) (1) increasing the public's awareness of health problems, (2) increasing the public's knowledge of the available community resources and services to resolve the problems, (3) preparing the public to self-refer to appropriate resources, and (4) preparing the public to become involved in preventing the factors that lead to the problem.

Secondary prevention strategies include facilitating self-screenings and referral to appropriate community resources. Tertiary prevention strategies include lobbying for adequate services and resources to meet the particular community health problems. An example is "health care reform by rethinking health policy and writing new health legislation at many levels of government" (Beddome, 1995, p. 571). The systems model presents a comprehensive approach when nurses serve the community as client. However, the systems approach uses the change as stability perspective.

A Human Field–Environment Model of Viewing Community as Client

From the paradigm of nursing in which change is directed toward growth, the following brief discussion uses the Rogerian framework for viewing the community as client.

Hanchett (1988, p. 128) said that, in this view, the community is seen as an energy field in process with the environmental energy field, and health is viewed as the dynamic well-being of the community–environmental process. Manifestations of these energy fields in process may be reflected in visible expressions such as motion, rhythms of quiet and activity, and the togetherness of the community people in participating in change.

For example, motion that is observable by the nurse is the speed of persons and traffic in daily life. Rhythms of quiet and activity may be seen in the sleep–wake patterns of the community. Everyone has heard about how the streets are "rolled up at night" in some communities. Gatherings of people in community settings can be observed to analyze togetherness. Other pattern manifestations of this energy process include the "number of cultural and ethnic groups of the community, the variety of lifestyles and ideas that flourish, and pragmatic, imaginative, and visionary approaches to change evidenced by the community" (Hanchett, 1988, p. 129).

The goal of nursing is to help the community achieve maximum well-being. According to Hanchett (1988), this is done by the nurse participating in the process of change, assisting community groups to move toward well-being. Rogers' definition of health as "dynamic well-being" means that the community must become more aware of factors that maximize well-being and minimize conditions that limit actualization or realization of full potential.

This view of health directs the actions of the nurse in this model. These actions all center on facilitating persons becoming more aware of their patterns of energy exchange with the environment and the evolving outcomes of these exchanges. Manifestations of field patterning include "diversity, rhythms, motion, the experience of time, sleep–wake and beyond-waking states, and pragmatic, imaginative, and visionary approaches to conscious participation in change" (Hanchett, 1988, p. 128). The nurse attempts to facilitate evolutionary change in the human field–environmental field process from lesser diversity, longer rhythms, slower motion, experiencing time as slower, pragmatic foci, and longer sleeping, to greater diversity, rhythms that seem continuous, motion that seems continuous, experiencing time as timelessness, visionary foci, and longer waking, perhaps even beyond waking, respectively (Hanchett).

The essence of this model for community nursing is that the community as a group–environmental field process determines the health of the community. In each community, the process unfolds at a unique pace and in unique patterns. The community's health is an expression of the mutually evolving process. Nursing's approaches to enhance the well-being of people–environment speak of community well-being. Influencing public policies to provide improved shelter, food, and clothing for all people is an example of approaches to improve community well-being. Nursing is "the science that the art of nursing uses in the conscious participation in the human–environmental field process toward the goal of maximum well-being" (Hanchett, 1988, p. 132).

In the Rogerian model of nursing, the community field–environmental field process integrates all other definitions of community; that is, it validates the community as a social system, as a place (space), and as a people. The resultant health of the client system (community) is more than the sum of these identified parts. Well-being is an integral process in which human beings and the environment evolve toward greater awareness of their being. Respect for both diversity and sameness in patterns of energy exchange is essential for the professional nurse to operate out of this conceptual model of nursing.

It is evident from the general nature of the discussion of this model that much research is needed to assist further development of the Rogerian model. Determining manifestations of patterning of life, identifying patterns that maximize health, and developing strategies that focus on the community field–environmental field process are necessary for fuller implementation of this model in community nursing practice in which the community is the recipient of the care.

Similar to the Rogerian perspective of community, Parse (2003) espoused the interconnectedness of the community and the environment. Parse (2003) defined community as "a oneness of human-universe connectedness incarnating beliefs and values" (p. 1) that is "objective, measurable and concerned with relationships, change, symbiosis, localism, cooperation and the commonality of interests and goals" (p. 5). Parse (2003) further explained that the community is "an ever-changing incarnated interconnectedness correlated with all that is" (p. 21). Parse also envisioned a community that is more than just an acreage or a location. Using her consistent method of what seems to be nearly polar opposites, she identifies two key considerations for the ever-evolving community. Anchoring–shifting deals with the phenomena of holding fast to some things while giving up others. Pondering–shaping refers to thoroughly thinking about how, dialoguing and listening to all community members, and considering all options before developing a means for change. Parse also specified that when one barrier to change is removed, others typically appear. Parse specified true presence serves as the core for nursing practice in the community and nurses need courage and confidence along with understanding of key community members in order to make changes. Co-creating rhythms occur within the community, thereby facilitating human interconnectedness that is ever changing and creating new possibilities.

To learn how to care for communities as clients, nurses may benefit most from participating in service-learning projects or clinical experiences in community agencies. Community-based nursing experiences enable nurses to appreciate the value of being an engaged citizen in a community while learning how to provide nursing services to larger groups of people. Community-based experiences offer situations where nurses give to the agency while they increase their repertoire of community nursing skills. When engaging in community nursing, nurses must expand their views to see how internal and external factors affect an agency while collaborating with community members to ensure that they offer relevant services (Narsavage, Batchelor, Lindell, & Chen, 2003). Nurses also work to build stronger communities as well as improving community health. Through role modeling, nurses can inspire community members to participate actively in the political process, increase participation in community activities, develop community goals, manage conflict effectively, attain consensus on goal priorities and how to reach them, use resources effectively, and obtain external resources for desired programs (Head et al., 2004). Finally, most importantly, nurses advocate for underprivileged community members so they gain access to health care and other basic services (McElmurry, Park, & Buseh, 2003).

Questions for Reflection 16-3

1. What additional professional nursing skills do nurses need when the community is the client?
2. What are current health concerns within my local community?
3. What are current health concerns within my academic community?
4. What health concerns can I identify in my clinical practice community?
5. Why are these health concerns important for each community?

SUMMARY AND SIGNIFICANCE TO PRACTICE

Conceptual models of the client–environment relationship provide frameworks to guide practice with family and community clients as well as individuals. Views of change reflected by the models underlie strategies to promote growth of the family or community or to facilitate return to stability. When working with the family or community as clients, nurses must develop an ability to think in multiple dimensions because more than one person becomes the client system. In most cases, the impact of an individual's health-related change affects a family system. The impact of a health change also may have implications for the entire community. As health care professionals, nurses must look beyond individual clients and develop strategies to provide relevant care for families and communities. Nursing models provide a theoretical foundation for guiding professional nursing actions as nurses work with individuals, families, and communities.

FROM THEORY TO PRACTICE

Review the vignette at the start of the chapter and answer the following questions:

1. List the individual as client, family as client, and community as client in the outlined school nursing situation.
2. Why is it important to expand the definition of client to include the family and community in this situation?
3. What do you think is the top priority in the vignette? Why do you think this issue should be addressed first?
4. What other issues do you see that need to be addressed? Why are these important?

WWW INTERNET EXERCISES

1. Visit the National Clearinghouse on Child Abuse and Neglect website at http://nccanch.acf.hhs.gov. Click on the words "General Resources." On the next screen, click on the underlined words "State Statute Search." Complete Step 1 by identifying your state. Complete Step 2 by clicking on the following words to check the boxes for Mandatory Reporters, Reporting Laws, Reporting Penalties, and Reporting Procedures. Complete Step 3 by scrolling to the bottom of the page and clicking the word "Go!" Read to find out if professional nurses in your state are legally required to report child abuse and neglect. Read the laws and find out if any provisions are made for immunity for reporters in your state. Share your thoughts with your colleagues.
2. Visit the Centers for Disease Control website at http://www.cdc.gov/nip/. Read information about this year's influenza season and national immunization guidelines.
3. Visit the Healthy People 2010 website at http://healthypeoplegov. Click on "Leading Health Indicators." On the next screen, click on the words "What Are the Leading Health Indicators?" Assess your family, academic community, clinical practice community, and neighborhood to see where improvements to health could be made. Outline a plan to assist family and community members to make improvements in one of the identified areas.

WWW INTERNET RESOURCES

For Family as Client:
  Children's Institute International: http://www.childrensinstitute.org.
  National Clearinghouse on Child Abuse and Neglect: http://nccanch.acf.hhs.gov.
  The Hudson Institute: http://www.hudson.org.
  Center for Health Care Strategies: http://www.chcs.org.
  Children Now: http://www.childrennow.org.
  Centers for Medicare and Medicaid Services: http://cms.hhs.gov.
  American Academy of Pediatrics: http://www.aap.org.
  March of Dimes: http://www.modimes.org.
For Community as Client:
  Healthy People 2010: http://healthypeople.gov.
  Centers for Disease Control and National Immunization Program: http://www.cdc.gov/nip.
  National Highway Traffic Safety Administration: http://www.nhtsa.dot.gov.
  The Substance Abuse and Mental Health Services Administration: http://www.samhsa.gov.

REFERENCES

Allen, C., & Easley, C. (2008). Ethics and human rights. In L. Ivanov & C. Blude (Eds.), *Public health nursing: Leadership, policy and practice* (pp. 359–389). Clifton Park, NY: Delmar Cengage Learning.

Anderson, E. T., & McFarlane, J. (2006). *Community as partner* (5th ed.). Philadelphia: Lippincott Williams & Wilkins.

Anderson, K. H., & Tomlinson, P. S. (1992). The family health system as an emerging paradigmatic view for nursing. *Image, 24,* 57–63.

Andrews, M., & Boyle, J. (2008). *Transcultural concepts in nursing care* (5th ed.). Philadelphia: Lippincott Williams & Wilkins.

Artinian, N. T. (1994). Selecting a model to guide family assessment. *Dimensions of Critical Care Nursing, 14,* 4–12.

Bailey, V. (2007). Satisfaction levels with a community night nursing service. *Nursing Standard, 22*(5), 35–42.

Beddome, G. (1995). Community-as-client assessment. A Neuman-based guide for education and practice. In B. Neuman (Ed.), *The Neuman systems model* (3rd ed., pp. 567–579). East Norwalk, CT: Appleton & Lange.

Blanes, L., Carmagnani, M., & Ferreira, L. (2007). Health-related quality of life in primary caregivers of persons with quadriplegia. *Spinal Cord, 45,* 399–403.

Bosek, M., & Savage, T. (2007). *The ethical component of nursing education: Integrating ethics into clinical experience.* Philadelphia: Lippincott Williams & Wilkins.

Canty-Mitchell, J., Little, B., Robinson, S., & Chandler, R. (2008) Racial and ethnic health disparities. In L. Ivanov & C. Blude (Eds.), *Public health nursing: Leadership, policy and practice* (pp. 529–552). Clifton Park, NY: Delmar Cengage Learning.

Chevannes, M. (1997). Nursing caring for families: Issues in a multiracial society. *Journal of Clinical Nursing, 6,* 161–167.

Christensen, P. J., & Kenney, J. W. (1990). *Nursing process: Application of conceptual models* (3rd ed.). St. Louis, MO: Mosby.

Clark, M. J. (1999). *Nursing in the community* (3rd ed.). Stamford, CT: Appleton & Lange.

Cody, W. K. (1995). The view of family within the human becoming theory. In R. R. Parse (Ed.), *Illuminations: The human becoming theory in practice and research* (pp. 9–26). New York: National League for Nursing.

Denham, S. A. (1999). Part I: The definition and practice of family health. *Journal of Family Nursing, 5,* 133–159.

Fawcett, J. (1989). *Analysis and evaluation of conceptual models* (2nd ed.). Philadelphia: F. A. Davis.

Forchuk, C., & Dorsay, J. P. (1995). Hildegard Peplau meets family systems nursing: Innovation in theory-based practice. *Journal of Advanced Nursing, 21,* 110–115.

Friedmann, M. L. (1995). *The framework of systemic organization.* Thousand Oaks, CA: Sage.

Friedman, M. M. (1992). *Family nursing: Theory and practice* (3rd ed.). East Norwalk, CT: Appleton & Lange.

Gilliss, C. L., Highley, B. L., Roberts, B. M., & Martinson, I. M. (1988). *Toward a science of family nursing.* Reading, MA: Addison-Wesley.

Hanchett, E. S. (1988). *Nursing frameworks and community as client.* East Norwalk, CT: Appleton & Lange.

Hanson, S. (1996). Family assessment and interventions. In S. Hanson & S. Boyd (Eds.), *Family care nursing: Theory, practice and research* (pp. 147–172). Philadelphia: F. A. Davis.

Head, B., Aquilino, M., Johnson, M., Reed, D., Maas, M., & Moorehead, S. (2004). Content validity and nursing sensitive community-level outcomes from the nursing outcomes classification (NOC). *Journal of Nursing Scholarship, 36,* 251–259.

King, I. M. (1983). King's theory of nursing. In I. W. Clements & F. B. Roberts (Eds.), *Family health: A theoretical approach to nursing care* (pp. 147–155). New York: Wiley.

Knoerl, A. (2007). Cultural considerations and the Hispanic cardiac client. *Home Health Care, 25*(2), 82–86.

Lapp, C. A., Diemert, C. A., & Enestredt, R. (1991). Family-based practice. In K. A. Saucier (Ed.), *Perspectives in family and community health* (pp. 305–310). St. Louis, MO: Mosby-Year Book.

Li, H., Melnyk, B., & McCann, R. (2004). Review of intervention studies of families with hospitalized elderly relatives. *Journal of Nursing Scholarship, 36,* 54–59.

Lundy, K., & Janes, S. (2001). *Community health nursing: Caring for the public's health.* Sudbury, MA: Jones & Bartlett.

Magnusson, L., & Hanson, E. (2005). Supporting frail older people and their family carers at home using information and communication technology: Cost analysis. *Journal of Advanced Nursing, 51*(6), 654–657.

McCubbin, M. A., & McCubbin, H. I. (1993). Families coping with illness: The resiliency model of family stress, adjustment, and adaptation. In C. B. Danielson, B. Hamel-Bissell, & P. Winstead-Fry (Eds.), *Families, health, and illness: Perspectives on coping and intervention* (pp. 21–63). St. Louis, MO: Mosby.

McElmurry, B., Park, C., & Buseh, A. (2003). The nurse-community health advocate team for urban immigrant primary health care. *Journal of Nursing Scholarship, 35*, 275–281.

McGoldrick, M., & Gerson, R. (1985). *Genograms in family assessment.* New York: Norton.

Mischke, K. M., & Hanson, S. M. H. (1995). Family health assessment and intervention. In P. J. Bomar (Ed.), *Nurses and family health promotion: Concepts, assessment, and interventions* (2nd ed., pp. 38–51). Philadelphia: Saunders.

Narsavage, G., Batchelor, H., Lindell, D., & Chen, Y. (2003). Developing personal and community learning in graduate nursing education through community engagement. *Nursing Education Perspectives, 24,* 300–305.

Neuman, B. (1983). Family interventions using the Betty Neuman health care systems model. In I. W. Clements & F. B. Roberts (Eds.), *Family health: A theoretical approach to nursing care* (pp. 218–230). New York: Wiley.

Neuman, B. (1989). *The Neuman systems model* (2nd ed.). Norwalk, CT: Appleton & Lange.

Newman, M. A. (1983). Newman's health theory. In I. W. Clements & F. B. Roberts (Eds.), *Family health: A theoretical approach to nursing care* (pp. 231–254). New York: Wiley.

Newman, M. A., Sime, A. M., & Corcoran-Perry, S. A. (1991). The focus of the discipline of nursing. *Advances in Nursing Science, 14,* 1–6.

Orem, D. E. (1983). The self-care deficit theory of nursing: A general theory. In I. W. Clements & F. B. Roberts (Eds.), *Family health: A theoretical approach to nursing care* (pp. 193–217). New York: Wiley.

Parse, R. R. (1996). The human becoming theory: Challenges in practice and research. *Nursing Science Quarterly, 9,* 55–60.

Parse, R. R. (1998). *The human becoming school of thought.* Thousand Oaks, CA: Sage.

Parse, R. (2003). *Community: A human becoming perspective.* Sudbury, MA: Jones & Bartlett.

Patterson, J. M. (1999). Healthy American families in a postmodern society: An ecological perspective. In H. M. Wallace, G. Green, K. J. Jaros, L. L. Paine, & M. Story (Eds.), *Health and welfare for families in the 21st century* (pp. 31–52). Sudbury, MA: Jones & Bartlett.

Pender, N., Murdaugh, C., & Parsons, M. (2005). *Health promotion in nursing practice* (5th ed.). Upper Saddle River, NJ: Pearson/Prentice Hall.

Peplau, H. (1952). *Interpersonal relations in nursing.* New York: G. P. Putnam's Sons.

Racher, F. (2007). The evolution of ethics for community practice. *Journal of Community Health Nursing, 24*(1), 65–76.

Rogers, M. E. (1983). Science of unitary human beings: A paradigm for nursing. In I. W. Clements & F. B. Roberts (Eds.), *Family health: A theoretical approach to nursing care* (pp. 293–316). New York: Wiley.

Rose, L., Mallinson, K., & Walton-Moss, B. (2004). Barriers to family care in psychiatric settings. *Journal of Nursing Scholarship, 36,* 39–47.

Roy, C. (1983). Roy adaptation model. In I. W. Clements & F. B. Roberts (Eds.), *Family health: A theoretical approach to nursing care* (pp. 255–278). New York: Wiley.

Saucier, K. A. (Ed.). (1991). *Perspectives in family and community health.* St. Louis, MO: Mosby-Year Book.

Schumacher, K., Stewart, B., & Archbold, P. (2007). Mutuality and preparedness moderate the effects of caregiving demand on cancer family caregiver outcomes. *Nursing Research, 56*(6), 425–433.

Shuster, G., & Geppinger, J. (2004). Community as client: Assessment and analysis. In M. Stanhope & J. Lancaster (Eds.), *Community and public health nursing* (pp. 342–375). St. Louis, MO: Mosby.

Spradley, B. W. (1990). *Community health nursing: Concepts and practice* (3rd ed.). Glenview, IL: Scott, Foresman/Little Brown Higher Education.

Stadnyk, R. (2006). Community-dwelling spouses of nursing home residents: Activities that sustain identities in times of transition. *Topics in Geriatric Rehabilitation, 22*(4), 283–293.

Taylor, S. G., & Renpenning, K. M. (1995). The practice of nursing in multiperson situations, family and community. In D. E. Orem (Ed.), *Nursing: Concepts of practice* (5th ed., pp. 348–367). St. Louis, MO: Mosby.

Tomlinson, P. S., & Anderson, K. H. (1995). Family health and the Neuman systems model. In B. Neuman (Ed.), *The Neuman systems model* (3rd ed., pp. 133–144). East Norwalk, CT: Appleton & Lange.

Walsh, S., Martin, S., & Schmidt, L. (2004). Testing the efficacy of a creative-arts intervention with family caregivers of patients with cancer. *Journal of Nursing Scholarship, 36,* 214–219.

Watson, J. (1996). Watson's theory of transpersonal caring. In P. H. Walker & B. Neuman (Eds.), *Blueprint for use of nursing models: Education, research, practice and administration* (pp. 141–184). New York: National League for Nursing.

Watson, J. (2007). *Nursing human science and human care, a theory of nursing.* Sudbury, MA: Jones & Bartlett.

Whall, A. L. (1986). *Family therapy theory for nursing: Four approaches*. East Norwalk, CT: Appleton-Century-Crofts.

Whall, A. L., & Fawcett, J. (1991). *Family theory development in nursing: State of the science and art*. Philadelphia: F. A. Davis.

Wright, L. M., & Leahey, M. (1988, May 24–27). Family nursing trends in academic and clinical settings. Paper presented at the International Family Nursing Conference, Convention Centre, Calgary, Alberta, Canada, in *Conference Proceedings* (pp. 29–37).

Zotti, M. E., Brown, P., & Stotts, R. C. (1996). Community-based nursing versus community health nursing: What does it all mean? *Nursing Outlook, 44*, 211–217.

CHAPTER 17

The Professional Nurse's Role in Teaching and Learning

KEY TERMS AND CONCEPTS

Teaching
Product
Experts
Learning
Process
Patient education
Readiness for learning
Validation
Feedback
Participant-focused teaching
Motivation

LEARNING OUTCOMES

By the end of this chapter, the learner will be able to:

1 Provide the rationale for identifying clients and nurses as "experts" in the client education process.

2 List the three main communication concepts that facilitate teaching–learning.

3 Explain how mutuality enhances client learning.

4 Outline the steps of the traditional teaching–learning process.

5 Describe each step of the traditional teaching–learning process.

6 Outline key strategies for effective client education.

7 Specify ways to validate client learning.

VIGNETTE

Lillian works as a staff nurse in a small rural community hospital. Frequently, she takes care of persons with poorly controlled diabetes, cancer, chronic obstructive pulmonary disease, back injuries, and a variety of conditions corrected with surgery. During her last performance evaluation, the nurse manager suggested that Lillian improve her patient teaching skills. Lillian acknowledges that her performance in client teaching could be improved. However, Lillian feels that client education is very time-consuming and that she must concentrate on providing safe, effective nursing care to clients who are physically unstable. Her heavy workload and unanticipated staff dismissals prevent Lillian from spending much time teaching clients and families. She knows that improved client education may likely prevent recurrent hospital admissions along with promoting the general health and well-being of all her clients. She wonders how she can deliver effective education to clients and families while frequently being the only registered nurse on her unit.

Teaching has been accepted as a leadership role for professional nurses for decades, even before the development of nursing models on which nurses could base their practices. **Teaching** is a process of imparting or sharing knowledge with another. Teaching involves instructing, coaching, and guiding another through unfamiliar content or procedures. In 1918, the National League for Nursing Education issued a statement that expressed the need to educate professional nurses to assume teaching responsibilities. Nurses acknowledge the importance of sharing information with clients about their medical conditions, their medications, and ways to carry out their prescribed medical regimens when they are discharged from the hospital, sent home from outpatient diagnostic and surgical centers, and leave clinics and offices. Historically, compliance to treatment plans served as the main reason for client education (Falvo, 2004). Current views of client education focus on empowering clients by providing them with knowledge and skills to manage their own health.

In daily practice, nurses share lots of information with clients. Some nurses have discovered that clients learn more effectively when health education emerges from a mutually determined process between nurse and client. Some nurses view each client encounter as an opportunity for sharing information on how to promote optimal health rather than just imparting information about a medical diagnosis, whereas other nurses simply follow standardized client teaching outlines found on client clinical paths or computer programs that address commonly encountered issues associated with a particular surgical procedure, diagnostic test, or medical condition. To make informed choices about health, clients need to know information about actual and potential health problems and options for prevention and/or treatment. In some cases, clients must make behavioral changes to avoid and manage certain diseases. As health care professionals, nurses serve as role models of good health for their clients and communities. Optimal education for lifestyle changes improves when client see that nurses follow healthy lifestyle habits.

Teaching–learning also has been considered to be a public duty of all the professions. For example: lawyers inform clients about the law, physicians teach clients about diseases, physical therapists teach clients how to ambulate safely, social workers educate clients about available community resources, and pharmacists teach clients about medications. Like other health team members, nursing has an obligation to present educational programs and lead public discussions on issues related to health. Professional responsibility goes beyond individual professional–client teaching–learning relationships. Nursing as a professional entity has the opportunity and obligation to educate the larger client system (the public) about the relationships between quality of life and health and to influence the mission of health care delivery institutions regarding the social ends they should serve. By listening to and learning from the public, the professional nurse becomes capable of providing relevant information that promotes health.

Likewise, many health care consumers want and need health education. Needs and wants vary according to clients. Some clients want to learn how to best promote personal health and to avoid illnesses. Other clients may not see the value of health information until they find themselves ill and in need of health care services (Rankin, Stallings, & London, 2005). When confronted with a health issue that involves early detection, some clients want to know the latest diagnostic techniques (Herzlinger, 2004). Clients also need to be aware of treatment options for health problems so they can make informed choices (Bosek & Savage, 2007; Falvo, 2004; Herzlinger; Rankin et al., 2005). Health care consumers also need to know about the complex health care delivery systems, health insurance options, and available community resources, and how to ask questions of health care providers to get desired information (Herzlinger). In many cases, clients need health care information to take medications safely, comply with complex treatment regimens, avoid potential complications of prescribed therapies, and know when to consult health care providers (Falvo; Herzlinger; Rankin et al.).

Sometimes, clients have more than one health care provider. Nurses become pivotal in ensuring client safety, especially in inpatient clinical settings. Nurses must learn about medications and complementary therapies that clients currently use to avoid any potential medication or treatment interactions. When clients and families are informed of prescribed medications and treatments, fewer errors occur (Joint Commission on Accreditation of Healthcare Organizations [JCAHO], 2008). Families and clients need to be educated about medications, and safe use of assistive devices and technology. For example, a client's level of consciousness determines optimal dosages of narcotic analgesics when patient-controlled analgesia (PCA) is being used for pain control. Clients and families need to be educated about the safe use of PCA pumps and that only the client should push the button. Well-intentioned family members have accidently overdosed (sometimes fatally) their loved one because no one educated them on the dangers of pushing the button when the client appears to be sleeping (D'Arcy, 2008). In addition, reduced length of inpatient hospitalization has been linked to increased hospital readmission rates without effective client education (Herzlinger, 2004).

 ## PHILOSOPHICAL ASSUMPTIONS ABOUT TEACHING AND LEARNING

The description of teaching–learning as a leadership function for professional nurses is based on the beliefs that teaching–learning is a process, not a **product** (or result); the process is implemented in a relationship between experts; and communication is the essential element of the process. Clients are **experts** in how health issues affect them and nurses frequently have information that helps clients to adjust to health alterations.

Process—Not Product

Believing in the significance of interpersonal relationships, the nurse must consider the possibility that the health of a person is determined to a large extent by the quality of the person's relationships with other people. Through relationships, growth can occur; that is, the person integrates new functions that lead to a more satisfying life. Thus, the nurse needs to provide the client with educative experiences that increase the integration of behaviors and attitudes that improve health. Teaching–learning in the nurse–client relationship is directed toward such growth.

Education involves personal growth and development. In professional nursing, the nurse–client relationships facilitate the educational process. Agnes (2005, p. 816) defined **learning** as "the acquiring of knowledge and skill." In recent years, neuroscientists have identified physiological processes that alter the brain to develop different types of memory for knowledge and skill acquisition. Lupien and McEwen (1997, as cited in Collins, 2007) described the **process** of memory in the following three phases: acquisition (exposure to knowledge to be remembered), consolidation (transformation of short-term to long-term memory), and retrieval (recall of knowledge or skill). Without long-term memory, learning cannot be recalled. Neurophysiological processes involved in the development of long-term memories include the Hebb rule (neuron cell efficiency improves with repeated firings of impulses), long-term potentiation (long-term improvements of neuronal synapses associated with changes in the length and density of the neurons triggered by the stimulation of hippocampal neurons), and cylic adenosine monophosphate responsive element binding protein (neuronal structural reorganization). Different neurons and areas of the brain are associated with different types of knowledge and skills. Some stress (low to moderate levels) enhances memory when persons are exposed to new ideas, skills, and situations (Collins).

If nurses view information as a product, they ignore the physiological and psychological processes required for long-lasting learning. When viewed as a process, the nurse offers clients information and educational experiences to reinforce the necessary information required for self-care and personal growth. The nurse also assesses the client for high stress levels and fatigue that might impair the learning process. In addition, the nurse can offer information in small chunks to facilitate knowledge acquisition and consolidation

(Collins, 2007). Client education culminates with the client receiving validation from the nurse that new knowledge, ideas, or skills have developed effectively. Teaching–learning is an interpersonal process in which both the teacher and the learner acquire and consolidate new information, experience new relatedness, and behave in new ways as a result of the relationship.

Current health care strives to facilitate the autonomy of health care consumers in making decisions. Many facilities strive to become centers of excellence for a particular disease, health condition, or procedure. Effective client education is a hallmark of a center of excellence. Typically, effective education facilitates learning by engaging clients in purposeful, sequenced learning activities while providing them support and guidance for mastering required knowledge and skills. The final outcome of learning becomes apparent when clients can recall key information and independently perform skills required for self-care.

When professional nurses believe that clients have these abilities, nurses view learning as far more than discovery by the client. Their educator role becomes focuses on "learning that leads to new action and new problem-solving, which enable individuals and systems to continue to learn" (Argyris, 1982, p. 160). Thus, teaching–learning becomes an ongoing dynamic process.

If learning is not the passive acceptance by the learner of information from the teacher, then nurses must commit themselves to collaborative relationships with clients to fulfill their teaching–learning role functions. This means that the teaching enables clients to participate, to define their own strengths and problems, and to construct their own meanings. Thus, teaching–learning is a collaborative process that is most effective when nurses fully engage clients as participatory learners.

Relationship Between Experts

Teaching–learning can be viewed as a relationship between experts. Experts are persons who have special knowledge and skills about a particular subject (Agnes, 2005). In the professional nursing process, nurses are the experts on health and clients are the experts on their experience of health and life circumstances. In the teaching–learning process, sometimes clients and professional nurses view nurses as the experts on knowledge about health and the information that enables people to achieve health, and clients as experts on the context of their life and the need for information and experiences to achieve their intentions to maximize health.

Nurse: Information and Knowledge Expert

Teaching–learning may be seen as a part of the healing process. Nurses who have reported that they believed their interventions made a difference in their clients' progress described several steps in that healing relationship (Benner, 1984, p. 49): mobilizing hope for the nurse as well as for the client; finding an acceptable interpretation or understanding of the illness, pain, fear, anxiety, or other stressful emotion; and assisting the client to use social, emotional, or spiritual support.

Viewing teaching as a coaching function, Benner (1984) proposed that "nurses become experts in coaching a patient through an illness. They take what is foreign and fearful to the patient and make it familiar and thus less frightening" (p. 77). The teacher also needs to have expertise in helping. Helping the learner become aware of learning and thinking processes and helping the person understand the nature of the problems may be equally as important as providing information.

To be an expert in the teaching–learning process, the nurse also must be an enabler. Learning is facilitated when teachers treat learners as responsible people. In addition, learning empowers clients to take action and assume responsibility for their health (Rankin et al., 2005).

In addition to coach and enabler, several other roles have been proposed for the nurse–teacher, including the following (Forbes, 1995, p. 99): (1) learning facilitator, who breaks down barriers to learning by listening, probing, and being aware of feelings; (2) authority, who sets up a teaching structure and rules; (3) ego ideal, who serves as a role model for the client's "altered existence"; (4) socializing agent, who acknowledges concerns and fears for the future; and (5) person, who relates to clients as people rather than just a disease diagnosis. Therefore, for the teaching and learning process to be successful, the nurse may need to assume multiple roles. Which roles should be assumed and outlining teaching–learning situations during which they would be most effective need to be validated through qualitative and quantitative research methods.

Client: Context and Need Expert

No one knows better the meaning of his or her life, individual health status, and full circumstances integral to life experiences than does the client. Thus, clients serve as the experts on the context in which they will be attempting to implement new health behaviors. They are the experts on individualized needs for information, support, and relatedness. When nurses appreciate their professional expertise and the personal expertise of the client, the teaching–learning process can truly be implemented as a mutual responsibility.

Questions for Reflection 17-1

1. How do I involve my clients and families during health teaching?
2. How frequently do I teach clients/families/communities about things that promote health?
3. What types of education strategies do I tend to use when providing client/family/community education?
4. What factors in my current working environment support my role as a client teacher?
5. What factors in my current practice environment prevent me from providing effective client education?

The Joint Commission has developed standards for client and family education as an essential element of nursing. According to the Joint Commission (JCAHO, 2006a), the purpose of **patient education** is to convey knowledge and understanding, create a different perspective or attitude, build self-care skills, and change behavior. The Joint Commission's educational standards (2006b) include the following elements for effective client education:

1. Facility plan, support, and provision of client education
2. Comprehensive learner assessment before education occurs (ability, readiness, literacy, preferences, cultural or language obstacles, physical or mental limitations)
3. Age and educational level; appropriate teaching methods and materials
4. Consideration of client preferred learning style
5. Education on safe and effective use of medications, medical equipment, potential food–drug medication interactions, therapeutic diets, and rehabilitation techniques performed by the best qualified member of the interprofessional health care team
6. Information on available community resources and how to obtain additional treatment (if needed)
7. Education on client and family responsibilities for ongoing health care needs and the knowledge and skills on how to fulfill these responsibilities (including personal hygiene while respecting client privacy)
8. Educational strategies that are interactive, provide detailed instructions, and present available and reliable resources for future use
9. Use of a medical translator when needed
10. Evidence that intended learning outcomes for education have been achieved

The Joint Commission standards provide a framework for nurses to follow as they plan and execute client educational activities. When providing clients with printed materials, nurses should consider client ability to read. In 2006, the Joint Commission (2006b) developed a client information brochure, *Patient 101*, that steers health care consumers to a variety of valid and reliable online sites for health education that includes governmental, disease-specific nonprofit organization, and academic websites. Frequently, published, printed, and posted Internet educational materials are written above the average sixth-grade reading level of Americans (Anhang, Goodman, & Goldie, 2004; Badarudeen & Sabharwal, 2008; Chang & Kelly, 2007; Edwardson, 2007; Hill-Briggs & Smith, 2008; Singh, 2003) and the fifth- to sixth-grade reading level of Canadians (Chiovetti, 2006). Some facilities offer client educational software programs that can provide printed materials in a variety of foreign languages to meet the educational needs of clients who do not have fluency in English.

Because the Joint Commission accreditation is required for federal reimbursement to organizations for delivered care, documentation of client education becomes very important. During accreditation visits, the Joint Commission surveyors examine client care documentation for evidence of client education. Ninety percent of client charts (paper or electronic) should contain this evidence to avoid facility receipt of a citation for improvement. In addition to documenting client education for reimbursement purposes, the professional nurse provides solid evidence of nursing's contributions to the interdisciplinary client care efforts. Documentation of education also may provide useful information regarding specific communication strategies that work well with individual clients and families.

Communication: The Condition for Teaching–Learning

Nurses who display empathy, respect, mutuality, and genuineness while teaching are likely to create environments for effective teaching–learning. By using empathy, nurses are more apt to understand client global situations and take full advantage of the expertise that clients bring to the relationship. Likewise, clients need empathy to perceive that nurses are sensitive to clients' human needs and will generate effective educational plans that include measurement of the cognitive, affective, and psychomotor (if needed) domains of learning.

If the teaching–learning process is to be accepted by both nurses and clients as a mutual responsibility, respect must be experienced in the communication between them. Perceptions of self-worth is based on this respect. Feelings of self-worth facilitate teaching and learning because teachers and learners see themselves capable of effectively fulfilling their roles. Teachers believe and know that they can create and execute meaningful learning experiences, and learners believe and know that they have the capabilities to master the content and skills being taught.

Full exploration and analysis of the health concerns and information needed to change behaviors cannot occur unless nurses and clients perceive each other as real, as genuinely human, open, honest, and caring in their responses to each other. Nurses must provide clients with accurate health-related information, and clients must perceive that nurses have information to facilitate health promotion, maintenance, or restoration. Clients display an authentic interest in the information being shared with them however they determine what, if, and when received information will be used.

Nurses empower clients to have control over their lives when they give them information or teach them skills to care for themselves. Rankin et al. (2005) outlined the following four-step counseling model for empowering individual clients: (1) identify the problem or issue (past), (2) explore feelings and meanings (present), (3) identify goals and choices (plan for the future), and (4) commit to action (future) (p. 75).

To identify the problem or issue and its impact on the client, the nurse uses holistic assessment skills. Once the issue or problem has been identified, the nurse uses the nursing process step of planning to specify goals and strategies to resolve the problem or issue in collaboration with the client. Once the client has committed to action, the change process begins.

 TEACHING–LEARNING PROCESS APPROACHES

Nurses can choose from more than one process when they provide education to clients. The traditional process has been used with success by many nurses and provides a structured approach. The traditional teaching–learning process is similar to nursing process. The steps of the traditional teaching–learning process are assessment, identification of learning needs, planning (including the development of learning objectives and selection of educational materials), implementation, evaluation, and documentation (Rankin et al., 2005; Redman, 1993).

The first activity on the part of the nurse–teacher is assessment: to gather facts and information that will help the nurse meet the client's or the family's needs for learning. Rankin et al. (2005) indicated that there are four steps in the assessment process: (1) selecting the areas to be assessed, (2) gathering the data, (3) sorting and categorizing the data, and (4) writing a summary statement (nursing diagnosis). Purposes of assessment can be found in Display 17-1 (Rankin et al.; Redman, 1993).

The assessment may be conducted by using the following behaviors: listening and questioning, observing, reviewing records, collaborating with the health care team, and integrating the client's verbal description with the nurse's observation. To fully understand the impact of the issue to be addressed in the educational process, the nurse must engage in active listening and validate perceptions with the client.

After determining the learning needs in the assessment stage, the nurse develops a plan that contains objectives for the client's learning that have been established together with the client and the family. These objectives clarify what is to be taught, what is to be learned, what and how to evaluate, and what to document. An objective must be singular to be specific, inclusive of all elements of content necessary to be understood, measurable, and realistic to the extent that it can be attained by the client.

After objectives are clarified and validated in the plan, implementation of the learning objectives is done by analyzing the information to be presented and selecting a method of presentation that maximizes the involvement of the client's senses. The nurse often can complement the presentation of information by using supplemental materials, such as audiovisual aids. Another major function of the nurse in the implementation phase is to observe the client's reaction to the teaching–learning.

In evaluation, the next activity in the teaching–learning process, the nurse and client determine whether or not the client has achieved the objectives. The criteria used in evaluation are the specifications of what the client will do and the particular behavior that

---

Purposes of Client Assessment for Education | DISPLAY 17-1

1. Identify what the client wants to learn.
2. Identify what information the client needs.
3. Establish a point of reference for learning (relate new information to preexisting knowledge).
4. Identify incorrect information and assumptions.
5. Determine what factors in the environment may pose barriers.
6. Identify potential client barrier to learning (language, cultural, educational level, cognitive or physical limitations).
7. Identify what will need to be evaluated.
8. Build trust and rapport.
9. Provide for involvement of family.
10. Set priorities for the needs and problems.

Source: Rankin, Stallings, & London, 2005; Redman, 1993.

the client will demonstrate, which are stated in each objective. The outcomes must be recorded on the client's official record. Using the objectives as a basis, the nurse should record client achievements and note client reactions on the record.

The holistic approach to the teaching–learning process offers another avenue for nurses to use for client education. Holistic teaching–learning espouses the use of active learning principles. Holistic active learning links the concepts of experiences (doing, see-ing, simulating), information and ideas (formal or informal acquisition of knowledge, learning them for yourself or from others, original ideas or ideas from others or resour-ces), and reflection (taking time to think about what is being learned, either alone or with others) (Fink, 2003). The holistic approach addresses the cognitive, affective, and psycho-motor domains of learning simultaneously and facilitates clients finding personal mean-ing in information that is needed for self-care and health promotion.

The holistic approach provides foundational knowledge for clients while paying atten-tion to human interactions, caring, and learning how to learn while learners work toward meeting intended learning goals (Fink, 2003). Self-assessment by clients toward achiev-ing the health education–related goals instills confidence in their ability to do what they need to do to care optimally for themselves or their loved ones. Taking time to reflect upon what is learned facilitates the development of the implicit memory that recalls sen-sory, emotional, and skeletal responses along with procedural skills (Collins, 2007). Cur-rently, there is little research validating that the holistic approach to client health education is better than the traditional teaching–learning process. Research Brief 17-1 provides evidence that acknowledges the benefits of a comprehensive, holistic approach to the teaching–learning process in women and their partners living the experience of breast cancer from baseline screening through recovery. It also provides evidence that effective client education encompasses more than sharing information and providing cli-ents with written health materials.

As nurses engage in the teaching–learning process with clients, they assist clients to become better informed about how to manage their own health. Thus, they are able to make informed choices about the type of health care that they receive. By eliminating the "mysteries" behind navigating the health care system, medical interventions, and com-plementary therapies, nurses assume the role of client advocate.

Research Brief 17-1

Budin, W., Hoskins, C., Haber, J., Sherman, D., Maislin, G., Carter, J., et al. (2008). Breast can-cer: Education, counseling, and adjustment among patients and partners: A randomized clinical trial. *Nursing Research, 57*(3), 199–213.

The investigators conducted a randomized clinical trial involving 249 breast cancer patients and their partners to compare the effects of disease management (DM), a physi-cian program of education and support, standardized psychoeducation (SE), viewing of psy-choeducation videos, telephone counseling (TC) by nurse interventionists, and SE with TC. Study data were collected to measure emotional, physical, and psychosocial adjustment during the following phases of their breast cancer experience: baseline, diagnostic, postsur-gical, adjuvant therapy, and ongoing recovery. Outcome measures provided data on emo-tional, physical, and social adjustment to the breast cancer experience.

Study results revealed that the DM had poorer adjustment over time. Participants receiving only TC had lower physical adjustment scores when compared to the SE with TC group. This study provides preliminary support that telephone counseling along with psy-chosocial education may enhance the physical, social, and emotional adjustment for women with breast cancer and their partners. The investigators caution that findings may be dif-ferent in other groups of women and their partners because the participants in this study were highly motivated, received their cancer care from private physicians in the New York City area, and were not culturally diverse. Replication studies are needed prior to changing the way education and support are given to women with breast cancer and their families.

TEACHING–LEARNING AS A RESPONSIBILITY OF THE ADVOCATE

The belief in advocacy as an appropriate role of the nurse has evolved in harmony with today's society characterized by consumerism, self-care, justice and human rights, equal opportunity for all, and individual accountability for health. People no longer believe that illness is an event over which the person has no control. Given these values, nurses today readily accept the obligation to act as advocates in their relationships with clients. One of the most significant activities of the nurse advocate is to provide informational support to assist the client to make the wisest possible decisions in the pursuit of well-being.

The Purpose of Teaching–Learning

The search for meaning in professional nursing should be focused on the clients' perceptions of their health situation. The phenomenologic model of curriculum proposed by Diekelmann (1988) fits the role conception of the nurse as an advocate for the client. In this model, "the central concern is the communicative understandings of meanings given by people who live within the situation" (Diekelmann, p. 142). Thus, the purpose for teaching–learning is to provide the opportunity for the nurse and the client to explore together the importance and meaning of the client's experience.

Applying Diekelmann's proposition, the essential aspect of the process is not transmitting or acquiring facts; rather, it is "making meaning and giving meaning ... through the initiation and maintenance of dialogue" (Diekelmann, 1988, p. 143). In addition, Diekelmann (p. 143) proposed that the teacher's role is to "link the contextual and conceptual worlds of students," who are, in this discussion, clients participating in the nursing process. In this kind of dialogue, clients retain the authority and responsibility for their decisions and health behaviors.

According to Babcock and Miller (1994), if nurses expect clients to take interdependent and independent responsibilities for decision making, they need nurses who can identify central issues, recognize underlying assumptions, recognize evidence of bias and emotion, solve problems, and think creatively.

The development of these abilities appears in definitions of critical thinking, a key cognitive skill for effective professional nursing practice. In client education situations, nurses guide the client to master knowledge and skills that are needed to make decisions. As clients begin to make informed choices for health and health care–related decisions, they look to professional nurses for support.

Functions of the Advocate in the Teaching–Learning Process

Providing the opportunity for dialogue to fully explore health concerns is the major function of the nurse acting as an advocate for clients, whether they are experiencing high or low levels of wellness. Within this exploration, nurses use their expertise to "not only offer information [but also] offer ways of being, ways of coping, and even new possibilities" for the clients (Benner, 1984, p. 78).

Benner (1984) proposed that teaching–learning transactions take on new dimensions when the learner (client) is ill. She cited the following competencies necessary for the nurse to assume the teaching–coaching function with a client who is ill:

1. Carefully time the interventions to capture the client's readiness to learn.
2. Help the client integrate the implications of the illness and recovery into the client's lifestyle.
3. Elicit and respect the client's interpretation of the illness.
4. Respond fully and cogently to the client's request for explanation of what is happening (within the limits of both the client's and the nurse's own understanding).
5. Make approachable and understandable any culturally avoided or uncharted aspects of an illness by exploring ways of being and coping for the client and the family and by identifying new possibilities.

Growth through learning is maximized if the nurse fulfills these functions with the client.

Mutuality in the Teaching–Learning Process

One of the primary characteristics of an advocate–client relationship is mutuality. Watson (2007), supporting the concept of mutuality, stressed that nurses must strive to develop interactions with clients that are liberating and empowering. Teachers and learners should learn from each other. Learning should be mutual, characterized by anticipatory–participatory behaviors, shared power, and knowing, doing, and being to become one. Watson's model of nursing is cited as one example of a model that mandates mutuality in the nursing process and places high priority on teaching–learning as a significant intervention mode in a reciprocal nurse–client relationship.

Mutuality can be defined as "a connection with or understanding of another that facilitates a dynamic process of joint exchange between people. The process of being mutual is characterized by a sense of unfolding action that is shared in common, a sense of moving toward a common goal, and a sense of satisfaction for all involved" (Henson, 1997, p. 80). Mutuality balances power and respect, encourages accountability, and "facilitates active involvement of both nurses and clients in effectively working toward mutually identified goals" (Henson, p. 77). Mutuality is consistent with any learning theory used to guide the teaching–learning process.

Questions for Reflection 17-2

1. Have I ever learned anything from a client, client family, or community? If so, what did I learn?
2. How do I feel when a client or family members learn a new skill or finally grasps key information regarding self-care for the first time?
3. How do I promote active participation by clients, families, and communities in the client education process?
4. Why is active participation important in the teaching–learning process?

LEARNING THEORIES

The process by which learning occurs has been described in several different ways. Learning theories and models explain how people learn. When nurses use models and theories to guide the client education process, they can use principles to structure meaningful client educational experiences, prevent overloading clients with information, and understand the reasons for unsuccessful client education encounters. In client education, educational effort should be focused on learners (individuals, families, significant others, and communities). Because of the vast amounts of information available on learning theories, the following section outlines Bruner's perspective, which encompasses five different learning models.

Bruner's Learning Models

Bruner (1986) cited five popular models of how the learner learns: empiricism, hypothesis generator, nativism, constructivism, and novice-to-expert. Empiricism is considered the oldest model. It is based on the premise that "one learns from experience" and that "such order as there is in the mind is a reflection of the order that exists in the world" (Bruner, p. 199). People need life experience for success in educational situations based on empiricism.

Unlike the rather passive view of the empiricism model, the hypothesis generator models include a major premise of intentionality. "The learner, rather than being the creature of experience, selects that which is to enter" (Bruner, 1986, p. 199). The characteristic of the learner is "active curiosity guided by self-directed projects" (Bruner, p. 199). A person is a successful learner in this model if the person has a good theory from which hypotheses are generated. This perspective of learning supports use of active learning educational strategies.

The nativism model proposes that the mind is innately shaped by "a set of underlying categories, hypotheses," both forms of organizing experiences (Bruner, p. 199). The task of the learner in this model is to develop a way of organizing perceived reality. Using the innate powers of the mind is the formula for successful learning in this model. Concept map use facilitates the organization of concepts to be learned under the nativism model.

The constructivism model was developed primarily by Piaget, who, according to Bruner (1986, p. 199), stated that "the world is not found, but made, and according to a set of structural rules that are imposed on the flow of experience." These structural rules provide boundaries for learning. The learner goes through stage-like progressions characterized by tension between previously assimilated structural rules and changes in the rules that come in later stage development. In accommodating these new rules, the learner is successful if his or her learning structure changes by moving to higher systems that subsume earlier structures. Thus, the constructivism model supports a holistic approach to teaching–learning.

Another learner model, according to Bruner (1986), is the novice-to-expert model. It "begins with the premise that if you want to find out about learning, ask first about what is to be learned, find an expert who does it well, and then look at the novice and figure out how he or she can get there" (Bruner, p. 199). In this model, the formula for success is to be specific and explicit in taking the steps to attain expertise. The novice-to-expert model substantiates the use of collaborative partnerships in the teaching–learning process.

Bruner (1986, p. 200) suggested that there is not just one kind of learning and that we would be better served if we understood that "the model of the learner is not fixed but various." When nurses appreciate the diversity in learner models, teaching–learning becomes "more than a scripted exercise in cultural rigidity" (Bruner, p. 200). In many health care organizations, nurses use standardized teaching guides, and frequently documentation consists of checking off items on a list. Nurses who use Bruner's learner models individualize client education, thereby maximizing client mastery of desired outcomes.

Types of Learning

Bevis (1988, p. 40) offered a helpful differentiation of six types of learning that may be useful in the teaching–learning process (see Display 17-2). Bevis suggested that different educational approaches work best for different types of learning.

Types of Learning   DISPLAY 17-2

1. Item learning: simple relationships between separate pieces of information, as seen in mechanistic and ritualistic lists and procedures
2. Directive learning: rules, injunctions, and exceptions, as seen in safety requirements
3. Rational learning: use of theory to buttress action, enabling logical decision making and logical judgments
4. Syntactic learning: seeing meaningful wholes, relationships, and patterns "addresses the lived moment and the relationships that ideas, concepts, have with each other" and enables the learner to develop insights and find meaning
5. Contextual learning: acceptance of culture, mores, folkways, rites, and rituals as ways of being; these learning transactions are "caring, compassionate, and positive"
6. Inquiry learning: investigating, categorizing, and theorizing in a way to generate ideas and develop a vision

Source: Bevis, 1988, p. 40.

Principles to Guide in the Teaching–Learning Process   DISPLAY 17-3

1. Focusing intensifies learning.
2. Repetition enhances learning.
3. Learner control increases learning.
4. Active participation is necessary for learning.
5. Learning styles vary.
6. Organization promotes learning.
7. Association is necessary to learning.
8. Imitation is a method of learning.
9. Motivation strengthens learning.
10. Spacing new material facilitates learning.
11. Recency influences retention.

12. Primacy affects retention.
13. Arousal influences attention.
14. Accurate and prompt feedback enhances learning.
15. Application of new learning in a variety of contexts broadens the generalization of that learning.
16. The learner's biologic, psychological, sociologic, and cultural realities shape the learner's perception of the learning experience.

Source: Babcock & Miller, 1994, pp. 45–48.

Bevis (1988, p. 45) suggested that syntactic learning, contextual learning, and inquiry learning are necessary for change that can truly maximize the client's abilities to gain the best control of his or her health. Syntactic, contextual, and inquiry learning incorporate personal meaning, cultural considerations, and discovery in the client education process rather than approaching learning as an exercise in mastery of relationships, rules, and logic.

Principles of Learning

Principles identified by Babcock and Miller (1994) are considered useful in any of these learner models or types of learning. These principles to guide the nurse in the teaching–learning process are listed in Display 17-3.

In addition, because clients vary in individual learning preferences, the professional nurse needs to understand the multiple models and types of learning to personalize the teaching–learning process effectively. Effectiveness is measured by the success the nurse and client experience in changing the client's health behaviors in a positive direction.

Questions for Reflection 17-3

1. How do I assess clients for preferred learning styles?
2. How do I learn best? Why is it important for me to know my preferred learning style?

 ## IMPLICATIONS OF CHANGE THEORY ON TEACHING–LEARNING

Growth is inherent in the definition of learning. Growth implies that change occurs. Because change is about the only thing that occurs constantly, change, growth, and learning happen continuously throughout life. Desired outcomes of education are changes in behavior, attitude, and psychomotor abilities (Bloom, 1974). However, in the process of learning, the human brain also experiences long-lasting changes (Collins, 2007).

Change as a Goal of Teaching: Growth

The mutually determined goal of the nurse and the client who are participating in the teaching–learning process is "becoming different than before" (Douglass, 1988, p. 226). Douglass noted that forces that influence change can be external or internal. The nurse is an intentional external force assisting the client to demonstrate different and better health behaviors.

In a series of sequential steps that are consistent with planned change theory, the nurse in the teaching–learning relationship needs to follow the list shown in Display 17-4 (Douglass, 1988). The sequential steps mirror nursing process because the initial step is exploring and identifying factors for the change (assessment), determining specific knowledge gaps (diagnosis), selecting an educational strategy (planning), executing the strategy (implementation), and determining the overall results (evaluation).

Outcomes of Knowledge Acquisition

The outcome of knowledge acquisition in the teaching–learning process may not always be satisfying to the nurse and client. Harmony within the human system results when the newly acquired information is congruent with previously integrated functions. However, if the new information is incompatible with previously integrated functions, clients and nurses may perceive disharmony. Feelings of being unsettled, restless, and uncertain frequently accompany periods of growth. Nurses often need to help clients understand that change may not be a painless process.

To reduce the discomfort that sometimes occurs in the teaching–learning process, nurses and clients together could analyze the current situation using a holistic perspective. The holistic approach would consider all aspects of the client's life, including how the change would affect the client as an individual, impact all persons involved in the client's life, and alter social structures along with the client's motivation for change. Both the situational context and the motivational aspects of planned change play a significant role in the client's ability to integrate information and develop new behaviors. The quality of the integration of new functions from the new information is affected by the perceived harmony or disharmony in the system.

For example, a single, working mother with newly diagnosed diabetes has many learning needs. In today's fast-paced society, eating regularly scheduled meals, making appointments for follow-up, securing insulin administration supplies, performing blood sugar checks, and performing special foot care may be difficult as she juggles multiple roles. Unless the client understands the benefits of controlling glucose levels, she may put taking care of herself behind caring for her children. The nurse needs to fully assess all learning needs for the client while considering the impact of lifestyle changes for optimal management of diabetes.

Readiness for Learning

A central issue for professional nurses in implementing the teaching–learning process as a strategy for changing behaviors is the client's **readiness for learning**. Benner (1984,

---

Sequential Steps Consistent with Planned Change Theory
DISPLAY 17-4

1. Explore the client's perceived need for change.
2. Identify the forces for change with the client.
3. Help the client state health concerns.
4. Identify constraints and opportunities in the situation.
5. Provide the information needed to analyze both the change needs and the potential strategies to achieve the desired change.
6. Critique each of the possible change strategies on the basis of both the information understood and the situational factors.
7. Select the change strategy to be attempted in the effort to achieve a different and better health behavior.
8. Plan the implementation, filling in all of the informational gaps perceived by the nurse and the client.
9. Design an evaluation process to determine success in changing health behavior.
10. Client: Implement the planned behavioral activities. Nurse: Offer feedback and facilitate opportunities in the delivery system environment to promote success of the client.
11. Evaluate the overall results of the teaching–learning interaction and the specific health behavior changes on the part of the client.

Source: Douglass, 1988, pp. 226–232.

p. 79) noted that teaching–learning interventions often are dictated by schedules in the health care delivery environment: "Assessing where a patient is, how open he is to information, deciding when to go ahead even when the patient does not appear ready, are key aspects of effective patient teaching."

Nurses frequently find themselves pressured to implement client teaching, especially in inpatient settings when they become aware of an unanticipated client dismissal. In the case of the woman with newly diagnosed diabetes, the nurse must determine how best to give the woman all the information she needs to know, which includes testing her blood sugar; following a complex method of determining how much insulin should be taken based on blood sugar results (basal insulin dose, bolus doses for high glucose results); preparing the injection; administering it; knowing the significance and symptoms of hyperglycemia and hypoglycemia; acknowledging the complications of poor glucose control; and understanding the role of diet, exercise, and medication on glucose control. However, all this information may overwhelm her, creating a situation in which she may be unable to absorb all required information for her safety and well-being. After a quick assessment, the nurse determines the capacity of the woman to learn, discovers any visual defects, identifies her preferred learning styles, sets learning priorities (ideally in collaboration with the client), and consults with the client to see if others need to be involved in the diabetic education prior to dismissal.

Most persons experiencing a newly diagnosed disease, illness, or surgical procedure experience some anxiety. Thus, learning readiness must be evaluated in terms of the degree of anxiety the client expresses. Minimal anxiety serves as a positive force for attention, alertness, or awareness, all of which are necessary for learning and integration of function to occur. Moderate anxiety usually is associated with selective inattention and decreasing awareness; extreme anxiety is associated with lack of attention and loss of awareness. Moderate or extreme anxiety usually is an indicator of the client's lack of readiness for learning. In these two anxiety states, the nurse's focus needs to be on reducing anxiety to enable the client to regain a sense of security and repossess the energy required for attention and awareness, which are prerequisites for learning (Collins, 2007; Rankin et al., 2005).

Validating Learning: Feedback

Validation is a necessary element of teaching–learning. Validation is a process of confirmation. In client education, **validation** means that the client understands the educational material, has mastered a particular health care skill, or uses the new information or skill effectively. For a behavioral change to become well integrated, it must be validated by persons significant to the client. Throughout life, a person requires validation through feedback from significant others to maintain the integrity of his or her self-system. Nurses frequently play a significant role in clients' lives. As teachers, nurses share their knowledge and expertise with clients. Learners appreciate feedback from teachers. **Feedback** is the transmission of information regarding how well learning outcomes are being met by learners. Frequently, constructive feedback stimulates learners to want to learn more. In client education, nurse feedback provides clients (and families) with specific information on how well they have learned information and skills to care for themselves (Rankin et al., 2005).

 ## STRATEGIES FOR EFFECTIVE TEACHING AND LEARNING

Nurses use many strategies and resources for effective client education. When nurses tailor the strategy to fit client-preferred learning styles, teaching is more effective. The subsequent discussion presents some strategies that may be used in planning and executing client education.

Focus on the Participants

In today's fast-paced delivery of health care, nurses frequently use standardized teaching plans. However, **participant-focused teaching** focuses on individual client learning needs and preferences. Client education works better when nurses and clients involved in the teaching–learning process know about each other. Nurses get to know clients as they use their repetoire of therapeutic communication skills and as they assess clients. However, clients may know very little about nurses other than information found on their employer name badges. Some health care facilities include professional licensure, earned academic degrees, and nurse specialty certifications on name badges. Some nurses carry business cards that they give to clients that specify academic degrees, certification, and scope of practice. In addition to providing these credentials to clients, nurses should communicate clearly their intentions in the teaching–learning process, share a clear plan of the time commitments to clients, and offer information about how contracts can be established if clients desire one.

For effective instruction, the professional should know the following information about clients involved in the education process: (1) how the client perceives the health situation; (2) physical, cultural, linguistic, or psychological limitations that may impede learning (anxiety or cognitive impairment); (3) intended learning outcomes; (4) interprofessional team members' plans for the client; (5) what the client's conscious intentions and desires are regarding health behaviors; and (6) what information the client perceives is needed to achieve the client's health goals. With this basic information, nurses and clients should be able to engage fully in the teaching–learning process.

Motivational Strategies

There are many teaching strategies to enhance the client's **motivation** (stimulus) to participate in learning, only a few of which are mentioned in this chapter. Additional motivational teaching strategies may be found in books devoted to teaching strategies.

In 1995, Theis and Johnson synthesized the existing research examining teaching strategies and found "66% of subjects receiving planned teaching had better outcomes than did control group subjects receiving routine care" (p. 100). Current literature also supports the effectiveness of structured approaches, reinforcement, independent study, and multiple strategies (Allen, Iezzoni, Huang, Huang, & Leveille, 2008; Budin et al., 2008; Chang & Kelly, 2007; Edwardson, 2007). Other teaching strategies are included in Display 17-5 (Babcock & Miller, 1994; Rankin et al., 2005; Redman, 1993).

Motivation for learning is enhanced if the student and the teacher trust and respect each other, the teacher assumes and expects that the student can learn, the teacher is sensitive to the student's individual needs, and both the student and the teacher feel free to learn and make mistakes in their own unique styles. Boswell, Pichert, Lorenz, and Schlundt (1990) reinforced the idea that active participation in learning is a strong motivator. Display 17-6 gives effective motivating strategies for learning, as outlined in Bevis (1988, p. 45).

Other Teaching Strategies

DISPLAY 17-5

1. Computer-based instruction materials
2. Observation and assessment scales
3. Demonstration
4. Lecture/discussion
5. Modeling
6. Programmed instruction
7. Role playing
8. Group activities
9. Use of media (posters, flip charts, overhead projections, videotapes, audiotapes, film)
10. Games and simulations
11. Concept maps

Source: Babcock & Miller, 1994; Rankin, Stallings & London, 2005; Redman, 1993; Fink, 2003.

Effective Motivating Strategies for Learning   DISPLAY 17-6

1. Engaging the learner in active analysis
2. Raising questions
3. Nurturing
4. Finding ways to make the learning meaningful and significant for the learner
5. Following the ethical ideal in giving clients all the information they need to make sound choices
6. Displaying a caring attitude

7. Using and encouraging creativity in the teaching–learning process
8. Encouraging curiosity and the search for satisfying ideas
9. Being assertive
10. Desiring to engage in and to seek dialogue

Source: Bevis, 1988, p. 45.

Contextual Constraints and Opportunities

Some contextual constraints, such as the dilemma of insufficient time and great need on the part of the client, have been mentioned. To attempt to control the environmental constraints that might be imposed on the teaching–learning process, the nurse should keep the following teaching strategies in mind: (1) try to arrange learning experiences when the learner feels relatively healthy, (2) provide time for learning at a comfortable pace, (3) have sufficient grasp of the subject matter to translate concepts into different terms for different learners, and (4) make sure expectations and standards are clear. Certain clients, such as the elderly, need to have a slower pace of instruction to allow for increased time for mental processing. The Hartford Foundation offers a vast array of resources for nurses working with elderly clients, including tips for effective teaching and learning (Fulmer, 2007).

Bruner (1986, p. 198) suggested that educators need to assist learners to perceive the value of the rich diversity in the world. He encouraged them to view the learner as "equipped to discriminate and deal differentially with a wide variety of possible worlds exhibiting different conditions, yet worlds in which one can cope." The nurse should perhaps heed this advice and have confidence in the client's ability to mutually participate in teaching–learning and to succeed in a diverse world, rather than trying to control all the contextual constraints that might interfere with learning. Power sharing would be more likely by nurses with this confidence in clients. Perceived abilities and learning are more likely in such relationships.

SPECIFIC CLIENT EDUCATION ACTIVITIES

Many routine nursing activities involve client (and family) education. When clients enter a health care institution, they frequently need instructions related to their expected role responsibilities. Health care professionals cannot deliver effective care unless clients are willing to provide them with information related to health problems and educational needs. During an initial client encounter, the professional nurse may learn more about the client needs and concerns, and the client actually assumes the role of teacher. To plan effective nursing care, the nurse needs to understand the client's perspective of the health problem or illness. Additional information related to specific care needs (special adaptive devices, cultural concerns) usually also surface during the initial encounter.

Nurses also assume the role of educator when they inform clients and families of the purposes behind nursing interventions and rationales for administered medications. Educational efforts such as these enable clients to understand the reasons behind care activities and learn why they must comply with the ordered medical regimen. Most teaching related to medication administration reinforces information clients have received from physicians. However, sometimes, as in the case of a client with newly diagnosed diabetes, the physician delegates the task of teaching insulin administration to a professional nurse or certified diabetic educator (who usually is a professional nurse). Educating families of unconscious or dysphagic patients to not attempt to give them food or fluids by mouth can help prevent the problem of aspiration pneumonia. In addition, the Joint Commission has a consumer education campaign for clients and families to speak up if they have questions or concerns about health care. Usually, clients and families must feel comfortable with health care providers before feeling free to ask questions.

Sometimes the roles of educator and client advocate become intertwined. As a client advocate, the professional nurse frequently verifies that patients understand procedures that are about to happen. Nurses frequently obtain signatures on consent forms before clients undergo invasive procedures. Informed consent requires that the client is competent, has had other treatment options disclosed to him or her, understands the treatment/test and its potential adverse effects, volunteers for the procedure without coercion, and consents to having the procedure performed (Bosek & Savage, 2007; Rankin et al., 2005). Nursing process is used to determine the multiple elements of informed consent. When assessing for the elements required for informed consent, questions related to the procedure may arise. The nurse who answers them engages in the process of client education. However, if the nurse discovers that the client fails to fully understand the anticipated procedure, the role of educator ceases, and the nurse assumes the role of advocate, informing the physician of an inability to obtain a signature on a consent form because the client fails to understand the risks and benefits of the invasive procedure.

Professional nurses also participate in community health education. Successful community education starts with the participation of community members. Professional nurses secure community input when planning community education programs by performing a needs assessment. In a manner similar to that used to identify individual client learning needs, the nurse asks community members to identify community learning needs. Methods for performing a needs assessment include individual interviews, informal polls, focus groups, or written surveys. Key community leaders must also be asked to identify group learning needs to ensure successful program development and implementation. Once a learning need has been identified, professional nurses secure credible resources and financial support for the program. Financial support may be secured in the form of grants or corporate sponsorships, or from the community. Involvement of community members during the program-planning process increases the chance that the program will appeal to community members. Teaching strategies that appeal to individual clients (videos, slides, and flip charts) may be highly effective for community education. However, the teaching strategies must consider the projected number of persons who will attend the program (Rankin et al., 2005).

Not all client education occurs in a formalized setting, such as a health care organization or community agency. Professional nurses reside in neighborhoods and are members of families. Family members, neighbors, and friends frequently consult the professional nurse when health care concerns or questions about a health condition arise. Sometimes, the questions fall within the realm of the professional nurse's area of expertise; at other times, they do not. Directing family, friends, and acquaintances to credible resources sometimes poses a great challenge for the professional nurse. As more persons use the Internet as a source of health information, the professional nurse should become aware of various websites and be able to assess the quality of information posted on each site. Professional nurses have an obligation to share accurate health-related information or refer the question or concern to another health team member when unable to provide the requested information.

Rankin et al. (2005) and Smeltzer (2005) outlined several factors that distinguish credible from less reputable information for client education and care. Hallmarks of suitable and unsuitable information are outlined in Table 17-1. The process of peer review increases the credibility of the information because the information has been appraised by experts in the field. Before suggesting materials for client education, nurses must review them to verify accuracy, readability, and ease of use.

TABLE 17-1

Determining Suitability of Information for Client Education

Suitable Sources	Unsuitable Sources
Peer reviewed	Use secondary sources of information
Primary source of information	May use editorial ideas as facts
Known experts in a field	Advertise products or information for sale
Editorial ideas clearly documented as such	Websites not updated on a regular basis
Government and higher education sources	No review of content by medical experts
Recognized nonprofit organizations for disease processes (e.g., American Cancer Society, Multiple Sclerosis Society)	For-profit organizations
Professional nursing organizations	Nonprofit organizations displaying narrow viewpoints
Websites updated on a regular schedule	High reading level required
Clearly delineate editorials, and advertisements from objective information	For elderly and visually impaired: print smaller than 12-point font
Display biographical information of all content authors (academic and professional credentials) as well as relationship to the organization	Websites that are poorly designed or are directly linked to advertising firms (automatic pop-up ads come when site accessed)
Disclaimer present that sends clients to physicians or other health care providers for their specific use	No disclaimer statement to warn clients of the need to consult with a health care provider to meet specific needs
Open disclosures if funds from companies were used to develop the study or website	
Hyperlinks to reports of original studies or primary sources of information	
Website design easy to navigate in order to reach desired information (internal search engines very helpful)	
Options for persons who do not read English	

Source: Rankin, S., Stallings, K., & London, F. (2005). *Patient education in health and illness.* (5th ed., pp. 280–282). Philadelphia: Lippincott Williams & Wilkins. Smeltzer, S. (2005). Is that information safe for patient care? *Nursing 2005, 35,* 54–55.

Questions for Reflection 17-4

1. How do I currently evaluate information that I give to clients for education?
2. Why is it important for nurses to determine the suitability of client educational materials before using them with clients?

 CLIENT EDUCATION AS AN INTERDISCIPLINARY PROCESS

Along with nurses, other members of the health care team make significant contributions to client education. Because nurses tend to spend more time with clients than other providers, they have the opportunity to assess client learning needs and responses to health teaching implemented by other team members. The nurse also has the ability to determine if the client has the capability to absorb teaching from other disciplines. Thus, the nurse may suggest that other health team members (such as dietitians, physical therapists, social workers, or pharmacists) refrain from educational activities until clients are in a physically stable condition and emotionally ready to benefit from detailed education for self-care.

In addition to determining the best times for client education, the nurse has the responsibility to coordinate educational activities and to verify that clients receive the same information from all health team members. Documentation of teaching by all disciplines (including nursing) serves as a key so that instructions from one discipline can be effectively reinforced. Documented teaching content also may eliminate duplicated teaching efforts and provide a detailed record to meet the Joint Commission standards for client education and for third-party reimbursement.

Within the past decade, nurses have participated in the development of client care paths. Care paths designate specific client educational activities so that client education does not occur haphazardly or at the last minute when the physician writes a dismissal order. Some institutions have formed multidisciplinary educational committees to develop guidelines for client education and identify continuing educational needs for the entire health care team.

SUMMARY AND SIGNIFICANCE TO PRACTICE

Teaching–learning is presented as a complex process among experts, the teacher, and the learner, in which all acquire new information, experience new relatedness, and change behavior as a result of the interaction. The nurse–teacher is an expert on health, and the client–learner is an expert on the client's experience of health and life circumstances. As the person who bears responsibility for developing and implementing effective client education, the nurse uses communication skills to assess learners and collaborate with them to develop relevant learning experiences. Cognitive skills prove useful when determining priorities, materials, and specific strategies to use during the teaching–learning process. When clients need to learn procedural skills, the nurse shares clinical skills with them. Effective teaching and learning result in increased confidence and competence for nurses and clients.

FROM THEORY TO PRACTICE

1. Reread the vignette at the front of the chapter. Using the information that you have read in the chapter, answer the following questions:
   a. What are the barriers encountered by Lillian to provide effective client education?
   b. What are the consequences when clients are dismissed without receiving detailed education about medications, diet, activity, and follow-up health care?
   c. What suggestions could Lillian make to the hospital to improve client education? What potential barriers might prevent Lillian's suggestions from being implemented? How would these suggestions be financed?
2. After reading this chapter, what ideas will you incorporate into your client education in clinical practice? Why are these ideas important?

WWW INTERNET EXERCISES

1. Look up a health topic of your interest using a general search engine found in your Internet software program. Scan the first ten websites that you can view from the results of your search. How many of these sites are trying to sell a product or products? How many of the sites are nonprofit organizations? How many of the sites are sponsored by a national or local government agency? Compare the quality of each website. Which websites would you recommend to clients for health information? Why or why not? Which sites would you use for personal health information? Why or why not?

2. Visit one of the recommended Internet websites listed in Internet Resources. Which sites contain health-teaching materials in more than one language? Print out information that you would like to use for client teaching and bring it to class. Analyze the information according to the following criteria:
   - Readability
   - Visual appeal
   - Accuracy of information
   - Ability to sustain interest and actively engage the learner

3. What types of policies does your current work setting have related to distribution of Internet resources for client education? Describe the materials for client education in your current work setting. Select a topic for which you frequently provide client/family education. Obtain your organization's teaching materials on this topic. Search the Internet to find teaching materials on the same topic. Compare and contrast the two resources.

INTERNET RESOURCES

The Joint Commission on Accreditation of Healthcare Organizations: http://www.jcaho.org.
American Medical Association: http://www.ama-assn.org.
American Cancer Society: http://www.cancer.org.
American Academy of Family Practitioners: http://www.aafp.org.
Lab Tests Online: http://www.labtestsonline.org.
NOAH: http://www.noah-health.org.
American Heart Association: http://www.americanheart.org.
National Institutes of Health: http://www.nih.gov.
Cancer Control Planet: http://www.cancercontrolplanet.cancer.gov.
National Women's Health Information Center: http://www.4woman.gov.
Office of Minority Health Resource Center: http://www.omhrc.gov.
Centers for Disease Control: http://www.cdc.gov.
Health Information Quality Assessment Tool: http://hitiweb.mitretek.org/iq/begguide.asp.
Canadian Women's Health Network: http://www.cwhn.ca/indexeng.html.
The Hartford Foundation http://www.hartford.ign.org.

REFERENCES

Agnes, M. (2005). *Webster's new world college dictionary* (4th ed.). Cleveland, OH: Wiley.

Allen, M., Iezzoni, L., Huang, A., Huang, L., & Leveille, S. (2008). Improving patient-clinician communication about chronic conditions: Description of an Internet-based nurse E-coach intervention. *Nursing Research, 57*(2), 107–112.

Anhang, R., Goodman, A., & Goldie, S. (2004). HPV communication: Review of existing research and recommendations for patient education. *CA A Cancer Journal for Clinicians, 54*, 248–259.

Argyris, C. (1982). *Reasoning, learning, and action: Individual and organizational*. San Francisco: Jossey-Bass.

Babcock, D. E., & Miller. M. A. (1994). *Client education: Theory and practice*. St. Louis, MO: Mosby-Year Book.

Badarudeen, S., & Sabharwal, S. (2008). Readability of patient education materials from the American Academy of Orthopedic Surgeons and Pediatric Orthopedic Society of North America web sites. *The Journal of Bone & Joint Surgery, 90*-A(1), 199–204.

Benner, P. (1984). *From novice to expert*. Menlo Park, CA: Addison-Wesley.

Bevis, E. O. (1988). New directions for a new age. In National League for Nursing, *Curriculum revolution: Mandate for change* (pp. 27–52). New York: National League for Nursing.

Bloom, B. (Ed.). (1974). *Taxonomy of educational objectives*. New York: D. McKay.

Bosek, M., & Savage, T. (2007). *The ethical component of nursing education*. Philadelphia: Lippincott Williams & Wilkins.

Boswell, E. J., Pichert, J. W., Lorenz, R. A., & Schlundt, D. G. (1990). Training health care professionals to enhance their patient teaching skills. *Journal of Nursing Staff Development, 6*, 233–239.

Bruner, J. (1986). Models of the learner. *Education Horizons, 64*, 197–200.

Budin, W., Hoskins, C., Haber, J., Sherman, D., Maislin, G., Carter, J., et al. (2008). Breast cancer: Education, counseling, and adjustment among patients and partners: A randomized clinical trial. *Nursing Research, 57*(3), 199–213.

Chang, M., & Kelly, A. (2007). Patient education: Addressing cultural diversity and health literacy issues. *Urology Nursing, 27*(5), 411–417.

Chiovetti, A. (2006). Bridging the gap between health literacy and patient education for people with multiple sclerosis. *Journal of Neuroscience Nurses, 38*(5), 374–378.

Collins, J. (2007). The neuroscience of learning. *Journal of Neuroscience Nursing, 39*(5), 305–315.

D'Arcy, Y. (2008). Keeping your patient safe during PCA. *Nursing 2008, 38*(1), 50–56.

Diekelmann, N. (1988). Curriculum revolution: A theoretical and philosophical mandate for change. In National League for Nursing, *Curriculum revolution: Mandate for change* (pp. 137–158). New York: National League for Nursing.

Douglass, L. M. (1988). *The effective nurse: Leader and manager* (3rd ed.). St. Louis, MO: Mosby.

Edwardson, S. (2007). Patient education in heart failure. *Heart & Lung, 36*(4), 244–252.

Falvo, D. (2004). *Effective patient education, a guide to increased compliance* (3rd ed.). Sudbury, MA: Jones & Bartlett.

Fink, L. (2003). *Creating significant learning experiences*. San Francisco: Jossey-Bass.

Forbes, K. E. (1995). Please, more than just the facts. *Clinical Nurse Specialist, 9*, 99.

Fulmer, T. (2007). How to try this: Fulmer SPICES. *American Journal of Nursing, 107*(10), 40–49.

Henson, R. H. (1997). Analysis of the concept of mutuality. *Image, 29*, 77–81.

Herzlinger, R. (2004). *Consumer-driven health care*. San Francisco: Jossey-Bass.

Hill-Briggs, F., & Smith, A. (2008). Evaluation of diabetes and cardiovascular disease print patient education materials for use with low-health literate populations. *Diabetes Care, 31* (4), 667–671.

Joint Commission on Accreditation of Healthcare Organizations. (2006a). *2006 hospital requirements related to the provision of culturally and linguistically appropriate health care*. Available at http://wwwjointcommission.org/NR/rdonlyres/A2B030A3-7BE-4981-A064-309865BBA6720/hl_standards.pdf. Accessed July 5, 2008.

Joint Commission on Accreditation of Healthcare Organizations. (2006b). *Patient 101*. Oak Terrace, IL: Author.

Joint Commission on Accreditation of Healthcare Organizations. (2008). *The Joint Commission hospital accreditation program 2009 chapter: National patient safety goal* (prepub. version). Available at http://www.jointcommission.org/NR/rdonlyres/3:23E-9BE8-F05BDICBOAA8/09_NPSG_HAP.pdf. Accessed July 5, 2008.

Lupien, S. J., & McEwen, B. S. (1997). The acute effects of corticosteriods on cognition: Integration of animal and human model studies. *Brain Research Reviews, 24*, 1–27.

Rankin, S., Stallings, K., & London, F. (2005). *Patient education in health and illness* (5th ed.). Philadelphia: Lippincott Williams & Wilkins.

Redman, B. K. (1993). *The process of patient education* (7th ed.). St. Louis, MO: Mosby-Year Book.

Singh, J. (2003). Research briefs reading grade level and readability of printed cancer education materials. *Oncology Nursing Forum, 30*, 867–870.

Smeltzer, S. (2005). Is that information safe for patient care? *Nursing, 35*, 54–55.

Theis, S. L., & Johnson, J. H. (1995). Strategies for teaching patients: A meta-analysis. *Clinical Nurse Specialist, 9*, 100–105.

Watson, J. (2007). *Nursing human science and human care: A theory for nursing*. Sudbury, MA: Jones & Bartlett.

CHAPTER 18

Leadership and Management in Professional Nursing

KEY TERMS AND CONCEPTS

Management
Leaders
Managers
Formal leaders
Informal leaders
Leadership
Empowerment
Leadership development
Leadership and management skills
Empowered caring
Transformational leadership
Strategic plan
Budgeting
Staffing
Marketing
Change
Change agent
Habits of effective leaders
Criteria for evaluating leadership

LEARNING OUTCOMES

By the end of this chapter, the learner will be able to:

1 Explain contemporary thoughts about the concepts of leadership and management.
2 Compare and contrast the concepts of leadership and management.
3 Identify the essential habits of effective leaders.
4 Outline the strengths of a feminine approach to leadership.
5 Specify the value of empowering others and oneself in professional nursing relationships.
6 Outline criteria to evaluate leadership effectiveness.

VIGNETTE

Alice is a registered nurse who, while attending a Parent/Teacher Association (PTA) meeting at her son's school, learned that the school does not have a full-time nurse. At the last meeting, many parents voiced complaints related to current health education and school health care services. The PTA forms a task force and elects Alice to be the chairperson because she is a registered nurse (even though she graduated from school a year ago). Uncomfortable with her new leadership position, Alice decides that she needs to read about principles of leadership and finds her nursing leadership textbook that she was supposed to read in her undergraduate nursing program.

Questions for Reflection 18-1

1. How would I feel if I were in Alice's position?
2. Do you think that the task force made a wise decision in selecting Alice as their leader? Why or why not?
3. What would you do if you found yourself in a similar situation? Why would you do these things?

Distinguishing leadership and **management** is difficult because business literature often uses the terms interchangeably. The concepts of leader and manager overlap. **Leaders** are persons who influence others. Leaders view things more globally, create visions of what might be, inspire others, tolerate chaos and ambiguity, do not fear taking risks, and work with others in a more connected way. **Managers** receive their title usually because of an appointed position within an organization. Managers tend to focus energy and efforts to ensure smooth workflow and efficient use of resources to meet the objectives of the organization. Effective managers and leaders possess expertise in working with people, understanding organizations as being authentic, and pursuing work with passion (Covey, 2004). **Formal leaders** are persons who hold a position of power (either in groups, organizations, or workplaces). Formal leaders get their positions via appointments or elections. In contrast, **informal leaders** emerge when members of a group recognize a person has special knowledge, expertise, communication skills, or other personality traits they respect and admire. Informal leaders do not have formal appointments to their position (Donnelly, 2003; Videback, 2008). In the vignette, Alice became the chair of the task force because the PTA members elected her to assume a formal leadership position.

All professional nurses are leaders because they influence others. Nurses influence clients and other members of the health care team as they fulfill professional nursing roles and responsibilities. A stongr knowledge base of leadership and management skills enables professional nurses to influence others (including clients) to make optimal choices for health care decisions. As leaders of the interprofessional health care team, professional nurses coordinate the efforts and inspire others to provide the best possible client care.

CONCEPTUAL AND THEORETICAL APPROACHES TO NURSING LEADERSHIP AND MANAGEMENT

Leadership is a complex term with multiple definitions but is normally defined as a process of influencing others or guiding or directing others to attain mutually agreed upon goals (Agnes, 2005). Leadership outcomes include those of transaction (relationships based on the exchange of effort or something valued by the followers) or transformation (empowering others to create and work toward achieving anything that is possible). Transactional leaders typically use strategies that exercise power over others, whereas transformational leaders use strategies that empower others (Burns, 2003; Bass & Riggio, 2005).

Perceptions of Power and Empowerment

The ideas of mutuality, empowerment, and transformation as key elements of leadership surfaced in the late 1970s (Burns, 1978). These ideas comprise a feminist approach to leadership because emphasis is placed on "power with" rather than "power over," which is a more masculine approach toward the world (Noddings, 1984). Table 18-1 presents some currently used leadership theories and classifies them according to their approach to the use of power. Leaders choose how they use power based on their philosophical

(Text continues on page 462.)

TABLE 18-1

A Feminist or Masculine Approach: Contemporary Management and Leadership Theories

Theory Name	Theory Creator(s)	Key Principles	Approach to Leadership/Management
Leadership styles	White, R. & Lippitt, R. (1960)	The style of the leader affects worker performance. Three basic leadership styles were identified:	
		Authoritarian: Leader exercises great control to get the work done	Authoritarian: masculine
		Democratic: Leader and group work together to get things accomplished	Democratic: more feminine than masculine
		Laissez-faire: Leader abstains from leading and lets subordinates lead themselves	Laissez-faire: feminine to empower workers, but no attention paid to relationships
Theory X	McGregor, D. (1960)	The manager must control, direct, and motivate workers by offering rewards or threatening punishment Workers avoid responsibility and seek security Workers cannot be trusted	Masculine
Theory Y	McGregor, D. (1960)	Managers can trust workers to do the best possible job Workers value their work, are motivated by rewards, contribute to the organization, and derive satisfaction from meeting goals. Workers can solve work-related problems with their own initiative and creativity Managers can create an environment to increase worker commitment and self-direction	Feminine
Managerial grid model	Blake, R., & Morton, J. (1964)	Five basic leadership styles based on balancing concern for task and concern for people:	
		Impoverished: Low concern for task and persons	Impoverished: neither
		Produce or Perish: High concern for tasks with low concern for persons	Produce or perish: masculine
		Country club: High concern for persons with low concern for tasks	Country club: feminine
		Middle of the road: Balanced, but not high concern for persons or tasks	Middle of the road: poor use of both
		Team: High concern for persons and tasks	Team: feminine

A Feminist or Masculine Approach: Contemporary Management and Leadership Theories (Continued)

Theory Name	Theory Creator(s)	Key Principles	Approach to Leadership/Management
Be–know–do	The United States Army (2004)	Leaders influence other people by providing them with purpose, direction, and motivation while operating to achieve the mission and improve the organization. Effective performance is the result of transforming human potential To be a leader means to have values and attributes of a leader (loyalty, duty, respect, selfless service, honor, integrity, and personal courage) To know involves knowledge and mastery of interpersonal, conceptual, technical, and tactical skills To do means to live out the values, use knowledge and skills to influence others to achieve the mission, and improving the organization by providing everyone with purpose, meaning, and motivation High level of trust among soldiers and officers Officers have a duty to protect their subordinates and subordinates have a duty to follow orders issued by officers	Masculine
Theory Z	Ouchi, W. (1981)	Leaders share responsibility with workers Leaders match work with employee strengths Work processes are designed and work problems are solved by using quality circles where workers and managers have equal status Democracy and consensus building are the ways decisions are made. However, leaders consider the long-term effects to evaluate management decisions	Feminine
Contingency leadership	Fieldler, F. (1967)	A leader selects a particular leadership style to best fit a given situation that includes the nature of staff–leader relationships, formal position of the leader, and the nature of the task	Masculine or feminine depending of the style of leadership selected by the leader to fit the specific situation

(continued)

A Feminist or Masculine Approach: Contemporary Management and Leadership Theories (Continued)

Theory Name	Theory Creator(s)	Key Principles	Approach to Leadership/Management
Leader participation model	Vroom, V. & Yetton, P. (1973)	Leaders choose from the following three leadership styles—autocratic, consultative, or participative—when needing to make decisions. The leader uses a list of questions to analyze the environmental contingencies that may affect the quality of the decision made	Autocratic: masculine Consultative: primarily masculine Participative: primarily feminine
Transformational leadership	Burns, J. (2003). *Transformational Leadership.* New York: Grove/Atlantic Inc.	Identifies two types of leaders: transactional leaders, who maintain daily operations using rewards to motivate subordinates; transformational leaders, who inspire and empower everyone with the vision of what could be possible. The transformational leader has a high level of trust, gets others to share common values and mission, shows a committed work ethic, defines reality, keeps the dream alive, examines effects of actions, and makes adjustments as needed	Transactional leaders use the masculine approach Transformational leaders use the feminine approach
Path–goal theory	House, R. & Mitchell, T. (1974)	Leaders coach, guide, and reward staff to select the best paths to meet organizational goals. Achievement-oriented approaches are used to set challenging goals for competent followers A directive style is used to set expectations and operational methods for followers A participative style is used when the leader wants follower suggestions A supportive style is used to build follower trust and confidence	Achievement-oriented and directive approaches use the masculine approach The participative approach uses a more feminine approach The supportive style blends the masculine and feminine approaches
Situational theory	Hershey, P. &, Blanchard, K. (1977)	The leader selects from four styles of leadership while considering the following three dimensions of a situation: (1) the amount of direction required, (2) specific factors about the situation, and (3) the maturity of followers Telling: High task/low relationship (leader needs to be in command in a situation with one correct response)	Telling: masculine

A Feminist or Masculine Approach: Contemporary Management and Leadership Theories (Continued)

Theory Name	Theory Creator(s)	Key Principles	Approach to Leadership/Management
		Selling: High task/high relationship (leader has most of the controls but assists followers to boost confidence)	Selling: masculine
		Participating: High relationship/low task (leader and followers share decision making)	Participating: primarily feminine
		Delegating: Low task/low relationship (leaders assume the follower are competent and are capable of assuming full responsibility for the decision or task)	Delegating: feminine
Transforming leadership	Anderson, T. (1998)	"Transforming leadership is vision, planning, communication, and creative action that has a positive unifying effect on a group of people around a set of clear values and beliefs to accomplish a clear set of measurable goals. This transforming approach simultaneously impacts the personal development and corporate productivity of all involved" (p. 270). Transforming leadership anticipates future trends; develops new leaders; assesses, plans and implements organizational-wide leadership and self-leadership development programs; and creates a community within the organization. The leader uses communication, counseling, and consulting to create the organizational community	Primarily feminine
Authentic leadership	George, B. (2003)	Leadership is not about style, but rather it is about authenticity. Five qualities of authentic leaders are "understanding their purpose, practicing solid values, leading with heart, establishing connected relationship, and demonstrating self-discipline" (p. 18). Leadership is more effective when the leader leads a balanced life with authenticity in each of life aspects	Feminine
Servant leadership	Greenleaf, R. (1977)	Leaders use their values to empower workers by providing them with all the needed resources and an environment that enables each one to achieve their maximal potential. The top priority for the leader is to serve others (employees, customers, and the community)	Feminine

(continued)

A Feminist or Masculine Approach: Contemporary Management and Leadership Theories (Continued)

Theory Name	Theory Creator(s)	Key Principles	Approach to Leadership/Management
Quantum leadership	Porter-O' Grady first presented the idea in 1997. Porter-O'Grady, T. & Malloch, K. (2007). *Quantum leadership: A textbook of nursing leadership* (2nd ed.). Sudbury, MA: Jones & Bartlett.	"…Leadership emerges from the combined active engagement of all members in the organization" (p. 261) because the group has a deep commitment to a shared mission. Effective leaders possess technical (having knowledge of service, skills, and abilities), relational (connecting interpersonally with others while remaining connected to the technical aspects), and intentional (possessing goals that are based on values and skills). Typically various group members assume leadership to achieve a group or organizational mission (or goal) based on their areas of expertise and skill. Leadership is shared among group members, who use systems thinking to thrive in a complex, chaotic, and constantly changing world.	Feminine
Trait theories	Evolved in the early history of man	Leaders are born. They inherit characteristics that make them suitable as leaders	Either, depending on how the leader uses power

beliefs while considering specific situations. For example, Alice, as task force leader, analyzes the situation, characteristics of task force members, and persons in key decision-making positions before deciding what approaches may work best. Thus, she is more likely to use strategies from the contingency, path–goal, or situational theories.

Mutuality empowerment and transformation serve as hallmarks of contemporary leadership. In health care, the interprofessional team and unlicensed assistive personnel (UAP) work collectively toward attaining optimal client outcomes. Professional nurses assume leadership roles when coordinating care and making recommendations to interprofessional team members. In an ideal world, all members of the health team assume leadership roles when needed because of their special expertise. Covey (1996) proposed that today's leaders must combine personal values and visions to develop a strategic pathway, and align organizational resources and processes to fulfill visions and missions, while empowering others. Leaders create a vision that inspires commitment and empowers people by sharing authority. Empowering leaders prefer to be transformational, thereby changing individuals, organizations, and societies.

According to Covey (1989, p. 222), the real test of interpersonal leadership is the leader's ability to permit others to validate themselves and realize that they will benefit more by working toward accomplishing goals that are shared by the leader and team members. In transformational leadership, there is "mutual learning, mutual influence, mutual benefits" (Covey, 1989, p. 216). Donnelly (2003) noted that all definitions of leadership contain the following elements: "relationship, context, purpose and accountability" (p. 40). For example, in the vignette, Alice's leadership position means that she needs to spend time on building and cultivating relationships to enhance teamwork and influence persons who make decisions about student health services and education.

Questions for Reflection 18-2

1. Think of your current manager (or faculty member if unemployed). Which of the leadership theories do you suppose they use to motivate workers (or students)? Why do you think that they use the identified leadership theory?
2. Identify a situation in which a masculine approach to power would best get the mission accomplished. Why would this approach be best in the identified situation?
3. List the pros and cons of masculine and feminine approaches to use of power. When would this approach best fit clinical practice situations? Why?

Leadership as a Process of Empowerment

Perceptions of power and power relationships have changed markedly in recent years. In the past, physicians dominated health care because they held a monopoly on the key medical information and refused to share it with others. In today's world, many persons have access to state-of-the-art information on health care advances. Health care professionals and consumers can watch either online or televised video clips on health conditions and how to to manage them. Online electronic databases can be readily accessed on the National Library of Medicine website. Anyone with Internet access can read posted information on a variety of health care professional association and academic medical websites. If knowledge is perceived as a power source, power becomes redistributed as more persons gain access to it.

Porter-O'Grady and Malloch (2007) proposed that power has conflicting connotations. People can think of power in terms of coercion and domination or influence and strength. All persons have the power and the right to exercise it legitimately. Instead of centralizing power to persons in administrative positions or to an elite group, Porter-O'Grady and Malloch suggested that power should be shared by all (decentralized) so that all persons can use their expertise in delivering client care. By sharing knowledge and expertise with others, nurses empower clients, families, each other, health team members, and communities.

Blanchard, Carlos, and Randolph (1996) perceived **empowerment** as a releasing of the knowledge, experience, and motivation that people already possess. They have identified the following three keys to empower persons within organizations: (1) sharing information (trust people with it, and they will act responsibly), (2) creating autonomy through boundaries (clearly delineate purposes, values, images, goals, roles, structure, and systems; thus everyone within an organization understands and executes his or her own role to meet the mission), and (3) replacing the traditional organizational hierarchy with self-directed teams (workers assume full responsibility for entire work processes and products).

Empowering leadership gives energy to the work of nursing. Empowerment becomes an outcome of leadership. Bennis (1989, p. 23) said that empowerment is evident in the four themes (adapted for nursing) shown in Display 18-1.

Thus, empowered nurses make each person with whom they interact feel important. Professional nurse leaders also value the knowledge and skills that each person brings to a health care situation. Finally, clients, nurses, and health team members collaborate to determine a preferred vision for the future, and everyone works together to attain optimal client care.

LEADERSHIP DEVELOPMENT

When nurses envision themselves as leaders, they embark on the journey of **leadership development**. Aspiring leaders need to realize that leadership does not automatically occur with position appointment, but rather leadership must be learned and developed (Barrett, 1998; Donnelly, 2003; Dotlich, Noel, & Walker, 2004; Porter-O'Grady &

Empowerment Themes Related to Nursing Leadership
DISPLAY 18-1

1. People feel significant. All feel that they make a difference and that what they do has meaning and significance. In the nursing process, the nurse and the client are equal in significance; both have meaning and what they do together is mutually significant.
2. Learning and competence matter. The nurse and the client value learning and mastery. The nurse makes it clear that there is no failure, only mistakes that provide feedback and tell us what to do next.
3. People are part of a community. The nurse, the client, and other health care providers are experienced as a team, a family, a unit. A person does not have to like another to feel a sense of community (striving for a common goal).
4. Work is exciting. The nursing process is stimulating, challenging, and fun. The nurse "pulls," rather than "pushes," a client toward a goal. This pull style of influence energizes the client to "enroll in an exciting vision of the future....It motivates through identification, rather than through rewards and punishments" (Bennis, 1989, p. 23). The nurse articulates and embodies the ideals of health toward which both the nurse and the client strive.

Malloch, 2007; Van Velsor, Moxley, & Bunker, 2004). Table 18-2 outlines two different approaches for leadership development and includes examples of how a nurse might experience it. Most of the approaches begin with establishing a personal leadership mission followed by self-analysis. Once the aspiring leaders envision the type of leader they want to become, then they engage in a process of mastering key leadership skills that fit with the desired leadership approach.

McCauley and Van Velsor (2004) specified that leadership development occurs from a variety of experiences. Leaders learn from challenging assignments, education, significant persons, hardship, and other unidentified situations. They proposed that through leadership development programs, aspiring leaders learn self-management capabilities (increasing self-awareness, balancing conflicting demands, learning new skills and ideas, and developing a personal set of values for leadership). Along with personal capacity for development, novice leaders learn social capabilities (building and maintaining relationships, developing effective work groups, enhancing interpersonal communication skills, and learning how to develop other people). Finally, leaders develop work facilitation capacities by learning management skills, how to engage in strategic thought and action, increasing the ability for creative thinking, and learning how to imitate and implement change (McCauley & Van Velsor). Porter-O'Grady and Malloch (2007) concurred with this leadership development framework, but also added that leaders must learn how to take risks.

Nurses embark on a career in nursing leadership for a variety of reasons. Some nurse leaders assume leadership positions because they displayed these qualities in childhood. Other nurses view an administrative position as being less physically taxing. Others find daytime hours and salaries attractive. Sometimes, nurses find themselves in a leadership position because no other nurse in the organization would assume it, whereas other nurses enter the profession with the intention of becoming a nurse adminstrator. Little is known about why and how nurses opt for a nursing leadership position. Research Brief 18-1 presents information about the paths to nursing leadership.

Questions for Reflection 18-3

1. What steps have I taken to develop leadership in professional nursing practice?
2. Have I encountered any obstacles toward developing leadership? If I have, what are they and how did I handle them?
3. What areas do I need to develop to improve my leadership abilities? Why are these areas important to develop?

TABLE 18-2

Approaches to Leadership Development

Barrett (1998)	Leadership Passages (Dotlich, Noel, & Walker, 2004)	Professional Nurse Experience
Becoming a facilitator by focusing on physical, emotional, mental, and spiritual balance and aligning a personal mission, vision, and values with an organizational one	Joining an organization or company and learning the organizational culture	Finding a first nursing job, learning work expectations, and the culture of the particular nursing department as well as the culture of the larger organization the organizational culture
	Moving into a leadership role that results in losing one's personal identity, losing one's status as the upcoming star, and learning how to balance tasks and people	Realizing that some client care tasks particularly enjoyed must now be delegated to other persons in order to provide efficient client care
Becoming a collaborator by developing one's emotional intelligence; learning effective interpersonal skills; building collaboration and team spirit; accessing the intuition, creativity of others; empathizing with others; and giving and receiving effective feedback	Accepting the stretch assignment resulting in the need for overcoming feeling like a victim, coping with skepticism and hostility from others, and realizing what is not known and when to seek out other trustful team members	Accepting the position of "charge nurse"
	Assuming responsibility for actions by valuing the unfamiliar, displaying a resilient mentality despite setbacks, and accepting the paradoxical characteristics of the work	Taking responsibility when the nursing unit fails to run smoothly, realizing that more tasks need to be delegated, deciding that more knowledge and practice are needed for managing coworkers effectively, and doing what is needed to improve job performance
Becoming a servant/partner or wisdom/visionary by increasing individual role awareness, understanding the role of the organization, creating a sustainable future, partnering, forming strategic alliances to attain long-lasting success, deepening and strengthening personal and professional growth as a leader	Dealing with significant failures one has caused or is responsible by examining decisions that resulted in the failure, sharing experience with a trusted boss, coach or advisor, reflecting on the failure and devising different actions for future situations, and rallying the energy needed for perseverance	Sharing personal frustrations with a trusted professional nurse with more experience; developing a mentoring relationship; generating alternative actions if similar situations are encountered in the future; and keeping oneself physically, emotionally and spiritually healthy to remain in professional nursing practice
	Coping with a bad boss or competitive coworkers by developing a strategy to manage the ineffective relationship, analyzing your reaction to the boss or peer as to what it tells you about yourself, and defining personal values	Finding effective strategies to manage an ineffective manager or jealous coworkers while learning their weaknesses mirror your own, and engaging in a process of clarifying one's personal values

(continued)

Approaches to Leadership Development (Continued)

Barrett (1998)	Leadership Passages (Dotlich, Noel, & Walker, 2004)	Professional Nurse Experience
	Dealing with losing a job or not getting an expected promotion by using the following strategies: not letting a job or event define you as a person, try to understand what occurred by contemplation, use a support network, devise a strategy to address "what next"	Engaging in conversations with other nurses who have survived similar circumstances, recognizing that professional nursing does not need to consume one's total being, and perhaps changing to a new area of professional practice (or leave the profession)
	Being part of an acquisition or merger	Learning new ways of working and learning a new organizational culture (this is true especially when a not-for-profit health care organization becomes part of a larger for-profit network)
	Living in a different country or culture	Learning alternative ways of living and working (some nurses may go on medical missions, travel abroad, relocate to a different area, or go to a different location to further their education)
	Finding and maintaining a meaningful balance between family and work	Achieving an effective balance between one's personal and professional lives
	Letting go of ambition by realizing that you do not have to be "the best" or "first," accepting that all persons cannot be the best forever, redirecting energy to other things, and redefining a personal definition of achievement	Acknowledging that "perfection" in nursing is impossible, developing a meaningful professional practice, becoming more involved in things outside of nursing and realizing that others need to be educated to fill nursing positions as you and some of your colleagues consider retirement
	Facing personal upheaval by accepting tragedy as a means for humanization by revealing personal vulnerabilities to others, being authentic, and accepting fate and carrying on	Using personal losses and challenges to connect more effectively with clients, colleagues, and other health team members
	Losing faith in the system by finding meaning in one's life and current work, sponsoring a protégé for a leadership position, finding fulfillment with a current project, achieving new skills, reconnecting with what originally lead you to your area of expertise	Being a mentor to a younger professional nurse, clarifying personal values, and finding joy and meaning with current professional work

Research Brief 18-1

Bondas, T. (2006). Paths to nursing leadership. *Journal of Nursing Management, 14*(5), 332–339.

The investigator sought to discover why nurses applied for mangement positions and decided upon nursing leadership careers. Sixty-eight Finnish nurses participated in the study, which used analytic induction and grounded theory method to identify paths to leadership. Data were collected using an investigator-developed, semistructured, self-reported questionnaire.

Results of the study revealed a variety of reasons and patterns for a nursing leadership career. The four paths identified were the *path of ideals, career path, path of chance,* and *temporary path.*

The *temporary path* resulted when nurses substituted for other nurse leaders, and viewed the experience as a trial to see if a leadership position worked for them. The *path of chance* occurred when either the nurses sought out a leadership position or it was the only available nursing position when they were seeking employment. Nurses following the temporary path or path of choice often had no formal leadership education. The path of chance was a more passive appoach in which the nurses felt that the choices were made by others. Over 50% of the study participants reported taking the path of chance. The *career path* was selected by nurses who used personal power in making the decision to assume a leadership position because they perceived themselves to have personality traits, skills, and previous experiences to offer. They perceived themselves as being very self-directed, wanting desirable daytime hours, and needing to have a less physically demanding job. The *path of ideals* was followed by nurses who had a desire to seek knowledge and education. They engaged in self-reflection and dreamed about making a professional difference. Previous positive and negative experiences with nurse leaders influenced their career decision.

Nurses following the career path and path of ideals were more likely to have formal leadership education. Findings from this study should be viewed with caution because it was conducted in one country, Finland. More research is needed to determine if these paths apply to other nurses, and to identify the effects of the various paths on leadership effectiveness.

 ## KEY LEADERSHIP AND MANAGEMENT SKILLS FOR NURSES

Because of the nature of professional practice, all nurses need to develop leadership skills Nurses use many leadership skills when engaged in the multiple professional nursing roles. Table 18-3 outlines key **leadership and management skills** for nurses. Some of the skills that appear on the table require more attention than can be covered in this chapter, so it may be helpful to consult additional resources.

 ## PROFESSIONAL NURSES AS LEADERS

The professional nursing roles of critical thinker, caregiver, client advocate, change agent, counselor–teacher, coordinator, and colleague require use of many leadership and management skills. Nurses must believe they have personal power to execute each role effectively. Hagberg (1994) proposed that the first step to establishing personal power starts with the perception of being powerless. Feelings of powerlessness occur sometimes when persons encounter new situations. However, as time progresses, all persons (including nurses) develop some power as they succeed in a particular arena. Huston (2008) offered the following 11 strategies for professional nurses to use to build "a personal power base" (pp. 58–61):

1. Become an expert.
2. Find positive role models and ask one of them to serve as a mentor.
3. Develop coalitions and network with other professional nurses.
4. Keep employment options open.

TABLE 18-3

Key Leadership and Management Skills for Nurses

Leadership Skills	Skills for Leadership and Management	Management Skills
Focused and intense approach to work	Expand one's self-awareness	Clarify organizational goals and expectations
Challenge others to expand thinking and actions	Maintain composure and a high energy level when encountering multiple competing demands (stress management)	Use established relationships to influence others in the organization
Deliver compelling messages	Learn from experience	Create a strong organizational culture
Take risks	Seek feedback from a variety of sources	Uses all incentives available to motivate others
Set personal goals	Find common ground with others	See that day-to-day operations are effectively executed
Deep, connected, and emotional involvement with followers	Demonstrate sincere empathy toward others	Set organizational goals
Strong concern and investment with ideas	Make self available to others	Low level of emotional involvement with employees to be fair
See the gestalt of situations	Ability to listen effectively	Concern with results
Inspire others	Express appreciation for the contributions of others toward goals	Strong investment with the organization
Tolerate ambiguity	Abide consistently and constantly to ethics and principles	Staff inpatient and outpatient departments
Tolerate diverse perspectives	Establish trust with all persons	Enhance productivity
	Establish and agree upon goals using collaboration	Budget to meet operations
	Use facts or evidence to clarify expectations rather than assumptions or rumors	Market the organization
	Identify rumors, clarify their truth, and dispel them if false	Reduce risks in the organization
	Display optimism in all situations	Write and deliver employee performance appraisals
	Analyze situations from multiple perspectives to identify issues and concerns	Follow organizational guidelines and procedures
	Network with others to identify issues and concerns that need to be addressed	
	Monitor the impact of change	
	Learn new things quickly	
	Set effective priorities	
	Generate multiple courses of action	
	Take decisive action but know when to change to a different course of action	
	Commit self to effective action plans	
	Attract others to assume leadership or management positions	

Key Leadership and Management Skills for Nurses (Continued)

Leadership Skills	Skills for Leadership and Management	Management Skills
	Share power with followers/ subordinates	
	Form alliances with key players in any given situation	
	Precise and consistent communication	
	Communicate in ways that are acceptable and clear to others	
	Manage resistance	
	Clarify roles of others and encourage them to assume a leadership role	
	Resolve conflicts	
	Motivate others to be their best	
	Manage the vast sea of information	
	Master computers and other high-tech equipment	
	Meet standards of professional nursing practice	
	Work to attain optimal client outcomes	
	Delegate tasks to others	
	Deconstruct 20th-century barriers and structures	
	Recognize future trends that will point to a need to change to meet the needs of the future	
	Celebrate all progress toward change to meet 21st-century health care demands	

Adapted from Blank, W. (2001). *The 108 skills of natural born leaders.* New York: AMACOM; Donnelly, G. (2003). How leaders work: Myths and theories. In Steltzer, T. (Ed.). *Five keys to successful nursing management* (pp. 31–60). Philadelphia: Lippincott; Porter-O'Grady, T., & Malloch, K. (2003). *Quantum leadership: a textbook of new leadership.* Sudbury, MA: Jones and Barlett; McCauley, C., & Van Velsor, E. (2004). *The Center for Creative Leadership handbook of leadership development* (2nd ed.). San Francisco: Jossey-Bass.

5. Develop self-awareness.
6. Keep focused on personal and professional goals.
7. Determine which battles are worth the effort and potential consequences.
8. Take risks, especially when confronted with situations or issues that are incongruent with personal and professional values.
9. Sacrifice some ego.
10. "Work hard and be a team player" (p. 60).
11. "Take care of yourself" (p. 61).

Like Huston (2008), Hagberg (1994) stressed the importance of self-awareness and the value of teamwork when establishing personal power. However, Hagberg proposed that true empowerment does not occur until persons no longer use power by association (hoping the power of strong persons or superiors will be transferred to you) or power by symbols (displaying signs of success such as having an extravagant lifestyle, the newest gadget, or the need to impress others). Empowerment truly occurs when persons have the freedom to be their true authentic selves (power by reflection), live out their life purposes (power by purpose), or have power by gestalt (turning to higher powers without the need for social prominence). Truly empowered persons give power to others by fostering in others their ability to share special gifts and make meaningful contributions to the world (Hagberg; Bass & Riggio, 2005).

Leadership in the Role of Critical Thinker

Most nurses engage in critical thinking as they engage in all aspects of clinical practice. Critical thinking prevents nurses from blindly following physician orders and jumping to conclusions about client care situations. Nurses use critical thinking to analyze situations, identify problems, set priorities, develop multiple possible approaches to a specific situation, and consider the consequences of a strategy before taking action. Therefore, nurses assume the role of critical thinker as they engage in each of the professional roles.

Leadership in the Role of Caregiver

As an empowered professional nurse, the nurse assumes a leadership role as part of an interprofessional team. When driven by the purpose of doing what is in the client's best interest, nurses use power to ensure that client care needs are met. Empowered nurses use a feminine approach to power and empower clients to manage their own health. When nurses understand levels of power, they use power more effectively. Rafael (1996) described three levels of power as it is exercised in caring. The first level, power in ordered caring, has the following characteristics: uses a patriarchal (male supremacy) ideology; fosters separation, strength, and control (esteemed properties of masculinity); relates to having control over others and nature; sustains organizational hierarchies; and is "vested in certain positions and legitimized as authority over nurses" (p. 8). Examples of ordered caring include physician dominance in health care settings or nurses using autocratic methods to delegate tasks to UAP (Standing & Anthony, 2008).

At the second level, assimilated caring, power is gained through "access to male power through assimilation of male characteristics, practices, and values" (Rafael, 1996, p. 12). Assimilated caring is ethically based on "maelstrom ethics," with its emphasis on application of universal principles, such as self-determination, beneficence, and rights-based justice. As client advocates and caregivers, nurses use this power level when manipulating the health care system to get clients access to needed services.

Empowered caring, the third level, is distinguished by equal power and knowledge distribution among all persons regardless of gender, organizational position, social status, and education. A deep respect for others and nature also is a hallmark of empowered caring. Empowered caring recognizes that expertise arises from practice and is closely linked to research. Persons act as colleagues rather than competitors, and all have a commitment to resolving social problems. With empowered caring, all participants in health care situations equally participate in determining mutual goals and become transformed in the relational way of becoming within the therapeutic relationship. Instead of using ethical principles to guide dilemmas, relational ethics within each context are applied (Rafael, 1996, p. 5). Nurses use empowered caring when they incorporate research results into daily clinical practice, share nursing knowledge with others, and treat clients as equal partners when planning and delivering nursing care. Professional nurses cannot effectively promote long-lasting changes in behavior if they wield power over others. Behavioral changes arising from an "empowerment" experience are more likely to be realistic, genuine, and well-integrated and become long-lasting habits.

Nurses use a variety of power sources while engaging in clinical practice in a variety of settings. Expert power is used when nurses bring their specialized knowledge and skills to any practice. Nurses use power based on legitimate right and authority (position power) in daily practice situations. Nurses use referent power (based on identification with the personal qualities of the nurse) to mobilize others to facilitate desired outcomes.

The professional nurse must be an activist in the work setting and in the community while setting an example of what it means to live a healthy lifestyle and be a health advocate for all persons. When assuming the activist role, the professional nurse exercises all power bases to improve the quality of and access to health care.

Leadership in the Role of a Client Advocate

When assuming the role of client advocates, nurses use power on the client's behalf. The concept of client advocacy has many different meanings. The following discussion attempts to clarify the concept of client advocacy by explaining its key attributes of mutuality, facilitation, and protection.

Meaning of Advocacy

Nurses who believe in advocacy share the following beliefs:

1. Clients have a right to a nurse–client relationship based on mutuality, shared respect, consideration of information and feelings, and full participation when solving problems regarding their health and health care needs.
2. Nurses have the responsibility to ensure that clients have access to appropriate health care services to meet their health care needs.
3. Clients are responsible for their own health.
4. Nurses are responsible for mobilizing and facilitating the strengths of clients in achieving the highest level of possible health.

An advocate "supports or defends someone or something and recommends or pleads in another's behalf … [and] works to change the power structure so that a situation will be improved" (Douglass, 1988, p. 259).

Nurses cannot be effective advocates unless they believe fully in their strengths. Power is shared among nurses and the persons they serve. Frequently, nurses serve as resource persons for clients, subordinates, or colleagues. Because advocacy requires conviction, it is important for the nurse to overcome personal feelings and beliefs about nurses' "powerlessness" to take the first step in the process of empowerment (Richardson, 1992, p. 38).

Key Attribute: Mutuality

Evidence is abundant that decisions made when all involved persons are actively engaged in the process have an increased chance of success. Nurses have expertise to facilitate health and healing. Clients are the experts of their bodies, minds, spirits, and life situations along with the knowledge of how to best control them. Decisions affecting clients must be made by the client, with full informational support, empathy, and respect from nurses.

Mutuality means that the nurse and the client collaborate to fully identify the client's health situation (strengths and weaknesses), agree upon needed changes, set goals, explore alternative ways to achieve the mutually agreed-on goals, and work together to meet them. At this stage, the advocate verifies that technical and informational resources are available to the client. If needed, the nurse assists the client in gaining access to the needed health care services and additional resources.

Two essential elements of mutuality are respect and sharing. Respect means that the client has the right to make decisions and find meaning in them. Sharing means that the client openly communicates information, needs, and expectations while the nurse freely provides information and services in an empathetic manner. Empathy is important to understand in the advocate role because "empathy involves feelings of mutuality with another" (Olsen, 1991, p. 67). Olsen also said that "empathy can exist simply because both parties share humanity" and that "justification of another's humanity would make little sense in the way that justifications of another's actions or feelings do" (p. 70). Thus, empathized humanity is the crux of the nurse–client relationship and the advocate's role.

The most important factor in mutuality is that the nurse and the client are seen as equally able and responsible for outcomes. Their areas of expertise vary, but their authority and significance in the relationship are equal. Each person's potential can be more fully realized in a relationship characterized by mutuality.

Key Attribute: Facilitation

Facilitation in the advocacy process requires that the advocate take responsibility to make sure the client has all the necessary information to make informed decisions and to support clients in the decisions they make (Snowball, 1996). King (1984, p. 17) suggested that an effective way for the nurse to facilitate growth in self and others is through values clarification; that is, to help the client think through issues and develop a personal value system that aids decision making. Hames and Joseph (1980) suggested that facilitation is enhanced by helping clients understand the tasks before them, ensuring that they experience some success when they are trying to accomplish something, providing an environment that is conducive to learning (one of trust and respect), and offering information and emotional supports.

Key Attribute: Protection

Client advocacy has been associated with an assumption that nurses have a responsibility to protect their clients. Since Nightingale, nurses have been called upon to protect clients from harm. In practice, nurses have been called upon to examine their roles in protecting the client's right to live or die. Bandman and Bandman (1995) reported that nurses often are caught in ethical dilemmas when working with persons who are terminally ill or hopelessly disabled, especially when physicians or family members want to force treatments on clients or withold livesaving measures. Bandman and Bandman concluded that morality tends to support a client's right to live over letting others decide that the client's life should be terminated. In addition, there may be cases in which the nurse can legitimately protect a client's wish to end life.

Perhaps the greatest need for nurses to act as protectors occurs when nurses identify the need to change a condition or situation in which clients are given inadequate care or the environment poses some hazard. As client advocates, professional nurses assume leadership roles in promoting access to health care for all, preserving the rights of persons to make health care decisions, protecting clients from situations that may result in injury, monitoring client care quality, and intervening in a nonadversarial manner when harmful (or potentially harmful) situations are observed. The nurse may have to take risks to protect clients. When nurses defend patient rights, they act as client advocates even if they must engage in an adversarial struggle against the forces of institutional oppression, including those arising from cost containment or discrimination.

Challenges and Rewards of the Client Advocate Role

For nurses to effectively carry out the role of client advocate, the health care delivery system must be restructured, especially in terms of professional nurse positions within health care organizations. In many delivery systems, nurse advocacy efforts are challenged by lack of equality with administration or physicians. A recent trend toward interprofessional education of health care team members has resulted in more equality and responsibility. Each discipline assumes full responsibility and accountability for its own practice. However, until health care organizations eliminate hierarchical approaches to authority, nursing will continue to occupy a position of disadvantage.

Thus, nurses attempting to operate as client advocates in a hierarchical system need to learn how to negotiate the hierarchical situations and to develop strategies that promote the significance of advocacy work. If nurses perceive the need for equal authority to fulfill the advocate's role as important, then they must demonstrate the effectiveness of the advocacy work (such as improved client outcomes, improved service, and affordable cost). Because many nurses entered the profession because they possess compassion, they

Ways for Health Team to Promote Self-Care in Clients

DISPLAY 18-2

1. Development of understanding of clients' responses to various threats to health and development of strategies to respond effectively to these responses
2. Refinement and further development of health promotion and illness prevention abilities, as well as restorative abilities
3. Re-evaluation of belief systems about the independent versus dependent role of clients and self
4. Assumption of collaborative responsibility for monitoring the effectiveness of the delivery system, as well as of independent responsibility for evaluating the effectiveness of the nursing interventions in responding to the client's health needs
5. Implementation of interdisciplinary dialogue, with all professional workers sharing equal responsibility and authority for meeting clients' health needs
6. Provision of opportunity for all members of the team to evaluate effectiveness in collaboration, thereby avoiding the establishment of adversarial relationships

become satisfied with their careers when they effectively execute the role of client advocate.

Emphasis should be placed on the knowledge and skills needed to assist clients to increase competence in assuming responsibility for their health. In such a restructured system, nurses and other health team members need to be supported as they use ways outlined in Display 18-2 to promote client self-care.

The challenge to professional nursing is to restructure the work in order to facilitate the role of client advocate. Display 18-3 lists the duties of a nurse advocate. By gaining acceptance of, demonstrating the effectiveness of, and placing emphasis on these key

Duties of Nurse Serving as an Advocate

DISPLAY 18-3

1. Interact with the client in a manner and quantity that permits:
   a. Exploration of the client's personal responses to health or threats to health
   b. Evaluation of the environmental circumstances in which the client exists
   c. Identification of strengths and limitations
   d. Identification of resources perceived to be needed
   e. Clear allocation of responsibilities of client and nurse, which ensures the client's assumption of responsibility for health and the nurse's assumption of responsibility for the informational and interactional supports needed
2. Prepare for and implement teaching programs needed by the client
3. Update technical skills as new therapeutic techniques and equipment are made available for health care
4. Discuss beliefs about the client's abilities with professional peers in an effort to evaluate own values about independence and dependence in various states of health
5. Update nursing care plans in an effort to evaluate outcomes of nursing care
6. Participate in nursing research as a consumer and assist in nursing studies conducted in the health care setting
7. Identify all units of the delivery system that need to be involved in the client's care
8. Coordinate efforts of the multiple health care workers involved in the client's care
9. Assess the adequacy of efforts of all workers involved in care, according to the client's stated needs
10. Resolve conflicts that might occur in relation to advocacy efforts for the client by:
    a. Respecting the position of all involved
    b. Gathering data that describe the whole system of client–environment
    c. Promoting expression of conflicts
    d. Participating in the problem-solving process
    e. Allowing the client to make decisions based on data, rather than on advice from others
11. Recognize and show appreciation for the contributions of team members to the client's health care
12. Periodically discuss and evaluate the quality of the interactions of health care team members and evaluate own interpersonal effectiveness with the client and team members

behaviors and duties of professional nurses, the role of client advocacy for professional nurses becomes legitimate and solidified.

To restructure their working conditions, nurses must be advocates for professional colleagues and for themselves. Chapters 7 and 10 suggest that an effective method for gaining control over practice is to develop and use evidence as a basis for recommending changes. Evidence, rather than opinion, strenghens the need for change. Advocacy for anyone is more effective if the advocate is working from a position of strength, armed with solid evidence and the steadfast belief that what one is trying to accomplish is vital to high-quality client care.

Leadership in the Role of Counselor-Teacher

Professional nurses provide emotional support and education to clients, which has been explained in Chapter 4 and Chapter 17. Along with providing client support and education, nurse leaders teach and counsel colleagues. Most nurse practice acts contain a clause that states that professional nurses teach others in any nursing care activities. Most institutions set basic standards for educating UAP in collaboration with nurses. As direct supervisors, professional nurses assess educational needs of staff and design educational programs. Nurses serve as role models for all health team members when they keep the client at the center of health care delivery. When nurses diligently follow care standards and take time with clients, other team members acknowledge the key contributions they make in health care.

As members of a nursing care team, professional nurses frequently find other members of the team experiencing distress. Nurses who spend time listening to the concerns of team members offer support to them. Because of their professional knowledge and therapeutic communication skills, some nurses informally counsel coworkers and refer them to community health resources as indicated. For example, a registered nurse (RN) finds a UAP crying in the nurse's lounge instead of performing delegated tasks. The RN takes time to listen as the UAP shares information that she discovered a breast lump during her morning shower and just knows that it must be cancer. The RN shares her knowledge about various breast tumors and available treatment centers, and helps the UAP make an appointment for treatment. The RN accompanies the UAP to a breast care center, where a needle biopsy is performed and the tumor is found to be benign.

Leadership in the Role of Coordinator

Nurses frequently find themselves in the role of coordinator. Nurses coordinate the efforts of others to provide safe, effective client care. Nurses assume responsibility for delivering basic client care, executing physician orders, and promoting optimal client outcomes. When competing demands are placed on the nurse's time, he or she frequently makes decisions as to which activity has priority over another.

The role of coordinator becomes more apparent when professional nurses assume administrative positions. Managers assume responsibility for using people, supplies, money, and systems to provide high-quality, cost-effective care. They coordinate the efforts of others so that the job is performed efficiently. To meet the challenges of management, nurse managers use a variety of skills. Key skills used by nurse managers are people skills, budgeting and financing skills, information technology skills (see Chapter 15), and quality management skills (Chapter 19). The following discussion focuses on interpersonal, budgeting, and financial skills for effective coordination of resources for client care.

Interpersonal Skills for Nursing Management and Supervision

Effective managers strive to bring out the best in their employees while providing them with required resources and support to provde effective client care. Nurse managers need to set expectations for their departments and communicate them effectively. Besides effectively communicating with staff, nurse managers must also interact with administrators, other department managers, physicians, and other interprofessional team members. Strategies for developing helpful and healing relationships outlined in Chapter 4 serve as the basis for developing effective communication with staff and all members of the interdisciplinary health care team.

Empowering Team Members: Decisions by Consensus

When decisions need to be made related to problems or changes in practice, decisions by consensus rather than those made by an individual tend to work better. A major tenet of **transformational leadership** is to inspire and empower others to achieve the best possible future state (Burns, 1978, 2003). In any clinical situation, all persons within it have a unique perspective and a specific skill set that must be used to facilitate optimal outcomes. Sharing power and responsibility for outcomes is facilitated when all stakeholders (persons who are affected by a decision) participate in the process.

Consensus provides an avenue for participatory decision making because it relies on all parties sharing key information, generating alternatives, listening to the views of others with respect, and taking time to explore all options and their consequences. In most situations, generating several options for action may be more effective than generating an exhaustive list. Singular solutions are rare in human health concerns or in work situations. Although reaching consensus takes more time than other decision-making processes, persons making the decision have a commitment to execute it (Porter-O'Grady & Malloch, 2007; Burns, 1978; McCauley & Van Velsor, 2004).

For example, because of low client census on a hospital unit, nurses have been sent home on a rotating basis as a cost-saving measure. If accrued, the nurses may use vacation time. The policy states that nurses each take a turn being sent home. A group of older nurses with more seniority (and vacation time) collaborate with younger nurses who have recently been hired. The nurses reach a consensus that the nurses with more vacation time will go home twice for every one time that a new nurse is sent home. With their revised plan fully designed, all the nurses meet with the nurse manager, who agrees to its implementation. In the process of working together to attain a common goal, these nurses developed more meaningful working relationships and feel more connected to each other.

Connectedness underlies the process of consensus. When a team works together for a common goal (e.g., optimal client outcomes), team cohesion is enhanced when decisions are made by consensus. Consensus means that everyone will try to implement the decision even though each person may not agree fully with it. All persons participating in the process feel that they played a significant role in decision making, especially if participants engaged in meaningful dialogue (Wesorick & Shiparski, 1997).

All persons in consensus equally share accountability and responsibility for the quality of the decisions made. However, when hierarchical relationships are established in the health care setting, health care providers (including some nurses) tend to use command styles rather than participatory styles when coordinating efforts of the health team (Porter-O'Grady & Malloch, 2007; Standing & Anthony, 2008) or attempting to influence client decision making (Taylor, Pickens, & Geden, 1989). Participatory decision making is a hallmark of transformational leadership (Burns, 2003; Porter-O'Grady & Malloch). Common themes and meaning between the characteristics of transformational leaders and the attributes of women who are constructed knowers are described in Table 18-4. Barker and Young (1994) indicated that constructed knowers participate in a network or web that includes caring, moral responsibility, positive self-esteem, and use of intuition and logic. Both transformational leaders and women seek to establish an environment that generates empowerment in self and/or others (Barker & Young, p. 20). Decisions made through consensus result in commitment by all parties who made the decisions to execute them. As a change agent, the professional nurse collaborates with clients and team members to identify when and what changes are needed for better health and positive work environments.

TABLE 18-4

Transformational Leadership and Feminine Attributes

Transformational Leaders	Constructed Female Attributes
Relationships engaged	Relationships networked
Individual consideration	Caring
Leader as moral agent: values and needs	Moral responsibility
Mutual dependence/trust	Reciprocity and cooperation
Communication	Integration of voices
Builder of self-esteem	Positive self-esteem
Listens to intuition, balances with analysis	Use of intuition and logic
Empowerment	Empowerment

Source: Barker, A. M., & Young, C. E. (1994). Transformational leadership: The feminist connection in postmodern organizations. *Holistic Nursing Practice, 9,* 20. Used with permission of the publisher.

Team-Building Skills

Positive work environments are enhanced when all workers display commitment to the work and work together as a cohesive team (Porter-O'Grady & Malloch, 2007; Wesorick & Shiparski, 1997). Effective teamwork enables all team members to use their skills. Effective teams have members who collaborate to set visions and goals while identifying how they will work together to attain them. Effective teamwork balances unity with diversity. If a group is too unified, new ideas and divergent thinking may become stifled. If a group has too much diversity, conflicts may impede progress toward attaining mutually agreed-upon goals (McCauley & Van Velsor, 2004).

Strategic Planning

A **strategic plan** provides a long-term road map for ensuring the future of an organization. Organizations must constantly change to keep pace with the ever-changing world. Strategic plan development requires a detailed analysis of internal and external factors affecting offered services. Strategic plan time frames typically range from 3 to 10 years (Calhoun, 2006; Marquis & Huston, 2009).

The strategic-planning process typically begins with a thorough analysis of the current situation followed by identification of an ideal future state. Organizational vision, mission, and philosophy are reviewed and revised as needed. Then the organization identifies goals to fulfill its vision and mission. Once the strategic goals have been finalized, the organization outlines a deployment plan. The deployment strategy includes providing a culture, structures, and resources for plan implementation. Some organizations manage the plan using a strategic planning matrix that includes departmental goals (broadly written statement depicting a desired state), objectives (things to complete within a specific time frame), measurements or benchmarks (targeted dates and data collection to verify objective attainment), target date (deadline), and persons responsible for achievement of each goal (Calhoun, 2006). Table 18-5 outlines considerations for strategic plan development and deployment.

Strategic plans work best when organizations hold individuals accountable for successful implementation. To track progress toward meeting objectives outlined in a strategic plan, a means to evaluate progress must be devised. Some organizations opt for the use of interlocking scorecards to ensure that strategic objectives are accomplished by all departments. Balanced scorecards collect and analyze data regarding the following four aspects of organizational performance: (1) financial, (2) customers, (3) processes, and (4) learning and growth. Balanced scorecards may be completed at the organizational,

TABLE 18-5

Components of the Key Elements of a Strategic Plan

Direction Statement	Strategic Objectives	Strategic Priority Issues
Mission statement: purpose and why	Statements used to measure performance on the direction statements	Broad issues that should be addressed to meet a desired future state
Vision statement: desired future state	Scorecard that measures success on meeting intentions	Internal changes to continue to hold a competitive advantage over competitors
Business definition: clear and concise presentation of products, offered services, target consumers, technology, distribution of products, and service and geographical area served	Frequently addresses performance on profitability, shareholder value (if a for-profit), market position, services, quality, and innovations	Target areas upon which to develop measurable action plans
Competitive advantage: what makes you better than other organizations offering the same or similar services		
Core competencies: key systems, assets, intellectual prowess, programs, and special skills to enhance the competitive advantage		
Values/beliefs: Philosophy and values that guide organizational behavior and processes		

Adapted from Fogg, C. D. (1999). *Implementing your strategic plan.* New York: AMACOM. Marquis, B. & Huston, C. (2009). *Leadership roles & management functions in nursing theory & application.* (6th Ed.). Philadelphia: Lippincott, Williams & Wilkins.

departmental, and individual employee levels. Balanced scorecards typically contain the measurement methods and action steps outlined by the strategic plan. When the annual action steps do not happen as outlined by the strategic plan, a detailed analysis to determine why this occurred takes place. If results indicate that step failure was a result of unpredictable events (such as a major economic downturn), the organization reviews and revises the strategic plan appropriately. However, if the analysis reveals that the action steps were not executed because of managerial inaction, the organization may demote or terminate the manager (Calhoun, 2006; Marquis & Huston, 2009).

Budgeting Skills

To implement a personal or organizational mission, resources must be acquired, mobilized, and used. Human and material resources are required to provide health care services. Viability of a health care organization (large medical center to the smallest office or clinic) relies on effective use of human and material resources.

Budgeting serves as a process to plan for operations required to attain material and human resources to accomplish an organizational (or personal) mission—for example, acquiring the resources needed to go to school required planning, determining the amount of money needed to finance educational costs, and developing a plan to verify that all personal responsibilities could be met. Likewise, an organization must be certain that it has the capital, equipment, and people to meet its mission effectively. The planning phase of the budgeting process is not an exact science, but rather a process in which nurse managers look at the current direction of health care, anticipate what future services may be needed, and make decisions based on sound business principles and education. The staffing budget projects the amount of money and the number of nursing personnel needed to provide safe, effective client care. Nurse managers use critical thinking skills when developing departmental budgets. The budget is determined for a 12-month time frame and includes costs for staff (staff salaries and fringe benefits), client care (supplies and equipment), and environmental maintenance. At times nurse managers also submit budgets for capital expenditures along with expected revenue (Marquette, Dunham-Taylor, & Pinczuk, 2006; Marquis & Huston, 2009). Capital expenditures include material resources that are expensive and have a projected lifespan (e.g., cardiac monitors, computers). The supply budget consists of inexpensive items that are used for a short time (e.g., syringes, dressings, and office supplies).

Once the budget is approved by a governing body (e.g., board of directors), nurse managers compare actual spending to the projected amounts outlined in budget reports. Periodic review of reports enables nurse managers to monitor resource utilization and control excessive spending. Nurse managers must account for budgeting variances. Simply, a budget variance occurs when there is a difference between estimated and actual costs, revenue, or activity. For example, more money was spent on nurses' salaries than projected on a cardiac unit. The nurse manager must discover why this occurred and then justify the reason for the variance. Sometimes reasons may be beyond the manager's control (Marquette et al., 2006; Marquis & Huston, 2009). For example, a nurse manager identifies the reasons for staff overtime but discovers that unit census was above projections because of increased numbers of invasive cardiac procedures due to a new staff cardiologist. If the overtime was the result of ineffective delegation of tasks to UAP, then the manager must submit an action plan to remedy the situation.

Staffing

Seeing that enough nurses are available to deliver client care seems to be one of the most challenging tasks for nurse managers. The **staffing** process involves finding qualified persons to fill positions, and proving to the finance department how many persons are needed to provide quality nursing care. Many staffing plans use the full-time equivalent (FTE) model to develop staffing plans. A FTE is defined as a person who would work 2,080 hours annually (if no vacations, holidays, or sick days were taken). The following formula is used to determine the number of FTEs:

$$\frac{\text{Number of hours worked per shift} \times \text{Number of shifts worked per week}}{40 \text{ hours}}$$

When nurses work less than 40 hours per week, the nurse manager must hire additional nurses to fill the gap in settings that provide services 24 hours a day, 7 days a week. Along with productive employee hours (hours actually spent working), managers must budget for nonproductive hours such as vacation, jury duty, holidays, education time, and other benefits (Marquette et al., 2006; Marquis & Huston, 2009).

To determine the daily staffing requirements, the nurse manager must consider client census, client acuity, and the number of nursing care hours needed for each client. To accomplish staffing projections, nurses calculate the nursing hours per patient day (NHPPD). The number of NHPPD varies across nursing units, with intensive care nursing units having more required hours of nursing care than a short-stay surgical unit. To determine daily staffing needs, the unit manager multiplies the average daily census times the NHPPD. With daily census fluctuations, some nurse managers prefer to use a staffing matrix, which is a staffing plan based on the number of clients needing nursing care. The matrix also presents a ratio of RNs, licensed practical/vocational nurses, UAP, and unit secretary/clerks for each shift (Marquette et al., 2006; Marquis & Huston, 2009).

Because nursing care needs cannot always be effectively predicted, nurse managers build overtime expenses into the staffing budget. Prudent nurse managers realize that in health care settings, staff workloads and the timing of essential nursing tasks cannot be predicted accurately. The following examples describe the unpredictable nature of acute care nursing and result in overtime: (1) a client may have a medical emergency as nurses are changing shifts, (2) a nursing unit could receive unexpected multiple admissions within a short time, (3) a family emergency may require a staff member to leave work, or (4) a staff member may experience exposure to a health hazard or sustain a work-related injury.

Marketing Skills

Many nurses find themselves **marketing** the facility (advertising and bringing clients to the facility) in which they work and/or marketing the profession. Goals of marketing include increasing volume, maximizing client satisfaction, and improving the quality of life for the community. The steps of the marketing process mirror the steps of nursing process, starting with assessing the current situation. Considerations for a marketing assessment include listing services offered, and assessing the community served by the facility. The next step is selecting strategies to inform potential clients about the organization and its services. Sometimes, health care organizations have marketing budgets that nurses can use. Marketing strategies are outlined in Table 18-6. Of all the strategies outlined in the table, personal recommendation tends to be the most effective (Hunt, 2003).

Leadership in the Role of Change Agent

One constant in the natural world and health care is **change**. When persons are actively involved in designing and implementing change, the change is usually sustained. Henriksen, Keyes, Stevens, and Clancy (2006) defined transformational change as the process of reinventing an organization or a single work unit to improve performance, thereby enabling it to respond more effectively to external environmental changes and forces. As

TABLE 18-6

Marketing Strategies for Nurses

Strategy	Description	Expense
Personal recommendation	Word-of-mouth compliment	None
Newspaper advertisement	Print ad	Rates depend on circulation of the newspaper
Radio or television advertisement	Broadcast message	Free for a public service announcement; charge rates vary
Printed materials	Brochures, fact sheets, catalogs	Printing costs Free distribution if volunteer time Mailing costs Fee for distribution racks housed in hotels, restaurants or businesses
Community outreach	Speaking engagements, health screenings at health fairs or contact agencies where potential customers may be	Free if services volunteered Work release time for employees Cost for health screening supplies, props, and printed materials
Introductory offers	Health promotion classes on a trial basis Reduced cost for a new service	Costs of running program and delivering services
Traditional sales call	Sell health-related services to other companies	Salesperson salary, supplies, and fringe benefits

Adapted from Hunt (2003a). Marketing your facility. In T. Stelzer (ed.). *Five keys to successful nursing management* (pp. 276–286). Philadelphia: Lippincott Williams & Wilkins.

health care organizations look for ways to continuously improve the quality and safety of health care, they seek ways to streamline work processes and to use resources more efficiently. Some persons find moving from a current, comfortable state (or process) distressing, whereas others find it exciting. The professional nurse confronts change on a daily basis. As change agents, nurses steer change while helping themselves and other cope with it.

Organizational change requires resources and energy (Perlman & Takacs, 1990). Change has an emotional meaning for people and often is associated with feelings of loss or pain (Davis, 1991). Based on the Kübler-Ross model of death and dying, Perlman and Takacs (1990) proposed a 10-stage model to explain the psychological problems associated with change, the signs and symptoms of each stage, and nursing interventions to help others grow during the change process (Table 18-7).

In another model, Carnall (1990, pp. 141–146) proposed five steps in coping with change.

1. Stage 1: Denial of the validity of new ideas
2. Stage 2: Defense (experiencing depression and frustration)
3. Stage 3: Discarding (acknowledging change as inevitable or necessary)
4. Stage 4: Adaptation (feeling anger)
5. Stage 5: Internalization

Bridges (2003) approached change from the perspective of psychological adaptation. Unlike other approaches to change, he proposed that transitions start with endings and end with beginnings. He acknowledges that during any change, people enter a period of uncertainty (the neutral zone) when they fail to understand fully the meaning of and their role in implementing the change.

The Perlman and Takacs, Carnall, and Bridges models of change are compared in Table 18-8. The models address various psychological responses experienced by persons when confronted with change. Before change can be internalized, persons tend to progress through various stages of acceptance. Pritchett and Pound (1995) suggested that, as persons progress through the various stages of acceptance of changes, they frequently make several mistakes when coping with organizational change (Display 18-4).

Team Roles in the Change Process
Roles of the Professional Nurse Change Agent
Based on a comparative analysis of the literature, Wooten and White (1989) identified five basic change roles: (1) educator/trainer, (2) model, (3) researcher/theoretician, (4) technical expert, and (5) resource linker. The **change agent** (the person who brings about a change) must model appropriate behaviors in an atmosphere of trust and openness, accept responsibility for getting data in an appropriate manner, provide skills and expertise, and link needed resources in ways that make the intervention effective. The selection and timing of particular roles depend on the specific needs of the situation.
Roles of the Client System
Effective change depends on the client system assuming various roles. Wooten and White (1989) also described four basic roles of the client system: (1) resource provider, (2) supporter/advocate, (3) information supplier, and (4) participant. The client system provides effort, time, and money resources; advocates the change; provides information involving self and others; and participates in the change process. It is crucial that the change agent and the client collaborate to promote effective change.
Mutual Roles
Wooten and White (1989, p. 657) indicated that "mutual role enactment is at the heart of the change process." The mutual roles include (1) problem solver, (2) diagnostician, (3) learner, and (4) monitor. Instead of investing the change agent alone with the responsibility for the entire change process, this model focuses on joint responsibility and action.

TABLE 18-7

Growing with Change: The Emotional Voyage of the Change Process

Charted Summary

Phase	Characteristics/Symptoms	Interventions
1. Equilibrium	High energy level; state of emotional and intellectual balance; sense of inner peace with personal and professional goals in sync	Make employees aware of changes in the environment that will have impact on the status quo
2. Denial	Energy is drained by the defense mechanism of rationalizing a denial of the reality of the change. Employees experience negative changes in physical health, emotional balance, logical thinking patterns, and normal behavior patterns	Employ active listening skills (e.g., being empathic, nonjudgmental, using reflective listening techniques). Nurturing behavior, avoiding isolation, and offering stress management workshops also will help
3. Anger	Energy is used to ward off and actively resist the change by blaming others. Frustration, anger, rage, envy, and resentment become visible	Recognize the symptoms; legitimize employees' feelings and verbal expressions of anger, rage, envy, and resentment. Active listening, assertiveness, and problem-solving skills are needed by managers. Employees need to probe within for the source of their anger
4. Bargaining	Energy is used in an attempt to eliminate the change. Talk is about "if only" Others try to solve the problem "Bargains" are unrealistic and designed to compromise the change out of existence	Search for real needs/problems and bring them into the open. Explore ways of achieving desired changes through conflict management skills and win–win negotiation skills
5. Chaos	Diffused energy, feeling of powerlessness, insecurity, sense of disorientation; loss of identity and direction; no sense of grounding or meaning; breakdown of value system and belief; defense mechanisms begin to lose usefulness and meaning	Quiet time for reflection; listening skills; inner search for both employee and organization identity and meaning; approval for being in state of flux
6. Depression	No energy left to produce results. Former defense mechanisms no longer operable. Self-pity, remembering past, expressions of sorrow, feeling nothingness, and emptiness	Provide necessary information in a timely fashion. Allow sorrow and pain to be expressed openly. Exhibit long-term patience; take one step at a time as employees learn to let go
7. Resignation	Energy expended in passively accepting change; lack of enthusiasm	Expect employees to be accountable for reactions to behavior. Allow them to move at their own pace
8. Openness	Availability to renewed energy; willingness to expend energy on what has been assigned to individual	Patiently explain again, in detail, the desired change
9. Readiness	Willingness to expend energy in exploring new events; reunification of intellect and emotions begins	Assume a directive management style: assign tasks, monitor tasks and results so as to provide direction and guidelines
10. Re-emergence	Rechanneled energy produces feelings of empowerment, and employees become more proactive. Growth and commitment are reborn. Employee initiates projects and ideas. Career questions are answered	Mutual answering of questions; redefinition of career, mission, and culture; mutual understanding of role and identity; employee's action based on own decisions

From Perlman, D., & Takacs, G.J. (1990, April). The ten stages of change. *Nursing Management, 21*, 34. Used with permission of the publisher.

TABLE 18-8

Comparison of Theoretical Stages in Coping with Change

Perlman & Takacs	Carnall	Bridges
Equilibrium		*Endings* Disengagement Disidentification Disenchantment
Denial	Denial	*The Neutral Zone* Disequilibrium
Anger	Defense	Disidentification
Bargaining		
Chaos		
Depression		
Resignation	Discarding	
Openness	Adaptation	*New Beginnings* Re-engagement
Readiness		Realignment
Re-emergence	Internalization	Reidentification

Problem solving involves identifying a problem, generating alternatives, and testing assumptions. Diagnosis necessitates sensitivity to issues in the relationship. Learning includes knowledge, skills, or new attitudes, and monitoring involves "remain[ing] aware of alternatives, ascertain[ing] the consequences of action, gaug[ing] the effectiveness of the change effort and relationship at each stage of the intervention" (Wooten & White, p. 657). Each role can be adopted independently or simultaneously.

Selecting a Change Strategy

As change agents, professional nurses select specific change strategies to use in practice situations. Different strategies work best with different types of change. Change strategies are classified into the following six categories: empirical-rational, normative-reeducative, power-coercive, facilitative, reeducative, and persuasive and power. The following discussion defines each major category and supplies the reader with examples of how they are used in professional nursing practice when working with clients or other health team members.

Empirical-Rational Strategies

The empirical-rational category assumes that persons will act in a way that is rational and in their own self-interest. These strategies focus on educating a person about the

---

Mistakes Made When Coping with Organizational Change   DISPLAY 18-4

1. Assuming that the role of management is to keep them comfortable
2. Expecting another or others to reduce their stress
3. Aiming for a low-stress work setting
4. Attempting to control the uncontrollable factors
5. Refusing to abandon the expendable
6. Facing the future with fear
7. Choosing the wrong battles to fight
8. Unplugging psychologically from their jobs
9. Avoiding acceptance of new assignments

available options, assuming that the individual will change behavior because he or she knows that the new behavior will be beneficial and desirable.

For example, inservice education may include a demonstration of the latest techniques available for a particular task, with the expectation that nurses will apply that knowledge to improve their care of clients. Another example is nurses who do not take breaks during work hours and have an increased chance of making an error in client care. Nurses who attend a staff inservice on the need to take breaks during their shifts may incorporate this idea into practice. However, if the nurses have the deep personal value that clients come first, they may not take breaks. Thus, sometimes the empirical-rational strategy may be ineffective in establishing and maintaining a desired change, especially if the change encompasses changing personal values and beliefs (Cummings & McLennan, 2005).

Normative-Reeducative Strategies

The normative-reeducative category assumes that sociocultural norms are fundamental to a person's behavior. In addition to rationality and intelligence, change must involve modification of attitudes, values, skills, and significant relationships. Thus, when working with clients and colleagues, the change process must be based on mutuality and collaboration. This allows for the problem solving and personal growth believed necessary to promote effective change.

For example, a young woman who needs to have surgery for ovarian cancer refuses to have it because of her firm belief that the purpose of a woman's life is to bear children. When listening to the client, the RN discovers that the client had a childless aunt who received the undivided attention of her husband, had a lavish lifestyle, and was considered by the family to be spoiled and selfish. Once widowed, the aunt became very demanding of other family members. The client expresses fear that she will become like her childless aunt. The nurse acknowledges the fear, and the two of them engage in meaningful dialogue about the purpose of life. The young woman's attitude changes, and she consents to having the surgery.

Power-Coercive Strategies

The third category, power-coercive strategies, is based on the use of power. It is believed that despite the need for knowledge and for modification of attitudes and values, change will occur only when it is supported by power that is based on potential punishment and rewards. This rationale is the basis for much political action, and it may imply the use of legitimate channels of authority or violent, nonsanctioned methods (Chin, 1976). This strategy effects change more quickly than do other strategies, but the change that results usually is not lasting (Haffer, 1986).

For example, a professional nurse working with a particular UAP notices that every time they work together, the UAP fails to complete delegated tasks in a timely manner. Because the professional nurse supervises the UAP, the nurse initiates the first step of a progressive discipline process, which is documenting the conversation held with the UAP about not fulfilling job responsibilities. For a month, the UAP completes delegated tasks quickly, but returns to previous habits thereafter.

Facilitative Strategies

Facilitative strategies are used to make clients and others aware of the availability of help in sufficient detail and clarity so that they know exactly how to access and use assistance. Facilitative strategies are appropriate when there is openness to change. Examples of this type of strategy are (1) simplifying data, providing feedback, and providing other necessary tools to help others recognize a problem; (2) providing multiple potential solutions to the problem; and (3) involving others in the decision-making process. These strategies produce greater commitment to change, but the change agent must be sure that there are sufficient resources, commitment, and capability to maintain the change after leaving the situation. For example, a nursing research consultant is hired to help staff nurses develop and implement evidence-based practice or nursing research on hospital nursing units. The consultant meets with interested nurses every other month, helps them develop research projects, and coaches the nurses on project implementation. When the consulting contract ends, the nurse researcher contacts doctorally prepared nursing faculty from a local nursing program to continue helping the nurses execute and publish their research projects. The unit nurses select the faculty with whom they will work to finish their projects.

Reeducative Strategies

Reeducative strategies are based on empirical-rational theory but are different because the person needs to acquire new skills and knowledge. They also facilitate change when resistance is prevalent, when persons have inaccurate information, when the change involved is a radical departure from past practices, and when the person lacks confidence about the ability to implement the new practices. However, reeducative strategies work to bring about change only when there is a strongly felt need and a strong motivation to change.

Reeducative strategies work slowly, so they are feasible only when time is not a pressing factor. Examples of reeducative strategies are creating awareness that a problem exists by indicating how much better things could be when symptoms can be connected with causes, and outlining the benefits of new practices. Reeducative strategies work well when persons receive a new diagnosis of a chronic illness, such as diabetes or renal disease, that requires special self-monitoring and compliance to strict regimens for optimal outcomes. Reeducative strategies heighten awareness of a problem and possible solutions, but they fail to increase the motivation to change.

Benefits of Change Strategies

Professional nurses who have knowledge of the basic types of change strategies may select the best way to proceed when confronted with situations where change is indicated. Different persons vary in responses to the various presented change strategies. Sometimes the power-coercive strategy may be met with lots of resistance, and other times it may be very successful. The professional nurse also must assess the ability of individuals to cope with change and how many changes are occurring simultaneously. When one strategy fails, the professional nurse can try another one to bring about the desired change. Sometimes, the professional nurse must prioritize changes for clients, health team members, or organizations to avoid extreme psychological distress with too much change in too little time.

Leadership in the Role of Colleague

Whether working with individual clients, client groups, or other health team members, or across the organization, the professional nurse must establish collegial partnerships with others. Collegial partnerships enable equality among all persons involved in an interaction. Over time, health team members develop collegial partnerships with each other in which each person acknowledges the contributions and skills that the other members bring to client service.

A collegial partnership is a relationship in which all persons view each other as providing equal contributions to a mutually defined outcome. Collaboration serves as the foundation for professional partnerships in health care. Collaboration begins when individuals realize that they need others to attain an envisioned goal (Porter-O'Grady & Malloch, 2007; Wesorick & Shiparski, 1997; Wilson & Porter-O'Grady, 1999). Collegial partnerships may occur between nurses and clients, nurses and UAP, nurses and other nurses, nurses and physicians, nurses and other health team members, and even nurses and a community group. Partnerships may be short-lived or last for an extended time. When working in partnership with others, various partners assume leadership when an issue arises that falls within the realm of his or her expertise. The development of clinical paths or client care maps within health care organizations represents one outcome of interdisciplinary collegial partnerships.

Various barriers undermine development of effective collaboration among health care partners. Old animosities, such as perceived physician superiority, sometimes prevent the ability of the nurse to trust and relate effectively to physicians. Incongruence of philosophy related to the partnership also may create tension among partners. However, when these philosophical differences are acknowledged and a new common ground is found, professional partnerships may flourish. Competitive behavior also limits the ability to form effective collegial partnerships. Social status and inequality in educational levels may also interfere with the development of partnerships. Information sharing is critical, and systems must be designed so that all partners have access to the same information so that responsible decisions and behaviors can occur. Finally, sometimes partners equate collaboration with total agreement on every issue, and processes must be in place for ways to negotiate differences between and among partners when disagreements arise (Wilson & Porter-O'Grady, 1999).

 ## LEADERSHIP EFFECTIVENESS

Professional nurses assume leadership in a variety of ways. They serve as health experts, care coordinators, client advocates, counselors, educators, and change agents. The sharing of power, rather than the wielding of power, characterizes the transformational relationship of the nurse with all members of the health care team, including the client. Display 18-5 outlines different forms of nurse influence in the nurse–client relationship. These forms of influence may also apply when the nurse works with UAP. For example, nurses make legitimate requests to UAP when delegating tasks to them. At times, nurses may use coercion or rational persuasion to get them to perform the delegated tasks. With time, UAP may recognize nurses as experts, internalize some of the values of nurses they respect, relinquish control of independence to comply with nurse requests, participate actively in client care decisions, and begin to imitate nurses whom they admire. Likewise, some professional nurses acknowledge the valuable and unique contributions UAP make to client care (Standing & Anthony, 2008).

Forms of Influence Within the Nurse–Client Relationship

DISPLAY 18-5

1. Legitimate request: responding to legitimate power; the client complies with the nurse's request because he recognizes her right to make such a request. The client's compliance represents internalized values of obedience, cooperation, courtesy, respect for tradition, and loyalty to the organization.
2. Instrumental compliance: responding to reward power; the client complies because the nurse has made an explicit or implicit promise to ensure some tangible outcome that the client desires.
3. Coercion: responding to the threat of aversive outcomes, such as economic loss, embarrassment, or expulsion. Because the influence is motivated by fear, it is most effective when it is credible.
4. Rational persuasion: responding to a logical argument. The client is convinced that the nurse's suggested behavior is the best way to satisfy needs or attain objectives.
5. Rational faith: acting out of faith in the nurse's expertise and credibility. Such a response is based on expert power.
6. Inspirational appeal: responding to expressions of values and ideals without any tangible reward. The client acts from obedience to authority figures, reverence for tradition, self-sacrifice, and so forth.
7. Situational engineering: responding to manipulation of relevant aspects of the physical and social situation. The nurse must have control, and the client must accept the situation.
8. Personal identification: responding to referent power. The client imitates the behavior of an admired nurse.
9. Decision identification: responding to involvement in decision making.

In transformational leadership, rational persuasion and shared decision making serve as the most valid forms of influence because they promote empowerment. Recent research findings and current literature suggest that transformational leadership promotes staff empowerment, improved job satisfaction (for staff and managers), increased staff job satisfaction, improved client satisfaction with care, supportive work environments, the development of mutual team goals, and an optimal mix of nursing skill and expertise (Laschinger, Spence, Purdy, & Almost, 2007; Proenca, 2007; Raup, 2008; Robbins & Davidhizar, 2007). Increased staff nurse retention saves money because recruitment and replacement costs for new professional nurse employees range from $46,000 (Robbins & Davidhizar) to as high as $145,000 (Attencio, Cohen, & Gorenberg, 2003). Thus, effective development of transformational leadership competencies in nurses can positively affect health care delivery.

Transformational Leadership Competencies

In a synthesis of research findings, Gurka (1995, p. 170) identified the following three qualities of the transformational leaders:

1. Individual consideration—exhibited by promoting others' growth, recognizing and supporting others' needs and feelings, and giving positive feedback and recognition.
2. Charisma—exhibited by inspiring and motivating, demonstrating enthusiasm, and communicating in a positive manner.
3. Intellectual stimulation—exhibited by creating a questioning environment, acting as a mentor, and challenging others to grow and learn.

Gurka (1995, p. 170) also identified three qualities of the transformational leader that have been proposed experientially:

1. Vulnerability—exhibited by communicating authentically and openly, expressing emotions as well as ideas, and sharing the self with others.
2. Knowledge, concern, and courage—exhibited by seeking knowledge through study and experience, showing concern and caring for others, and being willing to take risks.
3. Feminine attributes—exhibited by maintaining accessibility, paying attention to process as well as outcomes, and practicing balance in lifestyle.

Based on transformational leadership concepts (Bennis & Nanus, 1985), Display 18-6 lists examples of leadership competencies. These actions, when they become part of the

---

Leadership Competencies   DISPLAY 18-6

Acknowledging and using the inner wisdom of self and others

Setting goals and working to achieve them

Working with others to achieve a common vision and mission

Recognizing the interconnection of everyone on everything

Abandoning the hierarchical approach to leadership

Recognizing that persons performing the work are specialists

Engaging in systems thinking

Recognizing patterns

Synthesizing new ideas and processes

Committing to lifelong continuous learning

Adapting to and accepting chaos

Facilitating each team member's involvement and accountability

Empowering others

Being receptive to new ideas and the ideas of others

Facilitating group meetings and participation of everyone in organizational processes (especially decision making)

Coaching

Acting with immediacy and equality

Displaying technical expertise (organizational culture and design, financial management, economics, business ethics, evaluation methods, health care jurisprudence, information technology and strategic planning for the long term)

Practicing knowledge of relationship dynamics

Sharing administrative functions

Favoring collaboration over competition

Mentoring others to assume leadership

nurse's character, are called habits. Leadership habits of the nurse also determine the effectiveness of the nurse in practice.

Covey's Habits of the Effective Leader

Covey (1989) defined a habit as the intersection of knowledge, skill, and desire that has great power in a person's life (p. 47). Covey has described knowledge as the "what to do and why," skills as the "how to do," and desire as the motivation, the "want to do" (p. 47). He emphasized that without desire or motivation, essential, effective leaderships skills such as sharing knowledge confidently and listenting intently to others will never become ingrained habits.

Habits of effective leaders are the internalized principles and patterns of behavior that reflect the three interrelated factors of knowledge, skills, and desire. Seven habits that Covey (1989) designated for effective leadership are based on the theoretical premise of sequential growth moving people from dependence to independence and finally to interdependence, the phase in which true mutuality can occur.

In 2004, Covey (2004) added another habit of great leaders: the eighth habit involves hearing one's own voice and inspiring others to find theirs. Finding one's own voice means periodic analysis of values and beliefs and finding quiet time to listen to oneself. Once found, the voice must be expressed by developing a personal vision, practicing discipline, showing passion in action, and not doing anything against one's conscience. Inspiring others means being a trim-tab (a small rudder that turns the large rudder of a ship), modeling character and competence, instilling trust, and blending voices to develop shared vision. Once others have discovered their voices, the great leader aligns goals and systems to achieve desired results (the shared vision) while empowering others to use their talents and live out passions. Covey identified the four roles of leadership as modeling (inspiring trust), path finding (creating order), aligning (nourishing vision and empowerment), and empowering (getting others to internally unleash their human potential). Great leaders use their influence to serve others. The eight habits identified by Covey (1989, 2004) are listed in Display 18-7 and briefly described in terms of nursing leadership. Habits represent the integrated principles of the professional nurse while providing consistency in action. When leaders use effective habits, they earn the trust of their followers.

 ## EVALUATING LEADERSHIP EFFECTIVENESS

As a professional, the nurse engages in the process of self-evaluation and looks for ways to improve leadership performance. Unfortunately, not all leaders are effective. Competing demands force leaders (especially managers) to make difficult decisions, which may result in win–lose situations. Ineffective leadership takes many forms, including the person who assumes a leadership position without proper qualification, one who bides his or her time until retirement, or the person who received a leadership appointment because of success in a previous appointment. Frequently, personal insecurity of persons in charge may result in dysfunctional leadership (Fitzpatrick, 2004). Poor nursing leadership also may occur when the well-respected, competent, professional nurse gets forced into accepting a leadership position. The quality of leadership suffers when the person assuming the leadership position would rather be doing something different. When nurses know themselves as persons and have a clear idea of life passions, they can thwart the influences of others before assuming a leadership position that they really do not wish to assume.

McCauley and Velsor (2004) proposed that when persons assume a leadership position, they should conduct periodic evaluations of their performance. They suggest

Covey's Eight Habits, Adapted for the Nurse

1. Be proactive. Nurses need to set a goal and work to achieve it. They commit themselves to the client's perceptions and serve as a model for health, not a critic of those with expressed concerns. They accept their own ability to be "response-able" in dealing with clients' whole human responses to their health concerns. They believe that "it's not what happens to us, but our response to what happens to us that hurts us" (Covey, 1989, p. 73).

2. Begin with the end in mind. The nurse should identify what is really important and try to do what really matters the most every day. The nurse also must differentiate management from leadership: management, representing the bottom line, focuses on how the nurse can best accomplish certain things with the client, and leadership, representing the top line, focuses on what the nurse wants to accomplish. "Management is efficiency in climbing the ladder of success; leadership determines whether the ladder is leaning against the right wall" (Covey, 1989, p. 101).

3. Put first things first. The formula for the nurse who wants to stay focused on the important business of nursing and give less energy to the unimportant is to set priorities, organize, and finally, perform. The challenge for the nurse is to manage time in such a way that most of the time is used for urgent important activities, such as crises, pressing problems, and deadline-driven projects, as well as the not urgent but important projects, such as health promotion/illness prevention, relationship building, recognizing new opportunities, planning, and recreation (Covey, 1989).

4. Think win–win or no deal. Interdependence is the most mature goal for any relationship; thus, in professional relationships, interdependence would emphasize mutual benefits. Activities would reflect a commitment to both parties' growth, development, and satisfaction. For example, a client benefits from being empowered by the professional nurse providing informational support, and the nurse benefits by having the interventions validated and the sense of presence with the client valued. When such mutuality is experienced, neither person in the relationship loses or feels powerless (Covey, 1989).

5. Seek first to understand, then to be understood. Empathy is the habit reflected in this principle. The ability to focus on the client's reality as he experiences is vital to positive communication. Empathy is discussed in detail in Chapter 19, Professional Communication to Establish Helping and Healing Relationships. Credibility problems, such as the client's feeling that "you just don't understand," are prevented to the extent that the nurse empathizes with the client (Covey, 1989).

6. Value differences and bring all perspectives together. Respect is the characteristic that enables the nurse to develop this habit. Respect is discussed further in Chapter 15, Client Systems. To the extent that the nurse facilitates respect for differing perspectives, the client is likely to feel more free to seek the best possible alternative. If the nurse also experiences respect for his or her perspectives, synergistic relationships are enhanced. Using the principle of synergy, the nurse and client multiply their individual talents and abilities, and the outcome of their efforts is greater than the sum of the parts (Covey, 1989).

7. Have a balanced, systematic program for self-renewal. Consistency in having a regularly planned and balanced program for self-renewal prevents weakening of the body, mechanization of the mind, exposure of raw emotions, and desensitization of the spirit. Clearly, nurses' leadership ability is enhanced if they consistently participate in activities that renew four aspects of the self: physical, mental, emotional–social, and moral being. Renewal energizes capabilities that are necessary for productive helping relationships in nursing (Covey, 1989).

8. Find your own voice and inspire others to find theirs. Being truly authentic towards one's personal life mission, and helping others find themselves, fosters the development of new leaders and promotes deep satisfaction with life and work. Others quickly detect lack of authenticity in a relationship, especially when nurses establish helping and healing relationships with clients and health team members.

Adapted from Covey, S. R. (1989). *The 7 habits of highly effective people*. New York: Simon & Schuster; Covey, S. R. (2004). *The 8th habit*. New York: Free Press.

self-reflection and eliciting information from followers to provide a complete, accurate picture of one's leadership. Some pertinent questions to use as **criteria for evaluating leadership** are listed in Display 18-8. Periodic evaluation of one's leadership provides information for future learning and professional development.

Criteria for Evaluating Nursing Leadership	DISPLAY 18-8

1. Can the leader be trusted?
2. Does the leader use effective verbal and nonverbal communication skills?
3. Is the leader accessible?
4. Is the leader aware of issues encountered by nurses engaged in client care activities?
5. Does the nurse leader support staff when problems arise?
6. Can the leader initiate, maintain, and terminate effective relationships?
7. Does the leader demonstrate sensitivity to the impact of self on others, leading to effective use of self?
8. Can the leader effectively modify his or her behavior and that of others?

9. Does the leader effectively delegate tasks to others or does he or she micromanage everything?
10. Does the leader provide the needed resources to provide quality nursing services?
11. Does the leader set high standards and hold others and self accountable for them?
12. Is the leader willing to help others grow as professional nurses?

Adapted from McCauley, C., & Van Velsor, (2004). *The Center for Creative Leadership handbook of leadership development* (2nd ed.). San Francisco: Jossey-Bass.

SUMMARY AND SIGNIFICANCE TO PRACTICE

Effective nursing leadership is critical in today's complex, chaotic health environment. Because all professional nurses are leaders, they need to use cognitive and communication skills to empower others to make decisions, facilitate access to needed care services, share knowledge, coordinate care delivery, plan for the future, use resources judiciously, and facilitate adaptation to change. Effective leaders in nursing display caring, compassion, commitment, confidence, and competence in their roles and periodically conduct self-evaluations to discover additional areas for lifelong learning.

FROM THEORY TO PRACTICE

Reread the vignette at the beginning of the chapter and answer the following questions.

1. Which of the leadership theories would be most useful to Alice as she leads the group of parent volunteers to determine how to get a registered nurse in every school? Why do you think the selected theory would work best? What are potential outcomes for having a registered nurse in every school for students, faculty, school administration, the local school board, and school district taxpayers? What obstacles do you think Alice and the task force might encounter from achieving the goal of a nurse in every school?
2. How do you rate your effectiveness as a nurse leader? What are your strengths? What are your opportunities for future growth as a leader? Outline an action plan to facilitate your growth as a nursing leader.

WWW INTERNET EXERCISES

1. Visit the International Council of Nurses website "site map" at http://www.icn.ch. Click on the words "Site Map." Click on the words in the yellow oval labeled "Leadership for Change." Read this information and answer the following questions:
   How can nurses contribute to global health care reform?
   What perceptions about nurses held by others prevent nurses from assuming leadership roles in global health care reform?
   How can the nursing profession dispel the negative perceptions of others?
   What do you think about the vision and mission statements for the Leadership for Change Initiative?
   How would you like to change health care delivery in your locale?

INTERNET RESOURCES

American Academy of Nursing: http://www.aannet.org.

American Organization of Nurse Executives: http://www.aone.org.

American Nurses Association: http://www.nursingworld.org.

Transformational Leadership and Leader Effectiveness from Human Assets Limited in London, England: http://changingminds.org/disciplines/leadership/styles/transformational_leadership.htm.

Sigma Theta Tau International: http://www.nursingsociety.org.

Center for Innovative Leadership: http://www.cfil.com.

The Leadership Institute: http://www.leadership.org.

REFERENCES

Anderson, T. (1998). *Transforming leadership* (2nd ed.). Boston: St. Lucie Press.

Attencio, B., Cohen, J., & Gorenberg, B. (2003). Nurse retention: Is it worth it? *Nursing Economic$, 21*(6), 42–47.

Bandman, E. L., & Bandman, B. (1995). *Nursing ethics through the life span* (3rd ed.). East Norwalk, CT: Appleton & Lange.

Barker, A. M., & Young, C. E. (1994). Transformational leadership: The feminist connection in postmodern organizations. *Holistic Nursing Practice, 9*, 16–25.

Barrett, R. (1998). *Liberating the corporate soul: Building a visionary organization*. Boston: Butterworth-Heinemann.

Bass, B., & Riggio, R. (2005). *Transformational leadership* (2nd ed.). Mahwah, NJ: Erlbaum.

Bennis, W. (1989). *Why leaders can't lead: The unconscious conspiracy continues*. San Francisco: Jossey-Bass.

Bennis, W., & Nanus, B. (1985). *Leaders: The strategies for taking charge*. New York: Harper & Row.

Blake, R., & Morton, J. (1964). *The managerial grid: Key orientations for achieving production through people*. Houston: Gulf Publishing.

Blanchard, K., Carlos, J. P., & Randolph, A. (1996). *Empowerment takes more than a minute*. San Francisco: Berrett-Koehler.

Bondas, T. (2006). Paths to nursing leadership. *Journal of Nursing Management, 14*(5), 332–339.

Bridges, W. (2003). *Managing transitions* (2nd ed.). Cambridge, MA: Perseus.

Burns, J. (1978). *Leadership*. New York: Harper & Row.

Burns, J. (2003). *Transformational leadership*. New York: Grove/Atlantic.

Calhoun, S. K. (2006). Strategic management: Facing the future with confidence. In J. Dunham-Taylor & J. Pinczuk (Eds.), *Health care financial management for nurse managers: Merging the heart with the dollar* (pp. 607–645). Sudbury, MA: Jones & Bartlett.

Carnall, C. A. (1990). *Managing change in organizations*. Upper Saddle River, NJ: Prentice Hall.

Chin, R. (1976). The utility of systems models and developmental models for practitioners. In W. G. Bennis, K. D. Benne, & R. Chin (Eds.), *The planning of change* (3rd ed., pp. 90–122). New York: Holt, Rinehart & Winston.

Covey, S. R. (1989). *The 7 habits of highly effective people*. New York: Simon & Schuster.

Covey, S. R. (1996). Three roles of the leader in the new paradigm. In F. Hesselbein, M. Goldsmith, & R. Beckhard (Eds.), *The leader of the future: New visions, strategies, and practices for the next era* (pp. 149–160). San Francisco: Jossey-Bass.

Covey, S. R. (2004). *The 8th habit*. New York: Free Press.

Cummings, G., & McLennan, M. (2005). Advanced practice nursing: Leadership to effect policy change. *Journal of Nursing Administration, 35*(2), 61–66.

Davis, P. S. (1991). The meaning of change to individuals within a college of nurse education. *Journal of Advanced Nursing, 16*, 108–115.

Donnelly, G. (2003). Why leadership is important to nursing. In T. Stelzer (Ed.), *Five keys to successful nursing management* (pp. 2–30). Philadelphia: Lippincott Williams & Wilkins.

Dotlich, D., Noel, J., & Walker, N. (2004). *Leadership passages*. San Francisco: Jossey-Bass.

Douglass, L. M. (1988). *The effective nurse: Leader and manager* (3rd ed.). St. Louis, MO: Mosby.

Fieldler, F. (1967). *A theory of leadership effectiveness*. New York: McGraw-Hill.

Fitzpatrick, M. (2004). Facing challenges. In N. Holmes (Ed.), *Five keys to successful nursing management* (pp. 162–191). Philadelphia: Lippincott Williams & Wilkins.

George, B. (2003). *Authentic leadership*. San Francisco: Jossey-Bass.

Greenleaf, R. (1977). *Servant leadership: A journey into the nature of legitimate power and greatness*. Mahwah, NJ: Paulist Press.

Gurka, A. M. (1995). Transformational leadership: Qualities and strategies for the CNS. *Clinical Nurse Specialist*, *9*, 169–174.

Haffer, A. (1986, April). Facilitating change: Choosing the appropriate strategy. *Journal of Nursing Administration*, *16*, 18–22.

Hagberg, J. (1994). *Real power: Stages of personal power in organizations* (2nd ed.). Salem, WI: Sheffield.

Hames, C. C., & Joseph, D. H. (1980). *Basic concepts of helping: A wholistic approach*. New York: Appleton-Century-Crofts.

Henriksen, K., Keyes, M., Steens, D., & Clancy, C. (2006). Initiating transformational change to enhance patient safety. *Journal of Patient Safety*, *2*(19), 20–24.

Hershey, P., & Blanchard, K. (1977). *Management of organizational behavior: Leading human resources* (3rd ed.). Upper Saddle River, NJ: Prentice Hall.

House, R., & Mitchell, T. (1974). Path-goal theory of leadership. *Journal of Contemporary Business*, *3*, 81–97.

Hunt, P. (2003). Marketing your facility. In T. Stelzer (Ed.), *Five keys to successful nursing management* (pp. 276–286). Philadelphia: Lippincott Williams & Wilkins.

Huston, C. (2008). Eleven strategies for building a personal power base. *Nursing Management*, *39*(4), 58–61.

King, E. C. (1984). *Affective education in nursing*. Rockville, MD: Aspen Systems.

Laschinger, H., Spence, H., Purdy, N., & Almost, J. (2007). The impact of leader-member exchange quality, empowerment, and core self-evaluation on nurse manager's job satisfaction. *Journal of Nursing Administration*, *37*(5), 221–229.

Marquette, R., Dunham-Taylor, J., & Pinczuk, J. (2006). Budgeting. In J. Dunham-Taylor & J. Pinczuk (Eds.), *Health care financial management for nurse managers: Merging the heart with the dollar* (pp. 425–456). Sudbury, MA: Jones & Bartlett.

Marquis, B., & Huston, C. (2009). *Leadership roles and management functions in nursing: Theory and application* (6th ed.). Philadelphia: Lippincott, Williams & Wilkins.

McCauley, C., & Van Velsor, E. (2004). *The Center for Creative Leadership handbook of leadership development* (2nd ed.). San Francisco: Jossey-Bass.

McGregor, D. (1960). *The human side of enterprise*. New York: McGraw-Hill.

Noddings, N. (1984). *Caring: A feminine approach to ethics and moral education*. Berkeley: University of California Press.

Olsen, D. P. (1991). Empathy as an ethical and philosophical basis for nursing. *Advances in Nursing Science*, *14*, 62–75.

Ouchi, W. (1981). *Theory Z: How American business can meet the Japanese challenge*. Reading, MA: Addison-Wesley-Longman.

Perlman, D., & Takacs, G. J. (1990). The 10 stages of change. *Nursing Management*, *21*, 33–38.

Porter-O'Grady, T., & Malloch, K. (2007). *Quantum leadership: A resource for health care innovation* (2nd ed.). Sudbury, MA: Jones & Bartlett.

Pritchett, R., & Pound, R. (1995). *A survival guide to the stress of organizational change*. Dallas, TX: Pritchett & Associates.

Proenca, J. (2007). Team dynamics and team empowerment in health care organizations. *Health Care Management Review*, *32*(4), 370–378.

Rafael, A. R. (1996). Power and caring: A dialectic in nursing. *Advances in Nursing Science*, *19*, 3–17.

Raup, G. (2008). Make transformational leadership work for you. *Nursing Management*, *39*(1), 50–53.

Richardson, P. (1992, Spring). Hospital practices that erode nursing power by promoting job dissatisfaction. *Revolution: The Journal of Nurse Empowerment*, *2*, 34–39.

Robbins, B., & Davidhizar, R. (2007). Transformational leadership in health care today. *Health Care Manager*, *26*(3), 234–239.

Snowball, J. (1996). Asking nurses about advocating for patients: "Reactive" and "proactive" accounts. *Journal of Advanced Nursing*, *24*, 67–75.

Standing, T., & Anthony, M. (2008). Delegation: What it means to acute care nurses. *Applied Nursing Research*, *21*(1), 8-14.

Taylor, S. G., Pickens, J. M., & Geden, E. A. (1989). Interactional styles of nurse practitioners and physicians regarding patient decision making. *Nursing Research*, *38*, 50–55.

U.S. Army. (2004). *Be-know-do: Leadership the Army way*. San Francisco: Jossey-Bass.

Van Velsor, E., Moxley, R., & Bunker, K. (2004). The leadership development process. In C. McCauley & E. Van Velsor (Eds.), *The Center for Creative Leadership handbook of leadership development* (2nd ed., pp. 204–233). San Francisco: Jossey-Bass.

Videback, S. (2008). *Psychiatric-mental health hursing* (4th ed.). Philadelphia: Wolters Kluwer Health/ Lippincott Williams & Wilkins.

Vroom, V., & Yetton, P. (1973). *Leadership and decision making*. Pittsburgh, PA: University of Pittsburgh Press.

Wesorick, B., & Shiparski, L. (1997). *Can the human being thrive in the work place? Dialogue as a strategy of hope*. Grand Rapids, MI: Practice Field Publishing.

White, R., & Lippitt, R. (1960). *Autocracy and democracy: An experimental inquiry*. New York: Harper & Row. (Published after Lewin's death)

Wilson, C. K., & Porter-O'Grady, T. (1999). *Leading the revolution in health care* (2nd ed.). Gaithersburg, MD: Aspen.

Wooten, K. C., & White, L. P. (1989). Toward a theory of change role efficacy. *Human Relations, 42*, 651–669.

CHAPTER 19

Quality Improvement and Professional Nursing

KEY TERMS AND CONCEPTS

Quality
Quality health care
Total quality management
Continuous quality improvement
The Joint Commission
Quality assurance
Plan, do, check, act (PDCA)
Internal customers
External customers
Lean
Six Sigma
Benchmarking
Malcolm Baldrige National Quality Award
Total quality improvement (TQI)
Nursing-sensitive outcomes

LEARNING OUTCOMES

By the end of this chapter, the learner will be able to:

1 Define the term quality.

2 Outline hallmarks of quality health care.

3 Compare and contrast quality assurance, total quality management, and continuous quality improvement.

4 Explain the plan, do, check, act (PDCA) cycle used in quality improvement programs.

5 Identify internal and external customers in health care settings.

6 Explain Six Sigma and how it could be used to improve health care quality.

7 Describe the process of benchmarking.

8 Specify nursing-sensitive outcomes for clients and health care organizations.

9 Explain how recent quality and safety initiatives will improve the quality of health care delivery for clients and nurses.

VIGNETTE

Laura is a nurse working on a busy cardiac care unit. This evening, she has admitted two persons with chest pain, and transferred another one of her assigned clients to the intensive care unit. As she charts all of the medications that were routinely ordered on her assigned clients, she notices that she administered the wrong doses of warfarin to two of her assigned clients, who were roommates. She completes an incident report on herself after reporting the mistake to the physician, who yells at her. Because she is new to the unit, she wonders how the nurse manager and her colleagues will react to her mistake.

Questions for Reflection 19-1

1. How does the organization in which I practice nursing handle medication errors?
2. Am I afraid to complete incident reports? Why or why not?
3. Who is at fault when a nurse makes an error?

When analyzing quality in health care, the term **quality** means "a degree of excellence which something possesses" (Agnes, 2005, p. 1173). Quality in health care means different things depending upon individual perspectives. Consumers look for caring providers, timely services, technical competence, error-free care, accurate bills, and improved health status as indicators of quality. Nurses look at nurse–patient ratios, adequate time to spend with patients, availability of supplies, quality of ancillary staff, easy access to resources for procedures, and educational information and assistance as quality indicators. According to the Institute of Medicine (IOM, 2000), as many as 98,000 hospitalized Americans may die each year as a result of errors in care delivery. Errors occur when health care providers fail to complete planned actions as intended or use a wrong plan. Omitted and unintended interventions may result in no adverse client outcomes, in reversible client harm, in temporary or permanent disabilty, and even in death (IOM, 2004). In today's hospitals, nurses have the complex tasks of caring for more acutely ill clients that require them to change their thinking rapidly, keep a mental list of multiple tasks to accomplish, document all care activities, and supervise unlicensed care providers. According to a Safe Staffing Poll conducted by the American Nurses Association in 2008, responses of over 7,000 nurses reported that inadequate staffing compromised the quality of nursing care services. Over 5,000 of these nurses reported changing places of employment because of declining quality of care. Nearly 5,000 nurses also reported lacking confidence in the ability of their health care facility to provide needed nursing care should they or a loved one be hospitalized. In 2001, the Committee on the Quality of Health Care in America outlined the following hallmarks of **quality health care**: (1) safe, (2) timely, (3) efficient, (4) equitable, (5) effective, and (6) patient centered.

Companies that manufacture products would be out of business if they had as many errors as occur in the health care arena. Quality management became popular in business and industry after American manufacturers lost market share to Japanese competitors (Ouchi, 1981). The terms **total quality management** (TQM) and **continuous quality improvement** (CQI) are used synonymously in the business and health care–related literature. For years, health care providers and organizations rationalized higher margins of error because, after all, some patients entered the care system with fatal illnesses or injuries. Thus, saving everyone's life emerged as an impossible outcome for health care providers.

Questions for Reflection 19-2

1. What do I consider elements of quality of care when I receive health care services?
2. What do I consider elements of quality of care as a professional nurse?
3. How well do the lists of quality of care match?
4. What are the elements found in each list? Why are they important?
5. What elements are important to health care consumers that may not be important to health care providers? Why are these important to consumers?

HISTORY OF QUALITY IMPROVEMENT IN HEALTH CARE

Florence Nightingale can be considered the first nurse who engaged in quality improvement (QI) activities. During the Crimean War, Nightingale's work at the Barrack Hospital demonstrated the effects of nursing care on wounded and infirm soldiers. The mortality rate at Barrack Hospital was 60% when Nightingale arrived. It fell to just a fraction over 1% when she departed. Nightingale kept detailed records that included statistics about the effects of cleanliness, good nutrition, and fresh air on the survival of the soldiers (Kalisch & Kalisch, 2004). Her diligent attention to detailed records and continuous analysis of data provided evidence that nursing care by women could reduce mortality. She reported her success to the British government and documented her work in three books: *Notes on Matters Affecting the Health, Efficiency and Hospital Administration of the British Army* (1858); *Notes on Hospitals* (1858); and *Notes on Nursing* (1859) (Kalisch & Kalisch).

A group of surgeons concerned about the quality of care in American hospitals formed the American College of Surgeons (ACS) in 1913. By 1918, work of the ACS led to the implementation of the Hospital Standardization Program (HSP). The HSP evolved into an accreditation process that designated minimum standards for credentialing, privileging, and monitoring functions for medical staff. The HSP also developed minimal standards for medical equipment. To create a standardized system for record keeping, the HSP determined standards for health care recipient medical records (Koch & Fairly, 1993; Des Harnais & McLaughlin, 1999).

In 1951, the HSP evolved into the Joint Commission on Accreditation of Hospitals (JCAH), a private, nonprofit, voluntary agency that used ACS standards for accrediting hospitals. JCAH eventually expanded accreditation standards to include hospital administrative issues. Concerned about the quality of care received by subscribers during hospitalizations, Blue Cross required that participating hospitals be accredited for JCAH. Eventually, JCAH accreditation became a requirement for hospitals to receive payment under the federal Medicare program (Des Harnais & McLaughin, 1999; Koch & Fairly, 1993; Sultz & Young, 2004).

Hospitals began to develop health systems that also included primary care services for consumers. In 1987, JCAH changed its name to Joint Commission on Accreditation of Healthcare Organizations (JCAHO; Koch & Fairly, 1993). Along with its name change, JCAHO produced a new definition of health care quality that used quantitative approaches that emphasized patient outcomes. JCAHO, now known as **The Joint Commission**, currently accredits nearly 16,000 health care organizations that include hospitals, home health agencies, laboratories, and extended care and outpatient facilities. The Joint Commission uses standards, performance outcomes, and consumer perception of rendered services as criteria for accreditation (JCAHO, 2004). In 2006, the World Health Organization acknowledged the Joint Commission's contributions to ensuring quality health services, and today it internationally accredits health care institutions.

Quality assurance (QA) programs became part of the hospital accreditation process in the 1970s. The Joint Commission standards require that health care organizations (especially hospitals) regularly review the following data in quality assurance programs: (1) mortality rates by department or service, (2) hospital-acquired infections, (3) patient falls, (4) adverse drug reactions, (5) unplanned returns to surgeries, and (6) hospital-incurred trauma (Sultz & Young, 2004, p. 108).

Along with ensuring quality of services to health care consumers, The Joint Commission accreditation standards address efficacy of health care interventions and appropriateness of services delivered. The Joint Commission also looks at how well services are delivered to consumers. Aspects for quality services include the following: (1) availability of the needed health care intervention, (2) timeliness of services, (3) effectiveness of health care interventions, (4) continuity of health care services across various health care settings, (5) safety of patient and others, (6) efficiencies of provided care and services, and

(7) respect given to consumers and caring with which services are rendered (DesHarnais & McLaughlin, 1999; Sultz & Young, 2004).

More recently, the Joint Commission Standards (2008b) emphasize the importance of CQI or TQM. Success in CQI and TQM is based on the premise that if staff members who are closest to the point of service delivery are empowered and educated on the process of incremental change, the quality and efficiency of client care will improve (Sultz & Young, 2004). QI differs from QA in that QA programs tend to be reactive in nature, and focus on correction of specific identified causes of problems with limited responsibility using authoritative problem solving. In contrast, QI is a proactive program aimed at correcting common system problems, it holds everyone involved in a process responsible, it has leaders who actively lead, and actual and potential problems are identified and solved by all employees (Koch & Fairly, 2003). In the literature, QI, CQI, and TQM all basically mean the same thing. The concepts all mean processes used to improve all aspects of goods and services that are offered to consumers. QI, CQI, and TQM work constantly and continuously to improve consumer goods and services. Table 19-1 outlines the differences between QA and QI programs.

The Joint Commission sets annual National Patient Safety Goals for health care organizations. The goal of this program is to avert errors that compromise patient safety. For 2009, the following goals were set: for hospitals, improvement of patient identification, of effectiveness of communication among health team members, in safety of medication use, in reducing the risk of infections associated with health care, of accuracy and completeness in reconciling medications across the care continuum, in reducing risks of client harm from falls, in active client involvement as part of a patient safety strategy, of identification of safety risks in its patient population, in recognizing and responding to client condition changes, and in compliance to a universal protocol to increase the safety of surgical procedures (JCAHO, 2008a). The annual safety goals are broadly written. For most of the goals, the Joint Commission outlines elements of performance that typically include client and health provider education, and a series of critical steps to follow. For example, in the case of preventing central line bloodstream infections, 17 performance elements are identified.

To understand the TQM/CQI approach, key concepts related to this process are discussed in the following section.

 ## QUALITY IMPROVEMENT APPROACHES

Quality improvement approaches to business and industry began after World War II. In health care, providers rated quality in terms of mortality and morbidity. Health care

TABLE 19-1

Comparison of Quality Assurance and Quality Improvement Programs (QI, CQI, TQM, or TQI)	
Quality Assurance Program	**Quality Improvement Program**
Conformance focused	Improvement focused
Reactive in nature	Proactive in nature
Looks for special sources of variation within a system	Focuses on internal variations within a system
Variation results from actions of specific persons or work groups	Variation results from increased complexity of work processes or may be random in nature

Adapted from McLaughlin, C., & Kaluzny, A. (1999). *Continuous quality improvement in health care.* Gaithersburg, MD: Aspen.

institutions held "Mortality and Morbidity Conferences" on a regular basis. Even today, hospitals hold regularly scheduled conferences to analyze precipitating factors and outcomes of rescue efforts following cases of respiratory and cardiac arrest. In many cases, some providers consider a death as an indicator of poor quality in health care service. However, TQM/CQI offers an alternative way to measure, analyze, and control quality in health care.

W. Edwards Deming

Dr. W. Edwards Deming (a physicist, mathematician, and engineer) was responsible for postwar construction in Japan. In 1950, he presented a quality management workshop in Japan that emphasized the importance of statistical control for managers. To maintain a competitive edge, Deming proposed that dedication to quality and productivity was essential. Deming suggested that errors increased and productivity declined as a result of flawed work processes rather than from the results of individual actions. He also believed that productivity and quality would improve when workers became empowered to make decisions about work processes.

He developed a cycle, today known as the Deming cycle, to improve quality. The cycle is a continuous loop consisting of the following steps: **plan, do, check, and act (PDCA)**. When using the Deming cycle, organizations plan what improvements need to be made, do by implementing the plan, check results of plan implementation using statistical data, and finally act by correcting work processes to improve the quality of services or products.

Deming also emphasized that a successful QI program requires total commitment and accountability for all workers (including management). He created the following 14 points that must be applied for successful QI processes:

1. Create a constancy of purpose for improvement of products and services.
2. Adopt the new philosophy that poor workmanship and services must not be tolerated.
3. Cease dependence on mass inspection by enlisting the workers to develop ways to improve production processes and have them make decisions during the production process whether to discard or rework a product.
4. End the practice of awarding business solely on the lowest cost.
5. Work constantly and endlessly to improve the systems of production and service.
6. Institute training for all workers.
7. Reconfigure leadership based on supervisors to help workers perform better.
8. Drive out fear in the workplace because fear prevents persons from asking questions or expressing ideas and perpetuates error in job performance.
9. Break down barriers between staff areas by bringing various departments together to work toward the common purpose and find more opportunities for improvement.
10. Eliminate slogans, exhortations, and targets for the workforce by having the workers write their own slogans and targets.
11. Eliminate numerical quotas as they create the perceptions that employment status is based only on meeting quotas rather than producing high-quality goods and services.
12. Remove barriers to the pride of workmanship by providing workers with the best equipment and materials so that workers can improve offered products and services.
13. Institute a vigorous program of education and retraining so that all managers and workers understand statistical techniques and teamwork skills needed for an effective QI program.
14. Take action to accomplish the transformation by defining the action plan required to lead the quality mission with dedication (Walton, 1986).

Along with proposals for successful QI programs, Deming warned of the following seven deadly diseases and obstacles that could derail the process:

1. Lack of constancy of purpose (everyone works toward different goals and no strategic plan is developed to ensure continuation of the organization)
2. Emphasis on short-term profits (quality and productivity may decline if quarterly data are used because if great improvement is noted in one quarter, workers or managers may scale back efforts)
3. Evaluation by performance, merit rating, or annual performance reviews (potential for destroying teamwork, instilling rivalry, creating despondency, and encouraging management mobility)
4. Mobility of management (management must understand the work, and complete changes for improved productivity and quality, which means managers must be on the job long enough to accomplish these tasks)
5. Running a company solely on visible figures (the effects of a satisfied or dissatisfied customer remain unknown)
6. Excessive medical costs (reveal potential problems with work environment or that employees have no time for health promotion)
7. Excessive costs of warranty, fueled by lawyers working for contingency fees (high losses reveal that inferior goods or services are being provided to customers) (Walton, 1986)

Deming provided businesses with an innovative approach. He outlined strategies for success that empowered workers. In addition, his obstacles warned about potentially catastrophic effects arising from failure to develop strategic plans, relying on technology rather than people to solve problems, and generating excuses for less-than-optimal performance (Walton, 1986).

If Deming's principles are applied to clinical nursing practice, efforts would be made to streamline work processes related to direct client care. For example, nurses would not be blamed if errors occurred while taking care of clients. Each error that occurred would be fully analyzed to determine the contributing factors resulting in the error. Work processes would be changed to prevent the error's reoccurrence. Nurses would be empowered to make changes in clinical policies and procedures as well as assume control over their clinical practice environments.

Joseph Juran

Like Deming, Juran noted the importance of careful planning to generate product quality. In 1945, Juran took his concepts to Japan. Juran used statistical quality control as a management tool. He created the Juran Trilogy, consisting of quality planning, quality control, and QI. The process of quality planning consisted of identifying specific customers and their needs, developing products to meet customer needs, developing processes to produce product features, and transferring production plans and product features to operating forces. Quality control consists of evaluating actual performance, comparing it to product goals, and acting on the difference. QI consists of establishing an infrastructure, identifying specific improvement projects, establishing project teams, and providing the improvement teams with resources, training, education, and motivation. The QI team works to diagnose causes of less-than-desired quality, propose and simulate remedies to identified causes, and establish control systems to maintain the gains (Juran, 1989).

Juran (1989) also differentiated quality circles from QI project teams. Quality circles (QCs) serve primarily to improve human relationships and secondarily to improve quality. QCs usually occur within a single department where members volunteer to tackle many QI projects. Managers and workers hold equal status in QCs. In contrast, QI project team membership crosses departmental boundaries, has a primary mission of improving quality, is run by a manager (or professional), and disbands once the project ends.

Juran (1989) outlined the following eight factors that distinguish institutions that have improved quality and reduced quality-related costs:

1. Upper managers led the quality process and served on quality councils (QI teams) as guides.
2. **Internal customers**' (persons working within the organization) and **external customers**' (persons outside the organization but received products or services) needs were concerns as QI processes were applied to businesses and usual operating processes.
3. Senior managers were given clear responsibility to adopt mandated, annual quality improvement with a defined infrastructure that identified opportunities for improvement, and were held accountable for making the improvements.
4. Managers involved everyone who affects the plan in the QI process.
5. Managers used modern quality methodology rather than empiric methods in quality planning.
6. Senior managers trained all management team members in quality planning, quality control, and quality improvement.
7. Managers trained all workers in how to participate actively in QI.
8. QI became a major feature in the strategic planning process.

Juran's approach to QI stressed the importance of planning.

Philip Crosby

Philip Crosby (1979) proposed that quality is free. He specified that time, manpower, and resources cost money. Crosby advocated for doing things right the first time and that quality saves money, thereby increasing profits. He defined quality as "conformance to requirements" (p. 8). Crosby's emphasis on doing things right the first time holds very true to health care delivery because health care professionals usually get only one chance to deliver effective, safe client care (i.e., the nurse has only one chance to administer the right medication to a client). He proposed that organizations needed to create climates in which attitudes and controls could make error prevention possible.

Like Deming, Crosby (1979) saw the need for all within an organization to be committed to the QI process. However, Crosby believed that "management needs to understand their personal roles in implanting quality and engaging employees in the vision of the company" (p. 78). Crosby also identified 14 essential elements to a quality management program:

1. Management commitment to the QI process
2. QI teams to oversee actions
3. Measurement tools appropriate to specific activities going through the QI process
4. Considering costs of quality evaluation (using estimates as needed)
5. Quality awareness promotion from all involved
6. Corrective action as needed to correct measurement tools, and reducing costs associated with the QI process
7. Planning for zero deficits
8. Supervisory education and training for all management levels
9. Holding a zero defects day to celebrate the new standard of performance
10. Goal determination for individual workers and work teams
11. Worker rather than management removal of causes of error after notification
12. Recognition of all involved once performance goals are attained
13. Quality circle sharing of ideas, experiences, and problems
14. Constant repetition of all steps (after all, QI is a continuous, never-ending process)

Crosby's thesis of the importance of doing things right the first time has been recently expanded by Toyota's **lean** operations and Chowdhury's Six Sigma Design approach to quality management.

Toyota's Lean Operations

Since the 1980s, Toyota automobiles have been known for their quality construction and performance. The Toyota Production System involves creation of a learning environment that uses the following four key practices:

1. How people work: Workers follow strict production specifications, are encouraged to identify changes in work processes, and then perform controlled trials of new work processes.
2. How workers connect: Workers across all levels of the organization interact directly following standardized methods. These practices reduce ambiguity, prevent key issues from losing attention, encourage requests for help (to which assistance is provided immediately), set deadlines for problem resolution, and foster trust among everyone in the organization.
3. How work is constructed: Work processes are designed to attain maximum reliability, eliminate repetition, and follow principles to promote worker health and well-being.
4. How work is improved and errors are reduced: All workers are trained in how to effect change, assume responsibility for making errors and use the scientific method to identify and propose changes to improve productivity, product quality, and reduce errors.

Toyota also uses lean operation techniques that advocate the use of desired, value-added activities while eliminating undesirable activities and waste in all work processes. Lean techniques eliminate waste by using visual controls, streamlined physical plant layouts, standardized work processes, and point-of-use storage. If a health care organization operated using lean principles, operations flowcharts outlining steps for delivering various services would be posted in departments. Nursing units and other ancillary departments would be designed to promote the flow of activities required for client care. Routine work processes would be standardized (many institutions already use standardized clinical care pathways for commonly encountered diseases, surgeries, and invasive diagnostic and intervention procedures). Finally, supplies, equipment, information, and procedures would be housed in convenient locations where client services are delivered (IOM, 2004).

The lean system outlines the following seven categories of waste: (1) poor utilization of resources, (2) excess motion, (3) unnecessary waiting, (4) transportation, (5) process inefficiency, (6) excess inventory, and (7) defects/quality control.

When nurses go searching for equipment needed for client care, hospitals practice poor utilization of resources, excess motion, unnecessary waiting, and process inefficiency. Many times clients wait for long periods after undergoing diagnostic tests because of unavailability of someone to return them to their rooms (waste from transportation, unnecessary waiting, and process inefficiency). Nurses may make medication errors because they engage in multitasking to meet client care needs (waste in terms of process inefficiency). Hospitals frequently buy supplies in bulk to reduce cost per unit, resulting in a higher inventory of supplies than actually needed; some supplies may become outdated and have to be discarded (excess inventory) (IOM, 2004).

Six Sigma

In the late 1980s, Motorola developed the **Six Sigma** as a means to sharpen its focus on quality improvement and to help accelerate the pace of change in a highly competitive technological and telecommunications market (Pande, Neuman, & Cavanagh, 2000). The concept has been expanded by other companies, including General Electric, Allied Signal, and Honeywell (Pande et al., 2000). Six Sigma has its basis in quality principles outlined by Deming, Juran, Crosby, and lean but takes quality to a new level. "In a nutshell, Six Sigma is a management philosophy focused on eliminating mistakes, waste, and rework" (Chowdhury, 2002, p. 4). Sigma (the Greek letter for deviation) measures variation within a process. The standard deviation of a process quantifies how far a process functions from its ideal. Instead of using percentages (based on a system of 100 performances), Six Sigma looks at "defects per million opportunities" (Pande et al.; Chowdhury). Table 19-2 summarizes the levels of Six Sigma, translates the levels in terms of performance accuracy, and presents health care–based scenarios.

Six Sigma methodology strives to improve products and work processes during the design rather than the quality control stage. Like TQM, Six Sigma processes emphasize providing the highest possible quality of goods and services to consumers. Pande and colleagues (2000, p. 68) identified a Six Sigma Roadmap consisting of the following five sequential steps: (1) identify core processes and key customers; (2) define customer requirements; (3) measure current performance; (4) prioritize, analyze, and implement improvements; and (5) expand and integrate the Six Sigma System.

The steps apply to situations related to business transformation, strategic improvement, and problem solving. When transforming business, Pande and colleagues suggested limiting the scope of change to one or two core processes. However, in health care, Six Sigma may best be used for strategic improvement (finding out what key customers need and want, followed by implementation of initiatives to fulfill customer expectations) and for problem solving (looking for ways to improve delivery of effective health care while reducing costs).

Six Sigma uses a process similar to the PDCA cycle. The cyclical process used in Six Sigma involves the following five phases for improving processes:

1. Define: Identify the problem, determine requirements, and set goals.
2. Measure: Validate the problem or flawed process, refine problems or goals, and measure key steps and inputs.
3. Analyze: Develop causal hypotheses, identify the "vital few" root causes, and validate a causal hypothesis.
4. Improve: Develop ideas to eliminate root causes, test solutions, standardize to a single solution, and measure results.

TABLE 19-2

Six Sigma Levels, Performance Accuracy, and Implications for Nursing

Sigma Level	Performance Accuracy/Million	Defective Performance/Million	Implication for Nursing Practice
1	310,000 (30.9% accuracy)	690,000	309 of 1,000 clients interactions made the clients feel that the nurse truly understood their concerns
2	692,000 (69.2% accuracy)	308,000	692 of 1,000 IVs are inserted successfully on the first attempt
3	933,200 (93.3% accuracy)	66,800	933 of 1,000 postoperative complications are detected and treated effectively
4	993,790 (99.4% accuracy)	6,210	994 of 1,000 medications are accurately administered
5	999,680 (99.98% accuracy)	320	4,999 of 5,000 physician orders are transcribed accurately
6	999,996.6 (99.9997% accuracy)	3.4	Between three and four errors are made per million client care documentation entries on medical records

Adapted from Pande, P., Neuman, R., & Cavanagh, R. (2000). *The Six Sigma way.* New York: McGraw-Hill.

5. Control: Establish standard measurements to maintain performance and correct problems as needed.

An acronym DMAIC ("pronounced deh-MAY-ihk" [Pande et al., 2000, p. 37]) is frequently used as a shortcut to communicate these Six Sigma process improvement processes or process design/redesign processes. Six Sigma may be superior to TQM/CQI initiatives. Six Sigma has one definition: "a business system for achieving and sustaining success through customer focus, process management and improvement, and the wise use of facts and data" (Pande et al., p. 3). Six Sigma is tied to the bottom line of the organization because funding efforts for it are based more on fact than TQM funding, which is based on faith (Chowdhury, 2002; Pande et al.). Six Sigma sets a no-nonsense but ambitious goal of 3.4 defective parts per million opportunities (Chowdhury; Pande et al.) rather than using **benchmarking** (comparing outcomes or results with those of other similar organizations) systems as indicators for improvement. Six Sigma has the capability to detect incremental and exponential change. TQM/CQI initiatives focus on product quality, whereas Six Sigma solutions attend to all business processes. Six Sigma may hold the key to delighting both customers and nurses in health care environments (Morgan & Cooper, 2004). See Research Brief 19-1.

Questions for Reflection 19-3

1. What is the quality improvement approach used in my current clinical practice settings?
2. How have I participated in the quality improvement process in my current clinical practice setting?
3. Is it important for nurses to participate in the quality improvement process? Why or why not?

CELEBRATING SUCCESSES IN CONTINUOUS QUALITY IMPROVEMENT/ TOTAL QUALITY MANAGEMENT

One of Deming's 14 principles for quality improvement is to recognize participants once performance goals are attained (Walton, 1986). In the early 1980s, the American manufacturing industry was trailing Japan. President Ronald Reagan signed a bill to investigate ways in which the government could reward organizations for productivity improvement. A decision was made to create a National Quality Award, and Congress passed the Malcolm Baldrige Quality Improvement Act (Public Law 100-107). The **Malcolm Baldrige National Quality Award** was named in honor of the acting secretary of commerce and amateur rodeo rider who was killed in a horse-riding accident. Only two awards per category can be awarded in any year (Baldrige National Quality Program, 2004; Hart & Bogan, 1992).

The National Institute of Standards and Technology developed criteria for the award to provide meaning and legitimacy to the Baldrige Award. The Baldrige quality framework consists of the following criteria, known as the "7 pillars": (1) leadership, (2) information and analysis, (3) strategic quality planning, (4) human resource development and management, (5) management of process quality, (6) quality and operating results, and (7) customer service and satisfaction.

The Baldrige Award process reviews organizational approaches to quality, how organizations deploy their approach, and results of the deployed approaches. Criteria for excellence in an approach mean that the approach is prevention based; has multiple evaluation/improvement cycles; uses appropriate and effective tools, techniques, and methods; is systematic, integrated, and consistently applied; is quantitatively based; and appears innovative. The organization's deployment of the program is analyzed for its use by all work groups, the appropriateness of processes and activities, the characteristics of

Research Brief 19-1

Morgan, S., & Cooper, C. (2004). Shoulder work intensity with Six Sigma. *Nursing Management*, *35*, 28–32.

The investigators performed a pilot project designed to change the workload intensity for nurses working on medical, progressive-care, and women and children's units. Data were collected using staff surveys generated from information obtained with telephone interviews with nursing staff and leaders, and registered nurse (RN) focus groups. Persons completing surveys were patient care staff members, prescribers who admitted patients to the units, and patient care staff family members.

Results of the survey revealed that the two key contributors to work dissatisfaction were work assignments and unavailability of client care supplies and equipment. According to the family members of staff, arriving home late and a lack of satisfaction with daily accomplishments were major contributors to job dissatisfaction. The project also identified the following key drivers that prevented nurses from feeling closure with daily assignments: client room readiness, multiple attempts to start intravenous (IV) lines, issues with phlebotomy, inability to find equipment, missing medication, delays with equipment repair, unavailability of supplies, client transportation, and no time for breaks.

The drivers then served as the basis for a work group to develop a workload data collection instrument in which RNs and licensed practical nurses collected data daily (24-hour time frame) for 1 week. A baseline score was obtained. After focusing on missing medications, phlebotomy skills, and IV line–starting skills; standardizing location for supplies and equipment; and using color-coded tags for supply bins, data were recollected using the workload data collection instrument. After initiation of all changes in work processes, overall workload closure score increased, resulting in reduced job dissatisfaction.

Results of this pilot project reveal the complexity of nurse job satisfaction and how work-related problems increase nurse workload. Caution should be exercised when interpreting study findings because the investigators failed to specify the number of nurses participating in the project and the number of observations related to workload to determine baseline and resultant scores. Future studies using Six Sigma as a framework need to be performed to validate the effectiveness of Six Sigma as a means to improve the quality of work processes used in health care.

the products or services offered by the organization, the transactions and interactions with customers, and, finally, the internal processes and activities (including physical facilities and employees). The resulting criteria consider the following eight characteristics: (1) the absolute level of quality in the results (products, services, in health care–client outcomes), (2) comparison of results with others in the industry and world leaders, (3) quality improvement rate, (4) quality improvement breadth, (5) duration of quality improvement (maintenance of sustained gains), (6) significance of improvements to the organization's business, (7) company ability to demonstrate that the improvements made were derived from the quality approach (practices and actions), and (8) contributions of outcomes and effect on the quality improvement process.

At this time, three integrated health care systems (SSM Health Care, St. Louis, MO; Sharp Health Care, San Diego, CA; and Mercy Health System, Janesville, WI) and five hospitals (St. Luke's Hospital, Kansas City, MO; Baptist Hospital Inc., Pensacola, FL; Robert Wood Johnson University Hospital, Hamilton, NJ; Bronson Methodist Hospital, Kalamazoo, MI; and Northern Mississippi Medical Center, Tupelo, MS) have received the Baldrige National Quality Award (National Institutes of Standards, 2007). Along with the Baldridge National Quality Award, most states offer quality award programs. Winning a quality award serves as a valuable marketing strategy in a health care system driven by competition and health cost reductions (Sultz & Young, 2004).

Some institutions post baseline and improvement data in view of health team members and consumers to showcase the accomplishment of quality improvement goals.

Posters highlighting goal attainment frequently recognize members of process improvement teams. Sometimes, intraagency publications express appreciation to workers for gains in quality. Other institutions provide recognition ceremonies for nurses and other team members who achieve performance improvement goals (Sultz & Young, 2004).

KEY CONCEPTS OF TOTAL QUALITY IMPROVEMENT AND OTHER QUALITY MANAGEMENT APPROACHES

Total quality improvement (TQI) may be viewed as an organizational value and process to deliver the best possible goods and services to consumers. TQI works to improve constancy in actions while meeting (and exceeding) product and service standards. The International Organization for Standardization (ISO) is an international, nongovernmental organization composed of a network of national standards institutes of 146 countries. The goal of the ISO is to set international standards to meet business requirements as well as broader needs of a global human society. ISO standards benefit society by prompting fair trade; compatibility of technology; conformity of consumer products in terms of safety, quality, and reliability; scientific knowledge and technology for health; and guidelines to prevent global environmental contamination (ISO, 2004). The ISO outlines eight key principles for TQM known as ISO 9000. ISO 9000 ensures consistency among all international efforts aimed at TQM, CQI, and TQI. The eight principles are outlined in Table 19-3, with examples of how a health care organization might follow them. Key principles of TQI consider persons who receive services and attend to persons providing services. Therefore, TQI enhances the health care delivery experience for everyone.

To summarize, all QI programs focus efforts on the following four areas: (1) customer service (internal customers are those who work within an organization, and external customers are the consumers of the organization's service), (2) ways to improve the quality of key work processes, (3) development and use of quality tools and statistics, and (4) involvement of all persons and organizational departments that provide service to the consumer. Effectiveness of QI initatives relies on institutional benchmarking, a process that uses standardized performance evaluation tools and compares results within the institution (to track gains in quality) or with similar institutions (to determine how well the organization is performing against others). Recently tools used to evaluate quality use a balanced scorecard system that examines performance in the four following areas: (1) consumer satisfaction, (2) financial performance and stability, (3) use of clinical services and outcomes, and (4) change and system integration (Sultz & Young, 2004; Hall et al., 2007). When performance fails to reach the benchmark, all persons within the organization work together to fix the work process rather than blaming individuals or each other.

TQM/CQI PROCESSES IN HEALTH CARE

TQM/CQI places consumers first. Persons providing services seek to find ways to streamline work processes. Deming proposed that the more complex work processes have more chances of error. Consistency of action reduces error rates (Walton, 1986; Sultz & Young, 2004). TQM/CQI programs use a variety of instruments to identify variations in work processes. Some of these instruments are presented in Table 19-4. With the exception of regression analysis, most of the instruments diagram the steps of a given process, thereby providing QI team members with a picture, and thus facilitating identification of variations along with potential sources for error.

Once the work process has been fully described, participants in the TQM/CQI process can proceed in implementing the Deming PDCA cycle. Notice that the first five steps involve planning and the final step restarts the cycle by looking for ways to improve the

TABLE 19-3

Key Principles of TQI Based on ISO Principles and How a Health Care Organization Might Follow Them

TQM/ISO Principles	Examples
Customer focus: the goal is to delight external and internal customers	• For external customers (recipients of health care services), provide them with "the little" extras that make big differences, such as customized menus, backrubs, esthetically appealing rooms • For internal customers (physicians, interdisciplinary health care professionals, nursing staff members, and other supportive client services staff), create an open, trusting work environment that encourages collaboration and suggestions to improve work-related processes that are studied, and if feasible, implemented
Leadership: the goal is to provide vision, direction and understanding of the constancy of purpose among all members of the organization	• Empower all workers by inviting them to participate in departmental strategic planning • Provide education about the mission, values, goals and objectives of the organization to all workers
Involvement of people: all persons within the organization should feel ownership in the TQM values and processes	• Formation of nursing unit and other departmental-based quality circles • Form interdepartmental and interdisciplinary quality improvement teams to improve work processes that involve more than one department or discipline • Institute interdisciplinary shared governance systems for nursing and other professional disciplines
Process approach: desired results are more effectively accomplished when related resources and activities are defined and managed as a process	• Constant monitoring of organizational performance, comparing results with similar organizations (benchmarking), and sharing results on a regular basis with all organizational members • Consistent use of client care pathways
Systems approach to management: leaders and persons in the organization must look outside the organization to plan how best to use physical, monetary, and human resources	• Analyzing local, regional, and global trends to plan future services • Reviewing and analyzing current work processes to determine how to improve health care and health education services • Staying abreast of the latest scientific advancements in disease management, illness prevention, health promotion, and health care delivery
Continual improvement: constant improvement becomes a permanent organizational objective	• Always looking for ways to improve delivery of health care services • Continual reinforcing the importance of improving quality with staff via education, informing staff of performance results • Sharing data with all organizational members who deliver specific services
Factual approach to decision making: actual data, current trends, and other forms of objective information serve as the basis for decision making within the organization	• Staying informed of current trends and advances in health care • Using data generated by quality improvement processes to guide actions, changes and plans • Piloting new equipment before making purchases
Mutually beneficial supplier relationships: the organization forms partnerships with external contractors based on the quality of goods and services they can provide	• Identifying vendors that provide high-quality products • Securing exclusive purchasing contracts with identified vendors

Adapted from ISO (2004) and St. Luke's Hospital of Kansas City Organizational Manual (2008).

TABLE 19-4

Instruments Used in TQM/CQI Programs

Instrument	Description	Advantages
Flow chart	Graphic representation of sequence of events required to attain a specific outcome. Specific symbols depict steps of a process (rectangle = activity, diamond-shaped polygon = decisions, triangle = wait, large circle = file, small circle = go to another point, arrows demarking direction of the overall process.	Easily identify sources of variation and easily updated to keep current
Fishbone diagram	A horizontal line depicts the work process with the desired outcome appearing at the far lefthand side of diagram. Inputs into the work process are represented as lines (or spines) that intersect the horizontal line drawn obliquely from the base line in upward or downward directions. The diagram looks like a fish skeleton.	Great for depicting work processes during brainstorming sessions, readily stratified to show details
Run chart	Displays the frequency of events or a particular observation over time. Frequency counts are connected by a line.	Wonderful way to depict data alterations arising from changes and key for knowing if improvements have resulted from changes
Pareto chart	Displays data using a rank order. Factors with the most frequent observation appear first, followed by less frequent observations.	Ability to stratify causes, identifies the top causes, helpful to prioritize changes and useful to show results of change
Histogram	Bar-type graph that displays the frequency of something occurring.	Ability to detect frequency of root causes in a process and useful for tracking results of changes
Control chart	Depicted as a run chart, but has statistically determined upper and lower limits of variation above and below the average performance	Essential to see if process remains under control
Scatter diagram	A point is placed across a vertical and horizontal axis to demonstrate the relationship between two variables.	Useful to see if any relationships between two variables are occurring to detect causes and to monitor the effects of changes
Regression analysis	Statistical testing of correlational models.	Tests hypothesis used by organizations for decision making

Adapted from Koch, M., & Fairly, T. (1993). *Integrated quality management, the key to improving nursing care quality.* St. Louis: Mosby; McLaughlin, C., & Kaluzny, A. (1999). *Continuous quality improvement in health care* (2nd ed.). Gaithersburg, MD: Aspen.

process. The following is an example of how Laura, the nurse in the chapter vignette, and the nursing department where she works would use TQM/CQI to correct the problem.

Step 1: Identify a work process to be improved: Accuracy of warfarin administration.

Step 2: Organize a CQI/TQM team: Select members to serve on the team that are involved in the work process. In this case, members would include a physician who writes warfarin orders, a unit secretary who transcribes the physician order, a pharmacist who fills the order, a courier who delivers daily doses to the nursing units, and one or two nurses who note off physician orders and administer the medication.

Step 3: Clarify the current work process: The team meets and diagrams the current process from the time the order is written until the client receives the ordered medication.

Step 4: Identify and understand all variation sources: The team notices that there may be as few as four persons (if the nurse transcribes and gives the medication) to as many as seven persons involved in the process of daily warfarin administration. The team also notes that daily orders may be written at any time during the day and that sometimes a daily order may not be given. They analyze all the medication incident reports filed related to warfarin administration that confirm the information generated from the brainstorming session. In addition, they create a checklist for collecting data regarding administration of warfarin for 2 weeks before the next meeting.

Step 5: Select the improvement: The team discovered after its data collection that administration of the medication to the wrong client occurred infrequently, but delay in administration was a more prevalent quality problem. Therefore, the team decides that perhaps commonly administered dosages could be placed in the computerized medication-dispensing station and a nurse will double-check warfarin with another nurse before giving it to a client. The suggestion is made to institute a bar-coding device medication administration system at a future date.

Step 6: Implement the improvement: The nurses obtain ordered doses from the computerized medication-dispensing system, and check the doses with another nurse.

Step 7: Check and compare results with desired outcome: Within a month of implementing step 6, the number of incident reports filed related to warfarin administration decreases by 25%.

Step 8: Take steps to maintain improved performance and suggest ways to further improve the process: Proposal is made for a hospital-wide patient band/medication bar-coding system to be purchased and implemented within the next 2 years.

Using a TQM/CQI approach, Laura, the nurse, does not receive a reprimand from her manager for giving the medication to the wrong client; rather, work processes are found to contribute to her error and those made by other nurses. In health care, the professional nurse plays a pivotal role in TQM/CQI.

To recognize success in implementing the TQM/CQI project, the hospital acknowledges contributions of the QI team in the organizational newsletter. The team also posts graphs indicating reduction in warfarin administration errors in the staff lounge of the cardiac unit.

PROFESSIONAL NURSING ROLES IN QUALITY IMPROVEMENT

TQM/CQI provides professional nurses an opportunity to showcase the unique contributions they make to interdisciplinary health care delivery. Because nurses have always been concerned with client safety and quality of care, they can assume leadership roles in TQM/CQI processes. Data collection by nurses as part of routine care delivery sometimes identifies a quality initiative (an area for improvement). In addition, the professional nurse serves as a key player in developing work processes and strategies to improve care quality. The following discussion outlines how nurses might use professional nursing roles to promote QI.

The Role of Caregiver and Quality Improvement

Professional nursing continues to study the effects of nursing care on client outcomes. Client outcomes that arise directly from nursing assessment and intervention are known as **nursing-sensitive outcomes**. Display 19-1 displays nursing-sensitive outcomes that have been identified to date. Most of these outcomes have been identified through nursing research or comprehensive literature reviews of nursing research studies examining the impact of professional nursing care on client outcomes (Doran, 2003; National Quality Forum, 2004; Sunton, 2008). Recent research suggests that increased levels of registered

Nursing-Sensitive Outcomes

DISPLAY 19-1

Client Outcomes

Safety from medication and other treatment-related errors

Functional status

Self-care

Effective symptom management

Effective pain management

Satisfaction with received health care services

Effective management of fatigue

Effective management of nausea and vomiting

Effective management of dyspnea

Early detection and effective management of postoperative complications

Reduced incidence of urinary tract infections

Reduced incidence of pneumonia

Increased incidence of successful rescue following cardiac or respiratory arrest

Reduced injury from falling

Reduced rates of institutionally acquired pressure ulcers

Reduced incidence of physical or chemical restraints

Reduced incidence of bloodstream infections from central line use

Information from Doran, D. (Ed.). (2003). *Nursing-sensitive outcomes: The state of the science*. Sudbury, MA: Jones & Bartlett.

Dunton, N. (2008). Take a cue from the NDNQI. *Nursing Management, 39*(4), 20, 22, 23

Institute of Medicine. (2004). *Keeping patients safe*. Washington, DC: National Academies Press.

National Quality Forum. (2004). NFQ-endorsed national voluntary consensus standards for nursing-sensitive care. Available at http://216.122.138.39/nursing/. Accessed July 15, 2008.

---

nurses improve client outcomes, reduce hospital-acquired complications, and reduce health care costs (Newbold, 2007; Ridley, 2008).

In daily practice, nurses collect data that substantiate adherence to Centers for Disease Control (CDC) and institutional standards for care when they document routine care processes. Some institutions have a quality council that determines what work processes need evaluation to determine QI opportunities. For example, for hospitals to get third-party reimbursement for IV tubing and supplies, the information must be documented in client medical records. If a hospital is interested in determining how well nurses are following CDC and institutional standards for IV therapy, the practicing nurse performs chart audits (a review of records) to identify when nurses are changing IV sites and tubing. After audit data are tabulated, nurses receive the results. If results reveal that standards are not being followed, a QI team analyzes the work processes for changing IV sites and tubing. Depending on the outcome of the analysis, the team then determines how to change work processes and provides staff education to ensure that all nurses follow outlined processes rather than taking shortcuts. (The IOM [2004] identified shortcuts or workarounds as frequent causes of error in health care delivery.) However, if the chart audits reveal that performance meets or exceeds desired performance, some form of recognition is given to staff responsible for effective IV management.

Because cost-effectiveness of health care has been identified as an indicator of quality health care, nurses in clinical practice look for ways to use human and material resources judiciously. Professional nurses use cost-effective strategies when they take time to attend to little details associated with care delivery that, if ignored, could result in poor client outcomes. For example, the Centers for Medicare and Medicaid Services (CMS) eliminated additional payments to hospitals for the following complications associated with hospitalization: pressure ulcer development, preventable injuries, ventilator-acquired pneumonia, deep venous thrombosis development, urinary and vascular catheter–associated infections, designated surgical site infections, objects left in patients during surgical procedures, and blood incompatibility reactions (Kurtzman & Buerhaus, 2008). Meticulous attention to infection control guidelines, implementing interventions known to prevent infections, promoting safe administration of blood, and addressing client immobility improve client outcomes while reducing increased costs associated with hospital-acquired infections and conditions.

In 2007, the Institute for Healthcare Improvement (IHI) launched its Protecting 5 Million Lives from Harm Campaign aimed at preventing patient exposure to harm while receiving health care. They defined "medical harm as an unintended physical injury" arising from either the absence or result of medical interventions "that requires additional monitoring, treatment or hospitalization, or that results in death" (p. 4). The following interventions aimed at reducing harm affect nurses employed in 3,100 hospitals as they provide nursing care: (1) use of rapid response teams at initial signs of patient deteriorating condition; (2) use of evidence-based strategies for managing acute myocardial infarctions; (3) prevention of infections associated with central lines, surgical sites, and ventilators; (4) avoidance of harm from high-alert medications (anticoagulants, narcotics, insulin, and sedatives); (5) prevention of pressure ulcers; 6) use of scientifically supported infection control practice to reduce the incidence of methicillin-resistant *Staphylococcus aureus*; and (7) use of evidence-based protocols for congestive heart failure to avoid hospital readmissions. Like the CMS reimbursement schedule changes, many address the need for careful use of infection control measures. However, evidence-based protocols for disease management and safe medication use require effective communication among members of the health care team.

The Role of Critical Thinker and Quality Improvement

Critical thinking is an essential cognitive skill used by nurses as they make clinical decisions. To ensure safe and quality nursing care delivery, professional nurses engage in multiple activities requiring critical thinking, from determining what assessments are appropriate for a clinical situation to how well clients have met desired care outcomes.

The process of safe administration of medication provides a key example of how nurses use critical thinking to promote high-quality care and identify areas for QI. Medication administration, an activity frequently performed by nurses, poses great risks to clients. More than 770,000 persons die or suffer irreversible injury annually because of adverse drug events (including medication errors) (IOM, 2004). Causes of medication errors include prescription errors; increased nurse responsibility for knowing medication dosages, action and potential adverse effects; errors in calculated dosages; and nurse interruptions (Cohen, Robinson, & Mandrack, 2003; IOM, 2004). Work-related processes identified by the respondents as contributing to medication errors include being distracted or interrupted when administering medication, having inadequate staff, caring for high numbers of clients, reading illegible medication orders, working with medications with similar names and packaging, and having incorrect dosage calculations. The IOM (2004) reported these findings along with miscommunication, lack of patient information, infusion pump malfunctions, and problems with IV delivery (extravasations, incompatibility of medications, dilutants, and ordered fluids).

Nurses use critical thinking to develop theoretical approaches to evaluate and improve the quality of nursing care (Sidani, Doran, & Mitchell, 2004). The following five key factors interact to affect client outcomes (directly or indirectly):

1. Client characteristics: personal, sociocultural, and health-related factors
2. Professional characteristics: personal (dedication, commitment, and finding meaning in work), educational preparation, keeping current with new practice advances, and sociocultural factors
3. Health care setting: physical layout, availability of supplies, and organizational culture
4. Health care interventions for client: invasiveness, risks, type, and if individualized to specific client
5. Nature and timing or attainment of expected outcomes for health care interventions

The functions of all five characteristics produce direct effects on client outcomes, thereby accounting for individual and variable responses to nursing and health care interventions.

Sidani et al. (2004) also identified two forms of indirect effects: "moderating and media-ting" (p. 61). Moderating effects address the effectiveness of care to produce desired out-comes according to different levels of the five factors, and mediating effects explain variance based on all factor effects on the intervention provided to the client.

A nursing-specific theoretical approach to evaluate nursing care is more valuable to nurses than relying on approaches used by medicine or business. As critical thinkers, nurses who use a theoretical approach can generate questions to gather data for a holistic approach to nursing care concerns and choose instruments to consistently measure the effects of nursing care. A theoretical approach also fosters an understanding of the unique contributions nurses make in the health care setting. A consistent approach to evaluating nursing care fosters quality improvement initiatives because comparisons can be tracked over time.

The Role of Client Advocate and Quality Improvement

Nurses work endlessly to consider the client's best interests. When participating in qual-ity improvement activities, nurses advocate for all clients. Improvements in work proc-esses reduce care errors. Nurses who acknowledge the effects of physical and mental fatigue advocate for clients when refusing to work overtime. Nurses who provide direct client care services for time frames equal to or exceeding 12.5 hours triple the chance of making errors (Rogers, Hwang, Scott, Aiken, & Dinges, 2004). Working extra shifts also increases the chance of committing nursing care errors (Rogers et al., 2004; IOM, 2004).

Despite the research evidence linking long shifts and overtime to nursing errors, some nurses volunteer for overtime shifts to fill staffing shortages. Some institutions require nurses to work overtime. Many nurses consider long hours and overtime acceptable and agree to work them despite the effects of fatigue on judgment (Leighty, 2004). Nurses who refuse extra shifts may be perceived as not being good members of the nursing care teams. However, refusing to work long hours and overtime may be the best way to pre-vent nursing care errors, increasing the quality of health care services while ultimately looking out for the client's best interest.

The Role of Change Agent and Quality Improvement

Professional nurses act as change agents when they identify needed changes in work processes to improve the quality of nursing care. Change occurs rapidly in the health care arena. As new health care devices, medications, and treatment advances become avail-able, nurses need to change practice procedures. Nurses, as stakeholders in the delivery of health care, continuously examine which rituals and routines remain applicable and determine which ones should be discarded (Porter-O'Grady & Malloch, 2007).

As leaders of a nursing care team, professional nurses must clearly communicate changes in practice procedures to all team members. Some staff members (especially those who have worked in nursing for a long time) need to learn new approaches, learn how to operate new machinery, and learn new skills. Replacing traditional practice may create distress for some older nurses. Successful integration of change requires that the innovation fits well with the practice setting, has congruence with staff roles, improves client outcomes, and complements values and beliefs. Empowering staff for making work-related decisions and empowering clients to assume responsibility for their health increase the chance of successful change (Porter-O'Grady & Malloch, 2007). Because change requires unlearning old ways and learning new ones, the role of counselor/teacher becomes critical.

The Role of Counselor/Teacher and Quality Improvement

Before adopting an innovation, staff must be educated about the reasons for the innova-tion, changes in practice policies, and how to operate new equipment (if applicable). Staff educational programs may be planned using the teaching/learning principles outlined in Chapter 18. Interdepartmental educational programs provide staff with the opportunity to network, share successes with change, and support each other.

Along with education, nurses and unlicensed care providers need emotional support during times of nonstop change. Psychological effects of change have been delineated in Chapter 19. Staffs need time to grieve for the way things have been traditionally done before they can fully embrace innovations. When the innovation process becomes tough or stuck, staff relationships may be the only glue holding the nursing care team together. Taking time to deeply listen to peers and team members fosters capturing the messages and the meanings that surround ever-continual change processes associated with TQM/CQI programs (Porter-O'Grady & Malloch, 2007).

The Role of Coordinator and Quality Improvement

As care coordinators, nurses must assess work colleagues for their ability to perform safe, effective client care. Physical and mental fatigue impair work performance. Actual errors and near misses (errors caught just in time before they occurred) are more likely to happen when hospital nurses work longer than 12-hour stretches; work overtime, regardless of shift length; and work more than 50 hours per week (IOM, 2004; Rogers et al., 2004).

As coordinators of care, professional nurses must seek ways to provide quality of care while using resources effectively. Nursing unit characteristics directly affect client outcomes. Increased nurse perception of autonomy/collaboration has been instrumental in reducing incidences of urinary tract infections and failure-to-rescue events. When specialized nurses provide care with continuity, lower rates of pneumonia and cardiac arrests were reported along with shorter length of hospital stays. High levels of nurse manager support have been associated with reduced levels of pressure ulcer prevalence and client mortality (Aiken, Smith, & Lake, 1994; Aiken, Clarke, & Sloane, 2000; Boyle, 2004; Haven & Aiken, 1999).

The Role of Colleagues and Quality Improvement

The American way of life values independence and self-sufficiency. Nurses frequently have a strong sense of responsibility for individual vigilance that accentuates independence and self-sufficiency. Some nurses believe that asking for help with client assignments might be viewed as a sign of incompetence. Also, these nurses are afraid of being perceived as being weak if they need to ask for assistance with a problem (Tucker & Edmondson, 2003). However, the QI process discourages this form of thinking, as all health team members have the responsibility to point out work process flaws.

As a colleague on the interdisciplinary (multidisciplinary or interprofessional) health care team, nurses have an equal responsibilty to engage in collaboration with team members to promote safe, effective health care delivery. Nurses have the responsibility to share concerns about clients when they arise with other members of the health care team. Effective teamwork facilitates safety and quality in health care. Establishment of a culture of safety in health care organizations requires trust among nurses, physicians, hospital administration, and all health team members. A culture of safety uses errors as an opportunity for learning rather than blaming. Team training for client emergencies using simulated experiences helps team members identify each other's roles, learn how to best execute their roles confidently, create a venue to dispel stereotypes associated with each team member, and provide an opportunity for collegial networking (Barnsteiner, Disch, Hall, Mayer, & Moore, 2007; Finkleman & Kenner, 2007; Grey & Connolly, 2008; Weaver, 2008).

When flaws are identified with work processes, multidisciplinary QI teams are formed. Participation in the QI project team provides opportunities for nurses to network with other members of the health care team, thereby strengthening working relationships with them. During team deliberations, members of the QI team have opportunities to see and value the unique skills and approaches they bring to client health care delivery.

AN INTEGRATED APPROACH TO QUALITY IMPROVEMENT AND SAFETY IN HEALTH CARE

Improving the quality and safety of health care requires a fully integrated approach from all stakeholders. Quality improvement initiatives from various stakeholders tend to overlap. Table 19-5 compares and contrasts quality improvement and safety programs from the Institute of Medicine, reports (primarily physician-based), Quality and Safety in Nursing Education (QSEN) (nursing education's response to the IOM recommendations funded by the Robert Wood Johnson Foundation), and the Joint Commission accreditation standards and safety goals (a nonprofit, regulatory body). QSEN opted to separate safety from quality because nurses traditionally have assumed the role of client advocate. Since the inception of the profession, nurses have assumed the obligation of keeping clients safe. Nurse educators established desired knowledge, skills, and attitudes associated with each competency to provide guidance for basic and continuing nursing education. IOM and QSEN competences and the Joint Commission standards and safety goals cross the entire health care continuum. Although the competencies, standards, and safety goals differ slightly, improving the quality and safety of health care delivery is the ultimate goal.

Effectiveness and safety serve as two hallmarks of quality health care (Finkleman & Kenner, 2007). To ensure fiscally responsible expenditures of taxes, the federal government no longer covers expenses incurred from hospital-acquired injuries and illnesses. The government also bestows awards (the Baldrige Quality Award) and recognizes health care organizations by publishing lists for consumer use to facilitate decision making about where to access quality health care. The Joint Commission also publishes and posts online lists of fully accredited providers, along with deficiencies found in others. For-profit health care insurance companies sometimes follow the lead of the federal government in cutting health care costs.

Nonprofit organizations such as the Institute for Healthcare Improvement (IHI) provide the voice of health care consumers in improving the quality and safety of health care. The 5 Million Lives Campaign designed and implemented through the IHI has the leadership and financial support of America's Blue Cross and Blue Shield health plans, the Cardinal Health Foundation, Blue Shield of California foundation, the Aetna Foundation, Baxter International Inc., and Abbott Fund (charitable arms on nonprofit and for-profit companies; Institute for Healthcare Improvement, 2007). Frequently, newspapers and magazines read by the public publish lists of the best health care organizations for general care or care for a specific disease. Thus, consumers, like health care professionals, become capable of making evidence-based health care decisions for themselves.

Consumers also play a key role in quality improvement and safety in health care. When they enter the health care system, consumers need to communicate their needs to providers. Consumers also need to freely share all information (such as a complete list of all medications, including those obtained over the counter, herbal supplements, and other home remedies) that could impact the health care provider's decisions for a safe treatment plan. Consumers are more apt to share detailed information when providers develop helping and healing relationships with them (see Chapter 4). Along with freely shared information about themselves, consumers provide valuable input into health care delivery processes when they complete satisfaction questionnaires for rendered services.

Therefore, many persons play key roles in developing and maintaining a culture of safety and quality for health care. The development of a culture of safety and quality may mean that some stakeholders might have to change behaviors and attitudes. When all have access to knowledge and take time to listen to each other, health care safety and quality improve. Everyone involved in health care delivery becomes capable of making evidence-based decisions. Evidence ranges from individual client values and preferences to a meta-analysis of research studies and/or clinical trials to determine best practices.

TABLE 19-5

Comparing and Contrasting Recommendations of the Institute of Medicine (IOM), Quality Safety in Nursing Education (QSEN), and The Joint Commission to Improve the Quality of Health Care

Key Consideration	IOM	QSEN Competencies	Selected Joint Commission Standards and Goals
Keeping health care services focused on consumers/patients/clients	*Provide Patient-Centered Care* Pros and cons of decentralized care Fragmentation of care Self-management support Health care literacy Effective use of interpreters Patient health information Family and/or caregiver preparation Consumer perceptions of health care needs Care coordination	*Patient-Centered Care* Acknowledgment of the patient (or designated other) is the course of control Compassionate, coordinated care is delivered in full partnership with the patient (or designee) Care is planned and delivered considering patient values, preferences, and needs	Standards address the need for care, treatment, and services based on assessment of patient needs, individualizing the treatment or care plan based on identified patient strengths and weaknesses along with relevant health education for client self-care based on client ability, educational level, reading ability, and language. National Standards for Culturally and Linguistically Appropriate Services in Health Care Reconciliation of all medications across the care continuum Facilitate patients' active involvement in their care as a strategy to promote client safety Required screening for patient and family complaints
Use special expertise to foster the best possible care across the care continuum for consumers of health care services	*Work on Interdisciplinary Teams* Creation of a culture of safety Development of an environment of learning rather than blaming Team learning, education, and training Adaptation to constant change	*Teamwork and Collaboration* Team efforts aimed at attaining high-quality patient care. Nurses communicate and function as effective teams with each other. Nurses function effectively in interprofessional teams. Effective teamwork is characterized by open communication, mutual respect, and shared decision making.	A nurse executive serves as a senior leader and provides effective leadership to coordinate nursing care treatment and services. Nurse executives are licensed professional nurses, have advanced education (graduate or postgraduate degree in nursing or a related field), and have managerial experience. A nurse executive directs and establishes guidelines for nursing care, treatment, and services, while directing nursing standards, policies, procedures, and staffing plans. Improve communication among caregivers including written or computer-entered physician orders, read-back-order verification

(continued)

Comparing and Contrasting Recommendations of the Institute of Medicine (IOM), Quality Safety in Nursing Education (QSEN), and The Joint Commission to Improve the Quality of Health Care (Continued)

Key Consideration	IOM	QSEN Competencies	Selected Joint Commission Standards and Goals
			for telephone orders, and test results along with mechanisms to document the read-back procedure. Standardized hand-off communication procedures that include time for asking and responding to questions. Emergency Department guidelines for nutritional screening, immunization status, and repeated visits. Required screening for facility selection of human resource indicators (e.g., overtime, staffing plan, staff injury, and nursing care hours per patient day)
Decision making by using all possible forms of evidence to provide the best possible outcomes for recipients of health care services	*Employ Evidence-Based Practice* Use of evidence-based practice resources Involvement in quality and safety research projects Evaluating evidence (systematic literature reviews and research studies)	*Evidence-Based Practice* Integration of best current evidence, nurse clinical expertise, and client preferences and values to deliver optimal health care	Implement best practices or evidence-based guidelines to manage central lines and prevent surgical site infections Health professional access to the latest developments in health care delivery and methods to facilitate optimal client outcomes Evidence of multidisciplinary approaches to manage complex client situations
Provide the safest and best quality care possible	*Apply Quality Improvement* Error management (analysis of actual errors, human factors, generation of solutions, and legal issues) The Joint Commission and QI (informed about latest standards) Medication administration (increased use of drugs, multiple-drug use in a single client, medication administration processes, preventing adverse drug events, collaborative approaches to medication management, and effective medication management)	*Quality Improvement* Use data to assess outcomes of care delivery processes Use quality improvement method cycles (plan, do, check, act) to test proposed changes before making them standard practices for improving the safety and quality of health care systems *Safety (separated as a separate competency because of long-standing nurse professional responsibility to keep clients safe)* Analyze individual effectiveness strategies to keep clients and providers safe	Use of a minimum of two patient identifiers when giving medication, blood or blood components acquiring lab specimens, and providing treatments or procedures. Use of a standardized list of abbreviations that do not contain dangerous abbreviations, symbols, and designations for medication dosages. Procedures for reporting critical results and values along with processes for measuring desired outcomes. Limit the use of look-alike–sound-alike medication to a total of 10. Labeling of all medications, medication cups, syringes,

Comparing and Contrasting Recommendations of the Institute of Medicine (IOM), Quality Safety in Nursing Education (QSEN), and The Joint Commission to Improve the Quality of Health Care (Continued)

Key Consideration	IOM	QSEN Competencies	Selected Joint Commission Standards and Goals
	Safety in Care Plan (avoiding wrong-site surgeries, preventing falls, setting safety standards, containing infections, attending mortality and morbidity conferences, participating in risk management programs, accessing standards of care and clinical guidelines, and making safety an essential staff competency)	Analyze system process to keep clients and providers safe	and solutions (on and off sterile fields) Standardized protocols for anticoagulation therapy Compliance with CDC or WHO hand hygiene and infection control practice guidelines Root cause analysis of sentinel events Fall reduction risk program Programs for improved early recognition and response to patient condition changes Pre-procedure verification process following a universal protocol prior to invasive procedures that include a "time out" before a procedure is started.
Integration of available technology to provide optimal safe health care services across the health care continuum	*Utilize Informatics* Clinical computer information systems that share client information across the care continuum. Use computer-based reminder systems. Computers as a means to access comprehensive client information. Clinical decision-making support programs.	*Informatics* Utilize information systems to facilitate knowledge communication and management Use technology and information systems to prevent and mitigate errors Use technology and information systems as resources to support clinical decisions	ORYX™ is an outcomes and performance measurement system for monitoring client outcomes with an emphasis on optimal outcome attainment. Computerized system required to track errors and near misses that occur in care delivery Ownership or access to knowledge-based information using systems, resources and services for health care professionals to access the latest information, to produce optimal client outcomes, avoid adverse events in the facility, provide needed education and information to patients (and significant others) and satisfy professional research-related needs.
Ethical care delivery	*No Competency Outlined by IOM; However, One of the 10 Rules That Apply to the Core IOM Competencies, Need for Transparency*	*No competency identified*	Accreditation standards address ethical behavior in delivery of care services, patient decision making, patient rights, and need for effective communication

(continued)

Comparing and Contrasting Recommendations of the Institute of Medicine (IOM), Quality Safety in Nursing Education (QSEN), and The Joint Commission to Improve the Quality of Health Care (Continued)

Key Consideration	IOM	QSEN Competencies	Selected Joint Commission Standards and Goals
Privacy Leadership Safe workplace (handwritten)	Collaborative teamwork Privacy of protected health information Transformational leadership Maximal use of workforce capability, including safe staffing levels, knowledge and skill acquisition, collaborative skills, verbal abuse management, interdisciplinary team forums, and work processes and work space designs (work hours, medication delivery systems, transfers, paperwork, physical layout of work spaces, use of contingent workers, development of learning organizations, and revival of nurse internships and residencies)		Hospital standards for frequent repeated emergency visits by a single client and readmissions to confront access to and use of health care services. Short-term and long term planning for meeting the needs of consumer base such as continued service programs, plans to expand services, and/or considerations for and actual discontinuation of provided services

Sources of information:

Croenwett, L., Sherwood, G., Barnsteiner, J., Disch, J., Johnson, J., Mitchell, P., et al. (2007). *Teaching IOM: Implications of the Institute of Medicine reports for nursing education.* Silver Spring, MD: American Nurses Association.

Joint Commission on Accreditation of Health Care Organizations (JCAHO). (2008). *The Joint Commission Hospital Accreditation Program 2009 chapter: National patient safety goals* (prepublication version). Available at http://www.jointcommission.org/NR/rdonlyres?3:23E-9BE8-F05BD1CB0AA8/09_NPSG_HAP.pdf. Accessed July 12, 2008.

Joint Commission on Accreditation of Health Care Organizations (JCAHO). (2008). *The Joint Commission Hospital Accreditation Program 2009 chapter: Nursing* (prepublication version). Available at http://www.jointcommission.org/STANDARDS/SII?sii_hap.htm. Accessed July 18, 2008.

SUMMARY AND SIGNIFICANCE TO PRACTICE

The process of delivering high-quality and safe health care is highly complex. Professional nurses use cognitive, communication, and clinical skills when working as partners with clients and in multidisciplinary teams. TQM/CQI programs look for opportunities to change the processes of health care delivery in order to improve the safety, effectiveness, patient focus, and efficiency. When nurses and health team members subscribe to a TQM/CQI approach, they constantly look for ways to improve care delivery. Professional nurses bring a unique perspective and offer valuable skills to enhance health care quality. All health team members must be invested in developing and maintaining a culture of safety and quality.

FROM THEORY TO PRACTICE

1. Do you think that the health care industry should be held to the same quality of services as that of big business and industry? Why or why not?

2. How would you have to change your practice and practice environment to strive toward attaining the same level of quality that is required of the business and manufacturing industries?

3. How does your clinical practice setting view incident reports? What are the advantages of having staff complete incident reports for quality monitoring purposes? Are you afraid to complete incident reports? Why or why not?

WWW INTERNET EXERCISES

1. Visit the National Quality Forum website at http://www.qualityforum.org.
   Visit the Joint Commission for Accreditation of Healthcare Organizations at http://www.jcaho.org.
   Compare the information found on these websites.
   Which website do you think offers the best information for nurses? Why or why not?
   Which website offers the best health-related information for consumers? Why or why not?

2. Visit Toyota Corporation at http://toyota.com/planetkaizen./index.html. View the online presentation of Toyota's quality improvement process. If unable to access the program, you can access the program by visiting Toyota's home page at http://www.toyota.com, then click on the words "Planet Kaizen" at the bottom of the page. What do the Japanese words *kai* and *zen* mean?

3. Visit General Electric Corporation and read about how they use Six Sigma to ensure quality products and services at http://www.ge.com/sixsigma. Learn more about the concepts of Six Sigma.

WWW INTERNET RESOURCES

Joint Commission for Accreditation of Healthcare Organizations: http://www.jcaho.org.
Institute for Healthcare Improvement: http://www.ihi.org.
National Quality Forum: http://www.qualityforum.org.
GE—Six Sigma: http://www.ge.com/sixsigma.
Toyota Planet Kaizen: http://www.toyota.com/planetkaizen/index.html.
George Group—Six Sigma—Lean: http://www.georgegroup.com.
Baldrige National Quality Program: http://www.quality.nist.gov.
See a picture and hear Dr. Juran's voice at http://www.does.org. Just click on his picture once you get to the site.
W. Edwards Deming Institute: http://www.deming.org.
Juran Institute: http://www.juran.com.
Philip Crosby Associates: http://www.philipcrosby.com.

REFERENCES

Agnes, M. (Ed.). (2005). *Webster's new world college dictionary* (4th ed.). Cleveland, OH: Wiley.
Aiken, L., Clarke, P., & Sloane, D. (2000). Hospital restructuring: Does it adversely affect care and outcomes? *Journal of Nursing Administration, 30*, 457–465.
Aiken, L., Smith, H., & Lake, E. (1994). Lower Medicare mortality among a set of hospitals known for good nursing care. *Medical Care, 32*, 771–787.
American Nurses Association. (2008). Safe staffing saves lives-safe staffing poll results. Available at http://www.safestaffingsaveslives.org/WhatisANADoing/PollResults.aspz?css=print. Accessed May 21, 2008.
Baldrige National Quality Program. (2004). Available at http://www.quality.nist.gov/Improvement_Act.htm. Accessed July 13, 2005.
Barnsteiner, J., Disch, J., Hall, L., Mayer, D., & Moore, S. (2007). Promoting interprofessional education. *Nursing Outlook, 55*(3), 144–150.
Boyle, S. (2004). Nursing unit characteristics and patient outcomes. *Nursing Economic$, 22*, 111–123.
Chowdhury, S. (2002). *The power of Six Sigma*. Chicago: Dearborn Trade.

Cohen, H., Robinson, E., & Mandrack, M. (2003). Getting to the root of medication errors: Survey results. *Nursing, 33*, 36–46.

Committee on the Quality of Health Care in America. (2001). *Crossing the quality chasm: A new health care system for the 21st century*. Washington, DC: National Academies Press.

Crosby, P. (1979). *Quality is free: The art of making quality certain*. New York: Mentor.

DesHarnais, S., & McLaughlin, C. (1999). *Continuous quality improvement in health care* (2nd ed.). Gaithersburg, MD: Aspen.

Doran, D. (Ed.). (2003). *Nursing-sensitive outcomes: State of the science*. Sudbury, MA: Jones & Bartlett.

Dunton, N. (2008). Take a cue from the NDNQI. *Nursing Management, 39*(4), 20, 22, 23.

Finkleman, A., & Kenner, C. (2007). *Teaching IOM: Implications of the Institute of Medicine reports for nursing education*. Silver Spring, MD: American Nurses Association.

Grey, M., & Connolly, C. (2008). "Coming together, keeping together, working together": Interdiscipinary to transdisciplinary research and nursing. *Nursing Outlook, 56*(5), 102–107.

Hall, L., Peterson, J., Baker, G., Brown, A., Pink, G., McKillop, I., et al. (2007). Nursing staffing and system integration and change indicators in acute care hospitals, evidence from a balanced scorecard. *Journal of Nursing Care Quality, 2*(1), 1–8.

Hart, C., & Bogan, C. (1992). *The Baldrige*. New York: McGraw-Hill.

Haven, D., and Aiken, L. (1999). Shaping systems to promote desired outcomes. *Journal of Nursing Administration, 29*, 14–20.

Institute for Healthcare Improvement. (2007). *Protecting 5 million lives from harm*. Available at http://www.ihi.org/NR/rdonlyres/EB7886DB-0955-4C9C-A9BB-599E1E53DF6D/0/5MillionLiveCampaign Brochure2007.pdf. Accessed July 15, 2008.

Institute of Medicine (IOM). (2000). *To err is human: Building a safer health system*. Washington, DC: National Academies Press.

Institute of Medicine (IOM). (2004). *Keeping patients safe*. Washington, DC: National Academies Press.

International Organization for Standardization (ISO). (2004). Introduction. Available at http://www.iso.org/iso/en/aboutiso/introduction/. Accessed July 13, 2005.

Joint Commission on Accreditation of Healthcare Organizations (JCAHO). (2004). Facts about the Joint Commission on Accreditation for Health Care Organizations (JCAHO). Available at http://www.jcaho.org/about+us.jcaho-facts/htm. Accessed July 13, 2005.

Joint Commission on Accreditation of Healthcare Organizations (JCAHO). (2008a). *The Joint Commission Hospital Accreditation Program, 2009 chapter: National Patient Safety Goals* (prepublication version). Available at http://www.jointcommission.org/rdonlyres/3:23E-9BE8-F05BD1CBOAA8/09_NPSG_HAP.pdf. Accessed July 16, 2008.

Joint Commission on Accreditation of Health Care Organizations (2008b). *The Joint Commission Hospital Accreditation Program 2009 chapter: Nursing* (prepublication version). Available at http://www.joint commission.org/STANDARDS/SII?sii_hap.htm. Accessed July 18, 2008.

Juran, J. (1989). *Juran on leadership for quality*. New York: Free Press.

Kalisch, P. A., & Kalisch, B. J. (2004). *The advance of American nursing* (4th ed.). Philadelphia: Lippincott Williams & Wilkins.

Koch, M., & Fairly, T. (1993). *Integrated quality management: The key to improving nursing care quality*. St. Louis, MO: Mosby.

Kurtzman, E., & Buerhaus, P. (2008). New Medicare payment rule: Danger or opportunities for nursing? *American Journal of Nursing, 108*(6), 30–35.

Leighty, J. (2004, August 23). Test pilots. *Nurseweek* (Heartland ed.), pp. 15–16.

Morgan, S., & Cooper, C. (2004). Shoulder work intensity with Six Sigma. *Nursing Management, 35*, 28–32.

National Institute of Standards and Technology. (2007). Baldrige Award recipients. Available at http://www.quality.nist.gov/Contacts_Profiles.htm. Accessed July 16, 2008.

National Quality Forum. (2004). NFQ-endorsed national voluntary consensus standards for nursing-sensitive care. Available at http://216.122.138.39/nursing/. Accessed July 15, 2008.

Ouchi, W. (1981). *Theory Z: How American business can meet the Japanese challenge*. Reading, MA: Addison Wesley.

Pande, P., Neuman, R., & Cavanagh, R. (2000). *The Six Sigma way: How GE, Motorola and other top companies are honing their performance*. New York: McGraw-Hill.

Porter-O'Grady, T., & Malloch, K. (2007). *Quantum leadership: A resource for health care innovation* (2nd ed). Sudbury, MA: Jones & Bartlett.

Rogers, A., Hwang, W., Scott, L., Aiken, L., & Dinges, D. (2004). The working hours of hospital staff nurses and patient safety. *Health Affairs, 23*, 202–212.

Sidani, S., Doran, D., & Mitchell, P. (2004). A theory-driven approach to evaluating quality of nursing care. *Journal of Nursing Scholarship, 36*, 60–65.

Sultz, H., & Young, K. (2004). *Health Care USA: Understanding its organization and delivery* (4th ed.). Sudbury, MA: Jones & Bartlett.

Tucker, A., & Edmondson, A. (2003). When problem solving prevents organizational learning. *Journal of Organizational Change Management, 15*, 122–137.

Walton, M. (1986). *The Deming management method.* New York: Putman.

Weaver, T. (2008). Enhancing multiple disciplinary teamwork. *Nursing Outlook, 56*(3), 108–114.

CHAPTER 20

The Professional Nurse's Role in Public Policy

KEY TERMS AND CONCEPTS

Politics

Laws

Policies

The Kingdon model for political processes

Responsible citizenship

Grassroots effort

Lobbying

Legislative agenda

Lobbying strategies

Federal legislative path

Coalition

Political action committee (PAC)

Mutual recognition state compact licensure

LEARNING OUTCOMES

By the end of this chapter, the learner will be able to:

1 Define public policy, politics, political competence lobbyist, and political action committee.

2 Explain key concepts and relationships of the Kingdon model for agenda development and policy formation.

3 Differentiate between the roles of lobbyists and political action committees.

4 List strategies used to lobby elected officials.

5 Discuss key elements of effectively written letters to elected officials.

6 Outline a plan for a personal visit with an elected official.

7 Specify strategies to stay abreast of current legislative and public policy issues.

VIGNETTE

As a result of budget cuts, school districts in a state no longer have resources to provide registered nurses (RNs) for student health services. State law specifies that a licensed practical nurse (LPN) may develop health promotion classes and health programs for a school district. Since enactment of the budgetary cut, lack of preventive health care services has resulted in the increase of the following adolescent health problems: alcohol abuse, drug abuse, sexually transmitted diseases, teenage pregnancy, obesity, and immunization noncompliance.

Nurses with children in school band together to work to overturn state policy. By assuming the roles of client advocates and change agents, the nurses approach members of the state legislature and the governor to see if they would propose legislation mandating "a registered nurse in every school."

Working to lower the speed limits on public roads, petitioning the city to install stoplights in a busy intersection, visiting an elected official to persuade action on supporting legislation on unlicensed assistive personnel (UAP) in acute health care settings, organizing a group of nurses to develop a legislative agenda, and lobbying for a bill aimed at increasing governmental funding for nursing education are a few examples of how professional nurses can influence public policy. Governmental and institutional policies greatly affect nursing practice and health care delivery.

This chapter provides an overview of public policies, various levels of governmental influence on the development and implementation of public policies, and how professional nurses influence public policies. It offers strategies for professional nurses to use when working with persons in charge of public policy development and implementation. Finally, it presents examples of nurses who have influenced public policy development and strategies for nurses to learn the art and science of political action.

Politics plays a key role in policy development. *Merriam-Webster's Collegiate Dictionary* (Agnes, 2005, p. 1114) defined **politics** as "the science and art of political government." Being political means "taking sides or prudently crafting a plan." People use political activities to influence policy development, revision, and implementation. Some policies may evolve into law. **Laws** are a set of established rules that create a system of privileges and a process for persons to solve problems with minimal force. Laws outline and govern the relationships of individuals to other individuals, organizations, and their government. In addition, laws outline and govern the relationships of the government to its citizens. In democratic societies, citizens use political action to influence the legislative process required for law enactment.

Once laws become established, polices must be developed to ensure consistency in procedures to uniformly enforce the laws. **Policies** are formalized procedures that are followed by persons responsible for delivering governmental or institutional services (Stanhope, 1996). In most cases, the government acts as the ultimate authority within society for policy enforcement (except in cases of rebellions or coups). Most laws are public policies. However, not all public policies are laws. The processes of law passage and policy development are highly complex. Therefore, presentation of a model for agenda development and policy formation provides a conceptual approach to political action of nurses.

THE KINGDON MODEL FOR POLITICAL PROCESSES

Like nursing models, nursing experts in political processes identify and use models from political science. Political action that results in policy changes requires the cooperation of legislators, special interest groups, and administrative agencies (Mason, Leavitt, & Chaffee, 2007; Milstead, 2008). The research-based **Kingdon model for political processes** offers a conceptual approach to the development of legislative agendas and public policies.

Kingdon's model addresses how issues become part of the political agenda and how alternative approaches for resolving them are developed. Kingdon (1995) specified that persons within and outside of the government play key roles in the processes. The processes for agenda development and policy formation are dynamic and fluid rather than linear and sequential, and include three key streams: (1) problem streams, (2) policy streams, and (3) political streams. A window of opportunity affects each of the three streams, thereby influencing the development of an agenda. Sometimes, a group of persons interested in publicizing an issue can develop a media campaign to illuminate the public (Abood, 2007). A formal agenda represents all issues that the government is attempting to resolve (Kingdon).

The problem stream starts with the recognition of conditions (issues that ought to be solved). Conditions become problems when people believe that something ought to be done about them. Triggers for conditions to transform into problems might be a key study report, an unexpected crisis, media attention to an issue, or a thoughtful, well-executed plan from a special interest group (Kingdon, 1995). For example, if the unemployment rate happens to rise sharply, many more Americans would lose health care insurance benefits. Conditions affecting disenfranchised members of society or those without resources to grant political favors, however, are sometimes ignored (Kingdon).

The policy stream involves determining viable approaches to solving the identified problem. Stakeholders (persons who have an interest in how the issue is addressed) present their views on how to best resolve it. During this phase, multiple approaches are generated and studied. Experts from all areas provide testimony about the issues from the governmental, private, and academic arenas. Kingdon (1995) called these experts actors. The actors know each others' views because they have awareness of each other's publications, involvement in professional organizations, and networking activities. Before addressing the problem in the formal agenda, ideas must be "softened up," a process of getting people accustomed to new approaches, building support for new ideas, and gaining acceptance for new proposals (Kingdon). For example, if too many persons lose health care coverage, health care providers, insurance companies, public health officials, and special interest groups would collaborate to generate multiple alternative solutions.

The third and final stream, the political stream, aims at creating a political culture in elected bodies that support tackling the problem. This stream involves changing the public mood, using pressure group campaigns, influencing election results, and changing the partisan composition of the legislature and administration. During this phase, coalitions are built based upon negotiation and persuasion. Political parties reach consensus on campaign platforms. Frequently, trading favors becomes a key way to building coalitions (Kingdon, 1995). For example, if the numbers of uninsured Americans would spike, the political climate might point to the need for some form of nationalized health insurance plan. Public pressure and media advertisements might change prevailing views toward a government health plan for all. Thus, the outcomes of the next election might put into office elected officials who espouse adopting a universal health care plan to ensure access to health services for all.

Agenda formation occurs when streams couple together during a window of opportunity. According to Kingdon (1995), windows of opportunity rapidly open and close. Kingdon specified that the problem and political streams drive agenda formation, whereas alternative solutions tend to be driven by the policy stream.

Kingdon (1995) acknowledged the contributions that elected officials bring to the processes of agenda development and policy formation. Elected officials bring issues to legislative bodies that are merged to become the formal agenda. The ability of the elected official to influence formal agenda development depends on his or her position as a member of the body. A legislative committee chairperson determines which issues are brought before a committee, a ranking member of the minority party on a committee has power to influence committee proceedings, and a member with long tenure as an elected official may be viewed as being more powerful than other committee members. Because of their elected status, each elected official wants to serve constituent interests well in order to get reelected, enhance his or her reputation, and pass sound public policy legislation.

Kingdon's model attempts to make sense of the complexity of the American political processes. A political model such as Kingdon's provides a framework to understand the complex process and guide nurses as they engage in the art and science of influencing public policy.

THE NURSE'S ROLE IN INFLUENCING PUBLIC POLICY

Nurses have lots of knowledge about health and the delivery of health care. Practicing nurses frequently identify flaws in the current health care delivery system. Nurses represent the largest health professional group in the United States, but have failed to play a proportionate role in shaping health policies for Americans at all levels of government

(Abood, 2007; Bissonnette, 2004; Mason et al., 2007; Milstead, 2008). According to Wakefield (2004), nursing lacks the financial resources prevalent in more highly influential groups such as organized medicine, insurance corporations, pharmaceutical firms, and other organized businesses. In the United States (and elsewhere in the world), money determines how much political power and influence a group possesses.

The Nurse's Role as a Responsible Citizen

The U.S. Constitution ensures the right of American citizens to have a voice in the government. Americans have the freedom to ask questions, offer suggestions, and debate the effects of public policies. Nurses have a history of political activism. During the women's suffrage movement of the early 1900s, the American Federation of Nursing (now the American Nurses Association, or ANA) joined forces with other women's groups to win the right for women to vote. Nurses quickly discovered that they could affect public policy by working independently and with other women to exert pressure on elected officials to develop policies that supported health promotion and disease prevention (Feldman & Lewenson, 2000).

The degree of political action varies from nurse to nurse. In 1996, Cohen et al. outlined four stages of political activism in nursing that still apply today:

1. Buying in: Nurses become aware of the importance of political activism to attain professional goals, and they use the political system to have input into public policy development.
2. Self-interest: Nurses use the political system exclusively to advance their own agenda.
3. Political sophistication: Nurses engage in complex political activity, such as building coalitions and running for political office.
4. Leading the way: Nurses serve as influential persons by holding key governmental positions and in the process select the course for public policy changes.

Professional nurses participate in public policy formation in a variety of ways. However, most nurses tend to be in the first stage of political activism. Casting an informed vote during an election is the first level of responsible citizenship in a democracy. **Responsible citizenship** consists of being an active participant in the governing process. The second level of responsible citizenship is engaging in the process of affecting governmental policies. Once they are successful in affecting public policy by providing input, some nurses progress to higher levels of political activism.

Political involvement by nurses started with Florence Nightingale's efforts during the Crimean War (Abood, 2007) and fits with professional nursing goals of enhancing health and improving the quality of life for all. The public perceives nurses as being trustworthy and credible. Nurses advocate for large groups of clients when they use their specialized knowledge to influence policy makers to create and fund public health programs. Nurses also have well-refined communication and assessment skills that enhance the ability to determine what types of health programs are needed (and wanted). Because of their ability to understand nursing and health-related research, nurses can present strong cases based on solid evidence to document the need for new programs and to continue existing ones. Politically active nurses frequently use nursing process to guide their thinking for public policy development and evaluation (Abood; Mason et al., 2007; Milstead, 2008).

Feldman and Lewenson (2000) noted that some nurses begin political careers because of grassroots efforts to accomplish a particular public policy goal. **Grassroots efforts** start at the basic unit of society (local community or special interest group) and expand to reach more centralized areas of influence (Agnes, 2005). Grassroots efforts frequently start as action to improve a local community that snowballs into bigger action. Grassroots activities involve building coalitions, writing letters, telephoning officials, visiting elected officials, and testifying before governmental committees. When nurses successfully attain political action goals, they directly affect public policy (Abood, 2007; Feldman & Lewenson; Mason et al., 2007; Milstead, 2008). Successful action in grassroots efforts builds the nurse's self-confidence, and a reputation that he or she can be trusted to get the job done (Milstead).

To be aware of current legislation and policies, the professional nurse must have access to information. Information on legislative issues may be found in newspapers, news magazines, nursing publications and on the Internet. The second stage of political action is that of self-interest. An analysis of the current American government reveals that many times, small groups of people expend great resources and much energy to have their agendas approved (especially when competing for a piece of the federal budget). The final stage of political action involves working with other groups to attain what is best for all. During this stage, individuals and groups collaborate and reach consensus about how to best use available resources to better society (Abood, 2007; Feldman & Lewenson, 2000; Mason et al., 2007; Milstead, 2008).

A policy is an established course of action determined to achieve a desired outcome. Governments and institutions create policies to achieve their missions. However, policy development and implementation are not limited to governments and institutions. Any health care–providing agency, professional organization, nonprofit organization, or family may make policies for members to follow. When health care policies are developed and revised, nurses bring special expertise to this process.

Research Brief 20-1

Itzhaky, H., Gerber, P., & Dekel, R. (2004). Empowerment skills and values: A comparative study of nurses and social workers. *International Journal of Nursing Studies*, *41*, 447–456.

The investigators sought to discover the differences between nurses' and social workers' perceptions and reported actions using the skills and values of the concept of empowerment.

Two hundred thirteen social workers and 152 RNs participated in the study, which employed a cross-sectional survey design. Participants completed Frans' Social Worker Empowerment Scale, Alperin and Richie's Social Service Skills Scale, and Schwartz's The Values Scale.

Differences were analyzed using multiple analysis of variance techniques. The following differences were identified:

1. The nurses scored higher in knowledge, self-concept, critical awareness, and propensity to act than the social workers, who scored higher on the scale measuring collective identity.
2. Nurses also scored higher on therapeutic communication skills than the social workers.
3. Social workers were ranked higher in social action skills (including finding government resources, lobbying, and contacting elected officials) than the nurses.
4. Nurses reported having more emphasis on spiritual and material values than social workers.
5. Social workers had higher levels of political activity than nurses.

The significance of these findings reveals that nurses and social workers, even though they both are helping professions, have distinct differences. The investigators suggested that the differences could have arisen because nurses daily use therapeutic communication. Results also reveal that nurses tended to think of themselves as individuals rather than as a collective group. Results of this study must be interpreted with caution because the study was conducted in Israel. However, the study points to the need to increase nurses' awareness of the political process and how they could influence public policy. More research is needed to see how all members of the interdisciplinary health team perceive empowerment and how they use their influence in helping to shape public policy and health care delivery.

Governmental Role in Public Policy Development

The federal and most state governments are organized using three branches: the legislative, executive, and judicial. The legislative branch develops and approves legislation for executive branch consideration. The executive branch approves legislative acts and administers and regulates governmental policies. Once laws are passed, the government must develop policies to enact them. The judicial branch interprets laws and the meaning of approved policies.

Legal bases for legislative action in health care are found in Article I, Section 8 of the U.S. Constitution, which states that the government bears the responsibility to provide for the general welfare of its citizens, regulate interstate commerce, fund the military, and provide funds for governmental operations. Each state bears the responsibility to enforce national policies while protecting the safety, health, and welfare of its citizens. Local governments implement national programs and develop laws, regulations, and policies to ensure public health.

The Nurse's Role in Public Policy Development

Because laws govern professional nursing practice, nurses have a stake in public policy legislation and enforcement. Legislators pass laws and provide funding for health care programs, access, professional education, and research. Nurses shape proposed legislation by contacting their elected officials to influence actions during the legislative process. Some nurses engage in proactive political action by proposing legislation, persuading an elected official in the legislature to introduce a bill, devising public relations campaigns around their proposal, **lobbying** (attempting to sway an elected official to take a desired action) to get the bill passed by legislative bodies, and influencing the head of the executive branch to sign it. A national or statewide effort to pass legislation requires the participation of many for success. However, once legislation becomes law, some nurses continue to work with state or federal agencies responsible for devising the regulations and/or policies to implement the law.

Nursing's Legislative Agenda

The ANA develops and publishes a list of legislative and regulatory initiatives for each session of the U.S. Congress (every 2 years). A **legislative and regulatory agenda** outlines the goals and actions of an organization to exert its influence on passing bills and developing governmental policies. Legislative goals are developed and approved by the ANA board. Once approved, the organization publicizes its agenda. Its membership bears the responsibility for supporting the agenda, whereas the ANA staff advances it. State nurses' associations (SNAs) and the ANA also develop state legislative agendas and hire professional lobbyists to promote legislation that favorably affects the practice of professional nursing (Abood, 2007; Mason et al., 2007; Milstead, 2008). The ANA agenda for the 111th Congress contained the following legislative and regulatory initiatives: (1) nursing shortage (immigration issues and funding for the future nursing workforce), (2) appropriate staffing (acute care staffing, mandatory overtime, and nurse staffing reporting), (3) workplace rights (barriers to advanced practice registered nurse practice, and plan of care designations for home health), (4) Medicaid coverage of advanced practice nursing services and whistleblowing/patient advocacy protection for nurses, and (5) patient safety and advocacy issues (access to health care coverage, medical malpractice liability/tort reform, Medicare reform, genetic nondiscrimination, health care quality measures and information, and stem cell research).

The first step in publicizing a legislative agenda is the development of position papers on the legislative goals. A position paper is a one-page paper that specifies a goal. A position paper forces clear, concise communication of the rationale behind the agenda based on solid facts and persuasive arguments. Supportive evidence such as research findings, statistics, and published articles helps to solidify the position. Typically, nursing organizations print the paper using their official logo, thereby adding credibility to the publication.

The Art of Lobbying

The world of politics moves quickly. Sometimes a piece of legislation changes in less than an hour. To stay abreast of proposed legislation and its changes, nursing organizations hire lobbyists. The ANA has lobbyists for federal legislation. Most SNAs hire a lobbyist for state legislation. Lobbyists visit with elected officials in the hopes of influencing action on a piece of pending legislation. In addition, lobbyists are responsible for keeping their organizational membership informed of proposed changes to a piece of legislation. At the local level, nurses engage in lobbying activities by attending city council and other community organizational meetings.

In addition to hiring lobbyists, the ANA and SNAs offer the Nurses Strategic Action Team (N-STAT), a coordinated effort to ensure that nurses' voices are heard at the federal and state governmental levels. Nurses use **lobbying strategies**, activities aimed to get an elected official to take a desired action. When presenting information on a legislative or local issue, nurses and lobbyists must do their homework to develop expertise on the impending issue.

Before briefing an elected official on an issue, it is mandatory to develop expertise on it. Having facts and statistics related to an issue provides a solid foundation for the art of persuasion. Effective use of statistics involves (1) putting the numbers in human terms; (2) reporting the statistics in simple terms while avoiding the use of percentages; (3) including practical and statistical significance when reporting numbers; (4) using national, state, and local statistics (legislators concern themselves with the local impact of an issue); and (5) citing the source of information (Abood, 2007; Mason et al., 2007; Milstead, 2008).

Besides statistics, personal stories may be used effectively to influence elected officials. Effective use of personal stories involves (1) using a personal story about a citizen who resides in the elected official's district; (2) telling the true story in clear, concise, declarative, strong, and simple terms; (3) requesting a specific action by the legislator; and (4) emphasizing the importance of the issue (Abood, 2007; Mason et al., 2007; Milstead, 2008). Because elected officials deal with a list of issues that multiply daily, they appreciate a clear, concise, precise, and persuasive presentation when meeting with constituents.

Before effective lobbying can occur, nurses must be aware of current changes in proposed legislation. Along with printed and electronic media, legislative bodies offer websites to inform constituents of pending legislation. The U.S. Library of Congress has an electronic information site (http://thomas.loc.gov) to link citizens to federal legislative information. This Internet site posts the status of pending legistation and committee hearing transcripts, which may be studied, downloaded, and printed. In addition, legislative body websites have features for citizens to find the legislators representing them.

Professional nursing associations post legislative issue information on websites. Some associations post information for all nurses to view, whereas others reserve information for members only. The ANA (http://www.nursingworld.org/gova) and the Canadian Nurses Association (www.cna-nurses.ca) websites also contain information about pending national legislation affecting health care and professional nursing practice. The ANA offers an online Capitol Update and opportunities for its membership to participate in N-STAT, a nursing grassroots lobbying group. Availability of information regarding state issues depends on the state or provincial nursing association. Several SNAs reserve information on current state legislative issues for their members (Abood, 2007).

Elected legislators frequently provide constituents with periodic reports during the legislative session. Reports may be delivered to constituents via e-mail or the postal service. Reports sent to constituents before the end of the legislative session usually ask for voter opinions on pending legislative issues. When nurses return questionnaires addressing pending legislation, they participate in the legislative process.

The Federal Legislative Path

Because of the complex process set forth by the authors of the Constitution, the path of legislation provides ample opportunity for citizen input. The **federal legislative path** outlines each step of the process by which an idea becomes a law. A member of the House of Representatives or the Senate must introduce a bill before it can be considered. Once a bill is introduced, it goes to a committee, where it may be referred (passed to another committee), become the topic of a hearing, be marked up (rewritten and amended), or be reported out (sent to the House or Senate for floor action).

The chair of the committee considering the bill decides on its action. This person possesses much power because he or she may delay presentation of the bill to the committee (Kingdon, 1995; Mason et al., 2007; Milstead, 2008). During this phase of the legislative process, nurses may brief the committee chair to attempt to influence scheduling of the bill for committee discussion or action on the floor.

Once either chamber passes a bill, it goes to the other chamber and is subjected to the entire legislative process again. After the second chamber approves the bill, it is submitted to a conference committee that consists of members from both chambers. The conference committee negotiates differences between the two bill versions, adopts the conference bill, and submits (reports) the bill to both chambers for adoption or rejection. If both chambers adopt the conference bill, it becomes an Act of Congress.

Each congressional act (also known as an enrolled bill) is referred to the president (or governor in state legislatures), who signs or vetoes it. If the bill is signed, it becomes law. If the bill is vetoed, the House and Senate may override the veto by a two-thirds majority vote, and the bill becomes public law. If the veto is sustained, the bill dies (Mason et al., 2007; Milstead, 2008).

The U.S. Constitution provides the president 10 days (excluding Sundays) to act on an enrolled bill. The president has four possible options. The bill may be approved by signature, approved by inaction (i.e., the president takes no action within 10 days, an option used when it is considered unnecessary or politically unwise to sign a bill, or if there are questions regarding its constitutionality), pocket vetoed (used at the end of a legislative session when Congress adjourns before the 10-day expiration date), or vetoed (the president refuses to sign the bill, and presents both bodies of Congress a message stating his or her objections to it) (Mason et al., 2007; Milstead, 2008). When the enrolled bill is submitted for executive approval, nurses should contact the president or governor via a telephone call, fax, or letter (electronic or postal) to voice desired action.

Lobbying Strategies

Lobbying techniques are classified into two types: direct and indirect. Direct lobbying involves personal contact with elected officials. Indirect lobbying involves influencing public opinion on a particular issue. Table 20-1 outlines direct and indirect lobbying strategies.

Before implementing lobbying strategies, nurses should outline a plan that contains a timeline for recording lobbying activities and their results. By keeping records of reactions and responses from elected officials, nurses may use this information in future interactions. Appointment of a spokesperson helps to maintain a consistent lobbying approach and enhances public recognition of a particular issue viewpoint.

Constituent pressure is perhaps the most effective weapon for the lobbyist, and mobilization of a group of individuals for collective action provides numbers that influence

TABLE 20-1

Lobbying Strategies

Direct Strategies: Through a Legislative Body	Indirect Strategies: Through Public Opinion
Participate in party platform development	Publicize nursing organizational agendas
Contribute time and money to political campaigns	Use the media, especially television broadcasts, to further the agenda
Influence legislative committees by personally visiting or writing committee members	Write editorial pieces for written media, such as the newspaper or news magazines
Contact agency regulators in writing or by personal visits	Seek public opinion by polling members of the public and publishing the results
Engage in direct lobbying by visiting or writing elected officials or hiring a professional lobbyist	Use paid media advertisements: television, radio, and printed media
Attend social events at which elected officials appear	Print and distribute books or pamphlets
Develop an understanding of elected officials' key positions on issues	Develop and execute educational campaigns

Source: deVries, C., & Vanderbilt, M. (1992). The grassroots lobbying handbook: Empowering nurses through legislative and political action. Washington, DC: American Nurses Association. Mason, Leavitt & Chaffee, 2007 *Policy & politics in nursing and health care* (5th ed.). St. Louis: Saunders & Milstead, J. *Health policy and politcs, a nurse's guide* (3rd ed.) Sudbury, MA: Jones & Bartlett

action. Letter-writing campaigns are effective when a bill is pending in Congress or in a state legislative body. Mailing a form letter is superior to sending nothing. If a specific piece of legislation is supported by a nursing organization, the organization may have a sample letter drafted for membership use.

Because the elected official relies on voter support for reelection, each letter and personal contact counts. Follow-up letters of appreciation for action on an issue enhance relationships among elected officials and their constituents. See Display 20-1 for characteristics of effective communication to an official.

Using e-mail to lobby an elected official has advantages and disadvantages. It is economical and quick. Use of this technology enables users to send messages at any time. The message is not dependent on postal delivery or a receptionist relaying the message to the official. Some legislators, especially younger ones, may prefer e-mail messages rather than formal letters (Brian Yates, personal communication, February 16, 2004).

However, e-mail also has distinct disadvantages. The quality of messages sent depends on the software used to create them and the ability of the nurse to individualize the message. Some software programs feature ways to emphasize specific message points. However, the intended strength of the desired message may be impossible to achieve. Some special interest groups bombard legislators with e-mail messages, many of which may be written identically. Staff members quickly identify this practice. Because many elected officials receive large volumes of e-mail, some rely on staff members to read e-mail messages and relay crucial information to the legislator (Brian Yates, personal communication, February 16, 2004).

Because legislators tend to hear exclusively from dissatisfied constituents, they may be led to believe falsely that large numbers of their constituents disagree with a pending issue. A bill may be introduced for years before it is passed. "Persistence and patience are two key factors in lobbying" (deVries & Vanderbilt, 1992, p. 59). When nurses stay in regular contact with elected officials, the officials are more likely to remember them and work to help support nursing's agenda.

A telephone call offers a way to deliver a brief and quick message to an elected official. A legislator's staff members frequently keep a tally of how many calls support and how many calls disapprove of pending legislation. Many nurses calling officials find it beneficial

Characteristics of Effective Written Communication to an Official

DISPLAY 20-1

1. E-mail messages get to officials sooner than letters because of mail-screening processes.
2. Limit letter or e-mail message to one page if possible, but no longer than two pages.
3. Focus on one issue for each e-mail message or letter.
4. Identify the issue in the message heading if an e-mail is sent.
5. Correctly address for a written letter, referring to the elected official as The Honorable (first name followed by surname).
6. Greet the official according to title (e.g., Dear Senator _____, Dear Representative _____, Dear Congressman/ Congresswoman _____, Dear Mr. Chairman or Madam Chairwoman _____, or Dear Mr./Madam Speaker _____) using a colon for punctuation after the greeting.
7. Identify yourself as a constituent, a health care expert, a member of a large organization, and a credible source on the issue within the first paragraph.
8. Refer to the specific piece of legislation by title (H.R. [number] for a House bill; S. [number] for a Senate bill) in the first paragraph if the letter pertains to a specific legislative proposal.
9. Emphasize the local importance of the proposed issue.
10. Be brief and specific when presenting key information.
11. Add personal experiences and views, thus eliminating the tone of a form letter.
12. If a letter is sent, handwrite it; use a professional but personalized letterhead.
13. Verify that the e-mail message or letter is neat and free of spelling, grammatical, or typographical errors (if typewritten).
14. Be specific about the desired action on the part of the elected official.
15. Offer personal assistance or the organization's assistance in the closing.
16. Thank the official for his or her action.
17. Provide contact information as legislators pay attention to letters/messages from their constituents.

Sources of information:
Mason, D., Leavitt, J., & Chaffee, M. (Eds.). (2007). *Policy and politics in nursing and health care* (5th ed.). St. Louis, MO: Saunders.
Milstead, J. A. (2008.) *Health policy and politics: A nurse's guide.* Sudbury, MA: Jones & Bartlett.

to have the desired message scripted for reading when relaying messages to an elected official. A telephone call is superior to typewritten media because the urgency of an issue can be better communicated in speech.

All national elected officials have offices located in Washington, D.C., and in the state or district where they reside. When legislators return home during breaks, nurses can contact them to share views and avoid the expense of traveling to the capital. Telegrams and e-mail messages are effective tools to send quick messages requesting prompt action. Petitions containing large numbers of signatures usually are effective only for public relations because it is difficult for staff to verify whether all signatures on the document represent constituents.

In addition to written communication, a personal visit is a very effective method of lobbying. Constituents are invited to meet with elected officials in the local or governmental offices. A personal visit lays the foundation for future contacts. A scheduled appointment usually ensures a personal meeting with an elected official. Frequently, visits are limited to 15 to 30 minutes. Because of legislative emergencies, appointments may be canceled, especially if a floor vote is scheduled during the planned meeting. See Display 20-2 for suggestions that will facilitate a personal visit with an elected official.

Once reliable relationships are established with elected officials, nurses may be invited to testify at legislative committee hearings. When this happens, careful preparation is required, and a technical expert or attorney may accompany a witness. The ANA president frequently testifies at committee hearings when issues regarding professional nursing practice are debated. Rich sources of evidence for testimony include the Agency for Health Care Policy and Research (http://www.ahcpr.gov), the Center for Telemedicine Law (http://www.ctl.org), the National Council of State Boards of Nursing (http://www.ncsbn.org), and the Department of Health and Human Services (http://www.hhs.gov).

Steps for Facilitating a Personal Visit with an Elected Official

DISPLAY 20-2

1. Confirm the appointment and arrive on time.
2. Provide the official with a business card after greeting him or her with a firm handshake and a personal introduction.
3. Open the meeting by informing the official of an established tie between you.
4. Inform the official of the mission and how the visit represents it. Refer to pending legislation by bill number and title.
5. Present statistics and personal stories when appropriate, while emphasizing the issue's importance to the local community.
6. Request the name of the staff member who handles the issue and request follow-up.
7. Be concise and focus totally on the issue of the meeting.
8. Leave a one- or two-page fact sheet summarizing the issue and your position on it.
9. Conclude the meeting by thanking the official for spending time with you.
10. Write a thank you letter after the meeting.

Source: deVries & Vanderbilt, 1992.

Writing letters and visiting legislators are the best-known lobbying techniques. Traditionally, persons lobby officials they have elected into office while ignoring powerful legislators, such as party leaders and committee chairpersons. Different lobbying strategies work more effectively during different phases of the legislative process. Table 20-2 outlines specific lobbying strategies recommended for use during each phase of the legislative and regulatory processes.

Obstacles to Effective Lobbying

Major obstacles encountered by nurses include not knowing whom to lobby, where to contact officials, and the best time for contact. Some do not know the names of their elected officials. Before contacting elected officials, nurses should find out about their personal biographies, committee memberships, voting records, and introduced or cosponsored legislative activity. In addition to this information, knowledge of their personal causes or pet projects may be useful.

Legislative Staff Members

Because of their enormous responsibilities, all elected officials have staff. (Elected officials work with thousands of pieces of legislation during one legislative session.) Staff members routinely handle much of the elected official's work. Good relationships with legislative staff at the national and local offices provide invaluable contacts and advantages when engaging in lobbying activities.

An elected official's personal staff may include an administrative assistant, a legislative director, legislative assistants, legislative correspondents, a press secretary, caseworkers, a secretary, an office manager, and a receptionist. Nurses may be members of the staff. Staff members are responsible for scheduling appointments and activities. More importantly, officials fill staff posts with highly qualified persons who assist them in making decisions. For example, Sheila Burke, RN, MPA, FAAN, served as chief of staff for Bob Dole when he was the Senate majority leader (Goldwater & Zusy, 1990). Mary Wakefield was a member of Senator Tom Daschle's staff. Both of these nurses advised the senators on issues related to health care delivery and workforce development.

When nurses serve as staff members, they bring their expertise on health and safety issues to the team. To become a staff member, nurses should get to know political candidates, join political parties, donate time to work for election campaigns, contribute funds to campaigns, and market nursing expertise on issues related to health care and health promotion.

When lobbying for specific action on an issue, inviting an elected official for a personal tour of a local hospital or to participate in a local community service event may assist in advancing the cause. These activities increase the official's visibility and provide an

TABLE 20-2

The Legislative Process: Steps and Suggested Lobbying Strategies

Legislative Process: Steps	Suggested Lobbying Strategy
Legislation introduction	Hold a technical expert meeting to map out a strategy. Form a coalition of persons and organizations with the same goal. Identify a legislator in each chamber of Congress who would be likely to introduce the proposal. Schedule a staff meeting with the legislator's staff members. Initiate a letter-writing campaign to other congressional members who may wish to co-sponsor the bill.
Immediately following introduction before committee assignment	Meet with interest groups to map out additional lobbying strategies. Create a one-page fact sheet to distribute to interested parties. Initiate a letter-writing campaign to elected officials to urge bill co-sponsorship. Draft proposed amendments to bill.
Committee consideration	Write letters to all committee members to emphasize the need for a public hearing. Enlist a letter-writing campaign by members of other interested organizations. Submit written information about oral or written testimony if a hearing is to occur. Have someone monitor the mark-up session and share information with letter writers. Conduct a letter-writing campaign to committee members either supporting or disagreeing with bill amendments added in committee. Conduct a letter-writing campaign to elected officials from local district outlining support or disapproval of the revised bill, or to enlist their support by contacting committee members or testifying at a committee meeting. Call a meeting of interested persons to verify whether or not new amendments are tolerable. Work with committee staff in drafting the final draft of the bill. Notify the press about the bill.
Rules Committee action	Work with Rules Committee members to determine if amendments can be made while the bill is debated on the floor of either chamber.
Legislation on the floor of a chamber	Send short messages to all members of the chamber in great quantities (postcards, telegrams, e-mail messages, and telephone calls). Develop a swing list of officials. Initiate personal visits to officials on undecided, leaning no, and leaning yes lists.
Conference Committee action	Meet with other interested persons to verify which version (House or Senate) is to be supported. Write, visit, or call district officials and members of the Conference Committee.
Return to both chambers for approval	No lobbying strategies needed if work has been consistent. Write or call elected officials from district.
Presidential or gubernatorial signature	Call the White House or governor's staff, leaving a message for veto or signature.
Veto override	Write or call locally elected official. Intensify lobbying efforts at those who appeared on the leaning yes list.

Source: deVries, C., & Vanderbilt, M. (1992). *The grassroots lobbying handbook: Empowering nurses through legislative and political action.* Washington, DC: American Nurses Association.

opportunity for interaction with constituents. Because this may be viewed as an opportunity for press coverage, special attention to the press secretary at this time may increase the chances of future access to the elected official (deVries & Vanderbilt, 1992).

Maintaining a Working Relationship

Expressing appreciation frequently is an overlooked step in the lobbying process. Elected officials should be acknowledged for introducing and supporting legislation that enhances the practice of professional nurses. Some SNAs bestow honors on elected officials who have developed records for supporting "nursing-friendly" legislation. A thank you letter that includes a statement about informing other nurses living in the district about an official's action in supporting legislation increases support for an official running for reelection.

Honesty is perhaps the most important factor contributing to effective lobbying. When lobbying, nurses must be willing to spend the time to explore the issues and collect valid and reliable data surrounding them. When encountering questions that cannot be answered accurately with complete certainty, nurses should refer the question to another expert or offer to find the desired information and present it to the official at a later date. Attempts to "wing it" or inadvertently share untrue information could sabotage the personal relationships established with officials (deVries & Vanderbilt, 1992).

There are multiple ways to cultivate a working relationship with an elected official. Wakefield (2004) suggested that working for an election (or reelection) campaign and joining and becoming a member of a political party foster networking with elected officials. Attendance at events where legislators are scheduled to speak or fundraise serves as other opportunities for access. Some SNAs offer programs to meet political candidates at district meetings or during special programs held in state capitals. A political campaign contribution offers a token of appreciation (Wakefield). Taking time to listen to candidates running for office when they canvass neighborhoods enables nurses to meet candidates. Sometimes, the elected official may just happen to live in the nurse's neighborhood.

Without nurses' active participation in the legislative end election processes, public policy may not remain friendly to the nursing profession or health care consumers. In the United States, public policy development and implementation are affected by money, power, and societal position. To maintain their position and power, elected officials frequently strive for reelection. Because officials acknowledge the importance of pleasing their constituents, their acts are aimed at protecting and serving their voters. Politically astute persons acknowledge the importance of building **coalitions** (forming a larger group from smaller groups of people with similar goals and interests) and contributing resources to a political campaign to get their candidate elected to office.

Questions for Reflection 20-2

1. Do I know the number of the congressional district in which I reside at the national and state government levels?
2. Who are the senators serving in the U.S. Senate from my state?
3. Who is my House of Representatives member from my congressional district?
4. Who are my representatives in the state legislature?
5. Which of the lobbying strategies is most appealing to me? Why?

Coalition Building

Although difficult to establish and maintain, coalitions unite diverse groups, organizations, and people for a common specific purpose. Coalitions operate under the assumption that "there is strength in numbers." Many coalitions begin with an informal structure that formalizes as the coalition evolves and becomes more active. Once formal structure has been established, the coalition may need to hire employees in order to accomplish goals. Before extending an invitation for membership, a background check verifies any strengths or weaknesses individuals or organizations bring to the coalition. The goal of building a coalition is to capitalize on all members' strengths (Skaggs, 1997). Usually, the organization that started the coalition becomes its leader. When the ANA and American Medical Association (AMA) work together to support a piece of legislation, they build a coalition of health care providers.

Political Action Committees

Political action committees (PACs) are created by existing organizations for the purpose of financing campaigns for political office. Federal election guidelines prohibit nonprofit groups from contributing to political campaigns. Funding for PACs is independent of its founding organization's funding.

Federal election guidelines mandate that PAC donations may be solicited from an organization's membership only for candidates for public office. However, general organizational funds may finance a political education program for members of the PAC's founding organization. Sometimes candidates for office receive political contributions from the PAC. However, some candidates may request only a public endorsement of their campaigns.

The ANA PAC, founded in 1972, supports political candidates with "nursing-friendly" agendas (ANA, 2001). "The ANA-PAC is an unincorporated committee of the ANA Board of Directors" (Conant & Jackson, 2007, p. 24). Conant and Jackson reported that the ANA PAC has a separate fund dedicated for the sole use of supporting candidates running for federal office. In 2006, the fund amounted to $585,835 (Twedell & Webb, 2007). Before supporting candidates, the ANA offers them the opportunity to complete a questionnaire that poses questions about their positions on issues important to nurses. Based on candidate responses (or lack of), the ANA PAC contributes to their campaigns along with ANA candidate endorsement. The ANA PAC initially supported Hillary Clinton during the 2008 primary season; however, they endorsed Barack Obama for president because John McCain failed to complete the questionnaire. Many SNAs also have PACs, and each sets criteria for contributing to state candidate political campaigns.

Currently, the AMA PAC is ranked as the second largest PAC, the American Hospital Association ranks fourth, and the American Association of Retired Persons (AARP) is ranked fifth. The American Association of Nurse Anesthetists PAC is the top nursing PAC (Twedell & Webb, 2007).

Of the 101 candidates running for federal office in 2008 who supported the ANA PAC, 88% became members of the 111th Congress (Hansen & Conant, 2008). Membership of the 111th congressional session in the U.S. House of Representatives includes the following nurses:

- Eddie Bernice Johnson, RN, the Democratic representative from the 30th congressional district of Texas
- Carolyn McCarthy, LPN, the Democratic representative from the 4th congressional district of New York
- Lois Capps, RN, the Democratic representative from the 22nd congressional district of California (ANA, 2008a)

 CURRENT POLITICAL AND LEGISLATIVE ISSUES AFFECTING PROFESSIONAL NURSING PRACTICE AND HEALTH CARE

Laws regulate nursing practice and health care delivery. Each state regulates nursing practice by its Nurse Practice Act. Federal and state governments regulate health care access and indigent health care service reimbursement. Many issues confronting legislators affect citizen safety, health care policy, and the control of nursing practice.

Hundreds of bills addressing health care are introduced into Congress and state legislatures annually. If a bill is not passed during the session of Congress when it was introduced, it dies. However, the bill may be introduced during each successive session of

Congress until it passes. Issues that are current at the time of the writing of this chapter may become tomorrow's history. Through lobbying efforts and by serving as elected officials, nurses influence the future of health care delivery, public safety, and nursing practice.

In the recent past, nurses have been successful in influencing the passage of legislation related to patient safety, nursing and health care research funding, human immuno-deficiency virus programs, family leave, tobacco settlements, abuse programs, direct Medicare reimbursement to advanced practice nurses, Medicare prescription medication coverage, and nursing education funding. Many times a particular issue surfaces over several legislative sessions before legislative action occurs. For example, health care reform has remained on the legislative table for decades. The following section discusses pending legislative issues that may be of interest to professional nurses.

The federal government develops a budget for all expenditures annually. During budget formation and negotiation, before approving the budget annually by the end of October, nurses need to be aware of the funding of established health-related, nursing research, and nursing education programs (Wakefield, 2004). There are long-standing programs related to public health, nursing education, and nursing research that are reviewed annually for funding from the federal budget. Nurses can become aware of proposed program cuts or increases through efforts of the ANA and other specialty nurse organizations.

Improving Access and Funding of Health Care

Gaining access to and paying for health care for all in America remains a consistent problem. Approximately 44.8 million persons have no health insurance coverage in the United States (Cymber, 2007). Three key factors contribute to recent increases in the uninsured: the rising cost of insurance, low incomes of workers, and recent rises in the unemployment rate. Companies who provide health insurance to employees pass on increased rates to them. Workers with low wages cannot afford to purchase employer-offered benefits (Sultz & Young, 2004).

Access to health care means that services are affordable, available, and acceptable (ANA, 2008b). Current trends in health insurance coverage require consumers to pay higher premiums for less coverage. Retirees find themselves receiving less and sometimes even losing health care benefits that were included in retirement packages. With identified preexisting conditions, many retirees or unemployed persons may be able to find coverage, but not be able to afford the expensive premiums.

According to the U.S. Department of Health and Human Services (2008), Americans spent $2.1 trillon on health care, with most money being spent on expensive medical interventions. Current spending priorities seem to be intensive (expensive) care rather than primary care (ANA, 2008b). The ANA (2008b) proposes and supports "a single payer mechanism as the most desirable option for financing a reformed health care system" (p. 9). To make this proposal a reality, health care stakeholders need to dialogue about revising health care priorities, deciding what services would be covered, and examining the impact of a program on current health insurance providers.

Improving the Quality of Health Care

When the Institute of Medicine (IOM) released the report *To Err Is Human: Building a Safer Health System* in 1999, health care consumers and providers began questioning the general safety of health care delivery. An IOM follow-up report issued in 2001 offered suggestions to improve the quality of health care so that it would become safe, effective, patient centered, timely, efficient, and equitable. (See Chapter 19 for more about safety and quality in health care.) Nurses seized the opportunity to validate their contributions to quality health care by conducting studies and sharing results that demonstrated improvements in hospitalized patient outcomes with increased registered nurse hours per patient day (Agency for Healthcare Research and Quality, 2007; Altman, Clancy, & Blendon, 2004; Buerhaus et al., 2007).

Along with increasing the numbers of registered nurses at the patient's bedside in hospitals, evidence-based disease management programs (some of which manage care across the inpatient, outpatient, and home settings) also result in improved client outcomes. However, no legislation has been introduced at the national level to mandate nurse-to-client staffing ratios or standardize disease management in various health care settings.

The American government spends billions of dollars to monitor and improve quality of health care services. The federal government funds the Agency for Healthcare Research and Quality (AHRQ), the National Institutes of Health, the Centers for Disease Control and Prevention, the Food and Drug Administration, the Health Care Financing Administration, and the Health Resources and Services Administration. Without adequate federal funding, the quality of health and health care in the United States would suffer.

The Safe Nursing and Patient Care Act

Since 2003, the U.S. Congress has considered legislation for promoting safe nursing and patient care. Legislative initiatives on this issue have provisions that would prohibit mandatory overtime for RNs and other licensed members of the interdisciplinary care team, but would not set limits on voluntary overtime. Neither version of this bill moved out of committees of both legislative bodies despite support from the ANA and the AMA (Institute of Medicine, 2004; McKeon, 2008). Despite IOM (1999) evidence-based findings denoting increased errors made by nurses when they work more than 96 hours per week or longer than 12 hours, no federal legislation has been enacted to reduce the amount of hours that a registered nurse can work within a week's time frame. Passage of any law limiting the amount of overtime or hours nurses work might create a financial hardship for some nurses.

Nursing Workforce

In 2004, the U.S. Department of Health and Human Services reported a shortage of close to 139,000 RNs in the United States. By 2012, the figure is expected to rise to over 400,000 (Horrigan, 2004). To meet the need for RNs and to keep RNs active in the workforce, federal and state governments have introduced health care workforce legislation. Such legislation attempts to increase funding for nursing education, such as the Title VII Nursing Workforce Development Program for the fiscal year 2008, which increased funding by $6 million. Funding for the program for the fiscal year 2009 will be finalized in March 2009 (McKeon, 2008). However, there are no legislative initiatives to keep current nurses in the workforce.

Legislation for Advanced Practice Nursing

In 2008, the ANA successfully worked with Congress to expand federal government reimbursement for advanced practice nurses (APNs). Participating APNs are scheduled to receive a 2% increase in the amount of federal reimbursement starting in 2009. APNs also became able to sign for and certify plans for Medicare recipients to receive home health services. For the 111th Congress, the ANA will work to get the Medicare medical homes demonstration project to include APNs as primary care providers. (The current project calls for primary care providers to be physicians.) This project seeks to provide accessible, continuous, coordinated, and targeted family-centered care to persons receiving Medicare services (McKeon, 2008).

Nurses and Health Insurance Reform

Besides working for legislation that provides improved working conditions for professional nurses, nurses have been catalysts for change in improving access to care for all

American citizens. Nurses have worked successfully in the areas of insurance reform. Nurses played a key role in supporting the Genetic Non-Discrimination Act (P.L. 110-343), which makes it illegal for employers to use genetic test results in making hiring, termination, or promotion decisions (McKeon, 2008).

Nurses served as catalysts in legislation enacted to improve mental health coverage. Mental health parity became part of the compromised version of the $700 billion financial market rescue package of 2008. Under this legislation, insurers must provide the same benefits for mental health coverage as for medical or surgical insurance coverage if the plan offers coverage for mental health services (McKeon, 2008).

State Legislative Initiatives

States frequently address similar health care issues in legislative bodies. To track state legislative initiatives, SNAs monitor pending legislation that affects health care and professional practice. Some of the issues that are active in various state legislatures include the prohibition of mandatory overtime, minimum nurse–patient ratios, malpractice tort reform, whistleblower protection for nurses, mandatory development of valid nursing staffing sytems for acute and long-term care, state funding for nursing education, and passage of mutual state compacts for nursing licensure.

Mutual Recognition State Compact Legislation

Within the past few years, the National Council of State Boards of Nursing (NCSBN) developed a system with which professional nurses wishing to practice across state lines would not have to secure individual state licenses; this is known as **mutual recognition state compact licensure** (MRSCL). Under this provision, the RN holds a professional nursing license in the state of his or her primary residence, but would not have to hold another professional nursing license in states abiding by the MRSCL. Under the compact, the RN is held accountable to the Nurse Practice Act of the state where nursing practice occurs. The compact is quite attractive to nurses who live close to state lines and those who are employed by traveling nurse agencies (NCSBN, 2001).

Each state regulates professional nursing practice within its borders. For a state to participate in the mutual recognition program, the state legislature must adopt the MRSCL. In some states, such as Kansas, participation in a multistate compact violates the state constitution and requires a constitutional change (NCSBN, 2001). Some SNAs, such as the Missouri Nurses Association (MONA), failed to support the mutual recognition compact legislation against the desires of the Missouri State Board of Nursing. Reasons for the lack of support included projected higher professional nursing licensure fees, loss of local control of professional nursing practice, and failure of the State Board of Nursing to consult MONA.

Questions for Reflection 20-3

1. What are my views on some of the current legislative issues?
2. Do my views match those of nursing professional organizations to which I belong?
3. Do positions of nursing organizations prevent me from becoming a member? Why or why not?

EXAMPLES OF NURSES INFLUENCING PUBLIC POLICY

Although politics frequently is equated with corruption and abuse of power, the combination of political activity and professional nursing does not create cognitive dissonance. Nurses bring a caring perspective to the political process. Health care delivery and access are greatly affected by the political process. Becoming politically active is one way to assume the professional nursing roles of client advocate and change agent. The following examples provide evidence that nurses have fulfilled these roles by becoming politically active.

In addition to influencing legislation, nurses have assumed responsibility in the legislative process by becoming members of legislative bodies. The right to run for and hold public office is guaranteed by the First Amendment of the U.S. Constitution (Tammelleo, 1990). Ninety-seven nurses have been elected to serve as public officials (ANA, 2008a). Three nurses have been elected to national offices.

Eddie Bernice Johnson, RN, was elected to Congress in 1992 and won her most recent election with more than 65% of the popular vote (ANA, 2008a). Representative Eddie Bernice Johnson, RN (D-TX), currently serves as the Democratic deputy whip and holds membership on the House Committee on Transportation and Infrastructure and the House Committee on Science. Along with multiple House subcommittee memberships, Johnson also serves as the secretary of the Congressional Black Caucus.

Carolyn McCarthy, LPN, represents the fourth congressional district of New York. Although she had no previous political experience, she won her initial election by advocating for a ban on assault weapons after McCarthy's husband was killed and her son seriously injured in the 1993 Long Island Railroad massacre. McCarthy serves on the Education in the Workforce and the Small Business congressional committees. In 2008, Representative McCarthy won her reelection with more than two thirds of the popular vote (ANA, 2008a).

Lois Capps, RN, became a member of the House of Representatives in 1998 after winning a special election to succeed Congressman Walter Capps, her late husband. Capps serves on the Committee on Energy and Commerce and the subcommittees on Health, Commerce, Trade and Consumer Protection, and Environment and Hazardous Materials. Before being elected to Congress, Capps worked as a nurse and health advocate in Santa Barbara County in the areas of teen pregnancy and effective parenting. She uses her extensive health care background to influence health care legislative efforts (Capps, 2003). Capps has introduced and co-sponsored bills related to nurse staffing issues, whistleblower protection, and mandatory overtime. In 2008, Representative Capps received 65% of the popular vote in her reelection race to Congress (ANA, 2008a).

Many nurses have testified before congressional committees. The president of the ANA frequently shares nursing expertise before Congress. Barbara Blakeney provided testimony regarding the nursing shortage (ANA, 2004a). Jane Aiken, RN, PhD, testified about the impact of RNs on prevention and early detection of complications encountered by hospitalized patients (ANA, 2004a). Theresa Valiga, RN, PhD, provided testimony to Congress regarding the current and worsening shortage of nursing faculty (Murray & Corcoran, 2008). Anne Tan Piazza, RN (ANA director of governmental affairs); Sue Clark, RN (Illinois Nursing Association lobbyist); Jan Lainer, RN, JD (executive director of the Ohio Nurses Association); and Rebecca Patton, RN, provided information about safe staffing to the Congressional Nursing Caucus during a briefing held on May 1, 2008.

Nurses also can influence government reimbursements for health care. Linda Aiken, PhD, RN, FAAN, has served on the White House Physician Payment Review Commission, which was created to make recommendations about provider payments under Medicare and Medicaid. Carolyne K. Davis, RN, PhD, served as the administrator of the Health Care Financing Administration. She credited her appointment to her direct political involvement in Michigan politics (Goldwater & Zusy, 1990). The Kansas State Nurses Association successfully lobbied for the addition of an RN position to the Health Care Data Governing Board in Kansas.

OPPORTUNITIES TO LEARN THE ART OF INFLUENCING PUBLIC POLICY

There are many ways to learn the art of influencing public policy development and legislative activity. ANA membership and involvement provide an avenue to learn how to play the political game. The ANA has four political action specialists who educate nurses about the political process, communicate directly with elected officials about pending legislation, collect information about elected officials' voting records, identify politicians who are friends of nursing, and advise the ANA PAC Board on potential candidates for ANA endorsement. In addition to active involvement in national politics, some SNAs offer daylong or weeklong internships in the art and science of influencing public policies.

Fellowships and internships also offer nurses an opportunity to learn the process of public policy development through actual experience. Fellowships and internships inform participants about the complexities of health care policy and legislative priorities and provide knowledge and skills to function in the public policy arena. Nurses may participate in formal fellowships and internships or create their own Washington internship. Some colleges and university graduate programs offer college credit to students who complete the Capitol Hill practicum. Internships offer nurses the ability to network professionally with members of Congress and congressional staff. An internship may start a long-term relationship with a legislator or an influential staff member and increase political passion within the nurse.

Informal internships can be set up by sending a brief letter and résumé to an elected official. The letter should be sent to the member's administrative assistant or chief of staff. Formal public policy fellowships are offered by a number of groups (Display 20-3). Information about fellowship opportunities can be found at the local public library, obtained by writing to the foundations, or through the Internet and electronic communications.

SUMMARY AND SIGNIFICANCE TO PRACTICE

Nurses possess cognitive and communication skills to successfully navigate the complex political processes required to influence public policy. In these chaotic times, change is needed to provide safe, effective, patient-centered, timely, efficient, and effective health care. In order to change the health care system, nurses can use critical thinking to analyze issues, and communication skills to illuminate elected officials, policy makers, and the public about pressing health care issues. A model such as Kingdon's model for political processes provides nurses with an evidence-based framework to guide political action efforts. Developing expertise in influencing public policy requires dedication, time, practice, and a willingness to work with others. When nurses succeed with political action, they become confident in their ability to improve health care for all. Issues affecting personal and public health are too important to be left to the politicians. They and their constituents need nurses to ensure that future public health care policies are based on solid evidence and improve access to health care for all.

Groups Offering Formal Public Policy Fellowships   DISPLAY 20-3

The Robert Wood Johnson Foundation
The W.K. Kellogg Foundation
The Congressional Black Caucus Foundation
The White House Commission
The Women's Research and Education Institute
The Coro Foundation
The American Association of University Women Educational Foundation
The Business and Professional Women's Foundation

The Everett McKinley Dirksen Congressional Leadership Research Center
The Supreme Court of the United States
The Woodrow Wilson National Fellowship Foundation
The Employee Benefit Research Institute
The Office of Technology Assessment of the United States Congress

Source: Sharp, Biggs, & Wakefield, 1999

FROM THEORY TO PRACTICE

1. Do you think that all schools within a state should have a RN on the premises at all times during school hours?
2. List the benefits of having a RN on school premises during school hours.
3. What impact would having a RN on school premises during school hours have on students? Faculty? School staff and administration? Parents? Taxpayers?
4. Find a piece of legislation that you think may affect your nursing practice or client care delivery. Write a one- to two-page position paper on the pending piece of legislation using research and other evidence to support your position. Give the paper to a colleague, and have him or her critique it in terms of clarity, conciseness, and strength of your position argument. Revise the paper based on your colleague's critique.

WWW INTERNET EXERCISES

Exercise 1
Visit the following governmental websites: http://www.senate.gov and http://www.house.gov.

1. Visit the home pages of your two state senators and your representative to the U.S. House of Representatives. If you do not know their names, you can find them by entering your home zip code, clicking your home location on a map, or typing in the number of your legislative district found on your voter registration card in the information request section.
2. Search for current legislation affecting nursing and health care delivery by performing a topic search or typing in key words. You can read the full bill text or bill summaries.
3. Send an e-mail correspondence to your senators and House representative using strategies for composing letters and messages found in this chapter.
4. Find your state legislature by typing in "(your state's name) legislature." Most state legislative sites have search capabilities. Type in "nursing" and "health care delivery" as key words to find information about current legislative efforts affecting professional nursing in your state.

Exercise 2
Visit the ANA website at http://www.nursingworld.org.

1. Find on the menu bar the following words: "Nursing Issues and Programs."
2. With your mouse on "Nursing Issues and Programs," a menu drops down. Click on the words "Government Affairs."
3. On the Government Affairs page, see if the ANA has issued any Action Alerts. If so, click on one of them, and on the next page, find the menu and click on "Track Legislation."
4. After reading information tracking action on current legislative initiatives, hit the Back button on your toolbar twice to get to the Government Affairs page.
5. On the Government Affairs page, click on "Nursing's Legislative and Regulatory Initiatives for the 111th Congress" (the congressional session's number increases every 2 years following the even-numbered years of the federal election).
6. On the next page, scroll down and find a topic of interest. Summarize the topic and bring it to class for discussion.

Exercise 3
Visit the National Council of State Boards of Nursing website at http://www.ncsbn.org.

1. On the home page, find the words "Nurse Licensure Compact" and click them.
2. View "Nurse Licensure Compact: FAQ." What are the benefits of participation in the compact for states and nurses?
3. Hit the Back button. View the Nurse Licensure Compact Map. What states participate in the compact? Does your state participate in the interstate nursing licensure compact?
4. Scroll down the page to view a table of states that have introduced or passed this piece of legislation and see the enactment dates. As you scroll down, you can see a map of the United States of legislative action on the Mutual Recognition Compact.
5. Make a list of states that recognize the Mutual Recognition Compact.

WWW INTERNET RESOURCES

Agency for Healthcare Research and Quality: http://www.ahrq.gov.
Centers for Medicare and Medicaid Services: http://www.cms.hhs.gov.
Institute of Medicine: http://www.iom.edu.
U.S. Government Legislative Website: http://thomas.loc.gov.
American Nurses Association: http://www.nursingworld.org.
RN Activist Kit: http://www.nursingworld.org/gova/index.htm.
Canadian Nurses Association: http://www.cna-nurses.ca.
Occupational Safety and Health Administration: http://www.osha.gov.
American Hospital Association: http://www.aha.org.
For a database with more than 1.5 million U.S. government web pages, see http://firstgov.gov.

REFERENCES

Abood, S. (2007). Influencing health care in the legislative arena. *The Online Journal of Issues in Nursing*, *12*(10) Available at http://www.nursingworld.org/MainMenuCategories/ANAMarketplace/ANAPeriodi-cals/OJIN/TableofContents/Volume122007/No1Jan07/tpc32_216091.aspx. Accessed July 20, 2008.

Agency for Healthcare Research and Quality. (2007). *Nursing staffing and quality of patient care* (AHRQ Publication No. 07-E005). Rockville, MD: Author. Available at http://www.ahrq.gov/clinic/tp/nursesttp.htm. Accessed July 20, 2008.

Agnes, M. (Ed.). (2005). *Webster's new world college dictionary* (4th ed.). Cleveland, OH: Wiley.

Altman, D., Clancy, C., & Blendon, R. (2004). Improving patient safety—five years after the IOM report. *New England Journal of Medicine*, *351*, 2041–2043.

American Nurses Association (ANA). (2001). 2001 nurse state legislators and state administrative leaders. Available at http://nursingworld.org/gova/state/nurseleg#2.htm. Accessed July 10, 2005.

American Nurses Association (ANA). (2004a). *ANA and you: The house of nursing. The 2003 annual stake-holder's report*. Washington, DC: Author.

American Nurses Association (ANA). (2007). *Nursing's legislative and regulatory initiatives for the 110th Congress*. Silver Spring, MD: Author.

American Nurses Association (ANA). (2008a). ANA 2007–2008 Nurse State Legislators and State Admin-istrative Leaders. Available at http://www.nursingworld.org/MenuCategories/ANAPoliticalPower/State/Nurse-Legislators/nurselegislators.aspx. Accessed December 31, 2008.

American Nurses Association (ANA). (2008b). *Health system reform agenda*. Silver Spring, MD: NurseBooks.org.

Bissonnette, T. (2004). Passion, engagement, and political action. *Michigan Nurse*, *77*, 1.

Buerhaus, P., Donelan, K., Ulrich, B., Norman, L., DesRoaches, C., & Dittus, R. (2007). Impact of the nurse shortage on hospital patient care: Comparative perspectives. *Health Affairs*, *26*, 3853–3862.

Capps, L. (2003). Congresswoman Capps' biography. Available at http://www.house.gov/capps/aboutlois.shtml. Accessed July 10, 2005.

Cohen, S. S., Mason, D. J., Kovner, C., Leavitt, J. K., Pulcini, J., & Sochalski, J. (1996). Stages of nursing's political development: Where we've been and where we ought to go. *Nursing Outlook*, *44*, 259–266.

Conant, R., & Jackson, C. (2007). Brief overview of ANA political action committee. *American Nurse Today*, *2*(3), 24.

Cymber, R. (2007). Census Bureau revises 2004 and 2005 health insurance coverage estimates. Press release for the U.S. Census Bureau. Available at http://www.census.gov/Press-Release/www/releases/archives/health_care_insurance/0097898.2.2007. Accessed August 4, 2007.

deVries, C., & Vanderbilt, M. (1992). *The grassroots lobbying handbook: Empowering nurses through legis-lative and political action*. Washington, DC: American Nurses Association.

Feldman, J. R., & Lewenson, S. B. (Eds.). (2000). *Nurses in the political arena*. New York: Springer.

Goldwater, M., & Zusy, M. (1990). *Prescription for nurses: Effective political action*. St. Louis, MO: Mosby.

Hansen, H., & Conant, R. (2008). Exciting election comes to a close! *Capitol Update*, *6*(9). Available at http://www.capitolupdate.org/Newsletter/index.asp?nlid=209nlaid=1051. Accessed January 3, 2009.

Horrigan, M. (2004). Employment projections to 2012: Concepts and context. *Monthly Labor Review*, *127*, 3–22.

Institute of Medicine (IOM). (1999). *To err is human: Building a safer health system*. Washington, DC: National Academies Press.

Institute of Medicine (IOM). (2004). *Keeping patients safe: Transforming the work environment of nurses*. Washington, DC: National Academies Press.

Itzhaky, H., Gerber, P., & Dekel, R. (2004). Empowerment skills and values: A comparative study of nurses and social workers. *International Journal of Nursing Studies*, *41*, 447–456.

Kingdon, J. (1995). *Agendas, alternatives and public policy*. New York: Harper Collins College.

Mason, D., Leavitt, J., & Chaffee, M. (Eds.). (2007). *Policy and politics in nursing and health care* (5th ed.). St. Louis, MO: Saunders.

McKeon, E. (2008). Legislative updates: 110th Congress wrap-up. *Capitol Update*, *6*(9). Available at http://www.capitolupdate.org/Newsletter/index.asp?nlid=209&nlid=1054. Accessed January 3, 2009.

Milstead, J. A. (Ed.). (2008). *Health policy and politics: A nurse's guide* (3rd ed.) Sudbury, MA: Jones & Bartlett.

Murray, J., & Corcoran, R. (2008). *The National League for Nursing executive report, October 2007–September 2008*. New York: National League for Nursing.

National Council of State Boards of Nursing (NCSBN). (2001). Mutual recognition information. Available at http://www.ncsbn.org/mutual_compact.pdf. Accessed January 12, 2002.

Skaggs, B. (1997). Political action in nursing. In J. Zerwekh & J. Claborn (Eds.), *Nursing today: Transitions and trends* (2nd ed.). Philadelphia: W. B. Saunders.

Stanhope, M. (1996). Policy, politics, and the law: Influences on the practice of community health nursing. In M. Stanhope & J. Lancaster (Eds.), *Community health nursing: Promoting health of aggregates, families, and individuals* (4th ed.). St. Louis, MO: Mosby.

Sultz, H., & Young, K. (2004). *Health care USA: Understanding its organization and delivery* (4th ed.). Sudbury, MA: Jones & Bartlett.

Tammelleo, A. D. (1990). Nurse terminated for election to public office. *The Regan Report on Nursing Law*, *31*, 1.

Twedell, D., & Webb, J. (2007). The value of the political action committee: Dollars and influence for nurse leaders. *Nursing Administration Quarterly*, *31*(4), 279–283.

U.S. Department of Health and Human Services, Centers for Medicare and Medicaid Services. (2008). *National health expenditure data*. Available at http://www.cms.hhs.gov/NationalHealthExpendData/02_national-HealthAcountsHistorical.asp. Accessed July 20, 2008.

Wakefield, M. (2004). A call to political arms. *Nursing Economic$*, *33*, 166–167.

As a profession, nursing can count on change. Professional nurses have many nursing career options. A rewarding and satisfying career depends on the interests and passions of each individual nurse. Once nurses discover what they want to do, they can use specific career development strategies to ensure success. Many nurses move from one area of professional practice to another throughout a professional nursing career. To meet the future need for professional nursing and to secure a future for the nursing profession, nurses need to examine current trends, develop future scenarios, and envision a preferred future. Once a preferred future is envisioned, then professional nurses can work together to make it reality.

SECTION IV

Glimpsing the Future of Professional Nursing

CHAPTER 21

Career Options for Professional Nurses

KEY TERMS AND CONCEPTS

Universal job skills

Licensure

Certification

Advanced nursing practice

Graduate nursing education

Nurse practitioners

General nursing practice

Specialized nursing practice

Clinical ladders

Certified nurse-midwives (CNMs)

Nursing administration

Nursing academia

Nurse entrepreneurs

LEARNING OUTCOMES

By the end of this chapter, the learner will be able to:

1. Outline universal job skills.
2. Specify which universal job skills nurses possess.
3. Identify career options for nurses educated at the generalist level.
4. Explain the differences between general and advanced nursing practice.
5. Distinguish certification from advanced nursing practice.
6. Describe advanced nursing practice roles and responsibilities.

VIGNETTE

Laura is thinking about entering the nursing profession. As she explores professional nursing, Laura finds that there are many career options within the profession. Laura interviews three nurses and finds that one nurse remained employed for over 20 years as a staff nurse at a clinical agency that was part of the nurse's undergraduate nursing program. Another nurse that she interviewed shared her experiences with a nursing career that began as a nursing assistant, followed by several years each of hospital staff nursing, school nursing, and outpatient clinic nursing. The same nurse pursued a graduate nursing degree and currently works as a nurse practitioner in a small rural clinic. The last nurse Laura interviewed was a nurse faculty member who held a nursing doctorate and seemed to enjoy research and teaching. After learning about the diverse career options in nursing, Laura decides to pursue a nursing career, but will keep her options open until she finds her niche.

Setting career goals begins with self-assessment. Ideally, career goals should match personal values and acquired skills. As outlined in the vignette, nurses have many career options without leaving the nursing profession. This chapter explores career options in professional nursing that have not been presented in previous chapters.

UNIVERSAL JOB SKILLS

In 1992, the *Occupational Outlook Handbook* published by the Bureau of Labor Statistics delineated the following **universal job skills** for all types of work: (1) leadership/persuasion, (2) problem solving/creativity, (3) working as part of a team, (4) manual dexterity, (5) helping or instructing others, (6) initiative, (7) frequent contact with the public, and (8) physical stamina. Very few jobs involve all of the universal job skills. However, nursing requires all of them.

Many job skills mastered by nurses readily transfer to other fields (Waxman, 2005). The comprehensive skill set required by professional nurses may be a reason that career opportunities in nursing are quite different. Individuals rank the importance of job skills differently, and the ranking provides a clue to personal values. Personal values guide nurses in deciding in which areas to practice professional nursing.

Questions for Reflection 21-1

1. How do I use each of the eight universal job skills in my daily professional nursing practice?
2. How do other jobs use the skills differently than nurses?
3. Why does nursing require mastery of all eight universal job skills?

LEVELS OF NURSING PRACTICE

In the United States, state legislatures and state boards of nursing regulate practice. In Canada, provincial/territorial professional nursing associations assume responsibility for regulating professional nursing practice (except in the province of Ontario, where the College of Nurses of Ontario assumes this responsibility). In both countries, regulation of practice involves determining educational qualifications, setting standards of professional practice, limiting the use of the title "registered nurse," approving nursing education programs, determining the extent of continuing education and competency, disciplining professional members who endanger the public, and specifying the scope of nursing practice (McIntyre & Thomlinson, 2003; National Council of State Boards of Nursing, 2000). When nurses complete a preparatory nursing education program (associate degree, diploma, or baccalaureate degree), successfully pass the National Council of State Boards of Nursing (NCSBN) Licensure Examination for registered nurses (NCLEX-RN), and pay nursing licensure fees, they begin professional practice as registered nurses. **Licensure** is a process of legal authorization for nursing practice. Newly licensed nurses practice as generalists initially. However, with increased nursing experience in a particular area of practice, many nurses become specialized.

Professional nurse associations recognize professional nurse competence in a particular nursing field by certification. **Certification** means that an individual meets specified requirements, which usually include specialized knowledge and skill in a particular area of nursing practice. Most certifications in professional nursing practice require a specified number of years of experience within a specialty along with successful completion of a competency examination. Each nursing organization sets criteria for nurses to maintain specialty certification. Most organizations require a combination of clinical practice requirements along with a determined number of continuing education contact hours.

Some nursing regulatory agencies recognize certification from professional nursing associations as credentials for an advanced nursing practice licensure.

Advanced nursing practice extends the scope and responsibilities beyond those typically expected from a registered nurse. According to Hamric (2005, p. 89), "Advanced practice nursing is the application of an expanded range of practical, theoretical, and research-based competencies to phenomena experienced by patients within a specialized clinical area of the larger discipline of nursing." Hallmarks of advanced nursing practice include **graduate nursing education** (master's degree or doctorate in nursing), certification, and focused practice on patients and families (Hamric).

In the early days of nurse practitioners and nurse midwifery, graduate nursing education was not required for entry into advanced nursing practice. Many states used certification as credentialing. Depending on the nature of advanced practice (nurse practitioners and midwives), additional state nursing licensure is required (Keeling & Bigbee, 2005). In the case of **nurse practitioners** (who deliver primary, secondary, and tertiary health care services in collaboration with a physician), most states require that they enter into collaborative practice agreements with physicians licensed in the state of practice (Anderson, 2005).

GENERAL NURSING CAREER OPPORTUNITIES

The nursing profession offers a wide array of opportunities. Nurses have the flexibility to focus on one area of practice or work in several practice areas. In addition, nurses may work for an organization or for themselves. **General nursing practice** encompasses areas of practice in which no additional or specialized formal education is required. **Specialized nursing practice** occurs when nurses work in a specific clinical area (such as obstetrics, oncology, and intensive care) where additional education and training are needed to meet specific client concerns or master unique clinical nursing skills. In many specialty areas of nursing practice, nurses become certified in the area of practice, which means they have mastered specific skills and possess a unique knowledge to deliver client care. When a nurse identifies a problem in practice, a potential opportunity has arisen for a new area of nursing practice. Sometimes, an identified problem leads to the development of a personal business or an entirely new health service to be offered by a large medical center. The more common areas of nursing practice are briefly summarized in this section. Detailed information about specific nursing careers is in this and other chapters: advanced practice nursing (later in this chapter), nursing informatics (in Chapter 15), lobbying as a nurse (in Chapter 20), and nursing careers in community health nursing (in Chapter 14).

Acute Care or Hospital Nursing Options

The hospital nurse who provides direct client care is who most people imagine when asked to describe a nurse. In 2007, more than 60% of employed registered nurses worked in hospitals, with most of them engaged in direct client care (Bureau of Labor Statistics, 2007). Recent changes in the health care delivery system have resulted in a variety of career options for nurses working in acute care.

Staff Nursing

Nurses engaging in direct client care find themselves in a fast-paced and challenging position. Within the past decade, the acuity of hospitalized clients has dramatically increased. Now, nurses frequently care for clients who once would have been admitted only to intensive care units. As complex specialized skills become requirements for various types of staff nursing (such as oncology and cardiac specialties), many nurses become certified in specialty practice areas. Experience and certification in specialty areas of practice result in highly trained experts delivering client care. As nurses develop more technical expertise in specific areas, they cannot be expected to provide expert nursing care to clients outside those areas of clinical specialties. However, because basic nursing education effectively prepares professional nurses to assume safe care responsibilities as nurse generalists, hospitals sometimes assign nurses to work outside their clinical specialty areas.

Staff nurses in acute care settings seem like circus performers. They juggle multiple tasks simultaneously. They walk tightropes when confronted with competing client care priorities, such as quality client care, cost containment, supervision of unlicensed assistive personnel (UAP), and shared governance responsibilities. They serve as ringmasters when getting clients where they need to go for diagnostic tests, surgery, or rehabilitative therapy. They soothe disgruntled clients, families, and physicians like the lion tamer who gets lions to remain calm. They assume the role of spotter when taking steps to monitor the safety of the environment for clients and staff. Finally, they act as clowns when they use humor to defray highly emotionally charged situations. Staff nurses work in critical care, emergency, and specialty (e.g., oncology, nephrology, obstetrics, pediatrics, cardiac, and cardiovascular surgical) areas. Staff nurse specialization depends upon the size of the hospital.

Keeping nurse experts at the client bedside poses challenges for acute care organizations. Some hospitals have designed nursing **clinical ladders** as a means to keep highly qualified and experienced nurses at the bedside. Clinical ladders reward experienced bedside staff nurses for ongoing professional development activities. Rewards include more income, and job titles denoting professional accomplishments and experience. Frequently nurses who climb clinical ladders serve as mentors or preceptors to novice nurses. Many use educational status, specialty professional nurse certification, integration of nursing research in clinical practice, and participation in shared governance activities as criteria for promotion (Cutler, 2002; Davis & Bheenuck, 2003; Robitaille & Whelchel, 2005).

Questions for Reflection 21-2

1. What are the benefits of having clinical nursing ladders for nurses? For hospitals?
2. Would a clinical nursing ladder keep me at the bedside? Why or why not?

Staff Development

Recent concerns related to staff competency and improving care quality have provided support for hospitals to maintain nursing staff education and training departments (sometimes called staff development). Staff development roles vary from organization to organization. Typically, staff development personnel provide organizational orientation and continuing education programs. When a facility trains its own UAP, the department offers and coordinates training efforts to ensure consistency in UAP preparation. Staff development departments also become involved in offering education for professional nurses on new equipment. Verification of professional nurse competence to perform specific clinical skills may be centralized through this department or may occur within single nursing units. Some hospitals require graduate degrees in nursing or education for these positions. Titles for nurses working in this field include staff educator, clinical education specialist, inservice educator, and educational specialist. Some institutions (usually smaller ones) also use the staff development personnel to plan community education programs. When a hospital is used as a clinical site for multiple nursing programs, staff educators frequently coordinate clinical day availability, set up programs to verify clinical faculty competence, develop student clinical orientation programs, and keep records related to nursing program satisfaction with the agency as a clinical site.

Utilization Review

To verify the effective use of hospital services, many hospitals and insurance companies use nurses to streamline inpatient care. In response to Medicare regulations, hospitals have developed utilization review programs. Because nurses have the education and experience to understand effective use of resources, sometimes they obtain employment as utilization reviewers. Some managed care organizations employ nurses as preadmission coordinators who prepare clients for hospital admission by coordinating preadmission testing and providing clients with education related to the usual hospital course (especially for surgical procedures). In addition, some managed care organizations use nurses as case managers who act as the client care advocate to make care-related decisions, recommend medical treatments, certify insurance coverage, and listen to customer expectations and problems.

When working as a reviewer, strong clinical background, good research skills, and well-developed skills in analysis are required. Nurses in these positions frequently serve as liaisons among the provider, physician, and consumer.

Risk/Quality Management

Most hospitals have departments to monitor care quality, track unusual reported incidents, identify potential liability areas, provide staff education on the documentation and reporting of incidents, and assist staff when legal actions or malpractice suits arise. Risk management focuses on reducing institutional financial losses because of care errors and accidents. Nurses employed in risk management departments sometimes hold law degrees.

Although all nurses play a role in managing the quality of health care provided within their institutions, some larger organizations may have a centralized quality management department to assess the quality of services provided. Because a large portion of the services offered by hospitals is nursing care, nurses may be members of the quality department to monitor the quality of nursing care services rendered to customers. However, other organizations opt for a decentralized approach to quality management. In these cases, staff nurses assume a larger role in monitoring the quality of nursing care.

Travel Nursing

With regional and seasonal shortages of registered nurses, some nurses (especially those who like variety, taking risks, and traveling) elect to travel to different inpatient institutions to practice bedside client care. Travel nurses accept staff nurse assignments in all areas of the hospital. Travel nurses may contract with a travel nurse agency or work as independent contractors. Most traveling agencies require that a nurse have 1 to 2 years of acute care experience before offering him or her a contract.

Travel nurse agencies may contract with hospitals to fill vacant staff nurse positions. The agency offers nurses positions from which to choose, and assistance with housing, moving, and professional licensure expenses; and some may offer benefits (health insurance, life insurance, and retirement plans). Terms of contracts with travel nurse agencies vary greatly. Most temporary agencies require nurses to fulfill their current contract and then wait a time before accepting a position once held as a travel nurse (Kearney, 2003). For example, conditions of a contract may state that the nurse must not accept employment at a hospital where the agency sent the nurse for 2 years after severing ties with the nursing agency.

Extended Care Facility Nursing

The Health Resources Services Administration (2007) estimated that close to 155,000 registered nurses worked in extended care facilities. Most of these nurses were educated in diploma or associate degree programs.

Elderly Long-Term Care

For many years, nurses have viewed professional nursing in long-term care institutions (nursing homes or extended care facilities) as unattractive. However, for nurses desiring to escape the fast pace of acute care nursing and establish long-term relationships with clients, long-term care (LTC) nursing provides these opportunities. In most LTC facilities, professional nurses assume supervisory roles and delegate tasks to licensed practical/vocational nurses, certified medicine aides, and other unlicensed care providers. With the push for earlier hospital dismissals, complex care needs, such as mechanical ventilation, tracheotomy, hyperalimentation, and tube feeding, have become common in such facilities. Some LTC clients are residents only long enough to complete postoperative therapy or to regain strength after a hospital stay. Thus, the professional nurse can maintain some acute care clinical skills when working in LTC. Some LTC facilities offer assisted living services. Professional nurses conduct initial periodic client assessments, screen clients for health problems, see clients when health-related problems arise, develop the client care plan, manage client medications, supervise licensed and unlicensed personnel as they provide client care, and determine staff inservice educational needs (Mitty, 2003). Instead of an institutional approach to client care, most LTC facilities view themselves as the client's home.

Some nurses find great rewards in working with the elderly. Unfortunately, some elderly clients have no families or support systems, and members of the LTC staff become their only link to the outside world. Many elderly clients develop strong personal relationships with LTC staff. Because death is viewed as a normal part of life in LTC facilities, residents may not be subjected to many invasive procedures or become attached to technological equipment that is used only to preserve life. Most LTC facilities permit visits by hospice when death is imminent, enabling comfortable, dignified, and peaceful deaths.

With the projected increases in the elderly population needing assisted living, LTC nursing represents one of the fastest growing careers. LTC offers professional nurses the chance to make a big difference in individual lives.

Rehabilitation Nursing

Advances in trauma care and increases in chemical dependency have resulted in an explosion of rehabilitation facilities. Likewise, insurance companies have identified that transferring clients to rehabilitation facilities after bouts of acute illness or surgery saves money. Rehabilitation units have opened as part of acute care and LTC facilities, and freestanding rehabilitation centers offer services to consumers. Some centers specialize in specific rehabilitation needs for a particular health problem, such as stroke, head injury, spinal cord trauma, chemical dependency, chronic respiratory illness, amputation, cancer survival, or blindness.

In contrast to nurses working in acute care, rehabilitation nurses participate as equal partners of an interdisciplinary health team. Rehabilitation nurses need to be cooperative team players and have excellent organizational and communication skills. There is a strong focus on client education because the goal of rehabilitation is to get the clients to care for themselves or coach someone on how to care for them. Rehabilitation nurses may become very involved with clients and families and experience great satisfaction from being part of the client's journey toward mastering an independent lifestyle. The Association of Rehabilitation Nurses offers special certification in rehabilitation nursing.

Outpatient Nursing Opportunities

Besides acute care nursing, many nursing opportunities occur in outpatient settings. Some outpatient nursing opportunities demand specialized education and training.

Outpatient Clinics and Physician Offices

Nurses working in outpatient clinics and physician offices usually work with clients who have less acute conditions. In 2007, ambulatory care centers employed close to 400,000 registered nurses (Bureau of Healthcare Professions, 2007). Many nurses choose these settings because of better hours (usually daytime hours with no weekend shifts) and less stressful working conditions. Depending on the clinic or office, the professional nurse may be a specialized expert or a generalist. Some nurses work in clinic settings, where on specific days of the week, a specialized clinic may be held. Clinics and offices may be located close to a hospital, in a professional office building, or in a shopping mall. Some clinics offer services 24 hours a day, 7 days a week for illnesses and injuries not requiring emergency services.

Outpatient Surgery Centers

The number of outpatient or ambulatory surgical centers has exploded within the past 20 years. Many surgical procedures do not require a postoperative hospital stay. Although these centers do not have all the resources that are available in an acute care setting, they do have emergency equipment available and policies to guide staff if life-threatening emergencies arise. Many nurses working in outpatient surgery centers have operating room experience. In this setting, some nurses admit clients, assist with surgical procedures, provide care after anesthesia administration, teach clients about discharge instructions, and accompany them to vehicles for the ride home. Some outpatient surgery centers have nurses call to check on client progress the day after the procedure.

Special Care Centers

In addition to outpatient clinics and surgery centers, disease-focused centers provide expert care to persons with health problems such as diabetes, heart disease, renal failure, and cancer. Some large urban medical centers have opened breast care centers that provide a comprehensive approach to breast health. Services include screening mammography, self-breast examination education, a comprehensive library related to breast cancer, ultrasound testing, and breast biopsy. In these settings, nurses work as interdisciplinary team members to provide holistic, comprehensive client care.

Community Nursing Centers

Community nursing centers offer primary health care services to middle- and lower-class clients at reduced cost as compared to traditional clinics and physician offices. Nurse-run centers usually have a nurse practitioner and nurses with specialized skills in health education, stress reduction, weight issues, lifestyle management, and other wellness-focused health topics to deliver services. According to a literature review by Coddington and Sands (2008), nurse-managed clinics provide an important safety net for delivering health care services to the underinsured and uninsured. Along with removing barriers to care, clients using nurse-managed centers develop meaningful, therapeutic relationships with nurse practitioners; reduce the incidence of emergency use for primary care and minor illnesses; reduce hospitalizations; promote health; improve patient compliance to treatment plans; and have the same level of consumer satisfaction with care when compared to care received from a physician's office. Community nursing centers may be located in a school or church. Nursing centers often have an affiliation with a collegiate nursing program. If required care is not available at the community nursing center, nurses make referrals and sometimes arrange for services. Depending on the funding, the nursing center may pay for services arranged within a provider network.

Community Education

As consumers seek wellness education, professional nurses frequently find themselves volunteering for various community education groups to teach a variety of health classes. Local businesses, civic organizations, and churches frequently want to offer staff and members information regarding cardiopulmonary resuscitation, first aid, cancer self-examinations, parenting skills, babysitting, and healthy lifestyles. Some organizations request health screenings and may sponsor health fairs.

Cardiac Rehabilitation

Within the past 20 years, most cardiac clients have received offers to participate in cardiac rehabilitation programs after undergoing cardiac catheterizations, pacemaker implants, or open-heart surgery. Persons recovering from myocardial infarctions also qualify for cardiac rehabilitation. Cardiac rehabilitation centers can be found in hospital settings, physician offices, or fitness centers. These programs rely on the expertise of professional nurses and exercise physiologists to develop and supervise a physical workout for patients with cardiac disease.

Most cardiac rehabilitation nurses have a background in critical care nursing and have Advanced Cardiac Life Support (ACLS) certification. Cardiac rehabilitation nursing responsibilities include observing cardiac monitors as clients exercise, performing periodic pulse and blood pressure measurements, assessing for signs of overexertion, and teaching relaxation and stress reduction techniques. Some cardiac rehabilitation programs use the nurse for nutritional lifestyle counseling and mental health counseling when nutritionists (or dietitians) and psychologists are not part of the program.

Forensic Nursing

Forensic nurses provide care to victims of violent crime. Many emergency departments have a nurse who has special education in working with victims of violent crimes. Nursing care provided by forensic nurses includes the following: caring for the victim's injuries, identifying and documenting the injuries (including taking photographs), determining wound patterns, collecting evidence (samples of hair, tissue, and body fluids) for future trials, and testifying in court to present and explain evidence and examination findings. Victims of violent crime benefit from having forensic nurses because the nurse knows how to approach and counsel victims of violent crime. Some emergency departments have special rape crisis or abuse crisis programs in which victims receive care from forensic nurses in specially designated rooms. In these cases, the nurse makes referrals to social workers for arranging safe living arrangements and follow-up counseling (Stevens, 2004).

Business Opportunities

In addition to being involved with direct client care, nurses can find employment opportunities in the business sector. Business career opportunities enable nurses to make an impact on client care by bringing the care ethic to corporations that supply products and reimbursement for health care.

Insurance and Managed Care Companies

Insurance and managed care companies use nurses for evaluating care delivered to customers. Third-party payers frequently use nurses as gatekeepers to verify that company resources have been effectively used to provide services. Responsibilities for nurses employed by companies include reviewing medical records and activities to evaluate the need for care, ensuring that the appropriate level of care was received, and determining that quality care was delivered in a timely fashion.

Along with quality management, third-party payers use nurses to staff telephones to certify insurance coverage before service delivery. Nurses who fill certification positions need a strong clinical background and an ability to grasp a global picture of all the issues surrounding care delivery. However, nurses employed in this position frequently encounter many ethical dilemmas when working with complex clinical issues and deciding when to certify care. If a wrong decision is made, the nurse may be solely accountable for it, especially if the nurse is a company manager.

Telephone Triage and Health Care Advice Lines

Managed care companies, physician offices, clinics, and hospitals frequently use professional nurses to staff call centers devoted to determining the urgency of care, providing health information, referring clients to appropriate health care providers, scheduling appointments with health care providers, and offering health advice. Although triage and health care advice lines started out as a marketing strategy, they quickly demonstrated the ability to streamline the use of health care services, thereby reducing health care costs. Some managed care companies require that subscribers call the triage nurse to certify trips to emergency departments. Nurses use assessment and therapeutic communication skills to determine the extent of the health problems of callers. Because some clients become frequent callers, telephone triage nurses may develop long-term relationships with them. Some nurses report that they schedule time to call clients to follow up on decisions they made.

Marketing and Sales

Companies that sell products such as pharmaceuticals, IV equipment, and monitors often hire professional nurses as sales representatives. Nurses provide credibility for product promotion, especially when they have used the product in clinical practice. Nurses also provide an insight into product improvements and future products that may be useful in client care delivery. When complex equipment is purchased, the company often provides staff education in the use of the equipment. As sales representatives, nurses know how to approach other nurses and anticipate questions and problems that the nurse may experience.

Sales representatives must be energetic and self-motivated. Because most sales representatives work from their homes and travel a lot, they work flexible hours. Much time is spent meeting with prospective customers. Knowledge related to the business world and principles of operating a home office provides needed skills for nurses entering the corporate world. Some companies provide a base salary that does not meet the salary earned from clinical practice. However, significant bonuses can be earned when commissions arrive from successful sales.

Occupational Health and Worker's Compensation Programs

Many businesses have occupational health departments for which nurses work at managing workplace injuries, preventing work-related illnesses, screening for environmental or occupational hazards, providing employee educational services, and marketing employee health programs to other companies. Occupational health nurses frequently offer CPR training and health promotion education for company employees. They also respond to work-related injuries or medical emergencies that occur. Some companies rely on the occupational health nurse to track the progress of workers recovering from work-related injuries. Other companies use nurses employed by the worker's compensation insurance plan to monitor worker progress. Nurses often develop light-duty work programs for employees who cannot perform all regular job duties but can provide some work for the company.

Private Consulting

When a nurse identifies a problem, an area for consulting has surfaced. As companies outsource employee services, demands for consultants increase. Health care organizations use consulting firms to prepare for accreditation visits, apply for quality awards, meet employee educational needs, engage in work redesign, and look for ways to reduce operating costs. Some consultants have insider status, with which they provide special services within a system that employs them. Other consultants have outsider status; they work for a company that provides services to organizations or as an independent contractor (Norwood, 1998). For example, a hospital may employ an enterostomal therapist specifically to provide ostomy care and education for clients and families. However, when the need arises for staff education related to ostomy care, the hospital uses the enterostomal therapist to provide a staff program. Extended care facilities may use external nurse consultants for monthly client assessments or to provide client services such as foot or ostomy care. Health care consumers may use nurse consultants to assist in selecting an extended care facility for a family member, paying medical bills, or learning relaxation techniques.

The success of nursing consultants depends on personal proficiency in the area where consultation is provided; strong theoretical, business, and clinical skills; the ability to solve problems quickly; and the ability to compete with other consultants. Consulting or working as an independent contractor can be done part-time until the business becomes established and profitable (Norwood, 1998).

Medical-legal nurse consultants (MLC) have been in existence for many years. As our society grows more litigious, the demand for medical-legal nurse consults rises. Because of the nature of the work, skills required for MLCs include an ability to quickly find relevent nursing and medical literature pertaining to a case, effective computer skills (including Internet searching), well-developed critical thinking skills, and detailed knowledge of legal issues surrounding nursing and health care delivery. MLCs assume the following roles and responsibilities: (1) clarify medical terminology; (2) review medical records to determine if harm was caused directly by a health provider's actions or inactions; (3) review medical nursing and health care literature; (4) develop timelines and summaries to explain events of a case or claim; (5) locate or serve as an expert witness; (6) conduct interviews with clients, witnesses, or other parties; (7) assist in the development of case strategy; and (8) provide support to clients during legal proceedings. MLCs may be independent contractors or employees of a law firm. Community colleges, 4-year universities, and law schools have educational programs for nurses interested in becoming MLCs. The American Association of Legal Nurse Consultants offers certification; however, certification as a MLC is not required (Kopishke, 2007).

In recent years, many nurse consultants have become nurse entrepreneurs. Starting and running an independent business is a complex undertaking, which is discussed in the next section. Some nurses who have specialized education in complementary health care practices, such as massage, therapeutic touch, or aromatherapy or magnet therapy, may assume the role of nurse consultant when they actually use these practices or help others to incorporate them into client care.

 ## ADVANCED NURSING PRACTICE CAREER OPTIONS

Nursing offers areas of advanced practice. Most advanced nursing practice careers require some education beyond the baccalaureate degree. In 2007, the Health Resources Services Administration estimated that close to 10% of registered nurses (304,977) had the education and credentials to practice as an advanced practice nurse.

In the United States, the practice of nursing is determined at the state level. Some states recognize professional certification as a nurse midwife or practitioner as the credential to obtain an advanced practice nursing license. However, because of the multiple entry paths into professional nursing, the NCSBN and professional nurses have pushed for advanced practice nurses to obtain a second nursing license to provide assurance that a minimum set of professional competencies is met. In addition, licensure as an advanced practice nurse enables some nurses to prescribe medications and receive direct insurance (private and/or government policies) reimbursement for rendered services in most American states. As advanced practice nurses move across state and national borders, credentialing becomes increasingly important. Credentialing provides documentation that a person is recognized by some regulatory body and has met the standards to use a particular title. In health care, credentialing serves as a vehicle to protect the public against persons who fail to meet the set standards and preparation to execute the duties implied by the health care professional. Because of the variance of state nurse practice acts, some states require credentialing prior to attainment of the second advanced nursing practice license. Along with providing initial documentation of qualifications for advanced practice, most states require that the advanced practice nurse fulfills continuing education and specific practice requirements (a certain number of clinical practice hours) to maintain certification (Hanson, 2005).

Future arenas of clinical practice for advanced nursing practice emerge as nursing specialties increase in complexity. When the specialty identifies key knowledge and skills, the evolution of the specialty as an opportunity for advanced nursing practice has begun. As soon as formalized training and education begin within the specialty, then the practice area has taken steps to acknowledge the need for standardizing the educational process. Finally, once the certificate-level training programs enter the arena of graduate education, the specialty practice becomes a legitimate area for advanced practice nursing. Areas of emerging advanced practice include parish nursing, clinical transplant coordinator, childbirth educator, advanced diabetes manager, genetic advanced practice nurses, and wound, ostomy, and continence nursing (Salyer & Hamric, 2005). The following discussion presents information on the most common forms of advanced nursing practice.

Nurse Practitioners

Nurse practitioners (NPs) provide primary health care services to consumers. Nursing care services provided by NPs include assessing client health using a holistic framework; identifying medical and nursing diagnoses; planning and prescribing treatments; managing health care regimens for individuals, families, and communities; promoting wellness; preventing illness and injury; and managing acute and chronic health conditions. The NP role surfaced during a physician shortage in the 1960s. The first NPs attended certification programs that lasted from a few weeks to as long as 2 years. NPs carved out a distinct difference in practice from the medical model by using a holistic approach to care based on nursing theory. As recognition grew, mostly related to the reduced cost of primary care and to positive health outcomes for clients, NP programs in higher education settings proliferated. Education at the master's degree predominates the education of NPs. Specialty practice areas for NPs include family care, adults, pediatrics, geriatrics, acute care, and women's health. Primary care NPs typically practice in outpatient settings and provide health care services aimed at health promotion, disease prevention, and management of simple, acute, and chronic health conditions while establishing a partnership with their clients (Anderson, 2005). The acute care NP provides health care services to clients who may be hospital inpatients or clients seeking care in emergency room or clinic settings. They work in a variety of clinical specialties, including diabetes management, orthopedics, oncology, neurology, neurosurgery, and cardiovascular services. Acute care NPs frequently perform procedures that residents perform in teaching hospitals such as lumbar punctures (neurologic acute NP), bone marrow aspirations (oncology acute NP), harvesting saphenous vein grafts during coronary bypass surgery (cardiovascular surgery acute NP), or serving as first assistants during surgery. They also frequently work with physicians, or they may have independent practice privileges at hospitals (Hravanak, Kleinpell, Magdic, & Guttendorf, 2005).

Today, more than 102,000 NPs practice in a variety of settings (Anderson, 2005). Before qualifying for direct third-party reimbursement, NPs must obtain certification. Several bodies offer certification examinations, including the American Nurses Credentialing Center, the American Academy of Nurse Practitioners and Nurses, the National Certification Board of Pediatric Nurse Practitioners, and the National Certification Corporation. Most NPs are required to renew certification every 5 years. This process requires documented practice and evidence of continuing education (Anderson, 2005). By 2015, all nurse practitioners should be educated at the doctoral level of nursing and receive a doctor of nursing practice (DNP) degree (American Association of Colleges of Nursing, 2006).

Within their relatively short existence, NPs have earned the respect of clients and other health team members. Recent research has demonstrated the effectiveness of NPs in primary care, health promotion, decreasing hospitalization rates, and client satisfaction (Bunnell, 2007). Research Brief 20-1 provides evidence of the contributions that NPs make toward quality care in delivery of services to persons with chronic kidney disease. In addition to demonstrating the value of their contributions to health care, NPs provide health care services to the underprivileged and persons living in underserved areas (Anderson, 2005; Bunnell).

Certified Nurse-Midwives

Certified nurse-midwives (CNMs) independently manage women's health care with a special emphasis on pregnancy, childbirth, postpartum care, newborn care, family planning, and well woman care. Well woman care focuses on family planning, screening for female-related cancer, and management of perimenopause and postmenopause. CNM care supports the natural processes of birth, growth, development, and aging; CNMs intervene only if absolutely indicated. The Health Resources Services Administration (2007) reported that 73,254 registered nurses work as CNMs.

Research Brief 20-1

Lee, W., Campoy, S., Smits, G., Tran, Z., & Chonchol, M. (2007). Effectiveness of a chronic kidney disease clinic in achieving K/DOQI guideline target at initiation of dialysis: A single centre experience. *Nephrology Dialysis Transplantation, 22*, 833–838.

The purpose of the study was to compare any differences in the quality of care of persons with chronic kidney disease (CKD) when receiving care from nephrologists or a trained renal nurse practitioner. The investigators retrospectively reviewed the charts of 77 clients who received care in a CKD clinic and 36 clients who received care in a physician-run clinic renal-hypertension (RH) clinic. Both clinics were linked to a Veterans Administration Medical Center in a Rocky Mountain state. They looked for evidence of compliance to the National Foundation Kidney Disease Outcomes Quality Initiative, the guidelines used by providers in the clinic to manage CKD. Practice guidelines call for initial evaluation by a board-certified nephrologist, and then the client can be seen by a specially trained nurse-practitioner (NP) or rotating medical residents. The NP addresses the psychosocial and educational needs of all clients in the clinic as well as assumes a clinic caseload.

Data in regard to client demographics, disease process (CKD or RH), systolic BP, diastolic BP, hemoglobin erythropoietin use, serum calcium, serum phosphorus, use of phosphate binders, and serum albumin were tabulated and analyzed using Fisher's exact tests for categorical or dichotomized variables and Wilcoxan rank sum tests for continuous variables.

Clients followed by the NP in the CKD were found to have more favorable outcomes than clients receiving care from residents in the RH clinic. The NP clients had higher compliance rates to phosphate binder and erythropoietin use, thus having higher hemoglobin and calcium serum levels and lower serum phosphorus levels. They also had higher serum albumin levels. In addition, clients followed by the NP had fewer hospitalizations than other clients. The NP followed the exact same protocols as the physicians providing client care in the study.

This single study demonstrates that NPs can follow medical protocols as effectively as medical residents; however, no clear-cut reasons can be given for the NP's superior outcomes. The result of the study should be interpreted with caution because it was conducted in a single institution and only one NP followed clients in the CKD clinic. There might be something special about her ability to gain trust and rapport with clients that might not be present in all NPs. Also, physicians need to deal with more than one issue rather than just preparing clients for dialysis. Thus, the NP may have had more time to spend with clients than the physicians. The study does support the use of protocols based on best practices rather than consensus of providers in controlling CKD.

Of all the advanced practice roles, midwifery is the oldest. Records of midwifery practice are documented in the Bible. As the profession of medicine arose, midwifery declined. Mary Breckenridge, who received midwifery education in Scotland, became the first practicing nurse-midwife in the United States when she established the Frontier Nursing Service in 1925. In 1932, the first American nurse-midwifery education program opened in the Maternity Center of the Lobenstein Clinic in New York City. Slow growth in nurse-midwifery occurred, and in 1955, the American College of Nurse-Midwives was established. The reemergence of the modern midwife started with a pilot project in Madera County, California, in the early 1960s. In 1971, a national certification exam became the standard for entry into practice by the American College of Nurse-Midwives. CNM practice is regulated by individual states, thereby creating variances in prescriptive authority, educational preparation, employment contracts, and practice arrangements. By the 1970s, nurse-midwifery became a demand of consumers seeking a more natural approach to childbirth. By the 1990s, many CNMs graduated from university-based programs (Dorroh & Kelley, 2005). The American Association of Colleges of Nursing (2006) has adopted the DNP as the desired degree for CNMs by 2015.

Although they started as certificate programs, nurse-midwifery programs progressed to graduate nursing education. Forty-seven nurse-midwifery programs are housed in American universities, and all but seven programs are incorporated into master of nursing programs.

Research evidence indicates that CNMs contribute substantially to the quality of maternal-child health care. The Bureau of Health Professions (2003) reported reduced cesarean section rates and fewer medical interventions for women at low risk when compared with women at low risk who received care from physicians. Studies report significantly lower neonatal mortality and infant mortality, as well as higher birth weights of infants when women were attended by CNMs. Along with improved outcomes, CNMs provide women with health care at reduced costs (Bureau of Health Professions, 2003; Gaudier, 2003; Rosseter, 2003).

Clinical Nurse Specialists

Clinical nurse specialists (CNSs) are highly skilled clinical experts in a specialized area of nursing practice and use all the steps of the nursing process to promote health, prevent complications, and manage health problems. CNSs work in many settings, including hospitals, schools, extended care facilities, homes, and community agencies. In 1954, Hildegard Peplau established the first graduate-level CNS program at Rutgers University to prepare psychiatric CNSs. CNSs provide expert patient care, serve as professional role models, and act as client advocates. They also provide indirect care services when they act as consultants or resources to other health team members, supervise care delivery, act as liaisons between the client system and care providers, initiate and direct change for client care, and engage in research and evidence-based nursing projects conducting clinical research. Some CNSs have prescriptive privileges, and others do not. Second licensure as an advanced practice nurse is not required for CNS practice in some states (Sparacino, 2005).

Skalla, Hamric, and Caron (2005) noted that changing population demographics, health care cost containment issues, accessibility and affordability of care delivery, the ever-expanding knowledge base for specialty nursing practice arenas, and shortages of physicians and nurses have resulted in the blending of the role of the CNS and NP. When CNSs have prescriptive privileges, typically most states require a second advanced practice nursing license. Nurses who have merged the roles of NP and CNS usually have had graduate educational preparation in both roles. The blended roles offers nurses an opportunity to cross health care settings, provide comprehensive health care services to a narrowly defined clinical population, and serve as team members in primary, secondary, and tertiary care settings.

Early CNSs primarily worked in hospitals to provide support for patients and nursing staff. However, with the advent of managed care, many hospitals enlisted CNSs to serve as case managers. CNSs coordinate care of highly acute patients within the hospital and have been used as discharge planners. They practice in many subspecialty fields, including pulmonary, oncology, neuroscience, geriatrics, rehabilitation, diabetes, hospice, and palliative care. In the 1990s, advanced practice nurses assumed case management positions within their specialty area of practice. Case management by advanced practice nurses is expected to evolve and, perhaps, become more commonplace as elderly persons with chronic illnesses have complex health care needs (Mahn-Dinicola & Zazworsky, 2005). The American Association of Colleges of Nursing (2006) has proposed a new academic degree, the clinical nurse leader, a master's degree aimed at facilitating seamless health care delivery across the health care continuum.

Certified Registered Nurse Anesthetists

Certified registered nurse anesthetists (CRNAs) provide anesthesia and anesthetic-related services to health care consumers. Along with completing the 24-month program consisting of advanced study in anatomy, physiology, chemistry, and pathophysiology, and 90 hours emphasizing the principles of anesthesia, the nurse must administer at least 450 anesthetics before taking the certification examination (Faut-Callahan & Kremer, 2005).

All 50 states recognize CRNA practice. According to the American Association of Nurse Anesthetists (2008), CRNA practice includes preanesthetic assessment; anesthetic plan development and implementation; anesthesia induction; the selection, application, and insertion of noninvasive and invasive monitoring devices; anesthetic selection, acquisition, and administration; fluid and ventilatory support; the administration of medications and fluids to facilitate the emergence and recovery from anesthesia; patient discharge and follow-up care after anesthesia administration; airway support and management in medical emergencies; and implementation of various acute and chronic pain treatment modalities. Despite rigorous, standardized education, approximately 80% of CRNAs practice anesthesia with a group of physician anesthesiologists. The other 20% practice independently to provide anesthesia services to outpatient clinics and rural hospitals (more than 70% of rural hospitals rely on CRNAs for anesthesia services). Certified registered nurse anesthetists receive payment for services directly from third-party payers. CRNAs assume full legal responsibility for their actions (Faut-Callahan & Kremer, 2005). The American Association of Colleges of Nursing (2006) has identified the need for CRNAs to hold DNP degrees by 2015.

Registered Nurse First Assistant

Registered nurse first assistants (RNFAs) may be employed by hospitals and physicians or may work as independent contractors. Practice settings for RNFAs include hospitals, ambulatory surgical centers, and physician offices. RNFAs work collaboratively with surgeons during surgery. RNFAs prepare skin for incisions, hold retractors, assist with clamping vessels, perform suction, perform cautery, irrigate the surgical wound beds, and close incisions. Along with working in the operating room, RNFAs collect client histories, perform preoperative assessments, make client preoperative visits, educate clients about procedures, and conduct postoperative visits (Martinkus, 2004). RNFAs are widely used in rural hospitals.

The scope of responsibility of RNFAs varies according to employment setting. RNFAs working in surgeons' offices tend to have more autonomy and responsibilities than RNFAs employed by hospitals. The Association of Operating Room Nurses (AORN) published the first official statement on RNFAs in 1984, and then structured an educational and certificate program for RNFAs in 1985. Qualifications for certification as a RNFA include current licensure as a RN, certification from the AORN as a certified operating room nurse, a bachelor's degree in nursing or a master's degree in nursing with a bachelor's degree in another field of study, and 2,000 documented hours of RNFA practice with the first 120 hours being completed under the guidance of a surgeon preceptor (Martinkus, 2004).

RNFAs are reimbursed for their services at a lower rate than assisting surgeons. Medicare does not reimburse RNFAs for their services. Many receive payment from surgeons or hospitals for which they work (Martinkus, 2004).

Nursing Administration

Most health care organizations and systems employ nurses as administrators or managers. Positions in **nursing administration** range from departmental heads (head nurse or nurse manager) to chief nursing officers or chief nurse executives (director of nursing). In many hospitals, the traditional "head nurse" position has been replaced with a "nurse manager," who may have to manage more than one unit. Many hospitals require advanced degrees for management or administrative positions. Many colleges and universities offer graduate nursing education in nursing administration. Some nursing administrative personnel have opted to pursue graduate degrees in business or health administration to facilitate role performance. Complex budgetary considerations, institutional accreditation requirements, legal issues, strategic planning, and staff management concerns (including having enough staff for effective care) are some of the key dimensions of the nurse administration career option (Caroselli, 2008).

Nursing Academia

Teaching the new generation of nurses provides great rewards for nursing faculty members. A career in **nursing academia** (nursing education) enables experienced nurses to share their knowledge and expertise with future professional nurses. As a faculty member, the professional nurse has opportunities to polish clinical skills, expand knowledge of clinical nursing, engage in nursing research, and participate in community service while sharing knowledge and teaching skills with future nurses. Although most nursing programs require a master's degree in nursing and recent clinical experience for faculty appointment, some associate degree and vocational nursing programs may hire a baccalaureate-prepared nurse. Most programs preparing certified nursing assistants use baccalaureate-prepared nurses as faculty. Nursing programs offering baccalaureate degrees prefer to hire faculty with nursing or educational doctorates. The American Association of Colleges of Nursing (2006) has called for the doctor of philosophy degree in nursing to become the required degree for nursing faculty by 2015.

Faculty roles vary across various educational settings. Most nursing faculty members engage in scholarly activities, teaching, and community services. State- and privately sponsored research universities require faculty to develop a program of nursing research. In these settings, faculty members develop research proposals, write grants to fund projects, engage in research, disseminate research findings, and fulfill teaching responsibilities. Nursing programs in the community college emphasize technical aspects of nursing, and faculty members concentrate on teaching students clinical skills. Many faculty members practice nursing outside of the academic setting to maintain clinical competence (Penn, 2008).

Distance learning programs pose different challenges for faculty. In addition to being content and practice experts, nurse faculty must have the knowledge and expertise to run computer hardware, use software to engage learners, work with technology support staff, and establish online student relationships. Faculty also find that they can enter course information onto websites from any computer linked to the Internet. Students can access course information and electronically submit assignments at any time. If online discussions are part of the course, students and faculty must routinely check discussion boards. With new technology, faculty must remain more flexible with online instruction, especially if the required technology fails (Ryan, Carlton, & Ali, 2004; Penn, 2008).

Nurse Researcher

As health care facilities strive to deliver the best quality care, many of them have hired nurse researchers to fill director of nursing research positions. Director of nursing research roles vary across institutions. The IOM's recommendation to include the use of best practices to provide safe, effective, and efficient health care has created a climate that values the input of evidence-based practices and protocols. In many facilities, the director of nursing research educates staff about the research process and how to critique research studies effectively. The director of nursing research also guides, supports, and assists staff as they engage in evidence-based quality improvement and nursing research projects (Dumont, 2008).

Nurse Entrepreneurs

Because of the complex factors and education needed to establish and maintain an independent business, the career as **nurse entrepreneur** fits the description of advanced nursing practice. Most entrepreneurs follow similar career paths. Many nurses experience some form of trauma that serves as the reason for a career change. Traumatic events may be a singular event, such as reaching a personally significant age, changing marital status, or having a child or children, or they may be a compilation of factors, such as job boredom, frustration with administration, an unfulfilled need, or a general feeling that life is being wasted. First, such nurses discover an idea for a viable business. Frequently, the idea for a business appears while practicing professional nursing in a traditional institution. Second, the entrepreneur gathers more information about the idea to provide a solid foundation for the new business concept. Third, entrepreneurs develop the business concept by verifying the idea through the gathering of more information. The fourth step involves an initial test of the business concept for success. The fifth step consists of expanding the number and types of offered products or services. The sixth and final step involves business expansion to include organizational structures, employees, policies, and procedures (Vogel & Doleysh, 1997).

Not all nurses possess the personality characteristics needed to embark on the entrepreneurial career path. Key personality characteristics shared by successful entrepreneurs include a willingness for risk taking, self-confidence, internal locus of control, determination, perseverance, interpersonal communication skills, willingness to delay gratification, business awareness, desire for total control, ability to direct others, physical stamina, mental resilience, and a strong need for achievement. The four following steps serve as guidelines for discovering a niche for a business: (1) developing a business idea, (2) market service analysis, (3) market testing, and (4) trial run. Running a personal business requires detailed knowledge of the corporate world and governmental policies that guide small businesses (Vogel & Doleysh, 1997; Waxman, 2005).

Waxman (2005) identified advantages and disadvantages of being a nurse entrepreneur. Advantages include a high level of autonomy, flexible working hours, constant change, meeting lots of new people, using previously untapped skills (creativity and interpersonal), and being paid high hourly rates. Disadvantages include constant change, loss of employee-based fringe benefits, having to secure accounts payable, taking risks, loss of daily contact with other nurses, no paid time off, and loss of job structure. However, nurses, especially those who enjoy working independently, find being an entrepreneur very satisfying and rewarding.

Questions for Reflection 21-3

1. What further information about the career options presented in this chapter do I want?
2. Who would I contact to explore an appealing nursing career option?
3. What additional education or skills would I need to obtain to pursue another career option in nursing?

SUMMARY AND SIGNIFICANCE TO PRACTICE

Professional nursing offers many career options for committed, caring nurses. Nurses have opportunities to change specialty and practice areas that are not afforded to the other health professions. Many expanded and most advanced nursing practice roles require additional education. Currently, most advanced nursing practice roles require certification and additional licensure in some states, and, by 2015, educational preparation for these roles will be a nursing doctorate. Some nurses find that discovering one's personal niche in the profession can be a challenging and complex process. When nurses take the time to explore the various available career options, they can make career decisions with confidence.

FROM THEORY TO PRACTICE

1. How would I respond to Laura in the vignette if she asked me about my current nursing practice? Why would I respond in this manner?
2. Whom would I contact if I wanted to explore one of the nursing career options presented in this chapter? Why would I contact this person?

WWWINTERNET EXERCISES

1. Visit the Sigma Theta Tau International website at http://www.nursingsociety.org. Click on the career icon found in the left margin of the website and explore areas related to career information, career mapping, and retirement planning. Did you find this information useful? Why or why not?
2. Visit the American Nurses Association website at http://www.nursingworld.org. Find information about specialty practice certification and advanced practice nursing. Was this information useful? Why or why not?

WWWINTERNET RESOURCES

Sigma Theta Tau International: http://www.nursingsociety.org.

U.S. Department of Labor, Bureau of Labor Statistics, *Occupational Outlook Handbook*: http://www.bls.gov/oco.

All Nursing Schools: http://www.allnursingshcools.com.

Nursing Spectrum: http://www.nursingspectrum.com.

American Nurses Association: http://www.nursingworld.org.

Health Web: http://www.healthweb.org.

Johnson & Johnson's Discover Nursing website: http://www.discovernursing.com.

Health Resources and Service Administration: http://www.hrsa.gov.

American Association of Nurse Anesthetists: http://www.aana.com.

Travel Nursing: http://www.travelnursing.com.

Forensic Nursing: http://www.forensicnurse.org.

REFERENCES

American Association of Colleges of Nursing. (2006, October 20). *DNP roadmap task force report*. Available at http://www.aacn.nche.edu/DNP/pdf/DNProadmapreport.pdf. Accessed July 18, 2008.

American Association of Nurse Anesthetists. (2008). Nurse anesthetists at a glance. Available at http://www.aana.com/aboutaana.aspx?ucNavMenu_TSMenuTargetID=1798&UCNavMenu_TSMenuTargetType=4&NavMenu_TSMenuID=6&id=265. Accessed May 3, 2009.

Anderson, A. (2005). The primary care nurse practitioner. In A. Hamric, J. Spross, & C. Handon (Eds.), *Advanced practice nursing: An integrative approach* (3rd ed., pp. 447–463). St. Louis, MO: Elsevier Saunders.

Bunnell, W. (2007). A review of the merits of the nurse practitioner role. *Nursing Standard, 21*(18), 35–40.

Bureau of Health Professions. (2003). A comparison of changes in the professional practice of nurse practitioners, physician assistants, and certified nurse midwives: 1992–2000. Available at http://bhpr.hrsa.gov/healthworkface/reports/scope/scope1-2./htm. Accessed July 1, 2005.

Bureau of Health Professions. (2007). National practitioner data bank. Available at http://www.npdb-hiprdb.hrsa.gov/Public_Use_Data_File.pdf. Accessed May 3, 2009.

Bureau of Labor Statistics. (1992). *Occupational outlook handbook*. Washington, DC: Author.

Bureau of Labor Statistics. (2007). *Occupational outlook handbook*. Available at http://www.bls.gov/oco. Accessed September 15, 2007.

Caroselli, C. (2008). The system chief nurse executive: More than the sum of the parts. *Nursing Administration Quarterly, 32*(3), 247–252.

Coddington, J., & Sands, L. (2008). Cost of health care and quality outcomes of patients at nurse-managed clinics. *Nursing Economic$, 26*(2), 75–83.

Cutler, K. P. (2002). Clinical ladder protocols and nurse career development. *Long-Term Care Interface, 3*, 22–32.

Davis, N., & Bheenuck, S. (2003). A professional development pathways scheme. *Nursing Standard, 17*, 40–43.

Dorroh, M., & Kelley, M. (2005). The certified nurse-midwife. In A. Hamric, J. Spross, & C. Handon (Eds.), *Advanced practice nursing: An integrative approach* (3rd ed., pp. 551–581). St. Louis, MO: Elsevier Saunders.

Dumont, C. (2008). Nurse researcher: A career, not just a job. *American Nurse Today, 3*(5), 33–34.

Faut-Callahan, M., & Kremer, M. (2005). The certified registered nurse anesthetist. In A. Hamric, J. Spross, & C. Handon (Eds.), *Advanced practice nursing: An integrative approach* (3rd ed., pp. 583–615). St. Louis, MO: Elsevier Saunders.

Gaudier, F. (2003). Health encyclopedia: Special topics—certified nurse midwife profession. Available at http://www.henryfordhealth.org/12893.cfm. Accessed July 18, 2005.

Hamric, A. (2005). A definition of advanced practice nursing. In A. Hamric, J. Spross, & C. Handon (Eds.), *Advanced practice nursing: An integrative approach* (3rd ed., pp. 85–108). St. Louis, MO: Elsevier Saunders.

Hanson, C. M. (2005). Understanding regulatory, legal, and credentialing requirements. In A. Hamric, J. Spross, & C. Handon (Eds.), *Advanced practice nursing: An integrative approach* (3rd ed., pp. 781–808). St. Louis, MO: Elsevier Saunders.

Health Resources Services Administration. (2007). National sample survey of registered nurses 2004. Available at http://blpr.hrsa.gov/healthworkforce/reports/nursing/mbehindproctions/4htm. Accessed July 15, 2008.

Hravanak, M., Kleinpell, R., Magdic, K., & Guttendorf, J. (2005). The acute care practitioner. In A. Hamric, J. Spross, & C. Handon (Eds.), *Advanced practice nursing: An integrative approach* (3rd ed., pp. 475–513). St. Louis, MO: Elsevier Saunders.

Kearney, S. (2003). *Hitting the road: A guide to travel nursing*. Philadelphia: Lippincott Williams & Wilkins.

Keeling, A., & Bigbee, J. (2005). The history of advanced practice nursing in the United States. In A. Hamric, J. Spross, & C. Handon (Eds.), *Advanced practice nursing: An integrative approach* (3rd ed., pp. 3–45). St. Louis, MO: Elsevier Saunders.

Kopishke, L. (2007). Legal nurse consultant: A career at the crossroads of health care and the law. *American Nurse Today, 2*(12), 11–12.

Lee, W., Campoy, S., Smits, G., Tran, Z., & Chonchol, M. (2007). Effectiveness of a chronic kidney disease clinic in achieving K/DOQI guideline target at initiation of dialysis: A single centre experience. *Nephrology Dialysis Transplantation, 22*, 833–838.

Mahn-Dinicola, V., & Zazworsky, D. (2005). The advanced practice nurse case manager. In A. Hamric, J. Spross, & C. Handon (Eds.), *Advanced practice nursing: An integrative approach* (3rd ed., pp. 617-675). St. Louis, MO: Elsevier Saunders.

Martinkus, W. (2004, November). A cut above. *NurseWeek* (Heartland ed.), 8–9.

McIntyre, M., & Thomlinson, E. (2003). *Realities of Canadian nursing: Professional, practice and power issues*. Philadelphia: Lippincott Williams & Wilkins.

Mitty, E. (2003). Assisted living and the role of the nurse. *American Journal of Nursing, 103*, 32–44.

National Council of State Boards of Nursing (NCSBN). (2000). Mutual recognition: Frequently asked questions. Available at http://www.ncsbn.org. Accessed July 18, 2005.

Norwood, S. L. (1998). *Nurses as consultants: Essential concepts and processes*. Menlo Park, CA: Addison-Wesley.

Penn, B. (Ed.). (2008). *Mastering the teaching role: A guide for nurse educators*. Philadelphia: F. A. Davis.

Robitaille, D., & Whelchel, C. (2005). Take PRIDE in your clinical ladder. *Nursing Management, 36*, 16.

Rosseter, R. (2003). Nurse practitioners: The growing solution in health care delivery. Available at http://aacn.nche.edu/Media/FactSheets/npfact.htm. Accessed July 18, 2005.

Ryan, M., Carlton, K., & Ali, N. (2004). Reflections on the role of faculty in distance learning and changing pedagogies. *Nursing Education Perspectives, 25*, 73–80.

Salyer, J., & Hamric, A. (2005). Evolving and innovative opportunities for advanced practice nursing. In A. Hamric, J. Spross, & C. Handon (Eds.), *Advanced practice nursing: An integrative approach* (3rd ed., pp. 677–702). St. Louis, MO: Elsevier Saunders.

Skalla, K., Hamric, A., & Caron, P. (2005). The blended role of the clinical nurse speialist and the nurse practitioner. In A. Hamric, J. Spross, & C. Handon (Eds.), *Advanced practice nursing: An integrative approach* (3rd ed., pp. 515–550). St. Louis, MO: Elsevier Saunders.

Sparacino, P. (2005). The clinical nurse specialist. In A. Hamric, J. Spross, & C. Handon (Eds.), *Advanced practice nursing: An integrative approach* (3rd ed., pp. 415–446). St. Louis, MO: Elsevier Saunders.

Stevens, S. (2004). Cracking the case: Your role in forensic nursing. *Nursing, 34*, 54–56.

Vogel, G., & Doleysh, N. (1997). *Entrepreneuring: A nurses' guide to starting a business* (NLN Publication No. 41-2201). New York: National League for Nursing.

Waxman, K. (2005). *Nurse entrepreneurship: Do you have what its takes? 2005 pathways to success.* Hoffman Estates, IL: Nursing Spectrum.

CHAPTER 22

Development of a Professional Nursing Career

Values

Career goals

Passion

Envisioning

Vision

Vision statement

Mission statement

Networking

Mentoring

Linear career paths

Nonlinear career paths

Career mapping

Professional nursing résumé

Professional portfolio

LEARNING OUTCOMES

By the end of this chapter, the learner will be able to:

1 Discuss the relationship of values when setting career goals.

2 Use a process to discover a passion for a specific area of professional practice.

3 Compose personal vision and mission statements for professional nursing practice.

4 Prepare a professional nursing résumé.

5 Compile a professional nursing portfolio.

6 Specify strategies to develop a professional nursing network.

7 Explain how networking and mentoring enhance career opportunities.

8 Design a career map for a future professional career.

VIGNETTE

Glen and Patricia work together on an inpatient oncology unit. They both started as new graduates a year ago. During a shift report, Glen mentions that he is thinking about changing jobs because he no longer enjoys his work. In response to his statement, Patricia states, "Oh, I'm sorry to hear that you don't love the work the way I do. I feel so satisfied if I can get the patients to smile, even for a minute, or have them share how they are coping with cancer. I think that I want to spend my entire career specializing in oncology nursing. However, if you no longer enjoy the work, it might be best for you to consider something else."

The responsibility for professional nursing career development lies within each nurse. As the health care delivery system changes, new opportunities for professional nursing practice arise. Professional nurses live in an exciting time in which specialized and complex skills affect client care and outcomes. Developing required competence for effective professional nursing practice, especially in specialty areas of practice, takes many years. As a profession, nursing offers a wide array of practice areas. Nurses decide what type of nursing they wish to pursue and where they want to practice. How a nursing career develops depends on the individual nurse. Some nurses create detailed written career plans with established timelines for implementation. Other nurses rely on seizing opportunities as they arise. This chapter outlines the importance of matching career goals with personal values, discovering ways to instill personal passion into practice, considering factors to envision a future career, developing strategies to create and implementing a career map, and closing one's career with effective retirement planning.

Questions for Reflection 22-1

1. What steps does each of the nurses in the vignette need to take to establish a nursing career tailored to best meet their personal needs and desires?
2. How can other nurses support these two novice nurses as they pursue career goals?
3. Why is it important for nurses to support each other as they pursue career goals?

VALUES AND CAREER GOALS

Every person has an established set of values. **Values** denote what a person perceives as being important in life. Values provide guidance to persons as they interact with each other and the environment. When persons share values, communities are formed (Barrett, 1998). Even within the profession of nursing (a community), no two nurses share an identical set of values. Examples of values include truth, integrity, justice, peace, health, education, conservation, possessions, money, security, safety, career, and family. Life has many important values, and selecting which ones are the most important can be a difficult task. A clue to defining a personal set of values may reside in what people enjoy doing. Self-betrayal occurs when personal life behaviors fail to match a personal set of values. In early life, values are formed in families, but over time, personal values may change. Nurses learn professional values as part of socialization into the profession.

Certain areas of nursing cater to different sets of values. Nurses who value technologically complex skills tend to pursue critical care, emergency department, or perioperative nursing. Nurses who value long-term relationships and the wisdom of the elderly find great rewards in working in extended care facilities with a geriatric population. Hospice nursing provides rewards for nurses who value comfort and peace in the dying process, rather than preserving life at all costs. Nurses for whom the generation of knowledge is a cherished value may become nurse researchers or theorists. Unlike other professions, nursing offers many career opportunities that fit with a nurse's personal values. Most nurses use personal values when determining **career goals** (specific professional nursing accomplishments). Display 22-1 offers exercises for use when engaging in the process of values clarification.

DISCOVERING YOUR PASSION IN NURSING

Chang (2000) defined **passion** as a "personal intensity, an underlying force that fuels our strongest emotions" (p. 19), and passions as "activities, ideas and topics that elicit these emotions" (p. 19). When persons perform with passion, the world becomes full of opportunities, rather than obstacles, and they focus on personal abilities, rather than limitations. All persons have the capacity to live passionate lives. Persons who live out their life's passions follow their hearts. Passions change as life evolves. A life without passion becomes a life of regrets (Chang). When persons follow a career based on passion, work becomes play (Abrams, 2000). Nursing is a content-based and context-based passion because it

Values Clarification Exercises

Step 1 Find a quiet peaceful place where you can spend some time alone free from interruption.

Step 2 Close your eyes and answer the following question: What things in life are important to me as a person? Record the list of items you consider important.

Step 3 Close your eyes and answer the following question: What things in life are important to me as a professional nurse? Record the list.

Step 4 Identify the common entries found on both of your lists to identify similarities of your personal and professional values. Create a list for these results.

Step 5 Generate a list of activities in which you engaged during the past week and include the approximate amount of time spent in each

activity. Place each activity in a list according to how much time you spent on it, with the activity in which you spent the most time at the top of the list.

Step 6 Compare this list to the list generated in steps 2, 3, and 4. This represents the congruence of how you spend your time with your set of personal and professional values.

Step 7 Answer the following questions:
1. Am I living in accordance with my personal values?
2. Am I living in accordance with my professional values?
3. Are there any things that I could do differently to live out my personal and professional values?

centers on a highly specialized topic (client care) and centers on a theme that can be applied to several activities (helping others).

Chang (2000) outlined a seven-step process to develop a passion plan for living that requires feeling, thinking, and acting. The seven steps are:

1. Start from the heart: Acknowledge all emotions and desires and recognize their power. Engage in a gradual process that requires identifying things that inspire or elicit deep strong emotions. (This may mean rediscovering things from childhood.)
2. Discover all your passions.
3. Clarify the purpose of your passions: Identify the results of living out life's passions. The purpose of each passion helps to determine how it will be followed.
4. Define the actions to achieve each passion: Develop an action plan for each passion.
5. Perform with passion: Implement the action plan developed in step 4, which may require some form of risk taking.
6. Spread the passion: Share the passion and how it excites you with others, and let it permeate all your interactions with others.
7. Persist in the passion: Stay the course, despite any unexpected circumstances or obstacles that may arise.

Passionate nurses provide client care from the depths of their hearts and souls. They hold to high ideals and have no fear in confronting situations that compromise client care. Because of their excitement as they practice nursing, nursing colleagues and other members of the health care team catch their enthusiasm. Through acts of authentic caring, clients and significant others receiving nursing care from passionate nurses feel safe and important. Nurses and clients deeply connect with each other, and the fond memories of the nursing situation last a lifetime.

Questions for Reflection 22-2

1. What are the deep emotions that surface when I engage in nursing practice?
2. What activities in clinical practice result in extremely high levels of personal satisfaction?
3. What passions, other than nursing, do I have currently in my life?
4. Why is it important to have passions or interests other than nursing in my life?

ENVISIONING YOUR NURSING CAREER

Envisioning means picturing oneself in the future (Agnes, 2005). A personal **vision** specifies a future desired state for oneself. Developing a career vision statement assumes that change in one's career will occur. The ideal professional nursing career vision would include nursing-related passions. Because nurses progress through human life transitions, personal career vision statements may be revised to address changes in physical, mental, and spiritual health status. A nurse may leave a position to stay home with children. A nurse may reenter clinical practice because of a change in marital status, spousal unemployment, or reduced child care responsibilities. Because physical stamina declines with age, a professional nurse may decide to pursue a nursing position that requires less physical exertion. Reviewing personal values and strengths facilitates the development of a career vision. All visions start with dreams. When developing a personal vision, let ideas flow without inhibition. Visions may be articulated in the present or future tense. A **vision statement** is a written declaration of a desired future state and may incorporate ideas for future improvement (Barrett, 1998; Covey, 1992, 2004; Wesorick, Shiparski, Troseth, & Wyngarden, 1997).

Vision statements relate closely to mission statements. **Mission statements** specify how visions may be actualized (Barrett, 1998) or specify the meaning and purpose behind work (Covey, 1992, 2004; Wesorick et al., 1997). Florence Nightingale (1929) viewed nursing as a spiritual calling. Barrett (1998) presented the concept of "soul work" as activities to be performed by the energy field occupying a living human body. For some, professional nursing may be one way to fulfill one's life purpose. Mission statements clearly and concisely outline specific service using action verbs and the meaning behind them that comes from the heart (Wesorick et al.). Mission statements related to a professional nursing career usually focus on client care. Displays 22-2 and 22-3 present a sample personal nursing vision and mission statement.

When nurses create a career vision based on passions, they commit to living out a meaningful life as they engage in activities of the soul, rather than those of the mind. Passionate nursing practice enables nurses to live out their life purpose of caring for others. Once personal visions and mission statements have been developed, professional nurses need to find a nursing position to fulfill them. Nurses use a variety of strategies to find and get a desired position.

 NETWORKING

Networking consists of exchanging ideas and information among individuals, groups, or institutions (Agnes, 2005). Professional networks are interconnected groups of persons who share similar work roles. Professional networks may be interprofessional in nature or consist of persons within a single profession. When professional nurses network, they become cognizant of career opportunities, learn about nursing care practice variances across settings, and support each other. When nurses interact with each other, their professional networks expand. Strategies for the development of effective professional networks include courage and a willingness to call others, a genuine desire to help others, freely sharing information with others, distributing professional business cards, and actively participating in collaborative projects (Borgatti, 2008).

Sample Personal Vision Statement	**DISPLAY 22-2**
I envision myself to be a professional nurse who demonstrates authentic caring toward	and appreciation of all living persons and things.

Sample Mission Statement	DISPLAY 22-3

As an authentic professional nurse, my personal mission is take time to listen genuinely to clients, families, nursing colleagues, and other members of the interdisciplinary health team to provide them with the highest quality of service that is humanly possible.

Opportunities for networking occur at work, school, professional organizational meetings, and community service activities. Networking outside of the nursing community enables nurses to expand their knowledge outside the discipline of nursing, share information about professional nursing with those who are not nurses, and explore other career options. Many nurse consultants and entrepreneurs rely on networking (professional and community) to generate business. Nurses who effectively use networking typically have a goal when interacting in professional or community groups (Borgatti, 2008; Waxman, 2005).

Questions for Reflection 22-3

1. Why is it important to have strong collegial relationships?
2. What have I done during the past week to strengthen my relationships with nursing colleagues?
3. What networking opportunities are available to me as a nursing student?
4. Why is networking important in nursing education and practice?
5. Have I taken advantage of professional nursing networking opportunities? Why or why not?

MENTORING

For centuries, novices in various professions have sought the advice of experienced professionals. The term "mentor" has its roots in Greek mythology, when Odysseus entrusted the education of his son to his friend named Mentor (Agnes, 2005). In recent years, the word **mentoring** has come to denote the process of enlisting an experienced guide or trusted adviser who assumes responsibility for the professional growth and advancement of a less experienced person, called the protégé. Mentors open doors, create opportunities, and provide career role modeling for protégés while inspiring them. In nursing, mentors provide direction for nurses just entering the profession or a specialized area of nursing practice. Mentors provide wisdom to protégés and help them develop professional networks. Mentors often actively sponsor protégés when career opportunities in the selected field arise (Falter, 1997). In addition, protégés help mentors by serving as trusted assistants who help mentors clarify ideas (Malone, 1999).

Successful mentoring relationships require personal chemistry between the involved persons. Some nurses experience difficulty in finding mentors. Sometimes, novices do not want to impose on a potential mentor's time, fear relationship failure, and have difficulty identifying the right person. However, sometimes the mentoring relationship may just unfold over the course of a career. Persons become mentors for various reasons, including desiring to help another, admiring the novice's personal and professional goals and vision, being reminded of a former younger self, and having been a protégé in a successful mentoring experience (Abrams, 2000; Malone, 1999). Successful mentoring requires mutual respect, complementary personalities, open attitudes, proper timing, and appropriate quality and quantity of guidance (Abrams).

To ease the burden of professional transition to clinical practice for new graduate nurses, some health care institutions offer mentoring, coaching, or preceptor programs. These programs provide guidance for new nurses and those changing specialty practice areas. For nurses just entering the profession, coaching (or mentoring) typically eases the transition for the new graduate into independent, professional practice (Messmer, Jones, & Taylor, 2004; Sherman & Dyess, 2007). Sometimes, these programs result in effective mentoring relationships. However, mentoring requires reciprocal investment in the relationship. Because most mentors have years of experience within a given field, they have much wisdom to impart to protégés (Sherman & Dyess). Mentoring provides mentors with the opportunity of fulfilling developmental tasks related to older professional nurses. Sometimes the mentor finds a protégé willing to continue the mentor's professional contributions as the mentor retires or loses interest in them as part of a natural career trajectory.

Questions for Reflection 22-4

1. What are the characteristics of an ideal mentor?
2. Why are these characteristics important?
3. If I were to select a professional nursing mentor today, whom would I choose?

CAREER DEVELOPMENT STRATEGIES

Once nurses identify career directions on which to focus, they can use a variety of strategies to make their ideal career happen. Most authors addressing career development begin the process with a self-assessment of personal values followed by a period of dreaming about what a future career may look like (Chang, 2000; Donner & Wheeler, 2001; Malone, 1999; McGillis Hall, Waddell, Donner, & Wheeler, 2004). A career in nursing equips nurses with many life skills that can transfer to other professions. Basic nursing knowledge transfers to a variety of professional nursing specialty areas. No two nurses follow identical paths for career development.

Career Paths

No one career-planning process has been proven to be superior to others. The process may be linear or nonlinear, and nurses select which to use based on their ability to tolerate uncertainty and ambiguity (Bongard, 1997a).

Linear career paths require nurses to follow a sequential series of steps. For example, staff nurses working with students decide that they will pursue a career in nursing academia. They usually earn a master's degree in nursing prior to assuming nursing faculty positions. Once employed by a nursing program, they closely follow a tenure track system with specific criteria for advancement from instructor to full professor. Nurses who like structure and meeting designated deadlines prefer this approach to career development (Bongard, 1997b).

Nonlinear career paths rely on life circumstances and critical incidents that result in career changes. Nurses following nonlinear career paths frequently create careers by using their interests, outside experiences, and nursing skills. They seize opportunities as they arise. Nurses using a nonlinear approach to career development frequently create new nursing positions within a health care organization or become entrepreneurs. In today's unstable health care arena, nurses following nonlinear career paths have a better chance of professional survival, especially as health care organizations elect to eliminate nursing positions (Bongard, 1997b).

Career Development Model

Donner and Wheeler (2001, p. 2) viewed career development as "an iterative and continuous" process and combine linear and nonlinear approaches to career development. They have developed a five-phase career planning and development model, which starts with scanning the environment to understand current realities and future trends in society that have implications for nursing and create possibilities for new areas of clinical practice (Research Brief 22-1). They emphasize the importance of periodic self-assessments and reality checks related to self-identity and how others view individual nurses. If nurses find that current employment situations do not fit with attributes discovered from self-appraisal, Donner and Wheeler suggested that it may be time to pursue an alternative career path. They also advocated for the creation of a career vision to link current status with future possibilities. Nurses may then use the career vision as a motivating source for remaining in a current practice setting or making a change. Donner and Wheeler suggested that designing a strategic career plan around the career vision facilitates attainment of career goals. Finally, once a career plan has been established, efforts should be channeled into marketing professional skills by forming an expansive professional network, developing a mentoring relationship, and further refining verbal and written communication skills.

Career Mapping

Malone (1999) used the term **career mapping** to denote a continuous process of nursing career development in which career moves unfold as a person engages in professional practice and lifelong learning. This process starts with identifying values, determining the importance of each value, and envisioning a future. The future vision creates a blueprint for personal action to make that envisioned future become reality.

Research Brief 22-1

McGillis Hall, L., Waddell, J., Donner, G., & Wheeler, M. (2004) Outcomes of a career planning and development program for registered nurses. *Journal of Continuing Education*, 22(5), 231–238.

The investigators wanted to assess the outcomes of a registered nurse career planning and development program (CPCDP). The outcomes selected to measure were job satisfaction (JS), career self-efficacy (CSE), absenteeism (AB), and organizational commitment (OC). The career planning and development program consisted of nurses attending a career development workshop during which they learned the career planning and development model developed by Donner and Wheeler. The nurses also received individual sessions to coach them on career planning and development. The nurse participated in the CPCDP over a 3-year time frame. JS was measured by the McCloskey-Mueller Satisfaction Scale (1990); CSE was measured by the Taylor & Betz Career Decision-Making Self-Efficacy Scale (1983); AB was measured by data collected by the human resources department where the nurses worked; and OCC was measured by Mowday, Steers, & Porter's Organizational Commitment Questionnaire (1979). A total of 128 nurses participated in the study (64 nurses participating in the CPCDP and 64 nurses in the control group).

Results of the study revealed that CPCDP participants were more likely to develop a career vision ($r = .17; p = .05$) and design a career plan ($r = .19; p < .03$). However, the CPCDP participants reported lower levels on the following factors associated with JS: "satisfaction with coworkers ($r = -.023; p < 0.0006$) and work and family balance ($r = -0.29; p = 0.001$)" (p. 236). Results for CSE revealed that when nurses worked more hours in an additional work setting, their CSE were higher. OC scores were significantly higher during the first year of CPCDP participation, but fell as time progressed, and no relationships were discovered in program participation and nurse AB.

Implications for the study include that the CPCDP fosters the development of career planning, promotes nurse retention, and fosters individual responsibility for one's nursing career. However, the results of this study should be interpreted with caution because the nurses worked exclusively in one acute care teaching hospital, the sample had a higher proportion of baccalaureate-prepared nurses (compared to the national average) and, perhaps, only the highly motivated nurses participated in the 3-year-long program. Additional research is needed to include more employment sites and to perform a pre-post test design for measuring JS, CSE, AB, and OC.

To facilitate the preferred career vision, nurses can use a variety of resources that outline career trends. Areas of resources for learning about current and future needs for professional nursing include the U.S. Department of Labor, the Bureau of Labor Statistics, *Healthy People 2010* (2006; work on *Healthy People 2020* is in progress); the American Association of Colleges of Nursing; the National League for Nursing; and the American Nurses Association.

Once nurses select a preferred career vision based on need, specialty certification serves as an important step in the career-mapping process. Professional certification provides public acknowledgment of professional competence, enhances career opportunities, demonstrates the ability of the profession for self-regulation, and increases personal power (Malone, 1999). The American Nurses Credentialing Center offers 27 certification examinations across a variety of nursing practice areas (Malone). Nurses also can earn certification from a variety of nurse specialty organizations.

Malone (1999) identified networking and finding a mentor as key strategies for developing successful career maps. Along with networking with professional nursing colleagues, nurses frequently overlook the importance of networking with professionals from other disciplines. Networking with other members of the health care team and with other professionals within the community enables nurses to gain a more global perspective related to the meaning of health and the needs for future health care delivery. Malone specified that personal and professional mentors serve vital roles in the career-mapping process because mentors help shape professional values and instill confidence in young professionals to pursue their dreams.

MAKING A NURSING CAREER CHANGE

Nurses make career changes for a variety of reasons. Some nurses pursue part-time employment to spend more time with families or pursue outside interests. At times, nurses may become bored with a current practice area and decide to change specialties. Nurses also may experience intense value conflicts with an employer that results in an employment change. Some nurses follow partners when their employment situations change. During episodes of economic downturns, some nurses unexpectedly lose their jobs (Kelly, 2008). Nurses who earn advanced degrees frequently change jobs. Finally, when nurses get bored or burned out with their current position, they embark on a journey to either change jobs or pursue a different area of nursing practice.

Several strategies prove useful for the nurse wishing to remain viable in today's employment market. First, keeping a current résumé enables immediate action when an opportunity for an employment change surfaces. Second, refining personal interview skills provides confidence when interacting with future employers. Third, networking with other nurses at professional organizational meetings, career fairs, conventions, and community service activities enables acquisition of key information about employment opportunities. Fourth, making lists of personal assets, strengths, and preferred professional activities helps identify the type of position best suited to the individual nurse. Fifth, exposing oneself to motivational information in print, on tape, or on videotape arms the nurse considering change with a "can do" attitude. Finally, after accepting a new position, easing out of the old one gracefully makes it easier to return if the new job fails to be better than the old one (Cardillo, 2001). Some basic skills and strategies used for marketing oneself and finding the right job are described here.

Questions for Reflection 22-5

1. What is my ideal picture of my future nursing career?
2. How can I make this picture a reality?
3. What are the consequences of not envisioning an ideal future nursing career?

Finding Available Nursing Opportunities

When considering changing nursing positions, nurses can use a variety of resources to locate employment opportunities. Most organizations (hospitals and integrated health systems) post internal job openings in areas accessible to employees and in human resources departments. Along with internal job postings, many organizations list employment opportunities on organizational or company websites (The Editors of VGM Career Horizons, 1996; Kelly, 2008; Yate, 1998). The Internet also offers online job search commercial sites, such as Monster Board's Monster Health Care or Career Mosaic's HealthOpps (Enger, 1999). Nursing journals and periodicals contain classified advertisements with available nursing opportunities. Professional nurses learn about career opportunities from networking with nursing colleagues during professional nursing organizational events (Borgatti, 2008; The Editors of VGM Career Horizons). In times of nursing shortages, some health care agencies turn to radio and television advertising to recruit nurses. Finally, local newspapers publish classified ads related to employment opportunities in nursing.

Marketing Your Skills

Employers need to verify that applicants have the correct skills to meet the demands of the position. When applying for a specific position, nurses may find that tailoring cover letters and résumés to address specific skills outlined by a position may prove to be more successful in securing a new job. Documents showcasing professional skills may be saved as computer files and edited to fit the requested skills and previous professional experience delineated by the posted job. Special care must be taken to verify that all information sent to prospective employers and clients has attractive visual appeal and no spelling or punctuation errors. Poorly constructed documents readily find their way into the trash (Bongard, 1997b; The Editors of VGM Career Horizons, 1996; Yate, 1998).

Cover Letters

Cover letters provide a general introduction to a prospective employer or client. In addition, the letter provides an opportunity to shed light on the job applicant's personality. If the organization specifies in the advertised position a person to contact, applicants should send the cover letter to the designated person.

Two forms of cover letters provide information. The traditional cover letter provides reasons for contact, expands on the rationale for applying for a position, and details how to contact the writer to set up an interview (Figure 22-1). The second form for a cover letter actually matches job requirements with acquired credentials and skills (Figure 22-2). The second cover letter format saves time for persons who screen applicants for interview invitations because they can easily read specific applicant qualifications. Typewritten or printed addresses on all materials sent to prospective employers or clients also send a better impression than handwritten ones. Finally, the cover letter signature may be the last item that the Human Resources Department reads, so applicants should pay close attention to verify that is neat and legible.

Résumés

The résumé originated as a solution for employers who wanted to interview only qualified job applicants. Human resources persons who screen job applications find most résumés dull and boring. A good **professional nursing résumé** presents individual strengths, while showcasing special skills and professional accomplishments (The Editors of VGM Career Horizons, 1996; Yate, 1998). A good résumé will get the candidate an interview, and the résumé preparation assists in interview preparation, especially for the dreaded request for applicants to "tell me about yourself." Résumé preparation also provides time for reflection about a career. All résumés strive to showcase professional achievements, attributes, and experience while minimizing any potential weaknesses, and to stimulate enough interest in the applicant to ensure an invitation for an interview (Yate).

Jane Doe, RN, BSN
111 E. Lilac Avenue
Springfield, MO   65106

October 3, 2009

Mary Ashcraft, RN
Nurse Recruiter
Human Resources Department
Springfield Medical Center
803 North Maple Street
Springfield, MO   65107

Dear Ms. Ashcraft:

As I was reading the Springfield Daily News, I spotted your advertisement for a nursing position
on your oncology unit. I have recently moved to Springfield, Missouri and would like to work for
Springfield Medical Center, the premier hospital in the area. My professional nursing background
includes previous oncology nursing experience.

I am enclosing a copy of my résumé so that you may review my credentials. I would appreciate
the opportunity to discuss my qualifications in person. Please call me at my home, 417-888-6464,
at any time to schedule an interview. If I am not available to take your call, please leave a
message and telephone number so I can contact you.

Thank you for reviewing my credentials. I look forward to meeting you soon.

Sincerely,

Jane Doe, RN, BSN

Figure 22-1
Sample cover letter.

Most persons use chronological or functional résumé formats. Of the two forms, the
chronological format is used the most. Some persons opt to combine the two formats when
developing a résumé (Yate, 1998). Table 22-1 outlines the chronological and functional
résumé formats and highlights the strengths of each. Selection of format depends on
where a person is within a career trajectory, employment experiences, and the type of opportunity being considered. Figures 22-3 and 22-4 offer examples of both types of
résumés. Résumé preparation experts and publications disagree on many aspects of
résumé preparation. However, they do agree on several preparation principles.

Persons reviewing résumés in human resources departments spend little time reading
individual résumés. Résumés containing more than one to two pages most likely will not
be read. The typical résumé receives about a 30-second review. When a job or career

Jane Doe, RN, BSN
111 E. Lilac Avenue
Springfield, MO   65106

October 3, 2002

Mary Ashcraft, RN
Nurse Recruiter
Human Resources Department
Springfield Medical Center
803 North Maple Street
Springfield, MO   65107

Dear Ms. Ashcraft:

As I was reading the Springfield Daily News, I spotted your advertisement for a nursing position on your oncology unit. I have recently moved to Springfield, Missouri and would like to work for Springfield Medical Center, the premier hospital in the area. I have also read the exciting news about the current expansion of the oncology services at Springfield Medical Center.

My professional nursing background includes previous oncology nursing experience and the following summary outlines how my qualifications fit your nursing position requirements:

Your requirements	My qualifications
* Professional nursing licensure in Missouri	* Missouri nursing license for 6 years
* One year's experience in oncology nursing	* Five years' experience in oncology nursing at St. Luke's Hospital, Omaha, NE
* OCN certification	* Current OCN certification

I am enclosing a copy of my résumé so that you may review my credentials. I would appreciate the opportunity to discuss my qualifications in person. Please call me at my home, 417-888-6464, at any time to schedule an interview. If I am not available to take your call, please leave a message and telephone number so I can contact you.

Thank you for reviewing my credentials. I look forward to meeting you soon.

Sincerely,

Jane Doe, RN, BSN

Figure 22-2
Sample skill-matched cover letter.

objective is present, human resources department employees assume that if it fails to match the open position, the applicant does not want the position. The following suggestions make it easier for résumés to be efficiently processed:

1. Organizing categories in a logical manner
2. Using a font size of 11 to 14 picas from an easily readable print style (Arial, Bookman, News Gothic, or Times New Roman are a few suggested font styles) and

TABLE 22-1

Comparison of the Chronological and Functional Résumé Formats

	Chronological Résumé	Functional Résumé
Description	Lists job titles and responsibilities in chronological order	Highlights professional skills (also called skill-based résumé)
Components	Contact information Job and career objectives Career summary that highlights dates of each position Education Special awards or honors Community service	Contact information Job or career objective List of skills specific for job Dates of previous positions, usually at the end or in smaller type Education and skills acquired from employment or community service activities
Situations for best use	Documentation of personal career growth Continued employment in a field without too many job changes	Professional career established Beginning of a career Career change with the goal to focus on relevant skills Stagnant or declining career Returning to the workforce after a prolonged absence
When best not to use	Frequent job changes (every 1–2 years) Just finishing school Seeking a career change	No situations
Advantages	Showcases detailed employment history Outlines specific job responsibilities and previous employers	Highlights skills, rather than employment history Makes it easier for human resource personnel to determine if skills match posted job description Can include skills gained from outside areas of past employment

From: The Editors of VGM Career Horizons. (1996). *Résumés for nursing careers*. Lincolnwood, IL: VGM Career Horizons; and Yate, M. (1998). *Résumés that knock 'em dead* (3rd ed.). Holbrook, MA: Adams Media Corporation

keeping the font style consistent (larger size can be used effectively to present headings)

3. Using 8 1/2-inch by 11-inch paper because employers frequently photocopy résumés for distribution to department managers and human resources files
4. Selecting high-quality, white, cream, or pastel (avoid pink) paper of 16- to 25-pound weight
5. Limiting résumé blocks to five to seven lines
6. Using action verbs to describe current and previous job skills and responsibilities
7. Maintaining strict alignment of margins within sections
8. Keeping a free-flowing appearance without any noticeable breaks
9. Having a friend or family member proofread it

Professional nurses may develop a résumé independently, seek the advice of career counselors, or have it generated by a résumé specialist. Most personal computers have

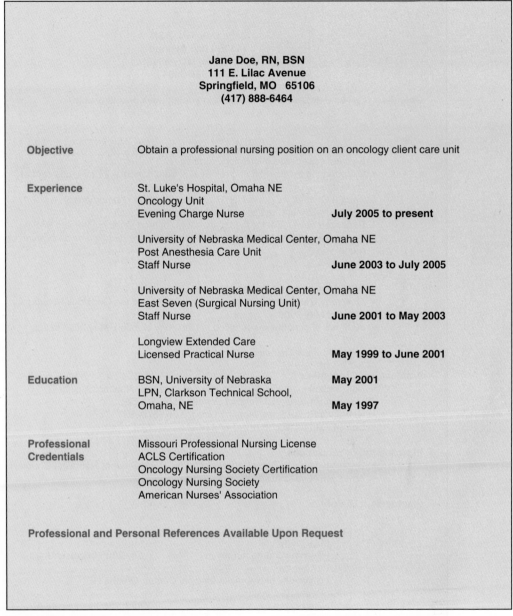

Figure 22-3
Sample chronological résumé.

the capability of accommodating résumé preparation software programs. The Internet has several electronic résumé preparation websites. State employment agencies also may have websites to assist with résumé generation. Yate (1998, p. 73) proposed using hypertext markup language to "create sharply designed and formatted résumés" that can be sent electronically to prospective employers and clients. Advances in computer software and electronic mail services enable job applicants to submit résumés via e-mail; some organizations prefer electronic submission of job application material over paper copies.

When providing contact information, the résumé should contain the person's name without any titles (unless it is a gender-neutral name), mailing address, telephone

Jane Doe, RN, BSN
111 E. Lilac Avenue
Springfield, MO 65106
(417) 888-6464

Objective: Full-time professional nurse position on an adult oncology unit

Skills

- Certification in oncology nursing since June, 2007
- 5 years' experience in oncology nursing
- Experienced in insertion and removal of percutaneous intravenous central catheters
- Taught Oncology Certification Review courses on chemotherapy administration and radiation therapy for oncology staff
- Published newsletter for the local chapter of the Oncology Nursing Society
- Supervised staff of two RNs and three patient care technicians as evening charge nurse

Education

- BSN, University of Nebraska Medical Center, May 2001
- Oncology Certification Course, Omaha Chapter of the Oncology Nursing Society, May 2006
- 30 hours of continuing education in Oncology Nursing, May 2005 to July 2007
- LPN, Clarkson Technical School, May 1999

Professional Credentials

- Certification in oncology nursing by the Oncology Nursing Society
- Missouri Professional Nursing License #556087352
- Nebraska Professional Nursing License #N6670889
- Current certification in ACLS and BCLS

Professional Organizations

- Oncology Nursing Society (past secretary of the Omaha, Nebraska Chapter)
- American Nurses Association

Employment History

St. Luke's Hospital, Omaha NE
Oncology Unit
Evening charge nurse   July 2005 to present

University of Nebraska Medical Center, Omaha NE
Post Anesthesia Care Unit
Staff nurse   June 2003 to July 2005

University of Nebraska Medical Center, Omaha NE
East Seven (Surgical Nursing Unit)
Staff nurse   June 2001 to June 2003

Longview Extended Care
Licensed practical nurse   May 1999 to June 2001

Professional and Personal References Available on Request

Figure 22-4
Sample functional (skill-based) résumé.

number, and electronic mailing address. If the telephone is connected to an answering machine, care should be exercised to specify this in the cover letter, and the applicant should frequently check the answering machine. Frequent reading of e-mail also should occur if potential employers use e-mail notification for scheduling telephone or personal interview appointments. Applicants should refrain from using current employment addresses and telephone numbers unless they have informed current employers of their search for another job (Bongard, 1997b; The Editors of VGM Career Horizons, 1996; Yate, 1998).

Finally, résumés lose power if they contain mistakes or possess certain characteristics. Yate (1998) offered the suggestions for what should never go into a résumé:

1. Giving the document a title, such as résumé, or fact sheet
2. Stating availability for employment
3. Specifying reasons for leaving previous or current job
4. Outlining references (employers have the legal obligation to obtain written consent from prospective employees before they can check references)

The résumé provides applicants with a written format to showcase professional skills and written communication abilities to prospective clients and employees. Usually, no verbal interaction occurs between the person screening the résumé and the applicant. Thus, utmost care should be taken when creating a résumé to create the best impression.

Reference Lists

Personal and professional references do not belong on a résumé (The Editors of VGM Career Horizons, 1996; Yate, 1998). The type and number of references vary across organizations (typically three to six are required). Position applicants usually find out the number of required references when they complete an employment application. When specifying references, common courtesy suggests that applicants inform the persons whose names appear on the reference list. In addition, if persons have used more than one surname while they have been employed, this information should be included somewhere because it can make verifying references difficult if a married name is given to a reference when he or she knows the person by a maiden name (Yate).

To make the absolute best impression, nurses should submit all materials printed with the same font and using the same type of paper (including the mailing envelope if possible). This creates a uniform package and presents an image of being detail oriented (Yate, 1998).

Professional Portfolios

Like artists, some nurses have developed **professional portfolios** to showcase professional skills and accomplishments. Some nursing programs have students generate nursing portfolios as part of the curriculum (Serembus, 2000). In clinical practice, the professional nursing portfolio is used by some health care organizations for professional promotion. In many Magnet-accredited facilities, a career ladder serves as a means for keeping experienced nurses at the bedside while offering them financial rewards for providing requisite nursing care and participating in shared governance activities. Professional portfolios provide documented evidence for meeting criteria of promotion. Nurses who have a nursing professional portfolio may elect to take it to interviews to display evidence of professional accomplishments. Some nurses leave the portfolio with a prospective employer for them to review after all interviews have been completed along with a specific time for the nurse to retrieve it (Bell, 2001).

Portfolio components vary according to intended use. Williams and Jordon (2007) offered the following suggestions for things to include in a professional porfolio: (1) résumé,

(2) nursing philosophy, (3) letters of recommendation or appreciation, (4) professional licensure, (5) professional certifications, (6) education diplomas and continuing education certificates, (7) special recognition such as honors or awards, (8) list of professional organizational memberships, (9) copies of publications, (10) photographs of podium or poster presentations, (11) evidence of organizational (such as shared governance committee participation) and community service, (12) list of inventions, and (13) written documentation of professional behaviors to facilitate client outcome attainment. Besides being just a vehicle to document professional accomplishments, Williams and Jordon specified that portfolio development provides nurses the opportunity to "reflect on" practice endeavors and to determine future career goals.

Interviewing Skills

A personal interview enables potential employers or clients to assess applicants to determine how they may fit with the organization. When an interview invitation is extended, applicants are one step closer to getting the desired position. Successful interview performance relies on adequate preparation. Table 22-2 outlines some tips for effective performance during an employment interview. Some nurses find the interview process stressful. However, interview skills improve with repeated practice. Some nurses find rehearsing with someone who assumes the role of interviewer to be an effective strategy for interview preparation. The interview allows employers and clients a chance to evaluate candidates on a personal level.

Prospective employers have legal limitations regarding specific questions they may ask during an employment interview. Some organizations have prospective employees interview with a member of the Human Resources Department, the department manager, and staff department members before an employment offer is extended. Nurses who inquire about the hiring process during the initial interview can prepare themselves for any future interviews. In times of nursing shortages, some employers offer large sign-on bonuses and other amenities to attract qualified nurses. When applying for positions with attractive bonuses and incentives, nurses should be aware of the risks associated with such enticements. Some incentives require nurses to sign contracts agreeing to a specified time commitment for employment. If nurses do not abide by conditions for the incentives, they usually must reimburse the employer for all or a portion of funds received.

Follow-Up Communications

After the interview, applicants who send a thank you note by the morning after the interview have extended common courtesy toward the interviewer. Manners mean a lot to organizations that value customer service and teamwork. A follow-up thank you note also gives applicants a chance to summarize interview highlights and to make a final positive impression.

SUMMARY AND SIGNIFICANCE TO PRACTICE

Development of a meaningful nursing career requires an open attitude, periodic self-assessment, lifelong learning, creativity, courage, and confidence. Along with personal characteristics, nurses rely on others for effective career development. Networking and mentoring offer effective strategies for career development. Both require commitment, caring, and effective communication skills. To live out a preferred career vision, professional nurses must develop a plan and market their personal and professional skills to make the vision become reality.

TABLE 22-2

Tips for Effective Interviewing

Tip	Rationale
Learn as much as possible about the organization.	Knowledge of mission and philosophy enable the ability to anticipate questions related to personal fit with the organization.
Dress conservatively in a business suit or well-tailored dress, not uniform or scrubs.	Present a professional appearance. The employment interview rule is to dress one level above the position being considered.
Avoid wearing fragrances, smoking, or filling your car's gas tank right before the interview.	Fragrances create impressions. Heavy perfumes may trigger allergies, and the smell of smoke emphasizes the habit.
Rehearse the employment interview with a friend or family member.	Allay interview nervousness and anxiety.
Bring nursing license and certification requirements with you.	Prospective employer may want to copy these for your file.
Prepare a set of questions related to the agency and position.	Asking questions may generate information to continue or stop pursuing the position. Questions also reveal interest.
Be armed with information related to the local market salary, bonus, and job expectations.	Verification that position is aligned with current market.
Arrive 5–10 minutes before scheduled time.	Extra time provides time to relax immediately before the interview, allays potential anxiety related to tardiness, and demonstrates punctuality. Arriving too soon may make the interviewer feel rushed with a previous appointment.
Look busy while waiting—read a magazine, look over a list of questions, or review your résumé.	Interviewer may accompany previous appointment to waiting area, and making use of waiting time creates a positive first impression.
Do not bring friends or relatives to the interview site.	Concern for them may keep you from being focused on the interview. Potential perception of lack of self-confidence.
Greet the interviewer with direct eye contact and a firm handshake.	Business etiquette dictates use of firm handshake when first meeting someone, and eye contact denotes assertiveness in Western culture.
Do not chew gum.	Disrupts articulation of words, and chewing motion creates an unprofessional appearance.
Always ask a question if asked if you have any questions.	Denotes interest in organization and also that you are focused on the interview.
Be honest and forthcoming with all answers.	Dishonesty or perceptions of covert information provide reasons for interviewer not to continue the job application process.
If asked about why you left previous places of employment, describe situation specifically using positive terms.	Chances are that if applicants speak negatively about previous employment experiences, they will do this when they quit this organization.
Wait for the interviewer to address salary, hours, and working conditions.	Usually not covered in the first interview. However, these must be discussed before accepting a position.
Limit answers to each question to three statements and share something about yourself related to the question.	Targeted and brief answers facilitate the interview process.

(continued)

Tips for Effective Interviewing (Continued)

Tip	Rationale
Come prepared to address professional experiences and include information related to teamwork.	The trend is toward behavior-based interviewing, in which applicants are expected to share specific examples of how they executed various aspects of professional nursing and evidence of working in teams.
Carry a briefcase to store evidence of accomplishments, extra résumés, reference letters, and reference list.	Briefcases keep materials neat and project an air of professionalism.
Conclude the interview with a question related to the next step of the interview process.	Communicates continued interest in pursuing the position.
Write a thank you note to the interviewer as soon as possible after the interview.	Shows appreciation and highlights courtesy as a personal strength; also provides one last opportunity to highlight a personal strength.

Source: Bongard, B. (1997b). Managing your career. In B. Case (Ed.), *Career planning for nurses* (pp. 69-73). Albany, NY: Delmar Publishers.

FROM THEORY TO PRACTICE

1. Review the vignette at the beginning of the chapter and answer the following questions:
   - What advice would you give to Glen as he looks for ways to change his nursing career?
   - Why is this advice important?
   - Why do you suppose that Pat is content in her current nursing position?
   - What are the positive and negative consequences of staying in a nursing position for a long time?
2. Develop a professional nursing résumé and compile a professional nursing portfolio. Analyze both projects. Are you on target to meeting your desired career goals? Why or why not?
3. Determine a nursing career goal. Design a career map to meet your desired career goal.

WWW INTERNET EXERCISES

1. Develop a brief professional nursing résumé using the 10-Minute Resume Website: http://www.10minuteresume.com. Print the résumé and then compare it to one you generate using a computer software program. Visit the Résumé Resource Center website (http://www.resumestore.com) and find how much it would cost to purchase a nursing and other types of résumés and cover letters. Would it be worth it to you to pay for a professionally generated résumé and cover letter? Why or why not?
2. Visit the Nursing Spectrum website at http://www.nursingspectrum.com. Click any of the entries under Jobs/Employers. Read about job openings, information on travel nursing, and prospective employers. Do any of these position openings appeal to you? Why or why not?

WWW INTERNET RESOURCES

1. For available professional nursing positions: Visit specific places where you would like to be employed, a local newspaper website, or a general job posting site such as http://www.monster.com.
2. For help with résumé preparation: http://www.10minuteresume.com or http://www.resumestore.com.
3. Nursing Spectrum: http://www.nursingspectrum.com.

4. Sigma Theta Tau International: http://www.nursingsociety.org.
5. The American Nurses Association: http://www.nursingworld.org.

REFERENCES

Abrams. S. L. (2000). *The new success rules for women*. Roseville, CA: Prima.

Agnes, M. (Ed.) (2005). *Webster's new world college dictionary* (4th ed.). Cleveland, OH: Wiley.

Barrett, R. (1998). *Liberating the corporate soul, building a visionary organization*. Boston: Butterworth-Heinemann.

Bell, S. K. (2001). Professional nurse's portfolio. *Nursing Administration Quarterly, 25*, 69–73.

Bongard, B. (1997a). Creating your own job: Using nonlinear strategies to reach your career goals. In B. Case (Ed.), *Career planning for nurses* (pp. 87–103). Albany, NY: Delmar.

Bongard, B. (1997b). Managing your career. In B. Case (Ed.), *Career planning for nurses* (pp. 59–86). Albany, NY: Delmar.

Borgatti, J. (2008). Networking for nurses. *American Nurse Today, 3*(4), 40–42.

Cardillo, D. (2001). Knowing when it's time to move on. *Nursing Spectrum, 2*, 20.

Chang, R. (2000). *The passion plan*. San Francisco: Jossey-Bass.

Covey, S. (1992). *Principle-centered leadership*. New York: Simon & Schuster.

Covey, S. (2004). *The 8th habit: From effectiveness to greatness*. New York: Free Press.

Donner, G. J., & Wheeler, M. M. (2001). Taking control of your career and your future. *Excellence in Clinical Practice, 2*, 2.

The Editors of VGM Career Horizons. (1996). *Résumés for nursing careers*. Lincolnwood, IL: VGM Career Horizons.

Enger, D. (1999). Making a difference. *Nursing Spectrum: New England Edition, 3*, 15.

Falter, E. J. (1997). The nurse-manager-to-executive track. In B. Case (Ed.), *Career planning for nurses* (pp. 203–217). Albany, NY: Delmar Publishers.

Kelly, K. (2008). Coping with unexpected job loss. *American Nurse Today, 3*(7), 24–25.

Malone, B. L. (1999). Career mapping: Visioning your future. In C. A. F. Anderson (Ed.), *Nursing student to nursing leader: The critical path to leadership development* (pp. 290–301). Albany, NY: Delmar.

McGillis Hall, L., Waddell, J., Donner, G., & Wheeler, M. (2004) Outcomes of a career planning and development program for registered nurses. *Journal of Continuing Education, 22*(5), 231–238.

Messmer, P., Jones, S., & Taylor, B. (2004). Enhancing knowledge and self-confidence of novice nurses: The "shadow-a-nurse" ICU program. *Nursing Education Perspectives, 25*, 131–136.

Nightingale, F. (1929). *Notes on nursing*. New York: D. Appleton & Co.

Serembus, J. F. (2000). Teaching the process of developing a professional portfolio. *Nurse Educator, 25*, 282–293.

Sherman, R., & Dyess, S. (2007). Be a coach for a novice nurse. *American Nurse Today, 2*(5), 54–55.

U.S. Department of Labor, Bureau of Labor Statistics. (2006). *Healthy People 2010*. Washington, DC: Author. Available at http://www.healthypeople.gov. Accessed April 1, 2009.

Waxman, K. (2005). *Nurse entrepreneurship: Do you have what its takes? 2005 pathways to success*. Hoffman Estates, IL: Nursing Spectrum.

Wesorick, B., Shiparski, L., Troseth, M., & Wyngarden, K. (1997). *Partnership council field book*. Grand Rapids, MI: Practice Field.

Williams, M., & Jordon, K. (2007). The nursing professional portfolio: A pathway to career development. *Journal for Nurses in Staff Development, 3*, 125–131.

Yate, M. (1998). *Résumés that knock 'em dead* (3rd ed.). Holbrook, MA: Adams Media.

Shaping the Future of Nursing

LEARNING OUTCOMES

By the end of this chapter, the learner will be able to:

1 Compare and contrast the terms "possible future," "plausible future," "probable future," and "preferable future."

2 Explain the implications of current trends on the nursing professions for each presented future scenario.

3 Outline strategies for professional nurses to plan for the future.

4 Specify ways for nurses to create a "preferable" future.

5 Outline how nursing education might better prepare nurses capable of meeting the challenges of future health care delivery.

6 Discuss the role of nursing scholarship in the future of the nursing profession and health care.

VIGNETTE

Jane is a registered nurse who just received word that the hospital where she has worked for 15 years is closing. Reasons for closing the hospital include declining economic forces in the community, less demand for services, increased competition for clients among health care providers, high unemployment, inability to meet financial demands, difficulty with nursing staff recruitment and retention, and movement of physician practices to the more affluent suburbs. Jane wonders why she did not foresee the hospital closure. Because Jane has worked for the past 10 years on the day shift in the postpartum unit, she knows that her work hours and special area of practice most likely will change. As Jane thinks about the situation, tears form in her eyes, and she wonders how she could have better prepared herself for the future she faces.

Questions for Reflection 23-1

1. How can I prepare myself so that I maximize the use of my knowledge, skills, and talents as a professional nurse?
2. Where would I like to be in the nursing profession 10 years from now?
3. What steps do I need to take to accomplish my future career vision?
4. What are the consequences for me as a professional nurse if I fail to consider what changes may occur within health care and the nursing profession in the next decade?

Humans have attempted to predict the future for many centuries. Pyramids in Egypt contain hieroglyphics that predict the future of the human race. Ancient Greek philosophers attempted to predict the future. Various religious texts, such as the Bible and Koran, contain prophecies. Mayan temple ruins foretell the end of the world. Fortunetelling has sustained the passage of time, despite an era in Western culture that highly values scientific evidence. Various aspects of human life confirm that the future repeats the past, such as the predictability of the changing of the seasons and recurrence of cultural holidays. When catastrophic events occur (such as terrorist attacks or natural disasters), many persons express the belief that some powerful external force is behind such situations. Recent technological advances have resulted in the development of sophisticated forecasting models and programs to aid humans in preparing for the future. However, because of the random nature of the universe, even the best forecasting methods cannot determine the future.

Throughout many generations, humans have come to realize that the only thing upon which they can rely is change. People age as time passes. Dramatic environmental and societal changes have influenced human health, health care delivery, professional nursing practice, nursing education, and nursing scholarship. Many of the forces influencing changes have been presented in detail in preceding chapters. Because the forces influencing professional nursing intertwine, an effort has been made to avoid redundancy. This chapter focuses on the future as a concept and outlines potential future scenarios so that the nursing profession and individual nurses can plan to meet the challenges during the 21st century and beyond. An entire book could be written about all of the issues that impact the future of the nursing profession. Therefore, this chapter provides a conceptual approach to the future, then uses it to address the following societal issues: an aging American population, disasters, and increased rates of obesity.

 A CONCEPTUAL APPROACH TO THE FUTURE

Depending on the context in which it is used, the word **future** means " that is to be or come; of days, months, or years ahead … the time that has yet to come … what will happen; what is going to be" (Agnes, 2005, p. 576). In a plural form, futures refer to contracts made for goods or commodities that will be delivered at a future date—for example, the rising price of crude oil in response to increased demand. In English (and many other languages), verbs have a future tense to communicate proposed actions. Whatever the definition, unless time ceases, the future will arrive soon.

Futurists use a variety of methods to forecast the future. Minkin (1995) proposed using a format that identifies and analyzes trends and determines implications of them before making predictions. Other futurists have used similar approaches in forecasting future trends with some success; these approaches include the writings of Naisbitt (1996), Aburdene and Naisbitt (1992), Naisbitt and Aburdene (1990), Johnson and White (2000), Sachs (2008), and Toffler (1970, 1990; Toffler & Toffler, 2006). Other futurists, such as

Thomas Alva Edison, started with a vision (the concept of electric lighting) and then took steps to make the vision a reality. In terms of the future, the meaning of **vision** expands to include forecasting or prophecy.

Scholarly debate has occurred about the ability of mankind to shape the future. Minkin (1995) said the future is the only part of life that persons can change from actions or inaction. Sullivan (1999, p. 5) identified two relevant assumptions about the future: "First, the future is uncertain.... Second, we choose and create major aspects of the future by what we do or fail to do." However, many religious faiths hold the belief that the future unfolds as part of a grand plan by a higher power.

Henchley (1978) specified four possible ways of looking at the future: (1) possible, (2) plausible, (3) probable, and (4) preferable. Henchley's approach considers the wildest possible ideas to probable concepts based on human history and trends. This chapter presents definitions and scenarios for the four ways to approach the future followed by selected key issues confronting the profession of nursing and health care delivery.

The **possible future** considers all potential things that may occur, including the wildest ideas that even violate current scientific laws (Henchley, 1978). Examples include unpredicted catastrophes, such as the catastrophic earthquake and tsunami disaster on December 26, 2004; potential, coordinated, multiple worldwide terrorists attacks; and a large meteor hitting and destroying the planet. Science fiction media and doomsday prediction exercises serve as sources for the possible future.

The **plausible future** focuses on what may occur based on current trends that may be combined to describe a range of potential futures (Henchley, 1978). Examples include increasing tensions between the United States and other nations, developing clean sources of energy, increasing disparity of incomes between the rich and poor, and increasing global warming and pollution by human beings.

The **probable future** presents a picture of what most likely will happen, with the future being primarily a mirror to the present with little or no actual change. Examples would include continued financial strain on health care providers and consumers in the absence of a reformed health care system and continued advances in technology and science, increasing the complexity of life and health care decisions.

The **preferable future** proposes the desired state for the future. Development of a preferred vision requires development of common visions, shared values, and strategic plans among many groups of persons. The preferable future starts by identifying a vision and taking steps to make the vision reality. Indeed, this future results from deliberate actions or inaction. Examples of this would include the unification of all health care providers (including third-party payers), consumers, and elected officials to develop a realistic comprehensive health care reform program and alleviation of culturally biased health care delivery by actively recruiting the best and brightest of all cultural groups into the health care professions.

Scenarios are forecasts, "an outline for any proposed or planned series of events, real or imagined" (Agnes, 2005, p. 1281). They raise awareness of the wide range of possible implications of external forces, sensitize people to potential threats and opportunities, and allow examination of alternative options for action. The scenarios presented in this chapter barely skim the issues that affect the future of professional nursing. Some of the presented scenarios are controversial. The scenarios without reference citations represent the author's predictions of what could possibly happen.

 ## FUTURE SCENARIOS FOR SOCIETY AND HEALTH CARE

Many forces that shape the future remain uncontrollable by the human race. Humans have yet to find ways to control acts of nature, such as weather patterns, earthquakes, certain epidemics, and famines. However, humans control governments, laws, and policies. Unfortunately, professional nurses have limited societal status and resources to become highly influential in the determination of laws, policies, and regulations. Professional nurses rely on building coalitions with more influential members of society and creating a solid united front to create change. The following scenarios related to society and health care contain factors that cannot be controlled by the nursing profession alone. However, nurses play a key role in being prepared to either confront these challenges or work collaboratively with others in hopes to steer action in a desired direction.

The Aging American Population Changes the Nature of Society

By the year 2030, the number of elderly Americans is projected to double, resulting in the need for increased nurses to provide health care services to them (Institute of Medicine [IOM], 2008; Cetron & Davies, 2008). For all health professions, especially nursing, providers need to prepare for the care of the special needs of geriatric clients. The IOM (2008) proposed a three-step approach that includes improving the way health care is delivered, increasing numbers of care providers specializing in geriatrics, and enhancing the geriatric competence of the health care workforce. Demonstration of essential knowledge and competence in the care of older adults may become part of licensure and certification exams. More home health nurses will be needed because increasing numbers of the elderly will live at home and need help with activities of daily living and management of complex drug regimens. Elderly clients (if they possess the cognitive ability to make sound, reasonable decisions) and their informal caregivers (family members and friends) need to become part of the health care team. Nurse geriatric consultants will help caregivers cope with the declining health of the elderly. Finally, nursing research will need to be conducted to determine needs and trends of the aging population along with ways to attract nurses to the field of geriatrics.

An aging nursing workforce compounds the issue of increased numbers of the elderly. A shortfall of 340,000 nurses is expected by 2020, and by 2010, 40% of the nursing workforce will be over age 50 years. Many nurses cut their working hours because of the physical demands of the job (Buerhaus, Auerbach, & Staiger, 2007). Perhaps, aging nurses might have an increased understanding of the needs of elderly clients as they experience caring for elderly relatives and recognize the decline in physical abilities associated with aging. To alleviate the nursing shortage, many health care organizations might look for ways to facilitate the employment of older nurses.

Clinical issues projected to arise will be prevention of infectious diseases (especially human immunodeficiency virus because sexually active seniors may refrain from condom use as pregnancy is not a potential outcome of intercourse). In addition, strategies for reversing the aging process may appear. Biotechnology also may create spare body parts and tissue transplants and implanted computer chips for disabled persons. Finally, gene therapy, herbal therapies, and more drugs will be used to cease or reverse the aging process or maintain sexual potency (Toffler & Toffler, 2006). In addition, lifestyle choices such as exercise (aerobic and weight lifting) have also been associated with an increased level of physical and mental fitness.

Frequently, the elderly with resources exhaust them to pay for health care services. As people age, they consume more health care services (IOM, 2008). By 2030, 20% of the American population will be over the age of 65 years and fewer than 50% will have defined pension plans. Unlike the past, economic downturns and uncertainty have resulted in some large corporations reducing and sometimes discontinuing health care benefits for retirees. Affected retirees find themselves scrambling to secure health care coverage (if they can get it because of preexisting conditions), or they have to pay much more for coverage than they did in the past. Because most retirees cannot afford to be without supplemental health care coverage, some of them make decisions about how to find resources to pay for some form of supplemental insurance. Decisions they face might affect their health, well-being, and quality of life. For example, some elderly persons make decisions to buy food or prescription medications, move in with children, buy less nutritious food (reduces grocery bill), or set thermostats to potentially dangerous settings (or not run air conditioners) in order to have resources to survive.

Forecasters predict that a possible intergenerational conflict may arise worldwide as Japan and several European nations have a similar problem with increasing elderly populations. Younger workers may revolt against paying high Social Security taxes to support the elderly (Toffler & Toffler, 2006). In the author's version of a worst case and possible scenario, societal values change and the elderly are perceived to have no value other than to use scarcely available health care and other valued resources. The aged have a new obligation to die in order to preserve precious commodities for younger, more productive world citizens. Governments enact laws to make euthanasia and assisted suicide legal, and the elderly who do not want to be a burden to their children or society willingly end their lives.

In contrast, a plausible scenario (especially for nations that have a democratic form of government and a large senior population) is that older persons with cognitive capability exert energy on political activism, resulting in massive reformation in available senior services sponsored by the government, business, and nonprofit agencies. For the financially solvent elderly, specialized residences and extended care facilities are built to provide desired, individualized, and culturally relevant services. Older persons without vast resources find themselves living with children who gladly offer their homes to them, thereby creating intergenerational family units. As working adults serve as primary caregivers for the aged, geriatric day care programs will increase and some may even be employer sponsored. The stress of caring for a debilitated aging adult might result in exhausted and depressed caregivers, resulting in neglect or some type of abuse. Caregiver programs will be developed to provide social and emotional support for them. Geriatric education, mental health, and respite care services will be available only for those who can pay for them. Legislation to provide funding for aging services, caregiver programs, medical care, and tax credits for home caregiving will be enacted. In this possible scenario, basic needs of the elderly are met and younger members of society value the elderly.

However, the probable scenario would be that the elderly might enjoy improved health from advances in medical science, remain a strong lobbying group, and demand increased governmental support for life and health care needs. In this scenario, society and governmental support for the health care of the elderly would remain similar to that in current times.

Finally, in the preferred scenario, the aging population makes health-promoting lifestyle choices (starting in middle adulthood) and develops strong ties with younger persons. Persons of all ages, governmental agencies, businesses, and nonprofit foundations and organizations work together to develop policies related to health care delivery that provides equal access to services for all who need it. The physically able elderly engage in volunteerism that results in a meaningful societal contribution. The elderly who have resources willingly assume financial responsibility for health care services and residential care requirements. Public funding use is reserved exclusively for the elderly and other societal members who cannot pay for basic life needs, including health care.

Questions for Reflection 23-2

1. How can the nursing profession prepare for the increased numbers of elderly who will need future nursing services?
2. What are the possible consequences for the nursing profession if it fails to address the aging population issue?

Disasters: Manmade and Natural

Any event resulting in great harm or damage can be considered a disaster. Manmade disasters occur because of human action. The very powerful or persons who are disadvantaged and disenfranchised act in violent ways that result in human and environmental catastrophes (government corruption, rebellions, wars, and terrorism). Natural disasters occur as the result of climate or geological events. In recent years, some climatic changes have been linked to the effects of people (see Chapter 13) (Sachs, 2008; Toffler & Toffler, 2006).

Before September 11, 2001, the United States considered itself immune to multiple terrorist attacks or acts of war. However, some persons forewarned of a coordinated terrorist attack plan (National Institute of Medicine and the National Research Council, 1999). Terrorist acts occur in many nations, and countless acts have been averted. The ease of securing plans for building bombs (some with nuclear, disease-producing, or noxious chemical capability) increases the likelihood of a large-scale terrorist attack. Technological advances such as nanotechnology, biotechnology, and robotics offer the possibility of destroying the human race while leaving buildings and infrastructures intact. Sources of energy production become prime targets because of the current reliance on power sources for health, safety, and business. Balancing societal need for safety while preserving individual rights provides challenges to persons entrusted to provide public safety. Terrorist attacks in the United States sparked a war on terrorism located primarily in Iraq and Afghanistan. At the time of the writing of this book, the results of the war remain unknown. However, as in all wars, much environmental destruction has occurred and many persons have died or have sustained physical and/or psychological injury. A possible scenario (and bleak scenario) is that terrorists obtain access to nuclear and biological weaponry. Within a short time frame (perhaps weeks), terrorists execute a well-coordinated series of attacks on American soil resulting in many civilian casualties and widespread destruction. A unilateral attack against terrorist cells by the United States with total disregard for national borders occurs. The American action fuels international opinion of the United States being a nation striving to conquer the world to force democratic and capitalistic values on all persons.

However, a more plausible scenario results in the strengthening of the coalition of countries engaging in the war on terrorism because of attacks happening in many countries. In this scenario, the United Nations (UN) becomes the place where strategic plans are made to rid the world of terrorist acts initiated by well-organized groups with global networks. The UN also develops a global response plan to chemical and biological attacks. However, acts of terrorism performed by individuals remain unpredictable, and the persons responsible for such acts remain elusive.

Unfortunately, the probable scenario results in a future not much different from that of today. The United States and certain allies develop stronger ties, and the war on terrorism lasts for many years. In response to identified biological attacks, the United States stockpiles medications and vaccines for future use, if needed. Most Americans refuse to be intimidated by terrorist threats and continue with their usual life practices, such as working, shopping, and attending sporting and other recreational events. A few anxious citizens stockpile supplies needed to prepare themselves in anticipation of a terrorist attack using nuclear devices. The government makes efforts to stimulate the economy while spending vast amounts of money to preserve homeland security. Less money becomes available to provide services to the poor and to repair infrastructure (roads, sewage systems, and power plants). American citizens live with minor inconveniences, such as having to arrive earlier and wait longer in lines when traveling by commercial airlines. Health care workers are asked to register voluntarily to serve as members of federal, state, or local medical response teams (Veenema, 2003).

The preferable future would be one in which all persons have no need for violent acts because diverse values and approaches to life become valued. Rich nations foster economic development of poorer countries. Agreement occurs on defining basic human rights and values across cultures while allowing for diversity when appropriate. All persons are valued. Persons with more resources than what they can use support persons who lack the capability for meeting basic human needs (food, water, shelter, and safety). Because all persons feel valued and respected, there is no need for violence.

Some natural disasters can be predicted, whereas other cannot. Natural disasters can occur quickly without warning (earthquakes, volcanic eruptions, some tornadoes, and flash floods), quickly with warning (storms, tsunami), or slowly with warning (downstream flooding, environmental contamination, or famines from prolonged drought). Hurricane Katrina revealed the lack of a well-coordinated disaster plan at the federal, state, and local state governmental levels. Predicted effects of global climate change include more intense storms, rising sea levels, and geographical climate shifts (tropical forests become deserts; temperate zones become tropical; tundra becomes fertile farmland). Infectious diseases would also follow climate changes (Sachs, 2008).

The possible scenario depicts a future during which humans show an ever-expanding disregard for the earth. The need for human survival and desire for extravagant lifestyles dominate all human activities. Humans ravage the planet and expand their residential areas with total disregard for wildlife and plant life. Environmental impact consolidates and results in catastrophic climate effects as depicted in the film *The Day After Tomorrow* (Emmerich, 2004), in which climate change produces rapidly rising sea levels and a series of massive storms that culminate with rapidly moving falling temperatures affecting Europe, North America, and the northern half of Asia. The falling temperatures result in deep freezes incapable of human existence. Not even the most powerful government can intervene to prevent the catastrophe.

In contrast, a plausible (and perhaps preferable) scenario would encompass increased human awareness of our impact on the environment. The United Nations spearheads a binding global environmental treaty for all nations (even the developing ones with fewer resources). The world works cohesively and collaboratively to reduce greenhouse gas emissions and air, soil, and water pollution, and facilitates action by offering incentives. Nature flourishes and counteracts the damage done by humans.

However, the probable future would be the continuation of existing international, national, and local environmental policies. Economic considerations supersede required actions for energy conservation and environmental preservation, with most persons abiding by them and other persons looking for ways around them because of increased personal expenditures. However, if (or when) sea levels begin to rise enough to threaten human life, storms become highly destructive, and plants and wildlife disappear, then the human race might develop and implement stronger, environmentally friendly global policies.

Obesity and Health Care

Currently, 65% of Americans are overweight, and, more than 25% of the overweight are obese (body mass index greater than 30 square meters). Obesity is linked to type II diabetes. Recent studies project that diabetes will develop in one in three Americans born in the year 2000 before they die. Ancient humans survived as hunter-gatherers, and efficient storage of energy promoted the survival of the human race. However, in modern times, Americans (and citizens of other developed nations) engage in a sedentary lifestyle and have unrestricted access to high-caloric foods (Centers for Disease Control [CDC], 2008). Besides diabetes, being overweight and obese contributes to the development of degenerative arthritis, hypertension, heart disease, stroke, gall bladder disease, sleep apnea, respiratory difficulties, and certain forms of cancer (CDC).

A possible scenario related to the problem of obesity is that science discovers ways to turn off the "thrifty gene," blocks chemicals responsible for hunger, and develops an effective weight loss pill that has few and insignificant adverse effects (Millett & Kopp, 1996). In addition, scientists realize that individual genetics determine how foods are metabolized and used by the body. Nutritional counseling based on individual genetic profiles becomes widespread (Underwood & Adler, 2005). A forecast by the author related to obesity includes government support to obese and overweight citizens for the following weight reduction efforts: prescription drugs for weight loss, memberships to health clubs, and psychological counseling. In return, governments impose taxes on "junk" food (unless the citizen is underweight), and initiate tax surcharges on obese citizens to defray projected increased health care costs. Many people lose weight and adopt a healthy lifestyle (to avoid increased taxes), which results in reduced demand for secondary and tertiary health care services.

A plausible scenario related to the incidence of obesity developed by the author reads as follows. In developed nations, affluent citizens keep getting larger and larger. They have access to unlimited food, engage in sedentary jobs, fail to exercise, and find comfort in passive entertainment (watching movies or television and spending endless hours engaged in computer activities). Health problems, once thought of as afflictions of aging, occur at younger ages (Trossman, 2005). Young, educated citizens find themselves incapable of performing any manual labor. They rely on housekeepers and gardeners to maintain a home or they live in condominiums or apartments where building and ground maintenance is provided. Because of their size and health problems, the young adults quickly find themselves unable to work because of their health, resulting in an increased incidence of worker disability. The obese young and the elderly consume health care services to the point of exhaustion. Nurses caring for the obese clients sustain more back injuries (Trossman). Nursing becomes one of the most dangerous professions because of the high incidence of permanent disability arising from work-related injuries.

A probable scenario related to increased obesity is that some obese and overweight persons recognize the impact of weight on their energy level, feelings of well-being, and health. Corporate America recognizes the problem and works to capitalize on the obesity epidemic. Numerous weight reduction products are developed and marketed to consumers. Obese and overweight consumers turn to science in hopes that it will discover a painless, quick way to lose weight. Persons with an external locus of control blame others for their weight. However, persons with an internal locus of control take steps to reduce their weight. Legislative efforts to pass regulations and laws protecting consumers from poor eating habits, knowing all unhealthful food ingredients in available foodstuffs, warning consumers about fraudulent weight reduction plans, and taxing "junk" food fail. Persons receive education on healthy lifestyles. Some persons (many who need psychological counseling) need the advice of health care providers and lose weight. However, others persons continue the cycle of temporary weight loss followed by weight gain. Persons (nurses and unlicensed care providers) caring for obese health care consumers have access to technological and other assistive devices to prevent work-related injuries (Trossman, 2005).

However, the preferred future would mean that more (ideally all) persons would adopt a healthy lifestyle. Health care professionals provide worldwide education programs that address the health hazards of being obese and overweight. Success at getting the message occurs. People lose lots of weight. They consume only the number of calories to maintain healthy body weight and follow the recommendations of getting 30 minutes of vigorous exercise daily (U.S. Department of Health and Human Services, 2000). Health care dollars are spent on health promotion, resulting in increased savings because of reduced consumption of secondary and tertiary health care services.

Questions for Reflection 23-4

1. How does obesity affect the health of consumers and nurses?
2. What are the potential adverse effects of caring for obese clients?
3. What are possible ways to minimize the health hazards for nurses working with obese clients?
4. What safety devices are present in my current clinical practice setting for nurses to use when caring for obese clients?
5. Do I use the safety devices available to me? Why or why not?

Genetics and Health Care

Findings from the Human Genome Project continue to have profound effects on society. Genes for various diseases have been discovered, and eventually these discoveries will lead to new detection and treatment techniques. Genomics or the reactions of genetics on body metabolism also plays a key role in the development of health-related problems. Genetic testing may result in determining suitable marriage partners, safe insurance risks, individualized diets, disease treatment interventions (certain medications or lifestyle changes), and human evolution. Persons also may receive genetically designed medication to prevent or treat illnesses. In addition, persons known to be at risk for a particular affliction may begin screening for a particular disease earlier in life than would be recommended for the general population. A RNA blood test has recently been determined to have 75% accuracy and 85% specificity for lung cancer diagnosis (Zander, Debey-Pascher Eggle, Staratshek-Jox, Stoelben, & Linseisen, 2008).

The completion of human genome mapping and the results of future genetically based research provide the foundation for various scenarios. A possible scenario comes from the movie *Gattaca* (Niccol, 1997), in which individuals receive genetic testing at birth to determine their future lives. The state selects the profession (or work), education, and genetic composition for all citizens. Marriage is no longer needed because new human life is created using artificial insemination in women genetically designed to thrive during pregnancy and childbirth. Individuals lose the freedom to choose their destiny.

However, a plausible scenario would be that persons would be genetically tested at birth to determine potential health risks. For the person with the genetic disposition to cancer, screenings would begin earlier in life than would be recommended for the general population. Drug companies would use genetic research to design effective medications against previously incurable forms of illness. In addition, genetically designed medications for individuals would enhance disease prevention and treatment efforts (Tariman, 2008). The cost of health care escalates as individually designed drugs increase costs for production and create more medications. Only the affluent have access to genetically designed medications. However, persons requiring earlier and more frequent disease screenings receive them only if they can afford them.

Finally, the probable scenario proposes that pharmaceutical companies and health care providers will use information generated from human genetic research to find treatments for and ways to prevent illness. All persons with familial tendencies for particular diseases will be offered genetic testing to determine optimal screening, prevention, and treatment modalities. Genetic testing will be performed only with voluntary consent. Nurses assume the key role of helping persons understand the results of genetic testing (Burke & Kirk, 2006; Tariman, 2008). For this issue, the probable scenario most likely is the preferred scenario.

Questions for Reflection 23-5

1. What impact will advances in genetic research have on the nursing profession?
2. What additional knowledge and skills will be needed by nurses in the future because of advances in genetic research and genetically based health care?
3. What are the potential hazards for consumers who undergo genetic testing?
4. What are the potential benefits of having a genetic health profile performed on all persons?

FUTURE SCENARIOS FOR HEALTH CARE DELIVERY

Health care delivery appears to be increasingly complex. Recent safety and quality inita- tives add to the complexity for all health care providers. Staying abreast of new discoveries about the human body (e.g., genetic, genomics, physiology, biochemistry, and stem cells), healthy lifestyle strategies, and technology creates distress for some health care pro- viders. Constant change seems to be the only thing upon which providers and consumers can rely. In 1996, Bezold identified possible health care delivery scenarios for the 21st century. For this chapter, Bezold's scenario titles are used, but updated information has been added based on current trends in health care delivery related to human physiology and disease etiology.

Hard Times Scenario

This possible scenario assumes that times are tough for the economy as a whole and for health care. Although health care costs currently have stabilized at 16% of the GNP, 47 million persons (11 million of them children) in the United States do not have health insurance (U.S. Census Bureau, 2007). As unemployment increases, citizens pressure the federal government to create a universal health care plan. Because of consistent increases in government deficits, the plan offers a very frugal benefit package. The gov- ernment refuses to pay providers for cost incurred from all preventable hospital-acquired conditions (Kurtzman & Buerhaus, 2008). Governmental controls increase the amount of documentation health care providers need to complete to justify reimbursement, and cost containment reduces the amount of federal funding for all forms of health care research. Health care innovations are dramatically slow. Heroic measures once used to prolong life are limited to patients who are younger and have something to offer society. A three- tiered health care system emerges, one for persons relying exclusively on the government program, another for those with resources for private insurance coverage, and another for persons who have the ability to pay for health care costs independently (who access care abroad because of reduced costs).

Nursing care of acutely ill clients would be important in this scenario, but nurses would be poorly paid and have little prestige. Consequently, most nurses would be from lower socioeconomic groups and from foreign countries. Some consumers of nursing serv- ices might have less confidence in receiving care from a foreign nurse, especially when the consumer may not understand the nurse's instructions because of her or his accented speech. Clients who could pay would be cared for in the home by private duty nurses (Bezold, 1996).

To streamline the use of limited resources, Herzlinger (2004) suggested that government- financed and insurance-covered health treatments would be limited to those with an established history of successful outcomes, based on reliable scientific evidence and docu- mented emphasis on promoting client comfort. Nurses would rely on standardized proto- cols for specific health care problems or concerns to shorten the time required for attaining the desired health outcomes. Standardized protocols would be followed by nurses and physicians for treating specific client health problems. Standardized protocols would reduce costs while enhancing client outcomes. Consumers with knowledge and resources would become empowered to act as equal partners with health care professionals. However, consumers without knowledge and/or resources might not be able to access needed or direct their health care services.

Buyer's Market Scenario

In this probable scenario, Bezold (1996) and Herzlinger (2004) proposed that the responsibility for health and health care expenditures has been returned to the consumer. Insurance coverage includes a tax to help pay for the cost of care given to the poor. Health care providers are certified by the state on the basis of knowledge and competence. Health care providers, especially nurses, use evidence-based guidelines for practice. Competition for health care consumers becomes fierce, and health care organizations work to delight consumers. People rely less on health care providers and have better tools for changing their lifestyles and preventing or managing illnesses. Consumers, rather than the third-party payers, choose from various types of providers and treatments. Because health becomes a highly valued aspect of human life, consumers seek health care for illness prevention, rather than disease treatment (Herzlinger, 2004).

This scenario offers real potential for nursing to achieve greater power and influence. Nursing practice based on scientific evidence elevates the level of professionalism for nurses. Nurses present solid evidence for optimal staffing patterns for positive client outcomes (Gordon, Buchanan, & Bretherton, 2008). Because nurses are seen by society as professionals who have altruistic concerns for clients and have reasonable workloads, more persons choose to enter the profession. Nurses develop independent practices and demonstrate superiority in primary health care delivery. By accessing consumers directly, nurses would have a major role in promoting health. Education would emphasize ways of teaching consumers how to promote individual, family, and community health. This scenario might be a preferable future for professional nursing because of its benefits for both nurses and consumers.

Business-as-Usual Scenario

Another probable future, the business-as-usual scenario, assumes continued technological ingenuity, proliferation of new pharmaceuticals, sophisticated communication, and high levels of consumption. Although most Americans are better off, the percentage of poor continues to rise. Health care reform has been left to the states, which in turn leave it to the marketplace. Advances in biomedical knowledge and technology make it possible to forecast, prevent, and manage illnesses earlier and more successfully. High-tech interventions such as performance-enhancing bionic implants and organoids (a new organ or organ part grown outside the body and then implanted) are widely available to those who can pay for them (Bezold, 1996). Small hospitals continue to close, patient acuity levels rise, early hospital dismissals become desired, and health care becomes more efficient. Wealthy for-profit and nonprofit hospitals develop integrated health systems and negotiate discounts with health insurance companies in order to obtain and maintain a stable patient base. Administrators rule and professional staff become employees of the hospital or integrated health care delivery system. Persons receive all health care needs within the developed health care systems that provide inpatient, outpatient, and home care services. Because long-term chronic care is expensive, no health system offers this service. Because innovations continue, health care costs continue to soar. Increased efficiency compounds the stress and strain on providers, who become forced to assume higher patient loads. Because health care is valued by consumers, the percentage of the gross national product (GNP) spent on health care continues to rise. The extension of the current environment additionally devalues the role of professional nursing and results in fewer persons entering the profession, and practicing nurses continue to seek employment outside of hospital settings. The nursing shortage continues to worsen.

Healthy, Healing Communities Scenario

This preferred and probable scenario involves a focus on "healing the body, mind, and spirit of individuals and communities" (Bezold, 1996, p. 38). Neighbors look out for each other, and people work together to eliminate problems such as drugs, teenage pregnancy, and the effects of poverty. However, as information and technology increase worker productivity (or replace workers altogether), unemployment grows to 25%. Health care organizations help to make communities environmentally and financially sustainable with the help of unpaid volunteers. Health promotion efforts begin in early childhood. Older persons find rewarding ways to contribute to the community, reducing disability and the time spent in long-term facilities. Advanced technologies lead to a comfortable life for most people, and bionics, robotics, smarter homes, and more caring neighborhoods allow disabled elderly individuals to remain in their homes. Consumers are involved in decision making regarding their health as they learn how to access and evaluate health-related information. The emphasis is on wellness and the development of full human potential, with rejection of anonymity, artificiality, manipulation, and unnecessary size or complexity. These factors closely mirror consumer-preferred preferences for health care delivery models.

Nurses would be full partners with consumers in this scenario, helping people with self-care and health promotion activities while providing information to support fully informed decision making. Consumers would select a "medical home," an outpatient office or clinic that would provide them with preventive and health promotion services in a coordinated care effort across the care continuum from primary care providers (including nurse practitioners). The medical home would offer specialized services based on life span needs (Vlasses & Smeltzer, 2007). Older persons would be valued and would be cared for at home. Various information sources to support health would be available at home through computer networks. Nurses would be recognized as highly educated professionals who make valuable contributions, such as providing psychosocial support to clients, engaging in surveillance activities to detect subtle changes in client health status, executing complex evidence-based clinical procedures and protocols confidently, and coordinating health care activities across the continuum of care (Formella & Rovin, 2004; Gordon et al., 2008).

 ## EVOLVING HEALTH CARE NEEDS AND HEALTH CARE DELIVERY

Along with the aforementioned issues, Cetron and Davies (2008) of the World Future Society have identified additional trends that impact consumer health care needs and the delivery of health care services in the United States. Demographic trends reveal an ever-increasing population with increased immigration in order to meet labor shortages. Immigration means a diverse workforce and more culturally diverse clients seeking health care services. Issues on the economic and occupational fronts include globalization, high unemployment (especially in the service sector), younger persons entering the workforce (influx of Generation X and Millennials), a shrinking industrial workforce, and the continued expansion of information-based organizations. The ever-increasing influences of Generation X and the Millennials, rising education levels, altered gender roles, increased political participation by all citizens, increasing technological sophistication and complexity, reliance on power, and knowledge dependency are societal trends that also impact health care needs and delivery. The United States will need at least twice as many physicians with specialization in geriatrics and between 340,000 to 500,000 more nurses by 2020 (Buerhaus, Auerbach, et al., 2007; Cetron & Davies).

Increased cultural diversity and immigration will force all health care providers to become more adept at delivering culturally sensitive and linguistically appropriate services. When people are ill or dealing with personal issues, they tend to prefer someone who looks like them. Health care providers must be attuned to signs of diseases never seen in the United States when working with persons who have lived in different lands. Differences in genetic profiles and genomics also must be considered when caring for culturally diverse clients. In an ideal world, health care provider demographics should match the demographics of health care consumers. In the United States, close to 90% of registered nurses are Caucasian, non-Hispanic women, very different from the demographics of the American public (Sullivan Commission, 2004).

Creating a culturally diverse workforce poses challenges to future health care delivery. Currently, the United States attracts internationally educated health care providers because of differences in income. The American health care system offers a higher income than what many health care providers can earn at home, and social status for nurses (especially from the Pacific Rim and Far East) is typically higher in the United States compared to the status of nurses in their homelands (Kirk, 2007). Thus, salaries for physicians and nurses far exceed what they can make in their homelands. Facilitating migration of nurses has been suggested as a remedy for the ever-growing nursing shortage. Currently, internationally educated nurses working in the United States come from the Phillippines (50.2%), Canada (20.2%), the United Kingdom (8.4%), Nigeria (2.5%), Ireland (1.5%), India (1.3%), Hong Kong (1.2%), Jamaica (1.1%), and South Korea (1%). Clusters of internationally educated nurses work in California, Florida, New York, Texas, and New Jersey (Brush, 2008). Nurses from Canada, the United Kingdom, and Ireland typically do not have difficulty speaking English. Unfortunately, nurse migration to developed nations creates nursing shortages in donor nations (Brush). Kirk (2007) proposed that the global migration of professional nurses results in an international flow of skills and knowledgeable health care workers. When working with a culturally diverse health care team, all members must demonstrate authenticity and encourage the full participation of everyone so that each person feels that he or she has a valuable contribution to the team's efforts. Little things such as failure to include culturally diverse team members in informal conversations or outside-of-work activities may "have cumulative and profoundly negative effects" (Myers & Dreachslin, 2007, p. 294) on a team member's overall well-being and professional performance.

Technological advances in health care also pose challenges to health care delivery. All health team members need effective computer skills to access client health data; find current evidence-based best practice protocols; order client medications, interventions, and supplies; and document client plans, interventions, and outcomes (see Chapter 15 for detailed information). In the future, persons may carry computerized identification cards that include protected health information. Identification cards will be useful to verify client identity to prevent health insurance fraud but, more importantly, provide a detailed, consistent health history, reducing the time spent for conducting a detailed health history for each health care service encounter. Summaries for each time the person accesses and uses health care services will be recorded on the card, thereby fostering integration of health care services across the care continuum. Computer order entry and client identification systems reduce errors in health care delivery.

Questions for Reflection 23-6

1. How do you think the current health care system will look in 10 years?
2. What knowledge and skills will be needed for effective nursing practice in 10 years?
3. How can nurses best prepare for the future health care delivery system?
4. What can the nursing profession do to help members prepare for the challenges in the future health care delivery system?

THE FUTURE OF PROFESSIONAL NURSING PRACTICE

Many issues confront the nursing profession as it works to maintain sustainable numbers to meet the needs of society. Recent initiatives calling for improved quality and safety provide an opportunity for nurses to present evidence demonstrating the valuable contributions that they make to health care. In addition, the profession needs to develop plans to accommodate a mobile society and increased geographical demands for nurses. If nurses fail to seize the current opportunities for leadership in health care delivery and continue to dissuade others from entering the profession, the profession may cease to exist. Nurses represent the largest percentage of all health team members. Current actions taken by the profession today have profound implications for future patients, health care delivery, nurses, and society.

Evidence-Based Nursing Practice

Nursing research findings, quality improvement data results, and clinical experience provide the foundation for **evidence-based nursing practice**. Evidence-based nursing practice uses the best available source of information to enable cost-effective and clinically effective client care. Systematic nursing research and detailed evaluations of health care interventions provide strong evidence that nurses can use as foundations for practice. Large databases such as those generated by the National Database of Nursing Quality Indicators (Dunton, 2008) and the Omaha System (Canham, Mao, Yoder, Connolly, & Dietz, 2008) facilitate the generation of solid evidence for use in quality management and clinical protocol development. In the past, nurses performed many tasks based on tradition and ritual. Evidence-based practice enables nurses to determine the effects of newly developed technology, alternative and complementary treatments, and the differences professional nurses make in client care outcomes. Nurses are doing a better job of producing and disseminating information about their impact in the delivery of high-quality care (Aiken, Clarke, & Sloane, 2000; Aiken, Smith, & Lake, 1994; Doran, 2003; Gordon et al., 2008; Havens & Aiken, 1999; Hinshaw, 2008). However, more needs to be done to inform the public and policy makers of the substantial contributions professional nurses make to health care.

Evidence-based practice enables nurses to be taken more seriously by other health care providers and society. Scientific justification for nursing actions raises the level of professional practice. In addition, evidence-based practice may serve as the vehicle for the nursing profession to clearly define the term "nursing."

Multistate Compacts for Nursing Licensure in the United States

Despite the recommendation by the Pew Health Professions Commission (1995) for the health care professional regulation to remain controlled by individual states, the National Council of State Boards of Nursing (NCSBN, 2000) has initiated an effort for a mutual recognition model for professional nurse registration. Under mutual recognition, RNs could practice nursing across state lines, provided that the states participated in the mutual recognition compact.

The interstate compact helps states with shortages of professional nurses by allowing nurses from bordering states to practice without needing to obtain additional nursing licenses. Electronic- and telecommunication-based nursing practice frequently crosses state borders. The nurse would obtain licensure in the state of legal residence. To protect the integrity of individual State Nurse Practice Acts, the professional nurse would abide by the Nurse Practice Act where the client receives care (NCSBN, 2000, 2001).

A single professional nursing license would facilitate interstate practice, improve tracking of nurses with disciplinary problems, increase cost-effectiveness, simplify the nursing licensure process, eliminate duplicate listing of licensed nurses, and enhance interstate commerce. In addition, interstate licensure simplifies the licensing process for nurses who are employed by traveling nursing agencies (NCSBN, 2000). Also, multistate compacts enable nurses to practice in diverse geographical locations, such as when many retired persons follow desirable weather and establish residences in the northern United States in the summer and in southern states during the winter.

Although multistate professional licensure may seem appealing, several disadvantages surface. State boards of nursing would need to raise licensing fees for professional nurses to replace the revenue generated by nurses who hold more than one state nursing license. Nurses with a disciplinary action record may not be able to obtain a fresh start in professional nursing after recovering from chemical addiction or after meeting the discipline requirements of a state board of nursing. Multistate licensure also would enable nursing agencies to provide professional nurses to institutions where nurses decide to engage in collective bargaining or strikes to improve working conditions.

To maintain state control of professional nursing licensure, individual states must pass state legislation to participate in the **multistate licensure compact**. By 2005, efforts to enact legislation have been successful in 18 states (Arizona, Arkansas, Delaware, Idaho, Iowa, Maine, Maryland, Mississippi, Nebraska, New Mexico, North Carolina, North Dakota, South Dakota, Tennessee, Texas, Utah, Virginia, and Wisconsin) but have failed in others (NCSBN, 2004a). Some failures have been the result of failure of all nurses to support the idea. For example, state nurses' associations oppose some elements contained in the language of the multistate compacts. In some states, participation in a multistate compact is prohibited by the state constitution, thereby creating another obstacle for multistate nursing licensure compact legislation.

The Demise of the Profession

The demise of the nursing profession is a possible future scenario. Within 10 years, 40% of working RNs will be 50 years old or older (Health Services and Resources Administration, 2004; Horrigan, 2004). Since 1985, more than 50% of new nurses educated in the United States have graduated from associate degree nursing programs (Hood & Leddy, 2006; NCSBN, 2004b, 2005). Associate degree nursing programs focus on the technical aspects of nursing practice. If the trend continues, the nurses providing care to elderly, infirmed, and disabled patients will be fewer, less educated, and older. As a way to prepare for the nursing shortage, some states are considering expanding the scope of practice of emergency medical technicians to include providing services that currently fall within the scope of professional nursing practice in emergency departments and intensive care units.

Increased pressure for health care organizations to make profits or stay financially viable results in professional nurses assuming a subservient role to health care administrators. Creative ideas to measure individual nurse productivity using wireless communication devices enable administration to track every move made by every nurse. Although the devices reduce the time for nurses to meet client care requests (Kuruzovich, Angst, Faraj, & Agarwal, 2008), nurses receive negative performance evaluations for spending too much time providing education and emotional support to clients, completing required documentation, reporting to colleagues during shift changes, and taking work breaks.

To combat the projected shortage, the federal government has increased funding for persons interested in pursuing a career in nursing. Hospitals are offering tuition reimbursement plans to recruit new nurses to fill vacancies (Henriksen, Page, Williams, & Worral, 2003). Along with federal initiatives, the Robert Wood Johnson Foundation has funded a variety of projects to develop a strong, highly educated, and diverse nursing workforce (Newbergh, 2005). However, despite these efforts, the U.S. Bureau of Labor Statistics projects a shortfall of more than 340,000 RNs in 2020 (Buerhaus, Donelan, et al., 2007). Unless the nursing profession can recruit and retain new members, professional nurses may not be available to care for clients. This will result in reduced client functional status. Clients will be unable to provide self-care. Pain and other symptoms will not be controlled as effectively. Finally, more clients will sustain injury as they receive health care services (Hinshaw, 2008).

Because nurses fail to produce a united front for resolving practice and educational issues, they continue to lose power and autonomy. The lack of unity confuses policy makers and members of society. Because of their marginalized status, nurses are denied participation in health care reform efforts and a system is created that encourages increased workloads, multiple practice entries, and division within the profession (Allan, Tschudin, & Horton, 2008). Nurses are seen as the reason why errors occur in health care. Thus, nursing becomes the weakest link in acquiring and maintaining high-quality and safe health care delivery.

Nursing Gains Clout in Health Care

A more optimistic approach to and preferred scenario for the future of professional nursing would be that the profession becomes cohesive, provides solid evidence for contributions made to health care, and is valued by society and other health professionals. Nurses have fought with each other for generations on issues such as entry-level education for professional practice, collective bargaining, defining professional nursing practice, and control of professional practice (for example, ANA versus NCSBN and staff nurses versus nurse administrators). Professional nurses work to safeguard the public against threats to health. As nurses provide solid evidence for the contributions they make to health care, society and other health team members will realize the value of professional nurses. Nurses have assumed the role of client advocate for many decades by protecting consumers from unscrupulous care providers and from serious treatment errors. The movement toward a multidisciplinary health team approach to client care provides nurses with an opportunity to showcase their knowledge and expertise.

Research efforts in recent years have demonstrated that increases in positive outcomes of client care are improved when they receive care from professional nurses. Reductions in failure to rescue, nosocomial infections, and adverse effects of immobility also reduce hospital costs (Aiken et al., 1994, 2000; Buerhaus, Donelan, et al., 2007; Doran, 2003; Gordon et al., 2008; Havens & Aiken, 1999; Unruh, 2008). However, executing studies does not mean changes in health care delivery automatically happen. Changes in health care public policy require an integrated and unified apprach by the public, government, and nurses (Gordon et al.; Milstead, 2008). Thus, professional nurses must determine a means to disseminate research findings to the public, to inform the government of their needs and desires, and to involve the elected officials who draft legislation for policy changes (see Chapter 20).

Along with improved societal status, professional nurses also become valued members of the health care team. Shared governance shifts from an exclusively nurse form of governance to an interdisciplinary form of governance (Porter-O'Grady & Malloch, 2007). Because of increased efforts of collaborative interdisciplinary teamwork, the health professions embark on providing interprofessional learning experiences that result in long-lasting effects. All team members understand their roles and they gain increased respect for nursing's contributions to the interprofessional team efforts (Hylin, Nyholm, Mattiasson, & Ponzer, 2007).

When nurses demonstrate specialized knowledge and expertise that make differences in client care outcomes, society and other health team members will greatly value the profession. Nurses will enjoy greater autonomy and higher salaries. Then, the profession of nursing will have no difficulty attracting the best and brightest young persons to the profession.

Questions for Reflection 23-7

1. What nursing knowledge areas need further development?
2. What is the current state-of-the-art knowledge on areas that need additional development and refinement?
3. How can nursing research affect the nursing profession and clinical practice?
4. How do I feel about a multidisciplinary approach to health and health care research?
5. What are the advantages of a multidisciplinary approach to health and health care research?
6. What are the disadvantages of a multidisciplinary approach to health and health care research?

THE FUTURE OF NURSING EDUCATION

The knowledge base and technology used in providing nursing care will continue to increase, as will nurses' need for skill and ability in (1) providing care to acutely ill clients; (2) monitoring for adverse effects of diagnostic tests, medications, radiation, and surgical interventions; (3) making critical clinical decisions; (4) using complex computer systems and technology effectively in clinical practice; (5) teaching clients, families, and caregivers how to manage health care needs effectively; (6) coordinating interprofessional health care teams; (7) delegating tasks to unlicensed assistive personnel; (8) collaborating with clients and health care professionals to improve the quality of health; (9) understanding and using research to provide a strong scientific base for nursing practice; (10) communicating to the public and health care providers the unique contributions nurses make to health care; and (11) participating in political processes for shaping health care policies.

In the future, more than ever, nurses will need a broad-based education, assertiveness skills, technical competence, and the ability to deal with rapid change. However, research and technology may provide the instruments nurses require for defining professional nursing, demonstrating that professional nursing care affects client care outcomes, and marketing professional nursing to the public.

Since the 1960s, there has been an intensive national effort to promote the baccalaureate degree as the entry level for professional nursing. In that time, although there has been an increase in the number of nurses prepared at the baccalaureate level, there also has been a dramatic increase in the percentage of nurses prepared at the associate degree level. More than 70% of currently practicing nurses are prepared at the technical level of nursing. In the United States, education for entry into professional nursing can occur at one of four levels: the associate degree, the baccalaureate degree, the master's degree, or the doctoral degree. Thus, there are at least four different patterns of education that create nurses with different levels of knowledge and expertise. In addition, the multiple entry levels into nursing create confusion for health care consumers, who consider that all nurses are alike.

The current pattern of more professional nurses entering the profession with associate degrees rather than baccalaureate degrees may continue. As a profession, nurses have been closely associated with upward mobility, especially for women. Most associate degree programs are located in community colleges, making them financially and geographically accessible. Demand can readily be met by an increased supply of licensed workers in a short time. Associate degree–prepared nurses frequently work in the same positions as baccalaureate degree–prepared nurses. However, some facilities require a minimum of a bachelor's degree for supervisory positions. As the complexity of professional nursing increases and nursing care moves to the community, where delivery settings have many uncontrolled variables, associate degree–prepared nurses may lack the theoretical knowledge to deliver safe, effective nursing care in these settings. The Pew Task Force on Accreditation of Health Professions Education (1998) proposed an educational ladder for RNs with associate degrees. Some nursing programs have developed creative approaches to advancing the level of nursing education. Examples of these programs include the RN to master's degree in nursing and the RN to nursing doctorate.

Before their baccalaureate studies, many RN students perceive nursing education at the baccalaureate level as additional and partially redundant, rather than as different and enriching. Little incentive for professional education is provided by the delivery system, which lacks differential salary structures or clearly articulated differences in job expectations. Licensure as an RN after associate degree education has reinforced this model.

However, in some states a bachelor's degree in nursing is required for professional licensure (e.g., South Dakota). Since more nurses are educated in community college settings and there is a serious nursing shortage, this requirement has yet to become the standard for professional licensure. Most major nursing organizations, including the ANA and the National League for Nursing, have endorsed this goal. An increasing number of nurses are seeking baccalaureate education because of increased opportunities for promotion, perceived increased professional marketability, and improved job security, and for personal reasons.

In response to recommendations in reports generated by the IOM, the Joint Commission, and the Robert Wood Johnson Foundation for reducing fragmentation and increasing safety and quality of health care, the American Association of Colleges of Nursing (2004) has developed the Clinical Nurse Leader (CNL) program. The goal is to provide a nurse generalist position with advanced education to provide leadership to clinical staff while coordinating client care across various health care settings. The CNL curriculum focuses on enhancing nursing leadership, managing clinical outcomes, understanding organizational and health care systems, facilitating change, and managing clinical environments using a complexity theory framework. Ideally, the graduate nursing program would develop partnerships with clinical facilities for clinical learning experiences while educating CNLs about needed services for a facility or health system (Begun, Hamilton, Tornabeni, & White, 2006; Gabuat, Hilton, Kinnaird, & Sherman, 2008; Magg, Buccheri, Capella, & Jennings, 2006; Rusch & Bakewell-Sachs, 2007).

Currently, there are four paths that lead to a nursing doctorate: the doctor of philosophy in nursing (PhD), the doctor of nursing science (DNS or DNSc), the doctor of nursing (ND) degree, and the doctor of nursing practice (DNP). Because of the increasing confusion with the multiple doctoral nursing degrees and the high number of credit hours required for advanced practice nurse preparation, the American Association of Colleges of Nursing has determined that doctoral preparation in the form of the DNP will serve as the entry level to advanced nursing practice by 2015. In 2007, 10 DNP programs were operating, and more than 190 DNP programs are being developed (Loomis, Willard, & Cohen, 2007).

The current faculty shortage has prevented tens of thousands of persons interested in pursuing a nursing career from gaining entry into nursing programs. In 2006, close to 63% of full-time nursing faculty in the United States ranged in age from 45 to 60 years old. By 2016, half of all nursing faculty are expected to retire. Besides age, the following reasons have been identified for the growing nursing faculty shortage: (1) profound gap in clinical and academic salaries for comparable or higher education, (2) the expense and time of pursuing a PhD in nursing, (3) the lack of effective educational preparation for assuming the full-time nurse faculty role (Fauteux, 2007), and (4) demands for nursing faculty to engage in research (sometimes, tenure decisions rely on the ability of faculty to secure extramural research grants), publication, service, and clinical practice. Like clinical practice, nursing faculty need to engage in evidence-based teaching. For some faculty, keeping up with these multiple demands seems impossible, especially if they strive for an effective work–life balance.

Because of its newness, the outcomes of these radical changes in graduate and post-graduate nursing education have yet to be determined. A possible scenario is an intense backlash against the revised model by current advanced practice nurses, a failure of higher learning institutions to provide required resources, a lack of available clinical facilities to develop service–education partnerships, increased nursing faculty shortages, and a failure of other health care professionals along with general and specialty nursing organizations to support the endeavor. However, the preferred future would be substantial improvements in client outcomes, professional stature of the nursing profession, wide support for the revised nursing education plan by all health care stakeholders, and an increased supply of nursing faculty. However, a more probable future scenario consists of mixed support and high criticism from other interprofessional health team and nursing profession members (Silva & Ludwick, 2006). Nurses who want a career in nursing academia may perceive the need to pursue a PhD, whereas nurses wanting a career in advanced nursing practice would pursue a DNP. DNP-prepared nurses would then be used as clinical faculty, leaving PhD-prepared nurses to assume classroom teaching and research activities (Loomis et al., 2007).

The nursing profession needs to better articulate and publicize (both internally and to the public) the contributions of professionally educated practitioners to health promotion and restoration and illness prevention. This book has identified the knowledge base and values that characterize the professional nurse in the hope that this will be the first step toward acceptance of scholarship and demonstration of professional competence in practice.

All educational programs must continue to modify their curricula to include changes in the theoretical and technical database for professional nursing practice. For example, computer technology is making an enormous impact on discovery, communication, information storage, and instructional techniques. Some nursing programs provide online distance education as the primary means for program instruction. Recent strides have been made in increasing the computer literacy of nursing students, professional nurses, and nursing faculty. Clinical simulation learning experiences using high-tech manikins, software programs to simulate client responses, and well-designed case studies provide students with the opportunity to practice clinical decision making and skills in a safe environment. Some programs have opted to use robotics to enable faculty to supervise students in laboratory settings. However, not all schools include computer courses and clinical simulations in their curricula. In addition, little attention has been paid to the moral implications of a computerized society that engenders feelings of isolation associated with impersonal communication and invasion of privacy.

To create a nursing profession to meet the needs of a multicultural population, nurse educators must work to recruit students from a variety of cultural backgrounds. However, more importantly, nurse educators must work to retain students from minority backgrounds once they are enrolled in nursing education programs. Special educational support systems may be required for remediation of reading and writing skills (especially for students who speak English as a second language). Curricular content and educational materials must include information regarding American and international cultural differences. Professional nurses from various cultural backgrounds can help faculty in the recruitment and retention of a culturally diverse student population. Finally, culturally diverse students rely on faculty of similar backgrounds for an effective connection within nursing programs. However, until faculties become culturally diverse, current faculty members need to make special efforts to connect with minority students to help them succeed in nursing education and perhaps attract them to the world of nursing academia (Sullivan & Clinton, 1999; Sullivan Commission, 2004).

As the multidisciplinary health team approach to health care delivery grows, nurses will need education related to other health care providers and information on how to work as a team. Some health professional schools have included interdisciplinary educational learning activities with some success and long-term effects (Hylin et al., 2007; Dinov, 2008). In an ideal world, all members of the health care team should learn together, beginning with the first day of their professional education. Faculty from all respective disciplines also would learn and work collaboratively to prepare students to grasp individual discipline content while assessing interdisciplinary processes during carefully designed and conducted seminars.

Ironside and Valiga (2006) outlined a preferred future for nursing education. Characteristics of ideal nursing education programs include (1) an open, flexible curriculum that responds to individualized student learning needs; (2) clinical practice focus in all nursing courses; (3) student selection of courses based on their individual interest (resulting in an individualized curriculum); (4) faculty teaching assignments based on areas of nursing in which they have great passion; (5) lively classroom discussions of significant issues; (6) students and faculty learn with each other; (6) course syllabi with suggested learning goals and activities; (7) elimination of required textbooks with the understanding that students would discover effective learning materials; (8) embracing and valuing diversity; (9) reciprocal challenges by students and faculty; (10) smarter, not harder, work habits of faculty; (11) visible thinking of faculty when interacting with students (including the admission of not knowing something); and (12) supportive deans and directors who provide rewards and required resources for faculty to excel in teaching. Unfortunately, this idea of nursing education would most likely not fulfill educational requirements outlined by most state boards of nursing. However, an egalitarian approach to learning the art and science of professional nursing would instill confidence in students as they master the cognitive, communication, and clinical skills required for effective professional nursing practice.

 ## THE FUTURE OF NURSING SCHOLARSHIP

Within the past 2 decades, nursing research has received increased support from professional nurses and policy makers. The National Institute for Nursing Research (NINR) celebrated its 20th anniversary in 2006 as part of the National Institutes of Health. The NINR provides grant funding for nurse researchers, including studies that look at specific clinical care situations, ways to improve patient safety, and strategies to increase the professional nurse workforce. Results of funded nursing research are disseminated at annual NINR meetings.

In addition, nursing research–based protocols have been developed for client care in the areas of skin management, cognitive impairment, culturally relevant care, pain control, and postoperative and chemotherapy-induced nausea and vomiting. Nursing research findings frequently cross health care disciplines. As interdisciplinary approaches to health care demonstrate improved client outcomes, nurses will be asked to participate in multidisciplinary research efforts. The National Institutes of Health's Roadmap to the Future offers opportunities for nurses to engage in multidisciplinary research projects.

Rapid development in nursing theory and research during the past 20 to 25 years points to a promising outlook for the future. Nursing needs to develop and explicate theories to predict nursing outcomes. Increasingly, nursing research has validated models and theories for nursing care to provide foundations for care. As this trend continues, nursing will develop a unique knowledge base to fulfill the criteria defined for a profession.

 ## SUMMARY AND SIGNIFICANCE TO PRACTICE

Although the future cannot be predicted with great accuracy, nurses can accurately predict that health care delivery and the nursing profession will change. Visualizing several possible futures and identifying a preferred future enable nurses to shape the future of professional practice while planning for potential problems. The preferred future is one in which health care consumers, policy makers, and providers value the contributions nurses make to health care. To create the preferred future, nurses must use cognitive skills (to develop research projects demonstrating the value of professional nurses, make effective clinical decisions in practice, and find meaning in their careers), clinical skills (to effectively execute safe client care and promote client comfort and well-being), and communication skills (to collaborate with all health team members, including clients and families; promote public awareness of nursing's valuable contributions to society; shape health care policies; and recruit future nurses and sustain them once they enter the profession). Competent nurses see opportunities to improve health care delivery and have the ability to work in the ever-increasing complexity of the health care environment while having the capability to cope with constant change.

FROM THEORY TO PRACTICE

1. Reread the vignette at the beginning of the chapter. What assumptions did Jane make regarding her nursing career? How did these assumptions create a future problem for her? What advice would you give Jane to help her deal with her situation? What are Jane's possible reactions to the advice that you would give her? Specify reasons for each possible reaction that you identify.
2. Make a list of the scenarios in this chapter that seem implausible and those that you do not agree with. Conduct a literature search to substantiate your viewpoints on the list of identified scenarios. Develop a more realistic scenario.
3. What actions can you take to promote a preferred future for the nursing profession? Why are these actions important?

WWW INTERNET EXERCISES

1. Visit the home page of Sigma Theta Tau International at http://www.nursingsociety.org. On the home page, click on the words "About Us." On the next screen, you will see the heading "Society Supported Initiatives"; click on the word "ARISTA" and on the next screen, click on the Executive Summary Report. Do you think that the preferred future outlined in this document is desirable? Why or why not? How can you contribute to the preferred future of the nursing profession outlined in this online document?
2. Visit the home page of the American Association of Colleges of Nursing at http://www.aacn.nche.edu. Scroll down the page and find the heading "Nursing Shortage Resource." Click and read information contained in the documents "About the Nursing Shortage" and "Strategies for Addressing the Nursing Shortage." What can we do collectively as a profession to alleviate the nursing shortage? What can you do as an individual to alleviate the nursing shortage? What are the potential consequences of inaction in this future crisis for health care and the nursing profession?
3. Visit the American Nurses Association at http://www.nursingworld.org. On the home page, click on "Nursing Issues/Programs." On the next menu, click on "Agenda for the Future." Do you agree with ANA initiatives for the future? Why or why not? What contributions can you make to fulfill the plan outlined in Nursing's Agenda for the Future?

WWW INTERNET RESOURCES

Sigma Theta Tau International: http://www.nursingsociety.org.
American Nurses Association: http://www.nursingworld.org.
National League for Nursing: http://www.nln.org.
American Association of Colleges of Nursing: http://www.aacn.nche.edu.
Institute for the Future: http://www.iftf.org.
National Institute of Health Future of Stem Cells: http://stemcells.nih.gov, then click on "Stem Cell Information" and type in the search terms to learn about the latest health research on a topic of interest.
Institute for Alternative Futures: http://www.altfutures.com.
The Bootstrap Institute: http://www.bootstrap.org.
Discover Nursing: http://www.discovernursing.com.

REFERENCES

Aburdene, P., & Naisbitt, J. (1992). *Megatrends for women*. New York: Villard.

Agnes, M. (2005). *Webster's new world college dictionary* (4th ed.). Cleveland, OH: Wiley.

Aiken, L., Clarke, S., & Sloane, D. (2000). Hospital restructuring: Does it adversely affect care and outcomes? *Journal of Nursing Administration*, *30*, 457–465.

Aiken, L., Smith, H., & Lake, E. (1994). Lower Medicare mortality among a set of hospitals known for good nursing care. *Medical Care*, *32*, 771–785.

Allan, H., Tschudin, V., & Horton, K. (2008). The devaluation of nursing: A position statement. *Nursing Ethics*, *15*(4), 549–556.

American Association of Colleges of Nursing. (2004). Working paper on the role of the clinical nurse leader. Available at http://www.aacn.nche.edu/Publications/WhitePapers/ClinicalNurseLeader.htm. Accessed July 21, 2008.

Begun, J., Hamilton, J., Tornabeni, J., & White, K. (2006). Opportunites for improving patient care through lateral integration: The clinical nurse leader. *Journal of Healthcare Management*, *51*(1), 19–25.

Bezold, C. (1996). Your health in 2010: Four scenarios. *The Futurist*, *30*, 35–39.

Brush, B. (2008). Global nurse migration today. *Journal of Nursing Scholarship*, *40*(1), 20–25.

Buerhaus, P., Auerbach, D., & Staiger, D. (2007). Recent trends in the registerd nurse labor market in the U.S.: Short-run swings on top of long-term trends. *Nursing Economic$*, *25*(2), 59–67.

Buerhaus, P., Donelan K., Ulrich, B., Norman, L., DesRoaches, C., & Dittus, R. (2007) State of the registered nurse workforce in the Unite States. *Nursing Econonic$*, *25*(1), 6–12.

Burke, S., & Kirk, M. (2006). Genetics education in the nursing profession: A literature review. *Journal of Advanced Nursing*, *38*, 228–237.

Canham, D., Mao, C., Yoder, M., Connolly, P., & Dietz, E. (2008). The Omaha system and quality measurement in academic nurse-managed centers: Ten steps for implementation. *Journal of Nursing Education*, *47*(3), 105–110.

Centers for Disease Control. (2008). *CDC behavioral risk factor surveillance system*. Available at http://today.reuters/com/news/articles.aspx?type=toNews/storyID=2008-07-17T170056Z_01_NI748843. Accessed July 17, 2008.

Cetron, M., & Davies, O. (2008). *Trends shaping tomorrow's world forecasts and implications for business, government and consumers*. Bethesda, MD: World Future Society.

Dinov, I. (2008). Integrated, multidisciplinary and technology-enhanced science education: The next frontier. *MERLOT Journal of Online Learning and Teaching*, *4*(1), 84–93.

Doran, D. (Ed.). (2003). *Nursing-sensitive outcomes: State of the science*. Sudbury, MA: Jones & Bartlett.

Dunton, N. (2008). Take a cue from the NDNQI. *Nursing Management*, *39*(4), 20, 22, 23.

Emmerich, R. (2004). *The day after tomorrow* [motion picture]. Los Angeles: 20th Century Fox.

Fauteux, N. (2007, April). The nursing faculty shortage: Public and private partnerships address a growing need. In *Charting nursing's future*. Princeton, NJ: Robert Wood Johnson Foundation.

Formella, N., & Rovin, S. (2004). Creating a desirable future for nursing part 2: The issue. *Journal of Nursing Administration*, *34*, 264–267.

Gabuat, J., Hilton, N., Kinnaird, L., & Sherman, R. (2008). Implementing the clinical nurse leader role in a for-profit environment: A case study. *Journal of Nursing Administration*, *38*(6), 302–307.

Gordon, S., Buchanan, J., & Bretherton, T. (2008). *Safety in numbers: Nurse-to-patient ratios and the future of health care*. Ithaca, NY: Cornell University Press.

Havens, D., & Aiken, L. (1999). Shaping systems to promote desired outcomes. *Journal of Nursing Administration*, *29*, 14–20.

Health Services and Resources Administration. (2004). *National sample survey of registered nurses*. Rockville, MD: Author.

Henchley, N. (1978). Making sense of the future. *Alternatives*, *7*, 24–26.

Henriksen, C., Page, N., Williams, R., & Worral, P. (2003). Responding to nursing's agenda for the future: Where do we stand on recruitment and retention? *Nursing Leadership Forum*, *8*, 78–84.

Herzlinger, R. (2004). *Consumer-driven health care*. San Francisco: Jossey-Bass.

Hinshaw, A. (2008). Navigating the perfect storm: Balancing a culture of safety with workforce changes. *Nursing Research*, *57*(1, Suppl. 1), S4–S10.

Hood, L., & Leddy, S. (2006). *Leddy and Pepper's conceptual bases of professional nursing* (6th ed.). Philadelphia: Lippincott Williams & Wilkins.

Horrigan, M. (2004). Employment projections to 2012: Concepts and context. *Monthly Labor Review* (127), 3–22.

Hylin, U., Nyholm, H., Mattiasson, C., & Ponzer, S. (2007). Interprofessional training in clinical practice on a training ward for healthcare students: A two-year follow-up. *Journal of Interprofessional Care*, *21*(3), 277–288.

Institute of Medicine. (2008). *Retooling for an aging America*. Washington, DC: Author.

Ironside, P., & Valiga, T. (2006). Creating a vision for the future of nursing education: Moving toward excellence through innovation. *Nursing Education Perspectives, 27*(3), 120–121.

Johnson, T., & White, A. (2000, February/March). Six business principles for the 21st century. *Civilization, 61*(2), 57.

Kirk, H. (2007). Towards a global nursing workforce: The "brain circulation." *Nursing Management, 12*(10), 26–30.

Kurtzman, E., & Buerhaus, P. (2008). New Medicare payment rules: Danger or opportunity for nursing? *American Journal of Nursing, 108*(6), 30–35.

Kuruzovich, J., Angst, C., Faraj, S., & Agarwal, R. (2008). Wireless communication in patient response time. *CIN: Computers, Informatics Nursing, 26*(3), 159–166.

Loomis, J., Willard, B., & Cohen, J. (2007). Difficult professional choices: Deciding between the PhD and the DNP in nursing. *Online Journal of Issues in Nursing, 12*(1). Available at http://search.ebscohost.com/login.aspx?direct=tru&db_cin20&AN=2009526632&site=ehost-live. Accessed July 17, 2008.

Magg, M., Buccheri, R., Capella, E., & Jennings, D. (2006). A conceptual framework for a clinical nurse leader program. *Journal of Professional Nursing, 22*(6), 367–372.

Millett, S., & Kopp, W. (1996). The top 10 innovative products for 2006: Technology with a human touch. *The Futurist, 30*, 16–20.

Milstead, J. A. (2008). *Health policy and politics: A nurse's guide* (3rd ed.). Sudbury, MA: Jones & Bartlett..

Minkin, B. H. (1995). *Future in sight*. New York: Macmillan.

Myers, V., & Dreachslin, J. (2007). Recuitment and retention of a diverse workforce: Challenges and opportunities. *Journal of Healthcare Management, 52*(5), 290–298.

Naisbitt, J. (1996). *Megatrends Asia*. New York: Simon & Schuster.

Naisbitt, J., & Aburdene, P. (1990). *Megatrends 2000*. New York: Penguin.

National Council of State Boards of Nursing (NCSBN). (2000). Mutual recognition: Frequently asked questions. Available at http://www.ncsbn.org.pdfs/FrequentlyAskedQuestions.pdf. Accessed July 20, 2005.

National Council of State Boards of Nursing (NCSBN). (2001). Mutual recognition information. Available at http://www.ncsbn.org. Accessed July 20, 2005.

National Council of State Boards of Nursing (NCSBN). (2004a). Nursing license compact implementation. Available at http://www.ncsbn.org/nlc/rnlpvncompact_mutual_recognition_nurse_.asp. Accessed July 20, 2005.

National Council of State Boards of Nursing (NCSBN). (2004b). 2003 NCLEX statistics. Available at http://www.ncsbn.org/pdfs/Table_of_Pass_Rates_2003.pdf. Accessed July 20, 2005.

National Council of State Boards of Nursing (NCSBN). (2005). 2004 NCLEX statistics. Available at http://www.ncsbn.org?pdfs/Table_of_Pass_Rates_2004.pdf. Accessed July 20, 2005.

National Institute of Medicine and the National Research Council. (1999). *Chemical and biological terrorism*. Washington, DC: National Academy Press.

. Newbergh, C. (2005). The Robert Wood Johnson Foundation's commitment to nursing. In S. Isaacs & J. Knickman (Eds.), *To improve health and health care* (Vol. 8, pp. 73–98). San Francisco: Jossey-Bass.

Niccol, A. (1997). *Gattaca* [motion picture]. Los Angeles: Columbia Pictures.

Pew Health Professions Commission. (1995). *Critical challenges: Revitalizing the health professions for the twenty-first century*. San Francisco: University of California, San Francisco Center for the Health Professions.

Pew Task Force on Accreditation of Health Professions Education. (1998). *Recreating health professional practice for a new century*. San Francisco: University of California, San Francisco Center for the Health Professions.

Porter-O'Grady, T., & Malloch, K. (2007). *Quantum leadership: A resource for health care innovation* (2nd ed.) Sudbury, MA: Jones & Bartlett.

Rusch, L., & Bakewell-Sachs, S. (2007). The CNL: A gateway to better care? *Nursing Management, 38*(4), 32, 34, 36–37.

Sachs, J. (2008). *Common wealth: Economics for a crowded planet*. New York: Penguin.

Silva, M., & Ludwick, R. (2006). Is the doctor of nursing practice ethical? *Online Journal of Issues in Nursing, 11*(2). Available at http://search.ebscohost.com/login.aspx?direct=true&db=cin208&AN=2009274044&site=ehost-live. Accessed July 17, 2008.

Sullivan, E. J. (Ed.). (1999) *Creating nursing's future*. St. Louis, MO: Mosby.

Sullivan, E. J., & Clinton, J. F. (1999). Achieving a multicultural nursing profession. In E. J. Sullivan (Ed.), *Creating nursing's future: Issues, opportunities, and challenges* (pp. 317–333). St. Louis, MO: Mosby.

Sullivan Commission. (2004). *Missing persons: Minorities in the health profession: A report of the Sullivan Commission on diversity in the healthcare workforce*. Available at http://www.amsa.org/div/Sullivan_Commission.pdf. Accessed July 13, 2008.

Tariman, J. (2008). Technologic advancements in cancer care. *ONS Connect, 23*(7), 8–12.

Toffler, A. (1970). *Future shock*. New York: Random House.

Toffler, A. (1990). *Powershift: Knowledge, wealth, and violence at the edge of the 21st century*. New York: Bantam.

Toffler, A., & Toffler, H. (2006). *Revolutionary wealth: How it will be created and how it will change our lives*. New York: Currency Doubleday.

Trossman, S. (2005). Obesity on the rise. *The American Nurse, 37*, 1, 4.

Underwood, A., & Adler, J. (2005). Diet and genes. *Newsweek*, 145, 39–48.

Unruh, L. (2008). Nurse staffing and patient, nurse and financial outcomes. *American Journal of Nursing, 108*(1), 62–71.

U.S. Census Bureau. (2007). Health insurance statistics. Available at http://pubdb3.census.gov/macro/032004/health-hol_001.htm. Accessed August 4, 2007.

U.S. Department of Health and Human Services. (2000). *Healthy people 2010* (Vols. 1 and 2). Washington, DC: Author.

Veenema, T. (Ed.). (2003). *Disaster nursing and emergency preparedness for chemical, biological and radiological terrorism and other hazards*. New York: Springer.

Vlasses, F., & Smeltzer, C. (2007). Toward a new future for healthcare and nursing practice. *Journal of Nursing Administration, 37*(9), 375–380.

Zander, T., Debey-Pascher, S., Eggle, D., Staratshek-Jox, A., Stoelben, E., & Linseisen, J. (2008, May). Predictive value of transcriptional changes in peripheral blood for future clinical onset of lung cancer in asymptomatic smokers [Abstract 1509]. Presented at the annual meeting of the American Society of Clinical Oncology, Chicago.

Index

Page numbers followed by *f* indicate figure; those followed by *t* indicate table.